1. Lawrenceville
2. Snellville
3. Lilburn
4. Duluth
5. Buford
6. Sugar Hill
7. Norcross
8. Suwanee
9. Dacula
10. Berkeley Lake
11. Grayson
12. Rest Haven
13. Auburn
14. Braselton
15. Loganville

Gwinnett:

A little above *Atlanta*

To Mary & Dexter Harrison

Enjoy Gwinnett History!

Elliott E. Brack

Elliott Brack

April 7, 2009

GwinnettForum
Norcross, Ga.
2008

Published by
The Brack Group (Ga), Inc.
dba GwinnettForum
Norcross, Ga. 30092
in conjunction with
United Writers Press, Inc.

ISBN: 978-1-934216-70-5

Printed and bound in the United States of America.

First Edition

Dedication

To the people of Gwinnett County and
to the memory of my friend,

Dallas Scott Hudgens, Jr.,
1923-2000

Contents

Preface xi

1 Those Who Made a Difference

Scott Hudgens 1
Hudgens in World War II 18
Alice Strickland 26
Rhodes Jordan 29
The Mason Brothers 31
John D. Stephens 49
The Williams Brothers 51
Mary Alice Juhan 69
Three Parsons Girls 72
Alice McCabe 74
Wayne Shackelford 76
Mary and David Kistner 80
William C. O'Kelley 83
Beauty Poole Baldwin 85

2 Early History of Gwinnett

1733: The setting as Georgia is founded 89
1818: Gwinnett founded 91
About Button Gwinnett 94
Other early settlements 97
All those Peachtree Streets began in Gwinnett 101
Early churches 102
Civil War times around Gwinnett 103
The coming of the railroads 108
Oldest city in Metro Atlanta 110
Why Buford became so important 116
How Gwinnett towns got their names 123

3 1900-1950

Why half a bridge at Jones Bridge? 127
Gwinnett's tie to early country music 128
Gwinnett's first hospital 131
Buford hospitals 136
How Lake Lanier came about 137
Major changes for Lawrenceville 143
E.R. Snell, Contractor 155

4 1950-1970

Perception of Gwinnett changes 159
Three policemen killed 162
Gwinnett's tie to the poultry industry 166
Gwinnett becomes a major part of the region 169
RC&D project provides benefits 172
Alcohol and the Gwinnett water system 178
Evil spirits 191
Early Gwinnett entrepreneur 193
One failed project: Merchandise Mart 198
Structural changes in government 201
Early growth rises from distribution 206
Early sporting activities 209
Sugarloaf Golf Classic 218
Playgrounds at opposite ends of county 218
Subdivisions spring up 230
Veteran realtor's view 235
Few mobile homes in county 237
Prolonged rapid growth 238
A daily newspaper helps guide the way 240

5 1970-1980

County-wide fire protection 251
Sewering the county 255
Innovative authority financing 258
Creating a recreation district 261
"Friendly" poker game is big news 265
Briscoe Field 268
Keeping engineers in Georgia 274
A new day for Gwinnett industry 276
High-tech comes to Gwinnett 284
A new dimension: modems 289
Scientific-Atlanta 297
National Football League comes to Gwinnett 299
Mountain Park gets a community center 303
Serving youth 305
Simpsonwood Conference Center 314
Modern medical facilities 317

6 1980-1990

Four major changes in one year 333
How Gwinnett got its courthouses 339
Gwinnettians value their libraries 342
A clean county is a better county 346
The New York trip–a bond adventure 350
Council for Quality Growth 355
Downtown development authorities 361
Gwinnett gets its own foundation 364

7 1990-2000

The arts in Gwinnett 367
The arts rejuvenate Buford 382
Gwinnett gets its own Civic Center 387
Charitable groups serve Gwinnett 399
Gwinnett gets hospice 409
Medical clinics 410
Public Health Clinics 414
Food co-ops 416
Fallen Heroes Memorial 427

8 2000-2008

Gwinnett lands a medical school 433
Public transit 435
Community Improvement Districts 441
Four-year college 450
Banking undergoes continued changes 454
Minor league baseball 467

9 School Systems

Schools are a major attraction 473
Innovation in school construction 477
Independent system in Buford 482
Private schools within Gwinnett 484

10 Working Together

Chamber of Commerce a catalyst 495
Five leadership programs 504
Gwinnett Historical Society 513

Historical groups and museums 517
Service clubs 525
United Peachtree Corners Civic Association 535
Business clubs 536
Woman's clubs 544

11 How, Why, When and Where It's Going

Why Gwinnett grew 549
Dramatic change: diversity 550
BAPS Hindu Mandir (Temple) in Lilburn 560
Diversity in the media 562
Diversity in politics 564
Diversity in local restaurants 566
Diversity in labor 566
What makes Gwinnett unique? 567
Something extra 570
More Gwinnett vignettes 581
Looking forward: Will growth ever end? 582

About the Author 584
Bibliography 585

Appendix A 589

Haynes Creek Primitive Baptist Church
By Sybil Deacon 590
Historical Outline of Lawrencville Female Seminary 594
Highlights of Dacula Banking Company, 1909-26 599
1944 Kiwanis Address Concerning Joan Glancy Hospital
By Kate Parsons 609

Early Norcross History 610
By Mollie James Jones

Norcross in the 1940s 612
By Col. (Ret) Clifford Jones Jr.

Gwinnett County Fair History 615
By Bill Baughman

Cover Letter from Attorney John Mobley to Wayne Hill 620
Memo to Hill from Mobley on early days of Water System

History of Gwinnett County Public Schools 624
By Nita Hallford

Condensed Gwinnett Police Dept. History 629
By Major Alan Doss

Dark Days For Gwinnett County as Three Officers Murdered 632
By Major Alan Doss

Time Line of Western Electric Plant, Norcross 635

American Cancer Society in Gwinnett 637
By Phylecia Wilson

Time Line of Gwinnett Parks Acquisitions 641
By Grant Guess

The Larry Flynt Incident 647
By Bryant Huff

Appendix B 652

Demographics 656
County Officials 678
City Officials 704
Community and Volunteer Leaders 736
Financial Data 764
School Data 777
Civic Clubs 811
Other Interesting Facts 822

Index 827

Calendar of Annual Events in Gwinnett 849

Preface

This history of Gwinnett in modern times has been some 40 months in the making. It's been enjoyable for me to work on, but at the same time frustrating, for as a newspaperman, I'm used to seeing what I write in print relatively quickly. Three years is a long time to wait!

Many people in Gwinnett have contributed to this book, and have been of immense help in ferreting out the details that are required when attempting a history such as this. People from all walks of life, and from every corner of Gwinnett, have been kind enough to take the time to answer questions I put to them, or to search the records for a mass of facts. Those reading this history will be indebted for ages to the good efforts of these many people. I thank them for the help, kindnesses, encouragement and detail that they have provided, especially to those to whom I sought information time and time again. The book could not have been written without them.

This book was originally conceived to be a very short history, one of about 100 pages. I even had a title: "A Short History of a Large Place," with a nod to a favorite author, T.R. Pearson. But as more time went into research, stories were added, and an extensive appendix was developed. It is to the point that the length is somewhat embarrassing, in that people will think the author cannot edit, nor cut out extraneous material. Yet the stories continued to come, the detail added color to the stories, people contributed new material, and the book kept growing. We finally gave up on a short book, and you see the results.

We realized that there was no modern, up-to-date objective history of the county produced in the last 50 years. And we resolved to produce such a book, one which people could enjoy, rely on, and use as a significant reference.

There still remains another void of written Gwinnett history. Most of the county's cities do not have an objective history about their city development, though Buford, Norcross and Lawrenceville have extensive histories. Those cities which have not yet seen the publication of a thoroughly researched book on their histories should move toward getting their town's history saved through encouraging some citizen to produce such a work. The cities could enhance the possibility of such a work if they would fund the cost of the publication.

A word about the title: *Gwinnett: A Little Above Atlanta*. Gwinnett's location northeast of Atlanta inspired the title. The idea for the title came from an Atlanta public relations executive, Tom Deardorff, who came up with this description of Gwinnett around 1980.

The book is primarily a collection of stories and the background and depth of people who have contributed to Gwinnett's fast growth since World War II. While there are some stories about Gwinnett from its earliest days, much of that has been covered in previous histories of the county. The focus of this book is the continual growth that Gwinnett has seen since 1950. The population of the county back then was 32,320, up 6,467 from its population of 25,853 in 1900. But after 1950, the enormous growth began, to its present population approaching 800,000. Few counties in the nation have seen such growth in so short a time.

What has amazed me is how well the county assimilated the onslaught of people moving within its borders. Oh, yes, there have been inconveniences. But all in all, from a back-road county of 1950, Gwinnett has moved smoothly to being the second largest county in Georgia in 2008. This book tells of the growth, development, problems and progress, who contributed to the county's development, and how it all came about.

We have relied upon current and previous interviews with the people who were associated with that growth. Some interviews were especially for this book. Others were with those with whom I had routinely talked and interviewed over the years in my newspaper career, since coming to Gwinnett in 1974. Many have since died.

There's one key person who was instrumental in the development of this history, though he died before he knew it was taking place. Let me take you back a few years. A telephone call in December of 1989 came from Minor Corley of Duluth, asking me to come have lunch with him and his wife, Winnie, at their home in Duluth. (Today this is known as the Payne-Corley house, where many parties are held.) The Corleys fed me a great meal of fried chicken and fresh vegetables, then Minor said: "Come in here and let me show you something." I had no idea what he would be showing me. Mr. Corley was a former mayor of Duluth, and had been an Allis-Chalmers tractor dealer---before his election as a county commissioner.

We went into the living room. He pulled from the corner a cardboard box crammed with papers, and said to me, "Look through this." It had all sorts of official papers, notes, records, etc. of his eight years as a county commissioner, from 1958 to 1964. As I looked at the material there, I remember saying to him. "This is good stuff," then asked in all innocence: "What are you going to do with it?"

His answer: "I'm giving it to you."

The answer so surprised me, that I blurted: "But what am I going to do with it?"

Minor's answer: "You'll find some use for it."

Skip ahead about 16 years, after I had retired. By then, I was just beginning writing what I thought would be the short Gwinnett history. One day, when up in a crowded upstairs closet, I spied the box that Minor Corley had given me. Taking the box downstairs, I started going through it again with renewed interest, and found much material that would be valuable—even germane---to the history. In particular, information about the early days of the Gwinnett Water System has proved invaluable, with much of the information perhaps not available readily, if at all, in other places. All this was thanks to Minor Corley's foresight, and to him the readers, and I, owe a debt of gratitude in his memory.

This cache of material led me to Atlanta Attorney John Mobley, who had been deeply involved with the Gwinnett water system in its formative days. You'll find great material from Mr. Mobley, who is still practicing law, and had recollections about his days virtually overseeing the county water system.

Some of the information in this book was in especially good shape when it came to me, as different people in the community had researched and published on various topics. Since the information was so good, and well done, I asked permission to include the material in a narrative appendix, under the byline of the person who wrote it. They deserve it for their time and effort in compiling the research for the agency or non-profit with which they have been associated. They had solid, often first-hand detail on that topic. What more can you ask?

It was about that time that we realized that to tell the real story of Gwinnett, there would have to be a lot of statistics on the changes going on in Gwinnett. It came about innocently enough. Seeking a list of previous county officials, we put a question to the office of the Probate Judge: "Send me a list of the previous probate judges," we simply asked. There was a pause, and the court official said: "I've seen that list around here somewhere." That's when we realized we needed a central depository for Gwinnett city and county officials of the past, for there was no such central location for those names. Hence came the idea for an Appendix. You will find that it has grown considerably, to the point where we have over 125 different tables about Gwinnett at the end of this book. We are indebted, again, to many people for these lists of past officials.

Some of these lists came from organizations with web sites. Some had histories and other data on the web, but few had a list of their previous officials on the Internet. When asking these different groups and cities to prepare a list of their past officials, or to send details of their history, we suggested: "Yes, do it now for this history book, but then put it on your web site for people to use when they visit your site." In this small way, we feel that the book has prompted these various groups and cities to enhance their web sites with this information.

The multiplicity of all or a part of 15 cities in the county only contributes to the difficulty of gathering of facts for a history. As a result of the compilation of information, particularly in the Appendix, we think we have the most complete and up-to-date information on both the cities and the county itself. We know of no other place where all such information is compiled together.

While Gwinnett has grown quickly in the last 50 years, this growth was primarily a homogenous growth, with mostly white newcomers moving into the county. But particularly since 1990, the influx of immigrants and minorities to this county from all over the world has grown exponentially. A study from Kennesaw State University in 2002 reported that the changing demographics in Gwinnett make it the most ethnically diverse county in Georgia, with one out of six adults born outside the United States.

Except for a section near the end of the book, this book addresses very little of the complexity of the diversity in the county. Gwinnett is the most diverse county in Georgia now. When someone sits down to write the next history of Gwinnett, we anticipate that individuals from what were once minority communities will be shown in positions of responsibility and leadership within the county. In recent years, few minorities have found themselves in these power positions in Gwinnett, as they focused more on becoming financially and socially self-sufficient in this modern day. Yet the impact of the diverse Gwinnett minority community is becoming more obvious each day, and will influence the history of the county more in the future.

While it is not always obvious, what has happened in Gwinnett is rather striking: moving from what was once a primarily farming economy, to the county's first major business focus, that of warehousing and distribution of supplies. Then came even more changes, the beginning of a booming home construction field, followed by wider choices of jobs within Gwinnett, then the rapid development of the metro area's first concentration of companies labeled "high tech," and finally to today's wide range of business activities, including those in international commerce.

Gwinnett has seen in the last few years a continually interesting series of events that have propelled the county forward. This book is an attempt to explain how all this happened.

One thing is for sure: it takes a lot of people helping you to produce a book, especially one concentrating on specific details of history. There are so many different stories you need more detail on, or to learn about from the very beginning, that many contacts with "those in the know" were necessary. We kept tabs on the people who have sent us detail, often via email, or in person, over the last two years. (Somehow, we lost the list, "the computer ate it," during the first year of research.) We still have details from more than 750 people helping us, and have over 2,000 emails to us from these people with helpful information. It blows our mind how many people have been of help.

However, we won't bore readers with that list. Yet the book could not have evolved without them. We thank them all for their individual contributions to this history.

A few people stand out whom we must mention. We probably would never have even attempted writing a book on Gwinnett history until after we met Vally Sharpe, who along with Jan Lowe owns United Writers Press, Inc., of Lilburn. They take manuscripts from authors, and do all the "back room" work, that is, looking at the text, asking all sorts of questions, designing, laying out the book, and preparing it for print. They even find the right printer and handle these sorts of details. Our thanks to Vally and Jan.

Then there's my "editor," my daughter, Betsy of Durham, N.C., who professionally goes over written materials in great detail. She can be tough on a writer, but she is fair and fast, and contributed immensely to this book and not just to editing, but with overall strategy. Another person usually initially reading the copy has been my wife, Barbara, who found all sorts of details to ask questions about, and greatly impacted and improved this work. These two have helped clean up the text and appendices that you see, and made the book far better with their thoughts and suggestions. In addition, my daughter, Catherine of Washington, D. C., was of great assistance with helping format the tables in the book, while my son, Andy of Charleston, S.C., contributed answers to problems with the Internet and computer, and designed the cover and web site.

Anyone setting out to write must also appreciate research librarians, for me, especially those with the Gwinnett Public Library. Often when stumped, these professionals found data which seemed unavailable. To Nicky Smith and especially to Neil Derksen, a great big "Thanks," while others within the system also helped at various times.

Helping make sure that the graphics, especially the photographs, in the book were of sound quality has been Nick Nicholson, with whom I share offices. He has scanned photos and other images, improved the quality of contributions, and provided expert advice.

Two people with deep ties in the community read some of the manuscript and made suggestions. They were Patsy Rooks, formerly with the Chamber of Commerce, and Attorney Jones Webb. We appreciate their direction and suggestions.

Thanks also to Mary Harris for meticulous proofreading of the entire book.

Early on in preparation for the book, publisher John Mellott of the *Atlanta Journal-Constitution* opened his files in the newspaper morgue for us, an invaluable contribution. Richard Hallman of the research department often was able to supply information perhaps not found anywhere else.

Now back to the bulk of people in Gwinnett who were so helpful. As said above, we won't mention them all, and if we did, we would likely leave several out. But those often providing multiple answers include Grant Guess, Lisa Johnsa, Lynn Ledford, Phil Hoskins, Amie Sakmar, Elvira Rogers, Teresa Lynn, Connie Wiggins, Jim Skinner of ARC, Jim Wilbanks, Bill Baugham, June Hawkins, Lisa Anders, Nancy Ward, Preston Williams, Rhonda Boyd, Bob Baroni, Shannon Coffey, Lillian Webb, John Adams, Scott Fuller, Sloan Roach, Sue Peterson, Wayne Sikes, Wayne Shackelford, John Hutchins, and many, many more people. We could not have done this without you.

Some thoughts on how to read this book: it's not a novel with a continuing story line. The events jump around considerably, though Chapters 2-8 are organized chronologically. The first chapter deals with a few key people of the county who had great influence in what happened in Gwinnett, with background about them. Sadly, it was not possible to include many people who deserved to be in this part of the book.

A reader might be confused about verb tenses used in the book. When the present tense ("says") is used, it means that the words came from a person living when the book was printed. When the past tense ("said") is used, this means that the person was deceased at the time of this writing. Hopefully, the back-and-forth use of the present and past tense will not cause the reader confusion.

We are happy to present this history of Gwinnett in its modern era for your edification and enjoyment.

Elliott Brack, Norcross, Ga.
August 8, 2008

1
Those Who Made a Difference

Scott Hudgens

Scott Hudgens grew up on a truck farm south of Atlanta during the Depression, fought as an enlisted man in a tank recovery unit with distinction from D-Day's invasion of Europe through France and Germany, met the Russians at the Elbe River, then returned home to become one of the most successful businessmen in Atlanta. Luckily for Gwinnett, he moved to the former Charles W. Summerour Farm in Duluth in the early 1970s, and, from then on, adopted Gwinnett as the focus for his work, and his philanthropy.

No one was more successful, nor wore the mantle of success with such dignity and grace, and, for years, as anonymously. Scott Hudgens shunned the limelight as he quietly gave enormous amounts of money to local charities while he was living. That work today continues through his Hudgens Family Foundation, one of the largest in Georgia, with assets of more than $100 million.

Hudgens had a reputation as a person able to make quick decisions on his own, and a person whose handshake was more solid than any contract. He also had a tremendous ability to make accurate financial calculations in his mind, garnered from his time working at a lumber yard. He could figure in his head, after looking at a house plan, the total board feet of lumber needed for building that house. "He thought in fractions, not decimals," said one of his proteges, Ben Carter, when explaining Scott's ability. Carter adds: "Fractions worked for him. He was a mathematical genius."

Jackie Hudgens remembers that on one of her first dates with Scott, he asked if she could do a mathematical calculation, which she could. But she says she thought: "I've never been on a date and had to do a math problem before. Scott was a real whiz at figuring matters in his head."

Another characteristic that typified Hudgens was his ability to see how land would develop. "He was a visionary," former Gov. Zell Miller says. "Scott defines the word visionary as well as anyone I knew. He would invite me to groundbreakings in broom-sage or corn fields. I would be thinking, 'How is this going to become what Scott thinks it's going to become?' But time and again he would be right. He was 10 years and sometimes more than 10 years ahead of us. I got finally to where if Scott says it was going to happen, it would, like it was pre-ordained."

Gwinnett County: A Little Above Atlanta

Jim Cowart, himself a successful developer who also grew up near Hudgens in South Fulton County, echoes a similar thought: "Scott was a visionary, and had as good a vision and foresight as anyone in the business."

Through his business transactions---and there were many---another quality stood out: Hudgens' ethical standard. His long-time employee and sometime partner, Tom Van Houten, a CPA and attorney, says: "Over the years, I never knew Scott to intentionally support anything which was even borderline unethical, or to take advantage of anyone. He was a tough businessman, and would do his best in negotiations, but once completed, he would do nothing unethical or illegal in any way." Another close associate in real estate transactions, Bruce Williams, summed him up in one word: "Integrity. He just wouldn't do things if he thought it was wrong."

Herman Russell, a partner with Hudgens in several ventures over the years, was close to Hudgens. "He taught me a lot, and was a role model for me. He was a genius, and also so kind. He gave his heart away to people. He was a man whose word you could take and did not have to have a contract. He would live up to what he agreed on. He was rare. He was closer to me than my brother." He adds: "He was just a caring individual. I don't think he ever got the recognition he deserved. He is one of the great heroes of Georgia who never was recognized as he should be."

Tall (6'3"), angular, somewhat slow in talking, and a good listener, Scott Hudgens easily gained people's confidence and respect by his demeanor. Hudgens had few hobbies, though he would tell people he enjoyed hunting and fishing. He doted on his family (wife Jackie and four children, Michael, Marsha, Mark and Dallas), but always kept focused on his long range business goals.

Some say his real hobby was not hunting and fishing, but driving around, especially on weekends, and looking at open land.....from the viewpoint of what it could become some day, and how people would gain access to that land.

Ralph Williams, a real estate attorney for Hudgens, recalls the time Hudgens spent driving around "recreational hours looking at property, mentally extending future roads, and trying to conceive of what the land would best be used for, and would become." Tom Van Houten says that he logged so many miles driving around that at one time the Internal Revenue Service questioned his auto tax deductions. "We finally convinced them that as a land developer, this was part of his business. For he would rack up enormous miles just driving around, often by himself, just looking at property." Williams says that Scott got an appreciation for the land from working on his father's farm before World War II, and as he fought going across France and Germany. "He once told me that during the war, as a tanker, he was always watching the contours of the land, for he said that once you got your tanks stuck, you could get killed. He was always visualizing the land, keeping in his mind how he would develop the land."

When Hudgens turned to developing shopping centers, his strategy was to get in and buy land quietly and quickly, and amass the land well before anyone realized that he was assembling it. He knew particularly where he wanted certain facilities. He picked the areas to locate major malls, for instance, because of the accessibility of roads, or because of the probability of future roads.

Hudgens' longtime associate, Tom Wheeler, also remembers Hudgens' ability to find the best road placement. "Scott fancied himself as a world class traffic planner. And he was really good at it."

* * * * *

Dallas Scott Hudgens Jr. was born August 13, 1923 in south Fulton County, near Stonewall, to Laura Scarborough Hudgens and Dallas Hudgens Sr. He was raised on what is described as a "two mule farm" near Union City as one of seven children. Mr. Hudgens said: "I learned about land from my grandfather, Frank Scarborough as we rode around together." The future developer would help survey the land from his grandfather's estate.

His father gave him his work ethic. Young Scott helped his father in farming and later, building houses on the side. He was also learning other aspects, as his father also told him: "All you've got to do is work hard, pay your debts, and tell the truth."

Father and son worked side-by-side before World War II. Hudgens told Hugh Merrill in a *Gwinnett Daily News* article on November 3, 1985: "My dad got interested in carpentry and building, so when we got through laying by, we'd cut down some trees and haul them to the mill and saw 'em. Papa had some acreage there with good timber on it, and we owned some land up and down the road. We started building those little houses on it. (That was) when I was about 12, back during the middle of the Depression." Scott added of his father: "We tried to outwork each other" in the family farming and house building. "We never would leave until it was dark. That's where I learned to work and get things done."

Scott Hudgens, Jr.

Scott graduated from Campbell High School in 1940 at age 16, and was on the baseball team. He later worked at Anderson-McGriff Lumber Company as a counter salesman. "We made $13.50 a week, if you came in and also worked on Saturday morning."

As World War II started, Hudgens and some of his friends from high school enrolled at what was then the Evening Division of the University of Georgia, which would eventually become Georgia State University. The idea was that after two years of college, they could volunteer for the Air Force. The group even passed the Air Force physical examination one morning --- only to learn that day that their plans were doomed. "We were sitting at the Varsity," Scott remembered. "We heard the news on the radio that Uncle Sam that day had abolished volunteer enlistments. We had just finished our exams and were going to volunteer the next day." So, like many others, Scott was soon drafted and went into the Army, being sent on February 1, 1943 to north of Sacramento, Calif., first for organizing, and then to the Mojave Desert for tank training.

By September of 1943, his unit was en route by train to New York for shipment overseas. Fourteen days after debarking New York, the 746th Tank Battalion arrived in Glasgow, Scotland. Later the unit was shifted to near Salisbury, England, before moving to Southhampton to join the invasion of Europe on D-Day.

The trip across the English Channel in heavy weather was in a small LCT (Landing Craft Tank), which held four tanks and their crews. Debarking in late morning of D-Day at Omaha Beach, the unit was put off in four feet of water. "I never looked back," Scott said. He also noted the fighting was still intense when his unit landed.

Hudgens commanded a tank retriever with five men in a spearhead unit. His tank recovery unit, which was in the forefront of an assault, cleared a path when tanks went out of commission. (More on this later.)

As the invasion progressed, Hudgens was always near the front, as the American Army crossed France, was stopped over winter near the Belgian-Dutch-Germany border, then broke out in the spring to speed across by then near-defeated Germany. Hudgens' unit was halted at the Elbe River, linking up with the Russians near Leipzig on April 20, 1945. He participated in five major military campaigns, and was awarded the Purple Heart with five battle stars. One of the members of Hudgens' company was a fellow Georgian, James Casey of Lawrenceville. This acquaintance led Hudgens to being introduced to Casey's sister, Jacqueline. These two were married in February of 1947.

Hudgens returned home on Nov. 28, 1945 and on the second day of January, 1946, Scott was back at work at Anderson-McGriff. Shortly afterward, he and his father sat down, discussed the future, and decided to build houses together. Getting materials for housing in the pent-up era following the war wasn't entirely easy. But with Scott working as an outside salesman at the lumber yard and handling procurement of materials, sales and loans, and his father supervising sub-contractors and construction, they soon finished their first house. It was in Union City, and sold for $5,500. "We made $1,200 on it," Scott said. He arranged for the financing of the house at the First National Bank of Atlanta, through a GI loan, recalling "The note was at four percent, and the monthly payment was $19."

Meanwhile, Scott and his father realized that the demand for homes was enormous. They built houses for five years, with Scott also building houses on the side with Anderson-McGriff. In that arrangement, Scott had eyed a "slab pile" of throw-away pieces of wood at the lumber yard. He went to Raymond Anderson, his boss, and suggested that some of the lumber could be salvaged into usable building materials. Scott volunteered to go into a partnership with Anderson, with Anderson allowing Scott to get from the scrap pile usable lumber, and Scott building the houses, a 50-50 partnership. The two built five houses out of the scrap pile. In 1949, his last year with Anderson-McGriff, Hudgens built 57 houses, while holding down his job at the lumber yard. He had also sold more material than any other salesman, though he admits, "I was buying most of it for myself."

The Scott Hudgens building was in College Park, on Interstate 85 near the airport, facing south, seen by those just arriving to Atlanta.

In 1950, Hudgens went out on his own. He formed his first company and continued to build houses on the south side of Atlanta. His first company was Scott Builders, and later on, Scott Development Company. From the start, Scott was always seeking to build a good house, but use the building materials efficiently. Jackie Hudgens says that when painting a house, if there was leftover paint, he would dump all the paint in a large bucket, with the mixture turning out gray, and would paint the inside walls of the house with this leftover paint. "It worked out fine, and he used all the paint that way," she says.

Around 1953, Hudgens also began apartment and duplex construction. By 1955, he also got into developing land for other contractors to build on. Before that, he was buying individual lots for himself to build out. He would later tell Hugh Merrill: "I don't even remember how many subdivisions we did down there." And by 1957, Hudgens realized he needed to get into commercial construction, with his first shopping center venture, Jamestown Shopping Center in College Park. In 1958, Hudgens ventured into a real estate firm, forming Tri-City Realty on Virginia Avenue in College Park. He bought a two-story, frame house for his office, adjacent to a cemetery. Ridley Nichol remembers: "Scott and I used the same desk. If one of us had an appointment to have someone come see us, the other one had to leave the room." His top real estate salesman was 22-year-old Cecil Day, formerly of Macon, the same Day who later became world famous for his Days Inn motel chain.

The year 1960 was a significant one for Scott Hudgens. That was the year that his financial statement net worth topped $1 million for the first time.

Meanwhile, in the late 1950s, Hudgens was finding one field more difficult: financing the houses he was building and the commercial activities he was getting into. Members of the financial community were more reluctant to loan money to developers and finance houses not on the north side of Atlanta.

Scott said: "Your biggest problem was that all your bankers and financial people had always lived on the north side of town. So in 1959, I got into the mortgage business. I still think it costs as much to buy a 2-by-4 on the south side as it does on the north side. And the bankers weren't paying us enough attention. That's why I got into the mortgage business."

Into mortgage business

The company was to become known as Scott Hudgens Realty and Mortgage Inc. (Scott always called the firm, "SCHRAM," his wife says.) But it wasn't easy. Ridley Nichol, who managed the mortgage company, says that "Everybody told us we didn't have the expertise to get into the mortgage business. On our first trip to New York, seeking to arrange financing, one banker listened to us, said we would never do what we said we would, added that we didn't know anything about the business, and threw us out."

At this time, the company had not made a single loan, and the pair could not get into a Mortgage Bankers Association meeting. "You had to have five years under your belt to become a member," Nichol says. At a restaurant that night, one guy overhead Nichol and Hudgens mentioning the mortgage business, and "had mercy on us. He told us to go to the old Commodore Hotel the next day. A group had a suite and hospitality room.

"One of them, an older guy, took us into a bedroom and closed the door. His first words were 'What kind of warehouse do you have?' We didn't know what he meant, and he proceeded to tell us. 'You guys can't do this without a warehouse,' he said."

A "warehouse" is a technical term in the mortgage business where mortgage companies have credit to make loans to individuals to buy houses. The builder gets paid off, and the company gets a security deed to give to the bank.

Nichol continues: "We talked to banks all over Atlanta, and every step we took was questions and answers. The only one to listen to us was Trust Company. They said they would give us a $250,000 warehouse line, adding that we would have to get a take-out for each loan. You get a commitment from another bank that they will buy the loan from you after it is closed. Then we would pay back the Trust Company."

Soon the pair had arranged with Charles Sandiford at Atlanta Federal to charge the Hudgens company one point for a letter to give the Trust Company. They also agreed to close the loan if the mortgage company did not find anyone else to sell it to. "That would be at a discounted rate," Nichol adds. Eventually Hudgens arranged for up to $4 million for such loans.

However, after all this, Hudgens was not pleased. He told Nichol: "There's gotta be a better way to make a house loan." He didn't like "having to stand in line, bow and scrape. We ought to change the approach, and sell money like you sell Fuller brushes," he said.

The result was staking out signs on streets that Scott Hudgens Mortgage would be the "originator" of loans, and they began contacting real estate firms and builders. Nichol says: "It was being done by one other firm, but we were the first mortgage company to do it and used salaried personnel to sell loans in Metro Atlanta."

Hudgens was calling on other Realtors. "So I went out and solicited loans and I shook up the mortgage business. I made all those fellows get out from behind their desks and dust themselves off and go to work." That mortgage company was the first one to be located south of Five Points in Atlanta, and became a fixture on the south side of Atlanta. People arriving in Atlanta and driving into town saw a giant red "Scott Hudgens Company" neon sign atop the building. The company was immediately welcomed by other area Realtors, and became successful, financing not only Hudgens-built homes and land, but for many others, too. The building would eventually become the home of not only the mortgage company, but also offices for Hudgens' move into insurance, property management, development as well as real estate sales. More than 300 people worked at the building.

Hudgens said it took until 1965 to get the mortgage business profitable. By then he had an $11 million warehouse line of credit from First Boston Bank.

However, for Hudgens, he wasn't entirely happy with the mortgage business. "It got wild," he said, "The REITs were getting back into it, and bankers were making all sorts of loans. We were asked to make construction loans, and Ridley Nichol said 'No' to that. And it employed a lot of people. We were making more money in building construction and apartments. When we were offered $9 million for the mortgage and insurance company, we sold it." Nichol was to remain with the new owners, the Bank of California, for three years to run the company.

Nichol says that "Scott had the damndest sense of timing" in his ventures. "We made a deal with the bank in October of '72, and closed it in January of 1973. In six months, real estate was in deep trouble until the later 1970s. Scott caught the market for selling at the peak." After selling the mortgage company, the number of Scott Hudgens employees went down to 15.

With the decline of the real estate market in the 1970s, Nichol found that working with the West Coast people was great, but that they could not control the sagging economy. By the spring of 1974, Nichol was spending all his time in the business, but was forced to let some workers go. By 1975, Hudgens was trying to buy back what he had sold. While he could not buy back the mortgage business, he was able to buy back the insurance element.

Around 1976, he and Nichol started a new mortgage company "from scratch." It was known as Scott Hudgens Company, not Scott Hudgens Realty and Mortgage, as before. By 1980, with the mortgage market more turbulent than ever before, he and Nichol sold the new mortgage company to Cameron Brown Company of Charlotte, N.C., a firm that eventually became part of First Union Corp. and Hudgens was out of the mortgage business for good.

By 1960, Hudgens was into even larger commercial centers, opening 85-acre Arrowhead Shopping Center on U.S. Highway 41 south in Jonesboro. A feature of the building was the largest supermarket then in Metro Atlanta, a 30,000 square foot Big Apple store. Later would come a discount shopping venture of Rich's, the 100,000 square foot Richway, and 417 apartments, an office building, nursing home and medical facilities.

Meanwhile, his real estate firm was booming. In the first six months of 1961, his firm led all other firms in Metro Atlanta, with $4.8 million in sales, $1 million more than the nearest competitor. By 1964, his real estate company sales surpassed all others in Atlanta, totaling $45,357,303.

Hudgens was beginning to spread his interest. He was into land assembly, something he loved to do quietly. He put together some 2,000 acres southwest of Atlanta, eventually selling this property to another developer, who would market the land as Fulton Industrial Business Park. His efforts at assembling 318 acres of land in another southside area also led to him selling the property intact to Trammell Crow Company, which developed it as Greenbrier Mall. He was also near this time getting out of the house building business. "It is so tedious and time consuming," he said, "if you do it right. You can't do it and commercial real estate at the same time."

While Hudgens was concentrating on several types of ventures on the southside of Atlanta, he was intelligent enough to spread his risks. Beginning in 1958, he began putting together land on the south side of Savannah, though for years little happened in this area.

By now Hudgens had heard of a new form of business activity, the retail shopping mall. He turned his attention to another part of the northeast side, assembling land in 1963 near the Stone Mountain Freeway for what would become the first enclosed, air-conditioned shopping mall in Georgia, called North DeKalb Mall. His major tenant for the mall was Rich's, the giant Atlanta department store. Mall strategy was different in those days, for President Dick Rich didn't want other department stores in the mall, and it opened with only one. The official opening was June 29, 1965. Note that with the mall sporting an air-conditioned building, it opened during the summer! Hudgens teamed with John Hancock Insurance Company in financing his first mall. Shortly after this mall opened, Greenbrier Mall opened, with Hudgens having assembled land for the first two enclosed, air-conditioned malls in Georgia.

First venture in north Atlanta

In 1960 came Hudgens' first land venture on the north side of Atlanta, buying 150 acres in North DeKalb County in what would become Dunwoody. Hudgens had learned from a planner that a perimeter highway, Interstate 285, would come through the area. He reasoned that it would bring both key commercial and housing growth. He purchased the land for $1,500 an acre. Knowing where the interchanges would be, in one transaction, he and Cecil Day sold to Texaco 20 sites around Atlanta in one day. The north tract sat with little interest for quite a while. In 1964, Hudgens opened Georgetown Shopping Center, to give the area a "community feeling," as the area blossomed. When Hudgens was marketing the Dunwoody land, he told his top salesman, Cecil Day, "Don't put Dunwoody on your signs. People will think we're too far out." Eventually, Jim Cowart bought 36 lots for $2,500 each and the area began to blossom as one of the more desirable executive housing addresses.

By 1962-63, Hudgens was tying up land, working with Cecil Day, in both North Fulton and Gwinnett County. In the early 1960s, Hudgens would often drive down Georgia Highway 141 headed for a get-away cottage on a point of Lake Lanier ("Las Brisas," or "The Breezes") off Georgia Highway 369 on the Gainesville side of Brown's Bridge Road. He appreciated the rolling, open acreage ("That beautiful land") he saw along the way.

It was during this time (1963) that the Atlanta Athletic Club was realizing it needed to move from its location as a downtown club, known as the East Lake Country Club. With many of its members in real estate business at that time, F. W. Bird of the legal firm of Alston and Bird, president of the country club then, picked Scott to look for property because, as Ralph Williams remembers, "Scott was an outsider." The club wanted to focus on the north side of Atlanta. The club had been looking for property in an area from Cobb County, through North Fulton County to Gwinnett County. But North Fulton was the obvious choice, since both Cobb and Gwinnett counties were dry counties for alcohol. Tom Van Houten says; "The North Fulton property, bordering the Chattahoochee River, though a Duluth address, was about as far east as they could locate the club." Scott optioned many acres of property and eventually assigned the club an option on the former 600 acre Ben Summerour Farm that the Summerour estate held in January of 1964. The Athletic Club paid $420,000 for its acreage. Soon the Athletic Club built on the site, creating a prestigious country club, as it disposed of its East Lake Club. The new Athletic Club site was the site of the U.S. Open in 1976, and the site for the 2001 PGA Tournament. The PGA is to return to the course in 2011. Altogether, the club has 36 holes of golf in its 425 acres east of Medlock Bridge Road, plus another 75 acres west of the road.

The other open land that Cecil Day had found in the area had Hudgens interests, as he optioned the 588-acre C.W. Summerour Farm on the outskirts of Duluth and 929 acres owned by Harrison Summerour, also near Duluth along the river. Total price for all three Summerour tracts totaled $1.172 million, a Scott Hudgens Realty and Mortgage spokesman told a newspaper. He also bought the 409-acre Vantress Farm west of Duluth at this time. Hudgens would in 1968 begin remodeling the former C.W. Summerour home and surrounding 110 acres for his personal use. In 1970 the family moved to Duluth from their home in Newton Estates off Roosevelt Highway in College Park.

With the assemblage of land, Hudgens owned what would become all four corners of the key intersection of Pleasant Hill Road and Peachtree Industrial Boulevard. He also owned three parcels toward Berkeley Lake. Interestingly, when Hudgens purchased these properties, there was no Peachtree Industrial Boulevard that far north as a north-south feeder. (That road stopped at Medlock Bridge Road then.) And to get from the eastern side of Gwinnett to cross the Chattahoochee River on State Bridge Road, a motorist had to drive through Duluth, down Howell Ferry Road and past Joan Glancy Hospital. One story is that Hudgens was the main contributor in donating right-of-way for Pleasant Hill Road to connect from Buford Highway to State Bridge Road (through the Peachtree Industrial Boulevard intersection). Those in Gwinnett for years also give Hudgens key credit for getting the Department of Transportation to plan Peachtree Industrial Road through Duluth to eventually connect with McEver Road north of Buford to form another key four-lane feeder road into Atlanta. Representatives of Hudgens got landowners between Duluth and Medlock Bridge Road to donate right-of-way for what would become Peachtree Industrial Boulevard. The road would cut through the Hudgens' property. The original plan of the Department of Transportation was for this road to go east of Duluth. By going on the west side, it provided a far superior feeder access road into Atlanta, since it would not be so close to Buford Highway as originally planned.

Eventually Mr. Hudgens owned 1,600 acres near Duluth.

Other land identified in the late 1960s which Hudgens purchased included 200 acres on the Chattahoochee River off East Jones Bridge Road, where in 1975 Simmons Mattress Company relocated from New York City. The firm built an award-winning headquarters on a bluff overlooking the river using environmentally-friendly building techniques. After Simmons was taken over by Gulf and Western Industries and its headquarters moved to DeKalb's Executive Park, the Simmons building sat vacant for several years before Jim Cowart purchased it, and sold it to Larry Dean for his new company, Stockholder Systems. Eventually Dean sold that firm to NYNEX, the New York telephone company, which sold the company and it became Check Free. In 2007, Check Free became a division of Fiserv of Brookfield, Wisconsin in a $4.4 billion cash buy-out.

By the mid 1960s, activities were picking up for Hudgens in Savannah. He built Oglethorpe Mall, with 250,000 square feet of shops in addition to its anchors. He got two major tenants, Sears and Belk, to anchor this mall, which opened in 1969. J.C. Penney would come in 1982, and Rich's (Macy's) in 1992. This was the first major mall to be located in South Georgia, part of a 240 acre Planned Urban Development, and it was enormously successful. For his far-reaching, visionary work in Savannah, Scott Hudgens was named Savannah's Citizen of the Year in 1969. Hudgens also "hit a home run," according to Williams, since he sold Oglethorpe Mall before the 1974 real estate crunch, clearing out much of his debt. Years later, the area would get Savannah Mall built even further south than the Hudgens mall.

Around 1970, Hudgens became interested in a venture with the Department of Housing and Urban Development, a 7,000 acre "new cities" program, called Shenandoah, near Newnan off Interstate 85. Hudgens soon brought in a new partner, Herman Russell, a minority drywall contractor, to the venture. HUD was to monitor and subsidize the development of the residential community.

The venture began with initial development of the commercial and multi-family aspects, including a 2,500 acre industrial park. But only 200 residential homes were built, as Hudgens and Russell found it took forever to get HUD approvals, and key decisions were constantly being made by new people coming to HUD. Besides Russell, Hudgens had brought the Union Bank of California into the project, and they had interested a REIT in Shenandoah about the time HUD decided to stop their participation in 1973, and terminated the program. The high cost of funds (financing was at 16 percent), and a downturn in the Atlanta real estate market at the time, had to be factors for Hudgens and Russell to get out of the project. Russell says: "We were the first in Georgia to take on a HUD project of this type, and originally we got a $47 million grant to develop the new town. We were ahead of our time, and we didn't lose money. We jump-started what you see around Shenandoah today. It just did not take off as fast as we wanted it to. I was proud of what we did, and know Scott was too. We were the first in the South with a new city that size under the HUD program." There were 2,800 people employed at the Shenandoah industries, including a two million square foot K-Mart distribution center, when Hudgens and Russell terminated their efforts there.

This initial effort between Hudgens and Russell led to many more ventures together, including purchasing the Equifax headquarters in Atlanta and leasing it back to them; buying the Rhodes Center in downtown Atlanta; and, venturing on some 5,000 acres in Cherokee County which turned into high-end residential development.

One of Hudgens' first commercial projects in Gwinnett was building the 145,000 square foot Lawrenceville Square shopping center in 1972 in an urban renewal area on the south side of town. Hudgens interested the Lawrenceville Belk store in locating from near the downtown square to the new location, and also pulled in another key tenant, Big Star supermarket, to the area. The Belk store was much larger, at 24,000 square feet, than the store uptown. Belk expanded to 32,000 square feet in the late 1970s.

A major development came for Hudgens in 1973: the sale of two Hudgens' companies, his giant mortgage company and his Spratlin-Harrington Insurance Service Company, which was the third largest independent agency in Georgia. The mortgage and insurance firms were acquired by Union Bank of Los Angeles, Calif. Included was the mortgage firm's $350 million loan portfolio. The sale of this firm, plus the sale of Oglethorpe Mall and the land nearby, allowed Hudgens to pay for all his vacant land and "not owe a dime" just prior to the recession of the mid-1970s.

Begins concentrating on Gwinnett

During the 1970s, Hudgens began to concentrate more on Gwinnett County, since the family had recently moved there. In 1972, he began developing Howell Station, a 1,600 acre planned unit development for some 2,000 multi-family dwellings in Duluth, plus some 300 single family homes. It also had three neighborhood shopping centers and multi-building medical facilities. He also began to focus on commercial tracts in River Green Industrial Park, a 290-acre business park, once Peachtree Industrial Boulevard came northward. Toward 1980, Hudgens also began selling off prime home lots along the Chattahoochee River at a subdivision called "Sweetbottom Plantation," where sprawling homes selling for between $350,000 to $1 million were built in low-country style, featuring garages on the lower level, and living on floors two and three, as seen at marsh and coastal areas along the Atlantic Ocean.

After the Sweetbottom development, Hudgens almost entirely concentrated on commercial development. He never forgot his roots. Very quietly, he began buying land near his boyhood home in Union City, and began assembling land in Gwinnett County, near Interstate 85. By 1978, Hudgens planned to build five more shopping centers. He would do more than that.

As Hudgens turned his attention to the area where he was raised, his goal was to open a mall at Union Point. In the meantime, Hudgens had been negotiating to open another mall in DeKalb County. But another real estate company, Carter and Associates, was also seeking to develop a mall in South DeKalb County. Hudgens held a key piece of land that Carter needed, and worked out a deal with Dick Rich that he would sell Carter the real estate for the South DeKalb Mall if Rich would agree to become a tenant at Shannon Mall at Union Point. Negotiations were successful, and Hudgens began efforts toward Shannon Mall, which he opened in 1982. It was at Shannon that Hudgens first became associated with Cadillac Fairview, the shopping center firm. Shannon Mall was opened at a bad time for business, and Hudgens brought Cadillac Fairview in to make it a joint venture project. Hudgens had assembled 800 acres for the site, and eventually developed 850 apartment units and other commercial activities there. The mall opened anchored by Rich's, Sears and Davison's. Later J.C. Penney would come to this mall.

Earlier, Hudgens' attention went far southward, as he determined that the Valdosta, Ga. area needed more retail shopping activity. In 1983, he opened a regional mall there of 450,000 square feet, anchored by Belk-Hudson, Sears and J.C. Penney. Hudgens also had periphery land consisting of 55 acres, which he also developed, an idea that came to him out of owning land around Oglethorpe Mall, which would serve him well later.

Hudgens' commitment to land along Interstate 85 at Pleasant Hill Road in Gwinnett was soon getting his attention. He had put together some 500 acres on what had been a mobile home community, having land on most of the corners tied up. Seeking to put a mall on this location was not easy. One of his key prospects, Dick Rich, thought the location was in the wrong place, and too far outside the perimeter highway. Tom Van Houten picks it up: "But Scott had driven all over Gwinnett, North Fulton and Cobb, and figured out where the mall would work best. He thought it was at Pleasant Hill Road." Hudgens, with his canny ability at locating facilities, held out, and signed three major tenants, Macy's, Sears and eventually Rich's, to locate at what would become known as Gwinnett Place Mall. Involved with Hudgens at the Gwinnett Place Mall as a 50-50 partner was Cadillac Fairview Shopping Centers.

Tom Wheeler tells the story of the zoning application for Gwinnett Place mall. "It was Scott's first big commercial venture in Gwinnett. At the zoning hearing, when the subject came up, Scott was the only person who stood up and spoke to the issue. Can you imagine how many people would pack a zoning of this significance today?" The Gwinnett County Commission was committed to the project, to the point of making inspections easier by placing a trailer office for a building inspector at the mall site, since so many inspections would be needed. That same process of having a building inspector from the county on site also took place when the Mall of Georgia was being built. "It was good for the county, making it easier to get to the inspections, and also helped speed the development of both malls," Wheeler says.

Before the mall opened on February 1, 1984, Gwinnett County was the largest county east of the Mississippi River without a mall within its borders. The mall opened at 1.1 million square feet, at the time the largest in Georgia. Hudgens got the key tenants to move the mall a considerable distance off the major thoroughfares, giving more room for outparcels on all four sides of the mall. The mall took up 108 of the 500 acre tract. It was the first time in Georgia, and one of the first in the country, to have the key mall location off the main streets, and when the land surrounding the mall was built out, it gave the area something of an urban center atmosphere. In came specialty shopping centers surrounding the mall, including financial institutions, restaurants, eventually hotels, and within a few years, one automobile dealer after the other, often locating next to one another. This was another Hudgens visionary concept, since auto dealers had not been bunched together near a mall before. Today that is commonplace around malls. Two more anchor tenants came to the Gwinnett Place Mall in expansions: Mervyns in 1986 and Parisian in 1993.

Tom Van Houten feels that Gwinnett Place was the big financial breakthrough for Hudgens. "When he sold the Savannah property, he had a clear $6 million. He had other properties in his wife's name, and decided to put that $6 million into land at Gwinnett Place. He told me 'I'm going to take a shot at buying property in Gwinnett County. If it fails, I'll be able to live on what I have already, and I can start over.'"

With the almost immediate acceptance of Gwinnett Place Mall by local and North Georgia shoppers, outparcel closings skyrocketed. Ralph Williams, Hudgens' real estate attorney, says that he and his associate, Jane Smith, closed $200 million in outparcel sales in one year alone. And major closings continued for several years, as first one chain store after another chose to have a Gwinnett location near its mall.

Even Hudgens admitted that Gwinnett Place was his most successful venture, prior to his development of the Mall of Georgia. But he also realized that "Savannah was just as good," for the amount of capital and size. "Savannah was the first shopping center where we kept the land around it to develop as a planned unit."

Just what impact Gwinnett Place had on Gwinnett County can be seen in looking at the county's tax digest. During the 1983-93 period, the county tax digest (the value of all property) grew a whopping 274 percent! But in the area where the mall was located, Martin's District, the tax digest grew 780 percent. Even the guy who started it all, Scott Hudgens himself, was overwhelmed. He said: "I have never seen any place develop like Gwinnett Place did."

Earlier, Hudgens had offered to include Cadillac Fairview in the outparcels at Shannon Mall, but that firm declined. They also declined to participate in the land surrounding Gwinnett Place Mall, though they were partners with Hudgens in the mall itself. Van Houten says that sale of the surrounding land at Gwinnett Place was good for Hudgens, and not participating taught Cadillac Fairview a lesson, for they participated with Hudgens on his next mall venture's surrounding land. "Scott got liquid and comfortable after Gwinnett Place. Prior to that he did not have liquid capital."

Hudgens stayed busy in the 1980s, as he expanded his scope in another direction, with the groundbreaking for a mall in Brunswick, Ga. in 1984. He opened Glynn Place Mall in February of 1985; it was a 507,000 square foot regional center, with three of his previous clients as tenants---Sears, J.C. Penney and Belk-Hudson. The mall itself was a 100 acre site, with 275 additional surrounding acres for future development, which soon came. Later would come an expansion of this mall area to include an eight-screen theatre, a 130-suite hotel and a K-Mart.

So, since 1982, Hudgens had opened Shannon, Valdosta, Gwinnett Place and Glynn Place Malls, just one away from his earlier stated goal. But he was far from done. A run-down Columbia Mall in DeKalb County got Hudgens' attention. Here's how.

Once Gwinnett Place opened, work was underway by another developer to open a second mall in Cobb County (Cumberland Mall was the first). Dick Rich asked Hudgens to look at the proposed site, which was off Barrett Parkway west of Interstate 75. Hudgens told Rich that it was "a good site, but not the best site." That prompted Rich to ask where was the best, and Hudgens showed him a site not too far away, but east of Interstate 75 and between there and Interstate 575. When Rich saw the site, he asked if Hudgens could put together the land, which Hudgens then began.

By then, the other major department store in Atlanta, Davison's, had been won over by the developer working on the site west of I-75. But Hudgens knew that Davison's, located at Columbia Mall, was interested in closing that location. He went to Sears, the owner of the mall, and asked: "If I can get the land between I-75 and I-575, will you come to that site? If so, I will buy Columbia Mall and let you out of your lease," he told Sears. They agreed. Then he picked up the telephone, told Davison's of the location in Cobb, and said that since he was buying Columbia Mall, he would let them out of their lease there if they would come to the Cobb County site, which would become Town Center. Bruce Williams remembers: "He did it all that day before noon." Together with Rich's, all three major tenants opened in February of 1986 at Town Center. Later, Mervyns would become the fourth tenant at Town Center in 1986, followed by Parisian in 1992. At Town Center, Hudgens put together around 150 acres, and had Cadillac Fairview Shopping Center as his partner, both on the mall and in the surrounding land.

By 1985, Columbia Mall, renamed now as Belvedere Mall, was ready to re-open, after an extensive $4.5 million renovation. It contained 325,000 square feet, anchored by Macy's Clothes Outlet and a theatre.

Among top malls in the country

Another aspect of the success that Hudgens and Cadillac Fairview had at both Gwinnett Place and Town Center: the two malls were among the top five percent of malls across the country in annual sales per square foot.

Keeping a strong running of mall openings, Hudgens had negotiated to purchase Lakeshore Mall in Gainesville with the owners, the Bank of Boston. Hudgens said of this venture: "I had been looking at Gainesville for 20 years, and went up there in one afternoon and bought it." Ralph Williams remembers hearing from Hudgens in 1986 on a Monday that he needed to go to Boston and close that purchase by the end of the week, four days away. "When our team went up there, we would work 18 hour days, and some would work overnight, to make sure we closed it by the end of the week, which was that company's fiscal year end. But we pulled it off."

Lakeshore had two anchors, Belk and J.C. Penney. Once renovated, Hudgens brought in Sears to the mall as it reopened in October of 1987, with Gov. Zell Miller heading the ribbon-cutting.

In his final effort in renovation of malls, Hudgens returned to where he had started, to North DeKalb Mall. He re-purchased the mall, renovated it and re-christened it in 1988 as Market Square at North DeKalb. This included expanding the mall in a joint venture with Cadillac Fairview, and bringing in new tenants, Lechmere and Mervyns, in addition to Rich's.

Hudgens had quite a run at bringing retail shopping to many areas of Georgia. Look at the chronology of mall openings and renovations Hudgens accomplished just in the 1980s:

- 1982: Shannon Mall
- 1983: Valdosta Mall
- 1984: Gwinnett Place
- 1985: Glynn Place and Avondale Mall
- 1986: Town Center at Cobb
- 1987: Lakeshore Mall
- 1988: Market Square at North DeKalb

In these short seven years, he opened five new malls, and redeveloped three. But he wasn't through. Enter Ben Carter, who remembers how he met Scott.

"I was out of college and getting into real estate, and decided to specialize around the airport, back about 1980. I saw Scott's name on his building, and picked up the phone. His secretary, Betty Wickes, set up a lunch at Scott's office. He asked what I was doing this afternoon, and for the next three and a half hours we drove around Clayton County, East Point and Forest Park. He would point out pieces of land, and tell me what he thought would happen, this as warehousing, another for hotels, which would be parking lots, or office space or housing.

"Ninety percent of the time he was dead-on true to what happened. I worked my business plan off what Scott had told me for three years. And I kept up with Scott. Once I got a contract on a property which Scott had listed, and he said to come see him the next day. Meanwhile, a snow storm hit Atlanta, and I went snow sledding the next day. But the following day I walked into Scott's office, telling him my contract was at the price he had listed the property, and the terms were acceptable to my client.

"Scott told me he had sold the property the previous day, when I had been snow sledding, when another Realtor had put snow chains on his tires and brought him a contract. The property was where the Ramada Renaissance hotel is located now. Scott said: 'Ben, let me tell you something. You're 24 years old and should have had chains on your car yesterday.' I'll always remember that."

Over the years, Carter and Hudgens often met. Later, when Carter felt he wanted to concentrate more on Gwinnett, he visited Hudgens at his farm near Hoschton. "We did the same driving around like we did on the south side of town, driving around Gwinnett for half a day. He took me to the county commission, introduced me to Lillian Webb and others, and gave me an introduction to Gwinnett. I worked that afternoon for the next five years. It was unbelievable what vision he had for what land would turn into what use.

"A few years later, I got an idea of locating major malls, visiting Scott and telling him where I thought they would be. He told me, 'I've already tied up the sites you mentioned in Canton and Fayetteville. You can forget Cumming, for there's a new site at North Point. But I'll work with you on the site in Gwinnett between I-85 and I-985.'"

That was the start of Hudgens' last mall, the Mall of Georgia, on which he and Carter were 50-50 partners, with Hudgens putting the land together. The two later brought in Corporate Property Investors, which owned Lenox and Northlake Malls, to purchase half of the Mall of Georgia interest. Carter says: "When Scott died, his estate and I continued to work on it, and together we sold our half of the Mall of Georgia to Simon Property Group, which by then had bought out Corporate Property Investors."

The Mall of Georgia at Mill Creek would become an even bigger venture, opening at 1.5 million square feet on 500 acres and landing even more major tenants than Hudgens' other malls. Original tenants included Nordstrom, J.C. Penney, Lord & Taylor and Dillard's. Rich's would open a year later, and eventually change its name to Macy's. The overall atmosphere was upscale. Meanwhile, outparcels continued to be key to this project for Hudgens, as major firms began to ring the mall with additional shopping. In total, Hudgens developed two million square feet of outparcel activity at the Mall of Georgia.

Interestingly, the Mall of Georgia opened on August 13, 1999, which coincidentally, was Hudgens' 75th birthday.

Meanwhile, Hudgens had originally tied up 500 acres of land in Cherokee County -- a project which later became known as Riverstone. He assembled 150 acres in Fayette County for what was completed as Fayetteville Pavilion. He sold both of these sites to other groups for them to develop. He also began work on a mall near Lithonia, but thought that area was growing too slowly, and sold his interest in this venture.

Turns more toward charity

Toward the middle of the 1990s, Mr. Hudgens began to have several health problems, primarily with his heart and back. But he never wavered in trying to keep going, and complete many of the projects he had in mind.

His efforts turned more toward charitable activities, though he once stated: "I find it easier to make money than to give it away." One reason it was so difficult to place charitable dollars was that he wanted his monies used in the most efficient and best manner to help others. He didn't want to throw any money away on unworthy causes.

He deliberately concentrated on larger projects, particularly for Gwinnett County. Among them were his funding to expand the Gwinnett Children's Shelter; the upgrading of facilities for 24-hour care at Annandale at Suwanee; and his complete funding of land, construction and the operation of Peachtree Christian Hospice.

A close friend over the years was former Governor George Busbee, who had moved to land near Sweetbottom Plantation. Knowing how extensive the Hudgens charitable efforts were, Busbee was among those who strongly suggested that Mr. Hudgens allow himself to come out of the anonymous category when giving to charities, and let his extensive charitable activities be known.

Busbee put it this way: "I told Scott that he owed it to his grandchildren and descendants. His giving showed that he was not only a successful developer and businessman, but that he demonstrated his real character. The nature of his gifts demonstrated that, aimed at children, the needy, and the less fortunate, including older people.

"I also told him that his gifts reflected his upbringing. He learned a trade, and now is trying to help people become skilled in an economic sense. Descendants need to know who the real Scott Hudgens was. I also suggested that his gifts would entice others to make similar gifts." That resulted in a report in *The Atlanta Journal-Constitution's Gwinnett EXTRA* that over the course of several years, Mr. Hudgens and his family foundation has given more than $25 million to local charities.

Hudgens' anonymity regarding his charitable giving was considerably different and ironic from the public persona of Hudgens, as he himself admitted. "While we have always in the past given to charity anonymously," he said, "For years, my name in neon lights was atop the length of a building I owned off Interstate 85 near the airport. That sign stayed up long after I sold my companies located there. Everyone saw it. But since we took the name down in 1978, we have been less public, and all our giving over the years was pretty much anonymous."

Recognizing Scott Hudgens' philanthropy, two organizations now give awards in memory of Mr. Hudgens. The Gwinnett Chamber of Commerce recognizes a charitable institution (or sometimes a person involved with humanitarian causes in the community) in memory of Scott Hudgens. The language says the award is to "the charitable institution which best exemplifies the spirit of compassion and generosity to which Scott Hudgens was so deeply committed." It was first presented at the annual meeting of the Chamber in January, 2004. Winners have included the Peachtree Christian Hospice, late Gov. George Busbee, Hi-Hope Service Center, Gwinnett Children's Shelter, and Annandale at Suwanee.

The second award is given by the Peachtree Christian Hospice of Duluth, which Mr. Hudgens conceived and funded. The Hospice established the "Scott Hudgens' Good and Faithful Servant" Award in his memory. That award goes to an individual who "exemplifies the unselfish spirit of love and caring for the people and the genuine interest in the community" that Mr. Hudgens showed. The first award was presented in 2003 to the Hudgens Family, in honor of the life and gifts of Mr. Hudgens. The awards in subsequent years have gone to the late George Busbee, Jim Cowart, Malon Mimms, Kathryn Willis and Dr. Jeffrey Nugent.

One final project

A trip to mark the 50th anniversary of D-Day that Scott took with youngest son, Dallas, would set the stage for another major Hudgens gift that he would make, this time to the entire nation.

Visiting the giant American cemetery on a bluff overlooking Omaha Beach in Normandy, France, Scott got an idea. He had earlier purchased 770 acres of undeveloped and pristine land near Canton in Cherokee County, Ga. Once visiting the American cemetery in France, he realized what he wanted to do with that land: make it a gift as a national cemetery for United States veterans.

One of the key individuals who worked with Hudgens on this venture was U.S. Senator Max Cleland. In an earlier stint in Washington, Cleland had headed the Veteran's Administration. With this background, he knew the need for a national military cemetery in the Southeastern United States. He says: "The National Cemetery in Marietta was full, and the average Georgia military veteran was having to go out of state in order to be buried in a National Cemetery." At one time, a 300 acre site at Ft. Gillem was under consideration, but political maneuvering scuttled that effort, Cleland says.

Hudgens invited Cleland to his farm near Hoschton in 1997, and showed him his plans, telling the Senator that he wanted "to do it for my war-time buddies." Hudgens had the area fully engineered, with drawings of the proposed plans and topographical maps. "He told me it was the most pristine, beautiful hardwood forest that he had ever seen. You could see the Blue Ridge Mountains from there, and it bordered the Etowah River, and you could see Lake Allatoona from there. He wanted to donate it as a National Cemetery." The land rises from 850 feet above sea level to more than 1,200 feet.

But it was only the beginning of what took four years before approval could be obtained from the Veteran's Administration. The VA had to determine if other sites were also available, environmental studies authorized by the VA had to be done, etc., as well as money had to be appropriated before anything could happen. Eventually, the Hudgens property was determined as the most desirable site.

In July, 2000, some months before Mr. Hudgens died, he completed the donation of the land to the Veteran's Administration. The VA included the project in the FY 2002 budget, and the family presented the deed to the land in a ceremony in Washington on April 3, 2001. Work was begun on the project in 2002, laid out primarily as Mr. Hudgens has initially conceived. It is anticipated that the cemetery will provide burial space to 135,000 veterans, and could be in use as a final burial spot for over 50 years. The first internment at the cemetery was on April 4, 2006. By mid-2008, more than 2,000 veterans had been buried in the cemetery.

Several associates of Scott Hudgens say that along with his funding of the Peachtree Christian Hospice, his donation of this land for a veteran's cemetery is his proudest accomplishment.

In a reflective mood one day, Scott Hudgens was talking about his ability to be successful. He said he looked upon his talent "As God-given, with a purpose." He added: "As a developer, God gave me the talent and the obligation to furnish jobs for people."

Scott Hudgens did so with an outright zeal, relishing in completing deals relatively quickly, always wanting to maintain high quality in his work, and continually moving forward. He did it happily with his God-given obligation in mind, maintaining, "I've never had a day off."

Hudgens in World War II

(Author's Note: Over the years, Scott Hudgens and I talked numerous times about his World War II military days. The war made a profound impact on Mr. Hudgens. His close comrades from the war became important to him. Mr. Hudgens often gathered together men who were in his unit during the war, having them visit him for weekends at his farm near Hoschton, or at times, even transporting them to New York, where they became virtual regulars at The Carlyle Hotel. This section will explore various aspects of the war as it related to Mr. Hudgens as his unit fought across Europe.)

Scott Hudgens and his unit, the 974th Ordnance Evacuation Company of the 746 Tank Battalion, First Army ("Big Red One"), under Gen. Omar Bradley, hit Omaha Beach on D-Day, June 6, 1944. Over the course of the next nine months, they would participate in campaigns at:

- Omaha Beach
- Hedgerows
- Battle of the Bulge
- Rhineland to Cologne
- Harz Mountains.

Eventually his unit was halted at the Elbe River, as they linked up with the Russian Army near Leipzig. There they were surprised: "The Russians were Cossacks, and they were riding horses," Scott remembered. "Not only that, but they had every kind of equipment there was to fight a war, and also brought along their women."

When the war was declared over, the thoughts of virtually every American were centered on getting home. The Army devised a point system to determine who would rotate back the earliest, with those in the heaviest fighting being ranked ahead of those with less intense combat. "You had to have 75 points, or else you would be on the list to go to the Pacific campaign, and with 85 points, you got to go home." Scott said, "And I had 86 points. My Purple Heart pushed me over the top" and he was expecting to come home soon. But he got delayed.

"They kept us near Kassel, Germany during most of the summer of 1945 with the Occupation, and re-classified us according to the number of points we had. We had been shipped back by train from Germany to Le Havre, France the last of August, to catch a ship home. There were a lot of delays in getting a ship for our outfit. In early October, I borrowed $40 from James Casey (his future brother-in-law) and got approval from a colonel for a pass to go to Paris." There he stayed several days where he found a friend running an Army hotel. "We had nice sheets, and good food. It was great there," Scott said. By the time he caught a bus back to Le Havre, his unit had shipped out. Going to see that same colonel, who was upset with Scott for overstaying his pass, Scott got re-routed, via a train all the way south in France to Marseilles. Six weeks later, he got on a "slow boat" (14 days) home. He arrived back just before Thanksgiving, 1945, and got out of the Army November 28.

As part of the invasion of France, Hudgens' squad landed on D-Day on Omaha Beach, after crossing the English Channel in a small British LCT, which carried two vehicles, and about 12 men. Scott said that "Waves were breaking over the LCT. The ship circled around once before we went in, and we drove off the ramp. We had as much ammunition and gas we could pile on. When we got in, the American troops had already gained the top of the hill at Omaha Beach. When we landed, we knew we had been put off in the wrong place. Everything on the beach was mixed up, and it took 3-4 days before they sorted it all out."

The drivers of vehicles being unloaded were told to drive as slowly as they could down the ramp, says Charlie Zammit, a member of Scott's unit from Lake Ronkonkoma, N.Y. "They had waterproofed the vehicle's exhaust and manifold, but the engine would be under water. Once the driver felt his wheels hit the sand of the ocean floor, he was to go as fast as he could to get up to the beach."

A model of the tank retriever Scott Hudgens drove in World War II in Europe.

Scott says: "Once on the beach, we went up in stages. But it wasn't cleared of Germans. How we got half the people up without getting all killed amazed me. Had it not been for a few non-coms and an officer or two, the whole operation would have gone to hell." It took members of his company several days to link up with one another.

The mission of Scott's unit was to recover tanks, shoving American or German tanks out of the way of the advancing Army, or retrieving tanks for repair to get them back into service.

His M-25 retriever was a massive truck, a 40-ton vehicle, with 10 wheels. It had armor plating, and pulled a 40-wheel trailer to haul recovered tanks. One description of it was "a gigantic, oversize truck with a long skeletonized trailer," with room for two tanks. Scott drove the vehicle, which had room for five members of the crew---himself, his sergeant, Virgil Schumacher of Waldo, Wis., and three riggers. The unit had a wench and boom on it for lifting the incapacitated tanks. "We were to push the tanks, German or US, though mostly German, or other large equipment, off the road. We didn't fool with the small stuff."

Hudgens' unit headed toward St. Mere Eglise, a small village nearby, where the 82nd Airborne had parachuted in, but first his unit had to cross a marshy area. There they ran across the first of the problems of the hedgerows, which for centuries had been routinely used as fences in this agricultural area of Normandy. "Many of the hedgerows would be six foot tall or more, and about that wide, and they were Hawthorne bushes, with lots of prickly stickers on them." The hedges were tightly ingrown "so thick that you couldn't shoot a rifle shot straight through them," Scott said. The hedges also resisted efforts of tanks to break through. "The tanks' front ends would bow up on the hedgerow, which would not give way, while the tracks of the vehicle were spinning," Scott said. Hedgerows would become more and more of a problem in the flat Normandy area for the entire Army, something the American planners had not counted on. This slowed the American advancement considerably.

Scott also explained one way the hedgerow problem was solved. "There was a PFC from upstate New York by the name of Drake who solved it. The Germans had taken steel rails, like you use on the railroad, and driven them down into the beaches all along the way to stop our vehicles from getting onto the beach. Somehow we got around them. But there the rails were on the beach.

"This PFC welded one rail across the front of a tank, then welded to that rail two rails sticking out in front, like a fork lift. Then the tanks would ram the hedgerow straight on with this fork lift-like tank and as it bowed up, lift the hawthorns out by their roots, clearing the way for vehicles or troops to get through. That PFC just figured it out, and it worked all across the front."

Slowly Hudgens' unit moved westward toward Cherbourg, where the Americans were trying to cut off the Germans, and gained control of the town and harbor. He had landed with a group of 64 from his company, with the bulk of his company coming in later. Hudgens says: "Our unit was always up there in the spearhead, near the first ones to enter an area. Cherbourg was a real battle. They slaughtered a lot of our guys there. We had a timetable to take Cherbourg and have its port in operation in 30 days, but it sure cost us a lot of men." Scott's team of soldiers "must have put 100 tanks back into action. We got 'em as quick as they got hit, pulling them back so we could check if they were salvageable. And virtually every tank we had to pull out of the way usually had two dead bodies in it. I pulled a lot of men out of them. We were between the infantry and the artillery, which meant we were right in the thick of things. We never were more than 10 miles off the front lines."

Lewis Thompson of Birmingham, Ala, a private first class with Scott in his truck, recalls a day that they were on a hill overlooking Cherbourg, and taking a break, watching German Messerschmitt fighter planes and P-47s engage in a dogfight.

"That's when Ernie Pyle, the war correspondent, caught up with us," Thompson says. Pyle wrote a dispatch which appeared in many American newspapers (and later published in his book, *Brave Men,* on page 425). It says about Scott: "(He) was a smiling, tall young fellow, with clipped hair---Dallas Hudgens, from Stonewall, Georgia. He was feeling stuffed as a pig, for he'd just got a big ham from home and had been having at it with a vengeance." (Stonewall is near Union City, on Roosevelt Highway, in Metro Atlanta.)

Scott explains: "By then, our company had finally caught up with us, since part of us went ahead of the main body. It was the first time since I landed that I had seen the rest of our company in two months. We had just returned from the front, and we had a shower. My mother had blocked (squared off) a big cured ham, and sent it. The mail, including the ham, caught up with us in Cherbourg. It was just as good as it could be. We were there fiddling around with our mess kits and a little bread and stuff when Pyle showed up and we shared some of it with him." He adds: "When my name appeared in a story Pyle filed from Cherbourg, my mother got copies of that article in different newspapers from people all over the United States." People wanted Mrs. Hudgens to know that her son was all right overseas. Pyle's dispatches were a vehicle for communications with the American people, relieving many parents of some of their anxiety over their sons being overseas.

The first time that Scott saw Pyle "was when the Ninth Division was fighting to get into Cherbourg. Pyle was a little guy, who was bent over running as fast as he could, without a rifle, and crossing a road when I saw him. This was near a German pillbox in the corner of the road in downtown Cherbourg. Pyle was with the infantry there, and always seemed to be up front with the fighting."

Scott said about sanitation during the early stages of the war: "I had worn the same clothing all the way from two weeks before D-Day until after Cherbourg, 6-8 weeks or more. That's when I got rough. You can really get 'seasoned' in such times. I was glad to get that shower!"

As Americans advanced through the French villages, Scott said that "the French were so happy to see us, crying and carrying on, shouting and singing. These people were real kind to us. You just sensed it, far different later in Germany than we saw in France or Belgium."

Soon the American Army had secured the Cherbourg peninsula, and turned eastward, toward St. Lo, where the Germans had holed up. "We worked at St. Lo to clear the roads, in marshes often, pushing the tanks off the road. That was about August 1 and after that time, we never got a day off much. We got into St. Lo with the First Division, but that Division was pulled back, I guess to give them a rest, and the 30th Division took their place. Soon after, they had to throw the First Division back in below us. I remember we were under continuous attack during August 13, my 21st birthday.

"At one time, the Germans got to within 200-300 yards of us at Mortain, and kept counter-attacking. That was the worst battle I ever was in, and the dead were stacked on top of one another for about two miles as we went in. They were mostly German bodies, but GI's, too. Our troops were up on the hill, and they came at us. That's why there were more German bodies. Even Ike (General Dwight Eisenhower) said you could not go for two miles without stepping on the dead. Along the way there was about every kind of equipment blown up or throw away."

Retrieving tanks was a different experience, requiring several skills. Scott said: "Several of us were trained to drive about every type of vehicle we had, including German ones, too.

The German Tiger tank was better than ours. I drove a captured one once down a road. I tell you, I was scooting. We wanted to get it back intact to the English Channel dock to send it home so our engineers could study it. I believe they used diesel for Tigers. Most of what Germans had was diesel, and we were gradually switching to diesel, for it didn't flame up real fast like gasoline, so was less dangerous in fighting."

There were constant calls for the retriever units. "Our job was to get the tanks back when they were hit, so they could be repaired and get back to fighting. We got 'em out and put hundreds and hundreds of tanks back into action."

Charlie Zammit was driving a reconnaissance Jeep and in Scott's unit. He adds: "Each morning my sergeant and I would go to Seventh Corps headquarters and get maps of where we were to keep the main supply routes open each day. We would then run back to the company area, where our heavy vehicles were, and determine where the units would be dispatched. We were to keep the routes open so that the advancing troops would not be held up. Our unit was created for the purpose of clearing the routes and recovering units. Our unit stayed together until V-E-Day."

Meanwhile, the American Army was moving. "You hear so much about the Third Army, and General George Patton," Scott said, "And we were attached to Patton for a while. But the First and Seventh Corps made the breakthrough to Cherbourg, then also made the breakthrough at Mortain."

Once the Allies fought their way through Normandy, the Army moved quickly across northern France. Lewis Thompson said that their unit went through Paris as it was being liberated. "The snipers were still there, but the people and the celebration were something else. People were laughing and hugging you, and trying to pour cognac down you. They had been mistreated so long by the German occupation, and they could not believe they were being liberated. Scott and a bunch of us went through there, though we didn't stay overnight in Paris, as our company moved on outside Paris."

By September, Hudgens' unit had been the first to The Netherlands, and was at Aachen, Germany by September 12, 1944. But the Germans repelled the Americans, and the forces retreated before Christmas from Aachen back over the Belgian border, setting the stage for Hudgens' third campaign, the Battle of the Bulge.

It was in the dead of winter that the Battle of the Bulge began. It started December 23, 1944, according to Scott, and continued until near the end of February, 1945. James Summerville, a sergeant in another squad in Scott's unit, from Gadsden, Ala., says: "They had us surrounded at one point, and they sent in the 101st Airborne to help us out."

Hudgens wins Purple Heart

It was in the Hertgen Forest, south of Aachen near the Siegfried Line, that Hudgens got hit by shrapnel in the back, and was awarded a Purple Heart. Years later, Hudgens was downplaying the wounds. "This was in November, and it got dark early there, about 4 p.m. The Germans would send up aircraft at dusk, and their pilots would spot any movement and attack. They had just brought up the chow truck and this German plane made a circle around us, then came back with anti-personnel bombs, which scattered into smaller bombs. It killed everyone around me. It really tore up the 28th Division there. It seemed like everyone in the squad was wounded, including Jackie's brother, James Casey. Four or five pieces hit me, but I had dived for a forked tree, and that saved me. They helped me get to an aid station by loading me on a truck. I was in so much better shape than the others that I was about ashamed to say anything. Finally, they patched me up, and I never did go to the hospital. They took James to the hospital, but another guy and I took a vehicle and went back for James. The wounds for me weren't all that bad."

Lewis Thompson remembers that attack. "Charlie Zammit and I were on reconnaissance that night, and I guess that's the reason we didn't get hit. We had spent the night in tents in the Hertgen Forest, or we would have been hit, too."

There was constant bombardment of the unit when in the Hertgen Forest, Thompson says. "When those 88s came in, they made the weirdest noise. You had to find a foxhole somewhere, but they could hit you there, too. Artillery was further away, but mortars were a real big problem, for you were near the Germans firing at you. They could see you and pinpoint you. If one mortar shell hit on one side of you, the second would hit on the other side. And if you were there when the third one hit, that would be the end of you."

Thompson says that for him, "The Battle of the Bulge was the hardest for us as a whole outfit. The biggest problem at the Bulge was that everything was so mixed up. The Germans had captured so much of our equipment and soldiers, and would take American uniforms and use Germans who spoke good English and knew about our country, and infiltrate us. They were infiltrating at Aachen in December, 1944, when we got orders to retreat. That was when they made their big push. Bad weather was in their favor, with snow and ice. We got orders to move back just before Christmas Eve, and I had never seen it snow so hard before. It was a real blizzard."

During the Battle of the Bulge, record cold temperatures and heavy snows hit the Hertgen Forest areas. Historians called it the "coldest, snowiest" winter people could remember. Scott told Ralph Williams that on many a night, it was so cold "We crawled under the tanks and all slept under there during the night, while we kept the engine running to keep from freezing to death." Charlie Zammit adds: "We didn't want to sleep on the icy, frozen ground, so our guys would get some boards from nearby buildings, and put them under the tank as insulation. The muffler exhaust would help keep us a little warmer, if you were lucky enough to have a tank to crawl under."

Scott said that it was February 20 when "we took our troops out of the Bulge, and headed for the Ruhr, getting to Duren on February 24. Our goal was to get to Cologne, and try to safeguard bridges for crossing the Rhine. The Germans stopped us and we got about two weeks rest. But then we went straight to Cologne on March 21. Then we crossed the bridge at Remagen about March 22, the first troops across. That's where I pulled a cable across the Rhine to the east side of the river. That cable was later used to secure a pontoon bridge after the Germans blew the Remagen bridge. We were fired upon as we went across. We got to the top of a hill, and had the higher bluff in a beachhead pocket. There was little resistance to start with on the East Bank. We kicked off 2-3 days later and headed toward Potsdam, going along the German autobahn. That's where we captured so many German prisoners."

The major battle in the Harz Mountains for Hudgens' unit took place at Kassel. But once past Kassel, the place that stuck in the mind of Hudgens, and others, was what they found when they took Nordhausen. Scott said: "We were going toward Berlin, but as we swung right near Patterhorn, the Third Armored Division got into a real dogfight in a forest nearby, with many casualties. Later, when the Division took Nordhausen, the Americans figured that the Germans put up such a defense to keep the Allies from seeing what was happening at Nordhausen.

"That was the first concentration camp we had relieved," Hudgens said, "And we never had proven that people were being cremated in gas chambers before we got there. One in my unit, PFC Kenneth Williams from Chester, W.Va., found a small German camera, and it had film in it, and we took pictures, which I still have, and though they were not good clear pictures, you could see that the Germans had stacked up dead bodies like cord wood. We found 4,000 corpses there. The Germans were trying to cremate the bodies in the ovens, but we got there before they could complete it. There were bodies dead in the yards, and others stacked up, four this way, four that way, by the ovens. The Americans put a tough Provost Marshal in command there, and threw up a cordon of MP's around the place. He ordered the German civilians to haul the dead people up to the top of a little hill outside town and bury them. He also ordered that they would put flowers on each of the graves." Scott also said that the German civilians in the town told the Americans that they were unaware of what was going on at Nordhausen, but Scott didn't believe it. Scott said: "It was bad. People just don't realize how bad it was."

Another member of Hudgens' truck crew, PFC Bernard Sipelstein of Brooklyn, N.Y., distinctly remembers Nordhausen, and in particular one incident. "A civilian German kid identified his mother and father as dead. We had the Germans dig a grave for them, and we lined the grave with an Army blanket, and put them together in the grave. I still get choked up a little bit when I think of it. Some of the German civilians handling the bodies of the dead wanted to use gloves, or take rags and put them around their hands, when handling the bodies. But we had them use their bare hands. I know it was a terrible thing for them, but our orders were to have them handle the bodies with their hands.....We saw the Holocaust right there."

Sipelstein and his wife were often guests of the Hudgens hospitality in Georgia, or visited with him on other occasions in New York. "Scott was a happy-go-lucky, fearless guy. I really miss him. He was a plain, down-to-earth man. There were no airs about him, in spite of his success."

It was at Nordhausen where the Americans captured V-2 rockets. Hudgens said: "The place was sealed off, and no newspapermen were allowed in. It never got in the newspapers. I think they shipped home 50 or more of the rockets for the scientists to test." One of the photos that Williams took with the German camera shows the front end of a V-2 rocket near the entrance to the salt mine where the V-2 work was going on.

After Nordhausen, the war slowed for Hudgens, as his unit moved to the Elbe River, where they were halted before crossing, and they met the Russians as the war ended.

Later, Hudgens' unit was pulled back to near Kassel, where they "lived like kings" for a couple of months. "When we took over this small village, we had it as good as you could get it. We slept in real beds, and were in houses. We had a chow line every day, and had beer stacked at the beginning of the line, at the end, and in the middle, too. Finally, one day they put us in a boxcar, and sent us to Le Havre, France. Charlie Zammit called Le Havre a "monster encampment. Units were waiting for the ships to take them home, and there were a lot of delays."

As bad as the war was, for Scott Hudgens, upon his return home, he got something else out of his friendship with one of his comrades, James Casey. Since Casey had shipped out with his unit in October, and Hudgens did not arrive back home until November, Hudgens wanted to look up Casey, and repay him the $40 he had borrowed to go to Paris.

Meets future wife

Hudgens said, "I found James in December of 1945, and he had left some clothes at a laundry, and was going by to pick the clothes up. His sister, Jackie, worked there as a bookkeeper." Scott also says, "When I saw her, James said 'Don't do it, Scott.' But I told him 'I am,'" and introduced himself to Jackie. At that time, Jackie was taking piano lessons, and that night, the two young war veterans accompanied her to a recital. Afterward, the three went out to eat. "On our first date," Jackie says, "They took me to The Varsity." Scott and Jackie began dating. The pair were married in February, 1947.

Hudgens and his Army comrades had reunions for 38 years. However, starting in 1983, Hudgens would personally get his closest mates from the war together, sending his Lear jet to pick them up from places around the country. They often went to Hillcrest Lodge, Hudgens' retreat near Hoschton. Several of them were spending the weekend there when Hudgens died unexpectedly.

Lewis Thompson was the last one of his comrades to talk to Scott. "We got there on Friday, and on Saturday did some fishing. That night the others had gone to bed, and Scott and I talked until about midnight, when he went to bed."

On Sunday morning, James Summerville remembers that he was surprised when Scott didn't get up early, just after him, as he usually did. "I knew he had stayed up late talking to Lewis, for Lewis was usually the last one to go to bed. That morning I didn't think anything about Scott not being up, though I looked in on him, and he seemed asleep, laying on his side, like he hadn't moved since he went to sleep." Later Summerville and Charlie Zammit checked on him again. Summerville says: "I hollered at him, and walked around his bed, and realized he wasn't breathing. I was never so shocked in all my life."

Three other former soldier-comrades of Scott were together that weekend: Besides Summerville, Zammit and Thompson, also present were Ken Williams of Chester, W. Va., and James Casey. By 2007, Williams and Casey were also dead.

Scott Hudgens had breathed his last, in the company of the people with whom he had bonded while in the war, and with whom he had been through many tough battles. He loved those guys for whom he would do anything. In their presence at the end, he went to rest.

Alice Strickland

Some people don't beat around the bush. Alice Strickland must have been like that. She was one of the most active citizens of Duluth, and the first female mayor in Georgia. Not only that, but she raised a family that became quite accomplished in their own circles.

Women weren't allowed to vote until the 19th amendment was ratified by sufficient states (the last being Tennessee) in 1920. The new law was enacted August 26, 1920. Women in Georgia first voted in 1921.

It was in 1906 that Duluth became incorporated as a city. By 1921, the local economy had slumped. A cotton shipping railhead, the town was suffering, since disease and insects had wrecked havoc on the cotton crop. The town was deteriorating, and Duluth found illegal liquor sales rampant.

Alice Harrell Strickland was from pioneer Forsyth County parents, having been born in 1859. At age 22 in 1881, she married Henry Strickland Jr., a lawyer and businessman, and moved to his home in Duluth, which had only been founded 10 years earlier when the railroad came through. Duluth, like some other towns, was "wide open" and had a problem with drunken brawls. (One of the reasons the Women's Christian Temperance Union had been founded in 1874 in Cleveland, Ohio, was because of such reputations and scenes across the country. The Georgia WCTS, comprised originally of mostly Methodist women, was founded in 1880. Mrs. Strickland was also Methodist.)

The Stricklands had seven children. All of them went to college, showing signs of their mother's pioneering spirit and courage. In 1897, the Strickland's home burned. She and her husband began to design a new home, which took eight years to complete. Theirs was a large Victorian house, on the east side of the railroad near the northern edge of town, a dominating, large, two story structure. It was completed in 1898. She continued to live in the house until her death in 1947. (The house was restored by her daughter, Ellyne, beginning in 1959. It still stands in 2008.)

In 1915, Henry Strickland died, when Alice was age 55. At this point, she was president of the local Civic Club. By now, only two of the children were still at home. Having a large house, Alice Strickland saw a need, and realized she could be of service. The need was for a clinic for the town. She offered the entire second floor of her home for this use. It included a prenatal clinic for women. Years later, old-time Duluth adults would remember "Miss Alice" putting them to bed upstairs when they had been sick as children.

The original clinic that Mrs. Strickland had started in her home later grew substantially, into first a stand-alone clinic, and in 1943, into Joan Glancy Hospital.

Mrs. Strickland was always a person who was known for her fierce determination and courage. She had become something of a conservationist. When linemen for a power company wanted to cut a path for power lines across her lands, she stood her ground. She sat holding a shotgun blocking the way. Later she would donate land for a community forest, to be used by children of Duluth for education and recreation. She led both children and adults in planting trees in the forest. This land became the first community forest in Georgia. Its outgrowth is today's millions of acres of conservation forests in Georgia, estimated at 10 percent of the forested land in the state. Mrs. Strickland was recognized by the American

Forestry Guild in 1923 on Mother's Day when a white birch tree was planted for her in the city park.

Her fame came from her opposition to alcoholic spirits. Some have called Duluth a bootlegger's paradise. There were routine drunken brawls and knife fights, and on most Saturday nights, the local "calaboose" (jail) filled. Often empty railroad box cars were used as a temporary jail.

Seeing all this, Alice Strickland determined a course. Though only recently registered to vote, she decided in the fall of 1922 to be a candidate for mayor. Her platform was simple: "I will clean up Duluth and rid it of demon rum."

According to the *News-Herald*, Mrs. Strickland defeated W.M. Dodson on Dec. 16, 1922, and served the following year as mayor. She took office at age 62. As mayor, she presided over city council and was the judge of the municipal court. She became known, as one person said, as "a very firm-minded person who stuck up for what she believed in." Jay Summerour, who later became Duluth postmaster, said she was "considerate of petty offenders but severe with those who willingly and flagrantly disregarded the rights of others."

Alice Harrell Strickland

Summerour told the story of how she dealt with one bootlegger:

"People in those days used to go riding in open touring cars. They called it 'airing out.' One day a high-powered car came through Duluth, down Main Street, going real fast, drawing attention (as a diversion) while a T Model Ford with a load of bootleg whiskey came down the road on the other side of the railroad tracks quietly....(but) the driver got boxed in and couldn't cross the railroad tracks. A policeman patrolling on foot saw him (the bootlegger) and arrested him. When he was brought before Mayor Strickland, she said, 'Young man, what were you doing?' 'Just airing out,' he replied. 'Well, just air out your pocketbook. That will be $99.99.' The legal limit for such a fine was $100."

On Dec. 16, 1923, Mrs. Strickland ran for a second term, but was defeated by H.B. Herron, with Mrs. Strickland receiving 15 votes. The Jan. 12, 1923 issue of the *Atlanta Constitution* reported that Mrs. Strickland was appointed to the town's Sanitary Committee.

About the Strickland children: look at their accomplishments:

Henry Jr.: Graduated from Georgia Tech, went to South America and built a road over the Andes Mountains. He later worked in Mexico and South Africa.

Harrell: Graduated from West Point, was in World War II and made the Army his career.

Glenn: Graduated from the U.S. Naval Academy, was a career Naval officer and later was one of the first Naval test pilots.

Anna Mary (Lewis): was a graduate of Wesleyan College.

Susie (McDonald): was a graduate of Brenau College and a teacher.

Charles: Attended Georgia Tech, but as World War I began, joined the Marines and never returned to college, but went to Florida. He was a real estate broker and sold Disneyworld thousands of acres of land.

Ellyne: Graduated from Duluth High at age 12; and a graduate of Brenau College. She was, at age 18, the second woman to obtain a degree from Emory Law School, and at age 25 received a Doctor of Law from Emory. She was a trial lawyer for the Department of Internal Revenue in Washington and eventually won conviction in prosecuting Al Capone for tax evasion.

* * * * *

Guy Ben Findley of Duluth, the great-grandson of Henry Strickland Jr., remembers that his grandfather went to South America to build sugar factories. He spoke several languages. But he told his offspring that he made more money unloading boats. Guy Ben reports: "They would get contracts to unload boats in a week. My grandfather would hire a gang and for every day they unloaded it before a week, he got a bonus." It must have worked. Guy Ben says Henry retired when he was about 40.

Alice Strickland would be pleased that in 1999, another female mayor of Duluth, Shirley Fanning-Lasseter, spoke at the unveiling of a historical marker in front of her home on Buford Highway. The marker reads:

"Alice Harrell Strickland (1859-1947) and her husband Henry built this home in 1898. The Stricklands raised seven children before Henry's death in 1915. Mrs. Strickland then became a community leader. With her service as Mayor of Duluth in 1922-23, she became Georgia's First Woman Mayor. Additionally, she served as Civic Club president, opened her home as a children's clinic since there was no hospital facility available, and led the community in forestry conservation with the donation of land for a community forest. Mrs. Strickland lived here until her death."

Yes, Mrs. Strickland was the first female to become mayor of a town in Georgia, and did so immediately after gaining the right to vote. Mrs. Strickland would be proud to know that, in 2008, there were more than 75 towns in Georgia with female mayors. Her efforts also led to women taking other positions in government. In the 2008 Georgia General Assembly, there were more than 46 female members.

Mrs. Strickland died in 1947, at age 88, leaving a rich legacy of civic duty.

Rhodes Jordan

Rhodes Jordan has an exemplary place in the history of Lawrenceville. He served off-and-on for eight terms as mayor of the city, winning and losing elections, but coming back again and again to serve as mayor.

Hilliard Rhodes Jordan, Sr. was a native of the city, born to Albert Barton Jordan, a farmer, and Maude Lee Jordan on October 16, 1918 in a house on Stone Mountain Street. His first name came from an uncle, and his second referenced a Dr. Rhodes, who delivered him during an influenza epidemic.

Rhodes' grandfather, Will Jordan, first moved his family to Gwinnett in 1909. His father, Albert Jordan, and grandfather eventually opened a general merchandise store, W.M. Jordan and Son, on the Courthouse Square in 1917. By age 12, Rhodes was working behind the counter, which gave the young man a front row seat to the busy activities of the community. After all, the store had one of the few telephones in town, and people came in often to use it. The store also served as the place where the fire call came, with young Rhodes often blowing the fire whistle!

Politics ran in the family. At one time, Will Jordan was appointed to run the pauper's home. Will was a Lawrenceville councilman in 1922. He served eight years. Albert Jordan served on the council in 1939 and won two terms and also won another term in 1946.

A significant year for young Rhodes was 1931, when he developed appendicitis, requiring hospitalization at Georgia Baptist Hospital. His mother stayed with him, but his father and sisters could not see him for three weeks. Even after returning home, he was still very sick, this time getting peritonitis, requiring a nurse to be with him. Soon after recovery from what was described as a "near death" experience, he joined the First Baptist Church.

He graduated from Lawrenceville High in 1936, with his studies including a class in "Expression" from Virginia Ezzard, an exacting teacher, where he learned to speak in public. Some thought he should become a minister, but he wanted to go to military school. He attended Georgia Military Academy, and later Emory University. He also continued to help his father in the store, but his father told him "You'll get nowhere working for me in the store." On the advice of his father, he entered Atlanta Law School. He was drafted in January of 1942 into the U. S. Navy and served as a signalman in the South Pacific during World War II. He worked his way up to Petty Officer, Second Class, by the time he was discharged in December of 1945.

When he returned from the war, Rhodes started back to law school in 1946. But he soon met Willela Allison from Cleveland, Ga., who had worked as a caseworker in Lawrenceville during the war. After an eight month courtship, they were married on August 30, 1946. Rhodes graduated from the Atlanta Law School and took the bar oath on August 11, 1947.

In 1947, he ran for the State House of Representatives as a Democrat and won. He served a term through 1948 and another term from 1953-54. Rhodes was best known for his eight terms as Lawrenceville mayor. In 1962, he was elected, and he won re-elections in 1964 and 1966. In 1968 and 1970, he was defeated by Bill Fortune. He won again in 1974 and 1976, was beaten in 1978, but was elected in 1980 and 1982. He continued to re-emerge as mayor, winning again in 1986. He was a local legend for his dedication to city politics, and for

Rhodes Jordan, Sr.

his memory. He frequently recalled events that occurred decades ago, remembering not only the day and the event but the time of day it occurred, what the weather was like that day, and who was there.

Rhodes was always active in his community. He was a member of the Lawrenceville Kiwanis Club for many years, and president of the club in 1950. He was a senior member of the Gwinnett County Bar Association and was the youngest deacon ever at First Baptist Church of Lawrenceville. He co-taught the Walter Alford Sunday School class for over 40 years; was a member of the Lawrenceville Masonic Lodge 131 and a life member of the American Legion Post 262. He was also a member of the board of directors of the Brand Banking Co. In 1988, Jordan received the Public Service Award from the Gwinnett County Chamber of Commerce, and in December 1989 received the Public Service Award from the Department of Health and Human Services. In the early 1980s, the city park was named Rhodes Jordan Park.

Except for short stints away at school and in the Navy, he never lived outside the city limits of Lawrenceville. He resided in a house on Culver Street from 1948 until his death in 1993. He was a staunch Democrat, but was known to vote Republican if he had strong beliefs in the individual or their cause. Rhodes enjoyed being a lawyer and considered himself a "people's lawyer." He family says that he never won any special big cases, but was content to handle legal matters and kept the door open for anyone who wanted to just come in and talk.

Jordan's office looked out onto the Courthouse Square on the floor above what was once his father's store. He watched the City of Lawrenceville from that vantage point from 1930 until his death, March 25, 1993. The former Jordan store and office building were restored in Lawrenceville and now houses the Lil' River Grill. There is a plaque with Rhodes' picture on the corner of the building.

The Mason Brothers

A pair of brothers from the Snellville area was a major reason for the quick spurt in housing and growth in Snellville in the 1960s and 1970s. The pair, Jimmy and Wayne Mason, are products of a family from the Centerville community which dates back to the early 1830s in Gwinnett. They built 1,800 single family houses from 1959-72, most of them in Snellville, leading to the town's fast population growth.

Snellville is centered at the intersection of two roads, U.S. Highway 78 and Georgia Highway 124. Listed as having only 468 residents in 1960, by 1970, Snellville counted 1,990 residents. But by 1980, the city had ballooned to 8,514 residents. So for two decades, it had 247 percent and 227 percent growth! By the census of 2000, Snellville had 15,351 residents and took its place among the larger cities of the county. By 2007, the city had an estimated 20,076 residents.

A Community Is Formed

Among the early immigrants to the area were two men from England, James Sawyer and Thomas Snell. Sawyer and his brother, Charles, left England in 1874, landed in New York, and traveled South that spring. Snell had planned to leave England with the Sawyers but was stymied when his parents learned of his plans. However, he soon sailed to New York and made his way South to join the Sawyer brothers. Eventually, the group arrived in Georgia to work on the A.A. Dyer Farm, near the present day Head Elementary School on Hewatt Road. Soon after, Charles Sawyer moved to Alabama. It was in 1879 that James Sawyer and Thomas Snell established a general mercantile store in what would become Snellville.

Eventually, the two Brits sought to have a post office at their location, as a way to attract business. They applied to the U.S. Postal Service, and between themselves, agreed to name the post office "New London." By chance, it so happened that on the day the postal official came to determine if the community should have a post office, Mr. Sawyer was away on business. The official asked Mr. Snell: "What is the name you want to call this post office?" And that's the story old timers tell on how the community got the name of Snellville!

Few remnants remain of the name "New London." In the late 1970s, one of the commercial strip centers south of U.S. Highway 78, within sight of the original Snellville post office, had the name of "New London Shopping Center." A W.T. Grant Company department store was one of the key occupants in the center, one of the last Grant stores to open before the company went out of business. (W.T. Grant had started "W.T. Grant 25 Cent Store" in Lynn, Mass. in 1906, and saw it grow into 1,182 stores by 1975. It declared bankruptcy that year, and closed all its stores in 1976.) Another legacy of that early designation is an acting company in Snellville that goes by the name of New London Theatre.

Little growth occurred in Snellville until the 1960s, as this community, like most in Gwinnett, was tied to the rural economy, never realizing the growth that was about to hit it. But then the Mason brothers started their careers in the homebuilding business. Jimmy and Wayne Mason were grandsons of a former sheriff of Gwinnett County, J.P. Mason.

With a deep family heritage in Gwinnett, the Mason boys formed a striking duo in business and politics. Jimmy was for six years on the Snellville City Council prior to serving for eight years as a state legislator. Wayne was on the county commission for two terms (1972-79), including four years as chairman, during the early days of Gwinnett's big growth spurt.

Wayne Mason is a flamboyant, colorful and successful Gwinnett businessman, known by all as a fast-talker and even faster thinker who can calculate in his mind precise and accurate complex financial transactions. He and Jimmy were equal partners until 1988, when Jimmy retired. Ten years later, Jimmy died after he had an accident while a member of the Georgia Ports Authority on a trade mission to Brazil.

The Masons had the ability to recognize the value and long-term potential of land in a growing market. Wayne Mason in 2008 was still seeking to buy and sell vast tracts of land. Those who work with him cite his business acumen, but also point out that the self-made businessman has a sterling character, with his word his bond. He's also known as a person who has a strong commitment for the underdog and those less fortunate, and one who has a big heart and makes gifts to those in need and to significant community causes, done usually anonymously.

Their firm, Mason Brothers Development Company, built and developed 1,800 houses, mostly in Snellville, from 1959-72. Later, the business partners branched into wholesale land and commercial development before Jimmy retired in 1988.

The 20 year period after Jimmy's retirement were even more successful for Wayne Mason, as he astutely parlayed his instincts and skills into a vast fortune. He switched from concentrating on Gwinnett to spreading his vision to other parts of Metro Atlanta and Georgia to seven other states. He did this through investing with many people in limited partnerships, often making millionaires out of his partners with his understanding, his foresight and his own financing of the projects.

Yet Wayne Mason remains relatively self-effacing, having not always found the going easy. He and Jimmy particularly found it difficult in the early and mid-1970s, when economic times, changes in banking regulations and his vast holdings of land caught up with them. He says that with their early successes, "I thought I was Rockefeller for a while, but shortly, I was flat broke for all purposes. But I worked it off, after losing a lot of money. And I ended up paying everyone off, and then came back myself even stronger."

What follows are notes from a 2.5 hour conversation with Wayne Mason, May 8, 2007.

The early years

Jimmy Mason was born in Centerville on January 26, 1937, and graduated from Snellville High in 1954; Wayne was born March 22, 1940, and graduated from newly-formed South Gwinnett in 1958. They were the sons of James Winston Mason and Ida Belle Moore Mason. The two brothers grew up with two sisters, Winifred Mason Herndon and Linda Mason Ewing. (John D. Stephens was in Wayne's class. He says of him: "We called him Dennis back then, actually 'Dennis the Menace.'") The Mason family had been in the Centerville area of Gwinnett area since 1838. "We have deeds from the Mason-Todd house back to then," Wayne says. The family went to church at the nearby Zoar Methodist.

One grandfather, Oscar Moore, was a Primitive Baptist minister at Friendship Church on Five Forks Road for 47 years. "He never lived long enough to see electric lights in the church." Another grandfather, J.P. Mason, was Gwinnett's sheriff in 1938-42.

Wayne Mason

When Wayne was 12 years old, his father, Winston, gave him $10. "That was the last money my father ever had to give me." Wayne has been working since he was that age, taking his first regular job at E.L. Juhan's grocery store in Centerville, near where the family lived. Jimmy had worked at the same store before him. Prior to that, Wayne had plowed and worked in the fields for a dollar a day. "I would plow gardens around Centerville, behind a one-eyed mule. I was so small that I had a sled to haul my plows. Before I went out, I had my three different type of plows fixed on the sled, since I was not big enough to rig them by myself. I had one plow for the middle of rows of gardens, one for beans and another for corn. I was not tall enough to reach the plow handles to pick it up, nor strong enough to lift the plow at the end of each row. So I would have to bend down and turn the plow around on the ground, then drag it to the next row. That old one-eyed mule would watch me and wait until I got the plow ready, and knew when to take off.

"Families had small gardens, with the men working in town most of the day, so they paid me to plow their gardens. I charged all of them the same thing, a dollar, no matter what the size of the garden. It might be a half acre or an acre. Everyone had gardens back then."

From the time Wayne began working, he was focused on making money, and always had money in his pocket. He bought his own clothes, and paid for his lunch at school. "On Mondays, I always made sure that I had a $10 bill to use to pay for my lunches for that week. Meals in those days cost at first 75 cents a week, then went eventually to $1.25 a week. Many a time the teachers had to run all around school to make change for my $10 bill," Wayne laughs as he says. "It made people think I had money, whether I had made $10 in the last week or not."

The brothers and their uncle, J.T. Jordan, at one time peddled eggs and other items from the country on a regular route in Atlanta to individual homes. "In the winter, your hands would get real cold, and turn red. At Christmas, it wasn't unusual for me to get from women customers several pairs of gloves. I didn't need the gloves, for I couldn't pick up the eggs, two or three at a time, with gloves on. I would take the gloves that the ladies gave me to school and sell them for whatever I could get.

"We sold eggs for 50 cents a dozen. We would also provide any other farm items the customers wanted: straw for their garden, mistletoe at Christmas, fresh butter or buttermilk. We also made wreaths at Christmas. We would get vines in the summer time, and tie them into a circle, and hang them up to dry. Then at Christmas you would strip some cedar greenery, and use the vines to tie the greenery into wreathes. I could easily make nice wreathes, and still can. We did anything to make money back then."

Wayne says that Jimmy was "smarter in school than I was. He jumped ahead one year at school, but I was held back one year. Later, I skipped the 11th grade, and hired a tutor, so that I would graduate on time with my class, with only three years of high school." Wayne enjoys telling people: "I was not voted most likely to succeed in high school!"

In 1955, 15-year old Wayne admits to lying about his age to get a driver's license. He later got a job working with an auto parts distributor in Lawrenceville, Hubert Brannen, (the uncle of Jimmy Brannen, who later owned auto parts stores in Lawrenceville, Lilburn and Buford.) Wayne ran a parts distribution route for Brannen. "I worked all over North Georgia when I was 17-18, spending three days a week delivering auto parts. Brannen didn't sell tires, so I could buy tires and sell them to the same places where I was delivering auto parts. Goodyear gave me the lowest price they had on tires, and I got a free re-cap every time I sold 10 tires. So I sold the tires at what I paid for them, and then sold that re-cap for $10. Every time I sold 100 tires for Goodyear, the re-caps made me $100."

Wayne adds: "Soon I was buying so many tires from Goodyear that they wanted me to go to work for them. I did, and soon I was their top salesman. I sold more tires than anybody for Goodyear in the Southern Region in 1959."

After high school, Jimmy first went to work at Sears, Roebuck Co. on Ponce de Leon Avenue in downtown Atlanta. (A family friend, Emmett Clower Jr., was working there.) Later, he switched to become a cable splicer's helper for Southern Bell. "He did it to make more money, and he worked in the manholes for several years," Wayne says.

That was in the days of the draft, but Wayne never served in the Army: "I don't join any organization, even the Boy Scouts, who wear uniforms," he quips. "I was too young for Korea and too old for Vietnam," he says. In reality, he had four children by the time he was 26, and was not required to serve. Wayne married Ann Biggers on September 5, 1959.

Jimmy had married Helen Elizabeth Phillips on August 3, 1956. Later Jimmy volunteered for the Army. He was sent to Korea and got out of the Army in 1959, when he and Wayne began to build houses in addition to their regular jobs. Jimmy remained at Southern Bell selling Yellow Page advertising until 1963, when he joined Wayne full time in the building business. Jimmy and Helen had three girls, Tracey, Teresa and Tina.

Jimmy stayed with Southern Bell "Until we were making enough in the company to support two families. Whatever Jimmy's salary was at the phone company was the amount I drew out of the company," Wayne says, as the brothers shared everything 50/50.

The first property that they bought, Wayne thinks, was on Lanier Mountain, in 1959, which they bought from Harvey Ewing. "We would buy the lot, and Harvey would give us a deed for the lot. Harvey didn't require us to pay him until we sold the house, so that deed was worth gold to us. We would take that deed to the bank and borrow money to build the house." Perhaps that's the reason, to this day, that Wayne calls Ewing "Moneybags." (Mason has nicknames for everyone. Ewing, in turn, calls him back, "Fireball.")

Wayne left Goodyear in 1961 to concentrate on house building. Jimmy continued at Southern Bell until 1963 when he joined Wayne full time in business. "Our business was making enough to keep both of us up by then," Wayne says.

When in home construction, the Masons built houses mostly in Snellville, though they would work in other places if someone wanted them to build for them. Wayne remembers that in 1963, when John Kennedy was killed, he was building a house in Vinings. "We were pouring concrete on this driveway, and we heard the news that Kennedy has been killed on the radio. I had a guy pouring concrete whose last name was Peters working with me, a black man, and I remember him saying of the Kennedy killing: 'Every time we get a good man, someone kills him.'"

When in business together, Wayne was usually in the lead with the decisions, while Jimmy went along. The brothers kept building, buying and selling houses until 1972, when they got out of house construction, and began concentrating on land.

When Wayne and Jimmy were building houses, these homes in 1959 sold for $11,750, later for $12,250 and by 1972 for $13-15,000. What the purchaser was getting was a home of 1,526 square feet, including a double carport. "That's less than $100 a square foot," Mason points out, "And they were good homes. Even if a buyer didn't add on to them, these same homes re-sell for between $160-170,000 today (2008)."

In 1972, the last year the brothers were in the home construction business, they had a stable of builders who erected 565 homes, and the two built 103 homes themselves. Why did they get out?

"We made $176,000 in 1972. But you have to put in a lot of work to make that kind of money. Meanwhile, we were buying and selling land, and would make more off the land than building houses. But we also had other businesses." That included, among others, a bonding company, Mason Brothers Ceramic Tile, Suburban Realty, and even a funeral home. And, with Three M Investments, they owned 700 acres on what would become Summit Chase Country Club.

The brother's first million dollar deal came in 1972, when they sold the Summit Chase Golf Club and surrounding property. "There were three of us in on the deal, including our uncle, Hilliard (Hill) Moore, who was in the auto business." (Wayne Hilliard Mason is named for that uncle.) They had purchased the land in 1965 by advertising with big signs saying: "We buy land for cash," which brought them lots of business.

At one time, the Masons owned 2,200 acres of contiguous land, running six miles from Rosebud Road east of Snellville, all the way to Georgia Highway 124 north of Snellville, with one parcel after another touching, though not always along U.S. Highway 78. There were 11 tracts altogether, including what is now most of downtown Snellville. This land was part of the several estates that the Masons often bought at auction, the Bryan, Williams, Sawyer, Smith, Johnson, Pate, and O'Kelley estates. "On several tracts, corn was growing when we bought it. We waited for the harvest that year before we took over the land," Mason says.

The Sawyer land also included the present Snellville Cemetery. The Masons soon donated the cemetery land to the Baptist and Methodist churches, and the churches eventually sold the cemetery to the city. (But first, the Masons retained cemetery plots on that parcel. This is where Jimmy is now buried, and Wayne plans to be buried some day.)

Mason likes to banter with his detractors, especially newcomers. One of Wayne Mason's quips to questioners, especially to newcomers, is to inquire of them how long they have lived in the county, and ask them whether they have a cemetery lot. He then comments: "You're not a very permanent resident unless you own a cemetery lot here and know where you are going to be buried." He also tells detractors who say that the local residents don't seem to like the newcomers: "I don't know where you got that idea. Before you moved down here, I was picking peas. You made me rich by moving here."

* * * * *

The brothers were also into developing shopping centers, putting in the first major center, Snellville Plaza, at the intersection of U.S. Highway 78 and Georgia Highway 124 in downtown Snellville. Eventually they landed their first chain grocery store, Winn-Dixie, for Snellville. Wayne tells that that grocery store chain signed what looked to the supermarket as a "sweetheart" contract with rent of less than one percent of gross sales. The grocery chain felt this was "insignificant" in the larger picture. But Wayne saw a larger picture: "Getting that supermarket to come to Snellville, the first one here, increased the price of all my land by $100 a lot. And when you own 2,200 acres of land, you stand to make some real money. For without the convenience of the supermarket, land is worth nothing."

Mason would later entice a doctor to locate in Snellville, then the only doctor in Snellville. "With that doctor in town, my land just went up another $100 per lot. There's no telling what I made off that."

By the early 1970s, each of the Masons brothers were worth $1 million, and had cash to buy land quickly.

Were the Masons thinking they were successful by then? Wayne Mason says: "We never ever did. After all, how do you measure success? Financially, we were very successful. But then, there are other measures, for instance, consider your family. You look at your family, your wife, and children. We have had no problems with our four kids, and now my wife and I have 11 grandchildren. We feel as a family we are very successful.

"Financially, we have been up and down. But now (2008), I get my monthly Social Security check and I am also on Medicare, so I'm set. These are ways to take care of me," Mason laughs.

By 1972, the two were still investing more into land. The biggest tract that the pair and an investor group ever owned was 5,518 acres in Smithsonia, in Clarke, Wilkes and Oglethorpe counties. The venture was subsequently the subject of a University of Georgia Press publication, entitled: "Smithsonia," Altogether, ten investors were involved. The land was sold in 1976, bringing in $2.8 million, and Mason adds: "We only owed $800,000 on it."

Mason says; "About that time, I owned 18,000 acres of land, and thought I was Rockefeller. But shortly after that I was broke for all intents and purposes." He adds: "Since 1959, I never experienced a shortage of money, just a shortage of collateral."

Several circumstances led to the Mason plight. First came a recession of the 1970s, plus changes in banking rules that hurt their ability to borrow money. Mason explains: "We had a lot of non-earning assets, which were listed as liabilities, so they could not be listed by the banking rules on the asset side. It stopped our borrowing and forced us to sell land at a virtual liquidation. We sold land, then had to take a mortgage back. We would service the first mortgage and take a second mortgage. But there was no way immediately to pay out the first or second. But we worked it all off, though we lost a lot of money. We ended up paying everyone off. But then we came back ourselves."

It wasn't the house building that hurt the Masons, but land got them. Hamilton Bank went bankrupt and was taken over by the FDIC. "We litigated with the FDIC and finally settled in 1983."

The Masons and politics

Back in the mid-1960s, the Masons realized that the county politically was at a void, with a lack of progressive leadership, and the county was at a standstill. "Our granddaddy had been the county sheriff, and our daddy, Winston, had been on the school board, and ran the Centerville school. It was not an unusual deal for us to think of getting into politics."

Jimmy had first been elected for three terms on the Snellville City Council, from 1961-1966. He later ran for the state legislator in 1966 and won. He continued to serve in the Legislature through 1974.

Wayne maintains that Jimmy was better at politics than he was. "Jimmy liked it, and stayed for eight years in the Legislature. I first ran for the district commission seat in 1968, and got beat by Carvis Williams, my cousin, by 455 votes. I lost my home precinct in Snellville by 228 votes. Hugh Snell liked to tell people that 'Carvis took two bushels of peas and beat me.' Another said that Carvis spent only $20 to run, while I spent $7,800 and had all types of items, from hats, bumper stickers, balloons, even put out a newspaper, and still lost. But if I had won that Snellville precinct, I would have won the election. I was 28 years old then, and people thought I was too young to be a commissioner."

What Jimmy brought was political connections. With his gregarious personality, he knew scores of key people at the state level, which was particularly helpful. The other Gwinnett state representative then was Norris Nash (a cousin of the Masons). Together, they could get local measures through the Legislature. That included such bills for Gwinnett as creating the Public Facilities Authority, Recreation Authority and Water and Sewer Authority, among others. These changes in structuring the county financially developed a basis that benefits the county to this day.

He continues: "Authorities were the only way to finance these big-dollar, long-range improvements. After all, the county commission didn't have much revenue then. We were operating the entire county on a budget of less than $7 million in those days. We would not have the water and sewer system today, which has been the backbone of our growth, without authority financing. I served myself for most of my term as a commissioner, until 1980, on the Water and Sewer Authority, since I understood finance. You must realize that Jimmy and I had a bigger budget in those days than the county had!

"We knew growth was coming. To finance the water and sewer bonds, we structured the Authorities so they could borrow money on anticipated revenue bonds based on the future growth. We borrowed the money for the Lake Lanier water plant, capitalized the interest for three years, and then went to full cash with interest for another three years. We back-loaded the bonds, paying interest-only in the early years and principal in the later years. Think what a dollar was worth in 1973 compared to what it was worth 25 years later. That way you could make the numbers dance. Everything was done based on the growth that we knew was coming. Without the growth in Gwinnett, and without the balance between commercial and residential development in the Gwinnett tax digest, we would not have the first class water and sewer system or top-notch schools we have today.

"If it was for the benefit of the county, we would find a way to do it. We did things in a different way from the way the county is run today."

Even after Jimmy left the Legislature in 1974, he continued to have contacts throughout state government, and to serve as an appointed official. For 17 years, he was on the State Properties Commission, which few people knew about. This is the state commission that buys land for state governmental purposes. Jimmy, with his real estate background, was perfect for the Commission, while at the same time, it kept him in touch with state political leaders. Later, he would serve for six years on the Georgia Ports Authority.

Though Gwinnett has changed to a heavily-dominant Republican county since the Masons got into politics, Wayne Mason remains a staunch Democrat. Mason explains:

"What sets the United States apart from any other country in the world is that we have a few very rich people, and a few very poor people. But we have a broad, no, a giant, middle class. Look at our standard of living. By any way they want to measure it, the United States is in better shape than any country in the world.

"The way we have done this is to use the tax structure to re-distribute the wealth of this nation. Before 1913, when the income tax was instituted, the big moguls had it all. We had the super-wealthy, the robber-barons, with money in few hands. The tax structure re-distributed the wealth." *(Editor's note: The 1913 beginning of the income tax had a rate of one percent on taxable incomes over $3,000, rising to seven percent on taxable incomes over $500,000.)*

"Now today, two-thirds of our economy is in consumer goods. Now tell me, how are the consumers going to buy the goods if they don't have money? The large middle class is better off, and can afford this, since we had the government creating the tax policy of re-distribution of the wealth."

He adds: "I tell my Republican friends that if you took all the money in this country, and divided it up equally among everyone, in a few days, the same people would have the bulk of their money back. I also like to tell my Republican friends that I am a Democrat, since I don't have enough money to be a Republican."

The Masons and Brand Bank

The Masons go back a long way with Brand Bank, which was their principal bank prior to 1972, and is again today. But there was a short break in their relationship. Wayne says; "I've been their customer since I was 12 years old. Back then I had one of those yellow passbook savings books, where you would take it in, and they would write in your deposit. We go way back." Later as adults in business, Wayne and Jimmy both dealt directly at the bank with Bartow Morgan III (this can be confusing; he is the father of Bartow Morgan Jr., who became head of the bank in 2002.)

After Wayne Mason became a county commissioner in 1972, Mrs. Louise Brand Morgan was president of the Brand Bank. She was the mother of Vice President Bartow Morgan III, who ran the bank on a day-to-day basis. But Mrs. Morgan was concerned about the Mason brother's financial position, and decided on her own to call in the Mason notes.

Wayne Mason picks up the story: "We had banked with Brand Bank all along. One day Bartow III's mother, who was the real power behind the bank, thought we had become over-extended, and Bartow called me up to the bank. He said: '....looks like our relationship has deteriorated. I want my money,' calling in all the notes we had at the bank. I asked Bartow how much they amounted to, and he said $476,000. I told him he would have it within a week."

Mason, who also had relationships with other banks, went to Gus Conley ("One of the best bankers I've known in my life") of C&S Bank in Tucker, who told him that Brand Bank could not legally call the notes. "I told him that they did it, and anyway, I wanted to pay them off. So the next morning, Gus came out and rode with me as I showed him property we had bought but still owed on at the bank, and after about three hours he said, 'Let's have lunch.' I told him I had more property to show him, but he said he had seen enough.

"We went to lunch at Country Manor in Snellville, the place run by the Frank Duke family. I told Gus that all the Brand notes were due on demand, and that they had called them. They had a mortgage on everything we owned, as collateral.

"Gus suggested that I come to his bank the next morning. There he asked me how much I needed to pay Brand Bank off, and I said $255,000, since we had some money we had saved. But then he asked how much I really needed. He said the worst problem of bankers was not loaning customers enough money. So I told him $355,000, and he loaned us the money, and we paid Bartow off."

Mason was on the county commission then, during the time Bill Atkinson was chairman. A few days later, Mason asked Atkinson "Didn't Brand Bank and Bartow III refuse to finance the house you were building?" Atkinson said yes, they did. Mason suggested why, then, did the county have all those accounts with Bartow's bank, saying: "If I was chairman, I would not keep all the county's money there." Atkinson didn't have an answer.

That must have set Atkinson to thinking. For Mason later learned that Atkinson went the next day to Brand Bank and closed all 11 of the county accounts and moved them to the First National Bank of Gwinnett, without the authorization of the commission. (Later, the action was ratified by the full commission.) Atkinson's brother-in-law, Richard Sikes, was vice president of the First National Bank.

That banking move by Atkinson produced a march up the hill to the commission office by Bartow Morgan III and his right-hand man, Harry Braselton. Atkinson asked: "What can we do for you, Mr. Morgan?" Mason, in his adjacent office, heard from the open door of Atkinson's office.

The banking pair wanted to know why Atkinson had closed all the accounts of the county at the bank. Atkinson asked them what percent of its funds did the bank loan out. Morgan replied 38 percent. Atkinson asked how much in federal funds, and Morgan answered. Atkinson then said he understood that the bank didn't offer any local auto loans, or loans to builders in the community, therefore, was not entitled to the people's money. "You weren't acting for the good of community," Atkinson told them. Mason remembers hearing Julian Archer, another commissioner, chiming in, "Damn right." Atkinson, adamant all the way, would not restore the accounts to the bank. Morgan is said to have turned red in the face, and the pair soon left.

Mason says that the ironic aspect is that it had been the Brand Bank that had virtually propped up the Gwinnett water system, by purchasing the water system bonds when it was going through its bad times in its early days in the late 1950s. Not only that, but the bank had dutifully served the county's other accounts for years. But Brand Bank had now lost the county accounts, and there was little that the Morgans could do.

About four years later, in 1976, shortly after Mason became chairman of the commission, and after the bank chairman, Mrs. Morgan, had died, Bartow Morgan III called up Mason one day and simply asked; "When you going to quit kicking me?"

Mason replied: "When you quit kicking me."

Bartow came back: "It's a deal!"

Soon, Brand Bank had some of the county's business again, and the Mason brothers themselves returned as customers of the bank. When Bartow Morgan Jr. (Remember, he is Bartow III's son) became chairman and CEO of Brand Bank in 2002, Mason was one of his staunchest supporters. Mason also feels that Bartow Jr. is "the smartest 32 year old banker I know. He built that bank up to a $1 billion bank in 2008, but his success doesn't go to his head. And his family business is into several income streams, not just one, and is going to go on and on." Mason said at one time that Morgan was "being groomed" to take over Mason's mantle as the "go-to" person in Gwinnett. "But (in 2008), he's already there. He's already taken my place," Mason yields.

Mason also feels that Bartow Jr.'s father, Bartow III, was one of the most astute bankers of his day. "He did not worry about your credit, but dealt mainly with security deeds and pine trees as collateral. If you wanted to borrow money from him, you put up your farm or the land you owned. That way, if you did not repay him, he could sell timber or your land. He was a collateral lender. There was always a shortage of collateral, but never with money with Bartow III. He was a great banker and a great individual. You could get along with him. I loved and respected him."

Other ventures

The Mason Brothers have been investors and operators in many business ventures in Gwinnett. Among them:

Funeral Homes: Once they were in partnership with Edgar Couch in a Lawrenceville funeral home. But Wayne disliked that business. "It bothered me, big time, for I did not like to make money on someone's miseries."

Banks: In the mid 70s, Atlanta banker Mack Robinson wanted to start a bank in Snellville, and was advised not to do it without involving the Mason brothers. Together, they started Gwinnett County Bank, the first bank headquartered in Snellville, with Robinson owning 62 percent and the Masons owning 18 percent.

Later, when Robinson wanted to get out of this bank, the Masons agreed to buy his share. But the Federal Deposit Insurance Corporation did not approve of the transaction, since Jimmy and Wayne were litigating with the FDIC over the Hamilton Bank of Chattanooga.

That's when the Masons brought in their cousin, Virgil Williams, to buy the Robinson shares in Gwinnett County Bank. The Masons also sold Williams their shares, giving Williams control of the bank. Wayne says: "I tried to sell it to John D. Stephens, but he had too much going on. So I called Virgil and showed the figures to him on a Friday, and Monday he said he thought it was a good deal. We set him up with Mack Robinson, and he bought Mack's stock. We sold him our stock at the same price he paid Mack."

Later, Williams would go more extensively into banking, and was the person who promoted the concept of putting banks in supermarkets. (See chapter concerning Virgil Williams for more details.)

Jimmy Mason

Years later, after Jimmy Mason's death, Wayne became more active investing in other banks. He has been the largest shareholder in the First Bank of the South (originally Button Gwinnett Savings and Loan), which later was bought by Blairsville's United Community Bank. He is also the largest shareholder in Georgian Bank. He considers his local bank holdings as among his most successful investments.

Liquor stores: The Masons, with partner Robby Sturdivant of Lilburn, were the owners of the first retail liquor store in the county. When the City of Lilburn passed an ordinance allowing the sale of bottled liquor in 1977, Mason told Lilburn Mayor Jack Sawyer that he would build a magnificent store that he and the city would be proud of, one they could place adjacent to the post office or City Hall. The store was subsequently built on Indian Trail Road. Later, Sturdivant sold his share to the Masons. "Roddy thought it was too slow a way to make money," Mason says. Eventually, the Masons would add liquor stores in Conyers and the second retail liquor store in Suwanee and one in Duluth. By 2008, Wayne Mason owns no store, but the Suwanee store is owned by Wayne Mason's children and Richard Tucker. It is the highest grossing liquor store in Georgia.

Closing a partnership

In 1988, Jimmy told Wayne that he wanted to get out of the business. "We were close as brothers, and we split everything as partners, 50/50. But Jimmy was never satisfied, with cars, wives or houses or anything. He was, as my mother, Ida Belle, told me he would be, continually searching. He was smarter than I was, and more forward, and he held me back in some way. But we worked well together."

Jimmy would say about a deal: "Ask Wayne. He'll change it." But Wayne says: "He let me take the lead in deals, and didn't pay all that much attention to details. One time when we had offices in the Gwinnett Federal building, we were coming down in the elevator and I told him we were going to a closing, and he asked: 'Are we buying or selling?'"

Jimmy was also more negative about possible deals, which Wayne calls a "black cloud." But Wayne listened to Jimmy. Wayne says that Harry Braselton of Brand Bank saw Jimmy far differently and not so negatively, calling him the "Voice of Reason."

Jimmy surprised Wayne in 1988, when Jimmy was by then worth $15 million, saying, "I'm quitting. I've got all I need." He wanted Wayne to buy him out in cash.

Another version of that story comes from Banker Tom Martin of Duluth. "Jimmy told me one time that he was richer than all the rest of his friends, richer than his brother, Wayne, or John D. Stephens or Virgil Williams," Tom says. "Not understanding the way he was thinking, and knowing the other people involved, I asked him, 'How is that?' Jimmy came back saying, 'I've got more than they have, for I have made enough for me, and they want to keep on trying to have more.'"

Before Jimmy and Wayne could close out the partnership, Jimmy said he wanted to keep the liquor stores. Wayne offered him $1 million for his share, which Wayne considered a reasonable offer. But then Jimmy came back and said Wayne offered too much, for the stores were only worth $900,000. Wayne adds that he virtually gave Jimmy the stores, since the stores had in cash $700,000. "So he got them for $200,000."After Jimmy's death in 1998, Wayne's children and Richard Tucker purchased the store in Suwanee from Jimmy's estate.

Fateful trip to Brazil

The circumstances of Jimmy Mason's death after he fell and injured his head in Brazil have not been fully chronicled until now. Gov. Zell Miller took Jimmy Mason off the Properties Commission in 1992 and named him to the Georgia Ports Authority, where he served for six years, including 1995-96 as chairman. It was while on a Ports Authority trade mission to visit potential clients in Sao Paulo, Brazil in 1998---which he told his wife it would be his final trade mission with the Ports Authority---that the fall happened. Two days following the fall, Jimmy lapsed into a coma from which he did not recover.

Along with Jimmy on the trip to Brazil were fellow Ports Authority members Smith Foster, Tom Dillon and Herman Russell. All except the Russells had arrived from Miami, on Saturday, May 9, 1998. (Mr. Russell and his wife arrived later.) The group had planned to go to other locations in South America on Georgia Ports Authority business after Sao Paulo.

Foster, Dillon and Mason took a trip on Saturday morning to visit a site about 50 miles away. Dillon says: "We found that no one was working on Saturday, as is their custom, so we saw some of the country that morning." After lunch on Saturday, the three joined a tour group with a guide, and were headed from their hotel to walk a few blocks, as the trio acclimated themselves.

Tom Dillon remembers that he, Smith Foster and Jimmy were out walking toward a monument. Dillon says: "We wanted to walk around the city, and familiarize ourselves about local activities and people, so we could have something to talk about to the business people on Brazil." Jimmy was ahead of the other two on the sidewalk, and turned his head while talking to them. Dillon says: "Without realizing it, his legs hit a utility pole guy wire about knee high, sending him falling and hitting his face square on the concrete sidewalk." He partially broke the fall with his left hand, which was also injured. It felt, Jimmy later told them, like he had been hit by a car. Dillon adds: "Jimmy was walking just in front of me, a couple of feet. He was walking backwards, talking to us. Had I not been walking forward, I might have hit the wire, too."

The group took Jimmy in a cab back to the Sheraton Hotel, and sought assistance at a "doc-in-a-box" medical outlet, but got little treatment. On Sunday, Jimmy felt well enough to visit a children's hospital with the others.

Doris Vincent O'Kelley Mason, Jimmy's second wife, picks up the story here: "I had talked to Jimmy on Saturday morning, but he did not call me on Saturday night nor Sunday, and he knew I was going to New York on Monday with the family. On Sunday night about 10:30, I called, woke him up, and asked what he was up to. He sounded bad, like he had a cold, but he did not tell me he had fallen. Meanwhile, I learned later, Smith Foster kept telling him that he needed to call me about the fall." Doris knew the other Authority members since she had been along on several trips that the Authority members had taken: China, Australia, Norway, Japan and Canada.

On Monday, May 11, Jimmy stayed at the hotel, while the others went out for a morning meeting. With Doris and the family still in New York, Jimmy called them around 3 p.m.. "We talked about 20 minutes," Doris says, "He said that the group had gone on Sunday to a medical foundation that Jimmy Carter was involved with. There I later learned someone had x-rayed Jimmy's injured hand, and put a cast on it. But he never said a word about falling." She adds: "That was the last time I talked to him."

In Sao Paolo, on Monday, Dillon said: "Jimmy was not feeling well. When we got back from a meeting, Jimmy was having a snack about 3 o'clock in the afternoon in the dining room, but still said he didn't feel well, and went up to his room." Dillon kept insisting to Mason that he tell Doris he had fallen. Jimmy told him: "There's no point in that. She will be real upset."

Herman Russell by then had arrived, and picks it up here: "When he came down for dinner on Monday, he stayed a while and said he did not have an appetite, and told us he was going to his room."

Dillon says: "I didn't like the way he said that, and in about 15 minutes, I decided to go check on him. When he came to the door, he still wasn't feeling well, and went to sit on the bed. Jimmy did not realize that he had a serious head injury, and coupled with him taking a blood thinner, we later learned that blood was escaping into his head cavity."

Later, Dillon would tell Doris Mason: "When he sat down on the bed, he told me that he thought he was dying."

In a short time, Smith Foster and Herman Russell came into the room. Jimmy had told them that it felt like "my head is about to blow off." With Jimmy not showing progress, the traveling companions decided to get him medical attention. They got a wheelchair and took him down to the lobby. But they had trouble getting an ambulance. The concierge at the hotel said that he would lead them to a medical facility recommended by the hotel, and called for two taxis. They got Jimmy into a taxi, and the concierge led them on a motorcycle about 15-20 minutes across town to what turned out to be another "doc-in-a-box" facility.

The Brazilian doctor there looked at Jimmy, who by then was groggy and not seeing well, and soon called an ambulance to take him to a hospital. Dillon says: "Jimmy told me, 'Tom, I feel horrible' about the time the ambulance came." Smith Foster got in the ambulance with Jimmy, and they went to the hospital, with Russell and Dillon following. Smith Foster later said that Jimmy had nothing to say as they drove to the hospital. "Jimmy became unconscious in the ambulance, went into a coma, and never revived," Dillon says.

Meanwhile, Herman Russell surprised Jimmy's daughter, Dr. Tina Mason. Tina had met Russell when Tina accompanied her father on a previous Authority trip. When Russell called her on Monday night, he told her that Jimmy was in a coma. She had been visiting in Dallas, had returned home and had talked to her father on Sunday. "He wanted to know how my trip was going. We had a really good talk. But he never mentioned that he had fallen."

Around midnight on Monday in New York, Doris was startled by a call from Smith Foster, who said Jimmy was in a hospital, and surgery was required.

With the news from Brazil of Jimmy's condition, his daughters hastily discussed the situation. They decided that Tina, since she was a doctor and had her passport with her, should go immediately to Brazil. The two other sisters wanted to go then, but their passports were in the bank safety deposit box. They would soon follow. But since Brazil required a visa, there were complications. Working with then-Gov. Zell Miller and U.S. Rep. Buddy Darden, a visa was waiting for Tina when she arrived in Miami on Tuesday morning, May 12. She flew that day to Sao Paolo. Herman Russell met her at the airport, and took her to the hospital where Jimmy was in intensive care.

On Monday night, Doris Mason, in New York, made plans to fly first to Atlanta, and then to Brazil. She had to go back to Atlanta and get her passport, and obtain a visa. Her son, Mark O'Kelley, met her at the airport Tuesday morning, and they went straight to the Brazilian consulate and both got visas for the trip. After packing, they left Tuesday night with Jimmy's daughters, Tracey Mason and Teresa Waters, for Brazil, getting in Wednesday morning. Tracey's future husband, Ron Blasi, also was on the trip; Teresa's husband, Gary Waters, had no passport and did not make the trip.

Earlier, Tina had talked to colleagues at Gwinnett Medical Center. They felt that Brazilian doctors should operate on Jimmy as soon as possible. Yet there were complications, since the Brazilian doctors realized that Jimmy was on a blood thinner, which concerned them, since it hindered the blood from clotting. They did not actually operate until after Tina was in Brazil.

Once in Brazil, when Tina saw the CAT Scans of her father's brain, though this was not her medical specialty, she knew Jimmy's condition was bad. "It was the worst I had ever seen," she says. In telephone calls to the family, Tina told them of the seriousness of Jimmy's condition.

Surgery was performed to relieve the pressure on Jimmy's head. A Brazilian internist thought there was a need to operate again, but the surgeon did not want to operate, thinking it would risk Jimmy's life. Tina talked for a second time with her cousin, Dr. Miles Mason III. He recommended that Dr. Charles Wood, a Gwinnett Medical Center neurosurgeon, who was familiar with procedures for operating on someone taking blood thinner, go to Brazil.

On Saturday, Dr. Charles Wood flew to Sao Paulo, and planned additional surgery. Prior to the surgery, he asked Tracey Mason what Jimmy's passions were. She responded: "People. People are his passion." Anyone who knew Jimmy saw his affability, his gregariousness. They understood he loved to meet people, and did so easily, relating to others so well, especially people from different cultures. Dr. Wood soon performed additional surgery May 17. Jimmy survived the second surgery, but there were problems controlling his blood pressure. There was no improvement in his condition.

Teresa Mason Waters remembers the time when Jimmy was in a coma. "Whenever I would talk to him, he would respond with a grimace. The nurse told me he could hear me and knew I was there. I like to think that." Doris adds: "He seemed to sense my distinctive perfume. Once when we were telling him we were going to eat, even the nurse in the room sensed a change, telling us he was trying to wake up. She told us to keep talking." But he never came out of the coma. Before Jimmy left the hospital, a second surgery was performed by Dr. Wood, with no change in Jimmy's condition.

Meanwhile, within the week, Teresa's husband, Gary, obtained a passport, and was planning to fly to Brazil along with Richard Tucker, but soon plans changed.

The family decided that Jimmy should return home. He was flown home May 19 in an air ambulance (arranged by American Express since Jimmy had purchased med-evacuation insurance for the trip), arriving May 20 at Peachtree-DeKalb Airport after a 12 hour flight, accompanied by Dr. Wood. He was transferred to Gwinnett Medical Center, where Jimmy was, at that time, a member of the hospital board. Doris and all but Tina and Tracey had flown home just before Jimmy left on May 19 and were in Gwinnett when Jimmy arrived. But his condition never changed and he never came out of the coma. Tina and Tracey were the last to leave Brazil on a commercial flight home.

Doris says of the Brazilian hospital: "Jimmy got excellent care. The hospital was very clean, and the people very nice. Their Intensive Care Unit had nurses for each patient. The nurses were very strict about the number of people in there." Tracey Mason Blasi adds: "While some of their equipment was outdated, our experience was so positive. The caring attitude they showed Daddy as a person, and to us as a family, was truly touching, from the nurses to the surgeons to the receptionists."

Once home, Tina says: "Eventually Dr. Wood told us there was not much hope. If the family had not agreed to stop life support, he could have died quickly, or could have gone on in a coma for years. We knew it was just the machines keeping him going, and that nothing was moving forward." Jimmy died at Gwinnett Medical Center nearly a month after falling, on June 5, 1998.

After his death, Governor Miller named Jimmy's nephew, Keith Mason (Wayne's son) to the Ports Authority. An attorney who himself is prominent in state Democratic circles, Keith Mason served for seven years on the Authority, including two years as chairman, from July 2001 to July 2003. However, when his father began buying land for warehouses near the port, Keith Mason resigned. With his resignation, his replacement was Lawrenceville banker Bartow Morgan Jr.

For Jimmy's years of yeoman service, the Ports Authority named a new ship-to-rail terminal in Savannah for him. It is the **James D. Mason Intermodal Container Transfer Facility**, and helps speed delivery of cargo in an efficient and faster mode, giving the Georgia terminal an edge with its competitors.

Best deal yet

Another investment which turned out to be super successful for Wayne Mason was his decision to purchase a major tract of land and the town of Braselton, a total of 1,740 acres. For years the domain of the Braselton Brothers of Braselton, the town gained national publicity when actress Kim Basinger was among those purchasing the town and adjoining land in 1989. Her financial partner was the telephone company of the Midwest, Ameritech. However, a few years after their purchase, little had been done to develop the area, and Ameritech, and in particular its pension arm, was eager to get the land off their books.

Mason tells the story of the Ameritech Pension Fund sending a young executive down to Gwinnett. "I think they told him just to get rid of the land at any price," Mason likes to tell. "The original purchase price that Basinger and her Ameritech partners paid for Braselton was $20 million."

Wayne says: "This young executive was in Atlanta at a lawyer's office, and they got me on the phone. I had made an offer to them of $4 million for the property, and he said he would not take one penny less than $5 million. I told him I would split the difference with him, but once we hung up the phone, my offer was off the table. I also asked him if he had looked out the window of the airplane when he came down here, he would have seen that the land had been vacant since the Braseltons bought it in 1840. I asked, since it hadn't been developed from that time, what was I going to do with it?"

Eventually, the young executive agreed on the $4.5 million price, and even went lower. Mason agreed to accept it without an environmental study on the land. "They were worried that the study might come back saying the land was contaminated, so they knocked off half what the environmental study would have cost, $300,000, or $150,000 off, and I bought it for $4.35 million."

Wayne relishes in telling this part of the story: "We got all that land, plus stores, houses, almost everything in Braselton, for $2,800 an acre in 1993. When I had the first sale of part of that land, going to Duke-Weeks, I made back my purchase price, for I sold them 100 acres for $4.6 million. It was several years before we made that first sale, but the Braselton property will be probably the finest deal we've ever made. In 2005, ten years after we bought the Braselton property, we sold an additional 300+ acres to Duke Realty." The *Atlanta Business Chronicle* confirmed that, in 2005, Duke Realty Corp. had paid $24.3 million for 318 acres of the property.

Turning to Atlanta

Another project outside Gwinnett which gained Mason far more publicity than he had ever gained before involved his purchase of a 70 acre, five mile railroad corridor in the City of Atlanta in 2004. Called the "Beltline Project," Mason had a vision for a public-private partnership of a pedestrian-oriented corridor with housing, mixed use retail, bike paths, parks and trails. Among his proposals was a plan to donate to the city 43 acres that the city could use at its own discretion for parks, trails and transit.

Mason went into this project after exhaustive research and extensive outreach with community and business leaders. His proposals even garnered support from two of the Neighborhood Planning Units. Before the formal hearing process began, their input was considered important by City of Atlanta zoning entities and elected officials. Mason's innovative approach of using the rail corridor for pedestrian-oriented development and green space received favorable support from different Atlanta media.

However, the Beltline Project ran into stiff opposition and zoning interference from the Atlanta Development Authority and some individuals within the city. Finally, after nearly two years, Mason sold the entire five mile corridor. As a result of decisions made by the City's Beltline entities, Mason says "It will cost the City of Atlanta $90 million more than it would have cost them if I had developed it."

While the Beltline did not progress as originally envisioned, Mason's proposals invigorated the City of Atlanta with a new way to look at abandoned rail property, and pointed the city in a new direction.

Mason has a certain affinity for land projects, and a distinct philosophy. "You gotta be patient. And you never get mad. People may treat you mean, but you keep your cool, for in the long run, you can get even. If you lay there and mess with me, there will come a time….. If you beat me, I will get it back ten-fold."

In all these concerns, Wayne says he is "just an investor. I will buy anything for a price. I am fortunate at being able to make a quick decision, and do what I have to do to bring people, those who become our partners, together. Then we share the wealth. We want to be 50 percent partners. For them to make $30, we have to do something to make $60. I keep 50 percent of all deals. And yes, I like the idea of doing business."

Mason doesn't talk about giving away money, though he has backed virtually every cause he considers good for the county with contributions, whether it is helping to promote an extension of the SPLOST tax, raising money for astute politicians, or funding projects such as the Chamber of Commerce, 1818 Club and Northeast Georgia Foundation.

He says: "I have given away lots of money, which people do not know about, and I want to keep it that way. I try to help people when I can, especially those who I know obviously need it. You are known for what you give away, not for what you try to take with you."

The Atlanta Food Bank is one of his key charities. He feels: "No one should go hungry in this country." Other gifts have been to schools and churches. Together with Virgil Williams, they gave land they bought from The Boeing Company, next to Interstate 85, for Crosspoint Church, valued at $18 million. "We gave them 74 acres of land, plus 280,000 square feet of building space, including 100,000 square feet for offices. The church gets

2,000 people attending services each Sunday." Wayne himself attends, routinely going to the 9:30 a.m. service, and staying afterward for Sunday School.

Of all his accomplishments, Mason remains proudest of his family. "My family is the biggest part of my life. I always knew I could come back in business, as long as I could keep a sound mind, I would be there. After all, I have an ability to make money. My family is the best thing I have. As long as your health is wonderful, money can come and go, but your friends are the most valuable and hard to replace. They will be with you when you die."

What does Mason see for Gwinnett's future?

"The county has major problems, and I do not know the answers. The key problem is that we have lost the core people who dealt in Gwinnett, and had a unity of purpose. These people are no longer around. Business is fragmented, with no focus. As for our leaders, today you see more professional politicians merely trying to get re-elected than be real statesmen or visionary while looking out for the long range future of the county. That worries me.

"I feel the diversity of people in Gwinnett is a big plus for us. It's the best thing that has happened to Gwinnett. We ought to recognize that all everyone wants, including the minorities, is to have safe streets and a better life for their family.

"If I were young again today, I would want to have children in the public schools and learn to speak Spanish. I would not want to be elitist. But as for Gwinnett, I now do business in seven states, plus many counties in Georgia. What can Gwinnett do for me?

"Would I do it again? Yes. I've had a great life, and yes, I would do it again. Of course, well, I've made mistakes, but as far as public office, I would do it again. I was the right guy at the right time for Gwinnett."

Major deals of the Masons

Over the years, the Masons have owned properties all over Gwinnett. When a county commissioner, Wayne Mason quipped that: "No matter where I pave a road, I'm going to catch the devil, for I own property all over the county, and about any paving project will help me in some way." In the eight years that Mason was a county commissioner, more than 800 miles of road were paved in Gwinnett.

Some key transactions of the Masons:

- Snellville Plaza Shopping Center (a first for Snellville).
- Development of 1,800 homes in Snellville.
- Sold land for Eastside Hospital, Presidential Market Shopping Center, and Summit Chase Country Club.
- Smithsonia, 5,518 acres in Clarke, Wilkes and Oglethorpe County.
- Presidential Crossings in Snellville (with Cousins Properties.)
- Development at Stonecrest in Rockdale County (with M.D. Hodges).
- Commercial property in Snellville (with Selig Properties).
- Discover Mills (with Mills Corporation).
- Corporate Lakes Park (with Connolly Real Estate Investments).

- Bluegrass and Pinnacle in Jackson County (with Solution Property Group).
- The 300 acre Scientific-Atlanta Corporate campus, originally purchased from Hayes Microcomputer.
- Global Forum, Gwinnett's first mixed-use property, on Buford Highway in Doraville.
- Crossroads, Duluth's first mixed use project.
- The 400 Commons development in Forsyth County.
- A total of 2,200 acres (other land was added later) in Braselton, developed with several partners, including Duke Realty Corporation, Solution Property Group, Southeast Investment Properties and Republic Property Group.
- Partnered with Solution Property Group in buying 800 acres in Savannah for warehouses in three business parks near the Port of Savannah.
- A total of 384 acres in DeKalb County near Stonecrest Mall for single family homes and townhomes.
- Mixed-use/retail show rooms on Peachtree Hills Avenue, after buying former Allied Ready Mix plant site.
- One Vining Mountain, with Vista Realty.
- Upscale townhomes on Roxboro Road, across from Phipps Plaza, with George Lane.
- Atlanta Beltline project, rail line property purchased from CSX Railroad, in Atlanta.

John D. Stephens

The Mason boys and John Dennis Stephens grew up together, with Wayne and John D. attending the same high school. Stephens was born on April 24, 1940, the son of Nick and Dovie Stephens.

After starting out installing septic tanks, he got a big job in Gwinnett repairing earlier-installed water lines running toward Norcross and Lilburn to shore up faulty Gwinnett water system lines. In 1975-76, he was part of the solution to water shortages in Snellville, as he helped installed the two-way water feed around the edges of the county to relieve low water pressures in several areas of the county.

After his initial work in Gwinnett, Stephens began to obtain contracts to install major water pipelines in other parts of the country, particularly in the West. His first out-of-state job was in Enid, Okla. in 1981. Not long after that job, he began contracting major work in Texas, where he continued to do large water pipeline work until 2005. He says: "All of our work out West was with water lines. Work out there is so big. At one time we ran a water line which was 156 miles long, to serve the Midland-Odessa area, much of it straight as an arrow across the countryside.

"The difference doing work out West is that it is wide open, and you do most of the work across country. You draw a line from Point A to Point B, and there is not much veering off that line. You don't have to worry much about people. We set up our operations in Amarillo, Tex. We would often go through towns where everything was boarded up. There was a town there once, but something happened, and about everything closed down, though some people lived there. These people there would give about anything for just part of the growth that we have had in Gwinnett."

Stephens is a real Gwinnett success story. After attending high school for 11 grades in Snellville, his 12th year was at the same school, but as a member of the first graduating class at the newly-consolidated (with Grayson) South Gwinnett High. After graduation, he worked his way through Southern Tech, then sold air compressors and rock equipment at an office on West Peachtree Street for "exactly one year." But it didn't satisfy him. He remembered young construction businessmen driving new pickups who had money in their pockets, as they put in septic tanks for housing projects.

John D. Stephens

Newly married, young, and unhappy with his work, he talked with his boss, who advised him to come back the next day. He sent him to the C&S National Bank, where "They loaned me every nickel on my first old used backhoe and I went into the septic tank business. Norris and Gartrell Nash sent me my first job, in DeKalb County." After doing septic tank work for five or six years, Stephens began installing water lines in Snellville, first for the city, then later for developers, "wherever I could get a job."

Joe Brand, who ran a convenience store in Mountain Park, likes to tell the story of how Stephens and other contractors virtually used his store as an office. "He would come by in the morning and use the pay phone to call his suppliers, such as the gravel company, to order what he needed for that day. And he would tell them to stop by my store and get directions for where he would be working. When the trucks came, I was glad to see them, for the drivers would often buy a sausage-and-biscuit and drink, and I loved having them as customers. I would tell them where John D. Stephens, or Dennis Billew, or others in the development business, would be working that day, so that they could make deliveries. That was well before anyone had cell phones, and they needed my store. I told them that the store was their business address."

Soon Stephens was getting bigger jobs, often in far-flung locations. At one time, Stephens had pipeline work going on in five states: Texas, Tennessee, Georgia, North Carolina and Virginia. "Some of the work in Tennessee was sewer work," he says. Stephens, no matter where the work took his company, always had Georgia supervisors on the job. They were long term employees of his, some eventually putting in 40 years with his firm.

At the height of his work, he at one time employed 400 people. "That was in 1986, when we had work everywhere, you might say. But we have found over the years, that when we had about 150-200 people, the bottom line was better. We started managing the jobs, rather than throwing darts at the wall. You can cover a lot of ground with 150-200 people.

"I was lucky," says the super-successful Stephens. "I got into something that I understood, knew how to do, and enjoyed it. It was hard work, and had many complications, but I enjoyed it."

It was often work with constant travel. "You got going each week, taking an airplane somewhere, working all day, then catching an airplane toward the end of the day to another place. The next day you were in another town, and by late afternoon, you were on another plane headed for another place. Many a morning I would wake up and have to take a few moments to remember what town I was in. Or what color the rental car was. It was sometimes hard."

Since 1978, Stephens has also been involved in contracting work at the Atlanta International Airport. "The first job I did down there was to put in some pipe at the west end of the Eastern Airlines parking lot. That's where a park-ride lot is now. We did a lot of work in the 1980s, but didn't do any for the airport in the 1990s."

Most recently, Stephens has been involved in moving tons and tons of rock at the airport, first for the fifth runway, and later for work on the new South and International terminals. "We've moved several million yards of rock." One of the main reasons for Stephens getting the job was his innovative conception of moving the rock not by truck, but by conveyor belt.

"That first contract was for $100 million. We provided rock for the runway, but now are providing rock for fill with dirt for the terminals. By adding rock to the soil, it makes good fill, better than just dirt. It just makes sense to move the rock by conveyor. We bought land in Clayton County in the year 2000 for the rock, and have been moving rock since June of 2002. We move it with a conveyor that is 4.5 miles long. We average moving the rock about three miles. It is so much cheaper and cleaner than moving it by truck, and there are no safety problems nor traffic problems.

"The airport work just keeps going. We will be there as long as they need fill materials. Once our conveyor work is over, we'll take down the conveyor and quit."

That conveyor belt used by Stephens at the airport was eventually 5.5 miles in length, spanned Interstate 285 and cost $13 million. It was capable of moving 3,200 tons of material per hour. He continued to operate it with moving dirt and rock until early 2008, when it was dismantled and sold.

Stephens says that by 2008, he had slowed down, working "only about 70 hours a week now." And his sons are now running his equipment and construction companies. Most people cannot tell that he has slowed, as he remains heavily involved with his company.

The Williams Brothers

Looking at a lifetime of activities in which the Williams brothers have been involved since 1955 will astound you. It's amazing how Jim and Virgil Williams, life-long business partners, could have started and run so many companies and have done it so well. Through it all, virtually all the hoopla around the brothers has centered on Virgil. He has been the up-front lightening rod, attracting the attention, being out front, cutting deals, and usually willing to talk openly about these ventures. Meanwhile, there's Jim, hanging back, virtually unnoticed and unknown, never being quoted, but adding his overall management guidance, with determination, strength and vision, to the vast and growing Williams empire. He's there, but the public never hears from him. Theirs has been a beautiful and beneficial partnership, one launched from the base given them by their father, Mercer Williams.

Former Georgia governors George Busbee and Zell Miller both saw in Virgil a key characteristic that tells a lot about how he succeeded. Both maintain Virgil's ability to "focus" was the key characteristic behind the Williams' success. Miller, speaking at a dinner when Virgil was given the Button Gwinnett Award by the Council for Quality Growth, said that Virgil is "the most focused, the most perceptive, the most resourceful and the hardest working man I have ever known." Jim was in the audience, but did not speak from the platform.

One aspect of the Jim and Virgil Williams' businesses is their diversity, focusing mainly initially on contracting, engineering and technology, but later involved with hospitality, the media, banking, real estate and, for Virgil, public service. After the brothers began to slow down, and sold off most of their jointly-owned companies, Virgil jumped into tourism and resort activities, as Virgil brought his wife and children into business with him. Jim, as usual, stayed quiet, retiring to a home between Snellville and Grayson, investing in some land deals, and remaining nearly unknown to the public.

Meanwhile, the new Virgil family venture, centered on Lake Lanier Islands, is a far cry from the day when the Williams brothers, out of their offices in Gwinnett County near Stone Mountain, had operations in London, Cairo, the Pacific Rim, Guam, and other corners of the earth. While averaging employment of 3,500 people over the years, the company at one time had 6,000 employees worldwide and had revenues of over $300 million a year in 26 companies. (The list of the Williams' companies continually changed. The vast scope of the Williams' ventures can be seen at the end of this chapter in a timeline.)

The Williams family started in Gwinnett in the 1880s, when one of their grandparents, William Pittman Williams, moved his family from Savannah to Gwinnett. He settled on what is now the Mountain East Industrial Park, east of Stone Mountain. The same land eventually was the headquarters for Jim and Virgil's company operations.

Jim is the oldest of three siblings and was born in 1932; Susan is the middle child (1937), and Virgil is the youngest (1939), all raised on the east side of Atlanta by Gertrude and Mercer Williams. Their father owned several small businesses, including a nationally active painting company, plus a swimming pool parts manufacturing firm. Virgil credits his father with teaching integrity and ethics in business, and his mother with teaching him an understanding of giving back to the community.

Through the years, the Williams children were close, playing together and supporting one another. As adults, they remained close.

Though Jim and Virgil were co-owners, Susan's husband, Jack Lane, was also involved with the companies, later trading his Williams companies stock for Atlas Manufacturing Company, a machine tool company.

Jim says of the relationship of the three men: "We tried to be good partners, and we talked about it. It was a lot of give and take. Sometimes it is easy for brothers to get crossed, or into the other's territory. I was flexible in this area. Our father, Mercer, taught us not to get into an argument with family members about money. It was a life principle

Virgil Williams

which we stuck to. I was more into field engineering. I don't know how it got along, but it helped that Jack and I didn't have egos. Virgil wanted to be the boss, and the face man. We let him be the boss, and he did a good job, being very innovative and creative. Jack was a good designer, engineer and implementer as an engineer. He could get things built. But I liked to stay in the background."

All three graduated from Georgia Tech, Jim in 1955 in chemical engineering; Jack in 1957 in mechanical engineering; and Virgil in 1963 in industrial engineering.

After graduation from Druid Hills High in 1958, Virgil went to Georgia Tech to study industrial engineering. While there, he got into real estate, supervising the building of homes and later commercial buildings.

The first subdivision he developed was Pendley Hills in DeKalb in 1961. Virgil would study in the homes he built on speculation during weekends while awaiting potential buyers. While in college, Virgil met a young nurse from Georgia Baptist Hospital, Sara Davis of Blue Ridge. They were married in 1959, and Sara kept the books for their initial businesses.

For 21 years, Jim and his wife, Barbara Covington of Atlanta, lived in a home near Northlake Mall. They had six children, two boys and four girls, and in 2008, 21 grandchildren. All their children continue to live within an hour of them. Barbara and Jim Williams moved to their home in Gwinnett in 1987, residing on a 100 acre tract.

Susan and Jack have lived in DeKalb County. They have three children.

Sara and Virgil Williams' first home was on Briarlake Road in Atlanta. Over the first years, they had four children. In the 1970s, they moved to an 80 acre farm on then-unpaved Webb Gin House Road in Gwinnett. Sara recalls thinking that it was in the "middle of nowhere." In 2001, the couple purchased a tract north of Suwanee once owned by Sherwin Glass, the person behind Farmer's Furniture's chain of stores, and moved there. It is a 40 acre site on the Chattahoochee River at the River Club.

Two months before Sara and Virgil were to wed in 1959, Mercer Williams died. He left the paint contracting and swimming pool supply company to his children. Though Virgil was still in college, he and Jim decided to take what their father had built and try to expand the business as new opportunities arrived. Using their technical background as their base, Virgil was the more creative person, in sales and planning and finding deals and acquisition for the company. Meanwhile, Jim focused on day-to-day operational management. Later Jack Lane would join them in the company. Virgil says of Jack: "He was the creative person who would figure out ways to get ideas workable. He put the bits and pieces together to make an idea come off. It was a three way partnership, flexible enough so that we could exchange roles, but we had our different roles."

Their first commercial project was simple enough, building a Texaco service station at the intersection of La Vista and North Druid Hills Roads in 1961.

Their operations expanded in the 1960s to include a munitions manufacturing company, producing weapon components for the Department of Defense during the Vietnam War. During this time, they also got into another field, with Jim and brother-in-law Jack Lane creating the largest slot-car manufacturing company of that day.

Working under Williams Contracting in the 1960s, Virgil remembers their first big job, taking on the interior painting of the First Union Bank Tower in Charlotte, N.C. This was under their Painting Services Inc. firm, a separate division, handling all the interior finishes.

During the Vietnam war, the three partners were in the munitions business, making two products at a machine tool plant on New Peachtree Road for the Defense Department. One item was producing a tip for a projectile out of bar steel stock. The other was producing a larger part, a tip for a mortar round, out of aluminum. The plant produced about a million of each tips a month. The production lasted five or six years, but in the late 1960s, deciding to focus on the painting and coating businesses, the three partners sold off their non-related firms, including those in manufacturing, munitions, and their high speed production facilities. Jim and Virgil concentrated on Williams Contracting, while Lane took Atlas Manufacturing Machine Corp., the machine shop, and continued to operate it.

Meanwhile, the parent company, Williams Contracting, was capitalizing on the base clients their father had acquired, working with large industrial clients such as Georgia Kraft, Florida Power and Light, and Georgia Power Company.

Innovative Approaches

The goal that the Williams sought was to look for emerging markets and tap into that niche with technical expertise and innovative thinking. It worked spectacularly.

One of their first large jobs came in Miami, Fla. at the Turkey Point Nuclear Plant of Florida Power and Light. It was their first nuclear project, a field where the Williams' companies would later become quite adept, in that they would develop a national reputation and have contracts from other parts of the country.

The initial job was to re-coat the inside of the nuclear reactor dome, which was made of steel. The coating on the steel had failed, was corroding badly, and needed replacement. The key to the job was to do the re-coating while the reactor was operating, a feat no firm had up until then accomplished. This was a perfect example of the type of projects that Williams became known for, tackling problems in a distinctive way.

Virgil adds: "We figured out an isolation system within the dome, whereby we completely grit-blasted the steel and recoated the interior finishing. And it was risky, since the reactor was continuing to produce heat all this time."

Jack Lane, who coordinated the nuclear projects, admits that the job was somewhat dangerous, with the crew having to don protective clothing at the site. Lane says that they came up with a false ceiling to partition off the upper part of the dome, where the work was going on, from the lower area. Each worker going inside the nuclear plant would have to dress in the protective gear, which was made of paper and impervious to the dust from the plant, and keep on when in the contaminated area. It was also very hot to wear. Afterward, when leaving the area, each worker would have to take off the clothing, shower before leaving the plant, and be checked for contamination.

Through using sectional modular partitions in the Browns' Ferry nuclear power plants, the same idea would be used later when doing similar work in paper mills, though the conditions were entirely different. Jack says of the isolation system: "It was a cordoned off area. We had to bring in all our pieces of equipment and materials through portholes, then re-assemble them inside the special area. We did this while the nuclear reactor was re-fueling and changing out its core rods, which usually took about 2-3 weeks. No one had ever done this, that is, re-coat the inside surface while the re-fueling was taking place. Each time we did a project, we got better, and did it in a shorter period, saving money for the utility."

The entire dome area, measuring 400 feet in diameter on the outside, and about 25 feet tall, was divided into bays. "We would work in 1-2-3 bays at a time, closing off three bays, and gritblast the steel of the torus. Then we had to apply the paint coating, and let it cure. We applied electric heaters to the surface to speed up the drying and curing process. There was a cooling fan so the workers could breathe easier. Once we finished a bay, we would leapfrog the modular partition around the inside of the torus to do other areas, using the same units on other bays. We could usually move the partitions in one or two shifts."

A continuing concern was safety. Jack says: "We had a quality assurance manager, who developed procedures to meet government regulations. There were also continuing inspections by the government."

Jim Williams

Because of their innovative approach, the Williams companies found that their nuclear-related work significantly broadened after that initial contract. "We went from specialty work at nuclear plants to general nuclear plant maintenance work. We did about every type of work needed, employing about every trade in this work. We often were hired to manage the plants year-round as their primary maintenance contractor. We did a lot of work for the Tennessee Valley Authority but had contracts for nuclear work up and down the East Coast and in the Midwest."

The company continued to do this type of work on nuclear plants in, among other areas, Illinois, Pennsylvania, New Hampshire, Florida, and often for the TVA projects in Tennessee.

One of these nuclear projects became what Virgil feels is one of his most rewarding efforts, and also one of the most complex. That was the initial coating and fire-proofing of Plant Vogtle, a nuclear plant of Georgia Power Company.

Meanwhile, the Williams were venturing into other projects, subdivision development, engineering, and getting broader contracts in the coating industry. They grew a national reputation within the painting and coating industry.

Another innovation in applying coating was a Portable Automated Coating plant to gritblast steel beams and plates prior to coating. This was a huge unit, some 240 feet long, with each unit built in Atlanta, and transported to sites on oversize flat bed trucks. Running down the middle, once set up, was a conveyor belt. Bridge cranes at each end would lift heavy steel beams into place for them to be grit-blasted. Earlier versions of such machines would require permanent facilities constructed with 20-30 foot deep holes, using large hoppers. The Williams system was entirely portable, able to be moved to new jobs on demand. They also had several different models of this unit. Later the company would sell Portable Automated Coating systems to other firms.

The device used centrifugal force from blast wheels to shoot small hardened steel shot onto the item being cleaned. This would knock off the corrosion of the steel, even cleaning out the small crevices, for coating. Meanwhile, the shot would fall onto the conveyor system, be cleaned, and be used again. Additional coarse shot would be added as the older shot was reduced by the blasting.

The Williams companies became known for their innovative techniques and engineering skills. Remember the "Scream Machine" roller coaster at Six Flags Over Georgia? The company took a novel approach to this venture. Working under Jack Lane's supervision, the entire machine was engineered in 1978 by Williams Engineering in a unique manner.

Jack Lane remembers this well. "The contractor for the Scream Machine shipped in fir wood from California to us at a warehouse downtown near Interstate 20. We would bring it to a conveyor line and automatically drill holes where needed, with pieces of various lengths. We then ran the wood through a dipping process as a quick way to give it a prime coat.

"They took the material to the job site, and assembled it like an erector set. They would give me the elevation line of the finished track, and the elevation survey of the ground under it. At each vertical leg section, I would calculate how long that piece needed to be, and how many pieces would be needed to get it to, say, 300 or 400 feet high, and figure the location of the holes. We numbered all these and bolted them together. We didn't do the assembly work, just manufactured the pieces, essentially pre-fabricating each piece, for the contractor to assemble. We had to do the supporting cross pieces, too."

A benefit to this pre-assembly: saving time. Where previously each piece had to be individually cut and fit, with the pre-assembly process, the job was finished in about three months, where other similar jobs had taken up to a year.

Going back to Jim and Virgil's father, the companies had worked closely with the pulp and paper business. One of the problems of such mills is that there is a corrosive atmosphere present, requiring constant repainting.

Jack Lane says that Virgil figured out an algorithm for predicting future failure times of steel at paper mills. Jack built a computer program from this, which proved invaluable to the mills in their preventive maintenance program.

Jack says: "We would do an inventory of every piece of steel in the plant, a Cyclic Environmental Maintenance Plan (CEMP). That might take a crew of three or four a month or so. From this we would determine whether each individual piece of steel was in a mildly or heavily corrosive environment, with gradations. We then would give the plant a 10 year schedule on when to repaint each piece of steel, and what it would cost."

He adds; "This would allow the plant to be smart about maintenance, not repainting every piece of steel, but only the ones that needed it. We would find pieces of steel that they didn't know were failing. We would also find steel that would be thin, or eaten away by corrosion, or find pieces that had fallen because of corrosion. We showed the plant the crucial areas, and saved them a lot of money."

The banking business

Working parallel with the growth of Williams Contracting Group, in 1979 Virgil and Jim got into the banking business, acquiring Gwinnett County Bank of Snellville. This led to the Williams boys helping revolutionize banking nationally and internationally, with their supermarket branch banks. This also proved to be the launching pad for Virgil's eventual seat on the board of Bank of America, one of the nation's largest banks.

Virgil's cousins, Jimmy and Wayne Mason, introduced the Williams brothers to banking. (The Masons' mother was a Williams, hence the relationship.) The Masons had invested in the early 1970s in Gwinnett County Bank when Mack Robinson, who had interests in some 30 banks in Georgia, wanted to locate a new bank in the growing town of Snellville. Later, with the downturn of the economy in the latter 1970s, Robinson needed to sell Gwinnett County Bank. When the Masons were stymied by banking authorities from buying his shares in the bank because of a lawsuit they were having with Hamilton Bank of Chattanooga, the Masons suggested that the Williams' consider getting into banking. Virgil and Jim Williams ended up with nearly all of the bank's shares, some 90 percent in 1979.

Two years later, in 1981, they purchased Fulton County Bank and combined the two banks into a bank holding company, and changed the names to Heritage Bank that same year. Next came the purchase, as individuals, of Rockdale Savings and Loan Association, which soon became Heritage Savings Bank, a "sister" company with the same name and logo, through owned privately from the banks. That purchase was key, for the Rockdale unit was a state chartered association, and could branch anywhere in Georgia. It was then the only bank in the state able to branch statewide. When Heritage Bank was sold to BankSouth in 1987, by then it had 34 branches in Georgia.

During this time, the innovations for which the Williams were known for in engineering began to be applied to banking. Virgil realized that the time frame for making a bank profitable was three years. Then came the idea that would change banking: put them in supermarkets.

Virgil says: "You could put mini-branch banks in supermarkets at reasonable and affordable costs, and you could expand quickly. You could put in 12 mini-branches for the cost of building one standard branch. We worked out a deal with Kroger to open three at one time, each in a different market, each with different demographics---North Atlanta, DeKalb and Gwinnett. (The first mini-branches were in Sandy Springs at the Kroger on Roswell

Road, on Memorial Drive in DeKalb, and at the Kroger in Peachtree Corners.) One area was white collar, another supermarket bank was in a mixed ethnic area, and the other was in a developing white-blue collar community." By having three locations in different types of community, the locations were test-marketed to determine different people's reactions.

Virgil says: "We found little negative reaction by people in any of these sections of town. We found demand and growth of deposits was just as good as at a branch bank. We learned that the average supermarket shopper went 1.2 to 1.5 times a week, and found that these shoppers accepted supermarket bankings' convenience, including late night banking, and even Saturday banking. We could offer the same products and services as regular banks. We got our market share in each area. We kept the supermarket branches open six days a week, usually 12 hours a day."

Traditional bankers, Virgil admits, "were laughing up a storm at us in the beginning of supermarket branches. Whoever heard of a bank in a grocery store? They asked if we were going to accept apples for cash. Then soon they started to realize we were on to something, and within a 10 year span, every one of them wanted to do it. Eventually old conservative banks like Trust Company of Georgia wanted in, and they started their own mini-branches."

Jim adds: "Before we opened the supermarket branch banks, the traditional banks were in the catbird seat at the time. They felt 'We're the top dog, and if you want to do business with us, you have to do it when it is convenient to us.' There was virtually no Saturday banking, and they closed at 4 p.m. or earlier."

Then Jim says: "We went in there and made it convenient for the customers. The bankers laughed at us. But we felt the people deserved more service than banks were giving them. So we had extended hours, for people to do business when it was convenient. When the supermarket banking really took off was when Virgil had the idea to sell it in other areas. And we created a new business in its own right. We had a lot of success which came from banking."

The Williams soon created a separate company to franchise the supermarket branch idea. This became, in 1985, International Banking Technologies, and got started on a fast track, out of a building at Indian Trail Road at Intestate 85. It became a national center for licensing, franchising and building branches in supermarkets.

Virgil says: "We would go to the national supermarket chains, Kroger, Safeway, Ralphs….anywhere in the country at first, then overseas, and agree to take down all the inventory they had to accommodate mini branch banks. We would take 100-200-300 at a time, having the exclusive right to market the sites to banks in the town where the supermarket was located. We would market the sites to the banks, then construct, promote and package a turn-key bank franchise. We soon had 100-150 people in training, sales, architecture, supervision and inspection. We brought people to the IBT building in Norcross and ran these people through training classes, showing them how to sell banking services in the supermarket environment, even how to effectively contact people in the aisles.

"Our company maintained the lease with the grocery chain, and then sub-leased to the bank. But we were still the leaseholder. We had to ensure that the local bank that got the space from us would operate within our standards. We were the franchisor for the concept."

A little more than one year later, in 1986, IBT had franchised 1,200 mini-branches around the nation, operated by local banks. That same year, IBT was sold to First Financial Management of Atlanta, and Virgil gained a seat on its board of directors.

A major development in the career of the Williams Brothers took place in 1987, when BankSouth acquired the 34 branches of Heritage Bank. With the purchase, Jim and Virgil did not take cash, but stock in BankSouth, becoming its largest stockholders.

As BankSouth continued to grow, it caught the attention of NationsBank, which was interested in growing its Georgia market. NationsBank had earlier acquired C&S Bank of Georgia, and in 1995, purchased BankSouth, with Virgil getting a seat on the NationsBank board. When NationsBank acquired Bank of America in 1998, it took the prestigious name of the bank it was acquiring, and Virgil also was on the Bank of America board. "It was the nation's largest bank by a long shot in terms of number of offices," Virgil says. Virgil retired from the board of Bank of America in 2005.

When in the banking business, the Williams' had acquired a Carrollton, Ga. firm that did data processing, and soon it was processing checks and doing accounting for 30 banks.

A similar firm was First Financial Management, which was originated out of the First Railroad Bank of Augusta. Virgil figured that handling work for 30 banks was not a critical mass, so went to First Financial and merged with it, getting a seat on the First Financial board. Later, when First Financial acquired Georgia Federal Savings Bank, Virgil, by then on the BankSouth board, had to resign from First Financial's board.

A few years later, First Financial had sold Georgia Financial, and bought IBT from the Williams. So Virgil went back on the First Financial board. This company later bought Western Union out of the New York bankruptcy court, which had changed from a telegraph company to one primarily involved with money transfers for major banks. First Financial operated the firm independently. It became a fabulous moneymaker not for delivering messages as before, but as a major conduit for wire transfer of money, often providing this service for immigrants. Soon Western Union was doing 93 percent of money transfers worldwide, often dealing with emerging market countries, such as China.

In turn, First Financial Management was sold in 1997 to First Data, a firm built around credit card authorization and transactional services. In the merger, it became the largest processor of financial data in the country.

Into communications

Virgil's venture into the media began in 1992, when Williams Communications bought *Georgia Trend* magazine from Millard Grimes. (Jim was not part of this venture.) The next year he bought *Business Atlanta* and merged it into *Georgia Trend*, and started *Business Augusta* later in 1994. Williams would re-sell the combined magazines to Grimes in April, 1994. During his ownership of *Georgia Trend*, Williams authored an editorial column on issues in the state. His years of owning the publication saw increases in circulation and advertising. In late 1997, Virgil also started *SOUTH* magazine, which he also sold to Grimes in April of 1998. Grimes combined it with *Georgia Trend* in the June edition. (In 1998, Grimes would sell *Georgia Trend* again, this time to Tom Cousins and Neely Young, who continue in 2008 to publish the magazine out of offices in Oakbrook Technology Park.

Williams Communications also obtained the rights to the three digit 711 telephone number in 1999, which Williams used to provide a telephone information service. He says: "We found out that the Public Service Commission would award three digit numbers to firms that would provide a public service with them. We applied and were awarded the 711 number. I thought that was something easily remembered, seven-eleven, and we would provide lots of information to people that way."

What emerged was a 711 system that people would call for all sorts of information. "They would push numbers and get information, with a lot of this automatic. If they wanted a job, they could get an operator, who in real time took their resume data down. We were building a data-base, but had to figure out how to distribute it. We were trying to match the resumes with firms needing people, and had to use more technology. Remember, this was before the Internet."

From this emerged the Career Network, an offshoot of 711, producing a resume data base. Later it would come Atlanta Employment Weekly, where resumes were distributed in print. Still later Career Network would distribute CDs of the data to companies seeking workers. "They could pop them into the computer and search through categories for workers, and contact us to get the name if they wanted to interview that person, for a fee, of course. Later we had a dial-in system, computer-to-computer, to search our data-base."

Yet Virgil did not take it one step further. He says: "I could have hit it big, but missed it."

Here's how that happened, as Virgil remembers: "We had this guy and his son who came in to see us, trying to get us interested in this new system called the Internet. He was unemployed at the time, and was a questionable character, both in appearance and by not having a job. But he seemed to know a lot about the Internet, which we didn't know much about.

"He wanted us to hook our data-base through the Internet, so that anyone anywhere would have that information available to them, without going through the telephone. I was suspicious from the beginning, what with the way they were dressed and all. I just didn't trust him, and told them that we would stick with what we had. This was several years before companies like Monster.com, back when people were not using the Internet like they do today.

"So I missed that boat, but came within a hair's breath of hitting it big if I had trusted those guys." He adds: "We also did not realize the implications of Internet advertising. The Internet was on its big beginning fringe, and I was an engineer, not a technical guru in any sense. We came close."

The upshot of the 711 number was that the Williams' gave their three digit enterprise away. They donated the rights to the three digit number in 1997 to United Way of Metropolitan Atlanta, with them supporting United Way's request to the Georgia Public Service Commission to use the 711 number for its "help line." (However, the 711 number was shortly thereafter assigned to the hearing impaired, and the Public Service Commission offered the Atlanta United Way the "211" number as a substitute for its Information Help Line.)

There has been an unusual impact from the Williams three-digit number gift to Atlanta's United Way. From a simple referral service for Atlanta's United Way, the three digit

211 number has become a full-fledged social utility number that connects people not only in Atlanta, but now 211 is used nationally for a United Way Help Line.

Five years after the donation of the three-digit number to United Way, Virgil said: "With over 300,000 calls expected this year, it is hard to believe how far 211 has come in such a short time. I am happy to see this easy-to-remember number has done so much good for so many people." The Williams' donation has become a permanent, lasting legacy of their commitment to United Way. The fist year of operation of 211 saw 104,674 calls to its Help Line, and those calls continued to grow to 349,830 in 2007.

Other media ventures of the Williamses included *Performance* magazine, a publication aimed at Williams industrial companies; and *Atlanta Employment Weekly.*

Other interests

Meanwhile, the Williams were active in other areas. Getting into real estate with Forest Adair in 1986, they formed Williams-Adair Realty Corporation, which manages, develops and brokers real estate in Metro Atlanta. Among its properties: the IBT building.

Other "big picture" engineering jobs became their focus. That included acquiring the 1987 acquisition of Moreland-Altobelli Associates, a major southeastern civil engineering, transportation and wastewater firm focusing on engineering and environmental services.

Adding to the Williams engineering firms, Law Engineering and Environmental Services was acquired in 1999. One of the premier engineering firms in the South, this firm gave the Williams tremendous entre into Law's international markets. Law had over 100 offices, 30 of them international.

Entering another aspect of business in 2001, Virgil Williams became a co-owner of the Nashville, Tenn. arena football team, moved it to Atlanta and changed the name to *Georgia Force.* He soon became the sole owner. The team played its first season in 2002 at Philips Arena in Atlanta. The next season, Williams moved the team to the Gwinnett Arena. During the three years that Williams owned the team, it had a 21-25 record, with a playoff appearance in 2003. Williams sold the *Georgia Force* to *Atlanta Falcons* owner Arthur Blank in the fall of 2004, and Blank moved the playing site back to Atlanta. However, in 2008, the *Georgia Force* returned to playing its home games at the Gwinnett Arena, where it began a five-year contract in 2008.

A decision by Virgil and Jim Williams in 1998 was to slow down, and basically get out of the businesses they had been in since the late 1950s. This came about gradually, with the last major sale of businesses taking place in 2007, as they sold Nitro Electric, a large heavy contracting firm in West Virginia.

Jim says of their decision: "Ours was not a briefcase contracting business with nine to five hours. The businesses were very complicated, and required an unusual amount of skill to run. We did little local business, in either Georgia or Atlanta. That meant a lot of travel out of state, pulling us away from our family constantly, and never ending. We had the many skilled craftsmen to work with, and constantly had to control quality. We employed about every skilled craft, the electrical, mechanical, heating and air conditioning people, a lot of different skilled crafts, which made it all the more difficult and meant a lot of exposure for us. We never sub-contracted work out, but had our own people performing the work.

"So that was the background. We realized that we did not want to subject our children to such working conditions. It would be best to have them in positions so that they could come home and be with their families each night. I did more travel, I guess, than Virgil did, but we both traveled and were away from home a good bit."

From this came the idea to sell the individual companies. It took about 10 years to sell the companies, with the last company being sold in 2007. Jim adds of his life: "I enjoyed most aspects of it. There were always new problems, but we would tackle them. In a way, I don't know how we did it, or where we got the energy to do it. But we had a good time and a good life."

Virgil slows down?

In 2005, Virgil Williams took a new direction, after he had sold off most of his contracting companies and other interests, usually to those running the companies. Virgil then turned his attention to Lake Lanier Islands, forming with his family the LLI Management Company to re-develop Lake Lanier Island facilities.

By happenstance, Virgil's participation in this project came about years after the commission he chaired recommended that such state groups be privatized. The original winner of the lease for the privatization rights to Lake Lanier Islands was KSL Recreation Corp. in 1996, which attempted to integrate the operations of the Islands into their overall company. When this did not work out well for KSL, it sold the lease to C&L REIT of Orlando, Fla., in 2003. This firm operated major large destination resorts in the country, with upward of 1,000 rooms per resort. Two years later, they realized that the Lake Lanier property did not fit into what they were doing worldwide. Williams' discussion with the REIT came in early 2005, and by September they had agreement. Williams' lease is for 50 years, which guarantees Lake Lanier Islands a minimum of $3.2 million a year.

Virgil's family began an extensive plan for redevelopment of the property, which started in 2006. Anticipated to take 7-10 years to be complete, it's estimated that the work will cost $300 million. The overall concept of his vision has approval of the Lake Lanier Islands Authority.

Initial work was a $50 million make-over of the Emerald Point Hotel, which got 42 additional rooms. The remodeled hotel opened in May of 2008. There's a possibility of adding 36 more rooms in new cottages on the hotel grounds. The golf course was also upgraded; the restaurants expanded; and other rooms and facilities were upgraded. Also included were a yacht club, major wellness center and spa and additional retail shopping space. The final phase of this makeover is scheduled for 2009.

Another aspect of the changes at the Islands was closing the initial hotel on the Islands, PineIsle, which was demolished in early 2008. It is scheduled for rebuilding to the standards of a four-star hotel on that site. This is Phase 2 of the overall project, which carries a $100 million price tag, and is expected to start in early 2010.

Ultimately, the scope of the Williams' stamp on Lake Lanier Islands will include 7.5 miles of new roads; 22 miles of additional walking trails; a new entrance and gates; plus infrastructure improvements for water and sewer lines. Out of these improvements, the Authority will have additional income streams from the lease. In early 2008, the Lake

Lanier Islands Development Authority took steps to replace the wastewater treatment plant when it got a $10 million loan from the Georgia Environmental Facilities Authority. The Islands were under a consent order with the Georgia Environmental Protection Division to replace the wastewater treatment plant by 2009. The Development Authority also secured a $10 million loan from Wachovia to help finance this project. Lonice Barrett, chairman of the LLI board, said that the move "puts a significant step into motion to work with our partner, the Williams family, at Lake Lanier Islands."

One of Virgil Williams goals in the Lake Lanier Island venture is to work closely with his immediate family on the venture. Williams notes that he is a minor stockholder. His wife, Sara, and his family are on the board of directors of the venture and are in key roles. Daughter Mindy oversees the decorating and artistic aspects; son Mike is the key day-to-day management person; and son Brad and Mindy's husband, David Bowling, oversee construction. A third son, Virgil Jr., sits on the board, but is not active day-to-day, since he has his own business, Williams Machine Works of Loganville.

Virgil's public career

Through most of his career, Virgil Williams had focused on private business, and became first involved with government in the mid 1970s. When on the county commission, Wayne Mason had named Virgil to the Public Facilities Authorities, which financed public projects in Gwinnett. It was Virgil's first foray into government. Mason says: "We had little business expertise on the Authority. Virgil did a good job for us."

In the late 1970s, Virgil chaired the Gwinnett Hospital Authority. This was at a time when the Authority sought to get Gwinnett voters to pass a bond referendum for funding a new central hospital. But the voters of the county handily turned this down in 1981, and the Authority at first was baffled on what course to take.

Led by its chairman, the Hospital Authority decided to build a new 190-bed hospital in Lawrenceville on a campus at the intersection of Georgia Highways 316 and 120. The Authority voted to guarantee the bonds from revenues of the hospital. In effect, the hospital funded its expansion itself. This was the only way the Authority found it could reasonably finance the much-needed new facility. However, it was both costly, and a little risky, with hospital revenues having to guarantee the bonds, since the voters rejected the less-costly county-guaranteed bonds. With this bold step, the Authority moved the Lawrenceville medical community forward.

Williams also brought in a new hospital president, Frank Rinker, out of Charlotte, N.C. to oversee the hospital development. Rinker remained with the hospital for 23 years, building the 190-bed central hospital, and developing plans before his retirement for a major, 155-room expansion in 2007.

Over the years, Virgil Williams had been friends with Lt. Gov. Zell Miller. Miller asked Virgil to head his gubernatorial campaign in 1988. Virgil worked tirelessly to raise money and gain support for Miller among the business community. Along with Wayne Mason's son, Keith, the pair brought in a little known Louisiana consultant, James Carville, to direct the political side of the campaign. It was a masterful stroke, as Miller won handily. Four years later, Williams again successfully headed the Miller re-election efforts.

Once elected governor, Miller turned to Virgil with another request: to become his chief of staff. He held that post during both Miller terms as governor. Among the jobs Miller initially tasked to Williams was to head a committee Miller called the "Governor's Commission on Effectiveness and Economy in Government." Miller later said of its work: "Because of the confidence and hands-on leadership that Virgil brought to that commission, it soon caused that long name to be forgotten and it was shortened to the Williams Commission."

Miller outlined why he thought this commission was needed. "Some people may have a notion that waste in government is concentrated in chunks out around the edges, sort of like fat is on a steak, where it can be easily identified and where you can quickly trim it off, leaving most of the meat intact. It's not that way at all. It's more like a round of beef, with the fat all mixed up and you have to put in a lot of effort to get the fat out. You may even have to cook it and turn up the heat a little and turn the meat into a different form. It's an ongoing process that takes time to achieve.....the Williams Commission recommendations.... continue to....make state government more efficient."

After one year of study, the Williams Commission report spelled out in detail how to improve state government operations with over 400 recommendations, with estimated savings of over $720 million. Among the recommendations: amnesty for overdue state income taxes, which netted $44 million relatively quickly; streamlining information technology; improving communications; creation of the Georgia Research Alliance; and sending state managers to seminars on how to reorganize for quality and efficiency.

However, perhaps the most far-reaching recommendation was to privatize many aspects of state government. Among them were privatizing key recreational facilities, those at Stone Mountain, Lake Lanier Island, and the Brasstown Valley Resort near Young Harris.

Some Georgia parks hotel organizations were included, but later went back to the state.

Parts of several state departments were privatized. These included contracting out three state prisons to private firms; that savings alone, over 20 years, amounted to an estimated $75 million. Another unit privatized was the Dept. of Veteran Services War Memorial Veteran's Home in Milledgeville. Maintenance of state vehicles was privatized as well, in private garages and service centers throughout the state as part of the Georgia Governor's Commission for a New Georgia. All this stemmed from the Williams Commission. Perhaps the greatest impact from this Commission was the realization by both politicians and state employees in following years was that there might be another way for state government to function instead of enlarging the number of state employees. The later day Commission for a New Georgia, for instance, approached some functions of state government with privatization in mind, and implemented new approaches in several departments which produced savings over the way the government previously operated.

It's ironic that after a long and successful career, Virgil Williams would move toward slowing down---if you call it that---by getting out of his many far-flung companies, and by gaining the lease to operate the privatized Lake Lanier Islands, and turning that into the focus of his new family-run business. That's the way Virgil Williams has spent his entire business life, getting into ventures where others didn't recognize the opportunities.

The Williams companies over the years

Individual companies that the Williams brothers have started, owned and operated through the years:

- 1955: Williams Photo Service: Film processing.
- 1956: Swimquip: Equipment sales.
- 1958: Atlas Manufacturing and Machine Co: Parts manufacturing for PoolQuip; also manufactured steel and aluminum parts for the defense industries.
- 1958: Poolquip Inc.: Pool equipment sales.
- 1959: Williams Contracting: Industrial coating for pulp, paper and power industry
- 1960: Virgil R. Williams, Builder: Residential homes and apartments.
- 1961: Pendley Hills: Subdivision development.
- 1961: Walton County Farm: Family farm.
- 1962: Old English Apartments: First apartment development.
- 1970: Williams Plan: First engineered, programmed maintenance approach for corrosion control and painting for heavy industries.
- 1971: Painting Services, Inc.: A Charlotte, N.C. company for interior wall painting.
- 1972: Upper Trace: Small family farm near Snellville.
- 1972: Florida Power and Light Turkey Point nuclear project: Nuclear decontamination and coating services for containment dome and other areas.
- 1977: Industrial Coating Services: Shop coating services for industrial construction projects and the Portable Automated Coating (PAC) Facility, a set of trailers designed to sandblast, coat, and cure steel on site for improved quality
- 1977: The Forest Subdivision: Subdivision development near Stone Mountain.
- 1978 Equipment Technology Inc.: Design and manufacturing of portable blasting equipment for large steel beams and small parts.
- 1978 PAC Systems Mark II: Smaller, single trailer design of the original multi-trailer PAC unit.
- 1978: Williams Engineering: Design and other types of technological support to both Williams Contracting and Equipment Technology.
- 1978: Six Flags Great American Scream Machine: Design and construct the roller coaster, using a system to pre-fabricate the parts and then assemble on site, saving 25 percent over normal wood-constructed roller coasters.
- 1978: Williams Plan with CEMP: Cyclic-Econo Maintenance Program (C.E.M.P.) was a computerized evaluation model added to the Williams Plan maintenance painting corrosion control system.
- 1979: Gwinnett County Bank: Purchased by Virgil and Jim Williams, had main office and two branches, set up ATMs in shopping areas to expand presence, also added 8 am-8 pm drive-in banking.
- 1980: Deposits Unlimited: Promote financial deposit incentive promotions for bank facilities.
- 1980: The Little People: First promotion program developed by Deposits Unlimited and implemented at Gwinnett County Bank (great success with Cabbage Patch Dolls and Designer Xavier Roberts.)

- 1980: Monolith Construction: General construction company for residential and apartments. Later produced commercial cabinets for banks and in-store banking units.
- 1980: North American Travel Bureau: Travel company located in Gwinnett County Bank facilities.
- 1981: Total Life Center: Insurance company located in Gwinnett County Bank facilities.
- 1981: Landmark Insurance Associates: Insurance company.
- 1981: Fulton County Bank: One-office bank, purchased and merged with Gwinnett County Bank.
- 1981: Heritage Bank: New name of merged banks; shortly after formation, started in-store banking program with Kroger stores.
- 1981: Metro Land Brokers: Real estate brokerage for commercial properties.
- 1981: Technology Graphics: In-house printing company.
- 1981: Southpoint: Plantation in Lee County, Ga.
- 1981: Williams Developers: Commercial development company.
- 1981: Williams Investment Realty: Investment rental properties; apartments, office and retail shopping.
- 1982: Heritage Savings Bank: Savings and Loan company acquisition with name change (Rockdale Savings and Loan).
- 1982: Eagle Pond: Plantation in Lee County, Ga.
- 1982: Mountain East Business Center: Office development in Stone Mountain (West Park Place); corporate office building for Williams companies.
- 1982: Williams Equity Corporation: Operational equity corporation.
- 1982: Williams-Adair Equity Corporation: Limited partnership real estate investment company, which became the leasing/brokerage agency for Williams/Monolith projects and a full service development and management company serving the Atlanta area.
- 1983: Financial Data Services: Data processing services for financial institutions including Heritage Bank.
- 1983: Williams Contracting Group Inc.: Expansion and reorganization of Williams Contracting.
- 1983: Williams Maintenance Services: Provide coating and industrial maintenance to the pulp and paper industry.
- 1983: Williams Mechanical Inc.: Provide mechanical services for power for pulp and paper industry.
- 1983: Williams Power Services Inc. Provide coating and industrial maintenance to the power utility industry.
- 1983: Pulpco Inc.: Manufacture and installation of pulp washers and other pulp and paper equipment.
- 1983: Paper Inc.: A mechanical contracting firm.
- 1983: Williams Service Group Inc., a holding company.
- 1984: Mountain Associates Inc.: Insurance brokerage.
- 1984: Heritage Bank building: Office building located at I-85 and I-285, corporate office for Heritage Bank.
- 1984: Alert Maintenance Plan: Special maintenance program as joint venture between Williams Contracting and Carboline Company (industrial paint manufacturer, St. Louis, Mo.).

- 1984: Heritage Village Shopping Center, in Snellville.
- 1984: Carboline-Williams: A joint venture in special maintenance program as joint venture between Williams Contracting and Carboline Company.
- 1985; Five Oaks Center: Strip shopping center with Heritage Bank branch as anchor (Five-Forks Trickum Road area).
- 1985: Country Quarters: Upscale apartment development.
- 1985: International Banking Technologies: In-store supermarket banking.
- 1985: Offshore Painting Contractors: Painting company for oil refinery and offshore oil rigs.
- 1985: One Seventy-Five Heritage Center: Office building with Heritage Bank office (Lawrenceville area).
- 1986: The Azcon Systems: Azcon Asbestos Control Services company programmed approach to asbestos removal in large office or industrial facilities.
- 1986: First Financial Management Corp.: Financial data services, acquired International Banking Technology (Virgil on board of directors of firm).
- 1986: Gulf Tech: Industrial painting services for pulp and paper, refineries and power industry in gulf region in Texas and Louisiana.
- 1986: Shaw Insulation Services: Industrial insulation and HVAC services for utilities, high-rise buildings, etc.
- 1986: Southern Heritage Plantation: Working plantation with restored 1850's home, near Albany, Ga.
- 1986: Williams Power Company: Contracting company (Williams Power Services).
- 1986: Pike Center at 316: Office Park.
- 1986: Williams-Adair Realty Corporation: Commercial real estate sales, leasing and management.
- 1986: Fulton Four Hundred Corporate Center: Office park (in north Fulton County).
- 1987: Bank South Corporation, merged with Heritage Bank.
- 1987: Home Cable Vision of Albany: Cable TV distribution company.
- 1987: Moreland Altobelli Associates: Civil engineers (Formed by Virgil and Jim Williams along with Tom Moreland and Dan Altobelli).
- 1987: Sentry Asbestos Abatement: Asbestos removal in northeast.
- 1988: Strategic Media: Marketing and design group.
- 1988: Harmon Engineering and Environmental: Environmental engineering and lab services (located in Auburn, Ala.).
- 1988: Williams Environmental Services: Provides environmental engineering plus environmental remediation services using therma desorption equipment.
- 1988: Benchmark Engineering: New name for Harmon Engineering.
- 1988: Asbestos Information Management and System: Computer-based system developed by Williams Environmental Services.
- 1988: Williams Industrial Services Inc.: Maintenance services primarily for pulp and paper industry.
- 1988: Block and Blevins: Heavy mechanical firm.
- 1988: Oakbrook Plaza: Office park.
- 1988: Williams Incinerator Services: Remediation services for on-site hazardous waste incineration at Super-Fund sites.

- 1990: Air Center Gwinnett: Aviation services company.
- 1993: Williams Communications: Georgia Trend magazine.
- 1994: Business Atlanta: Competitor to Georgia Trend, acquired by Williams, ceased publication 1994.
- 1994: Business Augusta: Competitor to Georgia Trend, begun by Williams, ceased publication 1994.
- 1995: NationsBank merger with Bank South.
- 1995: VISPRO: Occupational training and screening services designed to improve the client's safety performance and reduce costs.
- 1995: Employment Staffing Services: Temporary staffing services primarily for industrial technicians.
- 1996: Williams Group International Inc.: Williams service group.
- 1996: Williams Plant Services: Mechanical work for heavy industrial plants.
- 1996: Williams Specialty Services: Protective coatings division high end corrosion control.
- 1996: Williams Construction: Contracting division for commercial facilities.
- 1996 Bank of America merger with NationsBank.
- 1996: Datasphere Technologies Inc.: Software maintenance firm for large projects.
- 1996: Insight Maintenance Software: Proprietary software developed for comprehensive maintenance evaluation and tracking.
- 1996: Union Boiler American: Maintenance and installation of large power boilers.
- 1996: Nitro Electric: Heavy industrial electrical company in Ohio Valley area.
- 1996: South Magazine: Business/politics magazine.
- 1996: Pace Power Construction: Utility construction services in northeast US.
- 1996: Legge Steel Erectors: Mechanical maintenance services, including a unique approach to the straightening of steel beams (Ohio area).
- 1996: Wallace O'Connor: Offices in the Pacific, Caribbean and Middle East, primarily provides mechanical and electrical contracting services to the international market.
- 1997: Performance Magazine: Publication for Williams industrial companies.
- 1999: 711 Possibilities: Creation of information network.
- 1999: Career Network: Offshoot of 711 producing resume data base.
- 1999: Atlanta Employment Weekly: Resumes distributed in print with code number.
- 1999: MCC Commercial Cabinets: Banking, medical, class-A office facilities and specialty cabinet design, manufacturing and installation.
- 1999: Law Engineering and Environmental Services Inc.: Civil and environmental engineering in US and international markets.
- 1999: Computer Sentry Software: Computer security.
- 2000: Craftforce: Temporary craft labor services for heavy industrial (pipe fitters, electricians, welders, painters, boilermakers, etc.).
- 2001: Chateau Lyrah: Sara and Virgil Williams home, near Suwanee.

Virgil Williams' public career

- » 1958: Entered Georgia Tech.
- » 1963: Graduated Georgia Tech.
- » 1982: Gwinnett Public Facilities Authority.
- » 1983: Hospital Authority of Gwinnett County: became chairman.
- » 1984: Georgia Compensation Commission.
- » 1987: Georgia Tech Foundation.
- » 1988: Chairman, Zell Miller for Governor, 1990.
- » 1990: Heritage and Wildlife Conservation Council.
- » 1990: Chief of Staff for Gov. Zell Miller: for eight years.
- » 1992: Williams Commission: Governor Miller appointed Virgil to chair the Governor's Commission on Effectiveness and Economy in Government (which became known as the Williams Commission).
- » 1993: Governor's Development Council, chairman.
- » 1993: Georgia Board of Regents.
- » 1995: Georgia Gwinnett College.
- » 1996: Georgia Chamber of Commerce: board of directors.
- » 1999: 1818 Club: co-chairman.
- » 2001: Georgia Force: professional arena football team.

By the Virgil Williams family:

- » 2005: LLI Management Company LLC: Resort enterprise.

Mary Alice Juhan

Most communities have their distinctive citizens. Lawrenceville had its share. One of the most distinguished citizens of Lawrenceville in the 20th Century had to be Mary Alice Juhan. She died in 2002 at age 93.

Miss Mary Alice was a stalwart saint when it came to observing the Lord's Day. A staunch Presbyterian, she wanted to do no work, nor did she want any one else to do anything on Sunday, except glorify her Lord. People knew she was staunch in her church. Her banker, Bartow Morgan III, called her "the town's only Presbyterian nun." She was closely associated with, and helped fund, the national Lord's Day Alliance, and attended many of its conventions. She was even awarded its James P. Westberry plaque for her efforts to promote worship on Sundays.

She worried when seeing activity on Sunday: "You can't tell what day of the week it is," she would lament. Her hero was Truett Cathy of the Chick-fil-A restaurant business, because he closed all his outlets on Sunday.

Miss Mary Alice was of small frame, but tall in her beliefs. She was a school teacher who came from an old-time Gwinnett family. Her father, O.L., had operated a shoe shop in Lawrenceville. He was clerk of the Presbyterian Church session for 43 years, and he invested in real estate, including a 126 acre family farm west of town, but lost the land during the Depression. She grew up on North Clayton Street, up from her father's shoe shop and near the former site of the Lawrenceville Presbyterian Church.

She graduated from Agnes Scott College, taught for a while in Kentucky, but soon returned and became a teacher in the Gwinnett system.

Many old-timers in Gwinnett can recount their days with Miss Juhan in school. They remember her as a good and dedicated teacher, who would rap students on the hand with a big pencil when they misbehaved, or if they were slow to learn. One student recounted being told: "You're going to learn to read. I know you are not as dumb as your daddy, and I never did think I could get him to read."

Mary Alice Juhan

As she matured, she became more concerned about Sundays. When she would hear of a planned Sunday activity, such as a circus coming to town, she would follow around behind those tacking up circus signs, knock them down with her cane, and burn them. "They're illegal anyway," she pointed out. She also would go out on weekends collecting illegal real estate signs, sometimes gathering as many as 200.

Randy Simpson, whose father, Ralph, ran the projector at the Lawrenceville theatre, says that Claxton Jones, who then was running the theatre, was putting up signs for the movie on telephone poles. Miss Juhan followed behind him, ripping the signs off. It caused Jones to question: "Gee, I swear that I put signs up on this street," he later told Mr. Simpson. He got in his car, a Studebaker, and rode a few miles, and found Miss Mary Alice knocking down the signs.

Her most infamous effort was when the Thompson Theatre in Lawrenceville started opening on Sunday. This was in the early 1950s. To show her concern about being opened on Sunday, Miss Juhan tossed a brick through the ticket office window.

It was the talk of Lawrenceville. "They were going to lock her up," says Joe Ben Davis, a great-nephew, "but the town intervened." Miss Juhan paid for the theatre's plate window replacement, figuring she had made her point. One official told her: "You can't continue doing this stuff."

The story goes that Larry McClure, who operated the theatre, saw Miss Mary Alice on the street. "Miss Mary Alice, you should not have done that," he admonished. "Larry, you shouldn't be open on Sunday," she came back.

That next year, the Lawrenceville City Schools did not re-new her contract. Yet she soon landed a job of teaching in Grayson and later drove to Social Circle to complete her 42 years in the classroom.

When her father lost the family farm during the Depression, that hurt Miss Mary Alice. Over the years, she saved her money to re-purchase the land, and eventually succeeded. She later sold off some of the area for development, while the State Highway Department on three occasions took more of her land along the Lawrenceville-Suwanee Road. In 1995, she sold the remaining 17 acres of the farm that was left on Suwanee Road at Highway 316 for what would become a major shopping center, Lawrenceville Market.

Mary Alice Juhan nailed up signs like this on her property showing her true colors about Sunday movies.

She gave much of the proceeds to charities, but was still quite wealthy herself. That worried her. In her later years, when she was in most fragile health, and in a nursing home, she would ask Joe Davis, who handled her finances: "Do I have any money?" She did, and his answer would fret her. Davis says: "Finally, I just started telling her that she was broke, and the county might have to bury her as a pauper. That made her smile," he says.

Ben Davis, her great-great nephew, tells a story about Miss Mary Alice. "Whenever I brought a girl home from boarding school or college, the first thing Mary Alice would ask her was if she was a Presbyterian. Back then I was embarrassed by this.

"Right before Aunt Mary Alice passed, my wife, Clarissa, and I were visiting her. She kept staring at Clarissa. Mary Alice wasn't able to talk much at this point, and she just kept staring at my wife.

"Finally Clarissa went over and knelt down and said, 'Mary Alice, you know me. I'm Clarissa, Ben's wife.'

"All of a sudden, she looked up and said, 'I know who you are. I'm just trying to find out if you are a Presbyterian.' I miss her and her ways."

When he was a lad of 11-12 years old, Joe Davis was asked by his family to accompany Mary Alice to church each Sunday at Old Peachtree Road Presbyterian Church. "She would drive to church. Later she allowed me to drive back, and that was worth it to me. When we got to the church in winter, she would build a fire. Sometimes the attendance would be small, only four or five of us, but she would still teach the Sunday School lesson, and read Bible verses. She kept that church together when it was about to fall apart."

As Gwinnett grew, the church became substantially stronger. At her death, the church had grown to a robust congregation, with about 200 members and a full program. Its minister, Allen Johnson, along with Paul Ard of the Lawrenceville Presbyterian Church, preached her funeral.

Three Parsons Girls

Three native sisters of Duluth became key figures in the Gwinnett artistic and philanthropic communities. They are Margaret Parsons Andrews, Kathryn Parsons Willis and Ann Parsons Odum, the daughters of Kate Alford Parsons and Calvin Parsons. The sisters' parents continued a tradition started by Kate's father, Alvin Alford, who first opened a country general store in 1876 in the small community of Gloster, south of Lawrenceville. Through the years, Alvin Alford's nine children operated 12 Alford general stores in the Gwinnett area.

In 1925, Kate and Calvin Parsons joined the family business by operating a store in Duluth; they later started their own stores, and had five Parsons stores in Norcross, Lawrenceville, Buford, Cumming, and Flowery Branch. These were general stores, with groceries, hardware, farming supplies, shoes and dry goods. While growing up, the sisters all worked in the different Parsons stores.

As the sisters graduated from high school at North Avenue Presbyterian School for Girls in Atlanta (today's Westminster), they then each went to Wesleyan College in Macon. Margaret majored in speech, Kathryn in English and psychology, and Ann in education..

Ann Parsons Odum, Kathryn Parsons Willis, and Margaret Parsons Andrews

As the sisters married, their husbands joined the Parsons stores' business. Margaret married Agnew (Andy) Andrews of Tifton, who operated Parsons/Andrews Building Supply of Duluth. Kathryn married Gene Willis of Macon, who was with the grocery in Duluth. Ann married Wally Odum of Waycross, who became a partner in the hardware store in Duluth.

In 2008, these stores were continuing in the family, with Margaret's son Bill Andrews operating the lumber yard; Kathryn concentrating on stores in Cumming and Alpharetta with her three children, Gary, Kay and Tom; and Ann's son Cary and daughter-in-law Patsy working with a hardware and gift store in Duluth. The Cumming Parsons is the largest gift and collection store in Georgia. Kathryn remembers that her first job at the store, while a small child, was scraping chewing gum off the floors. Another early activity for the girls was throwing compound on the oil floors and sweeping it up, and retrieving Coca Cola bottles for return to the bottler. Ann says her early jobs at the store included grinding coffee and working behind the toy counter. Once a full time member of the store staff, she says her first job was working with Margaret on publishing a toy catalog. "We sold lots of toys there."

Besides their contribution to the stores, the Parsons sisters are known just as well for their other activities, including their creativity and devotion to the city of Duluth.

Margaret, as an artist in painting, concentrated on portraits at first, later went into landscapes, and finally to scenes using pastels. She has also been most involved with the Gwinnett Council for the Arts, as one of the early workers in establishing that organization. She has been president of the Council. Margaret was instrumental in gaining initial funding for the Art Center at the Civic Center in Duluth, which she called a "challenging experience." Margaret was also a key player in the establishment of the Jacqueline Casey Hudgens Center for the Arts adjacent to the Arts Center. Margaret has passed on her artistic genes to one of her daughters, Kathy Fincher, herself a successful artist.

Though all three sisters have been key players in the Duluth Fall Festival, this has become Kathryn's passion. As a girl growing up in Duluth, Kathryn had always "wished that Duluth had a downtown city park," and played a key role in establishing the Duluth Town Green. Barely a day goes by throughout the year that she doesn't have some activity involving the Fall Festival, which began in 1983.

The Duluth Festival Center on a regular basis is central to ongoing events in downtown Duluth. Funds from the Festival primarily paid for the $1 million Duluth Festival Center. The Festival provided the funds to purchase Taylor Park and gave it to the city. Other projects over the years included the bricking of downtown sidewalks and installing a sewer system downtown. From the early days of the Festival barely scraping by or even losing money, the Festival has grown to regularly contribute up to $100,000 or more each year to improvements in the area. From the 2007 Fall Festival, a record $172,000 in net profit was earned.

In 2005, Kathryn was recognized by the Festival with its "most valuable volunteer" award from Main Street Duluth. The Festival consists of up to 400 booths with a majority of the booths featuring art and craft objects. Food and sponsor booths make up the remainder. The Festival committees meet year-round to ensure the event's success. More than 350 people volunteered for work on the festival in recent years. The Fall Festival is the last weekend of September, while a Springtime "Barefoot in the Park" arts festival is held in April.

A second major project for Kathryn has been her service on the Gwinnett Hospital Authority, and later, on the Gwinnett Medical Center Foundation. She has served on the various hospital boards for 18 years, never missing a meeting. She has been instrumental in raising money and steering the activities of the Foundation's annual ball.

Ann, meanwhile, came to concentrate on art late in her career. "I saw an advertisement one day for the Famous Artist correspondence course. I got the material, and it gave me great basic background." At first, she was using oils and acrylics, but in 1984, she discovered pastels, and since then, this medium has been her concentration. She is a juried member of the Excellence in the Southeast Pastel Society, and has won awards in their international shows. Her work for years was featured on the cover of the Duluth Fall Festival promotional material. She is also a member of the Artists of Berkeley Lake. Her original work is on display at her gallery in Parsons Gifts and Cards in Duluth.

In her earlier paintings, Ann concentrated on historic paintings of scenes from Duluth and the surrounding areas. "I painted around Duluth because I loved it. Little did I know that most of the buildings I painted would be gone so soon." While she continues to produce local scenes, she is also moving into more impressionistic and multi-media activities.

Perhaps the most public display of Ann's work can be seen in blown-up murals at the Bunton Road Park in Duluth, and at one time, her work was also at the Kroger supermarket in Suwanee. Here artistic scenes were also the inspiration for the giant 10 foot tall mosaics of glassware, plates, salvaged brick and stone in the new Duluth City Hall. Ann has been voted the "best artist in Gwinnett" by *Inside Gwinnett* magazine.

All three of the sisters are also philanthropists, having donor-advised funds to benefit charities of their choosing at the Community Foundation of Northeast Georgia.

Alice McCabe

Alice Smythe McCabe has been a key volunteer for the Gwinnett Historical Society since she moved into the county in 1973, working in various areas, but mainly digging into the past of Gwinnett and producing invaluable records.

Alice McCabe

Mrs. McCabe was born in Chicago, Ill., and lived in New Jersey before moving to Florida. She moved to Gwinnett in 1973 from West Palm Beach, Fla., where her husband, John, was with the Internal Revenue Service. He was transferred to the Chamblee office, and they settled near Lawrenceville.

In the early 1970s, she began her fascination with Gwinnett history while on a bus tour conducted by the Historical Society. As a former reporter, she naturally took notes. John Hood, who was conducting the tour, noticed her jotting down information. Hood knew that the Society needed a replacement for a person who had been earlier nominated for secretary of the Society, but could not serve. He put Alice McCabe on the nominee list "even before I became a member of the Society," she says, laughing.

Later, Hood, who ran a tombstone company, often showed McCabe around the county, citing historic references "that I would never have known about otherwise." He also introduced her to the technique of rubbing tombstones to get information, something which would become handy later as she compiled cemetery records. "He had this blue paper, which would get darker when you rubbed across a stone," she says. He also told her of many uncharted cemeteries around the county, which eventually led to Alice authoring her invaluable book of cemetery records for the county. She was unfamiliar with family cemeteries in the South, since in her native New Jersey, her parents were buried in a perpetual care cemetery.

"We did not have family plots, nor did we have relatives going to a cemetery to make a day of cleaning up the plots, and actually holding picnics there, using the gravestones as tables. I thought it was a neat idea, and thought it showed how Southerners cared for their heritage, and also how tight families were and still are."

All of this led to the Society working on a Gwinnett family history book. "We were looking for families that had lived here in the first 150 years. If they left the county and moved elsewhere, we didn't go into what they did afterward." McCabe, working with Edith Green, began to put together information. They got great publicity from local newspapers, and families started sending in information. "I didn't write it," McCabe says, "But you might say I compiled it, and it took a lot of time. We finally got Edith and her cousin, Mildred Breedlove, to come in as typists. And Joyce Rovetta wrote a short history of the county to go in the front of the book."

Her journalistic skills were soon put to use as well, as she edited the Society's newsletter for 10 years, and began compiling records of Gwinnett's past. Her books include the 653 page *Gwinnett County, Georgia Families, 1818-1968,* which was published in 1980, and the 750 page *Gwinnett County Deaths: 1818-1989,* which came out in 1991. She also was a key participant in producing *Gwinnett Families (1918-2005).* She also was instrumental in the publishing of the two *Vanishing Gwinnett* books of period photographs of the county.

The "*Deaths"* book is "that big fat red book over there," she points out. "But it's out of print now." It is a massive compilation of the county's death records and where people are buried. The book took her and other volunteers 17 years to compile. Atlanta historian Franklin Garrett wrote an introduction that praised Alice's work, pointing out that, "Time, pollution, vandals, and careless builders have taken their toll. But Alice has done more then her fair share of preserving and honoring Gwinnett County's ancestors and the historic landmarks."

She often had to fight developers and construction people, intent on bulldozing a long-forgotten cemetery. Mrs. McCabe was the one person standing up and halting such construction, working "for the rights of those buried beneath." She has been instrumental in helping the government locate cemeteries on zoning maps, a move which helps save family plots from destruction. When one considers there have been over 400 identified cemeteries in Gwinnett, one can begin to understand the many hours it took to compile this information, and realize the importance of having this information to protect the history of the county.

Mrs. McCabe says that of her work with the Society, she has most enjoyed meeting the old families, hearing their stories, warts and all. "If they went to school without shoes in the old days, no one was embarrassed. Everyone was real, and not putting on a show. And even today, that's still true, though not to the extent it once was, with all the growth. But people here today are real, are honest, are approachable, and don't mind sharing their lives with you. I've loved working with the Historical Society, and would not have enjoyed living here as much if I had not become involved."

She has served in many volunteer offices for the Society, including being a Tour Guide at the Elisha Winn house near Dacula and held many leadership positions, including a stint as president of the Society in 1987. She has also been a member of St. Lawrence Catholic Church, worked as a Cub Scout den mother and Girl Scout "Wings" leader and has volunteered as a swimming instructor at the Tull YMCA in Gwinnett. She is also a founding member of the Gwinnett Writer's Club.

For her monumental efforts in compiling this information, the Gwinnett Historical Society presented to Mrs. McCabe its first Distinguished Service Award in 1988. In 1995 and 1997, she received the Preservation Award of the Society, and in 2000, its Legacy Award.

In 2008, the Gwinnett Historical Society is looking into printing a second volume of *Gwinnett Families (1818-2005).* The Society has been through three editions of *Gwinnett County, Georgia Families, 1818-1968,* which is currently out of print.

Wayne Shackelford

Few people have had the impact on Gwinnett's progress in the last 50 years as has Wayne Shackelford. A clean-cut, tee-totaling straight-arrow, he has participated in Gwinnett's growth from several angles, including serving the entire state of Georgia. He has emerged from it all without a scratch.

Wayne Shackelford

Besides his integrity, Shackelford brings his tremendous recall abilities---some say photographic memory---to every situation. Ask him to recall something, and he'll usually tell you not only the details, and other details of that day.

The future Gwinnettian was born in Carroll County on Nov. 3, 1933, the son of a sharecropping family. He went to Berry College in Rome, where as a sophomore, he helped organize the first student government association. He graduated from Berry in 1955. Then it was on to the University of Georgia for graduate studies. He served in the U.S. Army for nearly two years as a veterinary animal specialist, first at Fort Lewis, then at Fort Lawton, Wash., getting out a few months early to return to college to enroll in a class in animal nutrition that was taught only in the spring of 1958.

Shackelford's career took several turns after he left the University of Georgia. He joined the University's Extension Service in 1959, first as an assistant county agent in Haralson County. He came to Gwinnett as an assistant county agent in 1960, and was named county agent in 1963, upon the retirement of J.T. Alexander.

Then the unexpected turn in 1974, when he began to work in overall county government management, as the executive assistant to the county commission, something akin to being the county manager, though without title. This was during several years when Gwinnett was the fastest-growing county in the nation, as the county experienced the problems and opportunities of fast growth. Shackelford became the key person in county government to go to when anyone needed assistance from the county of any sort. His earlier experience with the Extension Service throughout the county was of immense help to him, since he knew the county highways and byways perhaps better than anyone in the area.

Another turn came in April, 1984, when he left county government, moving to the private sector. He took on an entirely different post, that as manager of land development for Cadillac-Fairview Shopping Centers, Ltd., the development firm that, with Scott Hudgens as their partner, had just opened Gwinnett Place Mall. His responsibility was to build relationships with governments, the business community and trade associations to monitor legislation. He helped the firm erect Town Center at Cobb mall. In 1987, he joined Alex Conroy as southern regional manager of property development of the Conroy Company, remaining in the development business until 1991.

Shackelford's understanding of the inner workings of government caught the attention of Gov. Zell Miller in 1991, who suggested and got approval of the Georgia Transportation Board to elect him the commissioner of the Georgia Department of Transportation. This position allowed Shackelford to share his abilities with the entire state, guiding the 5,900 employees of the DOT, with an eventual budget of $1.5 billion.

Zell Miller says: "Wayne Shackelford was not unknown to me. I had known him extremely well a long time, knew his work ethic, knew his mind and that great photographic memory, and knew what a great job he had done in Gwinnett. I had no qualms whatsoever about him. Too, he had lots of the same friends as I had, but it was not because of them that I appointed him. I would have appointed him anyway."

He adds: "I wanted someone who would grab that job by the nape of the neck like Tom Moreland had, and I knew that Wayne was that person. And look at the job he did! It was magnificent the way he led the Transportation Department. You can look all around the state and see the monument that he left. It's there."

While commissioner, he administered a budget of $1.5 billion. Among his proudest accomplishments: making sure that Metro Atlanta and Georgia had the most developed and up-to-date comprehensive traffic and incident management system in the world during the time of the 1996 Centennial Olympic Games in Atlanta. The smooth roads and the interactive roadway network, all on live television monitors to scan traffic, impressed many world-wide visitors to the city during and after the Games.

He gives insight about the transportation plan for the Olympics:

> *"The Intermodal Surface Transportation Efficiency Act, commonly known as 'IceTea,' had as a high priority to prepare Atlanta for the Olympics with a $58.5 million demonstration project. But it did not say who would run the program, and the thinking was that the money would come to the City of Atlanta. But all federal funds accrue to the governor, and the governor had executed an agreement saying that the Department of Transportation would act on his behalf to get the funds. Gov. Joe Frank Harris had originally signed that law, and by resolution it was continued.*
>
> *"Our job at DOT was to evaluate how to make Atlanta mobile. Intelligent Transportation Systems were just getting started then throughout the world. We did one of the first major system-wide ITS efforts in the world. We also built the Advanced Transportation Management Center on Confederate Avenue in Atlanta*

to bring together the state agencies who work in disaster, such as the State Patrol, National Guard, FEMA, etc., and of course, DOT. The ITS operations center works out of this building, and can help regulate the flow of traffic by monitoring traffic from here throughout Atlanta.

"We did some amazing things prior to the Olympics, spending $147 million on ITS by pulling down other funds. We identified $957 million in highway projects to be operable by the time the Olympics opened, and concentrated on them. We only spent $2 million on non-permanent infrastructure, primarily for signs directing people to the venues, which were taken down after the games. We even auctioned them off after the Olympics."

Two of the major projects accomplished prior to the Olympics which helped the flow of Olympic traffic, and still helps Metro Atlanta today, were adding another lane throughout the system to major interstate routes, and completing the High Occupancy Vehicle (HOV) lanes in the city.

Shackelford says: "We heard in May of 1994 of a California effort to add lanes to the freeways, and took a group out there to see it. What they were doing was adding a lane by shrinking the width of traffic lanes from 12 to 11 feet. We saw it out there, came back to Georgia and did it here to give us more lanes, and completed those additional lanes in two years. When the Olympics opened, we had 78 miles of HOV lanes opened to help speed the traffic during the Olympics, which are still serving us today.

"We had good, honest engineers who gave good reasons why they could not do this in the time allowed, but they soon came back and said it would work. Our contractors worked together to support the Intelligent Transportation System installation, and its network of fiber optic cable, signs and structures. It was complex work, for they could lay the cable easily along the asphalt shoulder, but at bridges, they could not sink the cable in concrete, but had to go under the bridges. It was complicated construction and it worked up and down the entire corridor. All this was happening at the same time other contractors were widening the road with the extra lane. It was amazing what was accomplished. There were contractors who normally would be at each other's throats, but they worked together beautifully."

The impact on Atlanta during the Olympics is that visitors rode on some of the smoothest and most up-to-date highways in the world**.** "There were great worries about traffic jams, but they never materialized," Shackelford says. "It went amazingly smoothly because of our prior planning."

Other Shackelford accomplishments in transportation included completing the Commuter Rail Study in 1995; the Intercity Rail Study in 1997; and interfacing with local, state and federal transportation officials on many issues. He had a keen interest in multimodal and intermodal transportation, focusing the Georgia DOT toward movement of people and goods, and not just vehicles.

While heading the transportation efforts in Georgia, Shackelford was also active in such efforts throughout the nation. He has been president of the American Association of State Highway and Transportation Officials, chair of the Intelligent Transportation Society of America, and chair of the Executive Committee of the Transportation Research Board. He also was president of the Southeastern Association of State Highway and Transportation officials.

Recognizing Georgia's leadership in road construction, the DOT won awards for both concrete and asphalt paving from the national associations. While he was commissioner, Georgia highways were named the "best maintained freeways" in the nation.

Finally, "Shack" retired from state government in 2000 and became senior vice president of Greshan, Smith and Partners, a consultative architectural, engineering and planning firm based in Nashville, Tenn., with 850 staff members in 18 cities in the United States and China. In Atlanta, their offices are in Alpharetta. Most recently, it became the architectural and engineering design firm of the new International Terminal at the Atlanta airport.

Ever since Shackelford's early days in Gwinnett, he has been active in Chamber of Commerce activities. He was on the Gwinnett Chamber's Agricultural Committee in 1963 which sought an application and won one of the 10 initial Resource, Conservation and Development pilot projects in Georgia. He has served for years on the Gwinnett Chamber board, but has also been at times on both the Cobb County and DeKalb County Chamber boards. Once retired from the DOT, he headed the Gwinnett Transportation Committee, which included environmental concerns. When Shackelford became chairman of the Gwinnett Chamber in 2006, he said: "....it was like coming home."

His Chamber activities come from a belief that "...as goes the relationship between the business community and government, goes success or failure. The Chamber, the business community, residents and homeowners associations must be in dialogue with government in openness and with transparency. That's the reason Gwinnett County has historically succeeded."

Along the way, Shackelford's abilities have been recognized with numerous local, state and national honors. He was the Gwinnett Citizen of the Year for the Gwinnett Chamber of Commerce for 2000. In state circles, he won significant honors, receiving only the third lifetime achievement award from the Georgia 4-H Club council. And he is one of the few people to have not just one, but two interstate interchanges named for him. One is near his native Carroll County, as the Department of Transportation board named the Carrollton Bypass at U.S. Highway 27 in his honor. The other interchange named for him is the Georgia Highway 316 intersection with Interstate 85 in Gwinnett County, including its distinctive "flyover" bridge from Georgia Highway 316 to I-85. In addition, in 1997, the state Transportation Board named the Transportation Management Center on Confederate Avenue in Atlanta the Wayne Shackelford Building.

Shackelford's first position in Gwinnett as an assistant county agent was a great training ground for someone who would become so intimate with county and state operations in his future. He got to know every nook and cranny of the county, which coupled with his tremendous memory, would particularly serve him well when working with county government, and even later as a developer and state official.

Wayne and his wife, Anna Nolan Shackelford, have three children, and seven grandchildren. The children are:

- Carolyn Gazda, whose husband David is regional manager of the American Angus Association, and live in Athens. She is a part time employee of the Animal Science Department of the University of Georgia. They have two girls, Katie and Taylor.

- Larry and his wife, Virginia, a stay-at-home mother, live in Marietta and have two boys, Matthew and Andrew. He is an attorney with Troutman, Sanders in Atlanta, specializing in banking and corporate securities.
- Steven and his wife, Nanette, live in Clay Center, Neb. He holds a Ph.D. and is a research scientist with the Meade Animal Research Center, specializing in meats and muscle biology. They have three children, Rachel, Lauren and Noah. Nanette is on the city council and a professor at Hastings Community College, teaching computer skills and management.

Through all his varied efforts, from working with youth in 4-H, to guiding the progress of Gwinnett County, to determining the state transportation plan, and giving guidance to many people, Wayne Shackelford charged ahead with gusto, enjoying it every step of the way. "Public affairs is my hobby," he has been quoted as saying, "My life has been study, get the facts, arrive at the truth and rally people around me to turn dreams and aspirations into reality."

Wayne Shackelford: he's done it beautifully!

Mary and David Kistner

A couple who would become significant contributors to the life of Gwinnett County moved to the county in 1950. They were Mary and David Kistner, who bought 500 mostly-wooded acres off Lenora Road east of Snellville. On it, they soon established Berkmere Farm, where they raised Beefmaster cattle, as David became active in community affairs..

David Kistner later became active in the Water and Soil Conservation affairs, including serving as state president in 1961 of the Georgia Association of Conservation District Supervisors. Three successive governors, Ernest Vandiver, Carl Sanders and Lester Maddox, appointed him to the State Soil Conservation Committee, with him serving from 1961-70. He was instrumental in Gwinnett becoming the only county in the South, and the only urban county in the nation, to obtain a pilot Resource, Conservation and Development designation to enhance soil conditions through improved water runoff techniques. He was appointed by President John Kennedy to the National Soil and Water Conservation committee. He also was chairman in 1962-63 of the Gwinnett Chamber of Commerce.

Meanwhile, Mary Kistner was active in the farm operations, particularly adept at keeping the bloodline records of their Beefmaster offspring. Later she would become more centered on the arts community, working particularly in fiber as a weaver and also in collage. As chair of the Visual Arts Committee, she curated and hung the exhibitions at the Gwinnett Arts Center.

Mary Straw Kistner was born in 1918 in Burr Oak, Mich., and spent much of her young years in Northern Indiana at the farm of her maternal grandparents. Her father died at an early age and her mother was a traveling nurse, staying with patients needing constant assistance for long periods.

The couple had met when they were both sophomores in college, and working on a cruise ship on the Great Lakes, says a niece, Ann Ortloff of Silver City, N.M. Mary was a waitress, and David was a purser on the cruise line. Mary graduated from Western Michigan University, majoring in English, and David graduated from Emory University.

Mrs. Ortloff, whose mother was David's sister, adds: "David and a twin brother were born in Silver City in 1919. His father was from Georgia, but had moved west because of tuberculosis. He died in 1927 a few years after David was born. His mother re-married the chief of the TB clinic, and in the 1930s moved to Detroit, Mich. When his twin drowned in a swimming accident in Detroit, his grandfather wanted him to come to Atlanta to go to high school. He would later take care of both his grandfather and great uncle. The family had a retail store, and in the 1920s, developed a row of shops on North Highland Avenue, which David inherited from his uncle, Byron Kistner." (Today the site has on it, among others, The Indigo restaurant.)

The week after Mary graduated from college, she rode the train to Atlanta, and in June, 1940 married David there. After graduation, David worked at Fulton National Bank, before enlisting in the Army, and serving in Europe. While he was in the service, Mary was furnishing coordinator at Rich's, where she worked with an interior architect, "who taught me how to look at and use space," she wrote later. She would take this talent and install rented art from the High Museum Art Shop, where she was a docent, with local corporations. She would also use this talent with the Gwinnett Art Center.

It was Mary's desire for the couple to move to the country, finally finding a 500-acre tract east of Snellville on Lenora Road, through which Big Haynes Creek runs. The story goes that they bought the land either, depending who you are talking to, for $15 or $25 an acre, with people telling them: "You'll never pay for that land bought at that price." Yet the Kistners proved resourceful, selling off the pine and mixed hardwood timber to pay off the land mortgage, and having enough left over to buy a bulldozer for clearing the land for pastures. The original plan was to raise Irish setters on the property, but David wanted to raise cattle.

Both were city folks, who thoroughly enjoyed the country. When friends in Atlanta would visit the Kistner farm, then only accessible by dirt roads, some upon leaving would cry with sadness over "David taking Mary to this god-forsaken wilderness!" But the Kistners were most enjoyed the country life. Mary taught English for one year at South Gwinnett High.

They immediately repaired and added to an ancient cabin on the property, where they would visit on weekends. Eventually they moved full time to the older house, where they lived for 20 years. Mary then designed a house, since David "didn't want a house to run him," which had many conveniences for ease. They moved into their new house in 1973.

Together, the couple read of different cattle breeds, not finding a breed they liked to any extent. Finally, they came across an article on a man in Texas raising a new breed of cattle, the Beefmaster brand. What they liked was that the offspring had small heads, making for easy births. They flew to El Paso, and met and became and remained close friends with Tom Lasater, who had developed the breed. They purchased one Beefmaster bull and 20 heifers to bring to Georgia. Over the years, they would visit and remain friends with both the Lasater family and with Watt Casey, Lasater's brother-in-law, and his wife Dosia. David, mainly interested in the genetics of the breed, would remain active with hybrid Beefmasters the rest of his life, including a term as president of a new Beefmaster association. He got his cattleman's mail through an address in Denver, Colo. since "...cattlemen didn't trust anyone east of the Mississippi." (David also used a Snellville post office address, after his farm address changed from Lithonia, to Loganville, and to Snellville, all within a short time. Every time he got new farm stationery printed, his address would change. So, out of desperation, David started using P.O. Box 278, Snellville, as his mailing address.)

Meanwhile, in preparing the land for pasture, early on Mary had researched with the Agricultural Department which type of native grasses were best for grazing at the farm. She later wrote that her purview "...was the Total Digestive Nutrients of various grasses and legumes being grown in the South at that time. We both were keenly interested in covering all the red clay with green grass."

David enjoyed telling people that he was basically "the PRAG-MA-tist of the family, while Mary is the AR-tist." Chris Snell, who became fast friends with the couple, said that "David looked at the dollars and Mary at the beauty."

Meanwhile, their herd was thriving, as they continued to improve their stock, culling out older ones, and selling bulls. A niece, Kathy Marcotte of Albuquerque, N.M., said the farm was a "virtual fertility clinic" for the Beefmaster brands, as the couple sold stock and semen to other cattlemen to improve their herds. Mary would often tell people that her job was that of "...only the gatekeeper. I ride with David in the truck and open and shut the gates," she would say, laughing. But those familiar with the operation knew that Mary was as deeply involved in the farm as was David. Mary kept hand-written records on each animal, and named each one.

More and more, Mary's artistic side showed itself. Ann Ortloff feels Mary "was a born artist." Her specialty was tactile art, weaving, hand looming, collages and mixed media, as Mary put it, "making ideas visible." She taught this art to students around Snellville, and was also busy raising wild flowers and herbs in her garden. She knew every plant species on the farm by name.

David Kistner took an active interest in civic affairs. Former County Commissioner Ray Gunnin remembers that David was on the original study commission in the 1960s seeking to change the three-man county commission. "He was a fine, intelligent man, always influential toward better government," he says.

Jimmy Beaver, who went to work on the Kistner farm when he was 13, remained working with them at various jobs for 31 years, and still lives adjacent to the Kistner house, spoke of David's interest in soil conservation, both for farming, and in other ways. "He was the one who got Gwinnett County to grade road rights-of-way, and sow them with grass seed, to prevent erosion of the banks," he said. It was a practical lesson David could suggest from his interest with the state and national water conservation services. Kistner is credited with being a prime force in the building of two dams on tributaries of the Alcovy River, forming the lakes in the 718-acre Tribble Mill Park.

Kistner was for about 30 years a member of the board of directors of Gwinnett Federal Bank. He was also a director of the Walton EMC for 12 years, and from 1982 until 1985 was vice president.

David Kistner died on April 13, 1991, when the couple had been married for almost 51 years. Mary died in 2001. She tried to follow the tenets she had learned from her

Pennsylvania-Dutch grandmother. Two of her favorite sayings were: "Brighten the corner wherever you are," and "Be better tomorrow than you are today."

Much of the land that the Kistners owned is still in large tracts. The late Richard Snell and his wife, Martha, bought land from the Kistners over the years, ending up with about 350 acres. Other parts of the property were developed in five or more acre increments. The remaining 42 acres and home at Mary's death went to the Georgia Open Land Trust for nature education. Mary's will also allocated $1.4 million to the Gwinnett Foundation for the Mary Straw Kistner Fund for support of the Gwinnett Arts Center, with her expressed will as "a legacy for future generations…giving back to the community in perpetuity."

* * * * *

The Gwinnett Community Foundation honored Mary as a citizen of the year and the Hudgens Center for the Arts named their lobby after her for her contribution to the arts. She specified in her will that her estate was to never be developed, but to be used to develop an appreciation of art and nature in the community. She believed: "If we educate adults, they will educate their children on the importance of preserving nature."

William C. O'Kelley

The highest-ranking U.S. government appointee in Gwinnett County is Senior U.S. District Judge William Clark O'Kelley of Norcross. He has served on the bench of the Northern District of Georgia since 1970, when he was appointed by President Richard Nixon. At that time, he was one of the youngest district judges in the country, and now has served for nearly 40 years on that court. He began senior status in 1996, though in 2008, he was still hearing cases at the court, mostly out of his office in Gainesville. He was chief judge of the district court for seven years.

William C. O'Kelley, Sr.

Besides his local duties, Bill O'Kelley was appointed to the Foreign Intelligence Surveillance Court by Chief Justice Warren Burger, and served from 1980-87. He has also been on the Alien Terrorist Removal Court, appointed by Chief Justice William Rehnquist, since 1996, and remained on the court in 2008. He was elected by district and circuit judges of the 11th Circuit to the Judicial Conference, and served from 1981-84.

Gwinnett County: A Little Above Atlanta

Judge O'Kelley is a native Atlantan, born on January 2, 1930. He is a product of the Atlanta schools, and was in the last class of the old Boys High, where he was editor of the newspaper, The Tattler. He obtained his bachelor's degree from Emory University, where he was a member of Sigma Chi and president of Omicron Delta Kappa. His law degree from Emory came in 1953. He passed the state bar in 1952. Nowadays, the law requires graduation first from law school before taking the bar exam.

From 1953-57, he received a direct commission as a first lieutenant in the Judge Advocate General Corps of the U.S. Air Force, serving in Albany, Ga., for six months in Japan, and for two years in Morocco. He remained in the Air Force Reserve, as a captain, until 1966.

For two years, he was an assistant United States Attorney for the Northern District of Georgia, beginning in 1961. For nine years, he was a partner in the firm of O'Kelley and Hopkins in Atlanta before his appointment to the bench. During his private practice days, he was an organizer and director of the Gwinnett Bank and Trust Company of Norcross; president of the Peachtree-Atlanta Kiwanis club; and a vice president of the Gwinnett Chamber of Commerce.

He was also active in affairs of the Republican Party while in private practice, including being general counsel for the Georgia GOP. He also attended the Republican National Convention in Miami in 1968 as an alternate delegate. However, once he went to the bench, attorneys practicing before Judge O'Kelley called him fair and square, not allowing politics to enter into his decisions. One said: "He's the epitome of a judge, playing it fair and square right down the middle." A former law clerk of his, Elizabeth Kohn of Birmingham, Ala., called the judge "What a Federal judge ought to be."

His law clerks and attorneys will also tell you that he runs a tight ship in court. "You wanted to make sure you were on time. He was well-respected by both sides." A close friend, attorney Julius Hulsey of Gainesville, says: "Every time I tried a case in front of him, he would not give me an inch. He's been a great judge, smart, quick of mind, and alert. You don't go into his court unprepared. He can see through you real fast, though he was always eminently fair. I think that instead of relying on his law clerks, he continues to read the law faithfully, and stays up on the law."

In talking with Judge O'Kelley, he says that the cases before him often run together. But he remembers several in particular which were of significance to the area.

One case involved the desegregation of the DeKalb County schools. He says: "I did not have that case originally, but had it handed to me and handled it for several years. It was a new area of the law, for no historical precedent had been set of a court taking over and running a school system." One key question was to determine when the constitutional wrong would be cured, and when he could justify terminating the court supervision. "The attorneys for the DeKalb school board were very creative, and gave me seven ideas of why the supervision should be terminated. These were items like elimination of segregation of faculty and students, per pupil spending for the northern and southern part of the county, etc. But these points all didn't sit well with me, and I added an eighth point, to me the paramount one, of quality of education for the students. I thought that was what it was all about."

Another case, one widely publicized, concerned the trial of William August Holmes Williams of Lilburn for kidnapping the Atlanta Constitution Editor Reg Murphy on Feb.

20, 1974 and demanding a $700,000 ransom, which was paid. The first trial went on for about two weeks in 1974, including weekends, and was held in Atlanta. Williams was convicted, and sentenced to 40 years in jail. However, on appeal, the Fifth Circuit Court reversed the decision. Attorney Fred Link, a former law clerk, remembers: "The court cited two errors, one a slight change in a wording in the statute, which on objective, had been read properly. They said that was not enough to reverse it. The Court also held that the pre-trial publicity in Atlanta was not enough to reverse the decision, but taken together, the two points were enough to reverse it." The defense won a change in venue.

The case was moved in 1976 to the most distant point in the Fifth Circuit, Key West, Fla., where Williams was convicted again and sentenced to 40 years with Judge O'Kelley presiding. Link adds: "When a case stays within the geographic area of the circuit when it is moved, the case judge goes with the trial and re-hears it."

Years later, Murphy remembers the trial vividly. He by then was the publisher of the San Francisco Examiner and had to commute to Key West for the trial. "Judge O'Kelley did a remarkably good job in keeping the court orderly in both cases. He had an interesting decision to move the trial to Key West and eliminate any question of pre-trial publicity affecting the outcome. And it got the same exact outcome!"

Link remembers another case where Judge O'Kelley gave a defendant a key message. It was a case involving the Reader's Digest and an Atlanta porno king. The defendant was seeking to get the editor of the Reader's Digest to testify. The editor demurred on the grounds of the First Amendment, even refusing to take the witness stand. This led to Judge O'Kelley telling the editor, and his prominent attorney, Hugh Dorsey, to return after the break for lunch with his "checkbook and tooth brush." After listening to his attorney over the lunch, the editor got on the witness stand and answered all questions thrown at him.

One of Judge O'Kelley's most prestigious honors came in 2005 when, in his 35th anniversary as a federal judge, his former law clerks quietly raised $126,000 to endow a scholarship named for him at Emory Law School, and surprised him at an outing with this announcement. One of his former law clerks, Chris Bly, said that "We thought this would be a way for his name to live on at the University, so that new law students would know about him." Funds for the scholarship came from friends, former clients and the law clerks. The first winner of the scholarship was Justin Victor, of the class of 2010.

Judge O'Kelley is a former member of the college's board of trustees and is an emeritus member of the advisory committee to the president and the chairman of the board.

Bill O'Kelley and the former Ernestine (Teeny) Allen of Atlanta were married in 1953. They have two children, Virginia Leigh O'Kelley Wood of Paris, Va., and William C. (Bo) O'Kelley Jr. of Norcross, and five grandchildren.

Beauty Poole Baldwin

Beauty Poole Baldwin has known since she was in elementary school that she wanted to become a math teacher. "When I was in the third grade at two-room Friendship School, the teacher would have the group of kids from first through third grade all together, and I would finish my math and go around helping others. It was fun for me to work with numbers. I knew right then that I wanted to be a school teacher, and to teach math," she says.

She not only became a teacher, but also went up the ladder, next becoming an administrator, then a school principal, and retired after serving for 10 years as the first black female superintendent in Georgia. Two months into her retirement, she was back in education, this time starting a school for her church. All the way, she was receiving honors, serving on local and statewide boards, and making significant contributions to the community.

But the job that she likes most of all is simply being a teacher.

Beauty Baldwin

Beauty Poole was born in Baldwin County, and attended elementary school there. Her family later moved to Sandersville, where she graduated from T. J. Elder High School in 1959. She then graduated from Savannah State College, in 1963, majoring, of course, in mathematics. Besides getting her degree at Savannah State, she also met there Lucious Baldwin, a student from Columbus. They were married in 1963, and both became teachers.

Her first teaching job was in Schley County, "where I was the entire math staff for the county" for two years. Later she would teach for 10 years in Columbus, where she began off-campus graduate classes of the University of Georgia.

The couple moved to Atlanta in 1973, where Beauty joined the staff at Central Gwinnett High, first as a math teacher. In 1974, she started taking classes at the University of Georgia, eventually getting a master's degree in vocational education, then a Specialist-5 and Specialist-6 certification from the school. Meanwhile, she was heading the Coordinated Vocational-Academic Education program at Central Gwinnett. "This was a program aimed at kids who were in danger of dropping out of school. It was a new program when I got to Central Gwinnett, and it included the math, reading and science together. We worked with these students to prepare them for the world of work. I did that for four years."

When a vacancy for an assistant principal's job opened up, the principal, Dr. Pat Mahon, encouraged Ms. Baldwin to apply for the job. Beauty says: "I was one of the first ever in Gwinnett to go through screening for that position. I was interviewed by six different people before I got the job of an assistant principal." She held that post for two years, when another educational opportunity came up.

That opportunity was for the post of principal of the independent Buford City System's Middle School, when the system's superintendent, Dr. Jim Puckett recommended that the School Board hire her for the middle school principalship. Beauty says: "I went there in 1980 and was principal of the school for four years before I was appointed the superintendent of the city system. The City of Buford really supports its schools, with 100 percent of the property tax going to the system. It's a small system, and run much like a private school. You get to know each of the students, and their parents, too."

Philip Beard of Buford, a city commissioner and school board member, says that the selection of Mrs. Baldwin as the superintendent "was one of the best decisions we made. She had her teaching and administrative background. She had earned that position. We interviewed some other good candidates for the job, but choose her for her experience and familiarity with the system. And in so doing, we found a diamond in the rough. She had paid the price and performed admirably with us."

While she and the Buford School Board did not realize it at the time, Ms. Baldwin was the first female black superintendent in Georgia.

Ms. Baldwin tells of how the Buford system operates. "The school system concentrates on having excellent quality in everything it does, in academics, literary and sporting events. It grows many of its own teachers, and can choose from among the best teachers since the system is well-known for its quality of education. Too, it takes a team approach on the academic side. While I was there, the system excelled in all areas." The system also responded to Ms. Baldwin's leadership. When she retired, the Peoples Bank and Trust began awarding the system's valedictorian and salutatorian with the Beauty P. Baldwin Award, to be given in perpetuity each year in recognition to Ms. Baldwin's years of achievement.

While Ms. Baldwin has been most active in educational circles, she is also active in the wider community. Many honors and awards have come here way. She has served on the Gwinnett Elections Board for 12 years, two years as chairman. She was on the initial Health and Human Services Board, has been on the Chamber of Commerce board for two terms, and has worked with the Red Cross for over 25 years, including a stint as a board member. She was also on the Leadership Gwinnett Founding Steering Committee, and has been on the board of Education Leadership Georgia. She is a graduate of Leadership Atlanta; a graduate of Education Leadership Georgia; worked with Big Brothers, Big Sisters; served on the Northeast Georgia Council of the Boy Scouts; and the American Business Women's Association.

The awards have been many, including the Distinguished Community Service Award from Greater Atlanta Christian School in 1986; an Outstanding Achievement Award in 1988 from West Georgia College; a Public Service Award in 1988 from the Gwinnett Chamber of Commerce; a Woman of the Year Award from the Gwinnett United Ebony Society in 1989; and in 2003, a Community Service Award from her alma mater, Savannah State University. Her sorority, Alpha Kappa Alpha, since 1994 has given the Beauty P. Baldwin Scholarship.

She says: "It makes me most proud when recognized, for I feel we are here to do but one thing, to serve, and when I get a service award or recognition, I am elated."

Ms. Baldwin has served at the statewide level, appointed by Georgia governors to the Georgia Council of Adult Literacy, and to the Board of Medical Assistance, where she was a member for 15 years, including four years as chair of the board.

After closing out her public education career, Ms. Baldwin was ready to sit back and relax. Two month later, her pastor at Hopewell Baptist Church announced that she would soon be starting a Christian Academy at the church. "It was news to me that I would be heading it, but we had discussed it," she says. Hopewell Christian Academy opened in 1997 with Ms. Baldwin as the headmistress. In 2008, it had pre-k-12 grades, and she is its superintendent.

Her husband, Lucious, also was a math teacher initially. He also taught in Columbus, is a former principal of a elementary school in Milledgeville, assistant principal at Central Gwinnett, and was a counselor at South Gwinnett High. He retired as the community school director at Shiloh High, and in 2008, was the assistant principal, part time, at the Give Center in Gwinnett.

The couple have one daughter, Geri, a certified public accountant in Duluth, who is married to Lorenzo Gonzalez; they have two children, a boy and a girl.

2
Early History of Gwinnett

1733: The setting as Georgia is founded

When General James Oglethorpe sailed from England to found the new colony of Georgia and landed at what would become Savannah on February 12, 1733, he arrived to find Indians atop Yammacraw Bluff. But these were no ordinary Indians.

Perhaps he had heard of the Indian chief, Tomochichi, and that the chief spoke English, having learned the language from the settlers of Charleston, S.C. Oglethorpe himself had stopped at Charleston first. He knew the South Carolinians had ventured into the land south of the Savannah River from time to time. For sure, it was mighty convenient for Oglethorpe to be able to speak through Tomochichi to the Savannah Indians.

With his ship packed with many people released from English prisons, Oglethorpe came to America to establish the English crown's 13th colony. The early Georgia grants from King George II stretched all the way westward to the Pacific Ocean. Later, it would extend only to the Mississippi River. Eventually, Georgia's western border would be the Chattahoochee River south of what would become Columbus.

As others before him in America, Oglethorpe was seeking to settle in what was Indian territory. Those arriving in Georgia were met with what initially were peaceful Indians. As the white man became more common throughout the vast area, often disturbances with the native Indians would erupt. The many embarrassments and downright criminal acts by the white man, including theft of the land and the rights of the Indians, is not a pretty picture, as has been told by others.

Yet the land in what was to become Georgia was fertile, the climate mild, and the white man found he could sustain himself and eventually thrive. A scant two generations after Oglethorpe arrived in Georgia, there were difficulties, not with the Indians, but with the British.

As the white man penetrated into the state, the frontiersman was, by his raw bone occupation, an independent sort, living without immediate community, dependent virtually entirely on what he could raise or do for his family, and not given to taking much direction.

It was a perfect setting for some who were seeking to be free from Mother England, to go it on their own, and succeed with little direction from others. Most had little time or need for governmental direction in their make-up.

While other colonies were more central in the fight for independence, Georgia was on the periphery. However, it still contributed men and materials for the Revolutionary War, though it had families backing both the Crown and other equally staunch families seeking independence. In an early maneuver during the Revolution, the port city of Savannah was soon occupied by the British in December, 1778, as it remained for most of the Revolutionary War. The British did not evacuate Savannah until July, 1782. Cornwallis surrendered at Yorktown in October of 1781, but the British continued to dominate some parts of the state for a time.

Eventually, after the difficult years of the Revolution, the War was over and the new nation got around to the task of forming itself into a government. Georgia, as the most Southern state between the new nation and Spanish Florida, developed at a slower pace than some other areas. Augusta, upriver from Savannah, was founded early on in 1736 but other parts of Georgia were slow to be occupied. Macon was settled in 1823 and Columbus founded in 1828. Augusta, Macon and Columbus were all three at the northern navigable point of rivers. In those days, the river was the chief means of moving heavy goods to the frontier, and of transporting products from the land back to the ports.

Another factor in the settlement of Georgia was its railroads, first coming out of Charleston to Augusta in 1833, followed by a line out of Savannah to Macon (the Central of Georgia) in 1840. The eventual City of Atlanta was founded as "Terminus" in 1837, with the City of Atlanta chartered in 1845. The city developed as a terminal point of the Western and Atlantic Railroad and was eventually the junction point of rail lines connecting the city with Macon, Columbus, and Chattanooga, as well as other points.

Rail historian Bob Hanson of Loganville says that a key date for the Metro Atlanta area was September, 1845, when the Georgia Railroad was completed from Augusta into what would become Atlanta. After came the Macon and Western Railroad being finished into the new city of Atlanta in 1846. From Atlanta, the railroad first known as the Atlanta and LaGrange (later Atlanta and West Point) began construction in East Point in the fall of 1849, with the first rail movement on the line starting on March 17, 1851. This line used the tracks of the Macon and Western between East Point and Atlanta.

(To provide an idea of the size of these cities, in 1820, Savannah had 7,523 people. By 1850, Savannah had grown to 15,312 residents, while Augusta counted 9,448. But by 1900, both cities had been surpassed by Atlanta, with 89,872 residents. Savannah had 54,244 in 1900, while Augusta had 49,441 residents. Details are from census data.)

It was in 1818 that the Legislature of Georgia decided to create more counties to honor the three signers of the Declaration of Independence: Lyman Hall, George Walton and of course, Button Gwinnett.

* * * * *

1818: Gwinnett founded

At the time that Gwinnett County was first formed by the Legislature in 1818, the area was part of the early frontier, as white settlers pushed westward from the Atlantic Ocean. The land essentially was all Indian territory, totally undeveloped, and quite sparsely populated. There were 42 counties in the state then, and with Gwinnett, along with Hall, Walton and Habersham counties all being formed at the same time, on December 15, 1818, the number grew to 46 counties.

As then, Gwinnett's western border is the Chattahoochee River, which, prior to the removal of the Indians from Georgia in 1838, was a dividing line between the Creek Indians to the south, and the Cherokee Indians north of the river. The two tribes respected their borders and lived somewhat peacefully, though from time to time skirmishes would break out between them.

To this area came mostly Scots-Irish white people to seek their fortune and establish families and a livelihood in the area. At first, they were nothing more than squatters, but resourceful, as they had to find either a way to support themselves off the land as hunters and trappers, or clear land for farming. It was a tough life. Commercial activities were far away, some 150 miles by horseback or over rough wagon trails in Augusta, or even more advanced and distant on the coasts at Savannah and Charleston. But the only route for travel in the founding days of Gwinnett was by horseback, wagon or on foot to Augusta, where irregularly-scheduled boats navigated the Savannah River to the coast.

The area which would become Gwinnett was initially part of a vast northeastern Franklin County, which stretched from today's southern border of Gwinnett all the way to the South Carolina line. Georgia's Legislature in 1818 decided to honor the three signers of the Declaration of Independence by naming counties after them in the northeast region of the state.

Why Franklin? Georgia's provisional government had before independence asked for the assistance of Benjamin Franklin to represent their interests in Europe, both before the French government, and in England. Citing an inability to adequately compensate him, the Provisional Government said it would give Mr. Franklin 1,000 acres of land in Georgia as payment.

Somehow, Mr. Franklin never got the Georgia land, nor did he ever visit the state. In 1777, the new Legislature formed the eight original Georgia counties: Burke, Camden, Chatham, Effingham, Glynn, Liberty, Richmond and Wilkes. These were much larger than the counties that bear these names today. Four were along the salt water, and four were upriver from Savannah. Only one county, Wilkes, was above present day Augusta.

Perhaps feeling guilty about not making good in its deal to Franklin, the state on February 25, 1784 named the ninth county for Franklin. (The 10th county, Washington, was also named that same date.) Franklin's land area was virtually all of Northeast Georgia including all of seven, and parts of four, present-day Georgia counties and three South Carolina counties. (Carnesville is the county seat today of Franklin County.) However, in 1796, the Assembly took away part of the land of Mr. Franklin's county, and created, among others, Jackson County, named for Revolutionary War general and eventual governor, James Jackson. Then in 1818, the Legislature carved land from Jackson to form Gwinnett, Hall and

Walton Counties. All three counties were named for signers from Georgia of the Declaration of Independence, Button Gwinnett, Lyman Hall and George Walton.

Those early pioneers coming to Gwinnett were mostly Protestants (Baptists, Methodists and a few Presbyterians) with English, Scots-Irish and Welsh backgrounds. Many came out of the Carolinas and Virginia, and nearly all basically were tillers of the soil, while very much people seeking opportunity on the frontier.

Once Gwinnett County was authorized by the Legislature, the early government was organized between Hog Mountain and present-day Dacula. The first meeting was at the home of Elisha and Philadelphia Winn. That building hosting the first meeting, the Elisha Winn home, still stands today and is maintained by the Gwinnett Historical Society. A festival with an old-time theme takes place each October at the Winn home.

Early records show that first session of what then was called the "Inferior" Court took place there. Later on, Elisha Winn would become a member of the Inferior Court. Gwinnett soon elected two people to represent them at the State Capitol, then in Milledgeville. John Threadwell was Gwinnett's first representative, and George Reid its first senator, both attending the session of 1819. this history is chronicled in great detail in J.C. Flanigan's History of Gwinnett County, Vol. I.

The business of getting the county organized began with naming of five justices of the Interior Court. They were selected on February 23, 1819, and were George Reid, Samuel Reid, John Cupp, William Towers and Joseph Morgan. In turn, they held an election for the county officers. The first officers of the county chosen were:

William Blake, sheriff;
James Wardlaw, clerk of Superior Court;
Thomas Dobbs, clerk of Interior Court and Treasurer;
James Laughridge, tax collector;
John Beauchamp, tax receiver;
John Wynn, coroner;
James C. Reed, surveyor.

A key element in this time was the Land Lottery of 1820, as many sought free land to homestead on the frontier. To be eligible for the lottery, it was required that the person be at least 18 years old, and a resident of Georgia for three years. Little else was required, and oral oaths were enough to get your name included. (Veterans of the wars were given an additional draw.) The lottery worked, with the county tripling in population in ten years, from 4,589 in 1820 to 13,289 in 1830. What the winners got was raw land, often covered, as the naturalist William Bartram found when he visited, with "the most magnificent forests I have ever seen….." The early settlers had to timber the hardwoods, cutting logs used for their first cabins, then clear the land and prepare it before they could grow crops. Overlay all this with the presence of Indians on this frontier, and it is obvious that the area was one needing hard-working, stout and enterprising people.

The Inferior Court justices were also given authority to pick a site for public buildings, primarily a courthouse and jail. A site was selected one mile west of the original courthouse, which appeared to be near the center of the county. It was on Land Lot 148 of the Fifth

District, and Isham Williams was paid $56 to build the first courthouse there in early 1820. The land today is in Lawrenceville, primarily on the east side of Georgia Highway 20, almost directly across from Gwinnett Drive. A Publix supermarket was once on the site. Once the first courthouse was built, the landowner decided to donate the land to the county, but later changed his mind so that the county had to look for another site for the courthouse.

They selected Elisha Winn, at whose house the county was initially organized, who was a land trader, and a former member of the Inferior Court of Jackson County, to buy one of three lots near the center of the county, 145, 146 or 147 of the Fifth District. One of these lots, which was of 250 acres, had been drawn in the land lottery of 1820 by John Breedlove of Hancock County. Winn journeyed on March 4, 1821 to the state capital of Milledgeville, which is adjacent to Hancock County. Winn paid Breedlove $200 for the land, with the deed transferred to Winn, who later transferred it to the county. The land was covered in forest.

Soon the land was surveyed by William Towers, and streets were laid out around the courthouse square. Tower was paid $23 for laying out four streets bordering the square. Buildings, stores, and homes were then erected, with one of the first structures to be completed being a boardinghouse.

William Maltbie, a former Hog Mountain storekeeper, moved to the new county seat and became the first postmaster, and later the second clerk of Inferior Court, a post he held for 20 years. It was Maltbie who suggested the name for the county seat, Lawrenceville, to honor one of the heroes of the War of 1812, Naval Capt. James Lawrence. He's the one known for uttering in battle the famous words, "Don't give up the ship, lads! Fight her as long as she swims," as he lay mortally wounded on his ship, the USS Chesapeake, engaging the British in a battle off the coast near Boston. (Lawrence, like Gwinnett and Franklin, never set foot in the county.) Lawrence's friend, Commodore Oliver Hazard Perry, took Lawrence's words and struck a flag to fly on the mast of his ship during patrols on Lake Erie.

Lawrenceville's founding dates from 1821, when the legislature issued the city charter. It is the oldest city in the five counties of Metro Atlanta. (Decatur is next oldest in the area, being founded in 1823.) It would be nearly 50 years before another city charter was issued in Gwinnett, to Norcross in 1870.

The town's first doctor was Philo Hall, Maltbie's brother-in-law, who was a native of Connecticut. He practiced in Lawrenceville until his death. The first attorney in town was Philip Alston, followed by N.L. Hutchins, who later became a circuit judge, state legislator, and had a large estate when he died.

The new county seat's first minister was the Rev. Dr. John S. Wilson, pastor of Fairview Presbyterian Church (1823), who was in charge of the first school, Lawrenceville Academy, a post he held for 12 years. Dr. Wilson was later also pastor at Goshen Church, near Norcross, for 10 years.

Those early pioneers coming to Gwinnett were mostly Protestants (Baptists, Methodists and a few Presbyterians) with English, Scots-Irish and Welsh backgrounds. Many came out of the Carolinas and Virginia, and nearly all basically were tillers of the soil, while very much people seeking opportunity on the frontier.

Modern Gwinnett has the distinction of having more cities (15) located or partially located within its borders than any other county in Georgia. However, only about 20 percent of the current total population lives in incorporated cities. The majority of Gwinnett citizens live in unincorporated areas of the county, and the county government is the key element for most citizens, providing many of the services one would normally expect in a municipality.

Gwinnett has a land area of 437 square miles, the second largest (after Fulton) in Metro Atlanta. Its altitude is from 800 to 1,200 feet above sea level. Rainfall averages 49 inches annually. It has a moderate climate, with mean average temperature of 61 degrees.

In 2008, Gwinnett County was governed by a five member board of county commissioners, and a five member School Board, with members of both boards elected on four year, staggered terms.

About Button Gwinnett

The name came naturally, though it sounds funny.

Both Button and Gwinnett are family names. One of Gwinnett's forebearers, Sir Thomas Button, was an explorer who set out in 1612 to seek the Northwest Passage through Arctic regions. Button rescued Henry Hudson, who was lost in the region. Near Fort Churchill, Canada, on Hudson Bay is Button Bay, named for him.

Button Gwinnett was born 1735 in England, in Glouchestershire, near Wales. His father was a minister of the Church of England. His father-in-law was a merchant and Gwinnett operated for a short career as a merchant there. He emigrated in 1765 to the new colony of Georgia.

Following his family tradition, he soon set himself up as a merchant in Savannah. But Button was found wanting as a merchant, so he got into a new venture, starting to farm and raise cattle on what is today St. Catherine's Island, off the coast, south of Savannah near Midway.

Button had an engaging personality, and the people in the Midway region elected him as their representative to the new provisional government of the colony. Remember, this was before independence, so the government was purely advisory, though it was inflicting consternation on the royal governor. Soon the colonies, upset over the manner in which the British Crown was ruling, began calling for action.

In 1776, heeding a call for a Continental Congress, Georgia's Provisional Assembly elected several persons to represent them at a meeting in Philadelphia. Besides Gwinnett, the body selected Lyman Hall, George Walton and Archibald Bulloch to be their representatives at the meeting. Three of them signed the Declaration of Independence, but Bulloch had been called back to Georgia before the document was complete.

There is little evidence that Gwinnett was a major factor in the discussions leading up to the writing of the Declaration. However, his simple act of signing the Declaration, on August 2, 1776, propelled Gwinnett into posterity in itself.

In recent years, his signature has become one of the rarest and most valuable of the signers of the Declaration of Independence. In 1979, a letter signed by Gwinnett brought $100,000 at a New York auction; its value was estimated in 1983 to be up to $250,000. More recently, Gwinnett gained more notoriety when his signature was auctioned for $270,000. There are less than 30 known copies of his signature.

Button Gwinnett

While Gwinnett is known primarily for his signature, his line soon played out, with no descendants, though he had with his wife, Anne, three daughters, two who died while children. Little is known about the third daughter, Elizabeth Gwinnett, who is said to have moved to South Carolina, and married Peter Berlin, but who died early. Georgia is the only place in the nation where his name appears, though in Pennsylvania there is a Gwynned Street in Philadelphia.

Gwinnett known four different ways

Being objective, we must assess Button Gwinnett as being known four ways.

First, he failed as a businessman. There is evidence that he was sued for not paying his bills.

Secondly, he failed as a farmer, in that his plantation for rice and other crops and cattle on St. Catherine's also was sued for lack of payment, and he lost the island to creditors.

Third, in politics, he had a stormy history, with limited initial success. After the months in Philadelphia and his signing of the Declaration of Independence, he returned to Georgia in 1777, served for two months as the provisional governor, then lost the next election.

Fourth, Gwinnett was also something of a hothead, quick to become upset over matters. He and another legislator vying for power, Gen. Lachlan McIntosh, had become major enemies seeking power and they often clashed in the chambers of government. Eventually one debate in the Legislature led to a challenge. McIntosh had publicly denounced Gwinnett "….a scoundrel and a lying rascal," which Gwinnett felt he could not ignore.

Historian Harvey Jackson picks up the story here:

"That put Gwinnett on the spot. To let the insult pass would be a permanent stain on his honor and render him unworthy in the eyes of others. He had no choice. He sent the note and challenged McIntosh to meet him at dawn the next day to settle the matter.

"On the morning of May 16, 1777, the two met, with pistols, in a pasture outside Savannah. When the seconds asked what distance they should stand apart, McIntosh suggested three paces, about nine feet. He did not want to miss.

"The seconds protested, added another pace, then the men took their posts, stood ready, and when the word was given, fired. Both men aimed for the thickest part of the body and the vital organs. Both men shot low.

"McIntosh was hit in the flesh of his thigh, but remained standing. Gwinnett fell, his leg broken.

"McIntosh suggested they take another shot. Gwinnett agreed, if someone would hold him up. But the seconds intervened and declared that both men had done their duty as gentlemen. The wounded shook hands and it was over."

While McIntosh was also hit in the leg, he eventually recovered. Gwinnett's wound festered in the hot and humid Savannah climate, and he died four days later. So it comes, that Button Gwinnett was also a bad duelist......but, since McIntosh was hit, a good shot, too.

One more twist

There's more. On July 4, 1848, the City of Augusta dedicated an obelisk on its Greene Street (the "Signer's Monument") to honor all three signers of the Declaration of Independence from Georgia. They re-interred the bones of George Walton and Lyman Hall under the obelisk.

It was a stirring day. *The Augusta Chronicle's* report on the event:

"The Masons, Odd Fellows and Son of Temperance, with their respective regalia and badges, attended by an excellent band of music, formed an imposing procession. It marched from the Masonic Hall down Broad Street to Centre Street: thence to Greene Street, and thence to the City Hall. The Rev. Mr. Rogers made an excellent ... prayer near which the Monument is to stand."

"... under (the cornerstone) were deposited the daily papers of the city. American coins of this year and other things supposed to be of interest to remote posterity - well protected by glass. W.T. Gould, Esq., acted as Orator of the day ... and delivered to a large and most respectable auditory, an address characterized by good sense, chasteness, eloquence and entire appropriateness to the occasion."

But note that Button Gwinnett's bones were not included. Here's why: when exhuming what was thought to be Gwinnett's grave at St. Bonaventure Cemetery in Savannah.....lo and behold, the bones in the grave did not have a shattered leg from his duel. It could not have been Gwinnett. To this day we don't know where his body is buried.

So, besides being a bad businessman, an unsuccessful farmer, a stormy politician, and a bad duelist.......now we find that Button Gwinnett is a bad corpse, too.

A monument was unveiled October 19, 1964 to Button Gwinnett in Savannah. It is located in one of the oldest parts of Colonial Park Cemetery. The Savannah Park and Tree Commission describes the tribute to Gwinnett:

"The monument is a 15 foot high structure of veined Georgia marble. Three rectangular marble platforms, each successively smaller, ascend to form the base and steps. Four attenuated Doric columns support an entablature, inscribed in gold with the name 'BUTTON GWINNETT'. Beneath this baldachin is a tabloid or pedestal of marble, with the bronze inscriptional tablet mounted on it."

This is perhaps the only stand-alone monument to Gwinnett, except for a figure cast on a pedestal at the Mall of Georgia, said to be Button Gwinnett. The only problem is that this statue is above the mall so high in the sky that no one can see the features of the person said to represent Gwinnett.

The respected historian Kenneth Coleman of the University of Georgia admitted that Gwinnett never "seemed to do very well financially, although he was very ambitious." Yet Coleman called Gwinnett "the foremost revolutionary in Georgia, and a leading figure in the colony for independence."

Button Gwinnett is a difficult person to comprehend in today's modern times. His legend lives as him having a lively and key role in pre-Revolutionary times in Georgia. He is best known today as having the most rare of signatures of the Declaration of Independence signers, and gaining new notoriety as the namesake of one of the most vibrant, diverse and fastest growing counties in the United States.

Other early settlements

Pinckneyville

Modern day Gwinnett is known as a place where private property developers play a key role in shaping the county. Early Gwinnett was made up primarily of independent farmers, and had but one major city up until 1870. However, a speculative investment from an outsider early on gave life to another community.

His name was Charles Pinckney, from Charleston, S.C. Essentially, he was investing speculatively on the frontier in the 1820s, for Gwinnett was raw, unsettled land, recently and often still populated by Indians. (Remember, "Terminus" was founded not until 1837, and got its charter as the city of Marthasville in 1843, when the railroad was extended from Augusta. It was well named, for it was the end of the railroad then. The city changed its name to Atlanta in a new charter in 1845.)

Back to developer Pinckney: there were two Charles Pinckneys, and no one has determined which of the two was the investor in Gwinnett. Both lived near the same time, and both centered their lives in Charleston, S.C. Either could have invested in the Gwinnett frontier land.

One was Charles Cotesworth Pinckney (1746-1825), a Charleston attorney, Revolutionary war general (and prisoner), state legislator, delegate to the Constitutional Convention, and later minister to France.

The other Charles Pinckney (1757-1824) was also a Constitutional Convention delegate, Revolutionary war soldier and also a prisoner of the British. He served at three different times as South Carolina governor, was a U.S. Senator and U.S. House member, and later was for four years minister to Spain.

No matter which, the Pinckney name lives on today in Gwinnett, in the populous Pinckneyville voting precinct. The community of Pinckneyville was in the western part of the county, near the present DeKalb County line, and two miles up a rise from the Chattahoochee River. That location was sound, for in those days the river routinely flooded each spring. Modern Pinckneyville is one of the most densely populated areas of Gwinnett. As of this writing, for instance, there are 27 voting precincts within this district (Pinckneyville A, B, C,…etc…X, Y, Z, to A-1.) In 2008, there were 45,464 registered voters in the entire Pinckneyville militia district.

Remember, however, there's one particularly notable aspect to the early Pinckney investment in Gwinnett: the settlers of the area thought enough of whichever Pinckney it was to name this community "Pinckneyville," termed the oldest white settlement this far west in frontier Georgia. (Early records list the name of the area as "Turkey Gizzard.") Land was acquired from a treaty with the Cherokee Indians in 1818. The area was never incorporated.

Today you can mark the location of the former Pinckneyville community at the intersection of Medlock Bridge Road, where Old Peachtree Road becomes Spalding Drive. The new Norcross High School is a few hundred yards away. The area was not far from the Hightower Indian Trail, a key trail in those days.

A church, Mt. Carmel Methodist (1826), is located nearby. In early days, the area had a stagecoach stop and post office and the Hunnicutt Inn, a landmark on the Augusta to Rome road. One of the first fee-based schools, Washington Academy, was nearby. Its site is at the location of today's Shiloh Baptist Church, on Spalding Drive.

Pinckneyville prospered as an unincorporated farming community for 50 years or more.....until the arrival of the railroad in the 1870s. At that time, the people of the area began to focus on the new town of Norcross, two miles away, with its ease of transportation and connections via the new railroad. Pinckneyville lost its identity as a community, when many of its people "moved to town."

Centerville Community

Another early center of settlement was in the very southern part of what is now Gwinnett, near Centerville. A former Indian path, the Hightower Trail, was one of the more important trails through this section of the country. In early Gwinnett, it began near the southern end of the county, crossed the Yellow River at a rocky juncture at the present Annistown Road bridge, wound northwesterly and eventually crossed the Chattahoochee River at the Shallow Ford. When DeKalb County was formed in 1822, the trail was the western boundary of Gwinnett.

The area south of Snellville around Centerville was settled in the early 1800s. The land was favorable to farming, and early settlers established homesteads there. Some of the oldest churches in the county were founded there, including Zoar Methodist Church (said to be founded in 1811, though no verifiable proof is available), and Rockbridge Baptist Church, which dates from 1819. Another church in the area, Haynes Creek Primitive Baptist Church, was founded in 1826.

At some time prior to the Civil War, the community was known as Sneezer. Under the name of Centerville, it had a post office from 1879 to 1903.

An early family moving to the area was Celia and Elijah Anderson, who came to Gwinnett in the 1820s. Celia died not long after the move and when Elijah passed away in 1840, their youngest son, David, inherited their land in the Rockbridge District. David's sister, Jane, married Thomas McGuire. Following Jane's death from blood poisoning in 1837, McGuire married another of David's sisters, Elizabeth. By 1860, David had a prosperous plantation of 670 acres. The Anderson family built a complex in the area known as "Pleasant Valley." It consisted of a church, general store, cabinet shop, blacksmith shop, cotton gin, grist mill and planing mill.

During the Civil War, the area had one of the largest plantations in the county, Thomas McGuire's "Promised Land." The plantation encompassed nearly 1,000 acres. McGuire kept a series of journals describing life on the plantation. A surviving diary at the Atlanta History Center, which chronicles the years 1859-66, tells of growing cotton, wheat, corn, vegetables, and fruit; and raising hogs, cattle and sheep. Activities on the plantation included carpentry, blacksmithing, ginning, tanning hides, milling flour, grinding cane, and making brick. McGuire's journal also records the effects of the Civil War on his plantation and the Atlanta area. In November of 1864, Union soldiers on their "March to the Sea" passed by the Promised Land and burned McGuire's gin house, stables, barn, and fences while McGuire hid out in the woods. The soldiers also stole or slaughtered his livestock. Fortunately, McGuire's house was spared and stands today in the Promised Land community.

Another prominent family of Gwinnett, the Masons, stem also from the Promised Land area. This family is reported in the area as early as the 1830s. In 1887, Ellery J. Mason acquired a house south of Centerville which was originally part of the Thomas McGuire plantation. For over 80 years, the Mason family has gathered at this site for their annual reunion each August.

Where the Hightower Trail crossed the Yellow River, giant rocky outcrops create shoals in the river. This is where an unpaved road got a steel bridge across the river in 1899. The bridge, now closed to traffic, is north of the modern concrete Annistown Road bridge (built in 1976-77), at a spot in Gwinnett where several people over the years thought would make a good manufacturing site, harnessing the waters of the river for power. The height of the fall of water in the river was 13 feet. Several mills were located north of the shoals to use this fall in the water.

The differing mills often took the names of their owners. The Maguire's Mill included a sawmill, lumber mill, flour and grist mills. The grist mill was operated with four turbines, each two feet in breadth, producing 45 horsepower, according to a study of prehistoric and historic excavations published prior to a road improvement in the area by New South Associates in 1998. The grist mill could produce 180 bushels a day. The sawmill was operated part time, but produced 150,000 feet of lumber and 40,000 shingles annually.

In 1897, John Maguire sold 370 acres including the mill to C.J. Haden. The deed lists a cotton factory and mill, run by water power, together with machinery and buildings, in the sale. It is Haden who is credited with naming the community "Annestown" perhaps after either his wife or daughter. The community even got a charter from the state in 1907, which was revoked (finally) by the state in 1995. Haden sold the mill tract to Annestown

Cotton Mill Corporation in 1900, but in 1901, the *News Herald* reported the "Cotton Mills seems to be dead....for want of capital." The next mention is with a new firm, in 1906, when Baxter Cotton Manufacturing Company was organized. Yet in 1908, the cotton mill was destroyed by fire, when it employed about 25 people. It closed afterward. Once again, the mill property was sold in 1913, but no additional production as a mill is evident, as records after 1908 refer to the area as a "former mill site." Much later, in the 1970s, would come intense subdivision development on high ground above the river.

The New South report of 1998 tells of an 1880 census in Gwinnett County that showed a total of 41 mills were in operation, six of them on the Yellow River. There were 27 flour and grist mills, and 14 saw mills. "Of the 27 flour and grist mills, 26 were powered directly by water and one by steam. Of the 14 saw mills, seven were powered by water, four by steam, and three by both. The water-powered mills included nine that were operated by turbines, 17 that had overshot wheels, four that had tub wheels and one with an unidentified wood wheel."

The "Promised Land"

In more modern times, reference to the "Promised Land" harkens back to the time when Robert Livsey bought 110 acres in the early 1920s, and began to farm the land. Mr. Livsey's family were light-skinned African Americans. After the purchase of the land for $2,500, this area became one of several African-American communities in Gwinnett County.

The 110 acres Mr. Livsey bought was on the route between Lithonia and Centerville, on the northeastern side of the Yellow River. Descendants of the Livseys continue to make their homes in the area in 2008.

However, interest in genealogy brought a recent twist with the realization that the black members of the Livsey community were related to white Livseys in the near area. This came about through efforts of Thomas Livsey and his son, Tom, in researching their family tree. Tom picks up the story: "For the first time, last summer [2007] the white and black Livseys celebrated a family reunion together. It was a wonderful occasion. No one owed any one an explanation or excuse for the past....(there was)....no animosity....no guilt. We must question our past in order to determine our own future. We all left with a whole new family tree."

As he says: "We all are cousins."

Members of the Livsey family now are seeking to determine if Green Livsey was a common ancestor. He came from Culpepper, Va. to Wilkes County, Ga. in 1815, married Barbara Poss and was an overseer on the Robert Toombs Plantation. In 1822 the couple had a son, Sandy, from whom Thomas and Tom are descended. Robert Livsey and his wife came to the Gwinnett-Walton area in 1840. The tracers of the Livseys know that their forebears were from Livsey County, Lancaster, in England.

Complicate all this with another blood mix: many of the Livseys now know that they also have Indian ancestors. So the family is tri-racial. They are seeking to tie in the other Livsey relatives. They continue to involve more "cousins," learning that they are related, but still have some loose ends of the Livsey family tree to tie up.

All those Peachtree Streets began in Gwinnett

Metro Atlanta is a city of many, many Peachtree Streets, Avenues, Chases and Walks. Developers, intent on naming streets with an Atlanta flavor, often resort to using the "Peachtree" name either in the name of their subdivision, or for streets of the development. But all the streets and avenues and usage owe their naming to the original Peachtree Road, which has a distinctive Gwinnett connection.

It goes back to the War of 1812, even before Gwinnett was founded. In that war, local Indians were often pledging their allegiance to the British, against the new United States.

Here in Georgia, garrisoned near present-day Hog Mountain was a "listening post" for the Army, called Fort Daniel. The United States had another such "listening post," in order to be alert to Indian movement, at the confluence of present-day Peachtree Creek and the Chattahoochee River. This was known officially as Fort Gilmer, but the common name given to it was the "fort at the standing peach tree." A road connecting the two forts, became known as "Peachtree Road." This road followed the Eastern Continental Divide ridge line. It was used first as an Indian trail, with its high ground and sight lines especially necessary in those early times.

Now you know where all the names of "Peachtree" in the Atlanta area originated from. But there is more to the story, as historian Franklin Garrett reports in his two-volume history of Atlanta (*Atlanta and Environs*).

As Garrett points out, a peach tree won't grow in a river bottom. It needs high, dry land to thrive. And where the "Standing Peachtree" Creek flows into the Chattahoochee River is surely a wet area. So that tree at Fort Gilmer wasn't a peach tree after all. It was a "pitch" tree, or pine tree, which thrives in wetter land.

What this should mean is that all these "Peachtree" names in Atlanta are incorrectly named, dating from the first one. The first road should have more accurately have been called "Pitchtree Road" or maybe "Pinetree Road." But "Peachtree" sounds more romantic.

There's another story of a mis-naming of a tree in Gwinnett. One of the premier communities within Gwinnett is Peachtree Corners, that sprawling section of Pinckneyville from Peachtree Industrial Boulevard and Norcross city limits westward to the Chattahoochee River. About 1970, Peachtree Corners was named by Paul Duke, the developer of the area, who wanted the area to have a distinctive identity, where people would live, work and play as a community. And for years, to help designate the area, a small tree was planted atop high ground near the intersection of Peachtree Industrial Boulevard and Peachtree Parkway, just north of Holcomb Bridge Road. (Today it marks the site of a shopping center anchored by Publix and Target stores.)

A ten foot square gray-painted box was built around the ten-foot-tall tree, with the large words "Peachtree Corners" on the box in white announced to all the name of this new community. It served as a landmark for years, until the present shopping center was built in 1994. But this tree, too, wasn't a peach tree. It was a Japanese Red Maple, imported by the Peachtree Corners development from North Carolina, at a cost of $8,000!

But most people thought it was a peach tree, and the tree and its distinctive signage helped promote Peachtree Corners in its formative years, before it got bulldozed for a shopping center.

Early churches

Even before Gwinnett was the name of the area, people were settling in the vicinity, which was then part of Jackson County. The earliest church in the county could have been Mt. Moriah Baptist Church, in the very northern tip of what is now Gwinnett. A large rock marker for years lay beside the Braselton Highway (Georgia Highway 124) pointing to the church, with the date of 1779 inscribed on the rock. With road maintenance, that rock is no longer there. No Baptist records at Mercer University show a Mt. Moriah church as active in those days. However, Silas King, who later moved to Buford, came to Gwinnett in the 1820s. He is reported to have lived near the church for a while, and to have served as a pastor of the Mt. Moriah Church. Another report showed that it had 200 members in 1828. The earliest church minutes are from 1835.

Mt. Moriah Baptist Church on Georgia 124 near Hamilton Mill. A plaque on the church wall says it was established in 1779.

Members of the church have passed down through the years that the date the church was started as 1779. Because of that, the church marked its 200th anniversary celebration in 1979, or as one member said, "We thought that was the date."

Another church, Zoar Methodist in the Centerville community near today's Snellville, says that it had its centennial in 1911, making its founding in 1811. Church officials admit that they can offer little proof of the founding date.

Let's mention a former minister of Zoar, the Rev. Nat Long, who around 1973 wrote an abbreviated church history in a most ethical and accurate way. Not having all his facts, the Rev. Long admitted this up front. He said:

"Tradition says that the Zoar Methodist Church was established in 1811, but there is very little authentic information about the Zoar Church for the first 60-100 years of her history." However, he has in the church possession the Zoar Sunday School Record book, covering the period of July 12, 1896 to June 2, 1902, its earliest records.

Flanigan, in Gwinnett County Georgia Churches, was at a loss to pinpoint the date of Zoar Methodist Church. However, he chronicles in his book that in 1911 Zoar was founded "about 100 years ago." Flanigan says the current (2008) location of the church dates back from "about 1848," and was the third site in the Centerville area for the church, though a new structure (apparently on the same site) was built in 1877, valued at $1,000.

At least two other churches date from the early days of the county. Rockbridge Baptist Church dates from 1819. Haynes Creek Primitive Baptist Church, in the southern corner of the county, was chartered on April 1, 1826. Among those at the chartering service included members of the Rockbridge, Bay Creek (now Shiloh) and Red Land Baptist churches.

Rockbridge Baptist Church dates from its founding under a brush arbor on the banks of the Yellow River on August 19, 1819. The next year it moved to a log house. The church has had several locations in Centerville and erected a large white frame building in 1879.

The Centerville community was a closely-knit one, and even cooperated in church matters. Since churches did not meet every Sunday, often members of one church would be visitors at the other's church. And until 1974, the Rockbridge and Zoar congregations worked together on a combined Vacation Bible School each summer.

In early 1983, Rockbridge moved to a new building, made of brown brick, and in 1985, the church called its first full-time pastor. Then in 2002, the church changed its name, becoming Hope and Life Fellowship, and now is a non-denominational, independent congregation. The church has also purchased the old fire station, now used as a youth facility. Altogether it has 16 acres of land. The former 1879 building is now the children's church. Attendance in 2008 on Sunday averaged 975.

Another early church in the southern part of the county was Flint Hill Methodist, later First United Methodist of Norcross, dating from 1818. The date on the cornerstone of another church, near Suwanee, that of Level Creek Methodist Church, is 1822. Its first building was completed in 1823.

You can tell many of the older churches from cemeteries near them. One of the finest examples of an old-time church and its adjoining cemetery can be seen today at Camp Creek (Primitive) Baptist Church of Lilburn, which dates from 1823. It continues to have regular services. Another old-time church with a cemetery is Sweetwater Primitive Baptist Church on Pleasant Hill Road, founded in 1824, which still stands today, but no longer has regular services.

Meanwhile as Lawrenceville was being formed, its First Methodist Church dates back to 1823, as does Fairview Presbyterian Church. Fairview was the first Presbyterian church in what is now Metro Atlanta. Out of this church, the Decatur Presbyterian Church was founded by the Lawrenceville congregation, and dates from 1825. Out of the Decatur church came the First Presbyterian Church of Atlanta in 1848, so Fairview is the grandparent of all Metro Atlanta Presbyterian churches.

A significant event took place in Lawrenceville in 1832, when five members of the First Methodist Church purchased 50 acres on Braselton Highway (Georgia Highway 124) north of Lawrenceville for a site for a camp meeting. The five were Elisha Wynn, William Maltbie, Isham Williams, George Brogdon and Buckner Harris. (See chapter on Lawrenceville history for more details on the continuing campground meeting.)

Civil War times around Gwinnett

Gwinnett is not the place for Civil War history. Though the area felt the war heavily, it did not see major battles within its borders, as only a few raiding parties took place. The Battle of Atlanta essentially bypassed Gwinnett, since it had no strategic rail line. The main thrust of the Atlanta campaign was along rail lines as the battle moved southerly from Chattanooga through Cobb County toward Atlanta.

Yet the Civil War took a heavy toll on Gwinnett, just as it did on most Southern counties. Its toll can be seen in two ways.

Gwinnett had 12,940 people in the 1860 census and was growing. That included 2,551 slaves and 31 "free blacks." By 1870, that population was 12,431, including 10,272 white and 2,159 "colored." By 1890 the population was 19,531.

More than 500 Gwinnett Confederate troops died during the Civil War, as the war had a devastating toll on the male population of Gwinnett, and the South. To put this into perspective, consider the memorial to "fallen heroes" who were from Gwinnett that was erected at the Gwinnett Justice and Administrative Center in 2003. Elegant gray granite monoliths list the names of those from Gwinnett killed in the various wars. In 2007, it listed the names of 502 Gwinnettians on three tablets killed in the Civil War. For a comparison, only one person from Gwinnett was killed in the Spanish-American War; 33 in World War I; 73 in World War II; four in the Korean Conflict; 25 in Vietnam; and 16 persons are listed in the 21st century War on Terrorism. (See more on the Fallen Heroes Memorial on page 433.)

The overall impact of the toll of the Civil War on Southerners can be seen by considering the Civil War in its totality. One historian says that the Confederate strength, which is less accurately known because of missing records, was between 750,000 and 1.25 million soldiers. Through battle deaths and disease, 258,000 Confederates died in the war....which would put the loss of lives at a minimum of 20 percent. As a comparison with other wars, during World War I, the number of Americans killed was 2.46 percent of those serving, while in World War II, 2.52 percent were killed. Only the Mexican War came close to the losses of the Civil War: 16.87 percent were lost in the war with Mexico. Sources for this are the Department of Defense and Historian Burke Davis.

The mass of names in the three monoliths at the left emphasizes the toll on Gwinnett during the Civil War.

The election of Abraham Lincoln to many in the South was a blow, and called for action. Gwinnett sent three delegates to a Confederate Convention in 1861. They were James P. Simmons, Richard D. Winn and Thomas J.P. Hudson. The convention pitted Southern plantation owners, needing lots of field hands and slaves, against the more conservative North Georgia farmers, who generally owned few slaves. Though the convention passed a resolution cutting Georgia's ties to the nation (280 to 89), the three Gwinnett delegates were in the minority with the mostly North Georgia farmer delegates. Soon Georgia and the rest of the Confederate States were at war with the Union.

Look at the Civil War another way. In his *History of Gwinnett*, J.C. Flanagan says that half the wealth of the county was lost in the Civil War. It would take years and years before the county could recover from what the Civil War had wrought.

The first troop to be formed was a company called Hutchins Guards of the 35th Regiment, in 1861. A company consisted of 12 officers and 100 enlisted men, locally recruited, who fought together. Gwinnett continued to supply other men for action in the war.

Just before the war, in 1858, the county's first newspaper, the *Gwinnett Herald*, was founded in Lawrenceville. During the war, once Union forces began a move on the rail center of Atlanta, the onrushing forces eyed the Gwinnett newspaper for the propaganda value of its printing press.

The publisher of the *Herald*, James T. Simmons, you might imagine, was a staunch Southerner, and didn't want his newspaper falling into "Yankee" hands. Word is that he felt threatened enough as Sherman moved toward Atlanta, that he systemically took his press apart, and buried the pieces bit by bit on the Terrell farm, two miles east of the city. As late as the 1930s, parts of his press were still being plowed up on that land. But the Yankees didn't get his printing press to use as a propaganda vehicle!

During the Civil War, the major physical loss for Gwinnett was its first industry, a cotton mill, which began in 1851 in Lawrenceville, just west of the present First Methodist Church. Yankee forces burned that plant in 1864. The plant during the war produced cotton bags used for salt for the Confederate troops.

In those days, armies usually lived "off the land," taking what they needed for food and forage. One Gwinnett diarist wrote of the War that "You had to watch out for North and South, too," as both side commandeered the supplies they found as they swept through an area.

There is a story from Civil War times that applies to one of the present Gwinnett communities. Near Stone Mountain in southern Gwinnett was a small community which had a general store. We know it as present-day Mountain Park. However, earlier the community was known as "Trickum." (This is not to be confused with another Georgia community called "Trickum" in Whitfield County, Ga.)

How the Gwinnett community got its name comes with two stories.

One story has it that the Confederates came galloping through only a few minutes ahead of a Yankee contingent. When the Union troops came by, stopping at a store where there are five forks to the road, the Yankee commander asked the storekeeper: "Which way did they go?" The proprietor pointed the direction and the Yankees sped off. But the storekeeper, a Southern sympathizer, had tricked the Yankees, for the Rebs had taken another fork of the road. Hence the name, "Trickum."

There's another version to the origin of the community name. When that same storekeeper at the five forks of the road gave customers change for their purchases, the customers had to be especially careful, and count their change! Or else the storekeeper would have shortchanged, or "tricked" them. Hence the name, "Trickum" and a second version to the naming of the area.

Two different versions of the community name: take the one you like best. To this day, many people in Mountain Park still call the community "Trickum." Interestingly, the area's middle school today bears the name Trickum!

Garrard's Raid

While Gen. William T. Sherman's campaign to take Atlanta kicked off on July 22, 1864, and while he occupied Atlanta beginning on September 1, 1964, Gwinnett was not in the direct line of the battle. Cobb County, on the other hand, was the starting point of the battle, and many of the key incidents took place within its borders before Sherman was able to successfully cross the Chattahoochee and enter the city of Atlanta. Kennesaw National Battlefield is, therefore, a perfect spot to learn about the battle.

Essentially, the Sherman attack was from the northwest into Atlanta. Gwinnett, lying northeast of Atlanta, therefore was not a key element in the direction of the campaign.

Though constantly under threat of Yankee intrusions into Gwinnett, there was only one major thrust into the county. It has become known as Garrard's Raid.

It came as Sherman moved to protect his eastern flank from Confederate reinforcements arriving from Virginia. He ordered Brig. Gen. Kenner Garrard, a West Point graduate of 1851, to head east and burn railroad bridges over the Yellow and Alcovy Rivers. Garrard's cavalry division set out on July 21, 1864, one day before the start of the decisive Battle of Atlanta.

Leaving their encampment in Decatur, Garrard's three brigades headed toward Tucker, and apparently crossed slightly into Gwinnett at a point called Choice's Store, near present day Lilburn. Then they turned southeasterly, and went to the Rockbridge crossing of the Yellow River, where they camped for the night.

During the night, the troops, hearing of the large plantation of Thomas McGuire called "The Promised Land" (south of present-day Centerville), set off hunting booty. They robbed McQuire personally of his watch and wallet, and took everything "not nailed down," returning to their encampment on the nearby Yellow River.

The next morning, the Garrard troops broke camp, burned the bridge over the river, and aimed for Conyers. Here the cavalry found a locomotive had just pulled into the station, and set it, along with the train depot, on fire. They rushed to the 555 foot rail trestle over the Yellow River, and soon had it in flames, along with a wagon bridge. Then they took aim at Oxford, where they did not linger long. Their more important target was Covington.

The troops terrorized the people of Covington, burned that depot, and bent rails on the railroad. They also stocked their wagons with provisions, including tobacco, a commodity always in demand by the troops. Then they turned their attention to the Alcovy River, galloping out of town and burning the train trestle.

That night of July 22, Garrard rested his troops at Sardis Church, north of Oxford. The next morning, they rode through Walnut Grove, destroying bales of cotton along the way, while outriders foraged on side roads. Another detachment headed to Social Circle and Monroe, where they ransacked the only commercial store. Meanwhile, for another thrust, Loganville was a few miles northwest of Walnut Grove, and here the Union forces found more bales of cotton to burn.

By now, Garrard split his forces, with one group going toward Lawrenceville. They initially met a group of about 50 Rebels, though this group scattered when the cavalry force advanced into the town. One person wrote that there was little to tempt the raiders except corn, which they gobbled up for their horses. A few weeks earlier, a large cotton mill had burned, with the town having no strategic resources. That night this group of Garrard's band camped on the banks of the Yellow River east of town.

Meanwhile, Garrard's other battalion left Loganville and headed for present day Mountain Park, bedding down at what was then called "Trickum Crossroads."

On July 24, as the Union forces marched toward Decatur from Trickum, expecting their own men, they were surprised to find Confederate forces in town, and a small skirmish ensued. They advanced into town on foot, and sent out patrols to protect their camp. The Rebels never re-attacked. Later, the Garrard troops re-grouped, and took inventory of their efforts. Garrard's efforts had brought in nearly 175 Confederate prisoners, with the loss of only two of his own men.

The raid was a quick move into Gwinnett, one of not key significance to the war. Bridges were burned in nearby counties, and Garrard's men came back loaded with supplies from the Confederate countryside. And in the meantime, they had burned two depots, destroyed three trains and six miles of track, and burned an estimated 2,000 bales of cotton. It was a good effort by the Union forces, which shut off the possibility of easy Confederates reinforcements from the East, keeping Sherman's left flank intact. He would need this protection, as the Battle of Atlanta started on July 22, and Garrard's efforts served to protect Sherman's left flank. But it would be six weeks more before Sherman could claim victory and occupy Atlanta.

Key Dates Leading to Sherman's 1864 March to the Sea

May 7: Sherman begins his drive toward Atlanta.
May 12: Sherman outflanks Johnston at Dalton.
May 14-15: Battle of Resaca, between Sherman and Johnston.
June 25: Battle of New Hope.
June 27: Battle of Kennesaw Mountain.
July 17: Confederates replace Joe Johnston with John B. Hood.
July 20: Battle of Peachtree Creek.
July 22: Battle of Atlanta.
July 28: Battle of Ezra Church.
Aug. 31: Battle of Jonesboro.
Sept. 1: Confederates evacuate Atlanta.
Sept. 2: Sherman occupies Atlanta.
Oct. 5: Battle of Allatoona.
Nov. 16: Sherman prepares for the March to the Sea.

Nov. 17: Beginning of the March to the Sea.
Nov. 22: Sherman occupies Milledgeville.
Dec. 13: Union captures Fort McAllister near Savannah.
Dec. 21: Sherman occupies Savannah.
Dec. 22: Sherman gives a Christmas present of intact Savannah to Lincoln.

The coming of the railroads

Early Gwinnett was a community cut off from the rest of the world by all means except horseback, wagon or foot until just after the Civil War. Unlike Augusta or Macon or Columbus, there was no navigable river. The Chattahoochee near Atlanta had low water most of the year, and was filled with too many rocks to make it navigable above Columbus. It took the coming of the railroads to give Gwinnett another access to areas and markets beyond its borders.

The railroads came after the Civil War. The first was opened in 1871, as the Atlanta and Richmond Air-Line Rail road, which received assistance and was controlled by the Richmond and Danville Railroad. Later, it was reorganized as the Atlanta and Charlotte Air Line Railroad, and shortly afterward, as the Georgia Air Line Railroad, and still later as the Southern Railway. This is the forerunner of the modern day Norfolk Southern rail line, connecting Atlanta northeasterly to Charlotte and other cities. In Gwinnett, train tracks ran near the western border of the county. This first railroad through Gwinnett followed much of the Eastern Continental Divide, or ridge line. This gave the railroad a relatively level course, and saved the cost of building trestles over lowlands.

As the railroad was built through Gwinnett, four communities sprang up: modern day Buford, Suwanee, Duluth and Norcross. And life in Gwinnett was changed forever!

In 1881, about 10 years after the first railroad came to Gwinnett, a second railroad, the narrow-gauge Lawrenceville Branch Railroad, connected the towns of Suwanee and Lawrenceville. This gave access by rail to the county seat. People in the edges of the county, in Buford or Norcross, could take a train to Suwanee, change trains, and steam on the Lawrenceville Branch Railroad to the county seat of Lawrenceville. It was a splendid, easy trip, compared to riding a mule or driving a buggy.

In 1891, the third railroad came to the county. It was first known as the Georgia, Carolina and Northern Railway, built by interests of the Seaboard Air Line Railroad. Today it is part of the CSX system. This railroad's tracks run through the center of the county, skimming modern Dacula, Lawrenceville and Lilburn, and on into Atlanta though Tucker and Emory University. In its early heydays, it also had stops at communities no longer operational: Luxomni and Gloster.

There is still one more railroad which contributes to Gwinnett history. That was the L&L Railroad, officially the Loganville and Lawrenceville, which began in 1898. This rail line made three trips daily from Loganville to Lawrenceville. Loganville is primarily in Walton County, though about one third of the town is in Gwinnett. The railroad ceased operations in 1932, by which time it was owned and operated as a branch of the Seaboard Air Line Railroad. It was a chronic money-loser.

That's the story of how Gwinnett came to have two major railroads, the Norfolk Southern and CSX, providing rail service in the county.

As this is written, there is renewed interest (which has been talked about for 40 years) in using the railroad rights-of-way for commuter passenger service into Atlanta. The main thrust is to connect Atlanta with Athens, with rail stops at Emory University, Tucker, at least three stops in Gwinnett, and on toward Athens through Winder, Statham and Bogart. The initial thrust took the name of "Brain Train," and began in 2006.

Whether this effort will be successful is unknown at the time of this writing. However, with highway congestion the major problem for many people in Gwinnett, some relief through commuter rail transit would be most welcome by all Gwinnettians.

In 1965, the Metropolitan Atlanta Rapid Transit Authority Act was passed by the state Legislature and subsequently approved for four counties (Fulton, DeKalb, Clayton and Gwinnett) and by the City of Atlanta, creating MARTA. Gwinnett and Clayton gained a seat on the MARTA board, which they retain today.

However, before the initial metro bus service could begin in the four counties, a vote was held in each county to see if voters would pay for the service through a sales tax of one penny.

The vote by counties on November 9, 1971:

County	***For***	***Against***
Fulton County	55,736	53,725
DeKalb County	39,565	36,207
Clayton County	3,300	11,147
Gwinnett County	2,500	9,506

Note that MARTA passed in Fulton County by a margin of 2,011 votes. The margin in DeKalb was by 3,358 votes. But both Clayton and Gwinnett turned down the proposal to have public transportation within their borders by significant margins.

Gwinnett County, with 10.3 percent of those registered voting, turned down the additional one cent sales tax to be a part of the MARTA service area. DeKalb and Fulton counties saw local bus service begin in 1972. The first MARTA train was put in service in 1979.

The MARTA question was put to another Gwinnett vote in November, 1990. Again Gwinnett citizens solidly were against any extension of MARTA into the county, voting 68,136 against, and 28,828 for the proposal.

Therefore, public referendums on extending the Metropolitan Atlanta Rapid Transit Authority through Gwinnett have been met with opposition the two times Gwinnett voted on this proposition. Heaviest opposition to MARTA in 1990 was in the corridor of U.S. Highway 78. However, it should be noted that in the 1990 vote, the people in the corridor from Norcross to Buford had the highest interest (43 percent voting yes) in extending MARTA through Gwinnett. This might point the way for a commuter line serving Gwinnett into Atlanta, perhaps starting in Gainesville, and serving Oakwood, Flowery Branch, and the four communities the first Gwinnett railroad caused to be founded…..Buford, Suwanee, Duluth and Norcross.

We'll see. In 2008, different but similar questions on Democratic and Republican primary ballots concerning MARTA and a possible sales tax drew different results from the two party polls. In general, Democrats favored mass transit strongly (70 percent for), while Republicans were against it, by 67 percent. The combined vote (though different questions) continued against the proposition, with only 46.3 percent of those who voted for it, in Gwinnett.

Oldest city in Metro Atlanta

Lawrenceville has the distinction of being the oldest city in the five-county Metro Atlanta area, dating back to 1821. It was laid out as the Gwinnett County seat, right in the middle of the county, with the town originally consisting of 250 acres. William Towers surveyed and laid out the courthouse square. The four streets around the courthouse were named for famous men of that era: Gen. Zebulon Pike, Maj. George Crogan, Naval Capt. Oliver Wendell Perry, and Judge Augustine Smith Clayton. Many of the initial streets in Lawrenceville are named for native trees. Hence, the Oak, Chestnut, Pine and Sassafras Streets, though Sassafras was later changed to Luckie, and Pine to Culver!

The city was located near several clear springs, for water. The importance of the springs is shown in the Inferior Court appointing five commissioners "to superintend and keep in order the springs belonging to the town of Lawrenceville." This gave the commission enforcement of powers concerning the springs. The five men were John Appling, John Brewster, Benjamin Ivie, James McClure and James Wardlaw.

Choosing a name for the city turned to relatively recent past events. One of the county's early settlers, Postmaster William Maltbie, suggested the name of U.S. Naval Capt. James Lawrence, who lost his life in the War of 1812 when he commanded the USS Chesapeake under attack by the British in the Atlantic near Boston on June 1, 1813. Wounded, Captain Lawrence uttered the words from the deck of his ship: *"Don't give up the ship lads! Fight her as long as she swims."*

However, the British won the battle, after Lawrence was first shot in the shoulder, and then squarely in the stomach. His ship lost, Lawrence was captured by the British, and perished en route to the British port of Halifax, Nova Scotia.

Commodore Oliver Wendell Perry used a shortened version of Lawrence's quote "Don't give up the ship!" on the flag of his ship, the brig USS Lawrence, in fighting successfully against British on Lake Erie in late 1813.

Though Lawrenceville was the county seat and first town, for most of its first 150 years, it was over-shadowed by Buford, which soon after it was founded in 1871, would become the largest city in the county, a title it held until 1970. Buford, with its key leather operations, was by far the most significant and largest city in the immediate area. While the courthouse and the courts were important to the development of Lawrenceville, it also had for many years the only newspaper in the county, the *Herald*, founded in 1858.

Lawrenceville's founding dates from Dec. 15, 1821, three years after the county was formed, when the legislature issued the city charter. It is the oldest city in the five counties of Metro Atlanta. (Decatur is next oldest in the area, being founded in 1823.)

After its founding, commissioners were to look out for the business of the town until an election could be held. The original town commissioners included James Wardlaw, Hugh B. Greenwood, James McClure, John Gaddess Sr. and Pascal Brooks. (Wardlaw was also the first clerk of Superior Court.) The town would be so governed from 1821 to 1883, when a new law allowed for a mayor and council. The first election for mayor was in 1884, when John Clay Smith won the position.

Growth in Lawrenceville was slow. By 1830, the town only had about 40 dwellings, 10 stores, ten machine shops, three law offices, three doctors, one academy and three churches. The city did not experience much growth in its first 100 years. By 1870, it had only 1,201 residents.

However, in 1851, the city got a boost when it landed the first industry, as a cotton bag manufacturing plant was built west of the city, between Crogan and Pike Streets, near the present First United Methodist Church. The Lawrenceville Manufacturing Company building was large for that day, measuring four stories high on a 220x50 foot base, made of granite. The mill had 3,050 spindles, 36 looms, and 80 operators, with the entire building powered by steam. The mill produced quite a handsome payroll for the only city in Gwinnett in that day, and was an outlet for the area farmers' cotton crops. In addition to the cotton mill, it also had a flour and grist mill, all powered by steam. It was a large venture for its day, with a capitalization of $90,000. Local housewives were no doubt pleased that a mill, for flour and corn, was attached to the building.

During the Civil War, about the only major physical loss for Gwinnett was its first industry, as Yankee forces burned the cotton bag manufacturing plant in 1864.

The war didn't find heavy battle engagements between the armies in Gwinnett. However, a small force of Union soldiers and rag-tag Confederates, consisting of teenage boys and older men, fired on each other near Lawrenceville in 1864, with little damage to either side.

One of the key dates in the history of Lawrenceville is 1881. That's the year that the railroad came to the Gwinnett county seat, as the narrow-gauge Lawrenceville Branch Railroad connected the towns of Suwanee and Lawrenceville. This gave Lawrenceville a modern connection to the outside world, and as a result, the city began its long period of slow growth.

That sustained growth was heightened when another railroad came to Lawrenceville in 1891. This time it was the main line of the Georgia, Carolina and Northern Railroad, which was building a rail line to connect Atlanta with northeastern cities. This rail line gave Lawrenceville residents a direct route (instead of having to transfer trains in Suwanee) into Atlanta to the south, and Athens to the north. In later years, it became the Seaboard Coast Line Railroad, and still later, part of the CSX system, giving Gwinnett two main-line railroads bisecting the county.

Early courthouse fence

All too often, elected officials have to tell their constituents: "We don't have the money for the project you want." This, in effect, was the answer the Gwinnett County Commission

Lawrenceville High School was at the highest point of the city, and that's why the city's water tank was erected nearby.

gave the judge of the Inferior Court in 1849 when he asked that a fence be constructed around the courthouse. He wanted the fence to keep livestock from disrupting his courtroom. In those days, animals had "free range" to wander as much as they liked, since modern fencing with barbed wire had not yet been invented.

So the commission came up with a novel idea. It proposed to the four attorneys in town that the lawyers build and keep up a fence around the courthouse, and if they did that, the county would grant them lots on the courthouse corners to build their offices.

That's how attorneys Charles H. Smith (Bill Arp), N.L. Hutchins, James P. Simmons, and T.W. Alexander received their courthouse lots for their law offices. The attorneys each built a brick building right on the four corners of the courthouse square, and the courthouse gained an eight-foot high fence. This fence had stiles on all four sides that gave people access to the courthouse. The attorneys could keep their lots as long as they maintained a substantial fence around the square to keep out wandering livestock.

By some logic, the fence kept out the animals. And the judge and his court had its decorum back. And it didn't cost the county government any hard cash.

In later years, the attorneys would all sell their lots, resulting in other commercial activities taking place on the courthouse square. At one time, one corner of Perry and Pike Streets was the office of Sam Brown and the Brown Bank and Trust Company, a bank that went out of business during the Depression. (That was the Simmons lot.) Over the years, the same building has been used by the State Department of Veterans Services, State Highway Department, City Water Department and the Gwinnett County Surveyors office. Its most recent use was as the Council For Seniors.

Now let's move to the modern day. Now you realize how two of the land lots on corners of the courthouse are owned privately. On the southeastern corner is the official headquarters of Brand Banking Company, which has recently enlarged their brick building on the corner from one to two stories.

The southwestern corner up until recently was a medical office, occupied by Dr. W.P. Ezzard and later his son, Dr. George Ezzard. Years before, the county got back the northeast and northwest corners. The building on the northeast corner (Clayton and Pike Streets) became the county library in 1951. Later on, it was the office of the county surveyor. In 1992, the county converted the northeast corner to restrooms when the Historic Courthouse was refurbished.

But back to the 1849 courthouse fence. By 1889, some citizens of the City of Lawrenceville, including its mayor and council, didn't especially like the fence around the courthouse. It was unsightly, and often in bad repair. The Council wanted the fence to be torn down.

J.H. (Jim) McGee Sr. came to the county in 1888 from Harris County, ran for many years a most successful department store, and later was executive vice president of the First National Bank of Gwinnett. He recalled an eventful time, chronicled in 1954 in the *News-Herald.* McGee writes that four years after the present Historic Courthouse was built, around 1889, many citizens considered the courthouse fence an eyesore and, he says, were ashamed of it. However, the county commissioners would not vote to take it down.

Therefore, writes McGee, citizens, along with the City Council in Lawrenceville, organized to tear it down. L.M. Brand was mayor of Lawrenceville back then, and he tore off the first plank. After that, other councilmen stepped forward to rip off a plank, and then McGee says, "....young fellows took over."

There's another ironic twist. McGee, who was 16 years of age then, had his own role in the event. He had moved to Lawrenceville to work in the store of his mother's late uncle, whose son, J.D. Spence (McGee's own uncle), was running the store, and was also the chairman of the county commission. Spence was a commissioner for 16 years. McGee's job during the fence caper was to keep his uncle, the county commission chairman Spence, who would not vote to take down the fence, "entertained" in the office in the back of his store "while all this was going on. The next morning there was no fence." Later, Jim McGee Sr. would himself serve as both a Lawrenceville city councilman and a county commissioner.

McGee doesn't give us the reaction of his uncle to the disappearance of the courthouse fence. But he says that the commissioners then built the present stone-anchored and iron pipe fence that is still around the courthouse today.

The 1885 courthouse, on the square in Lawrenceville, would serve until 1988 when the Gwinnett Justice and Administration Center opened, and is now is dubbed the "Gwinnett Historic Courthouse." It houses offices of the Gwinnett Historical Society and the Veterans Museum; it also has meeting and banquet facilities, with banquet seating for up to 200.

The first courthouse in Gwinnett had been built in 1824, at a cost of $4,000. It served the county until 1871, when it burned. The fire in the second Gwinnett courthouse is the key reason most Gwinnett County records only go back to 1871. The current Historic Courthouse was built in 1885, and cost $23,083.

A clock tower was added in 1908 for $4,000. The giant Seth Thomas clock still bongs away the time, thanks to a 1991 restoration by members of the National Association of Watch and Clock Collectors (NAWCC). They took the clock apart, cleaned and re-engineered its moving parts, and put this mechanism on display at the Gwinnett Justice and Administrative Center for a few months. Then they put the mechanism back together, and got the clock working in good order. Part of that work included taking parts down a 20-foot ladder from the clock tower itself, with some brass wheels weighing as much as 175 pounds. Of course, once refurbished, that meant hauling those heavy parts back up that ladder, then carefully putting those precise mechanisms back together in the courthouse tower! It was quite a job. Thanks, NAWCC members!

Restoration architect Jack Pyburn says that in 1935, during the Depression, the Historic Courthouse was greatly expanded. Built out the north entrance (onto West Pike Street) was a 42x50 (plus basement) brick "courthouse annex." Monies came from the Works Progress Administration, with most of the construction work done by convict labor. The total expenditure for the annex was $10,000.

A 1908 view of the Gwinnett Courthouse, with snow on the ground. Note this was before the clock tower was added.

A mainstay in Lawrenceville for years was a hotel at the corner of Crogan and Perry Streets, on the southwestern corner and opposite the courthouse. Documents traced the hotel back to 1895. It was known as the Cornett Hotel in 1912 and later as the Ewing Hotel. It was an imposing structure of four stories, and was the overnight residence of the man "drummers" (traveling salesmen) coming through the town on trains during the turn of the century.

The story goes that at one time the hotel was operated by the mother of comedian Oliver Hardy of Laurel and Hardy fame. As a young boy, Hardy, who was born in Harlem, Ga. in 1892, is said to have played around the hotel in the streets of Lawrenceville. Who knows? He may have acquired his comic skills from growing up in Gwinnett!

The hotel was owned by A.E. Ewing, and operated by Mrs. Hubert Ewing and her sister, Miss Myra Andrews.

On the "bitterly cold" night of Sunday, Jan. 9, 1927, with snow falling intermittently, the hotel burned. It was a big fire, and threatened the town. A frantic telephone call to

Buford brought its fire engine to help fight the raging fire, with reports that the engine arrived "just in the nick of time."

This also prompted a *News-Herald* story to report: "This conflagration has again demonstrated the need of a fire engine for Lawrenceville, and our citizens are loud in their praises of the Buford department in coming promptly to our rescue…." A photograph in *Vanishing Gwinnett* shows the city with firefighting equipment of its own in 1912, though it was not the 1925 American LaFrance modern fire truck which Buford had in 1927.

Nearly six months later, on July 8, 1927, another hotel, the Button Gwinnett Hotel, was on the site, under management of Ambrose T. Green and his wife, and their daughter Eva, who eventually became Mrs. James W. Magill. The property was owned by Dr. W. P. Ezzard, who leased the hotel to Green.

However, the first hotel in the city was "on the hill" on North Clayton Street, opened by Benjamin Ivie. There is no indication of the date, though it is thought to be before the turn of the end of the 19th century.

A prominent feature opposite the southwest corner of the square in Lawrenceville was the Cornett Hotel, later known as the Ewing Hotel, and later still as the Pharr.

Lawrenceville got another cotton mill in 1900, and it continued in production until 1939. At that time, the facility was purchased by the giant General Shoe Company (known locally as "Genesco.") Several Lawrenceville businessmen, including Mayor F.Q. Simmons and banker J.H. McGee, had visited the Genesco headquarters in Nashville, Tenn. in 1939, to entice the company to locate in Lawrenceville. It also had Georgia plants in Atlanta and Carrollton.

Genesco had 33 shoe plants throughout the nation, and was engaged in several other industries. It even owned Tiffany's of New York. The firm in Lawrenceville produced shoes, which by 1958 made 967,186 pairs of "stock shoes" at the Gwinnett facility for such firms as Sears, Roebuck and J.C. Penney. This mill was adjacent to the railroad east of town (adjacent to Georgia Highway 20 and CSX Railroad today). In 1941, the firm employed 370 people. By 1958, it had grown to 516 people employees, with a payroll of $1.3 million. The Lawrenceville site was closed in 1973, when 320 people were working there at an annual payroll of $1.5 million. The closing came because of labor problems and a shortage of skilled workers. The site lay dormant for years until it was demolished in the early 1970s. Today, the area is the location of Cofer-Adams Building Materials.

Another change in Lawrenceville in 1939 was the establishment of a plant to produce matched sets of cotton work clothes under the "Red Fox" brand. Officially the Charles W. Henson Garment Manufacturing Company, the plant was located on North Clayton Street adjacent to the railroad and employed 135 people in 1943. Henson built a plant in Monroe in 1955, and moved its operation there. His brother, Arthur Henson, opened Henson Inc., a sewing plant, in Lawrenceville and employed approximately 75 people, producing among other items, ladies' blouses. However, Arthur Henson died at age 39 in 1958. The plant continued to operate under the direction of Charles Henson. An expansion in Lawrenceville in 1966 doubled the size of its facility to more than 100 employees. Eventually the plant was sold, and discontinued operations in Lawrenceville about 1970.

Meanwhile, Lawrenceville, though important as the county seat, had little growth prior to World War II. Its population reached 2,156 in 1930; went to 2,223 in 1950; and 2,932 in 1950. It wasn't until 1970 that the county seat was larger in population than Buford, and by then had 5,115 residents, compared to 4,640 in Buford.

In 2007, Lawrenceville was the largest city in Gwinnett, with an estimated population of 27,043, up from the 2000 census figure of 22,397.

Why Buford became so important

In 1872, Bonaparte Allen, a 26-year-old Civil War participant, from what would become Barrow County in 1915, recognized that with the coming of the railroad to Gwinnett, there was opportunity. So the Confederate veteran left Rome, where he had settled, for two-year-old Buford, and began operating a tannery.

His brother, Robert H. Allen, had started a manufacturing company for horse collars, saddles, bridles and other leather goods in the area in 1867, before Buford was chartered as a town. After Bona Allen began his tannery, the brothers operated different and various businesses, sometimes together, sometimes separately. They appear to have discontinued any partnerships in the late 1870s. Robert Allen died in 1909.

After the turn of the century, Bona Allen Inc. began to thrive in tremendous proportions. What happened afterward is another American success story. For the Bona Allen family became tremendously successful and wealthy, even wealthy by any standard. Word was that the Allens would shop in New York.....but that they preferred Paris!

Bona (old-time Buford residents pronounced his name as "Mister Boney") Allen branched out from his initial tannery to include many products made with leather.....buggy whips, shoes, saddles, horse collars, industrial belts, and even glue. The tannery became the largest in the country. The family also had extensive farming operations, eventually 2,400 acres, particularly producing straw for stuffing horse collars. By the 1920s, the Allens had the largest horse collar factory in the world. His family was deeply immersed in the business, with profits continuing to flow for years.

The Allen workers were a close-knit bunch, and factories had relatively little turn-over of employees. Bona Allen Inc. official history says the employees "weren't pampered, nor did they get rich. But the company would pick up a hospital tab in emergency cases and even built homes for employees, renting them at very low cost." And on payday, for years, the company paid everyone in silver dollars and small change. There were no checks, no dollar bills.

During the Depression, the Allens employed more than 2,200 people at the peak in their Buford operations in 1932. The company to all intents and purposes did not feel the Depression. An official history of the company says that the firm was "Netting larger profits and gaining more workers." And one lady told this author: "Son, we didn't even know there was a Depression, for the Allens took care of us." Buford was very much like a mill town, with leather the driving force behind this empire. The Allens continued as a force in Buford through the 1960s.

But while tanning of leather was important to their operation, and the city became known in the nation as the "Leather City," the Allen operations were far more extensive. It produced shoes, horse saddles (even for Hollywood stars), harnesses, horse collars and about anything having to do with leather.

The key and first element for the Allens was tanning hides of animals, mostly cattle. At first, the hides were purchased from local farmers, but soon more hides were needed, and the Allen buyers spread out, first to the Midwest, and eventually to Argentina, to purchase thousands of hides. Once at the factory, the hides were soaked in a lime solution to loosen the hair. Then the hides were put in a huge, ground floor "tanning yard" where the hides were soaked in a bark liquor for at least 40 days….and some hides for up to a year. The leather-making process was a slow one, taking up to two dozen processes in converting the stiff hide into top grade, flexible leather. Thousands of dollars were tied up in the slow process.

Eventually the factory transferred the newly-smooth leather to other parts of the operation, for making harnesses, or saddles, bridles, halters and other implements used in the days of the horse and buggy. The company took particular pride in the saddles, producing 30-35,000 saddles in some years for sale worldwide. It was in the saddle-making area that skillful craftsmen could show their pride, even producing ornate and elegant saddles, each unique, for movie stars' horses. These were called "fully hand-carved" saddles, requiring hours and hours of intricate design and work. The Allens reported that an average saddle required 128 different manufacturing steps.

Meanwhile, other Allen operations turned leather into handbags, suitcases, even footballs, and a key element of the production line, shoes. By-products were important: the hairs from hides were sold for stuffing in upholstered furniture. Scraps and scrapings from the hide were made into glue, the only such factory in the South. Horse collars were stuffed with straw, with the Allen farm producing hay for the straw stuffing. In modern parlance, you could say that the entire Buford activities of the Allens was "vertically integrated."

In addition to the tannery, the shoe factory was located on West Main Street; the harness factory and saddle shop were on East Main Street, while the collar factory was behind the shoe factory on Elliott Street.

In 1925, Bona Allen Sr. died, leaving the empire in the hands of three of his sons, Bona Jr., Victor and John. They continued to operate profitably until 1941, when some of their workers encouraged a national union. Eventually, the CIO (Congress of Industrial Organizations) sent organizers to the shoe factory in Buford, and picketed.

The Allens had said that if the workers organized, they would close their operations. In August of 1941, the workers voted to unionize with the AFL-CIO Meat Cutters Union, Local 442, and a strike was called. In October, the Allens, true to their word, closed the shoe factory and the chrome-tanning area, which supplied the shoe leather. Two years later, in 1943, they closed the horse collar factory, and Allen employees in Buford dropped to 500. Operations ramped up during World War II, when the U.S. Army took over the

The original Bona Allen home in Buford
(from Bill Baughman/Gwinnett Historical Society)

former shoe factory to refurbish shoes, as 795 workers turned out 6,000 pair per day. The shoe plant closed after the war, though the tannery was still in production. The saddle and harness shop stayed open until 1972.

As a result of the Allens employing so many people in their operation, and being such a force in Buford, other industry shied away from Buford, since the labor market was tied up with Allen employees. However, in 1947, after the heyday of the Allens, Chicopee Industries, a subsidiary of Johnson and Johnson, took over the former shoe and horse collar plant on West Main Street. They were the first major industry to move into Buford since the Allens began operation.

Chicopee located its Lumite Division in Buford, and produced plastic screen. At the time, it was said to be the world's largest manufacturer of plastic screen. It expanded its presence with a new building. By 1963, the Chicopee plant was producing approximately 75 percent of the nation's fiberglass screening, Hansel Morgan reports. Chicopee continued to operate until 1976, when it closed the Buford plant. The building sat vacant until Barrington Industries made aluminum windows in the plant before closing in the early 1990s. The 13-acre site was bought by Don Arsenault and, in 2001, it was refurbished. It eventually became the home of the Tannery Row Artist Colony, providing studio space for about 13 artists in the restored building in 2007.

After John, the last of the three original Allen brothers, died in 1967, what was left of the vast family business, the tannery, harness and saddle factories, was sold in 1968 to the Tandy Corporation of Fort Worth, Tex. In 1981, the only operation still in Buford, the Tandy-run tannery, now down to 160 workers, closed after a fire on December 19.

What the Allens had built in Buford was no more.

Later on, the Allen family advertised their land for sale. Mobil Land Development officials saw an advertisement in *The Wall Street Journal*, and bought the property in 1978. The 1,820 acres of the Allen holdings were sold for $3.1 million.

The era of the Allens in Gwinnett was over.

That same property that the Allens once owned was developed by Mobil for several years, and later resold for $8 million. Eventually this firm sold to a third company which continued to develop it. All told, it's estimated that more than $40-50 million for land alone eventually came out of the $3.1 million that Mobil first paid for the property.

Buford still distinctive

Buford, meanwhile, as a result of the Allen touch, had for years been the largest city in Gwinnett, a distinction it held up until 1970. By then, development of other parts of Gwinnett outpaced the slower pace in the far northern part of Gwinnett, where Buford is located.

But Buford in its early days was far different from the way it is today in one key way: most of the town was located west of the railroad tracks, whereas today what is thought of as "downtown Buford" is located east of the railroad. Besides the downtown area, the first three schools were on the west side of the railroad, churches were there, the Masonic Lodge and the finer homes were there, while the east side of the railroad was virtual undeveloped land. It took some of the early Allen mansions locating east of the railroad tracks before significant growth came east of what was then Buford.

Something else took place early on: Buford became recognized as the key to politics in Gwinnett County. Lawrenceville may have been the county seat, but the political life of Gwinnett emanated from Buford. One Superior Court judge told the author that earlier, before he first ran for political office, "I went to Buford, took off my hat, and asked if they thought it was a good idea for me to run for judge."

They did. He won.

And he wasn't the only candidate getting thumbs up from the "Buford Crowd" to run for office. In effect, Buford controlled politics in Gwinnett for nearly a century.

One way to understand that control came in 1901. Bona Allen had a problem. Before then, if one of their employees happened to be incarcerated, they would be lodged at Gwinnett's only large jail, in the county seat of Lawrenceville. To bail an employee out of jail and get him back to work, someone from the Allen operation usually would have to make the trek to Lawrenceville. Such a trip in those days would either have to be made by horse or wagon down dirt and sometimes muddy, red clay Georgia roads from Buford to Lawrenceville. Or they could take a train to Suwanee, change trains to Lawrenceville....and return. Either venture would take most or all of a day.

"Can't you do something about it?" was the question from Allen forces to Gwinnett representatives in the Legislature.

Their solution was the creation of the "City Court of Buford," with jurisdiction limited to the Sugar Hill Militia District, where Buford is located. And with a court, you get a sheriff, solicitor, judge....and jail. So when the Allen worker was arrested in an altercation in Buford, the next morning an Allen employee could walk down the street to the jail, bail the person out, and have the guy back on the job before 9 a.m. This new court was created in the 1901 Legislature to commence January 1, 1902.

Don't think that such tactics applied only to Allen employees. All activity in the Sugar Hill Militia District worked on a fee system. Eventually, what happened throughout the county, no doubt with Allen involvement, was that if a person was arrested in other parts of Gwinnett, a canny policeman might ask: "Would you prefer to be tried in Lawrenceville (a county court), or in Buford (the militia district court)?"

A smart offender would pick Buford, benefiting both the offender and the Buford court system, which was on a fee system. And in the process, Buford became more entrenched in political power. Among other aspects, people in Buford always seem to vote in a bloc.

The powers of the Sugar Hill Militia District court and sheriff continued until December 31, 1970. By then, the political power had somewhat shifted as the population grew faster in the southern part of the county, and soon outnumbered the bloc controlled by Buford. That caused a young legislator from the southern part of the county, Jimmy Mason, to introduce legislation to eliminate the City Court of Buford for the Sugar Hill Militia District. Norris Nash, who was also a Gwinnett representative then, told Gov. Lester Maddox that the Sugar Hill sheriff set-up was "bleeding the little people," which convinced Maddox to sign the legislation. For the first time since 1901, Gwinnett reverted back to having only one sheriff and court system. The Buford fee system was gone forever, and the political power of Buford was no longer as dominant, though still powerful.

The Allens and baseball

Members of the Allen family loved baseball. In the early 1900s, many industrial companies across America had company baseball teams, often amateur, though sometimes semi-professional, operations. The Allens hired outstanding baseball players to work during winters in one of their plants, but in the summertime, they were full-time players. The Allens liked to win, hiring up-and-coming baseball players, or ex-major leaguers, to stock their team. (The Buford Shoemakers rivalry with the Norcross semi-pro team would ensure that most of the visitor's town would drive to the other town to cheer on their team.)

The Shoemakers were good. It's said that the Allens would offer a pair of shoes to any pitcher who beat them, and that the Allens did not give away many pairs of shoes. (Their record in 1933, for instance, was 56-5.) The Shoemakers were runners-up in 1936 and 1937 in the National Semi-Pro tournament in Wichita, Kan., then came back to win the national championship in 1938 with a 96-16 record. The Shoemakers fielded their last baseball team in 1941, as the semi-pro leagues were victim to World War II.

Buford also had the distinction of being one of the first towns in the South, and perhaps the smallest town, to have its own lighted ball park. The park was lighted on June 8, 1937, with 2,500 people overflowing the grandstands and bleachers to be at the first night game. Victor Allen flipped the ceremonial switch to beam light onto the field for this first night game north of Atlanta. Games continued at the field at night until the team was dissolved as World War II came. Even today (2008) you can see the tall steel girders with the rusted lights of the field on the west side of the railroad going north on Sawnee Avenue, but now the field is grown up in weeds, no longer the center of baseball action.

Naming the team the "Shoemakers" was good for business and a unique way to promote the Allens' business. At one time, the Allens outfitted an automobile, re-designed to resemble a man's shoe. This Big Shoe promotional automobile would cruise around Southern towns, often where the team was playing, and finally park near the store selling Allen shoes, with a sign proclaiming that the Shoemakers would play the local team at a certain time. People flocked to games.

The original Big Shoe was made by Lloyd Moore, who was a virtual do-everything handyman for Bona Allen. He took a shoe pattern, and used sheet metal to produce an exact replica of a shoe the Allens produced. It was dubbed "the largest shoe in the world on wheels," and was a size "300, width EEEEEEEEEEEE," measuring 15 feet 4 inches long. The Big Shoe was mounted on a 1932 Chevrolet Coupe chassis, and was a black oxford.

Later, the Shoe was mounted on the chassis of a 1936 Chevrolet pick-up, this time as a two-toned black and white Big Shoe, resembling the Allen's "Victor V" shoe. In 1939, Woodrow Tucker got a job driving the Big Shoe, traveling as far north as West Virginia, to Miami in the south, and across much of Georgia, Alabama and Mississippi. He got the job through Alton, his brother, who was later a probate judge in Gwinnett. (Alton Tucker was the in-house salesman for Bona Allen, and managed their warehouse. In 1948, he would run for probate judge, and lose the election. But four years later, the incumbent did not run, and Tucker ran unopposed He remained in the post over 30 years. Tucker was not a lawyer when he won the election, but attended Woodrow Wilson Law School at night to get his law degree.)

Woodrow Tucker recalls driving the Big Shoe in 1938-39 and making $12.50 a week, plus $50 a week for expenses on the road. "I would go into the town, and get permission to use the car's loudspeaker, play music on the car-mounted Victrola record player, and make a big hullabaoo about Bona Allen shoes. I would draw a crowd, and tell people you could buy these shoes, the finest in the world, for $2.98 for men's work shoes, or $5 for dress shoes. Bona Allen didn't go in much for ladies shoes, though they did sell them for $1.98. As a result of this promotion, lots of people would go inside the store and buy those shoes." Tucker was the Big Shoe's last driver. After 1939, the Allens discontinued using the Big Shoe for promotion.

After World War II, Woodrow Tucker became a lawyer himself, was president of the Atlanta Bar Association, and eventually was appointed to the State Court of Fulton County by Gov. Lester Maddox. He served for 20 years. He remembers: "Every Thursday, Attorney Glyndon Pruitt and I used to eat chicken at Maddox's Pickrick Restaurant. Glyndon said I was the only one who got anything out of it when Maddox appointed me to the state court."

National celebrity

Baseball and Buford got national attention in 1955, as a result of a television program, "The $64,000 Question." That was when Myrt Power of Buford was a contestant on the program, coming onto the show as a baseball fan. She had watched the Buford Shoemakers

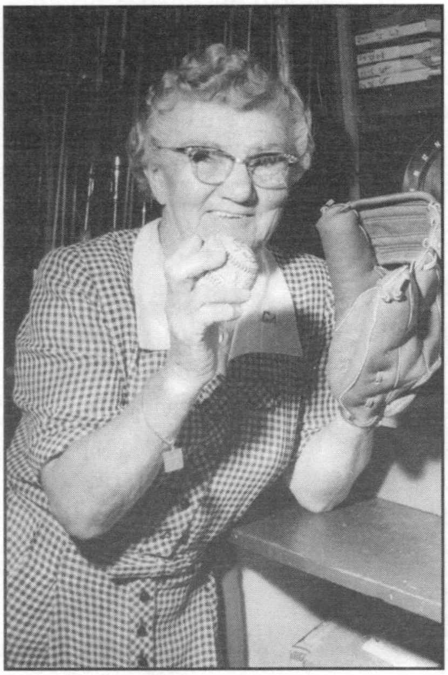

Myrt Power

over the years, and retained a lot of major league baseball lore. Her favorite team was the Brooklyn Dodgers.

She appeared on the TV program at the age of 72, and astonished viewers with her recall about baseball. She answered 10 straight questions over five weeks about baseball from the show's host, Hal March, before retiring by winning $32,000. The final question put to her was: "The official record books list seven players who are credited with over 3,000 hits in their major league careers. Ty Cobb heads the list with 4,191 hits garnered in his 24 years of play. Name the remaining six players who have a lifetime total of 3,000 plus hits."

Mrs. Power didn't miss a lick. She replied: "The 3,000 Club was small in 1955: Anson, Wagner, Cobb, Lajoie, Speaker, Collins and Paul Waner."

When she returned from New York, a hero's welcome awaited her in Buford, complete with a parade and presentation of the key to the city, with October 12, 1955 being proclaimed "Myrt Power Day" in Buford. She remained a celebrity the rest of her life. She was hired by the International News Service to cover the 1956 World Series. At the Democratic National Cnvention in Chicago in 1956, she carried the Georgia banner into the convention hall at the opening session. Mrs. Power died November 8, 1968 in Buford at age 84.

* * * * *

Today what also remains in Buford are several of the stately Allen mansions, now mostly private businesses, and one former warehouse converted to another use, lining Main Street in Buford. The Allen era has passed. In its heyday, the Allens in Buford were something else!

However, though Buford is no longer the largest city in Gwinnett (it was the largest until 1970), today Buford thrives, and has the largest budget of any city in Gwinnett, totaling $101 million in 2007. It retains its flavor as Gwinnett's most distinctive city, operating its own school system, maintaining a slow-but-steady population growth, keeping taxes low, and seeing a rush of industrial development within the city.

Part of the reason for its success is the laid-back style which its city government engenders. Led by Philip Beard, who has been on the city council continuously since 1975 (including 20 years as chairman in 2008), Buford residents take pride in their community, and also takes steps to ensure its continued success. In the early 2000s, Buford determined that future commercial buildings within its city should be of brick construction, ensuring a high quality presentation of its firms. That's a tie-in with the name that Mobil Land Development Company gave its development in Buford, "Brickton." Beard notes: "We've pretty much adopted brick construction, with strict landscaping and signage for new construction."

Beard remembers what Buford was like when he was growing up: "Back then, it was just a 10 block area along the railroad. But today, new Buford is all along Georgia Highways 13, 20 and 347, and Friendship Road. Our former uptown commercial district has been renovated. Culture and the arts have upgraded and dignified the area. We have nice large old homes which indicates what went on in the past. We keep them up and they look good. We've also improved our appearance with streetscaping, and will do more in the future."

Philip Beard

For his leadership within his city, the Georgia Municipal Association in 2007 surprised Beard by naming him to its Hall of Fame. He is the only Gwinnett resident in the GMA Hall of Fame who has not been a GMA president. (The other Gwinnettian in the GMA Hall of Fame is former GMA president Lillian Webb, who was the long-time mayor of Norcross and former county commission chair.)

As a result of its development efforts, 76 percent of the Buford tax digest is in industrial and commercial areas, with residences only making up 24 percent of its digest. This industrial expansion is done with little rancor and recriminations. As Beard puts it, "We zoned our property years ago, and haven't changed it. You don't see many fights over zoning in the Buford city limits."

Another major factor in the Buford overall impact is its enterprise funds. Buford has its own water, gas and electrical distribution systems. It distributes gas to areas of five counties: Gwinnett, Hall, Jackson, Barrow and Walton. Altogether, at the start of 2008, the city had 30,286 gas customers, another 3,198 electrical customers and 3,104 water customers.

How Gwinnett towns got their names

Here are the origins of the names of Gwinnett cities.

Auburn was named in 1892 for the red clay which abounds in the area. The late Russell Bradley related that, as a boy, he lived several miles from Auburn. There was a certain embankment whose red clay was used in dyeing cloth red. One cold winter morning his mother gave him a sack, told him to saddle the mule and go to Auburn to fill the sack with some of this clay so she could dye some cloth she had woven. He was just a youngster and was not at all keen about making such a cold trip. As he rode along he looked at the bank of red clay on each side of the road, which appeared to him to be just like what he had seen in

Auburn. He decided to shorten his trip and get the clay from the roadside instead of going into town. All went well until his mother tried to use the clay for dyeing-the color would not hold! So that red clay bank in Auburn had some special quality which other clay deposits did not have, according to *A History of Barrow County, Georgia*, published in 1983. Only a small portion of Auburn is located in Gwinnett.

Berkeley Lake began as a summer retreat for Atlanta citizens. In 1953, a Civic Association was formed, which led to incorporation in March, 1956 by the Legislature. The lake's name comes from Berkeley Blue Granite Quarries in Elberton, which the original property developer, Frank Coggins, owned. In 1952, Calvin and Kate Parsons, along with John and Dorothy Bagwell, purchased the Berkeley Realty and Investment Company and its 700-acre property. Today most of the city's land is developed, with residents buying 63 undeveloped acres of commercial timber for buffer and greenspace in 1996.

Braselton: The first Braselton person in this area was John O. Braselton, who came in 1884. The area prospered, but it wasn't until 1916 that the town obtained a charter from the state. It had the distinction of every member of the council being named Braselton when founded, for which it got mention in the *Guinness Book of Records*. The town functioned as a mercantile center around Braselton Bros. Store, which was far more, being not only a grocery and dry goods store, but also a bank, cotton shipper, feed and seed outlet and social center for the area. Today Braselton is fast growing, with its land area reaching into four counties: Gwinnett, Hall, Barrow and Jackson.

Buford is named for Algernon Sidney Buford, the president of the first railroad to come through Gwinnett, the Atlanta and Richmond Air-Line Railroad. The town was founded August 24, 1872. An attorney, Buford was a graduate of the University of Virginia, and served as a member of the state legislature. He lived in Richmond, though maintained an office in Atlanta when the rail line was being constructed in Georgia.

Dacula dates from August 7, 1905. It came into existence as a railroad stop about 1892, earlier called "Hoke." The name comes from scrambling letters from Atlanta and Decatur, determined by an early postmaster.

Duluth's name origin is interesting. It was earlier known as Howell's Landing for a crossing of the Chattahoochee River. When the railroad came in 1871, there was considerable discussion in Congress about extending a railroad to a newly-formed town in Minnesota, which was named Duluth. So Duluth adopted that name, and was chartered on February 28, 1876.

Grayson had a tough time getting named. The Rev. James Patterson McConnell secured a post office for the area in 1881, under the name of "Trip." This was the year the L&L Railroad came to the area. In 1901, the town was first incorporated by the Legislature as "Berkeley." However, another town had that name, so the town mayor, John E. Jacobs, suggested "Graymont." This, too, proved futile, as another Post Office already claimed the name. Meanwhile, a letter from his wife, visiting in Grayson County, Tex., gave him an idea. Finally, on December 17, 1902, the Legislature changed the name to "Grayson."

Lawrenceville, the oldest city in all of Metro Atlanta, dates from 1821, its charter being signed on December 15. It is named for the Naval captain of the War of 1812, who perished in a battle on the USS Chesapeake off Boston, and while dying, uttered the words "Don't give up the ship, lads! Fight her as long as she swims." One of the early settlers of

Gwinnett, William Maltbie, heard of this, and thought it would be fitting to name the town in honor of Capt. James Lawrence.

Lilburn was originally called McDaniel, which was the name of a land lottery winner who settled the area. Around 1900, the name was changed to Lilburn. It was named after Lilburn Trigg Myers who was the general superintendent for the Seaboard Air Line Railroad, which comes through the city. Its current charter dates from July 27, 1910. Its organized government ceased in 1937, one of the results of the Depression. It was reincorporated in 1955 as Gwinnett began to grow, with the purpose of bringing water lines to the area.

Loganville is named for James Harvie Logan, who moved to the area from Tennessee in 1842 and purchased 62.5 acres at a sheriff's sale for $150. Logan was a farmer and shoemaker. The city was incorporated for one-half mile from the center of town on Sept. 20, 1887.

Norcross gets its name from the second mayor of Atlanta. The town was founded by Atlanta businessman John Thrasher, who named it for his friend, Atlanta storekeeper Jonathan Norcross. It was the second town chartered in Gwinnett, on October 26, 1870. Thrasher Park, hard by the railroad, is named for the founding father.

Jonathan Norcross,
for whom the town is named

Rest Haven became incorporated on February 16, 1938, as a way to make more secure a place previously known for its bawdiness. It is located on the Gwinnett-Hall line above Buford, with its 320-acre corporate limits surrounded by Buford. The town sought to give up its charter in 2001, but was prohibited from this by a lawsuit. However, by 2008, about 100 acres of the town had been annexed by Buford, with the concurance of the county commission. The town voted to become part of Buford in 2008, but a court order has limited the acreage annexed into Buford. In the meantime, per capita funds Rest Haven gets from the SPLOST tax, are being paid to Buford to contract for road improvements in Rest Haven.

Snellville was an early settlement in the 1880s in Gwinnett, when it got a postal address. It dates its incorporation as a city to August 20, 1923. Two Englishmen, James Sawyer and Thomas Snell, opened a general mercantile location in its first days. The story goes that they agreed to seek the post office under the name of "New London," but on the day the postal inspector came to visit, Mr. Sawyer was away. Hence the name, "Snellville."

Sugar Hill: The "unofficial story" of its name comes from the city's web site: "Many years ago Buford was a railhead from which several freight wagons traveled regularly to Cumming, which even today has no rail lines. The story is that on one of the freight trips, a heavily loaded wagon lost a wheel on a high hill and spilled a part of its load, including several large bags of sugar. The wheel was repaired and the wagon reloaded - except for the sugar, which had broken open and spilled on the hill. The area became known as "The hill where the sugar spilled." It was shortened to "The Sugar Hill" and then just to "Sugar Hill." Sugar Hill existed as a Georgia Militia District for many years before it was chartered as a city on March 24, 1939."

Suwanee took the name of an old Indian community, which was centered there. The City's name is thought to derive from the English mispronunciation of Shawnee, a tribe of Algonquin Indians, who first settled along the banks of the Chattahoochee River. Shawnee is an Algonquin word for "Southerner" and was used because the Shawnee lived the furthest south of all the Algonquin tribes. The city was incorporated on February 25, 1949, though its post office was established in 1837. The city gained additional recognition as a rail stop with the arrival of the railroad in 1871.

3
1900-1950

Why Half a Bridge at Jones Bridge?

Even today, one of the most idyllic places in Gwinnett is Jones Bridge Park, located in Peachtree Corners off East Jones Bridge Road at the Chattahoochee River. It's a storied place, as rocks in the river once provided an easy crossing spot at low water for the Indians and early settlers. Today, its parkland is often full of children throwing Frisbees, of dogs enjoying the wide spaces, trout fisherman landing a prize, and people gazing at the shoals of the Chattahoochee River.

The area around Jones Bridge is some of the first land settled by white people in the area. John F. Martin is said to have purchased former Indian lands from the government on both sides of the river. He installed a ferry for ease of crossing. Upon his death, a niece inherited the land, who married a Jones, and hence the name. When the state built a bridge across the river on the Jones land, the name of Jones Bridge came into being.

Stories abounded as to why half a bridge is there.

Some say part of the bridge was washed away in floods.

Others maintain that the Yankees destroyed it. But could they burn half a bridge?

So, what's the story?

A steel-girder bridge connected this portion of Gwinnett to Fulton County, with the bridge built in 1904 by the Roanoke Steel and Bridge Company. It originally had three inch oak flooring planks. The bridge served the area for years, but required maintenance. During the Depression, with money short, neither Gwinnett nor Fulton kept up their bridges as they should. The upshot is that Jones Bridge became dangerous, as the thick planks of the flooring became worn, then rotted through. That's when both ends of the bridge were barricaded with dirt, so that vehicles could not gain the crossing. (A few brave souls continued to walk across the girders, but it was a tricky trek.)

Then, in 1945, when there were only six families living between Highway 141 (Peachtree Parkway) and the river, workmen showed up with heavy equipment one morning and began banging away on the bridge. A farmer, Otis Hamilton, lived in the closest house to the bridge, about 500 yards away. He said in a 1991 interview: "There were four or five of them tearing down the bridge. I thought they were from the county, and they worked there about two weeks before anyone said anything to them. They told us the county was going to put a concrete bridge across the river. The first thing I knew, they moved out their equipment and left the rest of the bridge."

No doubt the people of the area were pleased to see work on the bridge. As it was with the bridge barricaded, residents of the area had to drive from East Jones Bridge Road the few miles to what is now Peachtree Parkway to cross the Chattahoochee at Medlock Bridge to get to the Fulton side of the river.

Gwinnett at that time in 1945 was governed by a three member county commission. The commissioner for that part of Gwinnett was A.J. Corley, whose son, Minor Corley of Duluth, would later become a county commissioner himself. One Sunday in 1945, A.J. Corley was driving through the area, perhaps politicking, when he came to Jones Bridge, and saw the bridge dismantling that was going on.

He drove up to Mr. Hamilton's house that Sunday, knocked on the door, and inquired of him: "What are they doing to the bridge?"

Otis Hamilton told Commissioner Corley the story he had been told by the workmen: tearing down the bridge so that a concrete bridge could be built across the river. Commissioner Corley was surprised to learn this, saying:

"The commission hasn't voted for a concrete bridge."

Those workmen were stealing the bridge! Apparently they heard about the commissioner's visit, and vamoosed, never to be seen again. No one could identify them.

Later on, word is that the crew sold the steel for scrap in Charleston, S.C. But their identity was never determined, nor were there any charges made against them.

Mr. Hamilton philosophized: "What was gone was gone." And that's why you see half a bridge today at Jones Bridge Park.

Gwinnett's tie to early country music

Skillet Lickers

Ever think of Gwinnett in connection to hillbilly (today's country) music history? There is more to this line of thought than you might think.

It all started with fiddle players in Dacula. It was around the 1920s that Fiddling John Carson came to Dacula, probably part of the entertainment for a political candidate. (Carson later was a mainstay of the Gene Talmadge political rallies in the 1930s.) Carson had, in 1923, already made some early country music recordings.

Hearing him play the fiddle was James Gideon (Gid) Tanner, who was raised near Monroe and moved to Dacula around 1922. Tanner, a farmer, was himself a good fiddle player. (He won a fiddler's convention in Atlanta in 1915). In the early 1920s, a person

The original Skillet Lickers from Dacula included, from left, Gid Tanner, Clayton McMichen, Riley Puckett and Fate Norris.

from Columbia Records asked Tanner to come to New York and make a recording. Tanner said he would go if Riley Puckett, a blind guitar player, could go with him. They made several single records in New York in 1924. In 1925, Tanner and Puckett added Fate Norris on banjo and Clayton McMichen, also a fiddler, and adopted the name "Skillet Lickers." In 1926, the band recorded eight songs in Atlanta for Columbia Records and released them that same year, to an immediate receptive audience. One source calls the band the "most popular in the country" from 1926 to 1931. (Atlanta was a center in the South for recordings at that time.)

A big break came when WSB Radio in Atlanta put Tanner and his group on the air. The Skillet Lickers became favorites of the radio audience, and were soon performing in many towns of the area. The band was also on WCKY in Covington, Ky. in the 1930s, but afterward some members began to part ways. Others took the places of those who left, but the band soon stopped touring.

During the next eight years, the band, in various combination of artists, recorded more than 100 songs under the Skillet Lickers name. Among those joining the band in 1930-31 was Gordon Tanner, Gid's son, who took McMichen's place. Titles of some of the records were *Bully on the Town, Pass Around the Bottle and We'll All Take a Drink, Watermelon Hanging on the Vine,* and *Soldier's Joy*. The biggest selling record of the band was recorded at its last session in 1934, *Down Yonder*, with Gordon Tanner on lead fiddle. Some of the Skillet Lickers' releases were comedy records, alternating music with comic dialogue, such as *A Corn Licker Still in Georgia*. It was said that they were the premier band of their day. Figures talk: In 1934 in San Antonio, Texas, the band recorded *Down Yonder*, which sold more than a million records during the Depression. The Skillet Lickers preceded the Carter Family with their original recordings.

All through the 1930s, 40s, and 50s, the band continued to stay together, though with different members at times. Among its activities were bookings at school fundraisers. The band, under Gordon Tanner, had a regular program on an Athens radio station in the 1950s.

After Gid Tanner died in 1960, Gordon Tanner found interest in the group from his son, Phil Tanner, who joined as a fiddler. Gordon died in 1982, but Phil kept the group together. In 2008, the band was still playing regularly, appearing each Wednesday night at the Harvest Table in Dacula. They still get booking engagements, often at colleges in the

Members of the modern Skillet Lickers continuing the tradition of fiddling and country music in 2008 included, left, Joel Aderhold, Phil Tanner, Larry Holcombe, Russ Tanner, Brian Morgan and Fleet Stanley.

area. In 2008, the band had a group of members who would rotate in and out on different nights. Besides Phil Tanner, it was composed of another Tanner, Phil's son Russ, on lead fiddle; Fleet Stanley of Helen on resounding guitar; Doug Landress or Larry Holcomb, both of Lawrenceville, on bass; Julian McDaniel of Bethlehem, harmonica and mandolin; Brian Morgan of Winder, on mandolin; while banjo playing rotated between Art Rosenbaum of Athens or Joel Aderhold of Loganville.

Inducted into the Georgia Music Hall of Fame in Macon have been Riley Puckett (1986), and the original---Gid Tanner and the Skillet Lickers (1988).

Roba Stanley

Another early country singer to come out of Dacula was Roba Stanley, who had a short two-year recording career beginning in 1924, when she was "officially" 16, but may have been only 14 years old at the time (Some say she was born in 1908, while others say it was 1910). She found immediate success and was the first female country musician to record a song and be on the radio, appearing on WSB. She has been described as the first "sweetheart of country."

Her father, Robert Morland Stanley, was another accomplished fiddler out of Dacula, and had won several of the Georgia Old-Time Fiddlers conventions. As a child, Roba would play guitar on stage with her father and others, sometimes including the family's Dacula neighbor, Gid Tanner.

Roba's short career came to a halt when she married Frank Baldwin of Miami, Fla. in 1926. She then moved with him to Miami, and gave up music. She died in Gainesville,

Roba Stanley

Fla. in 1986. Interestingly, her entirely-original songs projected a strongly feminist point of view for those days. One reviewer called her songs a "spirited celebration of feminine independence."

Mrs. Baldwin was inducted into the Atlanta Country Music Hall of Fame in 1983. She was also honored at the Grand Ole Opry in Nashville, Tenn. An account of this ceremony said that she was so timid and shy that she received the accolades from her auditorium seat. It also said that her children did not know she had been a country musician.

Roba Stanley made only nine recordings, all done in Atlanta at different times for Okeh Records. She cut her first record a good three years before the famous Carter Family began its recordings. The guitar on which Roba Stanley learned to play is on display at the Female Seminary in Lawrenceville.

Gwinnett's first hospital

With Gwinnett County's proximity to a metropolitan center of population, that may be one reason why extensive medical facilities came late to the county. Gwinnett had nearly 30,000 people before the first rudimentary hospital, really a clinic, was built. As the county continued to grow, other medical facilities were built, but it was not until 1959 that the first substantial county-funded hospital was erected.

A hospital first came to Duluth in 1944, then to Buford in 1948, eventually to the county seat of Lawrenceville in 1959 and finally to the Snellville area in 1980. A more modern hospital was built in Lawrenceville in 1984. The Duluth hospital changed its name and saw a new campus in 2006, and the Lawrenceville hospital began a major addition to its facilities in that same year, 2006, which is expected to be completed in 2009.

After Gwinnett County began its spiraling growth in the latter part of the 20th century, coinciding with the opening of the new Gwinnett Medical Center in Lawrenceville, the county hospital facilities soon became among the top in the Metro Atlanta area. Three of Gwinnett cities now have modern hospitals, while Buford's medical facility has been closed since 1993.

First medical facility

It took the lives of two children hundreds of miles and 20 years apart to awaken the need in Gwinnett County for improved and modern medical facilities. The families of the two youths, who in dying proved instrumental for Gwinentt's first hospital, had no indication that the deaths of their children would become so important in the life of the county.

It was Christmas Eve in 1940 when Henry Burnett knocked on the door of his employer, Richard Hull at Irvindale Farms, a 409-acre dairy on the Chattahoochee River in Duluth. He told Hull about his six-year-old son, Olin. The boy had been feeling "puny" for several days and that day took a turn for the worse, and died of kidney failure.

Olin was one of 13 children born to Alice and Henry Burnett. Henry was a tractor mechanic at Irvindale Dairy, and also milked cows before mechanical milkers came along. The Burnetts lived by the calaboose (old jail) in Duluth, right off the railroad tracks. Young Olin had his sixth birthday in August, and was in the first grade when he became sick.

Mr. Hull was horrified by the thought that there were no medical facilities in Gwinnett County that could provide for the sick of the community, such as Olin. He called a town meeting in Duluth at the schoolhouse. At the meeting, he asked those present: "Why can't we have a clinic someplace in Duluth?" He added: "We need a clinic here, a place where people can take sick children even if they have no money."

These were hard times as the nation was coming off the Depression, and war was being threatened. Duluth area residents pledged their money, and $80 was collected, along with pledges for $450 more. In a story in *The Atlanta Journal*, Rosalyn Bradshaw reported that "Duluth residents will tell you that every person, from the poorest widow to the most well-to-do, contributed to that fund."

It took until 1941 before a clinic was located in an old frame house on the corner of the Duluth school property. It wasn't much: one room was an operating room, delivery room and clinic. There was a kitchen, and two patient rooms, one for whites in those segregated days, and one for negroes. They may have been segregated by rooms, but the medical treatment was equal.

A nurse was on call 24 hours a day. Physicians were available for certain days, and for emergencies. One of the first regular doctors for the hospital was Dr. Sylvester (Jack) Cain of Norcross. Later he would marry the first head nurse, Jeannie Pyron.

Local residents chipped in, volunteering to help around the clinic, with the cooking, washing and ironing, cleaning the floors, and keeping the yard neat and in flowers. Members of that early hospital committee included Mrs. Calvin (Kate) Parsons, Mrs. Guy (Clare) Findley Sr., Carl Johnson, J. Heard Summerour, Frank Mattison, Mrs. Mack (Martha) Pittard, Richard Hull and H.G. Herron.

Richard Hull's wife, Nora, was among those who were excited about the possibility of Duluth getting its own clinic. She wrote her parents in Detroit, Mich., where her father, Gen. A.R. Glancy, had been a vice president of General Motors' Pontiac Division and was retired. With the coming of World War II, Glancy was named a brigadier general, and put in charge of designing, procuring and maintaining military tanks, combat cars and automotive equipment. For his efforts, the government awarded him the Legion of Merit.

Glancy and his wife, Lenora, were touched when reading of the Burnett boy's death, and how the community wanted to have a clinic of its own. No doubt he and his wife thought back to Jan. 9, 1924, when the death of their four-year-old daughter, Joan, hit them hard. He wrote back to his daughter in Duluth:

"We are sending $500 now to help get things started, and every year we'll send $250 more on the birthday of your little sister, Joan, who died of pneumonia 17 years ago, because the drugs which might have saved her were not known. We make this gift in memory of her," he wrote.

Meanwhile, the contribution of General Glancy and his wife was deeply appreciated by the community, which was buoyed by their generosity. In appreciation, the clinic was named in memory of Joan Glancy. One of those working toward the clinic, Duluth Postmaster Heard Summerour, wrote a dedication in Joan Glancy's memory: "To Joan, who in swift transition achieved eternal spring, this hospital is dedicated, in the hope that through it the lives of other children may be enriched."

The people of Duluth invited the Glancys to visit, and see the facility. But in those war-torn years, a visit was not immediately possible. However, once able to visit Duluth, when seeing the clinic, General Glancy was impressed with the efforts of volunteers and local citizens, but also realized that the small clinic was not sufficient for the 30,000 residents of Gwinnett. So he, the industrialist, tackled the problem, and came up with a plan. He suggested that if the people of Duluth bought land and provided it with its own well water, he promised to build "the finest hospital in the country," not large, but complete with the most modern equipment. That promise was a major step-up from what Duluth had in its small clinic, and people of Duluth were surprised, pleased and impressed.

So Duluth got the first hospital in Gwinnett. It opened in July 9, 1944. More than 500 people were at its dedication that summer. The hospital was far larger, now consisting of 20 rooms, plus administrative, examination, emergency and operating facilities. Those in attendance heard the Rev. A.A. Phillips dedicate it "to Almighty God, to the memory of Joan Glancy, and to those who suffer that they might have health again."

Eventually, General Glancy realized that having a facility was not enough. Monthly bills for operating the hospital amounted to $4,000 or more, and there was not sufficient income. Now the Detroit industrialist came up with another plan.

He would build a small factory to manufacture products, and the profits would go to support the hospital. But what to build? The factory was initially known as the GKW, "Goodness Knows What" factory. It was through Glancy that the GKW plant got contracts for the products it would make. Through the years, the plant made buffing wheels and automobile seat covers. The buffing wheels were sold to several industrial customers, while the General Motors Olds-Pontiac plants were the customers of the seat covers.

The industrial buffing wheels were used for polishing or abrasive purposes to shine metal materials, says Alan Pittard, himself associated with the GKW factory for several years. "The base unit was a fabric made out of layers of rags, which you would continue to add up to 6-8 inches thick. These rags were cut into rough circles, and put on an automatic spindle on a sewing machine and end up with a fabric about 3/4 inches thick. Later on, rolls of fabric would be used instead of rags." The plant employed between 100-150 people at different times, primarily black women. Pittard's brother, Mack, ran the plant making buffing wheels.

There would be additional benefits: the plant would provide a payroll for the community, with good wages and steady employment. The area economy would be bolstered, as the factory eventually employed more than 150 workers. In addition, other plants were attracted to Duluth, providing more employment. Among them was at one time a lingerie factory, and another making jackets and rain coats.

On April 1, 1950, the story of Duluth gaining its hospital was known nationally, as Georgia journalist Harold Martin wrote an article for the *Saturday Evening Post*. A few years later, the DuPont Company put the story on their national radio show. Then on October 9, 1956, the new medium of the day, television, also featured Duluth and how the community got its hospital in the fifth season of the DuPont Calvalcade of America series.

After the television show, General Glancy wrote that "out of a clear sky (we never solicit) came from the Ford Foundation $10,000." That perhaps explained a plaque on the door of the X-Ray Department at the hospital: "In memory of Henry Ford."

An account of the hospital story in the *News-Herald* on March 22, 1956 noted that Glancy had invested (in 1940 dollars) a "half million dollars ….in the little hospital and the industries to support the 'experiment in humanity' in Duluth." He died in Atlanta on August 4, 1959.

The Joan Glancy Hospital was a private facility run by a local board of trustees until 1965, when that board was dissolved. In cooperation with the City of Duluth, the governance of the hospital was transferred to the Gwinnett County Hospital Authority. As part of the negotiations between the two authorities, a resolution of October 20, 1965 found that "the name of the hospital at Duluth would remain Joan Glancy Memorial Hospital," and it would remain a general hospital. In addition, as part of the agreement, the Gwinnett Hospital Authority would enlarge the hospital from 23 to 50 beds, but an action in December, 1965 officially changed the enlargement to 48 beds.

Joan Glancy Hospital was expanded to 99 beds in 1972, and had a five-bed addition in 1981, to 104 beds. But in 1985, when Gwinnett Medical Center opened in Lawrenceville, Glancy's capacity was reduced to 90 beds. In 1989, Glancy Rehabilitation Center opened, consisting of 30 beds in a new wing.

A highly-visible Glancy Outpatient Center was opened in 1995 on Pleasant Hill Road at Howell Ferry Road in a 75,000 square foot building. This would eventually be adjacent to the Gwinnett Medical Center-Duluth, when it began operations as an 81-bed, all-digital hospital in 2006. With the opening of the modern hospital, the name "Joan Glancy Hospital" was no longer in use.

First born

The first baby born in a Gwinnett medical facility was named appropriately. Born in Duluth on June 30, 1941 was Rachel Glancy Jones, daughter of Gladys and John Jones, who lived on Boles Road, not far from Duluth. She was named for two persons: the nurse (Rachel) helping deliver her, while the name, "Glancy" came from the hospital namesake, Joan Glancy. She was delivered by Dr. J.B. Chastain.

Most of her life, she has been known as "Glancy." The only time in her life when she was known as Rachel was in the first grade in Norcross, when "my teacher, Birdie Moore, insisted on calling me by my first name."

She first met General Glancy in May, 1948 by going to a birthday party the general was giving for children born at the hospital.

Glancy Dunn

The Glancys had earlier started providing education for children in Joan Glancy's name. The general writes in a remembrance he printed privately: "A financial record is always kept of the money spent on each student. Whey they finish school, a statement is sent to them, showing the total expenditure, and, with it a note saying they are not indebted to anyone for this money, but that we hope some day, due to the benefit derived from the college education, they can in turn give financial aid to someone, and when they do, they will express their indebtedness to little Jody (Joan)."

The Glancys incorporated the Lenora and Alfred Glancy Foundation in Atlanta to continue to support the hospital and other charitable commitments after their death. Then the general adds: "This is the story. Little Jody is living today."

General Glancy took an interest in the first-born of the hospital, and kept up with Glancy Jones' progress. Prior to her going to high school, General Glancy obtained permission from her parents to send the young girl to the private Westminster School in Atlanta for her high school education. The general's grandson, Gary Hull, was in her class. She was a boarding student at Westminster, and later graduated in 1963 from Rollins College in Winter Haven, Fla., with a degree in social work on a scholarship provided by General Glancy. Her first job during summers was working at the Duluth hospital. "I would ride the Greyhound from our home in Norcross to Duluth, and did about everything around there, cleaning up the emergency room or delivery room, or working with the autoclave or in the lab."

She met her future husband, Richard Dunn, after college while working at Georgia Tech. He was with the Georgia State Patrol, where he retired. The couple have lived in Snellville since 1972.

They have two children. Rick is named in memory of Richard Hull of Irvindale Farms, and got his master's degree from the University of Georgia, and for years was a professor at Dickerson College, Harrisburg, Pa. He became director of evaluation with the Georgia Department of Mental Health.

The Dunn's daughter also has a name with distinctive meaning. She is named Lenora, which was the name of General Glancy's wife. Lenora graduated also from the University of Georgia, and is an interior designer.

Glancy Dunn worked in social work for various agencies in Atlanta before accepting a job in 1980 with the new Snellville hospital when it opened. She became the director of social work, and retired after 27 years at the hospital.

On Glancy Dunn's retirement, one of her colleagues, Dr. Laurence (Lanny) Lesser, who has researched the history of Joan Glancy Hospital, said of her: "Glancy Dunn is a person who has extremely good values, is compassionate and probably has similar values as General Glancy. She was a hand-up, not hand out, social worker, always with a smile on her face and happy with patients, showing them a way to provide for themselves. She has a very strong religious faith without being evangelical about it. She shared values to capitalize on ways to bring people together. General Glancy would be very pleased in what she has done!"

Glancy Jones Dunn is a landmark figure in Gwinnett history, the first baby born back in 1941 at the Duluth Clinic.

Buford hospitals

The first major medical facility in Buford was also a clinic, a facility which was originally conceived as a maternity clinic. It was started by a father-son doctor team.

Dr. William Jackson Hutchins, who came to Buford about 1913, for years had offices on Main Street. He was a graduate of the Atlanta College of Physicians and Surgeons (later the Emory Medical School.)

Hutchins and his wife, Vivian, had four children. The oldest, William Jackson Hutchins Jr., was 16 years old and was about to enter college, when he was killed by a drunken driver when returning from a sandlot baseball game in Gainesville. When the clinic was opened, it was named Hutchins Memorial Clinic in memory of their son, who had wanted to become a doctor.

The Hutchins second son, Harry, became a doctor himself, and joined his father in the practice after World War II. Together the two organized and built the clinic in the pasture at the corner of Park and Scott Streets, behind where the doctors' offices had relocated.

The Hutchins' had two more sons, Jasper Dorsey Hutchins, who became a hospital administrator; and John Hutchins, who as of this writing remains in Buford and is an acclaimed expert on the Bible, including writing a book on how to read the Bible.

It was May of 1945 that work on a clinic began, and it officially opened Dec. 15, 1948, with a 22-bed capacity. It continued in operation until 1966, and during its years, served 19,972 patients, and had over 4,796 births recorded there.

The senior Dr. Hutchins continued practicing before his death at age 73 in 1958. His son kept the practice going, but died an early death from a heart attack at age 47 in 1969. By then the partnership had other doctors in with them. Among them were Cecil Miller and Tom Wages. This pair recruited Eugene Kennedy to come to Buford in 1970. In 1983, Kennedy began a solo practice which he kept open until 1998. His major assistant was a long-time black nurse, who had practiced with Hutchins and Miller, Katie Moore. Dr. Kennedy remembers her: "Katie was a stellar nurse, who was the backbone of my practice. People loved her, and she was invaluable to me."

Meanwhile, though the clinic served Buford well in its early years, town officials wanted to expand the medical facilities. That happened in 1965 when Buford General Hospital was begun by the Hospital Authority of Gwinnett County, under Hill-Burton guidelines. One third of the cost was split between the federal, state and local governments. Gwinnett

County contributed its share from the proceeds of a bond referendum approved in 1963 to build both the Buford and the Button Gwinnett Hospital in Lawrenceville. A 20-acre plot for the hospital was given by the Bona Allen family.

When Buford General opened, Hutchins Memorial Hospital was closed. When the hospital bond issue faced Gwinnettians in 1963, Dr. Harry Hutchins had said that the initial clinic was "inadequate" and had urged citizens to vote for the bond issue.

At its opening March 5, 1966, with Gov. Carl Sanders giving the dedicatory address, the hospital had 39 beds. In 1976, it was expanded by 20 beds, for a total of 59 beds.

Eugene Kennedy feels that his first 20 years in Buford practicing at that hospital were the "golden age of medicine. We had local people working there and we did a good job. However, when more specialization and the need for new and more modern equipment began later on, it got to the point that the hospital system could not duplicate or triplicate matters, and each hospital had to specialize. We tended to be more of a general practice hospital, but eventually, this hospital was forced to close."

Buford General Hospital closed on August 9, 1993, and its 23 by-then substance abuse beds were transferred to Summit Ridge, which had begun accepting patients on April 5, 1993. Summit Ridge occupies the facility once known as Button Gwinnett Hospital.

How Lake Lanier came about

People from all across Metro Atlanta today flock to Lake Lanier during the summer and winter. It's a premier playground, as the 38,000 acres of water are home to the "world's largest inland fleet" of play boats, power and sail, pontoon and fishing, canoes and kayaks.

Whether you want to fish for bass and other species, dive in for a swim, perform at the end of a tow rope on a pair of skis, or just enjoy the outdoors on the water, glancing up to see the start of Georgia's mountain range.....Lake Sidney Lanier tugs at people. It's both a resort and a playground, yet also home to more and more people as Metro Atlanta sprawls northward.

It's the most visited U.S. Army Corps of Engineers lake in the country, as 7.7 million people visit annually (2005).

The Lake provides for the region a continuing source of fresh water. The lake's deep—160 feet near the dam, and this helps keep the water clean, as it turns over twice a year, refreshing itself. It has a vital function for Gwinnett County: it's the source of water for the over three-quarter of a million people of Gwinnett. It is constantly replenished, as the Chattahoochee River basin gets an average of 48 inches of rainfall annually.

As an attraction, Lake Lanier is marvelous. But think of it in another way: it's a tremendous economic engine. Who would have imagined, before World War II, that one day you would have 10 marinas stretching around its 692 miles of shore? Or that more than 28,000 boats would be berthed at Lake Lanier? These many water craft must be purchased and serviced and sometimes re-sold somewhere. That's where the boat manufacturers, the repair shops, and associated gear suppliers come in.

Don't overlook those businesses along the shore which supply everything from fishing worms to overnight stays for those on or near the water. Lake Lanier's a tremendous economic engine for the region—an estimated $5.5 billion….and that's a 2001 estimate after a four year drought. In 2006 dollars, the economic impact of the lake is probably $6-7 billion…. that's billion with a 'b'….. dollars. The Gainesville/Hall County Chamber of Commerce says that the lake accounts for 30 percent of the total employment of Hall County.

The beginning of Lake Lanier

Even back before World War II, as Georgia began to grow, some people were thinking creatively about Georgia's future water needs.

One of these was an institution, the U.S. Army Corps of Engineers. Shortly after World War I, Corps officials viewed the Apalachicola-Chattahoochee-Flint River system, and considered its possibilities. No doubt they realized great possibilities could come from the Chattahoochee River -- at 436 miles long, the longest river in the state. Meanwhile, others in the growing city of Atlanta were thinking that the river could be more beneficial for that city. Since the Chattahoochee River flowed nearby, some of these futurists of yesteryear wondered about getting navigation channels all the way to Atlanta.

Such a task would be formidable, for Atlanta's elevation is one of the highest for big cities in the nation, at 1,010 feet above sea level. But that didn't faze the engineers or the big planners, who had a dream.

Eventually, the lower portions of the basin, where the Flint and Chattahoochee Rivers form the Apalachicola River, were dammed for barges. Over the course of years, the river became navigable all the way to Columbus.

Going upriver, first came the Jim Woodruff dam in 1957, forming Lake Seminole. Following that, the George Andrews and the Walter F. George Dams were formed in 1963, creating a water route up to Columbus. Then there are six small power company dams above Columbus before West Point Dam, which was finished in 1974. That would be the final Corps of Engineers flood control dam on the river.

There is one more dam on the Chattahoochee, one built much earlier. At the turn of the century, power officials dammed the Chattahoochee to generate electricity for the city of Atlanta. That was constructed at Morgan Falls near Roswell in 1904. The only other dam north of Atlanta before Lake Lanier was a power plant for Habersham Mills on the Soque River, a tributary, near Clarkesville. That dam affected the flow of the main river as far south downstream as West Point.

So, after World War II, planners were anticipating water to barge goods in a nine-foot-deep channel to Columbus. For barges to get to Atlanta, however, the channel would have to be elevated far beyond the 200 feet above sea level in Columbus, all the way to the 750 foot level at the river in Atlanta. Even engineers recognized that as difficult.

A proposal in 1930 was for a dam to be built near Roswell. But low terrain and more development in this area made this location less desirable. The Buford site, with the steeper banks and far less development, was by then an obvious choice. Just after World War II, in November, 1945, came the first Corps of Engineers' recommendation for a dam at Buford. The initial report called for much of what eventually happened, a dam creating a pool at the 1,065 foot elevation above the sea. This began a series of suggestions on justification for the dam. The obvious reasons were for flood control and downstream navigation. Others saw power generation (86,000 kw capacity for peak demand times), while some held out for navigation to Atlanta! Interestingly, there was little mention about development of recreation in the early proposals. Others recognized that the Buford site would be able to control the entire river system, with its large storage capacity.

It was about this time that significant developments began to take place on the political front. Leading the cause, and given recognition as the major advocate to build a dam at Buford, was Atlanta Mayor William B. Hartsfield. Recognizing what a dam near Buford could do for the region, he championed its cause everywhere he went, around the region, in Washington, and at any place he traveled. He had the vision to understand that although the dam was some 45 miles above Atlanta, it would have tremendous economic impact on the area. He also looked upon the creation of a reservoir as a major factor in the long-range water resources of the region.

Granted, Hartsfield had heard of the idea of making the river navigable to Atlanta. He liked the idea. Perhaps he looked upon the dam as the first step, built to regulate water, that could eventually lead to other dams and a river connecting Atlanta by barge to the Gulf of Mexico.

So Hartsfield labored on, getting more and more people on board. Among them were the leading officials of both Gwinnett and Hall counties. In 1949, Hartsfield led a delegation to Washington and included Buford figures Paul Hover, Weldon Archer, Jack Turner and Stanley Allen. Roy Otwell from Cumming was along, as was Lester Hosch of Gainesville, Jess Baggett of Lawrenceville, and John Cooper of Atlanta, who represented the Atlanta Freight Bureau. Maybe there was a glint of hope for barge traffic to Atlanta after all!

In 1947, $250,000 was allocated by Congress for planning only, not construction of a dam at Buford. This money went for core drilling samples and engineering surveys. By now, local enthusiasts and politicians were recognizing how difficult it was to get a big program such as a dam in Buford funded through the Congress.

But 1949 saw another $750,000 appropriated, for more planning.....yet some earmarked also for the start of construction. Glory be! The dam was to become a reality!

Eventually, ground was broken on March 1, 1950. What followed was a series of appropriations for portions of the work out of each successive Congress, with every allocation difficult and never entirely guaranteed. But it appeared the project was going to happen.

The actual earth dam work began in 1954, built between Gwinnett and Forsyth Counties, and extending 1,630 feet across what has been the valley of the Chattahoochee.

All told, some $45 million was spent on construction. Of that amount, 56 percent ($25 million) went to design and construction, while $19 million was for purchase of lands and relocation cost.

Land acquisition

When you tell farmers who have lived on their land for generations that you want to buy their land, and move them, they most always balk. The federal government and Corps of Engineers knew this, having years of experience with the Tennessee Valley Authority (TVA) and with water projects out west. Many questioned if the government had a right to require them to move, or take their land. Altogether, the government had to buy 56,000 acres to create Lake Lanier. It was a monumental task to get people to agree to sell their land. Many had lived on the same land their entire life. Many could not envision that a dam and lake would be worthwhile for the area, and particularly, not for them.

The purchases began in 1954, though negotiations were earlier, and rumors were rampant before the purchases. The newspaper in Gainesville warned about selling or optioning land early, which would allow speculators to gain major profits. Eventually, more than 700 families had to be relocated. They were paid an average of $50 an acre, as low as $25, and some as high as $75 per acre.

There were 1,532 individual tracts of property in the 56,000 acres that the Corps wanted. Gwinnett only counted 35 tracts, while there were 20 in Lumpkin County, 139 in Dawson, 386 pieces in Forsyth, and 952 tracts of land in Hall County. Six churches, 20 cemeteries and 15 businesses were affected.

Property owners were given the opportunity to remove structures, but only two did. Two historic buildings were saved from the waters. The Vann Tavern, built in 1805 by Cherokee Chief James Vann near the Old Federal Pike in Forsyth County, was disassembled, and moved in 1956 to the New Echota village site near Calhoun, where it was reassembled. The other structure which was saved from the Lanier waters was that of a home owned by Mr. and Mrs. R.C. Estes. The home had been built in 1825. Mrs. Estes had briefly lived on the property as a child.

Yet the land acquisition went relatively quickly. An article in the *Daily Times* of Gainesville on November 17, 1954, describing the land once the owners sold it, said that the land, previously cropland, was desolate, with the only sound on one farm the metallic banging of a piece of loose tin and the flutter of birds. Many of the buildings were sold "as is" by the government for movement to other locations. As expected, some landowners took the government to court, seeking more reward for their ownership. For sure, the government prevailed, and those living in the area had to relocate.

Groundbreaking

It was March 1, 1950, that groundbreaking for the dam took place. Fittingly, it was also the 59th birthday of the guy who had pushed so hard for the day, Mayor Hartsfield. As temporary chairman of ceremonies, he had arranged the program and sent out notices for people to come to a high bluff on the Gwinnett side, overlooking the Chattahoochee. Soon this location would be the site of the Operations Building for the project.

The day was cold, damp and windy on the hilltop above the river, with long topcoats a good idea. The dirt road was muddy from rain the night before, and a caravan of cars drove and slid, some into ditches, from Buford. An estimated 5,000 people were present.

The North Georgia College Band was there, and Mayor Hartsfield played the master of ceremonies. (In his remarks, the mayor mentioned navigation "first to Columbus, and eventually Atlanta." For him, it was a dream hard to extinguish.) The Rev. J. Thornton Williams, pastor of the First Baptist Church of Buford, gave the invocation.

Recognized were two Congressmen, Gov. Herman Talmadge, the keynote speaker, and Corps of Engineers officials. Afterward, 12 people (with almost everyone wearing a hat, as was the custom of the day) manned shovels and turned the dirt to signal the start of the project.

Following the groundbreaking, the dignitaries adjourned to a luncheon hosted by the Buford Kiwanis Club at a new school building. Mayor Hartsfield may have been surprised when he was presented with a cake marking his 59th birthday.

Thus began work on the lake.

A note about the current lake bed. As the waters began to be captured after the dam was finished in 1955, the reservoir began filling. Homes, farms, and other landmarks soon disappeared..

But there was one indication that remained visible a little longer to show that this has been fertile land. There was no effort made to harvest the trees of the lake bed, since these trees would provide a good habitat for fishing. Thus for several months, the tops of the trees, many pine, oak, sweet gum and hickory, were seen above the water line as the lake was filling. The inflow of the water was halted temporarily at 1,033 feet in 1957, so that the tops of trees could be cleared out from all around the shoreline. Trees were cut off below the water. At normal pool of 1,065, this would mean that there would be about 32-35 feet from the pool to the sawed-off tree trunks. Ever so slowly, as the rains came, these trees gradually disappeared.

However, as seen during the drought of 2007, this became more of a hazard, as the lake went down to a record low pool elevation of 1050.7, some 20 feet below the full pool level, and closer to the tops of the trees near the shore. Boaters, in particular at high speed, could hit the stumps and cause serious accidents.

Some 50 years after those trees were submerged, the trees have not tasted oxygen since. They are still under water, still a good habitat for fish. But....they are dangerous, too, for the trees preserved limbs can snag clothing and other debris. That's why when there is a report of a drowning at Lake Lanier...and you hear of divers searching for bodies....realize that the diving in itself is dangerous.

The dam intake gates were closed February 1, 1956, and the lake began to rise. It took three years for the waters to reach the normal pool level of 1,070 feet, marked on May 25, 1959. No longer was the red clay of the Georgia hills baking so brightly in the sunshine at the shoreline. Instead the azure-blue water was lapping at the shoreline as boats powered by.... and although the bass weren't jumping on the hook so fast in those early days, fisherman were dreaming of the day...

The big day: dedication

It was October 9, 1957 that Lake Lanier was dedicated. By then, the lake has swelled to 30,000 of its eventual 38,000 acres (at low elevation). The event was hosted by the Corps of Engineers and the Upper Chattahoochee Development Association, which had lobbied for the lake for years. Buford's Weldon Garner was the chair of the dedication committee. The event was held again in Gwinnett County, in the parking lot overlooking the dam. A special platform, draped in red-white-blue bunting, an estimated 30 feet wide, was constructed for key dignitaries.

Again Mayor Hartsfield was present, and was the master of ceremonies. This time, besides Gov. Marvin Griffin of Georgia, and Gov. "Big Jim" Folsom of Alabama, six Congressmen showed up, no doubt all claiming credit for some of the action. Both Georgia senators, Walter B. George and Richard Russell, were on hand.

A special presentation made all the dignitaries "commodores" of the Lake Lanier Navy, certified by Commodore Lamar Swift of the University Yacht Club. Early in the day, a "boatcade" of 50 small vessels, sponsored by Lake Lanier Power Squadron and Holiday on Lake Lanier, arrived. They beached their craft to allow their passengers to be part of the crowd.

You could look up to the sky to see part of the festivities. A fly-over by three Neptune Patrol bombers from the U.S. Naval Air Station at Atlanta entertained the crowd. A little later, the Air Force got into the act, as nine Lockheed C-130 airplanes flew in formation over the group.

Soon came the speeches by the dignitaries. The keynote was delivered by Sen. Richard Russell, who years later would have the bridge to Lake Lanier Islands named in his honor for his yeoman service in ensuring the funding for the lake.

Then it was time for the day's highlight, the christening, to officially dedicate the long-worked-for dam. With his usual flair, Mayor Hartsfield chose water from the three rivers, the Flint, Apalachicola, and Chattahoochee, in three Coca-Cola bottles, to smash against a ceremonial block.

It was a bang-up one and a half-hour ceremony. People left feeling accomplished, having done something for the region's future. But few, we suspect, would have anticipated just how powerful an impact Lake Lanier would eventually have.

Later, as the lake filled to full pool level, the waters would total 143 feet at its deepest point. The lake would back up water for some 45 miles, which was 51 percent of the entire length of the river above Buford Dam. (The Chestatee River would lose 18 miles of original shoreline along its river.)

Eric S. Garris, writing in The Heritage of the Gwinnett Historical Society in spring its edition in 2008, put it nicely. "Before the modulating effect of Buford Dam, the Chattahoochee was an inconsistent companion, low and unnavigable in dry times, and a raging flood spilling its banks in times of rain."

Naming the lake

While getting the dam authorized, funded and built were all difficult tasks, it wasn't an easy task to come up with a name for the lake backing up the river behind the dam.

The name of "Buford Dam" had come with little fanfare, as those interested simply relied on geography. The name evolved naturally. Not so naming the lake.

Some, including Jess Baggett of Lawrenceville, wanted to name the lake for William B. Hartsfield, saying he did more than anyone else to push for its funding and building. Hartsfield himself suggested Sen. Richard Russell.

Another name suggested for the lake was that of American cowboy humorist and newspaper columnist Will Rogers, whose family had lived across the river from Gwinnett in nearby Milton County before moving to Oklahoma. Another name floated for the lake was that of Georgia Tech Coach Bobby Dodd, who was tremendously popular in the state.

But it was the Atlanta chapter of the Sons of Confederate Veterans who first proposed the name of Macon native, Georgia poet, and Confederate veteran Sidney Lanier for the lake. They asked in 1954 in a letter to Senator Russell: "While Sidney Lanier has always been honored and loved throughout the South, to the best of our knowledge, this would be

Sidney Lanier

the first time that an honor, national in scope, would be given to him." They added what now seems a strong argument: "To give the name of the poet who wrote the beautiful 'Song of the Chattahoochee' to a lake formed by this river, seems to us to be a fitting memorial to Georgia's Sidney Lanier."

Later, the Georgia General Assembly asked Congress to name the reservoir after the Georgia poet. There was little opposition to the name.

Eventually, Rep. Phil Landrum in 1954 offered a resolution designating the lake created by Buford Dam to be called Lake Sidney Lanier. It took another session before the resolution got through both Houses, but on March 29, 1956, President Dwight Eisenhower signed the measure. The reservoir was now officially Lake Sidney Lanier. By then the gates had been closed only two months earlier, and the lake was beginning to rise.

What Sidney Lanier might have seen along the Gwinnett and Hall portions of the Chattahoochee River……the wild river……would be seen by human eyes no more. But his poem would live on for the stretches of the watershed in Gwinnett, upper Hall, Forsyth, Lumpkin, Habersham and White Counties….and his name would be associated with the lake for posterity. The naming of the lake for Sidney Lanier is a fitting tribute to the Georgian who penned such a beautiful, lilting poem, whose first lines read:

"Out of the hills of Habersham
Down through the valleys of Hall.
I hurry amain to reach the plain
Reach the rapid and leap the fall
Split the rock and together again
Accept my bed, or narrow or wide,
And flee from folly on every side
With a lover's pain to attain the plain
Far from the hills of Habersham
Far from the valleys of Hall."

Major changes for Lawrenceville

Two major developments have changed the face of Lawrenceville since 1950. The first was a government effort in the 1950s of two Urban Renewal projects aimed at ridding Lawrenceville of blighted areas. The second change came later, starting in 2002, was aimed at a better quality downtown business area around the Historic Courthouse, through innovations conceived by a private individual, Emory Morsberger. These two moves substantially changed the character of Lawrenceville, as both programs brought the city to a higher standard of development and benefited the tax digest with substantial increases in property values.

Those in the mid 1950s remember the areas targeted as "slums." The city clerk in those days, Rich Martin, wanted to upgrade two portions of the city. He convinced Lawrenceville city officials to apply for approval from the Housing and Home Finance Agency for an Urban Renewal program. Once gained, the city would be in a position to seek Urban Renewal Grants, whereby federal funds could be borrowed by the city to finance slum clearance, with the federal government paying two-thirds of the cost. As a requirement for the grant, the City had already established a Planning and Zoning Board and employed a planning engineer, who made a comprehensive survey of the town with a zoning map. The city would also join forces with the Lawrenceville Public Housing Authority to launch the slum clearance program.

(The city by then already had public housing which was begun in 1952. The Lawrenceville Memorial Apartments, 20 units, for white residents in those segregated times, were built off Georgia Highway 20, north of the railroad. Another 20 units, the Sally Craig Apartments, built for the African-American community, were at Neal Boulevard and Scenic Highway. T. L. Harris was chairman and John Green was director of the Authority when the work was begun. Subsequently, additional units were constructed in both areas.)

One tract the city focused on for additional public housing lay from Luckie Street along South Clayton Street back to Jackson and Green Streets, and down to Nash Street. The houses in the area were simply referred to as "slums." An account called the 33 acre area "mostly shanties and ramshackle housing," though several houses were in slightly-better shape. Two-laned Clayton Street, officially Georgia Highway 20, ran through the area. The streets in the area were mostly unpaved, and many residents only had water from outside spigots. Outhouses were common, and most residents rented their houses, though a few in the area owned their homes. The area was referred to as "Crosstown." Most residents were black, though a few white residents were in the area. This program was designated R-14, the 14th urban renewal program in Georgia.

A second area targeted for renewal was a 30-acre tract running parallel to the Seaboard Coast Line Railrod, from Georgia Highway 20 on the east to the railroad on the west side. Conditions were similar to the Crosstown area. This area became known as the Seaboard Urban Renewal area. It was the 32nd urban renewal program in the state.

In 1956, the city housing Authority program began seeking to build additional public housing units for people residing in the affected urban renewal area. Bryant Huff became director of the Housing Authority, serving until 1972 (when he became the district attorney. He later was a Superior Court judge.) Under the overall program, the city would acquire ownership of the area, pave and light the streets; provide water and sewer systems, sub-divide the lots and sell them to individuals. It would also initially build 40 units of public housing as part of the grant. Lawrenceville, on May 2, 1957, was the first city in the United States to sign a public housing contract under the Housing Act of 1956. (By 2007, the Authority had 212 public housing units under its supervision.)

Once the two Urban Renewal projects started and streets were paved, one of the first moves by the City was to propose relocating the previously small and cramped-in-one-room City Hall from Crogan Street to South Clayton Street. All offices of the city, including police and a jail, would be located in the 8,000 square foot facility. Residents were asked on April 9, 1958 whether a new City Hall should be built, funded through a $125,000 bond issue. The voting by the citizens of the city was closely divided on the measure, which eked by with a three vote margin, 285-282.

(Also on the ballot was a question on whether to build a larger "gymnatorium" (gym and auditorium) at Central Gwinnett High School for $20,000. This measure passed more easily, by 128 votes.) Bryant Huff says that drug store operator Clarence Monfort raised, he thinks, another $20,000 to match the county moneys for the facility. "Clarence could raise money like no one else. He came at you with a book of blank checks from either First National or Brand Bank, depending on where your account was. He would say, 'Sign your name right there. He had you covered."

The 30-acre Seaboard Urban Renewal project included much of the area around the railroad depot. Of the 51 buildings within the area, 49 were found to be sub-standard. This area included property along Eaton and Maltbie Streets, both sides of North Perry Street, crossing over North Clayton Street and continuing along Chestnut Street to Buford Highway. Not included in the project were businesses located in the vicinity of the depot.

Eligible for public housing in the area were 36 of the 37 families. (Fifteen of the 37 owned their property, and 22 were tenants.) Those residing in the affected area had first preference for the 40 units of public housing to be built. This area was known as Grady Holt Homes, named in honor of the mayor at the time. (Another 10 units for the elderly were built in the Omie Harris areas of Crossstown under the grant.)

Meanwhile, eventually as the slums were cleared by this program, businesses began to put bids in to purchase land in the area. In 1959, the City Hall was moved from Crogan Street to 18 South Clayton Street in the Crosstown area. Besides Holt as mayor at that time, the councilmen serving then included H. L. Cooper, P. V. Kelley, R.L. Norton Jr. and Hal W. Pentecost. L.R. Martin was the city clerk and Don Martin was supervisor of utilities.

For a while, the City Hall was the only business relocating to the urban renewal district. But in 1962, several firms began to purchase tracts from the city. One of the first to move was Lawrenceville Auto Parts, run by James F. Brannan. He had opened his firm on South Perry Street (in the present day Sherwin Williams location), and in January 1962, held the grand opening of his new facility adjacent to the property owned by the city. Mr. Brannan was a former two term mayor of Lawrenceville, and for three years headed the Gwinnett Chamber. At the time he relocated his Auto Parts, he was chairman of the Gwinnett Board of Education and also chairman of the Library Board.

Another person seeing opportunity in the cleaned-up area was Charles Brand. He had started out working at Monfort's Drugs when 13 years old, and later was the pharmacist for Williams Pharmacy on the Square, and decided to strike out on his own. His widow, Dot Brand, says townspeople were against Charles setting up a drug store in the new area, since they told him, "Nobody shops off the Square." But in June 1962, he opened his pharmacy on a corner of South Clayton Street and Church Street. The move immediately was termed a success. Soon locating adjacent to the drug store was the medical office of Dr. Donald Dove, who previously had his office at Williams Pharmacy.

Another to move to the area in 1962 was Tom Watson. He moved his Ford auto dealership from South Perry Street to a lot adjacent to the City Hall. And Ray and Tom Nash put their Chevrolet dealership down the street, at Nash and South Clayton Street. Soon other stores were opening in the area.

On the Seaboard Urban Renewal tract, interest in one property came from Bob Fowler, who had just purchased the News-Herald, and successfully bid for land on North Clayton Street, where he would erect the building that became *Gwinnett Daily News.*

In 1972, adjacent to the Crosstown redevelopment area, the Lawrenceville Square shopping center was opened south of Nash Street. The property had been a 60-acre home, farm and dairy site of J.H. McGee, with pastures around the home, and it stretched back across what is now Scenic Highway. The house faced South Clayton Street. Tom McGee went to the University of Georgia anticipating that he would take over his father's registered Jersey dairy farm, but he got called into the military during World War II. "When I got back from the war, my father had sold the dairy herd, and he wanted me to go into another business." His eventual career was with the Soil Conservation Service.

A requirement to sell pasteurized milk in Atlanta had been one reason the elder McGee limited his dairy sales in the Lawrenceville area. He also sold 50 of his 80-head herd to Berry College in 1937, when the college's Jersey herd had been wiped out because of brucellosis. Part of the herd was sold at auction in 1943, as the elder McGee rented a tent, served barbecue and auctioned off the rest of the milk cow herd. Eventually J.H. McGee sold his farm for the development of the shopping center.

One of the major firms in downtown Lawrenceville, Belk-Gallant Dept. Store, was the key tenant in the new center, which also included a Big Star supermarket, movie theatre, offices and Sears retail store. Belk opened in August 17, 1972, which corresponded with the retirement from Belk of its long-time manager, Clyde Roberts. Julian Franklin came from Decatur to become the store manager, and stayed in Lawrenceville until spring of 1983, when he was transferred to the Athens Belk Store, where he retired. Today, he lives in Highlands, N.C.

In effect, these two Lawrenceville urban renewal projects did exactly what the program was intended for, greatly improving and renewing the downtown area of the city, and bringing more employment and businesses, more modern facilities, and employing more people.

Revitalization of the Square

The idea for a revitalization of the downtown Lawrenceville Square area came from the creative mind of Emory Morsberger, and began in 2002. A Lilburn resident and former state legislator, Morsberger also was the driving force behind the idea of bringing community improvement districts to Gwinnett.

The Morsberger Group specializes in the development and redevelopment of communities. It was perfect for downtown Lawrenceville, setting the standard by establishing innovative pedestrian-friendly live, work, and play areas around the square.

Morsberger was initially put off by downtown Lawrenceville, feeling the place was a "dump" when he first looked at it in 1991. It worried him that the county seat was in such a state of disrepair. However, eventually Morsberger saw opportunity where no one else did.

It was in 2002 that Morsberger began to concentrate on the nine block area around the Courthouse, searched the records and compiled the history of each property tract in the area. Morsberger quietly began buying up property around the courthouse square in Lawrenceville, each purchase under a limited liability company, all under different names. Even the City Council was not aware of his concentrated activities.

By about 18 months later, word was out that Morsberger was behind the 25 property exchanges around town, and by 2007, he had purchased another 10 tracts. He admits that he "covered our tracks so that people would not find out much" about the sales. Once word got out that one person was assembling the land, he adds: "Then property prices jumped beyond what they are worth."

Meanwhile, Morsberger hired a design team (the architectural firm is Tunnell-Spangler-Walsh and Associates of Atlanta) to come up with a concept of how the area could be redeveloped. Included in the plans: attracting various types of firms, from retail and restaurants to service firms and even housing near the square.

By 2003, Morsberger started marketing the Square to firms he wanted to locate there. Morsberger began sprucing up the Square area buildings. One of the first new firms to arrive was Lil' River Grill, relocating from west of the city. By 2006, it was clear Morsberger's efforts were going to be successful. When people saw the quality of the redevelopment, and the landing of several key firms, the re-development turned around. In his promotion, Morsberger concentrated on mentioning ambiance of the exposed original brick facades and classic southern architecture of the spaces lining the Historic Courthouse, dating from 1885.

Emory Morsberger

Yet Morsberger wasn't satisfied, and wanted something to anchor the area, a big idea. "We didn't want any more junk on the square, such as a flea market, but wanted to upgrade what was coming to the area," he says. Morsberger mentions former Lawrenceville Mayor Bobby Sikes and former councilman Rick Johnson as having a vision for what the area could become. "And we had the cooperation of the Council," he adds.

Morsberger credits Lawrenceville attorney Bill Powell for having the first thought of locating a theatre near the square. Morsberger also admits that he was not familiar with the Aurora Theatre of Duluth, which was looking for a new home, but which had not considered Lawrenceville.

In 2003, Morsberger purchased the former Methodist Church on Pike Street, and began to search for a suitable occupant. By working with the city council, eventually the city and the Aurora Theatre came to an agreement, one that significantly changed the impact of the square revitalization, as it opened in mid-2007. Another big stroke: construction by the city of a parking deck, another first for the downtown area, on Crogan Street adjacent to the theatre, which added to the upgrading of the Square area.

Another feature of the revitalization of downtown Lawrenceville has been the construction of residential facilities at the former site of the First National Bank of Gwinnett at the intersection of Crogan and Culver Streets, one block from the square. The first units were to open in the fall of 2008, and consisted of 12 condos, 17 townhouses and four courtyard homes. The bottom floor of the approximately 30,000 square foot, three story building---designed to resemble the former Ewing Hotel---is for retail space. The concept was part of the Downtown Lawrenceville Master Plan of 2004.

Morsberger has also been active in other areas of Metro Atlanta besides Gwinnett. His investment company in 2003 also purchased the giant former Sears, Roebuck Company site on Ponce de Leon Avenue from the City of Atlanta to redevelop. The building is the largest in Georgia with two million square feet of space. Morsberger anticipates rehabilitating the building into both offices and housing units. He will take possession in 2008, and plans to have 1,600 housing units, plus commercial activities, within the building. It is anticipated that this project will take 10 years to complete.

Meanwhile, Morsberger and his associates continue to market the downtown Lawrenceville Square, and are finding success in attracting both individual retail firms, offices and residents to the Square area.

So two projects nearly 50 years apart, one government, the other private, set the tone for downtown Lawrenceville in the modern day.

Lawrenceville utilities

Another key factor in the growth of Lawrenceville has been its advantage of providing utilities for its residents. The first city electric power system was begun in 1903, with the first water and sewer system installed in 1912.

City voters were asked to vote on a proposition for a $500,000 bond issue on Nov. 21, 1950 to finance the gas line construction and bring natural gas (and its lower fuel charges) to city residents. In the referendum, the proposal passed overwhelmingly, with 680 approving it, and only six votes against the proposal.

Afterward, with a $5 deposit, residents in the city and along the pipeline route could connect to the system. The city would be able to serve customers along parts of Georgia Highways 81, 20 and U.S. Highway 78 rights-of-way. The line was built from Walnut Grove where the Trans-Continental Pipeline ran, which the city could tap on for its supply of natural gas. The City had franchise agreements with towns along the way (Grayson and Loganville) to supply these areas with natural gas. The city sold subscriptions to the gas service as a convenience for people along the route from Walnut Grove. The service area also extends eastward toward Covington, while the City of Lawrenceville also serves a portion of Rockdale County.

In 2008, the City had the second largest municipal gas distribution system in Georgia, after Austell, and had 39,641 residential customers, and another 2,666 commercial customers.

It also had the second lowest gas rates of any city in Georgia.

One of the mainstays of the City of Lawrenceville was Don Martin, who was its chief employee and utilities department manager for years. Martin later became the city utility system superintendent. It had been Martin's idea to extend the gas lines to outlying areas, a move which would later pay off handsomely for the City of Lawrenceville. The revenues from the gas customers would benefit Lawrenceville tremendously. The first month the city was able to bill gas customers was in late 1951.

With Gas Revenue Anticipation Certificates, the city was able to sell $500,000 in bonds to build the system. As a result, this has created a large geographic service area. Revenue generates a major margin for the city utilities to the present day. The geographic spread of the city's gas customers is basically from Interstate 85 on the west along Georgia Highway 20, to nearly as far north as Winder and Monroe on the east.

For 2008, the City of Lawrenceville was serving 10,312 electrical customers, mostly in and around the city limits, including 8,634 residential customers and 1,678 commercial customers. (There were approximately 9,071 households within the city limits in 2006.)

The Water Department had 5,864 residential customers and 993 commercial accounts. The city picked up garbage from 7,985 residents, and 1,448 commercial sites.

Altogether, the Lawrenceville utilities generated $72,907,923 in revenue during 2007.

Concerning electricity for Lawrenceville, Bill Fortune found when becoming mayor in 1968 that the city's electric system was antiquated. In Fortune's first term as mayor, days far different from now, Lawrenceville's utilities had over the years not been upgraded, and were in ancient shape. Fortune remembers: "We had thin, small electrical lines serving the city, and when there were surges along the lines from Georgia Power, those thin pencil-lead-size lines would sometimes burn out. Buzz Kramlich at his supermarket said that the surges also shorted out his frozen food freezers. Adding to the problem was that we had no regulators on the lines to boost or hold back the power surges. At one time, the electric lines burned through on the courthouse square, falling on the Brand Bank building." Fortune got the electric lines modernized, bringing in thicker 440-volt lines, and installing regulators and transformers.

The city's natural gas distribution system got its supply from the Georgia Natural Gas pipeline. However, the city had no gas storage facilities, and therefore paid the highest rate throughout the year, based on its peak usage on the coldest days. "Our rate was something like $1,000 a day at that time," Fortune says.

So Fortune, along with Don Martin, then the superintendent of utilities, came up with the plan to install a "peak shaving storage plant" using propane gas. With this system, the city could purchase propane gas at times of low rates, and store the gas for later use when gas cost more. That way, Lawrenceville could "shave" the high cost it was paying during cold times of the year.

"We paid for it in a heartbeat," Fortune says. The Lawrenceville residents benefited through lower natural gas rates.

The peak-shaving plant was built on Hi-Hope Road. Fortune's own company built the concrete pads and lifted the thick-plated tanks into place, at no charge to the city. Giant Cummins generators were used to push the gas through the system. "Then on cold days, the propane plant would be switched on, and our system had propane to supplement the natural gas. That way, we reduced the cost we were paying for our natural gas the whole year round, and saved tremendously."

Not only that, but Fortune found that the propane gas at that time was relatively cheap, compared to gasoline, so he put the police vehicles to run on propane also. "We caught the devil from the policeman, for the cars didn't have too much pick-up that way. But we didn't want the police in high speed chases anyway."

And, since the city was more efficient with both its electrical and natural gas distribution systems, it began to make more money from its proprietary funds. It ended up, during Fortune's years, in cutting the local taxes from 19 to seven mills. "And we could have cut it to zero," Fortune says, "But you have to have some taxes on property." These low property tax rates have continued. In 2007, the city's property tax millage rate was 2.20 mills.

Fortune, a civil engineering graduate of Georgia Tech, was head of a bridge construction company in Lawrenceville. He would serve as mayor for six years, from 1968-74, defeating incumbent Rhodes Jordan (his fellow church member at First Baptist) to become mayor. After Fortune moved to Marietta in 1974, Jordan was once again elected mayor, and would eventually serve eight terms, though not consecutive.

Jordan, an attorney, was one of the most colorful mayors in Lawrenceville's history. Jordan never let any defeat set him back and stop him from wanting to serve the city. As he said himself: "When you get defeated, you've only lost a battle. Some people never lose an election in 30 years and then come up and lose one, and it just kills them. I've always been able to readjust after the defeats… I want to be mayor of Lawrenceville as long as I am able and the people want me." He last served as mayor in 1988, and died at age 74 in his sleep in 1993.

A person long associated with Lawrenceville, Bob Baroni, came to town in 1971 from Ocala, Fla., hired as the first recreation director. He found undeveloped facilities, with one city park (the present Rhodes Jordan Park), with one playing field, a lake, and rough dirt roads around it. The former swimming pool had been closed.

Under Mayor Bill Fortune's efforts, the city acquired a Bureau of Outdoor Recreation grant, some $450,000, and redid its swimming pool, playing fields and paved the road in the park. The grants came before Baroni came, and allowed the creation of Lawrenceville Parks East and West, including eight Little League baseball fields. As a result of the new ball fields at Lawrenceville West Park, Lawrenceville hosted the first Dixie Youth World Series, August 18-23, 1975. Teams came from Florida, Virginia, Texas, Louisiana, Mississippi, Tennessee, North and South Carolina, Alabama and Georgia. As the host, Lawrenceville had a team in the tournament.

Once the Lawrenceville park program and its affiliated ball leagues were underway, the city invited other towns---Dacula, Grayson and Lilburn residents---to participate in its playground leagues. The other town residents had to pay a small fee to participate. This pre-dated the county-wide recreation department. Later Baroni would leave his position in Lawrenceville in 1972, but returned as its city clerk in 1974, and as of 2008, continues in that position.

Current City Hall dedicated

People can easily remember the date of opening and dedication of the new Lawrenceville City Hall. The event was Sept. 11, 2002, the first anniversary of the September 11 World Trade Center tragedy.

The new city building cost $8.3 million, and is a four-story, 64,800 square foot facility, done in classical Georgian style. This building is significantly bigger than the former City Hall just down Clayton Street, which was built in 1958, with the 8,000 square foot building financed by a $125,000 bond issue. The earlier City Hall once housed the entire Lawrenceville government, but eventually, the Police Department was relocated into the former Ford distributorship adjacent to the City Hall. Yet that 1958 City Hall had been the seat of government, though crowded, for 44 years. The 2002 building is a vast, spacious building, with built-in expansion space, as the fourth floor was intentionally left undeveloped for future use. (Another early City Hall was on Crogan Street, near the Square, and built in 1913.)

Speaker for the 2002 dedication was State Rep. Renee Unterman. After her talk, there followed a dedication of a plaque in remembrance of the 2001 tragedy.

Bartow Jenkins was the mayor that year, and says that the city picked September 11 for dedicating the new City Hall in memory of the events of the previous year. "We selected this date to show that our country stands ready to build on and keep this democracy going. We dedicated this building in memory of all those who died and who lost loved ones in the tragedy across our country last September 11. We're proud of this new building, but also we are proud of the way our country responded and continues to respond."

After the ceremony, Jenkins added: "What I loved best about the new building is that it is paid for, and will last us for years to come." The city used its reserve funds to build the facility.

Bill Dunn, project manager for the firm of E&C Integration Services Inc. of Lawrenceville, which designed and supervised construction of the new City Hall, says that the design is of "traditional courthouse style, with red brick and architectural stone and columns on the front. It's designed for functionality, with all the city offices in one building."

From Nash and South Clayton Streets, visitors enter onto the second floor, which is the main floor. Besides offices for payment of utility bills, there is also customer service (with drive-up windows), and offices for the mayor and council members. In the previous facility, only the mayor had a private office. Now, all council members have their own office and desk. The Council auditorium, with nearly 200 seats, is at the rear of the building's main floor.

The first floor, accessible off a large side street parking lot, houses the municipal court and its offices, plus a room for meter readers and a break room. The third floor houses computer services, the city engineer and other functions. The fourth floor is for expansion space, but was temporarily used for about a year by the Aurora Theatre before its renovated facilities were completed.

Bob Baroni, longtime city clerk, beams as he shows off the building. He says: "Now everyone in the building has more room to move around, and do their work more efficiently. And we think it could serve the city for the next 50 years."

Freeman's Mill

One of the key grist mills in the Lawrenceville area was Freeman's Mill, located on the Alcovy River east of town. In olden days, water was the key to a grist mill, as it continuously but slowly powered the mechanisms that ground the kernels of the grain into meal or flour.

Back in the days before supermarkets, when families produced most of their foods, one of the key units of any community was its grist mill. Farmers took their grain, whether it was corn or wheat, to the mill for it to be ground into meal, flour, grits or animal feed. As farmers gathered at the mill, it became something of a social occasion, with the farmers greeting one another and exchanging stories as their grain was milled.

Freeman's Mill has also been known as Swann's Mill, and also the Alcovy Grist Mill. It was probably named for W.S. (some say Winfield Scott) Freeman, of whom little is known. The exact date of the building of Freeman's Mill is not clear. Some connect it with the lottery of 1832, saying its wooden building went up in 1837. That makes sense with two accounts of the mill selling corn meal to the Confederate Army. However, others point to later years, either 1866 or 1879, as the time of the beginning of Freeman's Mill. Of course, both accounts could be right, with the possibility of the mill being somehow destroyed, perhaps by fire, and in need of rebuilding. One account has the mill built by John and Levi Loveless in 1866, putting the heavy timbers together with mortise and tendon joints, joined by pegs. Other operators at the mill included the Jackson, Freeman and Pharr families, with the mill eventually purchased by Dr. Lewis Swann, hence the latter name.

The mill itself has a sluice to bring in the waters of the relatively small Alcovy River and form a pond and raceway to drive the big wheel of the mill. Inside the mill are massive timbers hewn by hand, joined by pegs and mortises. The power of the water slowly turned the big drive shaft, moving its pulleys and belts. Finally, two slowly-turning, hand-sharpened stones would do the actual grinding of the corn or wheat into the useful meal or flour. The slow turning insured a good product, since turning faster would cause too much friction, heat up and "burn" the product, giving it a bad taste. As the wheel turns, you hear a soft rumble from the mechanisms, though loud enough so that a person has to talk in a raised voice. Feeling the ground meal or flour, you learn that the friction of grinding it makes the output a little warm. The mill was last used to grind corn in 1986.

The site of Freeman's Mill, 11.8895 acres, was purchased by Gwinnett County in 2001 with Georgia Greenspace funding. It is planned to open as a county park in 2008-09. It will be a passive park and will not be a demonstration mill, since operations would create vibrations, which could collapse the old wooden building.

Other grist mills were located throughout the county, notably a mill near Buford known to be a place not only to grind grain, but as a place for outdoor outings and bathing. That was known as Woodward's Mill, perhaps the earliest mill in the county, which dates back to 1824, built by pioneer Gwinnett citizen Shadrack Bogan. It was destroyed by a fire of undetermined origin in 1976.

Hopkin's Mill, off Beaver Ruin Road, was operable as late as 1950, but destroyed by fire. Brandon Mill was adjacent to the Alcovy River south of U.S. Highway 29, east of Lawrenceville. It was among the first water-powered mills in the county, and is mentioned as early as 1835. Tribble Mill, south of New Hope Road, was built near relatively smooth rocky outcrops, and had enough flowing water through a millrace to directly operate the mill wheel without having a mill pond. (One of Gwinnett's larger parks is located near this mill site.)

Honest Alley

Two places in Gwinnett have names associated with alleys. One was in Norcross, where "Skin Alley" had a checkered past associated with games of chance.

The other alley of note in Gwinnett is "Honest Alley" in Lawrenceville. It was a place where horse and mule trading occurred from about the beginning of the 1900s until tractors began to replace animals after World War II. Since such traders were not always known as straight forward gentlemen of transactions, to combat that attitude, perhaps with tongue-in-cheek, the name of "Honest Alley" came about, and stuck. For sure, Lawrenceville families warned their children to avoid the area, probably to no avail for many children. After all, such a place had a special allure.

Honest Alley also attracted traveling medicine shows to sell miracle tonics and other medications. The arrival of such traveling caravans didn't help give the alley an improved image, however, as these shows sometimes dealt with questionable potions, or perhaps sleight-of-hand tactics.

King Cotton was the chief crop in Gwinnett during the period when horses and mules were the primary locomotion for plows in the times after the Civil War and into the 1900s. Cotton had special properties making it attractive to farmers. First, it was a good bet for making money, with cotton in demand at good prices. As well, cotton could easily be grown in the Gwinnett area; cotton gins were in many local towns close to the farms; and cotton was not perishable. Mules were the standard in the fields where straight line plowing was necessary. "Farmers usually favored mules over horses since a mule, with their built-in smartness, would halt and just plain not move when it became exhausted. Horses would allow themselves to be worked to death," says former Gwinnett County Extension Agent Bill Baughman.

So into this picture comes Honest Alley. Eddie Oakes can tell about the alley in Lawrenceville. He was there when it was in its heyday.

"My daddy had a mule barn and livery stable on the property, and for a while, we lived next door. People would gather there on Saturday and trade for mules like people trade for cars now. And they usually drank a little liquor, I understand.

"My father was John Henry Hansford Oakes, and he built there about 1900. You entered the upstairs portion, which had a cement floor, and people kept their wagons and buggies up there. The back part was made of wood, and there was a chute down to the bottom floor, where they kept the mules and horses. He ran that mule barn until he died in 1944."

After Eddie's father died, the place was partially run by his uncles, known as Oakes and Higgins Garage, with a gas pump, wrecker service, etc. Then Roy Gunter had an Oldsmobile dealership at the location, before the site became Johnson and Sons Hardware Store.

Eddie also gives an insight of the Lawrenceville of years ago. "My daddy would go out West and buy several rail boxcar loads of mules and have them shipped back to Lawrenceville. Someone would hop up on an old gray mare, and would lead the mules from the box car up the hill from the depot through town and to the mule barn. There would be all sorts of mules there.

"He would put these wild mules out on farms of sharecroppers, where they would break them, then return them to the barn, where they would be sold. Most everybody in those pre-World War II days worked their farms with horses or mules."

Methodist campground

An institution that still stands today came out of the Lawrenceville Methodist Church, itself founded in 1823. Several years later, in 1832, five church members each put up $10 to purchase 50 acres for a campground to hold annual revival meetings. The five men were Buckner Harris, William Maltbie, Isham Williams, Elisha Winn and George Brogdon. (The Methodist Church is not sure all were Methodist members, with one suspected of being Presbyterian.)

The first camp meeting was held in 1833 in a brush arbor. The camp meeting was usually held during the warmer days of August, during "laying by" time, when crops were robust, but not ready to harvest. The site is about five miles north of present-day Lawrenceville, in an area shaded by hardwoods. One reason the site was selected was that it had two springs for water, on opposite sides of the tract, in which the attendees cooled their milk, butter and eggs. One of the springs is still active today.

In the early days, services would be held during the day, and again at night. Illumination for the night service would be provided by pine boughs (knots), elevated on poles piled with sand (for insulation).

This annual campground meeting became a tradition, and still continues each year, though in abbreviated versions and now held for five days in July. During the Civil War, the campground burned, according to a printed newspaper account, with members of Sherman's Army destroying it. (Another version had rowdy horse traders as the source of the fire.) At any rate, the site was dormant for about 10 years after the Civil War, but eventually was refurbished for the annual meetings. Other problems would sometimes cause cancellation for that year, because of economic conditions, the boll weevil, or once because of the threat of polio.

In those early days, people would stream to the campground to spend a week in revival, hearing several ministers who would speak sometimes for an hour or more. Those attending would go to great lengths to "dress up" in Sunday style for the services, the ladies donning their best dresses, the men in their coats and ties, even though the weather was usually scorching. However, ministers were said often to shed their coats when consumed with the heat of preaching.

The people would come to the campground in their wagons and on horseback. The wagons would be loaded down with bedding, clothing, cabinets and provisions for the week. Milk cows would be walked behind the wagon, and chickens in coops would be on the wagon. The cows and horses pulling the wagon would return to the homes or farms after the meetings, while the chickens would have been consumed during the week-long meeting.

Originally the attendees stayed in "tents," the term used by camp meetings for the housing. These were wooden, bare-bone cabins for lodging. All this centered around a large, open-air tabernacle or arbor, with a dirt floor, sawdust scattered between the benches for ease of footing and to keep down the dust. (The original worship area had been a brush arbor, made by lashing together bushes to keep the summer sunshine off the worshipers.) Today that "tabernacle" (chapel) remains, and has a tin roof on it, its wooden benches still ringed with sawdust during the revival.

In today's meetings, while the church continues the tradition of the campground meeting, no longer do people routinely live in the crude cabins. However, some drive up in their motor homes or pop-up tent trailers to stay during the revival. And no longer is it a Sunday-to-Sunday of services, but only held Monday until Friday.

In recent years, the Methodists have often focused on inviting different members of other denominations to participate at least one night a week during the services. Attendance remains good, usually filling the tabernacle with up to 150-200 persons.

E.R. Snell, Contractor

One of the oldest, continually operating firms in Gwinnett, with officers whose family was among the early settlers in Gwinnett, is E.R. Snell, Contractor, Inc. of Snellville. The firm stretches back to 1923 when G.F. (Gladstone Frederick) Snell, a rock mason, and his son, E.R. (Edwin Richard), started building rock culverts, bridges and walls in North Georgia. Today it is one of the largest privately owned highway construction firms in Georgia, employing more than 600 persons. The firm is involved in asphalt paving, grading, bridges, culverts and commercial grading projects. Most of its work is centered in and around Metro Atlanta, though it also has projects throughout North Georgia.

The company has grown rapidly in recent years, with sales of $20 million in 1989 to more than $250 million in 2008.

In the early 1950s, three more of his brothers, Tom, Cyril and Hugh, had joined with E.R. Snell in the company, as well as brother-in-law Thomas Briscoe. The start of the Interstate highway system solidified and expanded the company's position in the industry. The 1950s also saw the entry into the company of the next generation of family---E.R.Snell's sons, Earle, Ferle, Richard, Jack and son-in-law James Camp. On June 30, 1959, the company was incorporated as E.R. Snell, Contractor.

Most of the growth has been internal before the company made its first purchase of another company in 1978. ERS bought Stancil Grading of Snellville. Before that, the firm had not done grading work. Soon grading work became the largest income producer for the company, and greatly enhanced its presence in the highway construction industry, and elevating it from sub-contractor to contractor status in the late 1980s. Then in 1990, the company purchased Jasper Construction's Asphalt Division acquiring a liquid asphalt terminal in Lithonia, and four hot mix asphalt plants in Lithia Springs, Norcross, Stockbridge and Lithonia. Later it would add hot mix asphalt plants in Elberton, Jefferson, Athens and Good Hope. By 2008, it was operating 12 liquid asphalt plants throughout Metro Atlanta with the addition of plants in Grayson, Tyrone, Friendship and Paulding County.

With the purchase of Logan Paving Company of Athens in 1997 and Riverdale Paving Company in 2002, E.R. Snell significantly broadened its base in the private sector. The

Riverdale purchase targeted the growing south west Atlanta metro commercial market. In 2004, the company purchased Aamco Paving Company and their strong Gwinnett private commercial market.

The company is privately-owned, with the provision that each stockholder must be an employee working in the family business. Each family member that joins the firm must "start at the bottom," and work themselves up. Today 28 members of the Snell family are employed at the company.

The current president of the firm, Robin Snell, came to his post in 1996, after his uncle, Richard, retired. He started out in 1977 at the bottom, shoveling concrete, and building culverts for the company after graduating from the University of Georgia. In a 2007 newsletter to the firm's employees, Robin noted: "My father, Earle, had no intentions of me remaining with the company (when I started in 1977). He always insisted that my brother, David and I, find other occupations. I convinced him that I would return to the University of Georgia in the fall to work on my master's degree." He never returned to college.

"The work certainly wasn't easy that summer as my father instructed my uncle whom I worked for, James Camp, to make things as difficult as he could. However, I found that work interesting and satisfying," Robin stated.

"The greatest lesson I learned that summer occurred when the crew I worked with took a week off during July. A few of us summer guys worked that week and were determined to accomplish something. I think my uncle would tell you today that he was proud of what we did. However, I can't tell you how proud I was when the crew returned to work that following Monday. I learned that summer how important it is to have dedicated, skilled and loyal employees. Our company has changed dramatically since 1977, but the importance of what each employee means to our company remains the same."

David Snell, who is vice president and corporate secretary, in a 2007 talk to the "Success Lives Here" breakfast of the Gwinnett Chamber of Commerce, outlined some of the precepts that made their company successful. He said at the beginning: "Family is a big part of who I am. When growing up, my grandparents lived next door. And there are always a lot of cousins around. Our grandparents instilled ethics and morality in our work and the company. We knew right from wrong, with no gray areas. Our grandparents never lost sight of that, and conducted business in that manner." David Snell is a former chairman of the Gwinnett Chamber of Commerce.

Another key figure in the company is Chris Snell, a son of former president Richard Snell. He is the executive vice president and treasurer. Chris also started out shoveling concrete, but was injured severely in a dragline accident when he was 20 years old, in 1978, causing permanent injury, and making him a quadriplegic and wheelchair bound.

"I was standing on the back of a crane, helping dismantle it, when a cable came loose, and knocked me to the ground, with me landing on my head." Many did not think he would survive the accident, but he redoubled his attention to the business, and today is a key member of the leadership team at ERS-team.

"I was hurt in August, 1978, and was incapacitated, and in rehab until December. I started back part time in January, 1979, and worked up to full time, gaining my strength. It was mighty tiring laying on a stretcher or bed all day. But I wasn't out long." He moves

E.R. Snell

around in a specially-constructed wheel chair and has only limited use of his arms, using a brace on his arm to write or use his computer.

His cousin, David, says: "Chris didn't let that accident bother his effectiveness. He's vibrant, and works every day."

A friend describes his manner: "He barks orders and they get to it."

The work the Snells do can be dangerous, as people handle heavy equipment in tough outdoor conditions, often with traffic flowing near them. Two other members of the Snell family have been seriously hurt in accidents, and remain employed there.

Bryant Snell lost his right leg in a crane accident, from the mid thigh down. He is vice president for human resources for the company.

Bill Snell, who supervises the lowboy equipment and field trucks, had his foot run over with a crane. The foot had to be amputated from the ankle down. Other Snell personnel have also been hurt, though the company has a good safety record compared to other construction companies.

Today the company maintains its headquarters in Snellville, but also has offices in Athens, and a shop and office in Lithonia, Ga.

The Snells maintain a mission statement that is forthright: "E.R. Snell Contractor, Inc was built on Christian beliefs with honesty and integrity leading the way. Our goal is to build a safe and modern highway system while preserving the natural environment. Through quality production and high safety standards, we strive to be the best contractor possible, while continuing to be a positive influence on our employees and our community."

David, who first worked at Peachtree Doors, and later at American Charms furniture and Progress Container, came to work at E.R. Snell in 1989. "I was the new kid, and had to fit in. We purchased Jasper's asphalt company and I started in that division's operations." He is now vice president and corporate secretary.

Of their work at the firm, David says, "We work each day to accomplish our individual goals. All have to work to earn a place, and each is given responsibility and is expected to make the job work. The secret is that we share in the success of the company, with our employees, with the oldest and youngest sharing equally in our work."

One element of the company, even in the face of the company growth, remains the same at E.R. Snell. "There's more to business than just being successful," David says. Chris puts it this way. "We strive to leave every situation knowing we've done the right thing."

Robin sums it up: "My vision for the future of E. R. Snell Contractor Inc. is to continue the work ethic, values and principles on which the company was founded that have served us so well in the past."

PSST, LADY...
YOU WANT TO BUY PARTS
OF THE JONES BRIDGE?

4
1950-1970

Perception of Gwinnett changes

Before the significant growth of Gwinnett, which began seriously in the 1970s, the way others in Georgia in those days looked upon Gwinnett may surprise you. People thought of Gwinnett as corrupt, shady, and crime-infested.

A few elements gave Gwinnett this rough name. Here's how.

The first bad publicity Gwinnett received as a county didn't particularly have much to do with Gwinnett County's internal operations. But the incidents happened in Gwinnett and the county got its first black eye as a result.

The incident took place at the state prison at what was called "Buford Rock Quarry Prison for Incorrigibles," where prisoners worked from 6 a.m. to 6 p.m. breaking up rocks with sledgehammers. It was the summer of 1956, back when Georgia prisons were not the model of modern prisons. The Rock Quarry prisoners, upset with treatment they got from the corrections officers, rebelled by breaking their own legs with sledgehammers. In two incidents, a total of 41 prisoners injured themselves in this way, prompting a state investigation into the abuse of the inmates. The first incident took place in July, 30, 1956.

There were 189 prisoners at the institution, and the first incident took place when 36 prisoners, 29 white and seven black prisoners, broke their legs about 3:30 in the afternoon, when on a work break. These inmates took 10-pound sledgehammers used for crushing rock, placed their legs across stones, and maimed themselves. The next day, another five inmates also broke their legs in a similar fashion.

The action became nationwide news, and written in an August 13 issue of *TIME* magazine: "*...beyond dispute was the fact that inmates of (the) Rock Quarry had sunk so low on the scale of human hope that they had ducked out of the searing sun into the shadow of a rock pile, (and) had smashed each other's legs in a despairing gesture of mass protest.*" The magazine also said that the self-mutilators "*had been driven to their madness by the brutality of prison bosses.*" Officials denied mistreating the prisoners. *The Atlanta Journal* reported these words scrawled on a concrete and steel solitary cell: "*Thay is no God.*"

Governor Marvin Griffin ordered an inquiry. One prison account of the incident reported there was "nothing wrong" at the site, maintaining the incidents were merely in protest of work loads. The next week a joint House-Senate committee gave the prison a clean bill of health, saying "The allegations of brutality have not been substantiated….." The committee also added that "The prisoners are not being required to do any more work or to work longer hours than laborers in many types of industry." Another finding of the committee was that guards would no longer be able to curse prisoners. However, later the warden was transferred. Additional guards were provided for closer supervision, and new guard towers were built.

The Atlanta Constitution reported on August 11, 1965 that the Corrections Department Director, Jack Forrester, sent a report to the governor saying the investigation revealed "… no conduct on the part of the prison personnel strong enough to provide the sadistic acts committed by prisoners at this institution." It continued: "Acts of brutality and mistreatment of prisoners have been alleged, but we find no concrete proof that these alleged acts were committed. However, assuming charges of guards striking or slapping prisoners on four specific occasions to be true, such conduct was not sufficient cause for the prisoners to commit bodily mutilations on themselves and others."

Governor Griffin later was quoted as saying, "Incidents of this kind appear to set the prison system back a little."

"Chop shops" come to Gwinnett

The negative view of Gwinnett County corresponded with the arrival of the interstate highway through the county. As construction of Interstate 85 came out of Atlanta heading northeasterly in the late 1950s and early 1960s, crime came with it in a distinct manner.

Criminal elements would go into Atlanta, steal an automobile and drive like mad to the end of the Interstate. They would exit in the early days at Jimmy Carter Boulevard (then Norcross-Tucker Road). Later, as the interstate was extended northward, those making off with hot automobiles would zoom off the freeway at Indian Trail, then Beaver Ruin, and later at Pleasant Hill Road.

Tearing off into the back country, they would rendezvous with others at night in the backwood areas of Gwinnett, and immediately begin to disassemble the stolen automobile. A newspaper headline in January, 1964 asked, "Dumping Grounds in Car Thefts?" The headline added: "Four arrested in Crackdown by Lawmen; Suspect 'Ring.'"

Fred Banks, who retired as warden of the Gwinnett Correctional Facility after 10 years with the prison, was a deputy sheriff from 1961-1963. This department often found abandoned vehicles which were the victims of chop-shop operations.

Banks recalls about chop-shops: "At first I found it hard to believe, but I have heard individuals say that within five minutes after a stolen car arrived, they would have stripped it. These guys weren't after the incidental components of an automobile, such as the seats or radio. All they wanted to take was the motor and the transmission. After I watched stock car racing, where they can change four tires and fill the race car with gas in 13-15 seconds, I finally realized how they could strip a car in as short a time as five minutes."

When someone found the ravaged automobile in the woods, deputies would find the car complete….except for the engine and transmission.

Banks explains what would happen. "These were professionals, and they would be waiting for the stolen car to arrive at a rendezvous spot. They had with them a wrecker or tow truck. When the car pulled up, they didn't wait around, nor did they strip it with wrenches. They simply snatched off the car's hood, or bent it back, and started to work with a cutting torch. They cut the motor supports, then the wires, harness and hoses, cut the drive shaft, and with the wrecker hoist, yanked the engine out the front. They would use the wrecker to lift this heavy load onto the wrecker or pick-up, and be off, five or ten minutes after they began."

These criminals would take the valuable parts back to their garage, or warehouse. Banks says: "I understand they stored them, like at an auto parts store or dealership. People buying those hot parts would ask for a particular vehicle, and they would bring it off the shelf and sell it to them for cash. Or if they didn't have the exact engine or transmission a customer wanted, they would take an order for it, and tell them they would have it in a few days. Then they would send out someone to steal that particular car, and shortly, have the part the customer wanted."

Those were the days before serial numbers were stamped on major parts. Today chop shop operations are still around, but greatly curtailed in the USA because the parts are now numbered. Most chop shop output is bound for the overseas markets, often in high end sports cars, Banks says.

Moonshine drop-off point

These chop shops began to appear in the later 1950s, and picked up speed in the early 1960s on the heels of another illegal operation taking place in the county: running moonshine, which had been going on for quite some time in Gwinnett, even back to before World War II. Gwinnett had more than its share of moonshine operations.

However, Gwinnett was more of a major "drop off" place for moonshine. This whiskey was made in the mountains of North Georgia, then driven to points around Atlanta. Some moonshiners used Gwinnett for a temporary storage location, transporting the illegal liquor during the dead of night to a local citizen, who would in turn make deliveries to Atlanta. One present-day banker told me: "We knew that some of our neighbors were somehow in the moonshine business. It was just common knowledge." One Gwinnett woman remembers as a child talking often with one of her best friends on the telephone, and inviting her friend over often to spend the night. "But we never went to her house. We knew her father was mixed up in some type of different business, and we shouldn't go there."

For a while, running and making illegal whiskey took place in many counties, with the law enforcement officials of the 1950s and early 1960s well aware, if not involved, in its operation. Not only was moonshining prevalent in the county, but one Gwinnett sheriff, Dan Cole, was convicted in Federal court on two counts on Feb. 4, 1963, for possessing illegal whiskey and also for possessing jars and sugar for use in making the whiskey. Altogether, Cole faced seven counts in the court charge, but was convicted on only two counts. Mr. Cole was sentenced to one year in prison and fined $1,000 on the convictions.

The story of the moonshining conviction had several twists. The day after the conviction was read in court, the jury foreman called the chief deputy of the court and told him that the jury had made an error in the counts on which they had based the conviction. U.S. District Judge Boyd Sloan was quoted in the *News-Herald* of Lawrenceville. The foreman said that the jury meant to convict Cole on counts two and three of the indictment, instead of counts three and four. The foreman also said that he did not realize the mistake until he read the account of the conviction in the newspaper the day after the verdict. The jury deliberated seven hours before their verdict.

The *News-Herald* account reads: "Count two charged Cole with possession of some five tons of sugar intended for use in making distilled spirits, a misdemeanor under federal law. Count four, on which the jury reported a guilty verdict Monday night, charged Cole with possession of 192 gallons of non-tax-paid whisky last January. (Possessing illegal whisky is a felony, which carried a stiffer penalty.)

"The third count of the indictment charged Cole with possessing 3,612 half-gallon jars intended for use in making bootleg liquor, also a misdemeanor."

Judge Sloan also said to the newspaper that "after a jury is discharged, they can no longer change their verdict or re-convene." The account added that juries occasionally are polled in court before they are dismissed at the request of one of the parties to see if the verdict reported is the verdict all the jurors agreed upon. Judge Sloan added: "They waive (the) right if they do not make the request before the jury is discharged."

After conviction in court, Mr. Cole eventually resigned as sheriff on Sept. 6, 1963, with his uncle, Sam King, to serve as temporary sheriff until a special election was held to fill the office. Cole even sought to run in the resultant election for the unexpired term for which he had just resigned. However, he was disqualified as a candidate for the office. Frank Quill Sammon Jr. on Oct. 16, 1963 defeated four other candidates to win the office of sheriff in the special election. Sammon would only serve the rest of that term, from October, 1963, until December 31, 1964, as barbecue restaurant owner Hoke Huston (Hoke's, on U.S. Highway 29 south of Lawrenceville) would win the next election to serve a four-year term.

Three policemen killed

Along with the doubling of the population that Gwinnett was experiencing in the 20 years after 1950 (from a population of 32,250 in 1950 to 72,349 in 1970), came this wave of lawlessness. As a result, the people of the community first recognized the problem, then became concerned, as the county was singled out again and again for its illegal activities. Elected public officials were seeing all this, and were worried about it. But little was happening to curb this lawlessness.

Gwinnett's reputation as a haven for a notorious element, plus an uproar over the antics of the Sheriff's Department, eventually resulted in taking away police functions from the sheriff and creating the county police department for law enforcement.

In 1964, the impact of the stolen automobile operation in Gwinnett had been fortified in the minds of Metro Atlantans when three Gwinnett policemen were killed by members of a chop-shop operation. The community was embarrassed and outraged with this taking place within its borders----showing where inattention by law-abiding citizens to criminal enterprises can lead. However, careful police work quickly led to the capture and conviction of the criminal gang involved. (See Appendix A-14 for the official police account.)

One of the key persons working on the case of the three policemen killed in the stolen auto ring was the chief investigator from DeKalb County, John Crunkleton. Wayne Mason says that Crunkleton, through cultivation and conversation with one of the defendants, obtained statements instrumental in gaining conviction of the gang. "Crunkleton was the greatest factor in solving those murders." Crunkleton worked closely with the District Attorney, Reid Merritt, and Judge Luther Hames in the murders, and the three formed a bond, trusting one another. That was important, since there was an aura of criminality pervading law enforcement in those days in Gwinnett.

A policeman stands looking into the grave-like hole in the ground near Berkeley Lake where Barbara Mackle was buried for 83 hours.

Gwinnett breathed a little easier, only to be shaken again four years later with the Barbara Mackle abduction. A man and woman abducted Emory University co-ed Barbara Mackle, bundled her away in the night, drove to a wooded plot in Gwinnett, and buried her alive. Her coffin-like box contained a little food and water, plus a fan run on batteries, which soon gave out. The burial site was near what is present-day Berkeley Lake, just south of then-graveled South Berkeley Lake Road, and southwest of what is now Peachtree Industrial Boulevard. (That road did not exist in 1968.) The kidnappers demanded a ransom from her wealthy family, who had developed Marco Island off the coast of Florida.

Barbara Mackle

After the family made the ransom payment, the FBI swarmed in, catching the criminals, who led them to the burial site. Some 83 hours after being buried, Ms. Mackle was found alive. Eventually the perpetrators were tried and convicted. But the essential impact on Gwinnett was negative—she was found in Gwinnett, that place people remembered as where much other criminal activity was taking place.

By 1968, the county commissioners of those days, especially Chairman Dudge Pruitt, were fed up with the perception that people had about criminal activity in the county, and decided to do something about it. By 1968, there was now a five-member county commission, instead of a three-member commission. The other four commissioners serving in 1968 were Carvis Williams, Julian Archer, Ray Gunnin and Maron Buice.

Looking back, Pruitt flatly says "What I'm most proud of is hiring John Crunkleton one Sunday night to be our police chief. We met outside the county, at the Holiday Inn on Pleasantdale Road in DeKalb County. We interviewed him and Larry Puckett, who was police chief in Buford. But when Larry learned we were interviewing Crunkleton, who was with the DeKalb County detective's office then, Larry told us that he would rather work with John than become the police chief, and he was later Crunkleton's assistant." Crunkleton had come to the attention of Gwinnett authorities by helping solve the case when car thieves had murdered three Gwinnett policemen in 1964.

W.R. "Dudge" Pruitt

Pruitt says: "Crunkleton ran the police department. We didn't get involved with it. He did a mighty good job, and helped set the tone for the police and county government since that time."

Ray Gunnin remembers this: "When I went into office in 1968, people were real concerned about law enforcement elements, with lots of complaints. We met with the Superior Court judge, Charles Pittard, who strongly suggested that the police force not be under the sheriff's office. We also met with the new district attorney, Reid Merritt, and met with the FBI, even before we went into office. The FBI told the commission there was not a single Gwinnett police officer they would trust. There was a lack of confidence in the law, the leadership was poor, and we as commissioners knew we had to do something."

Pruitt put it more bluntly: "The police department was a mess. The first four years I was in office, we never could get the police department straightened out. But during my second term, we started the county police department, and assigned to the sheriff duties only as an officer of the court, with no police responsibilities."

Gunnin adds that the board needed a police chief who didn't owe any obligations to anyone, who would run his department on his own, and that the commission would give him complete control and not meddle into police affairs, as it had in the past.

Meanwhile, the FBI realized what was happening in Gwinnett, and as Wayne Shackelford said, "steered Crunkleton to talk to Ray Gunnin." Before taking office on

January 1, 1968, Shackelford said, Gunnin, a Southern Bell engineer, spent a period of months getting ready to be a member of the commission, making "vigorous analysis" of every function he was about to assume responsibility over.

Maron Buice, himself a new county commissioner, also realized something needed to be done. And with lots of study and planning, shortly "everything seemed to fall into place," he says. Pruitt, as chairman of the county commission, had the key role. Gunnin maintains: "Pruitt, our chairman, deserves the credit of bringing Crunkleton in as the new chief."

Gwinnett had made the sheriff's position that of only an officer of the court, and had taken away the sheriff's police power in 1959, when the Gwinnett Police Department was organized. By 1969, there had been four different heads of the department, though few saw major improvement in policing. Finally, the county commission took action.

It all came to a head in February of 1969. In one clean sweep, the Commission made major changes. After delays for years, the change was quite sudden. The commission asked Guy Stokes (in those days, he was Gwinnett's director of finance and would later become a county commissioner) how long it would take to get the police department payroll completed, giving all present policemen two week's severance, plus their vacation pay. Stokes remembers: "The next day we came in at 6 a.m., made out the checks, and by noon the commissioners had come to the courthouse. They went out on Swanson Drive, where the police headquarters was located, and fired the entire department and handed out the checks."

The commission immediately brought in John Crunkleton to head the police department. Crunkleton in short order, radically changed the department.

Stokes says: "Crunkleton rehired two of the officers on the old force, records keeper Gordon Parker and radio operator Charles Sorrels. He had arranged for the State Patrol to cover the county until he got his force established. He started hiring the next day, but always checked the backgrounds of the applicants." Crunkleton then allowed a few to reapply for their positions, but they had to have a background investigation if they wanted to reapply for the force.

Stokes continues: "John brought ethics and honesty into the Gwinnett police department, something we see to this day. The command staff he hired and promoted have stayed with us for long periods, even to today." One of the first to be hired was Carl White, who would later serve as county police chief.

Wayne Mason adds: "In all the years he was with the county, Crunkleton gave us no problems whatsoever. He was straight up. He was a fine person as well as a fine officer. He knew that politics and law enforcement don't mix. He never went around there."

Reid Merritt gave a similar view: "He knew how to deal with people. He was firm, stern, yet fair. People appreciated that. And it gave them confidence."

Crunkleton originally had a force of 32 people, including 27 sworn officers, two non-sworn, and three investigators. The department has had the continued backing of the county commission, even to this day. In 2008, the department, some 39 years later, had a strength of 729 officers and 391 non-sworn personnel, one of the largest police forces in Georgia.

One of the new chief's early decisions was to institute a distinct Gwinnett Police Academy. White says: "Crunkleton realized back then that it was necessary for the police to have more training than they had in the past." White was among the graduates of the first police academy in Gwinnett in 1972, as the chief used the Academy to establish its own espirit de corps. Gunnin recalls: "His attitude was to lift the county up, to move on, and do better things."

Another of Crunkleton's legacies to the county came early on. Shackelford remembers: "He had the understanding that each policeman needed to be assigned his own vehicle. The strategy was a sound business decision, with no longer having a cruiser rolling three shifts a day. You could fix responsibility. The policemen took pride in having their own vehicles." Crunkleton showed the commission that such a move would eventually pay for itself. It has continued to the present day, giving the county an efficient use of public money. It also gave the police an overnight presence, when the policeman parked his vehicle in the subdivisions or apartment complexes where each lived. It was visible law enforcement within the communities. (Those living outside the county parked their vehicles at fire stations near the county line.)

Maron Buice

Buice says: "Crunkleton sold us on how to pay for the police cars. The money part was difficult, but it was better than have the same car on the road 24 hours a day. There were more plus than minus factors, and John showed us how."

Another Crunkleton innovation: where previously prisoners had helped maintain police vehicles, Crunkleton stopped this practice. "No prisoner is allowed to work on any police vehicle," he ruled. He didn't want the guys who had put the prisoners behind bars to have to drive autos that the prisoners were maintaining. Crunkleton got his own professional mechanical shop for his vehicles.

Crunkleton was police chief up until 1985, when a new administrator wanted to change the leadership. (Crunkleton was a representative for the Regional Organized Crime Information Center after leaving Gwinnett. He died May 26, 1997.)

Today's Gwinnett Police Department continues to be highly regarded, and with virtually no major incidents among its key personnel. It is a legacy and tribute to John Crunkleton's early insistence of high ethical and professional standards in the initial hiring of its officers. (For an official police history, and detail on the 1964 murder of three police officers, see Appendix A-13 and A-14.)

Gwinnett's tie to the poultry industry

Before World War II, Gwinnett was far removed from Metro Atlanta, at least by thought and interest. Gwinnett was then more similar to most rural counties in Georgia, having little industry, dominated by small farms providing vegetables, meat and milk for Metro Atlanta, but earning its farmers more often subsistence living. As most counties, Gwinnett was generally considered not only rural, but also backward, and certainly far removed from major commercial activity or cultural activities.

Chickens fueled a change. After World War II, Gwinnett farmers tended their small farms. By 1950, some were going into "public work" and as they said in those days, "for wages," of some type, that is, working in commercial, or governmental activity with regular paychecks. (Large farms were never numerous in Gwinnett.) Around that time, a few farmers began to consider raising chickens to supplement their income. After all, a small chicken house would fit comfortably on their farm, take up little room, and bring in some regular money, they were hearing from farming friends who ventured into this new concept.

Gordon Sawyer has chronicled how one guy in Gainesville changed much of north Georgia. In his *Northeast Georgia: A History*, Sawyer relates how Jesse Jewell took over his mother's failing feed mill and started poultry farming in North Georgia, which eventually drastically changed North Georgia. Jewell began providing baby chickens ("biddies") to farmers, and then also sold them the grain to feed the chickens, all on credit. Providing credit was important, for up until then, farmers were not extended credit by feed mills for chicken operations. They were considered poor risks. But Jewell had the foresight to see beyond conventional thinking.

Soon, these small farmers found that raising chickens was easier than trying to grow row crops, particularly cotton. They could raise three cycles of chickens a year with far less work, with little regard to weather conditions, and make far more money. In just over a few years, by 1957, Georgia became the leading poultry producing state in the nation.

Jewell took the chicken industry forward. First, he started processing the chickens, creating a vertical operation, from biddy-to-market. More importantly, he took production of chickens one more step, pioneering the freezing and packaging of chicken, which housewives accepted. It was far easier to thaw a chicken than it was to wring a chicken's neck, pluck it, cut out the innards, and finally have something to work with. Jesse Jewell revolutionized the entire chicken industry, and is widely remembered as the father of the modern poultry industry, not just in Georgia, but with major impact in the nation and eventually, the world.

Another pioneer: Charles Vantress

Though Jesse Jewell is considered the genius behind the chicken industry in Georgia, another person had quite an impact in making the poultry industry what it is today, and he did it from Gwinnett County, in Duluth. That person was Charles Vantress, a geneticist. Moving to Gwinnett from California in 1954, he purchased the 409-acre Irvindale Dairy west of Duluth, and included all the land from the western city limits to the Chattahoochee River, between what would become Pleasant Hill Road and Abbotts Bridge Road.

Vantress was seeking to breed better chickens, though he used unconventional methods that poultry specialists thought unusual. His facilities were some of the first modern-day "clean rooms," where employees, upon arrival at the hatchery, took a shower and donned white uniforms to begin work. Vantress concentrated on selecting the genes of the male

Charles Vantress, who produced an improved rooster

chickens ("roosters") to produce a better and more healthy chicken, one he dubbed the "Chicken of Tomorrow." He won for three years running top prizes in poultry contests for roosters, and became well-known in the industry. Vantress kept the male line pure by destroying all female chickens. (Though the hatchery buried many hens, Vantress Farms donated oodles of broilers to Duluth High School, which paid for its football stadium primarily via barbecued chicken sales.)

Vantress employed Japanese workers, who cornered the market in determining the sex of the just-hatched chicks. They would separate the roosters from the females (approximately 12 out of 100 biddies are roosters.) Hulon Hall, who was hired to run the Vantress farm operation in Duluth, notes that later on, geneticists added one gene to the chickens, giving the newly-hatched males a slightly darker color when one day old. This cut costs since regular workers could separate the males from the females easily, instead of employing the higher-priced Japanese workers.

Early on in his research, Vantress found that the Vantress White Male Line chickens produced more white meat than other varieties of chickens, the New Hampshires (a red chicken) or White Rocks or other breeds. And as a result, what color chickens do people see in trucks being transported to chicken processing plants today? Virtually all white chickens. He was also interested in developing a chicken that would grow to maturity in the shortest time, have the lowest cost in feed, and could be easily dressed with mechanical equipment.

Vantress was incredibly successful in improving the breeding stock of his roosters. As Vantress' fame spread in producing superior flocks with his roosters, his prices rose. It was said you could buy breeding roosters from other producers for a dollar each, but soon farmers were gladly paying Vantress $1.65 to $1.80 for a Vantress baby rooster. Put another way by former Duluth Mayor Minor Corley: "The Vantress logo showed the rooster was so dominant that he wore a top hat and smoked a cigar!" The last year the Vantress farm was in operation in Duluth, Hall says, Vantress was shipping 90 percent of the chicken breeding stock in the States. "The only reason we didn't sell more is that we didn't produce any more that year," Hall says. The Vantress legacy lives on, as the Vantress White Male Line still is the dominant line in the industry. (If you eat chicken in the United States or Europe today, chances are you are eating Vantress chicken.)

There were several reasons why the Vantress chicken was superior. One was feed efficiency, for the Vantress chicken produced more white meat, on less feed, and in a shorter time. Prior to the genetically-selected Vantress roosters, a typical chicken would consume 4.5 pounds of feed to produce one pound of live weight. Vantress rooster's offspring consumed less feed and grew faster. Today's broiler chickens that descended from the Vantress stock need less than two pounds of feed to produce a pound of live weight. The time that it took to grow a chicken to market weight has been reduced from 12 weeks to today's six to seven weeks. Today the modern chicken weighs 4.5 pounds at six weeks of age. Sixty years ago it took 12 weeks to produce a 2.75 to 3 pound chicken. Researchers say this also resulted in more tender chicken meat

Besides its Duluth operations, where Vantress employed 125 persons, it also had production operations in Banks County and in Greensboro in Georgia, and also in Springdale, Ark.

Over the years, Vantress had a silent partner who financed the operation -- the Allyn Brothers of Chicago, who among other interests, owned baseball's Chicago White Sox.

Vantress sold his Duluth chicken operations in 1974 to Tyson Foods, which eventually moved most of their Gwinnett activities to Arkansas. To come full circle, at the same time, a businessman in Atlanta, the late Scott Hudgens, purchased the land where Vantress had his operation. One reason for the sale was that a new road, Peachtree Industrial Boulevard, was to split the Vantress operations in half in the mid-1970s. Eventually, Hudgens ended up owning 1,600 acres of land in the Duluth area, including land for the first mall (Gwinnett Place) in the county. The Vantress property west of Duluth was developed by Hudgens and is known now as the River Green Business Park.

Gwinnett becomes a major part of the region

Before 1950, Gwinnett citizens never considered themselves as part of the Metro Atlanta area. After all, going to Atlanta was difficult on two-lane roads. Telephoning Atlanta meant a long distance charge. Not only that, but the county was virtually all rural, sprinkled with several small cities, none over 4,000 population. Even Gwinnett cities were considered a great distance from one another, and a trip to the courthouse in Lawrenceville not only took people from the corners nearly an hour, but was a major trip. People just didn't move around much in those days, but stayed close to home.

An indication that Gwinnett would eventually get included in the Metro Atlanta area came on Oct. 2, 1960, when the cities of Norcross, Duluth and Stone Mountain were added to the Atlanta extended area telephone service area. These three areas then had direct distance dialing, and calling Atlanta was included in their service. However, calling from Duluth, for instance, meant customers first had to dial 476 (GReenleaf-6) before entering the seven digit Atlanta number. The Bell System did not go to all digital numbers until 1960.

On Oct. 14, 1964, Buford and Lawrenceville were included in the metro dialing area, giving most of Gwinnett direct access to the phones of Atlanta. The addition of outlying areas at this time meant that Metro Atlanta's telephone service had the world's largest toll-free dialing area.

A catastrophe took place on June 29, 1968, when the Norcross central office of Southern Bell was destroyed by fire. The company had to set up emergency phone service for the area. On July 16, fast-track construction began on a new building. The office reopened on October 26 on Buford Highway to replace the smaller central office. Another change for phone service came in 1966, when the Loganville area was added to the Metro Atlanta toll-free dialing area.

All this growth was coming, the Census Bureau realized, as it added Gwinnett to the metropolitan Atlanta area in 1958, when the area was expanded to five counties. At that time, the Metro Atlanta area counted 960,000 people. By 2007, the April 1 estimate of the 28 county Atlanta MSA (Metropolitan Statistical Area) was 5,278,904, or 55 percent of the state population of 9,544,750.

All around Atlanta, growth was beginning to be talked about in many circles. *The Atlanta Journal* in those days, said about growth of the entire area: "Atlanta is almost neurotically growth conscious…which is perfectly all right. As long as the city and the metropolitan area want to grow, it probably will."

In 1966, a specific reference to Gwinnett County came in a story in *The Atlanta Constitutio*n, saying: "Gwinnett County, which has suffered under national notoriety, some day may be the prestige area of metropolitan Atlanta." (The notoriety referred to was the slaying of three deputy sheriffs in 1964, and the reputation of Gwinnett as a lawless area prior to that time.)

As Gwinnett began in the 1960s to grow more quickly, its relative proximity to downtown Atlanta, plus Atlanta's growth toward its northern suburbs, made residents feel closer to Atlanta. Add to that the completion Interstate 85 all the way through Gwinnett in 1967, and suddenly, the time and effort to travel into Atlanta was shorter and easier. More and more Gwinnettians were finding work, if not in downtown Atlanta, along its outer suburban areas. (Interstate 285, the perimeter around Atlanta, was completed in 1969, though its northern portion from I-85 to I-75 was finished in 1964.)

Atlanta businessman Frank Neely, who for years headed Rich's Department Store, and who maintained a farm in the Norcross area by the Chattahoochee River near the DeKalb County line, warned Atlanta of what could happen with unregulated growth. He was chairman of the Fulton County Planning Commission, and had in 1941 told the Atlanta chapter of the American Society of Civil Engineers that in 20 years "one million people would be going to and from work in newly developed industrial centers, riding buses to new shops and stores and offices." He further said that "thousands more would be driving from home to half-a-hundred flying fields." (He got that wrong. They wouldn't drive to multiple airports, but thousands would be driving to one airport, Hartsfield International, which would become the busiest airport in the world.)

Neely warned "Unless some master plan could be devised, the city would be choked to death by its own traffic." By 2008, while still growing, Mr. Neely's words remind us of how clogged traffic has become in Metro Atlanta.

(Mr. Neely's granddaughter, Eve Parker Hoffman, would eventually live in the county on the property her grandfather once farmed, Neely Farms, now primarily a high-end subdivision. She served as a member of the Gwinnett County School Board and afterward became active in statewide educational circles.)

Atlanta Regional Commission

In 1947, the Georgia General Assembly created the Metropolitan Planning Commission (MPC), the first publicly funded regional planning agency in the nation. The MPC produced the first master plan for Atlanta's metropolitan area, which at that time consisted only of the City of Atlanta and Fulton and DeKalb counties.

In 1960, the Atlanta Region Metropolitan Planning Commission (ARMPC) replaced the MPC. ARMPC, as it was known, added Cobb, Gwinnett and Clayton counties to the region. In 1971, the Georgia General Assembly recognized the increasing growth of the region and it created the Atlanta Regional Commission (ARC) to succeed ARMPC. Gwinnett County became a member of the Atlanta Regional Commission in 1971.

The ARC is governed by a 39-member board: 23 elected officials and 15 private citizens, plus a representative of the Georgia Department of Community Affairs. Each chairman of the county commission is on the ARC, plus one mayor from each county chosen by a caucus of mayors in that county. The mayor of Atlanta is automatically on the council, plus two more mayors from Fulton County, one from the northern part and another from the southern part of Fulton. One city council member represents the City of Atlanta.

Commission chairmen who have represented Gwinnett on the ARC have included:

W.R. Pruitt, 1971-72; Bill Atkinson, 1973-76; Wayne Mason, 1977-80; Charles Ashworth, 1981-84; Lillian Webb, 1985-92; Wayne Hill, 1993-2004; and Charles Bannister, 2005-present. Other elected officials on the ARC have included Bill Fortune from Lawrenceville, 1971-74; Lillian Webb from Norcross, 1975-84; W. Emmett Clower, Snellville, 1985-99; and Philip Beard of Buford, 2000-present.

Citizen members have included Claude Roberts, 1971-91; Rick Porter, 1992-2001; Jimmy Brannan, 1992-93; Rick Chandler, 2000-2002; Harry Thompson, 1994-95; Rick Panyik, 1995; Scott LeCraw, 1996-2001; Judy Waters, 2001-present; Dave Williams, 2002-2007; Kerry Armstrong, 2008-present; and Julie Keeton Arnold, 2002-present.

The only Gwinnettian who has served as chairman of the ARC was Wayne Hill, from 1998 to 2002.

RC&D project provides benefits

Land practices have not always been scientifically managed. When a future president, Franklin Delano Roosevelt, saw the state's worn-out cotton fields and miles of eroded gullies while visiting Georgia, it registered in his mind. This was prior to Roosevelt becoming president, when his family owned land in Georgia. Years later, Roosevelt would return to Georgia and seek the curative waters of Warm Springs for his polio. He continued to see the problems that poor agricultural practices had created and the poverty of farms in Georgia. Once he became president in 1933, he began to put into place environmentally sound programs to restore the land.

Among Roosevelt's early programs was the Soil Erosion Service, which eventually became the Soil Conservation Service.

A soil scientist, Hugh Hammond Bennett of North Carolina, is considered to be the father of the Soil Conservation Service. He felt that the wealth of a nation could be seen in its soil and its ability to grow row crops. Bennett successfully promoted the passage of the Soil Conservation Act of 1935. While testifying before the Congress to improve conditions, dark descended on Washington in the middle of the day, as clouds of dust from the west turned the day into night. This assisted in making Congress more aware of the problem of soil erosion. When the bill establishing the Soil Conservation Service passed, the state of Georgia waited, out of courtesy to Mr. Bennett, for North Carolina to officially establish the first soil conservation district in 1937. Georgia immediately followed, eventually placing all 159 counties in one of 40 such districts. Gwinnett was included in the organization of the Upper Ocmulgee River Soil and Water Conservation District in 1938. A key factor in this program was controlling erosion of upland, and controlling flooding of lowlands, with effort to eliminate or reduce these hazards to a minimum. In 1994, the name of the Soil Conservation Service was changed to the Natural Resources Conservation Service, to focus on the agency's conservation mission to encompass water, air, plants, and animals in addition to soil.

How agricultural Gwinnett became prepared for the onslaught of growth partially came about when Gwinnett civic leaders in the 1960s recognized the inevitability that growth was coming. At one time, Gwinnett was the third largest cotton-producing county in Georgia. But after World War II, with its proximity to Atlanta, it was obvious that the city and its suburbs would grow, particularly northward. Altogether, some 279,000 acres in Gwinnett were defined to be in different watersheds, the largest being the Yellow River watershed, composed of 104,929 acres.

Gwinnett County commissioners, back in 1954, applied to the U.S. Agricultural Department for monies to help control flood waters, through the Watershed Protection and Flood Prevention, included in Public Law 566. Beginning in 1965, monies were included out of Congress to begin building a series of dams in Gwinnett for watershed protection and flood control.

Funding was eventually approved for six dams from PL 566 funds. These dams, their funding and when built included:

Dam	*Basin Acreage*	*Cost*	*Year*
Brushy Fork Creek No. 3	1,665	$28,792	1965
Brushy Fork Creek No. 22	745	$32,446	1965
Brushy Fork Creek No. 25	832	$35,565	1965
Brushy Fork Creek No. 21	1,030	$32,800	1967
Upper Mulberry River No. 11	4,100	$165,873	1976
Upper Mulberry River No. 7	1,798	$155,281	1980

About the time the funding was announced for these dams, an idea initiated by a Chamber of Commerce Agricultural Committee began brewing. Gwinnett became the only urban county in the nation to be included in a pilot program to study its land resources and to begin an early planning program for the quick growth the leaders saw coming. The pilot project, to be known as the Resource, Conservation and Development (RC&D) program, was out of the federal Food and Agriculture Act of 1962 suggested by Agricultural Secretary Orville Freeman. The program played a role in smoothing the way toward urbanization of the county. There were ten pilot projects throughout the nation, with the Gwinnett program the only one in the South.

An RC&D Dam on the Yellow River above Collins Hill Park
Photo from the Gwinnett Dept. of Water Resources.

Key people in Gwinnett had recognized that the county was in the path of inevitable growth. These included the county commissioners, top leaders of the Gwinnett Chamber of Commerce, and district supervisors of the Upper Ocmulgee River Soil and Water Conservation District. David Kistner, chairman of the Chamber for two years in 1962-63, was involved with many forward-thinking projects, and was also a supervisor of the Soil Conservation District, while operating Berkmere Farms in the southern end of the county. Kistner, along with Dr. W.A. Hartmann, the Chamber's agricultural committee chair, and the director of the Atlanta Metropolitan Planning Commission, Glenn Bennett, all understood that Gwinnett was about to face a period of extended growth. One report about growth said: "It is not meaningful to consider Gwinnett County apart from the region, and it is essential that Gwinnett's role in the region be clarified, established and understood by all.... (and that) resources, conservation and development be studied."

The three traveled to Athens, contacting the Soil Conservation Service office, and applied for the new federal program. Gwinnett became the only urban county in the program included in a "metropolitan sprawl" area in the nation. The federal funding for the Gwinnett RC&D Council amounted to $2.16 million over the initial 10 years, a relatively low figure for the scope of the program. These funds were primarily for technical salaries. Local input was $6.5 million, with much of this being "in-kind" contributions from individual landowners granting rights-of-way and easements in return for technical assistance on watershed lake construction. Kistner, quoted in a report in *The Atlanta Constitution*, said: "It (the program) brings together the latest governmental services in a package deal so that rural and urban people can avail themselves of them."

Among the questions that the organizers were seeking to understand back in the mid-1960s were:

- What are the sources for new markets and income for farmers?
- What should the county do to produce new revenues to finance the services so vitally needed?
- What are the effects of different taxation policies on land in the county?
- What new tax structures would be available?
- How can grass roots community action programs be organized?
- How can present agencies be used more effectively to achieve the proper relationship between the county and its surrounding region?

Among the reasons that the leaders listed as needing to start such planning studies was that Gwinnett's county seat "…is within 30 miles of Atlanta, with much of the first priority urban and industrial area within 16 miles of Atlanta." In a 1966 report, these early organizers recognized that the population was expected to "double by 1983." They were a little off. The 1965 population of Gwinnett was 56,125. By the year the study mentioned, 1983, there were 205,700 people in Gwinnett. This verifies just how strong the need for early planning in Gwinnett was, and indicates that the leaders of the county in its infancy of growth were seeking to be ready for what was to come.

The primary objective of the planning program was to outline a path toward orderly development in land use changes from a rural to an urban-rural environment. The efforts were recognizing that cropland was decreasing rapidly, and farmers were faced with converting to non-agricultural uses. The timeline for the work was not short, a minimum of 10 years. As the change came in Gwinnett, additional resources became available, initially through the RC&D Council, to help guide the county in its new role.

Controlling erosion

Newcomers to Gwinnett after 1980 seldom hear of any flooding in the county, but this was not always the case. Water runoff and soil erosion in rainy seasons once were routine---such as flooding of the Yellow River south of Lawrenceville, sometimes resulting in the closing of U.S. Highway 29 because of water over the highway. In those days, rainwater rolling off the low hills from the Eastern Continental Divide had no impediment, washed away topsoil, and caused periodic flooding and sedimentation problems.

One key purpose of the RC&D program in Gwinnett was to apply practical planning procedures in an area where growth was anticipated to help make an orderly transition from a rural to an urban area. After seeing the results over more than 40 years, the program must be deemed a success in Gwinnett, as it smoothed the way in many different arenas, becoming one of the fastest growing counties in the nation.

The program aimed at analyzing the physical and human resources of the county in nine general areas of conservation and development. They were:

- Soils;
- Land use and treatment;
- Water;
- Watershed protection and flood prevention.
- Forest improvement and management;
- Fish and wildlife development;
- Recreation;
- Industrial development;
- Education.

The overall goal in Gwinnett was to tackle the complex problems associated with land and people, problems that cluttered any transition from rural to urban living.

Lloyd Harris of Bleckley County was hired to run the Gwinnett RC&D program. The initial effort was to assemble information on the county's resources. The result was a 66 page book outlining the nine topics. In land use treatment, for instance, the report studied population trends, farm and non-farm ownership acreages, building projects and erosion, sediment control and drainage.

A chapter on water pointed out major problems, such as inadequate distribution of domestic water supplies in some parts of the county, at a time when the county water system was in its infancy, and facing financial problems. One reason: its expensive distribution lines had to traverse many areas where there were low concentrations of population and users, as it reached out to distant cities and their population concentration.

Other aspects of the early report suggested planning and zoning proposals to help the county avoid flood problems, and addressed problems farmers would face should they decide to sell their properties or put it to non-farm uses.

Much of the initial effort was best seen in the construction of six dams in Gwinnett County, mostly in the 1960s and 1970s, plus work from other federal-assistance programs in building dams in other parts of the county. Altogether, 12 watersheds were impacted..

The six dams funded by the RC&D project and the size of their drainage basins were:

Dam	***Basin Acreage***	***Cost***	***Year***
Yellow River	1,306	$61,109	1966
No Business Creek	2,611	$76,204	1967
Yellow River	1,933	$49,027	1968

Gwinnett County: A Little Above Atlanta

Dam	*Basin Acreage*	*Cost*	*Year*
Little Suwanee Creek	3,283	$49,027	1968
Wildcat Creek	3,674	$85,921	1970
Little Suwanee Creek	1,734	$92,092	1973
Tribble Mill-02	661	$574,278	1985
Tribble Mill-01	5,888	$1.246 million	1990

The dams were designed and constructed so that during the rainy seasons, they would collect and store the runoff, then slowly release this stored runoff over several weeks, instead of the runoff from the rainfall immediately flooding lower areas. These dams were built primarily for flood control to protect agricultural lands, prior to Gwinnett having a different annual crop----of new houses. As Gwinnett became a haven for new homes, many in these areas protected by the RC&D dams, the importance in conservation of resources and soil improvements, and in acceptance of the area in which to buy a home, became readily apparent.

Another major effort of the RC&D program in Gwinnett was allocating some $2 million in the 1980s toward the development of Tribble Mill Park. This 718-acre park obtained a full-time engineer and staff to design and supervise construction of a 100-acre and a 40-acre recreational lake.

Meanwhile, the initial "pilot" RC&D Council began to be expanded. In 1994, three other counties, Rockdale, Newton and Jasper, were added to the Gwinnett program, and the name was changed to the Upper Ocmulgee River Resource Conservation and Development Council, Inc. In 1995, Henry County became a member of the Council.

The Upper Ocmulgee River Council took the lead in 1997 in spearheading adoption of a program, which would eventually go statewide, the "Wheels-to-Work" program. This program assisted low-income Georgians by providing transportation to jobs. This program was initially begun from a $10 million fund created by the Georgia General Assembly. The 11 RC&D Councils partnered with the Georgia Environmental Facilities Authority (GEFA) in administering the program. It allowed individual workers to get a zero interest loan for purchase of low-cost used vehicles for transportation to work, improving local economies "one family at a time" in the process. The Upper Ocmulgee River Council assisted similar councils in Alabama, South Carolina and Tennessee in starting similar programs.

The original grant from the GEFA to the Upper Ocmulgee River Council was for $53,700 in 1997, with other grants totaling $92,000 through 2000. However, in 2000-2001, the General Assembly provided $514,076 to the Council for its program, through a program administered by the Department of Family and Children's Services.

Over the years, more than 200 individuals have been granted loans for these automobiles by the Upper Ocmulgee River Council, usually for 24-36 months, which they pay back in $150-225 monthly increments. Repayment of the loans from existing clients allows the program to fund other individuals for loans. The Council also raises funds from private sources to augment the program.

A more recent program, funded in 2000 for a three-year period, harkened back to the basic concept of the RC&D pilot project. The scope of this $565,115 project was to improve conditions in and around streams. It was a program funded by the Environmental Protection Agency to increase stream buffers at sites in Georgia. Some 29 buffer demonstration projects were built on private pastures, crop and forest land. The program cost-shares with landowners to fence cows out of streams, move back crop rows and widen silvicultural (forested area) buffer widths in 29 different counties throughout the state. Though the program was run by the Upper Ocmulgee RC&D District, none of these were in Gwinnett.

With the dams built earlier as part of the RC&D program aging, some being more than 30 years old, in 2002, the Gwinnett County storm water program began improvements to these dams, as required by the Georgia Safe Dam Act. The county had done maintenance on these dams, but for upgrading the dams, funds came through the Natural Resource Conservation Service. Altogether, the federal agency puts in 65 percent of the cost, and the county funds 35 percent. The cost of the rehabilitation of these 14 dams was $18.4 million, with the federal government providing $9.9 million and Gwinnett County contributing $8.5 million. It has a schedule to be completed in 2009.

Gwinnett leaders in project

The Upper Ocmulgee River RC&D project in Gwinnett has been one with a local leadership team, and presently includes a total of 20 individuals from the five counties. Those from Gwinnett who have been president of the program since its inception include:

- R.L. Vansant, 1964
- David Kistner, 1965-69
- Hughel Harrison, 1970-71
- Ellis Britt, 1972-87
- J.W. Benefield, 1988-90
- Robert Powell, 1991-2006
- Ellis Lamme, 2007-present.

In 2008, the Gwinnett representatives on the Council, besides Ellis Lamme of Dacula, included Jeremy Means and Jonathan Semerjian and Mark Brock of Lawrenceville, and Jim Scarbrough of Norcross.

The coordinators staffing the Upper Ocmulgee River RC&D office since inception were Lloyd Harris, 1964-86; Carol Harvey, 1986-1993; David Hinson, 1994-2006; and Jerome Brown, 2006-present.

Gwinnett has had its own Soil and Water Conservation District since the State of Georgia restructured the former Atlanta Soil and Water Conservation District in 1981. The Gwinnett District is one of seven Districts in the metro Atlanta area that is part of the Georgia Soil and Water Conservation Commission's Region III office. The other counties included are Clayton, Cobb, DeKalb, Fulton, Henry and Rockdale. The Region III office is in Conyers, where Russell Tonning is the regional representative.

The Gwinnett District has the distinction of being the first community in Georgia to pass an erosion and sedimentation ordinance. It also helped develop a new model for evaluating erosion and sedimentation efforts at the local level.

Three persons are elected by the county to serve on the Gwinnett District Board of Supervisors, while two are appointed. In 2008, elected members included Chairman Mark Brock, Bob Powell and Ellis Lamme. Appointed to serve by the county were Connie Wiggins and Jim Steele.

Nearly all of the work of the District centers on assisting local governments, both city and county, in the implementation of erosion control practices, to protect the state's streams and waterways. The District is an agency of the state. Under Georgia's Erosion and Sedimentation Control Law, the District, with the assistance of the Commission and NRCS, conducts overviews of local governments' erosion control programs. Anyone applying for a land disturbance permit must submit erosion control plans to the District before a local government can issue a land-disturbance permit. The District has in place an agreement with several municipal governments in Gwinnett County whereby the District has allowed those governments to review the erosion control plans in-house rather than sending the plans to the District for review. The District is an appeal agency when permits are denied by local governments prior to developers obtaining a land-disturbance permit. The District is also involved in an educational role with contractors and developers to insure good soil and water conservation practices.

Alcohol and the Gwinnett water system

It may come as a surprise to some people how and for what reason Gwinnett County government authorized the sale of beer. It was a pure emergency measure----of all things----to save the severely-underfinanced Gwinnett Water System. In effect, Gwinnett commissioners virtually turned beer into water.

Think about the Gwinnett of the mid-1950s. The county population was less than 40,000. Though county officials felt growth was coming, they did not recognize how quickly people would flock to Gwinnett and put pressures on the county for many services.

County officials realized that they needed a water distribution system to meet the growth. But back then, with Gwinnett a large county with a spread-out population, completing a first-rate water system would take time. After all, the best places to gain revenue from the system -- the population centers of the county -- were relatively small themselves. Plus, even the cities would produce little revenue when, or if, they joined the county system. (Most of them used their own wells back then.) Then, too, the cities were from five to ten miles from one another, and in addition, the far-flung, sparsely-populated areas between the towns would produce limited revenue.

As a result, any water system that the county operated was virtually assured of having meager revenues to offset the high cost of establishing the water plant and distribution lines.

Gwinnett commissioners had employed Vinson and Company, consulting engineers, of Atlanta, to appraise the situation for them. They issued a report in 1955 outlining how the county could go about funding and constructing such a system. ("Engineering Report, Water Supply Treatment and Distribution, Gwinnett County, Georgia.")

They pointed out how much of the county was served by individual wells on private properties, and that the city systems also got their water from wells. Much of their report emphasizes how a drought, which had happened in the area the year before, in 1954, could impact homeowners, and no doubt, this influenced the engineer's findings. Norcross had abandoned its wells early, in 1947, in favor of purchasing water from DeKalb County.

The engineers anticipated that the City of Loganville would also be served by the system. It had been operating its own system, supplied by two wells and a spring, pumping 70,000 gallons per day to 214 customers (1954). But in 1956, it found its wells were virtually dry, with the Georgia National Guard having to provide emergency water to its citizens. As a result, Loganville signed on early to be supplied by the Gwinnett water system, as did Lilburn, which had a critical water shortage because of the drought. These two cities were singled out to be the first two served by the new water lines.

The engineers proposed a water treatment plant on the Chattahoochee River in Duluth, 10 miles below Buford Dam. Engineers forecasted 16,050 customers by 1960, up to 22,800 customers by 1970, and 25,400 customers in 1980. The system would be financed by the county selling "Water Revenue Anticipation Certificates" (bonds) of up to $7 million. And, based on the projected customers of the system, including most of its cities, the county would earn a surplus each year to operate and pay off the bonds. Vinson and Company even said to the commissioners that it thought the projections for the county water system "…by the time the system is in operation, is quite conservative."

After all, they said, with the projected growth, it would be "very improbable" for wells in Gwinnett to supply more than four million gallons of water a day, when Gwinnett citizens would clearly need more than eight million gallons of water a day by 1985.

The engineers also said that lack of adequate water supply in the rural areas combined with the growing demands by the population for a better water supply system "leads us to believe that our estimate of 5,810 connections in the rural and residential non-urban areas of Gwinnett County by the time the system is in operation is quite conservative."

The consulting engineers also found interest from developers in having a Gwinnett County water system feed into the many new houses. One letter came in 1955 from E.R. Hawkins of Atlanta, who would develop Liberty Heights in Norcross. He sent with his letter another letter from First Federal Savings and Loan Association saying that they would supply construction and permanent loans for the 306 houses that Hawkins was proposing to build. That August another project, one off Pleasant Hill Road called "Sweetwater Estates," guaranteed that "at least" 300 customers would desire water in that subdivision.

Hearing this advice and counsel from their professional engineers, the Gwinnett Commissioners acted. They sold water bonds on Oct. 1, 1955. The amount was $5,925,000, though $7 million was authorized by a commission resolution. ("The balance of $1,075,000 certificates authorized to be sold could be issued subject to the restrictions contained in the authorizing resolution.")

The offices of the water system opened, with Frances Fortune of Lawrenceville its first employee. Engineering drawings were contracted for the plant and lines. Work began on the system in 1956. It took nearly three years before the water plant near Duluth was complete. The plant was to produce seven million gallons of water per day, and could, if operated 24 hours a day, produce10 million gallons a day. It was expected to meet Gwinnett's water needs for 15 years. The manager of the plant was Noye H. Nesbit of Norcross, a retiree from Standard Oil Co., who previously was in charge of that company's marine pumping operations in Savannah.

Eventually the system began extending distribution lines into the county. A 20-inch line was laid eastward to Lawrenceville. Other lines spread out to Norcross to the south, and toward Suwanee, Sugar Hill and Buford to the north. From Lawrenceville, a 12-inch line ran south toward Lilburn. The Gwinnett system bought its initial water pipe and hydrants from DeKalb County. The DeKalb system had previously piped water to parts of Gwinnett near Tucker and Norcross, which the Gwinnett system soon was serving.

Altogether, the county water system laid water distribution lines in many parts of the county. The initial lines included 180 miles of water mains in the county. Yet there was one consideration that the engineers apparently failed to take into account when projecting their proposal: every mile of water line in the county, and many miles even in the city, went past homes where most residents had their own wells. They could not see the wisdom of attaching onto the county water system, and having to pay for this installation, plus pay a monthly water bill, when they already had what many of them considered as essentially "free" water from their own well.

Therefore, the projections that the engineers made of the number of residents who would become water customers were far lower than the early estimates of people who would get their water from the new county system. A report in 1957 showed that a 1956 estimate anticipated 8,262 potential customers, while there were only 3,323 customers at the time of the report. The report blamed engineers for the exaggerated user estimate, citing "gross error" in the estimates. It concluded that the system was not taking in enough revenue to the bonds and interest when due. This report came from the new engineering firm of Havens and Emerson, whom the bondholders insisted to be used as the engineers for the system.

As the early projections for customers and revenue didn't come in as anticipated, the system got "behind the eight ball" from the beginning. There were many other problems with the fledging system.

Among them:

- Water rates were too low to provide the margins the system needed.
- The water pressures were low in certain areas.
- The system did not have enough customers.
- The system was having problems meeting its interest payments.
- Too, there were problems with the system's original contractor for building the system. Commissioners authorized an Atlanta law firm to seek redress.
- In addition, there had been problems with the piping of the system, which the attorney was also handling.
- Before it was all over, the county would also sue one of its attorneys that it had paid $93,000, seeking to recover $43,000, claiming that "fees paid to him were excessive and unreasonable, at least by that amount."

All these problems within the water system got the attention of the March, 1958 term of the Gwinnett Grand Jury, which recommended an investigation of the system. It said it found "gross mismanagement, organization and expenditure of funds" and recommended civil action. It sought possible recovery of $224,000 or more. Based on these recommendations, records show that "certain suits have been filed."

Paul Dover, O.D. Cain and Weldon B. Archer served on the commission from 1949 to 1956. Cain and Archer ran for re-election in 1956, but lost; Dover, who was chairman of the board, did not seek re-election.

In 1958, a civil action was filed against the three previous commissioners, Weldon Archer, O.D. Cain and F.P. Dover, that they "willfully, wantonly, unlawfully and malicefully conspired and confederated together to require Buchanan (Pipeline Company of Birmingham, Ala.) to pay to them a percent of sums by Gwinnett County to contractors for its water system as condition for performance of said contract." The sums totaled four percent of the payments, or $159,073.08, to be paid "secretly and in cash." Legal wrangling went on for years. However, the case never came to trial, and was closed after five years of dormancy.

The purchasers of the bonds that financed the early water system were headed by Connecticut General, a large insurance firm. Getting concerned about what they were hearing about the Gwinnett water system, the insurance company retained Atlanta attorneys John Mobley and his partner, Sumter Kelley, in 1956 to look out for their interests. Mobley, in an interview in 1997, recounted what was going on at the time.

"When we were selected, the water system was in a terrible shape. Plastic pipe was everywhere, and there were constant blow-outs. The system was often "on the blink," to the point that I got monthly reports, and they always showed the number of blow-outs. We inherited a poorly-constructed system."

Years later, Mobley told the story in a letter in 1993 updating the history of the system to County Commission Chairman Wayne Hill, pointing out that the system was improperly designed. "The water system was a gravity design flow system, composed in the main of plastic pipe laid uphill. The former commissioners who had approved the bond issue had been indicted by a federal grand jury. The improperly designed plastic pipe system has been poorly constructed. Numerous fire hydrants has been installed throughout the county and not one was connected to the water system."

Connecticut General, as the firm holding the bonds on the system, also insisted that the system get new consulting engineers, and suggested Havens and Emerson of New York. Glen Abplanalp came as their man on the job, "a superb engineer," according to Mobley.

In effect, the Gwinnett water system was in technical default, since it was behind on its debt service. Mobley says: "We were really robbing Peter to pay Paul, though the system would occasionally get more money, like $50,000 from the bondholders, to shore up the system. We were just trying to keep it afloat. When we finally got the water lines to the Southern Railroad property near Norcross, we were able to get some commercial customers, and we gradually did better, and the system started to make a little money."

Mobley says that the new engineers devised an interim system for replacing plastic pipes as they burst with steel pipes. "But all along, the bondholder's representative normally would call me once or twice a month to obtain progress reports. He would not deal with the county directly, but only through me. In no event would we permit any expansion of the water system except in accordance with the plans and recommendations of the engineers, this despite political pressure from the commissioners to extend the system to sparsely inhabited areas of the county.

"Often Glen Abplanalp would call me and tell me we needed pipe of maybe 12 inches. I would ask him how much more it would cost to lay a 24-inch pipe, and he would answer

'Not much more.' What we were doing, of course, was anticipating the growth of the county. Later on, one of the commissioners, Wayne Mason, was about the only one who could see the potential growth in Gwinnett.

"Meanwhile, the voters of the county approved a General Obligation bond issue to help the system. Later, we knew we had to have an added water supply, in addition to the Duluth plant. I showed the commissioners that the ridge line ran near Lake Lanier, and that became a second source of water for us, when Bo Callaway, as the secretary of the Army, signed a contract with the Corps of Engineers for a Gwinnett intake into Lake Lanier to buy water."

(Callaway signed the authorization on July 2, 1973 at Fort McPherson shortly after being named Army Secretary. The signing came after three years of negotiations between the county commission and the Corps of Engineers. Commission Chairman Bill Atkinson and Commissioner Ray Gunnin were present for the signing. Gunnin said that "A stipulation in the Congressional Act creating the Buford Dam project" served as the legal basis for Gwinnett being allowed to take water from the Lake.)

Another person who remembers the events around this time is Homer Stark, whose father, Hope Stark, was county attorney. (Homer Stark himself later was county attorney before he was named a Superior Court judge, where he sat for 22 years.) Stark says that naming of Havens and Emerson as the consulting engineer was "...the most fortunate thing that happened to our system. Glen Alplanalp was both an attorney and engineer, and had good experience working with governments. They stopped the system from extending 3-inch water lines in the county, and insisted on 6-8 inch lines as a minimum everywhere. The system had to get the approval for them to extend or change lines. It put a lid on political matters, for the county had to have a feasibility study to show it would produce more revenue for the system. You couldn't just lay pipe anywhere. It was an awkward system, but controlled, and got our system out of problems."

Over the years, the county refinanced the debt on the system several times. "In the early days," says Mobley, "we were doing it to postpone the debt service, for we did not have the money, and would not have been able to pay the principal and interest. Later on, we refinanced to remove restrictive covenants on the system, and also to get a lower rate of interest."

During the same time, says Mobley, Connecticut General was going through a bad time themselves. "They would call down here and ask how the water system was. I would invite them down, and they always declined, saying that's what they had me down here doing. They bailed us out of situations, and were pleased at what eventually happened. We said that it was done through 'main force and awkwardness.' We could not have done that today. Back then, Gwinnett was isolated, a two-lane-road county, with only one hotel, the Holiday Inn at Suwanee. We even met in the hallways of the old Courthouse for there was no other space to meet. The water system was 'on the blink' for a long time. But we finally got to going better."

It was January, 1959 when the county issued another $750,000 in water bonds after voters of the county approved it in the September, 1958 referendum. Cited in the reason for the bonds was the fact that "the Merchandise Mart and Industrial Park have not materialized." But matters would get worse. (See Merchandise Mart, page 198.)

The big problem was that the system just did not have enough customers, though its water lines passed enough homes of potential customers. In 1960, the Gwinnett system had laid mains totaling 1,053,280 feet, or just about 200 miles of water lines. But then it had only 3,637 "rural, residential and commercial customers connected to the system." (With 43,541 people in Gwinnett then, or about 10,000 households, that meant the water system was serving only 36 percent of county homes. Of course, not all homes had water lines passing nearby. Still, the situation was far from what was anticipated.)

The under 4,000 customers being served alone is enough to understand the financial problems that this would bring on, when the best estimate of professionals five years earlier had been that more than 16,050 (residential and businesses) customers would be tied onto the system. No wonder the system was having financial problems!

Scrappy Crowe of Lawrenceville, who worked for the system from 1958 until retiring in 1984, recalled "When they first floated bonds for the water lines, we virtually had nearly nothing in revenue to pay for the bonds. We had an understanding that after the system got started, it would soon be refinanced." That happened as current bondholders protected their investment by propping up the system with additional financing.

The system reached a crisis in 1961, when the Water Authority was about to run out of money. Havens and Emerson emphasized to the commission that the Authority, without drastic action, "will default on its obligations in Fiscal 1962." The engineers recommended finding additional funds by exploring "every possible way of lending monetary assistance to the System, and explore with present bondholders, the feasibility of deferring early bond maturities." They added that, should the county default on its bonds, it would certainly harm the bondholders, "but (in) the long term, far reaching damages which the County will suffer, outweighs greatly any bondholder's possible monetary loss." They even suggested a default would harm not only Gwinnett County and its Water Department, but would increase the cost of Gwinnett school financing, and adversely affect adjoining counties and perhaps even the state. It "would create a credit cloud over the County which will take many years to dispel."

Clearly, action was needed. But what? The eventual solution astounded many Gwinnettians, upset quite a few, and changed the way of life in Gwinnett forever.

Beer, please!

In March of 1956, the three commissioners in office when the new water system was started, Weldon Archer, O.D. Cain and Paul Dover, were about to go out of office. Coming into office in 1957 were Uhland Freeman, Dr. W.A. Elinburg Jr. and Gordon Franchisuer. Shortly after coming to office, Franchisuer died, and Minor M. Corley was elected to fill his unexpired term. The three, Freeman, Elinburg and Corley, were re-elected in 1961 to serve four more years.

It was Uhland Freeman, Wayne Mason remembers, who got the idea which eventually saved the system from default. Freeman suggested licensing the sale of beer within the county, giving the county the revenue to guarantee against the water system bondholders. Previously, Gwinnett County had been a dry county, with no alcoholic beverage sales. The commission used an obscure law that allowed them to issue licenses to sell beer. The commissioners did not call a referendum on this, but by resolution legalized the sale of beer in the county.

Prior to their passing the ordinance allowing the sale of beer, word got out what the commission was intending to do and the expected uproar came. There were several meetings between the commission and those opposed to licensing the sale of beer. Many opponents to beer sales wanted a referendum on the subject. The commissioners said they had no power to institute a referendum "at taxpayer's expense," and anyway, such a referendum was not binding.

John Mobley says: "The county eventually used the beer tax revenue, and whatever they could find, to pay the debt and operations of the system. Back when they voted the beer tax to pledge against the bonds, I told them that it was illegal, but of course, the bondholders didn't care. In effect, the commissioners 'gave their word' that bailing out the bondholders is what the revenue from the beer tax would go toward, and it helped give life to the system."

Moving to legalize the sale of beer in the county was a brilliant move, by a hard-nosed commission, since Gwinnett citizens were already drinking beer that they left the county to buy, giving the alcoholic beverage revenue to adjoining counties. By legalizing beer sales, the revenue would stay within the county, and in this case, get the county out of difficult times with guaranteeing its water bonds and insure the water system's viability, though this was merely an agreement, and not legally binding on the county.

Indeed, the commissioners, by guaranteeing the beer tax revenues to save the water system, had turned beer into water for its 4,500 Gwinnett water customers by then.

Freeman went to New York to get the plan approved by bondholders. The plan was to tax each 12-ounce can of beer five cents. The sale of beer became legal in Gwinnett on March 13, 1961, with each five cents per can starting an immediate revenue stream for the county. Revenue was projected to bring in $60,000 that first year, but collections actually totaled $85,000 from the beer tax in 1962. Minor Corley, who was a commissioner at the time, remembered in a 1989 interview. "That got us over the hump," he said, in having funds to guarantee the water department revenue bonds. (Interestingly, as attorney Mobley points out, it would have been technically illegal for the beer revenues from general government to prop up the water bonds of the Water Authority. However, the beer revenues were never needed for this purpose, as revenues began to rise from Gwinnett's growth for the Authority, avoiding a possible property owner suit. Think, too, of the disastrous effect to Gwinnett's financial reputation had the county been tainted with bankruptcy of its water system.)

The second year (1963), beer tax revenue for the county amounted to $184,000. By 2007, the annual revenue from malt beverages ("beer tax") brought Gwinnett County some $4.1 million. The total alcohol-related revenues for 2007 (beer, wine, distilled spirits, pouring licenses, and fees) was $8.8 million. (See Appendix B, page 770 for details.)

Wayne Mason says of the bold plan to save the water system. "Uhland had the sense to put a tax on beer, and guarantee that money for the water bonds. Without the revenue from beer, the county did not have enough water system revenue to pay the debt service, much less the principal, on the bonds."

Mason continues: "It took considerable political courage by Freeman, Elinburg and Corley to pass the beer ordinance in the county. They caught the devil from many."

And what happens in such situations? Yes, the three sitting commissioners fell at the polls. All three faced opposition, and were forced into a runoff for their posts. However, all lost in the runoffs to three newcomers to politics, as all three incumbents were replaced in the 1965 Democratic primary. The votes:

Felton Thompson 6,126;	W.A. Elinburg Jr., 4,548.
Ray Morgan, 6,287;	Uhland Freeman, 4,377.
Dudge Pruitt, 5,364;	Minor Corley, 5,261.

Yet the trio of commissioners who lost had found a way to save the county water system The fuel, if you can think of water as fuel, made the county ready for the explosive growth that Gwinnett County has seen ever since. Without the bold action of Freeman, Elinburg and Corley in propping up the county finances by having the beer revenue available, and unofficially making sure that the water system was protected, Gwinnett jumped over a big hurdle, and continued its early growth. Armed with this new set-up, Gwinnett continued with a progressive reputation. The three commissioners deserve to be remembered, if nothing else, for this positive and distinctive move, though it cost them at the polls.

With beer approved for sale in the county, Gwinnett commissioners followed with approval of the sale of wine on Sept. 29, 1970. During the early growth of the county in the 70s and 80s, the sale of distilled spirits of any kind (bottled liquor or mixed drinks) was against the law throughout Gwinnett. Some felt this was the reason that no major restaurants or hotels would consider locating in the county.

However, before the county got around to voting on the question of distilled spirits, three Gwinnett cities saw an opportunity.

These individual cities, first Lilburn, then Suwanee, and finally, Duluth, voted to allow packaged liquor. The vote in Lilburn on March 12, 1977 was close, 280-251. With the three cities' voters approving packaged distilled spirits sales, major tax revenues came to these three cities. Here's an indication of what this revenue is for these cities, with a history of when it happened.

City	*Beer Passed*	*Package Stores Passed*	*2007 Alcohol $*
Duluth	Oct. 13, 1969	April 11, 1977	$ 817,815
Lilburn	April 9, 1973	March 12, 1977	$ 505,031
Suwanee	May 27, 1974	April 26, 1980	$ 973,775

Then in 1982, Braselton approved the sale of alcoholic beverages in packaged form, along with wine manufacturing, and wine sales by the glass on premises. After all, Braselton was the site of the Chateau Elan winery, and eventually, its world-class Inn. Later, on July 21, 1992, liquor by the drink passed in Braselton by a vote of 73-24. The first license was issued to Chateau Elan Ltd. However, the first "true package store" did not open in Braselton until 2001.

Braselton gains considerable income from alcoholic beverages. For 2007, the town's revenue from these sales amounted to $486,246.

As might be expected, there was considerable rancor in some cities among the voters when proposals came for the sale of bottled spirits. In Suwanee, for instance, one pastor, Lamar Hansard at the Suwanee Church of God, put out a flyer to voters on April 17, 1980 appealing for a "No!" vote. He said in the letter:

"I know that there should not be one church member to vote for this liquor referendum. If there is such a person in Suwanee, then you should have the decency to request your name be removed from the church roll."

The Rev. Hansard also contended that the passage of packaged alcohol would not lower taxes, as some had contended. He added: "On your ballot, you will see the phrase 'controlling alcoholic beverages and liquor.' The phrase is misleading. 'Control' regulates conditions of sale, and nothing else. It does not control drunkenness, bootlegging, and disastrous consequences of over indulgence. Alcohol is as uncontrollable as quick-silver and just as deadly. Stand with us and join in the fight and let us together defeat this liquor referendum....and vote 'No!'"

Proponents of the measure responded in a letter signed by Howard Richardson, chairman of the Citizens for New Suwanee Revenue, and a former city councilman. He pointed out that property taxes brought in only $20,000 a year, which "isn't even enough to cover the $30,000 needed to operate our Police Department. If the police protection relied on property tax, it would have to be raised." He added: "Only one source of revenue, beer and wine, produces enough to more than pay the police cost."

Richardson maintained: "This is strictly an economic issue. Liquor is here, so let's tax the stuff. If you favor this plan, don't let any group or institution keep you from voting your belief. Vote YES this Saturday."

The vote for packaged liquor sales in Suwanee passed, 231-215. There was a heavy turnout, with 76 percent of those registered voting in the referendum. Though Lilburn was the first city to allow packaged sales, Suwanee was the first to allow the sale of mixed drinks within its borders, beginning in September, 1981. Two establishments there, the Falcon Complex and the Holiday Inn, had the early mixed drink licenses. The city had voted for mixed drinks in April 22, 1981, when it passed by a 238-162 vote.

The strategy in which the Suwanee mixed drink referendum was passed came after the hospitality industry hired a public relations man, Parks Rusk (brother of former Secretary of State Dean Rusk), to guide them. Rusk put together a sophisticated (for Gwinnett in those days) information and telephone campaign aimed at the registered voters in Suwanee, and was concerned about what he found out. There were only about 500 registered voters in the city then, and it looked like mixed drinks would not pass.

Then someone remembered that, in past Suwanee elections, among the voters were those living in the Annandale at Suwanee facility. This was a village where mentally disabled adults reside. Many had jobs within the community. Approximately 11 percent of the Suwanee voters were made up of people living at Annandale. Learning this, the hospitality industry made sure that the Villagers were well aware of the issue. As one hospitality official said, "We made sure that everyone at Annandale got to the polls that day."

A total of 55 Villagers voted in the following city election, and a flap was made of Annandale voters influencing the election, with some people asking that the village be de-annexed. The Council voted 3-2 to de-annex Annandale, but the measure was never introduced in the General Assembly.

A person who has been close to the activities of the Water and Sewer Authority for many years is developer Charles Wilder of Lawrenceville, who served for 17 years on the Authority at different times, more than anyone in Gwinnett, under four different administrations. "I would get off the Authority for a year or more and did this two or three times. Then the phone would ring, and people would want me to come back and serve," he says. Wilder was chairman of the Authority on two different occasions, for a total of five years.

Wilder explains the reason for the Authority: "It's a quasi-governmental entity that is comprised of appointed county citizens who assist and advise the County Commissioners on the management, planning, and financing of the county water and sewer department. Financing is achieved with the issuance of Revenue Bonds. Funds from the selling of Revenue Bonds are repaid by the actual customers purchasing water and sewage treatment.

"While the Authority may issue the bonds, the County Commissioners must agree. To the best of my knowledge, all bond repayments have been met from revenues paid by water and sewer customers. During my time on the board, the interest rate the Authority was charged has always been the lowest possible because Gwinnett enjoys one of the best credit ratings in the country.

"The advantages of this type of capital financing are many. Having water and sewage treatment capacity is essential in attracting industry that supports good jobs and a superior tax base for our county. No property tax is used to repay the bonds. Only revenues from the users of the improvements pay."

Wilder continues: "With the proceeds from the bond sales, the Authority continued to make improvements and expand the system. But it could be tricky. If you had an economic downturn, or a political attitude of no-growth, or perhaps environmentalists were using the Courts to slow down the growth, it would get rough for the Authority."

Wilder adds: "During the early years, it was like facing a two-edge sword. You had to sell more water and sewage treatment to get revenue, or else you could not pay down the debt on the bonds or continue with infrastructure improvements. The Authority was walking a tightrope for many years until the system got big enough to absorb the ups and downs of the economy and other factors."

When Wayne Mason came into office as a county commissioner in 1973, there were only 12,000 water system customers. "And the bonds were unrated," Mason remembers. "Wayne Shackelford and I went to New York twice a year for eight years to the three finance houses, Moody's, Standard and Poor's and Fitch. We got all our bonds, not just the water system, changed from B to BAA the first year. Gwinnett's bonds have steadily improved their ratings every since."

In fact, Gwinnett's financial health today is excellent. It got its first "triple-triple" rating from all three rating agencies in 1997, which it has kept since. That means that all three agencies rate Gwinnett's bonds as AAA. When Gwinnett got its "triple-triple" designations, there were only six counties in the nation with this distinction. Gwinnett and Cobb became the seventh and eighth counties in the nation with this designation. By 2006, Gwinnett was one of 24 county governmental systems in the nation having the highest ratings by all three bond rating systems. Having that AAA rank saves Gwinnett and its citizens millions of dollars over long-term financing for the county.

For instance, had Gwinnett financed $100 million in bonds at the "triple-triple" best rating, in August, 2006 the rate would have been at 4.34 percent. Had those bonds been rated AA instead of AAA, the rate would have been at 12 basis points higher, or 4.46 percent, so that the first year interest savings alone would be $120,000. Over the 20-year life of the bond, the savings would be $1.8 million. That translates, of course, into less cost for every taxpayer in Gwinnett, should the county borrow for roads, water and sewer improvements, even schools or other services.

Water system pressure problems

Gwinnett had to shore up the water system after problems occurred in 1974, as growth started to outpace the water system. People in the Snellville area, distant from the water production plant, were running out of water in the middle of the afternoon. There simply was not enough water in the small pipeline leading to Snellville to meet the needs of the growing population in that part of the county.

Snellville originally had two wells supplying it with water, one an artesian well near the present First Baptist Church. The city used the Gwinnett water system as back-up, and was served primarily by a small 10-inch line put in about 1968, which came from Lawrenceville down Georgia Highway 124. But there were pressure problems, which culminated in 1974 when Snellville on many days had no water in late afternoon.

Besides Snellville, the county water system was also having pressure problems in other parts of the county. There was a 16-inch line running parallel to I-85 to serve the entire southwest end of the county. It got to the point where Olive P. Ackerman, who was the water manager at the time, was hung in effigy by homeowners in the Rockbridge Road area, sensing that he was the problem with their lack of adequate water pressure.

That's when the idea came of serving water customers by providing water from two directions, in order to ensure adequate water pressure. The idea was to loop the county with major water lines. At the time, the water department had an old 16-inch main from Duluth toward Norcross running parallel to Interstate 85 to serve the Norcross and Lilburn areas. However, the pipes were always having problems, including serious leaks. That's when the water department hired Contractor John D. Stephens of Snellville to repair serious pipe leakages on the line supplying Norcross and Lilburn.

As Stephens remembers: "We would go in there at night to repair the places on that 16- inch line where they had leakages. You couldn't go in and shut them down in the daytime, for people would have no water. So we did the work at night."

Stephens had first done "bonded" pipeline work in Macon in 1968, and was busy with water pipeline work around Snellville. Previous to that, the Snellville native started out by installing septic tanks at subdivisions and for private residences throughout Gwinnett. (See page 5 for more detail on Stephens.)

Stephens explains: "We began in 1971 installing a 30-inch line from Interstate 85 that went down the then-unpaved Indian Trail Road, then followed Killian Hill Road, and finally went east on U.S. Highway 78 to the five million gallon water storage tank on Lanier Mountain in Snellville." This was Stephens' first big contract with the county water department, and it was for $800,000. The tie-in with Snellville was started in 1974, which eventually rectified the low pressure problem for the town, and assured Snellville residents decent water pressure with a two-way feed for water.

The lack of water had a tremendous effect on the Snellville housing industry, as people considering a move to Gwinnett were shunning what had been fast-growing Snellville, since the water pressure dipped to virtually a trickle nearly every afternoon. Many residents complained beginning in the summer of 1974, having to resort to getting in their autos and driving to the closest motels of that day, along Interstate 285, to take baths.

Those involved in the water system came up with a solution. As Wayne Shackelford related: "All of us---our consulting engineers, Havens and Emerson from New Jersey, headed by Glenn Abplanalp, our own water people headed by O. P. Ackerman, the Board of Commissioners and I---all of us knew of the need for a loop through eastern parts of Gwinnett to provide water feeds from two directions. The Havens and Emerson people spoke to Wayne Mason as chairman in 1977 before we opened the new plant about the need for the two-way loop feed and the fact that we could afford the bonding capacity to build it. We began construction of the loop in 1977 and ceremonially opened the valve completing the project in November of 1980. We opened the Lake Lanier water filtration plant in July of 1977 and dedicated it in October of 1977."

Meanwhile, the Water Department had been given authority from the Corps of Engineers for a water intake in Lake Lanier. This water filtration plant was 3.25 miles from Lake Lanier at one of the highest elevations in the county, and would become the main water production facility for the county. As this new plant was built, the county installed a 48- inch water main between the first filter plant at Duluth to the plant near Buford. The capacity of the Duluth plant (taking water from the Chattahoochee River) was small. By getting permission from the Corps of Engineers for the intake in Lake Lanier, it insured Gwinnett adequate water for the future. To this date, Gwinnett is the only county with a permit to take water from the lake.

In 1975-76, the Water Department came back to Stephens, hiring him to install a 48 inch loop main from the Lake Lanier plant along the eastern boundary of Gwinnett which looped and tied in to the 30-inch line near Snellville, providing even better pressure for that area.

Stephens says: "Most of that 48-inch loop line followed the roads of the county, though there were some places where we went across open land. Every time we crossed a place where there was a smaller water main, we made a cross connection there, to ensure good pressure for that area. By laying this main loop line, we finally got around to Snellville, and Gwinnett County residents had good water pressure."

Water capacity

In 2007, Gwinnett's Water Authority has a peak capacity of 225 million gallons a day, with a firm withdrawal permit of 150 million gallons a day. The daily average consumption for 2007 was 87 million gallons of water a day (MGD). Interestingly, Gwinnett consumes water as quickly as it is produced at its two plants. The county has stored 58.5 MGD at its filter plants, and 62.5 MGD at storage tanks around the county, all constantly replenished.

The Lanier Filter Plant of the Water Department, located off Peachtree Industrial Boulevard just north of Buford, was opened in 1977, and had a major expansion in 1986, adding a second filtering building. It then had a capacity of 100 million gallons a day, and with internal modifications in 1995, went to a 150 MGD capacity. The Shoal Creek Filter Plant, which came on line in 2004, and is located on Stewart Road in sight of Lake Lanier, added another 75 MGD, giving the entire water system a capacity of 225 MGD.

At the end of 2005, the Gwinnett Water Authority had 165 miles of transmission lines, and 3,295.66 miles of distribution lines for its customers. A total of 87 miles of 36 and 48- inch pipe circling the county maintains pressure from two directions, so if a line breaks, customers can get water from the other direction.

For the year 2007, Gwinnett's Water and Sewer Authority had revenues of $206 million, expenses of $158 million and an income of $48 million. The system then totaled 234,447 customers, including wholesaling water to Buford, Lawrenceville and Norcross. In recent years, the system easily covers its bond obligations, and continues to expand as growing Gwinnett needs its lifeline of water.

Meanwhile, the growth of the county has seen its water usage multiply. It was in 1961 that the system first averaged more than a million gallons a day. From pumping an average of 1.672 million gallons per day (MGD) in 1965, this usage jumped to 8.8 MGD in 1975, then to 31.8 MGD in 1985, to 63 MGD in 1995 and to 80 MGD in 2005. It is projected to hit 103 MGD in 2010.

The Gwinnett sewer system also has a healthy number of customers, 153,311 at the end of 2005. But note the difference in number of water and sewer customers, about 78,000 more water customers than sewer accounts. The county had issued 131,000 septic tank permits by 2006, though many of these homes have since connected to the sewer system. Estimates are that there are 90,000 working septic tanks in the county in 2008. This comes from the high number of septic tanks in primarily northern stretches of the county.

In 2007 Gwinnett was hit with an unexpected problem: low rainfall, the lowest since 1954. The rainfall during 2007 totaled only 31.85 inches (the record low is 31.8 inches, in 1954.) The drought sent the county's major water resource, Lake Lanier, to record lows, and for the first time, there were concerns for future years' water resources. Coming as it did in 2007 following several years of lower rainfall, it caused concerns and brought public officials to implement water restrictions throughout the Metro Atlanta area and the state.

Up until 2007, North Georgia thought that it had sufficient water, though the ever-growing population was beginning to tax the system. On average, the Atlanta area gets 48 inches of rain a year. Consider, too, that when Lake Lanier was built in the 1950's, Metro Atlanta's population was roughly 750,000. In 2008 the population of Gwinnett was that much alone, and the overall population of Metro Atlanta was 5.1 million people, a million more than the population of the entire state in 1960.

Another aspect of the concern is the relatively small watershed of Lake Lanier, a small triangle of land from the dam between Buford and Cumming and the Continental Divide above Helen, a distance of no more than 60 miles. Compared to other lakes in the Southeast, it is one of the smallest watersheds, meaning that in a drought, rain must fall in a relatively tight area to affect the water pool in the lake.

Today (2008), the Gwinnett water and sewer system is financially sound, as it expands with the growth of the county, through a continuing source of funds from its water and sewer customers. The system also benefits from the county's "triple-triple" bond rating, allowing lower rates on borrowed funds. It's a far cry from when the county thought it needed a nickel for every can of beer sold just to keep the water system afloat.

First water system in Buford

The first municipal water plant in Gwinnett County was in Buford, built in 1934. The city dammed up Big Creek, which flowed to the Chattahoochee River, to gain a water reservoir. The system initially had a capacity of 500,000 gallons a day.

All changed when Lake Lanier water started rising as the river was dammed. Buford's storage reservoir was flooded and the city gained a raw water intake into the lake for its raw water. The city's intake into the lake is about 150 yards from the plant on North Waterworks Road.

Cleveland Smith, Buford water superintendent, who started work at the plant in 1973, says that the plant was expanded to one million gallons a day in 1965, and later expanded to a two-million-gallons a day capacity in 1994. In 2007, Buford had a normal usage of 1.5 million gallons a day, from its 3,200 customers.

The City of Buford has a raw water storage capacity of 450,000 gallons at the plant, plus two water tanks in town with each having 300,000 gallons of storage.

Evil spirits

The sale of distilled spirits by the bottle takes place only in three cities in Gwinnett County -- Suwanee, Duluth and Lilburn. However, the sale of mixed drinks is legal in unincorporated areas, by permit, within the county. How did Gwinnett get to this position? It took years and years, and a couple of referendums.

A move came in the middle 1970s to get a referendum on the question of distilled spirits before the voters. To require a vote on that question was difficult, for in those days, Georgia law stipulated that a petition for a vote required the names of 30 percent of those who voted in the last election. Not only that, but the rules required that the referendum be in a special election with only the question of the sale of distilled spirits (bottled liquor) on the ballot. Should a "bottle bill" -- sale of bottle spirits -- take place, a referendum on mixed drinks could then be petitioned by only 15 percent of those voting in the previous election.

The deck was stacked, you might, say, in favor of the "dries." After all, this was the Protestant ethic of blue-stocking Georgia being reflected in the Georgia liquor laws of that day, prior to the heavy movement of people to Georgia from all across the country, where the alcoholic beverage laws were more liberal. For years on end, when these liquor laws were challenged, it was said that a Grand Coalition of "preachers and bootleggers" were the strange bedfellows joining to defeat any legal sale of alcoholic beverages. A vote on distilled spirits was to be a formidable task, as the laws were stacked in favor of those opposing liquor.

Meanwhile, Gwinnett was not merely growing, but was exploding in population. The fledging hospitality industry in Gwinnett in the late 1970s began work to secure a referendum on distilled spirits. (There were less than 300 hotel rooms in the county at that time. In 2007, there were more than 10,000.)

Eventually, forces in the county began a drive organized to start a push for packaged liquor. Leading the drive to have bottled liquor in the county was Norcross Realtor Larry Bradley. In a direct mail campaign, and by signing up people at shopping centers, eventually the names of 35 percent of those registered voters in the last General Election petitioned for a vote on the question. That in itself was a victory, just to get that many people to petition for the referendum.

But the pro-liquor forces didn't count on the strength of the churches against the measure. The Oct. 31, 1978 referendum to license the sale of distilled spirits failed by more than 2,000 votes, 11,813 to 9,199. All that effort fell to naught.

The upshot was a more organized hospitality industry effort. A Committee for Quality Hotels and Restaurants was created in the 1979-80 era, basically a regrouping of the industry. It was led by John Schwab of Peachtree World of Tennis. These forces lobbied for and secured a legislative change in Georgia law that had several important new wrinkles. First, the vote on such a measure could come during any election, effectively doing away with special, single-issue elections which typically had low voter turnout. Secondly, no longer was there a requirement that a sale-by-bottle vote had to pass before the mixed drink question could be raised. The pro-liquor forces got the legislature to change the law to allow a vote on the direct question of the sale of mixed drinks in a county.

Four years after the liquor-by-the-bottle vote, on Nov. 2, 1982, in a referendum, the county adopted in unincorporated areas legislation allowing the sale of mixed drinks. The vote was close, 21,988 for, and 20,222 against. Since that time, even until this day (2008), the sale of distilled spirits by the bottle is not allowed in unincorporated Gwinnett.

The key factor in this effort to legalize the sale of mixed drinks was Schwab and the owner of the Peachtree World of Tennis, Lamar Hunt of Dallas (one of the famous Hunt Brothers of Texas), who Schwab says "…..essentially funded most of the cost of the referendum, approximately $76,000." At that time, the Peachtree World of Tennis was the premier private club in the county, with Chamber of Commerce annual meetings held there, as well as other important county functions, in addition to events that brought famed tennis stars to the facility's eight indoor and 18 outdoor courts. Schwab adds: "Other private interests contributed perhaps another $20,000 to this referendum pool, but my boss, Lamar, provided the bulk of the money to get people to petition for the referendum, and he never questioned the expenditures."

Schwab might have had more incentive than anyone else in the county to see the sale of "legal liquor." He had been visited on Dec. 23, 1975, by two gentlemen at Peachtree World of Tennis, inquiring about club membership. Being the genial host, as they talked Schwab offered them a drink from the club bar. Then the two gentlemen asked for a second drink, only then to inform Schwab that he was under arrest for illegally dispensing liquor in a dry county. "Got me on a bootlegging charge," Schwab laughs when he tells of it years afterward.

Schwab posted a $500 bond, getting a receipt. Unofficially, Schwab was told that if he got to work on having a referendum on the liquor question, his club could continue to serve their members with mixed drinks in the meantime. All this, of course, was off-the-record and hush-hush, but this way, Gwinnett allowed the very popular private club to continue to operate in the face of Georgia laws being winked at by county law enforcement.

A few weeks later, Schwab was in his office one morning when two law enforcement men dressed in coats and ties walked in without asking, closed the door, and started talking about him being arrested on the dispensing mixed drink charge. Schwab had never seen the men before. They asked if he had posted bond, and when he said that he had, they asked for a receipt. Schwab produced this receipt, and the two were a little perplexed. "This is for $500?" they questioned Schwab. He said yes, since that was the amount he posted.

That's how Schwab learned that at the county sheriff's office, it listed him as posting a $400 bond. "That's how I learned about the $100 that was missing," Schwab says. And to this day, Schwab has never been called to court on the charge of him dispensing whiskey illegally in a dry county.

Schwab says: "I always thought that the missing $100 of my $500 bond as the cheapest insurance policy I could have on that charge. For had we gone to court, my lawyer would have been all over them on that missing $100."

After the vote on legalizing the sale of mixed drinks in unincorporated areas of the county, significant changes started in the hospitality industry. One of the key changes was the beginning of a larger hotel presence. It was in 1986 that the full-service Marriott Hotel opened at Gwinnett Place, a 17-story building consisting of 300 rooms. Its first guest registered on June 12. That same year, a second multi-story hotel, the 10-story Hilton Atlanta Northeast at Peachtree Corners with 175 rooms, also opened, providing a second area of Gwinnett with a full-service major hotel. Since then, the hotel industry has grown steadily. In early 2008, there were 10,558 hotel rooms in 98 hotels built throughout the county.

All this gives background on why, as late as 2008, Gwinnett County itself remains dry when it comes to the sale of bottled distilled spirits, though it's legal in establishments within the county to purchase mixed drinks. Meanwhile, Gwinnettians have the ability to stay within the county borders to purchase bottled whiskey, at three cities of the county!

It's all part of the patchwork quilt of regulations concerning "evil spirits" (alcohol) that can be seen all across the State of Georgia.

(For a look at revenue that Gwinnett County gets from alcoholic beverage sales, go to Appendix B, page 770.)

Early Gwinnett entrepreneur

Larry P. McClure was from Rabun County, and made a name for himself first in Gwinnett, then returned to his home county and did even more, primarily in partnership with Dr. Miles Mason Jr. of Duluth.

McClure had a ninth grade education, but those dealing with McClure recall him as a quick-thinking pure entrepreneur, a dreamer, who loved buying and selling, who did it often, then moved on to do it again. He was also able to envision projects from conception, though he was usually more interested in getting it going than running any dream. He made friends easily, was fun to be around, and had this capacity to win people over.

He was unconventional. For instance, when going to buy an automobile, he would borrow a friend's old truck, take cash in a paper bag, and wear old clothes. He didn't want a salesman to realize he had much money.

McClure was born Dec. 7, 1926. His brother, Bill, who was four years younger, remembers Larry at age 8 as having an eye for business. "In those days, the roads were not paved, and we lived east of Clayton. On Satolah Creek Road, we would take bamboo growing nearby and use this as a pipe to run water from a spring to the road, which was on a hill. People driving from Walhalla and Westminister. S.C. in their automobiles would get to this portion of the road, which was wet and slick, and not be able to get up the hill. Larry and I would push their A or T Model Fords out for a dollar. They would say to us, 'It's funny it ain't rained down the road.' Larry would say to them, 'You know how these showers pop up.'"

Like many in Rabun County, where there was little industry, Larry got involved in moonshine. Bill says: "Yeah, he had a steamer (moonshine still) on Charlie Mountain, which was owned by our grandfather, V.M. Burrell, who was the tax receiver for Rabun County. The other moonshiners got jealous and reported it, and we had to cut it up." Neither his father, nor his grandfather, knew of the still. Bill adds: "Papa (Larry Porter McClure Sr.) would have not stood for that." Larry later would transport moonshine in an automobile into Atlanta.

Another method: the innocent-looking young McClure would take the Tallulah Falls Railway into Cornelia, then switch to the Southern Railway, and get off in either Hall or Gwinnett County to make a delivery. Quarts of the illegal liquor were stashed in a big suitcase. Lee McClure Hussey of Marshall, N.C., one of his two daughters (the other is Melissa Ann McClure of Charlotte, N.C.) said her father told her it was easier to haul moonshine on the train "for you don't have to worry about the law and being chased."

Bill McClure of Duluth remembers being on furlough from the Air Force in Atlanta one time when visiting Larry, and the big heavy suitcase was having problems, and came undone. "Here I was near the bus station in my blue Air Force uniform, with half gallon jars rolling down the street, and me and Larry picking them up." The illegal spirits sold for $5 a quart back then.

Larry served in the Army toward the end of World War II, and was a staff sergeant on the way to the Far East when the war ended. He was in the 20th Infantry of the Sixth Division in Korea until he was discharged on December 24, 1946.

McClure's first legitimate business was **a** drive-in theatre in Tiger, just south of Clayton in Rabun County. McClure had been told by a relative in his native Rabun County that "If you're going to make something out of yourself, you've got to get out of Rabun County." He came to Gwinnett in the mid-1950s, and soon was the operator of walk-in movie theatres in Buford, Lawrenceville and Norcross. Then he opened the Starlight Drive-In in Sugar Hill, and later opened two other drive-ins in the county. He became a good friend of Jim Vic Hood of First National Bank of Lawrenceville, who bankrolled many of his ventures. His other drive-ins were in Lawrenceville (about 1954-55, off Pike Street near Old Norcross Road), and near Norcross, around 1957-58, as Gwinnett Drive-In (along present-day Jimmy Carter Boulevard and what would become Brookhollow Parkway.)

It was while he had the Lawrenceville Drive-in that Larry hired Sandra Coan as an accountant. The pair were married Dec. 26, 1960. They adopted two daughters in 1968 and 1970, with the assistance of Dr. Miles Mason Jr., who would deliver and accommodate the adoption.

About 1960, McClure started Metropolitan Mobile Home Park off Indian Trail Road, between Interstate 85 and the Vulcan Rock Quarry.

One of his early ventures in the early 1960s was a golf driving range on 16 acres in DeKalb County just inside what would become Interstate 285 on Interstate 85. Later he converted that driving range into a par-three golf course. He took part of the land to build Golfland Motel Lodge. There were few motels in the area then, and the place became profitable. It was also the motel closest to Gwinnett County. The lodge had a restaurant and lounge. This was before DeKalb started to legalize alcohol with pouring licenses. DeKalb police would routinely raid the lounge for serving alcoholic beverages. To combat this, McClure turned the lounge into a private club, complete with membership cards, etc., called The Duffer's Club. Those wanting to have a dinner could "buy" a membership, and be served alcoholic beverages. His brother, Bill McClure, who had come to Gwinnett as a teacher, would often help him in his interests, including acting as the bartender at The Duffer's Club. Bill McClure first taught school at Bethesda High, taught the one year that West Gwinnett High operated in Norcross, then started the football program and also coached basketball in Duluth High. (Larry and former Sheriff Crawford Pittard each gave $10,000 to help build the Duluth football field.)

Bill Mason, who with his three brothers had taken lessons in golf at the driving range, said that at the Golfland Lounge, Larry "got tired of being raided, and decided to make it legal with a private club." The par-three course was closed around 1973. Bill's brother, James, got his start at the par three course, and would later become a professional golfer. As of 2008, he was a member of the PGA Seniors' Tour.

In the early 1960s, McClure was assisting in building the North Druid Hills Country Club, which McClure wanted the group to locate in Gwinnett. That led to McClure beginning in 1963 to build Berkeley Hills Golf Club. W.P. "Willie" Jones, who would become mayor of Duluth in 1984, was a partner with McClure, operating the bulldozer. McClure seldom had drawn plans to build by, and that suited Jones fine, Claude Mason says. "Willie Jones didn't need a set of plans to go by to build anything. Once he conceived it, he just knew where to move dirt to get it done."

But about halfway through constructing the Berkeley Hills course, the pair ran into difficulties. Bill Mason says that one Friday afternoon as they finished building the first nine holes, McClure realized he had run out of money. McClure asked Jones: "Anybody in this town got any money?" Jones answered: "You might try "Foots" Mason," (his nickname for Dr. Miles Mason Jr. of Duluth).

McClure and Jones that same night got Dr. Mason out to see the work going on at the course. "We need $45,000 to finish the course," McClure told Dr. Mason. "When do you need it?" Mason asked. "Right now," shot back McClure. And Mason wrote a check. That was the start of a long and fruitful partnership between McClure and Mason. McClure said at one time that having Dr. Mason for a partner "was better than having a bank." McClure finished the balance of the course and the clubhouse, and Berkeley Hills was in operation beginning in 1965. The second nine was opened about a year later.

McClure often needed money quickly, to accommodate his many business deals. When he and Bill McClure went to see C&S banker Mills Lane once about a loan, Lane asked when he needed the money: "I'm double-parked right now," McClure said. Lane didn't buy that idea. But Larry and Atlanta Federal banker Billy Mitchell hit it off from the beginning; he told Larry: "I'm going to take a chance on you. I like the way you talk."

Miles Mason Jr.

Around 1968-69, McClure sold his interest in the mobile home park to Dr. Mason. About a year later, Dr. Mason swapped his half interest in the country club to McClure for half interest in the Golfland operation. Around 1971-72 Dr. Mason and Dick Lynott of Duluth totally bought out the McClure interest in the motel. Dr. Mason and Lynott continued to operate the motel until 1980, when they sold it to other interests.

McClure, who then owned all of Berkeley Hills, later would sell the club to a group of members called the "Berkeley Dozen." McClure was one of the dozen. The group operated it for several years. Eventually the golf course was sold to the membership, and by then McClure had moved back to Rabun County.

Soon McClure had another idea. "He was always coming up with ideas," says Bill Mason. It was in the mid-1960s that McClure and Dr. Mason as partners started work on the Kingwood Resort, which included a golf course, east of Clayton in Rabun County. McClure found that the Georgia mountain resort easily attracted wealthy Atlantans and upscale visitors to Kingwood. In 1971, even Hollywood discovered Kingwood, as the resort housed the cast for a movie, *Deliverance*, being filmed on the nearby Chatooga River.

McClure and Dr. Mason, in the meantime, had purchased some 500 acres north of Clayton near the North Carolina line at Sky Valley, for what they planned as part of the Kingwood club, its ski area. It opened its first ski season in 1968. In 1971, a group of developers, including Jimmy Bentley and a syndicate, purchased in cash from the McClure-Mason partnership the Kingwood resort (but did not include the ski area.) McClure and Mason began an extensive development at Sky Valley, which is located between Dillard, Ga. and Highlands, N.C. The attraction for this project was its higher elevation, ranging from 3,100 to 4,200 feet above sea level. Bill Mason notes: "People liked this area better, since it was cooler than the Kingwood Resort." Eventually the pair assembled some 2,200 acres for Sky Valley. The city is bounded on the north by the Georgia-North Carolina state line, and on the remaining sides by mountain ridges. Bill McClure was sales manager for Sky Valley.

The key idea McClure had was to make Sky Valley into the most southern ski resort in the United States. Improved machines could make snow whenever the temperature dropped below 28 degrees. McClure found that in some past years, there were 50-60 days when the temperature reached that level, though there were other years when there were only 10 days of the lower temperatures. Pumping water out under high pressure, making a mist, would freeze the mist as it hit the air, and enough snow could be made for the ski runs. And as a result, many Georgians got their first taste of skiing on the relatively tame slopes at Sky Valley. However, as a ski resort, the place never succeeded. The uncertainty of colder days for snow-making eventually caused a halt in the ski venture, as during their time of ownership, not enough days of lower temperatures materialized for the ski venture to become profitable.

McClure took another step at Sky Valley to make it more workable. He walked paperwork through the Georgia Legislature and got a city charter for Sky Valley, incorporating the town in 1978. Bill Mason says: "He did that to be able to sell alcohol at Sky Valley. Once incorporated, we called for a referendum on the booze question, when we had 33 permanent residents. Larry got his wife and a few others to vote against it, so it wouldn't look rigged. But it passed easily, since a majority was for it. The city had a water system from the resort, and had a tax base to maintain roads and the water system. Of course, the resort was the largest taxpayer in the city. Larry was the first mayor of the town. And I was the second mayor." Bill Mason had been involved with real estate in Sky Valley, though he had a degree in pharmacy. When he moved back to Duluth, he returned to pharmacy.

McClure bought out the Mason interest in 1980, but 18 months later Dr. Mason took the property back. He held it until 1989, when he released it to bankers, and got out of Sky Valley. Dr. Miles Mason Jr. died in 1994.

After Sky Valley, Bill McClure tells the story that his mother, Myrtice Burrell McClure, said to him one day: "Larry's gone crazy. He's going to these auctions and buying nothing but junk. Go with him and see what he's doing." Bill found that, indeed, he was buying up about everything at auctions. "I told mother she was right, he was going crazy. But a year or so later, Larry opened up an auction house of his own on U.S. Highway 441 in Dillard, was having sales, and about tripled his money on that junk mother thought he was buying."

Larry soon was into collecting antique automobiles, often purchasing them in run-down condition. At one time, he owned Elvis Presley's first limousine, and the vehicle used by Presidents Eisenhower and Truman. Eventually, he amassed more than 70 of these cars, and had so many that he stored some at first in former chicken houses. He restored the cars to pristine condition, and opened the Antique Dillard Mini-Mall, with a car museum, charging admission to view the automobiles. He eventually sold the restored automobiles.

Another venture McClure got involved with in later life was purchasing the Rabun County side of the land at Tallulah Gorge, adding it to land he owned in Tallulah Falls on the Habersham County side. He and his wife also operated a campground about three miles north of Tallulah Falls on U.S. Highway 441. At one time, the car museum was relocated in Tallulah Falls. McClure gave the former train depot in Tallulah Falls to the Tallulah Falls School. McClure eventually sold the Rabun side of the Gorge to the State of Georgia, which now operates Tallulah Falls State Park on the location.

Meanwhile, McClure had Graves' disease, complicated by diabetes, and was going blind. He died July 23, 1999. Sandra died Dec. 30, 2007, after being diagnosed with Lou Gehrig's disease some eight months prior to her death.

At the 2000 census, the City of Sky Valley had a resident population of 220, though it has more than 650 housing units, including many vacation homes. For 2007, the city had a budget of $1,676,930, including its enterprise funds, for its 3.03 square miles. The State Legislature in 2000 designated the Georgia Highway 246 from Dillard toward Highlands, N.C. as the "Larry McClure Highway." The measure, introduced by Rep. Ralph Twiggs of Towns County and Rep. Mike Coan of Gwinnett (his nephew) notes his Gwinnett County endeavors and partially reads: "...his foresight and commitment to his community brought unparalleled progress to Rabun County and the northeastern part of the state and has greatly enhanced the area's economy."

One failed project: Merchandise Mart

While Gwinnett County has been an area of tremendous opportunity for many people with its explosive growth, not every project that has been announced has succeeded.

With great fanfare in 1959, one such project had its groundbreaking in Gwinnett, offering great promise for much higher visibility for the county. Its location was a key element in the announcement, since it was to be at the point of land at the intersection of what would become Interstate 85 and Georgia Highway 316. Even before the official groundbreaking, work had already been contracted to begin clearing of a triangle of pine trees on the 293- acre tract. Bulldozers flattened the land for quick development, estimated to cost $20 million, in anticipation of being ready for occupancy in the fall of 1960.

At the groundbreaking on May 1, 1959, the world was told of the "Southeastern Merchandise Mart," a new wholesale marketplace, which would be the first such facility in the southeast. Dignitaries from as far away as Washington, D.C. were on hand, as well as Gov. Ernest Vandiver; Peter Garran, a representative from the British Embassy; Jaime Alba, a minister-counselor of Spain; Abit Massey, secretary of the Georgia Department of Commerce; the former chief of protocol of the Department of State; the Georgia adjutant general, George Hearn; Gwinnett Judge Joe Cheeley; and even the commissioner of baseball's Little League, John Lindemuth, who forecast the Mart becoming the "Yankee Stadium of Little League in the Southeast."

Listed as "sponsors" in the program were Weldon Gardner of Buford, representing the Upper Chattahoochee Development Association, who was master of ceremonies; Ken McMillon of Lawrenceville, president of the Gwinnett Chamber; and Gwinnett's three commissioners---Uhland Freeman, Dr. W.A. Elinburg, and Minor M. Corley.

Music came from the Athens High School Band. (Years later, one of those band members providing music that day, Dr. John Roark, would become pastor of the Buford Presbyterian Church.)

Among those on the program was Dr. W.B. Cockcroft, a representative from a relatively new company in Memphis, called "Holiday Inns of America," which was set to bethe developer of a giant 1,000-room motel at the site, which would be the largest in the world.

To ensure the world would know of this major event in Gwinnett, also in attendance were the media, newspapermen, TV crews and magazine people, from Buffalo, Cleveland, New York and Boston, and the major press services. Also present were prominent syndicated columnists. Many national journals sent their own photographers. The event was much ballyhooed!

Here's why this groundbreaking was taking place. This "Merchandise Mart" was to be a major new development for the South, an attraction which would pull retail merchants, but not the general public, to Gwinnett from all over the Southeast to see the latest goods in many fields. The mart would entice them to buy at the wholesale level the items that would stock their stores, similar to marts in New York and Dallas. At that time, there was no similar mart serving the Southeast.

The Southeastern Merchandise Mart would consist of:

- A giant market to display and market all sorts of goods to wholesale buyers of commercial products. It would be an 11-story facility of a million square feet, with entire floors devoted to different categories of goods.
- The world's biggest coliseum of that day, capable of seating 25,000 people and having space for a total of 38,000 admissions to exhibits or fairs, larger than San Francisco's Cow Palace or New York's Madison Square Garden.
- The world's biggest motel, to number 1,000 rooms.
- Parking for 10,000 automobiles.
- A penthouse club for fine dining.
- Its own airport landing strip.

Put simply, there was a lot of hoopla that sunshine-filled day in Gwinnett County, with Metro Atlanta's focusing on Gwinnett County for the second recent time, the first being the dedication of Lake Lanier, two years earlier. A few people were beginning to recognize that Gwinnett would be a major player in Metro Atlanta's future.

This wholesale showplace vision came from the expansive mind of one individual, an Atlanta real estate developer named Robert Holder Sr. He had been one of the key Realtors concentrating on an area in DeKalb County along Peachtree Industrial Boulevard, where he was said to have developed some 82 industries that, by 1959, were producing over $200 million in sales annually. Holder was successful in 1945 in enticing the giant General Motors to locate its Buick-Chevrolet-Pontiac assembly plant between the Norfolk Southern Railway and Peachtree Industrial Boulevard, hard by what would become Interstate 285.

Holder had begun to focus on the economic possibilities of the overall Southeast, recognizing that it did not have a major center for merchandizing that was found in Chicago, in New York, in Dallas and in California. But there was no merchandising magnet for the Southeast. He had researched the retail sales of the area, finding that the Southeast outperformed the Southwestern area around Dallas. He also found Gwinnett as the ideal spot for his dream of a merchandise mart and tied up the land in Gwinnett where he envisioned this new venture to be located. Mr. Holder also began to tie up land in options on key intersections along what would become Interstate 85 from DeKalb County northward to the proposed Mart site.

His statistics showed that the Southeast had far more potential for a mart than did the already-existing Dallas merchandise mart. The area, compared to the Southwest, had more retail sales ($24 billion compared to $17 billion), a higher percentage of total United States sales (12.4 percent compared to 8.6 percent), and nearly 50 percent more general merchandise sales, apparel sales and furniture and appliance sales. To Holder, it was obvious that Atlanta, with its central location, was overdue for such a merchandise mart, and he had found land he thought was the best location alongside two major four- lane highways in Gwinnett County, Georgia.

Abit Massey, later head of the Georgia Poultry Federation in Gainesville, remembers that groundbreaking. "Back then, we at the state level were promoting any and all new business we could. When Bob Holder Sr. came to the Capitol and asked us to be on the program, we went to represent the state. We were excited to come and welcome all those folks there." Massey, like many others, also remembers traveling up Interstate 85, which in those days had very little development alongside it, and then seeing the Holder location, abuzz with big bulldozers and other heavy equipment leveling the property for development.

A few more details of the proposed mart:

The major building would accommodate both manufacturers and their customers. Buyers of merchandise from hometown hardware stores and dress shops, sporting goods and jewelry, all across the South, were expected to make the trip to the Gwinnett site to buy inventory for their stores, rather than make a more difficult and more distant trip to New York. On the premises for these visiting buyers would be the motel and restaurant accommodations, all set amid landscaped, campus-like grounds.

The Mart itself would be 11 stories, with one million square feet of offices and showrooms. The adjoining coliseum would be 350,000 square feet, and have an unobstructed floor area equal to five football fields laid side by side. Both the coliseum and mart would be under the same management, with trade shows and conventions coordinated to Mart activities.

The Mart would become a mecca for some 14 states, where merchants would find under one roof leading lines of merchandise, a one-stop shopping experience. In short, Holder was promising, you could increase your sales and reduce your distribution costs by patronizing the new Southeastern Merchandise Mart in Gwinnett.

A $20 million contract was signed April 3, 1959 between Mr. Holder and the Beck Company to build the facility.

Whew!

But it never happened.

Though the bulldozers had flattened the triangle of land, yawning its rich red Georgia clay to passersby indicating something was about to happen, and awaiting the beginning of construction........there was a hitch.

Holder, seeking permanent financing on the project, heard from bankers what many developers hear: "Before we loan you the money, you need to get an insurance physical, as a precaution." They no doubt told Holder there was probably nothing wrong with him, but said, "You can never tell."

Indeed, Holder did not pass his physical. That stopped negotiations with his financial backers. Soon, work on the project itself was stalled first temporarily, then more prolonged, then indefinitely.

Meanwhile, Mr. Holder had been diagnosed with cancer. His health and his project were both collapsing around him. Just over two years from the big announcement about the Merchandise Mart for Gwinnett, on June 4, 1961, Robert M. Holder Sr., a power in the North Atlanta real estate market for years, died in Fulton County at age 59. And with his death, the dream for Gwinnett to house the Southeast's major merchandise mart imploded.

That was fine with powers in downtown Atlanta, who thought the Mart site in Gwinnett was too far from the city center. They pressed to locate such a mart in downtown Atlanta. Announced later that year (1959) was Atlanta architect John Portman's plan to build Southeastern Merchandise Mart in downtown Atlanta, almost identical in scope to what Mr. Holder had projected. Soon it was obvious that what Bob Holder had dreamed was on target, as the Southeast embraced what Portman had acted on. Portman's Merchandise Mart opened in 1961, and indeed became the major buying opportunity for retail establishments all over the Southeast. It has since expanded to include the Atlanta Apparel Mart, Atlanta Gift Mart and the Atlanta Decorative Arts Center.

The land that Bob Holder had identified for his own mart languished, and began to sprout small pine seedlings. Eventually, the only activity on this land was the growth of the pine trees, as they became full size. Soon the land was cleared once again for what would become warehousing and manufacturing facilities, where Bob Holder had envisioned a thriving merchandising center for the Southeast.

Mr. Holder's son, Bob Holder Jr., in the latter part of the 20th century, was a major figure in construction in the Metro Atlanta area and a prominent citizen of the area -- at one time president of the Metro Atlanta Chamber of Commerce.

Ironically, his firm, Holder Construction Company, built many projects in Gwinnett, many of them similar in scope to what his father had proposed for the county years earlier.

Structural changes in government

In the 1960s, Gwinnett County took several steps toward major changes that would help contribute to absorbing the tremendous growth that most believed was going to hit the county. It took a lot of effort to produce the change necessary to make sure that the county would adequately move forward.

The first step was a citizen-driven effort to enlarge the then three-man county commission. Gwinnett County had the only three-man governmental structure in Georgia. All three were equal in power, with the chairman gaining office by getting one other commissioner to vote for him. Essentially, the positions were all full-time, and the organizational structure was fraught with problems. There was no modern professional management of government, few professionals were on the county staff at any level, with most department heads essentially political appointees.

Gwinnett's Historic Courthouse, built in 1885, refurbished to its early glory.

This effort to change the structure came after a study instigated by the Gwinnett Chamber of Commerce in 1963 and done by the Institute of Law and Government at the University of Georgia. The study suggested ways that the county might change. ("A Study of The Government of Gwinnett County, for Planning Commission on Modernization of County Government.")

At that time, under this three-person county commission structure, all three commissioners were elected countywide and were equal in responsibilities and powers. Each commissioner was paid $6,000 annually. In effect, what Gwinnett had was three lone individuals, each with the same authority. Things did not always operate smoothly. If you could get another commissioner to go along with you, things got done. If not, your efforts on the commission fell by the wayside. It wasn't always pretty.

Some thought this was a terrible form of government. In election after election, those winning seats on the county commission were usually from either Buford or Lawrenceville, with other sections of the county getting little representation – and often, little attention.

In the early 1960s, all of this got a Southern Bell manager who lived near Norcross, Ray Gunnin, stirring for a more progressive government. Gunnin got his first taste of politics when president of the Pinckneyville Community Association. He participated in, and eventually headed, a study of county government, with the group calling for a referendum on whether to keep the three-man commission or institute a new five-man commission. Gunnin got help from an active Norcross Jaycees chapter. The new proposal for a five-man commission grew out of suggestions from many, and was supported by the report from the Institute of Government at the University of Georgia.

Changing the form of government wasn't easy. A Constitutional Amendment was necessary, which meant that the two local state representatives from Gwinnett, Tom Watson and Earl Story, plus the district senator, who was Dr. Al Minish of Commerce, had to put forward local legislation for the change in the General Assembly. For a while, Minish balked, but relented in February, 1966 and agreed to the proposed referendum.

In the meantime, there was much back-and-forth discussion on what the legislation would say. Finally, it was agreed that the wording to go before the voters would change the number of commissioners from three to five. In addition, the amendment would require the employment of professional management to run the county, through the use of a county manager. That provision was on the November, 1966 ballot. Prior to the election, there were meetings pro and con throughout the county, with both sides being highly organized and vocal.

The amendment for the change lost by 329 votes, the new daily newspaper in the county, *Gwinnett Daily News*, reported on November 3, 1966. There were 5,054 "Yes" votes, but 5,383 "No" votes.

In effect, the champions of change saw their five-year effort go down the drain with this election. However, there seemed to be more opposition to employing a county manager than in the change to a five-man commission. That caused efforts to be reignited for another vote on the change of governmental structure.

Meanwhile, additional overtures had to be made to the legislators, to get a new amendment set before the voters. Eventually, a new referendum on the question of enlarging the county commission went before the voters on April 10, 1968, in a special election. This time, the matter of a county manager was not mentioned. Instead, the effort concentrated on changing the number of commissioners from three to five. Four would run in areas of the county (districts), while the other office, that of the chairman, would be voted on county-wide. The chairmanship would be a full-time job, while the district commission posts would be part-time positions.

This time, there was overwhelming support of the measure, passing by 75 percent of those voting, 4,315 to 1,413. Only 19 percent of those registered voted and decided the election. In the fall of 1968, Gwinnett voters went to the polls to select their first five-person commission.

In the new governmental structure, the chairman in this arrangement is on the job each day. In reality, he has the same voting power on the board as the district commissioners. But because of being in the office each day, the chairman can exercise judgment that might be considered "power." But if the chairman moves too far ahead of the board's wishes, as a check-and-balance measure, the other four can out-vote him and override his actions.

Even with the key power of running a meeting, acting for the board between meetings, and being "out front," the chairman is also a "target" of the people of the county. In the eyes of many, the chair IS the county government, and gets the wrath as well as the glory. The five-member commission's method of operation is somewhat a measure to ensure balance, and in general, has worked fairly well since 1968.

The first new five-person commission took office on January 1, 1969. In the election, one of the three previous commissioners, W.R. (Dudge) Pruitt of Buford, had been elected chairman. The other four were new commissioners: Carvis P. Williams of Snellville, Maron Buice of Sugar Hill, Julian Archer from Harbins and Ray Gunnin of Norcross.

Pruitt is the only person who served on the Gwinnett County Commission both when it was a three-member body, and then when it changed to a five-person commission. Pruitt says that he enjoyed his years as commissioner. In his first four years in office, each commissioner had equal authority. Under the five man set-up, Pruitt won election as chairman, and worked with the four other district commissioners. "We used to meet every Tuesday. I let the district commissioners make the decisions, and daily carried out their ideas. I had no problems with them, though one commissioner once moved some equipment on a weekend. I only voted when there was a tie, which was seldom."

Later Pruitt would return to private business, buying and selling land, first with his brother, Glyndon. He sold out to his brother in 1975. Following that, he became associated with his nephew, Philip Beard, in real estate, and they "Borrowed money where we could, and bought and turned land."

Pruitt says that the commission should have made one decision when he was on the board that it made later: hiring Wayne Shackelford to essentially be the county manager. "The Commission did that when Bill Atkinson, who beat me in 1972, was chairman. We should have done that sooner." Pruitt feels that what defeated him from winning a third term is the same element that has defeated the commission chairman in races since then: "It is an anti-vote. That's what gets chairmen," he maintains.

Change was not easy, as the new five-man commission did not always appear to have the full confidence of the voters in its initial years. For instance, on July 29, 1970, the commission put to the people three ideas for bonds to help fund vitally-needed county infrastructure. The proposal was for (1) creation of a fire protection district throughout the county, a $2 million bond; (2) asking the voters if they would approve $850,000 in bonds for a new jail for the county; and (3) seeking approval of a $2 million bond program for roads.

The outcome surprised the commissioners. The voters were adamant: they did not like this method of financing these needs. All three proposals failed miserably, a solid 3:1 against them.

	Yes Votes	*No Votes*
Fire protection ($2 million)	1,709	5,546
For Jail ($850,000)	1,772	5,559
For Roads ($2 million)	1,556	5,686

One observer pointed out that the bond program was not "sold to the people very well." Another person noted that water mains were extended only to a small part of the county, and that the voters realized that proper fire protection with adequate water coverage was years away, and therefore, they would not support voting for fire protection with an inadequate water supply. Look, too, at the similarity of the vote against all three measures. The severity of the rejection of the three issues showed that the new five-member county commission government did not have the backing of those voting, and this had to concern the commission members, as the county was under-capitalized for what was projected to be imminent growth. So, little change came during the first term of the five-person commission.

One consideration in the early days of fast development of the county was that the county tax digest did not provide sufficient revenues for the operations that the county needed. For instance, in 1973, the county's total budget was only $6.5 million. And by that day's standard, this was good. The county budget in 1965 was only $1.7 million. That compares to the $1.675 billion that the 2007 county budget totaled.

On being on the new board, Gunnin says: "It seemed logical for me to try to help the government get started," since he had advocated the changes that brought about the five-man commission. As he was elected to the commission, Gunnin was the first person in 50 years to be elected from Norcross.

Gunnin would serve on the commission for 10 years. (He later resigned from the commission to make first one, then another, unsuccessful bid for the U.S. Congress.) However, Gunnin's efforts prior to and in the early days of the five-man commission were paramount in aiming the Gwinnett government along new routes to get things done. These efforts were vitally needed in the face of rapid change facing the county.

Once in office, the entire five-man commission had in mind several areas for improvement. These included fire protection, recreation for youth, garbage collection, animal control, business licensing and improvement in water availability. Over his 10 years in office, Gunnin innovated major change in all these areas, and compiled a record of outstanding accomplishments. Often Gunnin was in the forefront of studying issues and preparing his other commissioners on a variety of subjects. "I did a lot of the studies myself," he later admitted. "That was before the day when you hired consultants. We didn't have the money to pay for them, so I did the work myself." Gunnin even authored the initial policy and procedure manual for the county, as he understood the need for structure in government. Few found fault in his work, as the commission began instituting the changes Gunnin would suggest.

Bill Atkinson

A new day was headed Gwinnett's way. In the election of 1971, Bill Atkinson defeated Dudge Pruitt for the chairmanship. Another new face was Wayne Mason, who replaced Carvis Williams. The pace of change picked up after this election. Among the changes coming after 1972 were the adoption of modern management practices for county government, compared with the relatively backward and poorly managed system used before. Among the practices put into place relatively shortly were:

- Beginning of data collection system.
- Hiring a county engineer.
- Starting a land use plan.
- Implementation of a thoroughfare plan.
- System of franchise garbage collection, instead of bins.
- Modern policing structure.
- Leash laws.
- Business licenses.
- Development of modern water and sewer system.
- More progressive financing of county.

Eventually, other major changes would include a county-wide fire department and county-wide recreation authority. To put it in one word: the county government was being "modernized."

Some in the county kept alive the idea of professional management of the county, something the county commission badly needed. However, the commission also remembered the way that the voters of the county in 1968 rejected the idea of a county manager. After a lot of wrangling with the Gwinnett legislative delegation, which by then included Jimmy Mason and Norris Nash as the state representatives, finally a proposal was passed which allowed Gwinnett County to have an executive assistant to the board of county commissioners. Note the name: it was not officially a "county manager," but in effect, the "executive assistant," served in a similar capacity as a manager, but reporting to the board.

The key was picking the right person. That person, named on Jan. 1, 1973, was Wayne Shackelford, to be the executive assistant to the entire board. Shackelford was eminently aware of what was happening in Gwinnett through his previous work as the county agent of the Extension Service. He had come to Gwinnett County as assistant county agent on Feb. 1, 1960 and was named county agent on Aug. 1, 1963. At the county commission office, Shackelford worked closely with the chairman and district commissioners to insure that the county ran smoothly. He was "Mr. Inside," you might say, to the chairman being "Mr. Outside," and really, that's in many ways how the county has operated ever since.

Much later on, in 1987, under the administration of Lillian Webb, the county would eventually move to actually name someone to have the title and authority of a "county manager." By 1993, the position had been changed to the "county administrator," which in 2008 Jock Connell held. All departments of the county report to him, and he, in turn, reports to the county commissioners. The system works because of individuals who have been in the job having the trust of the commission.

Early growth rises from distribution

The major factor in the early commercial development of Gwinnett was its prime location in the Southeast with facilities for warehousing and distributing products. Initially, this could be seen in the long-range plan of the Norfolk Southern Railway in buying up land along its rail lines to locate industry that would use rail to bring in or send out its products. The railroad was buying land, particularly in the Gwinnett areas closest to Atlanta -- Norcross and Duluth. The railroad was paying what farmers considered high prices for what was essentially not the best farm land in the years following World War II.

The land the railroad bought sat fallow for years, but eventually paid big dividends for the rail system. With its resources, the railroad began amassing immense tracts of land near its rails in Gwinnett. The railroad then sat on the land for years, selling off portions at increasingly higher prices, with the land becoming more valuable the longer the railroad held it.

Today, most of the Norfolk Southern land in Gwinnett is fully developed, filled with warehouses from 100,000 to nearly a million square feet, storing and producing goods bound eventually for what was first the Southeast, and these days, often to ports throughout the world.

Work began on the expressway system in Atlanta in 1949. (It was initially labeled as a "$40 million expressway.") Slightly behind the early arrival of the railroad purchase of land for warehouses came the extension throughout Gwinnett of Interstate 85, opening Northeastern markets for faster distribution by truck. First, the expressway was completed to Norcross-Tucker Road (now Jimmy Carter Boulevard. Then, it opened to Beaver Ruin, then Pleasant Hill, then Old Peachtree Road and by 1967, I-85 ran throughout Gwinnett, a total of 45 miles of interstate highway. As each new segment of interstate opened, development began at a faster pace in adjacent areas. Virtually overnight, through-traffic left two-lane U.S. Highways 23 and 29 through Gwinnett for the faster interstate, which had no traffic signals and no slowing down when going through most towns. The last segment of Interstate 85 was opened to traffic on November 22, 1977, as a 27-mile portion between LaGrange and Grantville was completed. Altogether, I-85 runs 171 miles in Georgia.

Today, Interstate 85 is crowded morning and night, and constantly in use during the day and night. For instance, in 1990, traffic between Indian Trail Road and Jimmy Carter Boulevard on I-85 averaged 164,188 vehicles each day (going both ways.) By 2000, this average had grown to 236,400 vehicles, then to 264,120 in 2005, but dropped back in 2007 to 257,110, possibly because of an increase in fuel prices. (Figures from the Georgia DOT.) Interstate 85 is a main artery for commuters in Gwinnett, and for long-distance tourists and truckers.

As Gwinnett gained access to the Interstate route, land along I-85, the areas adjoining the railroad near Norcross, began to fill with businesses, often distribution facilities. Usually the new business in Gwinnett raised a one-story "office" building in front, with a two-story storage facility behind it, which, coupled with fork-lift trucks, made an efficient warehouse operation.

What started as a small segment of the business community in Gwinnett with a few warehouses, soon began to grow in capacity, as more and more companies needed Southeastern distribution facilities. They found the Gwinnett land close by, attractive, and relatively cheap, compared with Atlanta land.

Then, after a few years in Gwinnett, these companies often needed to expand, to add more warehouse space, or bring in another division, perhaps to add a sales office, or even locate a research and development unit. Since these firms had been treated kindly in Gwinnett by its people, its government and by its climate, why locate a sister unit far away?

What this meant, of course, was that much of the growth in Gwinnett was "from within," so to speak, in addition to Chamber of Commerce efforts of attracting new industry. Altogether, this allowed Gwinnett's commercial growth to expand even faster. This same mode of internal plus external expansion continues to work for Gwinnett even to the present day.

For a few years, in the late 1950s and 1960s, Gwinnett was quietly growing. Up until about 1970, the rest of Metro Atlanta paid very little attention to Gwinnett County. People drove through the county on the way to Athens, or Greenville or Charlotte, but seldom noticed what was happening. Then a blockbuster got their attention.

Getting the attention of all of Metro Atlanta in the early 1970s was Gwinnett's landing of its first major new industry, a most visible, and highly technical Western Electric plant and Laboratory at what is today Jimmy Carter Boulevard at I-85. It took an active county government plus significant innovations by forward-thinking county officials to snare the plant. These officials would later admit that the plant could just as easily have been located one exit south in DeKalb County, and Gwinnett would still have had to educate the children of the Western Electric workers living in the county. But since the plant was in Norcross, in 1973 it brought the couny's first $1 million check from a single company in ad valorem taxes.

Many consider Ray Gunnin, then a county commissioner from the Norcross area and a Southern Bell engineer in his vocation, as the key player in facilitating the location of Western Electric. Gunnin came up with an innovative agreement with DeKalb County to provide initial temporary sewer capacity and fire protection for the plant, until Gwinnett could provide its own services. (Shortly afterward, Gunnin guided the Pinckneyville Militia

District to establish its own fire protection district, the forerunner of today's fire department. Pinckneyville was the first area in Gwinnett to agree to fund through taxation its own district fire department, to guarantee Western Electric fire protection for its sprawling building.)

The plant eventually employed 3,800 people, and was the world's largest plant producing copper cable for the telephone industry.

(For more detail on the Western Electric plant, see the Appendix on page 635 for a time line of Western Electric activities in the county.)

Once Western Electric broke the ice with its location in Gwinnett, soon many other facilities, many of them high technology facilities, began to locate in the area around Norcross.

A key element in Gwinnett's growth of warehouse-distribution facilities was its early adoption of freeport legislation, a new element in Georgia's ad valorem taxing structure.

These inventory tax exemptions are for raw materials and goods in process, finished goods held by manufacturers, and finished goods held for out-of-state shipment.

Wayne Mason, who was on the commission from 1972-79, advocated with his fellow commissioners for adoption of freeport. "Some of the other commissioners at first were against granting this tax relief for warehouses, wanting to tax these firms on the goods awaiting shipment on their warehouse floor. But I told them that without freeport, we were not going to get these warehouses locating in Gwinnett, and that if they taxed them at 100 percent, that 100 percent of nothing is nothing. So they thought about it, and agreed, and we passed freeport, granting at first a 60 percent exemption, then added 20 percent for the next two years, to eventually have a 100 percent freeport. And as a result, coupled with the relative low cost of land in Gwinnett, and with both rail and interstate highway corridors in the county, Gwinnett in the 1970s got 70 percent of the location of warehouse-distribution facilities of Metro Atlanta. These firms provided industrial jobs at good salaries for us in Gwinnett, and helped give the county a more balanced tax digest, which also helped support and improve the schools of the county. It was a win all the way around."

Ray Gunnin's forward thinking on fire protection soon led him to propose a recreational tax for the Norcross area. Voters approved. Both the Pinckneyville fire and recreation districts were the first for Gwinnett. They paved the way to eventually extend fire and recreation districts throughout the entire county.

To show just how important the area around Norcross was to the county in its early industrial development, understand that there are18 militia districts in the county, from which precincts are drawn. In the 1970s, the Pinckneyville district (around Norcross) accounted for 40 percent of the entire county tax digest (which is the value of all real property, with improvements, in the county). That made the Norcross and Peachtree Corners area the job base for the county, with people driving from Snellville and Buford and Lawrenceville to work in Norcross.

Eventually, with industrial development extending to other parts of the county, Pinckneyville was no longer as dominant a part of the tax digest. But for 2004, that same area accounted for 20 percent of the Gwinnett overall tax digest, still a healthy figure. Meanwhile, four districts -- Lawrenceville, Martins, Duluth, and Pinckneyville---made up the bulk of the heavily developed commercial sector, accounting for 46.9 percent of the entire county tax digest.

Early sporting activities

In the modern day, sports play an important role at Gwinnett high schools. In years earlier, that was not the case. Up through the early 1950s, Gwinnett schools had a limited sports program, if any at all.

Gwinnett was first known as a power in high school circles for its basketball teams. One of the big events of the sports year was the Gwinnett basketball championship, pitting all the schools against each other.

One of the first Gwinnett teams to land a state title was the Dacula men's basketball team, which won a state basketball championship in 1938. The five-man squad included J.T. Bradbury, Carson Hogan, Horace McMillian, Willie Pharr and Luke Archer. The coach was H.J.B. Turner. Not only was the 1938 team good, but in 1939, the Dacula team was also in the state finals, losing the championship game by only one point.

Facilities were sometimes not the best for these early Gwinnett teams. For instance, by the time Dacula won a state men's basketball championship again, in 1945, the Dacula Gymnasium had been torn down, in anticipation of rebuilding another in its place. But by then, World War II had started, and materials were short, so the gym was not rebuilt until after the war.

The 1945 Dacula team, therefore, played only "away" games, winning every game they played, including the state championship. It was known as a team that practiced on an outdoor, dirt court! Those on the team included Julian Archer, Lonnie Etheridge, Roy Etheridge, Marlon Wages, Bernard Still, J.B. Gilbert, Joe Lovin, Aaron Johnson, Clinton Everett and Jamie Knight. (For a list of state champions from Gwinnett, see Appendix B on page 803.)

Bill Fortune, when playing basketball for Lawrenceville High, likes to tell the story of their team visiting in Suwanee around 1952-53 for the opening of a new gymnasium. "When we went out on the court, we found that in this new gym, the basketball goals were 12 feet high, not the regulation 10 foot. We went ahead and played the game with the goals at 12 feet. Later on, they changed them to 10 feet high."

While high school teams fielded baseball teams in the days before World War II, the major interest for Gwinnett in baseball was in the semi-pro leagues. (See chapter 2 about Buford for a glimpse at the Buford Shoemakers semi-pro team winning the national championship.)

Eventually, Gwinnett would have good high school teams in every field, and send its athletes into collegiate and professional sports. But Suwanee would also become the home for years of a professional football team (read about the Atlanta Falcons, page 300), and for a while, also home of an Arena Football League team, the Georgia Force. Later would come the Gwinnett Gladiators, an Eastern Hockey League professional team, with the Gwinnett Arena as their home rink. Then in 2008, a bombshell: Gwinnett would get its own Class AAA minor league baseball team starting in 2009, and more important for local residents, it would be called the Gwinnett Braves, and be the top farm team of the major league Atlanta Braves!

Held at the Gwinnett Arena are the Georgia High School Association basketball playoffs and wrestling championships. It also hosted Southeastern Conference basketball games, and the SEC women's basketball championship. Gwinnett has been the site for a major Professional Golf Association tournament, known for years as the BellSouth Classic before changing its name to the AT&T Classic in 2007 after the sale of BellSouth to AT&T. However, the Classic was last held in 2008, as AT&T dropped its sponsorship, and no other was announced.

First football team

Buford had the first football program in the county, though initially this was a sandlot football team, comprised of players from the community. During this era, sometimes the team was sprinkled with those who had graduated from high school, and other times, outside "ringers" were in the line-up. This amateur team was known as the "Austins," and was coached by Bob Lee, who later became a Federal Bureau of Investigation agent. John Hutchins tells the story that sandlot football jerseys with an "A" on them in the 1930s would be cleaned and stacked in front of the Bagwell Drug Store on Main Street. "Players, ages 13 to 30, would search for a jersey that they could fit into, and then you played," Hutchins says. The games were staged on the Buford Air Field, where Bona Allen Company kept its airplane. That field was at the intersection of South Lee Street and Buford Highway, the main office of Peoples Bank today.

It was during World War II, in 1945, that organized high school football began in Buford, which had the first high school football team in Gwinnett. The Rev. George Washington Sheffer, the Presbyterian minister in town, at age 69, and with no coaching experience, began the team and led the team to an undefeated season. He was an outspoken advocate for the youth, and also a major force in Buford, writing for the local newspaper, active in Kiwanis and a commissioner of the local softball league. He was pastor of the church from 1945-49.

After World War II, in 1946, when Tom Riden came to Buford as principal and coach, he generated interest in the high school sports program, including football. Riden's accomplishments as coach are legendary, as he remained in Buford in these capacities until 1960. The Buford football stadium was named for him on Sept. 1, 1995, at which time he and his family were present.

(The Buford baseball field is named for Gerald McQuaig, former player for the Buford Shoemakers, who taught school and was baseball coach at Buford High for many years.)

The second high school football program in Gwinnett was at Lawrenceville High, with many elements of the town uniting behind the idea for a team. In 1951, a joint meeting of the Kiwanis and Lions clubs decided to help raise money for the team, with a goal set of $3,000, but eventually they raised between $4-5,000 for equipment. It was noted that Buford had a team, with only 60 boys at their school, while Lawrenceville had no team but had 90 boys in the same grades as Buford. Reasons cited for fielding a team included breaking the monotony of the year-round basketball program, adding color to the overall school program; and helping keep boys in school who might otherwise drop out. The reasons also noted "character building" among the attributes of a football team.

Jack Britt coached his first year in Gwinnett at Lawrenceville High in 1952, and started that school's football program. He had a six-week spring practice session in 1952 to get the players familiar with fundamentals and to improve their physical conditioning. Just out of the University of Georgia in 1950, Britt had previously joined Dorsey Brooks at Tucker High to help take that school from 6 to 11-man football. Britt was the only coach for the Lawrenceville team, and also had to coach the Midget team.

Members of that first Lawrenceville High football team included Jimmy Brannan, Raymond Bradberry, Butch Britt, Glenn Bennett, Paul Brooks, Milton Cates, Travis Cooper, Dickie Corbin, Horace Corbin, Jack Craig, Freddie Dodson, Bill Fortune, Larry Gunter, Shirley Gunter, Jim Hood, Ken Hood, James Holt, Millard Davis, Hubert Hutchins, Kelly Guthrie, Robert Hutchins, Victor McKelvey, Bill Moon, Gerald Morgan, Keith Pharr, Larry Puckett, Ray Oakes, Barron Osborne, Randolph Simpson, Warren Swanson, Willard Swanson, Morris Langley, Maurice Cooper, Robert Fowler, Venoy Adams, Nelson Crowe, Marlon Wall, George Robinson, Lionel Hamilton and Robert McHaffey.

The co-captains were quarterback Scooter Adams and end Travis Cooper.

The Lawrenceville nickname in those days was the "Panthers," which it remained until the school in 1957 became the consolidated Central Gwinnett High, when the name was changed to the Black Knights. Bartow Jenkins was the first coach of the Central Gwinnett football team.

Besides starting the high school team in Lawrenceville, Britt also began a midget team of fourth and fifth graders, who would play area teams, such as Winder and the Athens YMCA team. Britt says: "We would go to Athens on Saturday to play football in the morning, then head to the Athens YMCA swimming pool, and later that afternoon, we would take the team to Sanford Stadium to attend the Georgia Bulldog football game." Among members of that midget team were Mickey Wages, Powell Smith, Doug Smith, Billy Corley, John and Wayne Patillo, Quill 'Smitty" Smith and George Pinion.

When the first Lawrenceville High School team began practice and was suiting up, only one member of the team had ever played football with protective equipment. Britt says: "My brother, Butch Britt, had played on the small Tucker team before, and was on the Lawrenceville team. When we gave out the equipment, Butch had to go around the dressing room to show the players how to strap on the shoulder pads and other gear. I remember Jack Craig came out with the tail protector in front, thinking it was more beneficial that way. He got kidded about that. He was a fullback."

Among the players on that first team was a student who would eventually become the mayor of Lawrenceville, Bill Fortune. Jack Britt remembers: "Bill was an all-around athlete, a big guy, 6 foot 2 inches tall, and good in baseball, basketball, and also track. He got a scholarship in track to Georgia Tech, as a miler, half-miler and relay runner.

"Bill had been injured in an automobile accident, and was not supposed to make contact in football. We could use him to punt and kick off, since he was better at this than anyone else on the team. I stressed to him that I would let him kick off, but he was not to make contact with the opposing players, because of back problems. And, as coach, I realized that I could not afford to get him hurt, for he was the mainstay in basketball, track and baseball."

Britt continues: "Well, the very first football game ever for Lawrenceville High was on Sept. 13, 1952 against Lithonia. In those days, the field was not lighted, so we played in the daytime. Bill kicked off, then ran as fast as he could down the field and made the first tackle ever for Lawrenceville High. But I had told him not to make contact. So I pulled him off the field, and told him he wouldn't be playing any more that day. I later used him to punt or kick off, for he kicked real deep. But I needed him healthy for the other sports, for he was a superior athlete." Lawrenceville lost the game 14-0.

Fortune remembers the incident well: "I made the first tackle in Lawrenceville High history that day," he says, "But it was also the last one I made."

After graduating from Georgia Tech, Fortune was a civil engineer for several firms, including E.R. Snell Contractor, Inc. out of Snellville. Fortune later started his own bridge building firm, and in 2008 was living with his family in Marietta.

Jim Hood was a 150-pound end on that first team. He says: "That first year, we were floundering, trying, and just learning the game. And we were such little guys in those days." The team would play eight games that year, and did not win a single game....until the final game of the year. On a bitterly cold Nov. 7, 1952 under the lights in Buford, Lawrenceville won 13-2. "That was exciting!" remembers Hood. Jack Britt had some bragging rights: "We say we won the county championship, because we beat the only other school in the county that had a football team!"

The Lawrenceville team, by Hood's senior year, had an all-state lineman in Class C, guard Ray Oakes.

And when you get a football team, you get cheerleaders. Members of that first football cheerleading team were Marie Freeman, Peggy Wages, Myrna Fountain, Betty Jo Mahaffey, Murlene Turner, Glenda Edge, Donna Fortune, Joanne Johnson, Jane Raney, Carol Storey, Jean Langston and Sybil Bramblett.

The cheerleaders had regular practice, just like the football team. Betty Jo Reepe, who kept a scrapbook of the year, remembers, "We had practice ever day, except game days. Not one of us had experience cheerleading for football, though some were cheerleaders for basketball, while others played. We all had a good time."

That first Lawrenceville High football team also didn't have a manicured stadium to play in, but played and practiced for the first few years at Rhodes Jordan Park, east of town. With the high school "on the hill" in Lawrenceville, the team would suit up for practice, then run together to the field at the park. After practice, they would walk back the mile up the hill to take off their uniforms.

Jack Britt says that appliance businessman Earl Story gave truckloads of soil to spread on the field, which was mostly red clay. "But even the soil had a lot of rock in it."

Jim Hood remembers that field for practice very well. "It was pretty much just a big graded rock pile, and we would practice football, then before we left, we would pick up rocks and throw them into the creek between the ball field and the swimming pool." Bill Fortune remembers that anyone who was tardy at school was punished by being given an assignment of throwing more of those rocks into the creek. That rock-tossing went on until the consolidated Central Gwinnett High got its new stadium near the school.

Jack Britt remained friends with his former players, many of whom he routinely plays golf with in his retirement. His former players remember one aspect, and often remind him: "Today football teams keep water jugs all around the field, but you wouldn't give us a drink of water." Yeah, Britt tells them, "But I gave you two salt tablets before each practice." Hood adds: "It nearly killed us, but that was the way we did it back then, and we still kid him about the salt tablets!"

Britt remained at Lawrenceville High for five years, then continued on for a total of 25 years in coaching. He retired in 1981. He was the second year coach at South Gwinnett High, and remained there for 12 years. He later also coached at Parkview High, where he taught construction in the vocational wing. “Bartow Jenkins was the principal there, and with it being a new school, the Booster Club wanted to build a stadium for the school. Bartow told me that we had $87,000 from the Club for the stadium and to ‘do as much as you can’ with it. They already had put in the football field and the track around it. My students poured about 100 yards of concrete after we built the forms, and put in the home field bleachers, the concessions stand and ticket office, for that $87,000. We didn’t have a penny left.

“But with the stands, Parkview could qualify for playoffs, since it could seat 3,000 on the home side. We didn’t have any money left to build the visitor’s bleachers.”

Britt was also involved in building several football fields in Gwinnett, as a result of being a member of a construction unit of the Georgia National Guard.

“We would use the equipment with operators from the Guard, and the school would pay for the fuel. The Guard members were veteran operators from World War II, and would either do it during the weekend drills, or if they missed the drill, could make it up during the week, by doing the grading then. We built the field at Lawrenceville that way, both the old and new one. Duluth already had a field, but we also used the Guard to grade the South Gwinnett field when I went there.”

Red Barron

Another name associated for many years with football in Dacula was David I. “Red” Barron, who became a football star at Georgia Tech under Coaches John Heisman and William Alexander. From Habersham County, he was an All-American halfback on the Tech teams of 1918-22, and won five letters in football, three letters in baseball and four in track. He captained both the 1922 football and baseball teams, and was named in 1959 to the Georgia Tech Hall of Fame.

Barron on two occasions was the coach of the Monroe A&M football team, and also coached at the Ninth District A&M in Clarksville. He also played professional baseball briefly with the Boston Braves, then joined the Atlanta Crackers, and managed that team in 1932. He returned to Monroe A&M in 1933, and eventually became president of the school, and after it lost state funding, turned it into a private school.

Always a friend with Gov. Eugene Talmadge, Barron was named to the Board of Regents in 1936. Two years later, he eventually obtained his degree from Georgia Tech, and through the efforts of the governor, was named a vice president at Georgia Tech, with Talmadge anticipating he could replace the sitting president. But faculty and students rebelled at the idea, and Barron remained at the Monroe school until it closed in 1942.

But there is much more to the story than that.

About that time, Barron and his wife had divorced, and in 1944, Barron married Helen Denny. From 1935 to 1952, Barron ran a football camp on a 265 acre tract in Rabun County. On the night of Sept. 5, 1952, he and his wife had been drinking, and the upshot was that Barron was charged first with manslaughter, a charge later changed to murder. He was convicted of the manslaughter charge, and sentenced to three to five years in prison. He served his time at the Alto Training Institute, now the North Georgia Corrections Academy on the grounds of Lee Arrendale State Prison in Alto. While there, Barron coached the prison football team. One person said of his incarceration: "Coach Barron was never locked up" or "...put in a cell and had the key turned." He was paroled after 20 months, and in 1955, was pardoned.

The Guthrie brothers operating Three Winds Farm off Club Drive in Gwinnett brought him to the county to manage their chicken operation. Meanwhile, Jack Britt says that Barron never drank alcohol again. Soon he married a woman 14 years younger, Dorothy Lyle of Maysville, who had been a student at the Monroe school while Barron was president.

Then one day, Barron got a surprise. He got a call from Carson Britt, who was principal at Dacula High. Britt suggested that Barron teach at his school. Taking the cue, Barron took courses at the University of Georgia, and obtained teaching credentials. Eventually he and his third wife built a brick home on a 10 acre tract on Sweet Gum Road, near Lawrenceville. He also joined and taught Sunday School at the First Baptist Church of Lawrenceville, where one person said the subject in Sunday school was often "Georgia Tech." He also peppered his history teaching with references to Georgia Tech.

Barron is remembered in Gwinnett for teaching history and coaching baseball at Dacula, but even better known as the person most responsible at starting the football program in 1963 at Dacula High. That first year, the team played a junior varsity schedule mostly with seniors, and never lost a game. However, while Barron was a coach or spectator, Dacula football never had a winning season after that first season. The football field at Dacula was dedicated to him on Sept. 9, 1965. Mr. Barron died in 1982.

Billy Britt, who was a "water boy" the year Barron started football in Dacula, and whose father brought Barron to Dacula, remembers him as someone who was outgoing and easily made friends. "He was always surrounded by children, for he would take time with them. And he had a contagious laugh, and was a jolly, red-faced fellow." Britt remembers that his father took a chance in hiring Barron. "Some folks in Dacula had known his wife's family, and my father really wanted to make sure that the community rallied around him. When the Dacula football field was being built, lots of people contributed to it, as a community effort. Local farmers helped plow, drag and seed the field."

Meanwhile, the Dacula football teams, eventually playing in the state's highest classification, are perennial powers in football circles, being in the state semi-finals in 1988, 1990 and 2005. Kevin Maloof has been the Dacula coach since 1991, compiling a record of 133-63.

Red Barron would have been proud.

Heisman winner

Gwinnett has produced one winner of football's Heisman Trophy. He is George Rogers, who began his football playing at Duluth High School, and later matriculated at the University of South Carolina, where he won the award in 1980.

Reported uneasy about contact when he began play in high school, he changed into a determined, skilled runner and hitter. He was both big and quick. At South Carolina as a tailback, Rogers led his team as they gained 21 consecutive victories. He led the nation in rushing with 1,781 yards and tied for third in TDs with 14. As the 1980 season opened, he was a Heisman long shot, but when the voting was over, he led decisively. The New Orleans Saints made him the top National Football League draft pick in 1981. Rogers later played with the Washington Redskins, who won the Super Bowl in 1987, a year he was one of the league's leading runners. He was elected to the NFL and College Hall of Fame in 1997.

Rogers also started the George Rogers Foundation, to provide scholarships to kids in need planning to attend USC. The foundation gives out more than $15,000 in scholarships each year. His jersey, number 38, is retired at the University of South Carolina.

First championship for Duluth

Duluth High School's first state championship in any sport came in 1951, when its baseball team won the state Class C title, beating Springfield High 4-3. This was the culmination of the team's season, as they finished with a 21-4 record.

That year's team has been playing baseball together in various leagues for several years. History teacher B.B. Archer of Dacula, was their coach, but all thought of him first as a basketball coach. One of the players on that team, the Rev. Lamar Hansard, said of Archer: "We mostly coached ourselves, for we knew each other's abilities real well since we had played together for several years. When there was a situation in a game, Coach Archer would call us together, and ask 'What ought we to do here?' and he pretty much let us guide him, since his love was basketball." Later Archer would return to Dacula as the basketball coach.

The team's regular season record was 14-4. The team was comprised of Hansard as the catcher, and Bobby Parker as the pitcher who ended with a 15-2 record. The infield was composed of Jack Mitchell at first base; Leonel E. (Stud) Barker at second; Jimmy Smith at third, and Richard Davis at shortstop. The outfield had Jerry Turner in left, Harold Robinson in center, and Ernest Mayes in right field. Their three subs were Charles Hansard, a pitcher and outfielder; Billy Daniel, a utility infielder; and Lamar Kelley, an outfielder.

There were seven games in the state single-elimination playoffs. In one of the games, Bobby Parker pitched a no-hitter in the afternoon against Johnson High in West Point, Ga. Since the winner had to play a second game that night, and in West Point there were no lights at this field, the teams drove across the Chattahoochee River into Lanett, Ala. for the second game that day at night.

The championship game was supposed to be played on a neutral field in Perry, Ga. However, heavy downpours left water standing on that field. Calling ahead, a playable field was found south, in Unadilla. Lamar Hansard remembers: "When we got there, about all they had was a backstop. But first we had to chase the cows off the field before we could start."

The opponent was Springfield High of Effingham County, winner of the southern division. Duluth scored first and held the lead the entire game. Richard Davis and Ernest Mayes each knocked in two runs, and the team won, 4-3. Bob Barker says that Davis was their best batter, particularly good at clutch hitting. "He could do everything, hit, bunt, steal a base."

First country club

Gwinnett had its first golf club in the 1920s in Buford, which continued in operation for 18 years. It was known as the Sawnee Golf Club, and the course consisted of 18 holes, Hansel Morgan reports in his *Historic Buford.*

The club was located in the southeastern quadrant of Bogan and Sandy Hill Roads. In those days, the greens were composed of compacted cottonseed hulls, an ample commodity from the many cotton fields of Gwinnett. That club eventually was closed before the major growth in Gwinnett came.

The first golf club of the modern era was organized by Doyle Johnson and Perrin Walker of Lawrenceville in 1961 on Camp Perrin Road. It was a nine hole course, at first called Perrin Country Club, which Walker laid out at his former camp for boys and girls. Walker had first built three holes, to see if any golfers would have an interest in a nine-hole course. Later, six more holes were built and the name was changed to Windy Hill Golf Course. It was a public course. The club operated until 1991, when the lease ran out. That land was purchased by Perrin Walker's son, Jimmy, in 1992, when the property was developed into Fairway Walk Subdivision. Where the club was located is adjacent to the site of the Collins Hill Library.

Perrin Walker in 1965 built an adjacent nine holes on Camp Perrin Road, and named it Walker Golf Club. In 1970, work began on an additional nine holes that was completed in 1971, and later became Pine Ridge Country Club. Besides the golf holes, the club had a new clubhouse, two swimming pools and two tennis courts, and was completed in 1973.

The club was sold to the county in 1988 for $3.4 million. The Springbrook Golf Commission was established in 2000 and the county issued a warranty deed for the property to the Commission in September of 2000. Shortly afterward, the Springbrook Golf Commission changed the name of the golf course to Collins Hill Golf Club.

What would become another 18 hole course was purchased off what became Club Drive, an extension of Shackelford Road, off Pleasant Hill Road, in 1959. A group of Buckhead businessmen, doctors and lawyers had purchased property known as Four Winds Farm, some 750 acres, and developed an initial nine-hole golf course, which they called Castleview Golf and Country Club. Though organized in 1959, the club did not begin operations until September, 1962, but its life was short. The club soon became bankrupt, and was bought by Country Clubs Inc. (CCI).

CCI bought the title to the club "for a song," and re-opened immediately as Northwoods Country Club. The original course had been designed by Willard Byrd and George Cobb. Eventually, they hired Charlie Underwood in 1964 to be their golf course superintendent. He opened up another nine holes in May of 1965. That began a 43 year association for Underwood with CCI, which later became Club Corp. He became the general manager of Northwoods in 1980, and was also the Southeast regional agronomist for Club Corp. He later became the regional manager, overseeing about 40 clubs owned by Club Corp. Even after retiring in 2000, Underwood remained active with Club Corp., going into the construction management aspect with them, overseeing building and renovations. Among the clubs he built were Bear's Best in Suwanee, Birch River in Dahlonega, and Eagle's Landing in McDonough.

More country clubs

• In 1964, Larry McClure and Dr. Miles Mason Jr. began Berkeley Hills Country Club, originally with 18 holes, later expanded to 27 holes. This began the era of country clubs built around homes.

• In 1973, the Snellville area got its first golf course, which was previously a 700-acre cattle farm. It became known as Summit Chase Country Club. About a year after the club was started by Nick Morgan and Charlie Hardy Jr., the club got into financial trouble, and the C&S Bank took over and ran it for several years. In 1979, Van Britt and Wayne Lisle purchased the club, and began operating it in early 1980. Meanwhile, homes were built in a subdivision on some 500 acres around the club, with the country club taking up about 200 of the acres. In 1995, Britt became the sole owner of the club.

• The era of the largest country clubs amid a major housing development started in 1989 when the Panos family began construction of a winery, golf course and subdivision of large homes near Braselton straddling the border of Gwinnett, Hall, Jackson and Barrow Counties along Interstate 85. The area became known as Chateau Elan. Panos, who became wealthy with the invention of the Nicotine Patch, poured millions into the development to create a major resort destination site. Meanwhile, larger and larger homes, many selling for more than $1 million, were built around the golf amenities.

• The first golf links at Chateau Elan were the Chateau course, followed by the Legends course in 1993 and the Woodlands course in 1996. The Chateau course was the site for four years (1996 to 1999) as a venue on the Ladies Professional Golf Association tournament.

• The City of Sugar Hill got into the golf business in 1992 when it opened its Sugar Hill Golf Club, a public course. The course was irrigated with treated wastewater. That continued until 1997 when Gwinnett County took over the Sugar Hill wastewater treatment facility. However the City of Sugar Hill continues to run the Golf Club as a public course of 18 holes.

• The year 1993 saw the start of two more clubs, Country Club of Gwinnett, located south of Snellville, and Peachtree Masters, bordering the Chattahoochee River in Duluth. With the fast growth in Gwinnett, more clubs began -- Trophy Club of Apalachee near Dacula in 1994, and, in 1995, the Hamilton Mill Golf Club at the vast Hamilton Mill development in extreme northern Gwinnett near Interstate 85.

• Perhaps the most well known course in Gwinnett emerged as the Duke Power Company-owned Crescent Properties began Sugarloaf Country Club in 1997. The club was known as the venue for the AT&T Classic of the PGA tour each spring. Crescent Properties added its second golf community in 2005 when it began the River Club near the Chattahoochee north of Suwanee.

• One Gwinnett course straddles the DeKalb-Gwinnett line. That is Heritage Golf Club, off Britt Road. The club consists of 27 holes, with 21 of the 27 holes in Gwinnett. It is owned by pro basketball player Julius Erving.

• Another public course in the county is The Hootch, another Duluth facility that is near the Chattahoochee River. It is an "executive golf course" of 4,200 yards, and includes an extensive driving range.

• A second Suwanee golf course is the Bear's Best club in Suwanee, dating from 2002, also built around an extensive selection of executive homes.

(For a list of golf courses in Gwinnett, see p 825 in Appendix B.)

Sugarloaf Golf Classic

One of the biggest events in Gwinnett for 12 years was the annual AT&T (earlier BellSouth) Golf Classic. It has been held at the Sugarloaf Country Club since 1997. The name was changed to the AT&T Classic in 2007 after the merger of BellSouth into AT&T, and discontinued for lack of major sponsor after 2008.

The tournament started in 1964, when businessman Jim Clay, along with six friends, purchased hundreds of acres of farmland near the Chattahoochee River in Cobb County. The Atlanta Country Club was built on this land, and it became the annual site of the Atlanta Golf Classic tournament. Clay and 50 of his friends put up money to establish the Atlanta Classic Foundation, to manage and promote the tournament.

In 1966, a two-day Pro-Am tournament was held at the Atlanta Country Club to demonstrate to professional golf officials that the Atlanta Classic Foundation could manage a golf tournament. Their first tournament was successful, despite the lack of a clubhouse, and despite a tornado hitting the course on the Thursday of the tournament. The Classic became part of the PGA tour in 1977.

In 1982, Georgia Pacific Corp. sponsored the tournament, and in 1989, BellSouth began as the title sponsor, a partnership that has produced more than $15 million donated to charity in 18 years.

When the Classic moved to Sugarloaf, the course was a par-72 course designed by Greg Norman, his first signature course in the United States, unveiled specifically for the BellSouth Classic. Scott McCarron was the first champion at the Sugarloaf course, and he also won in 2001. The only three-time winner of the tournament is Phil Mickelson.

Among the winners of the BellSouth Classic have been some notable golfers, including Jack Nicklaus, Tom Watson, Bob Charles, Calvin Peete, Hale Irwin, Larry Nelson, Tom Kite, Corey Pavin, John Daly, Tiger Woods, David Duval, and Retief Goosen. (See page 830.)

Dave Kaplan began his association with the tournament as the executive director in 1983, marking him as one of the longest-serving charitable organization directors associated with a charity in the area.

The year 2008 was the last year that the Classic was held, as the last prime sponsoring organization, AT&T, pulled their support. Anticipated to take place in 2009 was a PGA Seniors Tournament near the time the Classic was previously held.

Playgrounds at opposite ends of county

Two state authorities, anchoring opposite ends of Gwinnett County, oversee major recreational venues for not only Gwinnett residents, but for the state of Georgia and tourists from afar. At one time, the State of Georgia funded these authorities. For years now, neither of these state authorities have cost taxpayers a penny, as they have both generated sufficient revenue to be self-supporting. Though now both venues are privatized, there was no immediate savings of tax monies in this move, since the Authorities were already self-sufficient. Facility upgrades at the two authorities are now being paid out of private, not state, funds.

The two authorities oversee Lake Lanier Islands and Stone Mountain Park, both vast playgrounds of the area.

However, both of these authorities still get oversight from boards appointed by the governor of Georgia, which are charged with making sure that the entities are well managed. A list of the members of these boards is at the end of this section.

Lake Lanier Islands were created when Buford Dam backed up the Chattahoochee and Chestatee Rivers in 1956 to form Lake Lanier. The dam of the lake is between Gwinnett and Forsyth Counties, that is, between Buford and Cumming. The Islands were once hilltops, and these islands appeared as the lake's water rose. The state moved in 1962 to form an authority to govern the islands near the southern part of the lake, creating a man-made playground. The Lake Lanier Islands Development Authority is charged with developing the islands as a recreational venue for the people of Georgia.

The other local state-directed Authority, which is a recreational venue in Gwinnett, is the Stone Mountain Memorial Association. For years, Indians and early settlers all knew of Stone Mountain, a giant outcropping of granite 800 feet above the surrounding plateau. It is the largest known granite formation, one mile by two miles in size, and stands 1,683 feet above sea level. It is located on Gwinnett's southern edge. Only 35 of its 3,183 acres of land are actually in Gwinnett County. The Olympic Tennis facility, some 23 acres, is in Gwinnett, as is the 12-acre Stone Mountain Airport. The tennis venue was the only Atlanta 1996 Olympic site in Gwinnett County.

Besides being well known, Stone Mountain is one of Georgia's most visited attractions. It was in private hands until 1958, when the State of Georgia bought it. The Memorial Association operated Stone Mountain as a state park until 1996. That year, Gov. Zell Miller moved to privatize several state-run venues, including both Lake Lanier Islands and Stone Mountain.

Both areas are popular with visitors. In 2006, figures from the two authorities show that four million people visited Stone Mountain, and over a million people each year are counted at the gates at Lake Lanier Islands. The town of Stone Mountain and other suburban subdivisions surround Stone Mountain Park. Lake Lanier, however, when first built, was virtually in a rural area. The influx of new people into Gwinnett, Hall, Forsyth and Dawson Counties since the lake was built, plus the attraction of the lake, means that today Lake Lanier is also suburban and surrounded by subdivisions. Meanwhile, a vibrant recreational economy of marinas, boat manufacturing plants, and other tourism ventures have transformed the Lake Lanier area into quite a commercial engine.

Now a look into more detail about these two playgrounds near Gwinnett.

Lake Lanier Islands

On February 1, 1956, the U.S. Army Corps of Engineers started impounding the Chattahoochee River, as Lake Lanier started to back up behind Buford Dam. It took three years for the waters to form a full pool (1,071 feet above sea level) at Lake Lanier. The river must maintain a continuous flow below the dam, in order to preserve habitat and breeding grounds as the river winds through Metro Atlanta, then Western Georgia. It is the dividing line between much of Alabama and Georgia, and flows into Florida and finally on to the Gulf of Mexico. Lake Lanier itself is 26 miles long, covering about 47 miles of original riverbed, and at full pool, includes 38,000 acres of water.

Lake Lanier was authorized by the Flood Control Act of 1944, which includes language to permit water resource development around the lake "to minimize federal costs." It also encourages local interests to share the cost of providing recreational facilities and services.

When the state of Georgia created the Lake Lanier Islands Development Authority in 1962, plans for its first phase included a marina, campground, stables and a beach area. But access to the islands was only by boat until 1969, when Congressional funding provided a bridge to the main islands. The bridge is named for Sen. Richard Russell, who was in the forefront of seeking Federal backing for the entire project.

Long-range plans of the Authority from its early days called for a resort more extensively developed than traditional state parks. After all, the Islands, covering 1,041 acres, were a large water playground near Atlanta, with its perceived demand for advanced amenities. This multi-million resort became a destination attraction for many.

By 1975, an upscale 250-room hotel, Stouffer's PineIsle resort, had been opened, with its own golf course. This began a new wave of interest in the Islands, as visitors came from not just Atlanta and Georgia, but from a much wider area to visit. Meanwhile, for its summer beach improvements, tons of white sand from near Dublin, Ga., had been hauled to the Islands, creating a beautiful white beach in one of the red-ribbed clay coves near the PineIsle Hotel.

Another draw of the Islands from the beginning was a large campground, with 250 camping sites. This proved quite popular for visitors, many of whom arrived pulling "pop-up" campers to set up, some spending their vacation on the Islands. The Campground was operated year-round, and proved to be one of the most popular of the attractions, often completely booked for the day. It didn't take reservations, so often campers would arrive early in the day, to take the place of those visitors departing that day.

While PineIsle Hotel was a popular recreational and meeting facility for the Metro Atlanta area, and made money for the Authority, over the years, many of the other leased resort activities did not have a similar success. After all, the Island activity was mostly confined to the warmer months. Soon the horse riding stables, trout fishing and even the marina were not profitable, and it became necessary for the Authority to step in. Roy Burson, for years the general manager of Lake Lanier Islands, says: "Slowly, the Authority had to take over virtually all the amenities except for PineIsle Hotel and its golf course."

In 1987, the water park and beach found new life with the addition of water slides and a wave pool. One of the benefits of these features is that they could generate funds into the early evening, though not in the colder weather. In 1988, a second golf course was added, along with a second resort hotel, originally named Lake Lanier Islands Resort. This hotel was renamed the Hilton at Lake Lanier in 1990.

By 1989, the Authority reached a milestone. Up until that time, its operation had been to some extent subsidized by the state, though over the years, with smaller and smaller funding allocations, the state funds fell. But by 1989, Lake Lanier Island became financially self-sufficient. It still had on its payroll more than 600 persons, which included many summer part-timers, though about 200 people were on its year-round payroll. But operationally, it was not costing the state any money anymore.

One of the most forward-thinking and innovative ideas for the Islands came in November of 1993. Prior to that time, nearly all of the activities at the Islands were centered around water activities at the lake or the beach, primarily used in the daytime.

Little revenue was generated during the darker hours. But when the Authority invested $1 million to begin the "Magical Nights of Lights," all was changed. This became a popular night time destination during the Christmas season, as 32,000 cars in 2007, packed with parents and children, drove through the gates to see what was dubbed the world's largest animated light extravaganza. There were more than a million twinkling lights telling the story of the Christmas season to the delight of both youth and adults.

Families flocked through the gates of the islands to see the lights, taking a 6.5 mile drive through the islands. With each car coming onto the islands charged a higher than daytime gate fee, suddenly the light show created a big revenue source during the six weeks it glows each year. What began as a $10 entrance fee for the light show, grew to a $30 Monday through Thursday charge per vehicle by 2007 (and $40 for Friday through Sunday!) (See Appendix B on page 824 for visitors to Lake Lanier Islands.)

The popularity of the Islands as a playground for Georgians and visitors continues unabated. For 2007, a total of 77,054 vehicles paid to get on the Islands, with another 3,805 paying $38 for an annual decal to gain entrance to the Islands at any time.

All was changed, however, in 1996 during the administration of Zell Miller as governor. In 1995, the governor proposed that many state operations be privatized. Miller selected Joe Tanner, former head of the Department of Natural Resources, as his point man for privatization. Besides the Islands, other state-run activities under the privatization move included a veterans' home in Milledgeville, and smaller state operations, such as motor vehicle repair and sale of surplus property. Yet the two major entities that came under privatization were Stone Mountain Park and Lake Lanier Islands.

Tanner says that the overall privatization program was successful in saving the state money. "The pure reduced savings was in excess of $1 billion a year. But all were not complete savings. Some areas privatized earned money, like at Stone Mountain Park and Lake Lanier Islands, and funneled any income into maintenance and infrastructure improvements. Privatizing was more of a philosophical idea with these two authorities." It also allowed for private capital to fund new ventures at the two authorities.

For Lake Lanier Islands, soon nine bids were received on the property, with the state subleasing the property to KSL Lanier, a subsidiary of KSL Recreation Corp. This company operated major golf resorts in the nation, including Doral, La Quinta and PGA West. The Mobile District of the Corps of Engineers extended the state's lease to a full 50 years.

KSL agreed to pay the Islands Authority $9 million at closing, and $3 million per year plus 3.5 percent of all income generated on the islands over $20 million. At the outset, it also agreed to spend $5 million on new development in the first five years. For the nine years that KSL ran the property, it spent $10 million on improvements on the Islands.

Then in 2005, KSL was purchased by C&L Real Estate Investment Trust (C&L) out of Orlando, Fla. The Lake Lanier lease was on the market twice before C&L purchased it. C&L wanted the bulk of KSL's holdings, but found that the Lake Lanier property did not fit its profile of properties it wanted to operate. Officials from C&L met with the Lake Lanier Islands Authority only once, to tell the Authority C&L would sell its Lake Lanier Islands lease.

That's when Gwinnett businessman Virgil Williams and his four children entered the picture, closing on the lease in September 2005. C&L REIT held the property for less than a year.

Williams is the chairman of the board of the family-owned company, Lake Lanier Islands Management Company. His children own the majority of the stock, and three of the four children are active managers of the Islands company. The Williams' company agreed to pay $3.2 million a year to the Authority, with an additional percentage based on certain thresholds.

The new company plans a multi-phase improvement campaign, aimed at upgrading the Islands. Altogether, plans call for investing $300 million over 7-10 years. The first phase of $20 million began in 2006, adding 117 rooms to the Emerald Point Hotel (the former Hilton), and enlarging its meeting space, dining facilities and lobby.

The second phase of $100 million is envisioned within 7-10 years. It calls for tearing down the former PineIsle Hotel and rebuilding a new, four-star hotel on site. Before the upgrading is over, a total of five hotels are envisioned on the Islands, plus one more golf course (for a total of three). Other improvements in the plans include retail shopping, a yacht club, wellness center and spa.

Meanwhile, the Authority is a partner in this venture, taking its lease payments to upgrade the infrastructure of the Islands with 7.5 miles of new roads and streets, 22 miles of walking trails, new sewer and water lines and entrance gates.

By 2015, many of the improvements the Williams family is planning should be in place, aiming to make Lake Lanier Islands an even larger resort attraction not only for Georgians, but for people from elsewhere.

Ever since the work began on Buford Dam, and as Lake Lanier filled, and became a prime recreation area of Atlanta, the countryside around Lake Lanier changed radically. No longer did you see small farms and terraced fields growing crops. Land near the lake soon became quite valuable for homes, some second homes, some primary homes, for the Metro Atlanta area.

Not only that, but businesses thrived around the lake, often associated with the lake itself, as marinas, sailing schools, boat sales, boat manufacturing (even houseboat building) and similar enterprises flourished. All this activity directly related to the lake itself.

Then in the early 2000s, two different events began to affect the lake.

The most serious was a series of droughts in the Southeast, particularly over North Georgia, in three periods, 1986-1988, 2000-2002 and 2006-2008. The North Georgia area normally gets 48 inches of rain, but in 2007, saw only 31.85 inches of rainfall, the lowest since the record 31.80 inches in 1954.

Couple this with Lake Lanier having a relatively small watershed to catch rain, and the water pool at Lake Lanier was seriously impacted by the 2006-2008 drought. Lake levels were at record lows, and were threatening the water supply for Gwinnett, and the lake outflow to the Chattahoochee River. Since DeKalb, Fulton, Cobb and other counties pull water from the river, their supplies were being threatened, too.

The watershed at Lake Lanier has a 1,040 square mile drainage area. Another large lake in nearby Alabama, Lake Martin, has a 7,700 square mile drainage area, and therefore, would be less affected by a drought since it would have a bigger catch basin for water. With Lake Lanier having such a small watershed, any clouds must rain in exactly the right spot for the lake to rise. During periods of extreme drought, the small watershed exacerbates the problem of the level of the lake.

The other element affecting the lake was humankind. The level of Lake Lanier in the 2000-era was threatened by the three-state "water war" between Georgia, Alabama and Florida over the amount of water that should be released from the lake for downstream use. As of mid-2008, the states were still discussing the issues, though with no resolution of the conflict, court action seemed virtually a certainty. The future of the Lake Lanier water supply—which directly affects Gwinnett County—was at stake. Where are we now?

One mitigating factor in Gwinnett is that the county takes all of its water from Lake Lanier (in the Chattahoochee Basin). Before 2002, it was discharging a majority of its treated water to the Eastern basin across the Continental Divide, into the Yellow-South-Ocmulgee-Altamaha River systems. However, after 2002, more than half the Gwinnett wastewater was already being returned to the Chattahoochee River below Lake Lanier. A new plan by Gwinnett to begin in 2009 or 2010 is to return highly-treated recycled water to Lake Lanier after cleaning at the Hill treatment plant.

Gwinnett had been attempting this return of treated water to Lake Lanier for several years, and won this approval from the Environmental Protection Division of the Dept. of Natural Resources in 2000. Gwinnett officials had promised to return water to Lake Lanier "cleaner than it was when taken out" of the lake. This came about since Gwinnett had opened the F. Wayne Hill Water Treatment Plant in February, 2001, treating sewage to a new world standard. After protracted fights with the Lake Lanier Association, agreement was finally reached in April, 2000 for the return discharge to the lake. A return pipeline was begun from the treatment plant to Lake Lanier in late 2007, with the first return of water expected in 2009 or 2010.

This return of water from the lake from which it was taken will be a way to increase the lake pool. In 2007, Gwinnett water customers were consuming 87 million gallons of water a day from the lake. By returning the treated water to the lake at an anticipated rate of 40 millions gallons per day, the level of the lake would be raised, it has been calculated, by 15 inches when it is at full pool (37,000 acres). However, when the lake was at lower levels, such as 32,000 acres, the recycled water flowing into the lake would raise the lake pool by 17 inches.

Long-time director of the Lake Lanier Islands Development Authority was Roy Burson of Buford. He was succeeded by Lee Smith on July 1, 1996. Smith, in turn, was succeeded by Kevin Clark on July 1, 2007. Starting on January 1, 2008, Bill Donohue, who had been head of the Jekyll Island Authority, became executive director of the Lake Lanier Islands Development Authority. Meanwhile, Smith remains a consultant to the Authority.

In 2008, members of the Lake Lanier Islands Authority were:

Lonice Barrett, Dunwoody, chairman
Craig Dowdy, Atlanta, vice chairman
Elizabeth Brock, Athens, secretary-treasurer
Hank Burnham, Athens
Dorothy Burns, Gainesville
Donald Free, Perry
John Gibb, Buford
Connie Hagler, Gainesville
Robert Whitley, Cumming.

Stone Mountain Park

The sheer singularity of Stone Mountain accounts for its fame. This largest known exposed granite formation, rising more than 800 feet from the surrounding plain 16 miles east of Atlanta, the mountain is visible for miles and has attracted people for ages. Prior to the arrival of American settlers in North Georgia in the late 1700s and early 1800s, the mountain was part of the border between the Cherokees Indians to the north and the Creeks to the south, and served as a neutral meeting place.

Add to that an inspired idea from a member of the United Daughters of the Confederacy for a memorial to the lost cause of the South, then allow for the purchase of the mountain by the State of Georgia in 1958, and the result is Stone Mountain Memorial Park. It is one of the premier attractions of Georgia and the South. And with 35 acres of the vast park tract in Gwinnett, that's why it's included in this book.

**The "lawn" at Stone Mountain faces the carving.
This view gives an idea of the scope of the carving.**

Several years after the Civil War, the idea was floated for a commemorative monument at Stone Mountain. Letters to newspapers and columns revived the idea in 1914, especially in the mind of Helen Plane, a member of the United Daughters of the Confederacy (UDC), who though age 85 at the time, never shied away from leading the charge for a suitable memorial to the Confederacy. The "Lost Cause of the Confederacy" was never far from the minds of members of the UDC, of which Mrs. Plane made sure. She pushed through an endorsement of the idea at the UDC state convention in 1914.

Mrs. Plane soon had a Stone Mountain Memorial Association organized within the UDC Georgia Division. She even selected a well-known sculptor to design and carry out the project, well before getting approval of the landowners, who were the Venable family, and Samuel H. Venable in particular. Venable deeded in 1916 the "scarp of the mountain, 10 acres at the base, and a protective easement over the skyline of the mountain," according to David Freeman's *Carved in Stone, the History of Stone Mountain*. Holding the deed was the Stone Mountain Confederate Memorial Association.

The sculptor selected to do the memorial was Gutzon Borglum, a native of Idaho, who had just finished the sculptured head of Abraham Lincoln for the Capitol Rotunda in Washington. Borglum came to Georgia, won over critics with his ambitious idea of a carving, and providing carving models in 1917. His vision for the carving was not small nor limited.

Indeed, from the original idea of perhaps a carving depicting General Robert E. Lee, Borglum instead proposed a spectacular concept of groups of figures, as many as 700-1,000, all facing east (to greet the new day) with a central group consisting of Generals Lee and Stonewall Jackson, along with Confederacy President Jefferson Davis, and even others. The leaders were to be on horseback, the troops mostly marching. The total length of his proposed

The Stone Mountain carving features Confederate President Jefferson Davis, General Robert E. Lee, and General Stonewall Jackson.

carving would be 1,200 feet. Borglum also proposed more sculptured carvings at the base. This grandiose concept won approval of backers.

Work began on the carving in 1917. Then came delays, first from the entry of the United States into World War I, then from a lack of funds. Finally, in 1923, the work was resumed, and in 1924, the head of General Lee was unveiled.

Still needing funds, the project backers, in 1925, appealed to the U.S. Mint, and won approval for production of a Confederate Memorial half dollar (which sold for a dollar) to help raise funds. More problems arose, as new leadership and wrangling within the Stone Mountain Memorial Association created a virtual power struggle.

A man stands in Davis' horse's mouth, demonstrating the scale of the carving.

In addition, there were other difficulties, often financially related. In early 1925, Borglum's contact was cancelled. Borglum by then was also working on another project, his spectacular concept for the carving of four presidents at Mount Rushmore in South Dakota.

Stone Mountain had another connotation for many, one which is somewhat unsavory. It's a connection to the Ku Klux Klan. The mountain site was essentially sacred ground, where the Klan was resurrected, and for years, the group had meetings with giant crosses burning on the mountain. Sam Venable, himself a Klansman, granted an easement to the Klan to the top of the mountain for them to have their rallies. (This easement was cancelled in 1958 when the state bought the mountain.) Venable even worked to get the original sculptor, Borglum, to join the Klan. However, by 1970, when the sculpture was dedicated, James R. Venable, who was then the imperial Wizard of the Klan, boycotted the ceremonies, among other reasons, because a black minister, William Holmes Borders of the Wheat Street Baptist Church, gave the invocation.

After Borglum's departure, another sculptor, Augustus Lukeman, was hired to complete the work. Eventually, Borglum's original work was blasted from the face of Stone Mountain to make room for the new Lukeman design. But by 1928, all work on the carving had ceased, because of lack of funds. In 1935, Lukeman died, his work unfinished.

Work would not resume on the carving until 1964.

Meanwhile, little happened. Internal wrangling within the association and the conduct of World War II halted advancement of the memorial carving. However, the continued diligence of a few seemingly-lost souls, and eventually, the interest from state government, got the idea of a commemorative carving back on track in 1962.

Several civic leaders had sought to resolve the many difficulties surrounding the Stone Mountain carving and purchase of suitable land around it. It took the diligence of one such person, banker Mills B. Lane, to purchase on the same day 80 acres between Hugh Howell Road and the mountain for $90,000. Freeman writes: "To acquire the land, Lane approached each of the owners asking them to name their price. When they told him, he said 'You've got a deal.' He did this with each of the landowners in a single day so that no one would be able to discuss it with the others before he had gotten an agreement for the entire tract. He was concerned that in collusion they might hold out for more money." Eventually with other property, all this land was deeded to a state authority.

The Association also found an ally in Gov. Marvin Griffin, who convinced the Legislature to acquire the mountain, and also set up a governing authority of seven persons. The state purchased the 1,587-acre tract for $1,125,000. DeKalb County also deeded 409 acres to the Authority, and the Lane's property was given to the Authority. With other tracts added, the total acreage eventually became 3,183 acres, with the many parcels of land bought for $1.9 million. When Governor Griffin received deeds for the state, he is quoted as saying it was "....the happiest day in my whole tenure of office."

In 1963, Walker Hancock of Gloucester, Mass. was selected to complete the carving on the mountain. He was chosen over eight finalists, some of whom submitted bizarre and modern designs. Hancock finally chose the basic design that Lukeman proposed, consisting of three figures of Lee, Jackson and Davis. One change he suggested was eliminating the carving of the horses' legs and blending this carving into the mountain. Work resumed in 1964. New technology allowed the carving to progress much faster, by utilizing a thermo-jet torch. Roy Faulkner of Covington eventually was in charge of the actual carving of the figures, following precisely Hancock's measurements. Work began on the carving on July 11, 1964, and took six years to complete, being finished in the spring of 1970. The 90x190 foot carving was dedicated on May 9, 1970. Gov. Lester Maddox presented the carving to the nation on behalf of the people of Georgia.

The Stone Mountain Memorial Association had hoped to have a postage stamp commemorating the carving at the dedication. However, there was insufficient time. The stamp had its first day of issue from Stone Mountain four months later, on Sept. 19, 1970. It is a six cent stamp, the cost of mailing a first class letter in that day, printed in grey, commemorating the Confederacy.

Since the dedication in 1970 until 1997, activities at the Park were run by the Authority appointed by the governor. By 1973, the park was generating enough revenue that it sought no state appropriations, plowing the surplus into the maintenance of the park.

When in 1997, the State of Georgia sought interest from the entertainment industry about privatizing Stone Mountain Park, three firms were interested: the Herschend Family Entertainment Corporation (HEFC) of Branson, Mo.; Aramark of Philadelphia, Pa.; and Delaware North Companies International of Australia. All had extensive experience in the park management field. After proposals were evaluated, the Authority picked Herschend as seeming to be the best fit to run the park, and Herschend got the lease.

Herschend was begun in the Ozark Mountains in 1950, as it operated a small theme park at Marvel Cave, near Branson, Mo. In 1960, the small park (17 employees) had no advertising budget, and got the idea to give silver dollars as change instead of dollar bills. As the coins attracted attention with word-of-mouth advertising, eventually the park name was changed to Silver Dollar City. Meanwhile, the company expanded. These days, besides extensive attractions in Branson, the company operates the Dollywood theme park in Pigeon Forge, Tenn. and other attractions in Myrtle Beach, S.C., Orlando, Fla., Baltimore, Md., Memphis, Tenn. and Philadelphia, Pa. Herschend Family Entertainment is still privately held by the founding family.

HFEC's proposal in 1997 to the Stone Mountain Memorial Association (SMMA) was to pay rent for the park of $9.5 million a year, plus "additional rent" equal to three percent of gross revenues in excess of certain figures, with this additional rent guaranteed at no less than $600,000 a year for the first ten years of the lease. Because of Consumer Price Index escalators built into the base rent, the $9.5 million base rent had grown to $11.1 million in 2003. The agreement was deemed a good one for Stone Mountain, but by 2003, it was apparent that HFEC was struggling financially.

SMMA hired Price Waterhouse Coopers to do an evaluation of the firm and the basic financial agreement. Based on this report, the rent for HFEC was reduced by $3 million a year, in exchange for HFEC agreeing to pay a higher percentage of additional rent, that being raised from three to five percent. This rent concession was for a five-year period, after which the rent would revert to the previous level. By 2006, for the first time, SMMA began getting additional rent in excess of the guaranteed minimum of $600,000, and in 2007, the rent concession was extended for the life of the lease, unless HFEC is in default. (The original lease was for 30 years with four five-year renewal options.)

The new lease rejuvenated HFEC's interest in the park. The end result was an infusion of HFEC dollars, resulting in an initial $6 million expansion at the park's Evergreen Conference Center, which is operated for HFEC by the Marriott Corporation and which also runs the Stone Mountain Inn and golf operations within the park.

Back in 2002, HFEC had created Crossroads, a replica 1870 village, as an additional attraction. It is located near of the carving on the mountain, between the largest parking lot and entrance to many of the attractions of the park.

Curtis Branscome, CEO of SMMA, says, regarding the Crossroads area, that "Jack Herschend is a very creative person. He came to the park, and took a legal pad, and went around the area sketching, and the end result was Crossroads." The 30 acre Crossroads was designed to resemble an 1800s Southern town with a pleasant strolling atmosphere. Crossroads offers retail shops, plus era-specific crafts such as blacksmithing, candy making, and candle making. It also has activities for children, including a 4-D theatre, a "Treehouse Challenge" and the "Great Barn." Altogether, HFEC put in $35 million up front for Crossroads while adding new festival activities each year since it has been opened. Those included "Stone Mountain Christmas," "The Pumpkin Festival" and "Animal Planet Summer Adventure."

In its contract with Stone Mountain Memorial Association, Herschend also operates the hotel and motel at the park, through sub-leasing to Marriott Corporation. Its Evergreen Conference Center is a top-rated resort hotel in the Southeast, and also has a high occupancy rate. Many organizations holding functions in the park use the Marriott either for lodging, or for catering of their various events. The Evergreen Center is also a favorite with business and organizational groups for conventions and seminars, with the allure of meeting at Stone Mountain and its recreational possibilities, including golf courses, right at hand.

In addition, Herschend plans to add other ventures for winter, and in particular, for the Christmas season. Included will be a Festival of Christmas theme centered in the Crossroads area, where Christmas shows, food and shopping will bring in people, so that many visitors will want to come and enjoy "The Magic of Christmas at Stone Mountain Park," says Joel Manby, president and CEO of Herschend.

In late 2008, Manby also announced a new attraction aimed at stimulating business during the colder months. It would be Atlanta's first snow park, including a 400 foot tubing hill and a 30,000 square foot play area. It was to open on Dec. 31, 2008, and be operational through March 1 each year. The park would employ modern snow-making machines and use water from Stone Mountain Lake in a closed-loop system, in an environmentally-friendly manner.

It would be located on the area known as the "laser lawn" and include 11 tubing runs, special places to make snowballs and snow angels, and a play area for kids. There is a viewing area, warming chalets and bonfire area.

The idea behind the Snow Mountain at Stone Mountain is that surveys show that 40 percent of Atlantans has never experienced snow as a family outing, while 70 percent have not seen significant snow. It's aimed at providing a winter experience at the park for many Atlantans to enjoy.

Other ventures are not yet approved, but in the planning stage, to upgrade the park at other times of the year. One such project would be a $10 million upgrade of the water park, set for 2008, and already approved by the SMMA board. Manby says, "We want to put the beach back in play with some new attractions and activities."

Manby also envisions another type of attraction that Herschend will do which would attract people interested in recreation of a different sort. It would center around an outdoor activity he is tentatively calling an "Adventure Base Camp." Visitors could mountain bike, be on Zip lines, experience repelling and similar organized activities, and be out of their cars and in the outdoors. However, there would be no facilities for passive rides as the activities would concentrate on individual fitness activities.

All innovations conceived by HFEC must gain approval of the Stone Mountain board. Branscome notes that the board's guidelines are "very strict, from concept through specific design, and every step must be approved in detail." Then he adds: "HFEC understands this, and works well with our board. They appreciate what the park is about. I think it is the only company in the United States that could make it work out with the Association like it has."

While HFEC leases the attractions of the park, still two-thirds of the park is not included in the HFEC lease, but are in the natural, undeveloped area of the park. The SMMA, meanwhile, acts something like a municipality, maintaining the infrastructure of the park, such as roads, water and sewer, police and emergency services. The park in 2007 had 55 employees, two-thirds in public safety. The park employees are not state employees, nor included in the state pension program. Prior to privatizing, the park had 600 full-time employees (including 300 at the Evergreen Conference Center), plus 600 seasonal employees.

Meanwhile, HFEC lease payments have allowed the Association to embark in 2005 on a $25 million capital improvement program. Included among these items is a new pedestrian tunnel under the main roadway; a new and expanded parking lot; an upgraded water and sewer system; additional small parcel land purchase, plus fencing; and upgrading the security and radio system. Initially after the privatization, the Association also renovated its Confederate Hall main administrative building, and produced a geology exhibit about the mountain. It also hired a three-person education staff for environmental programs aimed at school children. "That helps build our future and is insurance," Branscombe says, "Since these students will some day become adults, visit here, and want to protect this place."

The close relationship between the park operator, Herschend Entertainment and the Stone Mountain Memorial Association got even closer in 2001, when Herschend moved its corporate offices from Branson to Triangle Parkway in Norcross.

What has happened at Stone Mountain since the area became a memorial park is nothing less than a continuing enhancement of the park for the enjoyment of local and far-away visitors. The park now sports a golf course, water recreation areas, cable car ride to the top of the mountain, a laser show at night, and numerous attractions to enhance the experience for a visitor, often themed around the Old South. Under privatization, it's anticipated that these offerings will continue to be enhanced to improve the park even further.

Yet one of the most remembered parts of visiting Stone Mountain for many has not changed since the day of the Indian. It is the simple 1.3 mile ascent up the western slope of the mountain, a trek that takes most people 45-60 minutes (and about half that time to descend.) The view from the top is spectacular, with the skyline of downtown Atlanta seen to the west, the subdivisions of Metro Atlanta in other directions.

The central theme of the mountain continues to be that magnificent carving, a memorial to the Confederacy, but an artistic and technological achievement for mankind. The carving is enormous, three acres, the size of three football fields. All this is 400 feet off the surrounding ground, and measures 90x190 feet, all being recessed some 42 feet into the granite. It's gigantic, and easily distinguishable from U.S. Highway 78, a mile away. At a distance, it commands awe; up close, it's overwhelming.

The carving is just outside Gwinnett's boundary. It's a magnificent memorial for one part of our country's history.

In 2008, members of the Stone Mountain Memorial Association were:

Mark Baxter, Macon, chairman
Greer Johnson, Duluth, vice chairman
Noel Holcomb, commissioner, Dept. of Natural Resources, Rome
Brent Brown, Atlanta
William Chappell, Atlanta
Michael Pentecost, Winder
Ray S. Smith, III, Atlanta
Joan Thomas, Monroe

Subdivisions spring up

Concurrent with job growth in Gwinnett came the growth in population and housing. When one realizes that the growth was essentially sudden, one can also recognize that most of the housing in Gwinnett today is modern and of high quality.

What you don't see in Gwinnett is much older housing. With only 32,250 people in Gwinnett in 1950, that would translate into no more than 10,000 housing units. And probably half those homes were not standing a half century later, meaning there may be only about 5,000 homes more than 50 years old in Gwinnett. To show a comparison, as of 2007, there were 261,052 households in Gwinnett, according to information from *Demographics Now.*

There are a few concentrations of older homes, mostly in cities where there is or was a railroad. So, one can generally find older homes in Buford, Duluth, Norcross, Lawrenceville, Lilburn and to a small extent, in Grayson and Loganville---all areas once served by the railroads.

The earlier boom in housing in Gwinnett until 1990 was primarily in single-family housing. Prior to 1984, there were few permits for multi-family housing. However, since then, multi-family housing has become a larger factor in the continuing fast growth in Gwinnett. Coupled with relatively low land prices for Metro Atlanta, Gwinnett is beginning to hear proposals of even higher buildings for both apartments and condo projects. (See table on building permits in Appendix B, page 661.)

Yet in the early days of Gwinnett's growth, it was individual smaller builders, not large-tract firms, which drove new home activity in the county. Therefore, the early subdivisions began to develop at a slow pace.

Among the early subdivisions were Young Estates and Beaver Ruin Estates in Lilburn, Waco Forest and Springdale Estates, on Norcross-Tucker Road. Most of the earliest housing development was in the area of the county along the DeKalb County line.

Cardinal Lake Estates is one of the oldest subdivisions, and was the largest when announced in 1959. It opened on August 9, 1959 as a 450 acre, 600-count unit of single family houses off Georgia Highway 120 near Duluth, and was by far the largest housing area in the middle of Gwinnett. Initially these homes were of the ranch style, but soon other types of housing began to appear. The first homes in this area were selling for under $20,000.

This subdivision featured a lake with a clubhouse, three miles of shoreline, and beach for swimming. It soon became a favorite of home buyers, and without realizing it, launched the subdivision housing boom which has continued for years in Gwinnett. Nearly 50 years later, this older subdivision continues to thrive, now the home of a large concentration of people with Korean heritage. (Nearby on Georgia Highway 120 is the Korean Community Presbyterian Church. It was started in 1985 on Clairmont Avenue in Atlanta, moved several times, and built a 72,000 square foot church and classrooms on 16 acres in Gwinnett in 2002. The church averages an attendance of 2,800 on Sundays.)

The problem of building homes in Gwinnett caught one builder by surprise. He was Pat Lewis, who had been in the construction business in Dekalb and Fulton Counties, and in the early 1960s, bought 40 acres of land just east of the city of Norcross, off what is now Jimmy Carter Boulevard near Goshen Springs Road. He called the subdivision Northeast Estates, and planned to build 84 houses.

But he found problems. His lenders, Fulton Federal and Decatur Federal Savings, were reluctant to make loans in Gwinnett, which they considered "too rural, too far out." Eventually, Mr. Lewis completed the subdivision, finally convincing the lenders that they could make money financing homes in Gwinnett.

He sold those houses, which he said had "right at 1,000 square feet, a little less," for $10,850. Mr. Lewis also later assisted members of Glover Baptist Church erect a structure on what is now Jimmy Carter Boulevard near Singleton Road. "We built that church for $16,000," he remembers.

Interestingly, Fulton Federal Savings later found the Gwinnett market attractive, building a modern, two-story banking facility in downtown Norcross, from which to originate loans. When Fulton Federal was absorbed by other institutions, the Norcross facility was for a while an office building, before it was purchased as an events facility for the catering firm which operated Flint Hill, called Magic Moments.

Pat Lewis would, in 1968, become the first Republican candidate in modern times to run for the chairmanship of the Gwinnett County Commission. He garnered 3,582 votes that year, but Democrat Dudge Pruitt won with 11,951 votes. The county was still safe in those days for Democrats.

Other areas seeing early development were in the southwestern part of the county, closest to Atlanta. That would include Tracy Valley and Casco Forest off Rockbridge Road not far from Norcross-Tucker Road east of what would become I-85; Edgemoor North near Norcross off Beaver Ruin Road; and Lockridge Forest off Winters Chapel Road. Most of these homes were of ranch style about 1,200 square feet, with two or three bedrooms, usually one and a half bath, with a single carport. Few of these homes sold initially for more than $15,000 in the 1950s and early 1960s.

Later on would see the building of Harmony Grove Estates off Harmony Grove Road in Lilburn, including many homes of the ranch and a style new then, the split-level house. When these homes were built in the mid-to-late 1960s, many of them were selling above $20-30,000.

In the Lawrenceville area, Western Heights, across from Central Gwinnett-Lawrenceville High school, was begun in the late 1950s, as was Craigdale Estates. Ray Lockridge was developing Lockridge Estates at the same time, while Charles Moore was introducing a larger house of higher quality, called Forest Hills. Homes in Forest Hills, offering differing styles, initially sold in the $30,000 and higher range.

Meanwhile, in Snellville, in late 1959 and the early 1960s two young brothers, Jimmy and Wayne Mason, began to construct ranch houses, usually of 1,526 square feet, which sold initially for $11,750, and by 1972 up to $15,000. The Masons virtually were a one-man show enlarging Snellville, and when they moved out of house construction, they had built 1,800 houses, and Snellville was no longer a small crossroads.

Becoming a major real estate developer and Realtor in Gwinnett in the late 1960s and 1970s was J. D. Caswell, who opened Caswell Real Estate in 1964 off LaVista Road in DeKalb County. He moved in 1968 off Rockbridge Road (near Norcross Tucker Road, later Jimmy Carter Boulevard.) By the early 1970s, he had the largest real estate business in Gwinnett, selling 60 percent of the houses, and had 120 real estate agents in five offices of Gwinnett. He also built a new main office in a modern two-story building on Jimmy Carter Boulevard at McDonough Boulevard.

Besides his Realtor activities, Caswell was also a homebuilder, starting Edgemoor North, a subdivision which in 1969-71 saw 204 homes developed by Caswell. "I would go in and build some houses, and then home builders would see that, and buy lots from me to build houses. Then we would market that house for them," he says. These houses were ranch and split-level style, selling for $19,900 to $24,900, They had between 1,550 and 2,000 square feet.

Two distinguished residents of Edgemoor North were Shirley and Zell Miller, who lived in the area for about 16 years, including the time Miller was lieutenant governor. At one time, Shirley Miller first worked at the C&S Bank in Norcross, and later opened with Margaret Greer a dress shop on Main Street.

Caswell built out Edgemoor North and immediately took aim at Stephens Hills off Pleasant Hill Road near Duluth. "I bought that land at auction for $1,300 an acre, as Harry Schaffer, Clifton Johnson and I went in together to develop this area. It had approximately 100 acres, and we built 180 homes there. This was my most profitable subdivision, since the market was so hot then."

Still active in the real estate business in 2008, Caswell has had his ups and downs over the years. The worst period for him came after the recession of the mid-1970s, when Hamilton Mortgage folded, a firm which had guaranteed a 107-acre subdivision in Loganville for $675,000, but would not deliver for Caswell. "And here I was stuck with paying interest at 16 percent, and they would not fund the development," Caswell remembers. "We finally settled after seven years. I figured it would take me five years to get even, and five more years to get back where we were. But we did it in seven years."

Looking back at 44 years in the business, Caswell figures he had himself built 3,000 homes, and sold to other builders lots for 10,000 homes. J.D. Caswell served as the finance and sales arm of his operation, while his brother, Carl Caswell, operated as the builder. J.D. Caswell first got into the business after being recalled to active duty with the Air Force during the 1962 Cuban Missile Crisis, just after his graduation from Georgia State. J.D. Caswell says: "It took 15 days to induct us, and then they sent us home, and that took another 15 days to get us out, and I didn't have anything to do. So I read a book on real estate, took the test, and got a real estate license."

Caswell began by selling houses for a friend, and first came to Gwinnett in 1964 to look at a four-bedroom, split-level house in Lilburn selling for $14,900. "I couldn't believe it, and had a client needing a house like that." While checking out the house, he ran across the builder, Horace O'Kelley, who began talking to him about selling houses. Their agreement was simple, as O'Kelley outlined the plan: "I'll build it, you sell it." That launched Caswell into a career into Gwinnett homebuilding and real estate." That career included key positions on the state and national home building scene. Caswell at one time journeyed to Poland as part of a National Association of Home Builders team to help that country on framing issues for housing.

Caswell likes to tell the story of one of his agents in the 1970s, Bob Wood, who was his new home sales manager. One Friday Caswell gave Wood a book, the 1937 self-help best-seller, *Think and Grow Rich* by Napoleon Hill. Wood read it over the weekend, and came in on Monday and resigned, to open his own office. Wood later succeeded Caswell in having the largest real estate team in Gwinnett County. Wood's method of hiring new agents was to train them at his own free real estate school, and then bring them on as agents in his firm. Wood also became a regular on election ballots for several offices. He served for four years on the Gwinnett County School Board. He met an untimely death in 2004 at age 65, though his firm still operates in Gwinnett County.

The larger housing boom in Gwinnett got its start in Peachtree Corners, as Jim Cowart Inc. began developing lots in the area, with a cadre of builders he had carefully picked. Previously Mr. Cowart had been a major player in the Dunwoody housing boom, in the area from North Peachtree Road, along Chamblee Dunwoody Road, to Ashford Dunwoody Road, on part of what had been the Spruill property. Most of the homes he developed were of brick veneer construction, and had a distinctive style about them. The Realtors dubbed the Cowart houses "Five-four-and-a-door." This meant that the front of the house had five windows on top of the two story house, four windows on the lower floor, and a door in between. (Later this style of house would spread throughout Gwinnett, and become a favorite with home buyers.)

Jim Cowart

Cowart related how he came up with the "five-four-and-a-door" concept. His first house for sale in 1957 was in the southeastern quadrant of Ashford Dunwoody Road at Interstate 285, where houses, with ranch or split-level design, were selling for $14-15,000 in those days. Cowart continued to build houses himself, then got the idea for a two-story house. He showed plans to his lender, seeking to get an OK to build a two-story house, and was turned down. "People won't buy a two-story house," the lender told him.

Shortly after that, a family approached Cowart to build a house for them with four bedrooms. The family had seven children, all under age eight. The family had been approved for a loan up to $28,800. Cowart showed the family his two-story plan, and they wanted that house. Though Cowart did not know what it would cost him to build such a house, he wanted to experiment with a two-story house, and agreed to that price. That's how the first "five-four-and-a-door" house began in the Oak Forest section of DeKalb County.

Afterward, Cowart started regularly developing subdivisions consisting mostly of two-story houses in Dunwoody. When he ran out of open land in Dunwoody, Cowart moved east across the Gwinnett County line, and began tying up land. Soon he had much of the open land in what is today Peachtree Corners bought or under option, and began to develop subdivisions there (and was no longer a builder himself). These houses were usually built speculatively and from the time construction began on the home, Cowart insisted that his builders first put in the lawn, and each day pick up building trash. As a result, when buyers came looking, they saw a neat subdivision, even when under full construction. This developed credibility for the Cowart subdivisions.

Cowart's first Gwinnett subdivision in 1977 was called Spalding Corners, with homes selling in the $95,000 range. Since then these houses have appreciated significantly. "Some of them have increased in value at the rate of $1,000 a month," Cowart says of the early homes he developed in Gwinnett. Often he would have more than 100 homes under construction in his subdivisions. One of the reasons for Cowart's success in Peachtree Corners is that there were no resale homes to compete with homes in his subdivision. He was developing on former farm or timber land. Another reason: Cowart built sidewalks in his subdivisions in 1985, something unheard of before. "When we started putting in sidewalks, Gwinnett County started copying us," Cowart says.

Other subdivisions Cowart developed in Peachtree Corners includes Spalding Corners II, Peachtree Station, Chattahoochee Station, Amberfield, Linfield and Riverfield.

Today the Peachtree Corners area is a prime housing center, particularly near the Chattahoochee River. Altogether, over a 30-year period, Mr. Cowart developed more than 14,000 lots in the north Metro area, besides also becoming involved with overall development of commercial and philanthropic aspects of the community. The Forum shopping center on Peachtree Parkway is one of the projects Mr. Cowart envisioned, sold to a developer, and eventually saw completed in 2004.

"Five-four and a door"

There have been several developments in housing in the Gwinnett markets during the county's heavy growth period. These included:

- 1975-80: The housing market in Gwinnett got a shot in the arm as Western Electric announced its massive new plant in Norcross. White collar workers wanted bigger houses, with first Lawrenceville, then Peachtree Corners, particularly benefiting from this plant's arrival.
- 1984: The opening of Gwinnett Place mall changed the market considerably. J.D. Caswell says "That did more to change the real estate atmosphere in Gwinnett than anything, as land prices skyrocketed. And the market moved much faster than I thought it would."
- 1996: The Sugarloaf development near Duluth. These mansions started off in the range of up to $500,000, and today sell for $1 million or more. Caswell says of this change: "I did not think the market was that deep for those types of houses, but I was wrong." Later this same firm, Crescent Resources, opened the River Club near Suwanee, also consisting of larger, upscale homes.
- 2000s: While the market became strong throughout Gwinnett, the new hot areas for substantial housing were along the Chattahoochee River north of Suwanee and in the Hamilton Mill area.

Veteran realtor's view

Back when Gwinnett was just beginning its growth in the 1960s, Realtors were not so numerous in the county as they were later. Jim Hood has had a 'catbird seat' to watch Gwinnett grow, having been born in Lawrenceville ("On Perry Street") in 1938. He's been in real estate in Gwinnett since 1964. "Back then there was no Board of Realtors, which was only started in 1970, when we had only six people in the business in the entire county." (At the end of 2007, there were 5,978 realtor-members of the Northeast Atlanta Metro Association of Realtors in Gwinnett.)

In those days, new homes were not marketed as such, but "developed as needed by the land owners, who sold lots to individuals, who contracted for the homes. Later J.D. Caswell opened a real estate office in 1964 and started to build some houses," Hood says, becoming the first Realtor with a large stable of agents. During the mid-70s, more than 120 real estate agents were with the five Caswell offices in Gwinnett.

Of modern day real estate in Gwinnett, Hood has thoughts about newcomers that readers might find educational. "Back in the 1960s, when Gwinnett had about 40,000 residents, there were no shopping centers as we know them. The first McDonald's in the county was in Lawrenceville on Clayton Street."

It was 1964 when Gwinnett joined the Atlanta toll-free telephone area, Hood remembers. "Some living in Atlanta found Gwinnett to be a beautiful, quiet and charming place to live, and said, 'This is just the place for us.' Since then, Gwinnett's population has doubled about every ten years since that secret leaked out."

Then he throws a new light on Gwinnett's growth: "By and large, newcomers have been welcomed into Gwinnett with open arms. But newcomers created the need for more and wider roads, shopping, water, natural gas, schools, parking, athletic facilities...to make this a better place for themselves and their children. Therefore, it's been the non-natives that caused the growth of the county."

Hood emphasizes: "Some of us were in business before most people in Gwinnett came to the county, while others went into business here because of the newcomers."

Hood also raises an issue about the perception of those in the development community: "How about a little slack for the developers, builders and Realtors who provided what the county needed so that newcomers could join the people that make up this great county? After all, they take the financial risk to provide products, and without their risk, this growth of people wouldn't be here! By the way, would you want a bankrupt developer to build your house? What's wrong with developers making money?"

The Gwinnett native adds: "Most of us are glad most of you (newcomers) are here. Just remember, we were here first, and you owe it to the next generation of new Gwinnett residents to be as kind and accommodating to them as we were to you. We didn't choose to live here, as you did. We were born here, and to us, Gwinnett's always been home."

Hood says several factors converged to allow for Gwinnett's growth. Among them:

1. **Lake Lanier Intake**: It was during the administration of Bill Atkinson that Gwinnett County got a permit from the Corps of Engineers to use Lake Lanier as its main source of water. It didn't hurt Gwinnett's chances that the Secretary of the Army at that time was Howard "Bo" Callaway of Georgia. Authorization for Gwinnett to have an intake for water in Lake Lanier was included in 1946 legislation pushed through by Sen. Richard Russell when he was in the Senate.

2. **Steve Reynolds Moving to Gwinnett:** The senator had been an oil distributor living in Commerce, and served on that city council and school board. After he moved his business to Gwinnett in 1964, he ran for and won election in 1968 to the State Senate, a post he held for 14 years.

Reynolds had a tremendous impact on decisions coming out of the State Highway Department, since he chaired the Senate Transportation Committee for 12 of the 14 years he was in the Senate. Later he would serve for five terms, until 2004, a total of 20 years, representing the Congressional district on the board of the Georgia Department of Transportation. Coupled with the Senate service, this meant that Reynolds served a total of 32 years with a continuing stamp on road activities in the state. His steady influence in transportation matters helped Gwinnett garner its share of road funds....if not more than its share. This, in turn, allowed Gwinnett to stay abreast of the curve as much as possible on movement of vehicles through the county.

While people have routinely complained about the movement of traffic and congestion in Gwinnett, the fact that Gwinnett has five major roadways into Metro Atlanta, which were constantly being upgraded, allowed traffic to flow more smoothly than could have been the case without the continual improvement program. (The five major transportation corridors from Gwinnett into Atlanta are, from the east, U.S. Highways 78 and 29, Interstate 85, Buford Highway and Peachtree Industrial Boulevard.) Hood continues:

3. **Two-Way Feed for Water**: Gwinnett's quick growth almost got shut down in 1974 when people at the end of the water lines, particularly in Snellville, were without water in late afternoons. House sales in this area came to an abrupt halt.

The solution was to encircle the county with a water loop, to provide a two-way feed for water for all the homes in the county.

What county commissioners did was to put in a 48-inch water main around the eastern portion of the county, to tie in with a 30-inch feed on the western side of the county. Coming together in the Snellville area, this gave adequate water pressure throughout the day, and ensured the continual growth of housing throughout the county.

These three factors were the key elements in the early growth of the county, which allowed for the future growth, Hood feels.

Few mobile homes in county

One type of housing that is rare in Gwinnett is individual mobile homes. Some nearby counties are heavily dotted with mobile homes.

Why are there so few mobile homes in Gwinnett? It goes back to the time of the first fast growth in Gwinnett, which happened in the Norcross area. Ray Gunnin, who was a county commissioner from that district, says he felt his district had more mobile homes than the rest of the county. "Some people didn't live in the trailers they owned, but rented them out, like apartments, and we had real problems with those areas." He adds: "Planners thought that mobile home land was merely a temporary use of the property, and that the homes would be moved when the land became more valuable for other purposes."

Opponents of mobile homes have pointed out that compared with conventional housing, mobile homes depreciate significantly from the first day of use. These people also note that the taxes that mobile home owners pay is substantially less than conventional housing, and that the mobile homes do not bring in sufficient tax revenues to pay for the services of the county, police and fire protections, recreation, schools, etc.

Former Commissioner Maron Buice says that the county had a public hearing on mobile homes while he was in office. "Everyone agreed to minimize them. It was in the Land

Use Plan. Mobile home parks could only be allowed in certain places, and had to have sewer to get such a park approved." Former Chairman Bill Atkinson said that the commission informally "agreed that you had to have five acres to get a permit for a single mobile home." That was apparently never written into the code.

Mobile homes are taxed as personal property, and require a decal to be placed on them each year. As of January 1, 2008, Gwinnett County counted 3,745 mobile homes. There were 26 mobile home parks, most of them located within Gwinnett cities.

The number of mobile home parks has declined in recent years, as land of the parks became more valuable for other purposes. That is a significant drop from the 4,919 mobile homes in Gwinnett in 2004, when it marked 2.3 percent of Gwinnett housing units.

Prolonged rapid growth

While Gwinnett grew little until after World War II, the major boom in Gwinnett's population has been since the 1970s. But this boom began shortly after World War II. The census shows this growth:

Year	Population
1900	25,585
1950	32,250
1960	43,541
1970	72,349
1980	166,903
1990	352,910
2000	588,448
2005	726,273
2006	757,104
2007	776,380 (July 1 estimate)

Gwinnett got its early notoriety in the 1970s from fast growth, leading the nation in percent of population growth for counties of less than 100,000.

The publisher of the Myrtle Beach (S.C.) *Sun-News* in the late 1970s called this author, with congratulations. "Why the congratulations?" he was asked.

"Because you are the fastest growing county in the United States under 100,000 population," he said.

"How do you know?"

"Because we (Horry County, S.C.) are second fastest," he said.

For the next several years, Gwinnett showed up as the top county in percent of population growth, within its population level. Later, Gwinnett had another distinction: it was among the fastest growing counties in the nation in real numbers of people moving into the county.

Between 1980 and 1990, Gwinnett averaged 18,684 new people a year, with its annual growth larger than the entire population of 84 of 159 Georgia's counties. And between 1990 and 2000, there was an even larger influx of people moving into the county, averaging

23,554 net residents gained each year. The fast growth has continued, with an average of 28,086 people moving into Gwinnett between 2000-2005!

Soon after his election in 1988, County Commission Chairman Wayne Hill realized that the fast growth was going to continue. He began telling people: "Where you see one person today, you will see two tomorrow." That simple thought quickly became true, as Gwinnett effectively doubled its population in the 15 years between 1990 and 2005. And the possibility arises that it will continue to gain population, with more and more people moving into what is still fast-growing Gwinnett, for the quality of its schools, for its safe, prosperous and vibrant communities, and more and more, for significantly good jobs from the ever-expanding industrial base in the county.

Hill had a comeback for those complaining about growth soon after they moved to Gwinnett, wanting to shut the floodgates and not allow others into Gwinnett: "I was born here. And I haven't asked anyone to move here." But people kept coming.

The consensus is that Gwinnett, with large portions of land area still not developed in 2008, will in a few years see its population top over one million people.....and maybe even larger, and perhaps become the most populated county in Georgia!

For years, the hobby of Gainesville Realtor Frank Norton Jr. has been to be alert to statistics on growth in all of Northeast Georgia. He compiles continuous, verifiable data, and monitors growth and real estate activity in this area.

His projection in 2006 was that Gwinnett will have a million people, maybe in 10 years. He says: "Leading from the top floor of the 1818 Club at the Gwinnett Chamber building, Gwinnett power brokers hold court on growth and progress, and drive new ideas to Gwinnett's ever-expanding vision.

"Gwinnett is still on target to break the million population mark by 2015-2020. To get there, we will see intensity of development in the four corners of the county, and densification and urbanization around the key nodes of Peachtree Corners, Sugarloaf, Chateau Elan, Mill Creek, Hamilton Mill, Lawrenceville and Duluth."

And while Lawrenceville has been the largest city in Gwinnett since 1970, Norton feels that, by the year 2020, the now-small town of Braselton (partially in Gwinnett, but also in Hall, Jackson and Barrow Counties), will be the largest city in Gwinnett. Norton predicts Braselton will have 80-100,000 people by 2020! (Braselton had 1,026 people in the 2000 Census.)

Here's another current view from economist Alfie Meek, who works as director of Economic Analysis for the county, and previously forecast his projections for the Finance Department. He projects that, by the year 2050, Gwinnett will reach 1.25 million people "if.....if current land use practices continue. If there is more density in development than in the past, that figure can only rise." (An amendment to the zoning ordinance in 2005 now allows buildings up to 25 stories in certain areas of the county.....perhaps a portent to a significant change in Gwinnett.)

Up until 2007, Gwinnett's anticipated growth seldom considered water resources, assuming that the county would take steps to provide sufficient water for its growth. However, the start of a drought in 2007 could signal a determining factor of just how much, and how fast, Gwinnett's future growth develops. While Lake Lanier up until 2007 was seen as a continuing supply of Gwinnett's water, now planners are wondering if the small Lake

Lanier basin watershed can adequately supply the water needed if the present curve of growth continues. Meanwhile, Georgia, Florida and Alabama continue to wrangle over water in Northeast Atlanta, with no solution in sight as of 2008.

Gwinnett became the second most populous county in Georgia in 2004. By the 2010 census, Gwinnett is expected to pass Fulton County as the most populated county in the state, with a projected 843,000 residents.

Gwinnett will also be more densely settled, since it has only 443 square miles, compared to Fulton's 529 square miles. Fulton is the largest Georgia county in land area, since Milton and Campbell counties were absorbed into Fulton after going bankrupt during the Depression.

A daily newspaper helps guide the way

Up until the early 1960s, Gwinnett had only weekly newspapers published within the county, a series of newspapers published at different times. *The Lawrenceville News* began in 1858, being the 15th newspaper to begin publication in Georgia. It ceased publication for a short time during the Civil War. Fearing a Union capture of its press, the equipment was taken apart and buried, then plowed over, in a corn field on the Terrell farm, two miles east of Lawrenceville. Once the hostilities were over, most of the equipment was dug up, reassembled, and the *News* returned to publication. But parts of the press were still turning up on the farm as late as 1906.

In 1875, the *News* acquired the *Gwinnett Atlas* and in 1898 it also bought out the *Gwinnett Herald*, and changed the publication to the *News-Herald*. One of its editors, J.A. Perry, was a long-time member of the Georgia Public Service Commission. Other editors and owners came over the years, including J.C. Flanigan, who served for a time as editor, and later was editor and owner of *The Winder News*, and a former president of Perry-Rainey College of Auburn. Mr. Flanigan is the author of a two-volume history of Gwinnett, and was the historian of Gwinnett County at his death in 1956.

In 1902, the newspaper published an account of the burning of the newspaper plant and four other building on East Crogan Street, using equipment of the *Gwinnett Journal* to publish its edition. The *News-Herald* then moved to South Clayton Street, where it remained until 1919. After several others either owned or leased the *News-Herald*, Attorney Marvin Allison purchased the newspaper in 1941. He later purchased in 1944 the *Gwinnett Journal*, and consolidated it into the *News-Herald*.

Hansel Morgan's book about Buford gives insight into the several publications which served what would have been for the most part the largest town in Gwinnett up until 1970. The first newspaper in Buford was *The Buford Gazette*, with Will Harris as its editor. In 1892 it became the *Alliance Plow Boy*, with W.W. Wilson as its editor. Ed A. Caldwell came to the Buford newspaper scene in 1895, with the *Buford Herald*. However, it lasted only until January 1897.

The *Alliance Plow Boy* continued publication until 1903, when it was sold to Oscar Wozencraft, and the name changed to *Buford Enterprise*. It folded in 1905. Then in 1906, Alma Kirby, the daughter of the editor of the *North Georgian* in Cumming, came to Buford and established the *Buford Journal* when she was 18 years old, using $500 her grandfather gave her for her 18th birthday. She married and returned to Forsyth County in 1914, selling the paper to Arnie Hendrix. The *Buford Journal* was succeeded by the *Buford Advertiser* in 1916. Early A. Wilbanks was owner of the *Buford Advertiser*, and much later, the newspaper was put out by E.W. Wilbanks, primarily a shopper.

In the 1960s, the official newspaper organ for legal advertising was the county-seat-based *News-Herald* of Lawrenceville, owned by attorney Marvin Allison. While Allison and the newspaper in Buford, the *Advertiser*, competed for news and advertising, and both were published on Thursdays, they primarily concentrated on their own towns. In 1963, the Georgia Press Association showed that the *News-Herald* had a circulation of 3,700 and the *Advertiser's* circulation was 1,600. Publishers of the *News-Herald* were Mrs. Jones Webb and Mrs. Marvin Allison, while Mrs. E.A. Wilbanks published the *Advertiser*.

Modern media changes in Gwinnett began when Charlie Smithgall, who since 1946 had owned a daily newspaper, *The Times* in Gainesville, entered the market. He purchased in 1963 the *Buford Advertiser* from Emma Mae Wilbanks, and at the same time bought from Roy Otwell the *Forsyth County News* of Cumming. He also hired Bruce Still, who had been the advertising manager for the *News-Herald* of Lawrenceville, published by the Allison Family. Marion Allison Webb was the editor of the Lawrenceville newspaper.

Soon Smithgall and Still began two more weeklies in Gwinnett, the *Duluth News Dispatch* and the *Norcross News Reporter*. The two weeklies were similar, except for the front page. Later on they combined the Norcross and Duluth weeklies into the *News of Gwinnett*. They kept printing the Buford and Cumming papers as stand-alone publications.

In June, 1964, Bob Fowler of Marietta entered the picture, buying from the Allison Family the *News-Herald*. Shortly after becoming the owner of the Lawrenceville newspaper, Bob Fowler recognized that, to become effective, he needed to have assistance.

Judy Fowler, his wife, remembers: "Bob got nervous. The *Times* was established, and had financial assets that we did not have. We had just bought the newspaper, so Bob started putting out feelers to have a joint venture with Smithgall, and got it going."

Robert D. Fowler

On November 1, 1964, Fowler and Charles Smithgall formed two companies, with each of the companies owning half of what was to become *Gwinnett Daily News*. Fowler's company was Gwinnett Publishing, while Smithgall formed Georgia Community Papers. By combining with Smithgall, Fowler had the financial backing to make the weekly the major success it turned out to be.

Janice Bullock, who was Mr. Fowler's key aide and newspaper business manager, says: "Mr. Fowler recognized that he needed a partner, and with the Smithgalls now owning the paper in Buford, thought it would be best to combine for all of Gwinnett."

After *Gwinnett Daily News* was judged Georgia's top newspaper, it didn't mind ballyhooing about the county *and* itself.

The following September 12, 1965, Fowler changed the publication frequency to daily and combined the weekly newspapers in Buford, Norcross, Duluth and Lawrenceville into *Gwinnett Daily News*. It would be printed six days a week, Monday to Friday afternoons and Sunday (though delivered on Saturday afternoon.) It was an immediate success, and well accepted by residents of the entire county. It virtually had no major competition for years, and was about the only media advertisers used to reach the growing Gwinnett market. It had the upper hand, though the metro *The Atlanta Journal-Constitution* would in the 1980s try to compete directly against it. Fowler was pleased to look back and admit of his flourishing newspaper, "We made money from the very first month."

Up until 1966, the newspaper was printed in Monroe, at the *Walton Press*. In late 1966, the newspaper purchased its own press, and began operations in a new building especially designed as a newspaper at 394 North Clayton Street in Lawrenceville. Over the years, the building would be added to five times as the newspaper continued to grow and needed additional space for its expanding operations. The building grew from 5,000 square feet when built in 1966 to more than 57,000 square feet when it moved out of that building to a new plant in Duluth in 1990, after new owners took over.

Gwinnett Daily News became one of the most successful of Georgia newspapers, continually growing both in circulation and esteem as the Gwinnett population expanded. It became a seven-day newspaper on October 1, 1983, prior to the opening of Gwinnett's first mall. The newspaper had a virtual monopoly in media in Gwinnett, with the Atlanta newspapers paying little attention to the county in the 1965-85 period. The newspaper continued to improve, was highly profitable, and was well thought-of by its readers. It constantly won key major awards from the Georgia Press Association. During the last several years of the Fowler leadership, it was judged the best newspaper of all dailies in the state, winning first place over both *The Atlanta Journal* or *The Atlanta Constitution*, a feat that particularly miffed the Atlanta newspaper's management team.

Meanwhile, *The Atlanta Journal* and *The Atlanta Constitution* were continuing to expand. In 1984, Cox Enterprises, which owned the newspapers, announced that it would build a satellite printing plant in Gwinnett County. (Interestingly, the first report of the new plant appeared in the rival *Gwinnett Daily News* on September 4.) The 30-acre plant would be on Best Friend Road in Norcross, and would consist of 350,000 square feet. It would house four giant offset presses, in addition to the four other presses, of the older letterpress design, which were located at their downtown plant. The cost of the new building was announced at $18 million, but with presses and other equipment, the outlay approached $50 million. The first newspaper came off the Gwinnett plant presses on October 28, 1985. Eventually, more than 1,000 people, including news, advertising and circulation staffs, plus the print and mail room operations, worked out of the plant, making it one of the largest employers in the county. The newspapers said they made the expansion of a printing plant into Gwinnett since press facilities at its downtown location were at full capacity, and that they needed the expansion to grow.

Over the years, others in the newspaper industry had recognized how well the *Gwinnett Daily News* was doing. In an industry hungry for good properties, the major newspaper chains came calling on Fowler and Smithgall. For years, they listened, but turned down all overtures. Eventually, however, the possibilities became virtually overwhelming. "The offers just became unrealistic, and it was time to take the money," one of the Smithgall family told this author.

So *Gwinnett Daily News* was sold in July, 1987 for what amounted to just over $100 million, the purchaser being *The New York Times*. Soon after the sale, newspaper talk around Atlanta centered on the Gwinnett "newspaper war" between the *Gwinnett Daily News* and the Atlanta newspapers. The *Times* management openly said that with its *Gwinnett Daily News* and potentially other properties, it was going to become the dominant newspaper property in the northern suburban area "from Interstate 20 on the west of Atlanta to I-20 on the east." Most observers felt that would include purchasing by the *Times* of the *Marietta Daily Journal*, to give the *Times* a base on the west side of Metro Atlanta to correspond to the *Gwinnett Daily News* base on the east, and help choke off the Atlanta newspapers in North Fulton.

It never happened. The Gwinnett newspaper operation was under the direction of the southern regional division of *The New York Times*, which by happenstance was located in Atlanta. From this office, New York kept a close eye on Gwinnett, which soon became something of an obsession with the regional office.

Meantime on May 2, 1988, the Atlanta newspapers halted distribution of their once-a-week publication for Gwinnett, which had begun in 1983, and began distribution with a six-day-a week *Gwinnett EXTRA*. A few months into 1989, on May 14, 1989, the newspaper began distribution of the *Gwinnett EXTRA* on a seven-day basis as part of the *AJC* in Gwinnett. In effect, the move to a daily Gwinnett section distributed in the *Atlanta Journal* and *Atlanta Constitution* meant a direct effort of Cox Enteprises to hold onto their Gwinnett distribution, in face of the expanded *New York Times* efforts with their *Gwinnett Daily News* subsidiary.

All this took place, of course, in Atlanta, which was the headquarters for Cox Enterprises, owners of *The Atlanta Journal and Constitution*, the major daily that the *New York Times* was competing against with its Gwinnett nameplate. The *Times* pronouncement of seeking to become dominant in the North Atlanta suburbs was akin to a slap in the face to Cox in its own backyard. The upshot meant that Cox made the battle with the *New York Times* in Gwinnett its prime concern.

It was a battle between equal media giants. At that time, one company was the 12th largest media company in the nation, the other the 13th largest.

But by changing the *AJC Gwinnett* section to first a six-day-a-week publication, and a year later in May of 1989 to seven days, the emphasis had changed mightily. Suddenly, there was a full-scale, all-out push for domination in Gwinnett, a battle of what the readers conceived as equals, with top coverage by the two newspapers in full evidence every daily. One day one newspaper would have a key story that the other did not have, and the next day the other would be dominant. It amounted to both newspapers wanting to cover every chicken dinner, or dropped handkerchief, complete with photos. It was overkill.

Subscriptions (to either newspaper) were not the normal $125 a year, but in Gwinnett were $75 a year. And, as allowed by the Audit Bureau of Circulation rules, either newspaper would sell a customer a year's subscription for half that, or $37.50 a year. As a result, the circulation of both newspapers rose, as Gwinnett readers enjoyed the bargains.

There was a major battle between the newspapers on the business fronts, with advertisers smiling at the low rates both newspapers were offering. It reminds a person of the Gwinnett-McIntosh duel of 1777 from four paces, since both sides "meant to hurt" one another, fighting as they were, virtually hand-to-hand on a daily basis. One result was that the *Gwinnett Daily News*, under the *Times* direction, was losing money. (Later it would be learned that under *Times*' ownership, *Gwinnett Daily News* lost $1 million a month for over 60 months.) The Atlanta newspapers maintained that their Gwinnett operation was profitable, but it was no doubt far less profitable than their other divisions.

Finally, on August 24, 1992, after five years in Gwinnett, *The New York Times* threw in the towel. They did it by invoking the Failing Newspaper Act, a technical provision enacted by Congress which protected newspaper companies in competing markets, which few people understood. Once invoked, a community is given 30 days in which to make comments concerning a newspaper coming under this Act's provisions, to determine if the government should allow a newspaper to fold. The failure of the readers to understand what was going on would make many of them say later, with perplexion: "They took our newspaper (*Gwinnett Daily News*) away from us!" And no one could do anything about it.

Since not enough of Gwinnett's residents complained about the invoking of the Failing Newspaper Act, as of September 6, 1992, *Gwinnett Daily News* published its final edition. The day it closed, *The New York Times* was legally able to sell the "remainder assets" of the *Gwinnett Daily News* to the Atlanta newspapers. Prior to the sale, under the terms of the anti-trust laws, the *Times* was prohibited from selling to a competing newspaper.

The upshot is that one morning, Gwinnett residents woke up and did not have their cherished and many-times-honored daily newspaper, the *Gwinnett Daily News*. The great Gwinnett newspaper war was over. People said of the *Gwinnett Daily News*: "They took our newspaper away from us!" How true!

Gwinnett Daily Post

After the closing of *Gwinnett Daily News*, another weekly publication changed to three times a week, then to daily publication, and is now the *Gwinnett Daily Post*.

The *Daily Post* grew out of a newspaper begun in 1970 by Bruce Still, who was once the advertising director of the *Daily News*. He called his newspaper the *Lawrenceville Home Weekly*, and had a circulation base in the Lawrenceville-Snellville area. It continued to operate as a weekly through 1992, with a circulation of approximately 16,000, published each Wednesday.

However, with the demise of the *Gwinnett Daily News* in 1992, Still changed the frequency of his publication the next month to twice weekly, and changed the name to *Gwinnett Post-Tribune*. Eighteen months later, in April 1994, he went to a thrice-weekly frequency, as his base of advertising grew. His circulation in 1995 was 15,447, according to the Georgia Press Association directory. In January, 1995, Still sold his newspaper to Gray Communications of Atlanta, whose principal owner was Mack Robinson, a high profile investment and banking executive, who owned the Albany and Conyers newspapers in Georgia.. That September the name of the publication was changed to *Gwinnett Daily Post*, with a five-day-a-week Tuesday to Saturday publication, and the following May the newspaper added a Sunday edition.

In late 2005, Gray approved a spin-off of its several newspaper properties, giving the newspapers a new owner, Triple Crown Media. It is closely affiliated with key figures at Gray Television of Atlanta. But old timers say this new product cannot be compared to the newspaper they fondly remember, one at which one time positioned itself happily as "a little above Atlanta," the *Gwinnett Daily News.*

Losing a daily newspaper again

Newspapers constantly change. Over the years, as the *AJC* published a daily section of Gwinnett news, it changed the names of the publication, from *Gwinnett EXTRA* to *Gwinnett News*. While it published weekly community sections in other parts of Metro Atlanta, Gwinnett remained the only area with its own daily community section.

However, the rapidly-exploding world of the Internet was drastically affecting newspaper circulation, as revenue flowed away from newspapers to the electronic media. In particular, newspapers felt this pinch from lower revenues as a result of the loss of advertising from automotive, real estate and help-wanted classified customers. The advertising base was also harmed by the reduction of the number of department stores and the amount of advertising that they ran.

The impact came to Gwinnett on August 10, 2008, when the Atlanta newspaper discontinued all community sections, including the daily Gwinnett section. The county had experienced its own daily section in the *AJC* for over 20 years, but now that section was being printed no longer.

Earlier the *AJC* had announced that it would close its downtown printing plant, and shift all printing to the Gwinnett plant. To do this, the *A*JC would invest $30 million in press improvements and capacity, and in doing so, would have a larger employment force in Gwinnett than before.

But again, just as the *Gwinnett Daily News* had closed, the discontinuing of the daily Gwinnett section of the Atlanta newspapers gave some the feeling that another newspaper "had been taken away from us."

Legal organ

There's not only a certain stature, but very much a financial return, when a newspaper is the official "legal organ" of a county. In Georgia, three Constitutional officials, the sheriff, clerk of court and probate judge, determine which newspaper should be the legal organ of the county. Any newspaper "of general circulation" published within the county may qualify for this distinction. In counties with no general circulation newspaper, those published outside the county but circulated within the county, may qualify as the legal organ.

As the legal organ, the newspaper is the official organ and newspaper of record, designated to publish court actions, such as sheriff's sales, clerk citations, incorporations, and other legal matters. By designating one newspaper for the office, citizens will know where to keep up with legal affairs of the county. The official organ is also a great place to search for historical records, from the legal perspective, of a county.

A sign near the microfilm storage cabinet of the Five Forks branch of the Gwinnett County Public Library, where microfilm of previous newspapers published in Gwinnett is located, helps researchers with the following chronicle of when various publications were the official organ of Gwinnett. It reads:

1946-64	*Lawrenceville News Herald*
1965-73	*Gwinnett Daily News*
1974-76	*Home Weekly*
1977-78	*Gwinnett Daily News*
1979-80	*Home Weekly*
1981-82	*Gwinnett Daily News*
1983-84	*Home Weekly*
1985-June, 1990	*Gwinnett Daily News*
July 1990-1992	*Home Weekly*
1993-Aug. 1995	*Gwinnett Post Tribune*
Sept. 1995-present	*Gwinnett Daily Post*

Once Bruce Still began the *Home Weekly* in Lawrenceville in 1970, and as long as he qualified to be the official organ by publishing for two years, he lobbied the three officials to become the legal organ of Gwinnett. From the time it was founded in 1965, the *Gwinnett Daily News* was the official organ, as a successor to the prior organ, the *News-Herald.* (Still's previous employer was the *Gwinnett Daily News.*) Finally, in 1974, the officials awarded Still's *Home Weekly* with the title of official organ, which his newspaper held for three years.

Beginning in 1977, the officials reverted the official organ label to the *Gwinnett Daily News*, and rotated it every two years until 1984.

Gwinnett Daily News held that designation until June of 1990, when its management under *New York Times* ownership, made a tactical error to lose the legal organ status. The *Daily News* had just moved its operations out of the county seat of Lawrenceville to a state-of-the-art newspaper plant by Interstate 85 on Shackelford Road near Steve Reynolds Boulevard. (Years later, in a retro-fitting, the building would become Louise Radloff Middle School.)

That relocation by the *Daily News* turned out disastrous from a legal view, as Bruce Still and the *Home Weekly* petitioned the three legal organ appointing officials, saying that by vacating the county seat of Lawrenceville, the *Daily News* was no longer eligible to be the legal organ, since law required the official organ to be published in the county seat. The officeholders agreed and in the middle of 1990, changed the official designation to the *Home Weekly*, since it was the only newspaper eminently qualified as the county organ by having its headquarters in the county seat. As the *Home Weekly* morphed into the *Gwinnett Post Tribune*, and later *Gwinnett Daily Post*, both still published in Lawrenceville, these newspapers held onto the title of official organ of Gwinnett.

Newspaper publishers eagerly seek to become the official organ of the county. In a booming county like Gwinnett, the weekly legal section could bring in substantial revenue. In 1988, for instance, the *Gwinnett Daily News* legal revenues were over $500,000. In 2006, for comparison, the *Gwinnett Daily Post* had over $1.5 million in legal revenues. For 2007, the legal advertisement section in *Gwinnett Daily Post* has averaged 40 pages a week, with a high of 48 pages.

Continuing newspaper changes: A timeline

1858: The *Lawrenceville News* debuts, with James Simmons the first publisher. Over the years, it merged with several weekly newspapers and becomes the *News-Herald*.

1871: A second newspaper, *Gwinnett Atlas,* opens in Lawrenceville with Dennis Boully as editor and Tyler M. Peeples, an attorney, as owners. In 1872, the name is changed to *Gwinnett Herald.*

1870-80: No precise dates are known, but the *Buford Gazette* was begun by Will Hendrix.

June 1, 1892: The *Alliance Plow Boy* began publication in Buford by W. W. Wilson. It continued to be issued until January, 1903, when Wilson sold the newspaper to Oscar Wozencraft, who changed the name to the *Buford Enterprise*. He sold the paper to an unknown owner, and the newspaper ceased in 1905.

Aug. 2, 1895: The *Buford Herald* began publication by Ed A. Caldwell. It folded in January, 1897.

1898: A round of changes begins. J.A. Perry and J.A. Bagwell take charge of *Lawrenceville News*, changing name to *News-Herald.* On December 1, 1899 Perry and Bagwell get the paper under a lease from the owners. Perry later sells his part of the lease to Bagwell in May, 1900. In June, 1900, J.C. Flanigan buys half-interest in lease from Bagwell. In October, 1900, Bagwell sells the other half of the lease to D.C. Morcock. Whew! It's hard to tell if this means the newspaper business is particularly good, or bad!

1902: The *Gwinnett Journal* started with J.C. Flanigan as editor. (There is no indication what happened to his half-interest in the *News-Herald.*) He was "succeeded" by E.H. Smith. Later on J.A. Bagwell re-enters the picture by buying the *Journal.*

December 18, 1902: The *News-Herald's* building, located on Crogan Street, was destroyed by fire. Though there is no mention in histories, the newspaper continued to publish.

1906: Alma Kirby, only age 18, comes from Cumming and starts publishing the *Buford Journal*. She sold the newspaper in 1914 to Arnie Hendrix, who changed the name to the *Buford Advertiser* in 1916.

1908: Bagwell sells the *Journal* to Flanigan.

1916: Flanigan sells the *Journa*l to C.M. Morcock.

1941: Attorney Marvin Allison of Lawrenceville purchases the *News-Herald.* He purchases *Gwinnett Journal* in 1944 and folds it into the *News-Herald.*

1963: The *Times* of Gainesville enters the market by buying the *Buford Advertiser* from Emma Mae Wilbanks. The *Times* begins publication of other weekly newspapers in Duluth and Norcross. In 1965 these three weeklies combined into the weekly *News of Gwinnett.*

June, 1964: Marion Allison Webb, who for 15 years ran and edited her father's weekly newspaper, sells the *Lawrenceville News-Herald* to Robert D. Fowler, former editor of the *Marietta Daily Journal.* On Nov. 1, Fowler and Charles Smithgall of the *Time*s jointly form a new company, with each owning half of the *News-Herald.*

Sept. 12, 1965: Fowler converts the weekly *News-Herald* into *Gwinnett Daily News,* published Sunday-Friday, though the Sunday newspaper is delivered Saturday afternoon.

1970: Bruce Still, former advertising director of *Gwinnett Daily News,* starts *The Home Weekly* out of Lawrenceville.

1983: The *Gwinnett Daily News* converts from sixto seven days a week with the introduction of a true Sunday edition.

July, 1987: The *New York Times* Co. agrees to buy the *Gwinnett Daily News,* which at the time had a circulation of 27,600.

May 2, 1988: *The Atlanta Journal-Constitution* expands its weekly *Gwinnett Extra* section to six days a week. That same day, the *Gwinnett Daily News* became a morning newspaper.

May, 1989: *Gwinnett Extra* becomes a seven day a week newspaper.

Jan. 14, 1990*: Gwinnett Daily News* opens $40 million newspaper plant in Duluth and moves its operation out of Lawrenceville.

June, 1990: Because it left the county seat of Lawrenceville, the *Gwinnett Daily News* suffers a revenue blow, losing its nearly $500,000 a year in legal advertising revenue to the tiny *Gwinnett Home Weekly.*

July, 1991: In a move to boost circulation outside its home county, the *Gwinnett Daily News* launches the "Metro" and "DeKalb" editions for Atlanta readers and drops "Gwinnett" from its name plate, now known as *The Daily News.*

October, 1991: *The Daily News* loses circulation for the first time in Gwinnett County since the *New York Times* Co. bought the newspaper. At the same time, *The Atlanta Journal-Constitution* widens its circulation lead in Gwinnett.

Aug. 24, 1992: *The New York Times* says it will close *The Daily News* and sell its plant and equipment to Cox Newspapers, leaving Gwinnett with only one daily newspaper, the *Journal-Constitution.* The last edition of *The Daily News* is published on Sept. 6, 1992.

The Daily News building, off Shackelford Road near the Steve Reynolds exit of Interstate 85, sits vacant for years. After retrofitting, it is recycled into the Louise Radloff Middle School.)

Oct. 18, 1992: After closing of *Gwinnett Daily News,* Bruce Still changes frequency of *The Home Weekly*. It now publishes twice weekly.

1994: After three years as a twice-weekly, Still changes publication of *Gwinnett Post-Tribune* three times a week.

1995: Still sells the *Post-Tribune* in January to Gray Communications of Albany, Ga., and publishes Tuesday through Saturday. On September 5, the name is changed to *Gwinnett Daily Post.* It begins expanded distribution through an alliance with a cable provider. Circulation rises to 48,000.

1997: On May 4, *Gwinnett Daily Post* prints its first Sunday edition, and is now a six-day-a-week newspaper. It begins expanded distribution through an alliance with a cable provider. Circulation rises to 48,000.

2001: On November 2, the last edition of the evening *The Atlanta Journal* is published. On November 5, the name of *The Atlanta Journal-Constitution* appears on the Monday-Friday newspaper, as it has on weekend editions for several years.

2005: On December 30, newspaper is spun off Gray Television and becomes under new owner, Triple Crown Media, based in Lexington, Ky.

August 10, 2008: After 20 years of publishing a daily Gwinnett-zoned edition, *The Atlanta Journal-Constitutio*n discontinued this section, and other weekly community editions. This came as a result of changes newspapers all across the country were experiencing, as revenue fell drastically as a result of Internet competition, and a major downturn in the economy.

5
1970-1980

County-wide fire protection

Modern day Gwinnettians enjoy virtual border-to-border fire protection and a Class IV fire insurance coverage. In effect, Gwinnett has the most modern of fire protection, with the county fire department covering the largest fire service district in the state with 715 (2007 figure) authorized personnel. It also operates the county emergency ambulance service. Each firefighter is cross-trained as either a firefighter-emergency medical technician, or firefighter-paramedic.

As of 2007, there were 27 fire stations with coverage of every homeowner within three miles of a station. A 28th station was to open in the fall of 2008 at Brushy Fork and Rosebud Roads, south of U.S. Highway 78. (See Appendix B, page 670 for location of fire stations.)

Fire protection wasn't always so up-to-date in Gwinnett.

One of the early issues Ray Gunnin tackled when becoming a county commissioner in 1969 was fire protection. Up until that time, no cities of Gwinnett had paid, full-time fire departments. Some of the cities had volunteer fire departments, though these gave scant protection for city residents, and virtually very little protection for any nearby residents who lived in unincorporated portions of the county. Some homes outside volunteer fire department cities paid a fee to be covered by that volunteer unit, but even this was inadequate fire protection.

A fire in the unincorporated area of the county near Norcross (Liberty Heights) in 1968 claimed the lives of four people in the same family. This hit Gunnin hard. A father and three children were killed in the house fire. "I went by there and saw the results of that fire," Gunnin remembers. "It convinced me we had to do something." Combined with the industrial growth in Norcross, adequate fire protection was missing.

Gunnin also knew that the county would not grow through commercial investment without fire protection. "Who would put millions of dollars at risk without fire protection?" he reasoned. "Those deaths in the fire, plus understanding the need for commercial fire protection, spurred me on."

A volunteer fire department, Gunnin realized, "was dependent on having people around to fight the fires, but you could not always get them together. They were heroes in fighting fires to lots of people, but this was inadequate in a county that was beginning to grow. We did the right thing at the right time. If we had not set up a fire department and expanded the water department when we did, Gwinnett would have been a backward county, for sure. But we had a board of commissioners who did the right thing."

Also on the county commission at the time was Maron Buice of Sugar Hill, who knew something about fire protection. "I was chief of the Sugar Hill Volunteer Fire Department for 16 years. We were the only fire department around that would go outside of the Sugar Hill city limits. We actually served all the way over to the end of Hamilton Mill Road and down to the Chattahoochee River at the Forsyth County line. We also served the homes around Lake Lanier and even answered some calls for assistance in Forsyth County.

"Having all that area where we would answer calls was a big problem, since there was so much territory to cover. It was hard for us to take care of it. After all, our firemen had regular jobs. Sometimes it would be hard to get them all together.

"But we never refused going when we were called. The county was growing so fast we could not take care of the large area we were serving. That also meant we could not get a good fire insurance class rating outside any of the city limits."

Wanting to offer fire protection throughout the county, the commission got Gwinnett's two legislators, Norris Nash and Jimmy Mason, to introduce a measure in the Legislature to allow Gwinnett militia districts to vote to tax themselves for various services. Put before the voters on July 29, 1970 was a proposal for a county-wide fire district. The proposal lost, by a three-to-one margin, as voters across the county, especially rural voters who lived where there were no water lines, and communities with volunteer fire departments, did not support the move.

However, Gunnin noted that fire protection had a majority of voters' approval in this 1970 vote in the area around Norcross, the Pinckneyville Militia District. Gunnin convinced Gwinnett legislators to allow individual militia districts to vote on individual services, such as a fire district. So in Nov. 3, 1970, citizens in all three precincts in Pinckneyville, voted 1,996 to 591 to tax themselves for fire protection. The new fire district immediately leased what had been Norcross' volunteer fire department equipment and station from the city. The county got two fire trucks: a 1942 Ford pumper (now parked at the Norcross Fire Museum in front of the new Station No. 1), plus the newer Ford-powered, American LaFrance modern pumper. This became the original Station No. 1 on College Street, which began operations March 29, 1971. There were no emergency calls that first day of operation.

Ray Gunnin

Gunnin remembers: "It was through the hard work of Norcross Mayor Leon Maloney that we worked out an agreement with the City of Norcross for the fire district to lease their equipment. Some on his Council didn't want to go into a lease with the county, but Mayor Maloney got the three votes the measure needed for passage, and we were in business. We had to agree to keep one of the two fire trucks within the Norcross city limits at all times."

Carl Garner, of Norcross, who would succeed Maloney as mayor, remembers that the county agreed to pay Norcross for the equipment over five years. Maloney further negotiated with Gunnin that the citizens of Norcross would not have to pay the fire district tax for a 10-year period. That lease agreement was later extended to another 10-year period, and actually went a few years beyond that. Eventually, the City of Norcross repaid the county for the additional years when they had not been taxed, and the county bought the property and station from the city.

After the vote on the fire district, Gunnin says: "The county commission approved Ray Mattison to be the first fire chief. He and I gathered around my dining room table at my house on Spalding Drive and hired Tom Griffin as a firefighter." (Years later he retired as the county fire marshal.) Mattison picked Richard Garner, who had been the Norcross volunteer assistant fire chief, to be the Department deputy chief. By February 15, 1971, Mattison had hired the entire 10-man force, which then went for training.

The date March 30, 1971 will mean nothing to nearly all residents of Gwinnett County these days. But it's an important date for the county, marking the date that the newly-organized Gwinnett Fire Department answered its first alarm at 10:15 a.m. out of Fire Station No. 1 in Norcross in the Pinckneyville Militia District.

The first station itself was a blue metal 3,000 square-foot building built inexpensively by the City of Norcross about 1968 for its city fire department. It was the first home of members of the county fire department in 1971, and remained in operation until January 18, 2008. At that time, the county constructed a new, modern 8,500 square-foot "Station No. 1," on Lawrenceville Street at Mitchell Road, near City Hall. It was built according to the standard plan used to construct several other fire stations in the county. That new Station Number One is a far cry in design and features than the blue metal building that got the fire district going in 1971. In addition, the date it was occupied, 2008, might confuse future researchers, in view of other similarly-designed fire stations built and occupied earlier.

Up until 1971, Gwinnett businesses and homeowners only had limited fire protection from volunteer fire departments within some of the cities. It wasn't until 1972 that any other city had their own professional fire department, when Snellville organized its own full-time department. As a result, fire insurance rates in Gwinnett were among the highest in the country.

Thus began the small department centered around Norcross that would expand eventually into coverage for the entire county. But the department would stay small only for a short time. Late in 1971, the city of Berkeley Lake voted to come under the fire department taxation and protection.

Adding another militia district to the Fire District was relatively easy, because of steps previously taken. Gunnin remembers: "I had talked earlier with other counties, principally Cobb, and found the legislation for the fire district needed to include a provision to allow other districts to merge into the system, if later on they chose to do so. That really helped matters later on, rather than having to go back and get additional measures through the State Legislature every time another district wanted to be included in the system."

The legislation allowed other militia districts to join the fire district upon a vote of the people. On Septenver 8, 1971, four other districts came together to vote on fire protection. The vote was:

	Yes	**No**
Berkshire	296	83
Cates	9	23
Garners	277	60
Rockbridge	32	40
TOTALS	614	206

Since the total vote was "Yes" for a fire district, the results were certified collectively, instead of by individual districts. Therefore, since the total vote was for a fire district, all four militia districts came into the expanded fire district, though a majority of voters in Cates and Rockbridge did not give their approval.

The second fire station was built in 1971 on Harmony Grove Road, followed by the City of Snellville building its own station. The third station came in 1972 on Five Forks-Trickum Road. All of these stations were built along the same lines as Station No. 1 in Norcross, using the same blue metal exterior material. The City of Snellville would get out of fire protection in 1980, when its fire department joined the Gwinnett system.

Gunnin also worked on how the county could finance an expanding fire protection district. "We got legislation passed to set up a Public Facilities Authority (see section on Public Facilities), which allowed us to finance the building of fire stations and equipment through revenue bonds guaranteed by the county fire district tax. The Republicans around here were opposed to authority financing, for they wanted all financing to require an absolute vote by the people. They felt we were going around the voters with an Authority, but on a district basis, people will vote for a measure that they know they need, like fire protection. An Authority was the only way we could do it." Harold Humphries of Norcross was first chairman of the Public Facilities Authority.

One more aspect: prior to the organization of the county fire department, ambulance service in Gwinnett was handled by funeral homes within the county. When the new department was formed in Norcross, its men were also trained in emergency medical technology. The funeral home in Norcross, owned by R.T. Patterson, donated a new van it had been using for emergency service to the department. So, from the day it began operations, the county fire department became the key component in emergency rescue, and eventually, for all of Gwinnett. That also meant that funeral homes throughout the county could stop answering emergency accident and medical calls at all hours, and concentrate their activities on the more lucrative funeral business.

Over the next several years, the more populous districts realized the need and voted for fire protection. Gunnin said that people in these districts "became jealous" that only

Pinckneyville had the protection and "realized we had set up a way for them to get fire protection by joining the fire district."

The City of Lilburn held a referendum on October 6, 1973 to have Gwinnett County cover the city rather than maintain a volunteer fire department. The vote was 172 yes, 31 no, with 4 votes void. The city council approved the results of that election at their regular meeting of October 8, 1973.

Meanwhile, other areas were beginning to understand the benefit that a Fire District could bring, not only in fire protection, but that of reducing significantly the fire insurance cost. So, in 1974, Duluth, in a straw vote of its people, voted 199-45 in favor of county fire protection. Its Council voted to join the district on June 10, 1974. Then on July 30, 1974, Goodwins District approved joining by a 78-11 margin, as did Lawrenceville by a 96-7 vote.

Then, using powers granted under State Amendment No. 19, giving governments a right to contract for services, the county voted to include areas in a special fire tax district, without a referendum. The remaining one-third of the county, primarily in the rural northern reaches, was added to the fire district then. The goal of having each Gwinnett resident within three miles of a fire station was reached.

Interestingly, by then the county water system had expanded significantly. It gave rural Gwinnett voters the confidence to know that, if there was a fire, not only would fire trucks come, but there would be sufficient water lines throughout the county (and water pressure) to fight a fire.

There was another benefit for the residents coming into the fire district. Those property owners in the fire district had found that the added tax for fire protection would be more than offset by far lower fire insurance premiums. By 1980, Gwinnett County had a virtual border-to-border professional fire protection, and an Insurance Service Office Class IV fire insurance rating, resulting in much lower fire insurance cost for property owners. (As of 2008, the only areas in Gwinnett not having a Class IV rating are near Norris Lake and around Lake Lanier, plus the City of Braselton, primarily because of response distances.)

In modern Gwinnett in 2008, the Gwinnett Fire Department is the largest multiple jurisdictional fire district in the state, serving all or parts of 13 cities. Only the cities of Loganville and Auburn operate independent fire departments.

Sewering the county

Gwinnett County treats its wastewater as extensively as any place in the entire world, making sure that the wastewater returns to streams cleaner than it was taken from Lake Lanier.

Treatment experts say that there are three places in the world that are rated exceptional for such treatment. Besides Gwinnett, they include facilities in the Truckee River near Reno, Nev., flowing into Lake Tahoe, and at Manassas, Va., near Washington, D.C.

For a community to have a sewer system, there must be a large concentration of homes in the area. That's because installation of infrastructure such as a sewer system is costly for individual homeowners in small areas. Financing such a system takes major up-front capital, which becomes affordable to a significant number of individual homeowners when paid for over many years.

Therefore, when developing rural land with homes spread far apart, sewer systems are often not initially used. It takes time for the household density to gain strength before removal of waste through sewers is economical. And in the meantime in the growth period, the homes and businesses rely upon individual septic tanks to treat sewer waste.

In Gwinnett County, where homes were far-flung in its early development, most of the homes prior to 1960 were on septic tanks. Some of the Gwinnett cities had oxidation ponds to treat waste from homes within their borders. This took place in Lawrenceville, Lilburn and Norcross, though the cities connected to the county sewer system once it was available in their areas.

Today (2008), approximately 40 percent of the county is still served by septic tanks. Estimates are that there are about 90,000 septic tanks in operation in the county, though 131,000 septic tank permits and repair permits have been issued. Many homeowners on septic tanks become sewer customers as sewer lines are extended to their areas, hence the disparity between the number issued and the number thought in use.

Buford had the county's first sewer system completed, in 1920, though it did not serve the entire city, and it dumped raw sewage into a branch, which fed Richland Creek. This first rudimentary sewer system came out of a 1919 bond issue which provided $30,000 for sewers and $10,000 for water improvements. The original sewers ran to a branch behind the Old Academy, Hansel Morgan tells us. A 1927 city ordinance required all property owners to connect to the sewerage system, with the sewers extended in 1927-28 to include most residents.

Buford's first sewage disposal plant came in 1949 on the northwest side of town. Buford in 1956 approved extension of the water and sewerage systems, which soon was serving 98 percent of the homes, where about 50 percent had service before.

In 1975-76, Buford built two sewerage treatment plants. Two plants were needed, since the city sat atop the Eastern Continental Divide, meaning that there are two watersheds in the city. The Chatham Road (Southside plant) is southwest of Georgia Highway 20 and Buford Highway on Suwanee Creek. The Westside plant is off Richland Creek Road.

The Southside plant, on Suwanee Creek, originally had a one-million-gallon capacity (MGD). The Westside plant, on Richland Creek, was a 300,000 gallon plant when originally built. Both plants were later upgraded, the Southside to 2 MGD, and the Westside to 350,000 MGD. The two plants in 2008 were not at peak usage, as Buford treats an average flow of about a million gallons of wastewater a day.

* * * * *

In Gwinnett County, the early sewer plants were built by subdivision developers. These were smaller "package systems," which would serve relatively tightly-drawn areas, usually of 100 homes or less. (Some of the few mobile home parks in Gwinnett were serving 200-300 families, but most have been phased out, as sewer came to the area.) These plants were installed as private systems, funded by the developer of a subdivision. Later, these plants were incorporated into the Gwinnett system. It wasn't until Gwinnett County started considering collecting sewage from a wider watershed that more modern and larger plants were built. This led to the construction of the vast Yellow River plant in 1979, and later, the construction of the sprawling Hill Plant.

The county government's first sewer plant was the Crooked Creek Water Reclamation Plant, located in the southwestern portion of the county in Peachtree Corners. Initial efforts for this plant came through Duke Enterprises, as developer Paul Duke was starting to develop Peachtree Corners. This plant was constructed in 1972, and had upgrading in 1987. Its original capacity was for 2 MGD, but the upgrade in 1987 sent its capacity to 6.5 MGD, and to 16 MGD in 1992.

Another key plant in the early sewer days of the county was the Jackson Creek plant, located off Indian Trail Road near U.S. Highway 29 in Lilburn. This plant was completed in 1973 as a 2.4 MGD facility, and later re-rated to 3.0 MGD. It is a constant flow plant with peak flows re-routed. It is anticipated this will be decommissioned in approximately 2010 when the Yellow River plant enlargements are finished.

In the lower end of Gwinnett, Snellville designed in 1973 and built in 1976 the No Business Creek Plant for its wastewater treatment. Shortly afterward, Snellville sold the plant to the county. It was decommissioned in 2006. Other plants once serving the Southeastern area include the Jack's Creek plant, the Big Haynes Creek plant and the one at Brushy Fork.

While at one time, these four other plants treated waste on site, now these plants' effluent is pumped to the Pole Creek plant in DeKalb County, which is a 20 MGD capacity plant. Gwinnett County owns 5 MGD capacity in that plant. A 2.5 mile underground tunnel sends waste from the Jack's Creek, to No Business Creek, to expedite the flow.

Other plants would come on line serving other basins, including the Beaver Ruin plant, which had participation from DeKalb County, since some of the drainage in the basin flowed to the Beaver Ruin plant. This plant began operation in 1978 as a 3.6 MGD facility, and was re-rated at 4.5 MGD in the 1980s. This is a constant flow plant, where peak flows are routed to either the Yellow River or Hill plants.

The largest water basin in Gwinnett is formed by the Yellow River, and naturally, this is the site of the first large wastewater treatment plant, located off Tom Smith Road in Lilburn. This plant collects sewerage from approximately 40 percent of the geographic area of the county. Construction started in 1979 and the plant came on line in 1981 as a 6 MGD plant, and later expanded in 1986 to handle 12 MGD. Other improvements have followed, including odor control, a centrifuge to dewater sludge and an ultraviolet disinfection system. The system is under more construction, expected to take its capacity to 22 MGD, so that smaller and less efficient plants in the basin can send their flow to the Yellow River plant by 2010. Afterward, these smaller plants can be decommissioned.

In the late 1990s, Gwinnett started thinking in a new direction as work began on the F. Wayne Hill Water Resource Center. This would be not only a vastly bigger treatment plant, but would incorporate the world's most modern filtration system so that water produced by the plant would be cleaner than the water pumped from the source, Lake Lanier. In 2009, Gwinnett County is expected to begin to return part of its wastewater from the Hill plant to Lake Lanier, in a recycling effort. This permit for returning the water to the lake came after several groups, notably one concerned with the quality of water at Lake Lanier, fought the discharge of treated water from the Hill plant, but eventually lost in the courts.

An interesting experiment with sewage took place in Sugar Hill in 1991. That city had a plant which treated waste to a tertiary level, and needed to dispose of it. The city council decided to build a golf course for its citizens, and use the effluent to irrigate the course and 70 acres of surrounding woodland owned by the city.

Later on, in 1997, the city sold their plant to the county, which closed the plant in 2005. It was in 2005 that the land application system was discontinued and the flow moved to county sewers. Sugar Hill's waste travels down Peachtree Industrial Boulevard and is treated at the Crooked Creek plant.

Gwinnett has set a world standard when it comes to treating waste. The Hill plant was drawing international visitors before it was opened, as sanitary engineers from all over the world wanted a glimpse of how wastewater would be treated at the highest level in the future. Although visitors flock to the Hill plant, each of the county's other major wastewater reclamation facilities are capable of producing the same high-quality effluent, because of improved methods of treatment through advancements in process and technology. In its commitment to watershed protection, Gwinnett County's permits for discharge back to the streams and lake require that the county treat the wastewater to near pristine levels so that it will have little or no impact to the overall quality of these bodies of water.

Treating waste to a world standard is expensive, usually exceeding the cost to produce potable water. Gwinnett County has always seen its wastewater cost exceed its raw water charge.

In 2007, the county charged $3.47 to households for each thousand gallons of water. The sewer charge is directly linked to the amount of water used. The charge for sewer treatment is $4.17 per thousand gallons of water coming into the house. In 2006, the average household had a combined water and sewer bill of $60.78 per month.

The Gwinnett County Water and Sewer Authority was created in 1970 to finance and construct water and sewer treatment and transmission facilities for Gwinnett citizens. The Act creating the Authority provides that the Authority shall consist of five members, all of whom shall be residents of the county. Each shall be appointed annually by the county commission, to serve for a term of one year from the date of appointment.

In 2008, Garland Smith was chairman of the Authority, but resigned effective June 30 when she moved out of the county. The commissioners named Charles Ashworth, himself a former chairman of the county commission, to become chairman of the Authority. Other members include Michael Sullivan, vice chairman; and members at large, Kevin McOmber, Tommy Hunter and Clint Dixon.

Innovative authority financing

Perhaps you have heard one wise man's thoughts: "I don't bet on sports games or politics!" In the National Football League, the phrase "On any given Sunday…." is synonymous with the possibility that even the lowliest football team can upset a top team.

And government has found that it's virtually impossible to determine what will happen in any election or referendum. The voters, it seems, can often be hard to read.

Back in 1972, Gwinnett's voters were certainly feisty and unpredictable, as they delivered what was a pretty severe blow to the local government. The county commission, seeking to fund much-needed facilities in what was then considered a fast growing county, put before the voters several propositions for General Obligation bonds.

Among the measures voted on individually were provisions for a new courthouse, expanded library and other major infrastructure improvements.

It was looked upon by the commission as the way to pay for facilities over several years through the use of bonds, rather than paying for these improvements out of raising taxes in the short term. The measures went before the voters on Saturday, December 14, 1974 in a special election, with only the eight bond referendum questions on the ballot.

Wayne Shackelford remembers the day: "It was a beautiful December day, bright, sunshiny and warm, and just before Christmas. While the young families went to the stores and shopped, it seems like every older landowner in the county turned out to the person at the polls and voted against every bond proposal on the ballot."

He adds: "That is the last time in my memory that we have had an election on Saturday."

There was no doubt about the mood of the voters that day, on the eight proposals for bonds for specific purposes. Every proposal went down to defeat. The scorecard showed:

Item	Yes	No
Roads and Bridges	2,102	7,607
Fire Protection	2,459	7,225
Public Safety Building	1,712	7,939
Library Building	2,201	7,477
Parks-Recreation	1,847	7,809
Juvenile Courthouse	2,186	7,471
Public Health Facility	2,097	7,592
Courthouse	1,644	8,027

The outcome stunned county officials, who had thought voters would give approval of these measures, and pave the way for funding the work without raising property taxes directly.

The question before them: how would they finance all these improvements that they needed. Shackelford recalls: "Someone said, 'Let's do it anyway with an Authority,' and we went that way."

Though the Commission could not get voter approval for bond financing of these needed new facilities, a provision of the Georgia Constitution gave counties the right to contract for services. Taking the idea to the county legislative delegation, the legislators came back and suggested two authorities.

From this in 1975 came both the Public Facilities Authority, and also the Gwinnett County Recreation Authority. It would allow the people moving into the county in the future to help pay for fire and recreational services of the county through debt services on bonds issued for building new facilities. Already in existence was the Water and Sewer Authority.

Appointed to the first Public Facilities Authority were Harold Humphries of Norcross, Virgil Williams of Snellville, and Maron Buice of Sugar Hill. Wayne Shackelford, the executive assistant to the county commission, was secretary of the Authority.

By funding capital projects through authorities, this would also allow equipping of buildings for fire and emergency medical services, even to the point of buying the actual trucks through the Public Facilities Authority. Two important benefits were clear: this could spread the cost of these facilities over several years, and at the same time, it would not require an up-front heavy ad valorem tax increase on property owners.

Soon the Authority was seeking bids on funding different buildings around the county. Shackelford, as secretary of the Public Facilities Authority, remembers: "We put these projects out to bid, and usually had bids from a number of local banks for the facilities. We did this funding relatively inexpensively, for we didn't have any of the normal cost associated with the issuing of bonds by dealing with local financial institutions."

Ray Mattison, the first Gwinnett fire chief and, in 2007, the fire chief in Winder, remembers those days of building fire department facilities. The Department had taken over the Norcross Fire Station, making it Station No. 1. New areas came into the district, with the next stations added being No. 2 on Harmony Grove Road (Berkshire) and No. 3 on Five Forks Trickum Road (Garners).

When the fourth station (on Spalding Drive) was under consideration, Mattison remembers that developer Paul Duke was concerned about the architectural design of the Peachtree Corners fire station. Mattison adds: "Neither of us liked the blue pre-fab stations that were built earlier in Berkshire and Garners. We wanted to design something different.

"The county was funding the early fire stations out of operational monies. I remember Ray Gunnin told me when we were designing the Peachtree Corners Fire Station that we had $70,000 to do it. The first price I got came in at over $100,000, and after about 30 days, I went to the contractor, Junior Duvall, and told him he could get in on the ground floor with this station, and it would work good for him and us, and his quote was $92,000. I told him that wouldn't work, and finally got him down to $79,960, and we built it for that."

It was a big day when the Peachtree Corners station was dedicated, as then Gov. Jimmy Carter landed in a helicopter to dedicate the station. He walked over to Ray Mattison, standing beside a fire truck, and told Mattison and Paul Duke: "Business is coming to Gwinnett because y'all (the fire department) are here." The future president's prediction proved true.

Two years after the Peachtree Corners station was built, metro area fire chiefs were meeting at Peachtree Corners station. Mattison says: "The Cobb fire chief took Polaroid photos of that station, and his department did drawings, and gave it to their engineers, who in turn gave them a ball park price of $412,000 to build a similar station. But we got ours for $79,960. It was quite a station, and built well."

After Station 4 was completed, the Public Facilities Authority began building fire stations. The county built other stations at low cost. Shackelford also says: "After the first stations were built, Ray Gunnin got Merv Seeley, who was the county engineer, to draw up the design for several fire stations, to save money on architectural fees. We built some of those buildings, which were often brick, for about $56,000." That was a turn-key price for smaller stations in Duluth, Grayson, Harbins and at Russell Road. Mattison adds: "These were great brick-faced stations, compact, and of good design. Later people said they could have cost $300,000 each."

But the Georgia chapter of the American Institute of Architects got upset with Gwinnett, Shackelford says, and sued the county for not having an architect design the stations. "The county won the case in court before Judge Reid Merritt, but the architects appealed. It went to the Court of Appeals, which sustained Merritt's ruling, and Gwinnett won the case."

Mattison picks up the story: "This came after we designed Fire Station No. 9 on Five Forks Trickum Road. Out of this, the architects got a law passed in Georgia that any building costing over a certain amount, I believe it was $50,000 at the time (which was raised later) must have plans from a licensed architect. But the law also exempts a city or county, saying they can use their own engineers for that."

Shackelford says: "When we started financing through the Public Facilities Authority, we went from three to 18 fire stations in the county before we had complete coverage of fire protection for the county in 1982. We also built the Fire Training Center on Jim Moore Road. We took all the cities of the county out of the fire business. We had stations in each major city, except in Buford where we covered Buford, Sugar Hill and Rest Haven with the station in Buford on the site donated by Mobil Land Development Company." Meanwhile, two cities straddling the Gwinnett line, Loganville and Auburn, have their own fire departments.

With the advent of Special Purpose Option Local Sales Tax as a means to finance projects, the need to issue debt for fire stations was no longer there. Fire services improvements have been paid by cash since then. Yet the Public Facilities Authority still exists, though it has not met in years. In 2007, the three members of the Public Facilities Authority included Rick Williamson, Michael Smith and Charles Bannister.

Other Gwinnett authorities, particularly the Water and Sewer Authority and the Recreation Authority, are still active.

Creating a recreation district

Soon after the Pinckneyville District opted for fire protection in 1970, its voters turned to a district-wide solution for another element of quality living: recreation activities, especially for its youth. This came after the county commission made it known that if the voters of an area were willing to pay for a service, they would provide it.

Pinckneyville area residents passed a recreation millage referendum on May 20, 1971 "not to exceed one mill." It soon found the move paying off. Before then, there were no parks within this part of the county. The first new park, to be called Best Friend Park, was designed with an outdoor swimming pool, recreational fields, picnic tables, gymnasium and open land, all on 43.38 acres of land donated by what was then the Southern Railroad.

On the heels of this, came an announcement of the purchase of nearly 30 acres of land as a park near Jones Bridge. The county purchased one-half of the land for Jones Bridge Park from Billy Orkin, and the other half was donated by Orkin (a son of the founder of Orkin Pest Control, which later was sold to Rollins Inc.). This beautiful tract of land, where once Indians and early settlers had crossed the Chattahoochee River on its shoals, was overgrown when the county took title to it. Soon this land blossomed into spacious fields for play, picnic tables, playground and a spot where fishermen could easily access the river to cast for the elusive trout. Shortly afterward, the county built on the tract a center for senior citizens, destined to become a popular meeting place. Altogether, Jones Bridge Park consists of 29.65 acres.

In 1973, the Recreation Department worked on a Master Plan, which was never adopted. Yet it set the tone for what the Department would seek over the years. One item from that report had a clairvoyant view of what the county would need when it stated:

"The larger the county grows, the more its citizens will need and seek open space. Today's open space will be tomorrow's subdivision or shopping center if Gwinnett fails to acquire land now. The projected growth in the county indicates the need for planning, acquiring and preserving open space today."

Unfortunately, the county was not generating the funds to buy recreational land economically in those early days. It would be nearly 20 years before the county started a massive acquisition of green and open spaces.

Just as happened in establishing the first fire district, in 1975 the Legislature changed the law to allow other militia districts to join the Recreation District by majority vote within that area. In 1976, Duluth and the Garners district (Mountain Park) voted to tax themselves for recreation.

On October 4, 1977, Dacula voted 198-92 to join the recreation district. Five other militia districts voted that day, with all the others voting against joining the recreation district. That included Goodwins, Harbins, Martins, Sugar Hill and Suwanee. Only in Harbins was the vote close, where the measure lost 95-71.

That same voting day, residents were asked another question in a "straw vote:" did they want to amend the Gwinnett County Public Facilities Authority bill to provide for a courthouse-administrative building? The people did not, though only 5,275 voted, with those voting yes totaling 2,344, and 2,904 opposing.

The turnout that day decided the courthouse issue. Only 10.2 percent of those registered actually voted. The recreational question seemed to carry the day, as the precincts that were the least populated turned out in large numbers to vote on both questions. However, the most populous areas of the county, nearer Atlanta, had only the straw courthouse question on the ballot, and did not have a high turnout, which may have doomed the courthouse question. As an example, in densely populated Pinckneyville, only 405 persons voted, while in Dacula, not densely populated, 287 voted in the straw poll.

Three years later, in1980, Suwanee residents changed their mind, as the City voted to join the recreational district. It had voted 148-110 against joining in 1977. The next turn for the recreational district came because of a change in 1981 in state law. This altered voting districts, making a vote in a specific Militia District virtually impossible.

Eventually, this led to the county adopting a county-wide recreation master plan, in February 1986. In that fall's election, voters of the county approved the county-wide Recreation District with its one mill recreation tax. The vote was 31,063 for the measure, and 21,362 against. The Recreation Authority was also expanded from five to nine members.

By January 1, 1987, the Gwinnett County Parks and Recreation Department was empowered to serve the entire county. Prior to this time, the Recreation Department served about 25 percent of the geographic area of the county, though 40 percent of the population.

The county's first 10-year comprehensive Master Plan for recreation was approved in 1986. The Authority also gave approval and started issuing revenue bonds for land acquisition and facility construction. What has happened since then is a story of continuing expansion of offerings by the Parks and Recreation Department. Operating as its own Authority, it has issued bonds for acquiring property and making improvements throughout the county. The first bonds, in August, 1987, were for $17 million to implement the first six years of the Master Plan.

Over the next few years, the Department relied upon revenue bonds for expanding its facilities. It issued $4 million in 1988, and $10 million in 1990.

Almost immediately, the county started acquiring park land. (See Appendix A-17 for complete list of key Recreation Department benchmarks.) Among the highlights:

- March, 1988: Acquires 50 acres on Britt Road.
- November, 1988: Springbrook Golf Course, consisting of 138.5 acres, is purchased.
- February, 1989, 141 acres on Bethesda Church Road came into the parks department.
- 1990: Among projects is the early development of Tribble Mill Park. Gwinnett is given 90 acres by the Adams family to become Vines Botanical Gardens, near Loganville.
- The county assumes operation of Lawrenceville city parks on March 28, 1992, expanding land and facilities.
- In 1996, a new vehicle for funding recreation came into play, as Gwinnett approved funds for recreation for the first time in a Special Purpose Local Option Sales Tax (SPLOST) vote, which included $60 million for land acquisition and project development for recreation. The county's general fund also made available $40 million for open space and park enhancement. In subsequent years, voters would again approve SPLOST funds for recreation, $192 million in 2001, and $162 million in 2005.

Since the first SPLOST vote in 1996, the Recreation Authority has not sought additional bond financing, but obtained funding either via SPLOST funds, or greenspace money and from the general fund.

* * * * *

Other significant projects expanded the county recreational activities even more.

- Gwinnett's 100-year Historic Courthouse in Lawrenceville was rededicated after extensive renovation and operates as the county's smallest park.
- October 4, 1994, Tribble Mill Regional Park officially opens, consisting of 650 acres.
- With assistance of the Trust for Public Land, 465 acres is acquired in 1998 for Little Mulberry Park, near Hog Mountain.
- The county's first Family Aquatic Center opened at Bogan Park. It is the first combined community recreation center and indoor leisure pool in 1997.

- The first Senior Golden Olympics was held in Gwinnett in the year 2000. That same year, McDaniel Farm, a 128-acre parcel near Gwinnett Place Mall, is purchased for greenspace and a future passive park.
- Historic Freeman Mill, also known as Swann's Mill and Alcovy Mill, was purchased. Operated as late as 1988 as a grist mill, funding was partially made with Georgia Greenspace Program funds.
- The Open Space and Greenway Master Plan was adopted in 2002, as a guide for future development. That same year, the Alexander property on Georgia Highway 124 between Snellville and Lawrenceville was purchased as a future open space park.
- Another distinction for Gwinnett: a free skate plaza and outdoor hockey rink opened at Pinckneyville Park in 2004.
- Gwinnett opened its first off-leash "dog park" at Ronald Reagan Park in 2004. This same year, the county set aside 3,700 acres of parkland as conservation easements, in nine parks of the county.
- Gwinnett assumed operation in 2005 of Lilburn Lions Club Park under terms of a 50-year lease with the city.

Since its initial development, the county parks and recreation district is a tremendously popular element of county government. It had a budget of approximately $29 million annually (2007), including $23 million from taxes and $6 million from department operational revenues. In 2007, it operated 33 parks, with plans for another 18 parks. The 2007 county's park system consists of 4,475 acres. Another 3,801 acres are earmarked already in 18 future parks, at present on hold until funds become available for implementation.

Little Best Friend Park, consisting of 43 acres, is dwarfed by mega-parks of the modern day. The largest of these holdings at 889 acres is Little Mulberry Park, while the smallest are the Gwinnett History Museum at 0.3 acres; the 1.5 acres of the Singleton Road Activity Building; and the 1.6 acres of the Historic Courthouse.

Other major parks in land size include:

- Tribble Mill Park, 700 acres.
- Yellow River Park, 566 acres.
- George Pierce Park, 303 acres.
- Environmental Heritage Center, 233 acres.

County officials identified the Little Mulberry area near Hog Mountain as a potential park in 1980, because of its pristine natural beauty. The county acquired part of the initial 485.27 acres in 1998 from the Trust for Public Land. It included a number of different land tracts which the Trust had assembled. The price was $5.2 million, or $10,861 an acre---a steal for such beautiful land.

The final 404-acre expansion came in 2001, through purchase from Mr. and Mrs. James Miller, who live nearby, for $6.6 million. More than 200 acres of this property is designated as the Karina Miller Nature Preserve, and opened to the public in 2006. This park is on one of the tracts of highest elevation in Gwinnett, and offers a large area left in a natural state, with passive activity, such as hiking and horseback riding trails, through the property.

Already on tap as a future park is the Harbins/Alcovy River site, anticipated to be open in 2008. The county purchased 1,895 acres in 2002, and came back and added another 106 acres to it in 2006 for a total park size of 1,901.79 acres, the largest in Gwinnett.

Through 2007, Gwinnett has spent over $85 million to purchase over 3,400 acres of greenspace through SPLOST monies. In addition to the greenspace purchases, the county acquired over 1,200 acres for active parks (those with a sports complex plus other amenities) for nearly $90 million, according to Phil Hoskins of the Parks and Recreation Department. (Gwinnett cities have also used SPLOST monies for park acquisition).

During the 12 years that Wayne Hill headed the county commission, more than 6,000 acres of greenspace were added to the county park land. In 2007, the county had 8,247 acres of park and greenspace land.

And as a result of extended land acquisition, Gwinnett County has one of the most modern and extensive county park systems in the nation. In 2005, the Gwinnett Park System was named as the only county government entity in the nation as a finalist for the National Recreation and Park Association's Gold Medal Award, for entities over 250,000 population.

The Gwinnett Recreational District maintains one of the largest, if not the largest, and more acres of greenspace, than any park system of a county in Georgia.

Both now county-wide operations, Gwinnett's parks and its fire department go back to the start that both systems had in the Pinckneyville area, back in the early 1970s.

"Friendly" poker game is big news

Casino-style gambling hasn't cropped up yet in Georgia, as it has in North Carolina, Mississippi and Louisiana. In Georgia, gambling as such is usually looked at askance---besides, it's against the law! Still there's a lot of gambling going on, whether it is betting on football games, auto or horse races, cock-fighting or, of course, the many local neighborhood card games.

One card game in particular was front page news in the *Gwinnett Daily News* for days and days back in 1972. One thing for sure: the story involved prominent citizens and politicians in Gwinnett. Besides newspaper accounts, this information came from one of the persons participating in the game, later a chairman of the county commission and perhaps the one single individual who has been the key person in Gwinnett's growth. That person is Wayne Mason.

We talked with Mason some 34 years after the game, and with his tight memory, he recalled the game as if it had been yesterday.

What follows is mostly Mason's account.

"Back in the 1970s, it was common knwledge that a bunch of us played poker every week, usually on Wednesday night, and often on Saturday afternoon. I had 700 acres off U.S. Highway 78 between Loganville and Snellville, which later would become Summit Chase Country Club. There was a boat house on J.B. Johnson Lake in the middle of those 700 acres, where we played.

"Everybody who was playing with me either worked for me or was kin to me. We had a $20 limit, and a person might win $2-3,000 any night. I wouldn't play with anyone if they didn't have as much money as I had, or else why play with them? We didn't play so as to hurt any of the players financially."

Mason reports that these days (2008), he does not play poker around Gwinnett, and when he does play, it is now only in Las Vegas. "I tell people I quit 'cause I don't like the competition,'" he laughs.

So on Wednesday after the Georgia Primary that year, on August 9, 1972, here sat a bunch of guys playing poker. Around the table were Doug McCurdy, a Stone Mountain Chevrolet dealer; Norris Nash, in real estate; Jimmy and Wayne Mason, the brothers who had been busily building houses in Snellville; Larry Smith, a Realtor from Snellville who later would own a Century 21 franchise; Hill Moore of Stone Mountain, an uncle of the Masons, who was in the auto business; and Warren Bush, a builder from Lithonia. Jimmy Mason was at the time a state representative representing the Snellville area in the Legislature, while Nash had previously been a state representative.

The night must have been something of a celebration for Wayne Mason, for the previous night, he had just won his first political race, the Democratic primary nomination (tantamount to victory in those days since he had no opposition in the General Election) to represent District 3 (around the Snellville area) on the Gwinnett County Commission. "I beat two guys without a runoff," Mason remembers. Four years earlier, in 1968, Mason had also sought that seat on the Commission, but his cousin, Carvis Williams, beat him for the post by 455 votes.

Politics ran in the family. Wayne's grandfather, James P. Mason, had been sheriff for four years, in 1938-42, in Gwinnett. Wayne's brother, Jimmy, was serving as one of two state representatives to the General Assembly.

Another of the players, Norris Nash from Lilburn, was also prominent politically, having served in the Legislature. The players at the table were old friends, who had been gathering in games like this for years.

Two of the poker regulars, contractor John D. Stephens of Snellville and the current (1972) county commission chairman, W. R (Dudge) Pruitt of Buford, were not present that night. Pruitt, who had been a county commissioner for four years, and chairman for another four years, had just been beaten in the Tuesday run-off primary by newcomer Bill Atkinson by a surprising 2,899 vote margin. Atkinson would serve one term as chairman, from 1973-77. And to show how politics got passed around in those days among friends, Mason would run against Pruitt, who was seeking a comeback, for the commission chairmanship, in the 1976 primary. Mason beat Pruitt by 376 votes.

So into this upbeat and celebratory setting, deep in what was a mostly quiet woody area five miles from Snellville, came a gunshot blast through a window.

Mason says: "About 10:30 p.m., three guys in masks blew out the window with a shotgun," as people ducked for cover. "The blast went past my left ear. I could hear it go by." The shot from a deer rifle hit Bush in the left arm, and he was hurt seriously, and lay in a pool of blood. "Three people blasted through a glass door, came in wearing masks, and told the players to get on the floor. They scooped up the cash on the table, later estimated at $1,500. They also demanded rings, credit cards and each person's cash. Included in the haul were some campaign checks, estimated at about $12,000, that Mason had in his wallet, and had not deposited." However, the robbery wasn't without effort, as poker players began battling back. Mason says: "I hit one with a 30-gallon trash can in the back of the head. He came back with a machine gun, and Jimmy had me duck behind a counter." But no one else was hit by the gunfire. Soon the robbers hightailed it away in Nash's car, which was later found abandoned 1.5 miles away. Detectives thought a fourth accomplice waited outside.

Bush and Wayne Mason were the only ones hit, with Mason having birdshot in his back. However, Smith received a slight injury in the holdup.

Before the robbers left, they slashed the tires on the players' vehicles, and took their auto keys. They also told the players to remain on the floor for 10 minutes. Eventually, a set of keys was found in Bush's pocket, and the players drove from the boat house to the Snellville police station on flat tires. The group was taken to the Button Gwinnett Hospital in Lawrenceville, with Bush bleeding badly. There they found Bush's wound was more serious. Meanwhile, doctors fished birdshot from Mason. Mason later that night went home and recovered, though Bush was transferred to Piedmont Hospital. Eventually, his arm had to be amputated. (He died from other causes about three years later.)

The police investigated, and the *Gwinnett Daily News* got wind of the game and robbery. Its headline the next day read:

Gunmen Crash Card Game Here;
Prominent Men Lose Thousands
Shotgun Victim Critical

The newspaper displayed pictures of both Wayne and Jimmy Mason and former State Rep. Norris Nash that day. It continued to pump the story in later days, adding new details as they became known. Mason had arrived at the boathouse about 20 minutes before the robbers came in. Speculation was that the robbers had followed him to the game.

But that's not all of the story.

The poker crowd figured that the only way to fight the group was with harsh tactics. "That's the way you fight crime, fight fire with fire," says Mason. It took several weeks to get the robbers.

Mason says: "We sent Maxie Price, then a used car dealer, down to 14th Street in Atlanta, where all the hippies were, to spread the word. He told them that there was a $25,000 bounty on each of the robbers, dead or alive." Mason says: "Once the robbers heard about this, they started finding ways of giving themselves up, in a public place, for they didn't want the police to shoot them and of course, possibly collect that reward."

Eventually five people were charged, all in their 20s. One gave evidence and helped convict the others. All got prison terms. Later the poker players learned that some of the robbers had been fishing at Johnson's Lake and realized the group was playing poker. One of the robbers was just back from Vietnam, and was on methadone. Mason says: "Once he got out of prison, he later tried to rob a Majic Market convenience store, run by Dillard Munford, who was head of the Atlanta Crime Commission. He put stakeouts behind glass at some of his stores, and when this guy tried to stage a robbery, he killed the guy." Mason adds: "That guy should have stayed in prison."

The upshot for the guys playing poker is that all but Bush, who was still hospitalized, were charged with a misdemeanor of gambling by District Attorney Bryant Huff. They could have faced a year in prison. However, appearing before Judge Charles C. Pittard, each pleaded "nolo contendere" and they were each fined $1,000. Newspaper accounts said that most gambling charges in Gwinnett resulted in fines of $50-100. Huff said he recommended the stiffer fines "because of the position they (defendants) hold in the community and what precipitated such a serious incident."

The group accepted their fate. However, Mason also says that the card playing was not necessarily something entirely limited to the group of persons at the game. "We had played cards with every judge and district attorney in the county," he adds.

* * * * *

There was one more political move coming out of this poker game. After this gambling incident, with steady news about a "crackdown" on gambling in the county, here came a new candidate running against Mason as a write-in Republican candidate in 1972 for county commission chairman. He was Jack Sawyer, the mayor of Lilburn at the time. Mason won easily. He says of Sawyer's Republican candidacy: "We had never seen one of them (a Republican in Gwinnett) before." Mason handily defeated him in the General Election. Sawyer would later serve as mayor of Lilburn, and eventually, for 12 years as head of the Gwinnett Chamber of Commerce.

Briscoe Field

Around 1972, when they looked at a forecast of the future of the Gwinnett County Airport, two of the first five members of the Gwinnett Airport Authority were incredulous. Cabinetmaker Wayne Hill and paving contractor Wiley Puckett were flabbergasted.

Puckett said in 2007: "We couldn't imagine that it would grow like they projected, since the report forecasted that the airport would have 10 times the number of planes it had in those days, when the airport then had about 30-40 airplanes. We couldn't believe it would have that many planes by the year 2000." The actual 2000 count for airplanes based at Briscoe Field was 352. And by 2007, this number had climbed to 466.

Wayne Hill adds: "The forecast blew our minds, but the airport really did grow just like that." The other three original members of the Airport Authority were Jones Webb, Robert Underwood and Hugh Britt.

While the county airport growth has paralleled the spectacular growth of Gwinnett County, some credit the airport as a key reason for the county's growth.

Gwinnett County's airport was created in 1966, an outgrowth of former Gov. Carl Sanders' program to situate airports within gliding distances as an extra safety measure when airplanes were flying at 10,000 feet altitude. That works out to have a landing strip for every 17 mile radius around the state. There were only 30 airports in Georgia when Carl Sanders became governor in 1962. A former World War II B-17 pilot, Sanders had campaigned for governor while flying a Commanche 250 single-engine plane around the state, landing in "cow pastures and mountain strips of less than 700-800 feet," he says. "Most of the airports we had in Georgia when I came into office were former military strips for pilot training."

Sanders went to the convention of the Association County Commissioners of Georgia (in about 1961), asking for support to build airports throughout the state. "They gave me a rousing no, and not only no, but hell, no," he says. "They wanted more money for roads." Sanders went to work, finding that there was a federal program for development of community airports. "The next year I went back to the county commissioners and said that the state would put up half the money, and the federal government would put up the other half if the counties bought land for the airport. They agreed to that."

During the Sanders Administration, Georgia had the top airport building program in the country. The former governor says: "We built over 70 airports during those years, to well over 100 airports. It provided an opportunity for aviation to Georgia, and also opened up the state for industrial development. As a result, during our four years, Georgia got over $1 billion in new industry to the state." And this in the mid-1960s! Meanwhile, by 2007, Georgia had 107 public-use airports, with 98 for general aviation, and nine commercial airports, an indication that most of the state's airports came during the Sanders' era.

Back in the mid-1960s, it took many back-and-forth negotiations between the county, the state of Georgia and the Federal Aviation Authority (FAA) to make the airport a reality. Little progress came until 1971, when the county commission asked the General Assembly to approve the creation of the Gwinnett County Airport Authority to assume management of the airport's activities. To this day, each of the five authority members is appointed by a county commissioner, and served a concurrent term with that commissioner. Jones Webb was elected as the first chairman of the Authority

When Gwinnett was seeking to have an airport, at that time there was a small landing strip on about 70 acres where the present airport is located. The grass strip was about 900 feet in length and was owned by James C. Grant and John (June) Clark, who worked to get the county to buy the airport. Grant had been a pilot for the Duluth-based Vantress Farms, flying both a DC-3 (two engine) and DC-6 (four engine) airplane for Charles Vantress. Both airplanes were housed at Peachtree-DeKalb Airport. Once Grant became involved with the Lawrenceville facility, he soon bought out Clark. He operated an air strip at the location, which was activated as LZU (Lawrenceville) airport on October 1, 1963. Upon recommendation of Lawrenceville's superintendent of public utilities, Don Martin, the county commission purchased the land of 70 mostly wooded acres from Grant in 1966. The site is located two miles northeast of Lawrenceville, alongside and north of the Seaboard Coast Line (CSX) rail tracks. Over the next few years, the county would continue to buy small parcels of land, as needed, from Grant to add to the airport acreage.

Around 1967, with state and federal assistance paying for the improvements, a 3,000 foot paved runway was laid, and the airport was in business. However, there were no taxiways, nor electronic assistance for airplanes.

Warren Chastain, along with a dentist, Dr. H.P. Edmonds, got a lease from the county to operate the airport. They operated two firms at the airport, Chastain Air Service, which primarily provided aircraft maintenance; and Lawrenceville Aviation, which was a Piper airplane dealer. Edmonds also offered flight training.

In 1971, the Airport Authority was created, and it sought to cancel the Chastain-Edmonds lease. Eventually, the two parties went to court, but in the meantime, Chastain died. Finally, the court ruled that the county could not cancel the lease. Shortly afterward, also in late 1971, Rob Mancini entered the picture. He had been a service manager for an aviation company at Peachtree DeKalb airport, and became interested in leasing the Chastain-Edmonds operation, wanting his own business. He and the Chastain Estate and Edmonds came to an agreement, and in 1973, Mancini obtained a 25-year lease from the Airport Authority, operating under the name of Roman Aviation.

Mancini was a key person in the development of the airport. The firm, privately owned, offered many airport services as its fixed base operator, including flight instruction, aircraft repair and fueling. With his general understanding of the local airport operations, Mancini was virtually a volunteer airport manager. Mancini says: "We began with 15 acres of leased airport land, two small buildings and two employees." Mancini could see a bright future in local aviation and helped put the Gwinnett airport on the map. He continued to be the leaseholder at the airport until the late 1980s.

In the early days of the airport, besides the paving of the runway in the late 1960s, the county built a 4,800 square-foot building for the fixed base operator (FBO), four paved tie-down areas, and put into operation a paved apron near the midpoint of the runway. The taxiways for the landing strip were gravel then, but were paved in 1973-74.

First airport in county

What is known today as the Gwinnett County Airport was not the first location for airplanes in Gwinnett. The first was in Buford, a small air strip on a farm owned by the Bona Allen interest. Though on some old maps a Buford airport is listed, the strip never operated as a functional airport, but merely existed as a landing strip for the Allen airplane and other airplanes. Air shows were held at the site, which was in the southeastern quadrant of the intersection where the home office of People's Bank is now at Hill Street and Georgia Highway 13. This air strip continued to function until the 1950s.

Lawrenceville was the site of another early air strip after World War II, which was operated by Sam Martin Jr. He and Ray Bailey, both from Lawrenceville and former pilots, had purchased 43 acres from Brand Bank. The field was located northwest of Georgia Highway 20 near the intersection of and parallel to the Lendon Lane subdivision and the present-day Georgia Highway 316 (which was not there at the time). After about a year, Martin bought Bailey out. Martin had flown P-47s in Italy in World War II, and had been shot down over northern Italy near Bologna. He was a prisoner of war, and was released in May of 1945.

Martin and Bailey named the landing strip Wages Field, in memory of Emory "Red" Wages of Lawrenceville, a Naval pilot who was killed in World War II. This grass landing strip was 1,600 feet in length, and Martin kept two J-3 Piper Cubs in a hangar at the strip. Two others, Paul Kelly and Joe Cooley, had planes parked there. Cooley had a single-engine World War II trainer, and flew airmail out of the airport on contract to the Post Office. The configuration of the airport was so tight that on take-offs northerly over Highway 20, the planes would fly under the power lines! Others report that landings would require halting automobiles on the then not-so-busy Highway 20, as the planes flew low to touch down on the short strip.

When in operation, Wages Field had a flight school and a five-lane bowling alley that Martin operated. When Martin returned to the Air Force in 1949, the field began to deteriorate, though it remained operational until the late 1950s. "We did not take care of it," says Sam Jr. His parents, Lucille and Sam Sr., continued to operate the bowling alley until the 1960s. It was a popular site, Martin says, "Some place to go at night." It served cold drinks and snacks, but no beer: "My mother would have had a fit," Sam Jr. says. Sam Martin Jr. retired from the Air Force in 1973. As of 2008, the family still owns the land of the former field, but were in negotiations to sell the property.

Since its beginning in 1966, Gwinnett's airport has been in a continuing chase of constant improvements. In the mid 1970s, the runway was extended from 3,000 to 4,000 feet.

* * * * *

After the Authority was formed, a series of improvements began which have continued without stopping since. In 1972, Tom Briscoe became chairman of the Authority, and was a key figure in the development and operation of the airport until his death in 1984. For his years of yeoman service, the airport was renamed Gwinnett Airport -- Briscoe Field after his death. Ironically, Mr. Briscoe was known for his strong personal fear and dislike of flying. Yet he gave the airport authoritative leadership, and spearheaded the direction of two major airport master plans, those of 1974 and 1983, and also directed its many improvements. His successor as chairman, Dr. Jim Davis, praised his work: "Without him, our realities would still be just a dream." The Briscoe family, in 2007, donated an airport observation area, consisting of a covered pavilion with picnic tables, granite marker and flag pole, located off Georgia Highway 316, in Tom Briscoe's memory.

In 1977, the airport conducted its first federally-supported development project, which included grading and drainage improvements for the runway, as well as clearing of land for proposed runway improvements. The funding came through a FAA Airport Development and Aid program.

A key event in 1986 was Rob Mancini's sale of the fixed base operation (FBO). Mancini had worked diligently, and gained the trust of those working in airport operations. When Mancini left, he says: "We went from less than 10 to over 150 aircraft based at the airport, including 10 corporate aircraft."

New operator of the FBO was Robert Wall of Lawrenceville, who bought the lease from Mancini, and operated as Wall Aviation. Over the next several years, a series of transactions began involving the FBO, with it having several operators in short time. At one time, Virgil Williams bought an interest in Wall Aviation, though later Wall repurchased the Williams' interest. About that time, the FBO's name was also changed to Air Center Gwinnett, as Wall renegotiated the lease with the Authority.

After Wall became embroiled with legal difficulties, the operation was taken over by RES Associates, a group of individuals who had previously worked for Hawthorne Aviation. In the mid-1990s, the giant Citibank became involved, owning the FBO for a time, though shortly selling their interest to Hawthorne Aviation, which later became Piedmont Hawthorne of Winston-Salem, N.C. This firm operated the airport FBO on the northern side of the runway until about 2002, when it was sold to Landmark Aviation, a part of The Carlyle Group of Tempe, Ariz., which had operations at 33 airports in the United States. The

Gwinnett site was managed by Shawn Harley in 2008, employed 14 persons at Briscoe Field, and provided ground support for personal and business aircraft for 350-400 customers.

In turn, in 2007, Carlyle sold their operation to Dubai Aerospace Enterprises (DAE). Before the sale was approved, DAE was required to divest itself of the airport FBO operations, since it was a foreign entity. In 2008, eight FBO operations of DAE were sold to GTCR Golder Rauner, LLC of Chicago, Ill. and they were brought under the management of Encore Aviation of Houston, Tex., which in 2008 had FBO operations at 42 airports, including Briscoe Field, all managed under the name of Landmark Aviation.

Professional management

In 1987, the Authority hired a 19 year aviation veteran, Scott Fuller, to become the first airport manager and director of the Aviation Division, Gwinnett DOT. He began to implement a set of improvements which would have significant impact on the airport and its operations.

As Fuller arrived, the airport was beginning a $25 million expansion, with 90 percent of the funding coming from the FAA, and five percent each from the State of Georgia and Gwinnett County. Part of the proceeds from the county came from a $4.2 million airport revenue bond of 1985, for property acquisition and construction of a replacement runway.

The way the Airport Authority actually gained control of the grounds from the county was creative. The Authority issued the $4.2 million bond, and used these proceeds to buy the airport from the county. That eliminated some question of who owned what, in that the Authority and the county, at times, had purchased different properties associated with the airport. The county then used the $4.2 million proceeds to provide matching funds for federal grants, thereby leveraging that amount to generate over $25 million in airport improvements. At the same time, the county hired the Authority to manage the airport.

Through the years, the Authority had been adding more land for airport operations. Between 1977-2004, the Authority had 13 land acquisitions, so that the site in 2007 totaled 507 acres. The largest expansions came in 1985 (175 acres), bought for $2.8 million, and in 1987, when 103 acres were purchased for $2.5 million. In 1989, a 39-acre plot cost $2.5 million. The last purchase was in 2004, when an 8.80-acre plot was purchased for $980,070. Altogether, the 507 acres of land cost the airport a total of $11.5 million over the years.

Several major improvements at the airport were most significant. A major step was scraping the former 4,000 foot runway in 1991 and building a new 6,100 foot runway to the south of the old one, with a few degrees change in runway alignment. The inaugural flight on the new runway was on April 4, 1991. This new and longer runway had a cost of $13,134,880 and gave the airport even more flexibility, as it gave Briscoe Field the capability to handle jet aircraft as large as DC-9 airplanes. And its addition saw the number of jets based at the airport increase.

Adding improvements has been a constant effort by the Airport Authority. Among them:

- 1990: Instrument Landing System.
- 1990s: On-site Automatic Weather Reporting Station (AWAS).
- 1991: Replacement and Expansion of Runway to 6,100 feet.
- 1997: Air traffic control tower manned 14 hours a day.
- 2004: Second taxiway, costing $7.5 million.

The AWAS transmitter allowed aircraft to land when the flying visibility was at less than a mile and cloud ceiling was 200 feet above ground. Prior to the weather station, the minimum was a 665-feet ceiling and one-mile visibility. The station can be accessed by pilots by phone when on the ground, or from the airplane when approaching the field. The continuous transmission of immediate weather includes temperature, altimeter setting, ceiling (how high above ground the clouds are at the airport), and the visibility (sight distance).

The south side is where a major portion of airport operations is now based. The expansion of the air traffic control tower cost $454,502. The tower is run under contract with the FAA by Robinson Aviation Inc. of Oklahoma City, Okla. Nationwide, the firm operates at 86 airports, and employs 450 air-traffic-control specialists. Subcontracting to operate the Gwinnett tower is Computer Intelligence Square Aviation Inc. of Marietta, Ga. Jerry Poole became the tower manager in February of 2008. The firm operates the tower with five full-time and one part-time employees.

Adding a second fixed-base operator came with the focus on the south side. The original operator of the second FBO was James Justice of Georgia Jet, which had won a bid to operate the system. In turn, Georgia Jet sold the operation to Atlanta Jet, which operated it before selling to a firm which eventually became known as Aircraft Specialist Jet Center, with John Gibbs as manager

In 2004 the Authority added, on the north side, a second taxiway at a cost of $7.5 million. This increased safety, and allowed for an increase in efficiency, with a shorter time between take-offs.

In 2007, some 16 years after commissioning the new instrument landing system at Gwinnett, the FAA has embarked on a 20-year massive program to convert the nation to a satellite-based traffic control, navigation and landing system. The program is slated to be completed in 2027.

Currently, the Airport Authority leases ground space for firms wanting to build facilities at Briscoe Field. The Airport controls the type and height of buildings that can be built. The buildings are used as hangars, airplane refurbishing sites, three flight schools, aircraft maintenance schools, airplane sales, and other aircraft work space and office buildings, most related to airport activities. In 2007, the county airport had 24 master leaseholders renting ground space at the airport, bringing in annual lease payments of $620,710. Its total revenue was $861,660. The airport also earns a seven-cents per-gallon fuel fee on all fuel sold at the airport and had sales of more than 2.5 million gallons for 2007. Overall, the airport had an operating margin of $113,309 for the year. (See Appendix B, page 671 for more detail.)

Any revenues over operating expenses are transferred to the Airport Renewal and Extension Fund for capital improvements. The Airport also receives funding from the federal and state governments for capital improvements. The Airport's six-year capital improvement program for 2007 was $22.2 million with over 72 percent of the funds coming from state and federal grants.

The Airport Authority periodically updates its Master Plan, the latest update finalized in 2006. Among the current recommendations is adding a parallel runway, suggested at 5,000 feet, which would cost approximately $12 million. This is not expected to be undertaken until substantial additional traffic is seen at Briscoe Field.

However, a more pressing problem in 2007 was the need for an additional taxiway, so that fewer airplanes had to cross the runway. In addition, another priority was to strengthen the current runway to a weight-bearing capacity of 100,000 pounds dual-wheel classification.

* * * * *

Gwinnett County Airport has a major economic impact for the county, bringing in significant tax revenue. Facilities and equipment based at the airport are part of the county tax digest. Aircraft based at the airport and buildings on its grounds, which are privately-owned, bring in significant ad valorem taxes to Gwinnett County. For 2007, the individually owned and commercial aircraft, hangars and equipment at Briscoe Field had a market value of $193,794,625, and an assessed valuation (40 percent of market value) of $77,517,850. The privately-owned craft, facilities and equipment brought in tax revenues to the county budget of $2,471,269 for 2007, according to the Tax Assessor's figures.

The Authority itself employs the airport manager and his staff, a total of five employees. After Fuller left as manager in 1997, John Ferguson was airport manager for about two years. Since 2000, the manager, as of 2008, has been Matthew Smith.

Gwinnett's Briscoe Field now ranks fifth in Georgia in the number of take-offs and landings. Ahead of Gwinnett are Hartsfield-Jackson (980,386 operations), Peachtree DeKalb (202,497), McCollum Field in Cobb (173,547), Fulton-Charlie Brown Airport (130,923). Lawrenceville (LZU) as of 2007 had 108,485 operations, while Savannah's commercial airport ranks next at 102,852 operations.

However, when it comes to the number of planes based at airports, Gwinnett ranks second in Georgia, with 466 based at its airport, to Peachtree DeKalb, with 565. Cobb County counts 358, Columbus totals 236, Henry County, 275, and Fulton County-Charlie Brown has 174, according to FAA data from February, 2008.

Keeping engineers in Georgia

It was a simple question: "Why do Georgia Tech engineering graduates leave Georgia?"

The Georgia Tech Foundation wanted to know. In 1966, it put up $100,000 to the consulting firm of Booz, Allen and Hamilton for an answer. And soon the answer came back: "Because there are not many engineering jobs in Georgia."

Well, yeah. But at least now the Foundation understood. The answer would lead to a significant change that would alter Gwinnett forever.

A 1945 Georgia Tech All-American football center, Paul Duke, heard this answer and mulled it over. He had not left Georgia himself, but was running a division for a Pittsburgh company (L.G. Foster and Co.) in Gwinnett County. Duke convinced 16 other alumni of his school to ante up dollars in the late 1960s, and tied up land west of Norcross. The goal: to create a community where people would work, live and play. He named this community "Peachtree Corners," with its centerpiece to be called Technology Park /Atlanta, a 300-acre tract., which started in 1971. The group hired as its key executive the president of the Research Triangle of North Carolina, Jim Shay, who was at the park one year.

Charlie Brown, who would become president of the park in 1979 and led the park successfully for 19 years, until 1998, explains what the founders were seeking. Readers should remember that the park became the leader for industrial park development within Metro Atlanta, but technology was not a by-word in those days. Brown says:

"Technology Park was started by a bunch of Georgia Tech alumni to provide real estate locations for technically oriented industry. In those days, technology meant mostly transistors. With the exception of a few large companies, technology did not permeate the economy at all like it does today. The result was that there were only a few possible potential tenants for the park. However, what was shown in other parts of the country was that these technical firms tended to bunch together, since it helped recruiting.

"There was another consideration. The type of space these firms needed was different, not just office, but with far more open spaces. They didn't need the tall ceilings of a warehouse. They filled up the open space with people. Normal warehouse space would not work for these companies, since buildings with warehouse space routinely did not have enough parking for the larger staffs that technical firms had.

"So Technology Park put together buildings with more open space, that is, more people space as opposed to product space and bulk storage. There was some manufacturing of tenant's products, but this did not take much space. Too, we had to offer the space with air conditioning, for some of the production required it. You don't think of that today, but it was new then."

With more and more companies joining the technical age through use of computers and other sophisticated gear, Brown says, "Before long, we could lease to anyone, since all firms needed to have high-tech engineers. Technology started to permeate everyone's business. It was the supporting base for most companies. And this meant that the market expanded for us. What Technology Park wanted to do was to provide jobs for people with technical backgrounds, especially for technical people in Atlanta."

Though slow at first, by the late 1970s, Technology Park/Atlanta began to attract firms moving into the campus-style grounds. The first tenant was Electromagnetic Sciences Inc., a firm that in 1971 built its own and the first facility in the park. Then in 1973 the Park put up a 14,000-square-foot multi-tenant building, soon followed by a 50,000 square-foot office for Ebasco Services, a giant engineering firm out of New York. Three more buildings followed in 1974, and the park was beginning to succeed. But it built only one building in 1975, because of the slow-down in the economy, none in 1976 and one each in 1977 and 1978. But 1979 saw a 40,000-square-foot office and manufacturing plant for Intelligent Systems, and a two-story office/laboratory for Perkin Elmer Corp., and the park became quite stable and attractive. Through 2007, Technology Park saw the coming of 97 buildings, totaling six million square feet. A total of 26 of these buildings exceeded 100,000 square feet, with the largest being 220,000, a twin four-story, multi-tenant office building, developed in 1991.

What Duke and his investors started eventually became the model high-grade industrial park in the area, and throughout the Southeast. National firms looking for locations recognized the beautiful landscaping, admired the quiet setting, saw the lakes providing serenity (also used to water the grass), and realized it was all happening in a county with a solid school system. Technology Park/Atlanta began to sign more and more tenants.

In 2008, more than 18,000 people were employed at elements of Technology Park. A total of 102 companies in the original Technology Park/Atlanta (near Norcross) employs approximately 7,000+ people in four million square feet, while at Johns Creek, 295 firms employ 11,000 persons, occupying five million square feet of space.

Indeed, what happened first at Technology Park/Atlanta, and then at other locations around Metro Atlanta, coupled with the need for most major firms to have engineers on their staffs, gave Georgia an ability to attract not only Georgia Tech engineering graduates, but people from schools all across the United States. Technology Park's timing was perfect, and greatly impacted the Gwinnett market.

A new day for Gwinnett industry

The type of development that Technology Park/Atlanta brought to the area was innovative and distinctive, and led the pace for the success of Gwinnett attracting so many high-technology businesses, which became solid employers.

Besides jobs, Technology Park gave Gwinnett much more. It became a model as a business park that has been replicated. All throughout Gwinnett today, and extending throughout Metro Atlanta, you see what was once farmland turned into business parks. In Gwinnett alone in 2005, high technology jobs employ more than 48,296 people, according to the county's Economic Development office.

While distribution facilities still dot the land throughout the county, today you see other higher-end industrial sites that owe their location to what first happened at Technology Park/Atlanta west of Norcross in unincorporated Gwinnett. These buildings are usually bricked for longevity, have long-term tenants or owners, are surrounded by flourishing landscaping, and provide far better-than-average jobs in technological industries.

Gwinnett also benefited from another aspect of Technology Park/Atlanta. It became known as a high technology center, as first one firm, then another, found facilities in the area to their liking. One reason for this understanding of Gwinnett as a high-tech center came when the Internet modem was invented by Hayes Microcomputer, which eventually was located in Peachtree Corners.

The development of Peachtree Corners and Technology Park/Atlanta and their many high quality, professional jobs is a direct benefit from Paul Duke and his vision of what Gwinnett could become. And today, as Duke envisioned, people work, live and play in close proximity in this area, and in many other high-tech centers in Gwinnett.

Presidents of Technology Park/Atlanta

1971	Jim Shay
1972	Brian Hogg
1973	Chappell Summers
1979	Charles Brown
1998	Rick O'Brien

In the early 1970s, on the western edge of Norcross, another area began to bloom. At the same time as Western Electric was opening, Peachtree Corners began as an area of upscale homes, and was being marketed as a future home for high-quality industry. Technology Park/Atlanta (TP/A) began as a place for excellent jobs. Nearby some of the first modern apartments were being built. Several subdivisions of large, two-story homes were beginning to rise near the Chattahoochee River. And on October 31, 1971, Technology Park/Atlanta got its first tenant as Electromagnetic Sciences Inc., a three-year-old company with ties to the defense industry, occupied its new facility.

Electromagnetic Sciences (EMS) was an offshoot of then DeKalb-based Scientific-Atlanta, a start-up founded and headed by scientist Dr. John Pippin. Few understood what this firm did, because of the nature of its high-tech business. Basically, EMS facilitated the communication between orbiting satellites by microwave transmission. Today the firm is still in Technology Park, with its name changed to EMS Technologies, employing 1,500 people. Some of its early work was with defense contractors, which is a major portion of its business today. Since then it has moved to commercial adaptations of its innovations, moving from military applications, especially for its wireless transmissions, into such fields as warehousing, inventory control, and aeronautical satellite communications.

As the original 13,000 square-foot EMS building was being completed, Technology Park itself was just beginning. Dr. Pippin recalls the firm moving into their Technology Park facility. "When we contracted for our building, we were the first company to locate there. We crossed farmland to get to the site, and sometimes left gates open and let cows out of their pasture before we realized it.

"We had to build our own construction road into the park, from Spalding Drive. Technology Park had a contract to get the road paved to our site by the time we moved, on October 31. Our land had lots of trees on it, and we brought in our own machine to grade the surface. The road builders were still packing down the first layer of asphalt on that day when our trucks arrived to unload our gear. We had to follow the packer at a slow speed to get to our plant's driveway. And after we arrived, we were virtually out here two or three years by ourselves. The first road came in off Spalding Drive, since the Peachtree Industrial entrance came much later."

Dr. Pippin found a surprising problem locating in the new technical park in Gwinnett: "During those first few months, Atlanta trucking firms would not make deliveries to our plant unless we paid an extra fee, for they thought we were so far outside Atlanta."

When Dr. Pippin left his job as CEO in 1994, the firm had 1,100 employees. By 1998, when he retired after having been its chairman since founding, it had over 2,000 employees,

Dr. John Pippin

and its facilities totaled more than 300,000 square feet. The firm researched, developed and designed all its products in Atlanta, ranging from defense products for the microwave transmission in the spacecraft industry to producing sophisticated antennas used in cellular phones and personal communication devices, which captured a large part of that market. Another division (LXE) was devoted to "real-time" data communication systems for warehouse and distribution centers, and became something of a standard for the radio-frequency field.

In effect, EMS took what it had developed for the military and governmental spacecraft markets, and focused on ways to use these technologies in the commercial marketplace. It changed from being a firm primarily devoted to defense and government work to a diversified company. Dr. Pippin's firm brought just what Technology Park wanted: a firm on the cutting edge of technology.

The second firm to land in the park was the Institute of Industrial Engineers, who moved to Norcross from the streets of New York City. The Institute was an outgrowth of the early time-and-motion studies of Frank and Lillian Gilbreth, made famous in the movie, "Cheaper By the Dozen." They are considered as pioneers of industrial engineering tools and techniques and the champions of work simplification.

Then-Gov. Jimmy Carter cut the ribbon for the Institute's 13,000 square-foot facility on December 1, 1971. When the move was made from New York to a 2.4 acre site in Technology Park in July, 1972, seven staff members relocated. However, over the years the number of employees grew to around 90 people as the business and the industrial engineering profession flourished. In the late 1980s, redundant positions were eliminated and all through the 1990s, lean management principles were instituted. It is able to manage processes and operations at a far more sophisticated level than 10 years earlier, but with a staff of only 26. Today the firm is in Royal Peachtree Corners, where it moved in 2002, across Peachtree Parkway from Technology Park.

More firms started to arrive at Technology Park, though attracting firms to this new type of park in Atlanta was slow when it first started. Technology Park officials were told that one major reason the park did so well was because of its natural setting, the landscaped grounds, its continuously blooming plantings during all seasons, all highlighted by the stately beauty of its many hard wood and pine trees. It was basically a forest punctuated with its own man made lakes, from which it would later draw water for irrigation (and initially for additional water storage for fire protection). Add in the wide landscapes of grass and colorful flower beds, and it was an idyllic campus-like atmosphere for industry.

And the eventual ease of access to the interstate highways through Peachtree Industrial Boulevard helped as well. The park caught the eye of commercial real estate specialists from national companies. They liked the serene setting of a campus-like park, where picnic tables were set outside for lunch, and joggers zipped around the wide streets safely.

Then another problem arrived: the recession of 1974-75, which was a financial setback for Technology Park. Yet the company remained above water during the lean days of that recession, and though one of its founders was forced to personal bankruptcy, Technology Park itself was spared.

Soon Peachtree Corners and Technology Park were being recognized for its innovative contributions to the county. In a February 19, 1978 issue of *Gwinnett Daily News*, the newspaper took an unusual step. In its Progress Edition of that date, the newspaper did something it had never done before: it dedicated that edition, the largest the company had then published, to Technology Park guru Paul Duke. It said:

"Duke came to Gwinnett many years ago to run one of the county's largest industries. Once here, he fathered a dream: to create the finest planned community imaginable, consisting of first-class industry, top-drawer corporate headquarters, and unexcelled residential development. After he invested his own fortune, the dream emerged as Peachtree Corners.

"Duke could not foresee the economic crunch of 1974, and the aftermath, which wiped out so many developers. Happily, though Duke suffered personally from the economic downturn, his dream remained intact. Peachtree Corners survived the ravages of the recession and is today viewed nationally as a standard of excellence worthy of emulating.

"There can be no doubt that its presence has had a profound effect on much of Gwinnett's other development. Peachtree Corners has not only attracted nationwide attention to Gwinnett, it has also become a standard by which subsequent local developments are measured.

"We are pleased to pay tribute to Paul Duke. Few, if any, business people have made the contribution to Gwinnett that he has. His personal fortunes would have prospered more favorably had he not dreamed so idealistically. Gwinnett, on the other hand, would not have reaped the harvest it has without Duke's dream.

"It is comforting to know that Paul Duke is still in Gwinnett and continues to contribute his know-how and talent to many worthwhile endeavors. He is a rare citizen, a great person to know and a tremendous ally to any cause.

"We can think of no one who better deserves tribute. It is our pleasure to dedicate Progress '78 to him."

Paul Duke

* * * * *

With Technology Park/Atlanta on target to supply real estate to technical companies, soon it became apparent that the firm was about to run out of its biggest asset---open land.

Charlie Brown picks up the story: "Once we got the Park going well, and our concept of having land for technical companies to locate got established, it became apparent that the best thing for the Georgia Tech Foundation was to sell the park, so it could gain from the rising valuation of the company. This was very difficult for the people who had started the park. But it was necessary, we realized, for the resources were not there for expansion we needed to make.

"A similar technical park in Denver had been acquired by a large English company, European Ferries, which later was to become the Peninsula and Orient Steamship Company. So with the similar park in Denver, and our people realizing Denver Tech understood us and would honor the commitment to develop the land for technical industry, and not be just a real estate land play, the sale took place. So the Georgia Tech Foundation and the investors sold a majority portion of their interest, to be repaid in 10-15 years. Denver Tech had control of the park, and several from Technology Park were on their board, and we were able to maintain the original goals of the group under the new ownership."

Georgia Tech itself benefited tremendously from the sale, since the original investors had over the years given part of their stock in the park to it and other area colleges. The windfall for Georgia Tech: $9 million. (Other local area colleges owned smaller amounts of stock donated by the original investors, and therefore also benefited.)

The Georgians found that growth was coming rapidly, and with the Denver Tech connection, they had the fiscal resources to expand as the market would allow.

Charlie Brown remembers going with Rick O'Brien to England the first time to see key British executives of the parent company. He wanted to explain a deal that was pending. His counterparts from other real estate investments in Denver, Houston, and officials overseeing operations for them in Southeast Asia, were present. The key element on Brown's mind: explaining a pending deal. Anxious to talk about the project, he found his English counterparts offputting, as they were showing the visitors around their offices, not getting down to business, but then going to nearby Bristol for an evening meal.

Sitting in a restaurant overlooking the English Channel, Brown finally blurted out to a superior: "Keith, I've got to talk to you about this." His answer, "Wait, Charlie, do you think we ought to do it?" Brown did. "Okay, let's do it," Keith responded, and Brown says, then immediately started talking about something entirely different. Charlie protested: "But it's a lot of money," with the answer from his superior: "But it's a lot of land. And anyway, that's what I've got you and Rick for, to look for deals like this."

Brown and O'Brien had been looking for more land, realizing that its Norcross park was finding faster development, and about to run out of land. About that time a Saudi Arabian prince, who had speculated in land northeast of Atlanta, was not paying his interest payments to C&S National Bank of Atlanta. Eventually, the bank alerted Technology Park officials about the land. In 1982, TP/A purchased from the bank 1,626 acres of land along the Forsyth-Fulton Counties boundary around the intersection of Highway 141 (Medlock Bridge Road) and McGinnis Ferry Road. The bank had taken the land deed back in lieu of foreclosure. Eventually, the area would be marketed under the name of Technology Park/ Johns Creek.

O'Brien, who had joined Technology Park in 1974, and in 1989, became president of the real estate firm, remembers: "We got this farmland for $1,964 an acre in 1982, while other land was selling for a little more back then." The firm then began a long process of putting in improvements. "We had to bring the sewer line all the way from the Fulton-Gwinnett line, several miles, to reach the Johns Creek property. We also put in the other infrastructure, which cost us millions to get the property in shape for development, for when we bought it, its use was primarily farmland."

Brown says: "So we had good relationships with our owners, and we bought the land. I concentrated on expansion of the business, and Rick concentrated on operations and making money for the company. "

Technology Park didn't realize it then, but in something of an ironic twist, the area surrounding the Johns Creek property would change drastically in the coming years. As the industrial park became more populated, the surrounding land was becoming an upscale area for subdivisions, and the place was growing rapidly. Soon it would begin recognizing itself as the unincorporated community of Johns Creek. After a few years, people in the area started lobbying to become a city, and with Georgia's changing political scene, that's exactly what happened. The City of Johns Creek was created, with an overwhelming approval of voters, on July 18, 2006, and incorporated as a city on December 1, 2006.

What started out as a real estate park for business, Technology Park/Johns Creek, developed into Johns Creek, a city of an estimated population of 59,580 in 2007.

* * * * *

Charlie Brown, himself a Georgia Tech architectural graduate, would join Technology Park in 1977. Prior to that, he was a real estate broker, having just successfully marketed the Atlanta Center, and was recommended to Technology Park. Brown was just what the park needed, and became president in 1979 and remained in that post for 19 years. However, one account goes that Brown would have never joined Technology Park if he knew how to read a balance sheet.

Brown himself laughs and admits this. "Three weeks after I came aboard, Rick O'Brien, who came to Technology Park before I did, asked me 'Why did you come here?' I told him the park was close to my house and golf course, and I needed a new job, so why not?"

There was reason O'Brien was worried. Sales had slowed during the last few months of 1977, and indeed, funds were being exhausted. O'Brien informed Brown: "But we don't have any money. We owe banks and other companies, and in a few days, those loans are due and we can't pay. The banks have been renewing the loans, but I don't think they will re-new again. After all, the Georgia Tech Foundation (who owned part of the park) won't guarantee them, and we haven't sold any land in a long time."

This surprised Brown, who did not know the financial interworkings. Yet Brown continued to be optimistic. "Soon we made a couple of more deals, one with Sangamo Weston and another that same day (Nov. 22, 1977) with another firm, which was a tremendous occasion for us. When the Sangamo deal closed, I had King and Spalding cut a check, which I personally hand-carried to the bank to pay off the loans. That was the end of the bad times for us, as the work started to turn around for the technical industries."

It was in 1980 that Scientific-Atlanta, which was originally started by Georgia Tech professors, signed a lease for a building in Technology Park. It was a manufacturer of satellite dishes and cable converter boxes for television sets. The company had been headquartered just over the DeKalb line on Pleasantdale Road. This Technology Park building remained as the company headquarters until 2001, when all the Scientific-Atlanta offices in the area were consolidated on a 280-acre campus off Sugarloaf Parkway in Lawrenceville. Up until then, besides the DeKalb location, the firm also had extensive manufacturing facilities in Gwinnett Park off Interstate 85 in Norcross.

Eventually Scientific-Atlanta would erect five large buildings on its massive campus, totaling 581,830 square feet by 2007. At that time, it employed 1,700 people at its facilities in Gwinnett. The firm was purchased by the giant technology firm, Cisco Systems Inc. on February 24, 2006.

More firms arrived, with Scientific-Atlanta in 1981 moving its headquarters to Technology Park, taking the key corner entrance off Peachtree Industrial Boulevard and Technology Parkway South. In came Data Supplies, General Electric, Travelers Insurance, the Technical Association of Pulp and Paper Industry, Georgia Power, NCR and other well known firms.

A key tenant of Technology Park came in 1981, as Travelers Insurance Company arrived to occupy a two-story office/data center of 160,000 square feet. The insurance giant's Norcross location purposely duplicated its computer storage facilities of its home office in Hartford, Conn. In order to provide Travelers with a secure continuous source of electricity, Georgia Power Company put in an alternative feed in case of emergency, further enhancing the facilities at Technology Park, and in effect, giving the park another marketing tool.

Those in business to help locate industrial sites told the story of how Technology Park was marketed. Charlie Brown, who became head of the park in 1979, said: "We would have a prospect coming to look at a site, often particularly from the Northeast. They might have a trip planned to look at land in Atlanta, Orlando and Dallas. When we drove them though Technology Park, and they saw the beauty and serenity, more than a few of them said, 'Stop. We don't need to see any more. We'll cancel the rest of our trip and we'll locate here. Where do we sign?' Now we thought we were good salesmen, but really, the park sold itself."

By 1990, some 5,000 jobs had been created at the original Technology Park. Still looking to expand its horizons, Technology Park turned its eyes south. Charlie Brown picks up the story here: "For years, the Standard Club had thought of doing something differently, but did nothing. So we started talking with them."

Technology Park entered into negotiations with the Standard Club, which with its predecessor, the Concordia Association, traces its history in Atlanta back to 1867. What the Standard Club and Technology Park agreed on in 1985 was a land swap. Technology Park would get 160 acres of prime property in Brookhaven just east of the Southern Railroad tracks and north of Roxboro Road near Buckhead and Lenox Square, where the Standard Club had its facilities since 1948. The Standard Club would gain a new country club on 303 acres off Medlock Bridge Road. Technology Park would also build the new Standard Club, including golf course and tennis facilities, and also design, build and furnish the new club, all the way down to the appointments, such as table ware, china, glasses, tablecloths and wall furnishing....in essence, a turn-key job.

Brown adds; "One of the reasons that Johns Creek was so invaluable to us is that we already had the property. The Standard Club did not have to find land, but as we worked it out, used land we already had. The Standard Club did not even have to hire an architect, since we designed it for them. We could offer then a good deal, and all that we had to do was to negotiate with them. Trades of land are good sometimes for both parties. It helped us, for there was not much located in that area then except for farming, and we got the club to anchor that area. And by the time they came, the growth was beginning to move into the Johns Creek area, so it made good sense to get it started with the land developing."

Simultaneously with designing the new Standard Club, Technology Park was going through re-zoning applications for the 160-acres of the old Standard Club, to change its zoning to mixed use. What was eventually built on the Standard Club property was over two million square feet of office buildings, a 300-room hotel, 200,000-square feet of retail space and 1,200 residential units. Later BellSouth would finish the development of this property and locate many of its employees at this desirable location. Altogether, more than 21,000 persons are now employed at this park.

The entire story of Technology Park/Atlanta has been beneficial to the area. At the original TP/A property near Norcross, some 2.8 million square feet was developed by Technology Park itself, plus other land was sold off for construction by others. At the Johns Creek site, 2.5 million square feet was developed by Technology Park. The most prolific years for Technology Park were 1997 and 1998, when the park began construction of buildings totaling 726,000 and 735,000 square feet, respectively.

The sale of the Johns Creek land turned into quite a profitable enterprise for Technology Park. Meanwhile, large firms were locating at Johns Creek. Among the major firms located there were State Farm Insurance, Novartis, Nordsen, Ciba Vision, Anheuser-Busch, J. Smith Lanier Insurance, Kodak, Saia Freight Lines, Exxon Mobil, Kraft, A. G. Edwards Financial, Fisher Scientific and Johnson Controls. For Ciba Vision, J. Smith Lanier and Saia, the park is the location of their headquarters.

Meanwhile, the initial site in Technology Park had over the years garnered some of the big names in industry to its locations, other than the ones previously mentioned. That would include Ebasco Services, Data Supplies Inc., Perkin Elmer Corp., General Electric (with three units), General Time Corporation, Traveler's Insurance, Beckman Instruments, Kawneer, Unisys Corporation, Alumax Corporation, Melita International, Sun Data, and many other firms, many of them in Class A multi-tenant mid-rise buildings.

While Technology Park/Atlanta initially owned the land in the park, many of the firms coming to the area bought their sites. Today the land at Technology Park locations is owned mainly by the firms occupying the land, or by private interests. An internal management team buy-out from P&O took place in 2004, and since then, it has been run by local interests, with Rick O'Brien the chairman and CEO of the firm, technically known as TPA Realty Services, LLC. Technology Park/Atlanta is currently developing in new areas of Metro Atlanta, principally in Cherokee County and east of Covington, and also in Bryan County.

The Cherokee County project consists of 750 acres, including a 24-acre facility for the Cherokee County government.

East of Atlanta, the activity near Covington is in cooperation with the development authorities of Newton, Morgan and Walton Counties, and totals 1,500 acres. In 2008, the firm was installing the roads and utilities for this investment.

Technology Park/Atlanta is also working on Georgia's coast, with a project in Bryan County of 600 acres. The firm is working on infrastructure on this project.

Technology Park/Atlanta has been a major success story, starting in Gwinnett County, and now spreading elsewhere.

Oakbrook Technology Park

While Technology Park was in its initial stages of development, another part of Norcross was undergoing its own development into what would eventually become known as Oakbrook Technology Park. This land is east of Interstate 85 and north of Jimmy Carter Boulevard. A key portion of the land was known as the 178-acre Salvation Army tract. In the early 1970s, another portion of this land had been the site of what the developers thought would be Gwinnett's first mall.

On August 15, 1972, a $150 million regional shopping mall was announced to be located on 178 acres of what was then Norcross-Tucker Road at the intersection of Singleton Road. The announcement came from C.L. Straughan of Straughan and Company, a firm which had developed substantial tracts in Atlanta. The new venture was to include high rise buildings, a hotel-convention center and a 15-acre hospital. The land had been purchased from the Salvation Army for $6 million. However, this first-announced mall never developed, as economic conditions turned down, and the land reverted to a New York bank which had financed the property.

Later on, Dick Gray had assembled part of what would become Oakbrook Technology Park, and wanted to develop it. He met with County Commission Chairman Dudge Pruitt. Gray says: "We met at a service station on Norcross-Tucker Road. Dudge told me what he wanted, and I told him what I wanted." The outcome of the meeting was the county's agreement to provide materials if Gray would construct a road from what was then Norcross-Tucker Road to Indian Trail Road, and install a water line along the road. Dick Gray remembers: "We had to get an easement from C.L. Straughan on property he had purchased from the Salvation Army. Altogether, we had to close with four different property owners on the property, all on the same day, before we could begin work." The entire assemblage was of 1,200 acres.

Gray obtained an acquisition loan from Cousins REIT, and eventually sold the land to Cousins REIT. After other developers bought into the area, a majority of the entire tract was developed as Oakbrook Technology Park, with Oakbrook Parkway bisecting it, and the area attracting a significant number of warehousing and high-technology firms.

High-tech comes to Gwinnett

Gwinnett County was similar in industrial development to other lesser-developed suburban counties until the 1970s. Then converging vectors propelled Gwinnett into high cotton, you might say, in terms of economic development.

This outlined tract of land was given to the Salvation Army. This photo, around 1972, was before the property was developed, or before Oakbrook Technology Parkway was cut paralleling Interstate 85. The relatively-new Western Electric plant is at the center right, and across what was then Norcross-Tucker Road can be seen the site of the Gwinnett Drive-In Theatre. Note in the bottom right what was then a single water tank with the "Gwinnett Is Great" phrase on it.

It came from an industry no one hunted. In fact, few people were even aware that this new sector, to be called "high technology," even existed, or could become what was on the horizon, with Gwinnett riding high for Metro Atlanta.

The first indication that something new was coming happened in June, 1969 as Western Electric announced it would locate a telephone cable plant on 175 acres at the intersection of Interstate 85 and Norcross-Tucker Road (which would become Jimmy Carter Boulevard), east of Norcross. The page-wide, two-deck headline in the *Gwinnett Daily News* screamed at the readers:

$20 Million Plant Here
To Employ Over 2,000

The plant would take three years to build. Groundbreaking was in October, 1969, and by June, 1971, the first section of the plant was completed. Workers began moving to the plant in September of that year, while others began moving into permanent offices in January 1972, with the final section of the plant finished in February. Western Electric shipped the first reel of copper cable in April, 1973. By then Western Electric was the largest real property taxpayer in Gwinnett, with its tax bill topping $1 million.

With the Western Electric plant now in operation, Gwinnett was on the map, industrially, with one of the biggest prizes of the time, the landing of what would eventually become its largest employer, with 3,800 workers at the site.

Though perhaps no one in Gwinnett recognized it at that time, the plant location in Norcross would eventually be recognized as in the high technology business, the first such location in the county.

About that same time, a Georgia Tech graduate named Paul Duke and 17 of his fellow Tech graduates and friends began to assemble land west of Norcross for a new entity to be called "Peachtree Corners."

This group's first venture came about 1969 to be known as Kaiser-Aetna Park, an industrial park of high-quality, brick warehouse-distribution facilities off what would some day become Jimmy Carter Boulevard, east of Peachtree Industrial Boulevard. Soon they would announce, in 1971, and open in 1972, Technology Park/Atlanta, to be a modern industrial park aimed at locating companies in this new field called "high technology." What they envisioned eventually became a model for industrial development in Gwinnett, and throughout Metro Atlanta.

Nearby sat the small town of Norcross (2,775 residents in 1970) between these two ventures, the new cable plant of Western Electric, and a proposed new concept, Peachtree Corners. Both were in unincorporated Gwinnett, though each had Norcross as its focus. Both areas were served by the Norcross post office. Eventually as Western Electric expanded, and Peachtree Corners began to attract new firms moving in, the Norcross area began to be viewed as the focus of this new type of industry, one grounded in "high technology" initially in Metro Atlanta.

How did all this happen?

To land the Western Electric plant, it took the involvement of an active county government, plus significant innovations by forward-thinking county officials, to snare the plant.

For instance, Gwinnett did not have sufficient water lines and its partner, fire protection, nor sewer capacity, to serve the Western Electric plant. However, by working with DeKalb County, with both water and sewer service at its border just a mile south of the plant, Gwinnett jumped over a big hurdle. The reason Gwinnett was able to secure these agreements was that DeKalb County had included the entire creek basin in its application for federal matching monies to build the sewer capacity for this watershed. So DeKalb would really be supplying what it had already said it was able to serve. Gwinnett was able to take advantage of this through the tie to the federal funding.

In addition, Gwinnett, by the time Western Electric opened in 1972, would also offer a professional fire department to protect the plant.

Western Electric was a boon in another way. Gwinnett officials would later admit that the plant could just as easily have been located one exit south in DeKalb County, and Gwinnett would still have had to educate the children of the Western Electric workers living in the county. As it was, Gwinnett got the ad valorem tax revenue for the county and schools, though hundreds of Western Electric employees lived in other counties. The arrival of the Western Electric plant would also prove a positive factor to upgrading and starting up of residential subdivisions, with many key plant officials settling in new (and somewhat more affordable and larger homes (than DeKalb County) in the Lawrenceville area.

While Western Electric's main plant was charged with manufacturing telephone cable, the company also located a Bell Labs Research Center adjacent to its facility. Soon patented out of this location was a new way to communicate, with something initially called "light guide," later called fiber optics.

In 1976, engineers at the Norcross Western Electric Bell Labs research facility would conduct a fiber optic telecommunication system experiment, demonstrating the first fiber optic transmission system for voice and data. Officials invited the media to the demonstration of the newly-invented cable, a hair-size strand capable of transmitting light ("fiber optics" or light guide) predicting it would eventually take the place of copper cable for communications.

At its announcement, people asked; "We've got copper cable; what use is there for this tiny light guide?" Attendees could not foresee the arrival of computers in every business and virtually every home, cell phones and other small devices needing that tiny strand to transmit voice and data. Eventually the Norcross plant became the largest fiber optic cable production plant in the world, as it provided work for thousands and was a solid rock in the Gwinnett business community.

In 1980, the Western Electric Norcross facility manufactured the first FT3 cable for light guide shipment. FT3 was the transmission system used in telephone lines in 1980, with a capacity of 45 megabits per second (MB). This was upgraded to 90 MB in 1984. In 2006, the technology had advanced to a rate of 10,000 MB, and approaching 100,000 MB by year 2010. (Scientists say that the theoretical maximum is 50 Terabytes/second, or 50 million MB, indicating that the industry is barely utilizing the theoretical maximum capacity of fiber optics.)

This FT3 cable was installed in Smyrna, Ga. to create the first standard communications fiber optic system. Later, in 1984, the Norcross plant provided fiber, cable and apparatus for the fiber optic system serving the Summer Olympic Games in Los Angeles, the first system to offer digital network broadcast quality video.

Looming on the horizon were circumstances no one in Gwinnett could forecast, which soon changed the Western Electric facility in a major way. It was the court-ordered breakup in 1982 of American Telephone and Telegraph. The Western Electric plant soon became part of AT&T, operating as AT&T Technologies. That lasted three years. Then with another move in 1995, AT&T would then spin off the Norcross plant and lab into Lucent Technologies.

In this time of high tech euphoria, the then-Lucent Technologies officials made another major announcement in October of 1997. The headline of that day read:

Lucent on Verge of Major Expansion

This announcement told of a planned two-year, $350 million expansion of the Norcross Lucent installation. Already the world's largest fiber optic plant, and consisting of

1.7 million square feet, officials talked of investing over the next two years to strengthen the plant's position in the fiber optic production, which was even promoted as a possible prelude to future expansion, perhaps up to $900 million.

At its height, the plant had 3,800 employees, and was the size of 29 football fields. Its property tax bill soon netted Gwinnett County $2.5 million annually, and the company spent $320 million each year with local manufacturers. The jobs were assumed to be the best in the county, with a yearly payroll of $164 million. Pay rates topped $17 an hour!

But something happened. Granted, Lucent built out the expansion as announced. Yet this was the time when the telecommunications market was about to implode. As one worker who was there remembered: "They built the expansion, but did not populate the plant."

The completion of the expansion marked the high point of the Norcross plant, for since then, everything has been downhill.

More change was on the way, as fiber optic demand fell substantially in the world, and the employee count at the plant was reduced. Lucent sold the plant in 2001. On November 16, 2001, Furukawa Electric Company, Inc., a multi-billion dollar global leader in optical communications, and CommScope, a world leader in broadband coaxial cables, completed the purchase of the Optical Fiber Solutions division from Lucent. On June 15, 2004 Furukawa acquired CommScope's minority shares and OFS became wholly owned by Furukawa.

With major advancements in robotic technology, in 2007 limited fiber optics manufacturing is underway at OFS in Norcross, and with far fewer workers, as the Norcross plant has gone through substantial changes. It is essentially the headquarters of OFS Brightwave and its corporate functions, and operates in Norcross with 300 employees. The scope of the Norcross operation includes designing and manufacturing high performance optical fibers. The firm also has a team of its OFS Labs engineers employed in Norcross, as well as OFS' North American sales team and product management. OFS Brightwave also operates another cable manufacturing facility in Carrollton, Ga., where it has shifted most of its manufacturing operations for Georgia.

Meanwhile, OFS Fitel, LLC was sitting on a valuable tract of 175 acres at the first interchange in Gwinnett County of I-85 north. Much of the site in 2008 was under-utilized, since the plant no longer employed thousands. Early efforts to market the land as a mixed unit development, including plans for high rise buildings, fizzled. However, approval of Gwinnett voters in 2008 of the Tax Allocation District proposal could improve the chances of re-development of the property. As of this writing, OFS officials are mum on what will happen to this sprawling facility. However, reading tea leaves and watching what has developed in other parts of Gwinnett, it could be forecast that a higher land use would be a mixed residential-retail development on the prize tract by this key intersection in Gwinnett, relatively close to downtown Atlanta. Another consideration for the property was for its inclusion in a tax-allocation district, the details of which were to be voted on by Georgians in the fall of 2008.

Should this high-rise development happen, the site could return to its days when it provided the highest ad valorem tax return within the county.

A new dimension: modems

In the mid-1970s, a scientific development was about to explode which would dramatically change the world, and in Gwinnett County, would solidify the position of Peachtree Corners as the key location for high technology firms within Metro Atlanta for the next decade.

This device came from the minds of two guys working at National Data Corp. in Atlanta. One was a former Georgia Tech co-op student with experience at Southern Bell, Dennis Hayes; the other was Dale Heatherington, who had a two-year technical college degree. One day, over lunch, the two cooked up an idea, and drew it out on paper napkins. The idea was a way for the earliest microcomputers, often kit-built infant computers from around 1975, to communicate with other computers via telephone lines with a device that would eventually become known as a modem. That was before the first popular computer, the Apple II, was unveiled, and several years before IBM introduced the Personal Computer.

Modem-like devices were already being used in science and industry, with the first units coming out of IBM through research that firm did for the government in the 1950s. Then from Western Electric Labs, the research arm of the Bell Telephone system, the first 103a type modem was developed.

What Hayes and Heatherington accomplished was that they were among the first to design a modem specifically for the new wave of microcomputers that caught on quickly with hobbyists, then educators, then businessmen in the latter 1970s, and eventually with the public in the early 1980s. The problem was that computers used digital systems, while telephones were on an analog system. The real breakthrough was that nobody specifically targeted an automatic connection which would allow the two different systems to communicate.

In reality, the two didn't so much "invent" something entirely new as much as create a specific microcomputer version of the existing invention. In addition, they were at the right place and the right time, that is, before Apple and later IBM popularized the microcomputer platform, commonly known as PCs and Macs. As the infant microcomputer industry took off, the Hayes organization was ready with a product, and gave that product better marketing and distribution support than competing, early microcomputer modem solutions. These actions combined to give Hayes early market dominance of the emerging microcomputer modem product category.

Heatherington says: "I'm not sure exactly what happened, but about 1975, we started experimenting, and I acquired parts and built a Mark 8 computer from scratch. We played around with Teletype machines, which ham radio operators used then to transmit over ham frequencies. All this was before we had cable modems."

With the idea on paper, Heatherington brought in all his life savings of $5,000, about 1976, and bought an IMSAI computer kit. Hayes didn't put any money in. "Dennis suggested that we build a modem for it, and we put together a design. He worked on the digital interface with the computer, and I did the analog work on the telephone side to interface with computers. After this collaboration, we put an advertisement in Byte magazine to see what would happen. We got 10 or so orders a month," Heatherington says. "Dennis handled the business end and I did the technical work," Heatherington says. Most of this was completed by April, 1977.

"Dennis was living with his family near Oglethorpe University in North DeKalb County then, and we hired a couple of guys to assemble the modems at his house. We were still working for National Data. After work, I would go by his house, pick up the units made that day, and take them to my house in Decatur, since I had all the machines for testing at my house. Later I would take the good ones back, pick up more, and they would ship the units from there. We were selling about 10-20 a month, for about $300 each. That went on for several months, and was very much a part-time deal."

What the two had invented was the first modern modem specifically designed for the small computer, which allowed the use of software so that computers could talk to one another, extract data, and display it for the user. The Hayes modem took out the complexity of hook-ups, and allowed the user to simply plug the modem to the telephone line and computer, and work away.

Dennis Hayes, about 1981, holding a 300-baud Smartmodem. The boxes contain Micromodem II modems for Apple computers. The Smartmodem 300 was introduced in June of 1981. A year later the Smartmodem 1200 was introduced.

The two quit their jobs at National Data in January of 1978. That same year, the operation grew large enough to move from the Hayes home to Perimeter Park, just off Interstate 285 across from what was then the Avon building, now the First Baptist Church of Atlanta.

It was in April, 1978 when Glenn Sirkis, another key person in the early days of Hayes, joined the firm. A Vietnam war veteran and recent industrial management graduate of Georgia Tech, Sirkis had been introduced to Hayes through a mutual friend, after hearing about the modem the Hayes team was making. "The idea immediately resonated," he says, "Since I thought that microcomputers would follow minicomputers in the way they would develop. I thought the microcomputer firms like Data General, Digital Equipment and Hewlett-Packard would not deal with modems initially, since like mini-computers firms had done, they had enough to do developing their own product."

When Sirkis and Hayes met in the spring of 1978, "We hit it off somehow and I went to work for him, with the understanding that I would not get paid at first, but would figure out how to get paid." What Sirkis brought to the table was a sense of organization, management and business skill.

What Sirkis found was a company not keeping books. "There were checks in shoe boxes, the books were not being balanced, and on top of it all, they were not making money," he says. "They were also promising more than they had. In April 1978, I figured they had two or three more months to go before they would run completely into the ground."

But Sirkis realized the modem had merit, and thought a company could be started around it. The firm moved from Hayes's home to a business park as Sirkis joined it. "Before, when they were working at Dennis' house, Dennis had retreated to one bedroom, the other two bedrooms were being used for manufacturing and for an office, the living room was for inventory and assembly, and the dining room was for shipping. It's amazing to me that the neighbors did not complain because of zoning violations."

New name for company

On January 3, 1978 the firm was incorporated as D.C. Hayes Associates Inc. Then in 1980, the name was changed to Hayes Microcomputer Products Inc. Sirkis thought the first corporate name was cumbersome, and wanted to get the word "microcomputer" associated with the firm. "I started in 1978 gradually making the word 'microcomputer' larger, and put it under the 'D.C. Hayes and Associates.' Eventually, by 1980, the two lines were the same size, so I went to Dennis and suggested that the switch to the shorter name of 'Hayes Microcomputer Products' was a logical one."

As it moved to its first industrial park location, at Perimeter Park, Hayes rented about 1,500 square feet the first year. "All we had," Heatherington says, "was a couple of folding tables in the assembly area, and some desks in other rooms. About a year later, the firm moved in the same business park to nearly double the space, as it added more people." The firm's eventual move to 15,000 square feet on Peachtree Industrial Boulevard in Gwinnett in 1980 was "because that was where industrial space was for lease," Sirkis says. By then, the firm employed about 30 people.

The firm in the early days was selling primarily modems, but also other products, such as green boards ("bare boards") to hobbyists for $50 a board. "It wasn't a good margin, but hobbyists would use them," Sirkis says.

The first modem was the 80-103-A (note the name, a throwback to the earlier Bell Systems design), Heatherington's first design. It could be plugged in the basic computers of that day, Altair and IMSAI products, though it took a certain technical skill to make it useful. Then in 1978, when Apple II came out, Hayes Microcomputer virtually bet the company on that computer, as its modem was a big hit with Apple owners from the beginning. Apple founder Steve Jobs invited the Hayes team to California in 1978, but then stood them up.

However, while in California, Hayes and Sirkis met with several Apple execs. One Harvard MBA, Trip Hawkins (then Apple's director of strategy and marketing), wanted Hayes to start selling the modem for $99 and seek the mass market. Sirkis says; "We told him at our price of $279 we could not make them fast enough, so why should we reduce prices?" (Hawkins eventually founded Electronic Arts Inc., a large video-game company, in California.)

One of the Apple execs provided Sirkis with a list of the Apple distributors, which he brought back to Atlanta and tacked on his office wall. He remembers: "One by one, these distributors came to Atlanta to see us, and I would check them off the list. These were start-up distributors, and they were looking for product. We didn't have a big marketing budget, except for a few advertisements in computer magazines. But these distributors recognized that we had a product they could put in their distribution channel. By the time we moved to Gwinnett in 1980, we had all the Apple distributors signed up to sell Hayes modems."

By then, Hayes Microcomputer was in a constant battle to build product, Sirkis says. "Literally, we could not get the parts fast enough. We had an 8-12-16 week lead time, and our job was to get people trained in that time to build products, running as fast as we could. When we moved to Gwinnett, we had about 30 employees, 10 in the office and 20 in the factory. We were doing all the manufacturing ourselves, instead of farming it out." Hayes was selling modems fast, and making a profit of about half of the $279 retail price. Sirkis admits: "We were making a profit hand over fist. We never had a bad quarter." About that time, Fulton National Bank provided the firm with a half-million-dollar line of credit. "It gave us room to grow," Sirkis says, "for we had good credit, and were making money."

Soon Hayes was improving his modem. It became known as reliable, and soon was regarded as the standard of the industry. At one time, it controlled half of the market for modems. Besides high speed modems, the firm was innovating with software, facsimile and local area networks, all designed for simplicity for the user.

The next breakthrough came June 16, 1981, with the development of what would become the standard modem, the Smartmodem, with a speed rated at 300 baud, and which sold for $299. Next came the Smartmodem 1200 (at 1200 baud), which sold for $599, giving users a faster connection. Later would come the 2400, introduced in 1984. This was able to work as easily on the IBM-PC, which opened up even much more of a market for Hayes.

What these two modems did was automate what was previously a time-consuming and slow process of linking two distant computers. In those days, connecting was difficult, compared to modern computers. A mechanical switch had to be set on each end of the connection for the two computers to communicate. An operator would set the switch for what he thought was the data rate on his end, and the person at the distant location would set his computer for the data rate on that end, and the two computers could "talk," or sometimes *not* talk, and the operators would have to set the switches for another rate.

The Smartmodem would find a signal, and set the data rate automatically. In verbage of the day, the modem would do a "handshake" between the two computers, and allow communications.

Much later would see falling modem prices, first getting down in 1988-90 era to $300, and even to $100. Eventually, as the chip could do a PC function, soon the modem became a commodity, and many people got into the PC business. Essentially, suddenly a lot of chip manufacturers decided to develop modem chip sets, so Hayes had a whole group of competitors.

But Hayes had set the standard, and many of these firms advertised that their modem was "Hayes compatible." Tom Campbell, who was with Hayes from 1984-95, starting out as purchasing manager and ending as vice president of manufacturing, remembers "For a while, we had a defense, and if they sold it as Hayes compatible, they were infringing on us."

All along, the company was growing. It soon outgrew its first Gwinnett location on 5923 Peachtree Industrial Boulevard, and had other locations nearby. A warehouse was located on Jones Mill Road, and eventually the research and development was at 330 Engineering Drive in Technology Park. In 1984, the Hayes administrative team, about 80 people, moved to its own building in Technology Park/Atlanta at Peachtree Parkway and Westech Drive. This was a three-story building of 70,000-square feet, loaded with an almost obsessive array of security measures to make sure its corporate secrets stayed within the building. (In 2007, the building Hayes leased on Westech Drive was occupied by S1 Corporation, a software supplier for the financial industry.)

The Hayes staff included teams of research scientists, many with advanced degrees. The firm also bought other technological companies. At the height of its staffing level, Hayes eventually employed 1,200 people, about 600 of them based in Norcross, with others in distant locations in California, Canada, Hong Kong, London and Beijing.

Impact on Gwinnett

Hayes Microcomputer was also making a terrific impact in the Gwinnett and Georgia business community. Hayes Microcomputer sought and cast an impressive aura. At one reception in Norcross before the move to their own building, the Hayes firm startled those attending a social function for some announcement by having music for the occasion provided by a string quartet. Observers said it was the first business cocktail party they had ever attended in Gwinnett with such high-class music.

Hayes also enjoyed the social scene with his wife, former journalist Melita Easters. They hosted elaborate parties, sponsored symphony concerts, and collected art, with Hayes at one time having the largest private collection of Ansel Adams prints in the country.

Dennis Hayes received recognition from many circles. He was the founder of the Georgia High Tech Alliance, composed of key execs of high technology firms. He enjoyed the glitter of accomplishment and recognition in the high tech community. As late as 2003, he was still highly regarded as a genius of his day, with election to the computer industry Hall of Fame.

Meanwhile, the company was thriving, especially after the IBM PC expanded the market tremendously. Modems were a new device on most computers, as it gave its owner ease of access in the days before the Internet to time sharing services of that era called "CBBS" (Computer Bulletin Board Systems).

By that time, 1982, Hayes and Heatherington had taken in Sirkis as a partner and named him executive vice president. He was also a stockholder, and owned a third of the company. His work concentrated on establishing the distribution network, and positioning the company as the dominant modem brand. He was well thought of by the industry, being named in 1982 by one magazine as one of the "distinguished members of the microcomputer community....pioneers who nurtured a technology into a thriving industry."

But it wouldn't last, as Sirkis found as he returned from the June, 1982 Comdex show. "I got a surprise when I got back," Sirkis says, "for Dennis fired me." Since he was no longer an employee, Sirkis had to sell his stock back to the company at the book value. He got $450,000 for his stock, though had the company gone public earlier as he had proposed many times to Hayes, he feels his one-third might have been worth $100 million.

"But I have no regrets. After all, I met my future wife at Hayes, as she applied for a job (which she did not take)." Sirkis eventually re-emerged in the electronics industry, and at one time headed Stradis, Inc. of Atlanta, a producer of digital audio products sold internationally and used by many television stations. He has since sold the company.

Sirkis says he doesn't know why Hayes fired him, but admits that he feels Hayes wanted "Yes" men around. "I wanted to bring in professional management, take the company public and cash out. Dennis, I feel, wanted to be Mr. Modem. He could have had that and money too, but the ego thing got him. He had the vision for the modem, but could not get past that until it was too late. There were so many opportunities that the company missed." Sirkis is now retired, and traveling the country in a large motor home.

Shortly after Sirkis left the company, Heatherington got antsy. "I was bored," he says. Never much attuned to helping run the firm after it became successful, Heatherington also recognized that competition was heating up. "Technology was moving faster, and I just wanted out of the rat race. Dennis enjoyed the rat race, so he stayed in."

Heatherington also proved to be smart in another way, recognizing the value of what he had helped create, and the consequences. "I knew what my stock in the company was worth, and realized it was all tied up in Hayes Microcomputer stock, and that I was not diversified as an investor. I also knew that high tech firms could be on top of the world one day and bankrupt the next. I knew I could take money and live the rest of my life with ease. Under the terms of the stockholder's agreement, I had to sell the shares back to the company over a 10-year time-frame. I figured in 1984 that it was a good time to go. And I did." He was 36 when he retired.

Heatherington timed it right. He received regular payments from Hayes over the next nine years and 10 months. "When Hayes declared bankruptcy the first time, they had two payments left to me. They put these two payments on hold, and when Hayes Microcomputer reorganized, I got the final two payments, plus interest, of all that they owed me."

How much? "Some numbers have been kicked around," he says, "Some saying $20 million. With principal and interest, it was close to that." Matt Kempner, in an article in *The Atlanta Journal-Constitution* on the Hayes company, said in 2003: "Hayes was always the one who got the glory. Heatherington was the one who got the money."

Heatherington moved to Roswell in 1987, and continued to work on various hobbies around a laboratory at his home, and to enjoy life. He doesn't seem to look back on how much more money he might have made. He once told a reporter: "But how much money do you need? You go through life once. You've got a certain number of years to live."

Meanwhile, events were starting to catch up with Hayes Microcomputer. From the time Heatherington "got out of the rat race," until Hayes first declared bankruptcy nearly 10 years later, in 1994, Hayes Microcomputer found increased problems. The high-flying Hayes team met with troubles. It started as the company moved to its new impressive headquarters in Norcross.

In one word, "competition." Other companies copied the Hayes idea, though often they would be met with squadrons of Hayes attorneys filing suit against them. By 1987, the industry was regarding modems as much of a commodity, with other models available. While the Hayes modem was regarded as reliable, others were coming on cheaper.

Dale Heatherington, around 1978. In the background is an IMSAI 8080 personal computer which was used to develop and test the first 300 baud modem, part number 80-103A. There is an early version of one of the modems mounted on an extender card sticking out of the top of the IMSAI 8080 computer, while on the wall are various schematic diagrams and drawings of the product. On the left are several modems waiting to be tested. The item with "INFAX" on it is a nine inch monochrome computer monitor. Under it is an eight inch floppy disk drive.

Hayes sought multiple means of surviving. At one point, about 1991, it even purchased two of its rivals, Practical Peripherals and Cardinal. Where the original Hayes modem had been highly-respected but never a cheap one, the company turned these two firms into low-cost brands, in order to compete with other competitors.

Yet some in the industry saw Hayes Microcomputer as increasingly becoming a follower of other firms, rather than leading the industry as it had when it first came on the scene. Interestingly, even years later, virtually all modems still use a variety of the Hayes command set first introduced in the Hayes Smartmodem.

In the late 1980s and early 1990s, Hayes did not respond quickly to the move of the computer industry to high-speed traffic. Neither did the firm seem to recognize the increasing widespread use of computers by business, creating a much larger market. Other industry changes in telephone networks eventually resulted in the basic Hayes concept being obsolete. Hayes had also bet the future on a new type of modem that the industry did not adapt. No new products were coming out of the Hayes shop that the industry adopted.

However, with the entrance of many other modem-making firms into the field, Hayes had to look to other products. Essentially, Hayes began to develop products that, unlike the first modem, did not become mainstream for the industry. Among some of the Hayes ventures at that time:

- An Integrated Systems Digital Network (ISDN): Hayes developed a product for ISDN, but the industry went to cable, rather than to ISDN, and to Digital Subscriber Loop, (DSL), which is the telephone system's answer to high speed. The ISDN product is no longer around.
- Hayes invested heavily in a product called LanStep, buying the company and technology out of Waterloo, Canada. Soon Hayes was realizing that it was a modem company, not a network company, and this venture fizzled.

- Perhaps the straw that broke the camel's back was an attempt by Hayes to manufacture modems in Mexico. Tom Campbell recalls shipping three months supply of raw materials to Mexico...."and Mexico did not produce a single modem, since the vendor selected was incapable of producing the product." The loss: $15 million for Hayes, which "sucked up most of our $20 million credit line, from which we could never recover," Campbell says.

The declining fortunes of Hayes eventually led the company in November 1994 to declare Chapter 11 bankruptcy. It emerged in October 1995 as Hayes Corporation, after selling 49 percent of the company to Nortel and a Singapore-based venture capitalist. Later would come more moves, merging in 1997 with Access Beyond, creating another company name, Hayes Communications. This eventually led to taking the company public. Stock went from $12 a share in early 1998 to pennies that year in October. This led to another Chapter 11 filing. But no new funding could be found. In 1999, the company was liquidated, and the years of Hayes being a player in the communication world were over.

For Dennis Hayes himself, even before the fortunes of the company went into a tailspin, so did his personal life. He divorced his first wife, married, and eventually divorced his second wife. He also found himself plagued with an inherited disease that began to surface when the company was doing well in Gwinnett. It was "Retinitis Pigmentosa," which makes it difficult for him to see clearly. That's one of the reasons he moved to New York, where he finds public transit easily available for him to move around. "It's one of the few cities where you can live and not own an automobile. With the taxis and subways, you can get around easily. When you cannot drive, like me, it's a lot better to be here with the available transit."

Today, Dennis Hayes is a management consultant, though most of his clients are in technically-oriented businesses.

* * * * *

Even though Hayes Microcomputer did not survive as a company, the mechanism this firm developed paved the way to modern communications as the world knows it. For Gwinnett County, the worldwide name recognition and notoriety that Hayes gave the county set in motion the perception throughout Metro Atlanta that Gwinnett, and in particular Peachtree Corners and Norcross, was the place to be if you were in any high tech business.

Something else was happening. Technology Park and the Norcross area were becoming crowded as traffic increased, so firms were forced to move up Peachtree Industrial Boulevard, to locations in Duluth, then Suwanee, then other portions of Gwinnett and in Metro Atlanta, to locate their plants and offices. Norcross may have lost its prime position as the key high technology center, but the jump-start that Norcross provided Gwinnett for about 10 years served the county well. High technology had put Gwinnett on the map.

The legacy: in Gwinnett in the fourth quarter of 2007, there were just slightly less than 50,000 jobs (49,483) with Gwinnett firms classified as "high tech." This translates into a high-dollar payroll, helping contribute to the high quality of living in Gwinnett.

Altogether, there are 4,204 firms in Gwinnett with SIC industrial codes relating to "high technology."

Yet the firm that brought the "high-tech" word to Gwinnett, Hayes Microcomputer, is not among them.

Scientific-Atlanta

A company that would become a major player in Gwinnett was founded in 1951 in DeKalb County by engineers from Georgia Tech. It would become known as Scientific-Atlanta. Today it is part of Cisco Systems, one of the key high technology firms in Gwinnett County. Some 1,800 of its more than 9,900 employees worldwide work in Gwinnett (2008).

But in its early days, Scientific-Atlanta was far from high-tech. It was a small firm making, among other items, plastic injection-molded food and beverage packaging; electronic equipment cabinets, and, more akin to what it is known for today, an early electronic test equipment producer for antennas and electronics.

Those responsible for starting the company included Georgia Tech employees Vernon Wilderquist, Lamar Widdle, Gerald Rosselot, Charles Griffin, Robert Honer, and Dr. James E. Boyd. To get the company off the ground, each contributed $100, as did Glen Robinson, the company's first employee, for a total capitalization of $700. Robinson left Georgia Tech in 1953 to become the full-time president of Scientific-Atlanta. It had its initial public offering of stock on July 29, 1959.

From its beginning, Scientific-Atlanta was heavily dependent on federal government contracts, and on work from the National Aeronautics and Space Administration (NASA). In the 1950s and 1960s, Scientific-Atlanta was helping NASA establish ground stations for communications, and helping the testing of communications equipment used by Project Mercury, Gemini and Apollo astronauts.

Then, Scientific-Atlanta turned a corner, and became more involved with a new product called "cable television." A key date for the company was Sept. 30, 1975, the famous "Thrilla from Manila" heavyweight boxing match between Muhammad Ali and Joe Frazier, in the Philippines. Setting up earth stations at cable systems in Mississippi and Florida, Scientific-Atlanta took the signal from the satellites supplied by RCA, while HBO provided the programming. American viewers witnessed the first satellite-delivered cable television programming, a breakthrough that changed the cable television industry. Another 1975 milestone: Ted Turner purchased a Scientific-Atlanta earthstation to launch his Atlanta superstation, WTBS.

Over the years, Scientific-Atlanta found forward-thinking engineers to develop its products. When Sid Topol became head of the firm in 1971, he began to reduce the company's dependence on military and aerospace contracts. Topol was able to guide the company toward the future, capitalizing on his vision for what the cable industry would come to mean for the country. In 1982, Topol clearly forecast what was to come:

"...I think eventually there are going to be three boxes in the home. The three boxes may be incorporated all in one box...the addressable 100-channel set-top terminal with tiering and pay-per-view....an interactive terminal for shopping, banking, security and that sort of thing….a modem will interconnect the cable system with personal computers---at high speed."

Topol, who is a Cable Hall of Fame inductee, had tremendous insight, helping guide Scientific-Atlanta along those lines, and even to higher technical advances in this industry. Only one year later, a Scientific-Atlanta cable box could deliver 128 channels. By 1985, the company was providing Holiday Inns with satellite earthstations to deliver cable systems to each guest room.

As president, Topol moved the headquarters of the company from Pleasantdale Road in DeKalb County to Technology Park in Gwinnett. The firm occupied a key location at 1 Technology Parkway South at Peachtree Industrial Boulevard, coming in early 1981to its new headquarters. Meanwhile, over the years, more of the company's manufacturing operations moved to Gwinnett Park, off Interstate 85 at Beaver Ruin Road.

Another key figure at Scientific-Atlanta was Jim McDonald, who became head of the company in 1993. He saw Scientific-Atlanta expand deeper into the cable industry, and into interactive digital networks and compression systems. He also led the company by helping sponsor the 1996 Atlanta Olympic Games, and consolidated operations at the company's modern campus on Sugarloaf Parkway. During his tenure, the firm also moved manufacturing operations to Juarez, Mexico and established a company charitable foundation.

Scientific-Atlanta began a move to a new campus headquarters off Sugarloaf Parkway near Georgia Highway 316 in October 2000, and completed the initial stages of that move in February 2001. This landed essentially 99 percent of Scientific-Atlanta employees in Gwinnett County at its campus of 280 acres.

Also in the 2000s, Scientific-Atlanta became a leader in television satellite set-tops, and a factor in digital video recorders (DVR), high-definition (HD) and Video-on-Demand (VOD) service for cable operators. The company was acquired by Cisco Systems in early 2006.

Though it didn't start that way, Scientific-Atlanta has been a virtual incubator for many other technical firms that trace their start to the Atlanta area. Many former Scientific-Atlanta employees have left the company to become founders of other firms. The Technology Association of Georgia produced a list of these firms in 2003. The amazing list of high technology firms coming in whole or part out of Scientific-Atlanta includes:

- Electromagnetic Sciences, 1968;
- Video Star Connections, 1980;
- Cirronet, 1983;
- Encom, 1983;
- Tridom, 1983;
- Digital Transmission Systems, 1984;
- EASI, 1984;
- E-Tech, 1984;
- Wegener Communications, 1984;
- American Technology, 1985;
- Eagleware, 1985;

- Lan Tel, 1985;
- AvData Systems, 1988;
- ANBC, 1989;
- ESP Technologies, 1989;
- Air Quality Services, 1989;
- D&D Enterprises, 1990;
- Business Television International, 1990;
- Pearl Associates, 1991;
- Home Networking System, 1992;
- Telecorp (Syntellect), 1992;
- Optima, 1993;
- Commetrex, 1994;
- Media 4, 1995;
- Simons Consulting, 1995;
- Chancellor Management, 1995;
- Digital Furnace, 1998;
- Medizeus, 1998;
- Highland Software, 1999;
- N2 Broadband, 2000;
- Wave7Optics, 2000;
- Aerias, 2000;
- Corporate Broadcast Services, 2000; and
- AlertPath Inc., 2003.

Today, the Scientific-Atlanta division of Cisco Systems concentrates on network-delivered broadband access to the home and to businesses. The company serves the markets indirectly by providing the products and services its telecommunications customers need to deliver to the ultimate consumers.

So the firm that started in nearby DeKalb County, soon moved manufacturing operations first to Gwinnett, then located its headquarters at Technology Park. Later Scientific-Atlanta would move its entire local operations to its new campus and headquarters in central Gwinnett and become a dominant segment in the world-wide communication business. Finally, it would become a major subsidiary of a giant of the industry, Cisco Systems. It continues to be a major player among industries and a large employer in Gwinnett County.

National Football League comes to Gwinnett

Though they don't call Gwinnett County home now, from 1978 until 2000, the Atlanta Falcons football team of the National Football League had everything except their game-day playing field in Gwinnett County---in Suwanee at the intersection of Interstate 85 and the Lawrenceville-Suwanee Road. The team offices, its training facility, practice fields, and even a lodging and conference facility, The Falcon Inn, were there. But except for some sleepy inner-city legislators, it might never have happened. Here's why.

In the middle 1970s, the football team had their complete operation, their ticket offices, and front offices, located in downtown Atlanta, and they played their games at Atlanta-Fulton County Stadium. For their training camp prior to the close of baseball season, the team traveled each day by bus to Snapfinger Field, off I-20. Once the Atlanta Braves completed their season, the football team held their practice sessions at Atlanta-Fulton County Stadium.

Wanting a permanent home and better facilities for the team, owner Rankin Smith went looking. Eventually, very much on the quiet, in 1977 Smith found land in Gwinnett that would work. It was a former Ramada Inn motel in Suwanee, with land around it that the team owners could acquire.

Meanwhile, the Falcons management turned to the Gwinnett Industrial Development Authority to help finance the move. After all, this was to be a major move, involving millions of dollars, and the Falcon owners wanted to have low-interest bonds to help finance the new location.

But there was a problem.

Under the industrial development law as written, sports teams were not eligible for such financing. Going the extra steps, Gwinnett legislators were approached about getting a change in the law. And here entered another problem.

The amendment to the industrial development financing had to be worded in such a way so as it would not signal what would eventually happen, should it pass: the move of the City of Atlanta's football….literally, out of the City of Atlanta.

If Fulton and DeKalb County legislators found out about the true intent of the proposed changes to Georgia law, they would see to it that the legislation would be scuttled. And with that, the Atlanta Falcons would not move their team facilities to Gwinnett.

What the Falcons were preparing to move to Gwinnett was everything except the playing field itself. They would move their team offices, the business department, the practice facilities and locker rooms to the county. They had preliminary plans to construct the practice fields with elaborate drainage facilities and ease of grass maintenance.

Meanwhile, at an August, 1977 Chamber of Commerce board of director's meeting, the possible move by the Falcons to Gwinnett was discussed as a prospective new business in Gwinnett. It was emphasized that this was to be held in strict confidence. After all, if in any way word slipped out about the true intention to amending the industrial development legislation, it would mean that the deal would be off the table, since the downtown legislators would work to kill it, and would probably succeed. If the word got out, no Falcons in Gwinnett.

Chamber directors, of course, were all for the location of the Falcons in Gwinnett. Those on the Chamber board at that time thought it would be a tremendous feather in Gwinnett's cap. They were eager to see the legislation passed, and determined not to mention it to others. The problem was that it was nearly six months before the Legislature could get the measure passed. That was a long time to keep anything hush-hush. Even after the measure passed, it would need the governor's signature, before the move could be announced.

That was a long time. Something could easily happen. A slip of the tongue here or there, and the whole proposition could be in jeopardy.

For at least one member of the Chamber director's board, this caused quite a quandary. Elliott Brack was on the Chamber board, and was the vice president and general manager of the county's daily newspaper, *Gwinnett Daily News*. And if his newspaper reported what he had heard at the Chamber meeting, not only would the Falcons not come to Gwinnett, but it could be a public relations debacle for the newspaper.

Taking the information back to the newspaper office, he met with editor Steve McMullan and publisher Bob Fowler. The upshot: since the news came out of a closed (to the public) meeting of the private Chamber of Commerce board of directors, and since it was not a public body such as a county commission (where the idea would been discussed openly), the newspaper would sit on the story.

So, from August on, the *Gwinnett Daily News*, in particular, was scanning *The Atlanta Journal* and *The Atlanta Constitution* each day to see if those newspapers had picked up this incidental information that could kill the Falcons move.

The news never got out. Somehow the Fulton and DeKalb legislative delegations never realized that the wording the legislation meant, in effect, that the Falcons were fleeing the City of Atlanta.

In 1978, Governor George Busbee (a future Gwinnett resident) signed the amendment to the legislation. And in the spring of 1978, it was announced that the Falcons would call Suwanee their home in the future.

Jim Hay was making a transition from the Atlanta-Fulton Stadium Authority, where he had been the stadium manager, to begin work with the Falcons, joining the Falcons on March 15, 1978. The Falcons started work on remodeling the former 102-room motel and site on April 15, 1978, and by August 15, the new training center, the offices and even the remodeled motel, were ready, built on an expedited basis.

Altogether, the Smith interests originally purchased the 37 acres around the motel, later adding other tracts to bring the total site to 148 acres. Built on-site originally were a two-story office building for the Falcons, three practice fields, three ponds for watering and water storage for recycling, and the renovated motel, the name of which was changed to The Falcon Inn.

One entered the red-brick-facade two-story offices on what was the second floor. The team offices were on this level. The back of the building, used mainly by the coaching staff, overlooked the practice fields. The lower part of the building was for the players' locker room, the training room, equipment room and exercise area. The players walked out of their dressing room to the practice fields on the same level.

Southern Turf Nurseries of Tifton installed the three playing fields. Two of the fields had sand bases over thick granite rocks under the grass, for quick grass growth, and for ease of drainage to ensure a dry field, even shortly after watering. The irrigated field drained into a lower pond, and the water was recirculated to an upper pond, from which water would flow by gravity for watering the fields. Hay remembers: "We had signed an arrangement to buy water from Gwinnett County during dry spells, but with our recirculation, even during droughts, we never needed their water."

On August 15, 1978, the Falcon's first year in Gwinnett, the team returned from its summer practice facilities at Furman University at Greenville, S.C. and found the remodeled quarters awaiting them. The Falcon Complex would become the team's spring and pre-season training camps. For home games, the team would spend the night before a game at The Falcon Inn, eating their dinner on Saturday night and pre-game meal in Suwanee. The team continued to hold its pre-season camp at Suwanee until the second year when Dan Reeves was coach, when, for "team building relationships," they opted to return to Furman for pre-season camp.

In 1979, the Falcons added another element at the Suwanee location. It was called The Complex, a family health-and-fitness club, centered around racquetball. There was also space in the facility for exercise machines, men's and women's locker rooms, and showers. Aerobics classes were taught at the facility. The Complex contained 11 racquetball courts, including a Plexiglass Exhibition Court, where onlookers in bleachers could watch matches. Racquetball tournaments were also held at The Complex.

Tommy Nobis, the first player drafted when the Falcons started, retired from playing in 1976, joined the Falcons the next year as an executive for the team, and managed The Complex. Nobis says: "There were not many health clubs then in Atlanta, and Rankin Smith thought this would be a good venture to get into. He knew the community was growing and there were no other health facilities in the area. I ran the place for three years, and we had lots of members from the surrounding communities. I still run into people who were members back then."

Tommy later managed The Falcon Inn and Restaurant, which by then was adding conference room space. It had one of the few large meeting rooms in Gwinnett at the time, and each month hosted the 200 or more members of the Gwinnett Chamber of Commerce for its "The Eye Opener Breakfast." It was a busy meeting facility for many county organizations. For years, the weekly meeting of the first Rotary Club in Gwinnett was there each Tuesday.

The Falcon Inn was full of football players and potential players each July and August, but for 10 months of the year, it was open to the public and run as a roadside motel and restaurant.

The Inn expanded its meeting room capabilities, using double-wide manufactured homes for conference facilities. Hay says: "We built eventually eight out-buildings for conferences, and had contracts with major companies to hold their training sessions at the site."

When the Atlanta Falcons were located in Suwanee, they were the toast of the NFL when it came to facilities. But over years, the place started to show some age. Too, land prices in Gwinnett were soaring, and other NFL teams had more modern facilities. Other National Football League teams could show off far more modern and expansive facilities to prospective players. The team first explored remodeling their Gwinnett location. But that turned out to be far more expensive than they first thought. So the Falcon management started looking around.

In addition, the employment at the team headquarters was also on an upswing. Where there were 50 employees when the team moved to Gwinnett in 1978, by 2000, as the operation moved to Hall County, the coaching staff was larger, as were other departments, and the staff had grown to 87 with office space at a premium.

In 1999, the team found 50 acres of land up Interstate 985 at Flowery Branch, initially developing 26 acres. There, the Falcons set up a much more sophisticated operation for offices, and expanded training rooms and weight room. By then, football observers said that the best training facility in the NFL belonged to the St. Louis Rams. The upshot was that the Falcons decided to have Clayco Construction Company of St. Louis, the firm that had built the Rams' complex, also construct a new home for the Falcons. Construction began in October, 1999, and the team moved into new facilities at Flowery Branch in August, 2000. Where their operation had encompassed 28,000 feet in Suwanee, the team moved into a new facility of 76,000 square feet. And though the team still had three practice fields, as in Suwanee, eventually one of the fields was a sprawling indoor facility, for inclement weather practices.

As the team got a new owner, Arthur Blank, instead of a former motel, Blank constructed what amounts to a dormitory for players' use during training and overnight times. It soon became the prototype for other NFL training centers.

Here's a final comparison of new and old facilities: the original Gwinnett Industrial Development bond to build the Suwanee location was $4 million, with another $1 million added later for a total of $5 million. The cost of the new Flowery Branch Falcon Training Center was $16 million, including the land. And yes, that same language that allowed Gwinnett to provide industrial bond financing for the Suwanee facility….also worked well in Hall County!

Mountain Park gets a community center

Ever wonder how the community of Mountain Park, not located on a rail line, has a former railroad depot as a centerpiece of its park?

For the answer, we go back to 1976, to when Mountain Park was an early Gwinnett hotspot of residential development. The source is the late Mike Barnett, who in 1976 became the president of a group very active then, the Mountain Park Jaycees. Mike told it his own way.

"There were many things we didn't have in Mountain Park back then. Our Jaycee chapter had to keep moving its meeting from place to place, since we had no permanent site to meet. We would move from Joe Brand's storage room, to the Gwinnett County Bank after they closed for the day, to attorney Jim Howard's basement, etc. We realized we needed a permanent meeting place, a community center.

"Then I read where Mary Beth Busbee, the governor's wife, was helping preserve old railroad depots. You see, the railroad was taking down abandoned depots because of the liability insurance. When approaching Mary Beth with the idea of a depot for our community center, she loved the idea, and started searching for the person I should approach. She was very helpful, and eventually suggested I talk to the Interstate Commerce Commission in Washington.

"It just so happened that this was the year I was taking our young daughters to Washington. While there after talking to bureaucrats all day, I finally found an ICC official I needed to talk to, of course with Mary Beth's help. He gave me a letter with his blessings to the Southern Railway officials in Atlanta.

"When I got to the Southern Railway official, he wasn't real happy with my idea, but since I had a letter from the ICC, and from the governor's wife, he said it might be doable. A few weeks later he sent me a letter with three depots they were going to demolish. If I was crazy enough to move one, he was crazy enough to allow it if I could get the paperwork and permits, he said."

Mike Barnett later was a five-term state representative from Gwinnett. He eventually moved to Forsyth County, with the engineering firm of Clark Rader and Barnett in Suwanee.

Mike continues with the depot saga: "I immediately hit the road to visit all three sites. One depot was too wide to make it over the highways. Another could not be jacked high enough to make it over a concrete bridge railing it would have to cross. And the third one was perfect. As soon as I saw it, I knew we had found our community center.

"There was one small problem. It was located in Shannon, Ga., above Rome, about 80 miles from Mountain Park. About this time a light bulb came on in my mind, remembering a grandfather of a girl I had dated who was a housemover in Atlanta. He agreed to help us, after we talked about his fine granddaughter.

"When he and a railroad official and I went to Shannon to inspect it before moving, another situation developed. One of the local residents inquired about what we were doing with 'their' depot? So I pulled out a letter showing that we had purchased it for one dollar, and it was our depot, and it was about to be moved.

"Then I was told that before he would see 'their' depot moved out of town, he would burn it down. The railroad official with us reminded him that the depot was now actually the property of the federal government, and since we had this guy's tag number and name, he would immediately be sent to a prison if the depot burned."

"But that didn't stop the nasty letters I got from the Shannon area. The county newspaper called me a thief and every other legal thing they could for days on end. The more they were determined to keep the depot, the more I was determined to move it.

"So we drew plans for all the bracing that it would take; then we cut the depot in half; and then it took two days to load it on two huge moving trucks. Earlier, the moving price had been quoted at $12,000, but the last night before it was moved, a four-man poker game at the depot, with the mover present, got the price reduced to $7,000.

"The Jaycees had previously obtained a loan for the move at the Gwinnett County Bank's Mountain Park office, with all the Jaycees signing the note along with the owner of a new Super Valu supermarket, Don Heathman.

"As we left Shannon, a little group of the town's citizens stood close by with tears in their eyes, waving their white handkerchiefs as the big moving trucks pulled away. We slowly made our way down the little back roads, with me riding in the front truck. You can only imagine the cold chills I had as 'their' depot rolled along and I waved at the people along the way who had never seen a railroad depot on wheels. Everything went fine until we reached the Forsyth County line.

"The sheriff stopped us saying there was no way he was going to allow 'that damn building' to proceed through his county and tie up traffic, or cause an accident, etc. We had to stop for the night anyway, so we figured the side of the road at the county line would be a good safe place to park a railroad depot.

"Then I set out and walked about a mile to the nearest little store and called the governor's mansion. After much ado, the trooper finally agreed to talk to Mary Beth about returning my call to the pay phone. Within minutes she was on the line wanting to know what happened, since she was following our efforts. The next morning we had a state trooper fore and aft, with blue lights and sirens. As we passed through downtown Cumming, I remember waving at the very mad Forsyth County sheriff.

"We finally arrived in Mountain Park, set the depot down on railroad ties, removed the bracing and patched the two halves back together. We now had our community center.

"Yes, we forgot a few minor costs, like a foundation, electricity, heat, plumbing, occupancy permits. But we soon held our first Jaycee meeting in the 'as is' condition. It took several years to get the depot in top condition, with lots of help from Wayne Mason, Jere Johnson and Wayne Shackelford. Later would be added a large room on the back and all the amenities. As I sometimes pass by the Mountain Park Depot, I cannot help but get a little teary-eyed about all the people that helped make the depot a reality."

Now you have the Mountain Park Depot story, from the guy who instigated its move to Mountain Park.

In the late 1970s, there was interest on the part of residents of the Mountain Park community to incorporate themselves as a city. A committee started looking into the proposition, then hit a stone wall: there was already a community in Georgia by the name of Mountain Park.

It is located in North Fulton County, near Roswell, and had operated as a city since 1927. Once residents of the Mountain Park community in Gwinnett learned this, it seemed to take the life out of the idea of being a municipality. Yet the area continued to thrive, thanks in part to the building of Mountain Park's 44-acre park, and its swimming pool.

Since 1977, the community had a small, cramped library in rented facilities in the basement of the building at 1304 Rockbridge Road. The addition of its own library building on December 19, 1987 also gave local citizens a sense of community, with little talk heard of the idea of incorporation. The modern new library branch was an instant hit and gave Mountain Park its own sense of identity when it opened as the first of eight branches in the county approved in a bond question before voters in 1986.

Serving youth

In a growing county such as Gwinnett has been since 1950, many of the social service organizations are not in place as people move into a county. Leaders of these organizations have to be encouraged to come into the county, and once they learn of the opportunity, have to be organized.

Two youth organizations which have blossomed with facilities in Gwinnett since the 1980s are the Young Men's Christian Association, and the Boys and Girls Clubs.

The United Way advisory board in Gwinnett played a hand in both the organization of first a Boys Club, then a Girls Club.

A major force in the YMCA movement in Gwinnett County was Bob Fowler, who published the *Gwinnett Daily News*. He gave the initial 22 acres near Lawrenceville where the first YMCA was built in the county, and also took the lead on organizing the second YMCA in the county; in Peachtree Corners, that YMCA now bears his name.

Boys and Girls Club

The Boys Club got started in Gwinnett slightly before the Girls Club. The idea grew out of a United Way County Development Committee, which had strategically set aside funds to develop agencies in outlying counties of Metro Atlanta. This group approached the Boys Club of Metro Atlanta, noting the need in the county for an organization providing service to boys. Executives Ron Osborne and Jerry Tipton, of what was only the Boys Club then, supported this move, and the United Way provided a $75,000 community development grant to launch the program. This program expenditure was for 1987.

Ronnie Jenkins, who at that time was a Boys Club executive in Atlanta, initially took the lead in the program. He was to determine which community in Gwinnett had the greatest need and density of population to support the planting of the first clubhouse.

Meanwhile, the advisory board of the United Way asked Elliott Brack to be an organizing leader of the project. He pulled together key members of the Gwinnett community to hear about the need for such a club, with this group holding its first meeting at a breakfast on March 24, 1987 at the Falcon Inn in Suwanee. From that meeting a board was formed. Those at the first meeting included Gene Ussery, Rick Paynik, Dave Foster, Bob Huttman, Hartwell Wash, Leonard Cyphers, Don Loggins, Boyd Duncan, Mike Hayes, Brenda Branch, Jim Crawford, Ted Elliott, Don McEnery, Kent Ryan, and Jim Walker.

Chairing the nominating committee was Hartwell Wash. Gene Ussery was selected as president. Other initial officers were Dave Foster, vice president for operations; Hartwell Wash, vice president for support; and Bob Huttman, vice president for resources.

The organization of the club went quickly. By mid-April, the group secured the two-story, brick Harris house at Perry and Nash Streets in Lawrenceville for the initial Boys Club site. After sprucing-up and making minor renovations on the house, the club was soon launched, with Buddy Skelton the first program director. Dedication of the Clubhouse was on May 30, 1987. This became the 16th site of the Boys Clubs in Metro Atlanta. In 2007, there were 33 sites of the Boys and Girls Clubs in Metro Atlanta.

In March 1995, the Lawrenceville Boys Club moved to a building owned by the City of Lawrenceville at 382 Stone Mountain Street, where it shared facilities with the Ezzard Charles Boxing Club and offices of city Parks and Recreation. The area was once Gwinnett County's Fairgrounds. (The boxing club was named for former heavyweight champion Ezzard Charles, who was born in 1921 in Lawrenceville.)

Meanwhile, in 1989 a group of women in Lawrenceville wanted to form a local Girls Club, and began meeting. Ms. Freddie Norman of Lawrenceville got a program started for teen-age girls, first calling it the Hooper-Renwick Girls Club, since it began in that area of the city. The girls would meet on Saturday afternoons.

Rather early, Ms. Norman approached the United Way, seeking to secure funding. She was encouraged to work with the Metro Atlanta Girls Club, who wanted to expand in the area, and tapped 21-year veteran Girls Club Director Mary Peavy to help with the program. It opened on June 19, 1989 with year-round activities. The club also secured a grant of $27,000 from the Gwinnett United Way. Julie Keeton, who was on the Gwinnett United Way advisory board, was the facilitator between Ms. Norman and her volunteers seeking the program and the Girls Club.

Keeton says: "The Lawrenceville group was a little suspicious of the metro organization, but we encouraged their cooperation. We wanted to enlarge upon what these Lawrenceville ladies had sought to do, and integrate them into the Girls Club organization. The United Way wanted the Metro Girls Club involved for financial stability. We got a little house at 241 Pike Street owned by Martha and Charles Ashworth. I remember that the local citizens came over one Saturday to help paint and fix up that old house. We began to get organized, with the staff director paid by the Metro Girls Club. We had very little money, and that first summer, we served 60 girls. By the time it ended as a separate organization, it had in excess of 250 members." That early group directing efforts for the Girls Club besides Ms. Norman included Eron Moore, Rubye Neal and Carol Burdges, besides Ms. Keeton, who was the president.

In the summer of 1990, the Girls Club moved to a larger location, the two-story former County Auto Tag Office "on the hill" at the former high school site. Mayor Rhodes Jordan and Butch Conway were among those helping spruce the place up. Later Mary Peavy remembers the Gwinnett Girls Club was to enter a decathlon competition in Atlanta, and practiced in the parking lot by the tag office. Practice paid off, for the Gwinnett Girls Club won the decathlon competition, which gave the members a tremendous boost of confidence so soon after being formed into a club.

A key element in the early funding of the Girls Club was an annual Walkathon put on by the Gwinnett schools. "The schools allowed the Girls Club to be the beneficiary one year, and that really helped get us on a sound financial basis, for we did not have much funding when we got started," Keeton says.

As the Girls Club program was beginning to get its feet on the ground in Gwinnett, negotiations were going on in Metro Atlanta to merge the Boys and Girls Clubs. The merger in Atlanta was accomplished in June of 1990. Keeton remembers that "the major funders in Atlanta and in Gwinnett didn't want to give money to both organizations, but wanted a single, strong program. Here we put a lot of volunteer committee hours in, and the merger eventually worked out well." The merger between the Boys Club and Girls Club in Gwinnett did not take place until the fall of 1991.

At that time, Keeton was president of the Gwinnett Girls Club, while Rich Panyik was president of the Boys Club. Keeton says: "When we merged, Rich and I both thought that neither of us should continue in office, and Bob Huttman of Gwinnett Federal became the first president of the merged group. He did a good job as the head of the merged Boys and Girls Club." When the two clubs merged, since the Boys Club had their own facility, the Girls Club activities also began to be worked out of the Stone Mountain Street facility.

Meanwhile, in 1994, the newly-merged Club began a $550,000 campaign to have the entire building on Stone Mountain Street for its larger operations. It purchased the building from the city, where it has operated since. The campaign was led by Curtis McGill, with Leonard Cyphers and John Robertson as co-chairmen.

After the Lawrenceville Boys and Girls Club got the use of its entire building, the board began to think broader in the county about its operation. The Boys and Girls Club had begun to conduct programs during the summers of 1995-96 at Norcross Elementary School. Interest stirred in 1997 in Norcross for its own club. The initial impetus for this came from Bradley Currey and Dave Nicholson at Rock-Tenn Corporation, the United

Way, and a wide cross-section of the Norcross community. The summer program at the elementary school had been expanded in early 2000 to also include an after-school program.

A campaign to raise $3.5 million, for a facility in Norcross began in the fall of 1997. Major funding, some $600,000, came from employees of Rock-Tenn Corp. and the A. Worley Brown estate contributed $500,000. The new club was named for Mr. Brown, a former Rock-Tenn chairman. The drive found an unexpected ally in the Kresge Foundation of Chicago, which liked the idea of merging of the Boys and Girls Clubs, and contributed $250,000 toward the Norcross building. Another foundation, the local Frances Wood Wilson Foundation, made available $50,000 for the drive.

A particularly key development in the Norcross Boys and Girls Club was the involvement of another United Way agency in the building. This was the Sheltering Arms of Atlanta agency, which specializes in care of young children for working parents. Deb Roberts, who was then with United Way in Gwinnett, was instrumental in getting the two agencies together. The upshot was for Sheltering Arms to have a location within the Boys and Girls Club building, some 12,000 square feet, for its local program. That agency in 2007 saw 100 children, age six weeks to 5 years old, being cared for in this program at the Norcross facility.

After the successful drive, a new 22,000 square-foot Boys and Girls Club, specifically built for that purpose, opened in May of 2000 on Old Norcross Road at Buford Highway.

Further development of the Lawrenceville Boys and Girls Club came in 2004, when the Gwinnett Board of the club felt the need to expand services to teenagers. Michael Guynn was chosen to lead the effort to build a 6,000 square-foot Teen Center, which cost $1.4 million. It is located near, but in a separate building, from the main facility in Lawrenceville. This new Center was opened on May 16, 2006, and named the James F. Pack Teen Center, in honor of the former banker's commitment and support to the Boys and Girls Clubs.

Two major changes came in 2007 and 2008. The first was, in 2007, when the Norcross Boys and Girls Club began a $1 million drive to erect a Teen Center at the Norcross facility. The second was winning a two-year grant for $216,000 from the Woodruff Foundation to fund a year-round Boys and Girls Club program at Radloff Middle School, starting in August, 2008. In previous years, the Club had run a summer-only program at the school.

The presence of the Boys and Girls Clubs in Gwinnett allows this organization to serve 3,000 youth throughout the county. In 2008, Rory Johnson was the Boys and Girls executive leading efforts in Gwinnett.

In 2008, members of the Board included Mike Guynn, chairman; Denise Townsend, president; Mary Galardi, secretary; Eric Ownby, vice presidenet of operations; Yoel Yohan, vice president of resources; Tom McBride, vice president of finance; Gregory King, resource development; and the following members: Renekia Strother, Laurie Attaway, Hector C. Baro, Carol Burdges, Harry Cardillo, Darryl Coleman, Russ Crosio, Randy Crump II, David Foster, David Haun, Paula Hill, Leslie Howell, Don Loggins, Darryl Moore, Eron Moore, Becky Munteanu, Rubye Neal, David Nicholson, John Pentecost, Jeff Stansell, Donna Tisdale, Charlie Underwood, Dick Wagner, Jean Walker, Gene Waterfall and Corbitt Woods.

YMCA comes to Gwinnett

There was excitement in the air in mid-1975, when about 45 people from throughout Gwinnett gathered in Lilburn at the Gwinnett Federal Savings and Loan Association branch to meet with representatives of the Metro Atlanta Young Men's Christian Association.

As the community youth leaders came together, they were saying among themselves: "Wow! Gwinnett's under consideration to get its own YMCA! We can't believe it!"

Earlier, on Jan. 31, 1975, after a request from families in the Lilburn area, a small exploratory committee met at the Decatur-DeKalb Branch of the Atlanta YMCA. The group discussed procedures and developed an organizational plan. David Kee, with Georgia Power Company, was appointed chairman of the group. Out of this grew an Advisory Board, which met at the Lilburn Middle School.

Then followed the general meeting of those interested in a local YMCA on July 21, 1975 at the Savings and Loan. After a presentation, the meeting sought questions from the floor. Tthe very first question was: "Where is the new Y going to be located?" Perhaps most people in the audience assumed that the building would go up soon, and were hoping it would be in their community.

Joe Bransby, who was president and CEO of the Atlanta YMCA from 1962-80, did not admit it, but at similar meetings in other counties, he had heard that same question usually raised first.

Joe had a ready answer: "We don't know yet, and may not know the location for 10 years. The Y first establishes programs in the community, using playgrounds which are available, churches, parks, donated fields, and any place we can find for our programs and classes. Then, years later, once we have the program fully underway, we'll concentrate on finding the best location for the YMCA."

That wasn't what those citizens interested in having a fully functioning YMCA in Gwinnett particularly wanted to hear. But they were pleased that the YMCA was taking notice of Gwinnett. After all, it was more than 20 miles from Lilburn to the closest YMCA, located on Clairmont Road in Decatur.

Thus began what soon became a major success story for the YMCA in Gwinnett County. The program flourished immediately. Besides Kee as chairman of the Advisory Board, it consisted of Luther Blackmon, Lewis Brinkley, Aggie Calder, J. D. Caswell, Lynn Csuka, Marsha Corbin, Lu Durden, Audrey Hardin, Mary Ann Hartman, George Hicks, Jim Howse, Ralph Pickwick, J.C. Schickedanz, Dr. Mike Soloman, Fran Topolski and Larry Yates.

The first YMCA staff director, working part-time, was Carl Mertz, a ministerial student at Emory's Candler School of Theology. First programs included Indian Guides/ Maidens/Indian Princess' (fathers and sons/mothers and daughters, meeting in homes); Gra-Y Clubs, identified with Gwinnett elementary schools, primarily boys, 10 to 12 years of age involved in sports and value-building activities; and Day Camping for younger boys, a summer activity. In the absence of a YMCA building, these initial activities were held in homes, school playgrounds and parks around the county.

The "Y" operated from an office on Perry Street in Lawrenceville, and moved to Clayton Street in 1981. Mr. Mertz was succeeded by Ms. Pat Hechenberger, the first full-time program director, in 1976. She was succeeded by David Stout, who was in turn succeeded by Tom Looby, who served from 1982 until 1989. He later was the YMCA executive in Nashville, Tenn., in Winston-Salem, N.C. and in 2008 was president of the Tampa, Fla. area YMCA. Looby was followed in Gwinnett by Randy Brown, who held the Tull directorship from 1989-1993, when he joined the Fowler YMCA. He later headed the Daytona Beach, Fla. YMCA and still later was president of the YMCA in Birmingham, Ala. As of mid-2007, Brown was the president of the Chattanooga, Tenn. YMCA.

Randy Brown

Meanwhile, soon after the 1975 meeting, the YMCA had programs chugging along in many parts of the county. It conducted a summer day camp, with 425 youth in attendance that first year. By 1979, more than 2,900 youth were participating in its activities.

By 1980, the YMCA had its first site-development committee, led by Fraser Duke. After taking the traditional route by investigating town locations near the center of the county, the committee found unexpected pay dirt in another location. Bob Fowler in 1981 offered to donate 21.5 acres of land on Scenic Highway at what would become Sugarloaf Parkway. It was close to the center of the county, and the committee deemed it a terrific location. It also had the additional benefit of being located between two key communities, Lawrenceville and Snellville. (Fowler would later donate three additional frontage road acres to the Y, making the complex a 25 acre site.)

Work soon began on a $1.4 million capital campaign to build a modern facility on that land. It would not be easy. Initial plans called for a 15,000 square-foot building but no indoor swimming pool. However, there was grumbling over the lack of an indoor pool, and eventually the local YMCA board upped the ante, determining that an indoor pool and health club were needed to assure the YMCA was a success.

Soon it was obvious that the fund drive was not going as they had hoped. In effect, it needed at least another $810,000. The pool was anticipated to cost $500,000, while the fitness facility was tagged at $310,000. But efforts at raising these big dollars lagged.

In those days, Lawrenceville attorney Gerald Davidson was chairman of the Gwinnett YMCA board of directors. He tells the story of getting a telephone call about 8 a.m. on Christmas morning in 1984. On the phone was Bob Fowler, who told Davidson: "I need to meet with you today."

"But Bob," Davidson protested, "This is Christmas Day and I'm here unwrapping presents with my kids."

"I know. But I really must meet with you today." Davidson agreed for Fowler to come out to his house that afternoon. When he arrived, Fowler began his story.

"I got a call this morning from an anonymous potential donor," Bob told Gerald. "This guy woke up this morning (Christmas Day), and realized that he had been very successful, and wanted to share his blessings with the community. He's willing to give the YMCA $500,000 to build that pool on two conditions.

"The first is that he must remain anonymous. And the second is that he told me he had studied the plans for the Y, and looked at it from the business side. He figures the indoor pool is necessary for generating membership, and that it is a great asset, but from a cost point, it runs a loss. He also said that he thought a health club is a profit center for the Y, and therefore an asset. Here's the proposition he made to me.

"If we will raise $310,000 by December 31, he'll give the YMCA $500,000 to build the pool. But we can't get it unless we raise enough for the health club to go with it. But we have just six days to raise that money, and I think we should go for it."

With that challenge, Fowler and Davidson jumped into action, having a breakfast at the Fowler house the next morning. About ten people were there, who divided up a list, and hit the streets seeking to raise the $310,000.

One target was the Tull Foundation, which had already given $500,000 to the original fund drive. Fowler sought a meeting the following day with the foundation folks, who included Chairman Walter Thomas and President George Smith, the key executives at the metals company in Norcross, who had additional duties at the Tull Foundation. Gerald remembers, "Bob called and said that we needed an emergency meeting with them at the Foundation the next day. We went downtown to the Hurt building to meet with them."

When the Tull officers heard the request, they were not only surprised, but stunned. "It normally takes us 30 days to process a request," the two soliciting the funding were told. Davidson adds: "Yet the Tull Foundation came through. They called back that afternoon and said they would give us $220,000 more. That meant we really had to go to work, but needed only another $90,000. We made that goal by December 31, and Bob was able to telephone the anonymous donor and tell him of our success. The donor said he would call his accountant and start processing his contribution, and would get us checks of $50,000 each from ten of his operating companies."

That anonymous donor had already given to many charitable causes in Gwinnett, and in Atlanta. Up until that time and most of the time before his death, his contributions were anonymous. Now it can be revealed that the anonymous donor was philanthropist and developer Scott Hudgens. His name comes up often as providing lead gifts and seed capital for many Gwinnett charitable purposes. His contributions continue today through the Hudgens Foundation. His son, Dallas, heads that foundation, which continues to support many worthwhile causes in Gwinnett.

Bob Fowler, though considering himself a mere member of the fund-raising committee, was the titular financial head, spearheading the effort and bringing the drive to its successful conclusion. With him the driving force, and since he gave not only the land for the first YMCA, but also contributed $1 million in cash, the YMCA board voted to name the facility for him.

This caused Fowler to seek a "face-to-face" meeting with Davidson. Fowler told Davidson that he did not work to establish a YMCA to get it named for him, no matter how much he had given and worked for it. Davidson said: "Bob told me in no uncertain terms, as he looked me in the eye, that in no way did he want the YMCA named for him. So the board soon rescinded its previous naming action."

The other large contributor was the J.M. Tull Foundation, which eventually led to the naming of the facility for J.M. Tull. That foundation's funding source was a company, J. M. Tull Metals, a distributor of metal products with many offices throughout the Southeast, which was headquartered in Norcross.

Groundbreaking for the Tull YMCA was July 30, 1985. When initially opened on October 16, 1986, it consisted of 36,000 square feet of office space, a gymnasium, the indoor pool, a health club, plus three outdoor soccer fields.

A key feature of the Tull YMCA was the construction of three soccer fields adjacent to the building. Soccer at that time was just emerging as a sport getting more attention in the county. The early YMCA soccer fields, since there were few sites specifically laid out for soccer fields then, were a key factor in the development of youth soccer in Gwinnett.

Since then, there have been continuing improvements. Tennis and racquetball courts have been added, a $750,000 teen center was built, an additional five acres was bought adjacent to the site, and a $900,000 outdoor swimming pool added. With additions, by 2007, the Tull Y consists of a 60,000 square-foot building. Altogether, over the years, the Tull location has seen nine expansions.

Today, the Tull YMCA serves 7,430 families, plus another 8-9,000 program participants. (The overall Atlanta YMCA is the fourth largest association in the United States as of 2007, with 260,161 members.)

Peachtree Corners YMCA

Plans for a second YMCA in Gwinnett began in 1990, when Peachtree Corners developer Jim Cowart donated a 10-acre parcel on Peachtree Corners Circle at West Jones Bridge Road.

Shortly afterward, Bob Fowler paid Jim Cowart a visit at his office in Peachtree Corners. Cowart remembers:

"There had been an article in the paper about me giving the land for a Peachtree Corners YMCA. I had heard of Bob Fowler, but did not know him, though I had been impressed with his attitude about doing things.

"He walked into my office with the newspaper article in his hand, asking me, 'Is this true?' When I told him it was, he said that what we needed to do was go about raising the money ourselves, and forget about the Metro Atlanta YMCA. But then he said that when we call upon people wanting contributions, the first thing they are going to ask is what we are contributing. He said that since I had contributed the land, he would give $500,000. Later I found out that he did more than what we had agreed to do. But before the drive was completed, Fowler died."

After Mr. Fowler's unexpected death at age 62 in June of 1993, the YMCA asked the Fowler family for their approval to name the Peachtree Corners location the "Robert D. Fowler Family YMCA," which the family granted.

At the dedication of the branch, Director Randy Brown had this to say about Fowler:

"Bob Fowler wanted the best for his community, and worked hard for that in many behind-the-scenes ways. His hand was in many Gwinnett activities, as people realized he knew and understood the community, and people sought his advice. His was an engaging personality, though Bob himself was a quiet and often reflective soul. Because of his love for the YMCA program, we feel there is no more fitting tribute than to name this Peachtree Corners YMCA for him."

Fowler and Cowart had similar visions for the growing Norcross/Peachtree Corners area that foresaw a gathering place for all "individuals, families and youth of all abilities, age, beliefs, cultures, faith and incomes" at the YMCA. (Cowart had in 1972 donated his former home on Ashford Dunwoody Road in DeKalb County, 18.53 acres, to the YMCA. Some 14 years later, the YMCA finally opened the facility, giving it the name of Cowart Family Ashford Dunwoody YMCA.)

The Peachtree Corners YMCA began a campaign in 1993 to raise $2.7 million for the Fowler Family YMCA in Peachtree Corners. Bradley Currey Jr. was the honorary chairman, while Elliott Brack headed the campaign. On the Steering Committee were William E. McLendon, local Y chairman, and Dan Cowart, Jim Cowart, Nick George, William Short, Robert Stedeford and Gerald Stephens.

In addition, the campaign committee consisted of Ralph Barber, William F. Brogdon, Janice Bullock, Mark Clay, Heyward Horton, L.N. (Bud) Mingledorff, James H. Nelems, Timothy Pakenham, Clayton H. Preble, Forrest W. Robinson, David Seago, G. Martin Shaw, Thomas T. Tate, Edward A. Thayer, Mickey Wages, Jim F. Watson and Monty Watson.

The money was eventually raised, with ground broken in late 1995, and the Fowler YMCA occupied in January 1997. This 35,000 square-foot Robert M. Fowler Family YMCA almost immediately reached its full capacity of 6,000 members and program participants. It was soon evident that more space was needed in the facility.

By 2002, the Peachtree Corners YMCA board was reconstituted, adding some 15 people. The Y kicked up its Partners with Youth campaign, and started a revised campaign for the first addition at the facility, to cost $6.4 million. Altogether, some $2.5 million was raised by the community, in addition to a $750,000 Community Block Grant that came from Gwinnett County to include a Senior Center in the addition.

John Manning was board chair then, and headed the campaign. On this committee were: Gerald Davidson, Louise Chernecky, Harvey Snider and Amy Massey.

A major contribution to this campaign came from the Northeast Georgia Community Foundation, from another Jim Cowart gift. Other responses came from some of Gwinnett's top corporations, foundations and individuals, including Scientific-Atlanta, Rock Tenn Corp., Atlanta Precision Moulding, Genuine Parts, Virginia and Gerald Davidson, and both the Cecil B. Day and Hudgens Foundations.

Some 10 years after the initial opening, on April 26, 2007, this expanded YMCA, now 53,000 square feet, was opened. It is able to serve up to 10,000 members and participants. The new space included a 5,000 square-foot Senior Center; 5,000 square-foot Wellness Center with 65 exercise machines; teen center; group exercise room; family locker rooms and space for babysitting, pre-school and school-aged programs. It also includes renovated adult locker rooms and a multi-purpose space and a spacious atrium.

Meanwhile, planning is already underway to expand the facilities at the footprint, as both a children's gymnasium and outdoor pool are on tap for the future.

In 2007, the Peachtree Corners YMCA was serving 8,376 people through 3,554 memberships.

The first director of the Peachtree Corners YMCA in 1993 was Randy Brown, who served until 1996. He was succeeded by Bill McKoy, who was the director until 2001, when he was named director of the Decatur/DeKalb YMCA. McKoy was succeeded in the slot by Debbie Sutton, who in 2008 was the director.

By all accounts, this Robert Fowler Family YMCA has become a center of activity for people, in particular, in the Peachtree Corners area---a testament to the foresight of Jim Cowart and Bob Fowler.

Simpsonwood Conference Center

Unless you belong to a certain church, many Gwinnettians do not know of one of the largest conference centers in Gwinnett, the Simpsonwood Conference Center of the North Georgia Conference of the United Methodist Church. It's located on a 227-acre tract by the Chattahoochee River near Norcross, bordering Peachtree Corners. Some 2,040 feet of the property is along the river itself.

The Lodge at Simpsonwood is an adult and family retreat center for worship, study, recreation and fellowship. The Lodge welcomes secular and non-profit groups for conferences.

The story of how this center came to be is a fascinating one. The Center is named for its benefactor, a remarkable, never-married former school teacher, Miss Ludie Simpson of Norcross. She was a graduate of what is now the University of Georgia (the Normal School in Athens in 1910), and also graduated in 1926 from Columbia University in New York, where she obtained her Master of Arts degree in 1928. Her first trip to New York was by train, but on all the other trips to that city she liked to take the train to Savannah, and then make the rest of the trip by boat.

Her first teaching experience was in North Carolina, and by 1929, she taught at Joe Brown Junior High in Atlanta, where she was head of the social science department. She retired from the Atlanta schools in 1953, taught for four years at Forest Park High then from 1957-62 taught history at Norcross High until she was 70 years of age. When teaching in Atlanta, she maintained a home in Norcross, where she would spend the weekends and summers.

The Simpson property had been in her mother's family for 120 years. Her parents, J.T. Simpson and Elizabeth Jane Sanders Simpson, came to Gwinnett in 1874, and had six children, though four lived to maturity. After J.T. Simpson deserted the family, Elizabeth Simpson ran the farm alone. The farm produced cotton, oats, wheat and peas, and there were fruit trees---apple, peach, cherry---on the property. Her parents had named her Lou Ann. She was quoted later as saying: "I think that is a beautiful name now, but I didn't realize it when I was growing up. I don't know where I got the nickname 'Ludie,' but it's on diplomas and everything I have."

After her mother died in 1931, Miss Ludie began an extensive hobby of traveling. Another hobby was hiking, saying at one time that she was "one of the best hikers around." She also was an accomplished gardener. In 1934, she made a grand tour of Europe and the British Isles, and followed this in 1935 with a tour of the Orient. Her master's thesis had been about China, and after visiting China in 1934, she produced a two-volume book on China, illustrating it with her own photographs. She told Pat Johnson of the *Gwinnett Daily News* in a 1973 interview that the trip "was when you could do all of China, Manchuria, Korea, Japan and the Philippines." Her book included descriptions of what it was like when Shanghai was under attack by the Japanese. Eventually, she would take 12 trips overseas, most of them after she retired from teaching. An around-the-world tour in 1971 lasted four weeks, and an African journey she took was of 56 days. Miss Ludie liked to travel!

But after she retired, she was perplexed about what to do with what she called "the river farm." She wanted to keep it intact, but believed tax laws and economics would force the land to be sold or divided. So, since she was Presbyterian, in 1971, when she was 84, she decided to give the land to her church. She made two provisions: that the church keep the land intact, and that it build a chapel in honor of her mother. When the Presbyterians didn't build a chapel on the property, Miss Simpson took her land back.

Unsolicited, Miss Simpson approached the Methodists (her mother was buried at Mt. Carmel United Methodist Church Cemetery), offering it to Wesley Homes Inc. for a retirement center. But the church thought that the land could not be used solely for retirement facilities. Miss Ludie told Pat Johnson of the *Gwinnett Daily News* in 1973: "I went down to see the bishop (John Owen Smith) myself when I decided to give the river farm to the Methodists." She asked that the Methodists keep the natural beauty of the tract and its size intact as much as possible. She also kept the provision in her deed to the conference that the Methodists build a chapel in honor of her mother. When donated, the value placed on the land was $2.3 million.

Unfortunately, though the Conference Center produced in 1973 a feasibility study on the land she donated, Miss Simpson did not live to see it become a reality. She died on April 29, 1975, and is buried in nearby Mount Carmel Cemetery alongside her mother.

The Methodists, good to their word, kept the property intact, and shortly erected a 100-seat chapel in an English style, keeping to the agreement to honor Miss Ludie's mother. The window in back of the pulpit in the chapel, of stained glass, is dedicated to the memory of her mother's parents, Thomas McGregory and Mariah Jackson Sanders.

Miss Ludie Simpson

People in Norcross fondly remember Miss Ludie Simpson. She would board the train in Atlanta to spend weekends in Norcross at her North Peachtree Street home. She never learned to drive, but would "walk like on tippy-toes, in short steps, always in a hurry, like she was going to break into a run," one person remembers. During her spare time, she sold the Encyclopaedia Brittanica.

The Rev. Jack Bozeman, who was the first director of the Simpsonwood Conference Center from 1984-87, had a prior connection with Miss Ludie: she had taught him English and math in junior high at Joe Brown School. "She was prim and proper, expected a lot from her students, and was a good teacher. By the time we started to build the conference center," he says, "Miss Ludie had died. But I oversaw the building of the first two lodges, and the chapel."

The entranceway to the Simpsonwood Conference Center in Peachtree Corners, with its "Christ doors."

The Rev. Bozeman recalls that "Mr. and Mrs. Peter Knox, Jr. and Mr. and Mrs. Robert E. Knox of Thomson in 1985 funded the chapel, and even sent workers from Augusta to help build it. They stayed in buildings there while working on the chapel. That was when we were cutting roads into the area. THe family also gave a Baldwin piano for the chapel, and the pews came from another church. One of the windows in the chapel is in the memory of Miss Ludie's parents. The Knox families also furnished a room for brides to dress at the chapel prior to weddings." Much of the wood in the chapel was from 100 year old hand-hewn timbers, secured by the Knox family from the former Arnall Mill in Elberton, Ga. The mill was owned by the family of former Gov. Ellis Arnall.

Mr. Bozeman described Miss Ludie as a "strong-willed woman in about everything. She had her own ideas. She once had been a member of the Presbyterian Church, and had visited in China. She was opposed to the views and actions of Chiang Kai-shek of Taiwan, and left the Presbyterian Church and became a Methodist over Chang's policies."

Once the Methodists began to construct facilities at the Center, they began a program of continually enlarging the center. The conference center included: a kitchen and dining room with the capacity to feed 240 guests at one sitting, two 150-seat conference rooms, and small meeting rooms for committee use. The first 32 room lodge, the Rollins Center, was consecrated on Sept. 21, 1985. A distinctive feature of the Center is its entrance, carved mahogany doors given by Lucille and Arnold Hughey. The carving of the thick doors, called the "Christ doors," depicts open hands and features glass panels; it was installed at the entrance to the Rollins Center in 1987.

A 32-room Hagan Lodge was completed in 1986. Then came several other facilities. Two other phases came in 1992 and 1996, another in 2001 and the last one in 2005. The last addition contained space for the North Georgia Conference offices.

Altogether, Simpsonwood can accommodate 350 people and has 168 overnight rooms and 10 campsites. It has three miles of trails through woods and beside the river, plus an outdoor swimming pool, tennis, volleyball and basketball courts, an athletic field, and the aforementioned 100-seat chapel.

Some may wonder where the suggestion for the name of "Simpsonwood" came from. At the funeral of Miss Ludie, John Wesley Pittman, who has been a volunteer caretaker of the property, spoke and "felt impressed" to propose the name of "Simpsonwood." That's been the way people have referred to it ever since.

Today the land Miss Ludie gave for the Conference Center also has on it the offices of the bishop and the North Georgia Conference of the United Methodist Church. The Conference allocated 12 acres of the property for the Simpsonwood United Methodist Church, which serves the Peachtree Corners community, leaving 227 acres of the 239 acre gift basically intact according to Miss Ludie Simpson's wishes.

Modern medical facilities

Button Gwinnett Hospital

Work for a hospital in Lawrenceville, to be Gwinnett's third, came in 1955, when county officials created the Hospital Authority of Gwinnett County. However, the other two hospitals were then not under the aegis of the Hospital Authority, but were run as local independent hospitals. At that time there were 49 hospital beds in the county, 32 in Duluth at Joan Glancy Hospital and 17 at Hutchins Memorial Hospital in Buford.

The Hospital Authority of Gwinnett County was established Oct. 3, 1955. The initial members of the Authority were Carson Smith Sr. of Lawrenceville, chairman; W.C. Britt of Snellville, vice chairman; Hubert Tucker Sr., Lawrenceville, secretary; and four others, Gaines Ivey representing Norcross; L.O. Hinton from Dacula; and V. H. Puckett and Chief Garner, from Buford. The Authority immediately began to launch plans for a hospital in Lawrenceville.

It was on August, 12, 1959 that the Authority's first hospital, the Button Gwinnett Hospital on Scenic Highway in Lawrenceville, had an open house. The hospital was funded by the Hill-Burton Act. Delivering the dedicatory address was Gov. Ernest Vandiver. The hospital consisted of 33,000 square feet, with 35-patient beds and was touted as being "air conditioned throughout." The Buford High School band provided music for the occasion. The official date for the hospital to begin operations was August 17, 1959.

By 1963, the Authority was taking a long-range view, planning several facilities, realizing the need for more beds in the county, and thinking of a large, central hospital.

In 1965, officials at Joan Glancy Hospital in Duluth voted to join the Gwinnett Hospital Authority, a move completed in 1966. The next milestone for the Authority came on March 6, 1966, when the Authority opened the 39 bed Buford General Hospital, as mentioned on previous pages. (The former Hutchins Memorial Hospital closed when Buford General Hospital opened.).

Speaking on that occasion on in Buford, then-Gov. Carl Sanders said: "Centralized management of the three Gwinnett County hospitals saves a lot of money, brings better care to patients more quickly, and allows the employment of highly-trained and hard-to-find specialists that one small hospital couldn't afford...Gwinnett can be proud of its pace-setting hospital system."

That same year, 1966, the capacity of the Button Gwinnett Hospital in Lawrenceville was increased with a new wing, which added 39 more beds, to a new level of 74 beds. In 1974, that capacity was increased to 79 beds with a new four-bed Intensive Care Unit and one additional hospital bed. Other new features added in 1979 were a new Emergency Department, cystoscopic operating room and recovery room.

In 1972, Joan Glancy Hospital's bed capacity was expanded to 99 beds, making it the largest hospital within the Gwinnett system. In 1981, Joan Glancy's capacity was increased to 104 beds, but was reduced to 90 beds when Gwinnett Medical Center in Lawrenceville opened in 1984.

Relatively early on, the Hospital Authority began to take into consideration the fast growth of Gwinnett. In 1969, the Authority chose a 54-acre site off Interstate 85 near Suwanee to be the location of a new central hospital for the county. In 1972, Gwinnett commissioners purchased 40 acres for the hospital tract, getting another 25 acres from the landowner as a donation.

By 1980, the Hospital Authority had drawn up plans for a new 250-bed, $30 million hospital on the property near Suwanee. There was a reason the Authority took this move. After all, on January 2, 1980, Gwinnett Community Hospital had opened in Snellville, which was pulling paying patients to its new modern facility. Meanwhile, the occupied bed count at the Authority's Button Gwinnett Hospital plummeted.

What the Authority sought was for voters all across Gwinnett to fund a central hospital near Suwanee. The vote may have been doomed from the beginning, since the three existing hospitals, the two operated by the Authority in Duluth and Buford, and the new private hospital in Snellville, all had parochial support from their communities. So neither Duluth, Buford nor Snellville area residents saw the need to pay taxes for a hospital in another part of the county. Snellville residents, in particular, recognized that they had a private hospital, one which had not cost them one red tax cent, making them generally opposed to the idea of a central hospital.

Yet the Hospital Authority proposed that a county-guaranteed bond would be the best way to finance and build a central public hospital for Gwinnett. Virgil Williams was chairman of the Authority at that time, and was flabbergasted when the Gwinnett citizens voted against the bonds for the hospital. There were 9,730 "No" votes, and 5,417 "Yes" votes, a devastating blow to the Authority. Yet the public hospital was desperately needed, the Authority felt, and soon sought other solutions to that problem.

Snellville gets its own hospital

As early as 1952, people in the Snellville area realized they needed better medical care in their community. There were not only no doctors in the area, but not even office space or a house for rent for a doctor. A group of men decided to take action, and in October of 1952, formed the Snellville Community Health Association, a non-profit organization, to finance a doctor's office. David Kistner was named chairman, with directors included Yulee Pharr, Ralph Head, Harold Britt, Colbert Brannon, Hollis Nash, Carl Hewett and A.W. Peters.

Soon $1,000 was raised, and land on Scenic Highway was donated on October 18, 1952 by T. Snell Johnson, grandson of one of the founders of Snellville, for a building. An eight-room rock building was planned, with various firms donating building materials, and individuals contributing their time in erecting the structure. Eventual construction funding cost $7,000 in cash, raised by many individual and civic contributions. The finished structure had an assessed value of $20,000. In November, 1956, the first doctor, Houston W. Kitchen, came to Snellville. He and his family lived in one part of the house, then he could cross a breezeway to get to the doctor's office. That's how Snellville got its first doctor.

After Dr. Kitchens, Dr. George Rawlins and several other doctors followed, living in one part of the building and practicing medicine in the other part. (Dr. Rawlins eventually used the entire house as his office.) This arrangement with the doctors lasted for a few years. Afterward, as doctors moved their practice, the city was again without a doctor living in town. During this time, the building was rented, as a residence, as a business location for a hearing aid clinic, and later Jimmy and Wayne Mason had their real estate office there.

Today the building no longer stands. On June 27, 1991 M&P Shopping Centers of Doraville, who had purchased the adjacent Snellville Plaza from Jimmy and Wayne Mason, made the Health Association an offer they could not turn down; $200,000 for the site. The income from earnings on what became the Snellville Community Health Trust continues to fund causes to benefit the community.

For instance, one year the Trust gave $5,000 to each of seven cemeteries in the area. That included the Snellville Historical Cemetery and the following church cemeteries: Zoar Methodist, Bethany Baptist, Cornith Baptist, Mt. Zion Baptist, Friendship Primitive Baptist and Chestnut Grove Baptist. It also funded improvements at the South Gwinnett Athletic Association, for playground equipment. One of its favorite charities has been the Gwinnett Community Health Clinic, founded by Dr. Lanny Lesser, located in the former hospital building on Fountain Square in Snellville, which has benefited from the Trust over the years. In 2007, the officers of the Trust include Richard Norton, president, W. Emmett Clower III as secretary-treasurer, and the following as directors: Clark Britt, Tony Britt, Leon Juhan, Gerald Rollins and Raymond Williams.

Again in the early 1970s, Snellville had no doctor living in town until another physician came in 1972. A chance meeting between Emmett Clower Jr. and young Dr. Edward Bowen was beneficial for Snellville. The two became acquainted while the doctor was shopping at a Sears retail store where Mr. Clower worked. He learned that Dr. Bowen had set up a practice in Loganville after graduating from Emory Medical School. Eventually, Mr. Clower attracted Ed Bowen to Snellville. The City of Snellville sold Bowen an acre of land for $15,000 on Lenora Church Road to build his office. He was the first doctor to own his office in town. Slowly, more doctors opened offices in Snellville, often coming to the community a few years out of medical school, and with their training up-to-date. As a consequence, when they opened their offices, their practices did well.

As Gwinnett began growing quickly in the early 1970s, soon there emerged a need for more modern medical facilities. Though the county had three hospitals by 1975, all were relatively small. They included a Hill-Burton Hospital in Lawrenceville, the Button

Gwinnett Hospital; Joan Glancy Hospital in Duluth; and another Hill-Burton hospital, Buford General Hospital. All were operated under the umbrella of the Gwinnett Hospital Authority, though there was little interaction between the hospitals.

What the county lacked was modern hospitals and the attendant cadre of physicians who would be attracted by modern medical services. Many Gwinnettians in those days felt that if you were sent to one of the three Gwinnett hospitals, you wanted to have a Band-Aid put on you, and be sent to one of the hospitals in Atlanta if there was anything seriously wrong with you. There was simply no first-class medical care in those days in Gwinnett, with its few doctors, and even fewer specialists.

The medical community was disappointed with the level of equipment in local hospitals. One Snellville doctor, M.T. Bagheri, tells the story of pleading with hospital officials to get a modern x-ray machine, and finding for a time, the hospital stonewalling against making such a purchase. Finally, he was told by the hospital: "OK, we'll get the machine on one ground: if at the end of the year, we have not made enough money from the machine use, you will have to pay the difference."

Dr. Bagheri, a thoracic and general surgery specialist, particularly needed the machine in his practice, and agreed to the twist-of-arms terms. But he had the last laugh. He says: "Before the year was up, this same hospital official came back to me, asking 'Is there any more equipment you need?' You see, not only did I use the specialized x-ray machine often enough, but so did other doctors, and the hospital was making more money from its use!" Dr. Bagheri laughs.

Yet there was still no hospital in the southern portion of the county. As time wore on, others had noticed this void in medical care, with one person approaching Snellville officials and doctors, bringing the town's doctors together to discuss a hospital. The upshot of that meeting in about 1975 was the doctors each contributing $500 to this consultant, who had approached them, to fund the process to get approval for a hospital.

The doctors told him, "Help us get the ball rolling." The consultant told the physicians: "I'll drive around town and see where we can put your hospital." It was, however, for naught. The consultant was a shyster, who skipped town with the money. Temporarily, efforts for the hospital were stymied.

Yet the incident put the idea of a Snellville hospital more in the minds for the seven doctors in town in 1976. They eventually talked with another consultant, and after first checking him out a little more thoroughly, and getting the nod of approval from the Snellville City Council, began an effort to secure a Certificate of Need for a hospital for their town. The consultant also had to get approval from two state agencies for the hospital.

The "original seven" doctors working to put the hospital together included Ed Bowen, M.T. Bagheri, Javad Deganian, Philip Edwards, Norman Freid, Robert Gadlage and Oscar Medina. For years all practiced in Snellville; Bowen died in 1998, and Medina moved out of state. The others continued to practice in the area or retired.

Many residents, when needing hospital services, were then being admitted to the closest modern hospital, DeKalb Medical Center, or other Atlanta area hospitals.

The key to the Snellville efforts was that there were no medical facilities of any description in the southern part of the county. With the area experiencing fast growth, more and better medical facilities were vital for the area's growing population.

Dr. Bagheri puts it stronger. "Working with the three hospitals in Gwinnett then in Gwinnett was a 'culture shock.' The system was definitely the 'good ole boys' who had done things one way for a long time. They resented us new fellows coming into the area. The people of the community were in need of a better hospital, and we as physicians were well accepted by the community in our practices."

This time, the efforts paid off. Working with Michael Sussman, a regional director for American Medicorp Inc. of Pennsylvania, after much paperwork and behind-the-scenes effort, state approval came and Gwinnett Community Hospital was formed. American Medicorp brought in as the first administrator David Harris, who had been working for them as administrator of the Sebastian River (Fla.) Medical Center. Harris came up for the groundbreaking, and began work in Snellville in January of 1978. This involved attracting the medical staff, selecting the equipment, and hiring the balance of the hospital staff prior to the opening of the hospital. The hospital rented quarters in a brick house at Wisteria Drive and Georgia Highway 124 until the hospital building was ready.

Harris was involved in continuous administrative detail, as he and the seven initial doctors in town met weekly at the Summit Chase Country Club to draw up the by-laws for the medical staff and hospital. The group went through by-laws from other area hospitals sometimes word-for-word. This group also was busy recruiting new doctors and interviewing physicians to staff the hospital's pathology, radiology, anesthesiology and emergency room departments.

Attracting new physicians to the new hospital was a major part of Harris' work. Harris says: "We started with a core group of seven well-qualified doctors, and we knew that attracting additional well-qualified physicians was the key to the eventual success of the hospital. Those seven doctors, plus the new facility, and the rapidly-growing population were all instrumental in attracting new doctors. Several physicians with offices near DeKalb Medical Center and Northside Hospital joined the medical staff, and were in Snellville at first for one or two or three days a week, but soon located their offices in the Snellville area." Several specialists were recruited directly from medical schools at Emory and Augusta. When the new hospital opened, there were over 50 doctors on the medical staff with 54 specialists, of which 35 had offices in Snellville. Through recruiting of medical specialists, by 1985 there were 98 doctors on staff, of which 55 had an office in Snellville.

Harris continued to attract medical doctors to locate in Snellville. He worked through local doctors, residents in training in medical schools or residence programs, and through the Humana Physician Recruitment Department in Louisville, Ky. Harris sent the Department a list of the key specialties that the Snellville hospital needed. In return, he got resumes of physicians interested in relocating to the Georgia area, and Harris would meet with these doctors. The majority of the new specialty physicians recruited to the Humana hospital in Snellville came directly from medical school residency programs.

Harris says: "Physician recruitment was rarely a problem for the Snellville Hospital, because of its modern facilities, emphasis on a well-qualified medical staff, and the expanding population of the area. These reasons insured that the prospective physician would be in successful practices in the South Gwinnett area."

Harris had another benefit in seeking physicians. "When our hospital was opened, we had a nicer hospital then than the other hospital in Gwinnett at Lawrenceville, since they were still in the Button Gwinnett building, and it made it easier to attract doctors. But then Gwinnett's Hospital Authority built a new hospital. Eventually we built our new hospital building, but then Gwinnett Medical Center expanded their facilities. The Medical Center is much bigger than Snellville is now." Harris would remain at the hospital through February, 1995, seeing it into a new building.

Groundbreaking for the first Snellville hospital was in October 1977, with Eighth District Congressman Ed Jenkins the speaker. The hospital located on the hill north of U.S. Highway 78 on Fountain Drive and was incorporated in March, 1978. But prior to the hospital opening, in 1979 the original owner, American Medicorp, was purchased by Humana Inc., the nation's second largest hospital corporation, and the hospital took on the name of Gwinnett Community Hospital when it was officially opened on January 2, 1980, with the first baby born there on January 2 to Mary and Larry Holcomb. He was named Eric Russell Holcomb. He and his mother still (2008) live in Gwinnett in Loganville. Mrs. Holcomb was the 13th patient admitted to the new hospital.

From the time it opened, the Gwinnett Community Hospital did well. Its beds were filled with patients, and the Snellville area began attracting many more doctors, including those with practices in such fields as gynecology, anesthesiology, and neurosurgery. Patients from all across Gwinnett started considering Snellville for any hospitalization.

With the success of the Snellville hospital, a major expansion was completed in 1985, and the name of the hospital was changed to Humana Hospital Gwinnett. This 1985 expansion served the community's medical needs until the early 1990s, when it was evident that another expansion was necessary. When hospital officials assessed the future medical needs of the community, they made a decision to replace the existing hospital facility.

Groundbreaking was April 7, 1993, for a new 245,456 square-foot hospital off Ronald Reagan Parkway. The property had once been the Clyde Williams farm.

However, just prior to the groundbreaking and during the construction period, another ownership change took place, and the hospital got a new name. In early 1993, Humana Inc. transferred ownership of the hospital to Galen Healthcare, but in September, 1993, Galen Healthcare merged with Hospital Corporation of America. It was at this time that the name of the hospital became Eastside Medical Center.

In 15 months after start of construction, an open house for the second hospital site in Snellville was held on Sept. 18, 1994, with the facility opening on September 21. Then in 1997, Hospital Corporation of America (HCA) became the sole owner of the hospital.

On February 1, 1999, HCA announced a partnership with Emory Healthcare for several Metro Atlanta hospitals. The change took place in 2000. With the restructuring, the Snellville hospital officially joined the limited liability corporation named EHCA, LLC. HCA was the owner, though it is operated under a lease from the LLC as Emory Eastside Hospital. Yes, it's confusing.

What the building of a hospital in Snellville did was attract a cadre of medical specialists to the area. From having a staff of approximately 50 doctors when it opened in 1980, as of January 1, 2007, there were 425 physicians on the staff of the hospital. It's a far cry from the early 1970s, when a handful of doctors found that their practices were limited because there was no hospital in the immediate Snellville area, and no specialists to take care of the needs of the growing population.

Les Beard became chief executive officer of Emory Eastside Hospital in 1995. He left the hospital in 2007. Then in early 2008, Kimberly Ryan, previously at Tulane Medical Hospital, became its chief executive officer.

Since being built, the Emory Eastside Hospital has been enlarged twice, and in 2007 had 200 beds. The hospital also continues activity at the former hospital site, the "Heritage" campus, which has 112,398 square feet, effectively operating as a dual campus. Among activities there are a Wound Clinic, Pain Center, Sleep Lab, and Mood Disorder Center, all outpatient services. Included as other services are a 20-bed in-patient Rehab unit, and a 61-bed in-patient senior mental health unit. The independent Gwinnett Community Clinic has space in the building. There is also Embracing Hospice, operated independently of the hospital, in the building.

An integral part of the hospital is its volunteer program. In 2007, Emory Eastside's 474 individual volunteers put in 62,193 hours of time to help the hospital and its patients in such areas as visitor waiting rooms, staffing the gift shop, operating coffee carts, checking blood pressures for visitors, and in health screening, among other areas of service to the community.

In early 2008, Emory Eastside Medical Center announced it was seeking a Certificate of Need for a $100 million expansion, which would bring the hospital 72 additional patient beds. Also included in the project was an expansion of acute care facilities, creation of additional parking, and construction of a third medical office building on the grounds of the hospital.

Gwinnett Medical Center

Recognizing the current serious need for additional public hospital facilities, and especially in view of the growth that was expected in Gwinnett, the Gwinnett Hospital Authority took a different path almost immediately after voters turned down the bond proposal for a new hospital. On Nov. 25, 1981, the Authority decided that since Gwinnett citizens would not support county-guaranteed bonds to finance a central hospital, the hospital itself would independently sell bonds backed by hospital anticipation revenues.

One guy said of this move: "The hospital went out on a big limb."

The upshot was that the Hospital Authority borrowed $37 million backed by hospital revenues it could generate, paying a higher interest rate than county-guaranteed bonds would have cost. Wayne Sikes, later chairman of the Authority, put it this way: "The voters didn't know what to do, and did not realize how seriously we needed the hospital. The Authority knew better, and saw the need and the opportunity."

Richard Sikes, who was on the Authority for 25 years, knew in his heart that the county needed the hospital, and went to the financial firm of Robinson-Humphrey in Atlanta, seeking the alternative financing. "They told us the only way we could sell bonds to build the hospital was to insure those bonds. Well, we didn't have money laying around for that, but we took some money we probably needed to use in other ways and backed the bonds. I think the insurance premium on the bonds cost nearly $1 million. But that way, Robinson-Humphrey could sell the bonds, and we could get a new hospital going."

Another former chairman, Jim Hinshaw, said it another way: "The Hospital Authority was in debt up to its ears. But this was the only real problem we had, and we went forward."

The chairman of the Authority in 2008, Wayne Sikes, says that the move back in the 1980s "…was an act of leadership by those hospital authority members of that day. After all, the voters had turned down the bond issue, and a politician would have said that they would not build a new hospital because the voters had spoken. But these were statesmen, people who were leaders, and they realized we needed to build a new hospital then for what growth they knew was coming."

Wayne Sikes

Sikes likes to point out to groups he speaks to around the county: "Twenty years later, the Hospital in just one year returned in indigent care alone to county residents $34 million (in cost), which was nearly as much as it cost to built the hospital in the first place. But we had to have the hospital first to provide that level of service. Those board members, Virgil Williams and Richard Sikes and Andy Andrews and all the rest, provided the good leadership that was needed, and serves us today."

Besides being chairman when voters made the decision to reject the hospital bond proposal, Virgil Williams in 1982 brought in Frank Rinker as president of the hospital. This was one of Williams' last acts as chairman, as Williams soon resigned from the Authority board. Rinker has been for 12 years vice president of the Charlotte (N.C.) Memorial Medical Center. A native of Augusta, he was a graduate of Emory University and had a master's degree and certificate in hospital administration from Queens College in Charlotte. Rinker, who would remain with the hospital for 23 years, found a hospital in desperate need of expansion, but he was not happy with plans that had been drawn for a central hospital.

Originally as designed, the hospital would have been a traditional horizontal, three-story red-brick hospital. Instead, the re-designed effort became an eight-story (plus equipment floor and basement) facility with 190 beds. Among the changes in the design were creating larger operating room and obstetrics facilities; arranging departments in a more efficient manner; putting the energy plant in its own facility for ease of expansion in the future; and adding a laundry for the facility.

Rinker brought in the architectural firm of Nix, Mann and Associates (later Perkins and Will) to redesign and enlarge the proposed hospital. As a result, a new Certificate of Need was not necessary. However, new plans had to be submitted to the State Health Planning Agency to make sure the plans complied with the previous Certificate. What came from the plans was the decision to build what became Gwinnett Medical Center.

The Authority had found a new site for the hospital in Lawrenceville. The Authority purchased 118 acres in Lawrenceville near Georgia Highways 316 and 120 for the new central hospital.

At its groundbreaking in August of 1983, then-Lt. Gov. Zell Miller told the audience: "Long ago, Hippocrates, the famous author of the Physician's Oath, said 'Healing is a matter of time, but it is sometimes a matter of opportunity.' Part of fulfilling that ancient oath is providing the opportunity, and that is what we celebrate here today."

The contractor hired to build the hospital was McDevitt and Street, which finished the building ahead of schedule and under budget. As with many projects, there were hitches along. An initial hold-up was obtaining a building permit. Since the hospital was to be in Lawrenceville, hospital officials sought a building permit from the City of Lawrenceville. But Lawrenceville officials balked, saying that they did not have staff expertise to inspect such a large project, and would not issue a permit.

Rinker asked for the city to give the Authority a letter rejecting their permit application. Since the hospital was under the jurisdiction of the state fire marshal, inspectors from the fire marshal's office came from the county and state as the hospital was being built. Prior to occupancy, another inspector, from the State Health Planning Agency, came to sign off on the new licensing of the hospital. Rinker remembers: "He asked to see our building permit, and I told him we didn't have one, and showed him the letter from the city. He knew the county fire marshal had been inspecting the construction as the hospital was being built. Finally, he said to me, 'Everything I can see is in order, and the state fire marshal has signed off on the entire project. Even though I've never done this before, I'll give you permission to open.' That's how we got our certificate of occupancy."

Shortly after the hospital opened, an elevator of the hospital lost electrical power and went into a controlled descent to the bottom floor of the hospital. One person claimed in a lawsuit against the hospital, which was dismissed, that she had been injured, and the story made the front page of a newspaper. The eventual cause was determined to be an interruption of electricity to the site. The computer controls sent the elevator, at normal speed, to the bottom floor. This became significant, for the hospital learned that the electrical power supplier, the City of Lawrenceville, had problems with supplying "clean" power to the site, which affected the computer controls. Eventually the City built an electrical sub-station near the hospital. A direct power electrical cable from the City's supplier, the combined Georgia Power-Municipal Electric Association of Georgia line, enters the substation, and a direct feed goes to the hospital. The city constructed the direct line underground, encased in concrete, to feed the hospital with power, insuring the hospital got "clean" power.

The new hospital completion time was set between Christmas and New Year's of 1984, the traditional time when the patient census is lowest, so that few patients would have to move. That day's entire Button Gwinnett Hospital bed census, a total of 20 patients, was transferred to the new Medical Center on December 29, 1984. The new hospital offered a broader range of services, with extensive medical facilities in Gwinnett, including medical, surgical, diagnostic and 24-hour emergency services. When the Medical Center opened, Button Gwinnett Hospital was closed.

The first birth at Gwinnett Medical Center was recorded the same day it opened, Dec. 29, 1984, at 4:52 p.m., as Courtney Lynn Bailey came into this world. Her parents are Mary and Glenn Bailey of Lawrenceville. The family got several gifts for her being the first born, including an engraved pewter cup. The first male born at the hospital was Cody Austin Maddox, the son of Runette and Gerald Maddox.

Before proceeding further, perhaps it is best to explain how the Hospital Authority operates. The Authority's nine-member board is appointed by the county commission. A change came in 1992, which many hospitals in Georgia have adopted: a lease of the publicly-owned hospital to a non-profit corporation originally created by the Hospital Authority Board. The Authority is the landlord and owns the property and originally leased the hospital to Gwinnett Hospital System, Inc. The Authority and non-profit Hospital System entered into a 40-year contract. This agreement was transferred to a unit of the System, called in 2008 the Gwinnett Health System Inc., a not-for-profit 501(c)(3) corporation, created to manage the hospital. This is a separately constituted legal entity whose sole mission is to operate the hospital. The Health System can enter into long-term contract and financing that the Authority, by law, cannot. The Health System gives the Authority quarterly updates on its efforts.

In 2008, the Health System board was composed of 16 persons, with two members of the Authority on the Health System board. Stephen Boyd is the chairman of the Health System board, the parent company of all the hospital activities and its subcorporations. This Health System Board is self-perpetuating and chooses its replacement members based on their qualifications and the expertise needed in certain areas.

The Gwinnett Health System has several subsidiary corporations, which perform different functions of the hospital, much like committees. Their members are appointed by the Health Systems board. (See Appendix B, page 740 for a list of members of these various entities.) By office, the Health System chairman (Boyd) is an ex-officio member of each of the corporate board. These subcorporations include:

• **Gwinnett Hospital System Inc.** This five-member body is appointed by the Health System chair. This is the group that essentially oversees 95 percent of the hospital activities, but owns no property. Steven Boyd is also chairman of this corporation.

• **Gwinnett Managed Care Inc.** This is another five-member body which deals exclusively with managed care for the hospital. The chairman is Dr. Jay Desai. It enters into agreements with insurance companies for bulk discounts.

• **Gwinnett Medical Services Inc.** A four-person body with Dr. Joseph Finley as chair. This company is the physician support and office management company, and employs medical doctors, nurses, and operates clinics.

• **Gwinnett Medical Properties Inc.** Another four-person body, this one chaired by Ed Radford, Ph.D., and is a real estate management firm for the hospital to lease space to doctors. From this income, this company must pay local taxes on its activities.

• **Gwinnett Medical Center Foundation.** This 22-person board is charged with raising money for the support of delivering health care. It is independent of any other corporations of the system. Chairing this board is Dr. Manfred Sandler. Mr. Boyd is not on this board, but the Health Systems is represented by Authority's chairman, Wayne Sikes, for continuity.

* * * * *

After its opening in 1984, a period of unprecedented growth began for both the Gwinnett Medical Center and the skilled, medical community around Lawrenceville. One of the early decisions was to work in creative ways to attract more medical specialty doctors to Gwinnett, since there were few medical specialists in the area immediately near the Lawrenceville hospital. The new Lawrenceville hospital, had, in 1984, a total of 205 doctors on its staff; in 2008, the hospital counted 767 medical doctors on its staff. Take a look at comparison budgets. The first full fiscal year operating as Gwinnett Medical Center, 1986, the budget was $45 million. For 2008, the budget was $562 million.

The Hospital Authority chose to work through its Foundation to construct a two-story office facility on its campus. The Foundation would use the building to attract doctors just out of residency programs and offer this space for their initial medical offices. The concept was that, after time in this building, the new doctor would feel his patient level was strong enough to go out on his own and open an office nearby and....most importantly.....remain in the community.

This is the way Gwinnett Medical Center drew many of its early cadre of medical specialists to the community. Tom Shepherd of the Medical Center was active in this effort. "We would tell them that we had space for them they could occupy immediately. We wanted to get them on their feet professionally, and use this building as an incubator facility. It worked beautifully for us to attract physicians for a while."

Though initially successful, the plan didn't last long. New regulations passed by Congress ultimately eliminated this method of attracting doctors. It was seen as a "patient steering" technique and forbidden by the Health Care Financing Administration, after action by Congress. But it served Gwinnett Medical Center well.

As a result, during the early days of the Gwinnett Medical Center, it was becoming a mecca for newly-minted doctors to locate their initial practice. Jim Hinshaw notes: "We were attracting doctors who saw that Gwinnett would be a fertile county for them to open their medical practice. Within two years after opening their offices, they would have a solid practice. Our incubator facility was a catalyst for them. We were attracting doctors from the Medical College of Georgia, Emory and other medical schools. Why, at one time, we had more new Emory Medical School graduates on our staff than Emory's hospital had."

Another reason for the success of the new doctors and for the Medical Center itself was its continued expansion. In 1988, the Authority opened Gwinnett Day Surgery in Lawrenceville. In 1988, it also converted a wing of the Joan Glancy Hospital in Duluth and retrofitted it into a rehabilitation center. It brought in Dr. Sunil Bnhole as a specialist in psychiatry (rehab medicine), who began a 20+ year stint with the Center and advanced the rehab program into a comprehensive inpatient program. Through his guidance, the program has won national acclaim and helped survivors of illnesses and injury return to their daily lives.

The year 1991 saw the construction of a 53,500 square-foot Women's Pavilion on the campus of Gwinnett Medical Center. It consists of 10 labor/delivery/recovery rooms, plus 34 private postpartum patient rooms. This was the first freestanding hospital dedicated to women's services in Georgia. It has been expanded four times and now consists of 70,808 square feet. In the first 10 years, 40,000 babies were born at the facility. Between 2001-2007, it saw the delivery of 40,826 more babies (in 40,596 deliveries, which means there were 230 multiple deliveries). In 1994, the Pavilion was expanded with a Neonatal Intensive Care Unit, while in 1998, a two-story 14,322 addition came with the re-designation of 15 existing acute beds at the Medical Center to the Women's Pavilion. The Women's Pavilion also houses the Breast Health Education and Resource Center for breast cancer patients, made possible by a grant from the American Cancer Society and the Gwinnett Hospital System Foundation.

With the explosive growth of Gwinnett's population in the mid-1980s, and the county not having sufficient space for governmental offices in Lawrenceville, the former Button Gwinnett Hospital was renovated to serve as the offices of the Gwinnett County commission and other administrative offices from the summer of 1986 to July 4, 1988. At that time the Gwinnett Justice and Administration Center (new courthouse) opened. Then the former Button Gwinnett Hospital sat vacant for two years. The 12.4-acre facility returned under the control of the Hospital Authority. On April 5, 1993, it changed the former hospital to a mental health and substance abuse treatment center, to be called Summit Ridge Center for Psychiatry and Addiction Medicine, the county's first psychiatric health care facility. The Center offers inpatient, partial hospitalization and outpatient programs.

Another innovation was begun in 1994 when Gwinnett Medical Center began a Parish (or Congregational) Nurse program, under the name of Congregational Health Ministry. The idea came to the hospital's president, Frank Rinker, from an old friend, Eugene Cochrane Jr., president of the Duke Endowment. The endowment had funded a parish nurse program in Charlotte, N.C. and Cochrane told Rinker about it. The Gwinnett Medical Center was the first non-religious hospital in the Southeast to begin the Parish Nurse program. Three churches at first participated in the program. Included among them was Hopewell Baptist Church, the first African-American church to have such a program. The Parish Nurse program has now been approved by the American Nursing Association as a specialty for registered nurses.

In 2008, there were 11 churches or groups participating in the program. The churches participating in the Congregational Health Ministry program include Duluth's First United Methodist, Snellville's First Methodist, Presbyterian Church of the Redeemer in Centerville, First United Methodist of Gainesville, First Baptist of Lawrenceville, Hopewell Baptist of Norcoss, Corpus Christi Catholic of Stone Mountain, First United Methodist of Norcross, Living Grace Lutheran of Tucker; and St. Pius X Catholic of Conyers. In addition, the hospital works with the Atlanta Baptist Association in a ministry for motorcyclists.

An addition to the Lawrenceville campus in 1997 was Gwinnett Extended Care, offering sub-acute and immediate care. The 33,375 square-foot facility came with nine private and 40 semi-private rooms, built to bridge the gap between levels of health care for those with acute illness or injury, but who do not need hospital care.

The Gwinnett Medical Center took a significant step on Oct. 11, 1994, when it joined with four other Metro Atlanta hospitals to form Promina Health Systems. This was a joint effort to consolidate services and pool purchasing to reduce costs. The System was also to negotiate for contracts with drug companies and health insurance providers under one umbrella for the five large hospital operations in Metro Atlanta. It also sought to attract system-wide managed care contracts.

Besides Gwinnett Health System, the other groups included were the DeKalb Health

System, Wellstar Health System (Cobb County), Southern Regional Health System and Piedmont Health System.

The amalgamation lasted 10 years. In the final analysis, the hospital executives could not work together as well as they had envisioned, and the combined efforts were abandoned. The Gwinnett system last operated as part of Promina in July 17, 2004.

Changes were about to come to the hospital facilities in Duluth. Beginning in 1995, the Authority opened a new facility called the Glancy Outpatient Center on a 27-acre tract off Pleasant Hill Road a mile from the Joan Glancy Hospital.

Some 11 years later, in 2006, the Authority built a new hospital for the Duluth area, on land adjacent to the Outpatient Center. This new facility was called Gwinnett Medical Center-Duluth. It consisted of 202,210 square feet, had 81 rooms, and cost $76 million. It was the first all-digital hospital in Georgia. It had expanded critical care and surgical facilities, a specialty-care Center for Orthopedics; wireless Internet for patients and visitors; filmless diagnostic services and an expanded emergency department. When this new hospital opened, the Joan Glancy Hospital, which had been the first hospital in the county, was no longer a hospital, though the Authority kept its 30-bed rehabilitation unit at that location.

By the year 2000, the hospital was continuing to grow, both in services offered, patient count and staff. Its staff had grown from 337 full-time and 546 part-time employees when it opened in 1984 to 3,166 employees by 2000, and by 2007, to 4,184 employees.

The year 2001 saw the Gwinnett Medical Center begin construction of a Support Services Building. It housed a Nutrition Center-Cafeteria; laboratory, outpatient treatment center and imaging facility, neuro-science center and administrative offices. Consisting of 75,108 square feet, it cost $23 million. Support Services forms the first three-floor base of the new North Tower, which opened in 2007.

With the continuing growth of the hospital and its staff, acreage became a new concern for the hospital. Seeing an opportunity, the hospital campus expanded across Pike Street to a former K-Mart location in 2003 to house non-medical aspects of the hospital, such as accounting, business, education and information technology departments. The 88,000 square-foot former retail center was on 7.56 acres, including a large parking area.

Another change in 2003 was the opening of the 575 Imaging Center on Professional Drive, which serves as the place for the outpatient diagnostic imaging activities. The hospital is a tenant in the facility.

In late 2006, the Authority announced the beginning of construction on a new 155-bed, 172,338 square-foot "North Tower" at Gwinnett Medical Center, scheduled for completion in 2009. Anticipated to cost $92 million, the eight-story tower features much larger patient rooms, including some rooms allowing family members to stay in rooms adjacent to patients. With the announcement of the new patient tower, plans were also put forward for renovation of the existing medical tower, to bring new health care advancement to the older rooms. There will also be decentralized nursing stations, four separate intensive care units in different specialties; and five specialty-care centers, in orthopedics and neuroscience, plus centers for joint replacement, spine and cardiovascular patients.

A breakthrough in relations between the Hospital Authority and the Gwinnett County Commission came in 2007, when the Commission voted to provide $5 million in

An architect's rendering of the nine-story Gwinnett Medical Center under construction in 2008

capital expansion funding for five years as part of the hospital expansion. The hospital also sought additional private community support from individuals and foundations.

Seeking to become a fully-functional hospital, the Authority in 2008 made application to perform open heart surgery. Though at first several other medical centers did not support the request, eventually opposition subsided. The hospital was approved for open heart surgery during 2008, with the program scheduled to be ready for patients as early as 2010. The hospital formed a collaborative relation with Saint Joseph's Health System to provide the program.

In September of 2008, the Gwinnett Medical Center sold its psychiatric hospital, Summit Ridge, to Universal Health Services of King of Prussia, Pa. Universal had operated six other similar hospitals in Georgia, in Atlanta, Dunwoody, two in College Park, Moultrie and Savannah. The Medical Center shed Summit Ridge in order to focus on acute care, diagnostics and outpatient care. The Medical Center had been operating at the former Button Gwinnett Hospital site as its psychiatric unit since 1993.

Hospital Auxiliary

Since 1984, Gwinnett Medical Center has an active Auxiliary program at both its Lawrenceville and Duluth facilities. In 2007, approximately 40,000 hours of time were logged by 250 members of its auxiliary, equivalent to having an additional 40 full-time staff. Volunteers cover the front desk, staff the hospital gift shop and the medical library, drive a courtesy cart for riders to the parking lot, and deliver flowers to patient's rooms. Proceeds from the gift shop are contributed to programs of the Hospital Foundation. Since it was founded, the Auxiliary has donated over $1 million to the system.

In 2008, officers of the Auxiliary were Phyllis Patterson, president; Carol Bullock, president-elect; Dorothy Walsh, vice president; Gloria Smallwood, recording secretary; Jodi Smith, corresponding secretary; Betty Walls, treasurer; Carole Martin, past president; and Cynthia Chandler, director of volunteer services.

One of the key volunteers of the hospital has been Ruth Ann Chapin of Duluth, who first became a member of the Auxiliary in 1997. She has been president of the Auxiliary on two occasions and is scheduled to be president again in 2010. She says of her activities at the hospital: "It's a way to give back to the community. My husband was hospitalized here on numerous occasions before he passed away. I saw the good that the Pink Ladies and the men in red vests do and joined them. Our volunteers are like an extra pair of hands for the nurses. We do whatever we're asked, whether it's help in admitting or discharging patients, taking samples to the lab, or just taking time to give people a smile, or to sit down with them, and hold their hand, and talk to them. The hospital staff does not have time do that. It's a way to give back and feel good about yourself."

The Auxiliary also raises money throughout the year, having special event sales for hospital associates for such things as uniforms or books. "It makes it convenient for the staff," Mrs. Chapin says. "We bring the vendors in, and the staff can buy at a discount, and the Auxiliary gets a commission." The Auxiliary raises approximately $150,000 a year in this manner, and puts the money right back in the hospital. Some of its purchases have included a Golf Cart for volunteers to use in transporting patients and visitors from the parking lot to the door, or vice versa; a see-through aquarium to decorate the Extended Care center; and a donation in 2007 of $50,000 toward the hospital's PATH project.

* * * * *

Dr. Miles Mason III, president of the medical staff of the Gwinnett Hospital System, is proud of the quality of the hospital system. He points out that the hospital ranks in the top five percent in the nation in clinical excellence and in pulmonary care. "The Gwinnett system was the first hospital in Georgia with a fully-accredited continuum of acute stroke care, and with an accredited chest pain center. We've won numerous awards, including the Beacon Award for critical care excellence. And this takes place while our emergency rooms see more than 100,000 patients per year. No other hospital in the nation has this many visits with the limited number of hospital beds we have."

Phil Wolfe, president of the Hospital system, foresees the need for even more hospital beds: "In 1984, when the Gwinnett Medical Center opened in Lawrenceville, the county population was 226,000 and there were 426 hospital beds. In 2008, in Gwinnett, with a population greater than 750,000, there are 611 hospital beds. That means there has been added only about 200 beds in 24 years. And we don't compare well with our neighbors in Cobb, for instance, with nearly 100,000 fewer residents, they have more than 800 hospital beds!"

Wayne Sikes, chair of the board of Gwinnett Hospital Authority, sees the continuing needs of the hospital: "We know that Gwinnett is growing faster than other counties, and it's the Authority's job to keep its health care facilities up to date with the latest procedures, techniques and facilities. We also must provide the service closest to population clusters, so we are constantly re-evaluating our priorities, and seeking to determine what we need to do next and where to do it. A hospital will thrive in a location for 50-75 years, much longer than commercial activities. We are now seeking where to locate the next hospital of our system to make sure that the people of Gwinnett have the best health care possible for years to come."

6

1980-1990

Four major changes in one year

1. Gwinnett gets its first mall

If ever there was a landmark year in Gwinnett's history, mark down 1984 as that year, as there were four major developments that substantially changed the county.

Perhaps most visible was the development of the first major shopping mall for the county -- Gwinnett Place. This opened on February 1, 1984. Scott Hudgens had put together land near Pleasant Hill Road and Interstate 85 for what would become the mall site. (It is located in the area which, before the mall, had been a mobile home park, and where a proposed area high school stadium had once been voted down in a bond referendum.) The site was highly accessible, and near the center of the county population – two major factors in its success. Anchor stores included Rich's, Macy's and Sears. Gwinnett shoppers also found that other major franchisees flocked to the land surrounding the mall, as it became a premier shopping destination for Gwinnett and Northeast Georgia. Another change: major restaurants flocked to the area, including some of the first in Gwinnett to sell mixed drinks. When the mall opened, Pleasant Hill Road had an average vehicle count of 3,500 automobiles a day. That figure in 2007 was 49,597 vehicles per day, according to John Karnowski of Street Smarts of Duluth.

Up until the opening of its first mall, Gwinnett had been the largest county in population east of the Mississippi River without a mall of its own. What the Hudgens interests opened was a 1.2 million square foot facility, with three major anchor stores -- at that time the largest mall in Georgia. It was incredibly successful from the beginning.

One reason was the loyalty that Gwinnett residents immediately gave the mall. After all, up until then, Gwinnett residents had to drive to distant Fulton or DeKalb County for major shopping purchases. With the new mall, they now had shopping close to home.

One saleslady at Rich's, one of the anchor tenants, and an Atlanta retail institution, told of a customer calling on the telephone soon after Gwinnett Place opened to ask if Rich's had a certain product at their Gwinnett store. "No, we don't have it here," she was told, "But we have it at another of our Atlanta locations." The customer replied: "But I don't want to buy it there. I want to buy it at my own mall." People felt an ownership in their new mall.

The mall developer, Scott Hudgens, had said that research had shown that a mall was needed for about every 250,000 people in a community. Mr. Hudgens had opened Gwinnett Place in 1984, when the estimated population of Gwinnett was 226,100.

Shortly after the opening of Gwinnett Place Mall, with other retailers seeing the throngs of people shopping there, out-parcels around the mall started filling. Soon most of the major retail chains and eateries in Metro Atlanta had a compelling central area in Gwinnett where they could locate their outlets.

Meanwhile, with Gwinnett continuing to grow quickly, before most residents realized it, developers began speculating on where another mall might be located in Gwinnett. There was speculation it could open in Snellville, the center of population most distant from Gwinnett Place. Without people realizing it, Scott Hudgens was already quietly purchasing land for a new mall.

This new mall was announced in March, 1995. It was developed as a partnership between Hudgens and an Atlanta Realtor, Ben Carter, who each owned 50 percent of the mall. As the mall was being built, they sold half their interest in the mall to Corporate Property Investors. However, prior to the opening of the mall, Corporate Property Investors sold their entire company to the Simon Property Group.

It was to be called the Mall of Georgia and would be built on Georgia Highway 20 between Interstate 85 and Interstate 985, near Buford. The location would be approximately 10 miles up Interstate 85 from Gwinnett Place, the distance mall operators deem acceptable from one shopping center to another.

The Mall of Georgia would be even bigger than Gwinnett Place. Its size was to be 1.5 million square feet, and would again give Gwinnett the distinction of having the largest mall in Georgia. In 2007, it is still the largest in the Southeast. This mall's anchor stores would be J.C. Penney, Lord and Taylor, Nordstrom and Dillards. Rich's became the fifth anchor store soon after.

The Mall of Georgia opened on August 13, 1999, which coincided with Scott Hudgens' 75th birthday. Hudgens had developed the first covered mall in Atlanta, North DeKalb Mall, in 1965, and had gone on to build malls in south Fulton County (Shannon), Savannah, Valdosta, Brunswick, DeKalb County (Belvedere), and Town Centre in Cobb County; plus he also remodeled Gainesville Mall. (See Chapter 1 for more about Scott Hudgens.)

A year after the Mall of Georgia was opened, when Gwinnett had approximately 600,000 people, another mall was soon to open, located between the Mall of Georgia and Gwinnett Place. It was located on I-85 at Sugarloaf Parkway, and would be called Discover Mills Mall. It was operated by The Mills Corporation, which has malls throughout the country, and has many discount merchants as tenants. Shoppers often arrive by bus from great distances to come to this facility.

This mall was built in a circular design. Walking its shopping circular corridor would take a person 1.2 miles. It consisted of 1.2 million square feet, and opened on November 2,

2001. One of its major tenants is Bass Pro Shops, which moved from Shackelford Road to the mall site. It is considered a "destination location," attracting customers from a wide area. Discover Mills opened with an 18-screen ATF motion picture facility, and many off-price outlets. A themed restaurant, Medieval Fair, opened at Discover Mills Mall in 2006.

In 1998, Simon Property Group (SPG) acquired 50 percent interest in Gwinnett Place Mall and the Mall of Georgia when it merged with Corporate Property Investors. This is also when Simon acquired Lenox Square, Phipps Plaza, Northlake Mall and 50 percent of Town Center at Cobb. Then in November, 2006, Simon acquired the remaining 50 per cent interest in the Mall of Georgia from Ben Carter, who was Scott Hudgens' partner, and had acquired Hudgens interest on Hudgens' death.

Then in early 2007, SPG acquired the Mills Corporation, which among other properties, included Discover Mills in Gwinnett. The Mills Corporation had also owned 50 percent of both Gwinnett Place Mall and Town Center at Cobb, giving SPG 100 percent of these centers. The upshot of the Mills Corporation purchase meant that Simon owned all of the three malls in Gwinnett County.

2. Three hospitals combined

Another change that 1984 produced was the combining of three different hospitals into one major central hospital system. The previous Button Gwinnett Hospital in Lawrenceville was closed, replaced by a 190-bed central hospital, now called Gwinnett Medical Center. The Joan Glancy Hospital in Duluth and Buford Hospital continued to remain open, though Buford was later closed. Eventually, the Duluth facility became a rehabilitation center.

Prior to 1984, the Button Gwinnett medical facilities were not considered up-to-date and modern by many residents. Many local citizens went to doctors in Metro Atlanta. However, the development of the new hospital in Lawrenceville, together with its many new advances in medical facilities, and its up-to-date equipment, began to attract more doctors and particularly specialists to the area.

The modern Lawrenceville Medical Center was a nine-story, 190-bed facility. In particular, with Gwinnett's fast growth, the hospital soon opened a wing of 49 additional beds in 1991 devoted entirely to childbirth. This Women's Pavilion soon began to set records in numbers of infants born there, and, since the year 2001, more than 5,000 births have been recorded each year.

The Medical Center opened its Summit Ridge Center for Psychiatry and Addiction Medicine in April 1993 on the campus on Scenic Highway in Lawrenceville where the Button Gwinnett Hospital once operated. It offers mental health and substance abuse programs for inpatient, partial hospitalization and outpatient programs for adolescents, adults, older adults and their families.

Gwinnett Medical System opened a second full-hospital facility in Duluth with a capacity of 81 beds in 2006, and is a replacement for the first hospital in Gwinnett, the Joan Glancy Hospital.

3. Opening of Gwinnett Tech

While the State of Georgia had technical schools in operation throughout Georgia, as late as 1983, there was no post-secondary technical school in Gwinnett County. With its fast industrial growth, businessmen in Gwinnett felt the need for their own technical college, but state officials gave them a deaf ear.

Under Superintendent Alton Crews, the Gwinnett School Board took action. It decided it would operate its own technical school, and in September 27, 1984, the system opened Gwinnett Tech on a 93-acre tract as a stand-alone campus alongside four-lane Highway 316 and what would become Sugarloaf Parkway, virtually in the center of the county. The first president of the school was Alvin Wilbanks, who later would become the county school superintendent.

From the beginning, Gwinnett Tech (as it became known) was a success. People in Gwinnett flocked to it to improve their skills, and enrollment grew quickly. Soon it would have the highest enrollment of any technical school in Georgia.

Launching its own technical school gave Gwinnett businesses an advantage by tailoring courses to local needs and producing graduates able to step directly into productive jobs with local employers.

Those graduating from Gwinnett Tech found jobs awaiting them. In one field in particular, those in medical-related training, 99 percent of students had jobs upon graduation, an attainment that has held for the last several years, and continues today.

Gwinnett Tech continued to expand course offerings and instructional facilities and buildings. Its vital role as a viable force in the community can be seen in this enrollment chart:

Year	*Credit Students*	*Others*	*Total*
1991	4,432	15,908	20,340
1995	5,461	15,083	20,544
2000	5,661	16,211	21,872
2005	7,380	14,476	21,856
2006	6,806	12,668	19,474
2007	7,102	12,985	20,087

The total enrollment also includes continuing education, GED and ESL students. The leveled rate of growth during recent years was affected by decreased funding for the college's English as a Second Language program and a decrease in contract training from 2002-2007, when companies were cutting their training budgets.

The percentage of growth in Gwinnett Tech's college credit courses from 1997-2007 has been 21.82 percent. The growth in online learning and in the health science fields has also been dramatic. Gwinnett Tech has one of the state's largest online enrollments among technical colleges, with more than half of all students in 2007 enrolled in online learning courses. The health care programs' enrollment has grown 121 percent in the last four years and constitutes 30 percent of the 2007 annual student population.

Gwinnett Technical College (GTC) plays a key role in workforce development for Gwinnett County businesses and industries. For more than 20 years, Gwinnett Tech has partnered with area employers to provide the highly skilled and trained workers they need to succeed. Gwinnett Tech met the workforce development needs of over 475 companies in one year (FY 06), training over 4,800 employees. GTC's customized training team and subject matter experts develop, deliver and monitor training programs specific to each company and industry, delivered on-site at the participating business or on the Gwinnett Tech campus and scheduled at the customer's convenience. Through Georgia's QuickStart program, many companies are eligible to receive free training through GTC.

Because of the increased cost of operating its own technical school, the Gwinnett School Board voted to transfer its technical school to operation by the Georgia Department of Technical and Adult Education in 2005. Today, all 34 technical schools in Georgia are under the direction of the state system.

In 1996, Sharon Rigsby Bartels who had been on the technical school staff as an administrator, followed Wilbanks to become the second president of Gwinnett Tech. The name of the college official changed in July, 2000, from Gwinnett Tech to Gwinnett Technical College, as other technical schools in the state system altered their names as well for consistency.

Gwinnett Technical College in 2007 was the largest technical college in the state, combining the students taking courses for credit, for continuing education and adult education. That totaled 20,087 students on its single campus. In that year, it had the largest program segments among the other state technical schools with 2,119 students in Health Sciences; 1,514 in Business and Finance; 548 in Computer Information Services; and 583 in its Construction program In 2007, it conferred the most certificates, diplomas and associate degrees in the state technical system (1,924), which was also the highest in Gwinnett Tech history. It also awarded the highest number of certificates (1, 345) and highest number of degrees (314) in the technical college system.

4. Major political upheaval

For many years, Gwinnett County, like most of Georgia, was governed by people tied to the Democratic Party. After all, most years there were few Republicans in Georgia, with the GOP being very much a minority party.

But it all changed in 1984. That election year, there were 17 positions up for election. Until that time, only a few Republicans had been elected in Gwinnett. (Louise Radloff was one of the first Republican office holders, being elected to the School Board in 1972. She was still in the same office in 2008.)

In 1984, Republicans, yearning for a change, fielded candidates for 16 offices in the fall election. Only Democratic Probate Court Judge Alton Tucker had no opposition. Few people gave Republicans much of a chance at victory. They were wrong.

Every Gwinnett Republican candidate, all 16, won their 1984 election, turning the Gwinnett political scene on its ear. Many were swept to victory in straight ticket voting, with Republicans having an 11,000 vote difference in straight party ticket voting. A new day had dawned for politics in Gwinnett.

The Republicans winning seats that year included:

- Clerk of Court, Gary Yates.
- Tax Commissioner, Katherine Sherrington.
- Surveyor, Carl McNally.
- Commission Chairman, Lillian Webb.
- District 1 Commissioner, Ken Suffridge.
- District 3 Commissioner, Mike Berg.
- District 1 School Board, Jeff Moore.
- District 3 School Board, Bobby (Bob) Wood.
- District 5 School Board, Louise Radloff.
- Coroner, Randy Simpson.
- Sherriff, Bobby Plunkett.
- District Attorney, Tom Lawler.
- House Dist. 60, Kerry Kay.
- House Dist. 61, Joe McLaughlin.
- House Dist. 62, Charles Bannister.
- Dist. 48 Senate, Jim O'Neill.

Charles Bannister

Since that time, few Democrats have raised their head to enter politics. And for years, every Democrat running was defeated. Democrats finally picked up a legislative seat in a heavily-minority area between Lilburn and Norcross in 1998. In the 2004 election, four Democrats won office, three state representatives and one state senator.

However, no Democrat has won county-wide office since 1984.

Interestingly, once it became evident that Gwinnett had become mostly Republican, many former Democrats suddenly changed parties. And as Republicans, they were in the majority and electable, which some had not been as Democrats.

While being a Republican worked in elections in Gwinnett up until 2004, those elected to the Legislature found that, with Democrats in control of both Senate and House, they could get little done for their county. Meanwhile, private businessmen used to access through Gwinnett Democratic officials, began to seek out state Democratic officials directly. Not only that, but these private businessmen began to be "players" in state activities, contributing heavily to statewide candidates, and becoming something of a force to be reckoned with in Gwinnett. For a while, with Democrats in control of the Capitol, there was more power exercised by private Gwinnett businessmen than elected officials.

All this changed, however, in 2004 with the election of the first Republican governor since Reconstruction in Georgia. While the state Senate had become a majority Republican body in 2002, now all three---the governor's office, House and Senate---were controlled by Republicans.

It brought smiles to Gwinnett Republican officials, now the gatekeepers of political power with access to state officials. Gwinnett had joined with other suburban counties to form a Republican "doughnut" surrounding the Democratic City of Atlanta.

How Gwinnett got its courthouses

The 1885 courthouse, on the square in Lawrenceville, was to serve until 1988, when the Gwinnett Justice and Administration Center (G-JAC, the new courthouse) was opened.

The first courthouse in Gwinnett had been built in 1824, and cost $4,000. It served the county until 1871, when it burned. The fire is the key reason most Gwinnett County records only go back to 1871.

It took until 1883 before a new courthouse was built. However, soon it was considered "inadequate." We know no more than that one word as the reason the local governing body tore down the 1883 building, and erected in 1885 the present Historic Courthouse, for a cost of $23,083. It would serve for 103 years as the seat of Gwinnett government through the early growth years, until 1988, when the Gwinnett Justice and Administration Center opened.

A modification to the Historic Courthouse came in 1908, when the county commissioned the building of a clock tower, housing a giant Seth Thomas clock. This new venture cost Gwinnett citizens $4,000, and completed the original building, giving it a new appearance with its tower and clock.

By the mid-1960s, Gwinnett governmental offices had long outgrown the courthouse. The county had expanded into many offices throughout Lawrenceville. The former school building "on the hill" on Oak Street began to be filled with offices for county governmental operations. The county commission moved its offices there. The county had even taken over the former gymnasium and other out-buildings for the office space the growing county government needed.

Other buildings in Lawrenceville found new uses, as county government spread to rent any available space. The courts soon had offices in a converted furniture store, in a former theatre and at one time in a former supermarket. It was obvious that the county courthouse was far beyond its capacity, and also obvious that the county could benefit by bringing its many offices under one roof.

But how to pay for such a structure? That was a major question.

The answer is still contributing mightily to Gwinnett's infrastructure today, in more than one way. It was the change in Georgia law on July 1, 1985 to allow counties to levy a penny in sales tax, under what would be called a "special purpose local option sales tax," or SPLOST. Up until that time, only the state could levy a sales tax, with no provision by law for counties to collect such a tax. As some form of the local option sales tax came into being, it has become a virtual fixture in counties throughout Georgia, with the monies dedicated to infrastructure purposes, not annual operating costs.

A key provision of the SPLOST programs is that the tax is for a specific period not to exceed five years, and that tax must be levied for specific purposes, a list which must be included in the vote on the provision. Not only that, the collection of the funds must not exceed the stated amount within this time frame.

With the county cramped for space in 1985, the county commission, while Lillian Webb was chairman, proposed a $57 million program for building a new courthouse, labeled the "Gwinnett Justice and Administration Center," which later had the handle

"G-JAC" applied to it. This proposal said that funds raised by the tax would be used to build a new courthouse on a 61-acre plot near the center of Lawrenceville. It was to be a four-level (three stories and basement) facility, a linear structure measuring 816 feet long and, containing 508,000 square feet. Anticipation was that the county would build a three-story building, but furnish only two floors in the $57 million proposal. The third floor was for expansion later.

When the initial sales tax vote were counted, the SPLOST passed overwhelmingly, 18,188 to 2,372. It was a major victory for the Webb Administration, and for Gwinnett, and was a forerunner of other victories for the one cent sales tax in years to come.

That's not the end of how Gwinnett got the funds to complete its G-JAC center, however. The robust economy in Gwinnett started pouring in the pennies to governmental coffers at a fast pace. Gwinnett and Georgia were new at SPLOST sales tax collections, and also new at knowing how to stop it. By the time Gwinnett realized it had collected the $57 million to erect the courthouse, and then by the time they took action at the end of a calendar quarter to stop its collection, the levy had produced $69 million in revenue. With interest, the collection was $72 million. With these added funds, the county could pay cash for the structure, finish the third floor, and occupy it. The county officially moved into the Gwinnett Justice and Administration Center on July 4, 1988, when a time capsule was sealed at the dedication ceremony.

(Figures on collections come through the State of Georgia Department of Revenue, and take several months after the actual collection for the collection statistics to arrive at county government level. Then, in taking action to stop the tax, it must come at the end of a quarter, and retailers must reprogram their procedures. Hence, the over-collection to $69 million.)

Since the first SPLOST, county government has had five more SPLOST programs, starting in 1988, 1992, 1997, 2001, and 2005. Through May 2006, this one-cent tax has brought in just over $1.5 billion from all six programs for county government operations.

Here is a re-cap of the SPLOST campaigns in Gwinnett:

Year	*Program*	*Projected Revenue*
1985	Construction of G-JAC	$65 million
1988	Road, Street, Bridge Projects	$92 million
	Construction of Civic Center	$30 million
	Historic Courthouse Preservation	$3 million
	Construction of Pre-trial Detention Center (jail)	$37.5 million
1992	Road, Street, Bridge Projects	$249 million
1995	Road, Street, Bridge Projects (defeated by 329 votes)	$675 million
1996	Parks & Recreation Projects	$60 million
	Public Safety Projects	$60 million
	Road, Street. Bridge Projects	$294 million
2001	Parks & Recreation Projects	$212 million

	Libraries	$12 million
	Public Safety Projects	$59 million
	Road, Street, Bridge Projects	$212 million
2005	Parks & Recreation Projects	$162 million
	Libraries	$12 million
	Public Safety Projects	$79 million
	Road, Street, Bridge Projects	$162 million
	Cities' Shared Allocation	$89 million

On one occasion, Gwinnett voters rejected a SPLOST proposal. That was in a Special Election on Nov. 7, 1995, when Gwinnett voters defeated an extension of the added penny, which was proposed only for road construction, by a thin 329 vote margin, 18,371 being against, and 18,042 being for the move. Only 17.78 percent of Gwinnett registered voters came to the polls that day.

County officials came back the next fall in the General Election asking approval of another SPLOST, and included not only roads, but also included public safety and recreation facilities in the proposal, which passed. Gwinnett citizens approved the plan, though not by a large majority. Of the 159,509 voting, some 53 percent (84,928) approved the 1997 SPLOST vote in Gwinnett. (Since the 1995 special election, where the SPLOST was the only issue on the ballot, Gwinnett County has asked voters for SPLOST approval only in General Elections, where a wider turnout is anticipated.)

Educational circles saw benefit in the sales taxes for county government, and in 1996, Georgia voters amended the law to allow the school board to have their own E-SPLOST to construct school buildings. This additional penny sales tax for educational infrastructure began in Gwinnett in 1997.

Through June of 2008, this penny has amounted to more than $1.3 billion to the

The Gwinnett Justice and Administration Center (G-JAC)

Gwinnett School Board for funding its continuing infrastructure needs for additional classrooms and schools. The approval of the 2006 E-SPLOST could net Gwinnett schools another $850 million through 2012.

In 2006, Gwinnett's courthouse was getting to be crowded, even though several departments had relocated to other space in town. The county purchased a building adjacent to the G-JAC at Crogan and Langley Streets (One Justice Square), a 100,000 square foot office building now housing several county departments, including Planning and Development, Fire Marshal, offices for the Georgia Department of Family and Children Services, and a state Office of Child Support Services.

A Court Annex on Stone Mountain Street houses the Recorder's Court and Juvenile Court. This building was opened in January 2006, and has 107,531 square feet. It is adjacent to the former Gwinnett Federal Savings building on Perry Street, which the county bought in November 1997, and it houses the Lawrenceville Tag Office, Business License, Police Permitting, Human Resources Training, Gwinnett Clean and Beautiful, GUIDE, the Coalition for Health and Human Services and other county offices. It has 34,424 square feet of space.

In 2005, the county purchased a former 134,982 square foot Wal-Mart on Clayton Street east of downtown for the departments of Elections, Records Management, Public Health Clinic, Environmental Health and for storage.

Meanwhile, constitutional officers (clerk of court, probate judge and sheriff) needed additional space, with some offices occupying former open and hallway areas. The exploding population creates more activities, which mean more personnel are needed, as well as space for them. It's a cycle Gwinnett's government has seen for the last 50 years, and will no doubt face in its future.

It brings to mind the response from the judges of Gwinnett in 1849 wanting a fence around the courthouse. "Where's the money to come from?" is still a big question in Gwinnett.

Gwinnettians value their libraries

People in Gwinnett appreciate their libraries. That can be seen by the continual strong use the Gwinnett libraries get.

In fiscal year 2007, for instance, there were 3.6 million visits to a Gwinnett County library, with these patrons checking out more than 6.4 million books, books on tape or CD, DVDs, videos, music CDs for children, and downloadable audio books, videos and music. They keep busy on more than 383 computers now available to library patrons. Joining the modern era, the Gwinnett County Public Library counts 2.4 million remote log-ins into the virtual library, its patrons going on-line for research of all kind!

This growth has been unusually spectacular. For instance, in 1968, annual circulation at the library was 261,968. Compared to 2007, that makes an increase in growth 25 times what it was in 1968. (See Appendix B, page 674 for library usage, and page 673 for growth of library facilities.) That's not all. Questions are routinely posed to the reference librarians, with 444,340 questions answered during a recent year.

Consider libraries in another manner. If all those people borrowing books, tapes, and other media purchased those items instead of borrowing them through the library, in FY 2007 that would have amounted to spending of $172.8 million. That translates into $221 per capita for Gwinnett, or $582 per customer. That compares to the tax for library funding per capita of $22.50.

For 2007, the library recorded 296,582 cardholders, with 63,500 new customers registered during the fiscal year. The average customer checked out 22 items during the year.

The usage of the library gives some hint about how popular it is with its cardholders. The group can be a powerful one in elections, with indications that this group participates in county elections to a high degree. Some even give the library patrons the credit for propelling Gwinnett County into the modern era by their support of overall county proposals. Case in point: in 1986, a $16 million library bond proposal was on the ballot for Gwinnett voters. Also on the ballot that day was a proposal for a $90 million road program.

The library bond proposal sailed through the election easily, 10,475 votes for to 6,004 against. While the road bond also passed, it had a smaller margin of victory, 9,511 to 6,964, showing 964 more "yes" votes for libraries than roads. Many felt the large number of people voting came primarily because of efforts by the library patrons to get their measure passed. The turnout that day was 17 percent of the voters registered.

Gwinnett has not always had fine library facilities. Its first library dates back to 1907, in Norcross, which was open on Friday afternoon in a small room of the Norcross public school. In 1909, it was relocated to the Masonic building, with free rent provided by the Masonic Lodge. Another move, in 1919, took the library to the Medlock building, with the rent of $13.50 a month paid by the Woman's Club. By then it was opened two afternoons a week.

The Norcross Woman's Club sought the help of a native son who made a fortune on Wall Street, Edward Buchanan, for their first library building. Mr. Buchanan contributed $100, a significant sum then, to help open the library in 1907. All along, he kept an interest in the library, later donating funds which helped erect the first library building in the county across from Thrasher Park, dedicated on June 21, 1921.

Mr. Buchanan later contributed $2,500, wanting the city to have a library building of its own. Then Mr. Buchanan's fortunes fell, and he died in 1910. It was not until 1919 that the library board secured a lot for a building on North Peachtree Street. When a year later work was begun, the original Buchanan gift had grown to more than $4,000. The library was dedicated on June 18, 1921. There were 2,500 books in the library when it opened. The Norcross Library joined the Gwinnett County Public Library system as a branch in 1957. By 1996, it housed 24,000 books and had 1,368 registered members of the library. This library was moved in 1971 to a former Southern Bell building on Carlyle Street, where it remained until Gwinnett voters passed funding for eight new libraries throughout the county in 1986, with the modern Norcross library opening in 1990 on Buford Highway. The former North Peachtree Street library is now owned by and houses the Norcross Woman's Club.

The first record of a library in Lawrenceville dates back to 1935, when the beginnings of a library were established----on a shelf at City Hall, through efforts of the Lawrenceville Parent-Teacher Association and its president, Mrs. R.H. Sams. This was during Depression times, when many could not afford to buy books. One person of the community told Mrs. Sams: "I liked to read; my children liked to read; the school library was not adequate; and the only way to get books was to buy them, which nobody could afford."

Hours of operation at the library were simple: 4 to 6 p.m. each Monday to Friday. Furniture for that library came from Parent-Teachers Association fundraising, including sponsorship of a basketball game and a "womanless wedding." The Lawrenceville Kiwanis Club helped in securing members.

Funds came slowly. Here's the method used to help pay for books for that early library. The newest books of the day were on a rental shelf, renting for 10 cents a week, or two cents a day, until the cost of the book was met. Afterward, the book was placed on the regular shelf, and could be checked out without charge. In its first annual report, it reported having 577 volumes, and circulated them 5,800 times to the 420 registered borrowers.

The library in Lawrenceville became the Gwinnett County Library, when, on Nov. 3, 1936, the County Commission and Board of Education jointly agreed to establish it. Two members were appointed by the School Board and one by the county. Its second location, secured in 1936, was at the Gwinnett County Courthouse, in one room on the ground floor (second room to the left when entering from the north entrance.) J. Heard Summerour of Duluth was the board chair, and the other two members were Marvin Allison of Lawrenceville and T.E. Johnson. In 1940, Mr. Allison became chairman, and served in this position until his death in 1959.

The county library began its bookmobile (originally called "Book Truck") service in 1940, traveling eight different routes around the county every two weeks. A new feature in 1942 was the addition of a Story Hour. The library qualified for purchase of books through the Georgia State Board of Education in 1944.

Space again and again was the major problem over the years for the Gwinnett library, as it sought to keep up with county growth. Even as far back as 1945, a report said of the library's one room at the courthouse: "Books fill all the shelves, are piled on tables, and placed under desks when no other space is found." The crowding of books into every nook and cranny available would be seen in Gwinnett County library facilities for years. By 1947, it had over 9,000 books in about 300 square feet.

After World War II in 1947, the library expanded -- to two rooms of about 600 square feet in the courthouse, moving across the hall. A further expansion came in 1951, when the library moved to its first dedicated facility, a completely remodeled building on the northeast corner of the Courthouse Square, which has previously housed *The Gwinnett Journal*. It had 920 square feet, and would soon become crammed with books.

The State Board of Education encouraged smaller libraries to merge into regional systems, which Gwinnett and Forsyth libraries did to form the Gwinnett-Forsyth Regional Library on June 1, 1956. Two years later, Dawson County came into the system, and since Lake Lanier was common to all three counties, it chose the name of Lake Lanier Regional Library.

In 1957, the Lawrenceville library found additional space near the American Legion post on Athens Highway, consisting of two buildings, one used primarily for cataloging, and the other for the new bookmobile. One official termed these facilities as "far from luxurious." Also in 1957, the Norcross Library joined the regional system.

By 1962, a newspaper article called Gwinnett's main library (in its 1951 building of 920 square feet) the "poorest housed library in the state." By then, Gwinnett had 48,195 residents.

Lawrenceville library officials and patrons were thrilled in 1965 when the library was moved to space 10 times its previous location…the former Lawrenceville Presbyterian Church at 221 Clayton Street. This location was just a half block from its former site at 103 Pike Street. It now had 3,854 square feet, and counted an inventory of approximately 39,000 volumes. Realizing the space would soon be full, the staff had a sign saying "Temporary Headquarters" at the front entrance.

The cities of the county needed more library services. The City of Buford agreed to join the system in 1967, and a branch was opened there. (*Flanigan's Gwinnett History* noted that in 1942, Buford had a library of 2,700 volumes. But that is the only mention of a library in Buford.) Library branches were opened in 1968 in Lilburn and Duluth, while additional branches were opened in Snellville and the community of Mountain Park in the 1970s.

Meanwhile, the Lawrenceville library continued to need more space, and soon moved to its sixth location. That move came in 1977, also to a former Southern Bell building, on Perry Street, which consisted of 4,546 square feet. This was more space that it had ever commanded which, with the growth of the county, was soon obviously also inadequate.

The start of the modern Gwinnett Public Library can be traced to the defeat of a library bond referendum in 1982. Voters were asked to approve a $4 million measure for library bonds, to provide for six libraries consisting of 7,500 square feet each, and another of 10,000 square feet to be the library headquarters. Voters rejected this proposal, to the surprise of many, by a vote of 2,570 against the proposal, to 1,438 for it.

However, that defeat in 1982 re-invigorated many library supporters. The Library Board four years later (1986) asked the people of Gwinnett to vote again on library bonds, this time on a package four times bigger, at $16 million. Voters easily approved this measure, by a margin of 9,511 to 6,004 (64 percent in favor). And, in effect, Gwinnett County was not only on the way to expand to eight new library facilities, but set the tone for years to come. It was also on the path toward progressive library developments since the county leaders understood how important voters thought libraries were. As more library buildings were needed, the county included libraries as part of the SPLOST programs in both 2000 and 2004.

In the 1986 bond vote, that $16 million library expansion included new libraries in Lawrenceville, Norcross, Buford-Sugar Hill, Lilburn, Duluth, Mountain Park, Snellville and Peachtree Corners. As the county grew more into outlying areas, libraries would be added in subsequent years on Five Forks Road near Ronald Reagan Parkway, and at Collins Hill, Centerville, Suwanee, Dacula and Grayson. In 2008, an ecologically-friendly, 20,000 square feet library in the Hamilton Mill area began construction and is expected to be open in 2009, to be located near the new Duncan's Creek Park at 3690 Braselton Highway. It will be the 15th library in the system. The county has also purchased land for a Peachtree Ridge Library, which will bring the number of locations for the library system to 16. This library site is at Sever and Lebanon Roads, on the Lawrenceville side of Interstate 85.

The Gwinnett County Public Library also has an intergovernmental agreement with Gwinnett Technical College to staff and operate the library at the college. Gwinnett Tech funds the positions and buys materials, but the staff is hired by the Library system.

Looking back on that 1982 referendum, in which the voters rejected a $4 million bond for libraries, some consider that rejection as good. They point out that had it passed, the smaller library program would have proven to be a disaster for the system, since it would have built much smaller facilities, which would have been inadequate by the time they were opened.

Meanwhile, the Lake Lanier Regional Library system was continuing to grow quickly. Items checked out exceeded four million in FY 1994, giving this library system the distinction of having the largest circulation of any library system in the state.

Then two moves came about. Dawson County joined the Chestatee Regional system on July 1, 1994, resulting in the Lake Lanier system becoming the Gwinnett-Forsyth Regional Library System again. But two years later, on July 1, 1996, the partnership between Gwinnett and Forsyth Counties was dissolved, and two independent public libraries were formed. So the name "Gwinnett County Public Library" returned. Another major change in 1996 was the Gwinnett library started to offer Internet access, including the virtual library, GALILEO, at all branches.

Persons who have headed the Gwinnett library include:

Mrs. J. Terrell Jackson, 1935-39.
Mrs. Bertha P. Sears, 1940-43.
Cora W. Holland, 1943-53.
Mrs. Ethlyn R. Rolfe, 1953-54.
Erwin E. Mapp Jr., 1954-62.*
Mrs. Robert L. Leroux, 1962 through August 15, 1978.*
John Shelton, August 15, 1978 until March 29, 1991.*
Jo Ann Pinder, April 1, 1991 until June 12, 2006.*
Nancy Stanbery-Kellam, began June 15, 2006.
* Also director of Regional Library

A clean county is a better county

One of the most innovative ventures in Gwinnett is a quasi-governmental endeavor, which operates as a 501(c)(3) non-profit organization, known as Gwinnett Clean and Beautiful (GC&B). Organized by the County Commission in 1980, it grew out of a 1979 meeting of 57 Gwinnett citizens, who discussed the problem of illegal dumping and littering in the county.

Since its official inception on March 19, 1980, with a 30 member, county-wide board of directors, it has put forth four broad goals to:

- Promote public interest in the environment of Gwinnett County.
- Initiate plans and coordinate programs for litter control.
- Improve the sanitation and cleanliness of the county.
- Recommend plans for improvements to beautify the county.

The program has been extremely successful, as the State of Georgia has adopted many Gwinnett programs and regulations for the entire state. In the meantime, the Gwinnett Clean and Beautiful efforts have been recognized often for state and national achievements by setting high standards and getting results.

These accomplishments have come as GC&B successfully partnered with key elements of the community to forge a team approach to attacking litter and striving for a clean community. These elements included government, schools, business and industry and a broad program of citizen input. Its early program for voluntary recycling has been recognized as a model for duplication throughout the United States.

GC&B took the initiative in promoting key quality of life issues, such as attacking graffiti and promoting more greenspace for the citizens. In its 25 years of existence, GC&B garnered more than 75 state and national awards for its efforts. It has been a leader in the Keep America Beautiful campaign, and has been recognized for helping to build and sustain practices, which benefit the community.

While about 27 percent of the budget for Gwinnett Clean and Beautiful comes from the county treasury, it generates funds through recycling and also gets corporate and individual contributions. Recycling alone generates roughly 55 percent of its $2.4 million budget, as of 2008, while private and corporate contributions are 18 percent.

While it has a small full-time staff, it runs an enormous program through two manpower sources: county prisoners and community service workers working out their sentences in court. In early 2007, approximately 60-70 prisoners were working each week, putting in 40 hours, while between 400-600 community service people were also contributing their time to the program. The GC&B's full time staff numbers 10 persons, plus another three correctional officers.

Gwinnett's Clean and Beautiful program began recognizing key firms and individuals of the county making significant contributions to the county in 1981.

Gwinnett Clean and Beautiful operates two recycling banks. The first one opened in 1986 on Satellite Boulevard near I-85 in Duluth, while a second center, primarily for commercial paper and cardboard, was opened in 2006 in Lawrenceville on Seaboard Industrial Way, near Briscoe Field. Recycled waste is sorted and bundled at these sites for resale.

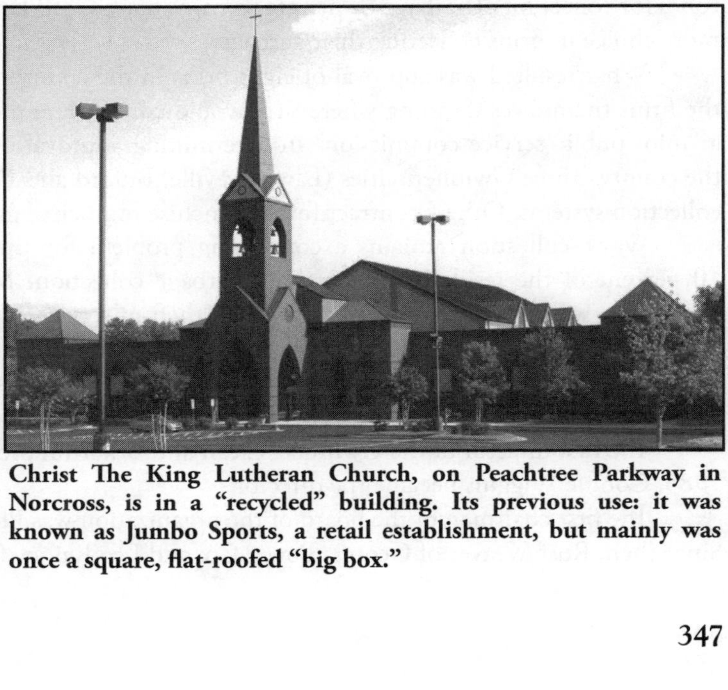

Christ The King Lutheran Church, on Peachtree Parkway in Norcross, is in a "recycled" building. Its previous use: it was known as Jumbo Sports, a retail establishment, but mainly was once a square, flat-roofed "big box."

Around 1985, two GC&B volunteers, Hill Jordan and Jim Steele, brought up the subject of litter in the community,

Connie Wiggins

and wrote regulations that Gwinnett County adopted concerning litter. Key elements of that wording became part of the state litter laws. One key feature, a new way of thinking for the state, is that if litter is found illegally dumped, and there's information that can be traced back to an individual, it's assumed that the person named is the person responsible for the illegal dumping, and court action can be taken. After the Gwinnett regulation was adopted, State Sen. Steve Reynolds of Gwinnett and Rep. Dewey Dobbs of Newton County introduced and passed similar language to combat illegal dumping statewide.

Around 1984, GC&B began a program of collecting Christmas trees for recycling. Two years later, in 1986, Gwinnett began a program of chipping those trees into mulch for use in parklands of the county. Ever since 2000, Gwinnett has led the state in the number of Christmas trees it recycles in its "Bring one to the chipper" program.

In late 1990, GC&B spearheaded the writing of the county's solid waste plan and developed a new system for garbage collection. Previously, Gwinnett had approved franchised zones for collection of garbage by private firms. What GC&B heard was that citizens wanted more choice in firms collecting their garbage.

What resulted was approval of eight firms in the county for garbage collection, with the firms themselves deciding where they would concentrate their efforts. GC&B serves as a "mini public service commission" in determining approval of waste collection firms for the county. Three Gwinnett cities (Lawrenceville, Buford and Dacula) run their own waste collection systems. Others contract for or franchise municipal garbage collection.

Waste collection remains a continuing problem for the county, as approximately 10 percent of the residents do not have garbage collection. Many dump in commercial containers, which is illegal, in effect, as it's a "theft of service." Illegal dumping, it has been found, also encourages and contributes to additional crime in a community. As of 2008, the garbage collection system was under review by Gwinnett C&B, with anticipation of additional recommendations to the commission for their consideration.

The first director of the Gwinnett Clean and Beautiful program was Tine Liegerot. In 1985, Connie Wiggins became the director.

The first chairman of the board of the organization was Philip Reed of Southern Bell. Since then, Russ Weaver of Georgia Power Co. and Leo Rainey (1988) of the First National

Bank of Gwinnett have been board chairs. Jim Steele, COO of the Gwinnett Schools System, has served since 1990 as board chair. A virtual who's who of Gwinnett leaders have been board members of Gwinnett Clean and Beautiful since it was formed.

In June 25, 2008, the Recycling Bank structure on Satellite Boulevard was destroyed by what appeared to be an accidental fire of an undetermined origin about 9:45 p.m. Three buildings were completely destroyed, with the loss estimated at between $5 and $6 million. Officials said they expected the Recycling Bank to be rebuilt at the same location.

The County Commission in 2008 also approved plans for a new recycling facility in Lawrenceville. It is expected to cost $14 million, and is designed to handle 100,000 tons or more annually. It will also increase, from 7 to 35, the type of recyclables handled. It will be built on Cedars Road between Georgia Highway 316 and U.S. Highway 29. GC&B anticipates erecting a third recycling facility in northern Gwinnett in the future.

* * * * *

Significant milestones of the Gwinnett C&B program are:

1980 Certified as a Keep America Beautiful affiliate.
Developed slogan, "Put the Lid on Litter."
1981 Began newspaper and aluminum recycling.
1982 Began glass recycling.
Formed teacher advisory board.
1984 Opened Recycling Center in Buford;
Initiated recycling at Technology Park.
1986 Opened Recycling Bank of Gwinnett.
1987 Held first Public Lands Day at Tribble Mill Park.
1989 Conducted solid waste handling strategic planning.
1991 Began curbside recycling with private haulers.
Developed solid waste collection system and ordinances.
1992 Expanded Recycling Bank to intermediate processing.
1994 Held grand opening of Tribble Mill Park.
1995 Expanded recycling to include junk mail and telephone books.
1997 Initiated first graffiti prevention program in Metro Atlanta.
1998 Opened paper sorting facility at Recycling Bank.
1999 Revised county tree ordinance.
2000 Began Annual Governor's environmental address.
First year recycled most Christmas trees in Georgia.
2002 Initiated "Graffiti Busters" program.
2003 Re-constructed Phase 1 of Recycling Bank.
2004 Conducted school waste stream audit.
2005 Launched Operation Fixing Broken Windows.
2006 Opened new commercial recycling facility in Lawrenceville.

The New York trip–a bond adventure

It started out innocently enough.

Seeking to ensure a good rating for bonds sold by Gwinnett County, representatives from the county commission would visit New York bond rating firms on selected bond issues, every year or so. On some years, representatives from the bond houses would visit with county officials in Gwinnett.

The county wanted the highest bond rating possible, so that the interest rate that the county was charged would be low, meaning a lower cost to the county treasury to service the bonds. Meanwhile, communicating was necessary so that the bond rating houses (Standard and Poor's and Moodys) would better understand the local situation. These communications and face-to-face meetings between the county and the bond houses had been going on since the county started bond issues. During the 1973-80 years, the chairman and executive assistant of the county commission had ventured to New York to make the presentation on one day trips.

In late 1984, just after she had been elected the chair of the Gwinnett County Commission, Lillian Webb was invited to make such a trip, suggested by then-chairman Charles Ashworth as a courtesy, since Mrs. Webb would be taking office January 1, 1985. Ashworth told her that while in New York, they would not only meet with the bond houses, but also take in some plays. He said that the cost of the trip "would be taken care of." Mrs. Webb says that even on that first trip in 1984, her husband, Jack, was concerned about who was paying for the trip. However, Mrs. Webb was assured that it had been done before, and was legitimate, and thought no more about it.

For the 1984 trip, the county was seeking to get a rating on a $35 million water-sewer bond being issued. On a trip in 1985, the bond was for $207 million, again for water-sewer projects. There were 14 people from Gwinnett on the 1984 trip, and 16 people from the county on the 1985 trip. The 1984 trip had the participants staying at the Helmsley Park Lane Hotel on Central Park South, while the 1985 trip participants were housed at the Waldorf-Astoria Hotel.

By the time a meeting with the bond houses was scheduled in February 1988, the number of people going on the trip had grown considerably. Details of the trip and reservations were handled by the county's bond counsel, Lex Jolley and Company of Marietta, including making air and hotel reservations. Those making the trip looked upon it as a "perk" of office being paid by the bonding company.

For the 1988 trip, four of the five county commissioners, Mrs. Webb, Mike Berg, Scott Ferguson and Ken Suffridge, made the trip, though Commissioner Don Loggins did not go. Loggins said that since he had a full-time job, and since the commission was taking a whole day out of his work each Tuesday, he didn't figure he had the time to go. And he also added, "I had just been elected and was brand-new on the commission, and did not feel like I could contribute anything. The other commissioners knew far more than I did, and I figured they could handle it."

Of the others on the trip, Mrs. Webb remembers: "One of the commissioners thought it would be a nice gesture, since we were to issue water and sewer bonds, and since the Water and Sewer Authority was so instrumental in making sure the needs and improvements of the county system were being met, that the Authority members also go on the trip. We seriously needed funds for major projects, because of the explosive growth of the county. Our sewer capacity was hurting, as some of the developers had even paid in advance for sewer capacity, only to find out that when they needed to hook onto the system, the capacity was not there. That was bad. So more people were on the trip than before. We thought we would bring them along to show support for our programs." The group was seeking at the time a rating on a $42 million water and sewer bond.

The entourage was composed of four commissioners; three Authority members, including Charles Wilder, Larry Bailey and J.D. Poole, and several county officials: County Manager Chuck Button; Charlotte Nash, who was finance director; County Attorney Richard Carothers; Bill Bush, head of the water department; and Bill Tanner, the Water and Sewer Authority attorney, and George Childers, with the Authority's consulting engineering firm of Havens and Emerson. Also on the trip were 11 spouses plus two members of the Lex Jolley firm, Gordon Mortin, who was president of the firm; and Mortin's son-in law, Edmund J. Wall. Altogether, there were 26 people on this trip. The county officials stayed at the Hemsley Palace Hotel. Two of the dinners were at the World Trade Center skyline restaurant and at the Four Seasons restaurant.

Lillian Webb

The details of the trip were handled by the Jolley firm. Most on the group headed out on Wednesday, and stayed through Sunday, in order to get the best air fare by staying over Saturday night. The Webbs flew up one day later, and had an engagement on Saturday, so came back on Friday. The others came home on Sunday.

But how did those making the trip think that the trip was being paid for? Many thought it was being paid for by the bond underwriters, similar to the way it had been paid in the past. The underwriter of the bond was selected on a competitive bid basis, giving the county the best rate when it opened the bids for the bond. The 1988 underwriter was the First National Bank of Atlanta. Built into the cost of the underwriting was an allowance for the rating service trips and other expenses. However, when the bills after the trip were totaled, the expenses of the trips exceeded the underwriting allowance, and the county had to make up the difference.

The average Gwinnettian knew virtually nothing of these detailed matters. Such visits received little publicity, since they were the "meat and potatoes" of administrative detail in selling the county's bonds, with most of the work handled by the Jolley firm.

While in New York, Mrs. Webb and the officials made presentations on successive days to the two firms. Mrs. Webb says that in her presentation, she stressed that "We were not using projections of future growth, but showing them that day's numbers, the actual figures. We knew we had to have additional capacity in all our systems, especially our sewer system, and have proper-sized lines in our water system. We also told them that we knew we could not throw up those heavy infrastructure projects quickly, but that they needed planning and construction time. The most frustrating part is that since we knew growth was coming, still we had to get the federal and state approvals, and later from EPA and other agencies. It took forever to get this added facility capacity approved by these agencies."

This infamous "New York trip" happened in February, 1988, during the first term of the Republican Webb administration. Remember, prior to 1984, Democrats had held most of the offices of the county, and the surprise-Republican sweep of every contested election in 1984 was a terrific blow to the Democrats. They were itching to get back into office, thinking that the 1984 election was certainly a fluke, and they would soon be returned to power. Meanwhile, Democrats were working to win in the 1988 election, a victory they soon would find has continued to elude them, and has not happened at the county commission level since, as the Commission remains continuously held by Republicans.

After the 1988 trip, little was heard of the meeting for several months. Then Democrats began either to hear or spread rumors about the trip. So the snooping began, as details emerged. The Democrats then alerted the media to the story. The Democrats were in hopes of getting the story in the newspapers before the November, 1988 election, thinking the airing of the story could put them back in power running the county.

However, the story did not break until November 22, two weeks after the General Election when Mrs. Webb was re-elected, and when W.J. Dodd and Curtis McGill came onto the commission. (Commissioners Mike Berg did not seek re-election, while Ken Suffridge was defeated in the Republican primary by W.J. Dodd, 2,393 votes to 1864.) The story broke on a Tuesday in the *Gwinnett Daily News*, citing the 26 people on the trip, and the $52,000 cost of the trip. The next day the story was in the Atlanta newspapers and all the key radio and television stations throughout Metro Atlanta. They had a juicy news morsel, and for days on end, would not let the story go. Soon coming out were full details, such as the plays attended (*Starlight Express*, for one); the use of limousines to transport the officials, with its $17,550 bill; the luxury hotel used; and even the food eaten at certain restaurants. The state attorney general, Michael Bowers, was asked an opinion, but cited that under current statutes, Gwinnett apparently broke no law.

Meanwhile, the uproar made Gwinnett the laughingstock throughout Metro Atlanta. Gwinnettians were stunned at the unfolding details. The "New York trip" was all the rage. Any adult living in Gwinnett in 1988 will tell you details should you mention the "New York trip" now years later.

Cloud over New York trip

One item to note: the three newly-elected commissioners had not even begun to serve a second time when the story broke. Yet, all during that second four year term, the cloud of "the New York trip" hung over their every deliberation. It was something that the commission could not get away from, and something Gwinnett residents continued to talk about.

Shortly after the story of the trip broke, the county commission took action to institute a new spending policy for the county. There were restrictions on travel, a limit on meals, and deluxe hotels would be off limits.

Mrs. Webb says: "When the ruckus came, we told Charlotte Nash to tally the cost, and we would pay our share. By then Jack had earlier told me that there were too many people on the trip." Altogether, the county determined that $20,000 of the trip cost was "inappropriate." Mrs. Webb said that the commissioners and their aides had agreed to reimburse the county for their expenses deemed inappropriate. She adds: "I think Jack and I paid either $2,600 or $3,600."

Two county commissioners who would go out of office on December 31, 1988, Mike Berg and Ken Suffridge, told the Atlanta newspapers that they would not reimburse the county for their wives' expenses.

Larry Bailey, who eventually would serve for 17 years on the Water and Sewer Authority, remembers the 1988 trip. "It was Mike Berg's idea for the Authority members to take their wives along. I had been on several trips to the bonding houses, but this was the first time I took my wife. At the hotel where we were staying, it would nearly cost you $10 for just a cup of coffee. I remember several of us went across the street from the hotel to a coffee house for breakfast at much lower prices. That, of course, didn't get any of the publicity once the story of the trip broke. But of all the trips I went on, and there must have been four or five, I probably spent more of my own money on the 1988 trip than any of the others."

Years later, Mrs. Webb agrees that "That New York trip was excessive, was overkill. We had too many people going up there, and certainly did not need the spouses. When the story broke, I began to get the phone calls, and was called all sorts of names. I remember one was 'Diamond Lil' and another was 'Mrs. Moneybags.' The public was fed up about it, and it was wrong. But we didn't realize it earlier.

"Our goal was to meet with the bond representatives, and to answer their questions to make sure we go the best rating we could on those bonds for the county. And we did that. Years later, when the county got its "triple-triple" rating from the three bond houses (the rating house of Fitch had become part of the picture by then), I think it stemmed from the time when the county started meeting with the bond houses. They trusted and understood what we were doing, and the triple-triple higher ratings we got saved the county millions of dollars in the lower interest rates. So, it was well worth it to be in direct contact with these bond rating houses. Yet the way it was handled, and the number of people on the trip were excessive."

Among the provisions that the county adopted later on when the bond representatives visited in Gwinnett, was not only for the bond officials to meet with county management people in person, but also to take the visitors on a helicopter tour of the county. Charlotte Nash says it "is a perfect tool to present a full range view of the county, so that they could see all the construction activity, and to focus on improvements and see the many projects involved in financing. It gave those visiting a real feel for the county." By using a county-leased helicopter, the representatives could easily and quickly see the growth and development in Gwinnett.

In face of the questions about the trip, Mrs. Webb sought a third term in 1992 as the chairperson of the commission in the Republican primary. However, voters had not forgotten the New York trip, and Mrs. Webb garnered only 11 per cent of the vote in the primary. She says of that election: "I probably should not have run. You lose and you win elections. It hurts to lose any election. But I did my best. We worked well for eight years when I was in office, and put in many new structures. We added a new runway at the airport and it held its first landing on the new runway in 1991. And we put in more water and sewer projects, and expanded the transportation activities. It was a good melding of the people, and Gwinnett remains a splendid place to be. But for sure, that cloud was over our heads the entire four years."

She adds: "That trip haunted me for years. It may be on my tombstone."

A former Democrat, Wayne Hill, won the Republican primary without a runoff with 58 per cent of the vote. The third candidate in the race was Donna Fisher, who herself garnered a respectable 31 percent of the vote. In the 1992 General Election, Mr. Hill defeated Democrat Bob Wood by a vote of 90,487 to Wood's 45,780. Mr. Hill would go on to serve for 12 years as the county commission chairman, and himself lose when he sought a fourth term to Charles Bannister.

In 2008, Gwinnett County had as its bond counsel the Atlanta firm of King and Spalding, with Woodrow Vaughan III of that firm as its key contact. They also use another law firm, Sutherland, Asbill and Brennan, as its disclosure counsel. The Sutherland firm has a long association with the county, back from the days when John Mobley was with that firm. In 2008, he was still working with the county on bond matters, as is another attorney from the firm, Matthew Nichols.

* * * * *

When Mrs. Webb won her first election to the county commission, she decided to visit a commission meeting prior to being sworn into office to find out how they conducted business. What she found was appalling to her.

She found a split county commission, which was fighting, and often recording votes a 4-1 split in public meetings and in internal meetings. The lone dissenter was the chairman of the commission, Charles Ashworth.

Mrs. Webb says: "When I went to that first commission meeting in their offices up on the hill in the old school building, I found them fighting all the time. And they would argue over the most trivial matters. The meeting started at 10 in the morning. They argued some, then took a break for lunch, came back and continue to fight over what seemed to be every issue. I also remember that there were visitors waiting to be heard before the commisison, one group seeking to get the commissioners to grant a proclamation. They kept those folks waiting until after lunch, when they could have disposed of them quickly. It was embarrassing…awful. There was no consensus, and they may not have even had a printed agenda. I must say that after that first meeting with the old commission, I was wondering what I had gotten myself into."

While mayor of Norcross, Mrs. Webb had instituted a "consensus agenda" in their meetings. "That was a way to dispose of trivial matters, and move the meetings along. You talked about items in your work session, and if there was agreement on housekeeping matters, you put them on the consent agenda. The big items were already discussed in the budget process. With the consent agenda, you could dispose of many of the items on the table with one motion. If one of the members of the board wanted to remove an item from the consent agenda, we could discuss it further in the open meeting.

"We knew when we went on the commission that we had to find a better way to resolve issues which we agreed upon, so that we would not be stalemated. Once in office as head of the county commission, we installed the consent agenda early on, and it sure worked well."

Council for Quality Growth

The early 1980s in Gwinnett saw a series of circumstances that would propel the county much faster into the future than most people thought possible. For a while, everything seemed to be lined up for spectacular growth, as the real estate market was hot, many new firms were choosing to locate in Gwinnett, the population was soaring, and smiles were on the faces of the growth community. Momentum seemed to be moving Gwinnett's way.

Consider the circumstances:

- The population had jumped from 116,500 in 1975....to 166,903 in 1980....to 259,028 in 1985. By then, Gwinnett was known to be the fastest growing county in the United States.
- Building permits had zoomed, from 2,250 in 1975 to 10,490 in 1985.
- Retail sales were setting records each year, highlighted by Gwinnett Place mall opening on February 1, 1984.
- And in 1985, showing confidence in the county, voters had approved the first local option sales tax for a much-needed new courthouse.

Yet this fast growth came with problems that many at first did not see. Among them was the inability for county government to keep pace with all this growth. In addition, the voters had made a change in the county leadership, bringing a new set of commissioners to the table. After the years of Charles Ashworth as chairman of the county commission, (1980-1984), and with the new department heads of the new chairman Lillian Webb administration in office, matters were sometimes topsy-turvy when it came to getting straight answers to questions. As a result, soon the development community was finding that though the market was "white hot," they could not get necessary permits quickly, building inspections were delayed, or sometimes, straight answers did not come from the overburdened county officials. One said: "What you would expect to happen in 30 days was taking up to six months, and getting worse."

"It got to the point," one developer said, "That one day you would get one answer, and the next day you would get another." It didn't help matters that the County Commission was wobbly, stemming from controversy during 1980-84 to different approaches in government by the chairman, Charles Ashworth. Many measures passed by a 4-0 or 4-1 vote, with the chairman in the minority, and the district commissioners always in the majority.

As a result, as Gwinnett was expanding at a rate unparalleled in the nation, it had problems. Gwinnett was faced with a seemingly irreconcilable set of circumstances: long-waited economic prosperity versus infrastructure shortfalls and rapidly changing public attitudes.

Gwinnett residential developer Frank McGowan remembers those days. "The county was not moving fast enough to handle the rush of development work that was going on in Gwinnett. Many times you would go for a building permit, and find there was a new regulation you knew nothing about. And then the following week, you would find something entirely different. This was a real problem for the individual developers. In addition, we as the development community were not organized and sometimes did not realize others in the field were having these same problems."

Overlay this with a new awareness of the environment---by individual citizens and state agencies. New concerns emerged in the residential building and in the commercial and industrial building communities. In addition, the Environmental Protection Division of the state was beginning to flex its muscles, causing those in the construction business to wonder what was going on.

This caused problems, as those in the building trades were unable to do their jobs in the same way as before.

Some individual firms, seeing a route for the county to solve some of these problems, began to approach the county about possible solutions. For several years, the Gwinnett Developer's Association, composed primarily of residential builders, had been meeting monthly. They gathered to talk about common problems, heard speakers, and occasionally, they would work on lobbying activities.

Mitch Peevy, then with Precision Planning, remembers one occasion. "I think Randall Dixon, my boss, raised my hand and I got made secretary of the group. I later learned that this meant that when we had meetings, I had to set up the place for the meeting, selected the food, and had to get a speaker. We meet at the Marriott Hotel every month. Occasionally we would raise some money for this cause or that. At first we had 25-30 show up, but toward the end of my three years as secretary, we were having 100 people or more at each meeting. Altogether, we met for about six years."

One development firm even went as far as conducting an extensive professional credible study of county problems, at their own expense, only to see the County Commission never even open the study, assuming the results were tainted, only because the study came from the development community.

Meanwhile, a few in the residential construction community, and others from the industrial and commercial development area, started talking among themselves and began to realize that they had common problems. An idea began to form in this group: perhaps they could band together under professional direction to solve the common problems. After all, many of them were already at an impasse with regulating officials of the county. What could it hurt? McGowan says: "We realized we would get stronger together."

Eventually out of this morass came the Council for Quality Growth. Ray Weeks and Frank McGowan were early leaders, along with others, including Tom Wheeler, Dick Myrick, Mitch Peevy, Randall Dixon, J.D. Caswell and Wayne Mason. The first meeting, comprised of about 15 people, was in Weeks' office, at what was called then Interstate Industrial Park, later to be known as Gwinnett Park. Weeks there laid out his vision for the new group. Some of these individuals opposed the idea of banding together, wanting to remain independent and believing they would lose their autonomy.

Charles Wilder remembers that the meeting included several developers who wanted to work individually with the county, or work through the Chamber. "Some thought another organization might hurt the Chamber. They didn't want an organization to be an in-your-face type group, for anti-zoning or anti-growth factions."

Mitch Peevy was present at those meetings. "We knew we needed to get more organized back then. The Gwinnett Development Association was meeting monthly at the Marriott Hotel, and there would be 80 to 120 of us present for meetings. And we had then about $25-30,000 in the bank, which we eventually rolled over as seed money to the Council.

"But we had no full-time person working for us, it being an all-volunteer group. We had no real direction; it was pretty much every man for himself. The developer's association was primarily to keep people talking, to have a level playing field. If we knew of something going on, we would tell the others. But it was not set up to be what the Council became. We were amateurs, but needed someone to guide us to take the group to a professional level."

Peevy credits Ray Weeks with "having the vision and being able to see what some of us could not see. We were going to a new level with professional oversight. It was an entirely new thought process for us."

So the idea of forming a developer-led group went forward. Wilder says: "These people felt that the developers needed a better platform, a group with some clout. As it was, we were being beat to death virtually one by one. We would hear one thing from the county one day, and another thing the next."

Those forming the group began meeting in different firms' conference rooms. Wilder says: "We were not trying to have one-upmanship, but wanted to get collective information that we could depend on."

After several meetings, the group organized in 1985, with Weeks the first president, representing the commercial side, and McGowan, representing the residential building group, as the vice president. Meanwhile, Weeks had contacted a relative newcomer to the county, Helen Tapp, about working with the development group.

Tapp had joined Gwinnett County government barely months before, as a "policy analyst." This was in the early days of the Lillian Webb administration, and she had a far-reaching job, delving into many aspects of governmental life. This would later come in handy for her in the Council job, as she knew the internal structure of government, and therefore had contacts---and was trusted---across the county operations.

At first Tapp balked at considering working with the development group, since she had been at the county only three months and felt a certain reluctance to leave. Eventually she approached Lillian Webb, was up-front on the matter, and told her she was considering the job, but would not do it if Mrs. Webb did not want her to do it. "You hired me and I have not been here that long," she told Webb.

Upon thinking about it, Mrs. Webb told her: "You could be exactly the person the development community needs for that job, for you know what we in government need. Not only that, we know and trust you. You could be the 'honest broker' between us." Then she told Tapp: "I would rather you stay, but if you want to do it, I will support you."

That's how Helen Tapp came to be the first director of the Council for Quality Growth. It became a tremendous fit for the young planner, as she brought the detailed skills to get to the meat of issues; she also had a professional, detached approach and the background (though short) in county government. She knew the right persons to contact at many levels of government to cut across red tape, which was an ability the Council needed.

Tapp says of the Council: "Developers, builders, bankers, engineers and others who were providing the spark for Gwinnett's economic growth responded by forming the council. While different in their perspectives, they united. They shared a common commitment. In short, competitors banned together for survival…to remain viable players in Gwinnett's future." She began with the council on Nov. 1, 1985. The new job was clearly along her line of interest.

Soon Tapp and the Council started making a difference. Among the many problems developers were facing were those in the area of water and sewer. To help finance the expansion of the Water and Sewer Department, developers for years had been buying reserve sewer capacity well in advance of their need, some writing huge checks with the guarantee that sewer would be available when they needed it. But soon the Gwinnett sewer capacity was at a limit, and on July 1, 1985, Gwinnett was hit with a sewer moratorium.

One of Tapp's earliest jobs was to work with Bill Bush, the head of the Water and Sewer Department, to figure out how much capacity the county actually had. She remembers: "Even while the county was extending the sewer system in many parts of the county, on a day-to-day or week-to-week basis, they were not able to say how much capacity was available. So we worked to determine the capacity basin-by-basin, sitting down with the staff, and going through the work orders, with tally sheets. We would see how many permits were outstanding, subtract from what we had before, add in the interceptor lines that were hooked up for more capacity…..all to determine the capacity. This was all done by paperwork, before the days of computers."

Council members tackled technically complex and tough issues. Tapp says: "We were committed to keeping standards high in tough times." These outcomes also proved helpful in building the credibility of the Council. Many detailed studies which the Council produced, in the sewer field and others, worked to build credibility for Tapp and the Council. The venture was, indeed, working as Mrs. Webb hoped, to help the county, as well as the development community, rather than the developers fighting the government every step of the way.

In about three months, the initial sewer moratorium was lifted. Gwinnett would face such issues on two other occasions, and resolve them quickly both times. (An interesting sidelight of the moratorium issue: years after the initial ban was lifted, people living in other Metro Atlanta communities, and not familiar with everyday Gwinnett, might ask: "Is the county still under a moratorium?" It was an example of just how much perception, not fact, often sticks in someone's mind.)

A sister issue facing the county (and the development community) was the previous use of packaged sewer plants by residential builders. Though something of an expedient stop-gap measure from builders, these plants had the early support of the county and state. However, packaged sewer treatment plants were a short-term measure, and not designed for long service. These plants, in general, were not well maintained. Not only that, each plant system required its own particular mechanisms and parts, which were not common to other packaged plants. Eventually, these systems had to be either by-passed or retrofitted and their capacities brought into the county system. What had been expedient early on did not work out in the long run. The Council was deep into working out solutions with the county in this area.

One technique used to develop rapport with Council members was a continuing and effective communications program. Soon after taking office, Tapp began to issue color-coded "FLASH" bulletins to Council members on important issues facing the Council. Chock full of detail about that particular problem, often the FLASH would ask members to attend hearings, or ask for input on this particular problem, or call for certain officials to be personally contacted by members. The FLASH reports went out (in those days before email) by postal delivery. One developer remembers that "We learned that when Helen said come to a meeting, that it was important. So you went there, and that way, we were able to achieve many goals, large and small."

Meanwhile, with the Environmental Protection Division (EPD) flexing its muscles on the subject of erosion control, the Council found itself involved. There was serious talk of additional clamping down on builders. One of the early issues involved "silt fences," which McGowan admits: "At first, we didn't know what they were."

On one occasion, concerning silt fencing, the proposition from the county was that, when working on a property, the silt fence should encircle the entire project. "Even at the top of a hill?" EPD officials asked a developer. "Why do you need it there?" The developer answered: "The county told us it was needed around the entire project." Soon that got sorted out so that silt fences were not required all around a property, but only on the downhill sides of projects.

Another example: in subdivisions during the early 1980s, developers were laying six-inch water pipes, though the county was pushing for eight-inch pipe. By talking and working with county officials, developers realized that with an eight-inch pipe, it would affect the water pressure, and that affected the homeowner's fire insurance cost. So subdivisions began getting eight-inch pipe.

Another time, county officials were concerned about sewer stub endings in a subdivision. The county wanted to have a device to determine where these stubs were, and came up with a plan to install a radio-controlled wire sticking out of the ground at each ending. Then, using radio equipment, the stub ending could be found, with developers having to purchase this high-priced radio unit. Developers countered by asking: "Can't we put in a post and paint it green?" The county was flabbergasted: "You would do that?" they asked. The green poles later on would allow the builder of the adjacent property to know where to locate a sewer line to tie onto the adjacent stub line.

As one builder says: "We were going through growing pains, but by talking and working together, we both came out ahead."

One of the county's toughest problems in those formative years was one that many developers did not at first realize would impact them. It was homeowner complaints about foul odors emanating from the county's new modern sewerage treatment plant on Tom Smith Road at the Yellow River.

Developers did not consider the problem to be theirs until it became evident that the problem had to be solved, or else broader sanctions might be imposed. Eventually, through better technical methods, the county was able to run and maintain the plant without complaint of odors, with the Council playing a key role in helping find an answer to this problem.

Meanwhile, as the Council gained stature in the eyes of the community and the county, it was also gaining strength with its own members. After a conversation one day with Lewis Tinley of the Environmental Protection Division, a matter came to the Council's attention about one of its members, a major national homebuilder, whose practices were so seriously faulty that the EPD was considering shutting down all building in the county until it was resolved.

Realizing the scope of the problem, a Council member contacted the local president of the homebuilding firm and brought him up-to-date on the matter. The president was not aware of the situation, since he was not getting information back from the field from his employees. Once apprised of the matter, the firm changed its practices immediately, and EPD was able to lift the threat to the building community.

EPD was stunned. "How did you do that?" a Council member was asked. He was told: "It's easier to hammer one of our own than all of us get hammered by you." Self discipline was alive and well within the Council for Quality Growth.

Tapp gives credit for a lot of what the Council was able to accomplish to a "chemistry between the senior county staff members and Council members." She adds: "People like George Black, Ron Seibenhener, Dick Carothers, all at the top of their game, worked well with the Council. We sparred, but there was a sense of 'Wow! We are headed somewhere, this is fun, and this community has the resources. We're growing faster than any other large county in the nation, and though we make mistakes, we have the ability to recover and learn faster than others.' They all had the will to improve. They knew it couldn't last forever, but it was an exciting time."

The Council eventually was firmly established as a partner in decision-making with the county. It was done through dissemination of credible research, through policy discussion, from expertise of members and by getting all parties to a common table. The Council became a forum for problem solving.

While the initial years of the Council for Quality Growth were concentrated on improvements in only Gwinnett County, eventually developers began to realize a need for a change in the geographic scope of the Council. After all, members who were once primarily concentrating on Gwinnett soon began to have operations in adjoining counties. Limiting the Council's work to Gwinnett meant it would not focus on many of the same issues that were going on in other counties.

So in 2003, the Council changed its direction, as problems of development became regional. Sam Olens in Cobb County was finding that the development difficulties he was having were similar to the problems that Gwinnett County was having. And as Council members spread their attention to other Metro Atlanta counties, the need for the change became apparent. The Council became the regional voice of the growth industry, with membership from all over Metro Atlanta.

Work of the Council, once almost entirely done only in Gwinnett, now is carried on in the other Metro Atlanta counties. The Council monitors the activities in these various counties and provides the platform for discussion, which often leads to a catalyst for consensus that is adopted across these counties. The work of the Council is now recognized as essential in regional decision making....and even state level decision making.

The Council continues to conduct numerous studies, on such diverse subjects as mass transit, road medians, impact fees, building codes, water and sewer capacity, fire codes, water reclamation, air quality, waste water, greenspace, stream buffers, school systems, river basins, and conservation overlay districts, to name some of them.

It's done through working committees, educational workshops, research, community forums, roundtables, and continual discussion with governmental officials, aimed at making the individual community a better place to live and work.

In 2007, the Council's membership came principally from real estate development (29%), engineers, planners and surveyors (20%), contractors and material vendors (10%), and the financial community (10%). Other members are builders, architects, law firms, real estate brokers, utilities and other miscellaneous firms and individuals.

Those who have been the key executives for the Council have been:

- Helen Tapp, 1985-1997.
- Kelly Love, 1998-2001.
- Laura Beall (interim), 2002-2003.
- Michael Paris, from September, 2003 to the present.

Now with the focus on the larger Metro Atlanta area, the Council for Quality Growth aims at an even wider future.

* * * * *

In 1990, the Council inaugurated an annual award, initially known as the Button Gwinnett Award. Though the event was started primarily as a fund raiser for the Council, it soon became a key mark of recognition in the county, honoring community members who exemplified the Council's mission of promoting balanced and responsible growth. The award is for life-long achievement. The list of these honorees (see Appendix B, page 742) represent some of the most outstanding Gwinnett citizens of the day. As the mission of the Council grew in 2003, the name of the recognition was changed to Four Pillar Award, and those honored began coming from the wider Metro Atlanta region.

As the first president of the Council for Quality Growth, Ray Weeks said: "Out of duplicated and unfocused efforts, the Council was born. Many of us breathed a collective sigh of relief. Amazingly, the model of the Council worked! We quickly earned a reputation as an important and credible coalition, and soon our work seemed endless."

Downtown development authorities

Gwinnett cities are interested in keeping their downtown areas viable, with many of them activating a quasi-governmental body, a Downtown Development Authority (DDA), for that purpose.

By 2008, such authorities had been established in Buford, Dacula, Duluth, Grayson, Lawrenceville, Loganville, Lilburn, Norcross, Snellville, Sugar Hill and Suwanee. Many of the cities were especially active in promoting the DDAs as a tool for their downtown redevelopment. The cities appoint their Authority members, and the Authority is a legally distinct body, able to enter into long-term contracts with individuals and companies, which the cities cannot do.

A 1981 Georgia law authorized all cities to have these authorities for revitalization and redevelopment purposes. It's a decision of the cities whether to activate these authorities. Once in business, the local DDA could make application to the Georgia Department of Community Affairs for partial funding, at below-market rates, of projects. The Department's Revolving Loan Fund could finance 40 percent of a total project, with 10 percent of the financing coming from the borrower's own monies, and 50 percent coming from conventional lenders. The monies could be used for new construction or redevelopment and rehabilitation projects, with a maximum from the Revolving Loan Fund of $250,000.

The DDAs can also get grants and loans from other sources, including the Georgia Cities Foundation. However, many of these projects are typically financed by local banks, with the arrangement made by the project developer. The DDA acts as a conduit between the Revolving Loan Fund and the individual.

Activities of DDAs include entering into contracts; acquiring property; financing projects; borrowing funds or issuing revenue bonds; extending credit or making loans; using, selling or leasing property; making long-range proposals in cooperation with the city; and even serving as an urban redevelopment agency.

Typically, DDAs have as their objectives:

- Revitalize and redevelop the central business district;
- Develop and promote for the public good and general welfare, trade, commerce, industry, and employment opportunities;
- Finance projects within the central business district that will develop and promote the public good and general welfare; and
- Issue bonds to finance projects.

Nationwide, DDAs were most active in the early 1980s, up until President Ronald Reagan curtailed their activities when he signed the Tax Act of 1986. This essentially stopped DDAs from making loans with tax exempt bonds for commercial projects. Opponents of this measure pointed to abuses in industrial development bonds. However, state governments had rectified many of the abuses, putting more restrictions on such projects. The Tax Act of 1986, however, brought to a halt the greatest period of downtown revitalization that blighted downtowns had ever seen.

As a result of changes in the Internal Revenue code in 1986, development authorities of all type were required to change their approaches. Now DDA projects must be set up for a public purpose, whether it be for a college, hospital, health facility, or even parking deck. In the case of cities, bonds may be issued for DDA purposes, as long as the project has a public aspect.

The cities, meanwhile, consider DDA activities beneficial for development, or re-developmental purposes. As an example of what type of projects can be financed this way, the City of Snellville in its early growth took advantage of this type of financing. Among some of its projects were the Wisteria Associates center on Wisteria Drive; a Haverty's furniture store; Heritage Village shopping center; Fountain Square center, including a Richway store; Gwinnett Ambulatory Surgical unit; a dental office of Kent Mattison; a McGee Road hardware store; and Heritage Bank's building.

Former Snellville Mayor Emmett Clower could speak for several Gwinnett towns when he says: "The authority gave us an avenue for development that we did not have before. It made us competitive, and increased the tax base."

In 1999, a new focus on downtown development came to Metro Atlanta as a result of Gwinnett sitting within the scope of the Atlanta Regional Commission (ARC). The ARC began a Livable Centers Initiative (LCI). A second reason for the new development focus was new leadership emerging in many of the towns.

The LCI was a grant program encouraging local jurisdictions within the ARC to plan and implement strategies that linked transportation improvements with land use development, to create livable, sustainable communities. The ARC committed $1 million annually for planning studies. Once complete, communities could apply for construction dollars to implement the plans produced. Through 2007, six planning projects were approved in Gwinnett for public improvements, after the studies showed the areas were complying with the study plans. Funds for these projects come through the Department of Transportation, with ARC committing $500 million to fund projects identified in the studies.

The planning grants approved through the LCI program include:

Year	Area	Amount	Project
2001	Norcross	$67,500	Historic District Study
2001	Gwinnett Co.	$90,000	Area of Ga. Highway 316 and I-85
2003	Snellville	$75,000	Town Center Study
2004	Buford	$75,000	Redevelopment, Sidewalks
2005	Evermore CID	$94,000	Corridor Strip Study on U.S. 78
2006	Gwinnett Co.	$100,000	Indian Trail-Lilburn Corridor

* * * * *

Several Gwinnett cities have not one, but two development authorities. These additional authorities have jurisdiction within the cities, but outside the downtown areas. Besides its Downtown Development Authority, Snellville also has the Development Authority of Snellville. Lawrenceville's Downtown Development Association focuses on the activities around the central business district or downtown historic area, while the Lawrenceville Development Authority has projects within the city but outside of the downtown overlay boundaries.

Buford has a Downtown Development Authority (1985) but an Industrial Development Authority preceded it in 1982. The Buford authorities have been dormant in recent years. And Suwanee comes with not only a downtown authority, but an Urban Redevelopment Authority (2003). Duluth has only one authority, but it is named the Urban Redevelopment Agency of the City of Duluth.

As the law was originally written, the local DDA entities had the power of eminent domain, though it was seldom, if ever, used. However, in 2006, the legislature removed that element from the books. In reality, the city in which the DDA was located has eminent domain rights, and could still obtain land, which could be sold to the DDA for development purposes.

The year the Gwinnett Downtown Development Authorities were founded and a list of their 2008 chairs:

Year	***Town***	***Chair***
1982	Snellville	Jimmy Norton
1983	Lawrenceville	Mike Reedy
1985	Buford	(being re-organized in 2008)
1985	Loganville	Edgar Brush
2001	Sugar Hill	Dawn P. Gober
2001	Suwanee	Kevin O'Brien
2003	Duluth	Ken Odum.
2003	Norcross	Bob Wilkerson (acting)
2006	Lilburn	Norman Nash
2008	Grayson	(to be named)

Duluth began the Urban Redevelopment Agency of the City of Duluth in 2003, with Steve Gaultney as chairman. Snellville began the Development Authority of Snellville in 1983, with Jimmy North as chairman. Suwanee began the Urban Redevelopment of Suwanee in 2002 with Alex Stone as chair. The Development Authority of Lawrenceville started in 1983, and Marie Beiser is chair.

Gwinnett gets its own foundation

Prior to 1984, there was no general community foundation in Gwinnett. A group of community leaders, working out of the Gwinnett Chamber board, strongly thought that some system was needed to get Gwinnettians to contribute in a more organized and aggressive manner to community causes. These people wanted a method whereby individuals and businesses could have a reasonable way to funnel funds to worthy community activities.

Meanwhile, with no foundation in the county, many non-profit groups were appealing to one of the few county-wide organizations, the Chamber of Commerce, for funding of different causes. These were legitimate projects, but causes which the Chamber did not feel came under the aegis of its mission.

A major impetus to the effort came from then-School Superintendent Alton Crews. Since the Chamber itself was limited in what it could do by its charter, the result from a committee recommendation was to develop a community foundation, necessarily independent of the Chamber of Commerce. The idea was that these causes could be helped better through a foundation than through the Chamber. However, many of those who were on the original foundation board were also on the Chamber committee studying the question.

The result was the start in March, 1985, of Gwinnett Foundation Inc. The first president of the foundation was Charles R. Brown, of Technology Park/Atlanta. Pat Brown was hired to be the first director of the foundation. (See Appendix B, page 745, for a list of the presidents, directors and end-of-year assets of the foundation.) One of the early projects which funds funneling through the Foundation helped get started was to purchase land across from Parkview High School for soccer fields for the community.

During its early days, the foundation held numerous fund-raising events and social activities, seeking to raise the profile of the foundation in the community's eye. (One memorable event: a dance at Peachtree World of Tennis featuring Chubby Checker.) The initial goal of the foundation was to be the one place within Gwinnett that people could go to find out key needs of the community, and raise money to meet such needs. The central purpose was to build a large and permanent endowment so that Gwinnett activities would be served even better. The foundation closed its first calendar year with assets of $170,700.

An initial capital campaign produced seed money, but the foundation got a major boost in 1987 from Robert Fowler. At the time when he and his partners sold the *Gwinnett Daily News*, they offered a $1 million challenge grant, which was eventually matched by the community. This new funding provided a solid base for the foundation to move forward.

J.D. Caswell was chairing the drive to match the $1 million challenge. He remembers an initial meeting of about 20 people at Peachtree World of Tennis to work on raising the matching money. "Once we talked about what we had to do, Wayne Mason put it simply: 'There are about 20 of us here in the room, so that makes $50,000 each of us has to either raise or pay.' And we went out of there and raised the money."

Caswell also relates another story of the drive: "About halfway through the campaign, the stock market dropped 508 points in one day. I got a call from Alton Crews, wondering if with this news, we needed to extend the time to raise the money. I told him that if Gwinnett County couldn't raise $1 million within the time, it wasn't worth it. We didn't extend the time, and still we raised the money in that bad business atmosphere." After the challenge gift, the foundation had $2.189 million in assets at the end of 1987.

One of the earlier supporters of the Gwinnett Foundation was the national Gannett Foundation. Among its reasons for supporting the local foundation was that the Gwinnett Foundation board members were active and contributing to the cause, and that the foundation was not spending for operations out of its corpus, but was covering the cost of operations otherwise.

In 2001, the foundation broadened its geographic scope and outlook, changing its name to the Community Foundation of Northeast Georgia.

By 2007, the assets of the foundation had grown to $32 million, up from $17 million the previous year. This major increase had come through the addition of 60 new individual funds between 2006-2008. In recent years, the Northeast Foundation has undertaken to handle back-office functions for the Gwinnett Foundation and other similar organizations, such as the Cobb County Foundation, while it remains as an independent entity. This allows such smaller foundations to reduce their overhead tremendously, and gives them in the long run a far better return on their monies.

By 2008, the foundation had more than 250 funds. That includes donor-advised funds, designated funds and administrative funds. Each one generates grants back to the community according to the donor recommendations. And since its founding, the Foundation has granted over $37 million to local not-for-profit organizations and programs, engaged in such areas as health and human services, the arts, education and environmental improvements. These grants are made to tax-exempt private agencies and public charities. The foundation seeks to fund innovative programs that address specific needs of the community.

It may be best to understand what the foundation does not support. That would include endowment and debt reduction of agencies; fund-raising campaigns; religious organizations; travel for individuals or groups, such as band, sports and school classes; services provided by the community, such as police and fire protection, welfare and library activities; lobbying activities; nor individuals.

The first executive director of the foundation in 1985 was Pat Brown. She was followed by Deborah Roberts in 1988; and by Joe Estafen in 1993. Since 2004, the director has been Judy Waters, a former county commissioner.

7

1990-2000

The arts in Gwinnett

Similar to Atlanta being a city "too busy to hate," Gwinnett seemed a landscape with not enough time to grow, much less invest in the finer arts.

With the rapid growth of commercial activity in Gwinnett, and with the continuing influx of new residents occupying the burgeoning homebuilding industry output, for a while there seemed little attention given to cultural needs---the theatre, fine arts, and other activities.

Had you moved to Gwinnett prior to 1980, you would seldom hear the topic of "fine arts" discussed in any way in connection with a Gwinnett angle.

Yet a few people were thinking about this topic. The development of cultural arts in Gwinnett County started out through the initial work of a member of a civic club -- Paula Bagwell, a member of the Lawrenceville Junior Woman's Club, which had been started in 1971.

Mary Louise Stark of Lawrenceville, herself an artist and former member of the Junior Women's Club, says: "Paula came up with idea for an arts council. I do not know how she came up with idea, but she had a real interest in arts, and felt a Council was needed." She adds: "In those days, you could not get a lot of elected officials in the county interested in matters like art. They said they had more vital concerns back then."

Rachel Bronnum of Lawrenceville remembers Paula Bagwell's efforts. "The formation of the Arts Council was somewhat a project out of the Junior Woman's Club, but it was not directly affiliated with the club. Paula visited other towns and learned about their Arts Councils, then got several people together from different parts of Gwinnett to talk about an arts council."

Talk started about formation of an arts council in 1980. The Gwinnett Council for the Arts Inc. was incorporated in 1981 as a non-profit foundation, and met initially at the Female Seminary in Lawrenceville.

The first president of the Arts Council was Eleanor (Lynn) Alford, and Ethel Andersen was president-elect, with Paige White as secretary, and Wayne Sikes as treasurer. Dues were set at $10 a year for general membership.

Members of the initial board included Betty Adams; Curtis Akers; Lynn Alford, Ethel Andersen, Tom Andersen, Martha Ashworth; Paula Bagwell, Barbara Brack; Rachel Bronnum; Charlotte Crosland; Jeanette Crews, Marlene Embry, James Garner, Joe Grizzel, Nancy Gullickson, Ed Heys, Tom Hitchcock, Connie Hudson, Richard Jewett, Winford (Buck) Lindsay, Dr. Jesse Long, Faye Moore, John Otwell, John Shelton, Wayne Sikes, Cyndae Sims, Mary Louise Stark, Paige White, Sherry Tennant and Marion Webb.

Its first project was a Poetry Reading by Dr. John Lewis, poet laureate of Georgia, at the Female Seminary in Lawrenceville. Another early project, done in conjunction with the Board of Education, was sponsorship of a locally-produced live musical, "A Broadway Melody." And there was talk of an "all-county theater" group in the making.

On July 3, 1983, Gwinnett County got a gift that it did not know what to do with, nor how to house it. The gift was a collection of fine furniture, art and antiques from George Williams, a Gwinnett native, who was a career official of the Treasury Department in Washington, D.C. At his death in 1982, he bequeathed his antique furnishings collection from his Washington home to Gwinnett County. Commissioner Wayne Mason, a distant cousin of Williams, had accepted the gift to the county while Williams was still living. A few years after Williams' death, the collection was moved in 1985 to Gwinnett. It had been expected to be on display at Gwinnett's Courthouse, but that was impossible, since it was before the new court facilities (G-JAC) were built. The old Courthouse was crowded, full of routine governmental services, with no space for the furniture.

George Williams in 1930 had designed a house on Crogan Street in Lawrenceville for his brother, Andrew David Williams, a family physician. Knowing the new Arts Council needed an office, the county got permission from the Dr. A.D. Williams Estate to use the house for the Arts Council office. The Council moved its offices into the 2,000+ square feet of the Williams home in 1983. Later, the county asked the Council to curate the Williams collection in the house.

Then, in 1989, after the new courthouse was built, more space became available for the Council. The former Lawrenceville Post Office had been used for court room space, but was no longer needed by the courts. Since the Council was in need of additional space, its offices were moved to this site. To the Council, the old post office seemed a massive space of 7,000 square feet, compared to the 2,000 square feet of the Williams house.

The move allowed the Council to have room for exhibits, besides its offices. The Council also kept the Williams house open for display of the furniture collection. It was after the Historic Gwinnett Courthouse was refurbished that the Williams Collection was moved to two rooms at the courthouse, a perfect setting for the elegant collection of George Williams.

Nancy Gullickson became the director of the Arts Council in 1983. She remembers those early days: "We had little funding at the outset. We got a $10,000 grant from the county to house, maintain and show the Williams collection. That first year we also received a $12,000 Georgia Community Development grant, which the next year was a matching $6,000 grant, to operate the center. By the third year that grant had disappeared."

Meanwhile, around 1990, discussion began on construction of a Civic Center for the county, to include a Performing Arts Center. Though sales tax monies were anticipated for funding the Civic Center and Performing Arts portion, there were no public funds earmarked for the Fine Arts Center.

County officials were in agreement that a Fine Arts Center would make a worthy addition to the overall focus of the Civic Center. They agreed on September 27, 1990 to lease one-third of an acre near the Performing Arts Center at the Civic Center to the Gwinnett Arts Facility Authority, which would, in turn, sublease the land to the Arts Council for a fine arts center, museum and art school. The span of the lease was to be for 50 years. In addition, the county on July 23, 1991 agreed to help fund site preparation and improvement costs, to include lighting, paving and building upgrades of $207,923. The Arts Council was to raise an additional $165,454 for this initial work.

About that same time, the Arts Council found, after discussion with its architect, that the price tag on a Fine Arts Center was right at $1 million. Being a relatively young organization, and with no experience at raising large dollars, the Arts Council had no idea where it might look for funding, as it began to seriously consider its future. Yet committees mulled ideas, and came up with one approach.

Nancy Gullickson remembers talking with Tom Wheeler, who had long been associated with developer Scott Hudgens, about the arts program. "Tom took a few pages in a booklet that we put together to Scott. Mr. Hudgens later called, and asked us to come over to his office and talk about our plans. He was recovering at the time from a heart attack. So Margaret Andrews, Carol Kendall and I went to Scott's home. While driving there, we discussed what we should ask for, and if we should mention a figure of what we needed. We really didn't know what we were going to say."

But Carol had another idea, and told them: "One thing is for sure. If you don't ask for money, you won't get it." Though they had estimates that the cost for building the art center would be about $750,000, Carol was adamant. "No sir, $750,000 just gets the building. It doesn't include the essentials, like equipping it. We need to ask for $1 million."

Nancy picks up the story: "Then as we talked to Scott, he asked what it would cost. When we said $1 million, he in the next sentence said, 'I would like to build this center for you.' We were floored! Scott then added a caveat: he wanted to do it anonymously. We happily agreed to keep his gift anonymous." Mr. Hudgens gave the money in 1991.

Margaret Andrews says: "We had not planned on him doing that, for we were dreaming. But we were so excited."

Carol Kendall adds: "We leaped ahead of the curve when Mr. Hudgens gave that money. But we would have languished without his help, and that of Bob Fowler, especially in the second half of the campaign. That got us going."

Thus began the Arts Center. The organizers had a lot of behind-the-scene help from Bob Fowler, who had also talked with Hudgens. Fowler recognized that funds would be necessary to keep up the museum, and started efforts to create an endowment.

Once the funds were assured for the building, Gwinnett County set up an Arts Facility Authority to provide a ground lease to the Arts Council. Carol Kendall ended up chairing the authority. "Faye Hinshaw was president of the Council then. And Sen. Don Balfour helped us with guiding the legislation for the Authority through the General Assembly.

He was very careful that the Authority could not have any debt. It was mainly an enabling group for the lease. Once all was set and done, we had a big signing party, and each of the commissioners appointed a representative to the Authority."

What was to come out of the ground was a 14,000 square foot Fine Arts Center, with gallery, gift shop, space for classrooms and offices. It opened in January, 1993. The first exhibit to be shown were the works of Steffan Thomas, an artist working out of Stone Mountain, who had died in 1990.

Shortly afterward, the Council was approached by developer Ray Weeks, whose father, A.R. Weeks, had just died. The senior Mr. Weeks had founded one of the first major office parks in the county, now called Gwinnett Park. This was a modern office park along Interstate 85, and was one of the first such parks to have extensive landscaped grounds in its conception.

Ray Weeks and his siblings all chipped in, giving the Arts Center $150,000 for a 28,000 square foot outdoor Sculpture Garden, in memory of their father, Al Weeks. With the Weeks organization providing extensive landscaping at its park, the gift also was much larger, since it included additional "in-kind" gifts for the garden.

Gullickson remembers another aspect: "We called it the '30 day wonder,' since they (the Weeks firm) built the outdoor garden in 30 days. We opened the garden in June, 1993."

Others in the community were interested in helping fund the Arts Center. In 1991, the Arts Council received a $250,000 gift from the Lettie Pate Evans Foundation for its original building. And, beginning in 1993, the Frances Wood Wilson Foundation became a steady friend of the Arts Center, generous with funds for equipment and programming. Over the years, the Frances Wood Wilson Foundation has given the Arts Center grants and funds for furnishings, education and accreditation. The first grant was in 1991, and through 2006, the grants totaled $427,424. Former County Commissioner Don Loggins is a member of the Frances Wood Wilson Foundation board.

Meanwhile, another generous benefactor was working behind the scene, providing guidance and encouraging others to give. This was former *Gwinnett Daily News* publisher Bob Fowler, who made a $300,000 contribution to the Gwinnett Foundation for the beginning of an endowment for the Arts Center. In 1994, the Arts Center named its main gallery in honor of Fowler. The $100,000 contribution from Carol and David Kendall, led to the Arts Center naming its entrance rotunda for the Kendalls.

Another large contribution came from another art patron and artist herself, Mary Kistner of Snellville. She had been a generous supporter of the Center during her lifetime. In her will, she gave $1 million to the Gwinnett Foundation to help fund special shows at the Center. One such show was a Picasso Ceramics exhibit, which brought distinction and tremendous publicity to the Center in 2006. The Atrium of the Arts Center was named for Mary Kistner in 1995.

The expansion of the Art Center came about again through interest by one of its earlier patrons. One day in 1998, Scott Hudgens stopped by the Art Center. Nancy Gullickson says: "Actually, Scott dropped by my office just to chat. Eventually, he and I discussed the idea of a Children's Museum addition. He stood at the window of my office and looked out over what was a vacant field opening between the Arts Center and the Performing Arts

Center. Scott commented that if he could talk his wife, Jackie, into letting him name the museum for her, he would build the addition of a Children's Museum. And that's how our Children's Museum got started...."

Then in 1999, a gift of $250,000 came from the Robert Woodruff Foundation to help fund the children's museum.

Hudgens wanted a center for the arts to benefit the youth of Gwinnett. It was at a time when the Arts Center was contemplating an expansion for use by children. Hudgens stepped forward, this time with a $2 million gift.

"On that project, we had some problems with contractors building that wing, which slowed down construction," Gullickson says. "And Scott was concerned. It was about that time that Rankin Smith, owner of the Atlanta Falcons, died. One day Scott called and asked about the building, warning me 'Don't let me die before you finish it,' and we laughed. We were able to complete the building and name it for Jackie when we opened the Children's Museum in January, 2000, just a few months before Scott died."

Today the entire Arts Center is known as the Jacqueline Casey Hudgens Center for the Arts. Altogether, the Fine Arts Center has 35,000 square feet under roof, including 14,000 square feet in the Fine Arts Center, and 21,000 square feet in the Children's Wing. The addition of the Children's Wing also connects the Fine Arts Center with the adjacent Performing Arts Center.

The key features of the children's wing include a black box theatre, which was added in 2005; a spacious play area with innovative interactive electronic toys and games for children as young as kindergarten; major space for hanging exhibits; and a promenade where receptions are often held.

Another significant art gift came from Mr. and Mrs. Frank Rowe. The promenade at the Hudgens Children's Center is named for Johnnie A. Rowe, who has been active on the Arts Center board for years, and has served as its president.

In its 25 years as the art conscience for Gwinnett, the Gwinnett Arts Council has become highly regarded by the arts community. It was designated by the Atlanta Olympic Committee in 1996 as a cultural venue, as it held a "Festival of Fire," honoring native Americans.

The Gwinnett Fine Arts Center was named as the "best suburban arts venue" by Atlanta Magazine in 1997.

Perhaps the Gwinnett Fine Arts Center's most important exhibit came in 2006, as it bid for and got a show of Picasso ceramics, created over 25 years, which explored the growth of the artist in this time. The exhibit gained wide publicity and tremendous notoriety, and vastly increased attendance for the Hudgens Center. The original show was to be on display for three months, then remained upon request of the Museum for six more weeks than originally planned.

Over the years, officials of the Fine Arts Center have been proud to say when people visit, "Everything you look at is paid for." It took more than 25 years of hard work from Paula Bagwell's original idea that Gwinnett ought to have its own fine arts council. Gwinnett's fine arts program has come a long way.

In 2008, members of the Arts Center board of directors included Lynn Agnes, Betty Atkinson, Carolyn Bagheri, Arlesia Crooms, David Cross, Janet Dunwoody, Ronnie Ford,

Bill Frech, Cheryl Gee, Terry Gordon, Laura Grams, Stan Hall, Demetrius L. Jordan, Kathy LaSelva, Don Loggins, Caryn McGarity, David McMullen, Christi Reeves-Tullis, Johnnie Rowe, Anne Soutter, Pat Swan, Lee Tucker, Judy Waters, and Peggy Woods. Officers were Hall, chairman of the board; McGarity, vice chair; Dunwoody, secretary; David Cross, treasurer; and Swan, immediate past chair.

Gwinnett Ballet Theatre

Gwinnett Ballet Theatre (GBT) has been nurturing young dancers since 1977. Founded by Lynn Snipes, this organization became a non-profit entity when Lisa Sheppard Robson took over as artistic director in 1995. The Gwinnett Ballet School, as well as the performing company, is the only combination non-profit ballet company and school in the region outside of the Atlanta Ballet.

GBT's mission is to develop young dancers and to provide a dance education that will allow students the ability to pursue a professional dance career upon graduation. As a result, approximately half of GBT graduates sign contracts with major dance companies across the United States.

One such graduate, Alessandra Ball (also a graduate of Greater Atlanta Christian School) was the recipient of the coveted Princess Grace Award in 2005. She later was a soloist for North Carolina Dance Theatre in Charlotte, N.C. GBT is also an Honors Company for the Southeastern Regional Dance Association.

Other notable accomplishments include the GBT Scholarship Program. Begun in 2005, this initiative allows 20 students between the ages of 7 and 14 the opportunity to take twice-weekly classes and perform in both The Nutcracker and the annual recital.

GBT has its own live music ensemble, the Gwinnett Ballet Theatre Orchestra under the direction of Predrag Gosta for selected productions. The Orchestra launched in March, 2006, with the premiere of A Midsummer Night's Dream. No other Metro Atlanta in 2006 had live music for The Nutcracker performance.

Gwinnett Ballet Theatre performed its Nutcracker on a stage at the convention center the Friday after Thanksgiving in 1992, and since then, has given their annual performances at the Performing Arts Center. It's still a fixture on the calendar now, and marked its 25th anniversary in 2006.

Gwinnett Philharmonic

The Gwinnett Philharmonic and its vision for bringing great music to Gwinnett County was born in the hearts of Gwinnettians as the Performing Arts Center was yet under construction in 1992.

It was during a lunch-time conversation between Forrest Robinson and Monte Nichols that the dream was first expressed. An active leader in raising awareness and funding for arts and other charitable causes in the county, Robinson spoke of the importance of "giving back" to the community through involvement in quality-of-life issues for the benefit of generations to come. Being a professional musician himself, Nichols was curious to ask Robinson if he could envision the day that an orchestra made up entirely of professional musicians would regularly perform on the stage of the new Performing Arts Center. Ever the visionary, Robinson replied simply, "It's inevitable." They agreed that the only questions were when --- and who --- would organize it.

Nichols had already been challenged to expand his musical activities beyond his full-time work as worship and music pastor at Peachtree Corners Baptist Church in Norcross. The senior pastor of the church at the time, Gerald Harris, encouraged him to not only begin building a small orchestra for the church's services, but also to serve the broader community by becoming involved in the founding of an orchestra for the county.

As the lunchtime meeting came to a close, Robinson suggested as a "next step" that some time be spent asking community leaders if they felt that the founding and sustaining of a professional orchestra would be a "doable" project. One of the first such meetings was held with Nancy Guillickson of the Gwinnett Council for the Arts, who had been involved in the design of the Performing Arts Center. Her response was immediately encouraging as she had maintained from the beginning a "build it and they will come" philosophy concerning the construction of a performing arts venue for the county. Nichols soon found himself a member of the Performing Arts Committee of the council's board, and the following year was asked to chair the committee. Many of the council's members became enthusiastic supporters of the orchestra's founding. It was during a meeting of the council's Performing Arts Committee that the name Gwinnett Philharmonic was first discussed.

After holding encouraging conversations with many other individuals from all corners of the county, the confidence to move forward began to emerge. At the same time, professional musicians expressed willingness to become involved. David Arenz agreed to become the founding concertmaster. From his position as a titled member of the Atlanta Symphony, his collaboration with Nichols brought immediate interest from a number of excellent musicians in the region.

In January of 1995, after three years of discussion and research----and much hoping, dreaming, and praying on the part of Nichols and those closest to the project----the Gwinnett Philharmonic Association, Inc. was formed as a 501(c)(3) charitable organization with the help of Chung Lee, a local attorney. A meeting of the founding board of directors included Robinson, Nichols, Ruth Strickland, Pam Ernest, and Kevin Regan. That same month, the mission statement was adopted: "The Philharmonic exists in order to make great music as accessible as possible to the people of Gwinnett and the surrounding region and encourages audiences to enjoy great music wherever it is found in metropolitan Atlanta."

It was decided that an open-house reception would be held in March of that year at the new concert hall where the vision of the Philharmonic could be presented to those interested. Several hundred citizens attended and many joined as founding, contributing members of the recently incorporated association. Robinson obtained commitments from several large corporations and the first season, consisting of three concerts, was fully underwritten.

The inaugural orchestral concerts were on October 5 and 6, 1995 with a trio of overtures which represented the orchestra's "overture" to the community. Gary Menzies was soloist for the Grieg Piano Concerto. The season continued with a winter concert titled "Beethoven to Broadway"---- an eclectic bill of fare from musical theatre, opera, and cinema. The season's spring concert featured the Rev. William Sheals as dramatic narrator in Aaron Copland's "Lincoln Portrait."

The Gwinnett Philharmonic has presented concerts of symphonic music to enthusiastic Gwinnett Performing Arts Center audiences in the fall, winter, and spring ever since. These concerts would not have been presented without significant annual support from season presenting sponsors, such as Primerica and Scientific-Atlanta, as well as broad community support of many other members of the community. That includes significant support from Ernest Communications, the Community Foundation for Northeast Georgia and the Metropolitan Arts Fund. The Philharmonic has received grants enabling it to add two staff members, an executive director and an operations/public relations specialist.

Along the way, performances of smaller ensembles and soloists have been added to each season. Patrons have responded to more varied offerings of classical chamber music in addition to the orchestral concerts. The Philharmonic's offerings were expanded to include its own Big Band Jazz ensemble with its first performance announced for May of 2007.

As support for the Philharmonic has grown, outreach into the community has been a growing part of its vision. Annual performances have been given for school children with the support of leaders such as Sylvia and Phillip Beard and Chris Fowler at the Buford Performing Arts Center. Also beyond the walls of the Gwinnett Center, outdoor patriotic concerts have been presented in the cities of Duluth and Lawrenceville.

The orchestra continued its outreach to students by sponsoring a mentoring opportunity in the form of annual side-by-side concert with the Gwinnett Youth Symphony Orchestra in which the young musicians gain valuable experience performing with the Philharmonic's professionals.

The Philharmonic orchestra was comprised entirely of professional musicians from Gwinnett and neighboring counties and includes players who are often heard in professional performance venues around Georgia. Many of the orchestra's musicians were also active as music educators. Many also performed in other top orchestras of the region, but all brought great skill and commitment to the goal of offering the best to Gwinnett's audiences.

* * * * *

In August, 2008, the Philharmonic's board of directors declared their 13-year run of presenting classical music a "success," but announced that because of higher professional costs, lower-than-expected underwriting support, and an economic downturn, the orchestra would close and not have another season.

The Philharmonic was no more. The loss was a blow to the cultural offerings of Gwinnett.

Aurora Theatre

While the Aurora Theatre is now comfortably housed in a retrofitted historic church in downtown Lawrenceville, it wasn't always located in such professional quarters. In fact, it wasn't always in Lawrenceville, though it is a key to the revitalization of downtown Lawrenceville.

When it originally started, it also didn't go by its present name, but was known as "Down Right Theatre," the brainchild of veteran theatre instructor Ray Ross, soon joined by his sons, Sam and Scott. They launched Down Right in a converted hardware store in Duluth in 1992.

The Aurora Theatre in Lawrenceville

Later on, the father and sons found that they had different interests, and the Ross group sold the Down Right theatre to four people: Barbara Hawkins, who had been a student of Ross in both high school and college in Ohio; her husband, John Scott of Decatur; and to Sharon and Phil Albert of Pine Lake. In June of 1996, the four purchased the assets of the Down Right Theatre from Ross, for a for-profit venture and changed the name to Aurora Theatre. Albert was named producer. For the 1996-97 season, in the former Duluth hardware store, the Aurora had an average attendance of only 27 in the 130 seat theatre, and ended the year with 120 season subscribers. (Later the theatre added more seats, to 197, at this Duluth location.)

However, during their second season, 1997-98, Barbara Hawkins and John Scott sold their interests to the Alberts. They, in turn, brought in Anthony Rodriguez on commission as the managing director. Attendance picked up during this season, with the theatre counting 420 season subscribers at the end of the year.

Attendance grew during the third season of the Aurora, but in May of 1999, there was a new wrinkle in the management of the theatre. Albert got an opportunity to run the *Reach of Song*, Georgia's official historical drama at Young Harris, and was not going to be around to direct Aurora operations.

Rodriguez, who had two successful seasons under his belt as the managing director, talked with Cindy and Randy Sutt. They had their business in Duluth and were theatre supporters, and wanted to keep theatre alive in the town. The upshot was the formation of a non-profit entity, eventually a 501(c)(3) corporation, to purchase from the Alberts the assets of the Aurora. Terms were $20,000 over three years, with no interest. Rodriguez was named producing artistic director for the final show of the season, *Catfish Moon*. Ann-Carol Pence was named resident musical director. Total subscribers at the end of the season hit a record 950.

The newly-reinvigorated Aurora continued its upward movement during the first complete season as a non-profit entity, 1999-2000. By then, Ann-Carol Pence was named associate producer, and for the first time, the theatre hired a part-time assistant for the box office. The theatre also got its first corporate grant, from Target Corporation, of $3,000. Season subscribers hit an all-time high of 1,200.

The theatre had put together a strong non-profit board, which has continued to be supportive. In 2008, the board consisted of Theresa Bullock, Laura Dennison, Randy Foster,

Laura Dennison, Barbara Howard, Terri Jondahl, Rick Johnson, Jay Markwalter, Ann-Carol Pence, Anthony Rodriguez, Cynthia Sutt, Randy Sutt, Mark Tyrrell, and Angela Woo. Foster is president, Randy Sutt is vice president, Tyrrell is vice president for finance, Pence is secretary and Johnson is capital campaign chair. (Rodriguez was chairman from 1999 until Foster became chair.)

Meanwhile, acceptance of the Aurora by the community has been continual. From the early days of having 120 season ticket holders, this number in 2007 is past 2,100, with anticipation that, with the new theatre, the count will go over 4,000. Season ticket holders now include people from 221 cities in 107 counties in Georgia and surrounding states.

The Aurora continued to offer top-quality theatre, under Equity guidelines, and for 11 years has scheduled six shows each of 25 productions.

Another feature: beginning in the 2003-2004 season, the theatre found sponsors for each production. Different corporations of the community have signed on as sponsors of individual shows since that time, in sponsorships ranging from $5,000-10,000.

The Aurora's budget for 2006-07 was $600,000, and the anticipated budget for the first season in the new theatre, 2007-08, has been projected at $825,000. (That's a far cry from the $100,000 first year budget for the Aurora.)

Perhaps the Aurora would never have moved to Lawrenceville had not Emory Morsberger been looking for a key anchor for the re-developed Courthouse Square in Lawrenceville. Aurora as a focus for the downtown area fit together hand in glove with Morsberger's goals, and suddenly, the revitalization had a new anchor.

Working with both Aurora Theatre and the City of Lawrenceville, Morsberger crafted an arrangement that made the deal come together. A key feature of the project is a city-owned parking deck adjacent to the theatre, which serves Aurora patrons well, but also enlarges the capacity for downtown parking during the day. The City of Lawrenceville's contract with the Aurora is for a 20-year period in a rent-free arrangement. There is an option to renew the lease for another 20 years. The cost of contract for the renovation of the original First Methodist Church into the Aurora Theatre was originally $3.5 million.

The Aurora Theatre itself launched an $800,000 fund-raising campaign for the new quarters, and surpassed that goal well in advance of the deadline. As part of the theatre's contribution, the audience will benefit from a state-of-the-art sound system in the new facilities. The Aurora has modern theatre technology-driven equipment, such as lighting, with 102 spotlights, and the most up-to-date rigging, stage curtains, lift systems, fixtures and equipment. The theatre also owns a fog machine to create illusions of mist or moor, or even clouds. There are four dressing rooms, and a big rehearsal hall (a former Sunday School room.)

What the Aurora offers is a theatre with a capacity of 250 main-stage seats, with 48 of these in the balcony. It is a far cry from the cramped former hardware store. There's no bad seat in the entire theatre, and no viewing obstruction for any theatre-goer. Attendees now have improved seating and state-of-the-art acoustics. Theatre lovers are even allowed to bring their beverages to their seats!

Another feature of the new theatre is the more intimate Black Box Theatre of 150 seats. This space is anticipated to be of use for concerts, children's theatre and for rental for small arts groups.

Highlights of other seasons:

- 2000-2001: Keith Hinze named production manager; an educational outreach, Learning Library, was begun, reaching over 6,000 students annually. Subscribers at the end of the season: 1,600.
- 2001-2002: A box office manager/Learning Library coordinator was on board. Aurora begin to hire Equity performers and pay union scale. Learning Library performs to over 20,000 Gwinnett County students.
- 2002-2003: Musicals by moonlight launched with *Guys and Dolls*. Teatro del Sol, with programs in Spanish and English, was launched in formative stage. Development director temporarily hired.
- 2003-2004; Teatro del Sol produced first show in March; Patrick Campbell named production manager; Cabaret series launched; Volunteer Guild began; first New Year's Eve Cabaret and Casino night held.
- 2004-2005: Director of sales and marketing, Al Stilo, hired. Randy Foster is named board chairman. Saturday matinees launched, and Gwinnett County Public Library becomes partner with its Pennies from Heaven effort. First *Barefoot in the Park* held in Duluth; first grant from Georgia Council for the Arts arrives, for $5,000. Aurora announces eventual move to Lawrenceville.
- 2005-2006: City of Lawrenceville hires Foreman, Seely, Fountain as architect for the theatre. New Year's Eve event at Hudgens Center for the Arts. Lawrenceville Ghost Tours begin, a 90-minute walking tour through the city, with storytelling -- this proves to be quite successful.
- 2006-2007: City of Lawrenceville approves temporary theatre on unused fourth floor of City Hall until new theatre operational. Geoffrey Brown is technical director. Three shows were presented here, allowing Aurora's seasons to continue without interruption.
- May 31, 2007: Opening of new Aurora Theatre in Lawrenceville, with first presentation on the vast, deep (and 30 foot tall) stage: *Camelot!* Adjacent parking deck funded by the City of Lawrenceville through the Special Purpose Local Option Sales Tax. Parking deck designed by architect John Heard and built by Foster and Associates. The parking deck adjoins the theatre, with patrons gaining entrance from the deck directly into the theatre.

New London Theatre

A production of *The Wizard of Oz* at the Snellville United Methodist Church was the springboard for a community theater developing in South Gwinnett, the New London Theatre. It came out of the work of Kirk and Jean Buis, who have taught theatre at South Gwinnett High for years.

The community theater started in 1999, through the efforts of the Buis couple. He remembers: "We had become involved in the production at the church of *The Wizard of Oz*, and even our daughter, who was then seven, was in the play as a munchkin. After that, we realized that the community needed something involving a lot of people. From that came the New London Theatre."

The first play produced was *Charlotte's Web*. "The reception we got encouraged us, and that's how we got started. Having a community theater like this is a way an entire family can come and get involved, on stage, back stage, in publicity, or in other ways, as we help each other out."

The company has produced a veritable catalog of top plays of all sorts over the years, including *Anne of Green Gables, The Music Man, Amadeus, Cotton Patch Gospel, Annie, Doctor Dolittle,* and *Man of La Mancha.*

The company, now a non-profit charitable institution, has been quite active, producing five plays each year, and often involving large casts in musical productions. It usually plans its big musicals during the summer, when there is more rehearsal time. For *Peter Pan*, there were 70 in the cast!

Most plays run for two performances on two weekends, and draw an average of 400-500 in attendance. However, the most successful of the plays was the 2004 performance of *Annie*, which drew an audience of 2,654. One reason *Annie* was so well received is that many, many young girls were cast as orphans, and with the large cast, lots of people, including many parents, were in attendance.

The Theatre ticket prices are attractive: $10 in advance and $12 at the door. A season ticket is $50. The company plans eight plays a year, with each having nine performances, or a total of 72 offerings.

Buis, who grew up in Kansas City and Pittsburgh, came to the area when his father was transferred to Atlanta. His work with New London Theatre is strictly part-time, while teaching drama and language arts full-time for 15 years at South Gwinnett High School. He previously taught for four years at Meadowcreek High. He graduated from Grove City College in Pennsylvania.

Buis is president of the company. The theater's board of directors meets monthly, approving operations and the plays to produce. The budget for 2007 was $35,000. There is little payroll, except for the pianist and director, with virtually all the others being volunteers from the area.

Members of the Theatre's board of directors in 2008 include Kathi Mardis, chairman; Kirk Buis, executive director; Lana Blaha, treasurer; and Jonathan Cates, David Clack, Beth Elam, Tonya Hensley, Leslie Raab and Kyle Simonis.

The theater maintains an interactive web site and accepts applications for parts and directors for upcoming plays online. The theater even allows visitors to its site to vote online to determine which plays will be presented.

In 2006, the Theater began a drive to raise monies for a new home for the company. It succeeded in finding a home at 2485 East Main Street, in the Snellville Plaza shopping center, at the intersection of U.S. Highway 78 and Georgia Route 124. One of the benefits of this location was the availability of parking.

The first performance in the new home was the musical *Godspell*, on February 15, 2008, the second the mystery, *Arsenic and Old Lace*. A different cast performed on alternate presentations for this play, one with the actors under 18, the other with actors over 18.

New London Theatre can entertain 125 patrons in stadium seating in the 4,000 square foot theatre, which previously was a rug outlet. The company's initial goal was to raise $35,000 for the refurbishing.

Please Read
Important Information Concerning Your Electric Bill

Beginning with your November 2009 bill, you will notice a four percent city franchise fee as an additional line item. Cities charge these fees to Walton EMC for access to and use of city property and right of way in conducting our normal utility operations.

For more information, call us at 770/267-2505 or log on to waltonemc.com.

GA00350G

Buis anticipates the continuation of children's theatre offerings, plus classes on acting and stagecraft classes. Currently the theater offers summer camp in theatre, and eventually plans to have classes year around, which it has done since 2005. Mostly, however, the new home for the New London Theatre will allow the company to have longer runs and give people more chances to participate in live theater.

Lionheart Theatre

Lionheart Theatre Company seeks to offer affordable entertainment, and encourages the participation of community members in all aspects of theatrical production. Lionheart's goal is to elevate the spirit of community by enriching the cultural experiences of its members and audiences.

Lionheart Theatre Company, based in Gwinnett County, is a nonprofit, 501(c)(3), all-volunteer, community theater. Its history is rooted in the drama ministry at Norcross Presbyterian Church (NPC). Offering theatrical productions in a number of formats, The NPC Players, as they were then known, also toured surrounding communities as the "Suitcase Players." In 2000, this dedicated group of actors, designers and stage technicians made the "leap of faith" into the community at large, and formally organized as Lionheart Theatre Company.

Michael and Tanya Carroll founded the company. Michael Carroll began his acting career with The Alliance Theatre before attending the University of Georgia as a drama major. He has appeared in more than 35 Atlanta-area stage productions.

Tanya Carroll is a graduate of Georgia Southern University in theatre. She produced and directed theatrical productions for both Norcross Presbyterian Church and Lionheart Theatre Company. Tanya is the producing artistic director for Lionheart Theatre Company.

In 2007, Lionheart located at the Norcross Community and Cultural Arts Center. Prior to that time, it was a roving theatre company at various venues around Gwinnett.

Lionheart seeks to keep ticket prices affordable for folks who hope to find quality, family entertainment in their own back yard. Lionheart's $15 ticket price, with discounts for seniors, kids and groups, includes a homemade dessert and beverage.

Lionheart has a track record of giving back to the community in a variety of ways. It has used its productions to solicit contributions for Norcross Cooperative Ministries. It has supported Plant a Row for the Hungry and The American Diabetes Association, the local foster children's program and Relay for Life.

One of the goals of Lionheart Theatre Company is to have folks who have experienced the theatre in high school or college to put there skills back to work and still have a day job and time with the family.

Red Clay Theatre and Arts Center

Plans for the Red Clay Theatre and Arts Center in Duluth were started in 2005. It was clear that the community wanted an arts center -- sustaining both culture and entertainment was important to the City Council. All this came up after it was announced that the Aurora Theatre was leaving downtown Duluth for a new home in Lawrenceville.

Town officials decided that a new theatre would be designed and built using the former Calvary Christian Church building on Main Street. A new building had been considered, but the existing structure (owned by the city) would provide excellent accommodations for an auditorium, and keep activities downtown.

The theatre was approved for design and re-fit by Duluth Mayor Shirley Lassiter, city councilman and Administrator Phil McLemore, and a 'Theatre Search Committee' of Duluth citizens. The committee consisted of 26 local citizens.

The theatre was designed by Mark Pitt, a local actor and former arts educator from the United Kingdom; Shelly Howard, a citizen of Duluth for whom the theatre represented an essential part of her community; and The Sizemore Group, who are architects. Working closely with city officials, they designed an elegant 280-seat auditorium and stage. Realistic Home Solutions of Cumming did the building conversion. Atlanta lighting experts Barbizon and In Time Productions, a sound company, provided sound and lighting technology.

The building received its certificate of occupancy in October, 2006, just days before the opening night of *Educating Rita*, the theatre's inaugural production.

The theatre also transferred the Horizon Theatre's hit, *Bad Dates*, to Duluth. This represented the first time that this in-town professional company had traveled to the suburbs. Additionally, Red Clay's community work featured local company New Dawn Theater, as they brought *Yes, Virginia, There Is a Santa Claus* to the theatre at Christmas 2006. The season ended with a co-production between Red Clay Theatre and Play Right Productions, as *Smoke on the Mountain* played to audiences in May, 2007.

For Red Clay Theatre, the permanent home will allow the company to have longer runs and give more people more chances to participate in live theater.

New Dawn Theatre

Another theatre group, New Dawn, was founded in 2003 by Sherry Ingbritsen from the disbanded Pelican Players, which operated from Westminster Presbyterian Church in Snellville. It later moved most of its presentations to the Historic Courthouse in Lawrenceville. Original board members included Sherry Ingbritsen, president; Bill Miller, vice president; Vince Lockwood, treasurer; Stephens Collins, recorder; and Beth Peters, publicist. Dawn Davis was later named treasurer when Lockwood left the board. The theatre applied for and obtained 501(c)(3) status in 2005.

Its first play was *Mousetrap* in March of 2003. It presented two more shows in 2003, one play in 2004; two in 2005; and three in 2006 on various stages around the county. Its 2007 season included four plays and the group began 2008 with their first presentation at the Red Clay Theater in Duluth. It now makes its home at the Second Stage at the Red Clay Theater, and has seen its audience size increase there. Funding comes primarily from its audiences. The company now includes casts of children to allow these young people to gain experience on the stage.

In 2008 the officers of the Theatre were Sherry Ingbritsen, président; Martin Gravely, vice president; Patricia Michko, treasurer; and the following board members: Jerry Knoff, Chuck Mason, Rebecca Knoff, Beth Peters, Martha Sosebee, Aliza Gravely and Mike Yow.

County Seat Players

County Seat Players was founded in 1993 to bring quality live theatre to Gwinnett County, making it one of the oldest community theater groups in the county. Since then it has produced several plays and musicals each year. It is a non-profit 501(c)3 organization.

It has been a continually producing company, with nearly 50 plays presented at different venues over the years. Among its efforts have included dinner theatre productions at Vines Botanical Gardens and The Flying Saucer Retro Café in Lawrenceville, as well as productions at several Gwinnett high schools, the Chapel at Berkeley Lake, the former Royal Gallery in downtown Norcross and the Pinckneyville Community Center, the 1818 Club, the Hudgens Center for the Arts in Duluth, and Summit Chase Country Club.

Button Theatre

The second professional theatre company in Gwinnett (after the Aurora) is the Button Theatre, founded in 2007, a name that harkens to the county's namesake. Founding members Celia Rosenblum, Mary Carolyn Conti and I.J. Rosenblum decided that there needed to be more quality theatre in Gwinnett County. From this small conversation, Button Theatre was born. Its first production, *Godspell*, was in July of 2007. The company presents performances at the Black Box Theater at the Hudgens Arts Center. I.J. Rosenblum is the managing director of the company, Conti handles marketing, and Celia Rosenblum heads the educational unit.

It seeks to offer affordable, quality musicals and plays that can be enjoyed by all ages, showcasing primarily local talent, and employing high production values. All its crew members are paid professionals. It also offers children's theatre classes and summer camps and cultivates local talent through workshops for actors and technicians.

Besides the three founders, the Button board members include Larry Larsen, Anne Lockhart, Carol Ann Stough, Joanne Taylor and Teresa Osborn. Officers are Larsen, president; Stough, secretary; and Lockhart, treasurer.

Spotlights on Center Stage

Spotlights on Center Stage is a non-profit community theatre founded by Marion and Michael Guyre of Grayson in the fall of 2006. Its mission is to provide quality family entertainment and to invite families to enrich their lives through the theatrical arts.

The emphasis of the group is to have a theatre community where old relationships are strengthened and new ones are formed. The group also stressed that the entire family can spend time together at the theatre, while each member does something he or she loves, whether they choose to be an actress or a guy with a hammer.

Spotlights' first production, *An Evening of Entertainment*, was hosted by Barnes and Noble at The Avenue in December of 2006. Since that time, Spotlights has presented shows such as *A Mad Breakfast, Death By Chocolate, An Evening of Fairytales,* and *The Elves and the Shoemaker*.

The group is a traveling theatre since they do not have a permanent home. In the past, performances have been staged at Ingleside Presbyterian Church in Lawrenceville. The theatre group is looking for a facility in the Grayson/Lawrenceville area to call their own.

The arts rejuvenate Buford

Downtown Buford lost its retail vigor in the 1970s as businesses moved from Main Street to the new Georgia Highway 20 four-lane between Interstate 85 and the Norfolk Southern rail crossing. Banks, auto dealers and retail stores all congregated around "Buford Mall" (really a strip shopping center), which opened near the intersection of Georgia Highways 20 and 23.

Yet Main Street in Buford in 2008 is alive with activity during the day and at night. What caused this dramatic change in business climate? How did it come about?

What rejuvenated Buford did not come from anything that city fathers did, nor was it planned. The revitalization was started by people who are not normally associated with economic development, but are creative people. In a word, by "artists."

It all came about because the downtown businesses had, one by one, closed, creating many vacancies along Main Street.

Then, in 1981, a couple who had moved nearby, heard that the Buford Grill served a good breakfast, and happened to go there to eat one Saturday morning. At the Buford Grill, they noticed long faces on many of the customers in the grill, who were grieving, practically crying. The guy who ran the diner told the couple, Sandra Sumner and Randy Wood, about the fire the day before, December 19, which destroyed the massive Buford Tannery. Many of those men at the diner had either worked there themselves, or had relatives who worked there. They all had memories of what at one time had been the Bona Allen Tannery and how it and its allied companies had driven the area's economy and had provided jobs for the people of the area. By then, the Tannery was owned by the Tandy Corp. of Fort Worth, Tex.

After breakfast, the couple drove to Main Street, and down to the fire scene. Sandra Sumner remembers: "We had never been down Main Street before. As we approached the Tannery, we could smell the smoke from the fire. The area had been roped off and the fire had been put out when we got to the scene."

The couple had just moved to a house on two-laned Georgia Highway 20 near the Woodward Mill (across from present day Mall of Georgia). She was operating a gallery in Mountain Park (Front Porch Gallery), and he was a vocational counselor at Stone Mountain High.

The downtown Buford area had their interest, which simmered in their minds for three years, until late 1984. Sandra says: "We were in the wholesale picture framing business in Lawrenceville, and renting our premises. Since we had just sold a retail business in Snellville, we had a little money, and saw that building at 9 Main Street in downtown Buford, talked to Venita Masters, the real estate agent, and found that the owners, who included Venita's mother, would finance the building. So we bought it. "

In December of 1984, the couple moved into the building. Sandra says: "We just fell in love with the place, and started fixing it up. We cleaned it up, painted the outside, and others saw what we were doing." Randy Wood adds: "We needed more space for our wholesale framing business and gift business, "Distinctive Collections." The place we bought had previously been Buford Hardware, then Tony Lord had run an air- conditioning business from there. It had about 7,000 square feet on three floors, and we were able to buy it for $45,000."

At the time, retail businesses were leaving the area. This was about the time that Buice Wallace closed N.W. Buice and Company. Many of the buildings were boarded up, and few spaces had occupants in them. Meanwhile, Randy had admired the building at 37 Main Street. "It had these arched windows on the second floor, which you could see from the back. I thought they would be spectacular fixed up. The top floor had been the Odd Fellow's Hall. We were able to buy that building in 1991, and move in after renovation about 1993."

Later on, Parsons Department Store closed its store at 39 Main. Bush says: "I had mentioned to Calvin Andrews that if they ever wanted to sell, to let me know, and we bought that building, a smaller one, for $30,000. We rented it to an antique store at first, and later leased it to a gallery owner, who eventually bought it."

The couple were not through. They bought from George White the No. 13 Main Street building, where Sandy moved her business. They eventually sold No. 9 Main Street to a stained glass shop, which had its pieces in many of the galleries along the street.

Then the couple met Rozelle Morton and Allen Bush, artists specializing in glass, who had their studio in a little garage besides their house. Allen Bush picks up the story: "We moved to Buford in 1984, and got to know Randy and Sandy as framers, as they did some of the larger pieces for us. We moved our studio to Main Street in 1988, across from Jay's Drug Store."

Soon another couple came, Petra and Deitrich Hecht. She was a potter, and opened her studio where Polly's Clothing had once been, and rented space to other artists.

Another artist, Lee Bomhoff, who specialized in pastels, moved in. And others followed. Eventually, there would be more than 30 artists at one time on Main Street, and since 1984, more than 100 artists have worked in Buford at one time or the other. Other early members of this community of artists included Ferdinand Rosa, Mary Pratt, Nancy Shaffer, David Kidd, Charles Dingler, Irven Penn, Michael Dierdorf, Vic McCallum, Geoffrey Johnson, Sarah Hatch, Mavis Stevens, Lynne McIntosh and Judith Surowiec.

Ferdinand Rosa got a building in downtown Buford about 1990. He was an abstract painter, specializing in mixed media, though most of his work is large art, in acrylic and oils. "I was in Atlanta," Rosa says, "and had moved to Lake Lanier, and was looking for a loft studio. A friend had family in Buford, and one day he showed me the space that once was Drake Furniture Company, which was a vast space.

"One day after we were open a while, a guy walked up the stairs to the studio, and we were scraping down the walls, getting it painted, and he wanted to take pictures. He told us that back in the 1930s, he had worked on the second floor for Bona Allen Company, hand-carving saddles for the cowboys in Hollywood. He said the whole second floor was covered with people working in leather, doing the lapidary work for the saddles. The Allen craftsmen built saddles for Roy Rogers and the Cisco Kid in Buford. They would even ship in the horses so that they could fit the saddles to them." Though the Allens closed their saddle making operations, remnants of the craft still flourish in parts of the area.

Also arriving at the scene by 1991 was businessman, Bob Bowden, who partnered with Lantz Caldwell and Mark Alexander to open the Contemporary International Museum of Art on Main Street. It attracted famed New York artist Robert Rauschenberg to visit. The Museum showed contemporary work, though was not a favorite of those visiting the area, and soon closed.

Rosa, originally from Bridgeport, Conn., and his wife, Catherine, realized that the local artists needed some method to attract people to the studios and galleries in the town. "We tried to get other artists in town to help, but most were not interested. So we organized and founded the Tannery Row Festival of the Arts, and the other artists said they would be available to sell their art work during the show on Main Street and on the square. We even formed a 501(c)(3) charity to put the show on."

The City of Buford became interested in helping the Festival. The city provided the festival funding from the hotel-motel tax money, and put up a stage and provided electrical power for the event.

Rosa says: "The first year we held the Festival (about 1990) people could not believe how many showed up. The City said it would fund it every year, and did for several years. It brought people into town. Eventually we got artists from all over coming, even from surrounding states."

Allen Bush puts it this way: "Everyone was in culture shock from the reception of people to the festival. People were coming to downtown Buford for the art. Sandra Sumner had the vision for what the place could become, and she had the drive to pursue that vision. Sandy and I would work together on projects, though we were not close. It gave the community a strength, and the artists had the vigor and drive. At one time we had 32 artists there."

One way the group bonded together was at a "rally in the alley" gathering on Friday nights. Bush says: "Every Friday we would gather at my loading dock in the alley, and have drinks, music and grill food. It was a celebration of that week, with the artists grateful for not having to have a regular job."

During the 1990s, more and more artists were settling into studios, and galleries were opening along Main Street. These newcomers to Buford created original art in many forms: paintings, pottery, photography, blown glass, in fiber and jewelry. Their styles were varied, from traditional to folk to contemporary. One, Dennis Primm, worked in functional iron sculpture, which now is seen in many of the doorways and restaurants. All this functioned to create a certain excitement -- a vibrancy -- along Main Street. Buford became a destination for authentic, original and collectible art.

This period was the height of the artist boom in Buford. Bush says: "It was about 10 years that were magical and special. It's rare for something like that to happen. I am glad I was a part of it, and yes, I miss it."

Wood encouraged other artists to buy their buildings, but many did not have the resources. "They were paying rent of maybe $150 a month for their space, and that was all many of them could afford."

Low real estate prices were one reason the artists first came. Rent was relatively cheap for the essentially vacant buildings. Some artists paid as little as $40,000 to $100,000 to buy their buildings. They were happy, producing art, and now people were visiting the area regularly to see their art, and for many, to buy their art.

Though the artists did not promote their efforts very much, one effort for the art colony was an exhibit for many years at the Piedmont Arts Festival in Atlanta. Allen Bush rented a 50'x50' tent to show creations from the Buford artists, an effort he dubbed "Passages," from 1988 to 1998. "Piedmont was a nine-day show, attracting two million people. We had displays from five or ten Buford artists to show, and it attracted people to Buford on subsequent weeks. That festival was in September, and we would give out invitations to a December show in Buford. We got people from Atlanta, not a huge turnout, but they came, and bought art, either for themselves, as gifts, or for clients. Everybody who came seemed to buy something."

People would come to Buford, and visit in the galleries and studios, and get hungry. But they had to leave the area to find a place to eat, and most of the time, they didn't immediately return to Main Street. That's when the artists sought restaurants to come to the area. Ellen Stevens operated a restaurant and did very well. Another restaurant arrived, also making a go of it, and in 1999, Laurie Attaway arrived on Main Street.

She had opened a restaurant in 1996 on Holiday Road, the route to Lake Lanier Islands, which Attaway called "Third Coast Grill." It prospered, bringing an upscale, new flavor to the dining offerings of the area. Attaway started the Aqua Terra restaurant in 1999 on Main Street, and hasn't looked back since. It was an immediate success. One native called it an "upscale restaurant, one without Buckhead prices." Later, she had opened a high-end boutique, Bella Luna, in 2001 on Main Street. "It lasted two years, but Buford had not come into its own yet. It wasn't pulling the people it needed; it was ahead of its time." In 2003 she opened a second restaurant, 37 Main, again to success, a restaurant which has since expanded. The secret of her success, Attaway says, "is having great people, a good chef, great service and a good menu." On top of that, the food must taste good, and people approved of Attaway's methods.

As one-time Buford City Manager Bobby Kerlin put it, "Business was dead in downtown before the artists came. You used to go uptown on a Saturday night, and no one was in town. Now the artists have generally left, but the restaurants draw people. You can't find a parking place there on Saturdays at about any time, even at night."

As the businesses began to thrive, the city responded. To improve the looks of the area, the City of Buford put in new sidewalks, created a park by the railroad on Main Street, and generally spruced up the area. But with the new looks, and improved business conditions, came higher rents.

Interestingly, the people who started it all, Sandra Sumner and Randy Wood, were the first to leave. Sandra Sumner says: "We had tried to get the artists to buy their buildings, and some did. But for the others, the rent got too high, and they moved out."

As happens in rejuvenated areas, real estate prices began to climb. Some artists who purchased their studios got $300,000 for their buildings, so the decision to move became an economic one. And prices continued skyward, Wood reports. "I sold one building for $300,000, and one guy kept it about a year and a half, and it sold for $450,000. Since then the same building has sold for $800,000, and artists cannot afford space in buildings because of their high cost."

Sandra says: "Too, development was all around us. Trees were coming down, and the esthetics were changing rapidly from when we moved there. Also, Randy and I yearned for the mountains, and finally moved to Robbinsville, N.C., which is surrounded by three lakes and mountains, and is the most northwestern city in that state. We felt at home immediately, and eventually opened an art studio there."

* * * * *

Randy Wood had amassed a large collection of mementos related to Buford history, and displayed the items in a corner of his location as a Buford museum to attract customers.

People started bringing him more items. In 1987, David Mabry and Pat Garner contributed items and tools of their fathers to jump-start the collection. John Johnson soon followed suit with leather-working tools he used from 1932-1965 working for Bona Allen. These hand tools, work bench, dies, patterns, and stamps, give a more complete look into the talent and craft required to hand carve and make saddles.

In 1988, Larry Bailey donated an extensive collection of memorabilia from the Bona Allen baseball team, the "Shoemakers," Buford's own "World Semi-Pro Champions." Included in this collection are photographs and trophies, among them the National Baseball Congress World Series Trophy and the 1940 Denver Post Semi-Pro Championship Trophy.

Randy Wood didn't want to move this collection of memorabilia out of Buford, and by happenstance, Buford native Lynn Bowman had returned to the area in 1997 from Macon, where he had worked since college at Mercer. He bought and then refurbished the former Victor Allen house on Sawnee Street. Bowman's ancestors had been some of the first settlers in Gwinnett in 1818, the same year the county was formed. Bowman showed an interest in the artifacts that Wood had. Eventually he agreed to purchase the items, with Wood insisting on certain restrictions, such as not moving them out of Buford.

Bowman is a real estate broker, and continues as custodian to operate the Museum of Buford at 95-B Main Street. It is open on Saturdays with free admission. Private showings are often held at other times. The Museum has an extensive web site, mostly built through efforts of students at Buford High School.

Bowman is hoping eventually to catalog the items in the Museum. There are more than 5,000 items in the Museum, including 80-120 page catalogs showing the product lines of the Bona Allen Company. Bowman says: "Bona Allen Company sold the same items over and over, so a catalog would last for years. They would put out new price sheets on each product from time to time. "

He adds: "Our plan for the Museum by 2012 is to double the collection in holdings, and also create a stand-alone division by 2017 which focuses on the fine arts from artists cycling through Buford. Some are well known, and we want to collect pieces from each artist who worked in Buford to have in a Fine Arts Museum. We also want to get the entire collection on electronic files to make them available to the public. All it takes is time and money."

Another artist who moved to the area took art to a new turn. When Anita Stewart moved to Main Street in 1998, she opened a gallery as an artist offering to do commission work in addition to selling her art work. As time went on, she found people interested in taking art lessons from her, and began to concentrate more on that aspect, soon forming the Buford School of Art. In 2006 she moved around the corner (to Moreno Street) and changed the name to Anita's ArtsCool, also adding more teachers, with classes for children, teens and adults. The school offers instruction in drawing, painting and pottery. The school was called "one of the crown jewels of Buford" by the *Gwinnett Daily Post*. Ms. Stewart continues as a professional artist, entering national competition.

Allen Bush remembers one item in the museum. "It's a photograph from when the Buford artists had a show at the Gwinnett Arts Center. Just before the show, we gathered and had the picture made, which is at the Buford Museum now. When I see that photo, I remember thinking how lucky we were to be a part of a vigorous and creative group. The relationships formed were on the strength and creative interest in each other's work. It was a good time."

Meanwhile, in 2001, Don Arsenault began renovating the former Chicopee building at 554 West Main Street, which had been the site of an Allen bridle and harness factory earlier. The 13-acre site included a four-floor, 115,000 square foot building, which had been the Allen shoe factory. The entire site had once been destroyed by fire, and had been re-built in 1903. As such, the building was before its time, with built-in sprinklers, massive fire doors, and it far exceeded the fire codes of that day.

As Arsenault began to restore the building in its earlier fashion, he sought artists to locate there. By 2004, some of the Buford artists migrated to his renovated facilities, dubbed the Tannery Row Cultural Arts Center. In 2008, there were 16 artists in the location in working studios, providing a distinctive blend of output for the arts, including paintings, pottery, figurative sculptures, mixed media, and wrought iron sculptures. "The artists like the space, as they have room for more of an individual studio than mere gallery atmosphere," Arsenault says. It is Buford's first art colony under one roof, and continues the atmosphere first seen on East Main Street in the last part of the 20th century.

In 2007, in the downtown Main Street area, there were only two art galleries, and limited space reserved for artists' studios. Yet the street remains bustling, with restaurants, boutiques and other businesses attracting good traffic.

Rozelle Morton and Allen Bush eventually moved to Monroe County. While Bush works in glass at Stone Mountain, Morton is the director of the Georgia Piedmont Art Association in downtown Winder.

Gwinnett gets its own Civic Center

Now a busy fixture just off Sugarloaf Parkway near Interstate 85 in Gwinnett, the Gwinnett Civic Center is the virtual nerve center for the county. Among its facilities are a giant indoor arena gaining wide acclaim in the entire metro Atlanta area, exhibition space for trade shows and corporate meetings, a major ballroom, plus both a Performing Arts and Fine Arts Center.

Located adjacent to the Center is the Gwinnett Chamber of Commerce, with offices for several major non-profit agencies all in the same building: The Gwinnett Convention and Visitors Bureau, the Council for Quality Growth, the Community Foundation of Northeast Georgia, and the American Cancer Society all call the building home..

Across Sugarloaf Parkway are the classically-styled offices of the Georgia Baptist Convention. Hotels, Class A office buildings, shopping centers and office parks are popping up nearby. Across Interstate 85 is Discover Mills Mall, now attracting restaurant, office and other out-parcel facilities. The area is a virtual core center for so much that happens in Gwinnett. It's somewhat an incubator for major developments in the county.

The idea for a civic center in Gwinnett all started in the late 1980s as a dream in the mind of Mike Berg, then a county commissioner, says former Gwinnett County Commission chairperson Lillian Webb. "Mike pushed it. There was no place large enough to hold high school graduations, corporate seminars, and other business meetings. We thought it would be a good use of Gwinnett County funds if we could get a sales tax approved for a Civic Center."

Berg remembers: "Besides needing space for graduations, there were many other groups that needed meeting space. We even had acrobatics classes needing a stage on which to perform, and we thought we were losing business the county could have had, since the meeting space was so inadequate and many groups went outside the county to meet. We were thinking of trade shows, conventions, exhibitions and other gatherings. Before deciding to put the question of a Civic Center on the sales tax measure, we had quite a big discussion wondering if including a Civic Center in a sales tax proposal would help it, or sink it. We talked to a lot of people, and decided it would help to have it on the ballot. I'll admit to pushing for the Civic Center. I felt we needed some place like that for key meetings."

With the rapid growth in Gwinnett of industries during the 1980s, and with the continuing influx of new residents, for many years there seemed to be little attention given to the needs of meeting spaces, or the visual and performing arts. But that was soon to be remedied.

The Civic Center

What eventually emerged was the Gwinnett Civic and Cultural Center, which opened in late 1991. Its location was superb, just off Interstate 85 at the four-lane Sugarloaf Parkway exit. On November 13, 1987, voters granted their approval for a Civic Center that would cost $30 million, the money to come from a one cent special purpose local option sales tax (SPLOST). In total, voters that day approved an aggregate sales tax measure of up to $162.5 million, to include building a new Detention Center (jail), renovation of the Historic Courthouse; and for road and bridge improvements.

What was first proposed for the Civic Center itself was a modern structure, consisting of several elements:

- 50,000 square foot exhibition hall,
- 700 seat Performing Arts Hall,
- 14 meeting rooms of 13,000 square feet,
- Parking for 1,500 vehicles.

What the commissioners envisioned was that Gwinnett could become the site of trade shows, conventions, exhibitions and other gatherings, and even high school graduations. That's proven to be true, as the Civic Center always seems to be hopping with first one group, then another, including heavy use by companies in Gwinnett hosting seminars or conferences in its many meeting spaces.

The Civic Center was designed by the architectural firm of Chapman, Coyle, Chapman. The work on the Civic Center began in 1990. The general contractor was Blount Contracting. Its new construction division, unfortunately, went bankrupt during the construction period, causing delays and considerable problems.

Construction was supposed to be complete in 18 months. But there were delays, some associated with the weather. With the prime contractor having financial problems, there were also payment delays, with subcontractors refusing to work until paid.

After many delays, the official opening was in November 1992, the day after Thanksgiving, though many of its functions were not in full operation until the following year. When the Civic Center was first opened, Sugarloaf Parkway had not been completed west of Interstate 85. Anyone going to the Civic Center in those days had to exit the expressway at Georgia Highway 120. Some early critics even called its location "in the boondocks," though in a few years, the center's location would be considered perfect.

Among the festivities of the opening ceremonies was a fireworks show.....during daytime. Yes, a fireworks show during daylight. The show fizzled, as people gathered at the opening could hear the "Boom!" of the fireworks being set off, but could see no burst of light in the sky. The big question on the minds of those attending the opening was: "Who came up with this idea?" No one has admitted to it.

Wayne Hill

As much planning as county officials did for the new Civic Center, at the first major event held at the center, those attending the function were surprised. The event was a "Festival of Trees," during the 1992 Christmas season. As attendees arrived for the event, they were directed to the parking lot, where they were astonished to find a $3 fee to park virtually adjacent to the trees in the woods. There was a reason for this charge, since the parking fees had been built into the budget and were important for the financial viability of the Center.

There was an uproar over the parking fee. More than one of the attendees sounded much like one disgruntled one: "I don't mind paying a little for parking when I go to downtown Atlanta, but it seems a little much to ask me to pay out here, in effect, to pay for parking in a corn field."

No one had thought of the attendees' reactions. But the Civic Center took action, and still had a good stream of revenue from parking. The difference is that the parking fee is hidden in the cost of renting the facility now, or hidden in the price of the ticket, giving the Center the added revenues it required from its initial plan.

Thus began the activity that had been virtually continual since the Gwinnett Civic Center opened in 1992. It has become quite a popular venue. Visitors like the open spaces, the ease of getting to the facility, and, more and more, the growing amenities surrounding the Civic Center.

Even though officially opened in 1992, much more work was needed before the Center was fully functional. In fact, it was well into 1993 before the Center was without some construction activity, with six months of punch list items after that. John Robison, director of engineering, who joined the Civic Center staff in the fall of 1992 as operations foreman, says: "We had to work around events already booked to get the final items finished."

One of the driving forces of having the opening in late 1992, after the General Election, was that County Commissioners responsible for starting the construction were leaving office. This included Chairman Lillian Webb and District Commissioners Curtis McGill and W.J. Dodd.

The incoming commissioners, who were replacing the people who had authorized the construction, at first were merely lukewarm to the idea that a Civic Center would benefit Gwinnett. However, once the new commission started realizing the potential that the Civic Center would bring Gwinnett, they understood, and got behind the Civic Center wholeheartedly.

The leadership at the County Commission from the 1992 election would include Chairman Wayne Hill and District Commissioners Tommy Hughes and Judy Waters. They joined Doug Williamson and Renee Unterman on the commission. When they took office, the Center had just had its grand opening, but was not up and running smoothly yet. After discussion about the facility with Hill, Hughes replaced Berg as the commissioner with prime interest in the Center, which also was located within Hughes' commission district.

Hughes says: "Wayne and I met before we took office, and realized we both shouldn't look after the same activities and facilities. I had heard from staff that the Civic Center had lots of problems as it opened. Wayne and I agreed that I would take this area and look after it."

When Commissioner Dodd did not seek to return to his post on the Gwinnett County Commission in 1992, Hughes ran against two opponents and won. Hughes was an unlikely champion. A former Buford councilman at age 23, he was a real estate investor at age 37 when he came to the commission.

Hughes will admit today that when he first heard of the $30 million Civic Center, he thought it was "the biggest waste of money that I had ever seen." But Wayne Hill remembers: "Soon Tommy turned around, and had a vision that Gwinnett needed its own civic center to attract outsiders to the county. He also saw the need for a performing arts center, and a fine arts center. He began to ride herd on the Civic Center, and became its advocate."

What Hughes found was the Center was not yet complete. He says: "It was a mess. We had a bankrupt contractor. We did eventually get a good building, but it was at about 80 percent of being finished. And on top of that, it lost money, nearly $1 million that first year from operations."

The county, through the Gwinnett Convention and Visitors Bureau (which Hughes soon sat on) had earlier signed a contract with Leisure Management Inc. of Houston, Tex. (now SMG of Philadelphia, Pa.) to manage the Civic Center complex. "We went through three or four general managers," Hughes says, "But the place came to life when we got Preston Williams as the key figure for managing it in May of 1995. We got comfortable with him being the manager, and he was the driving force behind our eventually getting the arena. He had built and run similar facilities in other places, and worked day and night to make it right. I give him more credit than anyone. He guaranteed me that it would be done right, and it was. If he had not shown up, I do not think the arena would have been built."

The initial operational years of the Civic Center were run at a loss. In 1995, the operational deficit was between $700-800,000 a year. This shortfall was covered by the Gwinnett Convention and Visitors Bureau (GCVB) hotel-motel tax. Williams says that "Between 1995 and 2002 we brought the deficit down progressively each year leading up to the opening of the ballroom." The ballroom's opening in October 2002 was followed by the Arena opening five months later, in February 2003. Williams adds: "In 2003, we became cash-flow-positive, with a $2.2 million surplus, which is plowed back into maintenance and upgrading. Our operations have generated over a $2 million margin each year since then." When you consider that less than 10-15 percent of public assembly facilities turn a profit, the Gwinnett Center's profitability is even more outstanding.

Richard Tucker, the 2008 chair of the Gwinnett Convention and Visitors Bureau, which operates the Center, notes that the Gwinnett facility is "one of the few such facilities in the country that operates in the black based on revenue generated, not on public subsidies."

Looking toward the future, the Civic Center is planning an expansion, so that it can attract larger meetings and conventions. Among the items on the drawing board:

- Partnering with a private developer to build a full-service, upscale hotel of 300-400 rooms adjacent and in front of the Center, in the present parking lot. That hotel would be connected directly to the Center.
- Adding 75-80,000 square feet to the exhibit space, more than doubling the current space, plus another 10-12,000 square feet of meeting rooms. There would be an expanded kitchen and other support structure.
- Enlarging the lobby of the Performing Arts Center, and tying this into the hotel and Civic Center in a more pronounced manner. Included in this would be integrating the lake into the design of the expanded complex, including lakeside walkway.

The key to this expansion is getting the interest of a private developer in the site slated for an upscale hotel. That, in turn, would give the Civic Center an ability to compete for more big meetings and attract them to the site.

Though key individuals familiar with the proposed expansion say this could happen over 3-7 years, with the interest in the Center, many would not be surprised to find the new facility built by that time.

The Arena

As the success of the Gwinnett Civic Center gathered steam in its early years, talks began about the need for a bigger venue, capable of hosting much larger events. By early 1997, after feasibility studies and much discussion, county leaders were told that Gwinnett could support both an arena and large ballroom of its own. There was even the possibility that a minor league sports team would locate in Gwinnett, if an arena would be built.

At first, local officials were skeptical about this direction, but its Civic Center operator, LMI, told county leaders of the success it knew from managing arenas in much smaller markets. The sheer size of the growing Gwinnett market drove the discussion. After all, when discussions began on this possibility (1997), Gwinnett numbered 516,032 people within its borders.

Preston Williams, the manager of the Civic Center for LMI, recalls: "We did a complete business model on the idea of enlarging the Civic Center, and even brought in a third party, one of the big accounting firms, to critique the model that we had devised. The upshot was that the numbers spoke for themselves, saying that an arena and a much larger ballroom would be feasible for Gwinnett."

As key leaders realized what Gwinnett could become, new thinking was the rule of the day. Maybe Gwinnett could have an arena and much larger meeting space in the ballroom of its own.

The Arena was a multi-purpose space that would seat up to 13,000 for such events as hockey games and as many as 12,500 for concerts-in-the-round. Not only that, but the arena would be designed with distinctive built-in innovations. One would allow smaller groups to be accommodated easily in a curtained-off arrangement in the arena so that those attending would not feel swallowed up by the vast internal space.

What was projected for the Arena was a facility that would contain:

- A total building of 366,000 square feet.
- Seating of 13,000 at full capacity.
- Intimate seating of 3,500 for curtained-off events in a theatre set up.
- Ability to convert the arena for hockey games with modern ice floor.
- A parking lot adjacent for 4,100 vehicles.
- A club level containing 36 corporate suites and two party suites, plus a 2,000 square foot club lounge.
- In-house video production with three cameras and instant replay abilities.
- Two "DiamondVision" video display boards of 16x9 feet each.
- Full 360 degree video ribbon board on upper level fascia.

The Arena is built northwest of the Civic Center, and also includes a parking lot for more than 4,000 vehicles, all built on 88 acres fronting Sugarloaf Parkway.

Since its opening on February of 2003, the Arena has become a vital force on the Atlanta meeting and entertainment scene. The first big event at the Arena took place on February 21, 2003---a live telecast of the Georgia Force arena football game, which the Georgia Force won.

The Arena's first big entertainment act was a George Strait concert, with many other big-name stars to follow. Since then, the Arena and Ballroom have become vital elements in the Atlanta meeting and entertainment scene, out-distancing the initial projections for both entities in events and attendance, and extremely successful by:

- Hosting more big-name concerts that planners anticipated;
- By having higher-than-projected per capita food and beverages sales;
- Having more sponsorships, with suite sales exceeding the business model by a substantial margin.
- Finding a wider scope of business: civic and church groups now want to come to Gwinnett; and
- Hearing from visitors to the arena and ballroom of a wider acceptance of the amenities of the two facilities.

Meanwhile, another element played into the Arena picture, much as promised before the Arena was built. The Gwinnett Gladiators, a minor league (Eastern Hockey League) team, relocated to Gwinnett from Mobile, Ala. in 2003. The Gladiators have made Gwinnett proud, gaining the playoffs four of five seasons played in Gwinnett, and making the finals of the Eastern Hockey League playoffs in 2006. The team plays routinely to an enthusiastic, roaring audience. Gwinnett has become a hot hockey locale, with one of the best attendance records in the league, which has been in the top 10 in the league (25 teams) all its seasons in Gwinnett.

Headliners have found the Arena for their Atlanta performances. In its first season in 2003, those coming to the Gwinnett Arena included Bruce Springsteen, Alan Jackson, Elton John, and many more. A partial list for five full seasons shows:

Preston Williams

- **2004:** A total of 33 shows, including REM, Gloria Estafan, Willie Nelson, Bette Midler, Cher, and Larry the Cable Guy. Plus there was the Georgia High School Association (GHSA) basketball, SEC Gymnastics championship, U.S. Figure Skating championship, and regular season games of the Georgia Force and Gwinnett Gladiators. Eleven Gwinnett high schools had their graduations at the Arena.
- **2005:** There were 29 big-name shows, among them, The Eagles, Jeff Foxworthy, Yanni, Dolly Parton, Bill Gaither, and the Backstreet Boys. The SEC Gymnastics returned, as did GHSA basketball tournament, Deep South Basketball,

a University of Georgia-Georgia State basketball game, plus the Gladiators home schedule.

- **2006:** Some 34 top-flight entertainment nights were marked, including Bon Jovi, George Strait, Mannheim Steamroller, Red Hot Chili Peppers, The Who, and Eric Clapton. The Gladiators had a solid season of 46 nights; also, there was the GHSA basketball championships, the UGA-Gonzaga basketball game, GHSA wrestling finals, Eastern Synchronized Team Skating and American Idol Live from the Arena. During this year, 12 Gwinnett high schools graduated at the Arena, plus two high schools from outside the county, and three different DeVry Tech graduations.
- **2007:** Out of 38 entertainment events, top performers included Justin Timberlake, Maroon 5, Bob Dylan, Cirque Du Soleil Delirium, Christina Aguilera, Ricky Martin, Martina McBride, Hannah Montana, and Blue Man Group. Among other events were the Russell Athletic Tournament featuring Women's Atlantic Coast Conference versus Southeastern Conference Women's Basketball tournament, SEC Women's Basketball Championship and the Georgia High School Association Basketball Championship. The Gwinnett Gladiators made it to the playoffs of ECHL (East Coast Hockey League).
- **2008:** George Strait, who was the arena opening headliner in 2003, returned to the arena with another sold-out show. Performers have included Keith Urban and Carrie Underwood, Van Halen, Kanye West and Rihanna, Lynyrd Skynyrd and Hank Williams Jr., and The Cure. Also, SEC Gymnastics Championship and GHSA Wresting Championship came to the arena, and the Gwinnett Gladiators made the playoffs again. Gwinnett welcomed back the Arena Football League's Georgia Force which made it to the AFL Playoffs. With the Master Redevelopment Plan being released, new construction started this year including an additional arena parking deck. A mark of distinction for 2008 was the Arena being named one of the 'Top 10 Minor League Venues' in the United States.

* * * * *

People from throughout Metro Atlanta and North Georgia pay top dollar to get seats to hear these performers, with many of the stars preferring the cozy Gwinnett Arena compared to larger venues in downtown Atlanta, as they demonstrate by returning to the Gwinnett Arena for their events.

When the Jehovah's Witnesses hold their summer conferences at the Arena, between 10-13,000 worshippers over each four-day weekend were in attendance. Meetings of the Episcopal Diocese of Atlanta, Free Chapel in Gainesville, Georgia Baptist Convention, and other churches have been or are booked for events at the Arena.

Tommy Hughes adds, "The arena is used so much more than just for concerts, or athletic events, and it helps the county. During the summer, the Jehovah's Witnesses come for their week of meetings, and that means something like 10,000 people paying for hotel rooms, and eating at our restaurants. We're making money from meetings like this from the back side, too, as the county gets our six percent hotel/motel tax, and two cents of our local SPLOST tax every time visitors spend a dollar."

Altogether, the Gwinnett Arena is much busier than many arenas across the country. It averages 111 days a year with event activity. Concerts usually move in and out the same day, but the other 75 events require one or two "move in" days. For ice shows, there are extra days needed to put the ice down and take it out. Altogether, the Gwinnett Arena is in use from 55-60 percent of the time, Cheryl Gee, director of sales and marketing, says. "That is phenomenal for the industry. When you check other arena event calendars, you will find that most are busy half that time."

Another way to show the impact of the Arena is by the "sell-outs." Each year since 2004, there have been at least 16 events with attendance of more than 10,000, including 24 in 2006. There were many more "sellouts" for shows that were curtained off for either a half house or three-quarter house. For 2009, the Arena has already booked the NCAA Women's Regional Basketball Tournament. The Arena at Gwinnett is ranked No. 56 out of 100 arenas nationwide (of all sizes) as of 2007. The arena has been a major success, making the Civic Center area one of the most identifiable in Gwinnett to people from Metro Atlanta.

Another improvement began in 2008. It was to add 970 spaces on six levels in a parking deck to be connected to the northwest corner of the Arena. Development cost were $19 million, to be funded primarily by revenue bonds paid for with hotel/motel taxes. Construction began in January, 2008, and was expected to be completed within the year. The parking deck is to be built over the stormwater retention area. The addition of the 970 spaces in the deck will bring to 5,300 the parking available at the Arena. It will be built on two acres with direct access to the Arena via a covered walk and will substantially improve the disabled/handicapped facilities by providing more spaces closer to the facility.

In addition, a 5,000 square foot meeting/banquet space on the top deck will be built. This facility will have direct access to the club level of the Arena. The new parking space will not mean a change in the "no charge" parking policy for the existing surface parking. However, there may be a parking fee for the covered deck on selected premium packages that will be included in the ticket prices for events at the Arena.

The Ballroom

After the initial opening of the Civic Center, which was primarily an exhibit hall, it soon became obvious there was a need for a large ballroom for seated gatherings or meetings. As plans went forward to add the arena, also part of that package for construction was the addition of the ballroom.

The first additional element to become a reality was a new ballroom. It would be of 22,600 square feet, the largest event ballroom in Gwinnett, with 7,000 square feet of gallery pre-function space. It can seat 1,500 for a buffet dinner, or 1,200 for a seated banquet. The ballroom is also equipped with the most modern audio-visual elements. In addition, the room can be subdivided into smaller meeting spaces and is wired for video and other electronic presentations. Construction began in the summer of 2000.

The ballroom is located between the Performing Arts Center and Exhibit Hall of the Civic Center and connects the two buildings. Prior to construction, an ornamental pond separated the two buildings. The ballroom site required an unusual bit of construction, since it would be built over the pond.

Opening in October, 2002, major functions of Gwinnett and Metro Atlanta organizations, such as the Chamber of Commerce's annual meeting, are held routinely in the expansive ballroom. The Chamber's event was once relegated to downtown Atlanta facilities since no similar spaces were available in Gwinnett. Now, many different groups regularly come to the ballroom. It was even the venue for the celebration of Pakistani Independence Day in the summer of 2006.

Ron Wynn of Holder Construction Co. remembers how the ballroom was built. "It was a tricky bit of construction, since most of the ballroom is built over the pond. The question was how we would span the pond. First, we had to dam up the pond, so that we could reach the rock on the bottom and get our equipment down there. Once it was dried out and firm, then we could put the building foundation in, as if no pond had been there. Once we were finished with working the equipment in the pond area, we took it out, and took down the dam and let the water come back. Most people attending functions at the ballroom don't realize that there is water under its floor."

Today the entire Civic Center is a continuously-connected structure, from the Fine Arts Center on the east end, to the Jacqueline Hudgens Children's Museum, to the Performing Arts Center, the ballroom, and exhibit hall on the north end. Past this, 320 feet away, stands the Gwinnett Arena. It's expected that in the future, the space between the Exhibit Hall and Arena will be used for more exhibit and meeting space.

In 2007, the Gwinnett Center had more than 891 event days, bringing in 179,606 people. Meanwhile, the Arena, hosting much larger functions, was bringing 899,344 people for events and performances during 2007, up from 849,526 the year before. Such acceptance by the wider Metro Atlanta community far exceeded initial projections, making the facilities financially viable. Three categories topped the list attracting people to the Arena, concerts (207,677), religious events (205,248).....and hockey games (200,677).

Funding and building the expansion

The enlarged dream for a bigger Civic Center was a daunting task for Gwinnett leaders, something vastly different for its leaders to contemplate. But how would the county get the money for such a place, what with sales tax revenues already allocated?

The money came from a new wrinkle. What eventually happened came after the county had passed a hotel-motel sales tax of three percent in 1985, charged when booking rooms anywhere in Gwinnett. That was increased in 1994 to six percent, and in 2000, to seven percent. In 1990 the commission authorized payment to the Convention and Visitor's Bureau to establish a reserve for the operation of the Civic Center. (Of the original tax, 25 percent was to be set aside for tourism and economic development, with the commission the sole determinant of how that money was spent.)

By 2000, there were more than 9,000 hotel rooms in the county. Though the county could not fund outright the construction costs of an enlarged Civic Center and a new Arena, it could finance the improvement over several years, and use the hotel-motel sales tax to pay back bonds for those purposes.

In 2001, the Gwinnett County Development Authority issued $65 million of variable rate bonds to be repaid from dedicated revenue of the hotel/motel tax. To complete the funding, the county made available out of its reserves $25 million from the General Fund for the expansion, renovation for the expanded ballroom, and for the Arena. So the price tag on the entire new package was $90 million.

The eventual price tag for the arena itself was $68 million, including its parking lot. The Gwinnett Convention and Visitor's Bureau gets 2.5 cents of the seven percent of the hotel-motel tax, which pays the debt service on the arena. The bonds are scheduled to be paid off by 2031. The original bonds had an interest rate collar that limited the exposure to increases for five years, with a floor of 3.14 percent and a ceiling of 5.0 percent. The main reason for entering into the fixed rate was not savings, but stability, with the county being able to budget and plan for a known amount of debt service over the years. As of 2006, after a rate swap put in through 2011, the interest rate on the bonds was 2.864 percent.

To design and build the Arena, local officials interviewed several firms to work on this big project. The county selected Rosser International of Atlanta to design the facility. Picked from the many contractors interested in becoming the builder of the two facilities was Holder Construction Company of Atlanta. (This firm was headed by the son of the person who had big dreams for Gwinnett County in 1959 in contemplating developing a southeastern merchandise mart in Gwinnett, a project that failed.)

The local person who had managed the Civic Center from 1995-2008, and who supervises the Arena now for the Convention and Visitor's Bureau, Preston Williams, had been involved in several major arena construction projects in other locations, and was perfect to oversee the plans and construction and supervised work on these sites totaling over $1 billion. His experience with the management company LMI included work on arenas, convention centers, stadiums, amphitheaters and performing arts theaters. These job sites were at the Greensboro Coliseum Complex in North Carolina, the Bank Atlantic Center in Sunrise, Fla., the Acer Arena in Sydney, Australia; the Telstra Dome in Melbourne, Australia, and centers in Pikeville, Ky., Charlottesville, Va. and the Northern Kentucky University Arena, near Cincinnati, Ohio.

He says: "For the ballroom construction and building the Gwinnett Arena, we did a design-build project. This delivery method allowed us to bring in the work in the most value-added way we could do it. It was entirely painless from the start in terms of controversy, or insurmountable delays in construction. It just went very well. We ended up bringing the total project in ahead of schedule, on budget, and no one got sued. That's saying a lot in a project of this size."

Ron Wynn of Holder Construction was senior project manager, and calls the work "difficult and challenging, but a great job." He explains why:

"There were several things. First, there was the delivery method. We used the GMP method, that is, "guaranteed maximum price," meaning that it had an open book, team approach. The owner (the county, with Gwinnett Convention and Visitors Bureau managing the job) got to see all our costs, files, etc. It was a cost plus job, but guaranteed maximum outlay. Both sides were comfortable sharing that way. It was a team approach, so we all lived through problems and triumphs, with the owner getting the benefit of the good aspects, but sharing in problem solving. That was one of the key things that made it successful."

Wynn continued: "Even more important was having Preston Williams overseeing the job. On a project of that size and complexity, you must have someone who can make decisions. He had good instincts, knew when to challenge, to trust, or ask questions of our team. And he had the trust of the GCVB and the county. So the project was not bogged down in bureaucratic wrangling. We knew who was running the show, and that he was attending our weekly meetings. So you had the owner, architect and contractor together for two hours each week. We laid out the issues and worked through them. We did not just handle problems, for we found ways for savings. That's another beauty of this approach.

"For instance, we might find that the specifications called for a certain product, but that since the specs were written, there was a new product which we thought was better than the specs, and less expensive. The team would look at it and see if we wanted to do it this new way, and we often saved money that way. It was more of a team approach rather than adversarial environment. This was a team pulling together. Preston was one great leader. He has built similar projects for his employer, then SMG, and knew what to expect. It is so important to have a person like him on a successful project."

Wynn also mentioned another element at the meetings, as represented by George Heckman, himself an engineer. "George attended all our meetings, and worked as County Commission Chairman Wayne Hill's special adviser. George could weigh in from the county's perspective, so we had all stakeholders represented. This was also helpful, for as we worked matters out, we were assured that the county was OK with it."

Preston Williams adds: "In such a process, the owner is more involved. When you have a savings in one area, you could move that savings around. If the job had been hard-bid, that savings would go to the contractor. We did it at a lower cost, but the Arena got an added value out of it. At the end of the project, we had a $65 million arena, but in most markets in normal construction methods, it would have cost considerably more. I've had people in the business who were astounded that Gwinnett could build the arena we have at that cost. Many told me that they thought we would have put $80-$100 million in it."

In 2007, a master plan was advanced for additional development at the Civic Center. A key element in the projection was to have additional hotel facilities built within the facility. A request for a proposal went out in late 2007, with anticipation that responses would begin to trickle in during 2008. Several firms had indicated interest in such a proposal. However, no firm has stepped forward so far with a proposal, no doubt because of the economic turndown of 2008.

* * * * *

Looking back over 15 years of development around the Civic Center, Tommy Hughes, who has had as much to do with the Civic Center as any Gwinnettian, is pleased at what happened: "The dream turned out exactly the way I wanted it to be, a place owned by people of our county where they can go and have a chance to play and enjoy themselves. Some of our people did not realize how big the county was, as big name stars started coming to the arena. My proudest moment is when they turn on the stage lights, and something like 12,000 people are there having fun. That was the reason we built it, for the people. And, many of those people attending events there are staying in our hotel rooms, and that's good for our economy, and helping pay for the arena, too."

In the space of 13 years, what emerged from the red clay soil and pine trees that once was owned by the Eastern Airline Pilot's Pension Fund is Gwinnett's showplace, where people congregate from all over Metro Atlanta and the Southeast for a variety of activities. They come to be entertained, to laugh, to worship, to see sports teams in action. They bring more traffic, but they also help create a booming economic impact that shows no sign of weakness, a situation projected to benefit Gwinnett well into the future.

Tommy Hughes

Charitable groups serve Gwinnett

In Gwinnett in 2008, charitable institutions offer a vast array of services to the people of the county, but these services were not always readily available. It took years and years for the development of these services, though each year additional activity seem to be needed. Luckily, Gwinnettians are a happy lot of volunteers, with different segments of the community stepping into the voids once they are noted.

A developing county such as Gwinnett doesn't come ready-made, with all services already available when the growth arrives. Rather, for years, many much-needed services simply just did not exist. Often Gwinnett residents found themselves having to go to adjacent counties for good quality child and senior care, for medical facilities and for many specialty services.

But over the years, those in need of the human services began to talk to one another, form committees, and band together to begin, often in small ways, these vital services. Eventually these small organizations began to form themselves into agencies and gained non-profit status, which often was an essential element in their growth. As more people found out about these offerings, the agencies that were being developed became stronger, and gained support of the wider community and of foundations.

In any developing community, forming credible charitable institutions can be slow. However, with Gwinnett growing so fast, often the need outgrew the capacity of these agencies, putting additional pressure on the community.

What follows in this section is a detailed look at many of the service agencies that have become a strong element for assistance to the people of Gwinnett.

Health and Human Services Coalition

By Ellen Gerstein

Gwinnett during the 1970s was a very rural area. There were not very many folks living in the county, so there was not a lot of need for many charitable organizations.

In 1991, when the Gwinnett Coalition for Health and Human Services (the Gwinnett Coalition) began, it conducted a needs-assessment about the health and human service needs in Gwinnett and where people could get assistance. This was a difficult task because the area had grown so rapidly that no one entity had a grasp of all the need or where to turn for help.

Most of the charitable agencies that were in Gwinnett at the time were Atlanta-based agencies. The Coalition was concerned about that, since decisions about funding and program expansion would not consider the needs of Gwinnett residents as a priority for the Atlanta-based organization. The Coalition felt that it would be better to have county-based charitable organizations that would be led by Gwinnett residents and serve Gwinnett residents as number one priority.

What a success this has proven to be in Gwinnett in the last decade!

In 2005, the Gwinnett Coalition conducted the first non-profit economic impact study to determine the scope of the non-profit sector in Gwinnett and its impact on the economy. Many will acknowledge the value of non-profits in a community for the good work that they do, but often in conversations about economic development, non-profits are overlooked.

However, the study found that the non-profit sector has tremendous influence on the economic well being of the community. From 1996-2004, the growth of the non-profit sector in Gwinnett has been 443 percent.

The non-profit sector in Gwinnett County is large, diverse, and growing. It spans the political spectrum of ideas and encompasses every aspect of human endeavor, from symphonies and Little Leagues, to homeless shelters and day care centers. While each non-profit is unique, all are based on the core value of people coming together around issues of mutual concern and common interest in pursuit of the common good.

Among the key findings:

- In 2004, there were 1,577 non-profit organizations located in Gwinnett County, an increase of 443 percent since 1996.
- The value of non-profit assets held reached over $1 billion in assets with over $1 billion in gross receipts.
- Annual budgets for Gwinnett non-profits totaled almost $774 million, including over $290 million in employee compensation.
- Health and education constitute the largest non-profit sectors in Gwinnett County.
- With a $290 million payroll, the non-profit sector is large both in absolute terms and relative to other sectors in the county. Gwinnett County non-profits have a greater local payroll than the state government, transportation and warehousing, or telecommunications sectors.

- Over the period of 2000 to 2035, an average of 13,900 jobs in Georgia are projected to exist because of the Gwinnett County non-profit sector. Approximately 11,600 of those jobs are forecast to be located in Gwinnett County. This indirectly results in the addition of three jobs in other industries for every one job in the non-profit sector.
- Gwinnett County non-profits are projected to provide an average of 5,966 jobs per year over the 36-year study period and an average of $260 million in additional personal income.
- If local county government were to assume the activities of Gwinnett County's non-profit sector, significant budget deficits would occur. That is, budget deficits of between $6.1 million and $18 million annually would occur depending on the financing approach.

Annandale Village

In 1969, Dr. and Mrs. Maxwell Berry located and purchased a 100-acre farm within the city limits of Suwanee for $50,000 and founded Annandale at Suwanee, Inc. or Annandale Village.

The Berrys, at the time residents of north Atlanta, had purchased the land in the hopes of creating a home with peers for their daughter, who was mentally disabled. The 100-acre site (a farm in disrepair) included many elements that the Berrys thought were essential for a village-like atmosphere, modeled after similar communities in Europe: a lake for recreation and scenic beauty, a garden to grow food for resident consumption, a pasture, walking trails and an orchard.

Most importantly, the site was convenient to local community resources such as churches and shopping centers and was only 35 miles northeast of Atlanta. To fund the Village, Mrs. Berry wrote letters asking for support, and arranged dinners and meetings with potential benefactors. A total of $250,000 was initially raised through the generosity of the Berry family, patients of Dr. Berry (a gastroenterologist and prime founder of West Paces Ferry Hospital), Elliot Haas of Atlanta's Haas and Dodd Insurance Company, and Harold Brockey, former Rich's chairman of the board.

After the purchase of a tractor and fencing, employment of a director, and conversion of an old farmhouse into offices, the first residence with space for 10 handicapped adults, two staff apartments and a large classroom was opened in 1974.

In 2007, some 38 years after founding, Annandale serves 117 adults with developmental disabilities in three different ways: (1) through a residential program, (2) through a day program, and (3) at a skilled nursing facility. All of Annandale's services are either licensed or certified by the state of Georgia. The program has 80 staff employees, and operates on a budget of $4 million.

The life of a Villager can vary, depending on functioning level, likes and dislikes of the Villager, and the wishes of his or her family. However, each day all of the Villagers participate in the Patricia M. Brown Center for programs. The Program Center is divided into three areas: Arts and Academics, Recreation, and Vocational Services.

When entering the Arts and Academics classroom, most people are drawn back to their first art class, as they are bombarded with a collage of colors and various forms of creativity.

Pictures of monkeys are a theme throughout the room as the Annandale Arts and Academics Villagers have enjoyed a partnership with Gwinnett Yerkes Primate Lab for many years. In cooperation with residents from a local nursing home, the Villagers pack up snacks for the monkeys in small Dixie cups. A brigade of Villagers then delivers the packed snacks to the lab and they often watch the monkeys enjoy each morsel.

Just past the Arts and Academics room begins Annandale's Recreation area with a specially laid gym floor and regulation basketball court. In the back, exercise bikes and Stairmasters are available. To the other side, through a set of double doors, is a universal weight set and two pool tables. Behind the gym, anybody can splash into Annandale's swimming pool. If a visitor arrived on a Wednesday, they can participate in water aerobics alongside many Villagers, led by a parent volunteer.

Just outside the gym is Annandale's Vocational Service area. Inside, assembly lines, lifts, pallets, and various other factory type items line this special workshop. Each Villager fills a bag with ancillary engine parts as the bag goes down the line. The last Villager weighs the bag and if one washer is missing or one extra bolt has found its way into the bag, the weight will be off and the Villager will send the bag back down the line. Quality is a priority in Annandale's workshop.

Through Annandale's Vocational Services, some Villagers may work off campus. Villagers have worked at local hotels, schools, and restaurants. Whether they are working off campus or in the workshop, all Villagers are earning real wages, giving them an unequaled sense of pride and accomplishment.

The Program Center also contains a media center and television room, which may be standing room only if the Braves are playing. To bridge the gap between Program Center time and evenings and weekends, activity sign-up sheets fill a bulletin board near the door, equipped with an extra large calendar. Villagers may sign up for various on and off campus activities, including, but not limited to: horse and carriage riding in Hoschton; mall walking; dinner and a movie; or watching Gwinnett's minor league hockey team, the Gladiators, at Gwinnett Arena.

In 2006, the Annandale Board of Trustees and management sold approximately 70 of its 124 acres and used half of the proceeds to either build or renovate every residence and Villager-utilized building on its newly configured campus. The balance of the proceeds were invested with Annandale's endowment fund to ensure the future success of the unique Village concept created 38 years earlier by determined parents of a child with a developmental disability.

One way Annandale raises funds, and keeps its visibility in the community high, is through the promotion and hosting of its annual spring Jazzy Thing, a Cajun-themed social/charitable event which started in 1994. Annandale raised $150,000 at the 2007 Jazzy. Since 1994, Annandale has raised $1.3 million through fund-raising at the Jazzy Thing. The money is used to offset the cost of care and allow Annandale to be affordable to families who otherwise would not be able to access services like those of Annandale.

Hi-Hope Center

One of the brightest chapters in Gwinnett County's history began on the darkest day of a young Lawrenceville mother's life.

The doctor couldn't tell Nell Moses the cause of her three-year-old son's developmental disability. However, he had no doubt about the boy's long-term prognosis or the need to institutionalize him: "This child will never be able to function in a normal society... It wouldn't be fair to him or to the other children to keep him at home."

The distraught mother contacted the Georgia Association for the Help of Retarded Children Inc. She didn't find a cure. She found a cause. The association told the 27-year-old housewife to start a Gwinnett chapter of the association to advocate for change. So was born the Gwinnett County Chapter for Retarded Children

Mrs. Moses turned for help to the Lawrenceville Jaycees. The group embraced the cause as their own, agreeing to sponsor a community meeting and then blanketed the county with meeting notices. The crowd was large, between 150 and 350, and the Gwinnett chapter was organized with Mrs. Moses as president and three Jaycees, Bob Powell, Walker Haywood and Troy Lee, as officers.

The Jaycees then joined parents in spearheading fundraising for a new school, with a spaghetti dinner, volunteers soliciting donations door-to-door and businessmen competing to see who had the biggest heart and the deepest pockets.

The Gwinnett County Chapter for Retarded Children received its charter on Jan. 30, 1960. Two weeks later, Gwinnett County became a pioneer in the community-based education and training of people with developmental disabilities. The school opened on Feb. 15, 1960, with Mrs. Esther Turner of Duluth volunteering to teach the five boys and girls in a nursery building behind Lawrenceville Baptist Church.

The classes were relocated in the fall of 1961 to a larger space inside the Masonic Hall. The next year, the chapter hired its first paid teacher, Mrs. Vinie Lowry, who had been recommended by Gwinnett School Superintendent B.B. Harris. She took the job for a monthly salary of $100.

Sometime after Mrs. Lowry's arrival, the teachers and parents decided it was time to name the school. Everyone agreed on the word "Hope." Teachers tacked on the "Hi."

It was officially the "Hi-Hope School."

In 1963, Mrs. Lowry and her husband George allowed the students' parents to convert their garage in a new home on U.S. Highway 29 south of Lawrenceville for Hi-Hope School. The community donated money, supplies and appliances for the three classrooms, two restrooms and kitchenette. The school remained there for seven years.

Mrs. Lowry, who directed the school until 1970, had a profound impact on many lives. With no previous exposure to developmentally disabled children, she developed her own techniques in the classroom. She learned it was best to treat each child as an individual and to take each one as far in education and training as he or she could go. She also actively involved the children in their community through regular outings and even long-distance travel. For several years, representatives from The University of Georgia traveled to Hi-Hope to observe her classroom. Today, this person-centered approach and community integration are the hallmarks of best practices for services to people with developmental disabilities.

In 1968, Lawrenceville businessman Ralph Saul was president of the chapter. He and a team of parents obtained federal funding to build a permanent facility. The community donated $100,000 that was matched by a $300,000 federal grant. The Hi-Hope Training Center opened in 1970 on Hi-Hope Road in Lawrenceville.

In 1972, the Lowry Building opened adjacent to the training center and later housed Gwinnett's first sheltered workshop. An annex for additional employment services opened in 1987. A capital campaign launched in 2002 paid for improvements and an Activity/ Senior Center and multiple group homes.

Hi-Hope began providing residential services in 1979 with the opening of one group home. In 1999, its adult foster care services began. Since 2000, four additional group homes have opened. The newest one, which opened in 2006, is totally handicapped -accessible. Twenty-one adults with developmental disabilities reside in these group homes.

In 2008, the Gwinnett County Association for Retarded Citizens, Inc., which does business as Hi-Hope Service Center, provides services to 140 adults. One of the oldest community-based programs in Georgia, it is a model agency that continues to pioneer innovative, person-centered services. The CEO in 2008 was Alice Cunningham.

A few years ago, Hi-Hope clients began giving back to the community that had nurtured them. These adult clients now volunteer year round, helping with holiday food drives, park maintenance, other non-profit organizations' packing needs, and enthusiastically participate in Gwinnett's Great Days of Service.

Two awards from the community demonstrate the recognized place that Hi-Hope and people with developmental disabilities now have in this community. The Center was given the "Together We Can" award in 2003 from the Gwinnett County's Coalition for Health and Human Services It was also recognized with the "D. Scott Hudgens Jr. Humanitarian Award" in 2006 from the Gwinnett Chamber of Commerce.

Rainbow Village, Inc.

by the Reverend Nancy Yancey, Executive Director

Rainbow Village began as an outreach ministry of Christ Episcopal Church in Norcross in 1991 and was known as Rainbow House. A generous parishioner provided $25,000 seed money to begin an outreach ministry for homeless families. These funds and $10,000 from Christ Church were used to renovate a home in Norcross owned by the Georgia Power Company. The home was leased for one dollar a year and converted into a duplex.

In 1995, six additional homes in the same community were leased from Georgia Power and Rainbow Village, Inc. was formed. As a nonprofit corporation, other churches, community organizations, businesses and foundations were solicited for funding and support. Because of the demolition of several of the homes, the Norcross community was reduced to two properties. (Rainbow Village could not afford the costly maintenance operations and renovation costs of these four 50-year old homes.) In 1999, a gift from Mr. and Mrs. Scott Hudgens allowed Rainbow Village to purchase an eight-unit apartment complex in Duluth, where eight families now live.

In addition to fully furnished homes, residents receive targeted case management. A case manager assists each family in setting and achieving realistic goals allowing them to break the cycle of homelessness.

Life skills classes address behaviors, parenting, nutrition, wellness, home ownership, and financial management, among other topics. Job training includes resume writing and computer training. Partnerships with DFACS, Consumer Credit Counseling, Kaiser Permanente, local schools and other community organizations allow Rainbow Village to offer programs to families.

Rainbow Village provides a comprehensive after-school program for all resident and "graduate" school age children and youth. Most of these children have attended many schools in their short lives due to the instability of the family. Rainbow Village provides a safe place to grow and learn after school.

Rainbow Village, Inc. has offered hope and a future of promise for families faced with a domestic or economic crisis who have become homeless. Rainbow Village provides the necessary assistance and resources for families to stay together in transitional housing while they become self-sufficient. By offering homeless families safe homes and a strong support system, Rainbow Village provides hope for today and the future.

Rainbow Village provides necessary assistance to families in crisis to enable them to overcome the devastation of homelessness and return to the mainstream as productive members of society. With the support of Rainbow Village more than 200 families have successfully transitioned back into the mainstream as productive members of our community. Rainbow Village is unique in that families are held accountable and must take initiative to overcome the obstacles of homelessness. Rainbow Village supports families in recovering from events of the past—the trauma of domestic violence, the loss of homes, jobs, families and friends. Rainbow Village offers families tools to support their transition but each family must do the work for themselves.

Homelessness frequently breaks up families. The physical and emotional damage, the effect on a child's growth, development and education, the probable separation of family members—all of these disruptive elements can tear a family apart.

A principal wage earner for the family may be suddenly unemployed. A mother flees an abusive relationship with children in tow. A medical emergency depletes a family's savings. Women fleeing abusive relationships are in battered women's shelters often separated from their teen sons. The majority of families who live at Rainbow Village are single mothers receiving little or no child support. Some are single fathers with children. Others are grandparents supporting their grandchildren.

Rainbow Village provides a home where people live as part of the larger community, not in isolation. Families that are accepted at Rainbow Village live in facilities in Norcross and Duluth. The Norcross village has two single family homes. In Duluth there is an eight unit apartment complex.

Families enter into a covenant with Rainbow Village to follow a closely managed plan to become self-sufficient. Once admitted, the family moves into a completely furnished home where they may live up to two years if in compliance with the program agreement, but most complete the program in one. Each family establishes a savings account with Rainbow Village and pays rent on a sliding scale. Financial accountability is required by reporting income and expenses weekly. A monthly budget, which includes a debt repayment plan and savings account, must be followed.

The financial goal for each family is that upon completion of the Rainbow Village program their credit score will be improved, they will have sufficient savings to move into a home of their own and a savings balance equal to at lease one month of living expenses.

Each family that comes to Rainbow Village enters into a covenant based on accountability, initiative, and the achievement of mutually agreed upon goals. Opportunities are offered for each family to become self-sufficient within one year. By being part of a supportive community families not only stay together but find hope and promise for the future. By forming new habits and lifestyles, acquiring better job skills and learning to live as healthy members of our community all are served.

Volunteer support is crucial to Rainbow Village. Volunteers donate home furnishings, assist with the after-school program, job training and life skills classes, provide meals for evening sessions and assist with the upkeep of homes and grounds. Among the churches regularly supporting Rainbow Village are:

Christ Church Episcopal
Perimeter Church
Duluth First United Methodist
Sugarloaf United Methodist
Norcross First United Methodist
Simpsonwood United Methodist
McKendree United Methodist

David Weekley Homes provided an opportunity for two of the graduate families to purchase a home of their own. A single mother and three children, ages 9, 10 and 11, are residing in the first home donated in 2005.

Revenue for Rainbow Village comes from numerous sources, and totaled $666,787 for 2007. For 2007, some 27 percent of the budget came through various fund-raising activities, while about seven percent came directly from supporting churches. It raised $175,322 from a gala and from a golf tournament in 2007.

Frank Rinker is chairman of the Rainbow Village board, Loretta Salzano is vice chair, J. Terry Gordon is treasurer, Celia McCarthur, secretary. Other board members include Mildred Armstead, Michael J. Ballenger, the Rev. Dave Fry, Lisa Moore, Pat Nelson, Judy Fowler Ottley and Joe Young.

Sheltering Arms

Another agency serving Gwinnett is Sheltering Arms of Atlanta, first established in Gwinnett in 1976. The original agency was set up in 1888 by women volunteering through the First United Methodist Church of Atlanta to provide child care and family support to help meet the needs of the working poor and to help them build stable homes and opportunities for their children.

At the request of the United Way of Metro Atlanta, Sheltering Arms established the David Kistner Center in Snellville in 1976. It sought to provide quality, affordable child care for the growing unmet needs in Gwinnett. The center was later moved to McClure Bridge Road in Duluth. In 1985, it moved again, to a location on Buford Highway in Duluth, where in 2007 it was providing services for 70 children.

After a service needs assessment determined that Gwinnett would need 20 similar centers by 2010, in 1993 County Chairman Lillian Webb formed a task force for a new Sheltering Arms center. A new center was opened in Lawrenceville that year and was named the Lillian Webb Center. Community Development Block Grant funds helped provide the funding. The Center opened at its capacity of 100 children.

In 2001, the third Gwinnett Sheltering Arms location was opened. It was located in Norcross on the first floor of the A. Worley Brown Boys and Girls Club. It also serves 100 children. Timothy J. Pakenham, a former Gwinnett resident who served as president of the Sheltering Arms board from 2002-2004, headed the $1.3 million capital campaign for the Norcross facility.

Gwinnett Children's Shelter

Around 1995, Gwinnett's Scott Hudgens asked several close friends: "What does Gwinnett need?" In essence, he was asking: "What can I give money to that will benefit the most people in Gwinnett, that is, something the county really needs?"

Two suggestions came back from several of those whom he asked: facilities benefitting children and senior citizens.

That opened Mr. Hudgens' generous heart again, with him giving $750,000 through the United Way to help fund the construction of a new, larger facility for the Gwinnett Children's Shelter, which shelters teenagers who were victims of abuse and neglect. He also opened the way to the founding of what became known as the Peachtree Christian Hospice, which will be discussed in another section of this chapter.

The Gwinnett Children's Shelter was started in the mid-1980s by three "PTA Moms," Barb Lewis, Joanne Culvern and Sherry Hague, who were concerned about what was happening to abused and neglected children in Gwinnett County. At that time, Gwinnett was the fastest growing county in the nation.

After finding that many children were spending the night in caseworker's offices or the youth detention center, these women decided to develop an emergency shelter for children and youth. With involvement from countless community volunteers and donors, in 1987 the dream of the Gwinnett Children's Shelter became a reality.

Since its beginning, the Gwinnett Children's Shelter has provided emergency shelter and counseling services to over 5,000 children and youth. In the late 1990s, the agency realized that the growth in Gwinnett County, as well as the increasing complexity of issues facing children in their care, necessitated agency expansion. A successful $2.25 million capital campaign in 1996, led by Jim Pack, was initiated to build a new adolescent facility housing up to 26 teenagers aged 12-17 on 40 acres of property owned by the county in the northern section of Gwinnett. This land was provided to the agency at a no-cost, 25-year lease, renewable for another 25 years.

The capital campaign was a success, and in September of 2000, the Gwinnett Children's Shelter moved into its new 19,000 square foot building. Programs provided to residents in the shelter include 24-hour supervision, community service work projects, individual and group counseling, an on-site classroom, recreational activities, and community outings.

While this development expanded space and services for teenagers, the agency's next focus was to build a home on the same property serving younger residents. In 2001, representatives of Bowen Family Builders visited the Gwinnett Children's Shelter, and were so moved by the work they witnessed with the youth, that they offered to build a home for the Young Residents as a full donation to the Gwinnett Children's Shelter. In November of 2002, the Gwinnett Children's Shelter opened the Jean Kirby Bowen home, a 4,000 square foot home for eight children, aged 5-11.

Also during the 1990s, the Gwinnett Children's Shelter began to expand its services to include programs for families and youth not in the shelter. In 1998, it became the first shelter in the metro-Atlanta area to sponsor Project Safe Place, a nationwide program funded at the local level by community-based agencies providing shelter, counseling and family support to runaway and homeless youth. In 1999, the Gwinnett Children's Shelter received a Federal grant that allowed expansion of services to runaway youth, as well as provide shelter and family counseling to youth placed at the shelter by their parents.

In an effort to involve youth in the planning, development and implementation of services, it began a Shelter Teen Board in April of 1999. This group is comprised of teenagers from local high schools that participate in a variety of activities including monthly service projects, monthly shelter events with shelter residents, and review of program material and procedures. The Gwinnett Children's Shelter board includes two youth board members with full voting rights. Other community outreach programs include weekly parenting classes in English and Spanish, volunteer opportunities, in-home family counseling services, and child and family assessments.

In 1998-2000, the Children's Shelter conducted a campaign that raised $2.85 million which was used for site development, including roads, sewer and water lines, power lines and construction of a 19,000 square foot, 26-bed emergency shelter for teens, counseling offices and meeting room space..

After almost 20 years as the only emergency shelter for children and youth in Gwinnett County, the shelter's dream is to expand services to provide long-term care to children for whom family reunification is not an option. To achieve that goal, in 2005-2006, the Gwinnett Children's Shelter constructed a 4,000 square-foot home to house eight adolescent boys in the Adolescent Boy's Independent Living Facility, which opened February 21, 2007. This was achieved through a campaign that sought $1.75 million, led by Herb Hamby, which actually raised $1,903,043. In 2008, a Young Resident's facility was converted to an Adolescent Girls Independent Living facility.

In addition, it is in the process of developing its own private foster home program, and has submitted an application to become a Child Placing Agency to the Department of Human Resources Office of Regulatory Services.

Board presidents since the founding include Robert Waller, Paul Steckenrider, Marty Shaw, Roger Willis, David Seago, Jesse Long, Susie Hite, Jim Hinshaw, Richard Myrick, Jr., Tom Andersen, Lynn Price and Brad Kendall.

The first director of the Children's Shelter was Donna Lane, who headed the program from 1987-1993. Nancy Friauf became the director of the Shelter in August, 1993.

Gwinnett gets hospice

Peachtree Christian Hospice

What eventually became the Peachtree Christian Hospice had a slow time getting started. In initial efforts, Scott Hudgens meet with two different non-profit organizations concerning the hospice, over about a three-year period, offering to each to fund its construction and initial operations.

The first group, after extended negotiations, would not agree to the terms Hudgens sought to operate a proposed hospice as a non-profit entity, as the group wanted more direct control, where Hudgens wanted a more independent body governing it. Turning to the second organization, it agreed to build a hospice, but never started activity. After a year of no action, Hudgens withdrew the second offer, and was back to square one.

That's when Scott Hudgens visited an old friend, Dr. Jim Collins, pastor of Peachtree Christian Church in downtown Atlanta, with the idea of building a hospice in Gwinnett. It was in the spring of 1998 that Hudgens approached Dr. Collins with his dream of a hospice. This coincided with Dr. Collins' desire to expand his church's ministry northward beyond midtown Atlanta. He had been focusing on the area along the Chattahoochee River corridor north of Atlanta, which happened to be in the same area that Hudgens was thinking to locate a hospice in Duluth.

Surveys showed the need for a hospice, since there were none in the fast-growing northeast area. Upon presentation of the idea to the Peachtree Christian Church congregation, in the summer of 1998, members Martha and Bill Todd began to lead a task force for the hospice.

Subsequently, their church's task force studied the matter, and began working on its plans. Included was a search for a healthcare organization to assist in making the hospice a state-of-the-art center. Early on, the committee selected United Hospice of Atlanta to run the operation.

A board of directors was formed in April 1999 with the Todds as co-chairs. The organization was incorporated as a non-profit entity. Groundbreaking came in August of 1999 on 8.7-acres of land and donated by Hudgens in Duluth.

Architectural design came from Stevens and Wilkinson Stang and Newdow Inc. of Atlanta. The contractor was The Griffin Company.

The initial design included 12 beds, with all-private rooms. The plans called for a building of 18,342 square-feet, surrounding a courtyard filled with trees, plants, two small ponds, a gazebo and seasonal flower gardens.

This first hospice opened on October 22, 2000, with Mr. Hudgens broadly smiling at the opening. This was seven days before Scott Hudgens died unexpectedly on October 29, 2000 at his farm near Braselton. His wife, Jackie, says that she thinks he was about the happiest she ever saw him at this opening of the hospice.

The entire project was funded by Hudgens. This included the $2.9 million cost of the facility, and Hudgens also paid the operational cost for the first few years. The value of the land donated was appraised at $1.015 million.

Since the opening, through early 2008, the hospice has served over 3,600 persons from more than 50 counties in Georgia. Because of the demand, it has converted four rooms to semi-private status, so that 16 persons can now get care at its facility.

Peachtree Christian Church continues to oversee the operation through its members on the hospice board of directors. As Martha and Bill Todd have said: "This hospice is committed to giving the best possible care to patients with a life-limiting illness, and to assure that they are surrounded by kindness. This care is also extended to their families by a social worker and chaplain staff for their emotional care and comfort. Ours is a group dedicated to continuing this mission and maintaining a beautiful and loving place of rest, comfort and hope to individuals at a most difficult time in their lives."

Embracing Hospice

Another hospice, also opening in 2000, was Embracing Hospice in Lawrenceville. It was opened in Lawrenceville in December of 2000, operating out of Life Care of Lawrenceville. It had 10 beds and was called Embracing Hospice. The facility was started by the Bennett family from New Jersey, who owned Life Care.

However, this hospice moved to Snellville in early 2001, to the Eastside Heritage Center, the original Humana Hospital. It operates 20 private rooms on two wings of the first floor.

In 2005, the hospice was sold to American Hospice, based in Jacksonville, Fla. It is one of the nation's oldest and largest hospice providers. Besides the palliative care offered in the Eastside Center, it also has an extensive program of in-home hospice assistance.

Over the years, the program has served 5,000 patients. At any one time, Embracing Hospice is normally caring for up to 300 people. It employed, in 2007, a staff of 180 professional nurses.

Georgia Rupert, who has been with the hospice since 2004, is the patient care coordinator for Embracing Hospice. She says: "What we do is to help patients by alleviating pain so that they can pass with dignity and the luxury of time with loved ones. Living without pain is the greatest gift we can give them."

Medical clinics

If you were among the uninsured or under-insured in Gwinnett County in 2008, you needed to pick carefully the days you got sick, as certain medical clinics were only open on specific days. There are several not-for-profit clinics in Gwinnett for those without insurance, but these clinics are often overwhelmed with patients. One estimate in 2008 was that there were 140,000 people in the county who were without insurance.

The large number of uninsured came as a result of the unparalleled growth in Gwinnett. These residents, often new to the county, have the same everyday medical conditions as everyone else. Those sick often show up at a hospital Emergency Room for care. It is both expensive and troubling for the hospitals involved. From these conditions, came the idea of community clinics.

There are 11 medical offices which have the word "Clinic" in their names, but in 2008, there were only six non-profit medical clinics operating in Gwinnett, each providing differing levels of care for the indigent. In addition, there are three traditional public health clinics and two public specialty clinics. While these clinics serve as many patients as possible, the need in Gwinnett for additional medical facilities for those least able to pay continues to be acute.

Each of the six non-profit medical clinics has its own methods of operation and each is run by its own non-profit board. They will be discussed individually.

1. Gwinnett Community Clinic

The first medical clinic started out of the Gwinnett Health Department in Lawrenceville. That was in 1989, when Dr. Lanny Lesser, who practices cardiology and internal medicine, talked with Pam Kramer, a nurse, and Madeline Estafan, a teacher who worked in education for the Gwinnett Medical Center, about the need for the medically uninsured to have adequate health care.

The three went to a focus group at the First United Methodist Church of Lawrenceville and discussed the idea. From this they were encouraged. Knowing nothing about medical clinics, Dr. Lesser worked for a year with clinics in Grant Park and at St. Joseph's Hospital, and came away with ideas of how a clinic should be set up. With the idea moving forward, Dr. Lesser got his medical colleagues to volunteer one night at week at a clinic to begin at the Health Department in Lawrenceville. Later, the clinic was open three nights each week. Ms. Kramer remembers: "We stored our equipment in the Health Department basement, and brought it up each night."

The idea was to give health care to people without an insurance plan or money for health care. "Most were working poor, but sometimes we found people just down on their luck, who eventually bounced back to a productive life," Ms. Kramer says. Patients paid on a sliding scale if they could afford it. They were given routine medical care, and supplied with drugs when they needed them.

Soon Dr. Lesser found that certain patients needed more than just simple medical care. "These patients needed to have a continuity of care, to get to triage with the correct doctor. We went to Administrator David Harris at the Snellville hospital and worked out a certain allocation for indigent care to be provided by the hospital, without charge. And our doctors helped out with patients in the hospital without fee. The doctors had a lot of enthusiasm to take care of seriously sick people without insurance. We wanted to be able to treat more than just episodic aspects of medical care."

The Health Department-run clinic continued until 1995, at which time the Eastside Hospital provided the clinic with space at its Heritage Center, the former hospital building. The key to this Clinic is that doctors, primarily from Emory Eastside Hospital, were continuing to volunteer their time. Since its opening, the Gwinnett Community Clinic has always had good cooperation from the medical staff in working at the clinic without charge.

Those receiving services at the Gwinnett Community Clinic must live in Gwinnett County with family income not exceeding 200 percent of U.S. poverty guidelines, based on a sliding scale and family size. Patients are asked for a $10 donation per visit, though no patients are turned away. The clinic in 2008 operated on Tuesday and Thursday nights. Over a year's time, it will see more than 3,000 patients. If patients have medical problems larger than the clinic can provide, they can be referred to physicians (without fee), and treated at Emory Eastside without cost.

The Gwinnett Community Clinic has wide support from the Snellville community, both from volunteer staffing and from financial contributions from the area.

2. Ob/Gyn Clinic

Another clinic, started in 1989 by the Gwinnett Hospital System, is the OB-GYN clinic in Lawrenceville. This clinic was begun in the late 1980s when the number of pregnant women going in labor and arriving at the Medical Center without adequate pre-natal care became untenable. A collaboration between Dr. Jim Crutcher, the District Health director, hospital leaders and physicians, the OB-GYN Clinic became the Hospital's commitment to providing quality pre-natal care.

Originally, residents from Georgia Baptist Hospital (now Atlanta Medical Center) and the then-Emory University School of Medicine were employed to provide comprehensive pre-natal care at the Lawrenceville Health Department. As the needs grew because of continued population growth, hospital leaders committed to a significant expansion of the clinic. Under the leadership of Dr. Greg Fourtain, the medical director, the OB-GYN Clinic was moved to the Medical Center campus, and grew to seven physicians and 12 midwives providing a full range of obstetrical and gynecological care for the uninsured and underinsured women of Gwinnett County. The OB-GYN Clinic averages 25,000 patient visits per year and delivers over 1,200 babies a year.

3. Kid's Clinic

With the growing number of indigent women having babies at Gwinnett Medical Center in the late 1980s, the Gwinnett Hospital System in Lawrenceville committed to providing dedicated pediatricians to give newborn care to the babies of the mothers delivering with the OB-GYN Clinic described above. Dr. Gretchen Prater was employed to be the first Medical Director and began a decade-long journey of developing comprehensive care for the county's indigent children. Initially, she worked in the local Health Department providing well-baby care. Hospital leaders realized there was no medical home for these children and that more than well-baby care was needed. As a result, The Kid's Clinic was opened on the Gwinnett Medical Center campus to provide comprehensive pediatric care for these children. The physician staff of The Kid's Clinic grew to six physicians and a nurse practitioner. The Kid's Clinic averages more than 26,000 patient visits per year.

4. Hope Clinic

Once a Lawrenceville physician in private practice, Dr. Bill Martin opened the non-profit Hope Clinic in Lawrenceville in 2002. The clinic is open five days a week to provide medical care for the working uninsured or underinsured "who previously fell through the cracks." It became a 501(c)(3) charitable entity in 15 months. It is the largest non-profit medical clinic in the county, serving 8,000 patients, of which 5,000 are uninsured. For 2007, 64 percent of its patients were uninsured or "self pay." It has 2,000 commercial insured patients, and another 1,200 on Medicare.

The target population of the clinic is the uninsured and those to whom access to primary care is limited by language, income or insurability. Its goal is to diagnose and prevent medical conditions of metabolic syndromes, such as diabetes, hypertension and heart disease. It offers specialty care referrals and prescription assistance when needed.

Its daily walk-in clinic (7:30 a.m. to 10:30 a.m.) provides patient care for non-life-threatening acute care, as an alternative to patients going to emergency rooms. In 2007, the clinic provided the equivalent of $635,000 in uncompensated care to patients, which is partially subsidized write-offs. The mix of its patient population in 2007 was 46 percent Hispanic; 26 percent Caucasian; 23 percent African-American; and 5 per cent other.

Altogether, the Clinic had receipts in 2007 of $738,000, of which $138,000 was in grants ($69,800) and donations ($68,200), and other income from patient, insurance and Medicare payments.

The clinic is limited in its ability to serve, with only one physician on staff. One of its goals is to increase its professional staffing. Many patients have to wait to see the doctor for up to three days. Often, when the Hope Clinic cannot see people with acute needs, the patient is referred to local Hospital Emergency Rooms.

In 2008, members of its board include Dr. Bill Martin, who is the Medical Director; Pam Martin, his wife and the clinic's part-time executive director; and John Mitchell, Michelle Holstad, Brian Thompson, Robert Beavers, Paul Tuggle and Claudia Diaz Kukucka.

5. Good Samaritan Clinic

Located on Club Drive near Pleasant Hill Road is Good Samaritan Clinic started in May of 2005. It originated out of a coalition of 70 Gwinnett churches. Also of assistance in its founding was the Norcross Cooperative Ministry, the Gwinnett Coalition for Health and Human Services, Gwinnett Medical System, and many other community organizations. It provides an alternative health care system for the neediest citizens. It is patterned after a similar clinic which opened in Atlanta in 1999 (there is a third similar clinic in Cobb County). It has both medical, dental, and optometry care, plus limited counseling. A cadre of volunteers continually assists the clinic in its operations.

Good Samaritan Gwinnett is a "private physician practice" model. Patients with insurance are referred to other physicians in the community. Those without insurance are eligible for a sliding fee schedule depending upon income and their family situation. The clinic is open each day, and has a physician and physician's assistant on staff.

Patients are seen on an appointment basis. During 2007, it served 1,100 patients in 3,000 patient visits. It accepts new patients, as it has openings on the first business day of the month. Established patients can book follow-up visits.

The mix of the clinic's budget for 2007 was 17 percent of revenue from patient fees; 30 percent from grants; 23 percent from individual donors; 19 percent from special events; and 8 percent from supporting churches. Its budget for 2008 was $660,000.

The clinic purchased its building on Club Drive in 2007. It consists of 6,500 square feet, and additional space will likely be needed by 2009. Curtis Tyler is executive director of the clinic and Dr. Jacob Varghese is the medical director.

6. Hebron Clinic

Hebron Baptist Church of Dacula operates a clinic in Lawrenceville. It was started in 2003 when a member of the church saw the lack of medical and dental services available to people who did not have the insurance or income to pay for medical services. The goal of the clinic is solve medical problems so that they can prevent larger problems.

The clinic is part-time, open two nights a month for medical care, and three nights a month for dental care. It operates out of a donated house in Lawrenceville. In 2008, it was serving 1,000 patients annually and staffed by doctors, nurses, dentists, hygienists, counselors, translators and office workers volunteering their time. The professional volunteer staff numbers more than 90 persons. During the day, new patients may make application for the program. Once approved, they are served at appointed hours. On an average night, about 30 people can be seen for medical services, but only 11-12 people per night for dental work.

The Clinic has a budget of $38,000, which comes from grants, individuals and company donations, and from the church. By 2008, it was almost self-supporting. It pays no rent nor salaries, and there is no charge for any patient, though many give a small donation. Most of the patients are from the northern part of Gwinnett, with an evenly-distributed grouping of patients from all ethnicities. When severely sick patients cannot wait two weeks for appointments, they are referred to Emergency Rooms.

The Clinic is governed by a board which meets monthly. Otis Jones is chairman of the board. Other members include Dr. Hoyt Gazaway, Mamie Outlet, Eon Brent, Paula Cady and Sam Brown.

Public Health Clinics

Three traditional public health clinics operate in Gwinnett—in Lawrenceville, Buford and Norcross. No physician care is provided at these clinics, which are staffed entirely with nurses. The clinics are open to all and give preventative care and health services, provide immunizations, medical counseling, and other services. While some programs at the clinics are funded by federal and state grants, such as Family Planning and Women's Health, the centers generate other revenue through charges for services, though generally much less than in private-sector medical offices.

During a year, nearly 250,000 visits are made to these three offices, with 83,000 unique visitors for 2007. That included 36,000 visits in Lawrenceville; 35,000 in Norcross; and 12,000 in Buford.

Four Corners Primary Care Clinic

A fourth element of public health opened on Nov. 1, 2007. This was the Four Corners Primary Care Center, funded by a $750,000 first-year federal grant in Norcross. It is located in the midst of census tracts whose residents are federally classified as medically underserved. It is a "Federally Qualified Health Center" as defined by the government. Its purpose is to provide primary medical care for non-emergency treatment for both insured and uninsured clients. These services include treatment for children and adults for chronic diseases such as diabetes, high blood pressure and asthma. Minor injuries, and well child check-ups, infections and joint disorders are also part of primary care. Charges are based on a sliding scale according to income and family size. The initial grant is expected to cover five years, with the Center anticipated to be self-sufficient at the end of the period.

The clinic was led by Dr. Gina Kalaitzidis, a family practice physician. The clinic, a 501(c)(3) organization, is run by a local board of directors, which is chaired by Dr. Gloria Stingley-Seals. Other members of the board include Jaime Valezquez, vice chair; Sheron Quinn, treasurer, and members Sondra Blue, Babatunde T. Loye, April Tillman, Brenda Ganaway; Sally Sherrington-Haggard, Stacy N. Collins, Karen Jackson, Mary Jane LaBonte, William A. Murrain, Dr. Lloyd Hofer and Laine Lawler.

WIC Clinic

A fifth public health initiative in Gwinnett is the Women's, Infants and Children's (WIC) Clinic opened in June of 2005 in Lilburn. It is located in the former Winn-Dixie shopping center on U.S. Highway 29 and only provides nutrition services to women and children. It averages 10,000 patients a month for children up to five years of age and their mothers. The idea behind this clinic is to get the children off to a healthy start in life. The Lilburn clinic, like all WIC centers, is funded by a federal grant. Half of all children born in the United States begin life with WIC support.

Mason Clinic

A clinic no longer in operation was known as the Mason Clinic. The Mason Clinic began providing primary care for indigent children under age 16 in 1996. Initially it was a partnership between the County Health Department and the hospitals in Snellville and Lawrenceville. For years, this clinic was given space by the County Commission at the former Post Office in Lawrenceville, but it eventually moved to the campus of Gwinnett Medical Center about 1998, when this hospital became the sole support for the Clinic. Its location near the hospital made it more convenient if patients needed additional services, such as x-rays or lab work.

Its name honors a physician for years associated with helping the uninsured, Dr. Miles Mason Jr., known as "Daddy Mason." Eventually, the hospital employed family practitioners to staff the clinic.

The Mason Clinic was closed Nov. 16, 2007. At the end, it was seeing 27,000 patients a year, while its nursing staff cared for 30 patients every day. The closing came as the clinic saw a decline in patients, and the Hospital System felt its resources could best be used elsewhere.

Food co-ops

Accompanying the growth in Gwinnett has been an at-first-overlooked imperceptible development of an underclass of society: those families and individuals who become homeless, or find themselves impoverished temporarily because of varying circumstances.

Prior to 1980, there was little recognized homelessness in Gwinnett. However, with faster growth of the county since that time, and with a much larger population within its borders, Gwinnett found more and more people in dire circumstances. There were few agencies in the county able to handle this situation. However, communities began to step up to the challenge as the need became overwhelmingly apparent.

Norcross Cooperative Ministry

In 1986, with more widespread hunger and homelessness in the community, two Norcross area churches saw a problem and banded together to address the question: "Wouldn't it be wonderful if all the Norcross area churches could combine their efforts to help those in need?"

This casual question came when representatives of Christ Episcopal and the Norcross First United Methodist churches met to discuss combining efforts to help a family facing eviction.

After discussions in the fall of 1986 with others, the two churches sent invitations to other area churches for a meeting on February 16, 1987 to discuss addressing poverty and homelessness in the community. Nine churches were present. Besides the host Christ Episcopal, there were representatives from the following Norcross area churches: First United, John Wesley and Mount Carmel United Methodists; First and Hopewell Baptists; Pilgrimage Presbyterian; St. James Lutheran; and from the St. Vincent de Paul Society of St. Patrick's Catholic Church. The Rev. Gene Lamb, associate pastor of First United Methodist, was moderator. The outcome was to pursue forming an ecumenical ministry to help the needy. A three person committee---the Rev. Bert Hahn of St. James, Barbara Kasbo of Christ Episcopal, and the Rev. Joe Williams of First United Methodist, were named to study existing community ministries in the area and report back.

Their report in April was presented to by now 11 churches, as Simpsonwood United Methodist and Northside Wesleyan had joined the group. The name chosen for the new organization was Norcross Cooperative Ministry (NCM). At a steering committee meeting on June 1, 1987, Christina Dean from Mt. Carmel Methodist and Cy Warren from First United Methodist were named co-chairpersons. Shirley and Jim Cabe of John Wesley Methodist were secretary and treasurer, respectively. Late in 1987, First Baptist of Norcross offered basement space in a building adjacent to their church, though the offer was not formally accepted until Spring of 1988.

The Co-op opened for business May 2, 1988, for four hours a day, three days a week, offering food, financial assistance, gas vouchers and funds for prescriptions to the needy. The staff was made up entirely of volunteers. By now, Virginia Tinsley of Mt. Carmel Methodist and Barbara Kasbo were chairpersons. Later, the steering committee became a board of directors, as the organization eventually got recognition as a 501(c)(3), tax exempt, non-profit group. Christina Dean was the first president, while Robert Pugh of Landmark Church was vice president.

In the first week of operation, only two families sought help. Less than a year later, eight families were helped in one day. By 2008, often NCM would serve up to 1,000 families per month!

Through agreement with other food Co-ops which have since organized in Gwinnett, the Norcross ministry only helps individuals who live in specific ZIP codes around Norcross. This geographic method has become a standard for the various assistance ministries within the county.

By 1990, the Norcross Cooperative Ministry had hired its first paid person, Shirley Cabe, who became a clerical assistant. (She would later see increasing duties, and by 1998 became the full time director.) Later in 1990, the NCM hired its first director, who was Amy Vickery.

Early support from churches was meager. Only two churches were pledging financial support in 1988, and that totaled only $550 a month. But by 1991, the NCM was receiving regular pledges from 18 churches. Meanwhile, many individuals were contributing time, canned goods and other items, including clothing. Churches organized donation programs and signed up to take certain months to seek regular food and other items from their members. It became a community affair, as help came from many sources. The Lutheran Brotherhood of Christ the King Church built a storage building in June 1994. The NCM board by then consisted of one representative from each participating church.

After 10 years in the initial location provided by First Baptist, NCM had outgrown that facility. It received more space at the Norcross Wesleyan Church in 1999. But that space was short-lived, as the Wesleyan Church Board of Governors sold their property, forcing a move in 2000. The new location was on Mitchell Road in a former auto repair shop -- a larger, 4,000 square-foot facility---but even that soon became inadequate. Thus began the realization that a new facility was needed. The ministry began a capital building program for a facility of its own.

In 2001, the NCM traded property that the NCM had acquired for a 1.5-acre site from the City of Norcross, which was also on Mitchell Road. Meanwhile, a building concept with anticipated construction costs of $900,000 was presented. Over $480,000 was raised in a capital campaign. That included $280,000 from the Jim Ellis family.

Groundbreaking was Sept. 12, 2002, as NCM began to erect a 12,000 square foot brick building, which it occupied Feb. 10, 2004. The building was named the Greg Ellis Center in memory of the son of Mr. and Mrs. Jim Ellis Jr. Many local firms donated materials, furniture and equipment for the new building, which was estimated to have a market price when finished of $1.2 million.

As space for the facility grew, NCM began to offer more services. From the initial food and financial assistance NCM offered, today it has developed a much larger program. Services include a clothes closet; toy collection at Christmas; Thanksgiving dinner for its clients; language classes; support groups; and job seeking assistance. Victory World Church has taken on leadership for Bible study classes.

Gwinnett County: A Little Above Atlanta

The facilities of the Norcross Co-op were put to the test in the Fall of 2005, when it saw a tremendous influx of people from the New Orleans area escaping Hurricane Katrina. Altogether, the ministry helped in excess of 1,000 evacuees during this difficult time in their lives. Perhaps as a result of that experience, Gwinnett County designated NCM as an emergency center for evacuees to receive aid.

A testament to the hard work of many volunteers over many years, the Norcross Cooperative Ministry paid off its debt on its building in 2006, and now operates debt free.

In 2008, a total of 21 churches made regular contributions to the Co-op, with each church naming a representative to the Co-op's board. The churches supporting the Co-op with regular contributions include Atlanta Vineyard Church, Campus Church of Christ, Atlanta Church of Christ - Gwinnett, Christ Church Episcopal, Christ the King Lutheran, Grace Church, John Wesley United Methodist Church, Johns Creek United Methodist Church, Mt. Carmel United Methodist Church, Norcross First Baptist, Norcross First United Methodist, Norcross Presbyterian Church, One Heart Church, Peachtree Corners Baptist Church, Peachtree Corners Church of Christ, Peachtree Corners Christian Church, Peachtree Corners Presbyterian, Perimeter Church, Simpsonwood United Methodist Church, St. James Lutheran Church, and Victory World Church.

With the success of the Norcross Co-op, the Gwinnett Coalition of Health and Human Services adopted the idea in 1991 to establish Co-ops throughout the county.

* * * * *

In June of 1991, the Coalition had released its first-ever needs assessment of the county, One of the recommendations was to duplicate the model of the Norcross Cooperative Ministry throughout the county to address the emergency assistance needs in the county.

As the board of directors were discussing implementation of these recommendations, Ellen Gerstein, director of the Coalition, said, "When this came up, I was very concerned. I told them if they thought that organizing all the health and human service agencies was a challenge, organizing the churches would be nearly impossible. We were looking for implementation partners and the Gwinnett Community Council's Education Committee agreed to take on this task with us. We hosted many meetings at churches in each community to help kick off the cooperatives. As a result, we ended up with six Co-ops, in Norcross, Lilburn, Duluth, North Gwinnett/Buford, Southeast Gwinnett (Snellville), and Lawrenceville."

Years later, in 2008, Ellen Gerstein looked back on the development of the co-ops with amazement: "I was pleasantly surprised that with our new partner, Gwinnett Community Council's Education Committee, and with the Norcross Co-op as a model, we were able to organize churches. These six co-ops have been a wonderful community asset. The co-ops have really guided the community, help thousands of people in Gwinnett, to prevent homelessness, hunger and other social ills. The six cooperative ministries were successful because the churches realized that alone they could not address these issues, but together, they could."

Lilburn Cooperative Ministry

The Lilburn Cooperative Ministry opened in October 1992 in a small brick house on the property of Mountain Park United Methodist Church. It shared space with a Habitat for Humanity group. The originating churches included Mountain Park United Methodist, Lilburn Alliance, First Baptist Church of Lilburn, and Berkmar Methodist Church.

Volunteers working to set up the Co-op were Donna Fisher, Doris Fowler and Bill Terry from First Baptist of Lilburn. They each volunteered at different times to help organize and run the start-up organization. Within nine months, they had hired a part-time director, Kay Whithear, who soon became the full-time director.

After the initial formation, several other churches in the area came on board. That included these churches: Pilgrimage Presbyterian, First Baptist of Mountain Park, Trinity Lutheran, Harmony Grove United Methodist and Good Shepherd Presbyterian.

The original building both leaked and flooded and was far too small. The churches, however, soon put on a new roof, solved the flooding problem, and volunteers built shelves for the items the Co-op would stock.

When Whithear first joined, there were few support churches and very little money or food. However, more churches soon joined. Melvin Everson came to the ministry to help spread a gravel driveway in 1997 while it was still in the tiny brick house. He soon became involved as a volunteer. He became president in 1999, and has been president for three terms. By 2007, the Co-op counted 40 support churches as well as support from Boy and Girl Scouts, businesses, schools, community groups and the Lilburn Business Association.

When the Olympics came to Atlanta in 1996, the Lilburn Co-op's volunteers worked concession stands at the nearby tennis venue. This effort raised the most money in the history of the Co-op, as it netted over $20,000. It also gave volunteers the realization that the Co-op could raise money to get it into larger quarters.

The Co-op directors remembered that, prior to the Olympics, Georgians had paid to have their name on bricks. From this came the idea to offer local residents a chance to purchase a square foot within the ministry in honor of or in memory of others. This was how the Co-op's new building fund began.

At almost the same time, in 1999, an individual supporter who had donated to the Co-op, Celia Slattery, explored the possibilities for the Co-op to expand. She offered to rent two bays of a building at Rockbridge and Five Forks Roads, in the center of Mountain Park, for a year. During that year, she reasoned, the Co-op could put on a fund drive to buy a building of its own. Thus began the Lilburn Co-op's move into the retail thrift store business. The Co-op opened one bay of the rented space for its ministry and office and the other unit as a retail thrift store with bargain prices on items anyone could buy. The Co-op soon added a third rental bay as an expanded thrift store. For 2007, that income was $130,000, which is used to pay overhead. Whithear says: "Using our retail income for overhead means that when people contribute money to the Co-op, all of it can go directly to our clients."

Meanwhile, information about the Co-op was getting out and support was coming in. When Whithear was invited to give a "Mission Minute" during the Sunday service at Good Shepherd Presbyterian Church, she was concerned. There was one big negative: it was the Sunday of the Fourth of July. Add that Whithear still spoke with her native English accent, and she was concerned that the effort might be in vain.

By this time, the Co-op had raised $150,000 by going to churches to suggest people buy a square foot of the building. The Co-op had found a building whose owner was willing to give a one-year lease to the Co-op. In addition, the owner would take $10,000 off the price of the $200,000 building if the Co-op bought it during that year.

It was when Whithear was speaking at the Good Shepherd Church on that fateful July the Fourth that she got affirmation that the Co-op was on the right track. After Whithear's "Mission Minute" at the church service, a person in the congregation came up to Whithear and said, "I am going to give you $50,000." Whithear says: "It was not a figure I had mentioned during the service, but it was the exact amount we needed to buy the building. And to make it even more unusual, that individual businessman had never been to Good Shepherd Church before, and the church tells me that he has not been back since."

With this $50,000 gift, the Co-op completed the building purchase in May 2001. The location is at 5329 Five Forks Road, just up the street from the previous location. The building had originally been built for a sporting goods shop, and in recent years had been a real estate office. Volunteers came from all of the participating churches to renovate the building to meet the needs for a food pantry, thrift store, and offices for ministry assistance. The Co-op moved into the building in May of 2001.

Whithear says of the operation: "Each year we help more people with their immediate needs. Originally, we would only see 10 to 15 families a week, but in 2007, we were up to seeing 150 families a week. We have a great support base in this wider Lilburn and Mountain Park community and now count more than 250 regular volunteers. We receive food from many restaurants and grocery stores in our community, to supplement the food donated by churches, Scouts, schools and community groups.

"We have added many other services, including a prayer room, financial counseling, car repairs, school supplies and Christmas assistance. The funds we distribute come from churches, individuals, groups and grants, as well as our own thrift store. Our thrift store, which provides free clothing etc. to families in need, added $158,000 to the ministry in 2006."

The Co-op's board of the ministry is made up of one member from each support church, a total of 40 individuals. The executive board consists of five persons selected by an overall board. In 2008, the board included Melvin Everson, president; Ronda Roberts, vice president; Jan Mahoney, secretary; Debbie Dowdin, treasurer; and Peggy Harris, president-emeritus.

North Gwinnett Cooperative Ministry

Since 1985, the Sugar Hill United Methodist Church had been providing a ministry called "Open Hands," which had outgrown the church's basement and moved on to a business location on Georgia Highway 20. For this effort, additional support came from the Sugar Hill Baptist Church, which provided volunteers and donations. It was from this combined group that the North Gwinnett Cooperative Ministry grew, says the Rev. Mary Lane Brooks, who was instrumental in starting "Open Hands."

In 1992, as the need increased, Ted Poole, pastor of Sugar Hill United Methodist Church, enlisted the help of Geraldine Cates and Carolyn Hill to expand the ministry in the Buford, Sugar Hill and Suwanee areas. These two visited the Norcross Cooperative Ministry for information and ideas.

Later, churches, cities, businesses and civic clubs gathered, and agreed that the group should include representatives from each city, with both business and church representatives. From this, a Board of Directors was elected including Geraldine Cates, Carolyn Hill, Kathy Williamson and Cheri Davis from business; Phillip Beard from the City of Buford; Gary Webster, City of Sugar Hill; and Mary Lynn Mobley, Ralph Davis, Wayne Smith and Betsy Stephens.

Additionally, there was a Church Council formed, with two representatives from each of the 12 participating churches. This council met monthly and included these churches: Bethlehem, Buford, Level Creek, New Prospect, Rock Springs and Sugar Hill United Methodist; Bogan Road and Sugar Hill Baptist; Buford Church of God; Buford Presbyterian; Epiphany Lutheran; and St. Mary and St. Martha of Bethany Episcopal.

Buford City Commissioner Phillip Beard made the old Buford City Hall available for the Co-op offices, as the City provided space and utilities. Under the part-time direction of Doris Poole, the ministry began to give support to even more people than before, providing a "hand-up, not a hand-out" on Monday and Wednesday from 10 a.m. to noon. Volunteers kept the office going. The Board, meanwhile, received the donated services of Dianne Frix and Jeff Forrestall, as its legal house was put in order. By now, the base of financial support was expanded to include businesses and civic clubs.

In 1994, Deana Moses was hired. Hours open were increased to include Friday mornings. By now, with more space needed, the City of Buford stepped forward and provided a building on Hill Street in a previous school.

More and more churches were joining the co-op. New member churches included Suwanee Parish Methodist and New Bethany Baptist. Several additional civic clubs were giving their support. They included Junior Civitan, Buford Kiwanis, Buford/North Gwinnett Rotary, Buford-Lanier Woman's Club, American Business Woman's Association of Buford, and the Buford Lions Club. New Board Members included Ralph Jones, Wayne Smith, Dave Wetherington and Von Hughes.

In January 1996, a parish nurse, Mary Riddett, joined the Co-op staff. This position was partially funded by the Gwinnett Hospital System. She provided blood pressure tests, counseled clients relating to their medications, and gave preventive medical advice. She also organized Health Fairs and Blood Drives and helped with information in Spanish. Also, in this year, the Easter Sunrise Service at Lake Lanier, which is sponsored by the Buford Ministerial Association, first gave the offering to the Co-op as volunteers from the Co-op staffed this event, a relationship which has continued.

By 1997, the Co-op was serving 890 families and receiving more support from the community. The City of Buford continued to provide space and utilities and new storage shelves when more room was needed. The Buford Post Office sponsored food drives, as did area schools. These activities helped fill the shelves. A number of fundraisers have provided good support over the years: golf tournaments, tennis tournaments, yard, bake and calendar sales. Clothing sales under the direction of Esther Jay showed an increase in dollars.

In 1997, Stephanie Crane became the executive director of the Co-op, bringing her United Way experience to the position. Grants were received from the Gwinnett Community Foundation, Primerica, United Methodist Homeless Council, FEMA Housing grant, Episcopal Charities Foundation and many others.

Doris Poole was succeeded as director of the Co-op in 1994 by Deana Moses, and in 1997 by Stephanie Crane. Donna Chrobak became director in April of 2002, after previously volunteering. Around this time, use of computers allowed for more efficiency. Maureen Kornowa succeeded as director in 2005, after also volunteering for two years on a regular basis.

In May 2007, it became necessary for another physical move, and again, the City of Buford helped by providing space at 70 Wiley Street in Buford. The North Gwinnett Co-op re-opened its doors on Monday, June 11, 2007. The Co-op was providing bread and bakery items to an estimated 410 people each month and food/financial services to approximately 300 people.

The statistics have grown steadily, from serving 4,677 people in 2000, to 7,757 in 2004 and to over 10,500 in 2007. It serves people residing in Buford, Sugar Hill and Suwanee.

The North Gwinnett Co-op board in 2008 was co-chaired by Geraldine Cates and Carolyn Hill. Other members include:

Steve Agee	Business
Phillip Beard	City of Buford
Caron Burnette	City of Suwanee
Terry Cohron	Church
Sandra Fisher	Church
Jeff Forrestall	Business
Jeff Garvin	Church
Bob Hail	City of Sugar Hill
John Marbury	Church
Scott Snedecor	Business
Jan Wells	Business

In 2008, churches supporting the co-op included Buford Presbyterian, Buford First United Methodist, Duncan Creek Church, Ephiphany Lutheran, First Baptist of Sugar Hill, Hamilton Mill Presbyterian, Level Creek United Methodist, Rolling Hills Baptist, St. Mary and Martha's Episcopal, Sugar Hill United Methodist and Suwanee Parish United Methodist, plus the Buford Ministerial Association.

Southeast Gwinnett Cooperative Ministry

The year was 1992. The Rev. Joel Davis of Annistown Road Baptist Church and Frank Latimer, a member of that congregation, visited a fellow church member with an idea of forming a food Co-op in the Snellville area.

Davis and Latimer, a retired Goodyear Tire dealer, went to see Don Ashworth of Loganville, but not at his home. Ashworth was sitting up in his hospital bed at DeKalb

Medical Center when the two visited. Ashworth remembers: "I had just had prostate cancer surgery and was in my hospital bed when Joel and Frank called. I didn't even know what a Food Cooperative was." The visitors must have been convincing, for after getting out of the hospital, Ashworth checked out the idea of a food Co-op, and started putting together a Constitution and By-Laws. It took him about eight months of leg work before he had six churches agree to open the Co-op.

The churches were Snellville First Baptist, Annistown Road Baptist, Evangel Community Church, Westminster Presbyterian, Maranantha Baptist and Trinity Lutheran. The first chairman was Ron Davidson of the First Baptist Church. For over 12 years, the Co-op offices were in two different buildings on the grounds of the First Baptist Church, provided at no cost to the Co-op---even utilities were covered.

After about a year, a total of 28 churches had signed onto the idea, and the Co-op had about $50,000 a year for operations. Ashworth says: "About 85 percent of the money went to funds given to the needy, and to purchase foods when enough donated food was not available." The Co-op serves the communities of Snellville, Loganville and Grayson.

Ashworth came to the post after 30 years in the U.S. Forest Service, plus another six years as director of the Lawrenceville Housing Authority. He served for 11 years as the director of the Southeast Gwinnett Food Co-op, leaving the post in 2003.

He says that "The early years were slim pickings. Eventually during my stint there, we helped more than 5,000 people a year. It was an interesting job, giving a feeling of really contributing something worthwhile. It really was a work of love, and I feel, blessed a lot of people, especially me and the volunteers who made it work by donating their time and energy."

Davis agrees: "We had struggles with it." He adds: "But his years with the housing authority gave him insight into how to deal with people on welfare. We were most fortunate to have him as the first director."

When Ashworth retired from the Co-op (his third retirement), Cindy Ridgedell was the director for about a year, after which Beth Moffat became the director of the agency in 2003. The South Gwinnett Co-op operated for about a year out of a storefront on a U.S. Highway 78 property of Snellville First United Methodist Church. However, after a land swap between the church and the city of Snellville, the Co-op had to find a new location.

One of the key strengths of the Co-op came in 2003 when it developed a close relationship with counselors from schools in the area. The schools, in turn, helped the Co-op with school food drives, finances and with manpower from volunteer teachers. It was a two-way street, since the Co-op helped families at schools within the boundary of the Co-op.

The Co-op then planned to move to property of the Community of Grace Lutheran Church, just outside the Snellville city limits on U.S. Highway 78 between Snellville and Loganville. The church's Vision Board voted to lease the land to the Co-op at a rental of $10 for three years. The Co-op rented two mobile homes to place on the property in July 2006, but soon found it had problems with getting a permit for the trailers. In effect, it was virtually out of business for more than a year, until it reopened on September 29, 2007.

Before that, in its last full year of operation (2005), the South Gwinnett Co-op had by then built up its annual cash contribution from all sources, mostly churches, to $102,188. In that year, it gave $60,375 in assistance to those in need; provided in-kind food assistance of $92,724; gave out in-kind clothing help of $8,238; and provided another $1,949 in school supplies to families. Its total cash outlays were $94,618, which included insurance, office supplies, moving and trailer rental. In the last year, approximately 8,000 people were served before the co-op temporarily ceased operations.

When the South Gwinnett Co-op got back in business October 1, 2007, it had the financial support from only 22 of the 35 churches that were previously serving it. However, it continued to get donations in gifts of money, clothing and food from 35 churches. In mid-2008, the Co-Op was providing an average of $15,000 in cash payments to the needy.

Dan Yoest, president of the Co-op, says that with the Co-op suspending services for 14 months, the South Gwinnett Co-op was slowed in its efforts to rebound. However, he anticipated to return to the same level of income from churches, businesses and individuals by the end of 2008. Its board in 2008 consisted of Yoest as president; Leola Harris, vice president; Sharon Richardson, secretary; and Cline Morrison, treasurer. In 2008, Laura Drake, formerly with the Lawrenceville Co-op, became the director of the Southeast Gwinnett Co-Op.

Lawrenceville Cooperative Ministry

It was May 3, 1995 when the first group of people got together in the Lawrenceville area to discuss what led to the formation of a Cooperative Ministry. Five churches were represented -- Lawrenceville Presbyterian, St. Lawrence Catholic, First United Methodist, St. Edwards Episcopal and Sola Fide Lutheran. The Rev. Paul Ard of the Presbyterian Church presided. The initial purpose was to provide a "clearinghouse function to relieve pressure on churches, coordinate church and community assistance, and direct people to the most expeditious help possible."

Those attending the first meeting included Carol Carlsen, Charles Kirkman, Julie McIver, Jan Lander, Pat Rydell, Sylvia Jackson, Donna Fisher, Judy Harper, Al Jordan, the Rev. Bill Payton and Ard.

By July, the group had picked officers, with Kirkman president; the Rev. Bill Payton as vice president; Carol Carlson, secretary; and Sylvia Jackson, treasurer.

The doors of the Co-op first opened on December 13, 1995, on West Pike Street in space donated by Virginia Ezzard. By its first full month -- January 1996 -- the Co-op had helped 29 different households, and by the end of that year, that figure was up to 100 households a month. Pat Shafer was the first director of the Co-op (a voluntary position), with Carol Carlsen as the volunteer office manager.

In May of 1996, Dacula was added as an additional area to be served by the organization.

At the end of the first full year of operation, 16 churches were listed as supporters. They included: Amazing Grace Lutheran, Central Christian, Christ the Lord Lutheran, Lawrenceville Church of God, Crossroads Community, Fairview Presbyterian, First Baptist of Lawrenceville, Hebron Baptist, First Christian Church, Lawrenceville First United Methodist, Lawrenceville Presbyterian, McKendree United Methodist, Prospect United Methodist, Sola Fide Lutheran, St. Lawrence Catholic and Sunrise Baptist.

In 1997, Faye Herrington became volunteer director of the Co-op. The Lawrenceville Co-op moved in 1999 to new space on Buford Drive in a former NAPA Auto Parts building -- space donated by Marjean Simpson. And on June 1, 1999, B.J. Griffin became the first paid director of the Co-op. He was succeeded in 2001 when Linda Freund became the director, a position she held in 2008.

The Co-op got a huge opportunity in 2002, as one of its key supporters, First United Methodist Church, asked it to outline what it hoped to achieve in a "dream letter." In a letter on December 2 to Jeff Poyner, chairman of the trustees of First United Methodist, the Co-op included six Dream points:

- A convenient, safe location of its own of 3,000-5,000 square feet.
- Continuous flow of canned goods year-round.
- Adequate financial resources from churches to help every household who qualifies for up to $100 assistance per year.
- Resources from churches to provide job training, temporary child care, computer training, counseling and other needs for clients to become productive members of society.
- More outreach to Co-op clients, and follow up through member churches.
- Hold a joint meeting by Co-op church members about its activities, and provide long-range planning.

By 2005, all the needs outlined in this letter had been met by the Co-op.

Perhaps the most basic need, that of having its own location, came about in ways the Co-op never envisioned. It came as the location that had been donated for five years, which the Co-op had long outgrown, had to be vacated by January 31, 2005.

Prior to moving, someone suggested starting a Building Fund, and contributed $7,100 to it, even before the Co-op knew it would have to relocate. Meanwhile, suitable rentable quarters were sparse, or would cost up to $2,000 monthly to rent.

At a Vision Team meeting on August 17, 2004, the group heard the Rev. Davis Chappell report a phone call he had that morning. Linda Freund picks up the story: "It came from Sandra Webb, whose husband, Fred, was the former director of the Gwinnett Family and Children's Services office. He had been instrumental in forming the Co-op back in 1995, and he'd also been a member of the Vision Team. He died in July of 2005. Sandra was unaware of one insurance benefit that Fred had. Sandra knew that Fred was concerned that the Co-op needed a home. She knew the money was from Fred and from the Lord for the Co-op. She pledged to give the Co-op $100,000!"

Later, the Team learned of a property and visited the former Pleasant Hill Baptist Church building in the middle of Lawrenceville at 176 Church Street. The church agreed to sell the building at below market value. The Webb money arrived at the Co-op the day before the closing, and the Co-op was able to pay an additional $110,000 at closing, allowing it to owe a smaller mortgage on the property. It first occupied the former church on March 4, 2005, and held an open house celebration to show off its new facilities there on May 1. (Pleasant Hill Baptist Church had moved previously to the corner of Moon Road and Scenic Highway in Lawrenceville, and had been renting its former building prior to the Co-op sale.)

Others directly affecting the relocation to the new facility included Chappell, The Rev. Ron Dunnigan, the Rev. Ken Reed of Pleasant Hill church, and Carol Millsaps, who was board president at that time. The Co-op's mortgage was "paid in full" on Dec. 28, 2005.

In its annual report for the year 2007, the Lawrenceville Cooperative Ministry had contributions of money, pantry items or volunteer hours from people in 61 area churches. Total financial donations from churches for 2007 were $188,250. The largest financial donation was from the First United Methodist Church ($54,415), though three other churches donated at least $10,000: 12Stone Church, Lawrenceville Presbyterian Church and McKendree United Methodist Church. Volunteers gave 11,620 hours of their time to the Co-op.

Benefits for the clients have increased to nearly 3,300 different households being served each year, with about half that number as first-time visitors. It found a tremendous increase in both donations and providing help during 2003, with the bulk of the increase coming in response to the Gulf hurricanes.

In 2008, there were 28 congregations in support of the Co-op. They were: 12-Stone Church, Amazing Grace Lutheran, Bethesda United Methodist, Central Baptist, Christ the Lord Lutheran, Collins Hill Baptist, Cross Pointe - The Church at Gwinnett Center, Gwinnett Church of Christ, Fairview Presbyterian, First Baptist of Lawrenceville, First Christian, First United Methodist of Dacula, First United Methodist of Lawrenceville, Grace Community, Gwinnett Community, Hamilton Mill United Methodist, Ingleside Presbyterian, Ivy Creek Church, Lawrenceville Presbyterian, McKendree United Methodist, New Hope Christian, North Metro Baptist, North River Community, Pleasant Hill Baptist, Prospect United Methodist, St. Edward's Episcopal, Sunrise Baptist, and The Church of the Way.

Hands of Christ Duluth Cooperative Ministry

It was in October of 1992 that representatives from 10 churches in Duluth met to discuss ways of meeting a growing need in the community. That was the beginning of the Hands of Christ Duluth Cooperative Ministry. The group soon organized into a 501(c)(3) non-profit organization. The Co-op at first was run out of a closet at the Duluth Masonic Lodge.

After organization, an effort began to enlist area churches in this effort. Those churches who came on board initially included: Calvary Christian Fellowship, Church of the Hills Presbyterian, Duluth Church of God, Duluth First Baptist, Duluth First United Methodist, Duluth Seventh Day Adventist, Johns Creek United Methodist, Meadow Baptist, Mount Tabor Baptist, Old Peachtree Presbyterian, Parkway Baptist, Perimeter Church, Pleasant Hill Presbyterian, Sugarloaf Community Church, Sugarloaf United Methodist, Trinity United Methodist and West Gwinnett Christian Church.

The Hands of Christ Duluth Cooperative Ministry is an ecumenical Christian organization which provides aid for people in the community with urgent physical, economic, social and spiritual needs, as local churches put faith into action. It is open by appointment three days a week.

The Co-op's first leadership team consisted of Judy Wiltshire, president, of Pleasant Hill Presbyterian Church; the Rev. Larry Richardson, vice president, of Holy Cross Lutheran

Church; Nancy Gormally, Victory Christian Church, secretary; and Susan Frye, Duluth United Methodist Church, treasurer.

By 1999, the Co-op was in need of more space. It moved to a 675 square foot space on Fox Street, by 2003, it outgrew this space and moved to 1,000 square feet on Georgia Highway 120, and finally, in December of 2006, it found a 9,000 square foot industrial building off Fox Street to purchase.

Mary Roberts had started as a volunteer with the Co-op, and, in 2000, she was named the director. She had scoured the foreclosures and found the building, which the Co-op was able to buy for $375,000 in 2006 with financing from Gwinnett Community Bank. (By mid 2008, it had paid down its debt to $165,000.)

One of the key moments for the Co-op came in 2004, when the Sugarloaf Tour of Homes designated its profits to the Co-op. Since that first year's donation of $40,000, the Tour has given an additional $132,000 to the Co-op. The Co-op has also been the beneficiary of other groups contributing funds.

The Duluth Co-op may be the smallest of the Co-ops in Gwinnett, serving residents of a relatively tight area around Duluth, covering just two zip codes, 30096 and 30097. It serves 100 to 125 families a month, though recipients may come only six times out of a 12-month period. Besides food, the Co-op also provides personal care and baby items, clothing vouchers, referrals for jobs, rent and utility assistance, and prescription medications when available.

In 2008, the churches supporting the ministry included: Bridge Church, Church of the Hills Presbyterian, Cornerstone Church of Christ, Duluth Seventh Day Adventist, Duluth Church of God, Duluth First Baptist, Duluth First United Methodist, Epic Faith Church, Meadow Baptist, Mount Tabor Baptist, New Life Worship Center, Old Peachtree Presbyterian, Parkway Baptist, Perimeter Church, Pleasant Hill Presbyterian, Stone Mill Church and Trinity United Methodist.

In 2008, the leadership consisted of Paul Kesmodel as president; Norm Liable, vice president; Kelley Steinbaum, secretary; and Matt Chandler, treasurer. Other board members include John Kitchens, Matt Blackburn, Naomi Vann, Marvin Platt, Sandra Ferrell, Jay Varner, Sue McIntyre and Marybeth Cook.

Fallen Heroes Memorial

One native Gwinnett couple's concept and tireless efforts are the major reason that the county has a singular memorial to "Fallen Heroes" who died while serving the nation and the county. This elegant semi-circle of 13 black granite monoliths, each nine feet tall, is engraved with the names of Gwinnettians who died while serving in military or public service. It is situated directly in front of the Gwinnett Justice and Administrative Center in Lawrenceville as a constant yet silent memorial to honor these individuals. The memorial honors not just fallen military personnel from the time Gwinnett was founded in 1818, but civilians from the fire, police emergency services and county employees who gave their lives for others.

Conceiving the memorial were Carolyn and Ron Buice of Buford. He was at the time a captain with the Fire Department, where he led the Underwater Dive and Rescue unit. (He

Fallen Heroes Memorial

retired from the Department in 1999.) On returning from a trip to Cumberland Island in January of 1993, they stopped in Savannah and were impressed with a memorial there to those who served in Vietnam.

Carolyn Buice says: "As we read the names of Chatham County's fallen heroes, we were moved to tears by the humility we felt and remembered the solemn phrase seen on many t-shirts: 'All Gave Some; Some Gave All.' We had no idea of the journey we were about to take. It was at that moment we knew what we had to do."

Ron remembers: "Carolyn said that three of our classmates of the class of 1966 at North Gwinnett High School were killed in Vietnam. They were Dicky Parker, Don Roy Wood and Jerry Jarrard. We realized that we needed to honor those from Gwinnett. All the way home, and for months afterward, we continued to talk about it. The idea kept being expanded to include the three policemen killed in 1964, and of course, those who died in World War II. Finally, we realized we needed to include everybody, even back to 1818 when the county was founded."

That began 10 years of research for the couple. "We never thought it would take so long," Carolyn says. In their research, the couple began talking to others, including the Veterans of Foreign Wars, the American Legion, and local police and fire officials. The Gwinnett Historical Society's Phyllis Davis got involved chasing down names, especially from the Civil War.

The Buices spent time at the Georgia Archives, putting on special gloves to handle original records at that institution, in seeking names to be listed from Gwinnett on the memorial. The couple went back into military records, though often they found a Gwinnettian might have joined the service in an adjacent county. Or a home town might not have been listed. Other names came by chance. They were working to insure that every person killed from Gwinnett from the various agencies who lived or worked in Gwinnett would be included. The research continued right up until the deadline before placement of the memorial. Meanwhile, the couple rode across Georgia and to other states and Washington, looking at other memorials.

A key decision was that the names would not be listed alphabetically. "That way, if we missed someone, the name could be added later and not seem out of place," Buice says. Yet since the memorial was dedicated, there has been "not one phone call from people telling us of names that were left off." Altogether, there are more than 700 names chiseled into the granite.

By the summer of 1993, the non-profit Gwinnett's Fallen Heroes Memorial Committee, Inc., was formed and fund-raising efforts were underway. During this time, the couple was recruiting others to get involved. One of their former school teachers, Kenneth McDaniel, a retired brigadier general with the Army National Guard, came on to help. Soon the couple had an entire committee helping out. That committee eventually included quite a team. Buice headed the group as president. Other officers and members included: Paige Hicks, secretary; Carolyn Buice, treasurer; James Argo Jr., legal counsel; Brig. Gen. (ret) Kenneth McDaniel, military adviser, Carlos Oliva, representing law enforcement; Michael Finch of the Georgia Vietnam Veterans; and Joann Shaw, representing POW-MIA.

Along with their concept, the couple sought a way to pay for the memorial. Among the early ideas was the selling of commemorative bricks, which the Buices picked up from the Savannah Vietnam memorial. The Buices and their committee would set up booths at city days and the Gwinnett County Fair, and tell people about the bricks. Carolyn Buice says: "People would look at you, and have no clue what we were talking about." Even after the Atlanta Olympics started hawking commemorative bricks, people in Gwinnett still did not pick up on the idea of bricks helping pay for the memorial. "We thought we could sell maybe 5,000 bricks and pay for the memorial, which we thought would cost about $250,000," Carolyn adds. "But the community spirit never caught on." Altogether, the Buices raised $75,000 toward the memorial.

Yet after several years of effort, not a lot of progress was being made to raise money for the memorial. The Memorial Committee had been selling T-shirts, caps, and other items, but to little avail. Ron Buice admits: "People did not feel the spirit of patriotism, and we were wondering if we had the strength to do it. We were about ready to quit." What finally got the project kick-started came from an unexpected source: the tragedy of 9/11.

"We got a call from Wayne Hill, and he said the county would put in the rest of the money," Carolyn says. "We were overjoyed. Without Wayne Hill's support, this memorial would still be only a dream." The 9/11 tragedy was symbolic. Suddenly many people understood the reason for the memorial. "People didn't question the memorial after that time," Ron Buice says.

Soon a measure funding the memorial sailed through the Gwinnett County Commission, and after eight years of tireless work but little progress toward raising the money needed, the project was funded by the county. Its eventual cost to the county: $490,000. Through 2007, the total expenditures was $522,796, which included some after-the-fact landscaping and sidewalks.

Now efforts turned to a memorial design. Don Still of Atlanta Architectural Design, a resident of Lilburn, wanted to contribute the design, after his two-year-old daughter was revived by a Gwinnett firefighter. He also did the design to remember a cousin who had been in Vietnam. Taking the overall concept of the Buices, he drew a plan to contain 13 tablets, arranged in a semi-circle, with a long walk leading to the memorial. Then Still gave the design concept to Jess Jiminez, an artist, who drew a rendering and made a model. In turn, the final design work was done by Rob Ponder, a Gwinnett architect, who was on open contract to the county for providing services for relatively small projects.

It was Ponder who determined the actual size of the tablets, so that they would be stable and functional. "When we got the design, the tablets were conceived to be relatively thin, only four inches. We started talking to the granite people on how to install them so they would be stable. We wrestled with the proportions to make them both aesthetically pleasing and structurally sound, and then, I remembered the movie, *2001, A Space Odyessey*. A little research found that the proportions of monolith in the movie were one squared by two squared by three squared (or 1x4x9) . These were the perfect size and proportions when translated into feet. Having each piece of granite one foot thick also gave them enough stability to just rest on the concrete slab (since each slab weighs 7,500 pounds and would be hard to tip over). Just to be safe, we pinned each granite slab with a steel rod into a footing in the earth."

To add a patriotic touch, another element at the Memorial is that of an American Eagle, clutching a rose in its talons, about to land. (The rose is a symbol of remembrance for fallen heroes.) The Buices contacted a local sculptor, Vic McCollum of Buford, a firefighter with the Gwinnett Fire and Emergency Services, who came up with a full size six foot-wide design of an eagle, which was cast in bronze and weighed over 200 pounds. The eagle is mounted on a pedestal, near the center of the memorial..

Ron Buice went to his first meeting at the American Legion, in Buford, to tell them about the idea for a memorial to fallen heroes. After he mentioned the plan to have memorial bricks, one man who had served in Vietnam came up and asked how many bricks had been sold. When Buice told him none so far, the guy said he wanted to be the first one, and handed Buice $90, but wanted to remain anonymous. He also told Buice he knew what he wanted his brick to say: "LZ Friendly." That stood for "Landing Zone Friendly" in Vietnam, a designation which meant it was a safe place for pilots to land.

The final memorial design consisted of 13 elegant black granite monoliths, quarried in Virginia, which have carved into them the names of those from Gwinnett killed in the various wars. One person from Gwinnett was killed in the Spanish-American War; 33 died in World War I; 73 perished in World War II; four were killed in the Korean Conflict; 25 died in Vietnam; and 16 persons are listed in the 21st century Global War on Terrorism, with the 16th name added on Veteran's Day, 2008. (Three persons are listed as prisoners of war or missing in action.) The granite also honors law enforcement officers, firefighters, emergency medical personnel, and county employees who died in the line of duty.

With tremendous impact are the three monoliths absolutely filled with names of men from Gwinnett killed in what, in the Southern vernacular, the memorial calls the War Between the States. Altogether, the memorial shows the names of 502 Gwinnettians who lost their lives to that war.

Consider this: in 1860, Gwinnett counted 12,940 people. By 1870, it had lost population for the first time since the census began counting, down to 12,431 people. (But by 1890, Gwinnett had grown back to 19,532 residents.) But the point is: far more people were killed from Gwinnett in the Civil War than the 152 people who have died since in wartime circumstances from all the wars fought for our country.

The Civil War took a grievous toll on Gwinnett, and throughout the nation, in the 1860s. In the South, which had a higher percentage of its men fighting what most considered a "just" war, the impact was particularly great. This toll on lives of Gwinnett families is typical of many Confederate communities, and contributed to Southerners recounting the troubles during and after the Civil War. Now newcomers may begin to understand why Southerners have talked so much about this war. It hit their families hard!

* * * * *

Besides the memorial itself, the Buices are also responsible for bringing another aspect to Gwinnett life: the Memorial Day observation. The first such service was held on Memorial Day, 1995, and held at the Gwinnett Justice and Administrative Center.

"We realized that there was no such service in Gwinnett, and someone needed to do it. It has grown each year. We are proud of it, and now Gwinnett has a Memorial Day and also a Veteran's Day parade, each year. The National Guard, plus veteran's groups, participate in the parades. On either Memorial Day or Veteran's Day more names may be added to the memorial, as the honorees are officially recognized. The public and families of those being honored by being chiseled into the memorial are invited to the services."

During that first Memorial Day in 1995, Secretary of State Max Cleland was the keynote speaker. Up until that time, public servants had not been included in such ceremonies, which had been limited to honor those serving in the military. However, Cleland commended Gwinnett for being the first to include those in public safety in such a service. Carolyn Buice notes: "After 9/11, people saw a need for public servants to be included in such remembrances."

The Buices are pleased to have seen the completion of this dream to honor others. Carolyn Buice tells the comments from Mrs. John R. Cooper Sr., whose son John R. Cooper, Jr., is among the names on the memorial. "She told us once, 'I know this won't bring him back, but thank you for remembering.' That comment says a lot. We hope it will bring comfort to those families whose loved ones' names appear on the memorial."

Members of the Fallen Heroes Memorial Advisory Committee in 2008 include the Buices, Mike Finch, Jim Argo, Phil Hoskins, Mike Plonowski, Connie Hinson and Joe Sorenson.

8

2000-2008

Gwinnett lands a medical school

Almost overnight, Gwinnett got its own medical school in 2005. It seemed even quicker, since the negotiations to locate a medical school in Gwinnett went on in private.

The opening of the four-year osteopathic medical school in August of 2005 was the culmination of a series of events evolving over several years. The first was the acknowledged need for additional physicians in the rural and underserved areas of Georgia and the surrounding states. Second was the desire of the Philadelphia College of Osteopathic Medicine (PCOM), one of the nation's oldest medical colleges (chartered in 1899), to reach beyond the Northeast and to offer additional medical education opportunities in the South. The third factor was an invitation from the Osteopathic Institute of the South (OIS), a Gwinnett-based 501(c)(3) not-for-profit corporation, whose task is to coordinate a multi-state network for pre-doctoral clinical medical education for third and fourth year osteopathic medical students.

The PCOM approach to medicine is to educate primary care physicians and allied graduate medical programs. The College says that it has 48,000 graduates in the profession now, primarily in the Northeast. On the Philadelphia campus, the College has a total enrollment of 2,090 graduate students, with 1,084 of them in the program to become a doctor of Osteopathy. The expansion into Gwinnett was to provide additional medical professionals in an area of the country basically underserved.

In April 2002, the PCOM Board of Trustees approved a strategic plan which included a vision for a PCOM Campus in the South. A year later, PCOM President and Chief Executive Officer Dr. Matthew Schure and OIS President Barry Doublestein met with the Georgia Nonpublic Postsecondary Education Commission and later filed a letter of intent (to establish a branch campus) with the commission.

A feasibility study was initiated and an application was filed with the educational accrediting arm of the American Osteopathic Association to open a branch campus. In November of 2003, the Georgia Osteopathic Medical Association, then headquartered in Grayson, issued a letter of support, as did the Gwinnett County Board of Commissioners.

Gwinnett County: A Little Above Atlanta

John Fleischmann, a Gwinnettian living in Lilburn, was selected in December of 2003 as Campus Executive Officer. Dr. Fleischmann had spent more than 30 years in executive administration with the University System of Georgia before joining PCOM. Paul Evans, DO, then a senior administrator at Oklahoma State University's College of Osteopathic Medicine following 26 years as a physician/administrator in the U.S. Army, was named Vice Dean in January of 2004.

By March of 2004, the school had located a 150,000 square-foot facility which would become GA-PCOM. The building, at 625 Old Peachtree Road, sits on a 19-acre site which originally housed an Upton's clothing store distribution center and was later used as an electronics company warehouse. Meanwhile, the Gwinnett County Commissioners approved a special use permit for the medical school. The sale of the site was concluded in August, 2004.

Permanent faculty officially began duties July 1, 2005, and set up temporary offices at the Osteopathic Institute of the South in Grayson, where the school's offices remained until August 1, 2005, when the College occupied its new facility.

That first year, a total of 1,682 applications came in for admission to the inaugural class at the Georgia Campus. Of these, 242 candidates were interviewed and 86 students (a full class) took their seats for orientation on August 10, 2005. Classes began August 15. In this first class, 30 were from Georgia. Of the remaining 56 students, 44 (78 percent) were from the Southeastern United States. In all, 74 (86 percent) of the 86 students were from Georgia and the Southeast.

The first "White Coat Ceremony" for students enrolled in the Georgia program was November 6, 2005, marking the beginning of their medical education. More than 500 parents and friends were present. That first class is scheduled to graduate and become osteopathic physicians on May 17, 2009.

The ribbon for the medical school was officially cut November 7, 2005 by the Honorable Paul W. McGloin, chair of the College's Board of Trustees. He was assisted by PCOM President and CEO Matthew Schure, and student Robert Hales, the first class chair.

The Honorable John Linder, the member of Congress representing Georgia's 7th Congressional District (which includes Gwinnett), delivered the keynote address. The Collins Hill High School Chamber Ensemble under the baton of John Harriman provided musical interludes.

An inspection team from the American Osteopathic Association's Commission on Osteopathic College Accreditation made a full site visit in mid-February 2006. The College was notified in May 2006 of branch campus accreditation by the American Osteopathic Association's Commission on Osteopathic College Accreditation.

Students at the school follow a curriculum similar to traditional (allopathic) medical schools, which grant M.D. degrees. However, PCOM students also learn the osteopathic approach to medical treatment. That includes a four point philosophy that: 1) all body systems work together; 2) that the body possesses self-regulatory mechanisms; 3) that structure and function are reciprocally inter-related; and 4) that rational therapy must be based on an understanding of the first three. Osteopathic medical students also learn the practice of hands-on care to diagnose, treat and prevent illness or injury.

Just as allopathic medical schools, PCOM students, after completing the course work in the first two years, then spend two years in hospitals making rounds with medical doctors before they are granted the Doctor of Osteopathic degree. Then follows residency programs, from three to seven years, depending on their specialty, before these new physicians can begin their practice.

In August of 2006, the medical college began its first graduate studies program on the Georgia Campus by offering a one-year certificate/two year master's degree program in biomedical sciences. A total of 51 students were enrolled. At the same time, the second class (86) of first year medical students began. With two classes of medical students and one class of biomedical science students, enrollment at the branch campus more than doubled from the first year.

In December, 2007, Brenau University of Gainesville approved a Physician's Assistant joint degree program in collaboration with PCOM. Graduates from this five-year program will earn a master's degree in Physician Assistant Studies from PCOM and a B.S. in Biology from Brenau University. The first class of this program was to matriculate in August 2008 and is anticipated to have 75 students, increasing by 15 a year for six years, or a total of 150 students by 2013.

In January, 2008, PCOM Trustees voted to establish a School of Pharmacy on its Georgia campus. The first class is to matriculate in August, 2010 with 75 students and expand by 15 students until a full complement of 150 students in this program by 2016.

In 2007-08, PCOM counted 340 full-time students at its Suwanee campus. For Fall, 2008, enrollment was anticipated to be 412 students on its campus. That would include 347 Doctor of Osteopathic Medicine students and 65 students working toward a certificate or degree in biomedicine. At current enrollment levels for the doctoral and master's programs, plus expected enrollment for the pharmacy program, the College anticipates by 2016 a minimum of 1,014 students and more than 100 faculty and staff.

The PCOM Branch Campus remains in a state of focused growth, exploring programs which are a mutual fit for the College and will serve to fill a need in Georgia and the surrounding states.

Public transit

As Gwinnett County's population grew each year at a quick pace, the problems associated with vehicular traffic increased. So did the cries of the public for relief from traffic congestion. Some called for public transportation. However, Gwinnett had voted on two occasions, in 1971 and again in 1990, against joining the Metropolitan Atlanta Rapid Transit Authority (MARTA)....both times by overwhelming majorities. Yet others in the community continued to call for Gwinnett to offer some alternative to the automobile for transportation.

In 1997, studies began on the feasibility of providing public transit for Gwinnett. At first, the effort found lukewarm acceptance by public officials. However, while some people questioned the need for public transit, enough people kept insisting that the county move in this direction that the county commission instituted a study.

The findings of the study established that it would be feasible for Gwinnett to provide public transportation, and more importantly, most residents would support some form of public transit. With this first study result, a second study phase began, to design and evaluate transit service options, levels of service for the money available, ridership and revenue forecasts, funding strategies, and operating/management options. The final service options were further refined, leading to a transit service plan.

The Transit Feasibility Study designed and evaluated alternative transit service plans that could (1) be implemented within the next few years; (2) would help to reduce traffic congestion and air pollution; (3) be compatible with suburban development patterns of the county; and (4) work within Gwinnett's current funding capacity. The board of commissioners approved the transit service plan on September 22, 1998.

As then-chairman Wayne Hill stated on many occasions, public transit was not the answer to the congestion problem: "But it is part of the answer to this problem, and it will be more of an answer for the future. That's why we need to have public transit in Gwinnett."

What came next was a series of decisions, large in scope, which led to the eventual establishment of a Gwinnett County Transit System Advisory Board.

Hill adds more background to this issue:

"Gwinnett County was in non-compliance with the Clean Air Act and our federal money had been cut off from the Atlanta region. We had response in the past that the public would support public transit, but heard that they did not want to be a part of the MARTA system. I proposed to the board of commissioners that we start a local system that would free up federal dollars and also help clean up our air by getting cars off the road.

"We looked out 50 years into the future with this plan at the projected population growth and saw a need in the future. We knew that the local service would take some time to be successful, but all the numbers said the Express Service would be a huge success.

"We had been to San Diego and saw that they had many systems that were managed at one central location that coordinates all of the systems together. We felt like that would happen sometime in the future by the state of Georgia, or a new agency created in the Atlanta region. After much discussion, we moved forward with the creation of Gwinnett Transit."

These steps in the plan included such items as:

- organizational and policy planning;
- capital and operations budgeting;
- securing federal and state funds;
- bus specification and procurement;
- detailed service plan development;
- contract operator procurement;
- paratransit service plans and procedures;
- fare policy development;
- marketing and customer service concepts; and
- facilities development including upgrading existing park-ride lots and constructing a new park-ride lot, a new transit center, a temporary maintenance and fueling facility, and bus stops.

In addition, there was marketing of the new service including its name, Gwinnett County Transit (GCT), the script GCT logo, and the customized bus colors -- Gwinnett County Transit Red and Gwinnett County Transit Gold, which were specially mixed and cataloged by PPG Industries. Whew! Starting up a transit system in a county as big as Gwinnett isn't an easy task!

Then came another determination. At first, it was thought that the county would begin by providing local bus service as its initial effort. However, after consideration, local planners thought that the Express Service into downtown Atlanta along Interstate 85 would gain the most riders the quickest, so the county began to focus on Express Service.

So the morning of November 5, 2001 arrived, with local transit officials and politicians keeping their finger crossed. What would be the level of acceptance?

Express Service

From the start, it was clear that the Express Service to downtown Atlanta, indeed, was popular. That first morning in November, some 560 passengers, perhaps all wondering if this would become their routine way to get to Atlanta, boarded on three express routes into the city. During the first month, 12,636 boardings were counted, but six months later, that had doubled to 24,546. By 2007, the trips into Atlanta on these three routes had stabilized at three times the original boarding level....to 37,094. However, by the end of 2007, the average monthly boardings had grown slightly to 39,437. By April, 2008, the monthly ridership was 42,384 passengers for GCT Express, plus 24,427 for GRTA Express, or 66,811 passengers in that month.

In order to provide Express Service, the Transit System had to provide 17 buses for its original service. The initial routes originated at three sites, at park-ride lots along I-985 in Buford; along the interstate at Indian Trail Road in Norcross; and along the expressway and Sugarloaf Parkway at Discover Mills Mall. In addition, three reverse commute routes were set up to haul inner city residents to workplaces in Gwinnett using the same buses for the reverse commutes.

At startup, for downtown Atlanta, a total of 17 morning and evening peak express trips and 14 morning and evening peak reverse commutes were operated Monday through Friday. The buses ran on compressed natural gas (CNG) engines. Passenger amenities included reclining seats, footrests, cup holders, reading lights and overhead storage.

Starting out, passengers paid $2.50 for each boarding. Discounts were available through ten-ride tickets and monthly passes. However, in November of 2002, the fare was increased to $3 for each boarding, and was increased to $4 on August 1, 2008. (The rate remained $3 for riders from the Indian Trail lot.) Passengers could pay slightly less by purchasing a monthly fare card. Those riders wanting to transfer to MARTA trains and buses do so for free. For travel from MARTA to the Gwinnett system, riders pay the MARTA fare and transfer free to Gwinnett Transit buses.

Since the beginning of service, the Transit System has increased the frequency of trips in response to the rider demand. In 2007, the System was operating 33 morning and 45 evening peak express trips each weekday. However, there has been no additional increase in reverse peak rides.

In February 2006, Gwinnett added more routes into Atlanta through a new partnership with the Georgia Regional Transit Authority (GRTA). Two of these express routes began from a second point at Discover Mills Mall, with destinations to the MARTA Lindbergh Station and the MARTA midtown station, and to downtown Atlanta. In addition, this GRTA partnership also initiated another route from Snellville to downtown Atlanta, via U.S. Highway 78, I-285 and I-20 into Atlanta. This route begins at a park-ride lot at the Snellville First Baptist Church, with a pick-up point at Hewatt Road, before proceeding into downtown Atlanta.

These three added routes in cooperation with GRTA provide 14 morning and 20 evening peak express trips each weekday. From an initial boarding of 1,241 in February of 2006, the boardings by July of 2007 had reached a high of 17,078 on these three routes. A total of 20 GRTA commuter coaches were in service, with nine of them CNG powered; the other 11 run on diesel.

In May of 2008, the county upgraded its commuter bus fleet to add nine 57-seat coaches. These additional coaches were augmenting the previous 37 or 40 seat buses. The new coaches were purchased to use low sulfur diesel fuel meeting EPA air quality standards. The new fleet amenities included overhead rack storage, individual reading lights and air controls. By enlarging the fleet, the Transit System was large enough so that it could perform routine maintenance on the fleet at normal levels, and improve its overall efficiency.

In September, 2008, the System made another step to essentially "change out" its fleet, purchasing 35 MCI coaches with 57 seats to replace 38-seat coaches. This gave the System an increase of daily seat capacity from 1,183 to 1,995 seats without substantially increasing its operating cost. This nearly 70 percent increase in seat capacity corresponded to a dramatic rise in the use on Express buses. This service usage increased from March, 2008 hauling 59,249 passengers, to 74,883 in July. This was during a period of rising fuel prices, when commuters were swapping their individual autos for the bus to commute into Atlanta. Delivery of the new fleet buses was expected to continue through mid-2009.

Altogether, the six Express service buses operated by Gwinnett County (three in partnership with GRTA) provide 61 morning and 79 evening peak express trips each weekday. In addition, there are three midday express trips. Added together, it amounts to an average of a minimum of some 2,250 passenger boardings on the express and reverse commute routes each day. Many of the Express buses have passengers standing on trips into Atlanta. (See Appendix B for detailed figures on ridership of the Gwinnett Transit System.)

Local Service

With the success of the Express Service under their belt, Gwinnett Transit began local service with two local routes one year later, in November 2002. The service uses a transit center at Gwinnett Place Mall as the hub of its operations. One route connects the hub with the MARTA Doraville station along Pleasant Hill Road, North Berkeley Lake Road and Buford Highway (Route 10). The other initial local route (Route 40) goes from Gwinnett Place Mall to Discover Mills, Gwinnett Technical College, Gwinnett Medical Center complex, the city of Lawrenceville and the Gwinnett Justice and Administration Center (courthouse).

These local buses run six days a week, from 5:30 a.m. until 10:30 p.m., Monday to Friday, and from 6 a.m. until 8:45 p.m. on Saturday. The passenger fare is $1.75 for adults and 85 cents for seniors, persons with disabilities and youth. The system also offers a para-transit service for qualifying disabled persons within 3/4 mile on either side of each route. Those wanting this service must telephone the Transit System 24 hours in advance to initiate the ride.

After the two initial local routes, three additional routes have been added. These are:

- Route 20: connecting Gwinnett Place Mall with the Interstate 85 Indian Trail Road Park-Ride Lot and the I-85 corridors south of Norcross.
- Route 30 connecting the Gwinnett Place Mall area with the I-85/Indian Trail Road lot, the city of Norcross and the Peachtree Corners/Technology Park area.
- Route 50 connecting Discover Mills, the Arena and Gwinnett Center, the city of Buford and Mall of Georgia.

As might be expected, Route 10 (the connection with MARTA at Doraville) is the route most ridden. It averages up to 2,000 boardings a day, nearly 45 percent of the total local boardings. Three of the four other routes average between 700-900 boardings a day, while Route 50 (through Buford and the Mall of Georgia) is the lowest route in ridership, averaging less than 100 boardings a day. Passengers are picked up on these local routes at more than 600 bus stops within the county.

Transit officials keep a close watch on each bus route, and tweak their use by regularity in service. The busiest route, Route 10, has a 15-minute frequency of buses, while the least used, Route 50, has a 90-minute frequency. Additional changes are anticipated in the future to gain peak efficiency of routings.

However, not all areas of the county welcomed the transit authority with open arms. In Snellville, for instance, the City Council is on record as opposing mass transit local service.

How the System Operates

Those in the planning process realized that the county itself did not want be in the business of operating a local bus service, but wanted to put the operation of the system up for bid to private providers. Bids were first put out in late 2000, and McDonald Transit Associates Inc. of Fort Worth, Texas, the oldest independently operated transit firm in the nation, won the contract. Employee-owned, it operates more than 25 different systems throughout the United States, including the GRTA system and the system in Hall County, Ga.

Employees of Gwinnett Transit System are unionized members of the same union as MARTA in Atlanta, the Amalgamated Transit Union Local 732. Altogether, Gwinnett Transit has 103 drivers who are part of the union. Drivers on the morning and evening Express Routes work a split shift, determined by seniority.

McDonald Transit had an initial one-year contract (the maximum under Georgia law), with four one-year extension options. Near the expiration of the five-year contract, it was rebid. In April of 2006, McDonald lost the contract. (With Gwinnett County owning the system and its buses, the operation is easily transferable.)

The new operator with a similar one-year contract with four one-year options is one of the largest transit operators in the world, the French firm of Veolia Transportation, with its USA headquarters in Oak Brook, Ill. The firm is the largest private transportation provider in the United States, having entered the North American market in 2001. It is an outgrowth of two American firms, Connex North America and ATC. In 2007, Veolia had 16,000 employees in the United States. Among the systems it operates are Yellow Transportation in Baltimore, Md., the commuter railroad in Boston, Mass., the Los Angeles Metrolink commuter rail, and two city bus operations in Denver, Colo.

Veolia Transport Worldwide, with world headquarters in Paris, first began operating buses in France 150 years ago. Over the years, it has operated a network of road, rail and maritime passenger services in 25 countries, employing 72,000 people worldwide.

When Gwinnett Transit began operating, its first maintenance and operations facility was in a temporary facility on School Board property on Scenic Highway. The facility was used until July of 2007 before it was moved to a new operations center at Remington Park, off Buford Highway in Norcross, for servicing of the 53 Express coaches, 26 local coaches and 8 paratransit vans in the fleet, a total of 87 units. (GRTA coaches not included in the totals.)

What it costs to run the system

Setting up a bus system in a heavily populated and geographically spread out county 30 to 40 miles from the major city isn't cheap. Fares only pay for a small portion of the total cost.

From 1999 through 2006, the Gwinnett Transit system's capital expenditures were $28,372,770. This includes the purchase of buses and bus-related equipment, such as fareboxes, radios and other items. It also includes the purchase of natural gas compressors and related fueling equipment. CNG buses in local service average 2.3 miles per gallon of fuel and many average routes covering 500 miles per day. CNG buses on the express routes average 2.89 mpg. Paratransit vehicles, using diesel engines, average 10 mpg. Buses are scheduled for service each 7,500 miles. The mean distance between break-downs for the Gwinnett system is 19,000 miles. The average commute time from downtown to the Indian Trail park-ride lot in the afternoon is 48 minutes. The average time from downtown to the Buford park-ride lot is 68 minutes.

Part of the initial fixed costs included the park-ride lots at Discover Mills and the Gwinnett Place Transit Center, plus upgrading of existing park-ride lots, shop equipment and bus stop and park-ride signs. Nearly all of the capital expenditures were purchased with 80-10-10 percent of federal-state-local funding.

For operations, about half the revenue for the system comes from Gwinnett County funding. In many other states, those more committed to providing public transportation than the State of Georgia, local systems get a higher funding participation from their state governments. There was no increase in local fares from the beginning of the second year until August of 2008. At that time, local fares went from $1.75 to $2, while Express Service into downtown Atlanta went from $3 to $4, with the exception of those catching the bus at the Indian Trail lot, which remained at $3. With most costs and labor going up each year, it's anticipated that there will be further fare increases, though the fare revenue will probably seldom exceed 30 percent of total operations.

In the year 2007, for example, the operational expenditures were $12.4 million, with the income breaking down this way:

Source	*Dollars*	*Percent*
Fare Revenue	$3,035,442	24.4
Auxiliary, Non-Transportation Funds	64,488	0.5
Federal Funds	2,383,579	19.2
State (GRTA) Funds	1,233,828	9.9
State (General) Funds	61,994	0.5
Local General Funds	5,641,707	45.5
Total Revenues	**$12,421,038**	

When the first Transit System Advisory Board was named, on December 31, 2001, Lloyd Baker was named chairman. Serving with him were Art Sheldon, Craig L. Newton, Garry M. Rhodes, and Richard Lazar.

Dwight Harrison was the second chairman, leaving the board in 2004, and Bob Clark became chairman through 2008. Other members on the board in 2008 were Art Sheldon, Craig Newton, Jon Richards and Gerald Richardson.

Community Improvement Districts

A housewife was out during the week doing her grocery shopping at Cub Foods in Norcross on Jimmy Carter Boulevard. This was about 1990. She regularly shopped at that giant supermarket. When at the cash register unloading her shopping cart, and while the clerk rang up the groceries, something suddenly was amiss.

A young man ran past the housewife, lugging a case of beer. He had not paid for the beer; he was in the process of stealing it, by crashing past the startled shopper and cash register operator. "Happens often," said the cash register operator, almost flippantly.

This event caused the housewife to vow: "I don't need to be shopping in such a lawless place." This comment, probably repeated by other housewives, was the beginning of the end not only of her shopping at that grocery, but perhaps signaled the start of the decline of that shopping center, and the entire former robust retail activity along Jimmy Carter Boulevard east of Interstate 85.

As Gwinnett grew, segments of the county often declined as retailers found greener pastures in other locations. Sometimes it was the need of a larger store that caused retail businesses to move. Other times, it could be traffic congestion that precipitated the move. It results in a upward spiral of other relocations, and eventually, vacant retail locations. Such areas can often be spotted by the fading store fronts, with a distinctive faded pattern where a store sign once proudly displayed its name.

All this caught the eye of one Gwinnett businessman, who realized that there was hope for such fading shopping centers and neighborhoods in legislation passed by the Georgia

General Assembly. Emory Morsberger knew that the Legislature had authorized counties to create special districts where property owners could get together and form an association to upgrade their holdings through taxing themselves a little more.....in the hopes of seeing a greatly-improved area.

Morsberger remembers: "It grew out of the Gwinnett Revitalization Task Force," which he chaired beginning in 2000. "This group was appointed by the Gwinnett County Commission and had on it about 20 members from the community. This group looked at the distressed areas of Gwinnett, and tried to figure out how to get them turned around."

That's how Emory Morsberger became a "re-developer," which lead to the initial efforts to organize a Community Improvement District.

> *"From the beginning, we realized we couldn't digest the entire southern third of the county, where we thought the problem was the worst, the large area that had been developed first in the county. What we did was to concentrate on three models of problems: a corridor, a shopping area and a neighborhood."*

Appointed in 2000 and serving through 2001 on the force were: Jack Bolton, Stephen Boyle, Wayne Chan, Nancy Smith Chandler, Bob Chapin, Terrilee Cooper, James F. (Jim) Durrett, III, Steve E. Gaultney, Kelly K. Herndon, Michael Lant, Emory Morsberger, Bert Nasuti, Marina Peed, Ana L. Ramirez and John W. Sexton.

A second group was appointed and served from 2002-05. They included Morsberger as chairman and John Sexton as vice chairman. Other members of the body were Joe Allen, Jack Bolton, Teresa Cantrell, Nancy Chandler, Bob Chapin, David Hirsch, Kook-Ja "Cookie" Lee, Jim Durrett, Steve Gaultney, Lance Hatfield, Mike Lant, Marina Peed, Mark Williams, and Jim Feldt as facilitator.

Others who served at some point in time on one of the groups included Rico Figliolini, Christopher Leersen, Amy Lynn Hoch, Bert Nasuti and M. B. Strickland.

From this Task Force came initial work on the U.S. Highway 78 corridor, later near the Gwinnett Place area, and last, the land along Jimmy Carter Boulevard, primarily east of Interstate 85.

Morsberger says that the idea for community improvement districts grew out of New York City. "In the 1970s, owners of skyscrapers were nearing bankruptcy in the economic downturn, and realized that they had to clean up the sidewalks and streets, or else they would have empty buildings. From this came the concept that property owners could pay extra taxes into a fund to provide security, plus clean up the area and propose plans to benefit the entire area."

The idea of the community improvement district migrated from New York to other parts of the country, where it also found success. "It allows property owners to take charge of their destiny," Morsberger says, "Without waiting for government to get around and help them sometime in the future. And this happens without ordinary citizens being taxed, as this is strictly a tax on commercial property owners." The regulations allow non-residential property owners to work together. They are required to pay the extra tax. The improvements can include work on roadways, landscaping, security, clean-up and planning. CIDs have a sunset provision, meaning that the project must get reauthorization from property owners every six years. So far, none in Georgia have failed to get the reauthorizations.

The first entity similar to a CID in Georgia was in downtown Atlanta, coming out of Central Atlanta Progress. In 1941, downtown Atlanta property owners with a commonality of interest voluntarily chipped in, even before legislation was on the books in Georgia, to allow community improvement districts, and formed Central Atlanta Progress. It is a private, not-for-profit corporation that strives to create a robust economic climate for Downtown Atlanta. In 1995, the CAP founded its CID, The Atlanta Downtown Improvement District. (The first official CID in Georgia was in the Cumberland-Galleria area of Cobb County.)

Creating the first CID in Gwinnett wasn't easy. "People laughed at me when we started working on the Highway 78 CID," Morsberger says. "They thought we couldn't get it done. And when we turned to the Jimmy Carter Boulevard area, the good old boys thought we could not get the various ethnic groups to work together. But we did and now have three CIDs, which are seen as the flagships of revitalization in the county, and depended on by both the county and the Chamber of Commerce to drive revitalization."

After the CIDs were formed, and began to find success, the leaders of the county began to turn to the three CIDs' leadership to spearhead redevelopment in the county. One reason for this is because each of the CIDs, once up and running, have made marvelous progress in a relatively short term. And interestingly, when the ideas first began to be circulated, there was very little support from the leadership of the county, either at the governmental or private business level. Today, that's all changed!

How the CIDs work

Three CIDs have been formed in Gwinnett since 2003. All are making substantial progress. The CIDs have been formed (1) along the U.S. Highway 78 corridor between Snellville and toward Stone Mountain; (2) on both sides of Interstate 85 at the Pleasant Hill Road intersection around Gwinnett Place; and (3) on both sides of Interstate 85 and the Jimmy Carter Boulevard and Indian Trail Road intersections.

In effect, declining areas like the shopping center where Cub Foods was once located on Jimmy Carter Boulevard can be spruced up through additional tax dollars. Community Improvement Districts are able to make older shopping districts new again, regenerate the neighborhood, and bring additional tax dollars to the county through higher property values.

The CID has the force of law when it meets two thresholds. The first threshold requires signing on of 50 percent of property owners in a defined area, who must represent 75 percent of the assessed value of that district. Once this threshold is met, every commercial property owner must pay the fee that the District votes to levy through the county tax office. Once approved by the appropriate governing body such as Gwinnett County, the CID is able to collect the additional revenue and put it to use for projects within the District, and to leverage fees collected to gain additional funds.

Throughout Georgia, though mostly in Metro Atlanta, CIDs are the new way to ensure that a declining commercial neighborhood is revitalized. From downtown to midtown Atlanta, from Buckhead to Cobb, from South Fulton to North Fulton, and also in Gwinnett, governments and the private sector join as partners to accelerate and initiate improvements in transportation, safety, and community revitalization. What was once a slow process can be speeded up through the CID process.

Every CID in metro Atlanta that has formed remains in existence and keeps its area competitive and brings new life to the community. It's the modern community version of pulling itself up by its bootstraps.

Gwinnett Chamber of Commerce President Jim Maran says that the presence of CIDs makes a strong statement that businesses care about their community. "These districts will be re-designed with the latest, most modern materials, new transportation concepts and new architectural beauty," he says. "This enables the community to feel good about the standards that our constituents believe make Gwinnett and our 15 cities a great place to live, work and play. It reinforces our motto that 'Success Lives Here.'"

"The real value of a CID comes in the long-term," says Dave Rosselle, director of operations of the Gwinnett Place CID. "If we can improve property values, it's going to benefit everyone. It's going to benefit the residences as well as the businesses."

But maybe there's an even bigger value. The real power lies in the organization's ability to stretch the tax dollars and give property owners more bang for their buck.

Brett Harrell, director of the Highway 78 CID, says: "We want the Highway 78 corridor to be an attractive, accessible place that is a destination for shoppers. The bottom line is that we want to make this a stable, viable community that continues to increase in property value."

Nationally, CIDs have become one of the key powerful public-private tools that can revitalize business districts and re-energize entire communities. Taking a geographically defined district in which commercial property owners vote to impose additional ad valorem real estate taxes on themselves, these stakeholders take the future into their hands by determining how the additional funds will be spent to benefit their immediate area. Today, CID funds enhance existing city/county services such as public safety and traffic solutions. In addition to leveraging their funds with federal and state monies, CIDs allow community leaders to chart a course they determine for an area's economic growth and lasting vitality.

"What CIDs do so well is leverage tax dollars," says B.J. Van Gundy, the first executive director of the Gwinnett Village CID. "We take $1 million and turn it into $10 million."

The ability of a CID to focus on projects specific to its area enables businesses to address issues of direct importance to them. Of course, a CID could not fund large-scale projects on its own. The role of the CID is to use its money locally to attract state and federal funds. The CID funds the planning studies, develops the design, and completes all the background work. When federal or state funds become available, the CID stands at the front of the line, ready to go. Without a CID, a project could take much longer, if it is ever even considered by government decision makers. By identifying issues of concern---mobility, streetscapes, personal safety, cleanliness---the CID allows for concerted advocacy in which projects can be placed on a fast track for completion. Acting as a unified corporate voice to champion a project for state and federal support and by working in concert with public-sector planning experts, the CID projects are more likely to move forward.

The goals of many CIDs are to:

- Leverage tax dollars to increase funding for transportation and other community improvement projects.
- Improve transportation to make businesses more accessible.

- Increase the long-term property values in a district.
- Handle aesthetic issues such as landscaping and design.

For more information on comparing the three Gwinnett CIDs, see page 668.

Here is a brief outline of how the three Gwinnett CIDs came into existence, and their major accomplishments through 2006.

Evermore CID

U.S. Highway 78 from the DeKalb County line in Stone Mountain through the center of Snellville to the Walton County line in Loganville has undergone tremendous change over the past 30 years. In 2006, more than 50,000 vehicles traveled this dangerous stretch of road each day. A daily traffic count of as many as 70,000 vehicles is expected by 2010.

In 1989, the Georgia Department of Transportation "temporarily" installed a reversible lane system in the section of U.S. 78 between Stone Mountain and Snellville. This was a system in which the two center lanes of the six-lane road change direction via overhead traffic signals twice each day to accommodate rush hour traffic into and out of Atlanta.

Though the reversible lanes were to be replaced by a safer system by 1993, public objections to medians or other methods of increasing both traffic count and safety were rejected by area residents and businesses.

Soon the accident, injury and fatality rate per mile in the seven mile stretch of U.S. Highway 78 between Stone Mountain and Snellville was among the highest in Georgia, and even highlighted on a nationally televised news report about the most dangerous roads in the United States. Many residents began to avoid the confusing overhead directional arrows and the chance of encountering head-on traffic in the "Suicide Lanes" on U.S. Highway 78.

Finally, in 2000, the Georgia DOT announced that a median would be installed on U.S. Highway 78 within five years. The consensus of folks attending a Summer 2001 hearing at Shiloh High School to review the proposed median was that it was far overdue, and even though their particular street or driveway may become less accessible, at least their families and customers would be safer.

In January of 2002, at a Chamber of Commerce transportation update meeting, a handful of U.S. Highway 78 property owners decided to organize as a single voice to address political officials. This core planning group included property owners W. H. Britt, David Hunt, Kenny King, Emory Morsberger, Art Mezzullo, Nancy Patel, Ramon Patel and Art Rilling. The core group planned an initial mass meeting of the 330 owners fronting U.S. Highway 78 between DeKalb County and Georgia Highway 124.

In February 2002, property owners along the U.S. Highway 78 corridor in Gwinnett County joined together to form the U.S. Highway 78 Corridor Improvement Association (the Association). On April 30, 2003, the combined efforts of 376 private property and business owners gained approval from the Gwinnett County Board of Commissioners and the City Council in Snellville and became the Highway 78 Community Improvement District. CID status provides the group self-taxing powers to raise revenues to enhance the seven-mile linear corridor from Snellville to the Gwinnett-DeKalb line near Stone Mountain.

The association set the following goals:

- Develop and aid in the implementation of a long-term positive plan for the U.S. Highway 78 Corridor.
- Coordinate the median installation so that it benefits surrounding business and residential areas.
- Investigate landscaping along the median.
- Turn U.S. Highway 78 into an upscale destination rather than a road to somewhere else.
- Investigate services to U.S. Highway 78 owners, possibly including security and joint marketing efforts.
- Maintain communications between property owners, business owners, community leaders, and state, county and local officials.

The first Highway 78 Corridor Improvement Association meeting on February 28 was attended by 75 property owners and officials. A vote to immediately incorporate passed unanimously. As discussion of association funding was beginning, Bill Gower, manager of the Brand Bank branch in Snellville, committed $10,000 as soon as the association was incorporated. Gower stated that Brand had a long-term commitment to its customers and neighbors, and wanted them to continue thriving as the U.S. Highway 78 corridor evolved.

Many of the U.S. Highway 78 landowners in attendance were even more eager than the core coordinating committee to upgrade the appearance of the corridor. Discussions of attractive medians and corridors in Alpharetta and upscale office parks and subdivisions went on for most of the meeting. The group voted to expand their membership to include owners of non-residential properties contiguous to Highway 78, as well as the initial 330 fronting owners. Only property owners will become members of the District association.

Since the Association was formed, it has leveraged $2.4 million in local tax funds into $27 million in federal, state and local funds. It provides weekly landscape maintenance to include litter and graffiti removal, plus it provides additional police patrols using off duty Gwinnett police officers. It had advanced numerous Department of Transportation projects, including landscaping of medians and enhanced landscaping at intersections at West Park Place, Lake Lucerne, Killian Hill, Highpoint and Georgia Highway 124. It has also gained inclusion for advanced technology within the construction project that will include cameras along the corridor, radar volume detection, decorative mast arms at intersections, illuminated street signs and synchronized traffic signals.

The Highway 78 CID also partners with Gwinnett County on the Corridor Overlay District and its Revitalization Study; partners with the City of Snellville on Economic Development; and with the Lake Lucerne homeowners on sidewalk, fencing and landscaping.

In 2007, the CID changed its name from the Highway 78 CID to Evermore CID. Officials said the change was "To align itself more closely with the vision for the district." Market research data revealed highly negative connotations with the U.S. Highway 78/Stone Mountain Highway Freeway names. The new name "Placed the focus on the good being done for the community," according to the Association.

The founding director of the Evermore CID was Dave Rouselle, who began the program in March 15, 2003. He started the grass roots efforts to explain the benefits to the property owners in the area and served until September of that year. (He later helped organize the Gwinnett Place CID.) Brett Harrell, former mayor of Snellville, has been the director of the Evermore CID since September, 2003.

Gwinnett Place CID

Created by a resolution of the Gwinnett County Board of Commissioners on March 15, 2005, the Gwinnett Place CID has taken the lead in championing projects to enhance the economic vitality and long-term sustainability of Gwinnett's central business district.

When it opened in February, 1984, Gwinnett Place Mall was the center of commerce for the Gwinnett community. However, over time, changing buying habits, additional competition, and its auto-dependent development strategy began to have an impact. As noted in the July 31, 2002 report to the Gwinnett County Commissioners by the Gwinnett County Revitalization Task Force, "several of the major tenants in the area.... have closed their doors and reopened in larger more prominent locations just a few miles away from their original locations. These relocations have created numerous large vacant commercial buildings that impact the economic viability of small tenants left behind....We found that the Gwinnett Place area exhibits many of the problems typical of other activity centers in Gwinnett. Problems in the area include lack of civic and greenspace, poor pedestrian connectivity, higher vacancy rates among surrounding retailers, high levels of traffic congestion, and poor integration of different land use."

In late 2002, the Gwinnett Chamber of Commerce realized that in a community of choices all competing for the customer's dollar, the Gwinnett Place area could be an area that would benefit from the CID legislation. Chamber leadership believed that the formation of a CID in the area would provide the commercial property owners with a tool to strengthen the area's existing assets into a new activity center with a new vision capable of capturing the imagination of the consumer.

Following a December 2002 meeting with then-Gwinnett Place Mall Manager Michael Lowery, the Gwinnett Chamber staff organized a meeting of key players in the area on January 15, 2003 to explore support levels within the community's commercial leadership. This meeting included key area stakeholders such as Tom Wheeler, Leo Wiener, Charles Lotz, Bruce Williams, Gary Eplan and Craig Hillyard. This core committee began meeting on a regular basis and raising funds necessary to inform other commercial property owners about the push for a CID in the area. Working on a strictly voluntary basis with support from the Chamber of Commerce staff over the next two years, these individuals became the back bone of the formation efforts.

On March 15, 2005, with 160 individual property owners representing 191 commercial properties valued at $500 million, the CID was officially created by the Board of Commissioners as Gwinnett's second CID.

Since the Gwinnett Place CID was formed, the organization has moved on several fronts. Perhaps the most visible for shoppers is the overall "clean-up" of the area, from picking up of trash at interstate intersections and along streets of the CID, to maintaining streetscapes and landscaping the entire area; and adding new sidewalks, including setting priorities for sidewalk construction.

Its other accomplishments include:

- Championing for approval of the Yamasaki La Belle Verde mixed-use high rises on Steve Reynolds Boulevard.
- Construction of the first gateway monument and pocket park.
- Completed a comprehensive transportation study.
- Delivering a comprehensive redevelopment plan.
- Finishing a feasibility study and layout for reconstruction of the I-85 and Pleasant Hill Road interchange.
- Maintaining a continuous communications program between businesses of the district.
- Submitted a Liveable Centers Implementation plan for funding.
- Coordinated sidewalk projects along several streets, a total of 7,900 linear feet of new sidewalks.
- Contracted for more than 200 hours of additional security patrols in the district, aimed at improving safety in the district. Coordinated a property owner's criminal trespass notification.

When visitors travel to this well-established business community in Gwinnett, they will find much is beginning to change for the better. Dave Rouselle was the first director of the Gwinnett Place CID, starting in October, 2003. He is now the director of operations for the Gwinnett Place CID. Joe Allen became the director in March, 2006, after serving at the Gwinnett Chamber of Commerce as the director of business resources and external affairs.

Gwinnett Village CID

Created by a resolution of the Gwinnett County Board of Commissioners in March 2006, the Gwinnett Village CID has taken the responsibility in leading the revitalization efforts in the southwestern portion of Gwinnett County, and is the largest CID in the state.

Located within the district is the landmark "Success Lives Here" water towers, the first signs of major development activity in the County, which began to develop during the initial growth explosion of Gwinnett County in the 1960s, 1970s and 1980s. However, most of the new growth began to creep farther north leaving behind aging facilities and infrastructure in what would become the Gwinnett Village CID area.

Following the lead of the early successful formations of the U.S. Highway 78 and Gwinnett Place CIDs, a group of community leaders, business owners, and property owners in the area began to meet and discuss the possibility of creating a new CID in the southwestern portion of Gwinnett in early 2004. This leadership team envisioned a future CID that would become an advocate for the area bringing new ideas, investment, focus, and energy to a once thriving community. The core group consisted of Emory Morsberger,

John Perlman, David Fincher, Senator Curt Thompson, Michael Deming, Shiv Aggarwal, and Louise Radloff. They officialy kicked off the CID formation initiative in the spring of 2004.

One of the first initiatives of the formation leadership team was to bring a sense of community back to the area. The area that makes up Gwinnett Village is tucked between two cities (Norcross and Lilburn) in unincorporated Gwinnett County and has generally been referenced based on road names in the area. The formation team branded the area Gwinnett Village to capture the international flare of the community and to encourage a general sense of pride for the area.

In March 2006, with six individual property owners representing over 400 commercial properties valued at $745 million, the CID was officially created by the Board of Commissioners as Gwinnett's third CID. At its formation, Gwinnett Village CID has the unique designation of being the largest CID not only in Gwinnett but in the entire state. Since Gwinnett Village's original formation, the organization expanded in 2007-8 with a Phase 2 campaign to just under 500 individual property owners representing over 650 commercial properties valued at $1 billion. Gwinnett Village by then represented over 5,000 businesses, 50,000 employees and 100,000 residents.

Gwinnett Village CID is expected to bring in over $100 million over six years in investments to the area through infrastructure improvements, redevelopment, and economic development, and jobs.

Accomplishments of the Gwinnett Village CID in its short life include:

- Secured funding and completed three studies on Jimmy Carter Boulevard, Indian Trail Road, and Buford Highway. Total cost was just over $600,000. CID contributed $5,000, making this a 125:1 ratio of leveraging tax revenue dollars for the area.
- Obtained $800,000 of landscaping of three interchanges along I-85: Jimmy Carter Boulevard, Indian Trail Road, and Beaver Ruin Road.
- Picked up over 3,000 bags of trash in 2006.
- Turned in over 350 code violations in the area in 2006.
- Successfully lobbied commissioners for new ordinances on Urban Camping and Taxi Cab establishments.
- Secured new Gwinnett County Police Quality of Life Unit to be housed in Gwinnett Village, bringing 35 officers daily to the area.
- Launched Village Blue: the public safety force that will be staffed by a rotational team of off-duty officers with full powers of arrest.
- This force will visit businesses every six months with the intent to raise the perception of police presence in the area.
- Complete conceptual design for reconstruction of the bridge at Jimmy Carter Boulevard and Interstate 85, with costs estimated at $40 million.

The Southwest Gwinnett Community Improvement Association was founded in 2005 to essentially perform the many tasks required to form the District, with B.J. van Gunby as the organizing director. On January 1, 2006, Chuck Warbington was named the head of the Association. When the Gwinnett Village CID became an official entity and became incorporated in March, 2006, Warbington was named executive director of the CID, and remains in that position at this writing.

Four-year college

Eventually, with the fast growth that Gwinnett was having, it became obvious: the county had the population to support its own four-year college. Thus began the effort to get the State Board of Regents to award a college campus to Gwinnett. It took 33 years from the first time that the Gwinnett Commissioners and, later, the Chamber of Commerce, appeared before the Regents in 1973, until Gwinnett was officially approved to get its own four year college, which opened its doors in August, 2006. The idea for Gwinnett to host a public college was first floated by a minister, Charles Goe of the Grayson Baptist Church, in a proposal to the County Commission and the Gwinnett Chamber of Commerce, as reported in the August 22, 1957 edition of the *News-Herald*.

By the time the college was authorized, Gwinnett County was by far the largest county in the state without a four-year college. By then, Gwinnett officials were beginning to feel like a bridegroom left at the altar, as first one state official, then another, agreed that Gwinnett needed a state-funded four-year college. But.......nothing had come of it.

At the time, candidates for governor, members or potential members of the Board of Regents, and other influential officials got the special Gwinnett treatment, often around a bountiful dinner table. But no college.

Meanwhile, there was movement toward providing higher education in Gwinnett, outside of the Gwinnett School Board's Gwinnett Technical School. Several units of the University System began offering courses in Gwinnett. First, in 1987, came DeKalb College (later renamed Perimeter College), offering junior college courses at a location in Gwinnett. Then in 1990, the University of Georgia started graduate classes in Gwinnett, primarily in education and business.

Before it was over, Southern Polytechnic College and even the Medical College of Georgia offered classes in Gwinnett. Professors from these state institutions made the trek to Gwinnett to teach the classes, which were held in leased facilities across Sugarloaf Parkway from Gwinnett Tech. Eventually, these courses all operated through a unique administrative unit called the "Gwinnett University Center." On Aug. 17, 1999, the Regents dispatched to Gwinnett one of its top administrators, Dr. James Muyskens, who had been the senior vice chancellor for academic affairs for the Regents. He was named president of Gwinnett University Center, which essentially hosted the other colleges at the Center.

Of course, all this time the college student population was growing year by year. Gwinnett soon had another distinction: it was the largest county east of the Mississippi River with no four-year college within its borders.

By the year 2000, Georgia Perimeter College had 15,372 students in Gwinnett. That figure would grow in 2005 to 20,461 students, making the Gwinnett campus the ninth largest of 35 units of the University System. Teaching all those students was a whopping job. Georgia Perimeter College had 3,160 employees in 2005.

Meanwhile, a Gwinnett banker, Glenn White, had become the second person from Gwinnett to serve on the Board of Regents. (Virgil Williams had served for less than a year in 1993.) White was a former president of the Gwinnett Chamber, and before this, had headed its education committee, with a goal of securing a state college for Gwinnett. White began the first of his eight years as a Regent in January 1997 with the intent of Gwinnett getting a four-year college. (Later another Gwinnettian, Richard Tucker, began his seven-year term on the Regents in 2005, and became chairman in 2008.)

But first, where was the college to go?

Former County Commission Chairman Wayne Hill tells a story about how the land came about. "We (the commissioners) were in an executive session," Hill recounts, "And my secretary said that I had a telephone call from Virgil Williams, who would not take an excuse, but just had to talk to me immediately. I left the meeting to talk to him.

"Virgil said he was in the governor's office (Zell Miller was governor then) and Virgil, who had been working on getting a four-year college in Gwinnett, said that the governor would approve it if the county would buy the land for a college.

"I said to Virgil, 'No bull?' and he said back 'No bull.' But he said that the college would require at least 100 acres. So I went back to the executive session with the commissioners and explained it to them, and we voted to buy the land. We didn't know where we were going to get the land, nor exactly how we were going to pay for it. So I called Virgil back and told him it was a done deal, and that put the wheels in motion to get the college.

"We employed an offshore realty company to buy the land so the price would not get out of line, made an offer on a piece of property, and they accepted it. I believe the price was $33,000 an acre, and it was a steal at the prices you see today. We had committed for the land blindly. The land cost $6 million, and we put in another $3 million in infrastructure for the roads, water and sewer. The money came out of the county's General Fund."

Hill added: "What I liked about the deal is that when you get something like a college, those institutions go on forever. We'll be forgotten, but people will look back and recognize the purchase and landing of the college as one of the greatest accomplishments during our time in office. I'm proud of it."

Therefore, on July 6, 1994, Gwinnett County commissioners purchased 180.1914 acres of land just off Georgia Highway 316 adjacent to Collins Hill Road in Lawrenceville for $5.958 million. On April 27, 2000, the commission deeded 160 acres west of Collins Road to the Board of Regents for a college campus. (The original land cost $33,066 an acre, and some people thought "we were paying too much," Commissioner Tommy Hughes remembers. That land a few years later would be considered a steal, worth perhaps five or seven times that amount.) An additional 22 acres east of Collins Hill Road was not immediately deeded to the college, though 17 acres were later set aside for the college. The remaining five acre tract is planned as a site for a future fire station.

Another 23 acres adjacent to the larger tract was added on June 27, 2001, costing $218,000, or $9,356 an acre. In 2006, a five-acre tract was also added to the college, making the entire campus 205 acres.

Meanwhile, in December 2000, with students flourishing in college classes off Sugarloaf Parkway in Gwinnett, the Regents approved a unique public-private venture for the land the commissioners had set aside for the college. The Regents entered into an agreement with

The University Financing Foundation for the first classroom facilities for the new Gwinnett University Center in Gwinnett. This one-story facility, of brick construction, consists of more than 40 classrooms, science labs, a student center, bookstore and student services. This first 120,000 square feet of space was built in 10 months for the new campus constructed off Georgia Highway 316.

On January 7, 2002, the first classes in the new quarters began at Gwinnett University Center, with over 5,000 students. Earlier, the Georgia Legislature had funded a $19.7 million "signature building" of 100,000 square feet for the University Center, which was occupied later in 2002. This was to become the nerve center of the college, a distinctive building built in dramatic round style, with soaring heights, designed by John Portman and Associates, It had 18 classrooms, a library, learning lab and administrative offices and cost $22 million.

Finally, on October 13, 2004, the Regents voted to change the Gwinnett University Center from a stand-alone institution to a full-fledged campus of the University System. The legislature endorsed it in March 2005, and the Governor signed the resolution in May 2005.

Jim Muyskens, during his two years at the head of this consortium of college offerings, had opened and molded the higher-educational University Center into its direction with anticipation of it becoming a four-year college. However, before the transition of the Gwinnett University Center into a four-year college of its own, Dr. Muyskens was named president of Queens College in New York on July 29, 2002. Many in Gwinnett wondered at the time if the four-year college would lose its momentum.

Yet progress continued. The third building for the campus, with a first phase of 25,270 square feet, was funded in December 2005 and was a classroom and office building. It was completed in 2006 and cost $5 million. Phase II of this building brought more office and classroom space, consisting of 24,720 square feet for classrooms and faculty offices, plus a 300 seat auditorium. It opened in 2007.

Dan Kaufman

The campus added five acres of land in 2007 when it purchased and was partially gifted the former Plumbing Distributors facility right off Collins Hills Road adjoining the campus, which serves now as its Student Services Building. The college also got another adjacent parcel, the former Fitness International building, consisting of 36,862 square feet, in 2008, which it is using for a physical educational and aquatic center. It is adjacent and in front of the original campus.

With recent property acquisition, the college in 2008 consisted of 212 acres.

The last major development in the early history of the college was determining the name of the institution. This significant change came at the October 2004 meeting of the Regents, when the Board voted to "ask the General Assembly to approve the creation of a state college in Gwinnett County." With this act, the Regents finally granted what Gwinnett had been wanting for years: the decision for designation of the Lawrenceville campus as its own four-year college. The General Assembly gave its approval in March 2005, and the Governor signed the resolution in May 2005. Later on, in October 2005, the Regents chose a name for the four-year college, after a focus group of the Gwinnett Chamber of Commerce submitted several names to them. The new name: Georgia Gwinnett College.

On September 7, 2005, came another milestone, as Daniel Kaufman, a retired Army brigadier general, was named the charter president of Georgia Gwinnett College. Originally from Brunswick, Ga., Dr. Kaufman came to Gwinnett after serving as chief academic officer and dean of the Academic Board at the U.S. Military Academy at West Point for five years.

Soon, Dr. Kaufman was organizing his staff, and preparing to open the new University to classes. On August 18, 2006, about 10:30 a.m., and with Gov. Sonny Perdue being one of several officials snipping the ribbon, Georgia Gwinnett College was officially opened. It was the first four-year college created in Georgia in more than 100 years, and became the 35th campus of the University System of Georgia. Then on Monday, August 21, 2006, the students began their first day of classes at the college, complete with Dr. Kaufman himself dishing up ice cream for the GGC students that afternoon.

The Regents approved in 2006 a $28 million library, expected to be completed in 2009. A key reason for early-on approval of a library is that significant library resources are required when a college seeks accreditation.

The year 2006-07 was seen as something of a ramp-up year for the college, as it enrolled 120 upper classmen for the first year of operations, and hired 11 full-time faculty. However, by the fall of 2007, a total of 788 freshmen were enrolled at Georgia Gwinnett College, as the college took its first big steps toward providing higher education for the county. That next semester, in the winter of 2008, a total of more than 900 students were enrolled. The school by then had a faculty of 94.

Georgia Gwinnett College anticipated a fall enrollment in coming years to be 3,000 in 2008; 5,000 in 2009 and 8,000 in 2010. The college also anticipated a special appropriation for use in hiring the expanded faculty, in the fall of 2008, to then total about 150 members.

Starting a college brings several first-time activities. Among the most important is gaining accreditation, so that its students will be eligible for federal student loans. A candidacy committee from the Southern Association of Colleges and Schools was to be on campus in the spring of 2008. Meanwhile, the college had worked toward achieving accreditation candidacy status in 2008, and had applied for accreditation status.

Other early-on activities include forming an honor society; opening a student services building; forming a student government association; and selecting a school mascot! Earlier, the school chose green and gray as its school colors. After a process of elimination, the mascot for the school was chosen in 2008. From the names submitted, officials said the school's mascot will be the Grizzlies, the 'Georgia Gwinnett Grizzlies.'

(You can twist your tongue when you say those three words quickly!)

Banking undergoes continued changes

While virtually every institution in Gwinnett has seen major changes in the last 100 years, one element of the business community has changed enormously. That field is banking. It has gone through a virtual 180 degree turn, from rural banks loaning mostly to farmers, to urban banks often today involved in major real estate developments and even international transactions.

At the turn of the 20th century, banks as we know them today did not exist. But many communities had banks, which were mostly depositories, making small crop loans to farmers of the area. Most were small operations, with few sophisticated techniques. Many went out of business in the Depression, or clung on for dear life in those hard times.

Work at a small town bank after World War II was far different from the automated posting of deposits and checks today. That's another major change in banking compared to modern practice. Howard Green, who went to work when in high school in 1946 for the Bank of Norcross, stayed with it about nine years, doing most of the everyday jobs of the bank. "We had but three employees, besides Colonel Clifford Jones Sr., who was the bank president. There was Joe Nesbit, Lottie Ewing and me. The bank was located prior to 1930 on South Peachtree Street at a location that became Thelma's Beauty Shop. Later the bank built a building at Peachtree and Jones Street corners. And even today, those at Thelma's can show you the old bank vault, now used as a closet."

Green continues: "Back then, we all did whatever job needed doing, manning the window, waiting on customers, etc. And each person did their own bookkeeping, and had to balance every day. It was a lot of work to do after we closed at 2 p.m. Each day you would have to file all checks alphabetically, and post both the statements and ledger on this big Burroughs machine. One of us would post the statement, and the other the ledger, putting in the checks and deposits to people's accounts.

"Then, at the end of the month, we would have to pull everyone's statements, match them with the checks we had for them, and make sure if they had 26 postings, they had 26 checks to show for it. People wanted their statements quickly, and we tried to mail by the first or second of the month. Businesses, especially, always had lots of checks, some for as little as a dollar. And when one check was filed wrong, in another customer's file, we had to find the missing check and put it in the right place. At the end of the month, sometimes for two days or three in a row, we wouldn't get away until 8 or 9 p.m., when we normally left the bank about 5 or 6 p.m."

Green would later be associated with American General Insurance for 30 years before retiring, all the while living in Norcross.

Early banks in county

At the turn of the century, there were only a few banks in Gwinnett. The first was the Bank of Buford (with its slogan "oldest in the county"), chartered in 1893. It was first located in the middle of the block on Main Street, north of a drug store. Later it opened in a handsome building designed for that purpose which still stands today (but is no longer a bank) on the corner at 3 Main Street. This bank folded in the fall of 1930 during the Depression.

The Bank of Buford had what were essentially two branches of that day, the Bank of Duluth, across from the railroad, and the Bank of Suwanee, a small brick building which was built in 1908 at 571 Main Street. Both these offices had to close when the Buford bank failed.

Shadburn Banking Company of Buford was the second bank in the county, backed by the Allen Family, and formed in 1901. For more than 30 years, Kate Allen Shadburn was affiliated with and ran the bank, with author Hansel Morgan of *Historic Buford* adding that she was the "actual founder."

In 1931, the Gwinnett County Building and Loan Association was formed by people primarily from Lawrenceville, though it had its first office in Buford. Years later, it was known as Gwinnett Federal Savings and Loan Association, and even later as Gwinnett Federal Bank. Among the organizers were Jess Baggett and Marvin Allison of Lawrenceville, Willis Burel, Mode Cole and Garland Wallace of Buford, and possibly others. Baggett was president for many years. Garland Wallace of Buford succeeded him.

The association was for years the only savings and loan association in the county. It did not open an office in Lawrenceville until the early 1960s at 150 South Perry Street.

Carl Perry was the first manager of the Building and Loan Association. He had been cashier of the Bank of Buford. Business was not thriving in those Depression days, and Perry was something of an entrepreneur, creating a welcoming atmosphere at the bank. Among his methods was selling peanuts out of a peanut roasting machine, which sent the roasting aroma up and down Main Street. He also used space in the Association offices for a retail jewelry case and to repair watches and jewelry. John Hutchins remembers those days: "You walked by the teller cages to the back of the building, where there was a line of showcases with rings, watches, necklaces and other items in them." Perry's wife did the bookkeeping for the Association, and also ran an insurance agency.

Perry remained as manager of the Association and became something of an institution until the 1950s. After Perry died, Mrs. W.V. Bolding became the manager of the Association. It was not until Mrs. Bolding retired that the headquarters of the Association was moved to Lawrenceville in 1962.

Jim Pack became president of the Association in 1967. He had been the treasurer and assistant vice president of Decatur Federal Savings and Loan. The Gwinnett association had deposits of $11 million when Pack came, and grew to nearly $300 million. It went from a mutual association to a public company, Gwinnett Federal Bank in 1990.

On February 17, 1995, Gwinnett Federal Bank was purchased by BankSouth, which in turn was purchased on September 18, 1995 by NationsBank. The acquisition was completed on January 9, 1996. (At that time, Gwinnett Federal had the largest deposit share of any bank in the county, approximately 15 percent.) NationsBank, in turn, merged in 1998 with Bank of America, and now operates under that name.

Brand Banking Company

The first bank in Lawrenceville was the Brand Banking Company, which dates back to April 29, 1905. The bank is a distinctive institution, with its headquarters located on the southeast corner of the courthouse square. It also has the distinction which few Georgia banks have, that of holding both a state charter and a charter from the Federal Reserve system, which it joined in 1921.

Brand Bank is the oldest continually operating bank in the county, and has always been an "independent" bank, with virtually all of its stock held by members of the founding family. It is the largest of the locally based banks in Gwinnett in 2008, with assets of more than $1 billion. It opened its first branch in Snellville in 1973. It has remodeled its courthouse square office at least twice, the latest in 2003, when a second floor was added to the building.

The Brands were in the loan business long before they established a bank. E.M. Brand started loaning money to farmers on the Lawrenceville Courthouse Square in the late 1800s. His great-great-grandson, Bartow Morgan Jr., who in 2008 was chairman of the bank, says: "He was basically lending money on crops," since agriculture was the primary business of the Gwinnett area back in those days. He adds: "E.M. Brand would take the land as collateral when lending on crops." Brand loaned the farmers money for the seeds and supplies until the end of the growing season. "So when they harvested their crops and sold them, they could pay off their loans," he says. "It seemed natural."

When the bank was first organized, E.M. Brand was the president. Other presidents of the bank, and the year they came to the office, were:

L.M. Brand, 1912.
C.H. Brand, 1928.
Ruben E. Smith, 1933 (first non-family president).
Bartow Morgan Jr. 1936.
Mrs. Louise Brand Morgan, 1954
Bartow Morgan III, 1967
Jon D. Birts, 1994
Christopher Smith, 2002-present.

Though C.H. Brand was president of the bank for a while and director for years, his home was in Athens. He represented the Gwinnett area in the U.S. Congress (the Eighth District in those days) from 1917 until his death in 1933. He was on, and at one time chaired, the Banking and Currency Committee, and was instrumental in establishing the Federal Deposit Insurance Corporation, which protects depositor accounts.

Five generations of the Brand-Morgan family have led the bank. In 2007, the chairman and CEO was Bartow Morgan Jr., the great-great-grandson of the first president. His brother, Richard Brand Morgan, also served on the board in 2007.

(Note: Bartow Morgan Jr. is listed as president in 1936. This Bartow Morgan Jr. named his only offspring Bartow Morgan III. In turn, when Bartow Morgan III named his first offspring, the name chosen was Bartow Morgan Jr., with the reasoning, "He's my boy and I'll name him what I choose." In 2002, the second Bartow Morgan Jr. became CEO and chairman of the board.)

* * * * *

To say that Bartow Morgan III ran the bank in his own distinctive manner is an understatement. He never required customers to provide his bank with a personal financial statement. "It's not worth the paper it's written on," he felt. One customer, who was near the limit on what Bartow could loan him, was sent to a bank in another Gwinnett town for a loan. When that bank president started proceedings by saying, "Let me see your financial statement," the customer was surprised: "Bartow never asked me for a financial statement!"

This type of management often caused trouble for bank examiners visiting Brand Banking Company. The story has been told often of one bank auditor questioning a particular loan at the Snellville branch which Bartow Morgan III had approved. When the examiner pushed for more documentation on the subject, Morgan took action. He whipped out his check book, and wrote a check to buy the loan on the spot for his own account and take the bank off the hook from the examiner.

Bartow Morgan III's office was just beyond the teller windows at the bank on the square and was noted for its sparse furnishings. Visitors sat in cane-bottom chairs, as Mr. Morgan did. Though one newcomer to the county did not have an account at Brand Bank, he had heard of Morgan's management style, and visited to seek a loan. After small talk and hearing the visitor's loan request, Morgan simply said:

"OK," said Morgan, "I'll make you the loan."

The customer, surprised at the speed and lack of protocol he was used to, protested: "But I didn't tell you how much money I need."

"Are you gonna pay me back?" asked Morgan.

"Yes."

Morgan's answer: "Well then, it doesn't matter how much I loan you, does it?"

Bartow Morgan III

For more than 50 years, Harry Braselton, a member of the family who founded the town of Braselton, was associated with Brand Bank. He joined the bank in 1946, and was continuously employed at the bank full time for 49 years, retiring in 1995 when he was chairman of the board. However, he remained on the board for five years after retiring, and died in 2000. Jim Henderson says in his history of the Brand Bank: "We now live in a day of specialization. Harry could do it all. He knew every facet of the banking business. He made loans, kept books, trained others and did whatever was necessary to run the bank.......Harry was a vital part of the bank's success."

In 1994, at age 22, Bartow Morgan Jr. joined the bank's board of directors. He became chief executive officer and chairman of the board in 2002. Since his coming home from college to run the family bank, the bank and the family have expanded their reach, branching into Hall and Fulton Counties, and opening a Securities Brokerage Division and insurance company. It is currently building a new facility for its recently-developed mortgages business. In addition, his brother, Brand Morgan, manages the family real estate holdings, while his mother, Patricia Bowden Thomas, continues to serve on the bank's board. For a three year period, Patricia McLaurin Farrior, the two brothers' sister, served on the board. She now lives in Florida and is no longer on the board.

First National Bank of Lawrenceville

In 1921, the First National Bank of Lawrenceville opened on Perry Street. That building, consisting of stone facing and the word 'BANK" in marble over the door, still stands across from the Historic Courthouse, and now houses an antiques shop. The bank moved to a new building at Crogan and Culver Streets on November 27, 1958 adjacent to the Lawrenceville Post Office. It had changed its name to First National Bank of Gwinnett in the mid-1950s, and had its first branch in Snellville, which opened in 1974. The bank was sold to First Atlanta Bank in 1985, when later that same year this bank became part of Wachovia Bank.

Richard Sikes, long associated with the bank, says that he remembers Dr. G.C. Kelley Sr. was president of the bank when he began there in 1952, with J.H. McGee Sr. as chairman of the board. Kelley was succeeded as president by long-time cashier, Jim Vic Hood, with Hulon R. Norton succeeding Hood as president. Leo Rainey became president and CEO in 1974. While president, Rainey was also chairman of the Gwinnett Chamber of Commerce for two terms (1978 and 1979) and headed the United Way drive in Gwinnett.

Bank in Dacula

On September 27, 1909, 27 people gathered to organize the Dacula Banking Company. This bank started out with $25,000 in capital stock, and found that on the first day of business, $21,000 was deposited in the bank. A.M. Wilson was the first president, and B. Ambrose was named the first cashier, with a salary of $50 per month. A month after it opened, the bank bought an adding machine for $200, guaranteed for one year. That same year it voted to erect a building at a cost of $1,500.

The bank did well. In 1912, it voted out of surplus a fourper cent dividend. Two years later, it even started paying directors $1 for attending each board meeting. The bank joined the Federal Reserve system in 1922.

But times got tough. On December 16, 1926, directors voted to close the bank, principally because of the low price of cotton, which precipitated poor collection of its loans. The directors also found that the bank lacked $9,000 for paying depositors in full. Therefore, the directors voted to levy (mostly themselves) a voluntary assessment of $75 a share to raise the $9,000. The First National Bank of Lawrenceville was named agent for the Dacula bank to pay depositors.

Allen Hood of Lawrenceville, whose father ran the First National Bank of Lawrenceville, says that the First National required the Dacula Bank directors to ante up the money before First National would take over the bank.

(See Appendix A, page 599 for highlighted notes of minutes of the Dacula Banking Company.)

Early Norcross banking

In October, 1903, the first bank in Norcross was organized, though it did not officially open for business until February 1, 1904, under the name of the Bank of Norcross. In 1930, it erected a classic building at the intersection of Jones and South Peachtree Street, a building still standing today, though no longer a bank. In 1965, the Norcross bank was remodeled and enlarged, and in 1967, it joined the Citizens and Southern National Bank. That bank built larger offices nearby and closed the Norcross branch in about 1988.

Allen Johnson, a cotton broker in Norcross, was one of the key bank officials, as vice president and also served on its board, though not a full-time employee. (He later was a director of Gwinnett Federal Savings and Loan Association.)

In 1944, Colonel Clifford Jones, a West Point graduate, retired from the military, and moved to Norcross. His grandmother, Mollie James Jones, was a director of the bank, and Allen Johnson invited Jones to be a vice president of the bank. He became president about 1947-48. He retired as a member of the board in 1969, and died in 1974.

During those early days of the 20th century, Norcross had two banks. The other bank was Bank of Gwinnett, located at Cemetery and South Peachtree Street, though little record is found of it. However, indications are that it operated as early as 1917, and went out of business in what is thought to be the late 1920s.

John Adams of Norcross likes to tell the story of the time young Reps Miller went to the Bank of Gwinnett one afternoon to make a deposit for his father, Monroe Miller. His father had an account in the Bank of Gwinnett, as well as in the Bank of Norcross. The next day, the Bank of Gwinnett was closed and out of business. Adams says: "Reps told me that he put his pistol on his hip, and went back to the bank. He told them, 'Yesterday you took my father's money and didn't tell me you were going broke, and could have. I would like to have the money back right now.' There were no questions asked. With that, the bank clerk handed over the money Reps had brought down the day before. There is no indication that Reps Miller even had to move the pistol off his hip."

New Norcross bank

Grady Coleman came to Gwinnett from Covington, where he had helped start the First National Bank of Newton County in 1963. A group of investors wanted to give the Norcross area more choice in banking, since only the C&S Bank was located in the Norcross area then. Coleman came in 1968 and formed the bank when C&S Bank "was not considered an aggressive bank. It didn't have a drive-up window then, but built one onto its building in downtown Norcross after our bank was formed."

As president, Coleman led efforts to form the Gwinnett Bank and Trust Company, which built its office south of Norcross on Buford Highway. Years later, this would become a prime and busy corner, as Jimmy Carter Boulevard was cut through the undeveloped land of the area, and tunneled under the Norfolk-Southern Railroad west of the bank.

Coleman says: "We had all people with local connections coming together to form the bank. Paul Duke, who was beginning to assemble land for what would become Peachtree Corners, was still with L.B. Foster Company, right down Buford Highway, then. He was the driving force behind the bank. Those who formed the bank and became directors included Ed Howard, Leon Maloney (then mayor of Norcross), Carl Garner Jr., attorney Bill O'Kelley (who would become a U.S. District Judge), Dan Shepherd, Harold Humphries, E.M. (Skip) Bishop, Walter Thomas, John Aderholt and myself."

The original capitalization was $500,000. In 1987, when Gwinnett Bank and Trust was sold to the Georgia Railroad Bank and Trust Company of Augusta, its assets were $130 million. (In 1987, Georgia Railroad was sold to First Union Bank, which later bought Wachovia Bank, though the bank now operates under the name of Wachovia. It still has an office at the original Gwinnett Bank and Trust site on Buford Highway.)

Coleman and his bank were eager to form other branches, but there was a problem: Georgia law would not allow branch banking at that time. After working through the Legislature to get the law changed, Coleman and his bank put in the first application in Georgia for a branch bank "the day they started accepting them. We were wanting to locate a second office in Snellville. But we got turned down," Coleman says, "And we immediately took that same application, changed the location to one on Jimmy Carter Boulevard at Norcross Tucker Road, and resubmitted it to the Banking Department. We got that application approved, and had the first branch bank in Gwinnett, and one of the first in Georgia."

Before it was over, Gwinnett Bank and Trust had four branches. Besides the Jimmy Carter Boulevard branch, the other branches were on U.S. Highway 29 at Lilburn Square; on Killian Hill Road; and another inside the Ingle's supermarket in Lawrenceville at Georgia Highways 20 and 316.

Banking in Loganville

One of the oldest continually-operating banks in the area started as the Bank of Loganville, back in 1946. Since 1998, it's been known as The Community Bank, and besides its headquarters in Loganville, there are branches in Snellville, Grayson and Covington.

The bank was started by Charlie Kelley, the father of the 2007 chairman. Charlie Kelley was a mechanical engineering graduate of Georgia Tech, and Naval veteran of World War II. He and his wife, Frances, had operated a general store in Loganville before the war. A customer, Loganville's mayor, Cliff Cowsert, suggested to Kelley one day: "We need a bank in this town." In those days, Loganville was a farming community like many in Gwinnett, with cotton merchants streaming in to buy the local farmer's cotton from the cotton gin in town. But they gave checks issued on other area banks. A group of people bought stock in the new bank to support Kelley with the idea for Loganville to have its own bank.

The charter was issued in 1946. Kelley headed the bank, being president and chairman of the board for 52 years, from the start of the bank until his death in 1998. His wife was also involved as a member of the board of directors for more than 30 years. Today their son, Stan Kelley, is the second chairman of the bank, while a third generation Kelley, Katherine Franklin, is lending officer and member of the board of directors at the bank.

Another bank was organized with headquarters in Loganville in 2005. It was known as Legacy State Bank, and had $18 million in capital when opened. Larry Garner was the organizing chairman, and J. Patrick McGoldrick was its president.

Duluth banking activities

In the early days of the 20th century, Duluth had two banks, one a branch of the Bank of Buford (the Bank of Duluth) and the Farmers and Merchants Bank, which was founded in the early 1900s. Little is known of this bank. It failed at the height of the Depression. Harris Bagwell remembers that "my dad, Everett Bagwell, got mixed up with it, and eventually lost a lot of money."

That first Bank of Duluth (owned by the Bank of Buford) was on the corner of Main and Lawrenceville Streets. A new bank was organized under the same Bank of Duluth name in 1944, and opened for business in 1945. It occupied the same premises at Main and Lawrenceville Streets that the first Bank of Duluth did, with prominent Duluth merchants and businessmen on the board of directors. John Summerour was the first president, with Guy Washington Findley as vice president, and Everett Bagwell as cashier. These three plus J.C. Bagwell Sr., Calvin Parsons Jr. and Merrill P. Wilson were directors. Later the directors would rotate the presidency. All together, $25,000 was subscribed as the initial capitalization, with 70 people owning stock, putting in as much as $4,800 or as little as $120 for their shares.

Everett Bagwell would remain as cashier of the Bank of Duluth until 1958. He also sold insurance at the bank. Harold Kelly was president until 1963. During his tenure, the bank moved to new facilities across Buford Highway on Georgia Highway 120. Donald Carroll was brought in as president until 1969, when Arnold Smith became president and served until 1973. Tom Martin, who had been raised near Duluth and went to school there, began working at the bank in 1963 and became its president in 1973. The bank was sold in 1981 to Fulton National Bank. It changed the name of the Duluth bank to The Bank of the South-Gwinnett immediately. Later on, Fulton National changed its own name to Bank of the South.

Tom Martin

In 1983, a new local bank was organized, the Citizens Bank of Gwinnett. It opened in 1984, with Tom Martin as its president. Its first office was on Buford Highway in a former branch bank of the First Commercial Bank of Buford. Citizens Bank erected a new and larger building a few blocks south. Citizens Bank was sold to Premier Bancshares of Atlanta in 1997, which sold to Branch Bank and Trust Company out of North Carolina in 1999.

In October, 1999, Mr. Martin led the organization of a new bank for Duluth again, to be called Gwinnett Community Bank, and became its president. The original directors were Woody Bell, Don

Phillips Jr., Dr. Miles Mason III, Terry Gordon, Frank Rinker, Dan Reeves, Jim Braden and Tom Martin. The original capitalization was $8.5 million. In 2008, it had three offices, including branches in Suwanee and at Hamilton Mill. In June 2006, Tom Martin became the chairman of the board and CEO of the bank, and his son, John Martin, became president.

Banking in Buford

In Buford, the Allen family bank, Shadburn Banking Company, became Buford Commercial Bank in the 1940s. About 1974, the name was changed to First Commercial Bank. The name was changed since directors wanted to put a branch in Duluth (which opened in mid-1975) and a name of "Buford Commercial Bank" did not seem appropriate outside of the City of Buford.

First Commercial Bank eventually consisted of three branches -- the original office was on Main Street in downtown Buford; a second location across from the Buford Mall on Georgia Highway 20; and the third branch on Buford Highway in Duluth.

In the 1980s, when First Commercial's assets were approximately $22 million, National Bank of Georgia (NBG) offered a premium for the stock. NBG reduced staff, changed policies and products, and began imposing new regulations for employees and customers. As a result, it no longer was operated as the community bank its customers were used to it being. Frustrated with the situation, several Buford businessmen got together to form an independent community bank.

In 1983, stock was sold in Peoples Bank and Trust Company. Jerry D. Hughes was charter president and led organizing the bank. Mr. Hughes was a native of Buford and had been president of First Commercial Bank. However, he died on October 17, 1984. The bank opened on Dec. 13, 1984, with Clayton Bartlett as president. Most stockholders were residents of Buford, Suwanee, Lawrenceville, and Flowery Branch, areas where the new bank would concentrate. Included in its early rules was that no household could own more than five percent of the stock. The bank had an initial capitalization of $2 million. By December 31, the bank already had $10 million in assets. By the fifth year, its assets were $45 million; the 10th year, they were $95 million, and in 2008, its assets were $457 million.

Peoples Bank had its first location at the corner of Buford Highway and South Lee Street. It reopened the old Main Street Branch in downtown Buford in the early 1990s on Friendship Road and planned another branch on Peachtree Industrial Boulevard.

Doug Nichols, president of the bank in 2008, explains why he thinks an independent community bank is so special: "First of all, the community bank supports all aspects of the community. This commitment includes the local schools, community development, housing construction loans for growth, business loans for area businesses and many other items. Contributions are made to various groups for the support of the local community. A community bank helps communities grow and prosper."

* * * * *

Georgia Trust Bank was incorporated May 20, 2004, and is owned by Georgia Trust Bankshares, the holding company. It has offices in Buford near the Mall of Georgia and in

Kennesaw on George Busbee Parkway. It began operating in Buford in May, 2005, and the Kennesaw office opened as a branch in September, 2005.

The bank's original capitalization was $18 million. Original directors of the bank were Ronald D. Adamson, J. Michael Allen, L. Myron Cantrell, Michael L. Jordan, C. Dean Robinson, William E. Smith, Marvin O. Tibbetts, III, James J. Tidwell and Michael E. Townsend. William E. Smith is chairman of the board, and Mike Allen is president and CEO, a position they have held since inception.

Snellville banking activity

In the early 1970s, an Atlanta entrepreneur, J. Mack Robinson, wanted to open a bank in Snellville, as he had done in more than 30 communities across Georgia. Along with Wayne and Jimmy Mason as key stockholders, Gwinnett County Bank began. In 1979, Mr. Robinson wanted to sell his shares, and soon Gwinnett brothers Jim and Virgil Williams, who had run a succession of companies, purchased a majority of the stock of the bank. Two years later, they also purchased the Fulton County Bank of Alpharetta, and changed the two banks' names to Heritage Bank. A year later, they bought Rockdale Savings and Loan, and ran the financial institutions under the name of Heritage Savings Bank.

By 1985, the Williams began something different in Metro Atlanta. The idea: to locate branch offices of banks in supermarkets. (This idea has been pioneered in Georgia by Community Bank and Trust of Cornelia.) Kroger in Norcross was one of the first three trial offices. The Williams brothers found that they could build a mini-branch in a supermarket for 1/12th the cost of a conventional branch bank.

Eventually, there were 34 Heritage locations throughout Georgia, mostly in supermarkets. Supermarket banking gave the Williams another opportunity which they mined in 1985. It was the setting up of International Banking Technologies (IBT), a firm which licensed and franchised banks nationwide in supermarkets, and was headquartered on Indian Trail Road in Norcross at I-85.

In 1995, the Williams sold IBT to First Financial Management Corp., and by that time, there were more than 1,200 supermarket banks operating under their franchise. And those conservative bankers who had been laughing at the idea of a mini-branch in the grocery store by then often had their own branches in supermarkets.

Modern banking in Norcross

First Security National Bank opened for business in Norcross on June 25, 1985. At that time, it was the first new national bank that had been chartered in Gwinnett County in ten years. Its capitalization was $3 million. The original members of the board of directors were: Ralph Barber Sr., James Hewell, Marvin Black, Sonny Ackerman, Robert Holbrook, Dr. Harold Holloway, Harold Medlock, Carl Howington, John Smith, John Adams, Jerry Gardner, Tom Phillips, Lillian Webb, Jim Ellis and Jack Conway.

In 2006, First Security Bank was publicized in the American Bankers Association Magazine as one of the top 50 most profitable banks in the nation.

First Security National Bank has four offices. Besides the main office in Norcross, its branches, and the year they opened, include Chastain Park, Atlanta, (1994); Vickery Village, Cumming, (2006); and Harmony Lakes, Canton (2006). A distinctive feature of the bank is that 39 percent of the stock in First Security is owed by the Employee Stock Ownership Plan. President Dan Baker says: "As such, all our employees are owners of the company." Bank officials view this as instrumental in success and employee retention. On average, employees stay 12 years with First Security National Bank.

A new national bank came to Gwinnett in 2008, when Touchmark National Bank opened, with its first offices in an office building at Technology Park in Norcross. Its first banking office was in Duluth, at the intersection of Peachtree Industrial Boulevard and Abbotts Bridge Road. Its initial capitalization was $34.7 million, with Tom Persons as chairman. It organized with 20 directors, who were Bill Short (CEO), Edgerton Burroughs, Bill Butler, Dan Cowart, Barry Culbertson, Howard Greenfield, Yuling Hayter, John Johnson, Dan Kaufman, Moon Kim, Hiluard Kitchens, Sudhirkamar Patel, Tom Persons, H.P. Rama, J.J. Shah, Meena Shah, Bill Williams and Vivian Wong.

In the fall of 2008, another Norcross area bank was in formation. Several people involved previously with The Peachtree Bank of Duluth (in Fulton County) were seeking to move a bank headquartered in Coweta County to Norcross. The move came after The Peachtree Bank was acquired by Alabama National Bank, which subsequently was acquired by RCB of Canada.

The group was seeking to acquire First Choice Community Bank 1874 of Newnan. They were planning to operate at two locations in Gwinnett, in addition to a branch in Newnan, and change the name to The Piedmont Bank. Those involved with the effort included Robert D. Cheeley, Paul Donaldson, John Howard, Paul Maggard and Monty Watson, who had previously been president of The Peachtree Bank. The group planned to have its headquarters in Norcross and a branch in Lawrenceville. The headquarters would be at the intersection of Peachtree Parkway and Peachtree Corners Circle, across from The Forum shopping area.

Suwanee banking

Quantum National Bank was opened Dec. 27, 1995 in Suwanee at Peachtree Industrial Boulevard and Suwanee Dam Road, with the expressed goal of creating a financial institution to serve both a mainstream and immigrant community. Its organizing chairman was Dr. Narasimhulu Neelagaru, a practicing cardiologist from Jackson County. The firm opened with a capitalization of $5 million. Its founding board consisted of Dr. Neelagaru, President Chris Fluehr, Dr. P. Makizhnan, Chandra Patel, Narender Reddy and Dr. Srinivas K. Reddy.

The bank opened a second office in Alpharetta in 2005, and constructed a building there in 2006. In addition, it purchased Southeastern Mortgage and Financial Services and now operates a local mortgage company as a wholly-owned subsidiary. Its core business is to serve the financial needs of ethnic groups in Metro Atlanta, with particular emphasis of meeting the needs of Indian and Asian populations with commercial concentrations in convenience stores and motels.

First president of the bank was Chris Fluehr, who retired after nine years with the bank in 2004. He was succeeded by Douglas Wren, who remained as president until May, 2008. Brad Day was serving as interim president in 2008.

Homestead Bank of Suwanee was organized in 2003, with Lee Weilhiem as CEO. Its original capitalization was $12 million. The current bank president is Heyward Horton.

The name was changed to Security Bank of Gwinnett County, when the bank was sold to Security Bank Corporation of Macon on July 31, 2006. Its assets in mid-2008 were $357 million.

Lawrenceville activity

Nine years to the date after Gwinnett Banking Company was formed in Lawrenceville and moved into its first building behind the Justice and Administrative Center on Nash Street (October 31, 1997), the bank was sold to First Charter Corporation of Charlotte, N.C., on October 31, 2006. It was First Charter's initial purchase of a bank in Georgia.

The original capitalization of Gwinnett Banking Company was $10 million. Larry Key organized the bank, and became its president. Its early directors included: Jim Ballard, Jerry Boles, W.H. Britt, Grant Hayes, Rich Combs, Doug Langley, Joe Powell, Bill Stanton, Norris Nash and Larry Key. Deposits at the time Gwinnett Banking became part of First Charter were $400 million.

However, on June 9, 2008, Fifth Third Bank of Cincinnati, Ohio, purchased First Charter Bank, which had 57 branches in North Carolina, and the two GBC locations in Georgia in Lawrenceville and Alpharetta. At that time, Fifth Third had $111 billion in assets in12 states, primarily in the Midwest. The company traces its origins to the Bank of the Ohio Valley, which opened in Cincinnati in 1858. That bank was purchased by the Third National Bank in 1871, which later merged with the Fifth National Bank near the turn of the century and became known as the Fifth Third Bank.

American United Bank opened its doors on December 20, 2004 near Lawrenceville at Cruse and Old Norcross Roads. The founding chairman of the bank was P.I. Joy, with Glenn Thompson its president.

The initial capitalization was $10 million. Directors included Surinder Bahl, James Jett, P.I. Joy, Palamalai Mahizhnan, Kati Patel, Naresh Parikh, Gursharan S. Pannu, David B. Poythress, and T. Glenn Thompson. Aiming at the immigrant market, the bank advertised, among other points, that there were "11 languages spoken" at its office.

In 2006, Republic Bank of Georgia was organized in Gwinnett. It had a Lawrenceville address, with Robert Ratliff as its chairman, and with a capitalization of $24 million. Scott Reed is its president and chief executive officer.

Its original directors included Bill Brantley, Wayne Bloodworth, Mike Buckman, Gary Byrd, Bill Eason, Charlotte Nash, George Oelschig, Robert Ratliff, Scott Reed, Jim Stephenson and Mike Tennant.

In 2007, the Embassy National Bank was organized in Lawrenceville, with initial capitalization of $18 million. Nitin Shah was chairman of the Board, and Chris Fluehr was president of the bank. Directors included Chris Fluehr, Larry Johnson, Steve King, Navin Shah, Nitin Shah, Chuck Thakkar and Philip White.

The First National Bank of Gwinnett in Lawrenceville was the largest bank in Gwinnett until it was sold in 1985.

One person who has seen the change in Gwinnett from the old rural style to the modern banks is Richard Sikes of Lawrenceville, who in 2007 had put in 55 years in the field. He says: "Mr. Jim Vic Hood, who was president of the First National Bank of Lawrenceville, hired me when I was 17 years old back in 1952. He told me that the main thing is that a banker is supposed to find a way to help people, and that stuck with me. I failed in helping some, but wanted to do it, and got satisfaction from working with people who banked with us. He also told me, and I heard it from him first, to surround yourself with good people, and it'll always make your job easier."

First National had only five other employees when Sikes joined it. He started to work directly after graduation from Dacula High. "Mr. Hood let me start interviewing people and hiring them shortly after I went to work there. I got promoted and put into positions before I was qualified, but we started growing, and he gave me the opportunity."

Back when Sikes went into banking, he says Gwinnett was "100 percent rural and a farming county. The only type of loans we made would be in the spring, when we would make $300-500 crop loans. You, the banker, made them in the spring, and took payments and worked to collect them in the fall. Our bank had assets of $2.9 million back then."

As growth came, banking started to change. "We started making loans to people who were operating businesses out of old houses, or small buildings, or a car dealership, but they were mostly people who lived here. We never did much with outside people. We tried to serve our community, and stayed as much local as we could.

"In the last 20 years, we have made lots of commercial loans to construct buildings, or put people in businesses which created new jobs. We've also been heavy into the construction loans of new residences, and starter homes. But when I started out, we never made those types of loans."

In July 1985, the bank was sold to First Atlanta Bank, when it had assets of $100 million. Shortly thereafter, in December 1985, Wachovia bought First Atlanta. Sikes remained with Wachovia for four years, and officially retired May 1, 1989.

Almost immediately, Sikes started raising capital for what would become the Commercial Bank of Gwinnett. Sikes was chairman of the board of the new bank. Then in December 1996, this bank was sold to Colonial Bank for $230 million. Sikes remained for one year with Colonial Bank, and remained on its board for six years.

Then on April 1, 2003, Sikes joined Peachtree Bank of Fulton County (with a Duluth address) and became president of The Peachtree Bank, Gwinnett, its branch in Lawrenceville. In April 2, 2006, when Peachtree Bank was sold to Alabama National Bank of Birmingham, Ala., Sikes remained at the branch in Lawrenceville. In 2007, Sikes was buying property for a new and expanded location of The Peachtree Bank, on Scenic Highway, at Gwinnett Drive and Georgia Highway 124.

When construction began, the bank was still called Peachtree Bank, though owned by Alabama National of Birmingham, Ala. However, on Feb. 22, 2008, Alabama National Bank was purchased by RBC Bank of Canada. So it was RBC Bank's name on the door when it held its official opening in August of 2008. Then the top officer of the Lawrenceville office was Vice President/Community Banker Judy McDaniel, a veteran banking official in

Gwinnett. By then Richard Sikes had retired, saying: "I've put 55 years in banking, all of it in Lawrenceville, but boy, there have been changes!"

* * * * *

From essentially country banks in the early 1900s, the Gwinnett banking community has seen a continuing tide of change. These came often as a result of new banks being formed as older ones were bought, especially in 1980-2000 era. There has been the merger of banks, and in the last part of the 20th century, the emergence of the mega-banks wanting a part of the expanding Gwinnett action. One element has been prevalent throughout it all: change. We'll see where this change leads in the 21st Century. (See page 768 in Appendix B for a list of local banks.)

Minor league baseball

Just how did Gwinnett get a Class AAA baseball team? The story has never been told in detail. Here is one account.

Up until the late 1990s, when one thought of baseball in Gwinnett, it was either of high school teams, or major league baseball in downtown Atlanta. No one had even thought that Gwinnett might one day have its own minor league baseball team, except one man….. the late Scott Hudgens.

Toward the end of his life, Mr. Hudgens, who enjoyed baseball, thought that if other smaller communities in the nation could support minor league baseball teams, Gwinnett might be big enough for that, too. So he broached the idea to several people in the Gwinnett community. However, Mr. Hudgens died before he could devote his attention to this idea.

Then in late 2006, a county commissioner, Bert Nasuti of Norcross, said that one of his goals was to bring minor league baseball to Gwinnett at that year's county commission retreat at Brasstown Valley Resort. The upshot of that retreat was interest by the Gwinnett Convention and Visitors Bureau. That group commissioned a $60,000 study by the sports marketing firm of Conventions Sports and Leisure (CSL International) of Wayzata, Minn. Working out of their Dallas office, they produced a 123-page study by June 6, 2007, which gave an amazingly positive report on minor league baseball possibilities for Gwinnett County.

Among the conclusions of the study:

- "Demographic and socioeconomic makeup of Gwinnett County and the surrounding areas provide one of the strongest markets in the country to support a minor league baseball team.
- "There is limited minor league sports competition in the Gwinnett County area that offers quality entertainment at a cost below current area professional sports franchises.
- "An independent minor league baseball team and ball park could generate annual operating income before debt service ranging from $890,000 to $1.5 million."

The report cautioned that with the Atlanta Braves being located close by, perhaps the best possibility for a Gwinnett minor league team would be to hook into an independent league, not a league sanctioned by major league baseball. It suggested that perhaps Gwinnett could become a site for a league like the American Association, or an independent league.

Overall, the study ranked Gwinnett sixth among the independent markets studied in terms of total population and said that the county was projected to grow at a rate nearly double the national average. It also showed that within a 15-mile radius of a proposed stadium, there were 1.2 million people, and within 25 miles, 2.6 million people. In addition, the income of the area was 60 percent greater than other independent league markets.

The study also took a survey of residents, who suggested that the reasons they attended few Atlanta Braves games were traffic congestion, distance to travel, and that these games were too expensive.

The study concluded: "After analysis, it appears that the Gwinnett County market is best suited to support an independent league team. It is unlikely that the Atlanta Braves will support an affiliated team in a county in which the team perceives to be of significant importance to their on-going viability." The study also said that the Braves were in anticipation of working toward a new stadium for their Class AAA franchise in Richmond.

While the study came back glowing, and was made public in June saying that the Atlanta Braves were not interested in Gwinnett, local officials did not stop there. It was no accident that key people within the Braves organization read the study.

Nothing happened for two months of 2007.

Then Preston Williams, who heads the Gwinnett Civic Center, and who was the lead person for Gwinnett in working with the study about a possible minor league team, got a call from the Atlanta Braves. The study had raised their eyebrows, and they wanted a preliminary conversation about Gwinnett. Williams had the first meeting with Braves President John Schuerholz and Mike Plant, head of business operations, on August 17. Preston remembers: "We felt each other out. At the end of the meeting, both sides seemed to have serious interest to make something work." It was at this meeting that the subject of the Richmond Braves came up, with the Atlanta organization telling Williams of the need to keep the discussions under wraps, so it would not harm the Braves in their current position in Virginia.

Soon the Braves were back in Gwinnett, talking to the five-member executive committee of the Convention and Visitor's Bureau: Richard Tucker, Bert Nasuti, Tommy Hughes, Tom Martin and Williams. Preston says: "The first word out of the Braves' mouths was that they wanted a non-disclosure agreement with them to start a dialogue. They did not want the issue to get discussed in the public forum because of their relationships in Richmond. After all, if something did not happen in Gwinnett, they did not want to jeopardize their Richmond franchise." But it was also obvious by now that the Braves were interested in moving their Class AAA franchise to Gwinnett! That got the attention of the five attendees from the Gwinnett CVB. Remember, the CSL study had said that Gwinnett could hope for, at best, an independent league team.

During the latter part of 2007, only the executive board of the Convention and Visitor's Bureau was in talks with Braves' officials. Other members of the CVB board did not know initially of these conversations, as the CVB five members held the proceedings close to their chests. Soon began the formulation of a concept, focusing on different sites. Eventually two different sites near Interstate 85 came into play. Each of these land owners produced their own mixed unit development and site plans. Finally one site was chosen. But so far, people of Gwinnett did not know of these plans.

The Class AAA Gwinnett Braves start play in April 2009.

That all changed on Jan. 15, 2008. The Braves and the Convention and Visitor's Bureau held a press conference at the Gwinnett Arena, announcing plans for the Braves' Class AAA team to begin their year as the Gwinnett Braves in the spring of 2009, after the Gwinnett Board of Commissioners earlier that day had approved plans and financing of the proposed new local ball park site. The location was southeast of Interstate 85 on Highway 20, a 44-acre site, west of Old Peachtree Road.

On hand to announce the plans were key members of the Atlanta Braves, including their chairman and CEO Terry McGuirk, Schuerholz, Plant and Jeff Francouer, a former Parkview High athlete who is an outfielder with the Braves. One of the reasons cited that the Braves were to moved their Class AAA team was "challenges getting a new AAA ball park built in Richmond. (It) made it attractive to have them in our own back yard," said McGuirk.

Richard Tucker, chairing the announcement from the CVB, said that "the Atlanta Braves' organization has no equal in major league baseball. The partnership with the Gwinnett Convention and Visitors Bureau will bring a new level of enthusiasm for the citizens of Gwinnett County." Nasuti added that what had been his "dream 14 months earlier had become a reality."

Interestingly, when Atlanta got the Braves as a major league team in 1966, that sent the minor league Atlanta Crackers' franchise to Richmond, where it became the Class AAA Braves. So, in a way, the Richmond Braves were returning home to Georgia.

Also announced at the meeting were preliminary plans for the new ball park. It would consist of 7,540 fixed seats, 150 wheelchair spaces conforming to the American Disability Act regulations, plus it would have 2,500 berm seats in the outfield, for a total capacity of 10,190. There would be parking near the stadium for 3,200 automobiles. The park would have 23 suites, plus party decks for corporate sponsors. Another feature would be 350 club seats behind home plate. There would be a kid's play area, and a restaurant on the main concourse. Around the park would be an "urban village" environment developed by Brand Partners, which had owned the land chosen for the site.

With the ball park housing a Class AAA team, where players might go up to the Atlanta parent Braves major league at any time, Braves' officials asked that the field be designed with the same playing dimensions as Turner Field in Atlanta, so players would not have to make an adjustment when called up. That means that the left field wall will be 335 feet from home plate; center field, 401, and right field 330. The warning track will also conform to the Turner Field track.

Soon after the announcement, ground was being cleared. However, no dirt was moved until early May of 2008, when a land disturbance permit was issued shortly after the closing on the land by the county.

The baseball park land and construction was expected to cost $40-45 million. The funding came from a $33 million, 30-year Gwinnett Industrial Development Authority revenue bond issue backed by the county. There was $12 million in funding from the Gwinnett Recreation Authority. The 12-acre park site was purchased for $5 million from Brand Partners. Another $7 million was planned for construction costs. The revenue bond issue closed on April 1, 2008.

A snag appeared in September, 2008, when earlier plans for the stadium were found to be greatly underfunded. Instead of costing $40 million, the new cost was $59 million. However, with little fanfare, the Gwinnett County Commission approved the change after the GCVB recommended it. Uproar in the media was immediate, though little could be done about it.

Actually, the county and the GCVB were in a tough spot, since they had already committed to the project, with major work underway. There could be no going back, since too much had already been committed, including sales of bonds.

Time will tell if the move by the county was a good one. Though some people in the community were vocal about the added cost, it appeared that most Gwinnettians were not squawking much, but looking forward to minor league baseball in the county, thinking it would be a good "quality of life" attraction for the community.

Revenue for repaying the debt will come from a per seat tax, from a rental car tax that Gwinnett imposed throughout the county, from naming rights, and from parking revenue.

Reaction from people in Gwinnett was overall positive, though some grumbling came from questions about the privacy of the negotiations and financing of the park. However, the non-disclosure agreement that the Atlanta Braves required with the Gwinnett CVB prevented early open negotiations and sun shining on the project.

Developing the private land around the ball park will be the Brand Properties, a partnership of the Brand Family. Anticipated to be complete within five years on the property is 200,000 square feet of retail space, possibly including restaurants; 150,000 square feet in offices; a 150-room hotel; and 400 residential units. The property sits on Georgia Highway 20 between Technology Center Parkway and the Publix supermarket at Old Peachtree Road.

The architect for the project is the firm of HKS of Richmond, Va., which also has offices in Atlanta. Mark Hults of Dunwoody was the architect overseeing the design. His firm had been involved in designing Miller Park for the Brewers in Milwaukee, Wis., the Texas Rangers park, and many other parks and sporting facilities around the country. It is also the firm picked for a new stadium for the Dallas Cowboys.

Hults says of the design of the Gwinnett park: "We are designing not just the park, but the parcel of land around the park, too. We envision this, over time, as a destination for people to come any day of the year, and not just for baseball. The whole feeling should be comfortable, a place you can get in and out of quickly, but also go to shops and enjoy the restaurants."

Fred Ortiz was the lead designing architect on the project. Part of his early work was to research baseball in Gwinnett and Atlanta. "If you remember the old Crackers' park on

Ponce de Leon Avenue, it was adjacent to a warehouse district, and we have been highly influenced by it, and are establishing a couple of long and linear buildings bordering first and third base, along warehouse lines.

"You will enter the ball park at grade level, and step down to the lower seating level. There will be concessions all accessible along the concourse, behind the seating, so that the spectator will never lose touch with the ball park. The suites will be above the concessions. Here will be 21 suites, each of 16 seats, plus a super suite that will seat up to 50, plus a party deck."

Ortiz says that the idea is to create an entertainment destination, a nucleus of a mixed use entertainment district. The concourse will run 360 degrees around the park, meaning that fans entering behind home plate could walk to the berm outfield area and be able to see the playing field the entire time.

An architect's rendering of the new Gwinnett Braves Stadium on Georgia Highway 20 near the Mall of Georgia.

The construction firm hired on a design-build basis is Barton Malon of Southfield, Mich, which has had a presence in Atlanta since 1986. The firm originally retrofitted Olympic Stadium into Turner Field, and was also involved in the Georgia Dome construction. The firm's first project was Oriole Park at Camden Yards in Baltimore. It also built Coors Field in Denver and PNC Park in Pittsburgh. It has been involved with minor league fields for teams in Jacksonville, Fla., Greensboro and Charlotte, N.C.

Len Moser of Snellville is the project coordinator for Barton Malon, the contractor, and he's the man who hired HKS as the design partner. Moser, who moved to Snellville in 1996 to work on the Turner Field retrofitting, said that when excavation was begun on the Gwinnett ball park site, what the firm found was an extremely sandy soil, one well drained. "It wasn't rock or Georgia clay," he said. "And it's most unique for the region."

Overseeing the work on the site as liaison with the county as project coordinator for the ball park was George Heckman, who retired as director of the Gwinnett Water Department. He previously also oversaw work for the Gwinnett CVB on the Gwinnett Arena.

The land where the ball park is located was once farmed by the Billew family. Hazel Billew, who moved to the county in 1928, brought her parents and two brothers to the area. The Billews owned 60 acres, with 10 acres, including a sawmill, being north of Georgia Highway 20. Miss Billew was a Gwinnett librarian, and drove the county bookmobile. When Hazel Billew died, her surviving brother, Dorris (Dot) Billew, inherited the land, and later deeded the land to his heirs, who sold the acreage on the south side of the highway in 1991 to the Brand Estate.

So for minor league baseball to come to Gwinnett, it was two people, a decade apart, who are the ones who are most responsible for Gwinnett even thinking about getting a minor league baseball team.

It comes after the early visions of Scott Hudgens, and because of Bert Nasuti, who had the foresight to push for a feasibility study at the right time and gained the support of the entire county commission to fund it. That's how the Gwinnett Braves were set to come into being in the spring of 2009.

9
School Systems

Schools are a major attraction

At the end of the 2007-2008 school year, Gwinnett had the largest school system in Georgia with 154,517 students. That requires 10,654 teachers, and another 9,049 bus drivers, maintenance workers, and other staff. By the year 2010, at least 175,000 students are expected to be enrolled in Gwinnett. (For an earlier recounting of the history of Gwinnett schools, see Nita Hallford's article in Appendix A-12).

Add to that---Gwinnett has the most diverse population of students in Georgia. More than 100 different languages are spoken in Gwinnett public schools by its varied student population. Gwinnett students represent a global community ... an A to Z community that includes students from Afghanistan to Zimbabwe.

Here are just a sampling of the countries some Gwinnett students used to call "home":

Afghanistan, Angola, Aruba, United Arab Emirates, Bahamas, Burundi, Bangladesh, Bulgaria, Bosnia-Herzegovina, Brazil, Botswana, Central African Republic, Cambodia, Canada, China, Cameroon, Colombia, Congo Democratic Republic, Congo, Colombia, Costa Rica, Cote D'Ivoire, Croatia, Czech Republic, Cuba, Dominican Republic, Ecuador, Egypt, Ethiopia, France, Gabon, Germany, Ghana, Guinea, Gambia, Guatemala, Guyana, Honduras, Haiti, Hong Kong, India, Indonesia, Iran, Italy, Jamaica, Kenya, Korea, Liberia, Saint Lucia, Malaysia, Moldova, Mexico, Nigeria, Nicaragua, Pakistan, Panama, Paraguay, Peru, Philippines, Poland, Puerto Rico, Reunion, Romania, Russia, Rwanda, Saudi Arabia, Sudan, Sierra Leone, El Salvador, Somalia, Slovenia, Togo, Thailand, Trinidad and Tobago, Turkey, Taiwan, Tanzania, Uganda, Ukraine, United Kingdom, Uruguay, Venezuela, US Virgin Islands, Vietnam and Zimbabwe.

Many regard the Gwinnett public schools as the best system in Georgia. Year after year, a number of Gwinnett schools were cited as being Blue Ribbon Schools of Excellence. The distinction Gwinnett garnered for its schools in statewide competition had a major effect on the county. Many parents cite the high-quality Gwinnett schools as one of the most important reasons they move to Gwinnett when they relocate to Metro Atlanta.

Another consideration: Gwinnett County schools retain 93 percent, on average, of its faculty from year to year. And it compensates its teachers well, paying an average of $5-6,000 more in teacher supplements than the state average salary.

There's more. In addition to the county school system, the City of Buford maintains its own independent school system with about 2,700 students (2007). (See Appendix B section on Buford City Schools on page 791.)

Gwinnett's education system hasn't always been regarded as highly as it is today. Yet a convergence of many factors propelled what was an average/above-average system into an excellent one.

One factor has been the overall support of the system by residents of the county. With Gwinnett's growth, the great majority of people moving into the county were well-educated, and demanded that the schools give their children an excellent education; they also expected their children to do well. They were happy to support education through taxes, and usually supported school board bond initiatives. They readily backed bond proposals put forth by the school board. For instance, from 1971 to 1993, there were 12 bond referendums to fund more classrooms. Voters backed all of these referendums except in February, 1990, when voters turned down a $75 million bond referendum by a 4:3 margin. However, the school board came back in November of that same year and passed a $129 million bond referendum with 63 percent of voters giving their approval.

A $225 million bond referendum in 1993 was approved by voters for school classroom construction. In 1997, county voters approved an additional penny in sales tax for school infrastructure in the first Special Purpose Local Option Sales Tax for Education (or E-SPLOST), which netted the Gwinnett School Board $529 million. This has been the primary method of financing additional classrooms and schools since that time. Voter approval of the E-SPLOST in 2001 brought to the Gwinnett System $667 million, and the E-SPLOST voted in 2006 was projected to raise for school construction a minimum of $1.08 billion. The 2006 vote also authorized a general obligation bond for the Gwinnett School Board in the amount of $425 million to help the system jump start and speed its building program. The bonds allowed the system to begin building additional schools and classrooms for its burgeoning and expanding enrollment, prior to collecting the sales tax. These bonds were to be paid back with the sales tax proceeds as they were collected.

Through 2007, the E-SPLOST one-cent sales tax has brought in for construction of schools in Gwinnett County a total of $1,248,401,951. That's $1.248 *billion*. You can see why Gwinnett school officials respect the one penny tax on retail sales for school purposes.

In 2008, Gwinnett voters also approved a $750 million general obligation bond for school construction. The vote to approve these bonds was 106,688 for the proposal and 38,858 against it. The funds were to build eight new schools and more than 500 classrooms at other schools. The bonds had a special appeal: they did not require a tax increase, since budgets in earlier years had been used to pay off previous bonds, freeing up additional monies to repay the new bonds.

A portion of each E-SPLOST has also benefited the independent Buford City Schools. That brought to the Buford system $14.8 million (by special agreement) from the 1997 E-SPLOST; $13 million from the 2001 vote; and an anticipated $18.7 million from the 2006 vote. (See Appendix B, page 787.)

How have the schools of Gwinnett maintained their quality in buildings, in instruction and in having a good relationship with the voters? It was done with inspired leadership by:

- elected officials and paid staff;
- continued improvement in teacher quality;
- ready-to-learn students;
- parents who valued education;
- parents making sure their students performed; and
- parents who were ready to pay for good schools by continually passing bond issues, and voting to tax themselves for school purposes.

Consider another factor. Gwinnett County has had since 1959 an appointed superintendent, not an elected one. This change in the way the superintendent came to the position happened to correspond with the beginning of Gwinnett's growth. In succession followed individuals picked by the elected school board to ensure that the schools would be operated in a professional manner. So, in succession came individuals with superior qualifications who guided the school system into a period of solid achievement and steady growth.

For years in Georgia, one element of society had advocated that the voters elect county school superintendents, while a more progressive element in the state advocated that an elected board should choose the superintendent. A key argument on the side of the progressives was that by the board picking the superintendent, they would go after the most qualified person, and it would remove the important post from one step further from politics. In some smaller counties, often with the lowest academic achievement, there could be few, if any people, qualified by professional standards to be a superintendent.

If ever an example of why an appointed superintendent and elected board of education works, look no further than Gwinnett County. By taking this step to appoint the superintendent back in 1959, Gwinnett's School Board launched a system into the modern era, long before Georgia adopted this (in 1992, as a constitutional amendment) as a requirement of each county. This early adoption of an appointed superintendent helped make the Gwinnett School System the high quality system it is today.

The change came from Gwinnett voters, who in the fall election of 1956 voted to retain the system of electing five school board members representing districts of Gwinnett, but to eliminate the elected school superintendent. In turn, the School Board would make an appointment of the superintendent. Gwinnett at that time was one of a few systems in Georgia adopting the appointed superintendent system.

Running for elected school superintendent that same year was B.B. Harris, a veteran school teacher. He was elected to serve only a two-year term as superintendent, as the voters in that election adopted the appointed superintendent system to begin January 1, 1959. Mr. Harris then became the first appointed superintendent, and served in that role through 1967.

Then came as the appointed superintendent a series of highly-qualified individuals:

- J.W. Benefield, also a vocational-agricultural specialist, 1967-77;
- Alton C. Crews, who was in the past superintendent of schools in Cobb County, Ga. and Charleston, S.C., 1977-90;
- George G. Thompson, a former principal who had been nurtured in the Gwinnett system, 1990-94;
- David Crews, an interim superintendent, January to July, 1995;
- Dr. Sidney Faucette, from Virginia, who stayed less than a year, 1995-96; and
- J. Alvin Wilbanks, who had previously been an administrator in DeKalb County and with the Georgia Department of Education as director of the Occupational Educational Center, 1996-present.

Starting in 1984 as its first president of Gwinnett Tech, Wilbanks also held concurrently a position of assistant superintendent of human resources and continuous improvement for the Gwinnett school board. Mr. Wilbanks was the chief education officer in Gwinnett during the period when it became the largest school system in the state, and gained national prominence for its achievements. In 2008, it had more than 158,000 students.

But there is more to why Gwinnett has a good school system. Another factor to consider is this: when you already have a good system, and you need to hire anywhere from 200 (in the early 1970s) to 1,100 (for 2006-07)) new teachers each year, who are you going to attract? Add to it that you offer a nice supplement for beginning teachers, in a county with high-performing students and a good reputation? And the results? You get a continuing number outstanding teachers from across the country making application, and you hire the best of them.

Add to that formula a substantially high number of students moving into the county each year, many from families who have a high regard for education. The students moving into the county often have high intelligence, and when taking tests, would help improve the county-wide test results.

Alvin Wilbanks

Then you have administrative personnel who ensure that you get a value out of each school dollar, such as erecting new classrooms far cheaper than most systems nationwide. "More bang for the buck" would be another way of saying how the school system shepherds its dollars.

Back this up with voter approval of school bond referendums for many years. Follow that with a new funding possibility, the Special Purpose Local Option Sales Taxes (E-SPLOST) for education, that easily won endorsement in Gwinnett with 70.72 percent of voters approving the measure. The first SPLOST for education passed on March 18. In effect, if you are a Gwinnett school professional, you are given excellent material to work with in facilities, in materials...and in students. And in the meantime, even in the face of continually spiraling enrollments, even with many students in temporary trailers awaiting new classrooms, and even with many diverse students propelling the school age population to minority white...the system continues to improve.

Gwinnett's school system is truly amazing.

Now it is possible to begin to understand why people move to Gwinnett County.... not only because of land values, good quality homes and jobs. Many decide before any of these other factors to move to Gwinnett County because of the high quality of its schools. After all, they value their children, and want the best for them, which the Gwinnett schools can give them. That's perhaps the key reason for all the success in Gwinnett in the last 30 years.

Innovation in school construction

A fast growing county has a constant need for more governmental buildings. In Gwinnett, that was especially true of classrooms, as the school system grew so quickly. Gwinnett Public Schools have an exemplary record of keeping construction costs low, yet quality high, in building new schools. In effect, they get more for their money that way.

Alton Crews, a former superintendent of the school system, was known as an innovative leader for the Gwinnett School System. He impressed a lot of people when he arrived by talking extemporaneously – without consulting notes -- yet was very detailed in his presentations.

Perhaps one of the most far-reaching achievements of his years as superintendent was the hiring in 1976 of a commercial builder with general contracting experience, not a former teacher, to head the school construction. That person was Jim Steele, who was named in 1995 as the chief operating officer of the school system. He is the one single individual most responsible for making sure that the school system got value from each dollar it invested in new construction.

Jim Steele, who was hired by Crews as an engineer to oversee construction of the system, said Crews always tried to make three points in his talks. "He didn't think you could communicate, nor an audience could absorb, more than three points. He was also big on having visual aids, but not more than one to three, for a talk. And he did a lot more preparation for speaking than some people might think. He prepared endlessly, and did his own research in searching out the detail. By the time for the talk, he knew his subject thoroughly."

Crews told Steele anyone could tell whether a teacher was successful in the classroom by simply observing:

- Was order being maintained?
- Did the teacher know the subject?
- Were the students on task, and not talking?
- Did the teacher embarrass the students in front of their peers?

Gwinnett County: A Little Above Atlanta

After graduating from the University of Georgia, Steele worked for six years in commercial construction prior to going to work for the school system. His last job prior to the school system was General Superintendent for Taylor and Elrod Construction Company, a general contracting firm. He oversaw superintendents on as many as 10-15 commercial construction projects at any given time.

What has evolved in the years as he has headed first construction, then other non-teaching elements of the Gwinnett schools, has been phenomenal. No single item accounted for this, except perhaps Steele's "approach" to his job. It was to build confidence and a public trust in school construction.

As COO of the public schools, he has nine departments reporting to him. They are responsible for:

- construction,
- facility planning,
- contracts for engineering,
- transportation,
- risk management,
- environmental and supply services,
- grounds and fleet,
- building maintenance, and
- continuing improvement.

His ideas essentially call for a "partnering" between the School Board and its architects, engineers and contractors, in a "design-bid-build" delivery model. It's aimed at building public trust between the suppliers, the School Board, and the community. The idea is to be fair and open to all "responsible, responsive architects, engineers and contractors" in order to get the best price for every job. As a result, the schools are often working with firms well known to the system, firms who have done Gwinnett school work before, a known commodity. Steele says: "We often work with a panel of people we have worked with over the years, so we're not re-inventing the wheel all over again. It's an age-old delivery system, and perceived as the most fair way to build."

With Gwinnett schools growing so fast, there are always a lot of buildings needed. Gwinnett builds enough schools so that many architects, engineers, contractors and sub-contractors stay busy working with the system. "We have on the drawing board," Steele says, "About 20-30 construction projects of all different sizes most of the time."

By working with a known group of firms, and by standardizing as much materials and equipment as possible, the System gets a savings in operation, maintenance and interchangeability of parts. In addition, the firms providing the service know what type of units the System uses in its construction before bids go out. "They can fine tune the price, since they have built for us before, and know what the units will cost them down the road."

A Gwinnett Public School project includes much up front work, to get a total set of plans and all specifications complete before the first work begins on any project. This work is done in order to "eliminate the unknowns" in any job. As a result of this, the System finds that very few expensive change orders take place on Gwinnett Public School construction sites.

Jim Steele

The few change orders that develop come most often from unknown site conditions found after construction begins.

A required part of each Gwinnett Public School contract is a monthly meeting between architects, engineers and contractors with the school professional staffers to iron out any problems that may arise. This has led to other efficiencies in building Gwinnett's schools.

Steele says: "It's not a wasted meeting, since it addresses problems before they get out of hand. Contractors come in with answers, since they know the agenda before the meeting. Meetings most often last an hour and then they're done. We don't let problems get big, we take care of them when they pop up. We force ourselves to communicate, and set aside time to partner."

Another key element in the Gwinnett Public Schools method of construction is its use of "infill professionals" on its own staff to guide the construction. These staff architects, engineers and former contractors supervise the ongoing construction. They are not just out of college, but industry-trained, experienced professionals. Steele does not hire former teachers for these positions.

He says: "This is a huge difference for us. The trend in many educational systems is to send their teachers to get degrees in educational leadership, and then to reward these teachers by placing them in places like Facility Management. This is one of the biggest mistakes the educational profession has been making, by putting non-building type of people into a field they know very little about. We don't operate that way."

Steele continues: "Construction time is money, and is the essence of all contracts. If you can't answer questions and participate at the table throughout a project in a knowledgeable way, the project will go slower and the school will cost more to build, for you will have more overhead. By having our own professional architects, engineers and construction people on staff, they talk the language, can solve problems right there, and we don't hold people up, or have many change orders."

This must work. The industry standard for change orders is five percent on new construction. For Gwinnett Public Schools, less than one-half of one percent in change orders has come in the last billion dollars of construction work.

Steele says: "Change orders are really a mess. Projects built with few changes are beneficial to everyone, and in essence, cost a lot less."

In its routine procedures, Gwinnett Public Schools have their own construction management people on staff, not contracted.. They use the CPM (critical path method) process, time-scaling each job from beginning to end, showing the shortest pathway through the job.

Steele explains: "First you start with the sequential part of the job, showing how much time there is to each element of work. Once you have that sequential schedule, you go back and add in the concurrent items that can be done at any time, but are at least concurrent with the critical path. For example, you must get up the walls before you can paint them. Or you cannot put finishes into the building until it is energized."

So armed with the critical path, the work begins. Then all key people on the construction team come together regularly for the partnering meeting. This meeting is essentially one encouraging communication, taking a team approach to any situation that might crop up. Steele calls it a "trust in team approach. When you really think about it, the owner (the school system), the designer, contractors and subcontractors all have a common goal. That is, we need to get in, do a quality job, get out, get paid and go on to the next project."

Part of Steele's approach is to have the same last two items on each agenda at each meeting. The next-to-last item is to ask if everyone is being treated fairly. This applies to the System, or to any of the group in the room working on the project in any way. If anyone has anything under their skin, they are encouraged to get it out immediately. Steele says: "What this does is open the communication. We want nothing to worry them, no matter how small. You would be amazed at what having this as part of our known agenda does for us. And in the long run, it ensures that everyone trusts us, knows that they are getting fair treatment, and in the long run, it allows them to feel good about working with us. It produces for the school system a better building." The last item on the agenda has Steele asking if the group has left anything out.....before scheduling the next meeting.

Unlike some public projects, the Gwinnett County Public Schools don't feel wedded to the low bid concept. "Cheaper is not always less expensive," is the way Steele puts it. "When you take the cheap route, you often end up spending more in the long run. The best bid does not have to be the lowest."

By using this team approach, it may appear at first to cost more. But Steele feels that by having key staff members on board, and working closely with all providers in the project, the Gwinnett schools save more than $3-4 million a year by managing projects themselves instead of hiring out the management.

There is a major indication that this system works. In comparing the construction costs for Gwinnett County schools to the Southeastern regional school costs, Gwinnett schools cost 30 percent less. This accounts for millions of dollars in savings for every large construction project. As a result of this outstanding record, Gwinnett school officials are asked to be on panel-after-panel at K-12 summit meetings across the country to explain just how it accomplishes such savings in its construction management.

Going down the construction list at Gwinnett schools, and looking at those built prior to 1976, there have been multiple additions to most of these schools. As the county system grew, every school has had at least one addition in the last 30 years. Often schools have more than doubled their original size. (See Appendix B School Data section for a list of school additions since 1976.)

The School Board has also for several years been involved with renovating commercial buildings into school facilities. In most cases, such properties have been vacant or undervalued properties, which the county was able to purchase at a less-than-market price. As a result, by buying these distressed properties, the School Board has saved millions on property costs.

It was something of a natural turn for Jim Steele, in that he has for years chaired the Gwinnett Clean and Beautiful organization, with has as one of its purposes the re-cycling of materials. In this case, it was re-cycling commercial properties into school facilities.

The first conversion was in Lawrenceville at the vacant Lawrenceville West Shopping Center. Where once a Roses Department Store, Winn-Dixie supermarket and Revco Pharmacy and other facilities operated, the School Board picked up this property for $2.7 million, and in 1996 rebuilt it as Phoenix High School, an alternative school. A major bonus was the large parking lot that came with the property, perfect for a school. Overall savings on this school was an estimated $3.7 million, compared to purchasing land and constructing an equivalent school from the ground up.

Other properties that have been or are planned to be converted to school usages include:

- Radloff Middle School on Shackelford Road in Duluth, where the New York Times erected a new building for *Gwinnett Daily News* in 2002, purchased for $9.2 million, and when renovated saved $2.2 million.
- The main office of the School Board, the Instructional Support Center on Old Peachtree Road, was previously OKI telecom's offices and electronics plant. The School Board bought the property in 2004 for $12 million, and now houses the support operations for the School Board, including the school system main offices. The savings on this renovation was $15 million.
- A future relief high school between the Berkmar-Central Gwinnett clusters, to be located on Old Norcross Road in a former Bridgestone Tires warehouse in Lawrenceville. The tract was bought in 2005 for a price of $19 million, and will save an estimated $26 million when completed. This high school is to be built adjacent to the Benefield Elementary School. The two schools occupy about 80 acres at the site.
- Two schools, a 140,000 square foot Peachtree Ridge Elementary and 200,000 square foot Peachtree Ridge Middle Schools, are planned for a former Panasonic 500,000 square foot warehouse near I-85 in Suwanee. The balance of the building will also be used as a major warehouse for the schools. The building was purchased in 2007 for $23 million, and stands to save the School Board an estimated $15 million compared to acquiring land and building the three separate facilities.
- A new GIVE (Gwinnett Intervention Education) West facility in Norcross is to be built on the former 100,000+ square foot SAMPO-Maltese Signs site on Peachtree Industrial Boulevard. The Schools bought the site in 2008 for $6.55 million. The School Board expects a savings of $2.7 million on this renovation..

Steele notes that purchasing of already-built facilities comes "out of necessity and economics. In some areas of Gwinnett, there is not enough open land for new schools. These commercial properties on the market, often at a bargain, are sometimes the only areas large enough for us to locate schools."

In 2001, Gwinnett Public School's Division of Facilities and Operations earned the prestigious Malcolm Baldridge Award for demonstrated Best Management Business practices. This is a significant honor, something that no other school systems' operations division in Georgia has achieved.

The system continually tests its benchmarks against both the construction industry, and against other school systems. Steele says: "We take the best firms or systems in the nation and call them our 'class competitors' and measure ourselves against the industry. We also are in a continuous improvement mode, producing key performance indicators, items we feel are our core business, and constantly checking them with trend analysis. When we do that, we feel we will exceed our expectations. Altogether, we have between 90-100 key performers that we continue to look at to make sure we stay abreast of our jobs."

This close attention to detail by the Gwinnett Public Schools produces a major benefit: the citizens of Gwinnett are proud of, and have confidence in, their School Board, the way it spends its money, and the way it educates the students of the county.

Independent system in Buford

Educating children parallel to the Gwinnett system, Buford has maintained a proud, independent school system. It is the only city-chartered school system in the state, and in 2007, had 2,700 students in four school areas: elementary (grades k-2), an academy (3-5); middle (6-8); and high (9-12).

The independent system is understandable, when it's remembered that Buford was the largest and most important city in Gwinnett up until 1970. It had for years Gwinnett's only significant industry. A news article in the *Gwinnett News-Herald* of December 18, 1902 referred to Buford as the "New York of Gwinnett" in paying tribute to its industry and activity.

Education was on the minds of people in the Buford area even before Buford was established as a town in 1871. Indications are that the first school in the Buford area operated in 1869, taught by a Mr. J.W. Mitchell. Six families paid tuition to Mr. Mitchell to teach their 25 pupils, though the school was held for only three months in that summer.

Buford's "old academy" was built in 1884 at the end of Spring Street. This was a two story brick structure, and was said to be the first all-brick school in Gwinnett County. The street name was significant, in that included in the deed was the use of a spring behind the school for obtaining water for the school.

The top story of the school was used as a Masonic lodge. When the building burned, the original bricks were used in the replacement Masonic lodge.

In 1906, a new school was built on Church Street. It was an imposing two-story building, with a parapet around its roof. A high school was built adjacent to it in 1924. Soon after came talk of erecting an auditorium. That was completed in 1926, and was 70x90 feet, with a raised stage, and had theatre seating for more than 800 people. It even had a ticket window and projection booth. This facility, though it had poor acoustics, was used for more than 30 years. The auditorium, now in other commercial use, is still standing on Little Mill Road in 2008.

Buford's schools are governed by a four member elected board, with the chairman of the Buford City Commission also chairing the school board.

Buford residents take pride in the achievements and facilities of its school system.The town built the first brick schoolhouse in the county in 1884, known as the Old Academy.

This school had a wide-ranging academic and cultural program, and a major auditorium. In 1951, the system completed the largest gymnasium in Northeast Georgia, designed to seat 2,400 persons. Parents from outside the city limits and other counties paid to have their children educated in the Buford schools. It was a prestigious diploma.

The Old Academy later became the Masonic Lodge, but was destroyed in a fire in 1987.

The Buford school system has seen its students achieve substantially, publicized most recently from its athletic achievements. But for years, Buford has also excelled in academic pursuits, including the fine arts and literary events.

Buford parents like the small and independent system. Teachers know the students well, and they also know the parents. There's a "family feel" to its system, with so few students. Buford residents maintain that the community is in touch with the teachers, students and parents of the system. As one said, "People feel comfortable talking to one another, with it easier to maintain the buy-in about the system."

Geye Hamby

More than half the Buford Schools budget comes from city taxes. The system also gets SPLOST money from both Gwinnett and Hall Counties, since part of the city's area is in Hall County. Its overall budget for the 2007-2008 year was $29.7 million (for 2006-2007, it was $27 million), plus getting $21 million (over four years) from SPLOST for infrastructure improvements. In 2007, Buford voters approved a referendum for a $10 million general obligation bond program for construction of a multi-purpose facility for the city's schools. The vote was 672 to 133 for approval, which gives an indication of the way Buford citizens think its schools are being run.

Dr. Geye Hamby was superintendent of Buford Schools in 2008. Buford, in 2008, was completing a 35-room addition at its Academy building, and also opening an auxiliary gymnasium. In 2009, it was to complete another 35-room addition at its high school, and also add another auxiliary gymnasium. It opened the 2008-09 school year with 2,963 students within its system.

From time to time since World War II, there have been moves to bring the Buford schools into the Gwinnett County system. During the early 1950s, there were efforts to locate a new high school for Gwinnett County within Buford, while still "guaranteeing the independent status of the Buford system."

For many in Buford, such enticements "were never really considered," the way one guy put it. "We would be backing up if we joined the Gwinnett system." The main enticement was that the Gwinnett System would put its North Gwinnett High School at the intersection of South Lee Street and Buford Highway---where Peoples Bank eventually was built.

But these negotiations were unsuccessful, and in July 1955, the Gwinnett system announced that a new high school in north Gwinnett would not be in Buford, but near Suwanee on Level Creek Road.

A few in Buford were upset. That led to an official referendum in December 1956, about the Buford system joining with the county. This came after a petition of 283 citizens was signed, with seven more names than the required 276. The question of consolidation lost miserably, 571-80.

By the early 1970s, just after the black schools of Buford were consolidated with the Buford white schools, there were more efforts to bring the Buford system into the Gwinnett schools. A fact-finding report came out in 1972, and in 1973, another referendum was held. This time more people were for consolidation, 275, but still 508 were against it.

The last time this measure came up for an official vote was the next year, 1974, when 680 people petitioned for a referendum. Hansel Morgan, in his history of Buford, says: "Many of the petitioners apparently signed (it), hoping simply to lay the matter to rest, for only 368 voted for consolidation, while 848 were opposed."

Students who do not live within the city limits of Buford can apply to become non-resident students. If accepted, the cost of tuition is $2,000 a year. About 15 percent of the student body were non-residents in the 2007-08 school year.

Private schools within Gwinnett

Gwinnett County has a healthy number of high quality private schools operating within its borders. With the growth that came to Gwinnett since 1960, there has been a corresponding growth in the number of private schools in the county. In 2007, a total of 8.3 percent of Gwinnett school-age students were enrolled in the several private schools in the county. Nationwide, about five percent of students are in private school.

For the 2007-2008 school, year, there were 8,671 students living in Gwinnett attending private schools. As of May 2007, there were 2,210 families in Gwinnett "home schooling" their offspring. This translated into 3,671 students in home schools. Add the two figures together, and there are 12,342 students in school in Grades K-12 in Gwinnett not in public schools. The combined home school and private school students total 7.8 percent of the 2008 public school enrollment of 154,517 students, and the 2,802 students enrolled in Buford, or 157,319 public school students in Gwinnett in 2008.

Gwinnett ranks below the national average in private school enrollment. For the years 2003-04, throughout the United States, there were 47,591,082 students in public school grades K-12, and 5,122,772 students in private schools for grades K-12. That amounts to 9.7 percent of students nationally in private schools.

This chapter takes an in-depth look at the significant private schools in Gwinnett. All Gwinnett private schools are not included, though the schools included account for 70 percent of the private school enrollment in the county. (See Appendix tables for details on private school enrollment and their facilities.)

Wesleyan School (1963)

Wesleyan School was established in 1963 as an integral part of Sandy Springs United Methodist Church. Originally known as Wesleyan Day School, the school began as a preschool providing a nurturing, educational experience guided by Christian principles.

By the early 1970s, the school emerged as an elementary school of excellence, grounded in Christian principles and offering a low student-teacher ratio and a strong academic program. Wesleyan Day School added its middle school in 1987. The church agreed to add a high school curriculum and in 1994, Wesleyan offered its first ninth grade class.

With the addition of a high school, the school needed a new campus and in the fall of 1994, a new corporation, Wesleyan School, Inc., was formed. In the spring of 1995, a divestiture agreement from Sandy Springs United Methodist Church was finalized. After an extensive search for property, coupled with a generous land equity donation by Dan Cowart, a 53-acre site in Peachtree Corners was put under contract in the fall of 1995.

In the winter of 1996, the Board hired Zach Young, a graduate of the University of Virginia and Harvard University and former vice president and assistant headmaster at The Westminster Schools, as the headmaster.

In 1997-98, Wesleyan secured accreditation from the Southern Association of Colleges and Schools. Another milestone of the 1997-1998 school year was the graduation of Wesleyan's first senior class of 17 students.

Under the new name and leadership, Wesleyan opened the 1996-97 school year with 556 students on its new campus. That year, the facilities consisted of 15 modular units, a soccer field and the school's first permanent structure, Marchman Gymnasium. In 1997, Cleghorn Hall, a high school building, was named after long-time Atlanta educator, Wesleyan principal and community leader, Gwen Michael Cleghorn. Other buildings would be added in coming years, including:

- 1997-98: Hoover Student Activities Center.
- 1998-99: Henderson Stadium and Robinson Field, which hosted the school's inaugural varsity football season. Modular units for a high school and middle school cafeteria were added along with units for the music department.
- 2000: 12 acres of land were purchased adjoining the campus along Peachtree Parkway to be used for physical education, soccer, football, cross country and lacrosse.
- 2001: Wesley Hall is completed, the largest facility on campus, and houses the middle school and high school classrooms. It also has a 465-seat theater, a dining hall for middle and high school students, a library for both middle and high schools, a prayer chapel, science and computer labs and office space.
- 2002: Warren Hall, the lower school building, was completed. The 73,000 square-foot building includes its own library, gymnasium and a combination dining hall/ auditorium.
- 2003: Davidson Natatorium, with a l0-lane indoor pool, was built. It serves middle and high school swim teams and lower and middle school physical education classes. Over 25 percent of Wesleyan high school students participate on the swim team.

- 2005: Donn Gaebelein Field was dedicated for baseball. This all brick, lighted facility with raised seating replaced the original field which became Agape Field, also all brick and lighted, used since 2006 for softball.
- 2006: Don and Ida Yancey Gymnasium was opened with seating for 1,500, large weight training facility, locker rooms, and offices for physical education and athletic administration. New land east of Hoover Center was acquired and the five Curley Tennis Courts (plus two) were relocated from the central campus mall.
- 2007: The new 57,000 square foot fine arts building opens with teaching space for music, visual and performing arts, with galleries and meeting space and also the Bobbie Lencke black box theater, providing a second performance venue on campus. Also finished was Gillfillan Hall which provides meeting and office space for admissions, finance, development, board of trustees, and other administration.

All of Wesleyan's buildings and land acquisitions have been made based upon pledges to give gathered before the commencement of construction. The campus has grown to 75 acres, having added a Spalding Drive office building, additional practice fields, parking, and faculty/staff housing to its original land.

Wesleyan seeks to be a relatively small, Christian, full-activity school for students with average and above average academic ability but a higher than average enthusiasm for doing what needs to be done at school, academically and extracurricularly.

There were 24 graduates in the class of 1999 and 40 in the class of 2000. Since then, the school has grown to its originally intended size of 1,075 students. Grades in the high school average just over 100 students each. Graduates attend the best colleges and universities in America. Georgia and Georgia Tech are perhaps the most frequent choices, but schools like Vanderbilt, Samford, Baylor, Davidson, Virginia, Wake Forest, Duke, Stanford, Wheaton, Auburn, Alabama and the three national military academies are also regular names on Wesleyan's annual college matriculation lists.

Wesleyan is governed by a 21-member board of trustees. Wesleyan's progress in all its dimensions has been remarkable and it has become a great asset to Peachtree Corners and surrounding communities like Alpharetta, Dunwoody, Duluth and Norcross, the towns where most of its students reside.

Greater Atlanta Christian School (1968)

For many years, members of Churches of Christ in Metro Atlanta had wanted to operate a Christian school.

Attempts to start a school in Metro Atlanta by members of the Church of Christ in the 1940s and 1950s failed. But efforts picked up in the 1960s.

A Realtor showed those searching for land a tract on Indian Trail Road in Gwinnett County. That road was a one-lane dirt road that would not be paved for several years. It was just off Interstate 85 in what was still very much a rural area, with little development. Rumors had it that the area was often used to strip stolen automobiles of their key parts. As well, Gwinnett in those days did not have the best reputation as a progressive community.

However, the group was serious about having its own school. Eventually in 1961, a group of 12 men incorporated Greater Atlanta Christian School as a non-profit educational entity.

In 1963, Jesse Long, an Atlanta minister, was appointed president. He had a rich background in Christian Education from having attended a Christian high school and both David Lipscomb College and Alabama Christian College (now Faulkner University); he also had a family heritage in Christian Education. He and the board began promoting high school offerings and the purchase of land. Long recalls telling the Realtor, who belonged to his church and who first showed him the property where the school would eventually be located: "Lady, take me back to town. We are not going to build our school out in the wilderness."

The board decided to purchase two farms (172 acres) on Indian Trail in 1964. At that time, Gwinnett had a population of 53,347, but soon was to become the fastest growing county in America.

Long says: "Our concept was to provide academic excellence in a Christian environment. We intended to be winners in curricular and extracurricular activities. We were not opposed to public schools. We just offered a different kind of school with daily Bible classes and a chapel with a Christian worldview."

The school opened in 1968 with 150 students in grades 7-11. It grew gradually to an enrollment of 1,950 (K-12) in 2008. Students come from 12 counties, with the largest number from Gwinnett. The faculty and staff have grown from eight that first year to 330 in 2008. The school originally had two buildings of 26,496 square feet. In 2008, it has nearly 500,000 square feet of space in 22 buildings, with a stadium, track and four playing fields, all covering 75 acres.

Meanwhile, Indian Trail Road has changed considerably, too. It was paved in 1974. It has grown from 40 cars a day on the one lane dirt road to five lanes accommodating 120,000 cars each day in 2006.

The first chapel speech announced that this school would be "God's school." Its goal was to be excellent and to be a school of winners. The students started by winning one trophy the first year. In the 38 years of its operation Greater Atlanta students have won 541 trophies, with 105 of these representing first or second place finishes in academic and athletic competitions. GACS won state championships in drama before it had a stage, in basketball before it had a gymnasium and in track when students had to practice on the school driveway.

As a part of its Christian orientation each year, 200 students go on 10 mission trips to different locations around the world. The school has experienced substantial growth in numbers of students, in buildings and in the quality of the educational programs offered in recent years. Dr. David Fincher was appointed president to succeed Dr. Long in 1998. Dr. Long remains with the school as its chancellor.

GACS has some outstanding teachers. Jackie Bradford, the school's first coach, is nationally known for his work in promoting high school basketball. Clif Jones has won 15 state championships and one Southeast championship in one-act play competitions. Dr. Dwight Love won 10 state championships in math competitions and coached the state of Georgia high school math team that won the national championship.

By the early 2000s, GACS was the second largest private school in Georgia. In 2006, 99 percent of its graduating class was admitted to college.

Killian Hill Christian School (1972)

In the fall of 1972, Killian Hill Baptist Church near Lilburn started a kindergarten at its church with 15 five-year-old students. It was started with the intention that eventually it would grow into a facility for more extensive Christian instruction by adding additional grades. The church furnished the facilities and paid utilities. Jenell Shaafer and Brenda Sailors were the first teachers.

The following year, K-3 and K-4 were added, with K-4 three days a week and K-3 two days a week. Altogether the kindergarten-only program went on for four years.

Then by the fall of 1976, not only did Killian Hill Baptist have three years of kindergarten, but also added Grades 1-3. This came while Jon Kent was the church pastor, as he led the school to elementary classes. David Purvis was the first principal, as the school offered its kindergarten students the school the church had dreamed of some day having.

Expansion of the grade offerings continued until the first high school senior class of 14 graduated in 1986.

By 2007-08, Killian Hill has grown to an enrollment of 545, with 32 teachers and 48 full time employees. Approximately 42 percent of the student population comes from ethnic minorities as the school serves a diverse population. Altogether, some 160 churches have students in the student body of Killian Hill School.

After David Purvis, the school has seen Frank Canaday, Tim Luther and at present Paul Williams serve as administrator. The school is the largest outreach of the Killian Hill Baptist Church.

Killian Hill has matured from a small school to an accredited college preparatory institution. The academic program has allowed its students to gain college scholarships and complete degrees in many areas, from medicine to law and other professional fields. The school's academic and athletic teams have won state championships within the Georgia Association of Christian Schools, and also been finalists and winners in competition through the American Association of Christian Schools.

From its original facilities in the church, today the school has expanded to where it occupies approximately 30,000 square feet of space in four buildings, and has extensive athletic and playground facilities on the 26-acre church campus.

St. John Neumann Catholic School (1986)

Founded January 5, 1986, St. John Neumann Regional Catholic School in Lilburn serves the elementary educational needs of Catholic families within the northeastern suburbs of the Metropolitan Atlanta area. The first Catholic school to open in the Archdiocese of Atlanta in 25 years, St. John Neumann fulfilled the dreams of parents in Gwinnett County and neighboring areas who desired a Catholic education for their children.

Operating first in existing classrooms and office space within the St. John Neumann Parish, the school was unique—a regional school serving families in eight surrounding parishes; a school that would be administered independently from the parishes it served. When the school first opened in August 1986, 160 students walked through the doors at SJNRCS.

From this initial enrollment of 160 children in Kindergarten through fifth grades in 1986, the school added sixth and seventh grades in 1987, followed by eighth grade in 1988. Expanded facilities, including a gymnasium, six new classrooms, cafeteria, library, administrative office space, science lab, music and art rooms were constructed and opened in 1989.

Accreditation came through the Southern Association of Colleges and Schools in December 1990. In May 1994, the United States Department of Education awarded St. John Neumann Regional Catholic School the National Blue Ribbon School Award for Excellence.

In May 1995, the school began a facilities expansion, enlarging the Library into a full Media Center. In addition, existing terrace space off the cafeteria was enclosed to provide office space for the finance and development staff. This allowed the designation of permanent office space to house the school's resource and enrichment services. St. John Neumann Regional Catholic School currently offers three classes each for Kindergarten through fifth grades and two classes each for grades six through eight. The initial enrollment of 160 has grown to over 567 in 2007-08. Faculty and staff hail from many parts of the United States, bringing with them a diversity of educational backgrounds, as well as a richness of culture, Catholic heritage, and Catholic values. Over one-third of the faculty hold Master's degrees, with others pursuing advanced degrees in various fields. Instructional aides give valued assistance to both faculty and students.

SJNRCS is fully accredited by both the Southern Association of Colleges and Schools (SACS) and by the Southern Association of Independent Schools (SAIS). St. John Neumann holds memberships in the National Catholic Educational Association (NCEA), the Georgia Independent School Association (GISA), and the Atlanta Area Association of Independent Schools (AAAIS).

The first two principals of the school were members of the order of the Grey Nuns of the Sacred Heart. Those who have headed the school include:

- Sister Dawn Gear, 1986-96
- Sister Mary Margaret O'Hara, 1996-1997
- Mrs. Maryann Radnovich, 1997-1999
- Ms. Terry Lonergan, 1999-2001
- James M. Anderson, 2001-present.

St. John Neumann Regional Catholic School counts each family as a member of the community. As a school community, its patron saint is St. John Neumann, who dedicated and devoted himself to the education of youth in a Catholic environment.

Providence Christian Academy (1991)

In the spring of 1991, several families believed there was a need for an interdenominational, parent-sponsored, independent, covenant Christian school in Gwinnett County. These founding families sought to provide a Christian school with the mission of "providing excellence in Christ-centered education as an extension of the

Christian home." An April 1991 public meeting at a local church produced several hundred interested families, with the result that Providence Christian Academy was born.

With 200 applications in hand by the first of July, the new Board of Directors and staff were still in need of a facility. After discussion on the former Lowe's building at 4575 Lawrenceville Highway in Lilburn, it proved to be unavailable. Eyes then turned next door to the Greenhill's Shopping Center. A bank agreed to a lease/purchase arrangement and Providence Christian Academy was off and running.

The summer of 1991 was a flurry of activity to convert the former shopping center into a school facility. During the months of July and August, 32,000 square feet of the 54,000 square-foot facility were converted into classroom space, with more than 200 volunteers contributing time and effort. Providence opened its doors on September 3, 1991 with 350 students spanning grades K-12.

The founders of Providence Christian Academy envisioned an interdenominational Christian school ministering to families from a wide range of Christian denominations and churches. In 2007, Providence had students from more than 160 churches, representing 20 Christian denominations. The Board of Directors has been made up of parents, grandparents, and alumni. Since the school is not affiliated with a particular church or denomination, the Board established a Pastor's Advisory Council, consisting of local pastors supportive of Christian education, to provide spiritual advice and guidance.

For six years, Providence Christian Academy operated on approximately seven acres with one classroom building. Athletic facilities included rentals from various churches, Mercer University, and the Soccer Academy. Enrollment growth required the completion of the Greenhill's facility. In 1996, the boys' basketball team qualified for the Georgia High School Association State Class A basketball tournament, receiving publicity for the level of success without a home gymnasium.

By the sixth year, classroom space was at a premium and the athletic program had grown to the point that the use of rental facilities was creating increasing stress on the ability to meet the needs of the program. The first capital campaign was for the construction of a gymnasium, which opened in 1997. A second gym followed in 2001 to handle the increased demand for physical education and athletic facilities.

After several years placing portable classrooms throughout the property, the school purchased two eight-acre tracts. One was the adjacent former Lowe's building that had been unsuccessfully initially pursued. The other tract was property behind the school. With classroom space at a premium, the former Lowe's building was converted to a high school facility with more than 80,000 square feet of classroom space. The property behind the school was developed as an athletic complex including soccer and baseball/softball facilities.

From its founding, Providence Christian Academy has provided a college preparatory program. The elementary students are challenged with a stimulating academic program through age/developmentally appropriate methods and materials in order to prepare them for the rigors of a college preparatory course of study. One of the more exciting aspects of the elementary program is the implementation of the Orton Gillingham Multi-sensory approach to language. It has revolutionized the ability to meet a wide range of student needs for grades K-5.

Incorporated within the elementary curricula is presentation of biblical principles teaching character traits and moral values. This approach to a biblical world and life view is continued in the high school through a wide range of semester long courses which allow students a choice concerning course selection. Both the elementary and high school provide weekly chapel programs involving student leadership, providing time for praise and worship, and seeking to emphasize that a biblical worldview incorporates all areas of life (academic, vocational, physical, and spiritual) as seen from Christ's perspective.

A heart for service is also encouraged. In the elementary, students serve others through an annual massive food collection for the Lilburn Food Co-op as well as individual class projects. Each high school student completes service hours with a variety of organizations including Operation Christmas Child, Teen Moms, Gwinnett Pregnancy Center, Special Olympics as well as supporting a variety of tutoring opportunities in the community.

The desire of the Providence family to serve is reflected in the growing support for the annual Carter Martin Classic. Beginning in 2004, the first home basketball game in December is designated as the culmination of a fundraising effort to support the fight against childhood cancer. The entire school family gets involved in fundraising projects with proceeds from the event going to the Carter Samuel Martin Experimental Therapy Research Fund at Children's Healthcare of Atlanta.

This effort is especially passionate for the Providence family since the Classic and the Fund are named for a Providence student, Carter Martin, who was diagnosed with Ewing's Sarcoma while in kindergarten. For almost two years, he battled as he taught the entire school what it meant to live your faith in God. The appreciation for what Carter Martin taught the Providence family is reflected in this unifying community effort, which produced over $103,000 alone during the 2006 Carter Martin Classic.

The high school program meets all of the requirements of the Board of Regents for the State of Georgia and includes Advance Placement as well as honors courses. Since the first graduating class in 1992, Providence alumni have been accepted by a wide range of top schools in the nation.

Providence has grown from a school of 350 students in 1991 to 824 in 2008-09 with more than 850 graduates through 2007. After opening with one building and six acres, Providence now has 24 acres, two classroom buildings, two gymnasiums, and athletic fields. Providence has earned championships for GHSA in girls' soccer and softball as well as individual championships in swimming, cross country, and track and field.

Hopewell Christian Academy (1997)

Hopewell Christian Academy opened its doors in August 1997. Dr. William L. Sheals, Senior Pastor of Hopewell Baptist Church said, "God has truly blessed us with the opening of Hopewell Christian Academy. We believe HCA will serve to successfully prepare our children for spiritual leadership in the school, home, church, community, state, nation and the world. The responsibility for laying this foundation is awesome, but we are confident that our resources of prayer, commitment, cooperation, hard work and parental involvement are adequate to meet the challenge."

Academy Administrator Beauty P. Baldwin, says: "We are truly blessed and excited about what God has done to make the opening of the Academy possible. We take seriously the mandate given by God to train up a child in the way he should go... (Proverbs 22:6)."

The purpose of Hopewell Christian Academy is to train Christian young people to meet their fullest potential spiritually and academically. The Academy uses the A Beka Curriculum. This distinctive, Christian-based curriculum developed at Pensacola Christian College is thoroughly Christian and Biblical in every aspect. It reflects the very best in scholarship, design, practicality, and scriptural fidelity. A working partnership between parent and teachers is formed so that together they can fulfill the requirements of the curriculum.

William Sheals

The 1997-98 school year began with grades K4 through third grade. The projected enrollment of 50 was exceeded by 15, for a total of 65 students. The PTO (Parent Teacher Organization) was formed with the purpose of aiding the school in providing extra incentives to help in the education process. The PTO helps spearhead fundraisers, coordinate teacher appreciation lunches, serve as classroom volunteers and work with many school activities. PTO is an active and supportive group for the Academy.

For 2007, the Academy has 215 students enrolled in grades PreK-4 through 12.

Academy students, like students all over the country, took the Iowa Test of Basic Skills and the results were outstanding. Tests were given to all students, kindergarten through third grade. At each grade level, students scored average or above at both the state and national percentile rank.

The Academy was been developed based on the standards of the Southern Association of Colleges and Schools accrediting agency. It was accredited during its second year of operation.

Hebron Christian Academy (1999)

First begun as Northeast Atlanta Christian School on Fence Road, Dacula, in June of 1999, the school was purchased by Hebron Baptist Church of Dacula. It was operated under a separate 501(c)(3) designation by Hebron Educational Ministries, and set up as Hebron Christian Academy. Northeast Atlanta Christian School had begun in 1986. There were 329 students in grades K-12 at the school when Hebron purchased it.

John Doran was first chairman of the school board, and Scott Smith joined the school on July 8, 1999 as its first president. (He became president of North Georgia Christian Academy in 2008.) Rick Burslem became the headmaster on July 1, 2008.

Tuition that first year was $3,960 for high school and $3,600 for grades 1-6. What started out that year with 153 students grew to 386 during the first year of Hebron Christian Academy. Tuition for 2008-09 is $5,825 for grades K-6; and $6,140 for grades 7-12.

Hebron has consistently grown so that by 2008, the student body numbered 1,105, operated on two campuses, and was the 14th largest Christian school in Metro Atlanta. It has consistently fielded top-notch sports teams in the Georgia High School Association competition, advanced courses are offered, and the junior class goes on mission trips in the States and in foreign lands.

The school's mission statement reads: "Helping parents prepare their children spiritually, mentally, physically and socially to become disciples of Jesus Christ." The school was accredited by the Georgia Association of Christian Schools in 1999, and has been accredited by the Southern Association of Colleges and Schools since 2003.

Among the Hebron highlights by the years:

- 2000-2001: Eight new modular classrooms were installed on the Elementary campus at 2975 Old Peachtree Road, while the high school met on the third floor of the main church building. The Junior Class went on the first mission trip, to Costa Rica.
- 2001-2002: A second middle and high school campus is built at 570 Dacula Road with two buildings of 12 classrooms, and a common area for library, lunchroom and assemblies. Work begins on a student activity center on the high school campus.
- 2002-2003: The first AP class is offered in English. Work begins on full accreditation by the Association of Christian Schools International (ACSI), and membership application is made to the Georgia High School Association (GHSA).
- 2003-2004: A new student activity Center is dedicated, consisting of four classrooms, 1,200 seat gymnasium, locker rooms, weight room and concession stand. Also, construction begins on additional modular units on the elementary campus. The 15-acre high school campus is deeded to Hebron Christian-Academy from Hebron Baptist Church.
- 2004-2005: In the first year of GHSA membership, the girls win the Region 8A softball championship, while the girls basketball team makes it to the Final Four in the state. The fall sees the opening of eight modular classrooms at the elementary campus.
- 2005-2006: The school is fully accredited by both the Southern Association of Colleges and Schools and ACSI. Construction begins on the first permanent classroom building to house 10 classrooms on the high school campus.
- 2006-2007: Ten new classrooms open on the high school campus, along with three practice fields. The parking lot is doubled, and the school reports it is debt free. A full-time director of development joins the staff. A new baseball complex is built. AP (Advanced Plaement) classes are offered in English, math and history. Major renovations take place at the Elementary library.
- 2007-2008: Under construction at Hebron Christian Academy is a 32,000 square foot Science and Technology Building, complete with six science rooms with labs specific for drama, art, and chorus rooms, two technology labs, and library. Installation is underway to provide interactive technology on all campuses.

Notre Dame Academy (2005)

With the permission of the Catholic Archbishop of Atlanta and sponsorship secured by the Marist Order of priests, Notre Dame Academy opened its doors on August 15, 2005 as an independent, Catholic school to serve students in grades Pre-K3 through Eighth Grade. The school is run by an independent board of directors. It is sponsored by the Marist Order of priests. Marist guides the policies and practices of the school in the formation of its Catholic identity. The school has attained its 501(c)(3) non-profit status.

Notre Dame Academy is located in Duluth in a 48,000 square foot leased facility in the River Green Office Park. The school serves parishioners from numerous Catholic churches in the area.

In 2007-2008, the 503 students were instructed in a hands-on environment with science, foreign language, and computer science labs, as well as Smart Board classrooms. The goal of Notre Dame Academy is to integrate the Gospel within the context of academic content.

Full-time students also receive age-appropriate Catholic instruction, art, music, Spanish, computer science and daily physical education. Students partner with local non-profit organizations to perform age-appropriate service projects and to pursue studies of specific societal problems related to the service partners' challenges.

The school is accredited by the Southern Association of Colleges and Schools and is seeking accreditation from the International Baccalaureate Organization (IBO).

Notre Dame Academy focuses on Christ as the foundation of human knowledge and prayerful work to fully educate the developing person. "Knowledge set in the context of Faith becomes wisdom and life vision."

From 23 on staff the first year, for the 2006-07 school year, the school employed 50 professionals. The average teacher at Notre Dame Academy has ten years of teaching experience with a Master's Degree.

Notre Dame Academy has provided financial assistance to 18 percent of its students through the school's Guardian Angel Scholarship Fund. Debra Orr has been the president since its inception.

The school prides itself in involving its students in community affairs. As an example, in 2006-07, its third and fourth graders partnered with the Hands of Christ Duluth Cooperative Ministries while its fifth grade students went to nearby The Parc at Duluth (a senior living community) to implement the school's service learning program. Even its kindergarteners are active, with PreK-3 and 4 participating in doing a tree for the Festival of Trees that benefited Children's Healthcare of Atlanta. In addition, 52 Notre Dame staff, parents and students volunteered on three of the five project days to construct playgrounds at The D. Scott Hudgens, Jr. Early Education Center located on the campus of the Gwinnett Technical College.

In 2008, Notre Dame Academy was in the process of seeking to re-locate its campus to a 38-acre tract on Moore Road in Suwanee.

10
Working Together

Chamber of Commerce a catalyst

It was in 1947 that Lawrenceville attorney Marvin Allison called several Gwinnett leaders to come together to discuss a key element in what he saw as Gwinnett's future: forming an organization to help build the business community, a Chamber of Commerce.

After all, with World War II now over, with Gwinnett's proximity to downtown Atlanta, and with anticipation that the entire country, and particularly the Atlanta area, would grow substantially, the formation of an organization to help guide the county's growth was important.

The growth did not come quickly for the Chamber. In its early days, the Chamber was little more than a committee of businessmen, who did not get together all that often.

Yet Mr. Allison, who also owned the weekly newspaper in Lawrenceville, persisted in the formation, was initially the temporary president, and was soon elected to be the first president until a part-time manager was hired in early 1948.

From 1948 until 1972, eight different persons were the part-time executive directors of the Chamber, while each year a different businessman was named to be the titular head of the group. Then in July of 1972, Leonard A. Gilbert, who had headed the Cobb County Chamber, took over as the first full-time Chamber executive director for Gwinnett.

During his eight years with the Chamber, Gilbert brought a professional approach to Chamber activities. He added staff, including a director of economic development, who assisted in Gwinnett's fast growth of the 1970s. He also invigorated routine Chamber life with a continuing series of events, including his "Eyeopener" breakfast meetings once a month, free to Chamber members. These drew audiences of up to 400 persons from all parts of the county, at which leading speakers addressed issues of concern to Gwinnett and Metro Atlanta. For years, those meetings were held at the motel in Suwanee which would eventually become The Falcon Inn. One reason it was held there: it had the largest meeting room in the county. Gilbert died unexpectedly in 1980.

After serving a short stint as interim director, Jack Sawyer, a retired Marine and insurance firm owner and former mayor of Lilburn, headed the Chamber from 1981 until

1992, during more years of major growth of Chamber activities. By then, the Gwinnett Chamber was making itself felt throughout Metro Atlanta, as it had an active membership of 3,500 individuals, and was a player in shaping the region's destiny.

A mainstay for years in the life of the Chamber has been Patsy Rooks. She joined the Chamber when it was in the Stark Building in Lawrenceville on April 1, 1970. She soon became the administrative assistant to the first full-time executive director, Len Gilbert, and to subsequent heads of the Chamber. She retired on April 1, 2007 as vice president for special affairs. When she left office, Mrs. Rooks had put in 37 years with the Chamber. She was the "glue" who held the Chamber together, and became the "go-to" person on questions of Chamber culture, personnel, membership and activities. More than any other person, the word "chamber" in Gwinnett has meant Patsy Rooks.

Patsy Rooks

The first offices of the Chamber were in leased space, at one time on the courthouse square, then across from the square in the Stark Building in Lawrenceville. In the 1970s the Chamber was growing, and moved first into 1,500 square feet on Langley Drive, later expanded to 2,500 square feet. In 1983, the Chamber moved to its first owned building off Georgia Highway 316 at Sugarloaf Parkway near Gwinnett Tech, and had 5,500 square feet. By 1997, it found the growth in the county had caused its own staff to expand, and it was bursting the seams; with its next building, on Sugarloaf Parkway near Interstate 85, it moved to a 20,000 square-foot floor of the three-story Chamber building. It has since expanded into the second floor of the 60,000 square-foot building.

* * * * *

Richard Tucker came in as president of the Chamber in 1996 when it was experiencing a downturn in its efforts, and successfully re-vitalized the Chamber. "It has lost some members, after taking a lead role on a vote about MARTA," Tucker says. "I also felt like the Chamber had severed ties with elected officials, and looked back to earlier days when I spent three years as an employee in the county commission's office. In those days, the county was periodically meeting with the school board and Chamber, working on specific fronts. I wanted to get the Chamber re-aligned with the educational and governmental bodies.

"We didn't need me around telling prospective members what we were doing; we needed people on our board who could establish contacts with key potential members. I wanted successful business representatives to be board members, people like Virgil Williams, John D. Stephens, Wayne Mason, Scott Hudgens, Brad Currey and former Gov. George Busbee."

It was a big undertaking. Tucker says: "When I went to the first meeting of the nominating committee to talk about potential members of the 1997 board, I came away unsatisfied with the results. I asked if I could come back with an alternate proposal. I called several successful business people, and got their cooperation. The only one who turned me down about being on the board was Scott Hudgens, saying he was too distracted with other matters. I later learned he was in the midst of completing the land acquisition for the Mall of Georgia. But he was a big supporter of the Chamber financially."

Tucker felt that getting a board made up of established business people was a "way to establish substance and quality on a timely basis. The results are there to show what happened."

Tucker created a new element for the Chamber, a Chairman's Club, at first seeking to enroll 50 firms as "super members" contributing at least $5,000 for membership. By 2004, the number of members of the Chairman's Club had grown substantially, to 163, creating a funding source to expand Chamber activities significantly. Then, by mid-2008, the Chairman's Club membership stood at an even higher figure, at 288 members.

When Tucker came in as president of the Chamber in May of 1996, the budget that year was $1.1 million annually. The by-then inadequate building at Georgia Highway 316 at Sugarloaf Parkway was paid for, "but the operating fund was month-to-month."

By 1999, as a re-invigorated Chamber, the operating budget was well over $2 million and there was $1 million in its bank account. "When I came in, we had 1,500 members and were losing more members than we were gaining. We turned that around in two years to 2,000 members and gaining."

Tucker remained at the Chamber until 2003, when he resigned and Jim Maran, a former Motorola official with extensive international experience, was named to succeed him. For his efforts at revitalizing the Chamber, the new building was named in Tucker's honor.

By June 30 of 2008, the Chamber had 2,874 member-companies, and more than 14,000 contacts from the companies on its rolls. Its budget for 2008 was $6 million and it had no debt on its building near the Civic Center. The Chamber also had operating reserves of over $900,000, says Finance Director Larry Johnson.

Bigger office needed

Just as the Chamber was reorganizing itself, it also needed more office space. Tucker remembers: "We were packed in that building near Gwinnett Tech, and desperately needed additional space." He and his board came up with a proposal to lease land from the county near what would eventually be the Civic Center.

Tucker recounts: "Sugarloaf Parkway had not been completed then, so there was no exit off the Interstate. I got with the district commissioner, Tommy Hughes, and told him we needed a place for a new building. The county had been given 60 acres from the Eastern Airline Pilot's Pension Fund on which to build the Civic Center. They were to be given another 35 acres when Sugarloaf Parkway was built."

Deed restriction on the land from the Pension Fund required use by either a governmental entity or a non-profit organization. With the Chamber being a 501(c)(6) entity, there was no problem for it. (Subsequently, the restrictions were entirely removed.)

Hughes and Tucker looked at the entire tract for a Chamber location, with the Satellite Road frontage appearing to some at that time (before Sugarloaf Parkway was built) to be the preferable land. But Tucker liked the proposed Sugarloaf Parkway frontage better, and finally settled on that site for a ground lease from the county for 25 years, with an automatic 25 year lease additional term.

Then it was planning time. What at first was to be a two-story building soon was termed too restrictive, and instead, the Chamber started planning for a three-story building to be built.

All along, Chamber officials had anticipated that a portion of the building would be used for a private meeting club, to occupy one floor of the building. It became obvious that if the Chamber would use all of its first floor for offices to begin with, and the private club would occupy another floor, the Chamber should build in some expansion space. So instead of a 40,000 square foot building of two floors, a 60,000 square foot building on three floors was designed.

With the land secured, the Chamber then set out to raise the funds or the building. Tucker says: "We hired John O'Kane of Cox-Curry Associates from Atlanta as our consultant on raising the money, and they put together a campaign."

Soon the big guns in Gwinnett were pledging for the building. Naming rights helped.

- One of Gwinnett's largest philanthropists, Scott Hudgens, donated some of the first funds, $400,000, and asked that the Board of Directors meeting room be named for former Chamber Executive Jack Sawyer and former state Rep. Jimmy Mason.
- Developer Wayne Mason contributed $500,000, and the Chamber named the Atrium for him.
- Contractor John D. Stephens donated $300,000, and found the Education Room named in his honor.

Others gave in the range from $100,000 on down. Soon, the $3.2 million was raised from 165 individuals and companies. Altogether, the new Chamber facility cost $6.5 million, with long-term financing from loans making up the up-front construction monies.

Forest Robinson of Weeks Corporation was chairman of the Gwinnett Chamber at that time. His firm agreed to help with construction of the new facility at a nominal fee. The Chamber also secured the assistance of Technology Park President Rick O'Brien to supervise construction, as an overseer from the Chamber board.

Construction began in early 1999 at 6500 Sugarloaf Parkway, with the Chamber occupying the building in March, 2000. When he became president in 2003, Jim Maran had three goals in mind:

1. To see that the Chamber was demographically reflective of the overall community in its membership.
2. To diversify the membership away from real estate and land development, and specifically seek members from the bio-science, technology, automotive and health care industries.
3. To be a regional entity.

By 2007, the Chamber had accomplished all three goals. More than 30 percent of the membership of the Gwinnett Chamber was from outside the county.

Maran continued and expanded the practices Richard Tucker had begun. In 2008, the World Chamber of Commerce Directory said that the Gwinnett Chamber had 3,000 members, the same number as Metro Atlanta's Chamber. (Cobb County was listed as having 2,500 members.)

However, as of June 30, 2008, the actual figures show the Gwinnett Chamber as having 2,874 companies on its rolls, and 7,244 members representing these companies.

The Chamber plans to accomplish its goals by bringing the area together in "Community Connections," to help integrate the community for economic growth. It has launched several groups, including the Bio-science Council, Medical/Health Care Council, Technology Forum, Manufacturing Council and CEO Council. It actively pursues key minority groups, attends key functions, and has minority members on its boards and councils.

Trying to think ahead, in the spring of 2006, the Chamber put together a study of what the Chamber needed to do in the short term to keep Gwinnett moving forward positively. The upshot was a program called "Partnership Gwinnett: A Shared Vision for the Future." When it was launched, the question asked was: "How can we do better tomorrow than we did today?"

The Chamber realized that Gwinnett County reached a crucial time in its history. Fueled by immense population growth, Gwinnett was maturing into a dynamic community and one of the fastest growing and most diverse counties in the country. The Chamber was moving to proactively reorient local and external perceptions to embrace the reality that, as the second largest county in Georgia, Gwinnett was a major economic player.

The new program that the Chamber came forward with, Partnership Gwinnett, beginning in 2007 was a five-year, $10-million community and economic development initiative to develop a consensus vision for Gwinnett's future growth, plus propose an action plan to achieve that goal. It represented a bold call-to-arms for Gwinnett's public, private, economic and community development leaders unmatched in the community's history.

The results anticipated a net increase of more than 65,400 new jobs and $5.8 billion in new wealth. Four goals were identified to achieving this success:

- Job growth and wealth creation;
- Education and work force development;
- Enhanced quality of life; and
- National and global recognition through marketing and outreach programs.

Partnership Gwinnett seeks to demonstrate that, indeed, "Success Lives Here" in Gwinnett.

Of the future at the Chamber, Jim Maran says: "We anticipate that the Gwinnett Chamber will have the largest membership of all chambers in Georgia. We also plan to increase our political and economic development stature with a shared vision of the community." He adds: "There are discussions underway to place satellite offices in Metro Atlanta and select locations in Gwinnett, aligned to market segmentation."

Primarily, Maran sees the Chamber as the "nucleus for connecting all aspects of the community. The Chamber connects the dots, representing the various groups in the county. And we are and will continue to be an international community."

Primarily, Maran sees the Chamber as the "nucleus for connecting all aspects of the community. The Chamber connects the dots, representing the various groups in the county. And we are and will continue to be an international community."

Non-Profits in the Chamber Building

When planning its new facilities, Chamber officials decided to invite other non-profits of the community to occupy the second floor in rental facilities, making the Chamber building much more of a central facility for several Gwinnett-based non-profit organizations. In April and May, 2000, the non-profits were in their second floor offices. The organizations which originally came into the building included:

- Gwinnett Convention and Visitor's Bureau.
- Gwinnett offices of the United Way of Metro Atlanta.
- Quality Growth Council.
- The Community Foundation of Northeast Georgia (then called Gwinnett Foundation).
- The American Cancer Society.

Richard Tucker says that he wanted "...the synergy that those non-profits brought," when including them in the building. "And they got their space for about 60 percent of normal rental space, for in those days, we were under the restriction of only having non-profits in the building." He adds: "If you looked at the Chamber board, the same names were on our board as theirs. It made sense that way."

* * * * * *

With the many activities at the Chamber building, and the space utilized fully from the start, now Chamber officials may be wondering why they did not make the Chamber building bigger! That's a refrain heard often in Gwinnett County, from businessmen, school officials and others.

Convention and Visitors Bureau

The Gwinnett Convention and Visitors Bureau (GCVB) was organized to promote tourism in the county. John Schwab, who had been chairman of the Gwinnett Chamber in 1988, became chairman of the GCVB in 1991. He remained as chairman for five years. Schwab explains why a GCVB was organized: "The legislation allowing the levy of a hotel-motel tax required that the funds not go to a governmental entity, but to a stand-alone, non-profit, private board."

In December of 1990, the GCVB signed a five-year, renewing agreement with Gwinnett County to manage and market the Gwinnett Civic Center and the Performing Arts Center. Through this agreement, the GCVB receives funds from the county generated by the county hotel/motel tax for the promotion of tourism and the operation of the center. In turn, the GCVB sought a professional firm to direct the operation of the Civic Center. One of the early moves was to seek a Request For Proposal from firms around the country to run the Civic Center. The Board received 10-12 proposals, and heard presentations. In turn, the GCVB eventually contracted with Leisure Management International (LMI) on May 14, 1991 as the operator of the Civic Center and its Performing Arts Center, expanded later to include the Arena. The county dedicated one cent of its then six cents of the motel-hotel tax to capital improvements of the Civic Center.

LMI had previous experience managing large arenas and exhibition centers around the country, including the Miami Arena, the Summit in Houston, The Pyramid in Memphis and the Palm Springs Convention Center, among others. After a series of managers were sent to Gwinnett, eventually Preston Williams became the general manager for LMI in Gwinnett in 1995. He has been the "go-to" person at Gwinnett Center for LMI and its successor, SMG of Philadelphia, a leading company in venue management, which purchased LMI in 2000.

The GCVB also oversees the budget for the Civic Center, which in 2006 was $13 million. The budget dipped to $10.3 million for 2008, but had an estimated net profit of $2.5 million. The agreement between the GCVB and the county is for the Civic Center budget to set aside $1.6 million each year to a capital improvement fund, to fund replacements when air conditioners and other capital systems mature. All this is funded through rentals and concessions and through a seven percent hotel-motel tax collected in Gwinnett. The Bureau gets 29.06 percent of motel-hotel sales tax collections to promote tourism in Gwinnett. (Bonds backing the Gwinnett Arena are also funded through a portion of the hotel-motel tax.)

The GCVB has a 12-person board which oversees its operation, and meets monthly. Four of the members are appointed by the county, with two county commissioners on the board. Four board members are recommended by the hospitality industry; one serves from the Chamber of Commerce, one member is recommended by the Arts Council, and two persons serve at large and are picked by the GCVB board.

The GCVB did not have a full-time director until 1993. The executive directors of the GCVB have been: Susan Cohen from 1993-1996; Christopher Walters, one year, from early 1996 to early 1997; Bob Harris, nearly four years, from early 1997 to late 2000; and Caryn McGarity, who became director in late 2000.

In 2008, GCVB itself had 12 employees and a budget of more than $2.2 million. The budget included $600,000 for sales and marketing support to promote the county.

The GCVB has had one success after another in promoting Gwinnett, and bringing new activities to the county. It won the Southern Tourism Society's "Shining Example" awards in 1993, 1995 and 1996. Its sports marketing division, the Gwinnett Sports Commission, was named as "Sports Commission of the Year" in 2005 by the National Association of Sports Commissions..

The make-up of the Convention and Visitor's Bureau board in 2008 was Richard Tucker, chairman; Lorraine Green, vice chairman; Meredith Mason, secretary; and Dave

Kaplan, treasurer. Others on the board were J.W. Benefield, Tommy Hughes, Bert Nasuti, Jim Maran, Tom Martin, Art Rilling and Jeannine Rispin.

* * * * *

Richard Tucker

Many people do not recognize the presence of a hospitality industry within the county. A 2004 study from the University of Georgia marked the hospitality industry's economic impact on the county at $1 billion. In 2008, Gwinnett had 98 hotels or motels within its borders.

The hotel business has seen an astounding growth in Gwinnett in recent years. The first overnight lodging motels were mostly along Interstate 85. In the early days of Gwinnett development around Peachtree Corners, high tech visitors to the county had to be lodged overnight in nearby DeKalb County. It was not until passage of the mixed drink referendum that the hotel growth in Gwinnett exploded. Since 1985, the industry has grown substantially throughout the county. Look at the growth of hotel rooms:

Gwinnett Hotel Growth

Year	***Hotels***	***Hotel Rooms***
1980	3	301
1985	9	1,608
1990	31	4,397
2000	81	9,479
2008	98	10,760

Source: Gwinnett CVB

In early 2008, another six hotels had been announced for Gwinnett, though none had broken ground. These six hotels had a total of 863 rooms, with the largest being a 259-room Embassy Suites on Sugarloaf Parkway.

Through 2008, Gwinnett hotels were the tallest buildings in the county, with the highest being the 17-story, 426-bed Atlanta Marriott Hotel at Gwinnett Place. Another hotel tower is the 10-story, 272-room Hilton Hotel at Peachtree Corners. Another 10-story hotel, the Embassy Suites, was scheduled to be located at the intersection of Satellite Boulevard and Sugarloaf Parkway.

The 1818 Club

Meanwhile, when the Chamber building was being planned, from the outset a factor in the planning was that there would be a private club on the top floor, aimed at attracting key business and professional people as members. Eventually this became known as the "1818 Club," commemorating the date of the founding of Gwinnett County. A group of 16 business individuals went together to guarantee the initial loan for funds to build out the 1818 Club. This loan got repaid as individuals joined the club and anted up their initiation dues of $2,500.

In 1989, businessmen from the community had sought to organize a private dinner and supper club in the county. Through efforts spearheaded by Ray Weeks of Weeks and Associates, a contract was entered into with the Gwinnett Commerce Center, located adjacent to the Atlanta Marriott at Gwinnett Place off Pleasant Hill Road, to have a club on the top floor of the 10-story Commerce Building. A canvass of key businessmen produced a substantial turn-out of membership, initiation fees were collected, and work began on the build-out of the club, to be called the "Commerce Club." During the build-out, while 2x4s were in place for the different rooms, yet before the sheet rock was added, there was even a cocktail reception in the space. The future members marveled at the view from the 10-story building, looking out over what was then still undeveloped land on Pleasant Hill Road. You could even see Stone Mountain from the facility.

A few days later, a bombshell was dropped. The Gwinnett Commerce Center went into bankruptcy, and with this development, the businessmen's club was doomed. Though its officers sought to continue the idea by renting space from an under-performing restaurant at the Marriott hotel, eventually that fizzled. The fee the members had paid for initiation was partially refunded, and the idea of a businessmen's club lay fallow for years.

But the idea didn't die. And that's where the idea for the businessmen's club at the new Chamber of Commerce building came into play.

In 1999, as the 1818 Club organized, it started a membership drive. The club was officially opened in October, 2000. The 1818 Club in the first year grew to 400 members, while from the outset the club's cash flow was positive as it grew and in 2007, it had 900 members. It set a limit of 1,000 members that the club figures it can serve in its present facilities. The club reached that mark in membership, but soon saw a membership decline with the bad business climate. In the fall of 2008, it numbered 915 members.

In mid-2006, the club completed an expansion of space, creating a larger dining room for the crowded conditions at lunch, and finishing off a more private setting for the grill and bar. Meanwhile, its three main meeting rooms stay in use often in get-togethers for many Gwinnett groups virtually each day. The club had a cosmetic overhaul in 2008, sprucing up its facilities.

The 1818 Club benefits from its prime location at the Chamber building, on Sugarloaf Parkway, and adjacent to Gwinnett Center. It has become the "power broker" center of the community, as key members of the county are routinely seen in meetings within its walls. In 2008, Diane Jones was the general manager and Tim Canterbury was the executive chef.

Five leadership programs

Perhaps in no place in Georgia are there more and better leadership programs than in Gwinnett County. Those who founded the programs came along during the 1980s and 1990s and understood the necessity of preparing up-and-comers today for leadership roles tomorrow. That planning has resulted in Gwinnett hosting five leadership programs, each crafted for a certain group of current and potential leaders. Each program is distinctive, and each successful.

From the beginning, the programs have been non-political and off-the-record, not aiming at creating a consensus, not promoting issues, but providing an educational experience intended to enhance the leadership skills of the participants.

The five programs are Leadership Gwinnett (1985), Teachers as Leaders (1989), Neighborhood Service Leadership (1994), Gwinnett Student Leadership (1995), and Senior Leadership Gwinnett (1998). Each of these programs will be examined in detail.

A list of participants in the programs may be found in the Appendix.

Leadership Gwinnett

Two Georgia leadership programs helped spark an interest for a leadership program in Gwinnett. In the 1970s and 1980s, several Gwinnettians participated in either Leadership Georgia or Leadership Atlanta. They realized how beneficial the programs were to them, their co-participants and to the community. They also saw how such a program could help the exploding, growing world of Gwinnett. Several leadership programs had been around. Leadership Atlanta dated from 1969; Leadership Georgia from 1972; and Leadership Cobb from 1983. DeKalb started its program in 1986.

It was in the early 1980s that those interested in Gwinnett having its own leadership program sought to attract interest in such a program. However, it wasn't until Jack Sawyer, then executive director of the Gwinnett Chamber of Commerce, went through the Leadership Atlanta program in 1984 that efforts began to come together for a program in Gwinnett.

Sawyer in the summer of 1984 got a group together who had been through other programs. Among them was a member of Sawyer's Leadership Atlanta class, Carolyn Collins. Others who were on the initial leadership committee of the Chamber were John Johnson, Mike Pope, Larry Edmundson, Art Dana, Thomas Mitchell, George Thompson, Beauty Baldwin and Elliott Brack. Later joining the group was Mike Hutchins. At the time, Mike Tennant was the Chamber's vice president of community affairs, and was on the committee through that position. (Tennant would later on himself go through Leadership Atlanta and the Regional Leadership Institute.)

All 11 of these founders met for a year to formulate the concept for the year-long program. What the group sought was to plan an in-depth program overview of the issues facing Gwinnett County, through day-long, intense focusing on particular issues. These future leaders of the county would get to know those in other parts of the county. In addition, the planners foresaw presenting a variety of experts and local elected officials to the potential class. The entire goal was to provide current information to the class members so that they could be in a position to make a viable contribution to the county. Besides monthly meetings and smaller study groups, the plan was to begin the program at a two-day fall retreat at a remote location, and after the monthly meetings, to have a wind-up retreat to culminate in graduation from the program in the spring.

The overall governance of the program lies in the Board of Trustees, and consisting of those initial 11 founders. Elliott Brack was the first General Chair and chairman of the Trustees. Mike Tennant would become the second chairman of the Trustees in 2003.

Leadership Gwinnett began its first class in the fall of 1985. The program quickly became a "must-attend" for potential leaders in Gwinnett, and it also became the flagship program of the Gwinnett Chamber of Commerce.

Initially, getting nominees to agree to apply for the nine-month-long program proved difficult. For the first year's class of 32, only about 60 people applied to the program. When the nomination time rolled around the second year, more applications came in, as more people wanted to be included in what was viewed as a worthwhile program. By the time the third class was forming, far more people wanted to take part in the program, but class size remained at 32. This increased to 34 in 2003, to 35 in 2004, and to 36 in 2006. By the 10th anniversary of Leadership Gwinnett and since, acceptance into the program has been more difficult, as up to 150-200 people apply for the now 36-member class limit.

Each year's class is under the direction of a Steering Committee chair, with Carolyn Collins having that slot the first year. In subsequent years, the chair of the Steering Committee moved automatically to a seat on the Board of Trustees. The initial selection committee chair was John Johnson, while the first program chairman was Art Dana.

Subjects of the program days that first year were:

October	Growth in Gwinnett
November	The "Other Side" of Gwinnett
December	Judicial System
January	Regional Day
February	Image of Gwinnett
March	Education
April	Simulated Society game

Perhaps the single issue that most bothered those guiding the initial planning group was how the class members would be selected. However that turned out to be relatively easy, after Art Dana learned of a similar program in Houston, Tex. that relied on an objective numerical scoring system. The outcome was a score for each applicant, which pointed the way to the selection, though a high scoring applicant was not automatically accepted.

The emphasis from the beginning was on a diverse class, with no one profession, race or gender dominating. Several professions, particularly banking and the law, have had multiple applicants in most years. The founding committee limited the number of class members in any one field to two participants, to "balance" the class, and to give the class more viability, scope and diversity. This diversity was in fact the beauty of the program and helped make the total experience for the class a vision-expanding one.

From the beginning of the program, the group stressed that attendance was required. Several people who participated in most sessions of the year did not "graduate" because of poor attendance. Another emphasis was that the group as a whole would not take political positions nor outwardly support any candidates. This became one of the strengths of the program. The overall purpose was to expand the thinking/vision/understanding of the participants and encourage their involvement in making positive impact in their communities and the county as a whole.

When planning the first retreat, the idea was to use the assembly to meld the class together in an away-from-the-county setting. While the members were addressed by key leaders in the county and state, it was also to be a "fun" outing. The Steering Committee planned an outdoor team-building program. This helped bring the group closer together and build confidence of team members. The first fall retreat was at Callaway Gardens, with the spring retreat at the Falcon Inn. Other retreats have been at Lake Lanier, Lake Arrowhead, the Fieldstone Inn, Amicalola Falls and the Lodge at Lake Chatuge. The fall retreat has held at Lake Lanier since 1996, while recently the spring retreat has been at Callaway Gardens.

Another hallmark of the Leadership Gwinnett program is its sense of propriety. Every Leadership Gwinnett program is "off-the-record" and not to be discussed outside the meeting, for both class members, staff, and those addressing the groups. This allows both the class and those speaking to them the freedom to talk openly in remarks and question and answer sessions, knowing that what is said is private and is "off the record."

Stressed at the onset of the program was that leadership is needed at all levels of society. The class members heard: "This is not a program to prepare you to run for office, but to prepare you for leadership, wherever you go. By your selection for this program, you are a leader already. This program will make you a better one."

From the beginning, Leadership Gwinnett provided an opportunity for its graduates to continue to participate in the program by forming an alumni association as the first class graduated in 1986. Primarily, the Alumni Association was seen as a tool to foster and maintain alumni networking, to continue to offer information about the activities of the community, and to support the program.

The Association is governed by an Alumni Council, consisting of a representative from each of the graduating classes, plus original founding steering committee members. It is chaired by a member of the Leadership Gwinnett Board of Trustees. Connie Wiggins has headed this program since its inception.

Among its activities is to maintain an alumni directory and conduct at least annual educational forums and seminars on important issues facing the county. The Association also holds an annual event welcoming new alumni to its ranks.

There are many reasons why Leadership Gwinnett has been successful. Peter Boyce, in that first class, says: "The icons of Gwinnett opened our eyes to what made Gwinnett so great. To have the opportunity to get face to face with the colorful Wayne Mason, the detailed oriented Wayne Shackelford, to have Governor Zell Miller come to our fall retreat and to get the benefit of a world of knowledge from local historians boosted most of our lives both professionally and personally."

From its inception in 1985, Leadership Gwinnett has graduated more than 700 people as of 2007 to become the "go-to" people in their various communities. During its existence, Leadership Gwinnett has become the most popular program of the Gwinnett Chamber of Commerce, and has contributed tremendously to the life of Gwinnett County.

Teachers as Leaders

After the larger Gwinnett community saw the initial success of Leadership Gwinnett, the Gwinnett School System saw a need, and stepped in to fill it. Out of this came "Teachers as Leaders," a group of approximately 35 teachers embarking on a nine-month program to learn leadership skills. This first class met in the fall of 1990 and consisted of teachers from Gwinnett and Buford school systems.

Gwinnett's second leadership program sprang partially from its first program. The program was begun to foster leadership skills among teachers.

George Thompson, with the Gwinnett School Board, then administrative assistant to the superintendent, (who himself was superintendent of the Gwinnett schools from 1990-1994) played a key role in setting up the program. He says: "The idea came from experience I had in both Leadership Atlanta and being on the steering committee of Leadership Gwinnett, and from other leadership initiatives that I participated in during the 1980s."

He continues: "At the same time, others with experience in leadership classes, notably Beauty Baldwin, who was superintendent of schools in Buford, and Carolyn Collins, thought that a similar program would be a good framework for developing leadership talent in teachers. Carolyn came on as a consultant for the program. Out of these conversations, came the program." From the inception, while most of the program participants came from the Gwinnett system, class members always included two teachers from the Buford system. Both systems provided funding.

Thompson lists four benefits he saw that could come out of the program.

1. "Recognizing that teachers work in silos, a leadership class would provide an opportunity to collaborate with other teacher-leaders across the county at all levels, elementary, middle and high schools. This would serve as a model for principals and schools to cause teachers to collaborate in their own schools.
2. "It would serve as a network for teachers to become colleagues with other teachers, and call on one another for support in what would become its own learning community.
3. "With the school district facing tremendous challenges, teachers did not always have an understanding of the Big Picture problems, as we did not provide an opportunity to learn about them. Teachers As Leaders would not be an initiative of what to do in the classroom, but to look at other aspects such as growth, demographic statistics, technical changes and the whole aspect of what to do with these elements as they impacted the community at large. This would include crime, economics, race and other aspects that, when studying, would increase a teacher's understanding and enhance their ability to be more effective teachers.
4. "And finally, the idea was selfish, for we wanted to retain great teachers, to see them challenged, become excited, and stimulated. It was a way to do it in partnership with the community. Our steering committee was made up of teachers, but also of key community leaders who came to have a greater understanding of the challenges facing the teachers."

Once the program was underway, in the fall of 1990, the feedback immediately was positive. As teachers completed the program, they began to nominate others to be in the program in subsequent years. Pat Mitchell, the first executive director of the program, reports that after leaving one session where detention facilities were toured, one kindergarten teacher stated: "I've been in the classroom for 22 years; after today, I will never be the same teacher. Today I saw first-hand what happens when I am not successful."

The program year consisted of a starting retreat of one and a half days, then three one-day sessions scheduled through the year at different county locations. Meanwhile, study groups between sessions allowed for small group interaction. The year ended with another day-and-a-half retreat.

The program had a strategic change in 2004, after a study in 2003 about the objectives and concept of the program was reviewed. Where previously the program sought to give teachers a heightened awareness of the community and connect them with community resources, the revised program had a different goal. It sought to focus the program on the teacher becoming more of a leader in the classroom and school. As an example, one goal sought to strive for teachers to understand the culture of the classroom, and to create a climate in the classrooms so that students would not want to miss a class session. The new curriculum would also seek to have teachers step forward and demonstrate leadership at all levels of the school. The program continued to bring in community leaders, but the new goal would be to create teacher-leaders at all levels.

Teachers as Leaders was established as a non-profit corporation, guided by a steering committee of representatives from the schools and the community. This board managed it as trustees, and employed an executive director.

Several private firms within Gwinnett helped provide additional funding. A grant from the BellSouth Foundation for $30,000, paid over three years, gave the program a kick-start that first year. This outside grant helped validate the program, and gave Thompson leverage with the school board. There initially had been some concern that such a program was "frivolous," with school officials wanting teachers to have more concentration on improved test scores. But gradually, people started seeing the program as a beneficial initiative, giving the teachers additional training in areas that would enrich them as not only teachers, but as leaders within their community.

Since its inception, over 500 teachers have taken part in the Teachers as Leaders program, and it has continually been seen as a key selective program for aspiring teachers.

As director of staff development for Gwinnett County Public Schools, Dr. Patty Heitmuller implemented Superintendent George Thompson's vision for Teachers As Leaders for the first few years. Pat Mitchell followed as the first executive director of TAL, Inc. With the new direction in 2003, Nancy Ward assumed the role of executive director of TAL, Inc.

Neighborhood Leadership Institute

Soon another group stepped forward wanting to instill leadership abilities in their constituents. After a county-wide needs assessment in 1989, one of the findings was that grassroots community members wanted more citizen involvement in activities. What resulted came in 1994, as the Gwinnett Health and Human Services Coalition began the Gwinnett Neighborhood Leadership Institute.

This was a leadership program for "ordinary citizens" from local neighborhoods, started to provide this segment of the community its own leadership training. One of the key goals of the program is to identify and address community problems. Since inception, nearly 300 people have graduated by 2008 from this nine-month program, empowering another part of Gwinnett with its unique program for community leadership.

The first program began in the fall of 1994. The Institute seeks to address leadership development on two levels:

1. Provide a curriculum that addresses leadership topics affecting the social and economic well-being of the county; and
2. Train participants in interpersonal skills so that they can build a network of leaders within the communities.

From the beginning, the Institute folded the curriculum developed by the Fanning Leadership Institute at the University of Georgia into each monthly session. Participants attend a two-day, overnight orientation, seven monthly programs on Saturdays, and graduate at a special session in May. The Saturday sessions are held in various areas of the county, giving the students a glimpse of many of the meeting facilities in the county. One program per year is usually a visit to the State Capitol.

During the year, the class members are divided into four to six member teams to study community improvement topics they select. The results of their study are presented to the overall class and community at large at the graduation in the spring. While doing the research and study on the project, the participants work together in teams as a key part of their leadership training, allowing the students to apply skills and resources to the group.

The team projects focus on a variety of issues, and are often the basis for long-term enhancement for the community. Among the topics presented include a Volunteer Interpreter program for the Gwinnett County police; a pet population control support for the Gwinnett Animal Shelter; neighborhood landscape enhancements; recruitment of bilingual foster parents; a teen pregnancy program; and a comprehensive (and first) Senior Resource directory.

During the monthly sessions, a key component of the program of the Institute is to have community leaders address the students at their Saturday sessions on their particular topic, which gives the students more in-depth understanding of the way that particular aspect of the community works. With this approach, the students are introduced to community leaders, then later have a productive back-and-forth question session with them.

Funding for the program has come through contributions of members themselves of $500 as tuition (with partial scholarship help available). Additional support has come through grants from corporations, plus through small Homeland Security funds through the Gwinnett Police Department.

The class members have been diverse in all aspects. Efforts are made to insure that those in each class come from many demographic elements of the community. The age scope has been from 18 to 80.

With years of classes under its belt, the Institute has an alumni association of nearly 300 graduates. The alumni serve as mentors to team projects, as well as comprise a network of practical experience in neighborhood projects. The Institute is governed by a board consisting of two-third alumni and one-third non-alumni from the community.

Gwinnett Student Leadership Team

The fourth leadership program to evolve was aimed at high school students -- the Gwinnett Student Leadership Team, which began its first class in 1995. This program was born as an idea during the initial retreat of the 1992 Leadership Gwinnett program. Today this program has extended beyond the boundaries of Gwinnett, as the program that the GSLT group put together has found application in other high schools throughout the nation.

Had Nancy Ward and David Seago not sat next to one another at the opening of the 1992 Leadership Gwinnett session, a program recognized as tops in the country might not have been born.

While sitting adjacent, Nancy and David asked one another: "Why isn't there a leadership program for high school students?" After all, they reasoned, there were the other leadership programs going on in the county: for up-and-coming leaders, for teachers, and for neighborhoods. Why no program for students?

That initial conversation eventually resulted in a core group working toward formation of a student leadership program. Besides Ward and Seago, early collaborators included Ari Russell of the Gwinnett United in Drug Education (GUIDE) program and John Upchurch of Scholastic Images/Balfour. Others later joining in assisting the formation of the program included Mary Ann Manley of Georgia Power Company, Richard Tucker of the Gwinnett Chamber; Superior Court Judge Richard Winegarden; and Norcross Police Chief Rick Hetzel.

The development team later included Bobby Crowson, who would become Gwinnett Public Schools' associate superintendent; Randy Dellinger, Jackson EMC; John Green, North Gwinnett High principal; Barbara King, Primerica; Bill McCargo of Scientific Atlanta; and Gail Macrenaris, Sam's Club and later, with Gwinnett Chamber.

Three years later, in October of 1995, and after much planning, the Gwinnett Student Leadership Team was begun. In the first years, two juniors and two seniors from each of the schools were included; that has since been expanded to three from each class at each school. Through 2007, some 500 students, from all 17 public high schools, have gone through the two-year-long, once-a-month program. The students have continually given rave reviews to the program. As new high schools are built, three additional students join the following year's class.

Afterward, students participating in the program take what they learn and pass it on to others at their schools. Some 7,735 students have attended leadership development sessions at individual schools, led by students in the GSLT program.

Then in 2004 came a new, broader experience, a Youth Leadership Summit for students, principals and adult leaders. That first year at Buford Fine Arts Theatre, 400 persons attended. In 2007 at Gwinnett Center, more than 750 were in attendance.

A key development came in 2002, when Mike Rutherford, now of Charlotte, N.C., spoke to the class. A respected staff development professional, Rutherford had designed experiences and events for clients across the nation. Working with Rutherford, the GSLT team sought a leadership curriculum for the program, but found none suitable, and made a decision: to create one. The Gwinnett GSLT board raised $200,000 for the project, which the program not only began to use itself, but marketed to other communities. The framework for its program has been adopted as a curriculum for many other high school leadership programs. It is called "LeaderNext," an interactive program designed for future leaders. The GSLT gets 10 percent of the profits when the program is sold to other schools. Meanwhile, in 2005, the GSLT board had moved to become a 501(c)(3) non-profit group.

What has been developed over the years in this unique Gwinnett program is a unifying student leadership experience. Students develop practical leadership skills and strategies in the LeaderNext program, and are integrated with local corporate executives. This introduces the students to the value of community service. Then the three students from each school take the skills learned, and apply them at their own school, extending the reach of the program tremendously. The GSLT team called their participants "Legacy Leaders," equipped to expose the keys of leadership to others. The overall goal is for the participating students to "Learn, Teach, Serve." Among the key goals of the program is for the student to realize their leadership skills, and leave a legacy that promotes student involvement and improvement at their school. These skills also pave the way for the students after they leave the local community and matriculate at college.

All this would not have been possible without the initial inspiration by Nancy Ward, who was language arts teacher at Shiloh High, and David Seago, region manager of Georgia Power Company in Gwinnett. From the beginning, the program was encouraged to develop by the solid support of Gwinnett businesses.

Seago says: "When Nancy and I were in Leadership, we saw it was so beneficial to bring in leaders of the county, and thought it would be a real loss not to offer this to a younger age of participants."

Among the program modules are such subjects as developing dynamic habits; mastering communications; overcoming resistance; being self-aware; working in teams; and setting a moral compass. While each year's program is similar, Ward points out: "Each year's program is somewhat unique."

Ward says: "From 1995-2002, it was an individual leadership program, but had no way for the school to get anything out of it. But we changed the program, and allowed schools to get impact from leadership skills of the participants." She adds: "With Gwinnett's large schools, which have many incredible students in them, GSLT provides its own leadership to the schools."

Graduates of the program credit GSLT with helping them along. One Collins Hill graduate tells of getting admitted to Stanford after using the "vocabulary of leadership" when being interviewed. The majority of that discussion was spent as the interviewers wanted to know more about his high school leadership program. Another graduate talks about his freshman orientation program being much of a repeat of the GSLT program.

That chance seating at a Leadership Gwinnett program was fortunate. It led to a innovative Gwinnett program now helpful to schools in the nation, and beneficial directly to more than 500 Gwinnett high school students through 2008.

Senior Leadership Gwinnett

The fifth leadership program in Gwinnett also was an outgrowth of Leadership Gwinnett, one aimed at people 55 years and older, to be known as Senior Leadership Gwinnett. The idea for this program is that seniors, those still working and those approaching retirement, have a wealth of experience, and can provide a substantial pool of background and abilities to address the many concerns in the county. By gathering together many individuals who had helped in birthing Leadership Gwinnett, Senior Leadership Gwinnett was started in 1999.

While Senior Leadership Gwinnett has been smaller, with classes averaging 20 to 24 members, it has proven so popular that when the original sponsor, the Gwinnett Chamber, dropped the program in the spring of 2007, its former leaders and alumni were appalled. They re-organized the program into a new alliance, with Gwinnett Technical College stepping forward as the overall program host. It resumed the Senior Leadership program, after the program was "on sabbatical" for one year, 2007-08.

In the beginning, those working toward forming the Senior Leadership Gwinnett program found that, in 1994, there were 63,371 seniors (those 55 and over) in the county. That large segment of older citizens, they figured, needed their own specialized intensive year-long program, similar to Leadership Gwinnett, but aimed at seniors. The two programs have similar objectives and initially, similar program days. The difference is the focus on a particular age group for Senior Leadership. Bringing seniors into mainstream Gwinnett by capturing their "energy and experience" would be beneficial to them, the organizers felt, but in addition, would also be a benefit to the county. The group later learned that Senior Leadership Gwinnett would emerge as the first program of its kind in Georgia.

Many of those who helped plan Leadership Gwinnett were in on the early planning. The program begins in August with an orientation, moves through monthly one-day programs in different locations around the county, and ends with a graduation in May.

The first program year was in 1998-99, when 20 seniors went through the program. General chair was Elliott Brack, while Connie Wiggins was chair of the Steering Committee. Co-chairing the program committee were Dr. Jesse Long, Shirley Tennant and Russ Weaver. Other members of the steering committee included Pam Hoffman, Barry Gage, Jack Gantz, Sharon Rigsby, Carolyn Hill, Sandra Walker and Richard Tucker.

Nominations come from others in the county, and even from the individual themselves. Cost of the program is $500 annually, with partial scholarships possible upon application. Support for the program comes also from people and companies in the Gwinnett community. As in Leadership Gwinnett, all programs are "off-the-record" to encourage openness on the part of the class members and presenters.

Among the objectives of the program:

- To identify and inspire or re-inspire existing or potential community leaders who are willing to get involved and explore community issues and respond through community involvement.
- To acquaint these leaders with major community issues and the complexity involved in finding solutions for ongoing challenges.

- To give participants the opportunity to meet and interact with other current community leaders.
- To assist participants in expanding their leadership skills and apply them to their maximum use.
- To investigate leadership ethics and values.

Those forming the program realized that many seniors moving to Gwinnett were not connected to community activities and would knew few people in the county. Many moved here in retirement, often to be near their children and grandchildren, and did not have a local background.

Once the founding committee began to seek nominations, there was a snag. It was far more difficult to recruit new members than was envisioned. Seniors were reluctant to get involved in a new program, they said. They also were aware of the commitment to good attendance at the meetings, which sometimes stymied them from signing on for the program. After all, the founding committee discovered that many seniors felt they were far busier in retirement than when working. Some felt they did not have the time for the program.

Therefore, the anticipated 30 class members did not materialize. Usually, classes of about 20-24 came on board. And those joining the classes found, indeed, that they did enjoy the program, and urged others to sign up and enjoy learning about the community as much as they had. Since the program's inception, more than 180 seniors have graduated from the year-long study by the year 2006. There was no class in 2007-08.

The program was guided by the Gwinnett Chamber of Commerce through the 2005-2006 year. When the Chamber did not choose to support the program for the following year, alumni of the program got together and sought another host for the program. Gwinnett Technical College thought that Senior Leadership Gwinnett would complement its offering, and became the host, with the program re-starting in the fall of 2008.

Those participating in reviving the program at Gwinnett include Betty and Bill Atkinson; Bill Barry, trustee vice chair; Donnis Bowman; Elliott Brack, trustee chair; Tim Dunn; Faye Hill; Carolyn Hill; Anna and Wayne Shackelford; Pat Swan, 2008 general chair; Mike Tennant; and Connie Wiggins. Lorri Christopher was coordinator of the program from Gwinnett Tech.

Senior Leadership Gwinnett alumni continue to be an active group, holding regular meetings, offering support for the current program, and serving on positions in each year's class.

Gwinnett Historical Society

Interest in the history of Gwinnett County may have simmered a long time after its creation in 1818, but it was 121 years before a compiled history would result.

The Grand Jury in September 1939 noted in its presentments: "Therefore let it be resolved by the Grand Jury that J. C. Flanigan be authorized to compile and assemble the history of Gwinnett County as early as can conveniently be done." James Cicero Flanigan (1871 – 1956), educator, newspaperman, and historian, was chosen to write the history.

The resulting book, *History of Gwinnett County, Georgia, 1818 – 1943*, was printed in 1943. A second volume was completed by his daughter, Miss Annie Frances Flanigan, after his death.

There was no organization dedicated to preserving the history of the county in this day, so the Grand Jury took the lead. In a few years, for a second time, others were supporting the founding of a historical society. Among them were Hope Stark, Solicitor-General Emeritus; Judge Charles C. Pittard; Commissioners Ray Morgan, Felton Thompson and W. R. Pruitt; and Mr. and Mrs. R. L. LeRoux, co-directors of the Lanier Lake Regional Library.

In early 1966, discussions about the forming of a group continued. Included were Mrs. R. L. LeRoux, Mrs. William Bentley, Mrs. Howard Coggins and Marvin Nash Worthy. And, later discussions involved Mrs. Larry Gunter, Mr. and Mrs. J. Walter Johnson, Mrs. John Martin, Mrs. Hubert Tucker, Mr. and Mrs. John Hood, Mrs. James Emerson, Mrs. Jack Webb, and Mrs. Robert Piper. With the help of Marvin Worthy, George W. Jacobs, former assistant historian for Gwinnett, and a past president of the DeKalb Historical Society, began advising the group.

So, a "loyal group of enthusiasts" gathered at Mr. and Mrs. John Hood's home on June 6, 1966. Those included Mrs. Hubert Tucker, Mrs. Robert Piper, Mrs. R. L. LeRoux, Mr. and Mrs. J. Walter Johnson and Marvin Nash Worthy.

Those attending became the "Organizing Committee for a Gwinnett Historical Society" with Marvin Nash Worthy as temporary chairman and Mrs. Hubert Tucker as temporary secretary. A total of 19 members were listed as of October 20, 1966.

The Winn House before restoration. From 1978 Structural Survey of Gwinnett County--Historic Preservation Section, Georgia Dept. of Natural Resources (Gwinnett Historical Society Collection)

The Elisha Winn House is owned by the county and leased to the Gwinnett Historical Society. This was the original site for Gwinnett's government in 1818. Photo by Shannon Coffey.

The officers of the organizing committee were: chairman, Marvin Nash Worthy; vice chairwoman, Mrs. Jack (Lillian) Webb; treasurer, John J. Hood; assistant treasurer, Mrs. Walter (Sara) Johnson; secretary, Mrs. Hubert (Annette) Tucker; and assistant secretary, Mrs. James O. (Katherine) Emerson, Jr.

The first meeting(s) were held at the home of Mr. and Mrs. John J. Hood, but soon moved to the Lake Lanier Library, at the suggestion of Mrs. R. L. (Marcia) LeRoux, the Hood's daughter.

The Gwinnett Historical Society was chartered on January 2, 1968. By 1979, over 500 members hailed from many states and England. (The English member was a distant relative of Button Gwinnett.) In 2008, the Gwinnett Historical Society had 449 members. Volunteers operate the Gwinnett History Center Monday through Friday on the second floor of the Historic Courthouse in downtown Lawrenceville, and also operate the 19.2-acre Elisha Winn Property, where Gwinnett County was organized, in Hog Mountain-Dacula area.

The Society hosts the county's only genealogy library of over 1,600 publications, an archive collection of assorted county and family records, a map collection, a book store for county-specific publications, a microfilm research room, a growing collection of vintage and historic family and Gwinnett locations photographs, and an office with assorted surname, church, cemetery, school, place, and subject files.

One of the continuing projects of the Society has been to encourage and publish books on various aspects of Gwinnett history. Its best-selling books have been the two large-format pictorial *Vanishing Gwinnett* books the Society published. This came after the

Georgia Archives published in 1982 its well-received *Vanishing Georgia*, a hardcover book of old photographs from throughout the state showing the way life once was in Georgia. That caused the Historical Society to undertake such a project about Gwinnett.

The Society published *Vanishing Gwinnett* in 1984, made up of a total of 186 photographs gleaned from citizens throughout Gwinnett. Its size and subject matter make it a companion to the Archive publication. All 2,000 copies were sold by 1990, and in 1993, a second printing of 2,000 copies was made. Once published, Gwinnett citizens continued to send old photographs to the Society, leading to the publication in 2001 of a companion second volume, *Vanishing Gwinnett II*, a total of 267 entirely different photographs, which was equally well received.

Gwinnett is the only county in the state to publish two "Vanishing" books. DeKalb County published one volume of old photographs in *Vanishing DeKalb*. In the last few years, a multitude of smaller books of photographs of cities and counties have appeared in a less expensive form, in soft cover.

The fastest selling book the Society has published is *Gwinnett County, Georgia: Families, 1818-2005*. It sold 750 copies the first year it was printed. The Society is anticipating that it will reprint this book.

The society has just published its 15th book, and is working on the next one, *Gwinnett Marriages 1833 – 1900*. Its volunteers are also involved in other program areas, such as publishing a quarterly news magazine and managing an extensive website. The Elisha Winn House is open by appointment and was the birthplace of Gwinnett County. The rehabilitated 1811-era Winn House was placed on the National Registry of Historic Sites in 1980. It sits on a 19.2-acre wooded tract, with picnic facilities, and a variety of other buildings of interest, including the Walnut Grove one-room schoolhouse, the old Lawrenceville Jail, a mule barn, and a blacksmith shop. Plans for a permanent museum at the Winn Home are underway and will include the pre-contact Native American artifacts recently discovered during a 2006 archaeological dig.

The list of books published by the Society and the cost when available include:

Year Printed	*Name*	***Cost***
1983	*Gwinnett County 1860 Census*	$10
1984	*History of Gwinnett, 1818-1960 Vol. II*	$30
1984	*Vanishing Gwinnett*	$35
1986	*Gwinnett County 1850 Census*	$10
1986	*Gwinnett County 1870 Census*	$10
1987	*Gwinnett Inferior Court Minutes 1818-1861*	$5
1991	*Gwinnett County Schools, 1923 (soft cover)*	$5
1991	*Gwinnett County Schools, 1923*	$10
1992	*Gwinnett County 1820-30-40 Census*	$10
1993	*Woodward's Mill*	$5
1999	*History of Gwinnett, 1818-1943 Vol. I*	$25
1999	*Gwinnett Book B Marriage Licenses*	$2
1999	*Gwinnett Churches*	$25

2001	*Vanishing Gwinnett II*	$45
2002	*Gwinnett County 1890 Tax Digest*	$10
2003	*Gwinnett County 1900 Census*	$25
2004	*Gwinnett County 1880 Census*	$25
2005	*Gwinnett County Families, 1818-2005*	$55
2007	*Gwinnett Marriages 1833 - 1900*	$30

In addition to these books, the recent *History of Gwinnett, Volume 3* by Marvin Nash Worthy, published in 1994, and authorized by the County Commission, is available for sale at the Female Seminary for $35.

The Society's quarterly newsletter, *The Heritage*, dates back to 1971. A collection of articles, pictures, genealogical inquires and a calendar, it usually is composed of 24 pages aimed at different elements of Gwinnett history. Over the years, it has won numerous awards and in 2008 was named the first place winner of the National Genealogical Society for the county/local genealogical category.

Historical groups and museums

Gwinnett History Museum

The Gwinnett History Museum is housed at the Lawrenceville Female Seminary on South Perry Street. It is open Monday through Thursday from 10 a.m. until 4 p.m. and on Saturday from noon until 5 p.m. Admission is $1 per person.

The building is listed on the National Register of Historic Places.

The Female Seminary was originally built as a "finishing school" for girls. It primarily taught academic subjects: history, English, math and "moral philosophy." The building was erected in 1838 by Daniel Killian, after it was incorporated in 1837 by the Georgia General Assembly. It opened for classes on Sept. 24, 1838. The structure was destroyed by fire some time between Oct. 23, 1850 and July 21, 1851. A new building was erected between 1853-55. The new structure was built in conjunction with the newly-founded Lawrenceville Masonic Lodge No. 131. The students were instructed on the first floor, and the Masons met on the second floor, and were caretakers of the building. The Masons have since erected their own building adjacent to the Seminary. Around 1856, boys under age 10 were admitted to the school, but had to stay at school an hour after the girls left. The last classes were held in the building in 1888.

Since that time, the building has served as a "community center" for various organizations. The building over the years fell into disrepair, and was considered for sale in 1971. However, local citizens, spearheaded in a campaign led by Mrs. Hubert Tucker, put up earnest money and got the building listed on the Historic Register. Through a matching grant from the Department of Housing and Urban Development, the Board of Commissioners restored the building at a cost of $113,216 to what was considered its original appearance. Today the first floor is a meeting facility and rental space, and the second floor houses the Gwinnett History Museum.

The Museum offers visitors a glimpse into the history of Gwinnett County and its inhabitants by housing a permanent collection specializing in the acquisition, preservation and interpretation of Gwinnett County historic and folk artifacts. It also has a limited collection of family, library, city, county, school, church and club records and photographs. Artifacts housed in the museum include furniture, farm tools and equipment, clothing, textiles, looming equipment, turn of the century kitchen exhibits, Gwinnett church exhibits, one-room schoolhouse exhibits and a bluegrass music of Georgia exhibit.

Some museum programs include: lectures, adult classes and workshops regarding different historical themes, guided tours (by appointment only); monthly Grounds and Sounds coffeehouse nights during spring and fall; monthly Scots/Irish Coffee Ceili; History Camps for children ages 6-12 that include heritage and archaeology; and a History Book Club (co-sponsored by the Gwinnett County Public Library). The Museum also offers Scout programs and monthly classes in Gwinnett history for home-schooled students.

Museum-sponsored special interest groups include the Northeast Georgia Civil War Roundtable, which meets the first Sunday of each month, and the Gwinnoters, a chapter of the North Georgia Foothills Dulcimer Association, which meets on the fourth Sunday.

The Snellville Historical Society

In 1992, in a comprehensive plan for the city, Mayor Emmett Clower and the City Council of Snellville advocated the creation of a Snellville Historical Society. However, it was not until 1996, when Deborah Rich took a seat on the city council, that such a society was organized. It was one of her goals on taking office.

The first meeting of the society was April 24, 1996. Those in attendance were Bill Baughman, Sherrie Rabon, Melia Beth Jones, Annette W. Tucker, Hubert E. Tucker, Jacqueline J. Thomas, Leah Jennings, Angela Trigg, DiAnn Bruce Cox, J. Paul Gilleland, J.W. Cofer, Randy Simpson and Deborah Rich.

Named officers were Deborah Rich, president; Thomas Hale, vice president; Sherrie Rabon, secretary; Brenda Baranto, treasurer.

The main objective was to create an oral history of Snellville by taping the stories of senior citizens who saw the transformation of Snellville from a rural community of a few hundred to a bedroom community of thousands. Two other objectives of the group were the creation of a photographic history of the town, and the documentation of the remaining historic structures.

By the year 2000, interest in the organization waned but was revitalized by a group of dedicated citizens. This group included Bob and Kate Allen, Tom Ewing, Sybil Pate Deacon, Al Herndon, Melia Beth Jones, Carolyne Kirkland, Gloria League, Sherrie Rabon and Ferle Snell.

Elected to lead the society into the 21st century were Sybil Pate Deacon, president; Al Herndon, vice president; Gloria League, recording secretary; Sherrie Rabon, corresponding secretary; and Carolyne Kirkland, treasurer. The directors at large were Tom Ewing, Ferle Snell and Melia Beth Jones.

The mission statement established by the society in 2000 was to research, document and publicize the history of Snellville and the Snellville community. The organization set as its first goals: to publish three newsletters a year; to conduct two general meetings each year; to participate in Snellville Days activities; to collect photographs for the purpose of publishing a pictorial history of Snellville; and to begin the writing of a book on the history of Snellville Consolidated School. The school history was published by the Society in 2008, as Thomas Ewing researched and authored the text.

Carolyne Kirkland created a mobile historic display that has been used for History Week at the Elizabeth Williams Library, Snellville High School alumni banquets, Snellville Days activities, Brand Bank's anniversary celebration and the dedication of The Snellville Senior Center.

Since 2000, the Historical Society has had three presidents: Sybil Pate Deacon 2000-2004; Thomas Ewing 2005-2006; and Elaine Roberts 2007-2008.

Offices of the Society are in the city complex in Snellville and are open Monday, Wednesday and Friday mornings. Under the direction of Wayne League, a collection of historic photographs has been recorded on CDs that are sold by the Society.

Snellville became famous with the phrase, "Everybody is Somebody in Snellville." The Snellville Historical Society is striving to educate citizens to the fact that one of the reasons they are "somebody" is because of Snellville's rich heritage.

Duluth Historical Society

In 1999, the Duluth Historical Society was incorporated to help preserve and promote the rich history of the city. It lists as its mission to "Recognize the value of our people's rich heritage." The city's motto is "Preserving our history, recording the present and reaching for the future."

From the beginning, its purpose has included developing and sponsoring programs about the city's history, traditions and culture. The Society also has a purpose to collect and preserve artifacts about the heritage of the area, and to provide a mechanism for researching the past and to collect contemporary information as the Society recorded history for the future.

The original officers of the Society were Margaret Gallow, chairperson; Paul Boat, vice chair; Shannon Edwards, secretary; and Glen Faulkner, treasurer. Others holding office included Janice Yarbrough, museum director; Beth Faulkner, archivist; Kevin Kuharic, membership chair; and an advisory board consisting of Don Alford, Beth Bragg, Charlotte Dispain, Maxine Garner, Ed Johnson, Desmond Martin and J.C. Nixon.

A key figure in this development of the Society has been Janice Yarbrough. Manager of the Festival Center and an employee of the city since 1986, she realized that people came to City Hall asking about the town's history, and realized there was no place to collect artifacts relating to the history. As she found people donating historical items to the city, Mrs. Yarbrough asked the Council to provide space in the adjacent former church parsonage for the growing collection. In September 2000, the City of Duluth opened its doors to the first Duluth History Museum located next door to City Hall at 3582 West Lawrenceville Street.

That's where items were housed through 2007. As the new City Hall was opened in early 2008, many of the artifacts were installed in cabinetry at the new location. In early

2008, the Society was seeking a permanent home to house its growing collection of items with an historical interest to the people of Duluth. The Society holds monthly meetings. It plans rotating exhibits and satellite exhibits as part of its program.

Officers of the Society in 2008 were Judy Ann Wilson, president; Woody Bell, vice president; Joy Norris, secretary; and Helen Jones, treasurer. Members of the board included Don Norris, Nancy Sturgis, Maxine Garner, Mark Williams and Candace Morgan.

Among the activities of the Society:

- Historical preservation on the local, regional and national level;
- Building strong relationships within the community;
- Preserving and promoting the city's heritage, customs and traditions;
- Compiling lost history and artifacts;
- Collecting photographs of old Duluth, families, and environs; and
- Developing programs of historic interest open to the public.

Historic Grayson

During the early 2000s, interest grew in the City of Grayson about preserving the city's heritage, primarily driven by the mayor and city council. Envisioned was a means to organize citizens interested in the area's history and preservation, and to work on artifact collection and references of Grayson's past.

Mayor Jim Hinkle says that the city fathers realized: "Grayson had very little left of historical significance, and what we had remaining, we needed to preserve. After all, when it is lost, it is gone forever."

In 2001, when Doug Wilkerson was mayor, the City of Grayson bought a white-frame, one story house on Rosebud Road, known as the Kennerly-Cox house. Mrs. Flora Cox had lived there from about 1950 until 2001, and was an employee of the nearby school lunchroom. This was a "working man's" farm house, with wrap-around porch. The house was partially remodeled in 2002 by the city, which initially restored the kitchen area to a circa 1900 setting. The house was designated as the Grayson Art and History Center, which was incorporated as a 501(c)(3) charitable body. It operates the center and gift shop. The house, adjacent to the Grayson city park, is staffed by volunteers and open from Tuesday through Saturday from 10 a.m. until 2 p.m.

It's thought that the home was probably built about 1890 by the Rev. J.P. McConnell, who had founded Grayson. The house was built for the T.T. "Doc" Kennerly family. Kennerly, who was the town blacksmith, had his shop behind the house. He bought the house from his uncle, the Rev. McConnell. When restoring the house, the city found square nails, now on display, used in its construction. Indications are that Mr. Kennerly forged the nails at the blacksmith shop on the property. Mr. Kennerly was also the town coffin maker, and would store the finished coffins on his front porch for all to see.

In 2007, the City did further remodeling on the house, restoring the older higher ceilings and changing out the linoleum flooring to heart pine floors. A gazebo was added as part of an Eagle Scout project. Another element at the house is a one-chair barber shop from the business begun in 1965 by William Farmer in front of his house. (He closed his barber shop morning and afternoons while he drove a school bus.). He retired from barbering in 1998. He is said to have specialized in flat-top haircuts; former Gov. Lester Maddox was among his customers.

Key proponents of the remodeling were Barbara Hinkle, who is the executive director of the Grayson Historic Preservation Society, and Steve Starling, who is the city historian. From the work on the house came the idea to start the Society in 2006. Starling says: "It grew out of the Arts Center. We have people here who want to share the history of this community. Many newcomers want to know more about the history of Grayson."

The Society meets quarterly and offers several levels of membership to those interested in Grayson's history.

Norcross History Center

The Norcross History Center, Inc. (an independent, non-affiliated non-profit board) was founded in 2007 from a cross-section of representatives of the Norcross Woman's Club, Save Historic Norcross, the African-American community, the Norcross Baseball Association, and others interested in historical preservation and education. Its purpose is to establish a museum for the City of Norcross, using senior citizens and others as volunteers.

The city in 2008 was anticipating to designate a brick structure at 189 Lawrenceville Street as quarters for the Center, which the city was leasing from Gwinnett County. It's anticipated that the city would provide the facility to the Center for $1 a year. The facility is expected to house the artifacts of the Norcross Baseball Museum, and also be used eventually as a Welcome Center for Norcross. The house is adjacent to the Norcross Fire Museum.

The History Center presented a three-year business plan to the City Council in 2007. The City Council approved $3,200 "seed" money for start-up expense and incorporation. The Center has been the recipient of funds from the Norcross Art Fest, and has obtained funds from the Norcross Woman's Club.

Officers of the center are Anne Webb, chair; and Catherine Cash, secretary-treasurer. The board of directors include John Adams, Ann Barker, Edna Berkshire, Catherine Cash, Dodger Deleon, Edie Riehm, Deborah Walker-Little and Anne Webb.

Two museums in Norcross

There are two specialized museums in Norcross, within a block of one another.

The Norcross Baseball Hall of Fame is in quarters at the Norcross City Hall. It honors a long-standing tradition of semi-pro baseball, and also honors players from Norcross who went to the major leagues.

Two classmates at Norcross High, both former baseball players, were instrumental in moving the museum idea forward. They were Col. John Adams and the Rev. Avery Graves. They got the City Council interested in 1993, after collecting memorabilia about Norcross baseball. Adams had played professional ball for the Waycross Bears and Graves had been on a college ball team.

Three former mayors of Norcross have played professional ball: Frank Simpson, Frank Robertson and Thurman Terrell. In addition, at one time, Norcross had three residents on major league teams at the same time: Roy Edward Carlyle and brothers Absalom Holbrook (Red) Wingo and Ivy Brown Wingo. Carlyle is credited with hitting the longest home run ever measured: some 618 feet. This happened in Oakland, Calif. In retirement, he operated a hardware store in Norcross.

The Norcross Baseball Hall of Fame opened November 6, 1993 at the Norcross Arts Studio and Gallery on Carlyle Street, a former library and BellSouth site. Later, it was moved to the Norcross City Hall. The Hall highlights the baseball careers of nearly 40 Norcross residents who played professional baseball, many in the major leagues. Memorabilia is still being added to the collection.

In addition, Norcross has an as-yet-unnamed "Fire Museum," housed in a specially-designed brick building in front of the new Fire Station No. 1 on Lawrenceville Street, about a block from City Hall. The building houses a 1942 Ford Fire Truck, which the City obtained as surplus property from the U.S. Army's Fort Gillem just after World War II. R. A. (Junior) Gant, who was once the Norcross volunteer fire chief, says that Gus Morton worked at Fort Gillem, and lived in Norcross, and was instrumental in helping the city buy the truck. The cost: $1.

The truck is a 250 gallon pumper, and for years, was the only fire truck of the Norcross volunteer department. Around 1961, the City added a new American LaFrance fire engine, and the 1942 Ford was used as back-up for a short while. When the City of Norcross Fire Department became the nucleus of the new county fire department in 1971, the new engine was transferred to the county, but the 1942 Ford was soon stored in an open shed, though it had a roof, and virtually forgotten.

Around 1999, former members of the Norcross Volunteer Fire Department wanted to restore the 1942 truck to working condition. Carl Garner Jr., Wayne Little and Lane Campbell led the restoration effort. Little says that they wanted to do something for the City of Norcross, since the city had allowed them to sponsor an Old Car Show uptown. When they started inspecting the fire engine, they found the block busted, requiring a new engine. The group found a replacement in Alaska, a government surplus engine still with Cosmoline on it, for which they paid $2,000. "But we had to disassemble the entire truck, put in new brakes, new tires, glass and a floor pan," Little says, adding: "After all, we wanted to restore it, for it was one of the first fire trucks around here."

The Norcross Car Show Committee paid $32,000 for the restoration. Others pitched in to do the work, including David Little (Wayne's son), brother Charles Little and his son, Chuck. Former Norcross City Clerk Betty Mauldin also pushed for the restoration. Altogether, the restoration took nearly five years. The sparkling restored fire truck moved into its own building in early 2008.

Buford museum

In 1984, a small group of artists started coming to Buford. Included in that group were the co-founders of the Museum of Main Street, A. R. (Randy) Wood and Sandra (Sandy) Sumner, who opened the first art gallery, Distinctive Collections, at 9 East Main Street. In the years to follow, many of the early, and in a few cases, original businesses to Main Street, began to transition away or close their doors for the last time. Realizing the enormity of these events, Randy and Sandy had the foresight to start collecting and preserving Buford memorabilia. Together in 1986, they started displaying artifacts in one corner of their art gallery.

The reputation of the makeshift museum grew and members of the community embraced the idea of preserving the Buford community's heritage and contributions to the collection began to flow in. In 1994, the museum collection moved to 37 East Main and remained there until 2002, when a space was donated at the complex of Tannery Row located at 545 West Main Street.

In 2005, Lynn A. Bowman agreed to continue the tradition of the museum and became the curator and custodian of the privately-run collection. His family dates back to 1818. Earlier, he was involved in historic activities while in business in Macon. He returned to Buford in 1997, and is involved in real estate.

In January 2007, the museum returned to the central business district at 95-B East Main Street. There Bowman began an active campaign to expand the collection. With the aid of Buford High School, the museum added a fully functional, interactive web site with over 100 historic photos, a comprehensive history, related links to Buford, and a museum store for items of interest. It is open, with free admission, on Saturdays from 11 a.m. until 5 p.m. or by appointment.

Southeastern Railway Museum

A veteran Atlanta newspaperman is given credit for the impetus to start what eventually became the Southeastern Railway Museum in Duluth. He is Leo Aikman, a columnist for *The Atlanta Constitution*, who lamented in the 1950s in print how steam locomotives were vanishing from the American scene.

The locomotive he championed was No. 290, an Atlanta and West Point Railroad workhorse of its day, a Pacific (4-6-2) type dating back to 1926. At one time, this engine had propelled the passenger train Crescent Limited on its journey from New York to New Orleans, through Atlanta. Engine No. 290 was primarily used on the route between Atlanta and Montgomery, Ala. The locomotive was retired in 1953.

Aikman began marshalling his railroad buffs in 1956, which led to the formation of the "Save 290 Committee," assisted by E.M. Ivie, a retired Southern Railway engineer. The committee assisted in pursuading the railroad to give the engine to the City of Atlanta in 1958. The engine was moved to the Fairgrounds by the Army Corps of Engineers as an exercise in 1958. There it went on display, along with other railroad equipment, at a small rail museum at the Lakewood Fairgrounds, where the Southeastern Fair was held. The museum was at first called "Cinderama," but later got the more formal title of "The Southeastern Transportation Museum."

Members of the 290 Committee then sought to become a legitimate rail group, and joined the National Railway Historical Society (NRHS), with a goal of establishing an historical organization to provide educational and museum service in Atlanta. They held their first meeting in late 1958, and got a charter from NRHS in March of 1959. Around this time, the chapter got its first donation of railroad rolling stock, which gave the members equipment to maintain.

Soon the organization was asked to take over the supervision and operation of the Lakewood museum, and made plans to grow into a museum. At that time, Lakewood had only two rail tracks with room for about six pieces of rolling stock. Meanwhile, by 1961, the club was incorporated legally as an educational institution and gained its tax exempt status. It got its 501(c)(3) status in 1983.

By now, members were beginning to realize they needed additional acreage for growth, as they had received other engines, passenger and freight cars. Not only that, but in 1965, the City was going to close the Lakewood museum, meaning a new location was desperately needed. The Southern Railway came to their rescue, giving the chapter 12 acres of land in Gwinnett County near Duluth, east of Buford Highway on May Road, south of Pleasant Hill Road. Georgia Gov. Carl Sanders, Southern Railway President D.W. Brosnan and NRHS national chairman Lewis Pardee attended a ceremony to commemorate the handing over of the land to the museum. Mr. Brosnan at this time also donated three Pullman cars to the museum. And in 1965, the City of Atlanta gave Engine No. 290 to the chapter. By 1970, after major fund raising, grading of land and track laying, the first pieces of rolling stock were on the tract of land. Almost all of the labor for the preparation was done by volunteers.

To help fund the museum growth, the chapter began a period of focus on excursion trains through Georgia. In the 1980s, the New Georgia Railroad, a State of Georgia operation, brought some of the museum's cars and locomotives back into service. This allowed the Chapter to begin regular third Saturday "Steam Up Weekends" during the summers. Engine No. 290 was rebuilt by the state and used on excursion operations. The engine was also in at least one movie, *Fried Green Tomatoes*.

The count of rolling equipment at the museum got up to 90 in the 1990s, and the museum became a popular site for family outings. In that same decade, rail excursions became expensive, and the New Georgia Railroad stopped operations. That required the Atlanta Chapter of NRHS to focus on operating as a museum again.

By the mid-1990s, the Museum's 12 acres were crowded with rolling stock. In late 1997, the Museum bought a 30-acre site about a mile north off Buford Highway in Duluth, the former J.J. Finnegan rail car repair facility. This location had 14,000 feet of track, plus three large buildings. It was perfect for the Museum, but needed heavy maintenance work to bring it up to standards, including laying tracks to the main building. The site also needed, for instance, over a mile of fencing. It became a prodigious job for the all-volunteer Chapter.

It took about 10 months to get the new (and present) location ready for moving the rolling stock. The big day was Sept. 26, 1998. The Norfolk Southern Railway, at no charge to the Chapter, provided a "hospital train" to move the museum's rolling stock across their tracks to the new location....all done without a hitch. It was a complex move, as the railroad actually closed their main line for most of one day and part of another. The railroad also sent locomotives and manpower to insure that the move was smooth.

Meanwhile, the Chapter was able to sell its former 12-acre site to its neighbor, Mickey's Lumber Company, gaining $1.2 million for the property, part of which helped pay for the move. The Museum placed most of the funds in the Gwinnett Foundation, and used it for collateral to borrow funds for improvements needed at the new location.

The Museum also got Transportation Enhancement grants to make improvements to its buildings.

Other key elements of the Museum:

- The Chapter houses a Pullman car, the "Superb," once leased by the Pullman Company for use by President Woodrow Wilson and later used to provide transportation for President Warren Harding. The car came to the Museum as Atlanta Coast Line office car 301, which once had been Car No. 100 of the Charleston and Western Carolina Railroad. When restoring the car, a volunteer spotted the word "Superb" on the underside of the car, which was used to determine its original Pullman use. After Harding's death in San Francisco, it was the funeral car used to transport his body to Washington, and then for burial in Ohio. The "Superb" was fully restored in 1999, and is the only surviving rail car that served as a presidential funeral car.
- The Duluth facility is the official "Transportation History Museum of Georgia," designated in 2000 in a bill signed by Gov. Roy Barnes, introduced by Rep. Brooks Coleman (R-Duluth). This designation helped the Museum secure grants and display collections, such as MARTA's collection of Atlanta buses and transit equipment.
- The museum added 3.85 acres from James Elliott in 2005, which is now being used for parking and long-term development. The property was between the Museum entrance and Parsons Andrews Building Supply, and was bought for $500,000.
- Tunneling of Pleasant Hill Road under Buford Highway to improve that intersection became a benefit for the museum, as it received hundreds of loads of fill dirt for its site, which was graded to specifications. This is anticipated to speed up developming of the acreage on the back side of the property.
- In 2008, plans call for installation of a railroad turntable; building of a roundhouse; construction of a new entrance building; obtaining a steam locomotive previously used at Stone Mountain Park; and moving of the former Duluth train depot from a location on Pleasant Hill Road to the Museum property.

The first president of the Atlanta NRHS chapter was Dave Austin in 1959. A list of the presidents may be found in Appendix B, page 823.

Service clubs

Part of the fabric of Gwinnett life is its many service clubs. These range from small neighborhood homeowner and condo associations to school PTAs to the highly-organized international organizations such as Rotary, Kiwanis, Civitan and Lions, and to clubs with other specific concerns, such as women's and garden clubs, or even high school booster clubs. These clubs provide many worthwhile services to their communities, while adding another overlay to life. This chapter will touch on the activities of a few of these organizations, while the Appendix lists many of these club's leaders.

There are many homeowner associations within Gwinnett. Only one will be mentioned here, that of Peachtree Corners, which has been widely recognized for its effectiveness, creativity and impact. The United Peachtree Corners Civic Association has been called "the gold standard for homeowners' groups" by *The Atlanta Journal-Constitution* (May 11, 2003). Presidents of service clubs by years are found beginning on page 811 in Appendix B.

Kiwanis Clubs

Cathy McNally of Suwanee Kiwanis defines her service club in this manner: "Kiwanis is a global organization of volunteers dedicated to changing the world one child and one community at a time." Kiwanis International, first organized in 1915 in Detroit, Mich. has 248,000 members in 8,000 clubs in 92 countries, and today is headquartered out of Indianapolis, Ind. Its mission is to serve children of the world. It has 320,000 youth members. Its name stems from an American Indian expression, which means "We share our talents."

The Lawrenceville Kiwanis Club got its charter on May 25, 1923, with 36 original members. It immediately sent two delegates to the International Kiwanis Convention, conveniently held in Atlanta that year.

F.Q. Sammon, a Lawrenceville funeral director, was the first president. He also served as president in 1924, 1925 and 1929. He was mayor of Lawrenceville for 15 years, at different times, and also served in the state legislature. He was a former president of the Georgia Funeral Director's Association.

Over the years, the Lawrenceville Kiwanis Club has been a major force in improving conditions in Lawrenceville and Gwinnett County. The club and its members have worked for better business practices and more modern education, pushed for better government, encouraged the youth of the area, emphasized the qualities of good citizenship, and sought more cooperation between the county and its cities. It has often sought better roadways for the area, and helped bring new industry to the county. For instance, in the 1930s, it sponsored Gwinnett County Developing Company, which purchased the mill village in Lawrenceville to encourage General Shoe Corporation to set up a shoe factory. Later on, the Kiwanians started a movement to found the Gwinnett Chamber of Commerce.

The Lawrenceville Kiwanis encouraged and assisted J.C. Flanigan in getting his history of Gwinnett published. It also endorsed the construction of Buford Dam, and sponsored the adoption of a city manager program for Lawrenceville. *And* when Gainesville was hit by a tornado on April 6, 1936, the Kiwanians of Lawrenceville donated $1,000 to help.

The Lawrenceville Kiwanians for many years have funded scholarships to local students who are strong academically and involved in school and community service. It supports the Lawrenceville Cooperative Ministry and the Gwinnett Medical Center. Its biggest activity of the year is a Christmas party for underprivileged children, often hosting more than 300 youth. The club annually adopts an elementary school class and members work with the teacher through reading and working with students. It also supports a local Key Club at the high school and Circle K Club at the college. Among its fund-raising activities are an annual pancake breakfast and golf tournament.

Kiwanis International began accepting women into its ranks in 1987. As near as can be determined, Kathy Williamson of Sugar Hill was the first female Kiwanian in Gwinnett, joining the Buford-North Gwinnett club on July 28, 1987. The first female member of the Lawrenceville club was Inez Walker, who joined on June 25, 1992. Her husband, Perrin Walker, had been a member of that same club since 1958.

Over the years, many Gwinnettians held office as lieutenant governors of the region of Kiwanis. Victor Hagood of Lawrenceville was the first lieutenant governor from Gwinnett in 1932. A father-son team was also lieutenant governors, Hubert Tucker in 1968, followed by Dr. Hubert Tucker Jr. in 1983. Randy Dellinger of Lawrenceville served twice, in 1994 and again in 1997. (See Appendix for complete list of Gwinnettians in this role.)

* * * * *

The second Kiwanis Club in the county came to Buford on May 3, 1939. Its name was changed later to the North Gwinnett Kiwanis. Its first meeting was in the basement of the Methodist Church, but shortly moved to the first floor of the Masonic Hall. The club was an early supporter of the Chattahoochee River getting a dam near Buford, and planned strategy and raised money for this purpose. It adopted the development of the dam and lake as a club project in 1942. The club hosted a luncheon in 1950 for 350 dignitaries from Metro Atlanta at the ceremonial groundbreaking for the dam.

There was a long period before another Kiwanis Club was formed in Gwinnett.

A Kiwanis Club was formed in 1983 in Lilburn under the name of the "Growing Gwinnett" Kiwanis, but ceased to exist in 2000. Duluth Kiwanis was chartered on July 11, 1984. In future years it would become the Suwanee Kiwanis, May 9, 1996; Norcross Kiwanis, March 28, 2006; and the last club to be formed in Gwinnett, Hamilton Mill, in July of 2007.

Lions Clubs

One of the largest civic organizations is Lions International, consisting of 1.3 million men and women in 202 countries. Lions' members work together to answer the needs that challenge communities around the world. Known for working to end preventable blindness, Lions participate in a vast variety of projects important to their communities. These projects range from cleaning up local parks to providing supplies to victims of natural disasters.

The organization was formed in Chicago, Ill. first as the Business Circle of Chicago. After contacting similar organizations in the United States, an organization meeting was held on June 7, 1917 under the name of "Association of Lions Clubs." It became an international organization in 1920. It was an address by Helen Keller before the Lions in 1925 that focused the organization's emphasis on service to the blind.

Lawrenceville Lions

The first Lions Club in Gwinnett was in Lawrenceville, when that club received its charter on February 18, 1941. Thomas O. Davis, a local attorney, was the first president.

However, the club was short-lived, since most of its members were also members of the Lawrenceville Home Guard. Most of these men volunteered for the Armed Forces after Pearl Harbor was attacked. The state Lions historian, Eugene Sanders, says the Lawrenceville Lions Club was "one of the few clubs which succumbed to patriotism."

Almost five years to the day, on February 19, 1946, the Lawrenceville Lions Club was reactivated, with R.P. Smith the charter president. Thus began a proud history of service to the community. In 1948, a project to help pay for the first swimming pool at the City Park involved raffling off a 1948 Oldsmobile. The winner was Mrs. P.D. Cash, who had never driven before. However, she learned to drive that automobile and before her health halted her driving, she had driven the automobile over 100,000 miles.

The Lawrenceville Lions sponsored an annual carnival until 1953 where Central Gwinnett High is now located, a predecessor to the Gwinnett County Fair and Livestock Association. Since 1954, the Lions have operated a short-order concession stand at the Gwinnett County Fair each year.

A project of the early 1960s was raising money to help form the Gwinnett chapter of the Association of the Mentally Retarded. In so doing, the Lawrenceville Lions were instrumental in the founding of the Hi-Hope Service Center for those with developmental disabilities.

The club has been a supporter of the Boy Scout Troop 54. One of its members, Bob Powell, has served for 54 years as its Scoutmaster. More than 500 boys have been members of the Troop over the years, with more than 45 making the rank of Eagle Scout.

Norcross Lions

After Lawrenceville, the second oldest continuous civic club in the county is the Norcross Lions Club, chartered March 14, 1944 with 31 members, when Carl Garner Sr. became the first president.

Over the years, the Lions in Norcross have been involved in many civic activities.

The club contributed the original stadium and football field at Norcross High School. The club constructed the original field house at the school. The club has also maintained a sports park near the previous Norcross High School on Price Place for baseball and football. Later on, it would erect its own Club House adjacent to the field. Over the years, it has sponsored track meets, a baseball team, and both a Girl and Boy Scout troop.

Other activities of the club have included sponsoring scholarships for high school graduates; providing eye examinations and glasses for needy people of the area; leader dogs for the blind, and continued support for the Georgia Camp for the Blind and the Georgia Lighthouse for the Blind. Among its achievements was the rewiring of the old Norcross High School with improved lighting. This was done all in one weekend. Dick Rich of Rich's Dept. Store contributed 150 fluorescent lights, and the Lions members installed them within 16 hours, as an element of a Lions International "Better Town" contest, part of the overall Lions sight preservation program.

Key members of the Norcross community have been members of this first service club. Roy Carlyle, a former major league baseball player who holds the record for the longest measured home run in the Guinness Book of World Records (618 feet), was a charter member. Former Gov. Zell Miller was a member when he lived in Norcross, back when he was lieutenant governor. The future governor was also once president of the club. Through 2008, six mayors of Norcross and 20 members of city council have been members.

The charter president of the club was Carl Garner Sr. Records are unavailable as to who was president in any particular year. However, the former presidents of the Norcross Lions include:

John Adams, Bob Herman, I.G. Bottoms, Vern Boucher, George Bruce, Howard Burton, Marty Bush, Claude Carter, Charles Chappas, Gary Cobb, L.D. Ewing, W. H. Ferguson, Ellis Garner, Carl Gresham, Bill Grogan, Frank Hamilton, Bud Hamrick, Ed Hashbarger, Martha Herman, Bill Heron, Harold Hulsey, E.R. Humphries, John Kimsey, Jim King, Harold Medlock, Bobby Miller, Zell Miller, Grover Morris, Ed Owens, Walter Owens, J.T. Patterson, John Rudert, Trudy Rudert, Jimmy Shore, John Smith, John Spence and Billy Vickers.

Snellville Lions

The Snellville Lions Club was chartered on Sepember 25, 1962 with 28 members. Jimmy Powell was the charter president. For years the club met at the intersection of Georgia Highway 124 and U.S. Highway 78, in the old Sawyer store. The club later met at the Snellville Police Station on U.S. Highway 78, and in 1983, moved its meetings to the Walton EMC building on Lenora Church Road. The club meets twice a month.

The club has supported Lions International projects over the years, selling brooms and mops. The club was part of a team that worked to get the first doctors to develop practices in Snellville. The club also gives a $2,500 scholarship (The Jimmy Powell Scholarship) to two high school seniors each year. The club has supported the Georgia Lions Lighthouse, the Camp for the Blind, Georgia Recordings for the Blind and the Emory Children's Eye Center with its projects. Among its fundraisers, besides a golf tournament, is a pancake breakfast and concession stand sales at the annual Snellville Days. In 2008, one charter member, Ralph Hewatt, a retired grocer, was still a member of the club.

Buford Lions

A Lions Club going back more than 50 years is the Buford club, which began on February 14, 1953 with Russell Phillips the first president. It continues as a small club in 2008. Over the years it has been an integral part of the Buford civic life, and for many years sponsored an area-wide horse show. Another project for years was an Antique Car Show.

Today the club continues its projects, including producing a birthday calendar for the community as a fund-raiser. The club over the years has been a supporter of the Georgia Lions Lighthouse for the Blind, and recycles eyeglasses, hearing aids and cell phones. For years the Lions, along with other civic clubs in Buford, met in a building behind the high school on Georgia Highway 23, one named for a Buford Lions member. It was the Harold Hannah Civic Center. That building was taken down in 2007.

Jean Kilgore was the first female president of the club, taking over for the nine months following her husband, Jimmy's, death when he was the president. She has been president of the club for several years.

Another Lions International club is in Loganville. Other Lions Clubs were started in Lilburn and at Mountain Park, but both of these clubs folded.

Rotary in Gwinnett

Rotary International was the world's first service club, founded in Chicago in 1905.

The Rotary name derived from the early practice of rotating meetings among members' offices. Today Rotary has 1.2 million members worldwide in 200 countries. Its mission and motto is "service above self," as its members work in their communities and contribute their resources and talents to projects to benefit mankind throughout the world.

Rotary members adopted a code in 1925 called the "Four Way Test," which has been translated into more than 100 languages, consisting of the "things we think, say or do," and asks:

- Is it the TRUTH?
- Is it FAIR to all concerned?
- Will it build GOOD WILL and BETTER FRIENDSHIPS?
- Will it be BENEFICIAL to all concerned?

One of the most far-reaching efforts of Rotary was launched in 1985 to eradicate polio throughout the world. Since then, polio has fallen by 99 percent, with polio found in only four countries in 2008, and efforts continuing to ultimately rid the world of this disease through vaccination. Since 1995, the advocacy efforts of Rotary and its partners have helped raise more than $3 billion in vital funding.

The first Rotary Club in Gwinnett was founded on June 29, 1973, by Troy Chatham, a Norcross insurance executive. The Gainesville Rotary Club sponsored the Gwinnett club. In its first full year of operation, Gwinnett was the club of the year in the Rotary district, a distinct feat. It has since been recognized over and over as the top club within the district.

Rotary has become the largest service organization in Gwinnett, with seven clubs in 2008 totaling 287 members. The various club meetings, held weekly on different days, feature prominent members of the wider community addressing topics of interest to its members. For instance, at a meeting in 1988, Gwinnett Rotarians heard an Atlanta attorney, Billy Payne, tell of his dream of bringing the Olympics to Atlanta in 1996. Few in the audience thought that possible at the time, but Payne held the podium that day and delivered.

Rotary clubs in Gwinnett all participate in international affairs, by sponsoring individuals to come to Georgia for study, and funding projects throughout the world.

The county's first Rotary, the Gwinnett Rotary Club, has been instrumental in forming or co-sponsoring nine Rotary clubs in North Georgia, including all of the clubs in Gwinnett. In 1975-76, it began a new club, taking Rotary International to Forsyth County. Other clubs it has sponsored include Morgan County, 1978; Peachtree Corners in 1981; South Gwinnett, 1982; Duluth, 1986; Snellville, 1990; Norcross, 1992; Buford, 1994; and Lawrenceville, 1997.

Rotary's motto is "service above self." Rotarians show this spirit in their support of activities within their community and worldwide. The Gwinnett club's first fundraiser, which was done annually for several years, was a chicken barbecue held at the Norcross City Park. Another long-term effort by Gwinnett Rotary has been hosting of a student to study for one year at a Georgia college, under the auspices of the Georgia Rotary Student Program. The first student was from Edinburgh, Scotland, Elizabeth Watkins, in the 1975-76 school year. As other Rotary clubs were formed in Gwinnett, they have each traditionally sponsored all or a part of the cost of students to study at Georgia colleges.

While service clubs often tout their efforts in the community, they are also social organizations. Since 1979, Gwinnett Rotary has sponsored an annual Oyster Roast, inviting all Rotarians in the county to attend, in an inter-club outing. The timing is the same each year: in the outdoors on the first rainy, cold and stormy Wednesday afternoon in March. (This description describes the weather as it often happens on the day of the Oyster Roast.) The main ingredient is served in three ways: raw, roasted and stewed.

Over the years, Gwinnett Rotary has taken on individual projects for the community, such as recognizing the High School Student of the Year, based on citizenship, scholarship and athletics; selecting the policeman and firefighter of the year; sponsoring a Wheelchair Sports Center at Shorty Howell Park in Duluth; spearheading a playground for handicapped children at Bay Creek Park in Grayson; and putting on a golf tournament to raise funds for these community projects. In 1997, the club began funding a veterinary scholarship at Gwinnett Tech in memory of Jack Wall, a former member.

One major project for Rotary came after eight lives were lost in a fire at Suwanee's Annandale Village in 1983. That next year, 1984, Gwinnett Rotary, along with the Rotary Clubs at Peachtree Corners and South Gwinnett, collaborated to personally hammer, saw and nail together and reconstruct one of the buildings lost in the Annandale fire. It is now known as the Rotary Building at Annandale, and serves as a dormitory.

Being an international organization, members of Gwinnett Rotary Club have participated in Friendship Exchanges with Rotary clubs in Portobello, Scotland and in Guildford, New South Wales, Australia. Its members have also hosted Group Study Exchanges within the district, welcoming Russian and Mexican delegations to the state, and international students from around the world. In 1992, Gwinnett Rotarian Buck Lindsay founded the Rotarian Action Group for Population and Development, which has become a moving force within Rotary International, with far-reaching ramifications. Based in Lawrenceville, its 20,000+ membership draws from 65 countries around the Rotary world, and implements projects to help poor communities improve their lives, seeking to bring balance between population and resources.

Among the Gwinnett club's international projects have been forming a sister-club relationship with Patan West in Nepal; and funding projects in Egypt, Samoa, Nigeria, India and Nepal. One example of this was funding a fresh water well for a village in Nepal, where the club also provided funds for a birthing center.

When it first began in Gwinnett, Rotary was an all-male organization. However, in 1987-88, Rotary International changed its rules, and allowed female members. The first women in a Rotary Club in Gwinnett were Carolyn Collins and Kathy McCurdy, who joined the South Gwinnett Club on August, 10, 1989. Then when the new Snellville (now Sunrise) club began on Nov. 19, 1990, Carol Miller, Gale Hulme and Marie Soracco were charter members.

In 1991, Jo Ann Pinder, administrator of the Gwinnett County Public Library, became a member of the Gwinnett Club. (She later was president of the Lawrenceville

Rotary Club.) In 2000, Connie Wiggins of Gwinnett Clean and Beautiful became the first female Gwinnett Rotary president.

It wasn't easy for females to integrate what had been an all-male domain. Jo Ann Pinder later shared her feelings about what to her was something of an ordeal in becoming the first female member of a club: "I joined Rotary in the fall of 1991. There were members who would not talk to me, even when I sat beside them at meals and asked a direct question. Many times as I drove to the Falcon Inn for the meeting, my stomach would be churning. I knew the entire female population was dependent on me representing them well. It is important to note that Buck Lindsay, who was district governor and Wayne Sikes, who was president then, felt it was important to have women in the Gwinnett Rotary. So I was only the fulfillment of their goal. I was the right person at the right time."

Five members of Gwinnett County Rotary Clubs have been district governor of Rotary, directing the activities of clubs in the North Georgia area. A member of the Peachtree Corners Club, Jim Smulian, in 1986-87 was the first district governor from Gwinnett. Three from the Gwinnett Club have served in this capacity: Buck Lindsay, Jim Hinshaw and Jimmy Maughon. A member of the South Gwinentt club, Rich Panyik, was also the district governor. The Rotary District is No. 6910, covering the northern third of Georgia.

One former Gwinnett Rotarian now sits on the 11th U.S. Circuit Court of Appeals. He is former Lawrenceville attorney James L. Edmundson.

Another distinction of Gwinnett Rotary Club is that it is the first club in the Rotary world to have its members as 100 percent participants in the Rotary International Benefactor Program, done in 1989-90 when Jim Hinshaw was the club president.

Another activity which all Gwinnett Rotary Club participate in is the annual Bellringing around the kettle for the Salvation Army at Christmas. This was started in 1999 and has become a tradition with Gwinnett clubs. The seven Rotary Clubs of Gwinnett annually volunteer to ring the bell at the kettles at retail locations throughout the county. Funds collected are used by the Salvation Army for its programs throughout the year.

All the Rotary Clubs in Gwinnett support the charitable activities of Rotary International, and are also supportive of the Georgia Rotary Student Program. This program is unique to Georgia Rotarians, and started after World War II to bring students from war-torn countries in Europe to study at a Georgia university for a year, with funding from sponsoring Rotary clubs. Since the program was begun in 1946, some 3,000 young people from countries all over the world have studied for a year at a Georgia college, then returned home as an "ambassador" for Rotary and Georgia in their countries. While in Georgia, each student has an "adopted" Rotary family to guide them through the year away from home, often becoming virtually a "member" of that family.

Some of the key local projects of the clubs:

Lawrenceville (Meeting: Noon Mondays): This club is heavily involved in the Lawrenceville Cooperative Ministry, giving a weekly contribution. It is also involved in the Gwinnett Children's Shelter volunteer service painting, planting and ground clean-up; and works with the Hi-Hope Center in keeping up its grounds. It has often annually sponsored the Laws of Life Contest at Central Gwinnett High, including highlighting the winners with a pizza party at the school.

Peachtree Corners/Norcross (Meeting: Noon Mondays): Members of this club enjoy "hands on" activities to serve the local community, and target financial assistance programs. This includes a Habitat for Humanity partnership with Scientific-Atlanta; an annual Christmas Holiday project for Rainbow Village children; volunteering for Relay for Life; recognizing the honor students of the month at four local elementary schools; sponsoring the Interact Club at Norcross High; and contributing to the Norcross Cooperative Ministry, Boy Scouts, YMCA Partnership with Youth; and Special Needs Children's School. It also partners with the Field of Dreams project and has mentored students at Summerour Middle School. It regularly nominates students for Rotary Ambassadorial scholarships.

Snellville Sunrise (Meeting: 7:30 a.m. Tuesdays): Most of the funding of this club comes from its annual golf tournament. Its projects include a $1,000 scholarship to a South Gwinnett student, plus a $500 scholarship to a student at Gwinnett Tech. It supports the Southeastern Gwinnett Food Ministry; participates in the Relay for Life and sponsors a South Gwinnett High Interact Club. It also helps clean up Snellville City Park in the Great Day of Service program, and contributes to the Tull YMCA Partner with Youth program, the Dream House for Medically Fragile Children, and Boy Scouts.

Gwinnett (Meeting: 12:15 Tuesdays): This club honors police and fireman of the year; supports Interact Club at Peachtree Ridge and Meadowcreek High Schools; and has an annual golf tournament to raise funds for charitable activities. That includes the Gwinnett Children's Shelter; working with South Gwinnett Rotary at Christmas for Foster Kids; and this club has led all Rotary clubs in Gwinnett in raising money each Christmas during the Salvation Army bellringing. The club also led efforts for a children's handicapped park, Unity Place, at Bay Creek Park. It annually hosts an Oyster Roast for all Rotarians in Gwinnett.

Duluth (Meeting: 7:30 a.m. Wednesdays): Club members provide not only hands-on support but financial support to the following organizations through the funds raised at its annual charity golf tournament. Some of the organizations the club supports are the Duluth Interact Club; Leah Morgan Scholarship Fund; Relay for Life; American Cancer Society Patient Navigator Society; Habitat House in Duluth; Minority Development for United Way; Rainbow Village; Boy Scouts; Operation One Voice Project in the Dominican Republic; YMCA Partnership with Youth; quilts for military personnel serving in Iraq, scholarships for children of fallen soldiers; and The Dreamhouse for Medically Fragile Children. Duluth club members are 100 percent Paul Harris Fellows of Rotary International.

Buford/North Gwinnett (Meeting: Noon Wednesdays): A hands-on club, members join together working on projects with Gwinnett Great Day of Service, the state Adopt-a-Highway program and Earth Day projects in conjunction with the Gwinnett Environmental and Heritage Center. The club awards annual scholarships to two seniors each at North Gwinnett and Buford High Schools. Partnering with the Gwinnett County Library System, the club funds the purchase and provides sweat equity to assemble "Littlest Reader Packets" distributed to new parents at two Gwinnett County hospitals. Other projects include donating books to the library in the name of each weekly speaker; purchasing products for the local food bank and providing funds to purchase a disaster recovery Shelter Box and supporting the Gwinnett Children's Shelter.

South Gwinnett (Meeting: 12:15 Thursdays): This club is paired with a sister club in Matasmoros, Tamaulipas, Mexico, and the two clubs have completed a water project that will provide for drinking water for citizens of Matamoros. The club has also refurbished a bus for the Lazarus project in cooperation with Trinity Lutheran Church in Lawrenceville, which is used as transportation for homeless people to become more self-sufficient. It has also been involved with the Women's Domestic Violence Center and the club for years has provided a Christmas Party for the Department of Family and Children's Service clients.

Civitans in Gwinnett

The Duluth Civitan Club is one of many clubs in the Atlanta area, but the only one currently serving the Gwinnett County area. The club was chartered May 20, 2003, and meets the first and third Thursday of each month at Kurt's Restaurant in Duluth. In 2008, it reported 35 members.

Among those chartering the club were Cheryl Adams (Crouch), Terry Swaim, Chuck Hartman and the then-Civitan Georgia North Governor, Terry Crouch.

From the beginning, Gwinnett Civitans have distinguished themselves, with the club receiving Civitan International's Honor Club Award in its first year. It has been an Honor Club winner since.

The Civitans have been an active group in Duluth, working in the Duluth Fall Festival (sausage biscuits that first year), both in a booth and on the clean-up crew. Since 2005, it has hosted the State of the City address by the Duluth mayor, which is used both as a civic event and fundraiser for the club. It also supports a junior Civitan Club at Norcross High School.

One of the Duluth Civitan members, Loren Brown, saw his father, Mike Brown of Birmingham, Ala., nominated to be Civitan International president in 2007-2008.

Stonehedge Garden Club

While there are numerous gardens club throughout Gwinnett, we will cite only one garden club in this history. The Stonehedge Club was founded April 7, 1970, becoming a member of the National Garden Club Inc. in April, 1972. The name was chosen since the founding members lived on Stonehedge Drive in Buford adjacent to the Shadburn Estate, which was surrounded by a stone wall and hedge.

The club meets monthly. Its purpose is to encourage an interest in gardening, flower arranging and a desire to enhance the community. In 2008, it counted 35 members. In 2008, one of its active members was a charter member: Mrs. Elfrieda Phillips.

Members have sponsored many civic and community improvement projects. One of the first was to landscape and plant the grounds at the Buford School, as well as the City Square. The club helped buy and plant cement urns along the main street area in Buford and planted flowers along the railroad tracks running through downtown.

One of the largest endeavors was the grounds of the restored Bowman Pirkle House, circa 1818, located at the Gwinnett Water Park on Buford Dam Road. The club planted and maintained herbs and perennial areas around the historic old house for many years. The club received the National Award for Preservation of Historic Grounds and Gardens for this project. For many years the club also had annual plant sales in April, bazaars and flea markets and sold cookbooks as money making projects.

Among its previous activities is hosting flower shows in Gwinnett County. Members have volunteered time to plant and tend a garden area at the Gwinnett Civic Center. The club also supports activities at the Gwinnett Children's Shelter. The club since 1996 has contributed approximately 90 table floral arrangements for the Hi-Hope Charity Ball. It also sews and decorates small Christmas stockings to send to patients at the State Hospital in Milledgeville.

Among its current activities is working with the Gwinnett Environmental and Heritage Center to furnish plantings around the Meditation Circle and its Memory Garden. Trees, shrubs and flowering plants to be planted will be native to the area. The club had hoped to have the work completed, but postponed final work until the fall of 2008 because of the severe drought in the area.

United Peachtree Corners Civic Association

The United Peachtree Corners Civic Association (UPCCA) was established in 1993 in response to land use concerns in the unincorporated part of western Gwinnett known as Peachtree Corners. Homeowners joined together to form UPCCA, an umbrella group of neighborhood homeowners' associations, and incorporated as a 501(c)(4) organization. Thus organized, UPCCA was able to contribute to the discussion of development on the main thoroughfare through Peachtree Corners --Peachtree Parkway -- and the surrounding areas.

UPCCA has evolved through the years from a group defined by "opposition to development" to a group that's now defined by its "vision" for Peachtree Corners. This meant UPCCA came to view developers and the County as potential partners and not necessarily as adversaries. Peachtree Parkway has been improved because of support for certain development and a consistent pattern of cooperation with the Gwinnett Planning Commission and the Board of Commissioners. A major achievement has been the Peachtree Corners Overlay District, established in 2007, as a result of tenacious work of UPCCA.

A key UPCCA program is the Peachtree Parkway Improvement Project. Begun in 2004, UPCCA now maintains the Parkway medians year-round to improve upon the twice a year mowing done by the Georgia Department of Transportation. The program is funded by voluntary fair-share contributions of landowners on the Parkway and other stakeholders.

As part of the Peachtree Parkway Improvement Project, a gateway monument sign announcing Peachtree Corners and the Paul Duke Parkway was erected in 2008. It is located where Peachtree Parkway veers off from northbound Peachtree Industrial Boulevard. This stretch of Peachtree Parkway to the Chattahoochee River was designated the Paul Duke Parkway in 1999, in honor of the founder of Peachtree Corners.

UPCCA is participating in the Gwinnett Chamber of Commerce's "Partnership Gwinnett" by branding Peachtree Corners through its sign topper program, through the landscape maintenance program, and through the construction of a gateway monument sign. All of these efforts signal that Peachtree Corners in Gwinnett County is, indeed, what Paul Duke envisioned----a good place to live, work and play.

Welcoming sign to Peachtree Corners. Photo by United Peachtree Corners Civic Association

General UPCCA meetings are open to all. They are held at least six times a year, usually at the Simpsonwood Conference and Retreat Center. In election years, those running for elected office are invited to a Candidates' Forum.

In 2008, the officers were: Mike Mason, president; Wayne Knox and Sandy Laszlo, vice presidents; Joan Porter, secretary; Allen Joiner, treasurer; and Pat Bruschini, past president. Directors included Chris Crock, Marlene Gaskill, Lynette Howard, L.C. Johnson, Mike Murphy and Gay Shook.

Business clubs

In the 1980-90s throughout Gwinnett County, business and merchants associations sprang up, centered on many of the county's cities. Here is a brief synopsis of these groups.

Snellville Commerce Club

The Snellville Commerce Club was established in 1984 by a small group of business owners. At that time, it was known as the Snellville Merchant's Association. From this initial effort began the growth toward one of Gwinnett's largest business associations. In 2008, it counted more than 90 members. It has as its motto, "Where Business Thrives."

Its members meet twice monthly for lunch. Its purpose is to establish and promote programs that strengthen the ties among members, their respective businesses, and the community. It is a completely independent organization, with no ties to a larger organization. The club is involved in philanthropy within its community and has contributed over $35,000 to causes in the community since its founding. In 2006, the club began a scholarship program for DECA and FBLA students at the local high schools.

Tony Webb was president from founding in 1984 through 1999, and Jimmy Norton and Joan Miller have been co-presidents since. The club meets on the first and third Tuesdays at noon.

Duluth Merchant's Association

The Duluth Merchant's Association (DMA) began in 1989. It was the brainchild of the late John Lynch of Michelin Tires in Duluth, who pleaded with Mayor Bobby Williams for such an association. The mayor asked Shirley Lasseter, then his assistant, to help get the group started. Along with banker Tom Martin and Lasseter, Lynch got the group registered as a non-profit 501(c)3 organization, with Lynch as the first president.

At its initial meeting, the Association showed a video about Duluth, which told of the town and its amenities. At most meetings, merchants donate door prizes. Shirley Lasseter likes to tell the story of Bill Head of the funeral home donating a casket as a door prize, though Head required that it be used within 30 days! Shirley says: "I was set up."

The DMA was conceived with the idea that as business people, they can best accomplish together what no one could do alone. It is an association for members to participate in and improve the Duluth community.

One of the key ideas behind forming the Association was to cultivate businesses remaining in the city. With Gwinnett Place Mall opening in 1984, some Duluth merchants were feeling business pressures. Another threat to the downtown area was the development of new businesses on the newly-expanded Peachtree Industrial Boulevard on the west side of town.

Early meetings were more social than business, but soon they developed into working sessions that gave back to the community. The first year, the Association held a successful health fair downtown. The Association early on began sponsorship of an annual 5K Run as a fundraiser, and has been a strong supporter of the Duluth Fall Festival. In 2007, the Association had 105 members. Dr. Marion Maloof was president in 2008. Over the years, it has given back over $150,000 to downtown improvements.

The Duluth Merchants meet monthly on the first Monday in the month. Meeting sites rotate among members, and are often arranged a year in advance.

Buford Business Alliance

One business association did not start out as such, but began life as an arts association. That was in Buford, where several artists had located in the late 1980s along Buford's once-dying Main Street.

Eventually, as art galleries began to open throughout downtown Buford, the organization morphed into the Buford Business Alliance. As other businesses, shops and restaurants came to the revitalized area, the artists floundered for a while, then later moved to the south end of town to another old building that once housed a Bona Allen shoe plant.

In an attempt to resurrect the remaining few art galleries and bring art and commerce back to the downtown area, Christina Truhe and Margaret Kolk of Carisma Gallery took the reins of the Business Alliance in 2006 and brought new enthusiasm to the Main Street merchants. With their efforts, membership grew from approximately 20 to 75 within one year. In 2008, it counted 240 members.

As it grew, the Alliance became a multi-faceted organization embracing the city of Buford and the surrounding area, operating as a marketing, tourism and network opportunity organization. Tim Koenning headed the association as president in 2008. Among its efforts is a sub-alliance, the Main Street Merchant's Association, which is headed by Christina Truhe. The Alliance's purpose is to enhance Buford's Main Street for tourism.

Suwanee Business Alliance

The Suwanee Business Alliance was founded in 1999 and works to foster communication and commerce among its members and help businesses prosper. It is a non-profit organization run by volunteers. Meetings are held the second Wednesday of each month at rotating locations. Its purpose is to facilitate interaction between members; to promote their businesses; to support local activities, and to help create a "sense of community" between member businesses.

During the year, the organization sponsors a number of events. Among them are support of various local organizations, awarding of scholarships, promoting free summer concerts, the upkeep of the Jackson Street Cemetery, and support of local charitable organizations. Eric Behning of Sun Trust Investment was president of the Association in 2008.

Dacula Business Association

The Dacula Business Association began in 2003, working as a network for support of local businesses. Membership is open to all firms in the 30019 ZIP code and meets the third Tuesdays at noon at City Hall. Its theme is "Doing it in Dacula," seeking to encourage doing business within the city.

Every other month, the Association has a "Muffins with the Mayor" meeting at 7:30 a.m. as its Tuesday meeting. It also hosts a quarterly "business after hours" and is a major supporter of the Dacula Memorial Day Parade. Shelley Cole was president in 2008.

Lilburn Business Association

In Lilburn, that town's Business Association sponsors two of the town's biggest events of the year, the Lilburn Christmas Parade and Music on Main.

The Association, formed in 1992, is a sponsor of the annual Christmas parade, dubbed the largest in Gwinnett, on the first Saturday in December. The parade has grown from 75 groups participating in 2002 to more than 115 groups with 1,000 participants in 2007. It includes bands from Berkmar, Parkview and Meadowcreek Highs, and draws close to 5,000 spectators. A "Festival of Christmas" is held in the park after the parade.

Music on Main is also sponsored by the group and takes place on the first Saturday in September. Funds raised from musical performances and food sales from local restaurants are donated to the Dream House for Medically Fragile Children, which is located in Lilburn. Another event, which the Association sponsors, is an Easter Egg Hunt each spring.

Meetings of the Association are on the third Tuesday of each month for lunch and features a guest speaker and offers a broad perspective of programs. The Association also has a B3 (Business Builder Breakfast) on the first Friday of each month, focusing on the nuts and bolts of business and solid business practices.

Once a quarter the Association also hosts a Business After Hours for casual networking, at member businesses. Thor Johnson has been president from 2005-2008.

Norcross Business Association

The Norcross Business Association was formed around 1990 to help local firms network and to promote the downtown business district.

Among the projects it is involved with is the annual Third of July Fireworks celebration in the downtown area. This event is attended by as many as 20,000 spectators and is viewed as one of the key events of the year locally. The association is also a sponsor of a "Corners to Crossing" 10K race from Peachtree Corners to downtown Norcross, held in the springtime.

Chuck Paul was president of the Association in 2008. Leaders over the years have included Jeff Hopper, Terry Robinson, Edna Berkshire and Jan Glenn.

Braselton Business Association

The Braselton Business Association (BBA) is a not-for-profit association, specifically designed to assist the Business Community in achieving their professional goals. The BBA is committed to the success of the business community and the free enterprise system. The mission of the BBA is to promote commercial and industrial growth in the Braselton area while preserving its heritage, and to provide support, leadership, fellowship, and unity to its business leaders.

The key project each year of the Association is the promotion of "Christmas in Braselton," which takes place on the first weekend in November. That may be soon for Christmas sales, but this was also the anniversary of the opening of the Braselton Brothers store in 1904, when the Braselton Brothers, so much a part of the community, traditionally marked their store's birthday.

This is a major festival for the entire town. This is also the weekend of the "Movie in the Park." The day's activities conclude with a Christmas parade, which ends at the park in time for the movie.

In 2008, Carlos Llorens was president of the group. It has 50 members, meeting the second Tuesday for breakfast at 8 a.m. at the Braselton Community Center. The Association began in 1991.

North Gwinnett Business Alliance

One Gwinnettian in 2000 saw the formation of the various business groups, and realized that they needed to be contacting each other. Julia Hall, a banking officer at the Peoples Bank and Trust in Buford, realized that the different business groups faced similar major challenges and shared common issues, such as how to preserve local business and promote their community's downtown area.

Hall, along with Lisa Zaken, then with the Gwinnett Chamber of Commerce, and businessman Armando Martinez, formed the Gwinnett Town Business Connection, working out of the Chamber of Commerce. This Connection aims to be a forum for associations to discuss successes and failures with one another to move their groups forward. The group met monthly at first, but has moved to meeting every other month.

The North Gwinnett Business Alliance was formed in 2000. Hall says: "There was no networking association of business people in this area, except for civic clubs. And everyone does not want to be in a civic club in order to do networking. So we got started and it worked from the beginning."

The Alliance represents businesses stretching from Sugar Hill to Auburn, to Flowery Branch and to Lawrenceville. Its function is to promote the common growth of those businesses in North Gwinnett/South Hall counties.

A key function of the organization, besides networking, is to fund scholarships for students in the area's six high schools.

Park Place Association

A combination homeowner-business group, the Park Place Association, was being formed in the Park Place area near Stone Mountain in early 2008. Members come from the surrounding community with a Stone Mountain mailing address. There are more than 400 businesses and approximately 10,000 people living within the area served by the association.

The overall goals of the Association are to improve the perception of the area and improve the economic development of the area.

The Association came about after a study by the Evermore Community Improvement District suggested such a group would be key to the area's development. On August 17, 2007, an initial meeting between County Commissioner Mike Beaudreau, Evermore's Brett Harrell and community activists Muriel Costabile and Frances Smith, who was president in the Corinth Hills Homeowner's Association, found interest in starting an association.

The first get-together of the group was a forum on October 4, 2007, with more than 100 in attendance. Overall goals of the Association were outlined, and a slate of directors were chosen. Named to the five-person board of directors were Muriel Costabile, Doug Cox, Arthur Farr, Amanda Soesbe and Frances Smith, with Mrs. Smith being named president.

Lawrenceville Tourism and Trade Association

Perhaps the most active local business association is in Lawrenceville, the Lawrenceville Tourism and Trade Association (LTTA). Unlike any of the other similar groups, this Association is partially supported by tax dollars from the City of Lawrenceville's hotel-motel tax, which makes up about half its budget. The other half comes from membership dues and from special events.

In 2008, the group numbered 110 members; it now meets every other month, after meeting monthly since its inception in May of 2004. It is a 501(c)(6) non-profit organization.

One of its goals, for which it uses its tax dollars, is to promote both short-and long-term tourism in Lawrenceville. It has succeeded in promoting several annual large events in Lawrenceville with these funds; it has also launched branding campaigns for the city, including highway billboards and brochures distributed state-wide.

Gloria Faulkner, appointed by the city, is chairman of the Tourism Board. The Board contracts with Downtown Management Services of Athens to provide its leadership, while

Jay Markwalter is the staff person and executive director of the Association. He is also the staff person for the two Development Authorities in Lawrenceville.

Markwalter sees the biggest accomplishment in the four years the organization has been active as laying the foundation for significant tourism-related events in Lawrenceville. He also notes the partnerships developed at the city, county, and state levels, all working towards the promotion of investment and economic development in Lawrenceville. From the local merchant or builder to the county government and even Georgia Department of Economic Development, Lawrenceville's Tourism and Trade Association has been building critical relationships for destination marketing.

Among the now-popular, free events which the Association runs:

- Spring Arts Festival, working with the Dunwoody Arts Guild.
- "Farmers' Market" Saturdays from June to September, with local growers selling fresh produce, flowers, jams, jellies, etc. in downtown.
- July 3's Prelude to Fourth: The Aurora Theatre performs productions on the Historic Courthouse grounds, followed by fireworks. Attendance at this event averages 3,000-5,000.
- July 4: The July Fourth fireworks extravaganza is held on the grounds of the Gwinnett Justice and Administration Center, with accompanying crafts booths, food, and music activities.
- Moonlight Concert Series: Five concerts, held on the fourth Friday of each month, from May to September, in partnership with Gwinnett Parks and Recreation Authority, on the Historic Courthouse lawn.
- "Festival of Leaves:" Held on the third Saturday in October, this arts and music festival complements Gwinnett's Annual Reading Festival for the whole family. It features prominent authors, and is done in partnership with the Gwinnett County Public Library.
- Thanksgiving's "Lighting of the Tree" on the Historic Courthouse ground.
- Lawrenceville Rings on New Year's Eve: This takes place in the entire downtown, turning area businesses into venues, with music from 12 bands spread around downtown. There are lots of children's activities on the Square, from puppet shows to face paintings, a food court, hay rides, and several live theatre groups performing. The night is capped off with a pyrotechnic and fireworks show to ring in the New Year. As many as 8,000 have turned out for the event.

In 2007, the LTTA began to hand out Golden Hammer plaques to business owners and developers who made significant renovations, remodeling or new construction projects in the downtown area. At the initial presentation, those who had worked on developing the downtown area from 1997-2007 were recognized. These individuals and businesses represented $21 million in redevelopment projects. The Association plans to continue to make this an annual awards program.

In 2008, Baybe Oakes Baggett, the daughter of a former Lawrenceville mayor, donated $50,000 toward renovating the former Oakes family home at 235 Crogan Street as a welcome center for the city. The city had purchased the house in 2006, and is leasing the house to the Lawrenceville Downtown Development Authority for a welcome center and offices of the LTTA.

Centerville Business Association, Inc.

In the spring of 2007, a few church and business leaders began meeting with local politicians and established association leaders to explore the possibility of forming a business association within the Centerville community. After many meetings, it became clear that for a business association to be successful, it had to meet the needs of the community as a whole.

The group began reaching out to schools, homeowners' associations, home-based businesses, churches and storefront businesses. Dan Curry, who would become president of the group, said: "It seemed the missing ingredient was the sense of community. Those of us who grew up here remember a time when we knew our neighbors. The simple fact of knowing people and the roles they play in the community seems to ground us with the warmth of friendship. As Centerville has changed from farmland to subdivisions, we have lost that sense of community."

The Centerville Business Association seeks to form relationships among the community, so that it will be able to lead discussions and resolve the issues confronting this area. It also seeks to establish a united voice that can be clearly heard by elected officials so that the community is one where people will feel comfortable to live, work, worship and play.

The founding board of the CBA was composed of: Dan Curry, administration pastor of Hope and Life Fellowship; Dean and Brent Robinson of Centerville Auto; Mark Foote, Shane's Rib Shack; Tony Morgan, State Farm Insurance; Ron Weber, Buck's Pizza; and Tony Brock, senior pastor of Hope and Life Fellowship; and John Byerly, senior pastor of Redeemer Presbyterian Church.

Loganville Chamber of Commerce

It was in 1994 that the business community of Loganville organized its own Chamber of Commerce. It became the first city in Gwinnett to have its own Chamber organization.

Behind this organization was the unique geographic location of Loganville, splitting the Gwinnett-Walton borders. What Loganville merchants found is that they were not getting the assistance that many Chambers provide from either the Gwinnett or the Walton Chambers of Commerce.

That first year, some 220 merchants and individuals became members of the Chamber. Membership has steadily risen without a special drive, and by 2008, numbered over 300. The main purpose of the Chamber is to serve the businesses in town. The Chamber says its goal is to be a "rock of stability needed by the community to make good things happen." It also says that the Chamber strives "to be the leader in creating, promoting, and sustaining a responsible, pro-business environment and enhance the quality of life in the Loganville area."

The Chamber is housed in a building on Main Street owned by the city, which provides the office without cost. The Chamber has only one employee, director Betty McCullers, a former Realtor. At one time, she was the events coordinator at Stone Mountain Park, noted for coordinating the Yellow Daisy Festival. She is a native of Loganville, and has been with the Chamber since 1998. In addition to her regular Chamber duties, she also oversees economic development for the city and Chamber.

There are several annual events of the Chamber, including both a fall 5K run and spring scholarship 5K race. The Chamber donates proceeds from the spring run to a scholarship program for Loganville High seniors, and pays for part of its operations from proceeds from the fall run and festival. The Chamber also brings seniors into the City Hall to observe government for a day.

It also hosts Logan Fest the third weekend in October; and a tree lighting and the annual Christmas parade on the first Saturday in December.

Among those early proponents of the Loganville Chamber were several people, including former Mayor Michael Jones, Janice Tribble and Tommy Wolaver.

Former Mayor Michael Jones says that what started out as a merchant's association soon broadened into a full fledged Chamber. "It keeps Betty McCullers, our director, busy promoting the town, sending out packets from inquirors, developing demographics and attending Grand Openings."

Wolaver, a Realtor who served on the board of the Chamber for 10 years, adds that one major benefit is having "somebody working conscientiously every day on all sorts of activities for the community."

A former council member when the Chamber began, Janice Tribble remembers back to when the Chamber had its first Logan Fest. "We had a 5K run on Friday night, and had the streets closed off that night and had the festival booths open that night, and had a dance, and ran it until midnight. Then we opened back up on Saturday morning and continued the festival that day. But we found that this was a hard way to do it, so we continue to have the 5K run at 7:45 p.m. on Friday, but only have the festival on Saturday from 10 a.m. until 5 p.m." She adds: "In 2007, we had between 4,500 and 5,000 people attending Logan Fest."

Greater Grayson Chamber of Commerce

It was March 7, 2006 when the Greater Grayson Chamber of Commerce was formed. At the time of formation, it listed its mission to serve as a "regionalized resource for community businesses of all sizes throughout Grayson, Loganville and Snellville." It seeks to combine strategic initiatives to help build a strong and viable community. Initially, it had 40 members.

In the fall of 2008, the Grayson Chamber had 206 members, mostly from very small businesses, and is today something of an "intimate" Chamber, with few corporate members. An ambassador program of 12 people promotes the GGCC and is key to the community relations program. The Chamber emphasizes communications in the area.

The founders and officers of the organization were Michelle Couch, president; Pamela Blatchford, vice president; and three directors: E.J. Lehman, Karen Cash and Gail Moore-Huie.

The Grayson Chamber maintains a continuing program of activities. That includes a Networking "Commerce and Coffee" the last Wednesday of each month at various locations;

a Network Lunch Hour the second Wednesday of each month; and a quarterly Business After Hours program. It also sponsors weekly meetings by industry on several topics; and a spring and fall business development workshop. Over the course of a year, the Chamber offers over 370 opportunities for business development, that includes AM Exchanges, networking lunches, business-after-hours times, referral teams, small business workshops; and an Executive Business Council.

The GGCC also supports local festivals and events, and promotes itself with courtesy bags for marketing material.

Woman's clubs

A significant impact on Gwinnett County comes from the several Woman's clubs within the county. The history is extensive, dating back to the first club in Norcross in 1906. The purpose of these clubs is to provide a framework for its members to improve the quality of life on a local, state, national and even international basis. The interest of the clubs is as varied as their membership.

The clubs are all affiliated with the Georgia Federation of Women's Clubs and the General Federation of Women's Clubs. The clubs work in six areas: the arts, conservation, education, home life, international affairs and public affairs. Over the years, the clubs have been supporters of the Tallulah Falls School in Tallulah Falls, Ga. It is an independent, co-educational boarding and day school serving approximately 150 students. It enrolls day students in grades 6–12 and boarding students in grades 7-12.

Woman's Club members feel the benefits of membership are many, as they offer a chance for service and action, broader contacts, and provide both leadership opportunities and a chance to mold public opinion on community interests.

The Georgia Federation of Women's Clubs was organized in Atlanta, Georgia, on October 28, 1896. It joined the General Federation of Women's Clubs in July of 1897. The motto of the Georgia Federation is "Wisdom, Justice, Moderation." The Federation colors are green and white, and its flower is the Cherokee Rose. Georgia has approximately 150 clubs with over 5,000 members.

Norcross Woman's Club

The oldest continuously operating civic organization in Gwinnett is the Norcross Woman's Club, which got its charter from the Georgia Federation of Women's Clubs in 1906, and was recognized by the National Federation in 1908. The club was organized by 18 charter members in October of 1905.

In 1963, the Woman's Club agreed to build an addition to the Norcross Library, a meeting room behind the library. The work was completed on October 17, 1966, and it became the meeting site for the Woman's Club and other civic groups. By 1967, the indebtedness of the club on the addition had been cleared. The Norcross Library moved to a larger site in a former Southern Bell building in 1971. As a result of this change, the Woman's Club began using the old library space for its activities.

One of its key projects came in 1967, when the club sponsored the publication of a book about Norcross. It got one of its member's husbands, Allen Philip Francis, to compile "fact and legend pertaining to the history of Norcross" into a 94-page book. The club sold advertising in the book to help pay for it, and hoped to make a lasting contribution to the history of the community with the book's printing. The book paid tribute in its preface to the founder of Norcross, J.J. "Cousin John" Thrasher.

People who read this in 2037 should remember that the Norcross Woman's Club buried a time capsule in Thrasher Park, with instructions to open it 50 years from the time it was buried, in 1987.

In 1999, two members of the Woman's Club, Irene Ewing Crapo and Martha Miller Adams, both natives of Norcross, compiled a history of Norcross, updating the 1967 version. It is a large book, consisting of 534 pages, and includes many family histories and narrative historical accounts of life in Norcross.

Key activities during 2008 include a yard sale of crafts and collectibles, participation in Art Fest and a Christmas lunch and bazaar. Included in its charities besides the Tallulah Falls School are the Norcross Cooperative Ministry, Annandale Village, the Norcross Police Department, Duluth High School Orchestra, and Norcross Elementary and High Schools. In 2008, the club counted 40 members. It maintains a web site at *www.norcrosswomansclub.org.*

Buford Lanier Woman's Club

The second Woman's Club in Gwinnett was founded in Buford in 1923 as the Buford Woman's Club with 67 members. It is now called Buford Lanier Woman's Club. Its aims are to foster mutual counsel and helpfulness within the community, to unite the influence of women in promoting education, civic, social and moral advancement, and to support the Tallulah Falls School. The club is non-partisan, non-sectarian, and non-profit. It became a member of Georgia Federation of Women's Clubs and also the General Federation of Women's Clubs.

The club has for years been a vital part of Buford life, and has a significant record of achievement in many areas. The club has, on the average, been a large one, with many varied interests. The membership in 2008 totaled 50 women. One member in 2008, Carrie Fishback, had been a member for more than 50 years, and she continues to be active, heading the Home Life Department.

In recent years, the club has hosted a Home Tour in the spring. The homes are varied and include mansions, cottages, lake homes, houseboats and traditional homes.

The club has a history of conservation, working to enhance the community through maintenance and seasonal plantings in the Grace Harris Garden on Main Street in Buford; recycling; holding a plant swap; planting trees in Buford parks in observance of Arbor Day; supporting Lake Lanier Association and participating in ShoreSweep. It also supports with monetary donations several groups in the county: Gwinnett Clean and Beautiful, Upper Chattahoochee Riverkeeper, Friends of the State Botanical Garden, and the National Arbor Day Foundation. The club provides camp scholarship money to Elachee Nature Science Center; and pays for subscriptions to KIND News, an environmental publication, for two local school libraries.

Some other projects the club is involved with include honoring firefighters and police officers with cookies and cakes during the winter months; providing scholarships for graduating female students who will be attending college in Georgia; providing donations to the Gwinnett Children's Shelter; giving parties for Grandparents' Day and Christmas for residents at Laurel Baye Health Care in Buford; special gifts for veterans; and giving support for the Gwinnett County Relay for Life, the Buford/Sugar Hill Library, North Gwinnett County Food Co-op, Camp Sunshine, and Hi-Hope Center. It also provides docents and other volunteers for the Buford Museum, participates in the Art Walk and other cultural activities, and even supports the AARP 55 Alive Driving Class.

The club also donates nationally and internationally to Child Outreach International, Operation Smile, Operation Christmas Child, Global Health Action, March of Dimes, and Juvenile Diabetes, among many charities. The club maintains an informative web site at *www.bufordlanierwomansclub.com.*

Loganville Woman's Club

One of the oldest Woman's Clubs in the area is the one in Loganville, which was begun by 30 ladies in 1939. It is also an independent club, not affiliated with the state and national Woman's club federations. It has as its objective the advancement of civic interests, educational pursuits, and social and moral good among its members, the town and community. Its first president was Mrs. S.A. Bowland, who served in office until 1943.

Some of the accomplishments of the club over the years have been the funding of street lights on Main Street; erecting a sign for the local library, installing welcome signs to the city on U.S. Highway 78, and arranging for installation of a gazebo at C.A. Kelly Park. The club has also landscaped Kelly Park and West Walton Park, and over the years, it led beautification projects at other locations within the city.

Members made a large donation for playground equipment at Kirkland Toddler Park, and made donations to the Walton Senior Center and Loganville Christian Center. It has annually sponsored the Fourth of July Parade, and traditionally presents two scholarships to seniors at Loganville High.

A fundraising venture of the club is a Tour of Homes each year.

Lawrenceville Woman's Club

The Lawrenceville Woman's Club dates from 1970, when it was organized with 20 initial members, led by Barbara Bohne as its first president. Its influence on Gwinnett County life has been major, providing the leadership to begin the Gwinnett Council for the Arts, Gwinnett Clean and Beautiful and Gwinnett Hospital Authority.

The club has been involved in many other projects. It has contributed time and funds to the Gwinnett Battered Woman's Shelter, Gwinnett Dept. of Family and Children's Services, Gwinnett Children's Shelter, Quinn House, Gwinnett Tech, Teen Help Line, Vines Botanical Gardens, Summit Ridge Hospital, the Female Seminary, Hi-Hope Center, Meals on Wheels, the Gwinnett Library System and many others. It has provided scholarships over the years, worked in voter registration drives, cited the animal shelter as one of its interests, and has supported the American Cancer Society and its Relay for Life, Cystic Fibrosis, Dreams Come True and other worthwhile entities. The club counted 24 members in 2008.

In 2007, the club raised $24,000 to contribute to Lawrenceville's Aurora Theatre fund for its new facility. The club has a web site at http://lvillewc.org.

Lilburn Woman's Club

The Lilburn Woman's Club held its first meeting in October, 1972 with 10 members present; it was not formally organized until 1973 with 20 charter members. The first president was Faye Moore.

The club has worked under a theme "Community Concern," offering many avenues for its members to participate in the community. Lilburn Woman's Club members also work at the grassroots level for community improvement. Members volunteer for many philanthropic organizations including: the American Cancer Society, CARE, Child Reach, the Dream House for Medically Fragile Children, Hi-Hope Service Center, Operation Smile, Operation Christmas Child, UNICEF and others.

Additional activities of the membership include support of Lilburn Cooperative Ministries; the historical Wynne Russell house, and the Atlanta Veteran's Administration Hospital. Its volunteers support the Hudgens Center for the Arts, and volunteer at the Children's Art Museum. Each spring, members sponsor "Spring into Art," a juried children's art show, showcasing the artwork of local elementary school children. In the fall, the LWC Art department sponsors a middle school photography contest, a high school senior all-media art contest, and an elementary middle and senior high school writing contest.

Perhaps the one event that the club supports which has the most impact locally is its organization of the Lilburn Daze Arts Festival, which began in 1973. Held the second Saturday in October, the event features 200 booths of arts, crafts, food, music and gatherings in downtown Lilburn, bringing thousands into the city. Proceeds benefit the Woman's Club activities. In early 2008, the club counted 40 members.

Snellville Woman's Club

In February of 1980, the Snellville Woman's Club held its first organizational meeting at the home of Carol Bagheri, as she and Courtney Bowen, Beth Sikes, Cheryl Wienges and Phylecia Wilson met with Lib Anderson, Ninth District membership chairman, to discuss requirements necessary for membership in the Ninth District Federation of Women's Clubs.

The club was officially charted on May 13, 1980, and named the Snellville Woman's Club. Carol Bagheri was elected the first president, with 13 charter members.

Significant projects the Woman's Club has sponsored over the years included establishing a library at the Snellville Nursing Home; Nursing Home Pat-A-Pet Program; Snellville Library Summer Reading Program; Adopt-A-Family, improved facilities for the handicapped; Save the Tree program; Exchange Student Cookout; Miss South Gwinnett Tea; Snellville Christmas Tree Lighting; support of Tallulah Falls School; Gwinnett Arts Council Cart Week; Pumpkin Art Projects in the Elementary Schools; and many others. After years of service to the community, the club disbanded around 1995.

I CAN ALMOST HEAR HER SPEWING STEAM AND WHISTLING!
290
McLemore

11
How, Why, When and Where It's Going

Why Gwinnett grew

An outsider once inquired about the development in Gwinnett, asking: "Did Norcross and Duluth grow because of the railroads?"

Hardly. After all, that railroad came in the 1870s, and 100 years later, Duluth had only 1,810 people, and Norcross, 2,755. And though Gwinnett has more cities and towns than any county in Georgia, a total of 15, the city populations amount to only about 20 percent of the county population (and still do in 2008.) Clearly, with 80 percent of the people living in unincorporated areas of the county, the major government is the county government.

Meanwhile, Gwinnett in 100 years, by 1970, had grown to 72,349 people. Clearly, though the towns and entire county developed, it wasn't the railroad that powered that growth. When people realize that Gwinnett by 2008 had more than 10 times its 1970 population (to nearly 800,000), other factors were involved in its growth besides the railroad.

What was it?

Several factors impacted why the county grew so quickly. Of course, Gwinnett's proximity to Atlanta and its airport is the major factor for its early and continued major growth since the 1950s. But what were the other major contributing factors?

Cheap land. Comparing the more developed parts of Metro Atlanta with Gwinnett in the 1960-90 period, people with foresight could buy Gwinnett land for not much money and either hold it for a while and get much higher prices later (still cheap by Atlanta standards), or go ahead and develop it immediately to make a quick profit. Many took profits, and turned to more land, rolling over their business again, and for some, even again. In this 30-year period, this wasn't unusual, as developers and real estate speculators had the major impact on Gwinnett business, and really drove the Gwinnett economy, even more than they do today.

Good schools. Perhaps the most influential aspect of Gwinnett life today is its very good school system, which has attracted parents to locate in Gwinnett for over 30 years. With many of these parents moving here from areas where they also had superior schools, and had super-achieving children, it meant that for years, Gwinnett's schools made huge strides in improvement, which only led to others wanting to move to Gwinnett. It was an upward spiral that is hard to beat. Amazingly, even with the recent rapid growth, Gwinnett schools have been able to continually upgrade themselves, and insure high quality education. Many consider it the top system in the state, even with its more than 150,000 students.

New jobs. With the growth in population has come a concurrent growth in good jobs in Gwinnett, as significant commercial development came alongside the population growth. The total labor force, that is, people who live in Gwinnett and have jobs at any location, numbered 407,074 in March 2007, according to the Georgia Department of Labor. More and more residents live, and work, within the county: 213,000 (58.4 percent of workers 16 and over) work and live in Gwinnett (2005 figures).

Industries were locating in Gwinnett for the superior work force, which routinely spawned more good jobs. In 2007, about 50,000 of its 326,400 jobs in Gwinnett (second quarter 2007 figures) were considered "high tech" jobs.

Upbeat feeling. Gwinnett offers a high quality of life, with those residents proud to be Gwinnettians. It's a county that grows on people, and in the long run, attracts others to live here.

Good government. Compared to some places, Gwinnett has had good government in the last 40 years. There has been no widespread corruption. Those within government aim to please, present a good image, and seem to do a good job. And.... compared to some communities, no elected Gwinnett official has been found guilty of any crime or kickback or similar shenanigan. That image of good government makes Gwinnett a place you want to live, and be part of a community.

The growth in Gwinnett has been nothing less than spectacular. It has been continual. Neither recessions, interest rates, moratoriums nor any other factor, has been able to substantially slow the growth in the years between 1950-2008. Again, it is amazing!

Dramatic change: diversity

A study in 2003 by the Burruss Institute at Kennesaw State University said that Gwinnett was the most ethnically diverse county in Georgia, with one out of six adults having been born outside the United States. Five years later, the diverse nature of Gwinnett was even more evident, as only 52.5 percent of the population was characterized as white, and in the school system, only 36.6 percent of the school-age population was white.

For the first 150 years of Gwinnett's history, the county was a homogeneous one, with few minorities settling in the county, and the makeup of the county was all very similar. Even before the Civil War, in 1860, Gwinnett had a 20 percent black population. The county's population was 12,940, including 2,581 blacks. Gwinnett was never a major slave-holding county, as 361 owners averaged seven slaves each. The largest slave owners and the number of slaves they owned included Evin Howell, 72; Robert Craig, 65; Nathan L. Hutchins, 63; and Thomas J. Waters, 55, according to the 1860 Gwinnett County Census originally taken by Benjamin Thomas, and on record at the Gwinnett Historical Society.

Gwinnett's black population continually went down over the years, and was at 12 percent in 1930. As late as 1980, Gwinnett was still homogenous. Its black population then was only 5.2 percent in 1970, and fell to 2.5 percent black in 1980 as the influx of newcomers was almost all white, and the white population grew very quickly. After World War II until 1990, the few black people in the county were concentrated in several areas: around the "Promised Land" south of Snellville, and in small pockets of the cities of Lawrenceville, Norcross, Duluth and Buford.

But in 1990 at 5.2 percent, the black population started to grow, as did other minorities. By 2000, the census showed 10.9 percent blacks in the county. By 2008, the black population was estimated at 19.8 percent.

Meanwhile, other ethnic groups were moving into Gwinnett, and its population mix was quickly changing. Since 1980, when whites made up approximately 95 percent of the county, the white population had fallen significantly, to 72.7 percent in 2000. By 2007, with minorities increasing the speed of their move into Gwinnett, the white population was only an estimated 52.5 percent of the population of Gwinnett.

By 2007, the Census Official Estimate showed Gwinnett to have 776,380 people. The most dramatic aspect of population has been the explosion of the Hispanic population in Gwinnett, from not even registering on the Census in 1970, to 0.9 percent in 1980, to 2.3 percent in 1990, and 10.9 percent in 2000. The Gwinnett Hispanic population, from 2007 reports, was the largest of any county in Georgia, according to Census estimates, numbering 129,381 persons, while the Asian-Pacific Islander population estimate was 9.1 percent. Blacks were 19.8 percent, and persons counting themselves as from two or more races totaled 1.3 percent.

One projection for Gwinnett in 2030, from a draft of the county's 2007 planning document, is that the county will have an estimated population of 1,040,000. Of that total, the number of whites is expected to drop to 390,000 (38 percent) by 2030, while the black population is expected to increase to approximately 260,000 (or 25 percent). The Hispanic population is expected to be near similar at 260,000, while the Asian-Pacific Islander population should be about 130,000 (12 percent).

By 2007, the dramatic growth of several minority groups led to a big change in the make-up of Gwinnett. More and more people from all over the United States, and increasingly from foreign countries, came to the county and were scattered throughout the entire Gwinnett area.

Look at another measurement: school age children. As late as 1991-92, only 12.5 percent of the Gwinnett Public Schools students were minorities. However, the predominant influx of Asian and Hispanic students has dramatically changed this picture, so that by 2008, the majority of the Gwinnett public school age population was from minorities (63.4 percent). The breakdown at the end of early 2008 showed the following make-up:

White	56,796 (36.6%)
Black	42,349 (27.3%)
Hispanic	33,609 (21.6%)
Asian	16,184 (10.4%)
Multi Racial	6,207 (4.0%)
American Indian	198 (0.1%)

This influx of non-native people into Gwinnett and surrounding counties has changed the area tremendously. Many Georgians were surprised to learn in 2006 that the state ranked fourth in the United States in immigrant growth between 2000-2005, gaining 38 percent and ranking only behind South Carolina, Tennessee and Delaware. Gwinnett was at the tops of immigrant growth in Georgia.

The growth came from many places. Gwinnett found its Korean population concentrating in the Duluth area; the Bosnians were mostly around Lawrenceville; Mexicans were along the county line near Doraville, Norcross, Lilburn and Tucker; other Asians were concentrated in the Duluth area, though often living in other parts of Gwinnett. People from many other countries settled throughout the county, as immigrants found Gwinnett a good place to live. Many, appreciating education, came for its excellent school system.

While many of these immigrants came for specific jobs, others found the explosion of the population of people from their country now living in Gwinnett as an invitation to come. As a result, in Gwinnett you see many new minority businesses thriving which appeal to the thrifty immigrant community. It may be a West African restaurant; the arrival of immigrant lawyers, accountants, doctors and Realtors; the success of immigrant radio stations and newspapers in their own language; and even the largest adult immigrant soccer league in Georgia, numbering 175 leagues in 2005, headquartered out of Lawrenceville. This make-up and impact of the immigrant community is the most visible sign of change in Gwinnett since the large-scale exodus of many blacks following the Civil War.

Diversity in worship

Gwinnett is the home of many different houses of worship, including a new diversity in types of worship, now from all over the world.

The county was settled by Anglo-Saxon Protestants, of principally Baptist and Methodist lineage. In its early days, some of the earliest churches were "old-time" Baptist, or Primitive Baptist, congregations, often meeting only once or twice a month. You can tell many of the older churches in Gwinnett by the fact that they have adjacent to them old-style cemeteries, many with angular tombstones dating back to 1850 and earlier. The first group of these Primitive Baptist churches were Camp Creek, founded in 1823; Sweetwater, 1824; Haynes Creek, 1826; and Ivy, dating from 1854.

Up through 1970, the church membership of Gwinnett continued to be concentrated in standard Protestant churches of the south: Baptist, Methodist, Presbyterian, the Church of God and a few other evangelicals.

In 2002, the Association of American Religious Bodies, in conducting a church membership survey, found in Gwinnett the following count of members in churches:

1. Southern Baptist Convention: 91,854
2. Catholic Church: 47,177
3. United Methodist Church: 40,623
4. Presbyterian Church: 7,474
5. Church of God: 6,657

But that was 2002. The Association conducts this survey every 10 years, so there are no figures of church membership produced since. Remember, many Baptist churches in Gwinnett are either independent, or do not belong to the Baptist convention. It's estimated that one out of seven residents, more than 125,000 people, are Baptist of one sort or another in Gwinnett.

In 2007, a telephone survey of Catholic churches found that the eight Catholic parishes in Gwinnett County were serving 14,600 families. Additionally, a former Gwinnett parish, the Prince of Peace Church once in Buford, had moved to Flowery Branch and was serving an additional 3,000 families, no doubt many of them residing in Gwinnett. To get an estimate of Gwinnett families, add half the families from the Flowery Branch parish, and this comes to 16,100 Catholic families in Gwinnett. If the average Catholic family had four members, that would mean that by 2007, there were 64,400 Catholic members in Gwinnett County.

Therefore, the leading church denominations in Gwinnett, from a survey contacting the various denominations in late 2007, would line up like this:

Baptist of all type	+125,000
Roman Catholic	+64,000
United Methodist	37,748
Presbyterian	9,492
Lutheran	8,195
Church of God	6,554
Latter Day Saints	5,480
Church of Christ	+4,000
Episcopal	3,500
Jewish	2,500

+ = Estimates.

Denomination Headquarters

Look at diversity in another way. Gwinnett also has become home to several church organizations, with their headquarters located within the county. These include:

Georgia Baptist Convention. This main Georgia Protestant denomination moved to Gwinnett in mid-2006 from DeKalb County. The convention built an elegant classic building, costing $43.5 million. It consists of 155,000 square feet in a handsome headquarters on 42 acres on Sugarloaf Parkway, west of Interstate 85, and across from the Gwinnett Chamber of Commerce. The work force at the Center includes 100 missionaries, with an equal number of support staff, or total of 200 in the facility. The building's multi-purpose area has a seating capacity of 350 for meal functions, with a full commercial kitchen. It also has an interactive museum and a 250-seat chapel. Dr. J. Robert White has been executive director/CEO of the convention since January 1, 1993.

North Georgia Conference of the United Methodist Church. This denomination built its offices off West Jones Bridge Road near Norcross on its Simpsonwood Conference Center site. It moved to Gwinnett in 2002. Its offices consist of 16,000 square feet in a traditional building among the tall trees near the Chattahoochee River. The staff of the Conference consists of 50 people. There are 921 churches in the conference that the church oversees, with a membership throughout North Georgia of 346,430. The conference in 2008 had a membership in Gwinnett of 37,748 in 39 congregations. Named the new bishop of the conference in 2008 was the Rev. Michael Watson. The North Georgia Conference is the largest of all the Methodist conferences, with 350,000 church members.

Presbyterian Church of America, which has a staff of about 200 persons, is also located in the Sugarloaf area, on North Brown Road. The office moved from DeKalb County to the Gwinnett location in 2001. It is the second largest (1,600 churches) and most conservative Presbyterian group in the United States, concentrated in the southeastern United States. Perimeter Church, with 4,534 members, off Old Alabama Road near Duluth, is its largest church in Georgia. PCA supports Covenant College near Chattanooga, Tenn., has a seminary in St. Louis, Mo., and a retreat center, Ridgehaven, in Brevard, N.C. Dr. Roy Taylor is the stated clerk.

North Georgia Church of God, which has its offices in Lawrenceville, oversees 280 churches with 89,258 members. It employs 14 people at its office, off Georgia Highway 120, and is led by David Walker, the administrative bishop. From 1947 until 2002, the church offices were in Gwinnett near the DeKalb County line on Buford Highway near Doraville. The church also operated a campground at this site, which was sold to developers for a mixed use project. The church moved its office to Lawrenceville, and has developed a new campground near Homer in Banks County.

The Mormons

Another fast growing denomination in recent years in Gwinnett has been the Church of Jesus Christ of Latter Day Saints, or as many call them, the Mormons. In recent years, the LDS church has been one of the fastest growing in Gwinnett, starting out in 1977 with its first congregation in Lawrenceville. In 2007, there were six Mormon stakes within the county, making up 13 congregations, including three Spanish-speaking congregations. Officials of the Mormon church estimate that in 2007, there were 5,480 members in the "stakes" (or churches) in Gwinnett.

While the growth of the Latter Day Saints Church in Gwinnett in recent years has been fast, Mormon missionaries were in Georgia as early as 1843. The meticulous records that the LDS church keeps tells us that the first convert to Mormonism in Gwinnett was Nancy McKisley, baptized on October 4, 1889. The churches' members in the early 1900s were encouraged to migrate to Utah and to other Mormon settlements in the West. Therefore, early congregations in the East were short-lived.

Missionaries of the church continued to preach in Georgia and until 1957, the church in Georgia was primarily under the jurisdiction of traveling elders. In the 1920s, Mormons living in Gwinnett attended services in Atlanta at the corner of North Avenue and Boulevard. In 1954, the church built a chapel on Ponce de Leon Avenue in DeKalb County, and in 1977, built another in Tucker.

LDS congregations in Gwinnett were founded in Lawrenceville (1977); Lilburn (1980); Snellville (1987); another in Lawrenceville (1989); in Centerville (1992); and in Mountain Park (1998). There are three LDS Family History Centers in Gwinnett: in Lawrenceville, Lilburn and Suwanee.

Episcopalians

Some main-line Protestant churches were not present in Gwinnett County until the growth began in the 1960s and 1970s. There was no Episcopal Church in the county until 1969, when St. Edwards was established in Lawrenceville with the Rev. Victor Nickelson its first vicar. In 2008, there were five Episcopal congregations within Gwinnett, totaling some 3,500 communicants. The other Episcopal churches include Christ Church, Norcross (1978), whose first rector was the Rev. Joel Hudson; St. Matthews, Snellville (1979), where the Rev. Edward Hanson was the first vicar; St. Mary and Martha of Bethany, which started in Buford (1992) with the Rev. John Dukes as its vicar, now with its sanctuary at Hamilton Mill; and Christ the King (2006) in Lilburn, which is a congregation made up primarily of members with an international flavor, begun by the Rev. John Ray.

Lutherans

The Evangelical Lutheran Church of America counted 10 congregations in Gwinnett in 2007 and had the vast majority of Lutherans (6,653) in the county. However, there are congregations from three other synods of the Lutheran faith in Gwinnett, for a total Lutheran population in Gwinnett in 2007 of 8,195.

The first Evangelical Lutheran Church was St. James in Norcross, founded in 1969, with Harold Koch as pastor. Trinity Lutheran in Lilburn followed in 1974, developed by the Rev. Donald Hanberry. The largest Lutheran church in the county is Christ the King Church in Peachtree Corners, founded in 1982, by Pastor Gary Christiansen. It had 2,026 members in 2008.

Other Evangelical Lutheran congregations formed include Christ the Lord in Lawrenceville, in 1979, led by Pastor William Quail; All Saints in Lilburn in 1982, developed by Pastor Matthew Ernst; Amazing Grace in Lawrenceville dating from 1986 with Pastor Jim Panos; Epiphany in Suwanee, in 1998, led by Pastor Nancy Padgett; and Community of Grace, in Grayson, which Pastor Matthew Henning developed in 2000. There was also an Abundant Life group in Braselton meeting in 2007 as a worshiping congregation under development, as well as a Messiah Korean church in Norcross also under development in 2007.

The Missouri Synod churches in Gwinnett include Oak Road in Lilburn, which Pastor Marlin Mentz developed; and Living Savior in Lawrenceville, which was led in development by the Rev. Michael Mast.

There is also a Wisconsin Lutheran Synod congregation, Sola Fide, near Lawrenceville, which was organized in 1977 by Pastor Larry Zahn.

And there is a Zion Lutheran Church in Lawrenceville from another synod, that of the Fellowship of Confessions Lutheran Churches. It is the only church of this synod in Georgia. This church was organized in Gwinnett in 1998. John Johannes was the first church pastor.

Roman Catholic Church

In 1970, the migration of Catholics to the South resulted in the Roman Catholic Church establishing St. Patrick's in the former Norcross First Methodist Church. Then came St. Lawrence Church in Lawrenceville as a dedicated sanctuary in 1973. A gift of land in Buford resulted in the establishment of the Prince of Peace Church in 1977. (Its congregation outgrew the Buford facilities and moved to a Flowery Branch location in 2005.)

These were the first of what in 2008 are nine Catholic congregations in Gwinnett. The nine congregations ministered to 16,000 families, a count in 2007 showed. These congregations:

Church	*Year Founded*
St. Patrick, Norcross	1970
St. Lawrence, Lawrenceville	1973
Prince of Peace, Buford (In 2005, re-located to Flowery Branch)	1977
St. John Neumann, Lilburn	1977
St. Oliver Plunkett, Snellville	1978
St Marguerite D'youville, Lawrenceville	1992
St. Monica, Duluth	1994
Mary Our Queen, Norcross	1994
St. Stephen, the Martyr, Lilburn	2000

Jewish congregations

Snellville had the first synagogue in the county, Temple Beth David, founded in 1980 by Rabbi Robert Kravitz. It remains the only synagogue in the county, though a Jewish non-profit organization, Chabad Enrichment Center, has offices in Norcross and Lawrenceville. It also operates Jewish schools for students age 5-13 in those areas. The center is led by a rabbi. It's estimated that the Jewish population of Gwinnett is about 10,000 persons, representing 2,000-2,500 families in 2007.

Other faiths

There have been significant congregations established by the Hispanic and Asian population in Gwinnett. Many of these new congregations are an outgrowth from the missionary activities of Protestant churches, which for years have concentrated on sending funding for missions in distant lands. Now with the people in these countries once supported by the churches coming to the United States, almost overnight the local churches found direct ways to assist these new immigrant populations, sometimes by membership in their church, or by sharing their church facilities. One Gwinnett church after another opened their doors to new congregations from other lands. Protestant churches in Gwinnett would have their regular services on Sunday morning, with the new immigrant congregation holding services in the same building later in the day. Many times these new immigrant populations would become strong enough to rent their own facilities, or erect their own sanctuaries and thrive as a congregation.

A good example of churches which host other immigrant congregations within their facilities is the First Baptist Church of Lilburn. Itself a historic church, founded in 1840 by nine former members of Camp Creek Primitive Baptist Church, the church was originally known as Liberty Baptist Church. Its name changed in 1965 to First Baptist of Lilburn. It was similar to many rural Gwinnett churches, in that at first it held church services only monthly, but began meeting twice monthly in 1933. Services every Sunday began in 1953 as it got its first full-time pastor.

By 2008, the Lilburn church had six immigrant congregations meeting in its building each Sunday, in addition to averaging 800 in attendance at its own morning English-language service. (The church has a membership of 2,600, with 1,800 "resident members.") Immigrant groups meet and have services in their own language in different areas of the approximately 100,000 square foot church.

Other congregations of First Baptist, Lilburn, are:

Group	*Meeting Time*	*Average Attendance*
Lilburn Chinese Baptist	10 a.m.	30
Vietnamese Baptist Church	2 p.m.	60
Asian Indian Baptist Community	6 p.m.	35
Hispanic Baptist of Lilburn	11 a.m.	65
Atlanta Love Korean Baptist	10:30 a.m.	38
Arabic Baptist	5:30 p.m.	28

MegaChurches

Perhaps the most dramatic change in church membership in Gwinnett which has taken place since 1980 is not in mainline churches, but from mega-churches, sometimes not associated with standard denominations. There are several such churches, each with large memberships and extensive program development. Among these churches are:

Victory World Church, Norcross, founded in 1990, began as a church seeking to bridge the gap between the different cultures and ethnic groups in Metro Atlanta. In 2008, it was averaging 5,600 in attendance from 95 nations at its three services on the weekend. It focuses on cultural reconciliation, building families, transforming community and impacting the world. It has expanded to include church plants in Kennesaw and Athens, Ga., and in Orlando, Fla. Senior pastors at Victory World Church are Colleen and Dennis

Rouse, who met while students at Rhema Bible Training Center in Tulsa, Okla. They are assisted by 12 additional pastors, and lead a total staff of 83 persons.

The church has an extensive outreach program, including supporting orphanages in India and Sierra Leone and a medical facility in Ethiopia. It also supports missionaries in other areas.

Locally, the church works closely with the Norcross Cooperative Ministry, a prison ministry, outreach to the homeless, and feeds the hungry on weekends.

Hopewell Baptist Church, Norcross, a primarily black congregation founded in 1865, counted 16,800 members in 2007, with an average Sunday attendance at 9,000 in its three services. The church began growing in 1980 as The Rev. William Sheals became its minister, when the church had only 200 members. He emphasizes old-fashioned Gospel teaching, and asks his members to be part of a movement, not merely be a member with their name on the roll.

Hopewell Baptist Church

At this church, "Movement connotes activity, involvement, commitment and not compromise," Sheals says. It began its own school, Hopewell Christian Academy, in 1996, which in 2007 had 200 students. It also has a "Christianomics Mall," consisting of credit union, community development corporation, job readiness program, restaurant, coffee shop, barber and beauty shops. The church is affiliated with the National Baptist Convention. The church also has a television ministry broadcast on Atlanta Interfaith Broadcasting on Fridays at 7 p.m. Its pastor, now Bishop Sheals, oversees 14 other ministers and their congregations.

Hebron Baptist Church in Dacula, is an old-line church founded in 1842, when it only had 10 members. It began quick growth in membership in 1978 when Larry Wynn was called as the church pastor. When he began his ministry, the church had 342 members, and in 2007, it counted 12,453 members, and averaged more than 5,000 in attendance in two services at church on Sunday. It has three Bible study hours on Sunday. It opened a new sanctuary in 2006 with a 4,000 seat auditorium. This church also operates its own school of nearly 1,000 students in grades K-12. Hebron Church is a member of the Mulberry Baptist Association.

First United Methodist, Snellville is the largest Methodist Church in Gwinnett, with 4,020 members at the start of 2008. There are two other Methodist churches with at least 3,000 members, the Cannon and Lawrenceville churches, while Duluth counted 2,916 members. Altogether, there are 39 United Methodist Churches in Gwinnett, plus several other Methodist-related congregations, including the Wesleyan Methodist churches and the Salvation Army.

Cross Pointe Church is located in Duluth, alongside Interstate 85. Its pastor is the Rev. James Merritt, who started the church in May 2003. Previously he was pastor of the First Baptist Church of Snellville, and while there, was president of the Southern

Baptist Convention. The church has a membership of 1,400 (2007) and averages 1,850 in attendance on Sunday. The land and buildings for the church were given to the congregation by the families of two of its members, Wayne Mason and Virgil Williams.

It was previously the Gwinnett campus of The Boeing Company, which had its plant located on the 72-acre site.

Church of God, Buford: This church has 1,624 members, and has had Edward Davenport as its minister for 21 years. It is located in downtown Buford on 12 acres, but has purchased 40 acres on Bogan Road near Thompson Mill Road for a future campus. Its present sanctuary seats 1,000, with an anticipated sanctuary capacity of 2,000 when it relocates to its new property.

First Baptist Church of Snellville is the largest church of the Gwinnett Metro Baptist Association, counting 5,270 "active people" on its rolls. The church dates back to 1882. It was first known as the Darien Baptist, and in 1883 became Snellville Baptist Church. The present name came in 1975. Its current auditorium was originally completed in 1977, and was remodeled and expanded to accommodate 2,100 in 1989. The church campus on Snellville's main street, U.S. Highway 78, consists of 250,000 square feet.

Voices of Faith is an African-American church of approximately 12,000 members, located on Rockbridge Road, south of U.S. Highway 78, in Gwinnett, near Stone Mountain. It opened a second congregation in Conyers in 2006 on Sigmon Road. The church has two services each Sunday at each church. The Stone Mountain service averages 5-6,000 in attendance, while the Conyers services average 1,500 to 2,000 worshippers. The church was founded on August 21, 1994, out of the New Birth Missionary Church of Atlanta. It moved to its Gwinnett location in 1999, with only 30 members. It has been labeled as one of the fastest growing churches in the nation.

The church pastor, Bishop Gary Hawkins, is a native of Louisiana. He was licensed to preach by Dr. William Sheals of Hopewell Baptist Church in Norcross. His work before the ministry was as a financial analyst. He was elevated to a bishop in 2005 and consecrated by Bishop Eddie L. Long.

The church has 30 associate elders (ministers), including Bishop Hawkins' wife, Debbie. Each of the elders is assigned a special ministry at the church. Its services are televised on the Atlanta Interfaith Broadcasting channel on Sundays at 10 p.m. At its Conyers location, which sits on 55 acres, the church was in 2008 erecting a 20,000 square-foot shopping center, and opened a 12,000 square-foot Day Care Center for 250 children in July, 2008.

12-Stone Church, originally known as Crossroads Community Church, is located north of Lawrenceville on Georgia Highway 20, off Buford Drive at Calvin Davis Circle. It moved there from adjacent property in 2007. The church is part of the Wesleyan denomination and was founded in 1987 by the Rev. Kevin Myers, originally from Michigan, who was trained at Indiana Wesleyan University. The church has a total of 15 pastors on its staff, each charged with a different responsibility.

It has an average attendance on Sundays of 4,000 in three services. The church attendance is unusual, in that it has more in attendance than in membership of 900 families. The church focuses on non-traditional church followers. In 2008, it occupied a 105,000 square foot, $30 million facility, moving from 42,000 square feet. The buildings are on 70 acres. The auditorium seats 2,600.The church ministers to people from many backgrounds.

It targets the un-churched, especially those who have not grown up in a church. The church also has a campus in the Hamilton Mill area.

BAPS Hindu Mandir (Temple) in Lilburn

Another recent development in Gwinnett has been the rise of non-Christian congregations in the county, often to serve people from parts of Asia, such as India and Pakistan.

One of the most significant developments within the Asian community in Metro Atlanta has been the construction of a 30,535 square-foot Hindu Mandir (temple) on Rockbridge Road at U.S. Highway 29 in Lilburn, designed to last centuries. It is the BAPS Shri Swaminarayan Mandir, of traditional Indian design with multiple columns reaching skyward. It is massive, 239x136 feet, built of stone in India. The main pillar of the structure, 74 feet high, was begun in March 2006, and the Mandir was complete 17 months later in 2007. (The word Mandir comes from the word for the mind ("man") and the word still ("dir"), so a Mandir is a place to sit at peace, meditate or pray.) Worship activities are in a Family Activity Center, an adjacent brick-and-mortar structure resembling the Mandir, which was scheduled to open in the fall of 2008. Prior to that time, the congregation worshiped at their previous site in Clarkston.

The temple is built on a 30-acre tract, which has quickly became a landmark in Lilburn before it was even finished. It is one of five Mandirs outside India, is the largest in the United States, and one of the largest Hindu Mandirs in the world. Construction cost was $19 million. The other Mandirs in the USA are in Chicago and Houston, with another in adjacent Toronto, Canada. The first BPS mandir outside India was in London.

The temple is made of 34,671 pieces of stone, painstakingly chiseled in 1.3 million man-hours of work. The stones were carved in India. Then each stone was marked with a bar code for assembling, and shipped to the United States. Made of 4,140 tons of Italian Carrara marble for the main floor interior, 4,500 tons of cream-colored Turkish sandstone

The Lilburn mandir is one of four BAPS Hindu temples in North America.

for the podium level and main level exterior, and 3,065 tons of Indian pink sandstone for the podium and basement levels interior, it features thousands of pieces of custom stonework.

The stone was hand-fashioned in India. Each of the pieces helps form a distinctive design of geometric patterns, or rosettes, leaves and feathers. Temple members maintain that its spires are reminiscent of the Himalayan hills, with its stairways reminding them of long treks followers make to similar temples in the mountains of India.

The Mandir's Grand Steps have a width of 73 feet. The central dome is 23 feet in diameter, while a tapered ceiling is 26 feet in diameter. There are 116 arches in the Mandir. The ground floor consists of 216 pink columns, while the first floor contains 162 columns. There are 86 decorative ceilings, including 42 different types of ceilings. Some 1,669 carved figures are from marble, and another 474 from limestone. That red-and-white flag on top of the Mandir is a symbol of good winning over evil.

The sect of temple followers are adherents of the spiritual leader Bhagwan Swaminarayan, who lived in the 1700s and 1800s. This sect's members take a lifetime vow of mental and physical purity, which means no alcohol, nor meat, and purity in sexual relations, with no adultery. There are more than one million people following these tenets, and in 2007, the Atlanta congregation had a membership of about 500. Forty percent the members of the temple live within Gwinnett, though the temple draws from throughout Metro Atlanta.

The Mandir in Lilburn has become something of a tourist destination. Tours are scheduled in advance on an individual basis for a minimum of 10 persons, seven days a week during the day. There is no fee, though many visitors often donate one can of fruit or vegetables per person to the Mandir. These items are then given to the Atlanta Food Bank, as a way for the congregation to give back to the wider community.

There are two more Hindu temples in Gwinnett:

The Hindu Temple of Georgia opened August 27, 2006 on Brookhollow Parkway in Norcross. It was founded by Sri Sri Selvam, known as Dr. Commander Selvam, who personally pledged $22 million for the location. The temple practices with Vedic rituals. The temple says it is the only Shirva temple in the world with 108 "shivji," or images depicting ways of calling to one person in a respectful manner. These are often elaborate statues about 12-18 inches high with many decorations.

The other Hindu temple is incorporated as the **Greater Atlanta Vedic Temple Society**, Inc. and was founded in 1986. It purchased four acres with two buildings in 1988 on Harmony Grove Road in Lilburn. The temple has about 50 members, mostly Asian Indians. Members speak Hindi and English in conversation, while the worship is conducted in Sanskrit.

Other worshipers

Gwinnett has become the home of quite a few other religious bodies. There is, for instance, a Bahai temple in Buford, a Buddist temple in Lilburn, Islamic centers in Norcross and Snellville; Messianic congregations in Loganville and Lawrenceville; Orthodox churches in Lilburn and Suwanee, and a Unitarian congregation in Lawrenceville. Most are small, but all seem to be growing. They all bring with them their own form of worship, reflecting the customs in the country from which their members came.

Diversity in the media

Gwinnett found that the new diversity of the county is also being heard---on its airways. Former Lawrenceville Radio Station WPLO (610 AM) became "Radio Mex" in 1996, then changed to Hispanic Christian in 2007. In Duluth, "La Raza" (WLQK, 102.5 FM) has broadcast in Spanish since 2003.

WPLO first began in Lawrenceville as WLAW on Oct. 2, 1958 and was operated by Bob McGarity at 1360 AM, a 500 watt station.

However, on the dial it was "shoe-horned" between stations at 1340 and 1380 AM, making it difficult for people to get a clear signal. In 1985 Lamar Nash, who sold a Pontiac dealership in Buford, purchased the station and changed the call letters to WPLO. (Previously an Atlanta station with those call letters had operated at 590 AM. But when WPLO changed its call letters to WKHX, Nash scooped up the familiar WPLO letters and beamed out as a country music station.) When the station was changed to WPLO, it soon switched to a better spot on the dial at 610 AM, and shortly upgraded its signal to 1,500 watts.

In 1996, Nash sold WPLO to Filiberto Prieto, which made it the first Hispanic signal in Gwinnett. By 2002, WPLO was first among Mexican listeners in Atlanta Arbitron ratings. Prieto ran the station under Prieto Communications, Inc. In 2002, with his purchase of a second station, WFTD in Cobb County, at 1089 AM, Prieto grouped the stations under a spin-off, Prieto Broadcasting Inc. (By 2007, he had also purchased the Raleigh-Durham, N.C., station, WETC, 540 AM.) Besides communications, Prieto himself is also involved in the restaurant, beer and banking businesses.

WPLO under Prieto became known as "Radio Mex." It operates 24 hours a day, with the signal going to 42 counties. However, with the growth of several Hispanic FM stations in Atlanta, in 2006 WPLO's format was changed to that of a Christian Hispanic station.

Prieto leased WPLO on January 1, 2007 to Ministero Camino de Santidad on U.S. Highway 29 south of Lawrenceville, led by Pastor Guillremo Bono, who is the station general manager. It is operated under the name Radio Uncion ("Annointing"). The director of the station is Roberto Angarita, who is also co-pastor of the church. The station follows a religious format throughout its 24 hours of broadcasting.

The first radio station in Gwinnett was in the Buford area, beginning on the air on Nov. 7, 1956, as WDMF at 1460 AM. The original owners were David and Madeleine Fleagle. and the call letters reflected their initials. Bob Thomas, a Buford resident, operated the 1,000-watt station. In 1964, Jacqueline and Bob Joseph purchased the station from the Fleagles. They came to Buford from Paducah, Ky., where they had run a station for the Lackey family, who helped them buy the radio station in Buford. The Josephs, who were both from South Florida and had met at the University of Florida, soon bought out the Lackey interest.

The Josephs changed the name of the AM Buford station from WDMF to WDYX and boosted the signal to 5,000 watts in 1968. The Josephs started a 1,000-watt FM station, WGCO, on Jan. 1, 1970 at 102.3 FM, and soon were simulcasting the Buford AM and FM signals. In 1985, the FM station's call letters were changed to WLKQ, and boosted its signal to 3,000 watts with the station beginning to concentrate on Lake Lanier ("Lake 102").

The AM station was sold in 1990 to Sam Zammeron of Austell, who already owned WAOS (1600 AM) of Austell and beamed his signal at the Hispanic market. He changed the Buford AM station call letters to WXEM. Zammeron also owns a Gainesville radio station, WLBA, 1130 AM. All three stations are simulcast under the "La Favorita" theme.

In 2003, the Josephs got out of the broadcast business when they sold the FM station, WLQK, to Davis Broadcasting Company of Columbus. Davis converted the FM station to a Spanish format, aiming at the regional Mexican community. Davis brought in Bill Yeager, a 35-year veteran radio official, to be the station manager. He created the market's first Hispanic language FM radio station, transforming it into "La Raza," a regional Mexican station. Davis also moved the studios to an office building on Satellite Boulevard near Gwinnett Place Mall.

The company simulcasts the signal also out of WNSY, 100.1 FM, of Canton. That station has 25,000 watts of power and has the third highest rated Spanish signal in the Metro Atlanta market.

Other radio languages

There are two competing Korean language radio stations located in Gwinnett. One radio station, WFTD ("Radio Korea") is operated by Kun K. Park, a native of South Korea. Its offices are near the Duluth Library. In Korea, Mr. Park was a reporter for a daily newspaper, and immigrated to the States in 1996, to New Jersey, and came to the Atlanta area in 1997.

He leased radio station WPBC in Decatur in 2005, and broadcasts from 1310 AM. WPBC had 2,500 watts of power. Mr. Park kept this station until 2007, when he leased the 1080 AM WFTD, upgrading to a 50,000 watt station, which has a transmitter in Marietta.

Mr. Park's first venture in Gwinnett was in publishing, producing the weekly *Korean News Today* beginning in 2000. In 2007 that newspaper had a circulation of 8,000, and averages over 100 pages per issue. Most of the circulation is in the Metro Atlanta area, though 1,000 copies go principally to the states surrounding Georgia.

WFTD radio is primarily broadcast in the Korean language, and reaches up to 50,000 people per day, the station says. It broadcasts during the daytime hours, and features primarily talk and news shows.

There is another Korean station in Metro Atlanta, WPBC, which beams into Gwinnett, focusing on Christian programming.

Beginning in 2008, Gwinnett listeners could hear an Indian sub-continent radio station in Atlanta. On January 14, 2008, Spice Radio 1040 AM began broadcasting from quarters on Jimmy Carter Boulevard. The call letters are WPBS, and its tower is located in Conyers.

Called an "all day Desi radio station," it offered talk shows, top 40 countdown of Indian music, plus Bollywood information in syndication with Mumbai's radio stations, along with news, Hindi classics, and music from Pakistan, Bangladesh, Sri Lanka, and West Indies. Mark Premji is the owner and president of the station.

Other language newspapers

Several different language newspapers began to be distributed and printed out of Gwinnett with the rise in the minority populations.

With a major concentration of Korean people in Gwinnett, there are four daily Korean newspapers circulating in the county. Note this---there are four daily Korean newspapers! And these newspapers are not small, struggling operations, but often large, and owned by major Korean newspaper interests. Here's a survey of one day in the spring of 2008. *The Korea Daily* counted 80 pages, including 53 pages of advertising. It has a printing plant off Jimmy Carter Boulevard in Norcross. *The Donga Daily News* on Berkeley Lake Road in Duluth had 72 pages, of which 42 were advertising; and *The Atlanta Times*, on Buford Highway in Doraville, had 60 pages and 33 of these pages were advertising. The tabloid *Korean Daily News*, with offices on Steve Reynolds Boulevard in Duluth, had 80 pages, 41 of which were advertising. That's 252 pages geared toward the Korean community in Gwinnett being printed each day.

Many other foreign language publications circulate in the county, as different ethnic groups are well served by their own media. These publications have carved out their own section of the market, and are usually printed in the native language.

Hispanic newspapers

The growth of the Hispanic market has also created an opportunity for Hispanic newspapers in Gwinnett. Victoria Chacon, a native of Peru, began *La Vision* in 2002 as a five-day daily newspaper, printing 60,000 copies, averaging 36 pages, and circulating in the wider metro Atlanta area. The newspaper continued to publish as a daily until 2005, when immigration issues caused her advertising base to drop. It then became a weekly operation, publishing out of Norcross, with 40,000 copies, averaging 32 pages, printed each week. Mrs. Chacon, who has been in the United States for 20 years, also operates a contracting and janitorial service.

Diversity in politics

Diversity can also be seen in the politics of Georgia and Gwinnett. Gwinnett and most Southern counties in the first part of the 20th century were wall-to-wall Democratic, which meant that winning the Democratic Primary was tantamount to election. There was little organized Republican opposition throughout much of the South and few, if any, local Republican candidates on the ballots.

A little background: the economic development of the South was about to change many traditional ways of the area, as newcomers to the South from all over the nation did not always automatically vote Democratic. Though political change would come slowly, but it came as realities of the South changed.

The first crack in Georgia's Democratic political climate, which indicated a change might be underway, came in 1966. Segregationist Lester Maddox surprised a lot of people by winning the Democratic Primary runoff, and faced former Republican Congressman Howard "Bo" Callaway, the Republican nominee, in the General Election.

A former governer, Ellis Arnall, was something of a spoiler in the General Election. He had won a plurality in the Democratic Primary, but lost to Maddox in the runoff. When a number of Georgians wrote-in Arnall's name in the General Election, it caused a problem. Though Callaway scored the most votes, no candidate had a majority of votes to claim the governorship outright. Arnall's write-in effort had captured over five percent of the vote, Callaway received 46.5 percent of the total vote to Maddox's 46.2 percent in the Nov. 8, 1966 General Election. With no majority winner in the three-man race, Georgia law called for the selection of the governor to be decided by the Democratic Party-controlled Georgia Legislature, which picked the second place finisher, Maddox, by a vote of 182 to 66, to become governor. As much of the public, which had given the Republicans a plurality in the election, could yell, "Foul," Maddox was the duly elected governor, and served a remarkably good four years as governor.

(A total of 36 of the 228 Democratic legislators voted with the 30 Republicans for former Congressman Callaway. Ten legislators, including nine of the ten black members, did not vote for either man.)

But this race, which gave Georgia Republicans an inkling of what it would be like to win the governorship, produced new hope that the GOP might capture the state. For the next 36 years they would send an increasing number of their party faithful to the legislature. In 2002, this culminated with the Republican Party gaining control of the Senate. In the next election in 2004, the GOP won control of both houses of the General Assembly. And in addition, 38 years after Bo Callaway came close to being governor, the Republicans finally captured the governor's office, with the surprise election of the veterinarian, Dr. Sonny Perdue, over a sitting Democrat, Roy Barnes.

Changing politics

Meanwhile, just as state politics were changing, so were local politics in Gwinnett. The first Republican to hold office in the county was Louise Radloff, elected as a district member of the School Board in 1973. She was still serving on the Board in 2008.

The big change for diversity in politics in Gwinnett came in 1984, when 17 out of 17 Republicans seeking local offices won, with Gwinnett becoming virtually Republican territory since. (One Democrat, Probate Judge Alton Tucker, had no opposition, and was the only Democrat in Gwinnett to win that year.) No Democrat won any office in Gwinnett for the next 14 years, until a legislative candidate won a single seat in 1998. In 2007, only four legislative seats were held by Democrats in Gwinnett, with one of these seats held by a Hispanic-American. No Democrat has held a county wide local office since 1984.

Gwinnett's growth caused the change. From what was once a traditional stronghold of Democratic office holders and voters, people were moving in from other sections of the country who had different political leanings, or remembered that their parents had voted for Republicans. So, wary of local Democratic office holders principally because either they did not know them, or because they thought differently from the Democratic Party, these newcomers cast their votes for Republicans. While this trend line should have been obvious, the Democratic Party in Gwinnett was absolutely floored when they lost every local race in 1984. Some 24 years later, the Democratic Party was still gasping for air, though fielding more candidates. However, it probably will be at least several more elections before there will be a parity between Republicans and Democrats in Gwinnett.

Diversity in local restaurants

Another way that average Gwinnett citizens know the county is changing is in the variety of restaurants located within its borders. Up until the late-1970s, Gwinnett had only American-style restaurants, with little variety at that.

The first Chinese restaurant (North China on Jimmy Carter Boulevard, east of Interstate 85) came in 1977. Two years later, in Duluth, Acapulco became the first Mexican restaurant for Gwinnett. These two eateries were signs that big change was coming.

Since those first two ethnic restaurants opened, Gwinnett has become a mecca of food tastes from around the world, with perhaps the most extensive line-ups of restaurants in the state. No matter what type of food you want, it's available -- from spicy Latin dishes, to the heavier Eastern European (Polish, Czech) to African taste treats, coupled with about every Asian food style you can imagine.

The interesting aspect is that the typical Gwinnett native, raised in the fried chicken and potato salad of the South, or the recent move-ins, more used to Kentucky Fried than home-fried chicken, all have flocked to enjoy these new ethnic restaurants. Their arrival has offered Gwinnettians a menu of tastes not seen in the county before 1980, as such words as "tacos, pad thai and falafel" have become standards of the food offerings. It shows that with food, Gwinnett has also become diverse.

Diversity in labor

The make-up of the Gwinnett labor force is another way change can be seen. The shortage of skilled workers such as brick masons, house painters, roofers, gardeners, bulldozer operators, carpenters and landscapers, has been largely solved by people from other countries contributing their abilities to Gwinnett.

Contractors found they benefited from hiring these workers because of their hard work ethic and good attendance. It's to the point that the construction industry doesn't know how it can produce without these often newly-arrived artisans to keep the booming construction industry upright.

While the county is known for its fast resident population growth, the growth of the labor force has been just as spectacular. For instance, look at 10-year growth of the labor force. (Additional details in Appendix B, page 667.)

Year	*Persons in Labor Force*	*Percent Unemployed*
1973	36,432	2.5
1983	107,045	5.0
1993	245,231	4.3
2003	370,742	4.4
2007	421,912	3.8

The greatest concentration of jobs in Gwinnett is in a few key industries. Retail trade leads in number of jobs in the latest year detailed figures were available, for 2006, with 48,970 jobs. This is followed by administrative jobs, 31,381; wholesale trade, 30,931; local government, 27,129; hospitality, 27,123; manufacturing, 26,406; and construction, 24,147. There were, interestingly, 5,392 in computer and electronic product manufacturing, and 2,268 in the printing trades.

In 2006, the five largest private employers in Gwinnett were Ciba Vision, Gwinnett Hospital System, Kroger, Publix and Wal-Mart.

* * * * *

It's easy to make the conclusion: about any way you look at Gwinnett County, in 2008 you see nothing but a dramatically diverse county!

Gwinnett better get used to diversity, now and in the hereafter. As P.J. Woodall, interim rector at Christ Episcopal Church in Norcross, observed in 2008: "The diversity of heaven will be far greater than anything we earth-bound humans can possibly imagine. If we plan on going to heaven, let us begin now to embrace with rejoicing and love the gift of diversity that is in us in our time and place."

What makes Gwinnett unique?

Gwinnettians are proud of their county for many reasons. It's suburban, but near a larger city, while each area maintains a close, small-town identity in many areas. It's close enough for a quick getaway to the mountains, or just a few hours drive to the beaches. And while in the South, it enjoys a moderate climate because of its location about 1,100 feet above sea level. Its many cities give each area of the county its own marked differences.

Gwinnett is unique in many ways, as can be seen below.

- It is the most diverse county in the state with people within its borders from many lands. For instance, the Gwinnett School System teaches English as a Second Language to students from over 100 countries, from Afghanistan to Zimbabwe. More than 20 percent of households have their primary language other than English.

- Gwinnett has a solid school system, some say the best in Georgia, with high scores, high graduation rates, and teachers wanting to come to Gwinnett. Many people in Gwinnett will tell you they moved to the county to have their children in its excellent school system. As a result of having achieving students wanting to learn, Gwinnett hires the cream of the crop in new teachers, a minimum of 1,100 each year for the last five years. The school system is also the largest in Georgia, with nearly 160,000 students, and is the most diverse school system in the state.
- It has 15 cities, more than any county in Georgia, but most people (74 percent) live in unincorporated areas of the county.
- Gwinnett has a stable financial basis, and is one of a few counties in the nation with an AAA bond rating from all three rating houses in New York.
- Growth is the byword. Gwinnett has seen its population base jump from 32,250 people in 1950 to an estimated nearly 800,000 in 2008.
- The county has been through 60 years with a tremendous influx of new people, but maintained a stable, high-achieving and growing public school system, now the largest in Georgia, with more than 158,000 students.
- Gwinnett's government is a leader in technology in Georgia, gaining efficiencies and immediate input of information from up-to-date application of technology.
- Gwinnett has 14 modern community public libraries, with two more on the drawing board, with nearly 300,000 persons holding library cards. The oldest library building dates only to 1988. The system uses more than 800 computers for its clients and staff. More than 6.4 million items are checked out of the library each year. In 2000, the Gwinnett County Public Library was named the library of the year in the nation by Library Journal magazine!
- Gwinnett has a county wide parks and recreation authority, with 42 public parks with 8,611 acres of parkland/greenspace, plus parks in most of the county cities!
- Only Gwinnett and DeKalb Counties in Georgia provide a public, non-contracted ambulance transport system, responding to both emergency and scheduled calls.
- Gwinnett has a county wide police department, though several of its cities have their own police forces.
- Gwinnett maintains 2,700 miles of roadways, much of it paid for through SPLOST revenues of more than $1 billion in the 20 years since this one-cent tax on retail sales began.
- Gwinnett set the world standard for the cleansing of wastewater, and now operates the largest water treatment plant in Georgia. It is the only county in Georgia with a water intake into Lake Lanier, where it gets its raw water.
- Gwinnett has the largest fire service district in Georgia for the number of legal jurisdictions (13) under one fire department. It covers an area of 437 square miles.

- Gwinnett's Correctional Complex is the largest county-owned and operated correctional facility in Georgia, with beds for 800 inmates. Among services provided by inmate labor to the community: roadside cleaning, graffiti removal and recycling.
- Gwinnett's Recycling Bank produces 14,000 tons a year of scrap material, which includes plastic, paper, glass and aluminum.
- Gwinnett has within its borders three Community Improvement Districts, including Georgia's largest in geographical size and number of property owners.
- Once prime suburban farmland, with more than 400 dairies, Gwinnett had only 312 farms (2002), comprising 17,557 acres, with most now called "gentleman's farms."
- Gwinnett has more leadership programs guiding people to positions as leaders than any county in Georgia. First came the highly-successful Leadership Georgia program. Seeing its success, other programs began to teach leadership skills at other levels. These programs include Teachers as Leaders, the Neighborhood Leadership Institute, Gwinnett Student Leadership, and Senior Leadership Gwinnett.
- Gwinnett has a pro-active Chamber of Commerce, which embarked in 2007 on a five-year, $10 million community and economic development initiative, called Partnership Gwinnett. It seeks a net increase of 65,000 new jobs and $5.8 billion in new wealth for the county. No other county in Georgia has attempted such an ambitious program.
- In 2009, Gwinnett will add another element, when the Gwinnett Braves of the Class AAA International League bring minor league baseball to the county, in a specially-designed new facility on Georgia Highway 20. This will provide high-quality sports activity for family outings at affordable prices, in addition to minor league hockey at the Gwinnett Arena.

All these, and much more, are reasons that, as the water tower says on Interstate 85, "Gwinnett is Great!" Indeed, it's part of why "Success Lives Here."

Something extra

Flying out of LOX

There's more. There's so much more history about Gwinnett, though not all could be included because of a lack of time and space. Some of the stories are more like vignettes, and they don't fit into other sections as a neat package. These are just small snippets that paint their own pictures of the way life once was in Gwinnett. We wanted to include them, anticipating you would enjoy these tidbits.

Take for instance, Dean King of Loganville, a marvel if there ever was one. He had many talents, and was pleased to show them off, for instance, on an ancient 56-inch "high-wheeler" bicycle to the delight of crowds, all decked out handsomely, sometimes in an Uncle Sam outfit. He rode several times at Disneyworld, and at local parades in the Atlanta area.

In addition, Mr. King was also an aviation advocate, who learned to fly his own plane in 1956, and had a relatively-short, 1,410 foot take-off strip behind his home in Loganville, which he dubbed "LOX -- Loganville International Airport." It was within the city limits behind his home on the western edge of the city on O.J. Floyd Road. Watching him take off in his 1958 Piper-Tri Pacer on that short strip, a narrow, grassed strip between tall pecan trees, was a sight, as he taxied under a pecan tree to get in position to take off. He said in 1993: "I can usually get off the ground in 700 feet if I am alone, depending on the wind. It is the only airport I know where you take off and land under a tree." But landing was even more difficult as he neared the tall trees, and braked to a halt behind his house. The house had been built by his father-in-law, John W. Garrett, a former Loganville mayor who operated a store in Loganville and also built the first brick house in town in 1920, out of yellow brick.

Mr. King was a retired wedding and aerial photographer and was a Naval photographer in World War II. He got permission from Mr. Garrett to build the air strip. He also has landed routinely on a 1,600 air strip off Lake Burton in North Georgia. "It's on top of the mountain," he adds. He had several slogans taped to the instrument panel of his airplane: "Airplanes make flying much easier," and "We fly to places other airlines don't."

Sometimes Mr. King's neighbors would see him rev up the airplane engine, taxi a few yards, then turn around and rev the engine again. Was he about to take off? Mr. King's told his neighbors later: "No, I was blowing pecans off the trees." Afterward, he picked up three bushels of pecans, maintaining he "scared the pecans off."

Mr. King's family had an early interest in flying. Lawrenceville Attorney Jones Webb has a letter in his files to his brother, Albert, from none other than Orville Wright, to whom Albert King had written for some technical materials on flying. Mr. Wright, who had a simple "Dayton, Ohio" for an address when he wrote back in 1917, signed the letter "very truly yours," in a neat Spencerian signature that is quite legible.

Mr. King was a distinctive character. At his death at age 81, in 1996, the mayor of Loganville said he was the city's ambassador of good will. We remember him fondly. He was one of the many people who gave Gwinnett part of its vibrancy.

Farming as a way of life

Prior to World War II, farming was the most common way of life in Gwinnett. The key crop was cotton, though the county was also populated with dairy farms. Many people raised vegetables, trucking them into the major market in Atlanta.

Talk to many Gwinnett older natives, and they can tell you stories about farming. Bud Webb, who farmed off Webb Gin House Road between Lawrenceville and Snellville, first saw a cotton gin near his parents' home, "But that gin closed about 1918-19 when cotton prices were so low." He adds: "I can remember toting cotton to throw in the gin's press." He also remembers the Rocquemore Cotton Gin, in Lawrenceville on East Crogan Street where Kramlich's Supermarket would later be located. "Wagons would form in lines all the way back up the hill, to past what was later Johnson's Hardware, and nearly to the courthouse. There would be two lines at peak times. A bale of cotton could be ginned in about 20 minutes."

Mr. Webb remembers that in 1919-20, the boll weevil was destroying cotton crops. "Persons who were making 30 bales were making two bales of cotton." The weevil would return again and again to harm the crops. "Before the boll weevil hit, you could hear people say that the boll weevil couldn't make it across the Mississippi River, and we would be saved from it in Georgia. But that boll weevil could fly for 40 miles non-stop. People would use all sorts of things to try and stop the weevil, like putting out guinea hens, thinking they would eat the weevil. We used calcium arsenic to poison them, but that didn't work well. Only thing that worked to kill the weevil was the cold, for if it got to 10 degrees F., it would knock it out for the next year. I remember 1950 when it got down to zero. I said the next morning that we can raise cotton in the coming year, and that next summer we made 16 bales on about 15 acres. Back in those days, cotton was about the only crop you had you could count on. You might raise something like butterbeans, which we would take to the Atlanta Butler Street market, but you couldn't always count on what you would get for it."

At one point in his life, Mr. Webb went to the Ford assembly plant on Ponce de Leon Avenue, looking for work. "Henry Ford paid $5 a day then, and about 100 men stood in a vacant lot when I went down. The plant would send out men to hire day laborers, and would come and look over the crowd, and point to a man to come in and work that day. Then they would say, 'That's all we have today. Come back tomorrow.' I only went one time, and they didn't point to me. So I didn't go back any more."

Over the years, Mr. Webb worked a 30-acre farm, raising vegetables: beans, peas, corn, onion, cabbage, tomatoes, okra, potatoes. "I would sell a lot here at home, and take some to Atlanta. You can make the money on corn, on 'roastnears.' Last year I had an acre of corn, and sold it cheap for $1 a dozen ears. I couldn't get it up there to sell fast enough."

Frank Mattison

Frank Mattison of Duluth, who went to work in 1922 at Law and Pittard Company, a general store, remembers the old days. In the late 1930s, while working at the store, he would take payments for Georgia Power Company from local customers. "I would take the money, and deposit it into my own account at the bank. Then I would send the payment stubs to the company, writing them a personal check for the amount I collected." He began collecting for the telephone company in 1952, and for the gas company in 1953. Eventually these utilities opened their own offices in the area, and Mattison "turned the last one loose in 1967."

Mattison says: "We had three cotton gins in Duluth at the same time. One was on what is now Georgia Highway 120, where Kathryn Willis built her home. Another was up on Buford Highway, and another was behind the former Methodist Church, near Taylor Park, on the other side of town. Two were run by electricity, but the one near the Methodist Church was powered by a gasoline engine. Sometimes during the season the gins would run all night.

"People would average about one bale for every two acres, and the bales would weight 450-550 pounds. I've seen them sell a bale for $30. Many times, stores, like the one where I worked, would put up a bale of cotton as a prize, offering chances to everyone who spent money with us, getting a chance for every dollar of merchandise they bought. It was something for them to win that bale of cotton for the family (which they then sold)."

Mr. Mattison also remembers the bridging of the Chattahoochee River. "The first bridge in the area was Medlock Bridge, then came McClure, then Abbott and finally Rogers bridges. With flooding, the river was often difficult to cross. "I've seen flooding where you couldn't see the tassles in the corn stalks across that river bottom."

Gartrell Nash

Over in Lilburn, Gartrell Nash operated a store on U.S. Highway 29. He says: "They diagnosed me as having sleeping sickness in 1939, and because of that, they would not draft me. Even now, when I am still, I will drift off to sleep. As a result of my illness, I've had lots of wrecks. But a handicap can turn to a blessing. I had never held a public job. But I sold my automobile and bought a country store in 1945.

"We sold everything, meat and overalls and gasoline and horse collars. If someone wanted it, we would get it. I would sit in my rocking chair when things got slow, and doze off. People would wake me up to do business. Sometimes, they wanted to sell me their farm, and I didn't have any money to speak of, but sometimes, I would buy land. I've always known a bargain, but did not take borderline deals. For most of the bargains, you paid cash. As farmers sold out, I would buy land from them. I never knew much about timber, so we would clear the land, and my brother, Norris and I, would build a few houses."

Nash was part of an old-line family of Gwinnett. His great-grandfather, born in 1824, built a log house with red mud grouting and stone off what is now Killian Hill Road and Nantucket Way. Nash is one of four Nash brothers: Howard, retired from the post office; Gartrell; Norris, his business partner since 1945, and a former state representative; and Lamar, who at one time had an auto dealership, then a radio station, and finally an auto auction. They also had two sisters, Roberta, and Vernice, who died of rheumatic fever at age 36.

He adds: "In the older days, Lilburn was a cotton market, and that was about all it was. I remember when wagons pulled by mules would be backed up in every direction waiting for cotton to be ginned. When growing up, our family would make about a bale an acre. You could sell a bale for $25 in those days."

It was around 1975 that Lilburn began to grow. "We shut down the store in the 1970s. I tried to buy all the old buildings in old-town Lilburn. Most of them have been torn down. I helped keep the post office down there as long as it was affordable. I hope to have helped in some of the preservation."

Gartrell himself was mayor of Lilburn in 1968-69, and later served for 16 years on the city council. He holds a law degree, but has never practiced.

The Two Graces

The Buford community called them the "two Graces," Grace Harris and Grace Holland. They were quite a pair, and became friends because of sausage and roses.

Grace Reed Holland and her husband, E.J., produced pork sausage out of their home and workshop on Bogan Road. Grace and Cleve Harris lived in downtown Buford on Bona Avenue. She was a community activist before that term was in vogue, while he worked as a mechanic for more than 40 years with the Buford Chevrolet dealership, and after retiring there, was nearly 20 years with Lake Lanier Islands. He died in 1999 at the age of 90. The Hollands were white, and the Harrises were black.

Their love of flowers was the big inspiration that got the Graces together. They both had fine gardens, and shared secrets of making their roses even more stunning. They often supplied roses for various civic and church activities in Buford. Their roses were the best around.

Mrs. Harris was one-quarter Cherokee Indian and was born in Gainesville, where her mother worked at a cleaners, often doing mending of clothes. Grace Harris said she got a good education in town, including learning piano from professors at Brenau. She was proud to have been admitted to Spellman, but apparently did not matriculate. She was an attractive person, who always had nicely coiffed hair. Along with her pleasant personality, she was most gracious.

Her garden also was crammed with flower bushes, at one time having over 400 rose bushes. But there were azaleas, daylilies, peonies, iris and many other different plants in her garden. She particularly enjoyed rooting plants to create new ones, which she often gave away. She converted a sun porch into a greenhouse, complete with its gas furnace.

Cleve and Grace Harris

She gardened according to the environment. A side yard, a dry area, was all rocks and moss, with a few plants that loved sunshine. She advised: "You can get moss to grow on rocks if you pour buttermilk over the rock."

And she had distinctive views. On advice for gardeners, she once said: "Don't get a flowering quince. It will take over. Get a wild cherry tree instead, for it does well and looks good all the time." She was a member of the Poplar Hill Baptist Church, where she was the pianist-organist for over 50 years.

The two Graces met around 1960, when Grace and Cleve Harris visited Grace and E.J. Holland's sausage-processing plant. Grace Holland put it this way: "We just fell in love with each other immediately. We've been close ever since." Years later, after Cleve died, Grace Harris, who was living alone, told what happened each day: "At 8 a.m., on the dot, I get a call from Grace (Holland), to see how I am. She's wonderful."

Known particularly for their roses, the pair agrees with strong opinion on how to care for them. Grace Holland said: "If you have a tall bush, then cut it back in February to two or three feet. Then put Tree Kote dressing on the canes."

Grace Harris agreed with one exception: "In mid-Februry, when it starts to turn warm, cut them back. But I always use Elmer's Glue on the canes." She added : "Keep only the healthy canes. Don't leave those small canes."

On fertilizing, the two recommended: "Wait until at least the first of March," Mrs. Holland said. "I learned the hard way that you can't fertilize when you cut back the canes, for the bush will start putting out new growth, and a hard freeze will kill the plant."

The two Buford ladies' reputation with roses got them seen on the nationwide Home and Garden Network in 1996, as the show featured their flower-growing techniques. The pair got calls from all over the country after the show ran. They were also featured in a Public Broadcasting documentary entitled the "Amazing Graces."

Buford recognized the two Graces in 2001. Planted on the grounds of Buford Academy was an October Glory maple tree in honor of the two ladies.

Mrs. Harris died February 6, 2004, at age 90, and Mrs. Holland died August 4, 2008 at age 94. E.J. Holland is the only one of the quartet living when this book was completed.

Honoring veterans

The City of Duluth began a distinctive program in 1989 to honor veterans. What began as a small program has grown into a major remembrance of deceased veterans from Duluth, or a deceased veteran relative of a Duluth resident, who have served in the Armed Forces. It was the first city in the county to start such a program.

Twice a year, just before Memorial Day and Veteran's Day, the City of Duluth puts markers along the streets of the city with an American flag on it. Each marker lists the name of a deceased veteran and the war in which the veteran served. What started out with 12 veterans being honored, has grown into a program that put out over 650 markers in 2008.

The idea came from former Councilman O. J. Howell, who saw flags and markers in a small town in Alabama, Duluth Public Works Director Audrey Turner says. "He brought the idea back to Red Fowler, our former public works director, who designed the markers that are placed around town now. The original 12 markers were placed along the railroad between the tracks and parking lot near what is now the Red Clay Theatre. These original 12 are still placed each year, now near Taylor Park, which adjoins the Town Green."

The work is a major undertaking by the Public Works Department. It takes about a week to put out the markers, and another week to take them down. The Department also services each marker, to make sure that they stay in good condition.

Alton Tucker

From 1953-85, Alton Tucker was a judge of the court of the Ordinary, later termed the Probate Judge. His was a distinctive career, though not always in politics. He was well liked and so popular that, in 1984, when Republicans won every contested office in the county, Judge Tucker was the only Democratic official who did not draw opposition.

Judge Tucker was born in Alpharetta in 1910, where he lived until he was 11, when his family moved to Clermont. They would move to Sugar Hill in 1929. He began work in 1932 at Bona Allen in the cutting room of the shoe factory, "for 10 cents an hour for 55 hours a week, which was good wages back then," he maintained. At the factory, he moved up to timekeeper, then worked in adjustments and later handled sales of shoes to wholesale customers. He remained at the factory until 1941. From 1928 until 1942, he was appointed by the Grand Jury as a member of the Gwinnett Board of Education.

Judge Tucker remembered that a one-legged Sugar Hill barber, James Mercier, got the idea to incorporate Sugar Hill into a city. The judge says that the Southern Railway was paying school districts a tax, which went to the Sugar Hill Elementary School. "Buford had their eyes on that tax, and was thinking about incorporating Sugar Hill into Buford. Sugar Hill people thought that they might lose their school, so the move to incorporation got started."

Before the group took action, Tucker visited with John Allen, who ran the tannery where Tucker worked, asking if he had any problem with the idea of incorporation. "Mr. Allen told me that he didn't give a damn about that part of the county, though he owned land in Sugar Hill. So we went ahead with the incorporation, getting Marvin Allison to introduce legislation for it. All of this cost $6 or $7 to get a certified copy of the charter from the Secretary of State. One of the ideas in chartering was that there would be no taxes for several years, since we didn't need anything."

After incorporation, the city met in Mercier's barber shop regularly. At its first meeting, Tucker was elected as mayor, and served for two terms. He joined the Navy in 1944, was stationed at Bainbridge, Md., went across the North Atlantic in a convoy, and served off South Africa before being discharged nine months later. He was a helmsman on a destroyer escort. He feels he got that post since he was a little older than most of the crew.

After the war, Tucker sold cereal all over North Georgia for Kellogg. He first ran for the constitutional post of County Ordinary in 1948, but was defeated. He came back in 1952, won the office, and remained there until 1985, when he resigned, and his assistant, Sue Williams, became the Ordinary for the balance of his term. Judge Tucker died August 30, 1997.

Winder once in Gwinnett

Prior to 1914, Winder was located at the juncture of three counties---Gwinnett, Jackson, and Walton. Barrow County was created in 1914 by the Legislature "as a way of settling a dispute among the citizens of the City of Winder." The spot where the three counties met is commemorated today by a marker on the sidewalk across the street from the Barrow County courthouse. It was said that a man standing in Jackson County shot a man standing in Walton who fell dead in Gwinnett. It would have been a complicated prosecution.

The new county was named for David Crenshaw "Uncle Dave" Barrow, long-time chancellor of the University of Georgia. The city of Winder itself had been incorporated in 1893, after the Seaboard Air Line Railroad was built through the town. It was named after the president of the railroad, John H. Winder of North Carolina. The village was first known as Snodon, then Jug Tavern.

Summerour Family

A prominent family in the area of the Chattahoochee River were descendants of a German who immigrated to this country in 1742, a line that now goes back 10 generations. It is the line of the Summerour family, who have been in the Duluth area since 1903.

Heinrich Summerour was born in 1722 in Germany in what is believed to be Westphalia. A village there is named "Sommerau." Heinrich landed in Philadelphia, Pa. with his brother, Johan, and sister, Suzannah. He married in 1749, and moved to Lincoln County, N.C.

The second of three Henrys moved in the 1820s to Lumpkin County, Ga., preceding the gold rush. Later descendants would live in the Warsaw area of Milton County, and later, in Duluth.

Charles A. Summerour, born in 1875 in Warsaw, and his son, Knox Summerour, formed a tannery (C.A. Summerour and Sons) in Duluth, in 1934, similar to the Bona Allen Tannery. They produced leather harnesses, saddles, dog collars and similar goods, selling them to hardware dealers throughout the South. The factory, which employed about 25 people at one time, was located west of Duluth on Abbots Bridge Road. The factory was closed in 1986.

Meanwhile, other Summerours were doing well:

- Ben owned a cotton gin in Norcross, and later developed a hybrid cotton seed that sold well in the area. At one time he owned a farm where the Atlanta Athletic Club is now, and later owned a magnificent brick home in Norcross at 237 North Peachtree Street, which is still inhabited.
- Harrison had an extensive farm west of Duluth, and his father, Charles William before him, which was eventually purchased by Scott Hudgens, and became the Hudgens home in Duluth.
- Then there were the Summerour postmasters of Duluth. A Summerour held that post from 1922 until 1978. First came Frank, who was postmaster from 1922-44. He was born in 1884, the son of John Heard Summerour. Next in line was his first cousin, Heard, son of Charles William Summerour. He held the postmaster position from 1944-58, and he also chaired the Gwinnett School Board. Finally came Jay, the son of Heard, who was the postmaster from 1958-78, who was a local historian and authority on the life of Indians in the Chattahoochee River area.

At his death, the *News-Herald* editorial said of John Heard Summerour: "He went about, doing good." He also wrote, with his wife, a column for the newspaper. He was a charter member of the Duluth Lions Club, vice president of the Gwinnett Chamber, served on the Planning and Zoning Commission, and was for 35 years superintendent of the Duluth Baptist Church Sunday School.

Jay Summerour was a man of many talents, in history, in photography, traveling, and repairing items in his workshop. Prior to becoming postmaster, he was a railway postal clerk and postal transportation clerk. When he learned that the U.S. Open golf tournament would be held within his post office service area at the Atlanta Athletic Club in 1976, he led efforts to get a Bobby Jones commemorative stamp issued during the tournament. He also built the "Calamity Jane" (named after Bobby Jones' putter) post office for the tournament, since it was the Bi-Centennial year, and postmarked items in it from the tournament. The Post Office gave him its Bi-Centennial Award for this effort.

George Holcomb

The construction of roads is always a key element in the development of a community. Gwinnett would not have become a highly-developed county without I-85 bisecting it.

At one time, two lane roads were the standard. George Holcomb, a stalwart in the Buford community for years, recalls that when the Dept. of Transportation wanted to extend a highway north toward Gainesville, and come through Buford, the DOT initially got rebuffed.

"John Allen was against the state putting the road through downtown Buford. He thought it would be too much of a traffic jam on the Buford streets," Holcomb recalled.

Instead, Allen worked it out so that the highway alignment was east of town, the current location of Buford Highway and Georgia Highway 13. "It was one of the first bypasses around a town in this area," George noted.

Holcomb had first come to Buford in 1933 as a baseball player, after being a teacher. "I made $16 a week working for the Allens, though we played ball at least 2-3 days a week." He remembered one of the first lighted baseball parks in the country at Buford as one "with weak lights, where you got used to playing at night." But there were a lot of guys who struck out, "because of the lighting." Holcomb played on the team until 1938. He remembered one game where he laid down a bunt, the throw to first was wild, and he circled the bases to score. "Mr. Vic Allen told me to go get myself a pair of shoes for that one." He later played out West, and once when in North Dakota, found the opposing pitcher was Satchel Paige.

After three years in World War II military service in the Pacific, ending up in Honolulu, Holcomb worked with the War Assets Corporation at the former Ford assembly plant on Ponce de Leon Avenue in Atlanta disposing of surplus property. Later he was a contract administrator for ammunition for 15 years at the Macon (Ga.) Naval Ordnance Plant. His last job was with the Defense Supply Agency helping procure and deliver military supplies for the Vietnam war. He retired from the government after 39 years of service in 1970 and moved back to Buford. He then headed the Gwinnett Merit Board for five years. Later he was on the Gwinnett Housing Authority and the Gwinnett Industrial Development Authority.

Retirement haven?

Ever think of Gwinnett as a retirement haven? Tom Wages, in 1984, did not either. Tom ran a funeral home in Lawrenceville most of his life, and died in 2005 at age 81. As Tom's business grew, he recognized the growth of Snellville, which at that time did not have a funeral home, and built a handsome new facility on U.S. Highway 78 west of town. It happened to be directly across the road from Eternal Hills Cemetery, and people used to joke about Tom having a tunnel under the road, which he greased to slide coffins over to the cemetery. Tom would deny this to his death.

At the time the Snellville funeral home was being built, Wages was averaging about 300 funerals a year in Lawrenceville. He thought that in Snellville, perceived as a younger community, he would not hold so many services initially.

Tom performed 84 funerals in Snellville in his first year of operation. (His first year in Lawrenceville, in 1949, he had performed 87 funerals.) And then the number of funerals started to increase in Snellville, and eventually that chapel had surpassed Lawrenceville in services. He told people: "There's a lot of old people in Snellville!" That's when Tom realized and began telling people that Gwinnett was something of a retirement county.

What was happening is that with all its growth not only in Snellville, but all around Gwinnett, these young families moving into the county were having children. These families had come into the county from all over the United States, leaving their parents back in their home communities. And as babies were born to these families, the grandparents back in their previous communities wanted to see their grandchildren.

With many of these grandparents reaching retirement age, and many of them from the colder Northern climes, they began thinking of moving to warmer weather. Many started settling in Gwinnett (and other Metro Atlanta counties), to be near their children....and grandchildren. They left the rusting industrial communities of the North where their families had lived for generations, to move South. By moving, they established closer relationships with their children---and grandchildren.

After the initial migration of their children, the arrival of grandparents was an early indication of the diversity that Gwinnett would see in future years. As Gwinnett got closer to the 21st Century, instead of Northern accents of grandparents, the accents became international in scope, as people moved here from Africa, the Far East and India. Today Gwinnett is widely accepted as the most diverse county in Georgia, and one of the most diverse in the nation. Today hearing routine Southern accents in Gwinnett is about to become abnormal.

The growth of the senior population in Gwinnett can be seen in census figures. In 2000, 5.4 percent of the residents, or 31,599, were over age 65. By 2006, that figure was estimated by the American Community Survey at 5.9 percent over age 65, or 44,832 residents. There has been a steady increase in this older segment of the population, thanks both to the Gwinnett population being healthier and older, and through migration of seniors from other parts of the country.

Tom Wages, who died in 2005, would be beaming today, were he still alive, at the growth of his business overall, particularly in Snellville. In 2007, his Snellville funeral home counted 459 funeral services, while the Lawrenceville unit performed 312 services. And Tom had thought that Snellville was populated with mostly younger people!

Other Gwinnett publications

Starting in the Dacula area in 2002, the tabloid monthly *Neighborhood News* sought to concentrate on a single area, distributing to 5,000 homes in the Dacula and Hamilton Mill areas. Andy Forde of Braselton, had started a direct mail coupon book, and approached a friend from his church, Glenn Matlock, with the idea of starting a community newspaper. Matlock provided much of the editorial copy before joining Forde as a full partner in early 2003. By midyear, Matlock had bought Forde's share of the business. He was joined by his wife, Renee as associate publisher, to produce the newspaper.

By October, 2002, *Neighborhood News* added another 5,000 distribution with the Buford-Chateau Elan edition. And by February, 2003, three zones in the Lawrenceville-Collins Hill area added another 25,000 issues per month.

By 2007, the *Neighborhood News* zoned-publication concept was being distributed to 58,000 addresses in North Gwinnett, south Hall, west Barrow and South Jackson Counties. Areas covered in Gwinnett also included the Discover Mills and Sugarloaf Country Club.

Matlock brought experience from his years with the *Gwinnett Daily Post* and *Gwinnett Home Weekly*, first beginning at the *Home Weekly* in 1990. He is a native of Atlanta, and also worked previously on newspapers in Perry, Warner Robins and Hawkinsville.

Snellville Citizen

The Gwinnett Citizen has been published as a monthly newspaper since 1990. It began as the *Snellville Citizen*, but now goes to over 35,000 households throughout Gwinnett.

Co-editors and publishers of the Citizen are Carolyn E. Bagheri and her daughter, Auveed B. Cawthorn. Offices are on Scenic Highway in Lawrenceville.

Accent Gwinnett

Accent Gwinnett magazine was the brainchild of Gwinnett transplant Pam Ledbetter, and was founded in 2004 as a free, bi-monthly publication. Issues of the magazine feature articles written by local writers with a distinct perspectives as well as restaurant reviews, recipes, family segments, citizen spotlights, business/community focuses and a calendar of events. Within its glossy pages, readers will find original photography and articles relating to the past, present and future of Gwinnett.

The magazine is distributed via direct mail to 10,000 Gwinnett homes, and is available at 500 newstand locations, and at booths at trade shows and other local events. Issues of this full-color publication averages 64 pages.

Inside Gwinnett

Inside Gwinnett magazine was founded in 2002 by Rico Figliolini as a monthly community-oriented, and family-focused product. The magazine focuses on people, places and events in Norcross, Peachtree Corners, Berkeley Lake and the city of Duluth with approximately 20,000 circulation.

The magazine was launched with just 12 pages and a few advertisers. In the seven years, the magazine has grown to as many as 68 pages. It was purchased by Peachtree Corners resident Raymond Cobb in 2007. Editor is Janice Scott. One of the keys to its success has been providing the small business owner a vehicle to get their message to the residents in the immediate community.

Gwinnett Magazine

In 1997, the husband-and-wife team of David and Kelly Greer launched *Gwinnett Magazine*. Their goal was to produce a publication that reflected the rapidly-growing Gwinnett community. Starting with a home office and two employees, the business and lifestyle magazine thrived. By the end of its first decade, *Gwinnett Magazine* had doubled its annual page counts, tripled its revenue and quadrupled its staff size.

Gwinnett Magazine now reaches 100,000 readers with each issue and is Gwinnett's key business and lifestyle publication. The magazine has won several awards for design and writing. "I looked at *Gwinnett Magazine* more as a community-building project than a publication," David Greer says. "And it's one that hit close to home, since I'd been here all my life."

Gwinnett Business Journal

In 2003, David Greer, president of the Lawrenceville-based advertising agency, Tillman Allen Greer, created the *Gwinnett Business Journal*, which is aimed at Gwinnett's local business community. Advertising and readership grew steadily during the journal's first five years – a period that coincided with the county's own booming business community. As of 2008, *GBJ* has a monthly circulation of more than 18,000.

The *GBJ's* readership consists of corporate executives, small business owners, public officials, and civic and community leaders. The Journal features a mixture of local news and practical business advice. Each issue includes a Special Focus section devoted to subjects such as commercial real estate, technology and healthcare. The *GBJ* also publishes an annual "How To" issue in December, where local experts give a wide range of meaningful business advice.

GwinnettForum

Begun in 2001, *GwinnettForum* is an Internet-based forum of public opinion published twice weekly. The *Forum* is a moderated site (which means not allowing content in without close editing) about activities in and about Gwinnett and Georgia, published by Elliott Brack after his retirement from years of newspapering.

Major segments of the *Forum* in each issue include 500 words from a contributing writer, plus a 500 word column on various topics from Elliott Brack. Other elements include letters to the publication, and stories of significant Gwinnett activities. There are also book and restaurant recommendations, a Friday cartoon, a segment on Georgia history and a thought of the day. The *Forum* is free to subscribers who sign up, or may be read by anyone via the Internet. It is supported by Gwinnett businesses, who underwrite its production. A key feature of this publication is its archive of all items since inception, which can be easily accessed through an on-site search engine.

More Gwinnett vignettes

Early female postmaster

Lawrenceville had a female postmistress from about 1920 until 1933. She was Susie Dunnigan Sims, who was Republican, and appointed to office during the Republican administrations of that era. During those days, the post office was in the southwest corner of Pike and Perry Street. Mrs. Sims had two daughters, Elaine Martin and Elizabeth Smith.

Norcross Civic Improvement Club

The Norcross Civic Improvement Club was organized in 1916, seeking to promote better homes and gardens and every phase of civic improvement.

One of its first accomplishments was the creation of a "Railway Park" in 1917 at the cost of $36.20, which many said "added much to the beauty of our town and (railroad) station."

Over the years, it became a continuing source for civic improvement and focus of community projects, even winning cash prizes for exhibits at the Southeastern Fair for three years running, garnering the club a total of $300. Among its civic improvements was financing construction of the north gateway to Thrasher Park around 1924. It built its own clubhouse in 1930 at a cost of $2,000. Eventually the club went out of existence. Many former members joined the Norcross Garden Club, which today continues to work for civic beautification.

Three road names

Naming a road calls for creativity, which sometimes happens. As a result, unusual names can be created.

About the time that Gwinnett Place Mall was being built in the early 1980s, the county decided to extend Davidson Industrial Way from Beaver Ruin Road northward. But there was a hitch.

You see, Rich's Department Store, which had announced it was to locate a major outlet at the mall, didn't want an address with a similar name as its competitive department store, Davison's. As a result, the county was seeking to come up with a new name for the road that would go by the mall.

At that time, a company out of Cedar Rapids, Iowa, Collins Radio, had announced that it would build a plant to supply the government with rocket components at a location near Interstate 85. The entrance for the new firm would face the extension of Davidson Industrial Way, which needed the new name.

From this came the new road designation suggested by Collins Radio: Satellite Boulevard. It put smiles on the faces of the folks at Rich's. Meanwhile, before Satellite Boulevard was completed, Collins had become a subsidiary of Rockwell International, which was in 1996 purchased by Boeing Integrated Defense Systems. It retained the Duluth plant and was a key employer at the site until April 17, 2001, when Boeing transferred its operations to another state. The location is now the home of Cross Pointe Church.

Earlier, in the mid-1950s, another road needed a name. The road was a continuation of Beaver Ruin Road at Lawrenceville Highway southward toward Stone Mountain. The three county commissioners at that time were Weldon Archer, O.D. Cain and Paul Dover. Hence the name, taking the first two letters of each commissioner's last name: "Arcado."

Another county commissioner was involved in naming a street in a new section of Lawrenceville. The commissioner was chairman W.R. "Dudge" Pruitt, who was developing a subdivision off U.S. Highway 29 South, and named the street "Regal Drive." Why this name? Pruitt told us, "'Cause that was the name of the Scotch [Chivas Regal] I was drinking then."

Looking forward: Will growth ever end?

The unyielding growth that Gwinnett has experienced over the last half century will not continue at its past rate. Yet there's every indication that the county will continue to grow substantially over the next 10 years.

By the year 2020, it's reasonable to expect that Gwinnett will top one million people. It could happen sooner, since many factors are already in place to see fast, continued growth.

After all, there are concrete reasons that people are moving to Gwinnett. The county has good schools, a solid job base with more jobs added each year, and an attractive housing market. Of course, the major reason for Gwinnett's continued growth is its proximity to other areas of Metro Atlanta and the Hartsfield-Jackson International Airport.

Into this mix of reasons we must add one more that is sure to become increasingly important in the future of Gwinnett. That is the diversity of people now calling Gwinnett home. This aspect of Gwinnett life has exploded since 1990, as people have moved to Gwinnett from all parts of the world. The presence of this diverse population will only attract more minorities in the coming years. We have already seen how this influx has rapidly changed Gwinnett, giving additional layers of life to a community that only a few years ago was virtually homogenous.

There are also negative pressures that could affect Gwinnett. The key element for people within the Gwinnett community will be to absorb all the changes that come Gwinnett's way while maintaining a high quality of life. This means that unsavory elements, such as crime, must be checked. It means that homelessness must be addressed. It also suggests that Gwinnett must adopt and use measures, such as the Tax Allocation Districts, to make sure that no part of the county is blighted with unused and unattractive buildings or housing areas. The growing scarcity of developable open land in the built-up areas of Gwinnett will attract investors seeking to upgrade the county's real estate by redeveloping these areas and providing more attractive sites.

All the positive elements in Gwinnett must continue to thrive so that the people of Gwinnett find qualified, progressive candidates for public office, so that good government continues to flourish in Gwinnett. This will insure that the residents of Gwinnett continue to trust their leaders, giving approval to such ballot-box issues as the continuation of both the SPLOST and E-SPLOST sales taxes, therefore providing basic funding for expanded infrastructure of the county. This good government must be a key element in not only county operations, but in the running of the many Gwinnett cities, so that no single city "falls behind" and has any deterioration of its community or its services. The county could also benefit should a competitive two-party system begin to flourish in Gwinnett, rather than the old one-party system, first Democratic, then Republican, that has been the norm in the past.

Meanwhile, we have confidence that American industries will continue to find Gwinnett attractive and provide new jobs, pulled by a resourceful, innovative county. These new firms coming to Gwinnett will supply high caliber employment for the county, and boost the economy to new levels.

In Gwinnett's past, the single most important ingredient has been quality of the people native to the county. These have been resourceful, hard-working and God-fearing people, honest to their bones. They moved from their hardscrabble start in life, by hard work, into the modern life. They have been successful at what they have done, proud and accomplished, and have given Gwinnett its solid character.

Now, they are joined by people in Gwinnett from all over the world. These people, too, are successfully meeting difficult challenges, sometimes having to master the English language, and they are finding that, by determination, hard work and innovation, they can achieve a good life, too, in Gwinnett. The rich mixture of both natives and newcomers in Gwinnett gives Gwinnett its character and bodes well for the future.

So, to the question of "When will it end?" the answer is not any time soon. The people of Gwinnett are the reason the good life will continue in Gwinnett. In the next 50 years, Gwinnett is primed to become a major player not only in Georgia and the Southeast, but in the nation and the world.

About the Author

Elliott Brack is a native Georgian who grew up in Macon, Ga., graduated from Mercer University, and served for three-plus years as an officer in the U.S. Army in Germany. He obtained his master's degree from the University of Iowa.

He began his newspaper work in Macon as a carrier when 12 years old, and has worked in newspapers his entire life. He was publisher of the *Wayne County Press* in Jesup, Ga., vice president and general manager of the *Gwinnett Daily News*; and held a similar position with the *Marietta Daily Journal.* He retired after being the associate publisher of the Gwinnett section of *The Atlanta Journal and Constitution.* He is a former president of the Georgia Press Association. He has also been an adjunct assistant professor of journalism for 10 years at the University of Georgia.

He has lived in Gwinnett since 1974, and after retirement, began two Internet publications, *GwinnettForum* and *GeorgiaClips.*

He and his wife, the former Barbara London, a native of Arkansas, met in Macon. They have three adult children, Andy, in Charleston, S.C.; Betsy, in Durham, N.C., and Cathy, in Washington, D.C.; Andy and his wife, Courtenay, are parents of two daughters, Avery and Ellie Brack.

He and his wife live in Norcross and are communicants of Christ Episcopal Church. They enjoy a cabin on the Chestatee River above Dahlonega.

Bibliography

Sources

Baughman, John W., Freeman, Walter J., McCabe, Alice Smythe, and Stenhouse, Pamela Burton, editors, *Gwinnett County, Georgia: Families, 1818-2005,* Gwinnett Historical Society, 2008.

Baughman, John W., and McCabe, Alice S., *Gwinnett County, Georgia Schools, 1923*, a reprint, Gwinnett Historical Society, 1991.

Bellury, Philip Rob, editor, *Georgia Flight: The History of Aviation in Georgia*, Wm. Robb Group, LLC, 2007.

Bentley, Jane, and Bachtel, Douglas, *Growing Gwinnett: Changes and Challenges*, The Cooperative Extension Service, the University of Georgia, 1960.

Boatright, Susan, and Bachtel, Douglas, editors, *The Georgia County Guide,* The College of Agricultural and Environmental Sciences, University of Georgia, several editions.

Brack, Elliott, *Do You Know? 101 Facts about Gwinnett County*, The Atlanta Journal and Constitution, 1994.

Brack, Elliott, *The Internet Is Responsible for Linking Us with Phil Gwinnett,* GwinnettForum, 2008; Added material when taking Mr. Gwinnett on a tour of the county named for his ancestor.

Cates, *Donald W., Index to J.C. Flanigan's Volume II, History of Gwinnett County, 1818-1960,* 1959.

Corley, Minor, former Gwinnett Commissioner, Papers relating to Gwinnett government, from years 1957-64.

Coughlin, Robert David, *Lake Sidney Lanier, A Storybook Site*, RDC Productions, 1998.

Crapo, Irene Ewing, and Adams, Martha Miller, *Norcross*, Norcross Woman's Club, 1999.

Flanigan, J. C. *History of Gwinnett County, Georgia: 1818-1943, Volume I.* 1943. Reprint, Lawrenceville, Ga., Gwinnett Historical Society, 1995.

Flanigan, J. C. *History of Gwinnett County, Georgia: 1818-1960, Volume II.* 1959. Reprint, Lawrenceville, Ga., Gwinnett Historical Society, 1999.

Francis, Allen Philip, *A Compilation of Fact and Legend Pertaining to The History of Norcross in Gwinnett County, Georgia,* Norcross Woman's Club, 1967.

Freeman, David, *Carved in Stone, The History of Stone Mountain,* Mercer University Press, 1997.

Garrett, Franklin, *Atlanta and Environs: A Chronicle of Its People and Events*, Volumes I and II, Lewis Historical Publishing, 1954, University of Georgia Press, 1969

Gibson, Frank K., *A Study of The Government of Gwinnett County, Part I and Part II,* Institute of Law and Government and Institute of Community and Area Development, University of Georgia, 1963.

Grimes, *Millard, The Last Linotype, the Story of Georgia and Its Newspapers since World War II,* Mercer University Press and Georgia Press Association, 1985.

Gwinnett, Philip, *Someone Named Gwinnett,* GwinnettForum, 2008.

Henderson, James, *History of the Brand Banking Company*, 1905-2005, privately printed, 2005.

Jenkins, Charles Francis, *Button Gwinnett, Signer of the Declaration of Independence*, Doubleday, Page and Company, 1926.

Keimer, Harkness T., *Appraisal of Stone Mountain Property*, DeKalb County, Georgia, Atlanta, Ga. 1913.

Kirby, Bill, *Dynamic Gwinnett, Legacy, Life and Vision*, Gwinnett Chamber of Commerce (Longstreet Press), 1993.

Leroux, Marcia H., *The History and Development of the Lake Lanier Regional Library*, master's thesis, Emory University, 1968.

Long, Jesse, *Greater Atlanta Christian School, the Early Days, A Memoir*, DSI Press, 2008.

Long, Mary Frazier, *About Lawrenceville*, Southern Lions Books, 2008.

McCabe, Alice Smythe, editor, *Gwinnett County, Georgia Families, 1818-1968,* from Gwinnett Historical Society Inc., Cherokee Publishing, 1980.

Medlock, John C., *The Illustrated Legends of Norcross,* privately printed, 1983.

Miller, Gene, and Mackle, Barbara Jane, *83 Hours 'til Dawn.* Doubleday, 1971.

Moore, McHoyt, *The Big Shoe, As I Remember It*, privately printed, 2007.

Morgan, Handsel Grady, *Historic Buford*, City of Buford, 1993.

Pyle, Ernie, *Brave Men,* by, Henry Holt and Company, 1944.

Sawyer, Gordon, *Northeast Georgia, A History*, Arcadia Publishing, 2001.

Smith, Faye McDonald, *The Man from Modem*, Business Atlanta, October, 1984.

Stancil, W. Dorsey, *Vanishing Gwinnett, Gwinnett County, Georgia*, Gwinnett Historical Society Inc., 1984.

Stancil, W. Dorsey, *Vanishing Gwinnett II,* Gwinnett County Georgia, Gwinnett Historical Society Inc., 2001.

Other Materials

100th Anniversary booklet, Bona Allen Company, a Tandy Corporation Company, 1973.

Annual Report, Community Foundation of Northeast Georgia, 2007.

Feasibility Study for Proposed Minor League Ball Park, from Convention Sports and Leisure International, 2006.

Gwinnett County Airport, Master Plan, by Pegasus Associates International Inc. Project Team, 2006.

Gwinnett Daily News, archives on microfilm.

Gwinnett Daily Post, archives.

GwinnettForum.com, Archives, 2001-2008.

Log Book, Station No. 1, Gwinnett County Fire Department, 1973.

News, Gwinnett Community Foundation, Winter, 2001.

Newsletter, Georgia State Soil and Water Conservation committee and Soil and Water Conservation Districts, September, 1968.

Prehistoric and Historical Excavations at Site 9Gw347, Annistown Road Improvement Project, Gwinnett County, Georgia, by New South Associates Technical Report 560, October, 1998.

Scripts from Button Gwinnett Award Ceremonies, Quality Growth Council, various years.

Signals Today, Lucent Technologies, July 1997.

The Atlanta Journal and Constitution, archives.

The Story of Simpsonwood, DVD, North Georgia Conference of the United Methodist Church.

Vantress, Charles, *Chicken of Tomorrow*, DVD

PEACHTREE...
DON'T YOU MEAN
PITCHTREE?
McLemore

APPENDIX A

Many people helped in the formulation of this book. Some submitted material that was distinctive and complete unto itself, or which had been published previously. Here are presented several such items, with bylines of the authors submitting them. We appreciate their participation in this venture and their agreement to have this material published here.

Haynes Creek Primitive Baptist Church
By Sybil Deacon

Historical Outline of Lawrencville Female Seminary
Highlights of Dacula Banking Company, 1909-26

Talk to Buford Kiwanis About Joan Glancy Hospital
By Kate Parsons

Early Norcross History
By Mollie James Jones

Norcross in the 1940s
By Col. (Ret) Clifford Jones Jr.

Gwinnett County Fair History
By Bill Baughman

Cover Letter from Attorney John Mobley to Wayne Hill
Memo to Hill from Mobley on early days of Water System

Gwinnett County Public School History
By Nita Hallford

Condensed Gwinnett Police Dept. History
By Major Alan Doss

Dark Days For Gwinnett as Three Officers Murdered
By Major Alan Doss

Time Line of Western Electric Plant, Norcross

American Cancer Society in Gwinnett
By Phylecia Wilson

Time Line of Gwinnett Parks Acquisitions
By Grant Guess

The Larry Flynt Incident
By Bryant Huff

Haynes Creek Primitive Baptist Church

By Sybil Deacon

When pioneers began migrating to the area now designated as Gwinnett County, they established homes near the creeks and rivers. One of the large creeks that flowed for miles through Gwinnett, Walton and Rockdale counties was the Big Haynes Creek. As the creek moved through the southern part of the county, communities developed on either side of the stream. Chester was the name of one community established east of the creek. A wagon road led travelers south to a general merchandise store. Eventually the area became known as Rosebud and the store, Rosebud Store.

After establishing homes, families felt the need to have a place of worship. As churches were chartered, usually the first place they gathered was in the homes of its members. This was true of the people who chartered Haynes Creek Baptist Church on April 1, 1826.

Sybil Deacon

Much preparation went into planning for this day. Elders from other established churches in the county came to assist in the organization of the new church. Elder John Landers, moderator, and brethren Rice, Hooker and Williams from Rockbridge Church, brethren John Barrett, Morgan, and Chandler from Bay Creek Church (now Shiloh), and Elder John Bennett from Red Land Baptist Church at Lawrenceville attended the service. Elder John Bennett used as a text for his sermon the quote from the Bible, "Upon this rock I will build my house."

The following people were charter members of the church: Richard Hutchins, John Lambert, John S. Head, Joseph Morrow, Mary Carruth, Elizabeth Brand, Charity Hutchins, Elizabeth Tribble, Barbara Head, Mary Lambert.

Part of the business of that day was the writing of the constitution of Haynes Creek Church. The writing consisted of three handwritten pages that first addressed eight theological beliefs of the congregation. The second section listed seven statements called the gospel order, and the final section about decorum had fifteen directives.

The constitution ended with the following resolution:

Resolved that the institutions of the day called Benevolent, The Convention, Bible society, Temperance Society, Sunday School Union, Theological Seminary and all other institutions contributory to the missionary plan now existing in the United

> *States are unscriptural and that we as a church will not correspond with any church that is united with them nor will we hold in our union or fellowship any member that belongs to them.*
>
> *Also we will not fellowship any male or female who have been divorced having two living wives or the woman having two living husbands.*

The church members were expected to attend monthly services. If a male member was absent, he was expected to have a valid excuse. If a member had two absences, he received a visit from some church members.

In the church minutes given to the Gwinnett Historical Society and recorded on microfilm, the church had a conference on June 4, 1826. At that time members expressed a need for the following items required for the Lord's Supper: a sacrament cloth, tumblers and wine. A member, Brother Hanks, was to build a table for the sacraments.

The early minutes contain wrong doings of some of the members. They were reprimanded for drunkenness and card playing. One of the female members was taken out to talk to, but the matter was too delicate to put in the minutes.

In the middle and later part of the 1800s the Baptist churches developed divergent opinions concerning missions and other man- made additions to the church such as Sunday School, Seminaries and Temperance societies. Those churches that chose not to endorse the new philosophies became known as "old" churches and the others "new" church or Missionary Baptist churches. The "old churches" were known as Primitive Baptist. It is not definite when this movement occurred because of the distance between the churches and the lack of communication, but it was during this transition time that Haynes Creek became known as Haynes Creek Primitive Baptist Church. The word Primitive means original. These churches attempt to retain primitive or original practices of the church such as family style worship, a cappella singing and foot washing.

Slaves of members of the congregation attended services with their owners. In a listing of members in the middle 1800s there were approximately one hundred names and included were the names of four slaves-Jim, Oney, Jim and Bettie.

Although the church members did not endorse foreign missions, they believed in home mission work and worked tirelessly to help anyone in need. In the early 1900s there were many cases of tuberculosis in the area. People were afraid to go to the homes of those who had the disease, but people from Haynes Creek Primitive Baptist Church went in to help. One man who contracted tuberculosis lived in the area now known as Summit Chase. A member of the church visited him regularly and frequently sat up at night with the ill man. The next morning, without rest, the church member went to work. He did not develop the disease.

In the latter half of the 1800s, Haynes Creek Primitive Baptist Church flourished, and at one time had over one hundred members. It is at this time that the present church was erected. The building cost $975.89. One of the members at that time was E.M. Brand, who was the founder of Brand Banking Company. He gave $500 toward the construction costs. Today the beaded interior walls and ceilings are original. The pews are the hand-made ones used for over a hundred years. In the latter part of the 1900s the present building was renovated with the addition of electricity and indoor plumbing.

Men who lead the church are called Elders or Pastors. They do not use Reverend before their names. These men receive training for this position through mentoring by another man of the church. They do not go to seminary or have formal training.

Many men have served as pastors of Haynes Creek Primitive Baptist Church. The following is a partial listing of these leaders: Elder John Landers, 1826-1831; Elder R. Chandler, 1831-1835; Elder William Lacy, 1835-1836; Elder Benjamin Still, 1836-1837; Elder Kinchin Rambo, 1837-1839; Elder Ellijah Moore, 1840-1842; Elder Alfred R. Smith, 1842-1849; Elder B.B. Shaw, 1849-1863; Elder William D. Almond, 1863-1903; Elder A.J. Webb, 1903-1906; Elder J.B. Brown, 1906-1907; Elder J.F. Alford, 1907-1911; Elder Josiah James, 1911-1930; Elder J.C. Hewett, 1930-1947; Elder T.L Huff, 1947- unknown. Elder Ernest Wade, 1958-1962. Today Elder E.H. Gunter of North Carolina leads the congregation and has done so since 1978.

When the congregation was larger, the men sat on one side of the altar in what was called the "Amen" corner. The older women sat on the opposite side. Younger mothers with their children and visitors sat in the center section of the sanctuary.

Music in the church is a cappella, which means the members have no instruments to accompany their singing. The small hymnals used contain only lyrics. The hymnals have changed little since the church began.

The church believes immersion is the only accepted method of baptism. Since the church was chartered, baptisms have been in the creek that runs in front of the church. During the 1900s, a section of the creek was damned up to provide a baptismal pool. Baptisms are held soon after a person "found the door open for the reception of his membership." Mrs. Nell Foster recalls one baptism held in October. Those observing were shivering from the chill of the fall day. The person being baptized and the elder were standing in cold creek water. When Eunice Brooks Wade joined the church, her husband, Ernest Wade, was the leader baptizing. Mrs. Wade was dressed all in white. Her husband recalled that time frequently and said Eunice looked like an angel walking toward him that day.

When the church had conference or hosted the association of other Baptist churches, dinner was served "on the ground." Early on in the life of Haynes Creek, families spread their food picnic style just for their immediate families. Some of the leaders of the church felt this isolationist policy was not an appropriate way for Christians to treat each other, and the men of the church built a large table under the trees where everyone spread their food together.

Before the days of automobiles, people drove their carriages, wagons and buggies to church. They hitched their mules and horses to trees in the yard and went into the lengthy service. After several hours the animals began feeling the need for food and water; the mules, particularly, would begin disruptive braying. This ruckus served as a message to the speaker that he had preached long enough!

At the time of this writing the church has only seven members. Most of them have been members for decades. Services are held at 2:30 p.m. the third Saturday and at 11a.m. the following morning. Pastor E.H. Gunter comes from North Carolina to lead the service.

A copy of the Constitution of Haynes Creek Baptist Church written on April 1, 1826 is on file in the office of the Snellville Historical Society and is available for anyone desiring to read it.

Haynes Creek Primitive Baptist Church

Haynes Creek Cemetery

As one travels south on Rosebud Road at a sharp bend in the road, a white framed church and a large cemetery appear on the right. This is Haynes Creek Primitive Baptist Church and Haynes Creek Cemetery.

Near the time Haynes Creek Baptist Church was chartered, Haynes Creek Cemetery was established behind the church for the use of any resident of the community. Mariah Rutledge who died in the 1820s is reported to be the first person buried in the cemetery. There are several markers in the graveyard with birthdates in the 1700s.

There is one special marker for John Rutledge who was a veteran of the Revolutionary War. The marker reads "John Rutledge, Pvt., 2 Georgia Bn., Rev. W."

Although all have not been identified, there are many veterans buried at Haynes Creek Cemetery besides John Rutledge from the Revolutionary War. There are four identified Confederate States of America soldiers, six from World War I, fifteen from World War II, three from the Korean War, and two from the Vietnam War.

Slaves are buried in one section of the cemetery.

Mounted in the cemetery is a bell that was given by the E.M. Brand family around 1910. In the early days the bell ringing was a summons for people to come and help dig a grave. In the quiet countryside the sound of the bell tolling could be heard for miles. The bell was never used in association with the church.

The cemetery covers seven and a half acres and has approximately 3000 gravesites. As of this writing, there are 1,164 burials.

In 1947, members of the community established the Haynes Creek Cemetery Committee. The committee's main objectives are maintaining the gravesites and identifying unmarked graves. At this time the committee is diligently working to complete a survey of the unmarked graves. They want to build a monument that will list the names of people known to be buried in this cemetery but who lack a formal marker. A plat of the grounds and this memorial will be placed near the front of the cemetery.

As they worked on the surveying, the committee members divided the cemetery into four sections. Section 1 is the oldest section and contains many unmarked graves. Graves in this section are marked only by a rock placed at each end of the grave.

Since the first burials, the community had workdays at the cemetery to clear the graves of weeds and debris, but descendants of those buried there felt that more attention should be given to the area.

In 1947 the committee provided a home for a caretaker for the cemetery. The building was located on the southern side of the church. This service is no longer provided. The committee now sponsors two workdays a year, one in the spring and another in the fall, although people are encouraged to remove old flowers throughout the year. The committee is encouraging owners of gravesites to put coping around their lots.

Each spring, the committee sponsors a Memorial Service for people who died the past year and were buried in the Haynes Creek Cemetery.

The committee is experiencing difficulty accomplishing their objective of identifying the unmarked graves. Members encourage anyone who knows of someone buried in one of these graves to contact a member of the committee. Larry Rutledge of Snellville is the chairman.

Since the early 1800s, this cemetery has been an important aspect of life of people who live in the area, and with the commitment of the fifteen members of the Haynes Creek Cemetery Committee it will continue to serve the community for generations to come.

Historical Outline of the Lawrenceville Female Seminary

(Note: the following historical outline was provided by the Lawrenceville Female Seminary. The author of this article is unknown.)

In the 19th century, the words "seminary" and "college" were used to describe schools at a variety of levels. A "college" might give instruction either to university students, or to those of high school age and even younger. A "seminary" could be a preparatory school, or offer a college education or graduate and professional training. The idea of a "college" for women was horrifying to many people in the 1830s. Seminaries were educational institutions that provided young women with an education comparable to that of college-educated young men. At the time of the seminary's founding, women were barred from colleges. Although academies for girls existed, their curricula were limited to such "female arts" as conversational French and embroidery.

The Female Seminary in Lawrenceville
From 1978 Structural Survey of Gwinnett County--Historic Preservation Section, Georgia Dept. of Natural Resources (Gwinnett Historical Society Collection)

Circa 1836 – 1838

The town of Lawrenceville was incorporated in 1821, and by the late 1830s the citizens of the county were beginning to feel that their county had changed from a rough frontier outpost, to something a little more settled. In keeping with this image, the leading citizens felt that it was necessary to provide a school for the young ladies of the county. Therefore, the Georgia General Assembly incorporated the Lawrenceville Female Seminary in 1837 and Daniel Killian, general contractor, erected a building. The building was completed on July 31, 1838, and the doors first opened on September 24, 1838.

The Female Seminary served as a finishing school for the young ladies from surrounding farms, as well as for the daughters of merchants, attorneys, and doctors in the area. It served as an alternative for girls who were typically educated at home. In the beginning, the girls paid $12 a year for instruction in Spelling, Reading, Writing and Common Arithmetic; $20 a year for English Grammar, Geography, History, Moral Philosophy, Rhetoric; and $30 a year for Latin, Greek, Algebra, and Geometry, or Natural Philosophy, Chemistry, and Astronomy. In addition to the initial fee, parents were required to supply one cord of wood for every four pupils, one-fourth of which had to be light wood, used to heat the school room during the winter months.

Miss Martha Wells served as the school's first teacher, as well as the first principal. However, as was typical in this period of history, the teachers were overwhelmingly male in number at the Seminary. Among those who taught at the school were:

George B. Atkisson
Miss Sophia Bliss
Rev. George Bright
Dr. Alexander B. Brumby
Rev. Mr. Downing
W.R. Grey
W.W. Griffin
Rev. J. Lawrence King
Mrs. J. Lawrence King
Rev. J.F. McClellan
R.E. Mitchell
James T. Newton
Rev. James Rosamond
Rev. William C. Smith
Ambrose Spencer, Jr.
Miss Maggie Stewart
Rev. William H. Strickland
William Wallace
Lyman F. Wilcox
Miss L.R. Williams
Rev. William M. Winn

December 14, 1847

The trustees of both the Lawrenceville Female Seminary and the Lawrenceville Male Academy agreed that both schools be united and given to one person. Uniform tuition rates and books were shortly voted on. It is unclear in records how long this agreement lasted.

October 1850 – July 1851

A fire destroyed the original Female Seminary building.

July 2, 1853

An apparent lack of concern delayed the construction of a new school building until 1853. The trustees entered debate as to how to rebuild the Seminary, ending with the decision to build a structure of "wood – one story high and of the original size – with three rooms." Concurrently, they resolved to allow the Lawrenceville Masonic Lodge, No. 131, founded in Lawrenceville in 1850, "to build a lodge room on the new building above the proposed. The Lodge paying all the increased cost of building in consequence thereof." The only conclusion one can draw is that the Masons were intimately involved in determining the size and use of the present building from the time it was built to replace the earlier structure. The minutes mention, however, of "disposing of the old brick," so was the original structure brick, or was this referring to the foundation? The trustees and the Masons later changed their minds and decided to use brick in construction rather than wood.

The girls were instructed on the bottom floor of the new Greek-Revival building and the Masons held their meetings on the top floor, acting as the caretakers of the Seminary building. The principal's office was on the top floor, as well, just to the right of the stairs.

The Masons acquired purchasing rights in 1853. Copies of the transaction were lost in the fire, which destroyed the original Gwinnett County Courthouse on September 10, 1871, so the sale date is an approximation.

Circa 1856

Apparently, boys were attending classes at the Seminary, which must have finally caused a stir, for the minutes of December 16, 1856 excluded all boys regardless of age.

March 1862

According to the minutes, males were permitted to attend regardless of age during the 1862 school year. The reason stated that the Lawrenceville Male Academy had not yet acquired a teacher for the school year and, "Whereas from the distracted and deranged condition of our County (due to the Civil War) the said Seminary will have but comparative few female scholars during the said year (March 8, 1862)."

October 1862

Enoch Steadman, a wealthy Gwinnett County Citizen, offered to pay $150 due for construction of the building if the school will prohibit boys over 10 years old from attending; the board accepted. However, it appears through the rest of the decade, they waffled on this issue. They seemed to react to whatever the Male Academy was doing. If the Male Academy were excluding females, then the Seminary would exclude Males over 10. If the Male Academy were admitting females, then the Seminary would vote to accept males of any age.

June 9, 1873

During recess time, a sudden thunderstorm rolled into the area. Seeing the dark clouds, a group of a dozen schoolgirls ran for cover towards the outhouse, but by the time they had all reached it, a deadly bolt of lightening hit the play yard. Antoinette Roberts was killed instantly; Ada Wilson died 19 months later; and Mary Jeanette Hood died of complications 3 ½ years later. Ten other girls were also injured. Dr. Mitchell, Dr. Shaffer, and Dr. O'Kelly all gave quick medical attention. The principal at this time was George B. Atkisson and the Assistant Principal was Miss Maggie Stewart.

July 1876

For "Grossly immoral conduct," Dr. Alexander B. Brumby was suspended as principal, after teaching for the Spring term only.

November 1879

The trustees asked the principal to keep the sexes separated "as much as practicable" and gave them separate hours for recreation.

November 1885

From annual report given by Professor James T. Newton it shows how commonplace child deaths were in this era. "It is with gratitude that I can report only one death in my school this year and very little sickness."

1888

It seems the building's function as a school for girls ceased. It was then used as the Hi-Hope School for Retarded Children. The Seminary building was then used over the next half-century as a "civic center" for the community, frequently housing Kiwanis and Lion Club meetings and dinners, as well as meetings for various garden clubs, historical organizations, the PTA, and the United Daughters of the Confederacy. At one time, a music studio made use of the former schoolroom space.

July 6, 1938

Gov. E.D. Rivers dedicated the Lawrenceville Masonic Lodge playground on the lawn to the right of the Seminary building. The marker was later moved to the edge of the concrete patio at the back of the building. Local citizens remember that a tennis court was on the southeast corner and a ball field in the east side (back).

1971

The Lawrenceville Female Seminary building was nominated by the Georgia Historical Commission and listed on the National Register of Historic Places following a heated debate as to whether the structure should be torn down to make room for a Dairy Queen franchise.

1972

The Gwinnett County Board of Commissioners purchased the building from the Lawrenceville Masonic Lodge No. 131.

January 20, 1973

The Gwinnett Historical Restoration and Preservation Board was appointed by the Gwinnett County Board of Commissioners to restore and preserve the history of Gwinnett County in cooperation with the Gwinnett Historical Society and other historical organizations. Their first project was the preservation and restoration of the Lawrenceville Female Seminary building which was made possible through the 50-50 matching grant secured through a U.S. Department of Housing and Urban Development's Federal Open Air Grant. The price of acquisition and restoration was $113,216.00. Half of this came from HUD ($61,000.00), the other half was raised locally. The goal was to restore the building as nearly as possible to its original state. The restoration work lasted about thirty weeks, under the supervision of restoration architect, Mrs. Gloria Kidd Brown.

The restoration uncovered various findings:

- Plastered walls, shed of years of paint, revealed penciled inscriptions of names, dates, and memories of long ago. One of the oldest dates seen on the restored walls comes from 1862. This has been preserved and can be found on the second floor foyer.
- Green paint was removed in the schoolroom downstairs to reveal an old blackboard – 1/8th of an inch thick and as "hard as concrete." Note the smooth texture of the slate – it is a remarkable example of the workmanship, which produced it.
- A foreman noted that the lumber for the building was "hand-dressed" (sawed with up and down strokes, rather than with the modern circular saws of today). Also, the original pine floors remain mostly intact throughout the building.
- The roof was repaired and a steeple was constructed to house the original bell.
- The corner of a second-story windowsill has century old iron tiebacks for the shutters. The original hinges on the doors and shutters remain intact.
- The building was constructed of brick with walls twelve inches thick.
- 75 percent of the glass panes in the windows are original to the building, which can be detected in the little imperfections in the glass.
- Original receded mantelpieces, which contain little cuts thought to have been made by little boys while the teacher wasn't looking.
- A Federal fanlight over the front door on Perry Street was discovered.

Also, the grounds surrounding the Seminary were planned so as to use nothing but shrubbery used in the 1850s. The lot contains magnolias, dogwoods and pine trees, and an area off to the back of the building contains a brick patio shaded by a mighty Southern red oak tree. The Garden Club Council Extension Horticulturalist, T.G. Williams, provided the work and landscape architect at the University of Georgia, Bill Baughman, created detailed plans for the restoration of the grounds.

September 9, 1974

The restored Lawrenceville Female Seminary building and grounds were officially reopened. Today, it is one of the oldest and most treasured historic buildings in Gwinnett County and houses the Gwinnett History Museum on the second floor.

Highlights from

Dacula Banking Company, 1909-1926

The first annual meeting of the 27 stockholders (names listed at last of article) of the Dacula Banking Company met on September 27, 1909, and thereafter annually. A copy of the by-laws and minutes from each monthly meeting of the Directors of the Bank has been found. The capital started out with $25,000, $21,000 of which was deposited on the first day.

Directors were T.A. Maynard, W.T. Hinton, E.G. Hogan, G.W. Sikes, A.M. Wilson, R.M. Stanley, S.E. Pharr and J.M. Wilson. At the first meeting, the elected officers were: A.M. Wilson, President; W.T. Hinton, Vice-President; James M. Wilson, Secretary.

B. Ambrose was elected cashier at a salary of $50.00 per month. Salary of President was fixed at $300 per year.

October 4, 1909: The Board of Directors met and approved that the Bank buy an adding machine at the cost of $200 with a guarantee for one year.

November 1, 1909: The Directors called for $1500 for the cost of building, and insured the bank building for $750. A separate motion was made and carried to buy one dozen chairs and a table.

December 1, 1909: The Directors ordered to pay Leonard Hinton $7.50 for work done for the Bank and to buy some suitable advertising.

July 1, 1910: The Directors elected J.G. Hood, age 44, as cashier, since B. Ambrose had tendered his resignation. B. Ambrose was voted to fill out the unexpired term of G.W. Sikes as Director. Directors were elected to serve for the second year. The directors ordered the Perry-Rainey College note be extended.

May 31, 1911: A motion carried that A.M. Wilson and B. Ambrose assist in auditing the books with Guy Kilgore, and found them correctly kept. Dr. W.T. Hinton gave an interesting report on a meeting of the Bankers Association at Savannah, Georgia which he attended.

March 27, 1912: The Directors motion to pay dividends of 4% to the stockholders out of surplus funds. Motion to thank J.G. Hood for good showing made in last 6 months for his earnest efforts. Directors voted to pay C. Hood $750 per year and ordered cashier that all past due papers be renewed or paid as soon as possible.

September 23, 1914: The Board re-elected the same officers and salaries, including a motion that each Director to be paid $1.00 for each regular meeting he attended.

January 5, 1917: Directors moved to pay cashier J.G. Hood $1350.00 salary from October 1917 until October 1918.

September 25, 1918: Directors moved and carried that they elect same officers for year and include J.V. Hood (23 years of age and son of J.G. Hood) assistant cashier at a salary for both Hoods of $125.00 per month. Directors moved in year 1919 to 1920 to increase Hood's salary to $150 per month. Of interest is the expense account for June 1922:

June 1 – cashier salary: $150
June 2 – Revenue stamp note: $2.60
June 6 – Postage: $0.50
June 13 – Express on stationary: $2.66
June 14 – T.R. Bennett for report: $3.00
June 15 – T.R. Bennett special exam: $25.00
June 16 – making door key: $0.50
June 16 –Telephone to Atlanta: $0.35
June 17 – Bill stationary Geo Barnard: $20.22
June 22 – P.O. Box Rent: $0.25
June 22 – Telephone to Atlanta: $0.45
June 26 – One Broom: $0.65

February 22, 1922: A meeting of the stockholders was held for the purpose of reorganizing the bank by election of a new set of Directors. A.M. Wilson and J.M. Wilson tendered their resignation as Directors; this was accepted. The following gentlemen were unanimously elected: C.R. Ware, President, salary of $500 per year; Dr. B.V. Wilson, Vice-President; J.G. Hood, Secretary and Cashier.

August 23, 1922: A motion was carried to make application for membership in Federal Reserve Bank and an examiner for Federal Reserve Bank came and made an audit.

December 31, 1924: A motion was carried to elect the same board for the coming year.

Letter of criticism from Mr. T.R. Bennett, Superintendent of Banks, was read. In reply, the minutes read: "We as directors are doing our best to arrange the past due notes and get them in proper shape."

November 24, 1926: C.R. Ware tendered his resignation as President.

December 16, 1926: The Directors of the Dacula Banking Company held a special meeting in the office of the bank. The following named Directors were present: J.H. Hamilton, J.G. Hood, E.G. Hogan, R.M. Stanley, Claud Hinton and C.R. Ware. Owing to the low price of cotton and very poor collections, the directors decided that it was advisable to close the Bank and go into voluntary liquidation. On examination of the books, it was discovered that the Bank was short a sum of $9000 to pay the depositors of the Bank in full. It was therefore moved that a voluntary assessment of $75 a share be placed upon the stockholders in order to raise the $9000 needed. The motion was carried. The resignation of C.R. Ware at the last meeting was accepted, and J.H. Hamilton was elected President. It was also moved and carried that the First National Bank of Lawrenceville would be appointed agent for the Dacula Bank to pay depositors and to liquidate the business of the Bank.

January 23, 1929: The Directors of Dacula bank met in the office of First National Bank of Lawrenceville. Members of the Board present were H.J. Hinton, J.H. Hamilton, J.G. Hood and R.M. Stanley. Motion was made and seconded to authorize C.R. Ware as Liquidating Agent to finalize the business of debts, loans and deeds.

H.J. Hinton moved that C.R. Ware be authorized to sell the Banking House, vault and vault door for the sum of $1250 in cash. It was also moved that C.R. Ware be authorized to accept any reasonable compromise on any notes belonging to Dacula Bank, noting that he exercise his best judgment and advise the Federal Reserve Bank of Atlanta of compromises he deemed to be good business. This was the last meeting recorded in the Bank.

Stock represented as follows – September 1909

Name	Shares
T. A. Maynard	20
G.W. Sikes	10
R. M. Stanley	10
W. T. Hinton	14
S. E. Pharr & brother	10
S. G. Hinton	5
J. N. Williams	5
B. Ambrose	5
G. P. Craig	10
J. A. Moore	5
E. R. and R. E. Neill	5
Bob Bradford	1
Wilsons	100
J. L. Sims	3
J. G. Hood	2
E. S. Wages	2
J. W. Hamilton	2
J. H. Hamilton	2
J. B. Freeman	2
J. E. Kilgore	2
E. S. Ethridge	1
E. F. McAdams	1
J. C. Pool	1
J. T. Greeson	1
J. C. Wall	1
William McDaniel	1

Highlights from Dacula Banking Company, 1909-1926

(Note: In the modern day, the fine art of penmanship has virtually disappeared. Less than 100 years ago, the free-flowing Spencerian penmanship was a standard of many teachers, both beautiful and easily read. To recall those days, we're presenting a copy of minutes of the Dacula Banking Company (above), produced by Martha Hood Hutchins. People in years to come will have no trouble in reading this information, since the penmanship is so legible. We present it to show the high art of fine penmanship, and at the same time, lament its passing. –eeb)

(1)

Highlights from Dacula Banking Company
1909-1926

The first annual meeting of the 27 stockholders (names listed at the last of article) of a corporation of Dacula Banking Company meet on September 27, 1909 and annually thereafter. a copy of the By Laws and minutes from each monthly meeting of the Directors of the Bank has been found. The capital started out with $25,000 — deposites the first day was $21,000.

Directors were T. A. Maynard, W. T. Hinton, E. G. Hogan, G. W. Sikes, A. M. Wilson, R. M. Stanley, S. E. Phurr and J. M. Wilson. At the first meeting elected officers were:

A. M. Wilson, President
W. T. Hinton, Vice President
James M. Wilson, Secretary

B. Ambrose was elected Cashier at a salary of $50.00 per month. Salary of President was fixed at $300 per year.

On October 4, 1909 the Board of Directors met and approved that the Bank buy an adding Machine at the cost of $200 with guarantee for one year.

On November 1, 1909 the Directors called for cost of building to be $1500.00 and insured the bank building

(2)

for $750 and motion made and carried to buy one dozen chairs and a table.

December 1, 1909 Directors ordered to pay Leonard Hinton $7.50 for work done for bank and buy some suitable advertising.

July 1, 1910 the Directors elected J. G. Hood, age 44, Cashier as B Ambrose had tendered his resignation. B Ambrose was voted to fill out the unexpired term of G. W. Sikes as Director. Directors were elected to serve for the second year. Directors ordered the Perry - Rainey College note be extended.

On May 31, 1911 motion carried that A. M. Wilson and B. Ambrose assist in auditing the books with Guy Kilgore and found them correctly kept. Interesting report from representive, Dr W. T. Hinton who attended Bankers Assoc. at Savannah, Ga.

March 27, 1912 - Directors motion to pay dividends of 4% to the stock-holders out of surplus funds. Motion to thank J. G. Hood for good showing made in last 6 months for his ernest efforts. Directors voted to pay Cashier Hood $750 per year

(3)

and ordered cashier that all past due papers be renewed or paid as soon as possible.

On September 23, 1914 relected the same officers and salaries included each Director to be paid $1.00 for each regular meeting he attended.

On January 5, 1917 Directors moved to pay Cashier J.G Hood $1350.00 salary from Oct, 1917 until Oct. 1918. On Sept. 25, 1918 Director moved and carried that they elect same officers for year and include J. V. Hood (23 years of age and son of J. G Hood) assistant cashier at a salary for both Hoods of $125.00 per month. Directors moved in year 1919 to 1920 to increase Hood's salary to $150 per month. Of interest expense account for June 1922.

June 1 -	Cashier salary	150.00
June 2 -	Revenue stamp Note	2.60
June 6 -	Postage	.50
June 13 -	Express on stationary	2.66
June 14 -	TR Bennett for report	3.00
June 15 -	TR Bennett special exam	25.00
June 16 -	Making door key	.50
June 16 -	Telephone to Atlanta	.35
June 17 -	Bill Stationary Geo Barnard	20.22

(4)

June 22 – P.O. Box Rent .25
June 22 – Telephone to Atlanta .45
June 26 – One Broom .65
$1980.71

Call meeting of the Stockholders was held on Feb-22, 1922 for the purpose of reorganizating the Bank by election of a new set of Directors. A. M. Wilson and J. M. Wilson tendered their resignation as Directors which was accepted. The following gentlemen were unanimously elected.
C. R. Ware, Pres – salary of $500 per year
Dr B. V. Wilson, Vice Pres.
J. G. Hood Secretary and Cashier

On Aug 23, 1922 a motion was carried to make application for membership in Federal Reserve Bank and an examiner for Federal Reserve Bank came and made an audit. On Dec 3, 1924 carried to elect the same board for the coming year.
Letter of criticism from Mr. T. R. Bennett Superintendent of Banks was read.
In reply the minutes read. We as Directors are doing our best to arrange the past due notes and get them in proper shape.

On Nov 24, 1926 C.R. Ware tendered his resignation as president.

On Dec. 16, 1926. The Directors of

(5)

the Dacula Banking Company held a special meeting this afternoon in the office of the bank. The following named Directors were present, J. H. Hamilton, J. G. Hood, E. G. Hogan, R. M. Stanley, Claud Hinton and C. R. Ware were present by invitation. Owning to the low price of cotton and very poor collections, the Directors decided that it was advisable to close the bank and go into voluntary liquidation. On examination of the books it was discovered that the bank lacks about $9,000 having enough money to pay the depositors of the bank in full, therefore it was moved that a voluntary assessment of $75 a share be placed upon the stockholders in order to $9,000. The motion was carried. The resignation of C. R. Ware at the last meeting was accepted and J. H. Hamilton elected President. It was also moved was carried that the First National Bank of Lawrenceville be appointed agent for the Dacula Bank to pay depositors and liquidate the business of the Bank.

On Jan 23, 1929 the Directors

(6)

of Dacula Bank met in the office of First National Bank of Lawrenceville Members of the Board present were H. J. Hinton, J. H. Hamilton, J. G. Hood and R. M. Stanley. Motion was made and seconded to authorize C R Ware Liquidating Agent to finalize the business of debts, loans and deeds.

H. J. Hinton moved that C. R. Ware be authorize to sell the Banking House, vault and vault door for the sum of $1250 in cash. Also C. R. Ware be authorized to accept any reasonable compromise on any note belonging to Dacula Bank when in the exercise of his best judgment, after advising with the Federal Reserve Bank of Atlanta he thinks would be good business to accept a compromise. This was the last meeting recorded in the Book.

(7)

Stock represented as follows - Sept. 1909

	Shares		Shares
T. A. Maynard	20	J. L. Sims	3
G. W. Sikes	10	J. G. Hood	2
R. M. Stanley	10	E. S. Wages	2
W. T. Hinton	14	J. W. Hamilton	2
S. E. Pharr & Bro.	10	J. H. Hamilton	2
S. G. Hinton	5	J. B. Freeman	2
Spurgeon Williams	5	J. E. Kilgore	2
J. R. Williams	5	E. S. Ethridge	1
B. Ambrose	5	E. F. McAdams	1
G. P. Craig	10	J. C. Pool	1
J. A. Moore	5	J. T. Greeson	1
E. R. & R. E. Neill	5	J. C. Wall	1
Bob Bradford	1	Wm McDaniel	1
Wilsons	100		

Parsons' 1944 Kiwanis Address Concerning Joan Glancy Hospital

(Note: this is the text of a talk given on August 8, 1944 by Mrs. C.M. "Kate" Parsons Jr. of Duluth to the Buford Kiwanis Club concerning the Joan Glancy Memorial Clinic.)

The greatest problem we have in rural sections and small towns is the health situation. Unfortunately, the biggest toll of death among our people takes place in such a manner as to be un-noticed by the general public. Each year in Georgia, approximately 30,000 people die as the result of preventable diseases.

The cost of illness and death is not restricted to individuals or even to families, but becomes a community concern. I believe that by wise and courageous leadership this problem may be largely solved.

If the people in the larger towns and cities could realize the dire need of the less fortunate, they could provide the necessary leadership for a constructive, sound, adequate health program.

If through proper leadership we can achieve better health conditions for our people, what a heritage it would be for our children and all the generations of the future.

Every person needs to be more conscious of the part each one can play in its solution.

The story of how our clinic came to be in Duluth is the story of a little town putting their hearts into a thing they thought was needed and a fine, firm faith that "where there's a will there's a way" to do what should be done.

It was four years ago that Olin Burnett died. This hurt the people of Duluth. We believe that he might have been saved if medical attention had been available in time.

Richard Hull asked that we meet together to discuss raising funds for a clinic. From all parts of the community, men and women met and pledged enough to operate a small clinic and to have a full time nurse for six months.

It wasn't easy going. There were times when it looked as if we had come to the end of the road, but each day something would give us courage to carry on.

Others heard of our efforts and sent in small donations. Giving odd pieces of furniture, linens, discarded hospital beds, etc. We converted a tumbled down old shanty on the edge of the school yard into a community clinic.

When our funds began to get low, Mr. Hull got a letter from his father-in-law, A. R. Glancy, of Detroit. "Dear Dick," it read, "I am enclosing a check for $500 for your Duluth clinic and as you get going, Mother and I will send you $250 each year, on the 4th day of April, which was the birthday of our Joan."

Joan Glancy died at four years old, seventeen years before Olin Burnett died just before his sixth Christmas. These two events, so far apart in space and time had fulfilled their destiny. Here was all that we needed to set plans surging ahead again.

When Gen. Glancy learned that the little clinic had made a success, he sent a message to the town. "If the people of your community will subscribe enough to buy the land and furnish water, I will pay for a modern building of steel and concrete. If a half dozen citizens furnish the money, I am not interested. The sacrifice must come from everyone in the town."

Every person, from the poorest to the most well-to-do, contributed to that fund. The sum amounted to a little more than $4,000 with which we bought 23 acres of land and drilled a well.

The new building includes 20 rooms, and is provided with servants' quarters in the back. We treat an average of 600 persons a month, either as in-patients or through the out patient clinic.

The clinic is, at present, doing a booming maternity business and is equipped for X-Ray, metabolism testing and emergency surgery.

After the war, the clinic will expand and will include a dental clinic too. We are planning to build a nurse's home in the very near future. Also, included in our post war plans are homes for a superintendent and a full time doctor.

Within the next few months, we will have a registered nurse, who has completed a special course in mid-wifery, and the community will have its first opportunity for good, cheap obstetrics.

The State Department of Health and our County Board have cooperated to the fullest extent, assisting in the venereal disease, well baby, and prenatal clinics that are held each month.

No one has ever been turned away from the clinic because he was unable to pay. Those who have 25 cents, give that, and those who are able, pay the regular Doctor's fee. The hospital committee passes on their financial ability.

We are proud of the wonderful work that has been accomplished in the past, and we know that there are greater things in store for all the years to come.

On a tablet at the front of the building is inscribed, "To Joan, who in swift transition achieved eternal Springtime, this hospital is dedicated in the hope that through it the lives of other children may be enriched."

Our doors are wide open to minister to all who need our help.

SIGNED/ Mrs. C.M. Parsons Jr.

Early Norcross History

(Editor's Note: This early history of Norcross is attributed to Mollie James Jones, wife of Col. Clifford Jones Sr. It was written in 1945.)

In 1872, Professor Vincent, a noted educator, came to Norcross and started a boarding school that became quite famous and attracted students from surrounding cities and states. He was the editor of the first newspaper, *The Norcross Tribune.* Professor Vincent encouraged the building of a high school, which was located on the south side of the railroad. It was finally replaced by a brick building and has been used as a school ever since.

The Norcross Methodist Church was located on the south side of town at Flint Hill. In 1871 the church moved to town and used the school house as a place of worship until 1875. The beginning of the new church was the donation of 10 trees for building purposes. The lot was given by M.C. Lively, who also gave the school lot, the cemetery lot and the Masonic Hall lot.

Col. Clifford Jones, Sr.

An Orphan's Home was built in 1871 on the Stone Mountain Road, about a quarter mile from the corporate limits. A year and a half later, it was moved to the place beyond the cemetery, and afterward to Decatur. It is now called the Decatur Methodist Orphans' Home. (In 2008, the name of the home was the United Methodist Children's Home of Decatur.)

The Baptist church was organized in 1872, and they also used the school house for worship until they built their present church at Jones and Peachtree Street.

The Presbyterian Church at Goshen, a few miles east of Norcross moved their membership to town in 1875 and used the Methodist Church for a place of worship until they built their present church nearby.

The Norcross Woman's Club was organized in October, 1905. In 1907, Edward F. Buchanan, a "Wall Street millionaire," donated money for a library, which contained 4,000 volumes. The books were furnished by the women of the club. The club is active in all the departments of the State Federation of Women's Clubs. The Library building is also used as a youth center at the present time. The Norcross Civic Club was organized in 1916 and joined the State Federation of Women's Clubs in 1917.

The Norcross Lions Club was organized March 14, 1944 with 18 members. By March, 1945, it had 48 active members.

The electric light system was completed in 1909 and was and still is owned by the town. The water and sewerage system was completed in 1927.

Leading industries in past years include a harness and leather factory, trunk factory, brickyard, creamery, Buchanan Plow and Implement factory, McElroy Chair and Furniture factory, and a belting company.

Prior to the beginning of the town, the court of the Justice of the Peace for the Pinckneyville District was held at the juncture of Peachtree Road and the Federal (or McAfee Bridge Road.) (*Editor's note: This probably should be Medlock Bridge Road, especially with the reference to Pinckneyville.*) At one time the juncture was called "Tickle-gizzard," but has been known as Pinckneyville for more than a 100 years. About the time of the founding of

Norcross, at Pinckneyville there was a store, bar-room, blacksmith shop, saw mill and one house. In 1875, W.M. Hunnicutt bought out the store, house and later the sawmill. He and a neighbor, W.N. Sanders, and others, had Mt. Carmel Church incorporated, so forced the bar-room to move. There was a post office, where Thomas H. Jones was postmaster for many years.

An act to incorporate the town or Norcross was approved by the Legislature on October 26, 1870. The Richmond and Danville Railroad had been started through this section before the Civil War, but work was stopped during the war. In 1868 work was resumed and the first train was run over this road in June, 1870. The foundation for the first depot was laid in November of 1870. People came from miles around to see the first train. The dirt fill just north of the present depot was hauled by wheelbarrows.

The town was named for Johnathan Crawford Norcross, the second mayor of Atlanta.

The first baby born in Norcross was Crawford Norcross James. He was given a gold cup by Mr. Norcross, who also gave the bell of the Baptist Church.

The town was founded by John J. Thrasher of Atlanta, familiarly called "Cousin John." Mr. Thrasher was the first mayor. The Council members were Stephen McElroy, M.C. Lively, Gorman T. Robertson and Mr. Autrey.

The early town had a number of bar-rooms, with considerable lawlessness because of these. The Council was given the authority to regulate the sale of whiskey by a high tax or refusal to grant a license. It is a matter of considerable pride that license was only granted for one year.

The location of the town was practically in the woods. A small log house occupied by Hiram Wilson was the only dwelling near the present business part of town. Mr. Thrasher bought him out and began the erection of a hotel, which he occupied and ran for several years. He divided up the central portion of the town into lots, which he sold, and a few he gave away. He also gave the park site.

The first store was erected by G.W. Wallace, while grading was done on the railroad. The Norcross Post Office was established Sept. 4, 1871. Mrs. M.E. Parks was postmistress and Thomas H. Jones assistant.

The Bank of Norcross was established in 1904 and has a fine record of growth. The first school building was erected in 1872 by public subscription on Church Street (Holy Row.) The first teachers were a Mrs. Bass and Miss Helena Jones.

Norcross in the 1940s

By Col. (Ret) Clifford Jones Jr.

(Editor's Note: The author spent several years of his youth in Norcross, the son of an Army officer who retired to his home of Norcross. The writer is a graduate of the U.S. Military Academy, and had a 32 year career in the Army, then joined private business in the Buffalo, N.Y. area. He lives in retirement at Orchard Park, N.Y.)

Col. Cliff Jones, Jr.

In 1944, I arrived in Norcross at the age of 11. My father, Clifford Jones Sr. had retired from the Army after 41 years of service and decided to return to the home of his youth.

For our home site, he selected a vacant city block bounded by Williams, Autrey, Spike and Peachtree Streets, one block back from the railroad and a five minute walk to downtown Norcross. In my brief life, I had lived in three different cities and two military posts, but Norcross was my first taste of "country" living. As I recall, the population numbered about 2,200, farming was the principal economic activity, and a trip to Atlanta was an occasion of sorts. The only way to get there was via the Buford Highway to its connection with Peachtree Road north of Doraville, and then down Peachtree into the city. I recall as an "event" the subsequent extension of Highway 23 (two lanes concrete) directly into Atlanta. This was our only hard surface connection to the rest of the world. Norcross village streets were mostly paved, but except for Highway 23, every other road out of town was gravel, which made a bicycle trip out to the Chattahoochee for a swim a real test of determination.

Our mailing address was "Box 5." Our phone number was "7W." We were on a telephone party line with my grandmother, Mollie Jones, whose house was directly to the east. If I wanted to call her, I would pick up the ear piece and turn the crank on the control box. The lady who serviced the town switchboard would come on with "Central." I would say, "7E, please." She might advice me that my grandmother was out for the morning. If you walked down the street running north from the rail station, you could see "Central" through the front window of her house, at her switchboard. It was a cozy phone system.

I remember those magnificent steam locomotives whistling through on the Southern's double track main line. Daily excitement was being at the station's mail transfer point when at full speed the mail car attendant would launch the incoming mail bag at the platform, and then extend the arm that would snatch the outgoing bag from its rail-side tower. (Years later, when the Bank of Norcross had become part of the C&S organization, this process would be repeated when at the day's end, the C&S helicopter would collect the day's transactions from a hoist over the bank on Peachtree Street.)

During the cotton harvest, it was fun to go to the gin and watch the process. The picked cotton would arrive in mule-drawn wagons, go through the most amazing series of whirring and clanking machines, and roll out a huge bale of cotton. That was in the days when plant foremen didn't worry much about kids roaming around rotating machinery. That was the way we learned about things.

Cotton was really King then. When the cotton was ready for picking, the Norcross school suspended classes so that the farm kids could help get the crop in. We town guys thought that was really great. Two of the town's most prominent businessmen were the cotton broker and the owner of the cotton seed company. The only other production business I can recall, the Webb Company, manufactured glue (synthetic stuff, not from old horses.) There was also a tannery, but it was south of town and sort of out of the mainstream.

It's easy for me to romanticize the Norcross of my early youth, to see it as a Norman Rockwell setting. We had three churches, Baptist, Methodist and Presbyterian, with ministers routinely being invited to various homes for Sunday dinner. Our two doctors made sit-on-your-bed house calls. We had a police force of two, the chief was the day force and another fellow covered the evening hours. There was one shop with two barbers. (My mother routinely directed me to "have the boss" do mine when I went. I always felt a bit embarrassed for the other fellow who could probably make a 12 year old look as good as he needed to look.)

Our fire department was a towed hose trailer. The town truck was its prime mover. If the fire siren sounded, the town crew would drop what they were doing, go to the fire house for the trailer, and there get directions for the fire. The system worked. One time our attached garage caught fire, but the house was saved.

There was about one of every kind of store: drug, feed, hardware, grocery, dry goods, general, variety…but four gas stations. We had a serious blacksmith, an operational train station and a bank. My father was for a number of years president of the bank. His desk was immediately inside the front door, the first person a customer would see on entering. The cashier, tellers and bookkeeper were further in, behind the traditional counter…and that was the bank. And finally, the Swan, a real motion picture theatre, was opened. It showed feature films plus serials. Norcross had arrived!

What we didn't have were any restaurants, bars, liquor stores, hotels or even a guest house that I can recall. There was a low building on the south side of the town park which residents referred as "the old hotel," but I remember it occupied by permanent residents and not in the business of accepting guests.

The most memorable event of my early days in Norcross was when a gasoline tanker wrecked at the gas station located on the highway down the hill from town. It was a big fire, involving both tanker and building, then the un-ruptured tanker compartments started exploding. The swarm of onlookers was suddenly in panicked flight back up the hill as the flames towered over us (or so it certainly seemed!)

I was a full time participant of the country culture of Norcross from grade 5 through 7. Out of town school, and then a career away, resulted in fewer and fewer trips home until finally there was no connection left. My last real visit was in 2000 to buy my stepmother, Mary Jones, age 99, in a plot in the Norcross Cemetery. There she joined my father, my grandparents, my great grandparents and a great uncle, Hilliard Clarke Jones. (Hilliard was killed at age 10 by a stray union bullet when a firefight between union and confederate forces developed on my great grandfather's farm.)

The village itself looked much as it did in 1944, a tribute to historic preservation. Our old home site, with our original house nicely maintained, now accommodates a dozen or so new-builds. I enjoyed lunch in the Station where I used to wait for the mail train to snatch the northbound pouch. The other side of things…I could not recognize much of the countryside. Gravel had changed to blacktop in my time, but much of that was now divided four-lane parkway roads, with development everywhere. There was no way to even guess where the houses of several old friends had stood.

I finally realized that Norcross had changed forever, when I bought a Saab and in reading the literature that accompanied it, discovered that the headquarters of Saab USA was....in Norcross.

Gwinnett County Fair History

By J. W. (Bill) Baughman

Fairs have always been a part of local history, as farmers, housewives, merchants and government officials saw holding a local fair as good for all their endeavors.

One of the earliest Fairs mentioned in Gwinnett history was in 1891, when what is presumed to be the first fair was held. Under the auspices of the "Gwinnett County Fair Association," the fair was held in Suwanee that year. Then next year, there was no fair, but in 1893, Buford hosted the fair. A newspaper article from 1894 stated that the fair that year was held in a church grove in Suwanee.

(Note: the following history of the current Gwinnett Fair was compiled by a member of the current Gwinnett County Fair and Livestock Association board, who consulted the Association records for this information.)

Bill Baughman

There is evidence in early Gwinnett newspapers that fairs have been in existence in Gwinnett County for over 100 years, under a variety of names. And, in at least one year, two fairs operated at the same time.

The current Gwinnett County Fair stems from 1952, when County Agent Roy W. Garren brought people in the community together to discuss forming a fair association. The previous fair property been taken by the school board for the site of the new Central Gwinnett High School. However, there appeared to be genuine interest in the formation of a new fair association, with the indication the county commission would provide initial funding to help purchase a site for a fairground. Vocational-Agricultural Teachers and a World War II Veteran's Farm Training Class offered to pay up to $200 to cover the cost of legal work, including a charter.

Directors were chosen from a wide area of the county. The first directors included T. T. Howington, Buford; David Kistner, Lithonia; Uhland F. Freeman, T. L. Harris, and John B. Guthrie, Lawrenceville; Harrison Summerour, Duluth; Troy Sharpton, Auburn; W. A. Cooper, Grayson; and Carvis Williams, Snellville.

The board was organized at a second meeting, with Kistner elected chairman. An old fairground was to become the site of a new Lawrenceville High School. Directors sought the attention of the Grand Jury, anticipating they would recommend that the commission furnish land for the fairgrounds. A few days later, the Grand Jury made a favorable report to the commission, recommended they help "The Gwinnett County Fair and Livestock Association" get organized and in operation. However, though the commission was favorable about the formation, they did not initially commit on how they would help fund the effort. It took another month before a majority of the commission agreed to make a donation toward land purchase.

Four different tracts were under consideration. The directors eventually selected an 11.4 acre tract on Old Stone Mountain Road, which was owned by director T.L. Harris. The price was $2,000, and the commission had approved up to $1,500 for the land, and had refused to ante up more. Eventually a loan from the First National Bank of Lawrenceville was obtained for the additional funds, with each director endorsing the note individually. By now a certificate of charter for the Association came from the State of Georgia.

Directors then began working toward holding the 1953 Fair. They set the initial admission at 50 cents for adults, 25 cents for children. Parking was 25 cents. Gov. Herman Talmadge would later commit to be the principal speaker at the dedication of the new Fair Association The Chamber of Commerce, led by Pete Sever, helped, donating $2,900 for a fence to the association.

A list of premiums was adopted. For cattle shows, the first prize was $8; second prize, $6; and third prize $4. Champions and reserve champions received ribbons only. Field crops prize was $1.25 for first place, 75 cents for second and third prize got a ribbon.

The first year commercial and industrial exhibits were in tents. Some 17 Home Demonstration Clubs participated in booths. Industrial exhibits were in a tent. In school booths, Dacula won first prize, while Rosebud won tops in Home Demonstration Clubs.

Fair officials were pleased that an estimated 12,000 people came to the fair, which lasted six days. And when it was over, the directors were doubly pleased to report a profit of $4,235!

The success of the first fair encouraged the directors, with the fair being held every year since, and the fair continuing to expand its scope, prize money and overall impact on the community. The attendance has soared over the years, to the point in 2005 where 200,000 persons came through its gates.

By spring of 1954, directors began discussion concerning erection of a livestock building. One director was opposed. Activities were held in tents the first year, with an exhibit building erected after that year. Kistner was named manager for the 1954 fair. Delivering the opening address was Congressman Phil Landrum.

By 1956, the board authorized the borrowing of $10,000 to construct an additional structure, a 60x160 foot livestock building. The board also approved a 30x160 foot addition to its Exhibit Building, including a fair office. The Fair that year had Lt. Gov. Ernest Vandiver as its speaker. A Buford student, Shirley Wheeler, was named the first Miss Gwinnett out of the 50 contestants.

Other highlights of fairs over the years:

1956: Uhland Freeman was elected manager. A Pony Show and FFA Fat Steer show were started. Judging standards were instituted.

1957: A new 70x160 foot Exhibit Building was built to replace an earlier structure destroyed by fire started by lighting. Attendance was 17,000. Thursday was instituted as free admission day. Authorization came to borrow $20,000 for another building.

1959: The Gwinnett cattle show was open to other counties. Sam Rawlins was new fair manager.

1961: A committee of Directors Francis McDowall, J.W. Benefield and Uhland Freeman were asked to be on the lookout for a new fairground property. By now, the Fair receipts were at an all-time high, and $3,000 was paid in premiums.

1963: The Home Demonstration Clubs asked for better protection of exhibits, and also sought added restroom facilities, to include shower space. The biggest news, however, was announcement that the Association was out of debt. Plans were told of new restroom and showers for show personnel.

1964: A check for $810 was issued to the Vocational Agricultural teachers to pay them back in full their loan to the Association when the Fair was first organized, 11 years before. By now entries came from 350 individuals and 13 clubs, with prize money totaling $6,450.50.

1965: A small part of the fairgrounds (.11 acres) was sold to the City of Lawrenceville for a sub-station for $2,000. A Little Miss Gwinnett contest was planned for Saturday afternoon during Fair Week. Gate admission advanced to $1 for adults and 50 cents for children, and for parking.

However, the most significant part of 1965 came when the directors agreed to purchase 224.88 acres from the A.T. Roberts Estate, on the Lawrenceville-Grayson highway. The price was $136,950, which works out at $608.99 an acre!

1957: A second corporation (for profit), to cover the development of property not used as fairgrounds, would have to be formed. The officers of the two corporations were the same.

1966: Directors borrowed $55,000 to do the site work at the new fairgrounds.

1968: Directors had determined that it would retain 85 acres for the fairgrounds, and seek to develop the remaining land as a subdivision. It was at this time that a 10 day fair was planned.

1969: Instead of developing the subdivision land, directors decided to put the land on the market, and use funds from its sale to develop the fairgrounds. The Association decided the pave the access boulevard from Georgia Highway 20 at a cost of $40,888. Directors also chose to investigate seeking a grant from the Georgia Department of Agriculture for a livestock exhibit building. Local legislators set up a meeting with Agriculture Commissioner Tommy Irvin and Governor Lester Maddox, who agreed to provide $25,000 to cover the cost of constructing the livestock building, providing the Fair Association anted up matching funds.

1970: Directors decided to sell the subdivision for $165,000. This would provide matching funds, a stipulation of the Department of Agriculture grant, for the livestock facility.

1971: A house trailer was approved for a guard to live in on the fair property. Meanwhile, discussion arose on whether to sell the old fairground to the Board of Education for $100,000 or to the City of Lawrenceville for $125,000. Eventually, the sale went to the City, which used the space for a park. The Exhibit building and Livestock building were constructed during the year.

1972: The Association contracted with two county policemen to provide security at the fairgrounds, in return for a place to park their mobile homes. Among new activities for the year would be a Youth Pet Show and Horse Show. A new ring west of the current barn was set for the Horse Show.

1985: A 330,000-sq. ft. livestock building, *The Memorial Arena,* was built. It cost $272,239. That year Congressman Ed Jenkins gave the dedicatory address.

1994: A large bathroom facility was completed.

1996: An entertainment building of 9,600 square feet was constructed to hold beauty pageants and other music entertainment. Dale Thurman was hired as the first full-time Fair Manager.

In the years since 1996 ongoing projects include barn improvements: adding more electricity and water services; an increase in the space of paving; adding a camping area with electrical, water and sewer hookups; and remodeling the bathrooms in the exhibit building.

2004: New office addition, with banquet facilities, new board room, and new spaces for the CEO, fair manager and reception area.

2007: New iron fence constructed at Gate No. 1 entrance. More air conditioning capacity provided to the main exhibit building.

Fair Board Members

None of the original directors were living in 2006. Directors more often, once elected, were re-elected once their term was up. From Association minutes, the following directors have been elected; noted by the year they joined the board:

1952: T. T. Howington, Buford; David Kistner, Lithonia; Uhland F. Freeman, Sr., T. L. Harris, and John B. Guthrie, Lawrenceville; Harrison Summerour, Duluth; Troy Sharpton, Auburn; W. A. Cooper, Grayson; and Carvis Williams, Snellville.

1953: Ronnie D. Shreve.

1954: Carson Britt, Sam Rawlins.

1956: Tom W. Moss of Buford.

1958: Francis McDowall

1960: Robert Jones.

1963: Jack Boggs.

1965: Ralph Head.

1966: J.H. Reddy.

1967: Hugh Snell.

1969: Hoyt Williams.

1973: Carroll Knight.

1975: Dennis Still.

1975: Wayne Shackelford.

1976: Harold Williams, Horace Lovin.

1979: J. W. Benefield

1982: Ron Davis.
1985: Fred Banks, Hughel Harrison.
1986: Howard Maxwell.
1989: John H. Lovin.
1990: Roger Sartor.
1994: Bill Baughman.
1997: James Freeman, Bill Atkinson.

Directors serving in 2008: Fred Banks, Bill Baughman, Robert Sartor, J.W. Benefield, Wayne Shackelford, Ron Davis, John H. Lovin, Bill Atkinson and James Freeman.

Aerial view of the Gwinnett County Fair

1993 Letter from John Mobley to Wayne Hill on Water System

Sutherland
Asbill &
Brennan LLP
ATTORNEYS AT LAW

999 Peachtree Street, NE
Atlanta, GA 30309-3996
404.853.8000
fax 404.853.8806

JOHN H MOBLEY
DIRECT LINE: 404.853.8128

April 20, 1993

The Honorable F. Wayne Hill
Chairman
Board of Commissioners of
Gwinnett County
75 Langley Drive
Lawrenceville, Georgia 30245

Dear Wayne:

It was good talking with you last week and giving you some of my background as bond counsel for Gwinnett County.

You requested that I furnish you with a memorandum of my bond counsel experience for Gwinnett County and I am enclosing five copies of such memorandum for you.

It was a pleasure meeting with you and I look forward to being with you again soon and, hopefully, of having the opportunity of being of service to Gwinnett County and to you.

Best regards,

JHM/ws
Enclosures

See text of memorandum beginning on the following page.

John Mobley Memorandum to Wayne Hill on Water System

MEMORANDUM

TO: The Honorable F. Wayne Hill
Chairman, Board of Commissioners of Gwinnett County
FROM: John H. Mobley
DATE: April 20, 1993
RE: History of the Role of John H. Mobley
As Bond Counsel for Gwinnett County

In 1956, after Gwinnett County had completed construction of an improperly designed water system, the purchasers of all of the bonds (headed by Connecticut General Life Insurance Company) asked my late partner, Sumter Kelley, and me to represent them as bond counsel in Gwinnett County. At that time and at the request of the bondholders, Gwinnett County employed the nationally recognized engineering firm of Havens & Emerson, headquartered in New Jersey, to act as its consulting engineers.

Virtually everything that could have been done wrong, had been done. The water system was a gravity design flow system composed in the main of plastic pipes laid uphill. The former commissioners who had approved the bond issue had been indicted by a federal grand jury. The improperly designed plastic pipe system had been poorly constructed. Numerous fire hydrants had been installed throughout the County and not one was connected to the water supply.

Havens & Emerson, the new engineers, devised an interim system for replacing plastic pipes as they burst with steel pipes. The County initiated a fire hydrant tax the moneys derived from which were placed in the water revenue fund to pay operating costs of the system and to help make debt service payments. Shortly thereafter, the voters of the County authorized the sale of beer and a beer tax was imposed. The revenues derived from such beer tax were used for debt service on the bonds. The use of these moneys and the fire hydrant tax moneys, although not authorized to be pledged under the Revenue Bond Law, enabled the County initially to produce funds to meet in large part its debt service requirements on the water revenue bonds.

With the assent of all of the bondholders, the County refunded that issue in order to lower the annual debt service cost. Thereafter, with the approval of all of the bondholders, the County was able to issue, from time to time, small issues of revenue bonds, none of which exceeded $100,000, to extend the system. This enabled the County to provide service for industrial users that would locate on property adjacent to Southern Railroad property, thus enabling the County to pick up more significant users.

Despite all of this, the system went into technical default and it was necessary to again refund the outstanding issues of bonds in order to obtain lower debt service requirement payments. During all of that time I met regularly with county officials and I was often in consultation with the representative of the bondholders. From the start and over a period of many years, the then County attorney, Homer Stark, and the various elected commissioners fully supported and cooperated with me in my efforts to effectively represent the bondholders. Compensation paid to me for this representation was negligible. Probably if I calculated the payments on an hourly basis, my compensation would have been $5 an hour or less. Nevertheless, we were beginning to make some progress due to an increase in customers and improvements that were constantly being made by our excellent consulting engineers. The bondholder representative normally would call me once or twice a month to obtain progress reports. He would not deal with the County directly, but only through me. In no event would we permit any expansion of the water system except in accordance with the plans and recommendations of the engineers, this despite political pressure from the commissioners to extend the system to sparsely inhabited areas of the County.

The County's water revenue bonds could not be rated. No purchaser of bonds of the County's water system could be found except the original purchasers of the bonds who made subsequent purchases of bonds to expand the system and thereby protect their investment. Under those conditions no difficulty was experienced in making certain that the expansion of the system was made in accordance with the recommendations of the engineers. The commissioners acceded to the demands of the bondholders. Homer Stark, the able and forceful County attorney, was extraordinarily helpful to me and to the bondholders in making certain that matters were handled correctly at the local level in accordance with the wishes of the bondholders. Later it became necessary that sewage treatment facilities be constructed as the County then depended on sewage treatment by small treatment facilities with limited capacity. Many of the residents depended on septic tanks for treatment of sewage. A basic sewerage system was designed for the County and with the help of an experienced underwriter from another state; Gwinnett County issued the first sewerage revenue bonds in the State of Georgia and probably in the United States.

Although the County's water revenue bonds were yet unrated, our revenues were beginning to increase and it became apparent that eventually we would need a large and readily available potable water supply. At a meeting in my office I indicated on a map of Gwinnett County that a water line could be built from Lake Lanier along the ridge line of Gwinnett County thereby assuring an adequate water supply for Gwinnett County and surrounding areas. We determined that there should be created a Gwinnett County Water Authority. The General Assembly passed legislation, which I wrote, creating the Gwinnett County Water Authority, later becoming the Gwinnett County Water and Sewerage Authority.

In the late 1960s, the voters of Gwinnett County approved a general obligation bond issue and we were able to secure an "A" rating on those bonds by Moody's Investors Service. Prior to that, after talking with Homer Stark and the commissioners, I recommended that the County employ a financial advisor as I did not feel comfortable in making market recommendations to the County and, in addition, they should get expert advice on ways in which to improve the County's credit rating. During those years I also served as bond counsel for the Gwinnett County School District. Jones Webb represented the School District and shortly after (we) were able to obtain an "A" rating for the County's bonds, we secured an "A" rating on the School District's bonds. The County's water revenue bonds and the County's sewerage revenue bonds were nevertheless unrated.

We determined that the water authority should issue revenue bonds to acquire and construct a water treatment facility at a site on the banks of Lake Lanier and to construct a water distribution system which would supply water to the County independent of its supply from the Chattahoochee River which was being treated by an antiquated water treatment plant. In order to obtain a water supply, the County was able to enter into a long term water supply contract with the U.S. Army Corps of Engineer which was signed by the then Secretary of the Army, Bo Callaway.

In order to issue bonds of the Authority, it was necessary that the County and the Authority enter into a water supply contract under which the County would make payments from its water system revenue fund for water supplied by the Authority, thus enabling the Authority to pay its operating costs and to meet its debt service requirements. Initially the bondholders threatened to bring proceedings in Federal District Court to enjoin us from taking any such action. I was able to work out a compromise and to persuade them to let us proceed by restructuring the then contemplated financing. After first resisting our action, the bondholders liked the new issue so much that the bondholders as a group bought a major portion of the new issue.

With this bond issue the Authority's distribution system was constructed. The County's water revenue bonds and its sewerage revenue bonds were refunded and those systems were combined into a water and sewerage system of the County. The engineers were able to complete the water distribution pipeline loop for Gwinnett County and the County then had a viable first class water and sewerage system in operation with a plentiful water supply furnished by the Authority.

Subsequently the County's outstanding water and sewerage revenue bonds were refunded as well as the Authority's bonds. Additional bonds were issued and under the financing method employed, the County's taxing power could be utilized if necessary to produce funds to make payments under a contract with the Authority. In its contract with the Authority, the County has covenanted to levy a tax to the extent necessary to produce funds with which to make payments to the Authority, thereby insuring the Authority's ability to make debt service payments on its bonds. As a result, the Authority's rating has been upgraded, and the bonds of the Authority now enjoy virtually the same credit rating as the bonds of the County.

Currently the County has been given an "AA+" credit rating. Certainly I make no claim for having been responsible for this rating, but I am the only one still active who originally helped bring all of this together and who guided the County on its course of action over many years. I helped pull the stumps, clear the land and first plow the fields, all to the benefit of the citizens and taxpayers of Gwinnett County.

Viewed from the prospective of where we started, if it had been suggested that Gwinnett County in a few years would be prospering as one of the fastest growing and richest counties in the United States, such a suggestion would have been dismissed as a pipe dream.

For having represented Gwinnett County these many years, I take no credit for the good result that has been achieved, but I take pride and satisfaction in knowing that I played a part in helping to make it happen. It is with great satisfaction that I have witnessed what Gwinnett County has accomplished. I salute Gwinnett County. My law firm would be honored to be asked to continue to be of service to the people of Gwinnett County.

History of Gwinnett County Public Schools

(Note: In 1989, Nita Hallford compiled a short history of the Gwinnett County Public Schools. It is a good short history, and will compliment the other parts of this book. Used by permission of Nita Hallford and the Gwinnett County Public Schools.)

By Nita Hallford, Editor

The history of the schools in Gwinnett County is at times diverse, yet it contains strands of similarities; at times controversial, yet it contains incidents of humor, at times filled with traditions, yet it is never dull. Since the early 1800s, the schools of Gwinnett County have been organized by people who value education and who desire to provide young people with opportunities to learn as much as possible in preparation for life's endeavors. Because schools are not mere buildings, but rather the community supporting the value of education, this history of Gwinnett County schools is about people. The local school historians who gathered facts on the history of each school researched diligently to provide the most accurate and thorough information possible.

Gwinnett County and its public school system are named for Button Gwinnett, one of the three Georgians who signed the Declaration of Independence. According to the research compiled by James C. Flanigan in *History of Gwinnett County, Georgia,* Volume I, the earliest date assigned to organized education in Gwinnett County is 1821, when an act was passed to provide trustees for a county academy. Those named as trustees were William Towers, William Turner, William Maltbie, Thomas Worthy and Jacob R. Brooks. Because of a lack of funds, no building was immediately erected, but more trustees were added in 1825: James Blackmon, Elisha W. Chester, Philo Hall, William Montgomery, William Green and Joseph Morgan. Ten acres of land on the hill northwest of Lawrenceville which is now the corner of Oak and Perry streets had been reserved for a county academy by order of the Inferior Court in 1822, but not until January 1, 1826, did the academy actually open after state tax money had been combined with previously issued state funds of $500 to erect the Lawrenceville Academy. Lawrenceville and the academy were named in honor of Captain James Lawrence, an American naval officer known for his courageous words during battle in the War of 1812, "Don't give up the ship."

The first superintendent of the Lawrenceville Academy was John S. Wilson, who was also pastor of the Fairview Presbyterian Church. Tuition was charged for instruction in orthography (spelling), reading, writing, arithmetic, surveying, English, grammar, geography, Latin, Greek, philosophy and rhetoric. Tuition fees ranged from an annual $10 for reading and writing to $24 for Latin and Greek.

Within the next 13 years, several other academies opened for instruction: Washington Academy in 1827, the Gwinnett Manual Labor Institute in 1835, the Female Seminary in 1837 and Center Academy in 1839. Washington Academy was located in the Pinckneyville district on the site of Shiloh Baptist Church on Spalding Drive, with Trustees Charles Gates, William Green, David Burge, Samuel Maloney, Henry Dunn, John Baker and

Thomas Morgan. The Gwinnet Manual Labor Institute was located on a farm near Fairview Presbyterian Church along what is now the Duluth Highway-Lawrenceville Highway (State Road 120), with John S. Wilson, James Gamble, R. Chamberlain, James Stratton, T. Y. Alexander, Thomas Robertson, Joseph Cunningham and Levi Willard as trustees. The Female Seminary, rebuilt in 1855 after a fire destroyed the first building and still standing on Perry Street in Lawrenceville, was served by Trustees John S. Wilson, N. L. Hutchins, R. S. Norton, James P. Simmons, B. S. Pendleton, Mathew Crawford, B. M. Powell, John B. Tripp and Henry P. Thomas. Center Academy was located in the Berkshire district with George W. Jones, William McDaniel, Thomas J. Watkins, J. W. Still and Humphrey D. Landers as trustees.

In volume two to Flanigan's *History of Gwinnett County, Georgia*, an effort to consolidate the Female Seminary and the Lawrenceville Academy is mentioned; however, Flanigan reported that no records show whether the consolidation took place. The proposed name for the consolidated schools was Lawrenceville Collegiate Institute.

While many Gwinnett County students were educated in the academics, mothers were able to gain an education because their parents contracted with a teacher to hold classes in their homes or in a nearby church. George Harrison Hopkins signed an agreement in 1830 to teach 25 students spelling, reading writing and arithmetic for a sum of $8 per pupil per year. From 1832 to 1860, Mr. Hopkins held classes in the Goshen meeting house located at what is known today as the corner of Indian Trail and Beaver Ruin roads in Norcross.

The education of a number of young men in Gwinnett County was interrupted in 1836 when volunteers were being enrolled all over the state to fight the Creek Indians, who were attacking settlers along the Georgia-Alabama border. The unrest of the Creeks was due to their removal to lands beyond the Mississippi River. According to letters of James C. Key, a student of the Gwinnett Manual Labor Institute, "The pomp and glitter of war had its effect upon my mind." Key enlisted as a volunteer, against his parents' wishes, and started with his company for the Creek Nation. In one letter he gave an account of "running for dear life" when the Creeks outnumbered his company in the Battle of Shepherd's Plantation 40 miles south of Columbus.

Another event of national importance drew young men of Gwinnett away from their studies in 1838, when the county was required to furnish two companies of volunteers to escort the Cherokee Indians to an assigned territory beyond the Mississippi. One mounted volunteer company was instructed to be in readiness to defend neighboring counties if the Cherokees were to become hostile. The ill-prepared Cherokees suffered greatly on their journey, known as the Trail of Tears, and as many as 4,000 died along the way.

The 20 years prior to 1860 and the Civil War were prosperous ones for residents of Gwinnett County. The principal occupation was farming; and because land was not expensive, the farmers were known as the wealthy class. Only approximately 25 percent of the farmers owned slaves; however, large plantations were located in all parts of the county. The education of slaves was prohibited due to a Georgia law passed in 1829, which stated that the penalty for teaching a slave to read or write would be based on the race of the offender and could be a whipping, a fine or imprisonment. The census of 1850 listed the existence of 31 one-teacher schools and a total attendance of 1,186 students in Gwinnett County.

The system of education prior to the outbreak of the Civil War continued to be provided through the academies or one-teacher schools. A diary kept by Lucretia Douglas, who lived near Suwanee, shows that in 1852, when she was 22 years old, she taught in what she called an infant school in one room of her family's home. Her pupils came from neighboring farms, and one even boarded with the Douglas family. In her diary, Lucretia Douglas stated that she could teach orthography, reading and writing.

Not until after the Civil War did the Georgia General Assembly provide for a system of public schools in the state. Even then, in 1870, the funds were diverted to members of the General Assembly to satisfy other obligations. The major portion of the state school funds came from rental fees paid by the Western and Atlantic Railroad.

The first Gwinnett County school commissioner (superintendent) was J. N. Glenn, who served during 1871. According to the annual report of 1871, Gwinnett County had 38 school houses and 41 teachers. The average monthly salary for male teachers was $48.70, and female teachers received a monthly average of $36.51. Student enrollment was 2,204. The number of days spent by Commissioner Glenn on official duties was 43.

A new commissioner, J. L. King, was elected by the board upon the resignation of Mr. Glenn. When no state funds were available in 1872, schools were suspended for the year; however, by 1873, the public school system began to function again. A two-story boarding school of eight rooms was built in Norcross. Soon 48 public schools were flourishing along with 20 private schools in the county. Four of the public schools were for black students,

In 1878, during Thomas E. Winn's service as commissioner, the commissioner's salary was increased from $150 to $156 for four months of work per year. Textbooks were adopted by the board of education for a three-year period with an explanation from the commissioner, "While a change of books may be objectionable to many, a beginning had to be made in establishing a uniform system." The boarding school administered by Norman Favius Cooledge continued to operate in Norcross in 1877, and Duluth followed with its high school in 1880 known as the Duluth Academy.

By the end of the 1800s, remarkable changes had taken place in the area of education in Gwinnett County. The method of paying teachers was changed by Commissioner William T. Tanner in 1897 from a system based on daily attendance to a salary system. Eighty-five public schools and four private high schools were operating. Lawrenceville had established itself as a local system in 1893, and in the next year, a college known as Perry-Rainey College was founded at Auburn, Georgia. The college was named for William T. Perry, a well-known farmer and merchant, and the Reverend Hiram N. Rainey, a Baptist minister. James C. Flanigan, author of the two-volume *History of Gwinnett County, Georgia* was a graduate of Perry-Rainey College and served as president of the college for two years.

Gwinnett County was first organized into school districts when James A. Bagwell was commissioner in 1900. Mr. Bagwell, commenting on the need for organizing districts, said, "The board of education...decided to lay off the county into school districts, and it is now high time that the school territories should be definitely known. When this work is done, the teachers will know where to find their children, the children will know to which school they must go, and the commissioner and board of education will be able to ascertain the reasons for non-attendance in any district in the county" (Flanigan, Vol. I, 305).

During the many years that C. R. Ware served as school commissioner, 1907-1920, he supported compulsory educational legislation. Not until 1919 did the compulsory attendance law become effective; however, the law was not enforced. Mr. Ware was responsible for changing the official title of school commissioner to school superintendent. Also during Mr. Ware's administration, the board of education took the position that it was not more schools that were needed in the county, but better schools.

In 1924, K. E. Taylor was elected school superintendent and served from January of 1925 until his death in 1933. While Mr. Taylor was in office, four employee positions were added to the school system: a home demonstration agent, an attendance officer, a supervisor of primary education and a visiting teacher. Both salaries and requirements for teachers were raised in 1931. The term for some schools was increased from six and a half months to nine months.

A major change that occurred during the mid 1930s was the consolidation of schools and the erection of better buildings. When R. S. Simonton became superintendent in 1933, there were 71 schools; however, when he retired in 1940, there were 18 schools for white pupils and 12 schools for black pupils. The accredited schools in 1934 were Norcross, Dacula, Duluth, Grayson and Snellville. Lawrenceville and Buford had accredited, independent school systems.

Many Gwinnett County residents had their high school educations interrupted in the 1940s due to World War II. Construction continued, however, in the '40s with the building of a new Suwanee School during 1942-43, the opening of Lilburn High School during 1942-43, the erection of a new facility in Dacula in 1947 to replace two buildings that were destroyed by fire in 1944, and the rebuilding of one of the Grayson School buildings after it burned in 1944. Howard Pool was the superintendent for most of the decade from 1941 to 1948, when the Lawrenceville system became part of the county school system. Major conveniences added to several schools in the 1950s were indoor restrooms and cafeterias. While R. C. Wilbanks was superintendent, a 1955 bond issue provided funds to erect four high school buildings: Central Gwinnett-Lawrenceville, South Gwinnett at Snellville, West Gwinnett at Norcross and North Gwinnett at Suwanee. The bond issue provided for the building of Hooper-Renwick School in Lawrenceville and Hull Elementary School in Duluth, which were for black students and which replaced several one-teacher black schools in the county. Construction of new schools at Harmony and Sugar Hill was also funded along with additions to Dacula, Lilburn, Duluth, Centerville, Norcross, Snellville, Grayson, Bethesda and Suwanee. By 1956, Gwinnett County changed its method of selecting the board of education by adopting the current plan of electing five board members from five districts, with the superintendent being approved by the board.

When B. B. Harris became superintendent in 1957, citizens of Dacula were taking court action to prevent Dacula High School from consolidating with Central Gwinnett, and citizens of Duluth were asking to have their children moved from West Gwinnett High School in Norcross back to Duluth. Both groups were successful in their pursuits, and a 1958 bond issue provided funds for a new high school in Duluth as well as additions to Dacula and Lilburn. Also under the Harris administration, Lilburn and Bethesda high schools consolidated to form Berkmar High School in 1966. (For more information on Mr. Harris, see "History of B. B. Harris Elementary School.")

The late 1960s marked the period of consolidation of many white and black schools in Georgia, and in Gwinnett County, Hooper-Renwick School in Lawrenceville and Hull

Elementary School in Duluth joined the existing schools in their communities. J. W. Benefield was superintendent from 1967 to 1977, a time of more new construction with the opening of the Parkview Complex in Lilburn, composed of Camp Creek Elementary, Trickum Middle, Parkview High and The Gwinnett County Vocational Education Center at Parkview. The method of grouping sixth, seven and eighth graders, known as the middle-school concept, was put into effect with Snellville Middle being the first Gwinnett County middle school. Middle schools constructed during Mr. Benefield's administration were Lanier, Lawrenceville, Sweetwater and Trickum. Also, the following elementary schools opened: W. C. Britt, Camp Creek, Centerville, J. G. Dyer, Gwin Oaks, Knight and Peachtree. (For more information on Mr. Benefield, see "History of Benefield Elementary School.")

The decade of the '80s had been a time of phenomenal growth in Gwinnett County. National attention has been given to the county as it has moved to the ranks of the top five fastest growing counties in the nation. Keeping up with the growth has been a demanding task for the school system. Twenty-two of the schools whose history is presented in this collection opened during the administration of Alton C. Crews, who became superintendent in 1977. The community has continually supported the public schools of Gwinnett County by passing bond referendums enabling the construction of three high schools, four middle schools and 13 elementary schools. Additionally, Gwinnett County now has an alternative school, Open Campus High School, and a post-secondary school, Gwinnett Technical Institute.

Under the administration of Dr. Crews, the community became involved in all aspects of education. Local school advisory committees, organized in every school, consist of volunteer citizens who help set school goals and priorities. Another method of teaming local schools with the community is through partnerships with local businesses interested in sharing resources. Also, enrichment courses are offered to the public through 10 community schools, thereby putting school buildings to use after regular school hours.

Since the first school commissioner's report showing an 1871 enrollment of 2,204 students with 41 teachers employed, Gwinnett County public schools have grown to an enrollment of 62,132 with 3,500 teachers employed. The history of the public schools of Gwinnett County is, however, more than a comparison of numbers; it is a resource exhibiting how much the public values education. Because this resource needs to be preserved, an appointed historian from every school has carefully documented points of interest in order to share each school's memorable past.

Sources

Flanigan, James C. *History of Gwinnett County, Georgia,* Volume I. Buford, Georgia: Moreno Press, Inc., 1943, reprinted 1975.

Flanigan, James C. *History of Gwinnett County, Georgia,* Volume II. Chelsea, Michigan: Book Crafters, Inc., 1959, reprinted 1984.

Condensed Official History of the Gwinnett Police Department

(Editor's Note: the following chapter is from the official history of the Gwinnett Police Department, which gives an overview of the growth of the unit. Major Alan Doss is a native of DeKalb County, who has been in law enforcement in Gwinnett County since 1977.)

By Major Alan Doss

In 1919, the Gwinnett County Grand Jury recommended the hiring of two officers because of increasing liquor traffic in the county. No action was taken. Again, in 1921, the recommendation was made for the hiring of a police force. October, 1921 is the first known documentation of police officers being hired by Gwinnett County, when "Messrs. Dowis of Duluth; Hugh Garner of Lawrenceville and Telford Yancey of Grayson" were named as Gwinnett police officers. At the time, Gwinnett was a sparsely populated 437 square miles, known for years for cockfighting, car theft and illegal liquor.

Minutes of a 1953 commission meeting record the first attempt to structure a department. "...The county commission March 2, 1953, to take up matters pertaining to the county. Motion was made by Weldon B. Archer and seconded by O.D. Cain to appoint Richard (Dick) Martin and George Barron as county policemen. Also included in discussion, salaries to be paid at $225 per month each and county to furnish one car." A variety of individuals served over the years.

Alan Doss

The department had originally been instituted without a chief being appointed. In January 1959, J.O. Bell, a U.S. Navy veteran, was named Gwinnett's first Police Chief. The department's primary job at that time was "traffic regulation," though news accounts continued to tell of frequent seizures of moonshine. It was not until 1963 that the department moved into its headquarters building on Swanson Drive – a building that was demolished in 2002 to make room for improvements associated with the Gwinnett County Comprehensive Corrections Complex.

Chief Bell retired at the end of 1964 and Havard Norred became chief on January 1, 1965. During his tenure, the department became a member of Metropol, mobile radios and surplus military guns were obtained, and firearms training was instituted. Citing the "constant pressure" of employee dissension and Grand Jury probes of "irregularities," Norred resigned three years later, in March, 1968. He was replaced by Bobby Plunkett, who resigned after two months (May 1968), after county commissioners didn't want to retain several of the officers he had hired. (Plunkett served later as chief of the Lawrenceville Police Department and was elected Sheriff of Gwinnett County in 1984 and served for two terms until beaten in a run-off with Jim Carsten).

Jimmy Kilgore was named to replace Chief Plunkett. Allegations of theft of confiscated property arose during his term, and commissioners said there was a "lack of cooperation" and "division and loss of public confidence in the police department." Kilgore resigned on February 19, 1969. That same day, all of the department's remaining police officers were fired as John Crunkleton, a lieutenant with the DeKalb County Police Department was named chief.

Crunkleton had come to the attention of Gwinnett officials when he was instrumental in the investigation of the three officers' murders in 1964. He started rebuilding the department of 33 people by hiring some of the former employees. Crunkleton began changes and improved the espirit de corps. Officer's uniform color went from mint green/black to tan/brown; and vehicles colors were changed to tan/brown. He established qualifications for employment of police officers and a period of probationary employment began a basic police training school and instituted regularly scheduled in-service training.

Gwinnett's new Police Academy was the first county academy to be certified by the state of Georgia. Among the graduates of the initial class of the academy in 1972 were Bill Dean and Carl White, who both later would be chief.

Other innovations under Crunkleton's time as chief:

- An aviation unit was established through acquisition of military surplus equipment.
- The detective division began, as was an identification unit (now the Crime Scene Unit).
- A chaplain program started.
- Intoximeters came into use.
- The "one man, one car" program was established. (Assigning a patrol car to each officer increased the number of cars needed but allowed the cars to be used over more years than would have been possible if they had been used around the clock.)
- Precincts were established in Sugar Hill and on Harmony Grove Road.
- Through grant money, the department's Headquarters building on Hi Hope Road was first occupied on March 28, 1978. The department had moved from a building of 3,624 square feet to a new one of over 42,000 square feet. (Employees, not yet aware of how rapidly Gwinnett County would grow, wondered how such a huge facility with so much vacant space could ever be used to its potential. It was not many years, however, before the building had been outgrown and modifications were required.)

From 1978 to 1985, Gwinnett's population increased from 137,200 to 249,600, making it one of the five fastest growing counties in the nation. The police department's authorized strength went from 173 to 283 employees during that time.

On February 22, 1985, the county commission removed Crunkleton from his position and named Kent A. Ryan, chief of the Fire Department, as director over a newly created Department of Public Safety. This move brought under one administrator the police, fire department, corrections and animal control department. Ryan assumed the duties of police chief.

Among Ryan's first moves was a change in the color of police cars. All cars were solid white with a "reflective gold" stripe running from front to back on each side, to increase police visibility through the reflection of the stripe. It also helped eliminate units in different hues when repainted after damage. (Some officers saw the "gold" stripe as being "yellow" and felt it to be what might be considered a 'stripe of cowardice.') A uniform committee was named to determine new uniform colors.

Ryan offered employment incentives to previously certified officers having experience in other departments. This allowed the county to hire relatively large numbers of police officers quickly to catch up with rapid manpower demands because of the county's growth.

Ryan opened the first Southside Precinct building in a doublewide, pre-fabricated office building off Hewatt Road.

On October 17, 1985, Ryan hired Steven F. Schildecker as police chief. He came from the DeKalb County Police Department and served until March 1, 1988, at which time the commissioners had terminated Ryan and put Schildecker in as the new director of Public Safety. As chief/director, Schildecker organized the department's SWAT team and an Explosive Ordnance Disposal (EOD) unit. The current 800 MHz radio system with portable radios was activated under his command and the enhanced-911 phone system was brought to Gwinnett. He established a K-9 unit and changed uniform colors to French blue/navy. He started the first attempt at a crime analysis function and was able to purchase two MD500E helicopters with forward looking infrared devices.

After a nationwide search for police chief candidates, C. Wayne Bolden, an assistant chief from Ft. Lauderdale, Fla. was selected to head the Department in March, 1989. (It was at this time that the "gold" stripe on police cars was changed to blue.) Bolden initiated an Employee Award program and the DARE program for Gwinnett's fifth graders, taught by Crime Prevention officers. He also initiated a COPS (Community Oriented Police Services) program, which offered training to neighborhood groups and is sometimes now compared to a "neighborhood watch on steroids." Bolden created the first formal Field Training Officer program, which trained experienced officers in methods of providing on-the-job training to new officers upon academy graduation. It was in 1993 that the department obtained national accreditation as a law enforcement agency. This effort was led by then-Capt. Bill Dean, serving at the time as accreditation manager.

From 1991 to 1993, Schildecker served concurrently as Public Safety Director and Acting County Manager. During this time the concept of a Public Safety Department in Gwinnett County faded from popularity and the Police Department became once again an independent department. Schildecker was removed from his roles in January 1993. (Chief Schildecker later served as a consultant for the Georgia Emergency Management Agency after he left Gwinnett. He died of a brain tumor on January 11, 1999.)

Bolden resigned in December 1993 as chief. (He later served as chief deputy of the Gwinnett County Sheriff's Office.)

Carl White, in the first Gwinnett Police Academy class, had earlier been Acting Chief, and was named to head the department in January 1994. He was the first of Gwinnett County's "home grown" police chiefs. In 1994, he organized a departmental anniversary program, at which time former John Crunkleton's badge, #001, was permanently retired and Chief Crunkleton was publicly honored for his service to the department.

Among the accomplishments as chief, White obtained the Gwinnett Training Center from the City of Buford, giving the Police Academy its own facility. He started a fifth precinct (what would become known as the Central precinct) and led the renovation of the headquarters building. White also established the Citizen's Police Academy in 1997. The Southside precinct moved to its new Stone Drive facility in 1998. Chief White retired in June 1998.

W.H. "Bill" Dean became the second member of the first Gwinnett Police Academy to rise through the ranks and become chief on June 6, 1998. Under his leadership the department was re-accredited and obtained certification through the state of Georgia. A video conferencing system was installed throughout the department. This system features 50" plasma screens and allows Headquarters, the Training Division and all precincts to be linked together for training or conducting meetings. In March 2002, the Central Precinct moved into its new building on Satellite Boulevard, a facility shared by the Crime Prevention Unit. Dean retired on October 1, 2003 and Charles M. Walters, a graduate of the ninth Academy, was named to succeed Dean.

Groundbreaking for the Northside precinct at the Mall of Georgia came March 2, 2004 and the building was put into use on July 11, 2005. A Westside Precinct was occupied in April, 2004. Groundbreaking came on April 19, 2005 for a $20 million training facility on Highway 29 at Sweetgum Road, scheduled to be occupied in 2006. A new Eastside Precinct on Alcovy Road, was occupied also in 2006.

The force serves Gwinnett's unincorporated areas and the cities of Grayson, Buford, Rest Haven and Berkeley Lake.

Dark Days for Gwinnett County as Three Officers Murdered

(Editor's Note: Modern Day Gwinnett got unwanted notoriety in 1964 when three of its police offers were murdered—-with their own weapons. Here is the official police report on the tragedy from a member of the police force.)

By Major Alan Doss

In the early morning hours of April 17, 1964, Gwinnett Police Officer Marvin Jesse Gravitt became ill while working an accident in Suwanee and needed to go home. Officers Jerry R. Everett and Ralph K. Davis, having just finished their meal at an all-night restaurant, drove together to the accident scene to pick up Jesse Gravitt and take him home. It was shortly after 1 a.m. when they arrived.

On their way to "Pop" Gravitt's home minutes later, they were diverted to a call of "suspicious activity" on Arc Way, a dirt road in what was then a remote area between Beaver Ruin and Pleasant Hill Road. The officers responded to this call as a "red light call." When they got to Arc Way they saw three men gathered around an Oldsmobile and a Chevrolet parked in the woods. One of the men got into the Chevrolet and sped away in reverse. Gravitt and Davis gave chase, leaving Everett with the two men at the scene. The Chevrolet driver was caught nearby. The two officers took the driver, Wade Levi Truett, back to where the Oldsmobile and police cruiser were parked.

The officers didn't realize at the time that the Oldsmobile had been stolen in Atlanta. The officers had interrupted three men in the act of hiding their crime: Venson Williams, 43, was changing ignition switches; Alex Evans, 38, was going through the glove compartment; and Wade Levi Truett, 33, was changing the license plate on the car.

When the two officers got back to Everett, they found him in the driver's seat of the Olds, checking the ignition switch, with Evans in the passenger seat next to him. Everett and Evans were already acquainted. (Evans had been the chief deputy under Sheriff Dan Cole. In April 1964 Cole was serving a federal prison sentence on a liquor violation.)

Everett had apparently trusted Evans, or perhaps Everett's confidence was gained by a convincing cover story. In either case, Everett was caught off-guard. Everett slid out of the car and Evans did also, producing two pistols and thus gaining a critical advantage over the officers. Evans had Truett disarm the officers and cuff them together, and then wondered aloud what to do with the three officers. Venson Williams' response: "When they put the uniform on, they automatically become dirty sons of bitches. It don't matter to me."

Truett suggested that they be cuffed to a tree. Evans and Williams put the officers in the Oldsmobile and drove a short distance further on Arc Way, while Truett moved the police car off the road where it wouldn't be seen. He then drove the Chevrolet to where the Oldsmobile was now parked and heard "firecrackers" when he drove up. Truett got out and saw the officers on the ground, Evans and Williams standing over them with guns drawn. One officer, apparently still alive, was "moaning and bubbling." Truett took two bullets from one officer's gun belt and shot the still-live officer. The moaning stopped.

The officers lay lifeless on the ground, side by side, cuffed together. Ralph Davis and Jesse Gravitt had each been shot five times in the head. Jerry Everett had been shot once in the shoulder, once in the thigh and twice in the head. The three had been killed by 14 shots with their own pistols.

The person who called to make the original report of the suspicious activity had witnessed part of the chase involving the Chevrolet and he reported having heard an argument. He had seen the police car leave where the chase had ended and saw the red blinker stop shortly afterwards. He surmised that the officers could use their radio to call for help if it was needed. What he didn't know when he saw the red light stop blinking was that the wires were being ripped from the police car so that neither the radio nor the red lights would be of further use.

The Oldsmobile was set on fire. Truett began to back the Chevrolet out, but it got stuck. Williams jacked the car up to get it out of the sand, and then he and Truett drove to South Carolina. They disposed of their clothing in a creek and then bought a set of recapped tires for the Chevrolet so that its tire tracks wouldn't match those left at the scene of the murders. They then threw the old tires into a creek as well.

A baby sitter in the home of the original reporting party noticed the police car around 8:30 a.m. and the homeowner reported it. The bodies were discovered when responding officers arrived. On Sunday morning, two days later, sightseers in the area found a pistol near the road. A search was initiated and police officers and Civil Defense volunteers combed the area, uncovering another pistol and a flashlight. All the items found had belonged to the officers and had been thrown out as the killers fled the area.

About a month after the murders, Gov. Carl Sanders signed an executive order granting police powers in Gwinnett County to the Georgia State Patrol and the Georgia Bureau of Investigation, thus allowing them to work independently of local authorities to investigate the murders. When it appeared in August of 1964, in the midst of the civil rights movement, that the investigation was going nowhere, Sen. Zell Miller offered a $15,000 reward and criticized the Federal Bureau of Investigation for not pursuing the case. He referred to the fact that many agents had recently been assigned to Athens to investigate the murder of a black educator and that a $25,000 payment to a government informant had led to the discovery of the bodies of three civil rights workers killed in Mississippi, but that nothing was being done by the FBI to solve the murders of these officers. Governor Sanders then asked the FBI to assist in the investigation.

The case had drawn the attention of law enforcement officials around the state. A lieutenant in the vice and intelligence unit of the DeKalb County Police Department, John W. Crunkleton, was among those who had taken an interest in the case and assisted the GBI and GSP in the investigation. He was able to develop leads in the case and indictments were brought against Venson Williams, Wade Levi Truett and Alex Evans over a year later, in July, 1965.

At the time of the indictments, Evans was in federal prison in Illinois on a charge involving illegal liquor. He was brought to the Atlanta Federal Penitentiary and testified later that he had not left home on the evening of the killings; that he didn't know Truett; that he had only a passing acquaintance with Williams, having spoken to him only three or four times; and that he, himself, had actually been investigating the murders and had come up with suspects. Venson Williams had lived in Alabama, Dawsonville and Atlanta before being arrested for the hijacking of a trailer loaded with liquor. Wade Levi Truett was a truck driver from South Carolina who helped operate a body shop before he was convicted of stealing an interstate shipment of liquor.

At trial, Truett agreed to testify against the others and was granted immunity from prosecution. Evans and Williams were convicted in separate trials for Everett's murder, and prosecutors saw no reason to try them again for the other deaths. Both were handed a death sentence. However, the Fifth Circuit Court of Appeals struck down Williams' sentence in August, 1968 and ordered that he be retried or that the sentence be commuted to a life sentence. The Court's decision was based on the exclusion of 33 potential jurors who had said they conscientiously opposed the death penalty. Williams' sentence was commuted to life. Evans' death sentence was commuted to life in 1972 when the U.S. Supreme Court struck down Georgia's capital punishment law.

Wade Levi Truett died in 1983. Venson Williams was paroled in 1989 and moved to Conyers. Surviving relatives of the murdered officers learned of his release through newspaper accounts and picketed his home after he was paroled. As recently as late 2003, Williams refused to discuss the case, believing that further media attention might negatively affect his parole status. Alex Evans has been denied parole several times, most recently in 2003. He remains at Men's State Prison in Hardwick, and maintains he is innocent, claiming he has information that will absolve him "when the time is right."

Timeline of Western Electric Plant, Norcross

January, 1970: Personnel move into permanent facilities in office.

February, 1972: Final section turned over to Atlanta Works officials. Open house held to commemorate completion.

March, 1972: CWS certified as exclusive bargaining agent for hourly-rated production and maintenance employees.

April, 1972: First reel of cable shipped.

December, 1973: Total employees to 2,317 at year end.

November, 1973: Justice Department files antitrust suit seeking to dismember the Bell System.

November, 1975: Employees pledge $105,000 to United Way Fund drive.

January, 1976: Works develop a laboratory fiber optic production line. Experimental lightwave system installed in ducts and manholes under the east end of Bell Labs building, 2,100 feet long, to study effects of environment and field test splicing techniques. Develops world's first large fiber optic cable carrying large quantities of voice, data and image signals.

December, 1977: Employment stands at 2,700. (550 who started at opening still employed.)

September, 1978: First WE produced standard lightwave communications system to be installed by Southern Bell in late 1980. Processes for the cable, connectors and closures developed at Atlanta Works lab.

February, 1979: CWA local 3263 dedicates new union hall on Singleton Road in Norcross.

April, 1979: Doherty Protective Services Center opens at Crescent Drive and Norcross Tucker Road. Built on land donated by Atlanta Works.

March, 1980: WE ships first lightguide cable to Southern Bell Smyrna FT-3 project.

November, 1981: Atlanta Works begin purchasing quartz tubes for lightguide from US supplier, saving $492,000 a year.

January, 1982: Justice Department and AT&T reach historic agreement on the seven year antitrust suit. AT&T agrees to a government proposed modification to the existing 1956 consent decree to divest itself of 22 local telephone companies, retain long distance services, and the Western Electric equipment manufacturing business, as well as Bell Labs. In turn, the government removes restrictions which limited AT&T to provide tariffed communications services and manufacturing equipment needed to provide those services and barred the company from entering other fields.

November, 1983: Atlanta Works lightguide cables used to link 26 widely separated Olympic sites to national TV networks.

January, 1984: Divestiture. Atlanta Works become part of AT&T Network Systems.

July, 1984: Fiber Optic network from Atlanta Works serves the 1984 Summer Olympics in Los Angeles.

September, 1984: Fourth major expansion of lightguide facilities since 1979. Expansion covers 100,000 square feet of manufacturing space, with major increase in production.

February, 1989: LITESPEC Inc. formed with Sumitomo Electric Industries of Japan, a joint venture to produce optic fiber in new process. 51 percent of firm held by AT&T.

May, 1990: Atlanta Works cable part of 22 mile fiber cable network installed by Northeast Gwinnett Cablevision of Suwanee.

December, 1991: Payroll for year at $143 million. Gwinnett ad valorem tax bill is $2.5 million.

May, 1993: Atlanta Works received International Standard Organization 9001 registration.

January, 1994: Ultra-tall draw towers building of six stories increases fiber production capabilities. Also that year: copper manufacturing ceases at Atlanta Works.

February 5, 1996: New name officially launches, Lucent Technologies.

July, 2006: Atlanta Works employees, about 200, participate as volunteers in 1996 Olympics in Atlanta.

October, 1996: Lucent officially spins off from AT&T.

Officials at Western Electric, Norcross and successors over the years:

1970-72:	Jim O'Neill, general manager
1972-75:	Stu Miller, general manager
1975-78:	Bill Hicks, general manager
1978-89:	Lee McClary, general manager
1989-91:	Peter Ballantyne, Mfg. Vice President
1991-98:	Jim Carboy, Fiber Optics Vice President (William Spivey was president of Network Products Group of Lucent Technology from 1997-2000)
1999-2001:	Denys Gounot, president of Optical Fibre Systems (Lucent Technology), reported to Spivey.
2001-2003:	Eddie Edwards, CEO, OFS
2003-2006:	Klyoshi Takeuchi, CEO, OFS
2006-2008:	Katsuhiko "Jack" Murota, CEO, OFS
2008-present	Timothy F. Murray, CEO, OFS

CWA Local 3263 Presidents

1972:	Donald Holly
1973-83:	Jim Stone
1983-84:	Mike Palmour
1985-89:	Ralph Maly
1989-93:	Joe Finn
1994-99:	Leon Gusek
2000-01:	Iven Todd
2001-03:	Eddie Christian
2003-current:	David Lasley

American Cancer Society in Gwinnett

By Phylecia Wilson

Phylecia Wilson at Gwinnett's Relay for Life

Gwinnett County is well known across the nation in American Cancer Society (ACS) circles. More money is raised at the Gwinnett Relay for Life than at any Relay in the nation. Gwinnett's Relay has set record-after-record, and keeps raising the bar, being the top earning Relay in the country for several years.

In 1994, the first year for Gwinnett's Relay for Life, the funds raised totaled $119,246, which at the time was the most ever raised by a rookie event. Teams, survivors and participants involved, as well as dollars, went over the top in subsequent years. Gwinnett was the first Relay for Life in the nation to net $1 million in a single Relay, coming in at $1.1 million for 1999. Three years later, in 2002, Gwinnett was the first Relay to raise and net $2 million, hitting $2.006 million. For 2008, Gwinnett's Relay raised $2.5 million By 2008, which was the Gwinnett Relay's 15th anniversary, the cumulative total raised in Gwinnett Relays has gone over the $20 million mark. This is a singular, unmatched accomplishment for the entire ACS organization. (See Appendix for details.)

It's a far cry from earlier efforts at raising money and awareness of the dangers of cancer. For several decades, ACS volunteers conducted annual door-to-door solicitations in the "Crusade Against Cancer." Canvassers, mostly homemakers, visited neighbors asking for donations, and handed out information about the seven warning signs of cancer.

As more women began to join the workforce, the Society began looking for new ways to raise money. Special events came into fashion. In 1975, the ACS held the first gala in Gwinnett a "Crusaders' Ball Against Cancer," which raised $110,000 for cancer research. Chaired by Lawrenceville's Marion Webb in the early years, that ball has become a Gwinnett institution. In 2006, the Ball raised $235,000 in the fight against cancer. Since its start in 1974, the Ball has raised more than $6 million for cancer research.

The Society began holding other fund-raising events in the mid 1980s such as golf and tennis tournaments, "Swim for a Cure," "Send a Mouse to College" (for the elementary school students) and also a "Jail and Bail" event. Jail and Bail was popular at the start, but after the third year, it lost its popularity.

Relay Comes to Gwinnett

Little known to Gwinnett during that time was what was happening clear across the country that would change not just the way the ACS raises money, but also the way it relates to survivors and to communities nationwide. In 1985, Dr. Gordy Klatt, a Tacoma colorectal surgeon, wanted to enhance the income of his local American Cancer Society office to show support for his patients who had battled cancer. He decided to personally raise money for the fight by doing something he enjoyed, running marathons.

In May of that year, Dr. Klatt spent a grueling 24 hours circling the track at Baker Stadium at the University of Puget Sound in Tacoma. He ran more than 83 miles. That first year, nearly 300 of Dr. Klatt's friends, family, and patients watched as he ran and walked the course. Throughout the night, friends donated $25 to run or walk with Dr. Klatt for 30 minutes. His efforts raised $27,000 to fight cancer.

While circling the track those 24 hours, Dr. Klatt thought about how others could take part in his mission to fight cancer. He envisioned a 24-hour team relay event that could raise more money to fight cancer. Over the next few months, he pulled together a small committee to plan the first team relay event, known as the "City of Destiny Classic 24-Hour Run Against Cancer."

In 1986, with the help of Pat Flynn, one of Dr. Klatt's patients, now known as the "Mother of Relay," 19 teams took part in the first team Relay event on the track at the historic Stadium Bowl and raised $33,000. An indescribable spirit prevailed at the track and in the tents that dotted the infield.

The idea for this type of fundraiser spread across the country and arrived in Gwinnett in the fall of 1993. By then, the ACS had adopted the Relay as their National Signature Event.

For the first year in Gwinnett, 1994, the committee's goal was to have 25 teams and raise $43,000. However, by recruiting Rotary Clubs, corporations, cities, schools and others, there were 43 teams that first year which raised the $119,246. It was the most ever raised by a rookie Relay event and Gwinnett received a National Merit Award from the National ACS.

The Gwinnett Relay, having outgrown the South Gwinnett High campus in one year, moved the second year to the new Collins Hill football field. Income for the event doubled to $242,242 and ACS officials began to speculate how much more might be raised.

Because of a state law limiting dates for spring football practice, the Gwinnett ACS committee had to find a new venue the third year and decided to go to the Gwinnett County Fairgrounds in Lawrenceville in 1995. New asphalt walkways worked perfectly for a Relay. It was like having two football fields in one venue and the Relay is held there to this day.

What a Relay is Like

It always amazes people how the Gwinnett Fairgrounds can turn into a small city on the Friday afternoon of the event. Nearly every Gwinnett County public school, from elementary through high schools, participates in the Relay, along with many private schools, Gwinnett Tech and Georgia Gwinnett University. Churches, corporations, neighborhoods, civic organizations—-you name it—and they are there Friday afternoon, setting up their camp site.

It's not just tents for shelter created in this born-overnight city. The "city" is created as tents and decorations go up one by one, until the "streets" around the fairgrounds are populated by a mixture of themed structures, such as a 1950s café with an Elvis impersonator, or a silver rocket, or a luau—as the Gwinnett teams show their creativity.

Teams have themes, many being cancer related; they decorate their campsites accordingly. For example, The "Kiss Cancer Good Bye" team might dress as Hershey Kisses and hand out the tasty morsels. Another team will build ships of plywood and called their team, "Cruisin' to a Cure." Gwinnett school bus drivers once used the back of a discarded school bus to decorate their camp site. With awards for "Best Team Theme" and "Best Spirit," the creativity and friendly competition is incredible. For years, one of the most creative teams was from Brookwood Elementary School. They once built a Paris sidewalk café scene, dressed as can-can girls with the theme, "We Can-Can Cure Cancer."

On-site fundraising is another big feature at the Gwinnett Relay. Georgia Power cooks and sells funnel cakes on Friday night and omelets on Saturday morning. The Gwinnett Sheriff's Department grills chicken and hamburgers. Teams sell raffle tickets for various items (even a play house!), and create activities for fun. It all started in Gwinnett the first year when Duane Downs (at that time with NCR) brought his bowling team "The Mixed Nuts" to the Relay. They had a mini-bowling lane where people could "bowl" for a quarter. At the Relay in 2007 this team went a step further and brought in a real bowling lane on a tractor trailer!

It's all about having a good time, raising money and raising awareness of cancer. Teams come to Relay often because of someone special they have lost or someone who is fighting their battle against cancer. At 7 p.m. on Friday, team members begin gathering around the track to cheer on survivors in the Survivors' Walk.

Up to 1,800 cancer survivors have participated in the Opening Ceremony "Survivors' Walk," most with their caregivers. Many are celebrating their victory over cancer; others are still in treatment; still others may have just been diagnosed with the disease. The Walk is a stirring, emotional display of human courage, which brings tears to the eyes of many watching. But mostly, it is a time of celebration. These are people who have "stared the beast in the eye and made it blink," as the late Terry Zahn, a TV broadcaster from Virginia Beach, used to say. Not only have most made the beast blink; they have brought it to its knees!

Entertainment follows the Survivors' Walk. For several years, American Idol first-runner-up to Fantasia, Diana DeGarmo, performed at the Relay as a child. Music and dancing are a basic part of the Relay, as team members begin walking the track after the Survivors Walks….for the next 12 hours.

Around 10 p.m. the Luminaria Ceremony begins. For months people have been putting together luminarias, bags with sand and candles inside, and written names of friends and loved ones on the front. As the candles are lit and bags are placed around the Fairgrounds track, the bags shine the names of those who lost their battle as well as survivors being honored. Bagpipers drone "Amazing Grace." Many participants take hand-held candles or their loved one's luminaria and silently walk around the track. It is a time for remembrance and meditation, and relative quietness.

Though the track is never vacant, matters pick back up around 11 p.m. Many team members continue circling the Faiground track in honor of those who battle cancer. This continues throughout the night, with people always walking, some with headsets on, some quietly conversing with their walk-mates, others walking in silence. After all, patients must deal with their cancer 24 hours a day. Those walking can show reverence for that fight by each team having a representative continually walking throughout the Relay.

The wee hours of night take on an almost eerie ambiance, with the track illuminated almost only by the luminaria, Many people prefer to walk for their team during this time, because of the quiet and the fact that it represents the darkness that comes before the dawn in the cancer patient's life. And after all, it's usually the coolest part of the night to walk!

The Gwinnett Relay ends mid morning with awards to teams and individuals for fund raising, spirit and creativity.

Back to History

The Relay got a boost in its fourth and fifth year when the Gwinnett County Schools become more involved. Previously, the school system had held its own "Walk-a-thon" for several years, raising money for charitable purposes, but had discontinued the walk for safety reasons. Instead, schools were encouraged to have their own walks at their schools, and donate funds raised to their choice of non-profit organizations. In the past, the school board chose a different charitable organization to receive the money each year. The ACS had never been chosen.

When one of the Gwinnett principals, Olivia Hodges of Dacula, lost a loved one to cancer, after having attended the Relay, she asked about donating the money her school raised to the ACS. The Relay committee suggested that she come to the event with some of her students and present the check. The following year she joined the steering committee as chair of school team recruitment. That year, Superintendent Alvin Wilbanks invited Phylecia Wilson to talk with staff and administrators about becoming involved in Relay. With those forces at work, there were numerous school teams from 1998 forward.

In succeeding years, more schools became participants in the Relay for Life. The schools have been a driving force for the Gwinnett effort. Altogether, monies raised by schools in Gwinnett account for 40 to 50 percent of the total monies raised. For 2007, the Gwinnett schools figure totaled $1,165,567 of the $2,571,681 total.

ACS volunteers have recruited key corporate firms in Gwinnett as sponsors. Support has been constant, as more companies come on board each year. Scientific Atlanta was one of the first sponsors and in the third year became the signature sponsor for the event. Primerica has been another perennial sponsor, as has Emory Eastside Hospital. Hayes Chrysler-Plymouth-Dodge has given $10,000 toward a car to give away for over 10 years. Another significant group participating in the Relay are the many Gwinnett churches, which have been a big factor since about year 3 in making the Relay a success.

Impact Nationally

Nationally, the ACS Relays For Life have raised more than $2 billion. It took 20 years to raise the first billion dollars, but with more than 4,600 community Relay For Life events across the nation, it took only three years to raise the second billion dollars. Money raised by the Relay goes to support the ACS programs for research, education, and patient services.

Today cancer organizations all over the world have adopted Relay For Life as a method to raise money, to promote awareness in their countries, and to do it all by having a grand, good time. And ACS officials point to Gwinnett as the Relay for Life event which has led the way in showing the world how to raise money to fight back against cancer.

Timeline of Gwinnett Parks Acquisitions

By Grant Guess

Grant Guess

- **1971** Legislation created establishing a special Tax District, known as Gwinnett County Recreation District #1, within the Pinckneyville Militia District. Legislation authorized a Recreation Tax levy not to exceed 1 mill. This legislation was enacted for Pinckneyville Militia District by Referendum on May 20, 1971.

- **1975** Authorization was passed allowing any Militia District within Gwinnett County to join the Recreation District by majority vote within that Militia District. Gwinnett County Recreation Authority was created to provide a funding vehicle to be utilized in conjunction with dedicated Recreation Tax to allow acquisition and development of parks and recreational facilities.

- **1976** On May 4, the Duluth and Garners (Mountain Park area) Militia Districts voted to join the Recreation District.

- **1977** October 4, the Dacula Militia District held a referendum and approved joining the Recreation District.

- **1980** The Suwanee Militia District on November 4, 1979 approved joining the Recreation District.

- **1981-82** Reapportionment altered voting district lines, making a true Militia District vote impossible. This ended the ability of individual militia districts to join the Recreation District.

- **1984-85** The Gwinnett Commissioners authorized a "Recreational Needs Assessment" to be conducted for the total county. This study indicated an overwhelming demand for parks and recreational facilities to be provided countywide.

- **1986** The Gwinnett Commissioners funded the development of "County-Wide Recreation Master Plan." This plan identified a specific 6 year plan, and a long-range plan for providing a parks and recreation system to meet the needs of the total county. This plan was adopted to guide the development of the park system by the Board of Commissioners and the Recreation Authority in February, 1986.

In response to the "Needs Assessment" and the "County-Wide Recreation Master Plan", the Gwinnett Board of Commissioners called for a referendum giving the voters the option of expanding the Recreation District to encompass the total county. On November 4, 1986, the voters approved the Countywide Recreation District and its one mill Recreation Tax. The vote was approved 31,063 to 21,362.

- **1987** On January 1, 1987, the Gwinnett County Parks and Recreation Department was legally enabled to serve 100 percent of Gwinnett County. Prior to this, the department was restricted to serving only 25 percent of the landmass and approximately 40 percent of the population. In August 1987, the Gwinnett County Recreation Authority issued $17,000,000 to implement the "Six Year Plan" of the Master Plan.

- **1988** March 19, 1988, 50 acres was acquired on Britt Road. This site combined with 18 additional county owned acres is to serve as the Service Area B Community Park. Acquisition Price: $2,000,000. November 15, 1988, Springbrook Golf Course was acquired as the County's first public golf course. On December 21, the Recreation Authority issued $4,000,000 in revenue bonds to finance the acquisition and improvements. Purchase Price: $3,418,000.

- **1989** State Legislators amended the Recreation Authority Act; expanding the Authority to nine members and placing a $50,000,000 cap on bond indebtedness. In February, condemnation of the Bethesda Church Road site, owned by Williams Brothers Lumber Company was completed. The 141.406-acre tract was acquired as Service Area F Community Park. Acquisition Price: $1,555,402. March 31, 1989 the 58.06-acre Collins Hill Road Property was acquired to provide the Service Area G Community Park. Acquisition Price: $1,422,470. On April 20, 35 additional acres were acquired to compliment the existing acreage at George Pierce Park. Acquisition Price: $489,314.

- **1990** On August 6, 1990, the Recreation Authority issued $10 million in Revenue Bonds. These bonds were issued to purchase three new community park sites, enlarge one community park, and begin development on Tribble Mill Regional Park, develop one community park south of Snellville, George Pierce Park in Suwanee and Lawrenceville's City Park East when an agreement is reached between the County and City. On December 26, 1990, a 90-acre tract of land with 12 acres of botanical gardens and a 22,000 square foot manor home were donated to the County by Charles and Myrna Adams. The donation was estimated at $3.9 million and will be named Vines Botanical Gardens in honor of Mrs. Adams father, Mr. O. O. Vines.

- **1991** February 6, 1991, 83.437 acres was acquired in Area "D" (south of Snellville) for $1,800,000. (Lenora Park) February 8, 1991, 24.979 acres was acquired in Area "A" (Norcross/Duluth) for $1,623,635 (South Old Peachtree property). August 9, 1991, 83.12 acres was acquired in Area "K" (Buford) for $706,426.50 (North Bogan Road property).

- **1992** Gwinnett County assumed operation of Lawrenceville City Parks on March 28, 1992. The 40-year lease agreement stipulated that the existing Rhodes Jordan/City Park East will be expanded and new facilities will be constructed. City Park West will be leased to the County for18 months to allow for replacement of the facilities from City Park West at the expanded Rhodes Jordan Park.

- **1992 (cont.)** On April 24, 1992, a dedication ceremony was held for the Gwinnett Senior Center at Bethesda Park. This $1.1 million, 34,706 square foot facility was constructed with Community Development Block Grant funds and offers recreational programs and events for seniors in Gwinnett. On July 3, 1992 the Gwinnett Historic Courthouse was rededicated and reopened for community use. The 100-year-old historical structure is managed by Parks and Recreation and is designed to serve a variety of community cultural and meeting needs. In December 1992, the Recreation Authority refunds $29,050,000 in Recreation Revenue Bonds creating a net savings to the Recreation Fund of $800,000+. On August 28, 1992 a 28.5 acre parcel was added to Dacula Park allowing the Park sufficient size to be developed as a community park. Acquisition Cost: $295,701.00.

- **1994** On April 9, 1994 new Baseball-Softball facilities at Rhodes Jordan Park and Lenora Park Phase 1 are dedicated on the same day. The completion of the facilities at Rhodes Jordan Park triggers the end of the 18-month lease of City Park West. On May 4, 1994, Vines Botanical Gardens is leased to a group of citizens who formed a foundation. The Vines Botanical Gardens Foundation, Inc. begins operations immediately to improve the facility while lowering the support provided by the county. In 1994, an Update of the Countywide Master Plan for Parks and Recreation is authorized. Plans call for a three-phase process including a Needs Assessment Survey, public meetings to gather citizen input, and a technical report to set development for six years.

- **1995** The Board of Commissioners authorize the construction of phase one of Bogan Park by appropriating $3.6 million in the 1995 budget. The Master site plan design firm is to be selected in February. Needs Assessment Survey completed by A. L. Burruss in preparation for the update of the Countywide Recreation Master Plan. Land swap was approved adding 19 acres to Bethesda Park for 4 acres to Gwinnett DOT for right-of-way at the Old Hospital Property near Suwanee. Citizens Steering Committee formed and public meetings held throughout the County to gather input of recreational needs as a part of the update of the Countywide Recreation Master Plan.

- **1996** In August of 1996, the Board of Commissioners approved the update of the County-Wide Recreation Master Plan to guide park development over the course of the next 8 years. In November of 1996, voters approved a Special Purpose Local Option Sales Tax (SPLOST) that includes $60 million for Parks and Recreation projects. The tax begins collections in April of 1997 and continues for four years. The vote for approval was 84,928 to 74,576. An additional 10.129 acres was acquired ($810,320) to supplement the existing 25 acres located at South Old Peachtree (Pinckneyville Park) and a master plan for the 35-acre site was begun. An additional 12 acres adjacent to Rhodes Jordan Park in Lawrenceville is jointly acquired by the County and the City of Lawrenceville for future development.

- **1997** Funds of $1 million is included in the 1997 budget for land acquisition and planning for natatorium for the Collins Hill area. An additional 14.9159 acres was acquired adjoining Pinckneyville Park was acquired ($1,342,431) for the new Pinckneyville Arts and Crafts Center. Land was acquired for the Collins Hill Aquatics Center. The County purchased 29 acres across the street from Collins Hill Park and subsequently sold 10.5 of these acres to the Board of Education. The remaining 18.5 acres will be developed for the Aquatics Center. Joint planning between the two staffs resulted in shared parking and an integrated multipurpose trail. A 14.9159-acre site was acquired for $1,349,491 next to the Pinckneyville Soccer Complex for a proposed Community Center.

- **1998** Green space is acquired for the proposed Little Mulberry. 485 acres was acquired $5,428,817 from a number of owners with assistance from The Trust for Public Land. Construction began on Dacula Park Redevelopment (a 1997 sales tax project). The Gwinnett Senior Center at Bethesda Park was expanded. Land was acquired on the opposite side of South old Peachtree Road from the Pinckneyville Soccer Complex. This 58-acre site ($4,431,438) is to provide space for a Baseball - Softball Facility and other amenities to complement the Pinckneyville Park Soccer Complex and proposed Community. Land (24,074 acres for $1,074,462) was acquired adjoining Rhodes Jordan Park for a Community Center - Outdoor Family Aquatics Center. Land was acquired adjoining Shorty Howell Park. This 6-acre tract, near the park entrance, was acquired for $881,467 for park expansion.

- **1999** Land acquired adjoining Lenora Park. This 24-acre site is to provide park expansion. Land acquired for the proposed Bay Creek Park in the South District, consisting of 140 acres. Tribble Mill Park Expansion - Approximately 50-acres purchased to increase total park acreage to 730 acres, the County's largest park at this time. Land expansions were added to George Pierce Park of 32.5 acres and to Shorty Howell Park of 19 acres. Joint project with National Park Service and Dept. of National Resources, 340 acres at Settles Bridge/ Chattahoochee River was purchased. County owns 217 acres. Rabbit Hill Park, 74-acres, purchased for future youth soccer fields.

- **2000** The Springbrook Golf Course Commission was transferred the management responsibility for the golf course. The first Gwinnett Senior Golden Olympics was held. Total of18.43-acre site on Rockbridge Road purchased for future pool/activity building site. McDaniel Farm, a 128-acre land parcel near Gwinnett Place Mall was purchased for greenspace. Land acquisition finalized for Bay Creek Park in the Grayson area, a total of approximately 154 acres. Passive community parkland purchased in West District. (The Graves family land tract, total of 70 acres). County owned property in Hog Mountain area (over 100 acres) designated for future community park. Gwinnett County and its cities received $3,330,892 for the first year of Georgia Greenspace Program. 2000 Sales Tax Referendum approved by voters of Gwinnett County. Minimum funding level of $192,375,000 for parks and recreation projects/greenspace. Vote was 100,838 for approval, and 82,345 against.

- **2001** Acquired Ewing Chapel (Palm Creek) Property (294.3507) acres for a future open space park. Acquired Five Forks Park Site (25.0180 acres) for a Passive Community Park. Acquired the Deshong property (208.246 acres) for a future open space park. Acquired the Alcovy Grist Mill Property (11.8895 acres). This property, also known as Freeman's Mill or Swann's Mill, contains an intact gristmill that was operable as late as the 1980s. This purchase was made with Georgia Greenspace Program funds. Added 404.4595 acres to the Little Mulberry Park. Included a lake and 200 acres to be designated as the Karina Miller Nature Preserve. Little Mulberry becomes the County's largest park at 889.7216 acres. Acquired 350.0260 acres upstream of Norris Lake along No Business Creek and Doc Moore Branch for open space. 210 acres of this purchase were acquired with Georgia Greenspace Program funds. Acquired Kanoheda Property (25.3632 acres) for future Passive Community Park. Added 31.6307 acres to Rhodes Jordan Park for future community park development. Applied for and received, along with cities, $3,142,726 for the second year of the Georgia Greenspace Program.

The Alcovy Grist Mill

- **2002** Added 65.9337 acres to Lenora Park for future community park development. Acquired the Alexander property (91.097 acres) for a future Community Park. Acquired 1,795.21 acres for future Harbins' Alcovy park. Added 15.2923 acres to Collins Hill Park for future community park development. Acquired 60.675 acres to preserve the view of Stone Mountain from Highway 124 near Centerville. Acquisition used Georgia Greenspace program funds. Began a statistically valid Needs Assessment Survey of Gwinnett citizens to determine their recreation interests in anticipation of updating the Parks and Recreation Comprehensive Plan in 2003.

- **2003** Expanded Settles Bridge Park site 51 acres bringing total acreage to 217 acres. Acquired Peachtree Ridge Park (155 acres) and West District Pool (Peachtree Industrial Boulevard Aquatic Center - 22 acres) sites. Completed stabilization of Yellow River Post Office historic site. A community advisory board was formed in 2003 to oversee the Newly created Mustang Athletics (formerly Lucky Shoals Athletic Association.

- **2004** The 2004 Parks and Recreation Comprehensive Master Plan was completed. Details from this plan were used to set the list of items on the November 2, 2004 SPLOST Vote. 35.75 acres of land was purchased from the Gwinnett County Water and Sewer Authority at the F. Wayne Hill Water Resource Center with Georgia Greenspace funds. This is land that will be part of the grounds for the Gwinnett Environmental and Heritage Center. A lease with the Gwinnett County Water and Sewer Authority adds an additional 197.4265 acres to the grounds for the Gwinnett Environmental and Heritage Center at the F. Wayne Hill Water Resource Center. The referendum for the 2005 SPLOST was passed on November 2, 2004 by a margin of 156,080 for to 83,449 against. 65.16 percent of the voters approved a $550 million program that included $180 million for the County Parks and Recreation Program: an additional $25.5 million was approved for use by the cities for Parks and Recreation facilities. The County and the Recreation Authority agreed upon Conservation easements covering almost 3,700 acres of parkland in the Gwinnett County System. Nine parks now have conservation easements held by the Recreation Authority to protect them for future generations. These Parks include: DeShong Park (208.1427 acres), Doc Moore Branch Property (140.026 acres), Graves Park (70.162 acres), Harbins Alcovy River Park Site (portion of site; 1183.7498 acres), Little Mulberry Park (890.249 acres), McDaniel Farm Park (128.114 acres) Palm Creek Property (294.3507 acres), Settles Bridge Park Site (217.1237 acres) and Yellow River Park (566.1007 acres). Total acreage = 3,698.0186 acres.

- **2005** The Lawrenceville Female Seminary celebrated its 150th Anniversary on September 18. Gwinnett County agreed to continue sharing Gwinnett school facilities until June 30, 2006, under an agreement with the Gwinnett County Board of Education. The joint-use concept makes school facilities available to the community for parks and recreation programs after school, in the evenings and on weekends. The first such agreement was 27 years ago. In November, Gwinnett County assumes responsibility for operating Lilburn Lions Club Park under a 50-year lease agreement with the Lilburn City Council approved by the Board of Commissioners. The County will lease the park for $10 a year. The Gwinnett Commissioners agreed to purchase the Vecoma property, 68 acres along the Yellow River south of Highway 78. The purchase price for the new passive park in the southern area of the county is almost $3.2 million.

- **2006** 2006 was a record-breaking year with a total of ten park and park facility grand openings and re-openings. These were: Lions Club Park, renovation; Yellow River Park, major improvements; Lenora Park, family aquatics center; Lenora Park, youth football field, dog park, trail, and other improvements; Bethesda Park, youth football field, and other park improvements; Best Friend Park, major renovation; Holcomb Bridge Park, renovation; Graves Park, new passive community park; and, George Pierce Park, new community center / senior activity center. Three new park groundbreakings were held. These were: West Gwinnett Park / Aquatics Center; DeShong Park; and, Peachtree Ridge Park. Commissioners bought 25 acres of land off of Pleasant Hill Road to devote to a new neighborhood park. The land adjoins other County-owned land, including two greenspace areas and the site of a former fire station. The Gwinnett Commissioners approved the construction of a new $5.8 million Community Center and Gymnasium at Lucky Shoals Park. The 68-acre park is located on Britt Road in western Gwinnett County. Acquired additional 106.578 acres at Harbins Alcovy site for future park, scheduled to open in 2008. Will be largest park in the county with 1,901.79 acres, GCPR purchases South Gwinnett Park from South Gwinnett Athletic Association on June 6 in order to preserve the land and facilities for future generations. The Gwinnett Environmental and Heritage Center was opened in October, 2006. The U.S. Green Building Council awarded a gold level Leadership in Energy and Environmental Design (LEED) rating to the Center (the first building awarded gold level in Gwinnett County). The LEED system is a nationally-accepted benchmark for design, construction, and operation of high performance green buildings.

- **2007** Two new county parks opened in 2007. Opened in July, 2007, the 25-acre Sweet Water Park is a passive community park located west of Lawrenceville. DeShong Park opened in August, 2007, and is a 207-acre park in southern Gwinnett County. In addition, the Bethesda Park Acquatic Center opened. The Mountain Park Skate Complex improvements were completed and opened. Funding from the 2005 SPLOST program allowed Gwinnett County to purchase several land tracts for new parks in 2007.

The Gwinnett Environmental and Heritage Center is an LEED-Certified building.

These include: 89-acres of land for a community park in the new Mountain View School Cluster; 66 acres of land for a community park in the new Lanier School Cluster; 58 acres of land for a passive park/greenspace near the Beaver Ruin / I-85 intersection; and 16 acres for a passive community park at Five Forks Road and the Yellow River (to be named "Lee Park"). Construction began on Duncan Creek Park and on a section of ivy Creek Greenway. Land acquisition started on 31 acres on Oak Road, and another 18 acres on Callie Still Road for the Tribble Mill Greenway. Master plans updates for Rhodes Jordan Park and Club Drive Park were completed, as was a plan for South Gwinnett Park. During 2007, Gwinnett County Parks & Recreation celebrated its 20th Anniversary as a County-wide Recreation District.

The Larry Flynt Incident

By Bryant Huff

(Editor's Note: The writer is a former Gwinnett County district attorney from 1972-85 and Superior Court judge from 1986-92 and was well aware of the activities surrounding Hustler Publisher Larry Flynt when he was shot in Lawrenceville. He gives this view, which has never been published before He is now retired and lives in Broxton, Ga.)

Larry Flynt, the publisher of *Hustler* magazine, had been convicted in Ohio for pornography and the case was on appeal. His lawyers were shopping to be tried somewhere in the Bible Belt and obtain an acquittal, thus arguing if the distribution of his magazine was OK in the Bible Belt of the South, then it was not pornography and he should be relieved of the Ohio conviction.

The State Court of Gwinnett County Solicitor Gary Davis was contacted and he agreed to try Flynt on pornography charges for distribution of his magazines in Georgia. I personally think that Gary wanted to impress Flynt's lawyers to the extent that he might get to join their firm.

The pretrial hearings were lengthy and the trial was also lengthy in order to bring in "experts" to testify that the magazines were not pornography. Gene Reeves, the Lawrenceville attorney, was hired by the Flynt team to be local counsel to assist in Georgia trial procedures and help select the jury and give general advice as the case was being tried.

The trial was in its third day, on March 6, 1978, when Gene accompanied Larry Flynt and others to the Britt's V and J Cafeteria on the corner of Lucky and Perry Streets. As they walked back up Perry toward the courthouse on the west side of the Perry Street, gunshots rang out. Flynt and Reeves were both wounded. Fortunately for them, an emergency vehicle was in the immediate area and was able to respond quickly and get them to Button Gwinnett Hospital. Again, luck was with them as Dr. M.T. Bagheri, a surgeon from Snellville, was at the hospital and immediately began treating them.

Bedlam took over the hospital waiting room and grounds.

Meanwhile, police from Lawrenceville and Gwinnett County took control of the east side of Perry Street between what was once the theatre and hotel annex in search of evidence. Rifle bullet casings were found. Other items, never disclosed, were also found, and indicated that the assailant had spent considerable time there awaiting his opportunity. (The trial had been going on for a few hours a day for three days, and Flynt and Reeves ate lunch at the cafeteria each day.)

At the time, I was District Attorney but had nothing to do with the State Court trial other than be aware of it. The Georgia Legislature was in session in Atlanta then and I was at the Capitol on behalf of the District Attorneys Association. A member of the prosecuting attorneys office found me having lunch and informed me of the shooting. I soon returned to Lawrenceville and met with county police in charge of the investigation. I went over the area where the assailant had fired the weapon and other portions of the old hotel and examined with the officers the evidence that they had located. The assailant had apparently left the scene down a passageway between the two buildings and went out the back, and around a wall to his vehicle, which had been in the public parking area behind the buildings, and vanished.

From Button Gwinnett Hospital, Police Chief John Crunkleton summoned me to come to the hospital. The Flynt organization had employed private guards in plain clothing, who were roaming the exterior of the hospital. The chief had several officers in uniform also at the hospital to insure Flynt and Reeves protection. The chief recognized the potential of conflict with the guards and his officers. I was asked to intervene with the person who appeared to be in charge of the civilian guards and coordinate their work with the county police.

An uneasy situation prevailed both inside and outside the hospital for hours. Many people were coming in and out of the hospital waiting room and milling around outside, mostly out of curiosity. One even brought homemade fig newtons and some kind of fruit and carrot juices for Flynt! This was not allowed to be delivered, of course.

To add to the scene, suddenly a helicopter arrived and landed at the hospital pad. Out stepped Flynt's wife in a sack dress loosely fitted, totally at odds with the local dress. Also arriving at the hospital was Ruth Carter Stapleton, the evangelist sister of then-President Jimmy Carter, who Flynt had been previously having prayer and religious meetings. (Even Larry Flynt's brother, Jimmy Flynt, his wife and the magazine's staff, felt that Larry was indeed having a religious conversion and wanted to tone down his magazines.)

Chief Crunkelton came to me and was so concerned about President Carter's sister's safety that he asked me if I knew how to get in touch with his Press Secretary, Jody Powell. He knew that I had been active in Carter's election to be governor and that Carter had appointed me District Attorney after Reid Merritt was named a Superior Court judge.

I got a phone number where I could relay to Jody Powell a request that President Carter should call his sister and request her to leave the area, so she was not at risk in such a volatile situation. I worked through my first cousin, Herky Harris, who went to Washington with Bert Lance to the Office of Budget Management. I related to Herky the necessity to get Ruth Carter Stapleton out of the hospital and away from the area. I asked him to contact Powell, who had direct access to the President, and to have the President call his sister to "get the hell out of Dodge City."

We escorted his sister into a room and within minutes the phone rang and she answered. To this day, I do not know who was on the other end of the phone, but she left the area pronto.

Flynt had been shot twice. One shot went through Flynt, and the other lodged on impact into his spine, which severed nerves and paralyzed him from his waist down, and doomed him to a wheel chair. The force of the shots knocked both Flynt and Reeves down on the sidewalk. Reeves says that the shots "knocked Flynt over like an elephant." Reeves staggered a few steps, but also collapsed on the sidewalk. The bullet which went through Flynt struck Reeves in the right arm, liver and gall bladder. He was hospitalized for 28 days. Thirty years later, he says that the only effects are the scars from the wounds. Flynt's organization paid the expenses of Reeves' care.

Flynt was transferred to Emory University Hospital, where he was under his personal guards. His lawyers would not allow anyone to speak to or interview him, including me as district attorney nor Gwinnett investigators. We did, however, interview him to some degree later at a hospital in Cleveland, Ohio, but he was reluctant to talk about his personal life or who he thought might have a reason to try to assassinate him. However, he felt that his investigations into the shooting of former President John F. Kennedy was the motive for him being shot.

Years later, while I was still in office, a hardened criminal and white supremacist, John Paul Franklin, called Gwinnett County. One of the investigators interviewed him. Franklin had been convicted in Federal Court of murdering a man in St. Louis, Mo. and was serving in the maximum security prison in Marion, Ill. Franklin confessed to Gwinnett investigators to the Flynt shooting. We think he did this in order to get tried in Gwinnett in hopes he could effect an escape. He revealed in his statement that he had stayed at the old Golfland Inn off I-85 in DeKalb County under a certain particular name.

I was able to recover through a subpoena the registration cards for ten days prior and ten days after the shooting and found a registration card that bore that name for several days prior to and including the day of the shooting, and a check-out date after the shooting. Subsequent review of all prior registrations for a year did not reveal that name again. I submitted an indictment to the Grand Jury and obtained an indictment, but never tried the case because he already had a life sentence in the federal system. The indictment was later dismissed without trial by District Attorney Tom Lawler, and rightfully so.

Later I attended Franklin's trial for bombing a church in Chattanooga, Tenn. One day he refused to come to court. He was a specimen of physical strength and could easily have overpowered guards and made a dash if given even a slight opportunity. We, as visiting officers of the court, were able to get into the courtroom. There he was also convicted and sentenced to life. So there was absolutely no reason to try Franklin in Gwinnett. I later related these reasons to my good friend, Gene Reeves, who agreed with me.

My last conversation with Larry Flynt came after he sent me a letter requesting me to come to the federal prison at Butner, N.C. and sent a check for a large sum payable to me.

I called his brother, Jimmy Flynt, at his magazine office and informed him of his letter and check and then returned a copy of the letter and the check to Jimmy. My investigator, James Burton, and I traveled to the federal prison at Butner, where Flynt was being held for being convicted on contempt of court for wearing only a U.S. flag as a diaper to court. Guards told me how Larry was trying to make their life miserable by not bathing, and being totally uncooperative with them.

When we began to talk, Flynt wanted to talk about the Kennedy Investigations. Later I pointed out to Larry that he was misdirecting his behavior at the guards, who were only doing their job, and that they were just ordinary guys trying to eke out a living and they should not be the object of his protest over being jailed.

He looked at me and said, "You're right."

YOU ARE NOW ENTERING
AND LEAVING
PINCKNEYVILLE, GA
McLemore

APPENDIX B

Demographics

Gwinnett County Population, 1820-2007	656
Live Births, 1990-2007	656
City Populations by Decade	657
Early Population of Gwinnett Towns	657
Police Statistics in Gwinnett 1969-2007	658
Crime Statistics, 1980-2006, for Gwinnett	660
Building Permits Issued, 1966-2007	661
Area Labor Force in 2007	662
History of Labor Force, 1973-2007	663
Registered Voters in 2008 in Gwinnett County	664
Registered Voters by Cities and Ethnicity	664
Topographic Details of Gwinnett Cities	665
Water Resources in Gwinnett, 2006-2007	665
Miles of Water, Sewer Lines	665
Roads, Vehicles and Signals in Gwinnett	666
Metropolitan Atlanta Rapid Transit Authority (MARTA) Votes in Gwinnett	666
Interstate 85 Traffic	666
Gwinnett Transit Total Boardings, 2006-07	667
Gwinnett Transit Average Daily Boardings, 2006-2007	668
Commuting Patterns in Gwinnett	669
Fire Department Statistics	669
Fire and Emergency Services Locations	670
Farming Activities in Gwinnett	671
Gwinnett Airport Operating Data, 2006-2007	671
Briscoe Field Operations, 1966-2008	672
Type of Aircraft Based at Briscoe Field	673
Facilities of Gwinnett Library System	673
Library System Usage Data, 1987-2007	674
Community Improvement Districts (CIDs) in Gwinnett	674
Georgia Lottery Sales, Prizes, Commissions in Gwinnett	675
Georgia Lottery Capital Outlays in Gwinnett	675
Park Land Acreage in Gwinnett	676

County Officials

County Commissioners of Gwinnett, 1873-2007	678
Gwinnett Constitutional Officers, 1819-2007	679
County Agents of Gwinnett	681
Recreation Authority Members, 1985-2007	681
Key Executives of Gwinnett Government	682
Elections Board Members since 1985	682
Judges of Superior Court of Gwinnett	683
Judges of State Court of Gwinnett	683
Gwinnett Court Administrators	684
District Attorneys	684
Solicitors of the Gwinnett State Court	684
Gwinnett Magistrate Court Judges, 1983-2008	684
Gwinnett Senior Magistrate Judges	686
Police and Fire Chiefs of Gwinnett	686
Medical Directors Serving Gwinnett	686
City Court of Buford Officials, 1902-1970	687
Senators Serving Gwinnett in Georgia General Assembly, 1819-2008	688
House Representatives from Gwinnett from 1819-2008	692
Membership in County-Appointed Boards, 2008	696

City Officials

Auburn City Officials, 1993-2008	704
Berkeley Lake City Officials, 1956-2008	704
Mayors of Braselton, 1916-2008	706
Braselton Council Members	706
Buford City Officials, 1899-1938	707
Buford City Officials, 1939-2008	709
Dacula City Officials	711
Duluth City Officials, 1950-2008	712
Grayson City Officials, 1951-2008	714
Lawrenceville City Officials, 1884-2008	716
Lilburn City Officials	719
Loganville City Officials	721
Norcross City Officials	724
Snellville City Officials	727
Sugar Hill City Officials, 1939-2008	731
Suwanee City Officials, 1962-2008, Mayor & Posts 1-3	733
Suwanee City Officials, Posts 4-5, Clerk, City Manager	734

Community and Volunteer Leaders

Chairmen of the Gwinnett Chamber of Commerce, 1947-2008	736
Gwinnett Chamber Executive Officials	737
Gwinnett Chamber of Commerce Citizen of the Year Award Winners	738
Public Service Award Winners of Gwinnett Chamber	739
Hospital System and Related Boards Members, 2008	740
Gwinnett Medical Center Auxiliary Presidents, 1961-2008	741
Leaders of Council for Quality Growth	742
Button Gwinnett - Four Pillar Winners of Council for Quality Growth	742
Gwinnett Bar Association Presidents, 1961-2009	743
Gwinnett Historical Society Presidents, 1966-2008	744
Gwinnett Historical Society Trustees	744
Officers of Northeast Georgia Foundation	745
Gwinnett Convention and Visitors Bureau Board Members	746
Gwinnett Realtors Presidents, 1970-2008	747
Chairs of Gwinnett Relay-for-Life, 1994-2009	748
Presidents of Gwinnett Children's Shelter	748
Leadership Gwinnett Alumni	749
Leadership Gwinnett Committees	752
Senior Leadership Gwinnett Alumni	753
Trustees of Senior Leadership Gwinnett	753
Senior Leadership Gwinnett Committees	754
Teachers as Leaders Alumni, 1991-2009	754
Neighborhood Leadership Institute Alumni	756
Members, Gwinnett Student Leadership Team, 1995-2010	757
United Way Campaigns in Gwinnett	763

Financial Data

Gwinnett Millage Rate, 1994-2008	764
Gwinnett Budget Comparisons	764
Gwinnett Tax Digest of 2007	765
Gwinnett City Government Budgets and Registered Voters	765
Top Ten Taxpayers in Gwinnett County for 2006	766
Top Ten Taxpayers in Gwinnett County for 2007	766
Gwinnett County Special Purpose Local Option Sales Tax (SPLOST)	767
Banks with Headquarters in Gwinnett in 2008	768
Gwinnett Revenue from Alcoholic Beverages, 1990-1997	770
Gwinnett Revenue from Alcoholic Beverages, 1998-2007	771
Industrial Development Authority Financing, 1967 - 2007	772

School Data

Gwinnett Public Schools Enrollment by Decade 777
Enrollment at Gwinnett Public Schools as of May, 2008 777
Superintendents of Gwinnett Public Schools, 1871-2008 779
Gwinnett School Bond Referendums since 1971 779
Naming Source for Gwinnett Schools 780
Proposed Names for New Gwinnett Schools, 2007 786
E-SPLOST I, II, and III Comparison of Results 787
Size, Classrooms of Gwinnett Elementary Schools 787
Size, Classrooms of Gwinnett Middle Schools 789
Size, Classrooms of Gwinnett High Schools 789
Teachers of the Year in Gwinnett Public Schools, 1980-2009 790
Teachers of the Year in Buford City Schools, 1983-2009 791
Buford City School Superintendents 791
School Board Members, Gwinnett Public Schools, 1906-2008 792
Buford City School Board Members, 1912-2008 795
Educational Foundations of Gwinnett Schools, Colleges 798
Private Schools in Gwinnett 799
Private School Enrollment by Years in Gwinnett 799
State High School Champions from Gwinnett, 1938-2007 803

Civic Clubs

Kiwanis Clubs in Gwinnett and Presidents 811
Kiwanis Lieutenant Governors from Gwinnett 813
Lions Clubs and Leaders of Gwinnett 814
Presidents of Rotary Clubs in Gwinnett 816
Governors of Rotary District 6910 from Gwinnett 818
Duluth Civitan Club 818
Woman's Club Officers in Gwinnett 818
Buford-Lanier Woman's Club Presidents 819
Norcross Woman's Club Presidents 820
Loganville Woman's Club Presidents 821
Stonehedge Garden Club Presidents 821

Other Interesting Facts

"Miss Gwinnett" Winners, 1955-2008 822
Museums Within Gwinnett 823
Southeastern Railway Museum Officials 823
Properties on National Register of Historic Places in Gwinnett 824
Visitors To Lake Lanier Islands 824
Golf Courses in Gwinnett 825
Classic PGA Championship at Sugarloaf Country Club 826

Annual Calendar of Events in Gwinnett

Annual Calendar of Events in Gwinnett 849

Gwinnett County Population, 1820-2007

Year	Population	Year	Population	Year	Population
1820	4,589	1949	31,981	1979	149,000
1830	13,289	1950	32,320	1980	166,903
1840	10,804	1951	33,298	1981	177,800
1850	11,257	1952	34,305	1982	190,800
1860	12,940	1953	35,343	1983	205,700
1870	12,431	1954	36,412	1984	226,100
1880	19,531	1955	37,513	1985	249,600
1890	19,899	1956	38,648	1986	274,400
1900	25,585	1957	39,817	1987	298,200
1910	28,824	1958	41,022	1988	316,200
1920	30,327	1959	42,263	1989	330,300
1930	27,853	1960	43,541	1990	352,910
1931	27,974	1961	45,809	1991	362,800
1932	28,096	1962	48,195	1992	370,600
1933	28,218	1963	50,706	1993	387,000
1934	28,340	1964	53,347	1994	409,800
1935	28,463	1965	56,126	1995	438,400
1936	28,587	1966	59,050	1996	456,900
1937	28,711	1967	62,126	1997	478,900
1938	28,836	1968	65,362	1998	499,200
1939	28,961	1969	69,074	1999	523,900
1940	29,087	1970	72,349	2000	588,448
1941	29,395	1971	76,900	2001	614,500
1942	29,707	1972	86,500	2002	638,800
1943	30,021	1973	99,500	2003	658,200
1944	30,339	1974	109,600	2004	670,800
1945	30,661	1975	115,400	2005	693,900
1946	30,986	1976	120,700	2006	719,600
1947	31,314	1977	127,500	2007	740,200
1948	31,646	1978	137,300		

Source: US Census

Live Births, 1990-2007

Year	Total Live Births	Gwinnett Hospital System*	Emory Eastside*	Number out of Hospital
1990	6,436			
2000	10,556	5,057	2,109	26
2001	11,202	5,325	2,158	30
2002	11,788	5,523	2,038	38
2003	12,503	5,713	2,079	42
2004	12,971	5,569	2,195	31
2005	11,788	5,665	2,141	unavailable
2006	14,395	6,020	2,445	unavailable
2007	unavailable	6,330	2,503	unavailable

Sources: Ga. Dept. Human Resources, Univ. of Ga. and local hospitals
**** Number of live deliveries at hospital includes residents of other counties.***

City Populations by Decade

City	1960	1970	1980	1990	2000	Est. 2007	% Growth 2000-2007*	Land Area in Acres
Auburn	374	361	692	3,139	6,904	7,447	8%	3,417
Berkeley Lake	94	219	503	791	1,685	2,064	23%	645
Braselton	255	386	308	418	1,206	3,072	155%	4,611
Buford	4,168	4,640	6,582	8,771	10,668	11,532	8%	9,408
Dacula	440	782	1,577	2,217	3,848	4,636	20%	1,847
Duluth	1,483	1,810	2,956	9,029	22,122	25,953	16%	5,603
Grayson	282	366	464	529	765	1,471	92%	1,124
Lawrenceville	3,804	5,115	8,928	17,250	22,397	28,969	29%	8,296
Lilburn	753	1,668	3,765	9,301	11,307	11,526	2%	3,938
Loganville	926	1,318	1,841	3,180	5,435	10,242	88%	3,860
Norcross	1,605	2,755	3,317	5,947	8,410	10,490	25%	2,605
Rest Haven	167	188	231	176	151	146	lost pop.	259
Snellville	468	1,990	8,514	12,084	15,351	20,076	31%	6,182
Sugar Hill	1,175	1,745	2,340	4,557	11,399	16,725	47%	5,863
Suwanee	541	615	1,026	2,412	8,735	14,878	70%	6,278
Gwinnett Co.	43,541	72,349	166,903	352,910	588,448	776,380		**276,900
(change)	11,292	28,808	94,554	186,007	235,535	187,842		
(Percent)	35%	66%	131%	111%	67%	32%		

Note: Buford, Loganville, Auburn, Braselton and Rest Haven are partially in Gwinnett though these figures show total population of these cities.
**** Census Estimates as of July 1, 2007, ** Translates into 437 square miles***
Source: Census; www.gadata.org/information_services

Early Population of Gwinnett Towns

(All Years Not Available)

Town	1900	1910	1920	1930
Auburn	161	216		
Buford*	1,352	1,683	2,500	3,357
Carl		164		
Dacula	not a city	169	244	304
Duluth	335	469	600	608
Grayson	not a city	278	322	245
Lawrenceville	853	1,518	2,060	2,388
Lilburn	not a city	not a city	157	179
Norcross	797	968	993	901
Snellville	not a city	not a city	not a city	105
Suwanee	247	250	246	214
Winder **	174	247		

**** For 1900, another 211 residents were in West Buford; For 1910, another 250 people were in West Buford.***
***** Winder was partially within the Gwinnett borders until 1917 when Barrow County was founded.***
Source: Early U.S. Census figures, through Gwinnett County Public Library.

Police Statistics in Gwinnett 1969-2007						
Year	**Service Population**	**Gwinnett County Population**	**DUI Arrests**	**General Calls**	**Traffic Calls**	**Total Collisions**
1969	unk	unk	unk	3259	1352	unkn
1970	unk	73,498	unk	6,185	2,773	1,205
1971	unk	78,964	unk	unk	unk	unk
1972	unk	84,117	685	10,586	5,013	1,759
1973	unk	99,907	482	13,895	5,473	1,949
1974	unk	110,801	681	19,008	5,059	1,873
1975	unk	118,468	614	20,635	4,887	2,030
1976	unk	126,486	573	25,209	6,423	2,562
1977	unk	135,409	824	30,909	9,004	3,073
1978	unk	145,186	622	35,152	10,480	3,449
1979	unk	156,350	708	39,848	11,634	4,004
1980	unk	169,344	1,017	49,091	12,558	4,153
1981	unk	179,135	1,002	53,305	15,387	4,678
1982	unk	192,057	1,390	55,264	19,015	4,688
1983	unk	208,337	1,200	58,931	22,121	5,946
1984	unk	229,270	1,129	65,351	25,104	7,822
1985	192,781	253,023	1,397	75,179	29,754	9,848
1986	191,010	277,263	unk	unk	unk	unk
1987	223,673	301,620	unk	unk	unk	unk
1988	246,287	323,528	2,101	34,063	12,146	11,991
1989	258,353	341,985	1,874	116,185	38,857	12,222
1990	288,347	356,979	1,958	130,585	37,423	11,658
1991	292,325	374,266	2,489	140,671	38,409	11,371
1992	297,975	394,210	2,459	150,266	41,958	12,981
1993	323,030	417,581	1,178	151,496	42,252	14,489
1994	329,474	441,474	1,322	166,575	50,492	16,416
1995	358,089	467,292	1,325	181,658	54,245	17,705
1996	365,648	489,382	1,119	203,403	59,083	19,556
1997	372,262	516,032	1,839	199,585	53,133	18,673
1998	419,404	540,954	2,401	212,030	66,493	19,325
1999	437,463	567,569	2,410	224,757	96,206	19,805
2000	484,143	596,659	2,790	276,372	143,237	34,280
2001	499,516	623,903	3,050	302,040	141,619	25,002
2002	510,024	649,355	3,023	319,121	155,861	24,973
2003	548,617	673,526	2,170	331,035	147,549	26,428
2004	569,827	700,502	2,903	359,362	159,754	28,130
2005	601,375	726,790	2,487	373,813	140,657	28,734
2006	625,988	757,104	2,132	360,690	149,291	29,030
2007	unk	776,380	1,406	466,767	184,076	29,603
Source: Gwinnett County Police Department						

Police Statistics in Gwinnett 1969-2007

Year	Number of Fatalities	Traffic Citations	Collisions w/Injury	Criminal Arrests	Ordinance Violations	Mileage
1969	27	unk	unk	unk	unk	630,725
1970	33	unk	unk	unk	unk	919,783
1971	unk	unk	unk	unk	unk	unk
1972	30	unk	675	unk	unk	1,010,599
1973	32	unk	603	unk	unk	1,048,584
1974	15	unk	549	unk	unk	1,393,589
1975	16	unk	603	unk	unk	1,761,944
1976	20	unk	731	unk	unk	1,647,599
1977	27	unk	860	unk	unk	1,935,647
1978	32	unk	1,036	unk	unk	2,250,769
1979	38	unk	1,248	unk	unk	1,948,637
1980	34	unk	1,224	unk	unk	unk
1981	36	unk	1,626	unk	unk	unk
1982	36	unk	1,515	unk	unk	unk
1983	40	unk	1,845	unk	unk	unk
1984	52	unk	2,234	unk	unk	unk
1985	30	unk	2,540	unk	unk	unk
1986	unk	unk	unk	unk	unk	unk
1987	unk	unk	unk	unk	unk	unk
1988	50	31,903	1,903	unk	unk	unk
1989	53	31,008	2,114	unk	unk	unk
1990	61	unk	1,801	unk	unk	unk
1991	52	37,421	1,572	unk	unk	unk
1992	41	38,703	1,657	unk	unk	unk
1993	50	24,604	1,675	unk	unk	unk
1994	44	unk	1,976	unk	unk	unk
1995	48	45,165	2,165	unk	unk	unk
1996	46	42,825	1,611	unk	unk	unk
1997	48	unk	1,593	unk	unk	unk
1998	53	unk	1,279	unk	unk	unk
1999	67	unk	1,327	unk	unk	unk
2000	65	64,205	4,020	9,916	3,719	unk
2001	69	72,816	4,130	9,600	5,764	unk
2002	63	95,449	3,974	10,458	4,030	unk
2003	68	89,165	3,721	11,901	4,131	unk
2004	79	103,020	4,196	13,238	4,448	unk
2005	75	90,091	4,417	12,917	8,461	unk
2006	83	97,629	4,260	14,116	7,146	unk
2007	65	119,127	3,833	18,071	9,128	unk

Source: Gwinnett County Police Department

Crime Statistics, 1980-2006, for Gwinnett

Number of Crimes by Offense

Year	Murder	Rape	Robbery	Agg Assault	Burglary	Larceny	MV Theft
1980	8	35	115	314	2466	4018	583
1981	4	31	140	274	2667	4232	595
1982	4	38	118	373	2677	3957	571
1983	4	38	89	365	2226	4210	617
1984	7	47	102	464	2571	5397	805
1985	8	43	143	449	3082	6752	1113
1986	4	65	188	412	3494	7982	1210
1987	4	59	229	449	3397	9157	1162
1988	2	73	197	489	3836	10684	1344
1989	1	82	302	528	3700	13010	1628
1990	11	85	343	621	3709	11414	1540
1991	13	121	319	416	3778	11732	1202
1992	18	117	355	405	3613	12840	1266
1993	10	14	322	444	3580	13213	1425
1994	9	36	372	412	3081	14268	1349
1995	17	19	357	445	3142	14347	1505
1996	6	96	385	666	3541	16735	1893
1997	11	84	513	514	3853	14719	2140
1998	17	115	500	562	2999	13103	2006
1999	36	202	683	844	4781	16029	2725
2000	22	146	463	625	3042	11066	1822
2001	16	148	680	735	4149	11860	2092
2002	26	163	710	641	4130	11941	2115
2003	42	171	760	728	4764	12190	2449
2004	32	164	851	853	5159	12886	2664
2005	31	141	958	848	5731	13269	2847
2006	43	109	1248	953	6283	13920	2931

Source: Georgia Bureau of Investigation

Building Permits Issued, 1966-2007

Year	Population	Residential Permits	Multi-Family Permits	Other Building Permits	Total Building Permits
Building Records Unavailable Before 1966					
1966	59,050	481		231	712
1967	62,126	751		248	999
1968	65,362	968		287	1,255
1969	69,074	912		226	1,113
1970	72,349	1,453		243	1,686
1971	76,900	2,195		557	2,752
1972	86,500	2,950	256	440	3,646
1973	99,500	2,173	240	500	2,913
1974	109,600	1,372	138	609	1,981
1975	115,400	1,774	18	458	2,250
1976	120,700	2,152	50	578	2,780
1977	127,500	2,510	98	703	3,311
1978	137,300	3,347	11	855	4,213
1979	149,000	3,984	55	1,035	5,074
1980	166,903	3,680	18	1,348	5,046
1981	177,800	2,671	396	1,528	4,595
1982	190,800	3,580	525	1,402	5,507
1983	205,700	5,847	918	1,923	8,688
1984	226,100	5,849	1,575	1,342	9,766
1985	249,600	6,923	895	2,612	10,430
1986	274,400	5,746	595	3,855	10,196
1987	298,200	4,710	174	4,195	9,029
1988	316,200	3,893	315	4,050	8,258
1989	330,300	3,184	42	3,712	6,938
1990	352,910	2,856	56	3,846	6,758
1991	362,800	3,448	15	32,886	6,749
1992	370,600	4,790	224	3,448	8,262
1993	387,000	5,823	73	4,346	10,242
1994	409,800	5,544	118	4,437	10,199
1995	438,400	5,482	191	4,733	10,406
1996	456,900	6,098	115	5,376	11,589
1997	478,900	5,772	94	5,473	11,339
1998	499,200	6,385	111	6,982	13,478
1999	523,900	7,246	214	7,419	14,879

Building Permits Issued, 1966-2007

Year	Population	Residential Permits	Multi-Family Permits	Other Building Permits	Total Building Permits
2000	588,448	7,121	214	7,419	14,754
2001	614,500	8,440	41	6,488	14,969
2002	638,800	8,202	131	8,413	16,746
2003	658,200	7,915	21	8,686	16,622
2004	670,800	8,291	15	9,095	17,401
2005	693,900	8,194	6	8,950	17,150
2006	719,600	6,615	35	9,345	15,995
2007	740,200	3,526	98	8,585	12,209

Source: Gwinnett Planning and Development Department

Area Labor Force in 2007

County	***Labor Force***	***Employed***	***Unemployed***	***Percent of Total***
Gwinnett	421,912	405,850	16,062	4%
Barrow	33,040	31,675	1,365	4%
DeKalb	396,858	378,698	18,160	5%
Forsyth	82,291	79,680	2,611	3%
Fulton	485,620	463,339	22,281	5%
Hall	90,114	86,993	3,121	4%
Jackson	26,822	25,764	1,058	4%
Rockdale	40,584	38,630	1,954	5%
Walton	40,341	38,516	1,825	5%
Gwinnett Area	1,617,582	1,549,145	68,437	4%
Georgia	4,814,831	4,602,947	211,884	4%
United States	153,124,000	146,047,000	7,087,000	5%

Source: Ga. Dept. of Labor; U.S. Bureau of Labor Statistics

History of Labor Force, 1973-2007

Year	Labor Force	Employed	Unemployed	Percent Unemployed
1973	36,432	35,527	905	3
1974	36,363	35,106	1,257	4
1975	36,267	33,967	2,300	6
1976	37,456	35,167	2,289	6
1977	39,002	37,052	1,950	5
1978	68,927	66,400	2,529	4
1979	71,285	68,969	2,316	3
1980	86,237	82,430	3,897	5
1981	90,993	86,977	4,016	4
1982	97,548	92,455	5,093	5
1983	107,045	101,665	5,380	5
1984	118,787	114,802	3,985	3
1985	139,794	135,273	4,521	3
1986	158,415	153,325	5,090	3
1987	171,710	165,675	6,035	4
1988	183,976	177,352	6,626	4
1989	186,727	179,370	7,357	4
1990	215,601	207,148	8,453	4
1991	219,438	211,093	8,345	4
1992	231,819	220,116	11,703	5
1993	245,231	234,799	10,432	4
1994	261,616	252,090	9,526	4
1995	276,315	267,724	8,591	3
1996	291,898	283,853	8,045	3
1997	308,351	300,553	7,798	3
1998	325,492	317,516	7,976	3
1999	340,143	332,543	7,600	2
2000	347,878	338,494	9,384	3
2001	358,390	345,677	11,713	3
2002	366,780	350,282	16,498	5
2003	370,742	354,574	16,168	4
2004	382,501	366,559	15,942	4
2005	400,881	382,554	18,327	5
2006	411,736	395,110	16,626	4
2007	421,912	405,850	16,062	4

Note; The big jump in the labor force between 1977-78 came as methodologies in the Atlanta MSA were changed.

Source: Bureau of Labor Statistics

Registered Voters in 2008 in Gwinnett County

	Black	White	Asia-Pac Isl	Hisp.-Latino	Indian	Other	Totals
County-wide	65,098	214,943	13,288	10,386	37	24,380	328,132
Percent	20	66	4	3	-	7	
Percent of Population	20	53	9	17	-	2	
Total Statewide Percent Population	27	66	1	1	-	4	
Total Voters In Gwinnett Cities	10,921	52,111	2,463	1,866	10	5,041	71,412

Source: Secretary of State, as of March 1, 2008

Registered Voters by Cities and Ethnicity

City	Black	White	Asia-Pac Isl	Hisp.-Latino	Indian	Other	Totals
Auburn	140	2776	34	63	0	156	3,169
Berkeley Lake	46	858	66	8	0	71	1,049
Braselton	173	2,534	44	96	0	158	3,005
Buford	567	3,283	33	117	2	228	4,230
Dacula	168	1,650	17	50	0	133	2,018
Duluth	1,837	7,154	796	265	2	890	10,944
Grayson	163	915	31	19	0	85	1,213
Lawrenceville	2,466	5,843	216	359	0	782	9,666
Lilburn	724	2,970	324	177	1	340	4,536
Loganville	757	3,810	48	66	0	351	5,032
Norcross	747	1,523	210	101	0	252	2,833
Rest Haven	0	15	0	0	0	1	16
Snellville	1,805	7,283	124	142	1	578	9,933
Sugar Hill	686	5,988	171	258	1	490	7,594
Suwanee	642	5,509	349	145	3	526	7,174

Source: Secretary of State, as of March 1, 2008

Topographic Details of Gwinnett Cities

City	Height Above Sea Level (ft)	Latitude	Longitude
Auburn	1,050	34.013N	83.827W
Berkeley Lake	1,056	33.983N	84.186W
Braselton	909	34.109N	83.762W
Buford	1,184	34.120N	84.004W
Dacula	1,050	33.988N	83.898W
Duluth	1,096	34.002N	84.144W
Grayson	1,096	33.894N	83.955W
Lawrenceville	1,066	33.956N	83.988W
Lilburn	951	33.89N	84.143W
Loganville	1,001	33.838N	83.9W
Norcross	1,047	33.941N	84.213W
Rest Haven	not listed		
Snellville	1,060	33.857N	84.02W
Sugar Hill	1,148	34.106N	84.033W
Suwanee	1,001	34.051N	84.071W

Source: US Topographic Service

Miles of Water, Sewer Lines

Year	Water Lines	Sewer Lines
1970	463	10
1980	1,175	268
1990	1,749	927
2000	2,732	1,797
2005	3,215	2,368
2007	3,345	2,595

Source: Gwinnett County Water, Sewer Dept.

Water Resources in Gwinnett, 2006-2007

	2006	2007
Water customers	230,850	234,447
Sewer customers	138,289	141,807
Water meter connection permits sold	8,045	3,962
Miles of water main installed	94	81
Total miles of water mains	3,230	3,346
New sewer connections	2,346	4,440
Miles of sanitary sewer installed	111	116
Total miles of sanitary sewer	2,480	2595
Fire hydrants installed	1,351	1139
Total fire hydrants in county	38,916	40,038
Water treatment capacity	225 mgd	225 mgd
Water use - average day	87.4 mgd	86.9 mgd
Water use - maximum day	129.8 mgd	126.3 mgd
Raw water storage (mg)	45 mg	45 mg
Wastewater treatment capacity *	71.62 mg	71.62 mgd
Wastewater treated - average day	52.21 mg	49.36 mgd

**** Includes contracted capacity in other jurisdictions***

Source: Department of Water Resources Annual Report

Interstate 85 Traffic	
Traffic both ways on Interstate 85 beween Jimmy Carter Boulevard and Indian Trail Road	
Year	Traffic Count
1990	164,188
2000	236,400
2005	264,120
2007	257,110
Source: Ga. Dept. of Transportation	

Metropolitan Atlanta Rapid Transit Authority (MARTA) Votes in Gwinnett			
Year	For MARTA	Against MARTA	Percent For MARTA
1965	2,500	9,506	20.8
1990	28,828	68,136	29.7
2008	24,469	27,667	46.9
Note: 1965 and 1990 were binding votes. 2008 was a straw poll by political parties. Source: Election Returns			

Roads, Vehicles and Signals in Gwinnett				
Year	Miles Of Roads	Miles Unpaved	Vehicles Registered	Signalized Intersections
1960	*	*		0
1970	*	*		0
1980	*	*		75
1990	1,750	149	323,647	245
2000	2,310	55	470,803	515
2005	2,650	30	605,546	580
2007	2,750	30	647,952	626
Source: Gwinnett Transportation Department				
**** Unknown numbers. Prior to 1987, approx 1,600 miles of road and approximately 160 miles of paved roads.***				

Gwinnett Transit Total Boardings, 2006-07

Total Boardings By Route

2006	Route 10	Route 20	Route 30	Route 40	Route 50	Mo. Totals
January	55,879	20,033	23,407	19,971	1,566	120,856
February	50,640	18,213	21,608	19,154	1,608	111,223
March	60,945	23,652	27,953	24,501	1,220	138,271
April	55,052	22,514	24,165	23,149	1,595	126,475
May	43,109	28,765	30,580	22,898	2,116	127,468
June	54,641	23,120	26,867	22,155	1,773	128,556
July	50,677	20,587	22,171	20,587	1,584	115,606
August	56,294	21,791	25,423	21,791	1,816	127,115
September	52,527	18,720	22,538	21,066	1,610	116,461
October	54,532	19,767	24,912	223,427	1,761	124,399
November	46,812	18,267	21,799	20,646	1,846	109,370
December	42,331	18,589	21,082	19,143	1,673	102,818

2007	Route 10	Route 20	Route 30	Route 40	Route 50	Mo. Totals
January	45,486	19,035	22,538	22,455	1,632	111,146
February	39,871	17,844	19,955	19,213	1,964	98,847
March	42,939	19,180	22,942	22,528	2,071	109,660
April	45,200	20,574	23,391	20,479	1,713	111,357
May	46,049	22,893	25,220	23,447	2,085	119,694
June	43,160	20,709	24,402	19,203	1,722	109,196
July	45,971	22,178	23,199	19,606	1,798	112,752
August	43,848	21,189	24,504	22,697	2,007	114,245
September	38,197	19,441	19,519	21,360	1,932	100,449
October	42,687	14,319	26,160	20,221	2,044	105,431
November	34,836	16,843	21,973	19,401	1,841	94,894
December	29,392	15,055	19,168	16,505	1,105	81,255

Source: Gwinnett Transit System

Gwinnett Transit Average Daily Boardings, 2006-2007

Average Daily Boarding By Route

2006	Route 10	Route 20	Route 30	Route 40	Route 50	Mo. Totals
January	2,235	801	936	799	63	4,834
February	2,110	759	900	798	67	4,634
March	2,257	876	1,035	907	45	5,120
April	2,202	901	967	926	64	5,059
May	1,658	1,106	1,176	881	81	4,903
June	2,102	889	1,033	852	68	4,944
July	2,027	823	887	823	63	4,624
August	2,085	807	942	807	67	4,708
September	2,101	749	902	843	64	4,658
October	2,097	760	958	901	68	4,785
November	1,872	731	872	826	74	4,375
December	1,693	744	843	766	67	4,113
2007	Route 10	Route 20	Route 30	Route 40	Route 50	Mo. Totals
January	1,749	732	867	864	63	4,275
February	1,661	744	831	801	82	4,119
March	1,590	710	850	834	77	4,061
April	1,808	823	936	819	69	4,454
May	1,771	881	970	902	80	4,604
June	1,660	797	939	739	66	4,200
July	1,839	887	928	784	72	4,510
August	1,824	785	908	841	74	4,231
September	1,592	810	813	890	81	4,185
October	1,591	530	969	749	76	3,905
November	1,393	674	879	776	74	3,796
December	1,178	602	767	660	44	3,249

Source: Gwinnett Transit System

Commuting Patterns in Gwinnett

EMPLOYED RESIDENTS OF			PERSONS WORKING IN		
County Where Employed	Number	Percent of Total	County of Residence	Number	Percent of Total
Gwinnett	169,000	55	Gwinnett	169,000	60
Fulton	57,737	19	DeKalb	34,737	12
DeKalb	51,481	17	Fulton	21,211	8
Cobb	8,648	3	Cobb	8,723	3
Forsyth	3,977	1	Barrow	8,229	3
Hall	3,015	1	Hall	7,189	3
Clayton	1,913	0	Walton	7,037	3
Rockdale	1,611	0	Forsyth	5,663	2
Other	12,223	4	Other	22,283	8
Total Employees	309,605		Total Residents	284,082	

Source: Ga. Dept. of Labor; U.S. Census

Fire Department Statistics

Year	Stations	Hydrants	Calls Answered
1972	4	1	*
1980	13	7,383	10,950
1990	18	14,859	1995/12,147
2000	23	28,187	35,865
2005	25	36,870	54,369
2006	27	38,916	57,916
2007	27	40,038	60,426

**** Unavailable***
Source: Gwinnett County Fire Department

Fire and Emergency Services Locations			
Station No.	Location	Date Built	Equipment Assigned
1	165 Lawrenceville Street, Norcross	* 1968	Engine, Ambulance
2	12 Harmony Grove Road, Lilburn	1971	Engine, Ambulance
3	4394 Five Forks Trickum Road, Lilburn	1972	Engine, Ambulance
4	5550 Spalding Drive, Norcross	1974	Engine, Ladder, Ambulance
5	3356 Club Drive, Lawrenceville	1974	Engine, Ambulance
New 5	3001 Old Norcross Road, Duluth	2004	Engine, Ladder, Ambulance and Division Chief
6	3620 Highway 124, Lithonia	1974	Engine
New 6	3890 Johnson Drive, Lithonia	2001	Engine, Ambulance
7	3288 Highway 120, Duluth	1976	Engine, Ambulance
New 7	3343 Bunten Road, Duluth	2008	Engine, Ladder and Ambulance
8	2244 Highway 20, Grayson	1975	Engine, Ambulance
New 8	2295 Brannan Boulevard, Grayson	2007	Engine, Ambulance
9	1900 Five Forks Road, Lawrenceville	1976	Engine, Air & Light, Medical Supervisor, Ambulance
10	842 Russell Road, Lawrenceville	1977	Engine, Ambulance
11	5885 Live Oak Parkway, Norcross	1979; 2000	Engine, Ladder, Ambulance and Battalion Chief
12	2326 Lenora Church Road, Snellville	1972	Engine, Ladder and Ambulance
New 12	2815 Lenora Church Road, Snellville	2007	Engine Ladder, Ambulance and Battalion Chief
13	343 Highway 23, Suwanee	1968	Engine, Ambulance
14	1600 Highway 23, Buford	1981	Engine, Ladder, Ambulance, Med. Supv., Swift Water Unit
15	275 Perry Street, Lawrenceville	1981	Engine, Ladder, Ambulance
16	195 Dacula Road, Dacula	1981	Engine, Ambulance
17	2739 Brooks Road, Dacula	1983	Engine
18	3600 Braselton Highway, Dacula	1983	Engine, Ambulance
New 18	1509 Mineral Springs Road, Dacula	2008	Engine, Ladder, Ambulance
19	3275 N. Berkeley Lake Road, Duluth	1993	Engine, Ambulance, Air and Light
20	1801 Cruse Road, Lawrenceville	1995	Engine, Ambulance, Haz-Mat Squad, Water Tender, Battalion Chief
21	470 Old Peachtree Road, Suwanee	1996	Engine, Ladder, Air and Light
22	2180 Stone Drive, Lilburn	1998	Engine, Ladder
23	4355 Steve Reynolds Blvd., Norcross	2000	Engine, Two Ambulances
24	2735 Mall of Georgia Blvd., Buford	2005	Engine, Ambulance, Tactical Rescue Squad, Battalion Chief
25	3575 Lawrenceville Highway, Lawrenceville	2004	Engine, Ambulance
26	6075 Suwanee Dam Road, Sugar Hill	2006	Engine
27	2825 Old Fountain Road, Dacula	2007	Engine
28	3725 Rosebud Road, Loganville	2008	Engine
29	2800 Thompson Mill Road, Buford	2009	Engine
30	Scheduled for Ozora Road area, 2010	2010	Engine, Ladder, Ambulance

**** First located on College Street; moved to Lawrenceville Street in 2008, still called "Station No. 1."***

Source: Gwinnett County Fire Department

Farming Activities in Gwinnett

Year	Number of Farms	Acres in Farms	Harvested Crop Acres	Net Farm Income	Crop Receipts	Animal Receipts
1945	3,452	239,494	83,244		all unavailable	
1949	3,104	206,669	52,827			
1954	2,659	186,052	32,400			
1959	1,345	118,695	17,183			
1964	991	93,967	9,542			
1969	591	51,615	5,791			
1974	449	38,530	5,137	$250,000	$711,000	$6,442,000
1978	413	34,882	5,443	$1,342,000	$991,000	$9,247,000
1982	492	33,762	5,661	$5,129,000	$4,524,000	$10,974,000
1987	441	29,435	3,866	$3,856,000	$8,911,000	$9,042,000
1992	345	24,239	2,635	$3,179,000	$5,718,000	$9,945,000
1997	436	37,882	2,969	$91,000	$5,649,000	$6,111,000
2002	312	17,557	1,627	$288,000	$6,521,000	$4,933,000
2005		unavailable		$1,485,000	$9,421,000	$6,822,000

Source: Georgia County Guide

Gwinnett Airport Operating Data, 2006-2007

	2006	2007
Land Lease Payments	$599,315.00	$620,710.00
Fuel Flowage fees	$160,036.00	$178,633.00
Tie down rental	$25,901.00	$28,420.00
Hangar lease payments	$29,161.00	$30,407.00
Interest	$27,727.00	$3,490.00
Total Revenue	$842,140.00	$861,660.00
Operating Expense	$609,902.00	$748,351.00
Margin	$232,238.00	$113,309.00
Misc		
Capital Improvement Program	$11.7 million	$22.2 million
Number of Lease holders	25	24
Gallons of fuel sold	+2,000,000	+2,500,000

During 2007, the airport continued to earn a $0.07 cents per gallon fuel fee.

Source: Gwinnett Department of Finance

Briscoe Field Operations, 1966-2008

Operations (Landings)				Based Aircraft			
1966	12,000	1988	141,100	1966	13	1988	180
1967	not available	1989	141,100	1967	not available	1989	180
1968	25,000	1990	157,600	1968	29	1990	187
1969	28,750	1991	161,380	1969	37	1991	210
1970	28,750	1992	165,200	1970	37	1992	233
1971	28,750	1993	165,240	1971	44	1993	251
1972	not available	1994	not available	1972	not available	1994	not available
1973	35,140	1995	not available	1973	48	1995	not available
1974	not available	1996	not available	1974	not available	1996	325
1975	not available	1997	99,738	1975	not available	1997	not available
1976	not available	1998	107,518	1976	96	1998	not available
1977	107,400	1999	115,345	1977	not available	1999	280
1978	110,000	2000	108,430	1978	not available	2000	352
1979	82,250	2001	106,421	1979	not available	2001	373
1980	83,325	2002	105,345	1980	144	2002	447
1981	not available	2003	89,965	1981	131	2003	not available
1982	121,200	2004	108,159	1982	148	2004	432
1983	121,100	2005	96,365	1983	162	2005	not available
1984	133,200	2006	87,676	1984	187	2006	466
1985	121,100	2007	87,707	1985	186	2007	433
1986	130,000	2008	not available	1986	195	2008	not available
1987	130,000			1987	159		

1998 is the first full year an Air Traffic Control Tower was in operation.

Information Sources:

1974 Gwinnett County Airport Master Plan by Mayes Suddereth and Etheredge

1983 Gwinnett County Airport Master Plan by Hayes, James & Associates, Inc., and Fehner, St. John & Associates, Inc.

1992 Gwinnett County Airport Master Plan by Rosser International, Wilbur Smith Associates and Duckett Associates

2006 Gwinnett County Airport Master Plan by Pegasus Associates International Inc.
Gwinnett County Airport Division Director Records and Files

Type of Aircraft Based at Briscoe Field

Aircraft on Airport						
Year	Single Engine	Multi Engine #	Turbo-Prop	Jet	Helicopter	Total
1991	144	45		0	21	210
1992	147	45		3	38	233
1993	179	43		3	26	251
1994			Not available this year			
1995			Not available this year			
1996	264	44		10	7	325
1997			Not available this year			
1998			Not available this year			
1999	164	92		13	11	280
2000	277	47		14	14	352
2001	292	37	12	22	10	373
2002	347	38	14	31	17	447
2003			Not available this year			
2004	324	46	11	35	16	432
2005			Not available this year			
2006	323	44	40	32	27	466
2007	324	26	31	36	16	433

 # Prior to 2001, turbo-props were included in milti-engine counts.

Source: Gwinnett County Airport records.

Facilities of Gwinnett Library System

Location	Date Site Re-Opened	Square Footage	Info
Lawrenceville	Jun.18,1990	28,309	First Opened 1935 in City Hall
Norcross	Aug.18,1990	10,624	1907: First Library in County Joined System 1957
Buford-Sugar Hill	Dec. 7, 1989	10,624	1967, third location in Gwinnett
Lilburn	Aug.22,1988	10,260	1968, fourth location in Gwinnett
Duluth	Jun.24,1989	10,499	1968, fifth location in Gwinnett
Snellville	Apr.15,2006	10,260	Sixth location; first opened, 1975
Mountain Park	Dec.19,1997	10,260	Seventh Location*
Peachtree Corners	Jan. 3,1989	14,852	Eighth location
Five Forks	Mar. 2, 1995	20,135	Has County Microfilm for Newspapers
Collins Hill	Oct. 19,1999	20,750	Tenth location
Centerville	Jul. 6, 2002	12,040	11th location
Suwanee	Oct.30,2004	20,447	12th location
Dacula	Apr. 15,2006	20,055	13th location
Grayson	Oct. 28,2006	20,055	14th location
Hamilton Mill			15th location in 2010
Peachtree Ridge			

**** Mountain Park's first library opened June 11, 1977.***

Gwinnett's Library System also staffs a library at Georgia Gwinnett College

Source: Gwinnett County Public Library

Library System Usage Data, 1987-2007

	Door Count	Check Outs	
FY87		834,729	
FY88		1,059,401	
FY89		1,660,567	
FY90		2,135,061	No. 8, Peachtree Corners, opened January, 1989
FY91	1,476,348	2,666,200	
FY92	1,681,866	3,023,554	
FY93	1,778,330	3,306,054	
FY94	1,740,500	3,555,315	
FY95	1,727,609	3,795,112	
FY96	1,853,812	4,075,471	No. 9, Five Forks, opened March, 1995
FY97	2,116,767	4,287,830	
FY98	2,147,192	4,692,967	
FY99	2,465,208	5,158,149	
FY00	2,354,412	5,307,572	No. 10, Collins Hill,opened October, 1999
FY01	2,532,141	5,524,651	
FY02	2,714,275	5,714,056	
FY03	3,030,031	6,100,381	No. 11, Centerville, opened July, 2002
FY04	3,526,510	6,172,537	
FY05	3,366,585	6,376,188	No. 12, Suwanee, opened October, 2004
FY06	3,444,597	6,020,455	No. 13, Dacula, opened April, 2006
FY07	3,654,886	6,491,754	No. 14, Grayson, opened October, 2006

Source: Gwinnett County Public Library

Community Improvement Districts (CIDs) in Gwinnett

Organization	Evermore CID*	Gwinnett Place CID	Gwinnett Village CID
When Established	April, 2003	March, 2005	March, 2006
Property Owners	380	187	500
Parcels	469	238	650
Number of Businesses	1,585	3,100	5,000
Geographic Size	7 Linear Miles	1.562 Square Miles	17.5 Square Miles
Property Value	$465 million	$683 million	$1 billion
Business Employees	16,913	35,700	60,000
Director	Brett Harrell	Joe Allen	Chuck Warbington

**** Initially known as US Highway 78 CID***

Georgia Lottery Sales, Prizes, Commissions in Gwinnett

Fiscal Year	Statewide Sales	Gwinnett Sales	Percent of State Sales	Gwinnett Population	Average Sale per Resident
FY94	$1,119,277,000	$34,328,071	3.06%	441,474	$77.75
FY95	$1,421,500,000	$41,928,418	2.94%	467,292	$89.73
FY96	$1,591,891,000	$49,036,604	3.08%	489,232	$100.20
FY97	$1,720,241,000	$50,071,848	2.91%	516,032	$97.03
FY98	$1,736,089,000	$52,035,229	2.99%	540,954	$96.19
FY99	$2,034,308,000	$65,634,973	3.23%	567,569	$115.64
FY00	$2,313,551,000	$77,618,608	3.35%	596,547	$130.11
FY01	$2,193,807,000	$75,758,329	3.00%	623,517	$121.50
FY02	$2,449,363,000	$88,402,049	3.60%	648,808	$136.25
FY03	$2,604,422,000	$98,237,251	3.77%	673,651	$145.82
FY04	$2,710,459,000	$106,486,807	3.92%	700,577	$151.99
FY05	$2,922,332,000	$124,913,257	4.27%	726,273	$171.99
FY06	$3,177,596,000	$146,794,770	4.62%	757,104	$193.88
FY07	$3,421,698,000	$171,840,390	5.00%	776,380	$221.33

Source: Georgia Lottery

Georgia Lottery Capital Outlays in Gwinnett

Fiscal Year	HOPE	Pre-K	Technology	Prizes Paid	Retailer Commis-sions	Total Returned to Gwinnett
FY94	$1,015,583	$616,234	$3,215,290	$14,595,311	$1,828,268	$21,270,686
FY95	$4,935,037	$1,297,421	$15,955,949	$14,707,299	$2,255,114	$39,150,820
FY96	$9,735,724	$9,872,236	$111,500	$16,114,269	$2,819,008	$38,652,737
FY97	$12,070,609	$15,582,479	$22,510,395	$19,648,835	$3,248,626	$73,060,944
FY98	$15,151,272	$15,352,011	$2,506,073	$20,752,207	$3,296,809	$57,058,372
FY99	$16,662,782	$16,167,003	$9,473,912	$26,297,120	$4,134,232	$72,735,049
FY00	$19,150,996	$16,512,642	$9,977,390	$34,620,073	$4,925,098	$85,186,199
FY01	$24,084,453	$16,633,041	$38,065,787	$35,260,713	$4,816,944	$118,860,938
FY02	$28,017,123	$17,094,173	$0	$41,693,435	$5,635,807	$92,440,538
FY03	$31,785,928	$18,605,860	$0	$49,643,607	$6,238,400	$106,273,795
FY04	$35,419,000	$19,852,220	$0	$53,779,841	$6,712,353	$115,763,414
FY05	$39,178,000	$21,575,753	$0	$66,417,998	$7,955,188	$135,126,939
FY06	$42,230,000	$22,991,123	$0	$80,079,112	$9,321,881	$154,622,116
FY07	$39,308,959	24,743,789	$0	$95,598,782	$11,006,945	$170,658,475

Source: Georgia Lottery

Park Land Acreage in Gwinnett

	Park Open or Opening in 2008	Acreage
1	Bay Creek Park	154
2	Best Friend Park	43
3	Bethesda Park	159
4	Bogan Park	83
5	Cemetery Field	6
6	Collins Hill Park	95
7	Dacula Park	76
8	DeShong Park	208
9	Environmental and Heritage Center	233
10	George Pierce Park	304
11	Graves Park	70
12	Gwinnett History Museum	0
13	Harmony Grove Park	18
14	Historic Courthouse	2
15	Holcomb Bridge Park	12
16	Jones Bridge Park	30
17	Lenora Park	178
18	Lions Club Park	17
19	Little Mulberry Park	891
20	Lucky Shoals Park	68
21	McDaniel Farm Park	134
22	Mountain Park Park	44
23	Mountain Park Aquatics Center & Activities Building	18
24	Pinckneyville Park	109
25	Rabbit Hill Park	108
26	Rhodes Jordan Park	162
27	Ronald Reagan Park	25
28	Shorty Howell Park	67
29	Singleton Rd. Activities Building	2
30	South Gwinnett Park	23
31	Sweet Water Park	25
32	Tribble Mill Park	718
33	Vines Gardens	79
34	Yellow River Park	566
	Sub-Total	4,761

Park Land Acreage in Gwinnett		
Property for Future Parks		
1	Duncan Creek Park	110
2	Norris Lake (Doc Moore Branch) Park Site	350
3	Settles Bridge Park	268
4	Freeman's Mill Park (Alcovy River Grist Mill)	12
5	Ewing Chapel (Palm Creek)	294
6	Alexander Park	91
7	Harbins Park	1795
8	Yellow River Post Office	5
9	Centerville Highway Park Site	61
10	Rock Springs Park	113
11	West Gwinnett Park	23
12	Peachtree Ridge Park	156
13	Bent River Property	48
14	Ross Road (Vecoma) Property	68
15	Highway 29 (Lilburn) Property	11
16	Club Drive Park	18
17	Hovis Property (Lilburn)	31
18	Beaver Ruin Park Site	58
19	Peachtree Industrial Blvd. - Lanier Cluster Park Site	67
20	Mountain View Cluster Park Site	91
21	Hospital Site (Old P'tree at I-85)	36
22	Lee Park Site	21
	Sub-Total	3,841
	Total	8,602

Souce: Gwinnett Deprtment of Community Service

County Commissioners of Gwinnett, 1873-2007

Year	Chairman	District Commissioners			
1873	R. D. Winn	Burton Cloud	E.J. McDaniel	W.W. Parks	D.M. Byrd
1877	W.E. Jones	B.A. Blakey	J.H.C. Maguire	W.I. Woodward	J.T. Lampkin
1881	J.D. Spence	J.H. Hopkins	J.E. Cloud	Nathan Bennett	Jefferson Britt
1885	J.D. Spence	J.R. Hopkins	J.E. Cloud	Nathan Bennett	Andrew Garner
1889	J.D. Spence	J.W. Mitchell	A.J. Vaughan	J.R. Espy	S.L. Hinton
1893	J.D. Spence	J.T. Lampkin	J.S. Dobbins	J.C. Carroll	W.T. Perry
1897	S.L. Hinton	J.T. Lampkin	J.S. Dobbins	M.A. Born	J.T. Jourdan
1901	T.C. Burton	A.A. Martin	J.H. Hutchins	D.M. Clower	J.A. Ambrose
1905	O.O. Simpson	A.E. Ewing	W.P. Crosby	D.M. Clower	J.P. Byrd
1909	A.T. Green	W.T. Knight	W.M. Jordan	J.H. McGee	J.L. Brand
1910	H.D. Miller	M. S. Cornett	T.A. Pate	S.J. Busha	J.L. Brand
1913	W.J. Tribble	R.E. Hill	C.A. McDaniel	J.A. Deaton	J.H. Britt
1916	C. A. McDaniel	L.P. Patillo	J.H. Britt		
1917	V. H. Allen	L.J. Phillips	J.H. Britt		
1921	J.K. Jackson	J.D. Miller	T.L. Harris		
1925	T.L. Harris	S.J. Busha	Paul Sims		
1929	T.L. Harris	S.J. Busha	W.R. Hurst	Note: Format changed to three commmissioners between 1916 and 1968	
1933	T.L. Harris	Paul Dover	W.R. Hurst		
1937	T.L. Harris	Paul Dover	W.R. Hurst		
1941	T.L. Harris	Paul Dover	W.R. Hurst		
1945	T.L. Harris	A.J. Corley	W.R. Hurst		
1949	Paul Dover	O.D. Cain	Weldon B. Archer		
1953	Paul Dover	O.D. Cain	Weldon B. Archer		
1957	Dr. W.A. Elinburg	Uhland Freeman	Gordon Franchiseur*		
1961	Dr. W.A. Elinburg	Uhland Freeman	Minor M. Corley		
1965	W. Ray Morgan	W. R. Pruitt	O.F. Thompson		
1969	W.R. Pruitt	Ray W. Gunnin	Carvis P. Williiams	Maron Buice	Julian Archer
1971	W. R. Pruitt	Ray W. Gunnin	Carvis P. Williams	Maron Buice	Julian Archer
1973	Bill Atkinson	Ray W. Gunnin	Waye Mason	Maron Buice	Julian Archer
1975	Bill Atkinson	Ray W. Gunnin	Wayne Mason	Maron Buice	Guy Stokes
1977	Wayne Mason	Ray W. Gunnin	K.C. Bowen Jr.	Maron Buice	Guy Stokes
1979	Wayne Mason	Edwin Howard	K.C. Bowen Jr.	Maron Buice	Guy Stokes
1981	Charles Ashworth	Edwin Howard	Jere Johnson	Maron Buice	Guy Stokes
1983	Charles Ashworth	Edwin Howard##	Jere Johnson	Maron Buice	Guy Stokes ##
1985	Lillian Webb	Ken Suffridge	Scott Ferguson **	Mike Berg	John Frank/Bartow Jenkins ***
1987	Lillian Webb	Ken Suffridge	Scott Ferguson	Mike Berg	Don Loggins
1989	Lillian Webb	W.J. Dodd	Scott Ferguson	Curtis McGill	Don Loggins
1991	Lillian Webb	W.J. Dodd	Doug Williamson	Curtis McGill	Renee Unterman
1993	Wayne Hill	Tommy Hughes	Doug Williamson	Judy Waters	Renee Unterman
1995	Wayne Hill	Tommy Hughes	Patti Muise	Judy Waters	Kevin Kenerly

County Commissioners of Gwinnett, 1873-2007

Year	Chairman	District Commissioners			
1997	Wayne Hill	Tommy Hughes	Patti Muise	Judy Waters	Kevin Kenerly
1999	Wayne Hill	Tommy Hughes	Patti Muise	Judy Waters	Kevin Kenerly
2001	Wayne Hill	Marcia Neaton	Patti Muise	John Dunn	Kevin Kenerly
2003	Wayne Hill	Marcia Neaton	Patti Muise	John Dunn	Kevin Kenerly
2005	Charles Bannister	Lorraine Green	Bert Nasuti	Mike Beaudreau	Kevin Kenerly
2007	Charles Bannister	Lorraine Green	Bert Nasuti	Mike Beaudreau	Kevin Kenerly
2008	Charles Bannister	Shirley Lasseter	Bert Nasuti	Mike Beaudreau	Kevin Kenerly

***** Franchiseur died March 14, 1958 and Minor M. Corley was elected to fill his unexpired term.**
Edwin Howard and Guy Stokes served until September, 1983, because of litigation over district changes.
**** Scott Ferguson and John Frank took office on October 11, 1983.**
***** Frank resigned in late 1984, and on April 16, 1985, Bartow Jenkins filled his unexpired term.**
Source: Gwinnett County Commission

Gwinnett Constitutional Officers, 1819-2007

Year	Sheriff	Court Clerk	Probate Judge	Tax Commissioner
1819-20	William Blake			
1820-21	William Nesbit			
1822-23	James Loughridge			
1824-25	William Nesbit			
1826-27	James Loughridge			
1828-29	William Nesbit			
1829-30	William Martin			
1830-31	Thomas Worthy			
1831-32	William Brewster			
1832-33	Gilbert Coffey			
1834-35	F.L. Brandon			
1836-37	Levi Loveless			
1838-39	L.M. Cates			
1840-41	Nelson Roberts		Blank Years Unavailable	
1842-43	R.S. Foster			
1844-45	Nelson Brooks			
1846-47	J.W. Maltbie			
1848-49	M.C. Malone			
1850-51	G.T. Rakestraw			
1852-53	J.L. McElvaney			
1854-55	James A. Bracewell			
1856-57	Henry Allen			
1858-59	Walton Camp			
1860-61	W.W. Brand			
1862-63	J. L. McElvaney			
1864-65	J.R. Bracewell			
1866-67	William J. Born			

Gwinnett Constitutional Officers, 1819-2007

Year	Sheriff	Court Clerk	Probate Judge	Tax Commissioner
1868-1870	J. T. McElvaney			
1871-72	M.V. Brand			
1873-78	J.M. Patterson			
1879-1880	R.M. Wheeler			
1880only	R.M. Wheeler		Cyris A. Allen	
1881-84	J.M. Patterson		Cyris A. Allen	
1885-90	William P. Cosby		James T. Lawkin	
1891-92	T.A. Haslett		James T. Lawkin	
1893-96	T.A. Haslett		R.B. Whitworth	
1897-1902	T.A. Haslett		John P. Webb	
1903-06	R.T. Martin		John P. Webb	
1907-08	J.G. Brown	R. N. Holt	John P. Webb	
1909-10	J.G. Brown	R. N. Holt	G.G. Robinson	
1911-14	E.S. Garner	R. N. Holt	G.G. Robinson	
1915-16	J.W. Boss	Francis Maddox	G.G. Robinson	
1917-20	E.S. Garner	Francis Maddox	G.G. Robinson	
1921-24	E.S. Garner	Grady Holt	G.G. Robinson	
1925-28	W. T. McGee	Grady Holt	G.G. Robinson	
1929-36	C. F. Griswell	John Langley	E.S. Wages	
1937-40	J.P. Mason	John Langley	E.S. Wages	
1941-44	W.R. Hutchins	Henry Wages	E.S. Wages	
1945-48	J.L. Morgan	Henry Wages	E.S. Wages	
1949*	W.H. Hutchins*	Henry Wages	E.S. Wages	
1949-52	T.J. Johnson	Henry Wages	E.S. Wages	
1953-60	C.K. Pittard	Henry Wages	Alton W. Tucker	
1961-63	Daniel C. Cole**	Henry Wages	Alton W. Tucker	
1963-63	Samuel King	Henry Wages	Alton W. Tucker	
1963-64	Frank Q. Sammon	Henry Wages	Alton W. Tucker	
1965-68	Hoke Huston	Henry Wages	Alton W. Tucker	
1969-83	W.J. Dodd	Henry Wages	Alton W. Tucker	Lamar Wages
1984 only	W.J. Dodd	Henry Wages	Alton W. Tucker	Katherine Sherrington
1985 only	W.J. Dodd	Henry Wages	Alton W. Tucker	Katherine Sherrington
1985-86	Bobby G.Plunkett	Henry Wages	Sue Williams	Katherine Sherrington
1987-1992	Bobby G. Plunkett	Henry Wages	Fred P. Meyer	Katherine Sherrington
1993-96	Jim Carsten	Henry Wages	Walter J. Clarke II	Katherine Sherrington
1997-current	R.L. "Butch" Conway	Tom Lawler	Walter J. Clarke II	Katherine Sherrington

Four officers of the county are required by the Georgia Constitution to maintain their offices at the courthouse. They are the sheriff, clerk of court, probate judge and tax commissioner.

**** Hutchins died in office; his wife temporarily succeeded him until an election in 1949.***

***** Cole resigned, and Samuel King won an election to succeed him.***

Source: Gwinnett County Government

County Agents of Gwinnett

Years	Name
1917	H.H. Kemp
1918-49	A.G. Robison
1950-54	Roy W. Garren
1954 -59	Ned W. Shirley
1960 - 1963	J.T. Alexander
1963 - 1973	R. Wayne Shackelford
1973 - 1994	J.W. (Bill) Baughman
1994 - 2001	Rosalyn V. Joseph
2001 -	Robert Brannen

Note: The title of the job changed over the years, but these were those heading the extension office.

Source: Retired agents

Recreation Authority Members, 1985-2007

Name	Years Served	Name	Years Served
Allen, Lois	2003 – 2007	Little, Jeff	2005 – 2007
Berg, Mike	1988 – 1996	MacArthur, Ken	1985 – 1989
Black, Mike	1985 – 1993	McKenney, Bill	2001 – 2003
Bowen, Rudy	1987	Maloof, Glenn	2007
Bowers, Bob	1989 – 1990	Nash, Charlotte	2005 – 2007
Brown, Doug	1993 – 1995	Nasuti, Bert	199l
Byrd-Lewis, Renee	2003 – 2006	O'Brien, Peggy	2003 – 2007
Carroll, Randy	1985 – 1986	Payne, Robert	1989 – 1992
Cato, Rodney	1989 – 1992	Pearce, Phyllis	1987 – 1989
Chastain, Linda	1986	Pereira, Alisia	2002 – 2004
Crowell, Alan	1989 – 1990	Queen, Bobbie	1993 – 2000
Culberson, Leon	1987 – 1989	Randall, Chip	2005 – 2007
Curry, John	1997	Salter, Charles	1991 – 1994
Dodd, Teresa	1995 – 2003	Shumate, Greg	1996 – 2000
Durrance, Justin	1992 – 1994	Smith, Edith	1989 – 1992
Ferguson, Scott	1995 – 1996	Strickland, Dot	1991 – 1994
Ficco, David	2005 – 2007	Sutor, Wayne	2002 – 2007
Figliolini, Rico	1999 - 2002	Thompson, Kathy	1993 – 2000
Gardner, Charlotte	1985 – 1990	Tucker, Lucille	1992 – 1993
Gerwin, Joe	1995 – 2001	Underwood, Charlie	2007
Houston, Jan	1985 – 1986	Williams, Mark	2001 – 2006
Hunt, Lamar	1995	Williamson, Greg	1991
Johnson, Billy W.	1993 – 1997	Wilson, Mickey	1987 – 1990
Joiner, Thad	1987	Wilson, Phylecia	1993 – 2004
Kenney, Tom	1995 – 2002	Wood, Bob	1991 – 1992
Kesler, David	2001 – 2004	Zeigler, Tammie	1997 - 2000
Klen, Jan	1987 – 1989		

Source: Gwinnett County Dept. of Community Services

Key Executives of Gwinnett Government

Name	Dates	Title	Administration
Wayne Shackelford	Jan. 1, 1973-April 1, 1984	Executive Assistant to Commission	Arkinson, Mason, Ashworth
Bob Witt	1984-Sept. 15, 1986	Executive Assistant to Commission	Ashworth
Winford Gower	Sept. 1986-May, 1988	Administrative Coordinator	Webb
Chuck Button	March 9, 1987 -1991	Exec. Assistant; County Manager	Webb
Steve Schildecker	Feb. 1991--Sept. 1991	Interim County Manager	Webb
Sam Brownlee	Sep. 3,1991-Dec. 31,1992	County Manager	Webb
Bill Northquest	Jan. 1,1993-Aug. 15, 1995	County Administrator	Hill
Charlotte Nash	Aug. 1995-Dec. 17, 2004	County Administrator	Hill
Jock Connell	January 2005 -	County Administrator	Hill; Bannister

Source: Gwinett County Government

Elections Board Members since 1985

Year	Chairman	Member	Member	Member	Member	Elections Supervisor
1985	Mae Bell Britt	Rick Flemming	Robert Joseph	Dr. Tom Price	Shirley Sommerville	Mae Bell Britt
1986	Lloyd N. Harris	Rick Flemming	Robert Joseph	Dr. Tom Price	Shirley Sommerville	Lloyd N. Harris
1987	Lloyd N. Harris	Robert Joseph	Rex Millsaps	Dr. Tom Price	Shirley Sommerville	Lloyd N. Harris
1988	Lloyd N. Harris	Robert Joseph	Rex Millsaps	Dr. Tom Price	Shirley Sommerville	Lloyd N. Harris
1989	Robert C. Sacks	Don Butler	Robert Joseph	Rex Millsaps	Sandra Scott	Grant Guess (acting)
1990	Robert C. Sacks	Don Butler	Robert Joseph	Rex Millsaps	Sandra Scott	William Northquest
1991	Don Butler	Ralph S. Cline	Samuel H. Harrison	James K. Purcell	Sandra Scott	William Northquest
1992	Don Butler	^Ralph S. Cline	Samuel H. Harrison	James K. Purcell	Sandra Scott	William Northquest
1993	Sandra Scott	Don Butler	Samuel H. Harrison	James K. Purcell	Joan H. Zellner	Wayne K. Brown
1994	Sandra Scott	Don Butler	Samuel H. Harrison	James K. Purcell	Joan H. Zellner	Wayne K. Brown
1995	Joan H. Zellner	Don Butler	SaSandra Fischer	Samuel H. Harrison	James K. Purcell	Wayne K. Brown
1996	Joan H. Zellner	Don Butler	>SaSandra Fischer	Samuel H. Harrison	James K. Purcell	Wayne K. Brown
1997	James K. Purcell	Beauty P. Baldwin	Don Butler	Beth S. Gibbons	Joan H. Zellner	Norma Lyons
1998	James K. Purcell	Beauty P. Baldwin	Don Butler	Beth S. Gibbons	Joan H. Zellner	Norma Lyons
1999	Beth S. Gibbons	Beauty P. Baldwin	Don Butler	Beth S. Gibbons	Joan H. Zellner	Norma Lyons
2000	Beth S. Gibbons	Beauty P. Baldwin	Don Butler	James K. Purcell	Joan H. Zellner	Norma Lyons
2001	Beth S. Gibbons	Beauty P. Baldwin	Don Butler	Joseph Buckner	Joan H. Zellner	Norma Lyons
2002	Don Butler	Beauty P. Baldwin	Joseph Buckner	Beth S. Gibbons	Joan H. Zellner	Lynn Ledford
2003	Beauty P. Baldwin	Beth S. Gibbons	Michael Muntean	Ray Street	Joan H. Zellner	Lynn Ledford
2004	Beauty P. Baldwin	Beth S. Gibbons	*Michael Muntean	Ray Street	Joan H. Zellner	Lynn Ledford
2005	Joan H. Zellner	Beauty P. Baldwin	Beth S. Gibbons	Ben Satterfield	Ray Street	Lynn Ledford
2006	Joan H. Zellner	Beauty P. Baldwin	Beth S. Gibbons	Ben Satterfield	Ray Street	Lynn Ledford
2007	Beth S. Gibbons	Beauty P. Baldwin	Deborah Ellis	Ray Street	Joan H. Zellner	Lynn Ledford
2008	Beth S. Gibbons	Beauty P. Baldwin	Deborah Ellis	**Joey Chapman	Joan H. Zellner	Lynn Ledford

^Joan H. Zellner replaced Ralph S. Cline in July 1992.
> Beauty P. Baldwin replaced SaSandra Fischer in September 1996.
< Lynn Ledford appointed Acting Elections Supervisor in September 1996.
**** Ben Satterfiield replaced Michael Muntean in April 2004.***
***** Joey Chapman replaced Ray Street in January 2008.***

Source: Gwinnett County Elections Department

Judges of Superior Court of Gwinnett

Note: Prior to the Gwinnett Judicial Circuit, Gwinnett was part of the Piedmont Circuit, which included the counties of Barrow, Jackson and Banks, which still form that circuit.

Name	Date Began	Served Until
Charles Pittard	Jan. 1,1961	1985
Reid Merritt	July 1, 1972	1986
Homer M. Stark	July 1, 1977	1999
Dawson K. Jackson	Dec. 1, 1982	
James Henderson	May 27, 1983	1993
Bryant Huff	Nov. 3, 1986	1992
Richard Winegarden	July 9, 1987	
Fred A. Bishop Jr.	July 17, 1991	2005
James W. Oxendine	Dec. 21, 1992	2002
Michael C. Clark	Jan. 1, 1993	
Melonie Snell Conner	July 1, 1998	
Debra K. Turner	Jan. 1, 1999	
Timothy Hamil	Jan. 14, 2002	
William M. Ray II	Jan. 14, 2002	
Ronnie K. Batchelor	Jan. 1, 2005	
Thomas N. Davis	Jan. 1, 2006	
Warren Davis	Jan. 1, 2008	

Judges of State Court of Gwinnett

The State Court of Gwinnett was established by the Legislature to handle increased caseloads of the Circuit judge. In 1962, the State Court of Gwinnett replaced the City Court of Gwinnett. It was a part time position until 1979.

Name	Date Began	Served Until
A.G. Liles	1952	Nov. 4, 1954
W. White Edmundson	June 15, 1956	
Joseph E. Cheeley Jr.	Nov. 24, 1958	Mar. 31, 1978
C. Hughel Harrison	Nov. 7, 1978	Jan. 8, 1979
Dawson K. Jackson	April 5, 1979	Dec. 1, 1982
Richard Winegarden	May 17, 1983	July 9, 1987
Howard E. Cook	Jan. 1, 1985	Jan. 1, 2005
Paul M. Hoffman	Aug. 24, 1987	
Fred A. Bishop Jr.	Aug. 24, 1987	July 17, 1991
Robert W. Mock Sr.	July 23, 1991	
David Fuller	Jan. 1, 1993	Sept. 1, 2003
Melonie Snell Conner	Oct. 28, 1993	July 1, 1998
Timothy R. Hamil	Jan. 1, 1999	Jan. 14, 2002
Pamela D. South	Feb. 2, 2001	
Joseph Iannazzone	Jan. 14, 2002	
Carla Brown	Nov. 7, 2003	
Randy Rich	Jan. 1, 2005	
John F. Doran Jr.	Jan. 1, 2007	

Gwinnett Court Administrators

Name	Years Served	
Arthur V. O'Neil	1988-2003	
Philip M. Boudewyns	2003-	

District Attorneys

Name	Years Served	
Jack Holland	1961-1965	
Reid Merritt	1965-1972	
Bryant Huff	1972-1985	
Tom Lawler	1985-1993	
Danny Porter	1993-	

Note: Name changed to District Attorney from Solicitor General during Merritt's term

Solicitors of the Gwinnett State Court

Name	Years Served	
Herbert Jenkins Jr.	1983-1986	
Samuel H. Harrison	1986-1987	
Gerald N. Blaney Jr.	1987-2007	
Rosanna Szabo	2007-	

Source: Gwinnett Court Administrator

Gwinnett Magistrate Court Judges, 1983-2008

Name	Start Date	Ending Date	Of Note
Alexander, Richard	February 12, 2001		
Argo, James	August 14, 2006		
Bishop, Fred Jr.	July 1, 1983	September 3, 1987	First Chief Magistrate, To State and then Superior Court
Bachelor, Ronnie	March 1, 2002	December 31, 2004	To Superior Court
Blum, Kristina	May 13, 2005		
Brogdon, William	September 26, 2000		
Brown, Ivory T.	October 15, 1991	October 15, 1993	First African-American Magistrate
Cantrell, Gene	June 18, 2002		
Clark, David E.	September 14, 2007		
Clark, Michael C.	July 16, 1991	December 31, 1991	To Superior Court
Collar, Richard E., Jr.	July 1, 1982	September 1, 1988	
Conner, Melodie	January 1, 1993	October 28, 1993	First of two full time magistrates (1993), then to State, Superior Court
Conway, R.L. (Butch)	July 1, 1983	March 31, 1991	Current Sheriff of Gwinnett County
Davis, Warren	October 16, 1984	December 31, 2007	Second Chief Magistrate (as of August 24, 1987; Later to Superior Court)
Duncan, Angela	June 18, 2004		
Gaskill, Don	July 1, 1983	July 1, 1985	
Greene, Michael	January 1, 1987	October 10, 1991	To Recorders Court

Gwinnett Magistrate Court Judges, 1983-2008

Name	Start Date	Ending Date	Of Note
Gullickson, John	June 1, 1987	March 2, 1994	
Head (Elbaz), Valeria	October 18, 1991		First of two full time Magistrate Judges, as of January 1, 1993.
Hinkle, James	August 5, 2003		Also the Mayor of Grayson
Hopkins, Sharon	February 12, 2001	June 14, 2002	
Hutchinson, George	December 1, 2004		Third Magistrate Court Judge, as of Dec. 1, 2004; Became Chief Jan. 11, 2008
Iannazzone, Joseph	October 3, 1988	January 14, 2002	To State Court
Jacobs, John	July 1, 1983	December 31, 1984	
Knight, Michelle	June 18, 2004		
Layng, Mark	February 13, 2001		
Lee, Chung	August 12, 1999	August 11, 2004	First Asian-Amerian Judge
Lewis, Mark	May 6, 1993		Began full-time March 21,2001
Mann, Jennifer	June 19, 2002		
Martin, Glenn	July 1, 1983	December 31, 1992	
McKinney, Janice	September 20, 1997	November 23, 2004	
Mitchum, Robert	February 8, 1987		
Moja, Jan	June 18, 2004		
Naughton, Frances	January 13, 1986	December 31, 1992	
Nguyen, Angela	May 13, 2005	August 11, 2006	
Norton, Albert	May 13, 2005		
Pierce, Robert	October 12, 1984	March 17, 1986	
Powell, Emily	July 1, 1983	January 1, 1987	
Powell, Emily	July 1, 1990	December 31, 2004	
Randazzo, Joseph	November 3, 2005	July 1, 2007	
Reeves, Gene	March 11, 1994	November 30, 2004	
Robinson, George	July 1, 1983	December 31, 1984	
Russell, Phyllis	May 3, 2007		
Smith, Macklyn	July 1, 1983	October 1, 1985	
South, Pamela	January 1, 1999	February 2, 2001	To State Court
Tate, Laura	September 16, 2002		Began full time
Thorpe, Michael	May 3, 2007		
Turner, Debra	Nov. 15, 1993	December 31, 1998	To Superior Court
Walker, Robert	March 7, 2008		First Full-Time African-American Judge
Waller, Robert	October 1, 1986		
Williford, James	December 15, 1990	June 3, 2005	

Source: Gwinnett Magistrate Court

Gwinnett Senior Magistrate Judges

Bennett, Ernest	November 3, 1989		
Holman, Patricia	July 1, 1983	December 18, 2004	
Peevy, Wendell	July 1, 1983		
Powell, Emily	January 16, 2008		
Reeves, Gene	January 1, 2005		
Sissel, Kenneth	September 10, 1985		
Williams, John	December 7, 1987	April 25, 2005	

Source: Gwinnett Magistrate Court

Police and Fire Chiefs of Gwinnett

Police Chiefs of Gwinnett County	
Years	Person
1959-1965	J.O. Bell
1965-1968	Harvard Norred
1968	Bobby Plunkett
1968-69	Jimmy Kilgore
1969-1985	John Crunkleton
1985-1985	Kent A. Ryan*
1985-1988	Steve Schildecker
1989-1993	Wayne Bolden
1993-1998	Carl White
1998-2003	W.H. "Bill" Dean
2003-	Charles M. Walters
Fire Chiefs of Gwinnett County	
1/1971- 1/1984	Raymond J. Mattison
4/1984-2/1985	Kent A. Ryan
4/1985-2/1988	John S. Holland
2/1988-9/2001	Michael H. Buice
10/2002-2/2006	Jack K. McElfish
3/2006 -	Steve Rolader

**** Ryan was fire chief, then became the director of public safety and acting police chief for the county after Crunkleton left. He remained head of public safety until 1988.***

Source: Gwinnett County Government

Medical Directors Serving Gwinnett

Year	Person
1966?	T.O. Vinson*
1972- ?	Charles Teal
?	Elizabeth Blanton
? - 1984	Herbert Hudgins
1984-1996	James Crutcher
1996-1997	Claude A. Burnett.
1997-2000	Patrick Meehan
2000-2001	Alvin Sievert
2001-	Lloyd M. Hofer

**** Gwinnett was in Metro East District with DeKalb County.***

***** A county health department is said to have been formed in 1941, with two nurses, Electa Kimbrough and Adele Saxton, heading the agency.***

Source: Gwinnett Health Department

City Court of Buford Officials, 1902-1970

Year	Judges	Clerks	Solicitors	Sheriffs
1902	J.O. H. Brown	W.M. Shelley; W.B. Brogdon	Burton Cloud	J.H. Hawkins
1903	J.O. H. Brown	Walter B. Brogdon	Oscar Wozencraft	J.H. Hawkins
1904	J.O. H. Brown	W.B. Brogdon; W.M. Shelley	Oscar Wozencraft	J.H. Hawkins
1905	F.F. Juhan	W.M. Shelley; C.H. Smith Sr.	D.K. Johnston	O.M. Bennett
1906	James W. Green; E.O. Dobbs Sr.	William M. Shelley	J.V. Pool	O.F. Pharr
1907-10	Emmett O. Dobbs Sr.	William M. Shelley	J.V. Pool	O.F. Pharr
1911-22	I.L. Oakes	William M. Shelley	Emmett O. Dobbs Sr.	J.R. Shadburn
1923-24	I.L. Oakes	William M. Shelley	A.G. Liles	J.R. Shadburn
1925-28	I.L. Oakes	William M. Shelley	A.G. Liles	W.H. Hutchins
1929-30	I.L. Oakes	William M. Shelley	A.G. Liles	Frank Y. Light
1931-32	S.M. Ledford	William M. Shelley	A.G. Liles	Frank Y. Light
1933-34	S.M. Ledford	William M. Shelley	A.G. Liles	T.C. Samples
1935-38	S.M. Ledford	William M. Shelley	E.W. White	T.C. Samples
1939	A.G. Liles	William M. Shelley	Emmett O. Dobbs Jr.	J.L. Morgan
1940-44	Marvin A. Allison	Maude G. Tapp	Emmett O. Dobbs Jr.	J.L. Morgan
1945-47	Marvin A. Allison	Maude G. Tapp	E.O. Dobbs Jr.; J.R. Merritt	J. W. Hosch
1948-50	Marvin A. Allison	Maude G. Tapp	J.Ray Merritt	J. W. Hosch
1951-52	E.W. White	Maude G. Tapp	J.Ray Merritt	Journey Phillips
1953-54	E.W. White	Maude G. Tapp	J.Ray Merritt	Willie Garrett
1955-58	J. Ray Merritt	A.R. Bramblett	Joseph E. Cheeley Jr.	G.R. Leak
1959-62	J. Ray Merritt	A.R. Bramblett	Glyndon C. Pruitt	G.R. Leak
1963	Reid Merritt	A.R. Bramblett; Betty Jo Reepe	Glyndon C. Pruitt	R.L. Smith
1964	Reid Merritt	Betty Jo Reepe	Glyndon C. Pruitt	R.L. Smith
1965-66	Handsel Morgan	Betty Jo Reepe	Glyndon C. Pruitt	G.R. Leak
1967-70	Handsel Morgan	Betty Jo Reepe	Glyndon C. Pruitt	Howard Stephens

Note: Court abolished by Legislature as of Dec. 31, 1970.

Source: Historic Buford, by Handsel Morgan

Senators Serving Gwinnett in Georgia General Assembly, 1819-2008

Year	Senator	Senator	Senator	Senator
1819	George Reid	John Tredwell		
1820	George Reid	Luke Robinson		
1821	George Reid	Luke Robinson		
1822	Thomas Worthy	William Green		
1823	Thomas Worthy	William Green		
1824	Thomas Worthy	Edward Featherstone		
1825	Thomas Worthy	William Green	John Park	Nathan Hutchins
1826	Elisha Wynn	Edward Featherstone	Nathan Hutchins	John Boring
1827	Thomas Worthy	William Green	John Park	John Brewster
1828	Thomas Worthy	John Park	William Green	John Boring
1829	William Nisbet	John Boring	Nathan Hutchins	John Ezzard
1830	William Green	John Brewster	Elisha Winn	Zachariah Gholson
1831	William Green	Zachariah Gholson	Nathan Hutchins	John Ezzard
1832	William Green	Zachariah Gholson	John Ezzard	
	Nathan Hutchins	William Martin		
1833	William Nisbet	John Boring	William Russell	
	John Gresham	Elisha Winn		
1834	Zachariah Gholson	William Martin	John Ezzard	
	Stewart McMullin	Kinchen Rambo		
1835	James Blackman	William Martin	John Ezzard	
	Robert Hamilton	Kinchen Rambo		
1836	James Blackman	John Ezzard	Robert Hamilton	
	Samuel Shipp	Kinchen Rambo		
1837	Hamilton Germany	Elisha Winn	Daniel Pittman	
	Samuel Shipp	George Reid		
1838	Levi Loveless	Thomas McGuire	Daniel Pittman	
	John Stell	Mathew Hamilton		
1839	Levi Loveless	John Stell	John Baker	Mathew Hamilton
1840	Levi Loveless	Samuel Martin	Daniel Pittman	George Reid
1841	Daniel Pittman	James Simmons	George Reid	
	James Blackman	Daniel Pittman		
1842	James Austin	Samuel Martin	John Whitworth	
1843-1844	Daniel Pittman	Samuel Martin	Madison Mitchell	John Whitworth
1845-1847	Charles Murphey	Samuel Martin	John Whitworth	
1847-1848	James Simmons	Joseph Brandon	John Whitworth	
1849-1850	Charles Murphey	Joseph Brandon	John Whitworth	
1851-1852	James Simmons	Levi Loveless	R.D.Wynn	
1853-1854	Henry Thomas	John Whitworth	Thomas Hudson	
1855-1856	J.Brown	John Whitworth	Thomas Hudson	
1857-1858	Henry Thomas	G.H.Hopkins	E.J.McDaniel	
1859-1860	M.L.Lenoir	Nathaniel Reeder	B.H.Blakely	

Senators Serving Gwinnett in Georgia General Assembly, 1819-2008				
Year	Senator	Senator	Senator	Senator
1861-1863	Samuel Alexander	Thomas Hudson (died)	Joshua Glenn	L.A. McAfee
1863-1864	James Polk			
1864-1865	Walton Camp (died)	A. Pool	Adam Robinson	
1865-1866	F.E. Manson			
1867-1868	F.E. Manson	T.H. Mitchell		
1868-1870	Milton Candler	Louis Nash	R.M.Parkers	
1871-1872	Milton Candler	W.E. Simmons	G.H. Jones	
1873-1874	Samuel Winn	J.W. Baxter	R.A.Blakely	
1875-1876	Samuel Winn	T.M. Peeples	A.A.Dyer	
1877	George Bryan	Nathan Hutchins	William Born	
1878-1879	William Born	Nathan Hutchins	George Bryan	
1880-1881	William Bond	Nathan Hutchins	Robert Mitchell	
1882-1883	Tyler Peeples	Robert Mitchell	James McElvaney	
1884-1885	James E. Brown	James Andrews	W.R.Poole	
1886-1887	J.C. Smith	W.L. Vaughn	E.M.Word (died)	J.L. Hamilton
1888-1889	William Smith	George Clement	George Jones	
1890-1891	C.T. Zachary	Henry Peeples	Nathan Bennett	
1892-1893	Charles W.Smith	William Smith	L.F.McDonald	
1894-1895				
1896-1897	Thomas Stewart	George Clement	L.F.McDonald	
1898-1899	William Morrison	Nathan Hutchins	Thomas Pate	
1900-1901	Nathan Hutchins	James Perry	W.T. Smith	
1902-1904	James Flanigan	Thomas Pate	Paul Turner	
1905-1906	C.M. Candler	O. Nix	W. Wilson	
1907-1908	E. Winn Born	W. Wilson	O. Nix	
1909-1910	S.C. McWilliams	O. Simpson	J.P. McConnell	
1911-1912	J.W. Mason	O. Nix	W. Wilson	
1913-1914	M.D. Irwin	G. Pharr	T.C. Shadburn	
1915-1916	E.M. Smith	G. Pharr	A. Johnson	
1917-1918	Alonzo Field	Giles Kelly	A.T. Green	A.T. Green
1919-1920	Walter Lenoir Bell	A.T. Green	Giles Kelly	
1921-1922	Oscar Nix	John Houston	J.S. Shettesworth	
1923-1924	Ed Gilstrap	John Houston	J.S. Shettesworth	
1925-1926	Walter Lenoir Bell	John Kelly	Francis Nix	
1927-1928	John Inzer Kelly	Francis Maddox	W.L. Nix	
1929-1930	Marcus Mashburn	William Holt	Edward McKelvy	
1931-1932	Lanie Eugene Jones	Mack Pittard	Frank Sammon	
1933-1934	Jesse Jackson Baggett	Mack Pittard	Frank Sammon	
1935-1936	Allen W. Darded	Frank Sammon	Edward McKelvy	
1937-1938	Frank Quill Sammon	Marvin Allison	Glyndon Tapp	
1939-1940	Royston Albert Ingram	Otis Pharr	Marvin Allison	

Senators Serving Gwinnett in Georgia General Assembly, 1819-2008				
Year	Senator	Senator	Senator	Senator
1941-1942	John Chapman Houston	Glenn Roberts	Marvin Allison	
1943-1944	Royston Albert Ingram	Marvin Allison	Andrew Williams	
1945-1946	Jesse Jackson Baggett	Andrew Williams	Charles Griswell	
1947-1948	William Thomas Dean	Emmet Oliver Dobbs	John Hutchins	Hilliard Rhodes Jordan
1949-1950	Aubrey Mell Turner	James A.White	Charles Griswell	
1951-1952	R.F.Duncan	Paul Kelly		
1953-1954	William Thomas Dean	Edmonson White	H.Rhodes Jordan	
1955-1956	Aubrey Mell Turner	Paul Kelly	Willie Kilgore	
1957-1958	Frank Quill Sammon Jr.	Tom Moss	Earl Story	
1959-1960	Clarence R Vaughn	Earl Story	Handsel Morgan	
1961-1962	W.Hugh McWhorter	Earl Story	Handsel Morgan	
1963-1964	Harold Harrison	Earl Story	Handsel Morgan	
1965-1966	J.Albert Minish	Earl Story	Tom Watson	
1967-1968	J.Albert Minish	Norris Nash	James Mason	
1969-1970	Steve Reynolds	Norris Nash	James Mason	
1971-1972	Steve Reynolds	Gib Dean	James Mason	
1973-1974	Steve Reynolds	James Mason	Gib Dean	Vinson Wall
1975-1976	Steve Reynolds	Tom Phililips	B.B.Harris	Vinson Wall
1977-1978	Steve Reynolds	Tom Phililips	B.B.Harris	Vinson Wall
1979-1980	Steve Reynolds	Tom Phililips	Charles Martin	Vinson Wall
1981-1982	Steve Reynolds	Tom Phililips	Charles Martin	Vinson Wall
1983-1984	Joe Wood	Bobby Lawson	Jerry Jackson	Thomas Phillips
	Mike Barnett	Charles Martin	Rex Millsaps	Donn Peevy
1985-1986	Joe Wood	Bobby Lawson	Jerry Jackson	Mike Barnett
	Charles Martin	Vinson Wall	Charles Bannister	Thomas Phillips
	Bill Goodwin	John Russell	Donn Peevy	
1987-1988	Joe Wood	Bobby Lawson	Jerry Jackson	Mike Barnett
	Ron Pittman	Vinson Wall	Charles Bannister	Thomas Phillips
	Bill Goodwin	John Mobley	Donn Peevy	
1989-1990	Wyc Orr	Bobby Lawson	Jerry Jackson	Mike Barnett
	Keith Breedlove	Vinson Wall	Charles Bannister	Thomas Phillips
	Bill Goodwin	John Mobley	Donn Peevy	
1991-1992	Wyc Orr	Bobby Lawson	Jerry Jackson	Mike Barnett
	Keith Breedlove	Vinson Wall	Emory Morsburger	Thomas Phillips
	Bill Goodwin	John Mobley	Donn Peevy	
1993-1994	Scott Dix	Charles Bannister	Ron Crews	Bill Goodwin
	Brooks Coleman	Ralph Johnston	Vinson Wall	John Dickenson
	Jere Johnson	Kieth Breedlove	John Mobley	
1993-1994	Joe Burton	Don Balfour	James Tysinger	
	Clinton Day	Sallie Newbill		

Senators Serving Gwinnett in Georgia General Assembly, 1819-2008				
Year	Senator	Senator	Senator	Senator
1995-1996	James Mills	Scott Dix	Charles Bannister	Ron Crews
	Bill Goodwin	Brooks Coleman	Ralph Johnston	Vinson Wall
	Jeffrey Williams	Jere Johnson	Kieth Breedlove	John Mobley
1995-1996	Joe Burton	Don Balfour	James Tysinger	
	Clinton Day	Sallie Newbill		
1997-1998	James Mills	Scott Dix	Charles Bannister	Ron Crews
	Tom Rice	Brooks Coleman	Ralph Johnston	Mike Coan
	Jeffrey Williams	Jere Johnson	Kieth Breedlove	Warren Massey
1997-1998	Joe Burton	Don Balfour	James Tysinger	
	William Ray	Thomas Price		
1999-2000	James Mills	Scott Dix	Charles Bannister	Mary H.Squires
	Tom Rice	Brooks Coleman	Eugene Callaway	Mike Coan
	Jeffrey Williams	Renee Unterman	Bobby Reese	Warren Massey
1999-2000	Joe Burton	Don Balfour	Charles Barton Ladd	
	William Ray	Thomas Price		
2001-2002	James Mills	Scott Dix	Charles Bannister	Mary H.Squires
	Tom Rice	Brooks Coleman	Mike Coan	Eugene Callaway
	Jeffrey Williams	Renee Unterman	Bobby Reese	Warren Massey
2001-2002	Joe Burton	Don Balfour	Charles Barton Ladd	
	William Ray	Thomas Price		
2003-2004	Ron Sailor	Earnest Williams	Billy Mitchell	Tom Rice
	Brooks Coleman	Pedro Marin	Mike Coan	David Casas
	Curt Thompson	Hugh Floyd	Charles Bannister	Scott Dix
	John Wilson Heard	Len Walker	Donna Sheldon	
2003-2004	Mary Hodges Squires	Don Balfour	Lane Levitan	Steve Henson
	Renee Unterman	David Shafer	Gloria Butler	
2005-2006	Tom Rice	Billy Mitchell	Robert Mumford	Pedro Marin
	Brooks Coleman	Bobby Reese	Hugh Floyd	Brian Thomas
	Mike Coan	Clay Cox	David Casas	John Wilson Heard
	Donna Sheldon	Phyllis Miller	Len Walker	
2005-2006	Curt Thompson	Don Balfour	Dan Weber	Steve Henson
	Renee Unterman	David Shafer	Gloria Butler	
2007-2008	Tom Rice	Billy Mitchell	Robert Mumford	Pedro Marin
	Brooks Coleman	Bobby Reese	Hugh Floyd	Brian Thomas
	Mike Coan	Clay Cox	David Casas	John Wilson Heard
	Donna Sheldon	Melvin Everson	Len Walker	
2007-2008	Curt Thompson	Don Balfour	Dan Weber	Steve Henson
	Renee Unterman	David Shafer	Gloria Butler	
Source: Georgia State Records				

House Representatives from Gwinnett from 1819-2008

Year	Representative	Year	Representative
1819	John Tredwell		Robert Hamilton
1820-1821	Luke Robinson	1836	John T. Ezzard
1821	Luke Robinson		Robert Hamilton
1822	William Green		Samuel M. Shipp
1823	William Green		Kinchen Rambo
1824-1825	Edward Featherstone	1837	Elisha Winn
1825	William Green		Daniel N. Pittman
	John G. Park		George Reid
	Nathan L. Hutchins		Samuel M. Shipp
1826	Edward Featherstone	1838	Thomas McGuire
	Nathan L. Hutchins		Daniel N. Pittman
	John Boring		Matthew T. Hamilton
1827	William Green		John W. Stell
	John G. Park	1839	John W. Stell
	John Brewster		John Baker
1828	John G. Park		Matthew T. Hamilton
	William Green	1840	Samuel Martin
	John Boring		Daniel N. Pittman
1829	John Boring		George Reid
	Nathan L. Hutchins	1841	James P. Simmons
	John Brewster		George Reid
1830	John Brewster		Daniel N. Pittman
	Elisha Winn	1842	James Austin
	Zachariah Gholson		Samuel Martin
1831	Zachariah Gholson		John C. Whitworth
	Nathan L. Hutchins	1843	Samuel Martin
	John T. Ezzard		Madison R. Mitchell
1832	Zachariah Gholson		John C. Whitworth
	John T. Ezzard	1845	Samuel Martin
	William Martin		John C. Whitworth
	Nathan L. Hutchins	1847	Joseph P. Brandon
1833	John Boring		John C. Whitworth
	William J. Russell	1849-1850	Joseph P. Brandon
	Elisha Winn		John C. Whitworth
	John H. Gresham	1851-1852	Levi Loveless
1834	William Martin		R.D. Wynn
	John T. Ezzard	1853-1854	John C. Whitworth
	Kinchen Rambo		Thomas P. Hudson
	Stewart McMullin	1855-1856	John C. Whitworth
1835	William Martin		Thomas P. Hudson
	John T. Ezzard	1857-1858	G.H. Hopkins
	Kinchen Rambo		E.J. McDaniel

House Representatives from Gwinnett from 1819-2008

Year	Representative	Year	Representative
1859-1860	Nathaniel Reeder	1900-01	Nathan L. Hutchins, Jr.
	B.H. Blakey		James A. Perry
1861-62-63	L.A. McAfee	1902-03-04	James C. Flanigan
1861-62	Thomas P. Hudson (died 1862)		Thomas A. Pate
1862-63	Joshua N. Glenn	1905-06	O.A. Nix
1863-1864	A. Pool		W.W. Wilson
1863	Walton Camp	1907-08	W.W. Wilson
1864	Adam Robinson		O.A. Nix
1865-1866	T.H. Mitchell	1909-10	O.O. Simpson
	Samuel Martin		J.P. McConnell
1868-70	Louis Nash	1911-12	O.A. Nix
	R.M. Parkes		W.W. Wilson
1871-72	W.E. Simmons	1913-14	G.W. Pharr
	G.H. Jones		T.C. Shadburn
1873-74	J.W. Baxter	1915-16	G.W. Pharr
	R.A. Blakely		A.A. Johnson
1875-76	T.M. Peeples	1917-18	Giles F. Kelley
	A.A. Dyer		A.T. Green
1877	Nathan L. Hutchins	1919-20	A.T. Green
	William Jasper Born		Giles F. Kelley
1878-79	William Jasper Born	1921-22	John C. Houston
	Nathan L. Hutchins		J.S. Shettesworth
1880-81	Nathan L. Hutchins	1923-24	John C. Houston
	Robert E. Mitchell		J.S. Shettesworth
1882-83	Robert E. Mitchell	1925-26	John I . Kelley
	James T. McElvaney		Francis Bartow Maddox
1884-85	James W. Andrews	1927	Francis Bartow Maddox
	W.R. Poole		W.L. Nix
1886-87	J.C. Smith	1929-31	William Grady Holt
	W.L. Vaughn		Edward L. McKelvey
1888-89	William T. Smith	1931	Mack Wheeler Pittard
	George C. Clement		Frank Quill Sammon
1890-91	Henry L. Peeples	1933	Mack Wheeler Pittard
	Nathan Bennett		Frank Quill Sammon
1892-93	William T. Smith	1935	Frank Quill Sammon
	L.F. McDonald		Edward L. McKelvey
1894-95	Henry L. Peeples	1937-38	Marvin A. Allison
	J.F. Espy		Glyndon P. Tapp
1896-97	George C. Clement	1939	Otis N. Pharr
	L.F. McDonald		Marvin A. Allison
1898-99	Nathan L. Hutchins, Jr.	1941	Glenn R. Roberts
	Thomas A. Pate		Marvin A. Allison

House Representatives from Gwinnett from 1819-2008

Year	Representative
1943	Marvin A. Allison
	Andrew D. Williams
1945	Andrew D. Williams
	Charles F. Griswell
1947-48	Emmett Oliver Dobbs, Jr.
	John Hutchins
	Hilliard Rhodes Jordan
1949	James Austin White
	Charles F. Griswell
1951-52	Paul V. Kelley
1953-54	Edmonson W. White
	Hilliard Rhodes Jordan
1955-56	Paul V. Kelley
	Willie L. Kilgore
1957-58	Tom W. Moss, Jr.
	Earl P. Story
1959-60	Earl P. Story
	Handsel G. Morgan
1961-62	Earl P. Story
	Handsel G. Morgan
1963-64	Earl P. Story
	Handsel G. Morgan
1965-66	Earl P. Story
	Tom O. Watson
1967-68	Norris J. Nash
	James D. Mason
1969-70	Norris J. Nash
	James D. Mason
1971-72	George G. Dean, II
	James D. Mason
1973-74	James D. Mason
	George G. Dean, II
	Clarence V. Wall
1975-76	Robert T. Phillips
	Billy Banks Harris
	C. Vinson Wall
1977-78	Robert T. Phillips
	Billy Banks Harris
	C. Vinson Wall
1979-80	Robert T. Phillips
	Charles C. Martin
	Clarence Vinson Wall

Year	Representative
1981-82	Robert T. Phillips
	Charles C. Martin
	Clarence Vinson Wall
1983-84	O. M. Barnett
	Charles C. Martin
	Rex A. Millsaps
	Thomas H. White
	Willard F. Goodwin
	John Russell
1985-88	O.M. Barnett
	Ronald W. Pittman
	Charles C. Martin
	C. Vinson Wall
	Charles E. Bannister
	Willard F. Goodwin
	John O. Mobley, Jr.
	John Russell
1989-90	O.M. Barnett
	Keith Roscoe Breedlove
	C. Vinson Wall
	Charles E. Bannister
	William F. Goodwin
	John O. Mobley, Jr.
1991-1992	O.M. Barnett
	Keith Roscoe Breedlove
	C. Vinson Wall
	Emory Morsberger
	Bill Goodwin
	John Mobley, Jr.
1993-94	Scott Dix
	Charles E. Bannister
	Ron Crews
	Bill Goodwin
	Brooks P. Coleman, Jr.
	Ralph Johnston
	Vinson Wall
	John David Dickinson
	Jere Johnson
	Keith R. Breedlove
	John O. Mobley, Jr.
1995-96	Charles E. Bannister
	Keith R. Breedlove

House Representatives from Gwinnett from 1819-2008

Year	Representative
	Brooks P. Coleman, Jr.
	Ronald A. Crews
	Bill Goodwin
	Jere Johnson
	Ralph Johnston
	Vinson Wall
	Jeffery Williams
1997-98	Charles E. Bannister
	Ron Crews
	Tom Rice
	Brooks Coleman
	Ralph Johnston
	Michael Coan
	Jeffery Williams
	Jere Johnson
	Keith Breedlove
	Warren Massey
1999-2000	Charles Bannister
	Mary Squires
	Tom Rice
	Brooks P. Coleman, Jr.
	Gene Callaway
	Jeffery L. Williams
	Renee Unterman
	Bobby Reese
	Warren Massey
2001-02	Scott Dix
	Mary Squires
	Brooks P. Coleman, Jr.
	Tom Rice
	Gene Callaway
	Michael Coan
	Jeffery Williams
	Renee Unterman
	Michael Muntean
	Warren Massey
	Len Walker
2003-04	Ron Sailor
	Earnest "Coach" Williams
	Billy Mitchell
	Tom Rice
	Brooks Coleman
	Pete Marin
	Mike Coan
	James Mills
	David Casas
	Curt B. Thompson II
	Hugh Floyd
	Charles Bannister
	Scott Dix
	John Heard
	Len Walker
	Donna Sheldon
2005-06	Tom Rice
	Billy Mitchell
	Robert Mumford
	Pete Marin
	Brooks Coleman
	Bobby Reese
	Hugh Floyd
	Brian Thomas
	Mike Coan
	Clay Cox
	David Casas
	John Heard
	Donna Sheldon
	Melvin Everson
	Lynn Walker
2007-08	Tom Rice
	Billy Mitchell
	Robert Mumford
	Pete Marin
	Brooks Coleman
	Bobby Reese
	Hugh Floyd
	Brian Thomas
	Michael Coan
	Clay Cox
	David Casas
	John Heard
	Donna Sheldon
	Melvin Everson
	Lynn Walker

Source: Georgia House of Representatives

Membership in County-Appointed Boards, 2008

Board Name	Representing and/or Appointed by	Member and City
Airport Authority	Chair Appointed	Eric "Tip" Cape, Duluth, Chair
	District 1	Mark Grams, Lawrenceville
	District 2	Frank Lombardi, Duluth
	District 3	Emory Geiger, Snellville
	District 4	Dustin Hewatt, Lawrenceville
Animal Advisory Council	BoC Appointed	
	Gwinnett County Domestic Feline Interests	Dennis Kronenfeld, Lawrenceville
	Gwinnett County Extension Service	Tricia Wallace, Lawrenceville
	Gwinnett Humane Society	Gloria Kennedy, Dacula
	Gwinnett Municipal Association	Allison Wilkerson-Rooks, Grayson
	Lawrenceville Kennel Club	Gail LaBarge, Buford, Chair
	Member At Large	Carla E. Brown, Dacula
	Member At Large	Clara P. Seals, Snellville
Arts Facility Authority	Chair Appointed	Lynn Thorndyke, Duluth
	District 1	Anthony Rodriquez, Duluth, Chair
	District 2	Judy S. Floyd, Norcross
	District 3	Dave McMullen, Lawrenceville
	District 4	Paula Hastings, Lawrenceville
Board of Construction Adjustments & Appeals	BoC Appointed	
	Barrier Free Gwinnett	Abbey Shirley, Lawrenceville
	General Contracting Industry	Charles Anderson, Lawrenceville
	Architect	James R. Lankford, Lawrenceville
	Civil Engineer	David Leonard, Lawrenceville
	Electrical Engineer	Ronald L. Bolden, Lawrenceville
	Fire Protection Engineer	Michael W. Banham, Duluth - Chairperson
	Registered Mechanical Engineer	Jiles A. Singleton, Atlanta
	Structural Engineer	Roger S. Lingerfelt, Snellville
Board of Health	BoC Appointed	Libby Anderson, Lilburn
		Mike Beaudreau, Lawrenceville
	Physician	Dr. Todd Williamson, Lawrenceville
	Superintendent of Schools	Alvin Wilbanks, Lawrenceville
		Louise Radloff, Norcross, Chair
	City of Lawrenceville	Tom Karr, Lawrenceville
	City of Lawrenceville	Rex Millsaps, Lawrenceville

Membership in County-Appointed Boards, 2008		
Board Name	Representing and/or Appointed by	Member and City
Board of Registration and Elections	BoC Appointed	Joey Chapman, Lilburn
	Democatic Appointment	Beth Gibbons, Stn. Mtn. Chair
	Democatic Appointment	Beauty Baldwin, Dacula
	Republican Appointment	Debbie Ellis, Buford
	Republican Appointment	Joan H. Zellner, Buford
Board of Tax Assessors	Chair Appointed	Norma Holliman, Dacula
	District 1	Robert W. Chaapel, Norcross
	District 2	Sue Seibenhener, Lawrenceville
	District 3	David Kesler, Duluth
	District 4	Norman Nash, Lilburn, Chair
Development of Advisory Committee	Chair Appointed	David Van Landingham, Snellville
	District 1	Carol Hassell, Suwanee
	District 2	Mark McClure, Lilburn
	District 3	Jerry Oberholtzer, Snellville
	District 4	Paula Hastings, Lawrenceville
	BoC Appointed	
	Architect	Greg Dechko, Lawrenceville
	Commercial Developer	Walter S. Rekuc, Jr., Norcross
	General Contractor	Burgess Baird, Lilburn
	Home Builder	Glen Wellborn, Dacula
	Industrial Developer	Jay Puckhaber. Atlanta
	Landscape Architect	Terry Baker, Duluth
	Land Surveyor	Dennis Billew, Duluth
	Multi-Family Developer	Mark Richardson, Lawrenceville
	Office Developer	Chris Stanley, Atlanta
	Planning Commission	Peggy Boydston, Lawrenceville
	Registered Engineer	Ed Myers, Gainesville
	Single Family Developer	Don Woods, Lawrenceville
	Utilities Coordinator	Terri Rosamond, Atlanta
	Zoning Board of Appeals	Marcia Bumbalough, Buford, Chair
	Planning & Development Director or Designee	Jennifer Peterson, Norcross
Development Authority of Gwinnett County	Chair Appointed	Richard Chandler, Buford
		W. David Leonard, III, Lawrenceville
		Jeff Mahaffey, Lawrenceville
	District 1	Sidney Theus, Duluth
	District 2	Johnny DiBartolo III, Suwanee
	District 3	Brian Martin, Lawrenceville
	District 4	Judy Waters, Snellville, Chair

Membership in County-Appointed Boards, 2008		
Board Name	Representing and/or Appointed by	Member and City
Family and Children Service Board	Chair Appointed	Pat Swan, Lilburn
	District 1	Suzanne Geske, Duluth
	District 2	Davida Baker, Tucker
	District 3	Marvin Harris, Snellville
	District 4	Gerald Mitchell, Lawrenceville
	BoC Appointed	
	Law Enforcement	Sgt. Larry Bright, Lawrenceville
	School Counselor	Catherine Garcia-Brake, Lilburn
Georgia Bio-Science Joint Devel. Authority	BoC Appointment	Charles Bannister, Lilburn
		Chris Brown, Duluth
		Eric Decker, Sugar Hill
Gwinnett-Rockdale-Newton Community Service Board	BoC Appointment	Beauty P. Baldwin, Dacula
		Angelo Harris, Suwanee
		Virginia W. Harris, Stone Mountain
		Nancy Hyde, Suwanee
		Gail H. Macrenaris, Berkeley Lake
		Louise Radloff, Norcross
	ExOfficio Member	Charles Bannister, Lilburn
Gwinnett Clean and Beautiful Board	BoC Appointed	Sheila Adcock, Ethel Andersen, Sharon Bartels, Carole Boyce, Chuck Button, Keith Carnes, Dick Carothers, Carla Carraway, Nancy Chandler, Butch Conway, Randy Dellinger, Mike Guynn, Karen Hill, Paula Hill, Lloyd Hofer, L.C. Johnson, Terri Jondahl, Stan Jones, Pat Kien, Berney Kirkland, Pam Ledbetter, Nick Masino, Alicia McCart, Caryn McGarity, Bartow Morgan Jr., Sean Murphy, Rick O'Brien, Jose Perez, Paige Powers, Diana Preston, Louise Radloff, Patsy Rooks, Mary Root, Bill Russell, David Seago, Tammy Shumate, David Snell, Melodie Snell-Conner, Vicky Sweeny, Richard Tucker, Charlie Walters, Chuck Warbington, Phylecia Wilson, Philip Wolfe Jim Steele - Chairperson
	Executive Director	Connie Wiggins, Sugar Hill, Ex. Director
Gwinnett Convention and Visitors Bureau	BoC Appointed	J. W. Benefield, Lawrenceville
	BoC Appointed	Lorraine Green, Lawrenceville
	BoC Appointed	Tom Martin, Duluth
	BoC Appointed	Bert Nasuti, Norcross
	Hospitality Representative	Dave Kaplan, Atlanta
	Hospitality Representative	Art Rilling, Lilburn

Membership in County-Appointed Boards, 2008		
Board Name	Representing and/or Appointed by	Member and City
Gwinnett Convention and Visitors Bureau (cont.)	Hospitality Representative	Meredith Mason, Snellville
	City Representative	Jeannine Rispin
	Gwinnett Chamber	Jim Maran, Duluth
	Council for the Arts	Vacant
	At Large	Tommy Hughes, Buford
	At Large	Richard Tucker, Suwanee, Chair
Gwinnett County Public Employees Retirement System	BoC Appointed	David Crews
Gwinnett Transit System Advisory Board	Chair Appointed	Bob Clark, Lawrenceville
	District 1	Art Sheldon, Duluth
	District 2	Craig L. Newton, Norcross
	District 3	Jon Richards, Lawrenceville, Chair
	District 4	Gerard Richardson, Lawrenceville
Gwinnett Historical Restoration and Preservation Board	Chair Appointed	Kim Hall, Sugar Hill
	District 1	Carol Hitchcock, Duluth
	District 2	Col. John Adams, Norcross
	District 3	Ben Satterfield, Dacula, Chair
	District 4	Phyllis Davis, Lawrenceville
Gwinnett United in Drug Education (G.U.I.D.E.)	BoC Appointed	
	Executive Director	Ari Russell, Lawrenceville
	Safe/Drug-Free Schools	Mary Flint, Lawrenceville
	Coalition	Ellen Gerstein, Snellville
	Law Enforcement	Deputy John Irvine, Lawrenceville
	Youth Organization	Mahuli Jakubek, Lawrenceville
	Buford City Schools	Teresa McCord, Buford
	County Chairperson	Steve North, Lawrenceville, Chair
	Non-Profit	Marina Peed, Duluth
	Board of Education	Chuck Truett, Lawrenceville
	Business/Chamber	Carolyn Wheeler, Snellville
	Parent Representative	Bobby Jean Moore, Lawrenceville
	Youth Representative	Schyler Cain, Lilburn
	Youth Representative	Jeniece Edwards, Grayson

Membership in County-Appointed Boards, 2008

Board Name	Representing and/or Appointed by	Member and City
Hospital Authority	Chair Appointed	Bruce Still, Lawrenceville
	District 1	Dr. Keith Carnes, Duluth
	District 1	Dr. Gale Hey, Lawrenceville
	District 2	S. Scott Batterton, Lilburn
	District 2	Gay Wiley Shook, Norcross
	District 3	David Peterson, Snellville
Hospital Authority (cont.)	District 3	Wayne Sikes, Snellville, Chair
	District 4	Roy Beaty, Lawrenceville
	District 4	Edward W. Radford, Buford
Housing Authority	Chair Appointed	Jann Moore, Lawrenceville
	District 1	James L. Thompson, L-ville, Chair
	District 2	L.C. Johnson, Duluth
	District 3	John McCauslan, Dacula
	District 4	Ron Foster, Lawrenceville
	Legal Counsel	Steven A. Pickens, Lawrenceville
Human Relations Commission	BoC Appointed	Melvin Emerson, Snellville W.C. Fields, Lawrenceville Rebecca Gonzales, L-ville, Chair Connie C. Jee, Suwanee The Rev. Erven Kimble, Norcross Koo-Ja Lee, Norcross Doretha Livsey, Snellville Theresa M. Livsey-Lemons, Lithonia Joseph L. McCarty, Lawrenceville Vacant Position Vacant Position Mushir Ahmed Siddiqui, Lawrenceville Kenneth Sissel, Lilburn
Library Board	Chair Appointed	Phyllis Oxendine, Duluth
	District 1	Brett Taylor, Lawrenceville
	District 2	Dale Tood, Norcross
	District 3	Lloyd Breck, Snellville, Chair
	District 4	Margaret Tiller, Lawrenceville
Licensing and Revenue Board of Appeals	BoC Appointed	Mark Newton, Snellville, Chair
	Grand Jury	Barbara Martin, Lawrenceville
	Gwinnett Convention and Visitors Bureau	Preston Williams, Duluth
	Board of Health Director	Richard Radloff, Norcross
	Planning & Devel. Director	Glenn Stephens, Lawrenceville
MARTA Board	BoC Appointed	Bruce LeVell, Lawrenceville

Membership in County-Appointed Boards, 2008

Board Name	Representing and/or Appointed by	Member and City
Merit Board	District 1	Betsey Dahlberg, Norcross
	District 2	Michael C. Murphy, Duluth, Chair
	District 3	Dick Lowing, Dacula
	District 4	Mitch Peevy, Buford
	Legal Counsel	Dick Carothers, Buford
	Employee	Jesse Jones, Lawrenceville
	Executive	Harry G. Mason, Marietta
Municipal-Gwinnett Planning Commission	Chair Appointed	Julianne Thompson, Suwanee
	District 1	Peggy Boydston, Lawrenceville
	District 1	Eric Johannsen, Suwanee, Chair
	District 2	Lynette Howard, Peachtree Corners
	District 2	Jose R. Perez, Norcross
	District 3	Teresa Cantrell, Dacula
	District 3	Chuck Warbington, Dacula
	District 4	Paula Hastings, Lawrenceville
	District 4	Floy Jumper, Buford
Partnership for Community Action	Chair Appointed	Garry Guan, Duluth
Public Facilities Authority	BoC Appointed	Charles E. Bannister, Lawrenceville Michael Smith, Lawrenceville Rick Williamson, Lawrenceville
Recreation Authority	Chair Appointed	H. S. "Chip" Randall, Suwanee
	District 1	David Ficco, Duluth
	District 1	Glen Malool, Lawrenceville
	District 2	Jack Bolton, Lilburn
	District 2	Wayne Sutor, Duluth
	District 3	Jeff Little, Auburn
	District 3	Charlotte Nash, Dacula
	District 4	Lois Allen, Lawrenceville, Chair
	District 4	Charlie Underwood, Buford
	Department of Community Services Director	Phil Hoskins, Lawrenceville

Membership in County-Appointed Boards, 2008

Board Name	Representing and/or Appointed by	Member and City
Mental Health Developmental Disabilities and Addiictive Disease Region Three Planning Board	BoC Appointed	Jon E. Baio, Lawrenceville
		Walter J. (Jim) Clarke, Lawrenceville
		Barbara Diefes, Lilburn
		Jean Kinard, Lawrenceville
		Virginia McVay, Snellville
		Vacant Position
		Vacant Position
		Karen Rawls, Lawrenceville
		Linda Lou Rickerson, Lawrenceville
		Carolyn Sword, Lilburn
		Evelyn Triana, Duluth
		Elizabeth Williams, Norcross
Springbrook Golf Course Commmission	Chair Appointed	B.J. Van Gundy, Norcross, Chair
	District 1	Leonard Buck, Duluth
	District 2	John Dunn, Stone Mountain
	District 3	Michael Tritschler, Lawrenceville
	District 4	Margaret (Peg) Murray, Lawrenceville
Stormwater Authority	BOC Appointments	Edward Sullivan, Lawreceville
		Chad Baker, Duluth
		James Orr, Bethelem
		William Puckhaber, Duluth
		Lewis Young, Duluth
	City Representative	Scott Batterton, Lilburn, Chair
	City Representative	Vacant
Tree Advisory Committee	Chair Appointed	Herman Pennamon, Lawrenceville
	District 1	Theresa Schrum, Suwanee
	District 2	Julie Stuart, Berkeley Lake
	District 3	Marguerite Whitwell, Lawrenceville
	District 4	
	BoC Appointed	
	Development Advisory	Dennis Billew, Duluth
	Gwinnett Cean & Beautiful	Paige Powers, Snellville
	Registered Forester	Dale Higdon, Stone Mountain
	Registered Landscape Architect	Terry Baker, Duluth

Membership in County-Appointed Boards, 2008

Board Name	Representing and/or Appointed by	Member and City
Upper Ocmulgee River Resource, Conservation and Developmental Council, Inc.	BoC Appointed	Jonathan Senerjian, Lawrenceville
		Jim Scarbrough, Norcross
		Jeremy Means, Lawrenceville
	Gwinnett Soil & Cons. District	Ellis Lamme, Dacula, Chair
	Gwinnett Soil & Cons. District	Mark Brock, Lawrenceville
	Gwinnett Soil & Cons. District	Bob Powell, Lawrenceville
Water and Sewerage Authority	Chair Appointed	Charles Ashworth, Suwanee
	District 1	Kevin McOmber, Suwanee
	District 2	Michael Sullivan, Lilburn
	District 3	Tommy Hunter, Dacula
	District 4	Clint Dixon, Chair, Buford
Zoning Board of Appeals	Chair Appointed	Jim Nash, Duluth
	District 1	Marcia Bumbalough, Buford, Chair
	District 2	R. Wayne Knox, Norcross
	District 3	Mike Royal, Lawrenceville
	District 4	Joseph Hughes, Buford

Source: Gwinnett Board of Commissioners, as of July 31, 2008

Auburn City Officials, 1993-2008

Year	Mayor	Council Member	Council Member	Council Member	Council Member	City Clerk
1993	Tom Riley	Brian Dunsha	Ray Hunter	Chris Stovall	Michael Churchill	Virginia Greeson
1994	Billy Parks	Judy Doss	Pete Gaudino	Chris Stovall	Harriett Schroeder	Barbara Frazier
1995	Billy Parks	Judy Doss	Harriett Schroeder	Chris Stovall	Pete Gaudino	Barbara Frazier
1996						
1997	David Hawthorne	Judy Dodd	Chris Autry	Ray McCulley		Patricia Adkins
1998	Len Cooper	Lewis Cooksey	Rick Roquemore	Terry Starry	Dewayne Metheny	Janet Bonner
1999	Neil Woolever	Lewis Cooksey	Richard Boutelle	Terry Starry	Dewayne Metheny	Fred Johnston
2000	Stephanie Grenier	Jean Bennett	Richard Boutelle	Terry Starry	Charles Sewell	Cheryl Gudz
2001	Stephanie Grenier	Lewis Cooksey	Charles Sewell	Terry Starry	Jean Bennett	Kirk Nylund
2002	Stephanie Grenier	James Shackelford	Charles Sewell	Jean Bennett	Len Cooper	Kirk Nylund
2003	Stephanie Grenier	James Shackelford	Jean Bennett	Charles Sewell	Len Cooper	Jessica Snyder
2004	Harold Money	Dorissa Shackelford	James Shackelford	Charles Sewell		Terry McElwee
2005	Harold Money	Dorissa Shackelford	David Hawthorne	Charles Sewell	Billy Parks	Terry McElwee
2006	Harold Money	Dorissa Shackelford	Donna Scouten	Charles Sewell	Linda Blechinger	Patricia Matthews
2007	Harold Money	Dorissa Shackelford	Donna Scouten	Charles Sewell	Sally Brown	Patricia Matthews
2008	Linda Blechinger	Dorissa Shackelford	Donna Scouten	Peggy Langley	Sally Brown	Rafael Avalos

Note: Where there are blanks, there is no information available

Source: City of Auburn

Berkeley Lake City Officials, 1956-2008

Year	Mayor	Council Member	Council Member	Council Member	Council Member	Council Member
1956	H.A. Grumann	E.H. (James) Bryant	Frank Kinnett	Jack Liles	John Bagwell	
1957	H.A. Grumann	Gene Willis	Mark K. Toalson	Robert Berkey	Roger Jacobs	
1958	H.A. Grumann	Cleve Farabee	Mark K. Toalson	Robert Berkey	Roger Jacobs	
1959	H.A. Grumann	Cleve Farabee	Mark K. Toalson	Robert Berkey	W.B. Dalton	
1960	H.A. Grumann	Cleve Farabee	Mark K. Toalson	Robert Berkey	W.B. Dalton	
1961	H.A. Grumann	H.S. McCurry	Mark K. Toalson	Robert Berkey	W.B. Dalton	
1962	H.A. Grumann	Thurmond Hood	Paul Wynn	Robert Berkey	W.B. Dalton	
1963	H.A. Grumann	Thurmond Hood	Paul Wynn	Robert Berkey	W.B. Dalton	
1964	H.A. Grumann	Joe F. Jones	Paul Wynn	Robert Berkey	W.B. Dalton	
1965	H.A. Grumann	Joe F. Jones	Paul Wynn	Robert Berkey	W.B. Dalton	
1966	H.A. Grumann	R.W. Richards	Paul Wynn	Robert Berkey	Clayton Buford	
1967	B.O. Greene	R.W. Richards	Bernard C. Maltby	Robert H. Cook	Clayton Buford	
1968	B.O. Greene	Robert Conk	Bernard C. Maltby	Calvin Carroll	Herbert Davis	
1969	B.O. Greene	John Wilkerson	J.E. Clements	Calvin Carroll	Herbert Davis	
1970	John Wilkerson	Jodie Buford	J.E. Clements	Calvin Carroll	F.E. Carlton	
1971	John Wilkerson	Warren Coleman	Paul Wynn	Calvin Carroll	F.E. Carlton	
1972	Warren Coleman	E.C. Simmons	Paul Wynn	Robert Conk	L.J. Dennison	
1973	Warren Coleman	E.C. Simmons	Bess McCorvey	Robert Conk	L.J. Dennison	
1974	Warren Coleman	Bess McCorvey	John McBride	Otis Phillips	L.J. Dennison	
1975	Bess McCorvey	Rick Arnold	John McBride	Otis Phillips	L.J. Dennison	
1976	Stephen Withers	Bess McCorvey	Taz Jack Crider	Warren Coleman	L.J. Dennison	

Berkeley Lake City Officials, 1956-2008

Year	Mayor	Council Member	Council Member	Council Member	Council Member	Council Member
1977	Stephen Withers	Ed Heath	Bobby Appling	Robert Conk	L.J. Dennison	
1978	Ed Heath	Bobby Appling	Sam Godsey	Robert Conk	Lour Cumbee	
1979	Ed Heath	Doc White	Sam Godsey	Warren Coleman	Bill Jostin	
1980	Ed Heath	Doc White	Sam Godsey	Donald Baranowski	Bill Jostin	
1981	Ed Heath	Bob Smith	Sam Godsey	Donald Baranowski	Bill Jostin	
1982	Ed Heath	Bob Smith	Mike Barganier	Donald Baranowski	Bill Jostin	
1983	Ed Heath	Bob Smith	Mike Barganier	Donald Baranowski	Bill Jostin	
1984	Ed Heath	Bob Smith	Mike Barganier	Donald Baranowski	Bill Jostin	
1985	Ed Heath	Bob Smith	Bill McLane	Donald Baranowski	Bill Jostin	
1986	Bill Jostin	Bob Smith	Bill McLane	Donald Baranowski	Gary Jones	
1987	Bill Jostin	Lyndon Eubanks	Bill McLane	Donald Baranowski	Gary Jones	
1988	Gary Jones	Lyndon Eubanks	Ric Hutchinson	James Pierce	Vasta Lucas	
1989	Gary Jones	D.W. (Pete) Rolader	Ric Hutchinson	James Pierce	Vasta Lucas	
1990	James Pierce	D.W. (Pete) Rolader	Bernard Cohen	Ed Nigh	Gary Jones	
1991	James Pierce	Leslie Cardin	Bernard Cohen	Ed Nigh	Gary Jones	
1992	James Pierce	Leslie Cardin	Bernard Cohen	Judy Archer	Rick Schmidt	John Strobko
1993	Bernard Cohen	Leslie Cardin	John Skrobko	Judy Archer	Rick Schmidt	Walter Rehm
1994	Rick Schmidt	Leslie Cardin	Bernard Cohen	Charlie Robson	Walter Rehm	Marion McDugald
1995	Rick Schmidt	Leslie Cardin	Bernard Cohen	Charlie Robson	Walter Rehm	Marion McDugald
1996	Rick Schmidt	Leslie Cardin	Bernard Cohen	Doug Dowdy	Walter Rehm	Marion McDugald
1997	Rick Schmidt	Rober Schutt	Bernard Cohen	Boulton Mohr	Walter Rehm	Marquerite Cook
1998	Marguerite Cook	Kelly Goff	Tom Kitchens	Boulton Mohr	Anthony Arakawa	Sherry Ruys
1999	Marguerite Cook	Kelly Goff	Tom Kitchens	Sherwin Levinson	Anthony Arakawa	Sherry Ruys
2000	Lois D. Salter	Elizabeth Branstead	Phil Cuttino	Ken Massaroni	Anthony Arakawa	Delicia Reynolds
2001	Lois D. Salter	Elizabeth Branstead/ Frank Lombardi	Phil Cuttino	Ken Massaroni	Anthony Arakawa	Delicia Reynolds
2002	Lois D. Salter	Frank Lombardi	David Steventon	Ken Massaroni	Anthony Arakawa	Delicia Reynolds
2003	Lois D. Salter	Frank Lombardi	David Steventon	Ken Massaroni	Delicia Reynolds	Betty Covington
2004	Lois D. Salter	George Sipe	Bernard Cohen	Marci Zielazienski	Delicia Reynolds	Ken Massaroni
2005	Lois D. Salter	George Sipe	Bernard Cohen	Marci Zielazienski	Delicia Reynolds	Debbie Guthrie
2006	Lois D. Salter	George Sipe	Bernard Cohen	Tom Kitchens	Walter Anderson	Debbie Guthrie
2007	Lois D. Salter	George Sipe	Bernard Cohen	Tom Kitchens	Walter Anderson	Debbie Guthrie
2008	Lois D. Salter	Frank Lombardi	Rebecca Spitler	Tom Kitchens	Walter Anderson	Debbie Guthrie

Note: Another Council seat added in 1992

Source: City of Berkeley Lake

Mayors of Braselton, 1916-2008	
Year	Mayor
1916-1956	William Henry Braselton
1956-1987	James Lewis Braselton
1987-2001	Henry Edward Braselton
2001-	Pat Graham

Braselton Council Members
John O. Baird
Green Braselton
Herman H. Braselton
H.E. (Brassie) Braselton
John O. Braselton, Jr.
H.B. (Kit) Braselton (1960's-2001)
Kyle Bryant
Tom Clark (2002-2003)
Elise Cotter (2002-2004)
J.A. Davis
Tony Funari (2008-curent)
T.S. Hartley
Pam Braselton Jackson (?-2001)
Don McLean
Richard Mayberry (2004-current)
Dudley Ray (1998-current)
Ralph Richardson, Jr. (2003-current)
Phil Spivey (2004-2007)
James Stevens (?-1997)
Don Webster (1995-1998)
Bruce Yates (1998-2003)
Source: City of Braselton plus cemetery markers.

Buford City Officials, 1899-1938

Year	Mayor	Council Member	Council Member	Council Member
1899	W. W. Wilson	J. G. Blackwood	W. L. Pirkle	J. V. Tapp
1900	L. R. Martin			
1901	L. R. Martin			
1902	Thomas C. Shadburn	J. P. Neese	J. E. Cloud	E. W. Vance
1903	Thomas C. Shadburn	S. J. Busha	O. M. Bennett	N. G. Deaton
1904	W. W. Wilson	J. P. Neese	S. J. Busha	O. M. Bennett
1905	L. R. Martin	H. W. Christian	T. C. Burton	George L. Brogdon
1906	John Q. Allen	W. Tom Power	J. Loss Shadburn	O. M. Bennett
1907	John Q. Allen	John M. Sewell	H. W. Christian	O. M. Bennett
1908	John Q. Allen	G. W. Thompson	V. H. Allen	W. L. Shadburn
1909	John Q. Allen	V. H. Allen	J. Loss Shadburn	N. S. Robinson
1910	John Q. Allen	H. W. Christian	V. H. Allen	O. M. Bennett
1911	S. J. Busha	T. C. Shadburn	V. H. Allen	O. M. Bennett
1912	J. Loss Shadburn	W. L. Shadburn	N. G. Deaton	J. W. Tidwell
1913	J. Loss Shadburn	W. C. Drake	W. E. Sears	V. H. Allen
1914	S. J. Busha	L. P. Pattillo	A. J. Pirkle	C. W. Power
1915	S. J. Busha	John Q. Allen	W. C. Drake	T. C. Shadburn
1916	V. H. Allen	C. W. Power	L. P. Pattillo	A. J. Pirkle
1917	V. H. Allen	R. L. Lawson	E. W. Vance	T. C. Shadburn
1918	L. P. Patillo	N. G. Deaton	H. L. Edmondson	W. E. Sears
1919	J. Loss Shadburn	A. J. Pirkle	W. C. Drake	John Q. Allen
1920	J. Loss Shadburn	H. L. Edmondson	G. L. Bowman	S. J. Busha
1921	J. Loss Shadburn	P. J. Cates	W. E. Sears	V. H. Allen
1922	John Q. Allen	H. B. Brogdon	W. T. Power	C. J. Pirkle
1923	S. J. Busha	H. Allen	W. E. Sears	W. H. Hutchins
1924	D. A. Irwin	G. P. Tapp	C. J. Pirckle	H. W. Strickland
1925	S. J. Busha	V. H. Allen	H. H. Beard	W. L. Shadburn
1926	S. J. Busha	H. W. Strickland	C. J. Pirkle	Robert G. Vance
1927	J. Loss Shadburn	H. H. Beard	W. L. Shadburn	E. A. Banks
1928	J. Loss Shadburn	W. C. Drake	C. J. Pirkle	E. A. Wilbanks
1929	S. J. Busha	G. P. Tapp	E. A. Wilbanks	Henry A. Puckett
1930	S. J. Busha	N. W. Buice	H. W. Christian	W. C. Drake
1931	G. P. Tapp	E. A. Wilbanks	Pat Greer	N. G. Deaton
1932	G. P. Tapp	C. D. Pirkle	L. H. Kelley	W. C. Drake
1933	G. P. Tapp	N. G. Deaton	C. W. Power	E. A. Wilbanks
1934	G. P. Tapp	H. G. Jett	Logan Kelley	Elbert L. Whiting
1935	D. A. Irwin	C. W. Power	G. P. Tapp	E. A. Wilbanks
1936	D. A. Irwin	C. D. Pirkle	W. L. Brogdon	E. L. Whiting
1937	C. J. Pirkle	N. G. Deaton	C. W. Power	E. A. Wilbanks
1938	C. J. Pirkle	C. D. Pirkle	W. L. Brogdon	A. K. Holbrook

Buford City Officials, 1899-1938				
Year	Council Member	Council Member	Council Member	City Clerks
1899				
1900				
1901				
1902	Dr. W. J. Rowe			
1903	N. W. Buice			
1904	N. G. Deaton	J. V. Tapp	J. Q. Allen	W. B. Brogdon
1905	J. P. Neese	J. V. Tapp	J. Q. Allen	W. B. Brogdon
1906	H. W. Christian	G. L. Brogdon	Sam B. Hoyt	W. B. Brogdon
1907	W. T. Power	G. L. Brogdon	J. L. Shadburn	W. B. Brogdon
1908	W. T. Power	John M. Sewell	G. L. Brogdon	W. B. Brogdon
1909	W. T. Power	W. L. Shadburn	G.W. Thompson/Bennett	W. B. Brogdon
1910	J. V. Tapp	W. L. Brogdon	J. Loss Shadburn	W. B. Brogdon
1911	J. V. Tapp	W. L. Shadburn	H. W. Christian	Lewis A. Hardman/ W. A. Pirkle
1912	A. J. Pirkle	T. C. Shadburn	V. H. Allen	V. L. Shadburn
1913	N. G. Deaton	A. J. Pirkle	J. W. Tidwell	M. E. Brogdon
1914	W. E. Sears	V. H. Allen	W. C. Drake	E. W. Tullis
1915	C. W. Power	L. P. Pattillo	A. J. Pirkle	E. W. Tullis
1916	T. C. Shadburn	W. C. Drake	John Q. Allen	E. W. Tullis
1917	A. J. Pirkle	L. P. Pattillo	C. W. Power	E. W. Tullis
1918	T. C. Shadburn	E. W. Vance	R. L. Lawson	E. W. Tullis
1919	W. E. Sears	H. L. Edmondson	N. G. Deaton	E. W. Tullis
1920	W. C. Drake	A. J. Pirkle	John Q. Allen	E. W. Tullis
1921	S. J. Busha	H. L. Edmondson (resigned)	Succeeded by G. L. Bowman	E. W. Tullis
1922	P. J. Cates	W. E. Sears	V. H. Allen	William M. Shelley
1923	H. B. Brogdon	W. T. Power	C. J. Pirkle	William M. Shelley
1924	W. H. Hutchins	W. E. Sears	Victor Allen	William M. Shelley
1925	G. P. Tapp	C. J. Pirkle	H. W. Strickland	William M. Shelley
1926	H. H. Beard	W. L. Shadburn	V. H. Allen	William M. Shelley
1927	C. J. Pirkle	R. G. Vance	H. W. Strickland	William M. Shelley
1928	H. H. Beard	W. L. Shadburn	H. W. Strickland	Johnnie K. Hamilton
1929	W. C. Drake	H. W. Strickland	C. J. Pirkle	Johnnie K. Hamilton
1930	E. A. Wilbanks	G. P. Tapp	H. A. Puckett	Johnnie K. Hamilton
1931	N. W. Buice	H. W. Christian	W. C. Drake	Johnnie K. Hamilton
1932	E. A. Wilbanks	Pat Greer	N. G. Deaton	Johnnie K. Hamilton
1933	C. D. Pirkle	L. H. Kelley	W. C. Drake	Johnnie K. Hamilton
1934	N. G. Deaton	E. A. Wilbanks	C. W. Power	Johnnie K. Hamilton
1935	H. G. Jett	Logan H. Kelley	Elbert Whiting	Johnnie K. Hamilton
1936	G. P. Tapp	E. A. Wilbanks	C. W. Power	Johnnie K. Hamilton
1937	C. D. Pirkle	W. L. Brogdon	E. L. Whiting	Johnnie K. Hamilton
1938	N. G. Deaton	C. W. Power	E. A. Wilbanks	W. C. Greer

Buford City Officials, 1939-2008					
Year	City Commissioner	City Commissioner	City Commissioner	City Clerks	City Managers
1939	John Q. Allen	N. W. Buice	W. L. Brogdon	W. C. Greer	Vernon W. Crawford
1940	John Q. Allen	N. W. Buice	W. L. Brogdon	W. C. Greer	Vernon W. Crawford
1941	John Q. Allen	N. W. Buice	J. Earle Simpson	W. S. Allen	W. L. Brogdon
1942	John Q. Allen	N. W. Buice	J. Earle Simpson	W. S. Allen	W. L. Brogdon
1943	John Q. Allen	N. W. Buice	J. Earle Simpson	W. S. Allen	W. L. Brogdon
1944	John Q. Allen	N. W. Buice	J. Earle Simpson	W. S. Allen	W. L. Brogdon
1945	John Q. Allen	N. W. Buice	J. Earle Simpson	W. S. Allen	W. L. Brogdon
1946	John Q. Allen	N. W. Buice	J. Earle Simpson	W. S. Allen	W. L. Brogdon
1947	John Q. Allen	E. E. Robinson	J. Earle Simpson	W. S. Allen	H. Jack Turner
1948	John Q. Allen	E. E. Robinson	J. Earle Simpson	W. S. Allen	H. Jack Turner
1949	John Q. Allen	E. E. Robinson	Chief Garner	W. S. Allen	H. Jack Turner
1950	John Q. Allen	E. E. Robinson	Chief Garner	W. S. Allen	H. Jack Turner
1951	Lionel Drake	E. E. Robinson	Chief Garner	W. S. Allen	H. Jack Turner
1952	Lionel Drake	E. E. Robinson	Arnold E. Hamner	Imogee Jett Mathis	J. C. Dover
1953	Lionel Drake	E. E. Robinson	Arnold E. Hamner	Carlton Sisk	J. C. Dover
1954	Lionel Drake	E. E. Robinson	Arnold E. Hamner	J. C. Merritt	J. C. Dover
1955	Lionel Drake	E. E. Robinson	Stanley Allen	J. C. Merritt	J. C. Dover
1956	Lionel Drake	E. E. Robinson	Stanley Allen	J. C. Merritt	J. C. Dover
1957	Lionel Drake	E. E. Robinson	Stanley Allen	J. C. Merritt	J. C. Dover
1958	Lionel Drake	E. E. Robinson	Stanley Allen	J. C. Merritt	J. C. Dover
1959	Lionel Drake	E. E. Robinson	Stanley Allen	J. C. Merritt	J. C. Dover
1960	Loss Sears	E. E. Robinson	Stanley Allen	J. C. Merritt	J. C. Dover
1961	Loss Sears	E. E. Robinson	Stanley Allen	J. C. Merritt	J. C. Dover
1962	Loss Sears	E. E. Robinson	Stanley Allen	J. C. Merritt	J. C. Dover
1963	Loss Sears	E. E. Robinson	Stanley Allen	J. C. Merritt	J. C. Dover
1964	Loss Sears	E. E. Robinson	Stanley Allen	J. C. Merritt	J. C. Dover
1965	Loss Sears	E. E. Robinson	Stanley Allen	J. C. Merritt	J. C. Dover
1966	Loss Sears	E. E. Robinson	Stanley Allen	J. C. Merritt	J. C. Dover
1967	Loss Sears	E. E. Robinson	Stanley Allen	J. C. Merritt	J. C. Dover
1968	Loss Sears	E. E. Robinson	Stanley Allen	J. C. Merritt	J. C. Dover
1969	Noah Herrington	E. E. Robinson	Stanley Allen	J. C. Merritt	J. C. Dover
1970	Noah Herrington	E. E. Robinson	Stanley Allen	J. C. Merritt	J. C. Dover
1971	Noah Herrington	E. E. Robinson	Stanley Allen	J. C. Merritt	J. C. Dover
1972	Robert P. Joseph	E. E. Robinson	Stanley Allen	Judy Puckett Martin	J. C. Dover
1973	Robert P. Joseph	E. E. Robinson	Charles Martin	Judy Puckett Martin	J. C. Dover
1974	Robert P. Joseph	E. E. Robinson	Charles Martin	Judy Puckett Martin	Bobby Kerlin
1975	Hubert S. Higgins	E. E. Robinson	Charles Martin	Judy Puckett Martin	Bobby Kerlin
1976	Hubert S. Higgins	Phillip Beard	Charles Martin	Judy Puckett Martin	Bobby Kerlin
1977	Hubert S. Higgins	Phillip Beard	Charles Martin	Judy Puckett Martin	Bobby Kerlin
1978	Hubert S. Higgins	Phillip Beard	Charles Martin	Judy Puckett Martin	Bobby Kerlin

Buford City Officials, 1939-2008					
Year	City Commissioner	City Commissioner	City Commissioner	City Clerks	City Managers
1979	Hubert S. Higgins	Phillip Beard	Robert M. Perkins	Judy Puckett Martin	Bobby Kerlin
1980	Hubert S. Higgins	Phillip Beard	Robert M. Perkins	Judy Puckett Martin	Bobby Kerlin
1981	Thomas Hughes	Phillip Beard	Robert M. Perkins	Judy Puckett Martin	Earley Biffle
1982	Thomas Hughes	Phillip Beard	W.R. (Gene) Wiley	Judy Puckett Martin	Earley Biffle
1983	Thomas Hughes	Phillip Beard	W.R. (Gene) Wiley	Judy Puckett Martin	Earley Biffle
1984	Thomas Hughes	Phillip Beard	W.R. (Gene) Wiley	Judy Puckett Martin	Earley Biffle
1985	Thomas Hughes	Phillip Beard	W.R. (Gene) Wiley	Judy Puckett Martin	Earley Biffle
1986	Thomas Hughes	Phillip Beard	W.R. (Gene) Wiley	Judy Puckett Martin	Earley Biffle
1987	Thomas Hughes	Phillip Beard	W.R. (Gene) Wiley	Judy Puckett Martin	Earley Biffle
1988	Thomas Hughes	Phillip Beard	W.R. (Gene) Wiley	Judy Puckett Martin	Earley Biffle
1989	Thomas Hughes	Phillip Beard	W.R. (Gene) Wiley	Judy Puckett Martin	Earley Biffle
1990	Thomas Hughes	Phillip Beard	W.R. (Gene) Wiley	Judy Puckett Martin	Mitch Peevy
1991	Thomas Hughes	Phillip Beard	W.R. (Gene) Wiley	Judy Puckett Martin	Mitch Peevy
1992	Chris Burge	Phillip Beard	W.R. (Gene) Wiley	Judy Puckett Martin	Mitch Peevy
1993	Chris Burge	Phillip Beard	W.R. (Gene) Wiley	Judy Puckett Martin	Bobby Kerlin
1994	Chris Burge	Phillip Beard	Michael Smith	Judy Puckett Martin	Bobby Kerlin
1995	Chris Burge	Phillip Beard	Michael Smith	Judy Puckett Martin	Bobby Kerlin
1996	Chris Burge	Phillip Beard	Michael Smith	Judy Puckett Martin	Bobby Kerlin
1997	Chris Burge	Phillip Beard	Michael Smith	Judy Puckett Martin	Bobby Kerlin
1998	Chris Burge	Phillip Beard	Michael Smith	Judy Puckett Martin	Bobby Kerlin
1999	Chris Burge	Phillip Beard	Michael Smith	Judy Puckett Martin	Bobby Kerlin
2000	Chris Burge	Phillip Beard	Michael Smith	Judy Puckett Martin	Bobby Kerlin
2001	Chris Burge	Phillip Beard	Michael Smith	Kim Wolfe	Bryan Kerlin
2002	Chris Burge	Phillip Beard	Michael Smith	Kim Wolfe	Bryan Kerlin
2003	Chris Burge	Phillip Beard	Michael Smith	Kim Wolfe	Bryan Kerlin
2004	Chris Burge	Phillip Beard	Michael Smith	Kim Wolfe	Bryan Kerlin
2005	Chris Burge	Phillip Beard	Michael Smith	Kim Wolfe	Bryan Kerlin
2006	Chris Burge	Phillip Beard	Michael Smith	Kim Wolfe	Bryan Kerlin
2007	Chris Burge	Phillip Beard	Michael Smith	Kim Wolfe	Bryan Kerlin
2008	Chris Burge	Phillip Beard	Michael Smith	Kim Wolfe	Bryan Kerlin
Source: City of Buford					

Dacula City Officials

Year	Mayor	Post 1	Post 2	Post 3	Post 4	Clerk/ Administrator
1905	Samuel L. Hinton, MD					
1970	Jimmy Wilbanks					Jean Otis Sims
1971	Jimmy Wilbanks					Jean Otis Sims
1972	Jimmy Wilbanks					Jean Otis Sims
1973	Jimmy Wilbanks					Claudia Bradberry
1974	Claude Holcombe					Claudia Bradberry
1975	Claude Holcombe					Pat Parr
1976	Claude Holcombe	John Huscusson	Dale Bystricky	James Williams	Bobby Rooks	Joyce Norman
1977	Joyce Pharr	James Williams	Dale Bystricky	John Huscusson	Walt Justice	Joyce Norman
1978	Joyce Pharr	James Williams	Wendell Holcombe	John Huscusson	Golmar Waters	Joyce Norman
1979	Larry Fleeman	Wendell Holcombe	Sam Venable	Travis Murray	Golmar Waters	Joyce Norman
1980	Larry Fleeman	Wendell Holcombe	Sam Venable	Travis Murray	Golmar Waters	Joyce Norman
1981	Larry Fleeman	Wendell Holcombe	Sam Venable	Travis Murray	Golmar Waters	Joyce Norman
1982	Larry Fleeman	Wendell Holcombe	Sam Venable	Travis Murray	Golmar Waters	Joyce Norman
1983	Larry Fleeman	Wendell Holcombe	Sam Venable	Travis Murray	Golmar Waters	Joyce Norman
1984	Larry Fleeman	Wendell Holcombe	Sam Venable	Travis Murray	Joe Houston	Joyce Norman
1985	Larry Fleeman	Wendell Holcombe	Sam Venable	Travis Murray	Joe Houston	Joyce Norman
1986	Travis Murray	Wendell Holcombe	Sam Venable	Tommy McDaniel	Joe Houston	Joyce Norman
1987	Travis Murray	Wendell Holcombe	Sam Venable	Tommy McDaniel	Joe Houston	Joyce Norman
1988	Travis Murray	Wendell Holcombe	Sam Venable	Tommy McDaniel	Joe Houston	Joyce Norman
1989	Travis Murray	Wendell Holcombe	Sam Venable	Tommy McDaniel	Joe Houston	Joyce Norman
1990	Travis Murray	Wendell Holcombe	Sam Venable	Tommy McDaniel	Joe Houston	Joyce Norman
1991	Joe Houston	Wendell Holcombe	Sam Venable	Tommy McDaniel	R. G. Hale	Joyce Norman
1992	Joe Houston	Wendell Holcombe	Sam Venable	Tommy McDaniel	R. G. Hale	Joyce Norman
1993	Joe Houston	Wendell Holcombe	Sam Venable	Tommy McDaniel	R. G. Hale	Joyce Norman
1994	Mike Moon	Wendell Holcombe	Willard Sims	Tommy McDaniel	R. G. Hale	Joyce Norman
1995	Mike Moon	Wendell Holcombe	Willard Sims	Tommy McDaniel	Trey King	Joyce Norman
1996	Mike Moon	Wendell Holcombe	Willard Sims	Tommy McDaniel	Reed Miller	Joyce Norman
1997	Mike Moon	Wendell Holcombe	Gene Greeson	Tommy McDaniel	Trey King/Reed Miller	Joyce Norman
1998	Reed Miller	Wendell Holcombe	Gene Greeson	Trey King	R. G. Hale	Joyce Norman
1999	Reed Miller	Wendell Holcombe	Gene Greeson	Trey King	R. G. Hale	Joyce Norman
2000	Reed Miller	Mike Moon	Gene Greeson	Trey King	R. G. Hale	Joyce Norman
2001	Reed Miller	Mike Moon	Gene Greeson	Trey King	R. G. Hale	Joyce Norman
2002	Reed Miller/ Jimmy Wilbanks	Wendell Holcombe	Gene Greeson	Mike Moon	R. G. Hale	Joyce Norman
2003	Jimmy Wilbanks	Wendell Holcombe	Gene Greeson	Mike Moon	R. G. Hale	Joyce Norman/ Jim Osborn
2004	Jimmy Wilbanks	Wendell Holcombe	Gene Greeson	Mike Moon/ Hubert Wells	R. G. Hale	Jim Osborn
2005	Jimmy Wilbanks	Wendell Holcombe	Gene Greeson	Hubert Wells/ Tim Montgomery	R. G. Hale	Jim Osborn
2006	Jimmy Wilbanks	Wendell Holcombe	Gene Greeson	Tim Montgomery	Greg Reeves	Jim Osborn
2007	Jimmy Wilbanks	Wendell Holcombe	Gene Greeson	Tim Montgomery	Greg Reeves	Jim Osborn
2008	Jimmy Wilbanks	Wendell Holcombe	Susan Montgomery	Tim Montgomery	Greg Reeves	Jim Osborn

Source: City of Dacula

Duluth City Officials, 1950-2008

Year	Mayor	Council Member	Council Member	Council Member	Council Member	Council Member	City Clerk
1876	Charles A. Howell, founder of town						
1880-1885	John Bruce Knox First Mayor						
1907	D.W. Wilson	J.L. Moor	J.A. Cook	J.A. Dodds	J.H. Summerour	Mack Pittard	
1908	D.W. Wilson	J.L. Moor	Lee Payne	T. A. Lewis	H.T. Knox	Mack Pittard	
1909	D.W. Wilson	J.T. Brown	C.S. Strong	S.M. Fossett	D.E. Flowers	Mack Pittard	
1910	D.W. Wilson	J.L. Moor	J.A. Dodds	A.M. Simm	Dr. J.E. Christian	F.E. Seay	
1911	Mack Pittard	J.H. Summerour	S.G. Dodson	J.L. Moor	D.W. Wilson	F.E. Seay	
1912	Mack Pittard	J.H. Summerour	J.A. Dodds	H. Strickland, Jr.	D.W. Wilson	E.F. Hall	
1913	W.B. Rutledge	S.W. Gresham	J.E. Lowe	W.R. Settle	J.A. Payne	W.E. Jones	
1914	D.W. Wilson	M.W. Pittard	Sam Dodson	J.A. Payne	H.N. Taylor	F.E. Seay	
1915	D.W. Wilson	M.W. Pittard	Sam Dodson	J.A. Payne	H.N. Taylor	D.P. Langley	
1916	W.E. Jones	M.W. Pittard	S.G. Dodson	W.M. Dodson	J.C. Bagwell	T.A. Lewis	
1917	W.E. Jones	T.A. Lewis	G.P. Findly	W.R. Jones	L.E. Payne	D.W. Wilson	
1918	W.R. Jones	J.H. Summerour	F.E. Seay	T.A. Lewis	L.E. Payne	S.A. Dodd	
1919	J.E. Lowe	J.H. Summerour	Frank Summerour	I.M. Suddeth	S.A. Dodd	J.C. Bagwell	
1920	J.W. Knox	H.G. Herron	J.C. Bagwell	I.M. Suddeth	C.H. Pittard	T.L. Huff	
1921	H.G. Herron	J.H. Summerour	D.E. Bennett	J.A. Dodds	C.H. Pittard	T.L. Huff	
1922	C.E. Strickland	John H. Pittard	H.G. Herron	D.W. Wilson	O.A. McGee	D.B. Phillips	
1923	Alice Harrell Strickland	J.H. Summerour	J.S. Brown	F.C. Brannon	J.C. Bagwell	D.B. Phillips	
1924	H.G. Herron	D.E. Flowers	F.C. Brannon	J.S. Brown	Mack Pittard	Grady Wright	
1925	H.G. Herron	Mack Pittard	T.A. Lewis	J.C. Bagwell	W.R. Jones	D.W. Wilson	
1926	H.G. Herron	Mack Pittard	D.W. Wilson	W.R. Jones	J.C. Bagwell	T.H. Roberts	
1927	H.G. Herron	Mack Pittard	D.W. Wilson	W.R. Jones	J.C. Bagwell	T.H. Roberts	
1928	J.C. Bagwell	Q.H. Roberts	D.W. Wilson	S.A. Dodd	J.A. Payne	E.A. Brown	
1929	J.C. Bagwell	S.A. Dodd	J.A. Payne	E.A. Brown	A.J. Corley	H.P. Wynn	
1930	H.G. Herron	L.R. Echols	H.P. Wynn	E.A. Jones	J.A. Payne	E.A. Brown	
1931	G.B. Strickland	H.G. Herron	E.A. Brown	J.H. Summerour	C.M. Parsons, Jr.	L.H. Jones	
1932	J.C. Bagwell	A.J. Corley	L.R. Echols	L.H. Jones	Joe Payne	Harrison Summerour	
1933	H.G. Herron	Harrison Summerour	L.R. Echols	L.H. Jones	Joe Payne	A.J. Corley	
1934	L.R. Echols	Joe Payne	Guy Findley	George Bennett	Charles Pittard	Bill Jones	
1935	L.R. Echols	T.L. Smith	A.J. Corley	W.M. Jones	H.T. Pittard	Noel Summerour	
1936	W.B. Shirley	D.E. Flowers	William Dodson	Charles Pittard	John Jones	E.A. Brown	
1937	W.B. Shirley	D.E. Flowers	H.G. Herron	Charles Pittard	V.G. Roberts	E.A. Brown	
1938	W.B. Shirley	D.E. Flowers	H.G. Herron	Charles Pittard	V.G. Roberts	J.A. Parsons	
1939	D.E. Flowers	LH Jones	H.G. Herron	Charles Pittard	G.W. Findley	J.A. Parsons	
1940	D.E. Flowers	Henry Seoy	H.G. Herron	Charles Pittard	G.W. Findley	J.A. Parsons	
1941	See Below*	William Jones	J.C. Bagwell	Charles Pittard	G.W. Findley	J.A. Parsons	
1942	L. Roy Echols	William Jones	N. Summerour	Charles Pittard	G.W. Findley	J.A. Parsons	
1943	L. Roy Echols	Joe Payne	B.F. Mattison	Charles Pittard	Hulon Jones	J.E. Ellis	
1944	Jack Parsons	WM Jones	B.F. Mattison	E.A. Brown	Hulon Jones	G.W. Findley	
1945	G. W. Finley, L. Roy Echols	Roy Echols	M.M. Corley	E.A. Brown	Hulon Jones	J.K. Mitchell	
1946	L. Roy Echols	T.F. Reese	M.M. Corley	G.W. Findley	B.T. Littleton	C.P. Johnson	
1947	L. Roy Echols	T.F. Reese	M.M. Corley	G.W. Findley			
1948	L. Roy Echols	*					

Duluth City Officials, 1950-2008

Year	Mayor	Council Member	Council Member	Council Member	Council Member	Council Member	City Clerk
1949	L. Roy Echols	*					
1950	Y.J. Harrington, Sr.	Ralph Burnside	M.M. Corley	W.M. Jones	B.F. Mattison	W.B. Latimer/ W.B. Shirley	William Jones
1951	Y.J. Harrington, Sr.	C.P. Johnson	M.M. Corley	W.M. Jones	B.F. Mattison	W.B. Shirley	W.M. Jones
1952	W.H. Vaughn	Alvin Davis	Joe Mitchell	Everett Bagwell	B.F. Mattison	W.B. Shirley	W.M. Jones
1953	W.H. Vaughn	Alvin Davis	Joe Mitchell	Everett Bagwell	Hulin Jones	J.A. Parsons	W.M. Jones
1954	W.H. Vaughn	Alvin Davis	J.K. Mitchell	Everett Bagwell	Hulin Jones	Jack Parsons	W.M. Jones
1955	W.H. Vaughn	Alvin Davis	Joe Mitchell	Knox Summerour	Hulin Jones	Jack Parsons	W.J. Jones, Knox Summerour
1956	Oliver J. Murphy	Alvin Davis	Troyce Jackson	Knox Summerour	W.M. Corley	H.D. Barker	Knox Summerour, Hillian Barker
1957	Y.J. Harrington, Sr.	O.H. Boles, Sr.	J.A. Parsons, Sr.	Frank Mattison, Sr.	A.J. Corley	Hillian Barker	Hillian Barker
1958	Mose D. Hamrick	Alvin Davis	George Bishop	Wilson Jones	Minor Corley	Oliver Murphy	Hillian Barker
1959	Mose D. Hamrick	Alvin Davis	Sam Jones/Barker	J.D. Archer	Ott Thompson	D.H. Boles	Hillian Barker, E.H. Moulder
1960	L. Roy Echols	Alvin Davis	Moses Hamrick/ Shaw	J.D. Archer	Ott Thompson	D.H. Boles	E.H. Moulder
1961	L. Roy Echols	R.J. Bagley	J.H. Cook	J.D. Archer/C.J. Shaw	Ott Thompson	D.H. Boles	E.H. Moulder, Max Summerour
1962	L. Roy Echols	R.J. Bagley	J.H. Cook	Lee Brown/S. Barker	Ott Thompson	W.H. Dove	Max Summerour, Jacquelyn Summerour
1963	L. Roy Echols	Harrington/Mose Hamrick	W.L. Brown	W.P. Jones	W.M. Jones	W.H. Dove	Jacquelyn Summerour
1964	Robert E. Bennewitz	M.D. Hamrick	W.L. Brown	W.P. Jones	W.M. Jones	Ivan Barker	Jacquelyn Summerour
1965	Robert E. Bennewitz	M.D. Hamrick	W.L. Brown	W.P. Jones	W.M. Jones	Ivan Barker	Jacquelyn Summerour
1966	Robert E. Bennewitz	Jim Bruce	O.A. Thompson	Minor Corley	W.M. Jones	Ivan Barker	Jacquelyn Summerour
1967	Robert E. Bennewitz	R.M. Burns	O.A. Thompson	Minor Corley	R.A. Ingram	Ivan Barker	Jacquelyn Summerour
1968	James Marlon Corley	Ray Burns	T.L. Smallwood	Minor Corley	RA Ingram	W.M. Jones	Jacquelyn Summerour
1969	James Marlon Corley	Ray Burns	T.L. Smallwood	Minor Corley	Paul Kesmodel	W.M. Jones	Jacquelyn Summerour
1970	James Marlon Corley	Ray Burns	W. Ray Bethune	Minor Corley	A. Edwin Barker	Lawrence Johnson	Jacquelyn Summerour Rembert A. Green
1971	James Marlon Corley	Robert Scott	Ray Bethune	C.E. Pittman	Edwin Barker	J. Gordon Orr	Rembert A. Green
1972	James Marlon Corley	Robert Scott	Marion Wood**	C.E. Pittman	Edwin Barker	J. Gordon Orr	Rembert A. Green
1973	James Marlon Corley	Edward Dispain	M.Wood/Claude Mason	C.E. Pittman	Edwin Barker	James Dispain	Rembert A. Green, Mary Lou Swansy
1974	Don Wilson	Edward Dispain	Claude Mason	C.E. Pittman	Edwin Barker	James Dispain	Mary Lou Swansy, Edward Dispain, W.M. Jones
1975	Don Wilson	Dispain/N. Summerour	Claude Mason	W.M. Jones	A.E. Barker	W.B. Shirley	W.J. Jones, Helen Banks
1976	Don Wilson	Summerour	Claude Mason	W.M. Jones	A.E. Barker	W.B. Shirley	Helen Banks
1977	Don Wilson	Joseph Pratt	Claude Mason	James Semple	A.E. Barker	W.B. Shirley	Helen Banks
1978	Claude D. Mason	Ken Pittard	Joseph Pratt	James Semple	A.E. Barker	W.B. Shirley	Helen Banks
1979	Claude D. Mason	Ken Pittard	Joseph Pratt	James Semple	A.E. Barker	W.B. Shirley	Helen Banks
1980	Claude D. Mason	Ken Pittard	Joseph Pratt	James Semple	Walace Lail	W.B. Shirley	Helen Banks
1981	Claude D. Mason	J.M. Corley	Joseph Pratt	James Semple	Walace Lail	Tom Wood	Helen Banks
1982	Claude D. Mason	J.M. Corley	Joseph Pratt	Bob Crowe	Walace Lail	Tom Wood	Helen Banks, Kenneth Pittard
1983	Claude D. Mason	J.M. Corley	Joseph Pratt	Ronald Patchen	Walace Lail	Tom Wood	Kenneth Pittard
1984	W.P. Jones	J.M. Corley	Billy Hinson	Ron Pittman	Dick Hyslop	Tom Wood	Kenneth Pittard
1985	W. P. Jones, Richard Hyslop	Charles Meagher	Billy Hinson	Ron Pittman	Dick Hyslop/ Ron Peterson	O.J. Howell	Kenneth Pittard

Duluth City Officials, 1950-2008

Year	Mayor	Council Member	Council Member	Council Member	Council Member	Council Member	City Clerk
1986	Richard Hyslop	Charles Meagher	Robert Harris	R Pittman/ Charles Barrett	Peterson	O.J. Howell	Kenneth Pittard
1987	Richard Hyslop	Charles Meagher	Robert Harris	Charles Barrett	Peterson	O.J. Howell	Kenneth Pittard
1988	Bobby Williams	Richard King	Jason Moore	Charles Barrett	Peterson	O.J. Howell	Kenneth Pittard
1989	Bobby Williams	Richard King	Jason Moore	Charles Barrett	Richard Hyslop	O.J. Howell	Kenneth Pittard
1990	Bobby Williams	Richard King	Jason Moore	Charles Barrett	Tim Loftin	O.J. Howell	Kenneth Pittard
1991	Bobby Williams	Richard King	Jason Moore	Charles Barrett	Tim Loftin	Victor Gerber	Kenneth Pittard
1992	Bobby Williams	Richard King	Jason Moore	Maxine Garner	Tim Loftin Billy Jones	Victor Gerber	Kenneth Pittard Teresa Lynn
1993	Bobby Williams	Rod King	Jason Moore	Maxine Garner	Suzanne Britt	Victor Gerber	Teresa Lynn
1994	Shirley Fanning Lasseter	Rod King	Jason Moore	Maxine Garner	Suzanne Britt	Victor Gerber	Teresa Lynn
1995	Shirley Fanning Lasseter	Rod King	Jason Moore	Maxine Garner	Suzanne Britt	Robert Peterson	Teresa Lynn
1996	Shirley Fanning Lasseter	Rod King	Doris Kirouac	Doug Mundrick	Suzanne Britt	Robert Peterson	Teresa Lynn
1997	Shirley Fanning Lasseter	Linda Hutchinson	Doris Kirouac	Doug Mundrick	Maxine Garner	Robert Peterson	Teresa Lynn
1998	Shirley Fanning Lasseter	Linda Hutchinson	Doris Kirouac	Doug Mundrick	Maxine Garner	Robert Peterson	Teresa Lynn
1999	Shirley Fanning Lasseter	Jim Dugan	Doris Kirouac	Doug Mundrick	Maxine Garner	Robert Peterson	Teresa Lynn
2000	Shirley Fanning Lasseter	Jim Dugan	Doris Kirouac	Doug Mundrick	Maxine Garner	Robert Peterson	Teresa Lynn
2001	Shirley Fanning Lasseter	Jim Dugan	Doris Kirouac	Doug Mundrick	Maxine Garner	Robert Peterson	Teresa Lynn
2002	Shirley Fanning Lasseter	Jim Dugan	Doris Kirouac	Doug Mundrick	Maxine Garner	Jim Hall	Teresa Lynn
2003	Shirley Fanning Lasseter	Jim Dugan	Doris Kirouac	Doug Mundrick	Maxine Garner	Jim Hall	Teresa Lynn
2004	Shirley Fanning Lasseter	Jim Dugan	Doris Kirouac	Doug Mundrick	Maxine Garner	Jim Hall	Teresa Lynn
2005	Shirley Fanning Lasseter	Jim Dugan	Doris Kirouac	Doug Mundrick	Maxine Garner	Jim Hall	Teresa Lynn
2006	Shirley Fanning Lasseter	Jim Dugan	Doris Kirouac	Doug Mundrick	Marsha Bomar	Jim Hall	Teresa Lynn
2007	Shirley Fanning Lasseter	Jim Dugan	Doris Kirouac	Doug Mundrick	Marsha Bomar	Jim Hall	Teresa Lynn
2008	Nancy Harris	Jim Dugan	Greg Whitlock	Doug Mundrick	Marsha Bomar	Jim Hall	Teresa Lynn

In 1941, four persons served as mayor, Mitchell, Parsons, Strickland, Echols

Source: City of Duluth and Duluth Historical Society

Grayson City Officials, 1951-2008

Year	Mayor	Council Member	Council Member	Council Member	Council Member	City Administrator*
1951	T.P. Jenkins	T.A. Downs Jr.	W. V. Brownlee			H.V. Jones
1952	T.P. Jenkins	Hill Cox	Clarence Bedingfield	John F. Bennett		H.V. Jones
1953	Clarence Bedingfield	J. H. Cox	M.D. Brownlee Jr.	John F. Bennett	T.A. Downs Jr.	Hazel Jacobs
1954	Clarence Bedingfield	W. F. Greene	M.D. Brownlee Jr.	John F. Bennett	T.A. Downs Jr.	Hazel Jacobs
1955	Bedingfield/Brownlee	W. F. Greene	M.D. Brownlee Jr.	T.P. Jenkins	T.A. Downs Jr.	Hazel Jacobs
1956	M.D. Brownlee Jr.	Mrs. J.H. Cox		T.P. Jenkins	T.A. Downs Jr.	Hazel Jacobs
1957	T.P. Jenkins	Mrs. J.H. Cox	M.D. Brownlee Jr.	L.J. Williams	T.A. Downs Jr.	Hazel Jacobs
1958	T.P. Jenkins	J. Doyle Cox	M.D. Brownlee Jr.	Troy L. Holcomb		Hazel Jacobs
1959	T.P. Jenkins	J. Doyle Cox	M.D. Brownlee Jr.	Troy L. Holcomb	Mrs. W.V. Gaffney	Hazel Jacobs
1960	T.P. Jenkins	J. Alfred McDaniel	M.D. Brownlee Jr.	J.B. Reese Jr.	Mrs. W.V. Gaffney	Hazel Jacobs
1961	D.D. Carroll	W.V. Brownlee	M.D. Brownlee Jr.	J.B. Reese Jr.	Troy L. Holcombe	Hazel Jacobs
1962	D.D. Carroll	W.V. Brownlee	M.D. Brownlee Jr.	J.B. Reese Jr.	Holcombe/Hunter	Hazel Jacobs
1963	D.D. Carroll	W.V. Brownlee	M.D. Brownlee Jr.	William C. Farmer	Eugene Hunter	Hazel Jacobs
1964	D.D. Carroll	J. Doyle Cox	M.D. Brownlee Jr.	Harold S. Smith	Eugene Hunter	Hazel Jacobs

Grayson City Officials, 1951-2008						
Year	Mayor	Council Member	Council Member	Council Member	Council Member	City Administrator*
1965	D.D. Carroll	William C. Farmer	M.D. Brownlee Jr.	Harold S. Smith	Eugene Hunter	Hazel Jacobs
1966	D.D. Carroll	William C. Farmer	M.D. Brownlee Jr.	A. M. McCart	Eugene Hunter	Joan B. Hunter
1967	T.A. Downs Jr.	J. Doyle Cox	Wayne C. Jordan	A. M. McCart	Eugene Hunter	Joan B. Hunter
1968	T.A. Downs Jr.	J. Doyle Cox	Wayne C. Jordan	A. M. McCart	Tom Kinney	Joan B. Hunter
1969	Downs/Jordan	John Wayne	Jordan/T.P. Jenkins	A. M. McCart	Tom Kinney	Joan B. Hunter
1970	Wayne C. Jordan	John Wayne	T.P. Jenkins	A. M. McCart	M.D. Brownlee Jr.	Joan B. Hunter
1971	Wayne C. Jordan	John Wayne	T.P. Jenkins Jr.	A. M. McCart	M.D. Brownlee Jr.	Joan B. Hunter
1972	Jordan/Wayne	Wayne/Don Vail,Jr.	T.P. Jenkins Sr.	Ernest Puckett	M.D. Brownlee Jr.	Joan B. Hunter
1973	John Wayne	Don Vail Jr.	T.P. Jenkins Sr.	Ernest Puckett	M.D. Brownlee Jr.	Hunter/Doris Vail
1974	Wayne/Vail	Vail/Voight Starling	T.P. Jenkins Sr.	Ernest Puckett	M.D. Brownlee Jr.	Vail/Judy Folger
1975	Don J. Vail Jr.	Voight Starling	T.P. Jenkins Sr.	Ernest Puckett	M.D. Brownlee Jr.	Judy Folger
1976	Don J. Vail Jr.	Voight Starling	Jenkins/Steve Allen	Ernest Puckett	M.D. Brownlee Jr.	Judy Folger
1977	Doug Wilkerson	Don Vail Jr.	Linda Jenkins	Ernest Puckett	M.D. Brownlee Jr.	Judy Folger
1978	Doug Wilkerson	Don Vail Jr.	Linda Jenkins	Taylor Jenkins Jr.	Jimmy Brownlee	Judy Folger
1979	M.D. Brownlee Jr.	Charles Powell	Linda Jenkins	Taylor Jenkins Jr.	Jimmy Brownlee	Judy Folger
1980	M.D. Brownlee Jr.	Charles Powell	Linda Jenkins	Walter Clark	Jimmy Brownlee	Frances Butler
1981	James (Jim) Hinkle	Taylor Jenkins Jr.	Linda Jenkins	Walter Clark	Jimmy Brownlee	Butler/Gail Hill
1982	James (Jim) Hinkle	Taylor Jenkins Jr.	Linda Jenkins	Walter Clark	Jimmy Brownlee	Gail Hill
1983	James (Jim) Hinkle	Julian Bateman	Wanda O'Neal	Walter Clark	Jimmy Brownlee	Gail Hill
1984	James (Jim) Hinkle	Julian Bateman	O'Neal/McDonald	John Hollinger	Buddy Brownlee	Hill/Jeanie Thomas
1985	James (Jim) Hinkle	Vance Vermilya	Doris McDonald	John Hollinger	Buddy Brownlee	Jeanie Thomas
1986	James (Jim) Hinkle	Vance Vermilya		Jimmy Brownlee	Buddy Brownlee	Jeanie Thomas
1987	James (Jim) Hinkle	Vance Vermilya	David Mudd	Jimmy Brownlee	Buddy Brownlee	Jeanie Thomas
1988	James (Jim) Hinkle	Vance Vermilya	David Mudd	Michael Ayers	Buddy Brownlee	Jeanie Thomas
1989	James (Jim) Hinkle	Ronald Clark	David Mudd	Michael Ayers	Buddy Brownlee	Jeanie Thomas
1990	James (Jim) Hinkle	Ronald Clark	David Mudd	Michael Ayers	Buddy Brownlee	Jeanie T. Reagan
1991	James (Jim) Hinkle	Ronald Clark	Stacey Britt	Ayers /	Buddy Brownlee	Reagan/Cecila Hicks
1992	Hinkle/Stacey Britt	Clark/Powell	Laurie Anderson	Doug Wilkerson	T.C. Parker/ Shumate	Cecilia Hicks
1993	Stacey Britt	Charlie Powell	Laurie Anderson	Wilkerson/Durden	Tammy Shumate	Cecilia Hicks
1994	Doug Wilkerson	Stacey Britt	Anderson/Payne	Kathi Durden	Tammy Shumate	Hicks/L. Anderson
1995	Doug Wilkerson	Stacey Britt	Peggie Payne	Kathi Durden	Tammy Shumate	Laurie Anderson
1996	Doug Wilkerson	Britt/Darron Britt	Peggie Payne	Kathi Durden	Tammy Shumate	Laurie Anderson
1997	Doug Wilkerson	Darron Britt	Peggie Payne	Kathi Durden	Tammy Shumate	Laurie Anderson
1998	Doug Wilkerson	Darron Britt	Peggie Payne	Kathi Durden	Tammy Shumate	Laurie Anderson
1999	Doug Wilkerson	Darron Britt	Peggie Payne	Kathi Durden	Tammy Shumate	Laurie Anderson
2000	Doug Wilkerson	Darron Britt	Peggy Payne	Kathi Durden	Suzanne Hawkins	Laurie Anderson
2001	James (Jim) Hinkle	Darron Britt	Jimmy Adams	Tammy Shumate	Suzanne Hawkins	Laurie Anderson
2002	James (Jim) Hinkle	Allison Wilkerson	Jimmy Adams	Tammy Shumate	Suzanne Hawkins	Laura Paul
2003	James (Jim) Hinkle	Allison Wilkerson	Jimmy Adams	Tammy Shumate	Suzanne Hawkins	Laura Paul

Grayson City Officials, 1951-2008

Year	Mayor	Council Member	Council Member	Council Member	Council Member	City Administrator*
2004	James (Jim) Hinkle	Allison Wilkerson	Jimmy Adams	Tammy Shumate	Suzanne Hawkins	Laura Paul
2005	James (Jim) Hinkle	Allison Wilkerson	Jimmy Adams	Tammy Shumate	Suzanne Hawkins	Laura Paul
2006	James (Jim) Hinkle	A. Wilkerson-Rooks	Jimmy Adams	Tammy Shumate	Suzanne Hawkins	Laura Paul-Cone
2007	James (Jim) Hinkle	A. Wilkerson-Rooks	David Schroder	Tammy Shumate	Suzanne Hawkins	Laura Paul-Cone
2008	James (Jim) Hinkle	A. Wilkerson-Rooks	David Schroder	Tammy Shumate	Marcus Hinton	Laura Paul-Cone

***** In 1951, the title was "Clerk-Treasurer." It was changed in 1960 to "City Clerk" and changed to "City Administrator" in 1995.**

Source: City of Grayson

Lawrenceville City Officials, 1884-2008

Year	Mayor	Council Member	Council Member	Council Member	Council Member	City Clerk
1884	J. C. Smith	A. L. Moore	E. D. Herrin	W. J. Brown	W. E. Brown	
1885	J. C. Smith	A. L. Moore	E. D. Herrin	W. J. Brown	S. A. Townley	
1886	J. C. Smith	A. J. Vaughan	J. C. Houston	S. A. Townley	W. E. Brown	
1887	C. S. Winn	A. J. Vaughan	J. C. Houston	M. E. Ewing	F. T. Pentecost	
1888	C. S. Winn	A. J. Vaughan	L. F. McDonald	M. E. Ewing	F. T. Pentecost	
1889	C. H. Brand	A. J. Vaughan	W. J. Born	F. T. Pentecost	S. A. Townley	
1890	C. H. Brand	A. M. Winn	G. D. Elliott	A. T. Patterson	W. E. Brown	
1891	L. F. McDonald	A. T. Patterson	M. M. King	M. E. Ewing	M. S. Cornett	
1892	S. J. Winn	J. D. Spence	W. E. Simmons	A. T. Patterson	M. V. Brand	
1893	S. J. Winn	J. D. Spence	W. E. Simmons	M. E. Ewing	A. T. Patterson	
1894	S. J. Winn	J. D. Spence	W. E. Simmons	M. E. Ewing	C. H. Brand	
1895	L. M. Brand	J. A. Ambrose	M. S. Cornett	T. R. Powell	C. U. Born	
1896	M. S. Cornett	A. W. Moore	G. A. Almond	M. E. Ewing	J. A. Ambrose	
1897	M. S. Cornett	A. W. Moore	J. D. Rutledge	M. E. Ewing	J. A. Ambrose	
1898	M. S. Cornett	A. W. Moore	J. D. Rutledge	M. E. Ewing	J. A. Ambrose	
1899	Oscar Brown	R. J. Bagwell	J. D. Rutledge	J. A. Ambrose		
1900	J. A. Perry	T. B. Bush	M. S. Cornett	W. M. Sasser	J. A. Ambrose	
1901	W. O. Cooper	L. M. Brand	W. H. Powell	A. T. Patterson	R. W. Peeples	
1902	R. W. Peeples	L. M. Brand	M. S. Cornett	R. L. Robinson	A. T. Patterson	
1903	M. S. Cornett	J. M. Jacobs	J. D. Rutledge	R. L. Robinson	T. L. Evans	
1904	M. S. Cornett	J. M. Jacobs	J. D. Rutledge	R. L. Robinson	T. L. Evans	
1905	L. M. Brand	J. M. Jacobs	F. Q. Sammon	R. L. Robinson	T. L. Evans	R. L. Robinson
1906	L. M. Brand	J. M. Jacobs	F. Q. Sammon	R. L. Robinson	F. T. Pentecost	R. L. Robinson
1907	J. M. Jacobs	G. L. Veal	F. Q. Sammon	E. L. McKelvey	F. T. Pentecost	R. L. Robinson
1908	J. M. Jacobs	G. L. Veal	J. D. Wallace	E. L. McKelvey	G. W. Clower	G. W. Clower
1909	J. G. Vose	B. L. Patterson	J. D. Wallace	W. P. Johnson	G. W. Clower	W. P. Johnson
1910	J. G. Vose	B. L. Patterson	W.P. Johnson	G. S. Kelley	V. G. Hopkins	Dr. V. G. Hopkins
1911	L. R. Martin	J. H. McGee	G. S. Kelley	E. L. McKelvey	V. G. Hopkins	L. L. Ewing
1912	L. R. Martin	J. H. McGee	J. H. Britt	E. L. McKelvey	J. P. Webb	J. H. Britt

Lawrenceville City Officials, 1884-2008

Year	Mayor	Council Member	Council Member	Council Member	Council Member	City Clerk
1913	L. R. Martin	Frank Taylor	F. Q. Sammon	J. H. Britt	J. P. Webb	
1914	L. R. Martin	Frank Taylor	F. Q. Sammon	D. C. Kelley	J. P. Webb	
1915	N. S. Robinson	B. L. Patterson	R. N. Holt	J. C. Houston	D. C. Kelley	
1916	N. S. Robinson	B. L. Patterson	R. N. Holt	J. C. Houston	D. C. Kelley	
1917	O. A. Nix	L. L. Ewing	D. C. Kelley	J. C. Houston	J. A. Ambrose	
1918	O. A. Nix	L. L. Ewing	C. T. Williams	G. S. Perry	J. A. Ambrose	
1919	O. A. Nix	L. L. Ewing	C. T. Williams	E. L. McKelvey	G. S. Perry	
1920	O. A. Nix	L. L. Ewing	C. R. Thompson	E. L. McKelvey	H. C. Smith	
1921	F. Q. Sammon	W. M. Jordan	J. F. Langley	C. R. Thompson	H. C. Smith	H. G. Robinson
1922	F. Q. Sammon	W. M. Jordan	G. C. Montgomery	J. J. Baggett	J. F. Langley	H. G. Robinson
1923	F. Q. Sammon	W. M. Jordan	G. C. Montgomery	C. R. Thompson	J. F. Langley	H. G. Robinson
1924	F. Q. Sammon	J. J. Baggett	R. L. Robinson	W. M. Jordan	W. S. Sims	H. G. Robinson
1925	M. D. Irwin	J. M. Langley	R. L. Robinson	J. J. Baggett	W. S. Sims	H. G. Robinson
1926	M. D. Irwin	W. M. Jordan	F. Q. Sammon	G. S. Kelley	W. S. Sims	H. G. Robinson
1927	J. C. Houston	W. M. Jordan	F. Q. Sammon	G. S. Kelley	G. W. Clower	Claude G. Craig
1928	J. C. Houston	W. M. Jordan	F. Q. Sammon	W. M. Wages	G. W. Clower	Claude G. Craig
1929	J. C. Houston	W. M. Jordan	F. Q. Sammon	W. M. Wages	Clower/Montgomery	Claude G. Craig
1930	J. C. Houston	C. W. Clower	J. A. Richardson	W. M. Wages	G. C. Montgomery	Claude G. Craig
1931	G. C. Montgomery	C. E. Monfort	J. A. Richardson	W. M. Wages	W. G. Holt	Claude G. Craig
1932	G. C. Montgomery	C. E. Monfort	J. A. Richardson	W. M. Wages	W. G. Holt	Claude G. Craig
1933	G. C. Montgomery	J. C. Oakes	J. A. Richardson	W. M. Wages	W. G. Holt	Claude G. Craig
1934	G. C. Montgomery	J. C. Oakes	W. B. Alford	L. R. Martin	W. G. Holt	Claude G. Craig
1935	W. G. Holt	J. C. Oakes	W. B. Alford	L. R. Martin	J. F. Green	Claude G. Craig
1936	W. G. Holt	J. C. Oakes	W. B. Alford	L. R. Martin	J. F. Green	Claude G. Craig
1937	J. J. Baggett	W. B. Alford	F. Q. Sammon, Jr.	L. R. Martin	J. F. Green	W. Guy Green
1938	J. J. Baggett	W. B. Alford	J. W. Garner	M. V. Frazier	H. F. Wages	W. Guy Green
1939	F. Q. Sammon	W. B. Alford	J. W. Garner	M. V. Frazier	H. F. Wages	W. Guy Green
1940	F. Q. Sammon	A. B. Alford	P. V. Kelley	M. V. Frazier	H. F. Wages	W. Guy Green
1941	Jesse A. Richardson	A. B. Jordan	P. V. Kelley	F. A. Sims	D. Y. Carter	Green/Martin
1942	Jesse A. Richardson	A. B. Jordan	P. V. Kelley	F. A. Sims	D. Y. Carter	L. R. Martin
1943	J. Frank Green	A. B. Jordan	P. V. Kelley	F. A. Sims	D. Y. Carter	W. Guy Green
1944	J. Frank Green	T. T. McGee	F. A. Sims	M. V. Frazier	T. H. Edwards	W. Guy Green
1945	Jesse A. Richardson	T. T. McGee	F. A. Sims	M. V. Frazier	T. H. Edwards	W. Guy Green
1946	Jesse A. Richardson	T. T. McGee	J. N. Tanner	U. R. Still	J. V. Hood	W. Guy Green
1947	F. Q. Sammon, Jr.	W. B. Alford	A. B. Jordan	T. T. McGee	J. V. Hood	W. Guy Green
1948	F. Q. Sammon, Jr.	W. B. Alford	A. B. Jordan	T. T. McGee	J. V. Hood	W. Guy Green
1949	J. C. Oakes	G. A. Huff	J. F. Brannan	T. T. McGee	J. V. Hood	W. Guy Green
1950	J. C. Oakes	G. A. Huff	P. V. Kelley	J. O. Whitworth	J. F. Brannan	Green/Fortune

Lawrenceville City Officials, 1884-2008

Year	Mayor	Council Member	Council Member	Council Member	Council Member	City Clerk
1951	H. C. Smith	G. H. Tanner	P. V. Kelley	M. V. Frazier	J. O. Whitworth	Frances Fortune
1952	H. C. Smith	G. H. Tanner	J. F. Brannan	M. V. Frazier	P. V. Kelley	Frances Fortune
1953	J. F. Brannan	U. F. Freeman	Russell Peeples	Hugley Cooper	P. V. Kelley	L. R. Martin, Jr.
1954	J. F. Brannan	U. F. Freeman	Russell Peeples	Hugley Cooper	P. V. Kelley	L. R. Martin, Jr.
1955	J. F. Brannan	U. F. Freeman	U. R. Still	Hugley Cooper	P. V. Kelley	L. R. Martin, Jr.
1956	J. F. Brannan	U. F. Freeman	U. R. Still	Hugley Cooper	P. V. Kelley	L. R. Martin, Jr.
1957	W. G. Holt	John Hood	U. R. Still	Hugley Cooper	P. V. Kelley	L. R. Martin, Jr.
1958	W. G. Holt	John Hood	U. R. Still	Hugley Cooper	P. V. Kelley	L. R. Martin, Jr.
1959	W. G. Holt	Robert Norton	Hal Pentecost	Hugley Cooper	P. V. Kelley	Martin/Archer
1960	Grady Holt	Robert Norton	Hal Pentecost	Hugley Cooper	P. V. Kelley	Archer/Mosley
1961	Grady Holt	Robert Norton	Hal Pentecost	Hugley Cooper	P. V. Kelley	Wiliam Mosley
1962	Grady Holt	Robert Norton	Hal Pentecost	Hugley Cooper	Oliver Harris	Mosley/Archer
1963	Rhodes Jordan	Cliff Brand	John Wilson	Hugley Cooper	Oliver Harris	Hazel Archer
1964	Rhodes Jordan	Cliff Brand	John Wilson	Hugley Cooper	Oliver Harris	Hazel Archer
1965	Rhodes Jordan	Cliff Brand	John Wilson	Hugley Cooper	Oliver Harris	Hazel Archer
1966	Rhodes Jordan	Cliff Brand	John Wilson	Hugley Cooper	Oliver Harris	Hazel Archer
1967	Rhodes Jordan	Cliff Brand	John Wilson	Hugley Cooper	Oliver Harris	Hazel Archer
1968	Rhodes Jordan	Cliff Brand	John Wilson	Hugley Cooper	Oliver Harris	Hazel Archer
1969	Bill Fortune	C.L. Brand	John Wilson	Hugley Cooper	Oliver Harris	Hazel Archer
1970	Bill Fortune	C.L. Brand	John Wilson	Bobby Sikes	Jimmy Brannan	Hazel Archer
1971	Bill Fortune	Bill Atkinson	Carl Herrington	Bobby Sikes	Jimmy Brannan	Hazel Archer
1972	Bill Fortune	Bill Atkinson	Carl Herrington	Bobby Sikes	Eddie Oakes	Hazel Archer
1973	Bill Fortune	Sonny Brand	Carl Herrington	Bobby Sikes	Eddie Oakes	Hazel Archer
1974	Bill Fortune	Sonny Brand	Carl Herrington	Bobby Sikes	John Wilson	Archer/Baroni
1975	Rhodes Jordan	Sonny Brand	Carl Herrington	Bobby Sikes	John Wilson	Robert P. Baroni
1976	Rhodes Jordan	Sonny Brand	Carl Herrington	Homer Sims	John Wilson	Robert P. Baroni
1977	Rhodes Jordan	Sonny Brand	Stanley Gunter	Homer Sims	John Wilson	Robert P. Baroni
1978	Rhodes Jordan	Sonny Brand	Stanley Gunter	Homer Sims	John Wilson	Robert P. Baroni
1979	Tom Cain	Joyce Humphries	Stanley Gunter	Homer Sims	John Wilson	Robert P. Baroni
1980	Tom Cain	Joyce Humphries	Stanley Gunter	Mahlon Burson	John Wilson	Robert P. Baroni
1981	Rhodes Jordan	Steve Pate	Stanley Gunter	Mahlon Burson	John Wilson	Robert P. Baroni
1982	Rhodes Jordan	Steve Pate	Stanley Gunter	Mahlon Burson	Bartow Jenkins	Robert P. Baroni
1983	Rhodes Jordan	Steve Pate	Ray Oakes	Mahlon Burson	Bartow Jenkins	Robert P. Baroni
1984	Rhodes Jordan	Steve Pate	Ray Oakes	Mahlon Burson	Bartow Jenkins	Robert P. Baroni
1985	Steve Pate	John Wilson	Ray Oakes	Mahlon Burson	Bobby Sikes*	Robert P. Baroni
1986	Steve Pate	John Wilson	Ray Oakes	Mahlon Burson	Bobby Sikes	Robert P. Baroni
1987	Rhodes Jordan	Butch Conway	Sonny Brand	Mahlon Burson	Bobby Sikes	Robert P. Baroni
1988	Rhodes Jordan	Butch Conway	Sonny Brand	Mahlon Burson	Bobby Sikes	Robert P. Baroni
1989	Bartow Jenkins	John Wilson	Sonny Brand	Mahlon Burson	Ray Oakes	Robert P. Baroni
1990	Bartow Jenkins	John Wilson	Sonny Brand	Mahlon Burson	Ray Oakes	Robert P. Baroni
1991	Bartow Jenkins	Mike Crow	Sonny Brand	Mahlon Burson	Ray Oakes	Robert P. Baroni

Lawrenceville City Officials, 1884-2008

Year	Mayor	Council Member	Council Member	Council Member	Council Member	City Clerk
1992	Bartow Jenkins	Mike Crow	Sonny Brand	Mahlon Burson	Ray Oakes	Robert P. Baroni
1993	Bartow Jenkins	Eddie Oakes	Sonny Brand	Mahlon Burson	Ray Oakes	Robert P. Baroni
1994	Bartow Jenkins	Eddie Oakes	Sonny Brand	Mahlon Burson	Ray Oakes	Robert P. Baroni
1995	Bartow Jenkins	Eddie Oakes	Sonny Brand	Mahlon Burson	Ray Oakes	Robert P. Baroni
1996	Bartow Jenkins	Eddie Oakes	Sonny Brand	Mahlon Burson	Ray Oakes	Robert P. Baroni
1997	Bartow Jenkins	Eddie Oakes	Sonny Brand	Mahlon Burson	Ray Oakes	Robert P. Baroni
1998	Bartow Jenkins	Eddie Oakes	Sonny Brand	Mahlon Burson	Ray Oakes	Robert P. Baroni
1999	Bartow Jenkins	Bobby Sikes	Sonny Brand	Mahlon Burson	Ray Oakes	Robert P. Baroni
2000	Bartow Jenkins	Bobby Sikes	Sonny Brand	Mahlon Burson	Ray Oakes	Robert P. Baroni
2001	Bartow Jenkins	Bobby Sikes	Sonny Brand	Mahlon Burson	Ray Oakes**	Robert P. Baroni
2002	Bartow Jenkins	Bobby Sikes	Sonny Brand	Mahlon Burson	Rick Johnson	Robert P. Baroni
2003	Bobby Sikes	Judy Jordan Johnson	Sonny Brand	Mahlon Burson	Rick Johnson	Robert P. Baroni
2004	Bobby Sikes	Judy Jordan Johnson	Sonny Brand	Mahlon Burson	Rick Johnson	Robert P. Baroni
2005	Bobby Sikes	Judy Jordan Johnson	David Rodriguez	Mahlon Burson	Rick Johnson	Robert P. Baroni
2006	Bobby Sikes	Judy Jordan Johnson	David Rodriguez	P.K. Martin	Bob Clark	Robert P. Baroni
2007	Rex Millsaps	Judy Jordan Johnson	Mike Crow	P.K. Martin	Bob Clark	Robert P. Baroni

**** 1984 - Bartow Jenkins left office at end of 1984 to run for County Commissioner. Bobby Sikes was appointed to finish 1984-85 term beginning January 1985.***

***** Ray Oakes died in June 2001. Rick Johnson was appointed to complete his term.***

Source: City of Lawrenceville

Lilburn City Officials

Year	Mayor	Mayor Pro-Tem	Council Member	Council Member	Council Member	Council Member	City Clerk
1955	O. B. Rowell		Hoyt Gresham	Norris J. Nash	H. C. Peevy	R. B. Pickens	R. E. Corley
1956	O. B. Rowell		Hoyt Gresham	Norris J. Nash	H. C. Peevy	R. B. Pickens	R. E. Corley
1957	O. B. Rowell		Norris J. Nash	H. C. Peevy	Russell Smith R.G. Hopkins	R. B. Pickens	N.R. Hughes
1958	O. B. Rowell		Norris J. Nash	H. C. Peevy	R. G. Hopkins	R. B. Pickens	
1959	O. B. Rowell		Norris J. Nash	H. C. Peevy	R. G. Hopkins	R. B. Pickens	
1960	O. B. Rowell		Norris J. Nash	H. C. Peevy	R. G. Hopkins	R. B. Pickens	
1961	O. B. Rowell		Norris J. Nash	H. C. Peevy	R. G. Hopkins	R. B. Pickens	
1962	J. W. Pursell		Wendell L. Jones	H. C. Peevy	Norris J. Nash	R. B. Pickens	
1963	J. W. Pursell		Jerry W. Griswell	H. C. Peevy	Jimmy Ray Morton, Jr. Mar-Dec	R. B. Pickens W. L. Jones	
1964	J. W. Pursell		Wendell L. Jones	Jimmy Ray Morton, Jr.	H. C. Peevy	Lindsey Smith	
1965	J. W. Pursell		Wendell L. Jones	Jimmy Ray Morton, Jr.	H. C. Peevy	Lindsey Smith	Doyle Grice
1966	J. W. Pursell		Wendell L. Jones	Jimmy Ray Morton, Jr.	H. C. Peevy	Lindsey Smith	

Lilburn City Officials

Year	Mayor	Mayor Pro-Tem	Council Member	Council Member	Council Member	Council Member	City Clerk
1967	J. W. Pursell		W. B. Hopkins	Jimmy Ray Morton, Jr.	H. C. Peevy	W. E. Meason	
1968	Gartrell A. Nash		W. B. Hopkins	Jimmy Ray Morton, Jr.	H. C. Peevy	W. E. Meason	Brenda Bailey
1969	Gartrell A. Nash		W. B. Hopkins	Jimmy Ray Morton, Jr.	H. C. Peevy	Troy Bailey	Brenda Bailey
1970	J. W. Pursell		W. B. Hopkins	Charles Shafer	Marvin Nash Worthy	Troy Bailey	Brenda Bailey
1971	J. W. Pursell		J. R. Bryson	Charles Shafer	Marvin Nash Worthy	H. Lee Lewis	Brenda Bailey
1972	J. E. Dotson		J. R. Bryson	Richard Hendrix	Gartrell A. Nash	H. Lee Lewis	Jean Cole
1973	J. E. Dotson		Tommy Caudell	Richard Hendrix	Gartrell A. Nash	H. Lee Lewis	Jean Cole
1974	Jack Sawyer		Tommy Caudell	Richard Hendrix	Harold Holloway	H. Lee Lewis	Jean Cole
1975	Jack Sawyer		Gartrell A. Nash	Richard Hendrix	Harold Holloway	H. Lee Lewis	Jean Cole
1976	Jack Sawyer		Gartrell A. Nash	Charles E. Bannister	Gene Lockhart	H. Lee Lewis	Jean Cole
1977	Jack Sawyer		Gartrell A. Nash	Charles E. Bannister	Gene Lockhart	H. Lee Lewis	Jean Cole
1978	Jack Sawyer		Gartrell A. Nash	Jimmy Ray Morton, Jr.	L. N. Hendrix	H. Lee Lewis	Jean Cole
1979	Jack Sawyer		Gartrell A. Nash	Jimmy Ray Morton, Jr.	L. N. Hendrix	H. Lee Lewis	Jean Cole
1980	Jack Sawyer		Jimmy Ray Morton, Jr.	Charles E. Bannister	Gartrell A. Nash	H. Lee Lewis	Jean Cole
1981	Jack Sawyer		Jimmy Ray Morton, Jr.	Charles E. Bannister	L. N. Hendrix	Gartrell A. Nash	Jean Cole
1982	Charles E. Bannister		Jimmy Ray Morton, Jr.	Jimmy Ray Morton, Jr.	Gartrell A. Nash	Bill Head	Jean Cole
1983	Charles E. Bannister		Jimmy Ray Morton, Jr.	Jimmy Ray Morton, Jr.	Gartrell A. Nash	L. N. Hendrix	Jean Cole
1984	Charles E. Bannister		Jimmy Ray Morton, Jr.	S. Scott Batterton	Gartrell A. Nash	L. N. Hendrix	Jean Cole
1985	Jimmy Ray Morton, Jr.		S. Scott Batterton	Diana Preston	Gartrell A. Nash	L. N. Hendrix	Jean Cole
1986	Jimmy Ray Morton, Jr.		S. Scott Batterton	Preston/W.C. Fitchett	Gartrell A. Nash	L. N. Hendrix	Jean Cole
1987	Jimmy Ray Morton, Jr.		S. Scott Batterton	W. Calvin Fitchett	Gartrell A. Nash	L. N. Hendrix	Jean Cole
1988	Jimmy Ray Morton, Jr.		S. Scott Batterton	W. Calvin Fitchett	Gartrell A. Nash	L. N. Hendrix	Jean Cole
1989	Jimmy Ray Morton, Jr.		S. Scott Batterton	W. Calvin Fitchett	Bill Barry	H. Michael Donald	Jean Cole
1990	Jimmy Ray Morton, Jr.		Helen Morriss	W. Calvin Fitchett	Bill Barry	H. Michael Donald	Jean Cole
1991	Jimmy Ray Morton, Jr.	W. Calvin Fitchett	Helen Morriss	Bill Barry	Diana Preston		Jean Cole
1992	W. Calvin Fitchett	Bill Barry	Helen Morriss	Gartrell A. Nash	Diana Preston		Jean Cole

Lilburn City Officials

Year	Mayor	Mayor Pro-Tem	Council Member	Council Member	Council Member	Council Member	City Clerk
1993	W. Calvin Fitchett	Gartrell A. Nash	Helen Morriss	Bill Barry	Diana Preston		Jean Cole
1994	W. Calvin Fitchett	Bill Barry	Morriss/Morton/ Bolton	Gartrell A. Nash	Diana Preston		Jean Cole
1995	W. Calvin Fitchett	Diana Preston	Jack R. Bolton	Gartrell A. Nash	Bill Barry		Jean Cole
1996	S. Scott Batterton	Bill Barry	H. Michael Donald	Diana Preston	Jack R. Bolton		Jean Cole
1997	S. Scott Batterton	Jack R. Bolton	H. Michael Donald	Diana Preston	Bill Barry		Jean Cole
1998	S. Scott Batterton	H. Michael Donald	Jack R. Bolton	Diana Preston	Bill Barry		Jean Cole
1999	S. Scott Batterton	Diana Preston	Bill Barry	Jack R. Bolton	H. Michael Donald		Jean Cole
2000	S. Scott Batterton	Bill Barry	Diana Preston	Jack R. Bolton	H. Michael Donald		Jean Cole
2001	S. Scott Batterton	Jack R. Bolton	Diana Preston	Bill Barry	H. Michael Donald		Kathy Maner
2002	S. Scott Batterton	Jack R. Bolton	Diana Preston	Bill Barry	H. Michael Donald		Kathy Maner
2003	S. Scott Batterton	Diana Preston	Bill Barry	Jack R. Bolton	H. Michael Donald/W.K. Swaim		Kathy Maner
2004	Jack R. Bolton	Bill Barry	S. Scott Batterton	Diana Preston	W. Kenneth Swaim		Kathy Maner
2005	Jack R. Bolton	S. Scott Batterton	Bill Barry	Diana Preston	W. Kenneth Swaim		Kathy Maner
2006	Jack R. Bolton	W. Kenneth Swaim	Diana Preston	S. Scott Batterton	Eddie Price		Kathy Maner
2007	Jack R. Bolton	Diana Preston	W. Kenneth Swaim	S. Scott Batterton	Eddie Price		Kathy Maner
2008	Diana Preston	Eddie Price	Tim Dunn	S. Scott Batterton	Johnny Crist		Kathy Maner

Source: City of Lilburn

Loganville City Officials

Year	Mayor	Council Member	Council Member	Council Member	Council Member
1961	T.C. Cowsert	Harbin	Dyal	McCart	Hodges
1962	T.C. Cowsert	Garrett	Dyal	McCart	Hodges
1963	Aubrey Harbin	Garrett	Dyal	McCart	Hodges
1964	Aubrey Harbin	Lee	Dyal	McCart	Hodges
1965	Aubrey Harbin	Neal Byrd	Ben Hodges	Everett Johnson	Morgan Hodges
1966	Aubrey Harbin	Neal Byrd	Ben Hodges	H.E. Cooper	Opal Cown
1967	Bob Wood	Jimmy Crawley	J.A. Hall	H.E. Cooper	Opal Cown
1968	Bob Wood	Dan Garrett	J.A. Hall	Emmett Stephens	Aubrey Harbin
1969	Aubrey Harbin	Dan Garrett	J.A. Hall	Emmett Stephens	Odis Moon
1970	Aubrey Harbin	Bob Wood	Mahlon Garrett	Emmett Stephens	Odis Moon
1971	Bob Wood	Max Guinn	Mahlon Garrett	Emmett Stephens	Odis Moon

Loganville City Officials

Year	Mayor	Council Member	Council Member	Council Member	Council Member
1972	Bob Wood	Max Guinn	Everett Johnson	Aubey Harbin	James Towler
1973	Bob Wood	Harold Tribble	Jack Stephens	Aubey Harbin	James Towler
1974	Bob Wood	Harold Tribble	Jack Stephens	Richard Tucker	James Towler
1975	J.A. (Junior) Hall	Carolyn Moon	W.J. Maxwell	Richard Tucker	James Towler
1976	J.A. (Junior) Hall	Carolyn Moon	W.J. Maxwell	Jim Fischer	James Towler
1977	J.A. (Junior) Hall	Carolyn Moon	W.J. Maxwell	Billy Stephens	James Towler
1978	J.A. (Junior) Hall	Carolyn Moon	W.J. Maxwell	Billy Stephens	Phillip Johnson
1979	J.A. (Junior) Hall	Tommie Lee Fuller	Melvin Cown	Billy Stephens	Phillip Johnson
1980	J.A. (Junior) Hall	Tommie Lee Fuller	Melvin Cown	M.C. Garrett	Lamar Johnson
1981	J.A. (Junior) Hall	Mike Jones	Morgan Hodges	M.C. Garrett	Lamar Johnson
1982	J.A. (Junior) Hall	Mike Jones	Morgan Hodges	M.C. Garrett	Richmond (Rick) Burrell
1983	J.A. (Junior) Hall	Henry Hammond	Morgan Hodges	M.C. Garrett	Richmond (Rick) Burrell
1984	J.A. (Junior) Hall	Henry Hammond	Morgan Hodges	M.C. Garrett	Doug Dollar
1985	Michael R. Jones	Adrin (Kelly) Perkins	Richmond (Rick) Burrell	M.C. Garrett	Doug Dollar
1986	Michael R. Jones	Adrin (Kelly) Perkins	Richmond (Rick) Burrell	Deborah Cohran	Doug Dollar
1987	Renee S. Unterman	M.C. Garrett	Morgan Hodges	Deborah Cohran	Doug Dollar
1988	Renee S. Unterman	M.C. Garrett	Morgan Hodges	Richard Woodall	Henry Hammond
1989	Renee S. Unterman	M.C. Garrett	Morgan Hodges	Richard Woodall	Henry Hammond
1990	Renee S. Unterman	Clint Rice	Morgan Hodges	Richard Woodall	Henry Hammond
1991	Julian R. Sellers	Clint Rice	Juanita Barnes	Richard Woodall	Henry Hammond
1992	Julian R. Sellers	Phillip Johnson	Juanita Barnes	Richard Woodall	Henry Hammond
1993	Michael R. Jones	Phillip Johnson	Juanita Barnes	Richard Woodall	Henry Hammond
1994	Michael R. Jones	J.L. Davis	Juanita Barnes	Richard Woodall	Clint Rice
1995	Michael R. Jones	J.L. Davis	Juanita Barnes	Richard Woodall	Clint Rice
1996	Michael R. Jones	Juanita Barnes	Janice Tribble	Sue Bailey	Pam Williams
1997	Renee S. Unterman	Greg Staffins	Bill Jones	Sue Bailey	Pam Williams
1998	Renee S. Unterman	Greg Staffins	Bill Jones	Sue Bailey	John Hartley
1999	William T. (Bill) Jones	Sara Bacon	Gene Matthews	Sue Bailey	John Hartley
2000	William T. (Bill) Jones	Sara Bacon	Gene Matthews	Sue Bailey	Pam Williams
2001	Michael R. Jones	Sara Bacon	Gene Matthews	Sue Bailey	Pam Williams
2002	Michael R. Jones	Sara Bacon	Gene Matthews	Sue Bailey	John Ferrara
2003	Gene A. Matthews	Sara Bacon	Tim Barron	Sue Bailey	John Ferrara
2004	Gene A. Matthews	Sara Bacon	Tim Barron	Jerry Price	John Ferrara
2005	Timothy Barron	Jerry Price	Mark Kiddoo	Ray Nunley	John Ferrara
2006	Timothy Barron	Jerry Price	Austin Jones	Ray Nunley	Mark Kiddoo
2007	Timothy Barron	Jerry Price	Austin Jones	Ray Nunley	Mark Kiddoo
2008	Timothy Barron	Jerry Price	Austin Jones	Ray Nunley	Mark Kiddoo

Source: Loganville City Government

Loganville City Officials (cont.)				
Year	Council Member	Council Member	City Clerk	City Manager
1961	Cooper	Griffin	Hilda Sanders	
1962	Byrd	Griffin	Hilda Sanders	
1963	Byrd	Griffin	Hilda Sanders / Opal Cown	
1964	Byrd	Johnson	Opal Cown	
1965	Harold Byrd	W.L. Johnson	Opal Cown	
1966	Bobby Boss	W.L. Johnson	Opal Cown	
1967	Bobby Boss	H.E. Cooper	Opal Cown	
1968	Bobby Boss	Frank Allen, Jr	Mary Alice Baker	
1969	Bobby Boss	Lamar Johnson	Kate Needham	
1970	Bobby Boss	Lamar Johnson	Kate Needham	
1971	Bobby Boss	Julian Sellers	Kate Needham	
1972	Bobby Boss	Julian Sellers	Kate Needham	
1973	Bobby Boss	Julian Sellers	Kate Needham	
1974	Kenneth Cloud	Julian Sellers	Kate Needham	
1975	Kenneth Cloud	Phillip Johnson	Kate Needham	
1976	Mike Jones	Phillip Johnson	Kate Needham	
1977	Mike Jones	Clint Rice	Kate Needham	
1978	Max Allgood	Clint Rice	Kate Needham	
1979	Max Allgood	Clint Rice	Kate Needham	
1980	Max Allgood	Clint Rice	Kate Needham	
1981	Max Allgood	Clint Rice	Kate Needham	
1982	Max Allgood	Clint Rice	Kate Needham	
1983	Max Allgood	Phillip Johnson	Kate Needham	
1984	Max Allgood	Phillip Johnson	Kate Needham	
1985	Max Allgood	Phillip Johnson	Kate Needham	
1986	J.A. Hall, Jr.	Phillip Johnson	Kate Needham	
1987	Jean Hall	Stephen Noel	Kate Needham	
1988	Jean Hall	Stephen Noel	Kate Needham	
1989	Jean Hall	Julian Sellers	Kate Needham	
1990	Phillip Sims	Julian Sellers	Kate Needham	Jim Dikin
1991	Janice Tribble	Harry Hinton	Michelle Deaton	
1992	Janice Tribble	Harry Hinton	Michelle Deaton	
1993	Janice Tribble	Wendell Geiger	Michelle Deaton	
1994	Janice Tribble	Wendell Geiger	Michelle Deaton	
1995	Janice Tribble	Wendell Geiger	Michelle Deaton	Lee Garner
1996	Bill George	Wendell Geiger	Michelle Deaton	Kenneth Cloud
1997	Bill George	Wendell Geiger	Michelle Deaton	Kenneth Cloud
1998	Danny Byrd	Wendell Geiger	Michelle Deaton	Kenneth Cloud
1999	Danny Byrd	Wendell Geiger	Michelle Deaton	Kenneth Cloud
2000	Danny Byrd	Wendell Geiger	Michelle Deaton	Kenneth Cloud
2001	Danny Byrd	Wendell Geiger	Michelle Deaton	Kenneth Cloud

Loganville City Officials (cont.)

Year	Council Member	Council Member	City Clerk	City Manager
2002	Danny Byrd	Wendell Geiger	Michelle Deaton	Bill Jones
2003	Eileen Waring	Danny Byrd / Mark Kiddoo	Michelle Deaton	Bill Jones
2004	Eileen Waring	Wendell Geiger	Michelle Deaton	Bill Jones
2005	Chuck Bagley	Wendell Geiger	Michelle Deaton	Bill Jones
2006	Chuck Bagley	Wendell Geiger	Michelle Deaton	Bill Jones
2007	Chuck Bagley	Wendell Geiger	Michelle Deaton	Bill Jones
2008	Chuck Bagley	Wendell Geiger	Michelle Deaton / Kristi Ash	Bill Jones

Source: Loganville City Government

Norcross City Officials

Year	Mayor	Council Member	Council Member	Council Member	Council Member	Council Member	City Clerk
1870	J.J. Thrasher	S.T. McElroy	J.A. Miles	G. Robinson	Mr. Autrey		
1874	W.H. Johnson	J.N. Vincent	J.A. Miles	W.G. Wigby	N. Arendalls		
1878	M.L. Lively	J.N. Vincent	J.A. Miles	W.G. Wigby	N. Arendalls		
1882	E.G. McDaniel	J.N. Vincent	J.A. Miles	W.G. Wigby	N. Arendalls		
1886	S.T. McElroy	J.N. Vincent	J.A. Miles	W.G. Wigby	N. Arendalls		
1890	Dr. O.O. Simpson	J.N. Vincent	J.A. Miles	W.G. Wigby	N. Arendalls		
1892	J.M. Holbrook	J.N. Vincent	J.A. Miles	W.G. Wigby	N. Arendalls		
1895	H.M. Lively	J.N. Vincent	J.A. Miles	W.G. Wigby	N. Arendalls		
1897	A.A. Martin	J.N. Vincent	J.A. Miles	W.G. Wigby	N. Arendalls		
1899	J.E. McElroy	H.V. Jones	E.C. Dean	A.A. Martin	F.B. Nesbit	C.P. Lively	
1900	E. Winn Born	H.V. Jones	E.C. Dean	A.A. Martin	F.B. Nesbit	C.P. Lively	
1902	C.A.McDaniel	H.V. Jones	E.C. Dean	A.A. Martin	F.B. Nesbit	C.P. Lively	
1903	S.T. McElroy	J.B. Hopkins	A.A. Johnson	A.A. Martin	F.B. Nesbit	C.P. Lively	
1906	D.K. Johnson	J.B. Hopkins	A.A. Johnson	A.A. Martin	F.B. Nesbit	C.P. Lively	
1907	A.A. Martin	J.B. Hopkins	A.A. Johnson	A.A. Martin	F.B. Nesbit	C.P. Lively	
1907	T.E. Johnson	E.L. Barrett	S. Cain	W.M. Keady	T.E. Summerour	W.P. Walker	
1908	T.E. Johnson	E.L. Barrett	S. Cain	W.M. Keady	T.E. Summerour	W.P. Walker	
1909	W.M. McElroy	E.L. Barrett	S. Cain	W.M. Keady	T.E. Summerour	W.P. Walker	
1910	W.M. McElroy	E.L. Barrett	S. Cain	W.M. Keady	T.E. Summerour	W.P. Walker	
1914	Ben Clement	E.L. Barrett	S. Cain	W.M. Keady	T.E. Summerour	W.P. Walker	
1914	Dr. O.O. Simpson	J.R. Garner	W.A. McGinnis	T.A. Rainey	D.B. Wall	W.P. Walker	
1918	T.E. Johnson	J.H. Kinnett	A.H. Leitch	E.G. McDaniel	W.C. Wall	T.E. Summerour	
1919	L.H. Letson	A.C. Maloney	W.R. Leitch	E.G. McDaniel	W.C. Wall	J.A. Webb	
1922	L.H. Letson	N.J. Guthrie	A.S. Johnson	D.F. McKinney	B.F. Summerour	J.A. Webb	
1925	J.T. Simpson	N.J. Guthrie	A.S. Johnson	D.F. McKinney	B.F. Summerour	J.A. Webb	
1926	J.T. Simpson	Frank Robertson	T.E. Johnson	F.A. Medlock	B.F. Summerour	D.B. Phillips	
1927	D.B. Phillips	Frank Robertson	T.E. Johnson	F.A. Medlock	B.F. Summerour	D.B. Phillips	
1928	D.B. Phillips	Frank Robertson	T.E. Johnson	F.A. Medlock	W.D. Flowers	W.M. Keady	

Norcross City Officials

Year	Mayor	Council Member	Council Member	Council Member	Council Member	Council Member	City Clerk
1929	D.B. Phillips	Frank Robertson	T.E. Johnson	F.A. Medlock	W.D. Flowers	W.M. Keady	
1930	D.B. Phillips	Frank Robertson	H.A. Martin	F.A. Medlock	W.D. Flowers	W.M. Keady	
1931	D.B. Phillips	Frank Robertson	H.A. Martin	F.A. Medlock	W.D. Flowers	W.M. Keady	
1932	D.B. Phillips	Carl A. Garner	B.F. Simpson	R.J. Merritt	W.D. Flowers	W.M. Keady	
1933	B.F. Simpson	Carl A. Garner	Frank Robertson	R.J. Merritt	W.D. Flowers	R.J. Dejarnette	
1934	B.F. Simpson	Carl A. Garner	R.J. Merritt	J.R. Dejarnette	W.D. Flowers	H.D. Meadows	
1935	B.F. Simpson	Carl A. Garner	R.J. Merritt	J.R. Dejarnette	Gaines B. Ivy	H.D. Meadows	
1936	B.F. Simpson	Carl A. Garner	R.J. Merritt	J.R. Dejarnette	H.D. Meadows	Gaines B. Ivy	Joe S. Nesbitt
1937	W.M. Doff	Carl A. Garner	R.J. Merritt	J.R. Dejarnette	H.D. Meadows	Gaines B. Ivy	Joe S. Nesbitt
1938	W.M. Doff	Carl A. Garner	Allen M. Johnson	J.R. Dejarnette	Roy E. Carlyle	Gaines B. Ivy	Joe S. Nesbitt
1939	W.M. Doff	Carl A. Garner	Allen M. Johnson	R.J. Merritt	Roy E. Carlyle	Gaines B. Ivy	Joe S. Nesbitt
1940	W.M. Doff	Carl A. Garner	Allen M. Johnson	R.J. Merritt	Roy E. Carlyle	Gaines B. Ivy	Joe S. Nesbitt
1941	W.M. Doff	Carl A. Garner	Allen M. Johnson	R.J. Merritt	Roy E. Carlyle	Gaines B. Ivy	Joe S. Nesbitt
1942	Gaines B. Ivy	Carl A. Garner	Allen M. Johnson	R.J. Merritt	Roy E. Carlyle	Gaines B. Ivy	Joe S. Nesbitt
1943	Gaines B. Ivy	Carl A. Garner	Allen M. Johnson	R.J. Merritt	Roy E. Carlyle	J.A. Davenport	Joe S. Nesbitt
1944	Gaines B. Ivy	G.W. Morris	Allen M. Johnson	R.J. Merritt	Roy E. Carlyle	J.A. Davenport	Joe S. Nesbitt
1945	Gaines B. Ivy	Geo. H. Verner	Allen M. Johnson	R.J. Merritt	Roy E. Carlyle	J.A. Davenport	Joe S. Nesbitt
1946	Gaines B. Ivy	Geo. H. Verner	Allen M. Johnson	W.L. Maloney	H.J. Reynolds	Jas. S. Cochran	Thomas H. Fallaw Sr.
1947	Frank Robertson	G.W. Morris	Minor P. Garner	W.L. Maloney	H.J. Reynolds	Jas. S. Cochran	
1948	Frank Robertson	G.W. Morris	Minor P. Garner	W.L. Maloney	H.E. Reeves	C.E. Kirkpatrick	
1949	Carl A. Garner	G.W. Morris	Minor P. Garner	W.L. Maloney	H.E. Reeves	C.E. Kirkpatrick	Hubbard T. Baxter/T.H. Fallaw
1950	Carl A. Garner	G.W. Morris	Minor P. Garner	A.M. Johnson	Joe S. Nesbit	C.E. Kirkpatrick	
1951	Carl A. Garner	W.D. Flowers	J.H. Webb	A.M. Johnson	Joe S. Nesbit	C.E. Kirkpatrick	Margaret Holbrook
1952	Frank Robertson	W.D. Flowers	J.H. Webb	A.M. Johnson	Joe S. Nesbit	C.E. Kirkpatrick	Margaret Holbrook
1953	Frank Robertson	A.F. Champ	R.A. Grant, Jr.	A.M. Johnson	Joe S. Nesbit	C.E. Kirkpatrick	Margaret Holbrook
1954	Frank Robertson	A.F. Champ	R.A. Grant, Jr.	J.H. Webb	John T. Paden	C.E. Kirkpatrick	
1955	Frank Robertson	Kenneth Warren	D.B. Phillips	J.H. Webb	John T. Paden	C.E. Kirkpatrick	
1956	Frank Robertson	Kenneth Warren	D.B. Phillips	J.A. Parsons	John T. Paden	C.E. Kirkpatrick	
1957	Dudley S. Hancock	John H. Adams	D.B. Phillips	J.A. Parsons	John T. Paden	C.E. Kirkpatrick	
1958	Dudley S. Hancock	John H. Adams	D.B. Phillips	M.O. Nesbit	John T. Paden	C.E. Kirkpatrick	G.W. Morriss
1959	W.L. Maloney	John H. Adams	D.B. Phillips	M.O. Nesbit	John T. Paden	C.E. Kirkpatrick	
1960	W.L. Maloney	W.H. Ferguson	D.B. Phillips	J.A. Parsons	H.C. Youngblood	C.E. Kirkpatrick	Betty Mauldin
1961	W.L. Maloney	W.H. Ferguson	L.D. Ewing	J.A. Parsons	H.C. Youngblood	C.E. Kirkpatrick	Betty Mauldin
1962	W.L. Maloney	L.D. Ewing	D.B. Phillips	J.A. Parsons	Carl Garner	C.E. Kirkpatrick	Betty Mauldin
1963	W.L. Maloney	L.D. Ewing	D.B. Phillips	J.F. Mitchell	Carl Garner	C.E. Kirkpatrick	Betty Mauldin
1964	W.L. Maloney	L.D. Ewing	D.B. Phillips	J.F. Mitchell	Carl Garner	C.E. Kirkpatrick	Betty Mauldin

Norcross City Officials

Year	Mayor	Council Member	Council Member	Council Member	Council Member	Council Member	City Clerk
1965	W.L. Maloney	L.D. Ewing	D.B. Phillips	A.P. Francis	Carl Garner	C.E. Kirkpatrick	Betty Mauldin
1966	W.L. Maloney	L.D. Ewing	R.A. Hamilton	A.P. Francis	Carl Garner	C.E. Kirkpatrick	Betty Mauldin
1967	W.L. Maloney	L.D. Ewing	R.A. Hamilton	A.P. Francis	Carl Garner	C.E. Kirkpatrick	Betty Mauldin
1968	W.L. Maloney	R.A. Hamilton	J. Stevens	R.M. DeLeon Jr.	A.P Francis	L.D. Ewing	Betty Mauldin
1969	W.L. Maloney	R.A. Hamilton	J. Stevens	R.M. DeLeon Jr.	G.L. Welden	R.A. Grant	Betty Mauldin
1970	W.L. Maloney	R.A. Hamilton	J. Stevens	R.M. DeLeon Jr.	G.L. Welden	R.A. Grant	Betty Mauldin
1971	Carl Garner Jr.	R.A. Hamilton	J. Stevens	R.M. DeLeon Jr.	Lillian H. Webb	R.A. Grant	Betty Mauldin
1972	Carl Garner Jr.	R.A. Hamilton	J. Stevens	R.M. DeLeon Jr.	Lillian H. Webb	R.A. Grant	Betty Mauldin
1973	Carl Garner Jr.	R.A. Hamilton	J. Stevens	R.M. DeLeon Jr.	Lillian H. Webb	R.A. Grant	Betty Mauldin
1974	Carl Garner Jr.	Daniel Marshall	J. Stevens	R.M. DeLeon Jr.	Lillian H. Webb	R.A. Grant	Betty Mauldin
1975	Lillian H. Webb	Daniel Marshall	J. Stevens	R.M. DeLeon Jr.	Charles Hollifield	Glenn R. Martin	Betty Mauldin
1976	Lillian H. Webb	R.A. Hamilton	C. Darrell Johnson	G. Robinson	Charles Hollifield	Glenn R. Martin	Betty Mauldin
1977	Lillian H. Webb		C. Darrell Johnson	R.M. DeLeon Jr.	Charles Hollifield	Glenn R. Martin	Betty Mauldin
1978	Lillian H. Webb	R.A. Hamilton	C. Darrell Johnson	J.F. Mitchell	Charles Hollifield	Glenn R. Martin	Betty Mauldin
1979	Lillian H. Webb	R.A. Hamilton	C. Darrell Johnson	J.F. Mitchell	William F. Bryant	Glenn R. Martin	Betty Mauldin
1980	Lillian H. Webb	Glenn R. Martin	William (Bill) Bryant	W.R. (Dick) Newton	R.A. Grant Jr.	Robert (Bob) Peach	Betty Mauldin
1981	Lillian H. Webb	Glenn R. Martin	William (Bill) Bryant	Patrick Corleto	R.A. Grant Jr.	Robert (Bob) Peach	Betty Mauldin
1982	Lillian H. Webb	Glenn R. Martin	William (Bill) Bryant	W.R. (Dick) Newton	Gary S. Cobb	Robert L. Barrett	Betty Mauldin
1983	Lillian H. Webb	Robert M. Brown	William (Bill) Bryant	W.R. (Dick) Newton	Gary S. Cobb	Robert L. Barrett	Betty Mauldin
1984	Lillian H. Webb	Robert M. Brown	William (Bill) Bryant	W.R. (Dick) Newton	Gary S. Cobb	Ruth Dodd	Betty Mauldin
1985	William F. Bryant	R.A. Grant, Jr.	Ray Garmon	W.R. (Dick) Newton	Gary S. Cobb	Ruth Dodd	Betty Mauldin
1986	William F. Bryant	R.A. Grant, Jr.	Ray Garmon	Patrick Corleto	Gary S. Cobb	Barry D. Payne	Betty Mauldin
1987	Gary S. Cobb	Ruth Dodd	Maurice Allen	Patrick Corleto	Ray Garmon	Barry D. Payne	Betty Mauldin
1988	Gary S. Cobb	Ruth Dodd	Maurice Allen	Patrick Corleto	Ray Garmon	Barry D. Payne	Betty Mauldin
1989	Thurman Terrell	Ruth Dodd	Maurice Allen	Patrick Corleto	Ray Garmon	Barry D. Payne	Betty Mauldin
1990	Thurman Terrell	Ruth Dodd	Maurice Allen	Patrick Corleto	Ray Garmon	Daniel Lay	Betty Mauldin
1991	Maurice Allen	Ruth Dodd	John A. McFarland	Patrick Corleto	Ray Garmon	Daniel Lay	Betty Mauldin
1992	Maurice Allen	Ruth Dodd	John A. McFarland	Andre Debski	Ray Garmon	Daniel Lay	Betty Mauldin
1993	Maurice Allen	Gary S. Cobb	John A. McFarland	Andre Debski	Ray Garmon	Daniel Lay	Betty Mauldin
1994	Maurice Allen	Gary S. Cobb	John A. McFarland	Andre Debski	Barry D. Payne	Daniel Lay	B. Mauldin/K. Bradley
1995	Maurice Allen	Gary S. Cobb/ Craig L. Newton	John A. McFarland	Andre Debski	Barry D. Payne	Daniel Lay	Karen Bradley/ Linda Brown/ S. Dennen
1996	Lillian H. Webb	Craig L. Newton	John A. McFarland	Andre Debski	Barry D. Payne	Daniel Lay	Sue Dennen
1997	Lillian H. Webb	Craig L. Newton	John A. McFarland	Joyce Howington	Barry D. Payne	Julie A. Barks	Sue Dennen
1998	Lillian H. Webb	Craig L. Newton	John A. McFarland	Joyce Howington	Barry D. Payne	Julie A. Barks	Sue Dennen

Norcross City Officials

Year	Mayor	Council Member	Council Member	Council Member	Council Member	Council Member	City Clerk
1999	Lillian H. Webb	Craig L. Newton	Faye McFarland	Joyce Howington	Barry D. Payne	Julie A. Barks	Sue Dennen
2000	Lillian H. Webb	Craig L. Newton	Tim J. Hopton	Joyce Howington	Barry D. Payne	Julie A. Barks	Sue Dennen
2001	Lillian H. Webb	Craig L. Newton	Tim J. Hopton	Joyce Howington	Faye McFarland	Julie A. Barks	Sue Dennen
2002	Lillian H. Webb	Craig L. Newton	Tim J. Hopton	Joyce Howington	Faye McFarland	Julie A. Barks	Sue Dennen
2003	Lillian H. Webb	Craig L. Newton	Tim J. Hopton	Bruce W. Smith	David McLeroy	Barry D. Payne	Sue Dennen
2004	Lillian H. Webb	Josh J. Bare	Tim J. Hopton	Bruce W. Smith	David McLeroy	Barry D. Payne	Sue Dennen
2005	Lillian H. Webb	Josh J. Bare	Tim J. Hopton	Michael Lovelady	David McLeroy	Bruce W. Smith	Susan Brooks
2006	Lillian H. Webb	Terry Bowie	Michael Lovelady	David McLeroy	Charlie Riehm	Bruce W. Smith	Susan Brooks
2007	Lillian H. Webb	Jeff Allen	Terry Bowie	David McLeroy	Charlie Riehm	Keith Shewbert	Susan Wuerzner
2008	Bucky Johnson	Jeff Allen	Craig L. Newton	David McLeroy	Charlie Riehm	Keith Shewbert	Susan Wuerzner

Source: City of Norcross

Snellville City Officials

Year	Mayor	Council Member	Council Member	Council Member
1923	Gladstone F. Snell			
1940	W. C. Britt	Jewitt W. Williams*	W. Raymond Williams*	
1941	W. C. Britt			
1942	W. C. Britt			
1943	W. C. Britt			
1944	W. C. Britt			
1945	W. C. Britt			
1946	W. C. Britt			
1947	Arthur H. Stancil	W.E.Buchanan/Ctlnd	Gerald Brownlee	Fred C. Snell/M.W. Howard
1948	Arthur H. Stancil	William S. Courtland	Gerald Brownlee	Martin W. Howard
1949	Cofer/Williams	William S. Courtland	Gerald Brownlee	Martin W. Howard
1950	Ernest J. Williams	William S. Courtland		Martin W. Howard
1951	Ernest J. Williams	William S. Courtland		Martin W. Howard
1952	Ernest J. Williams	Harold Bird	Hoke S. Nash	E. R. Snell, Sr.
1953	Ernest J. Williams			
1954	Ernest J. Williams			
1955	Ernest J. Williams	Juhan F. Leon	James D. Cofer, Sr.	
1956	Ernest J. Williams	William H. Norton		Martin W. Howard
1962	Henry B. Clower, Sr.	Randol P. Britt	Horace N. Nash	Walter W. Gresham
1963	Henry B. Clower, Sr.	William Ross Kirby	Jack S. Dillard, Sr.	Walter W. Gresham
1964	Henry B. Clower, Sr.	William Ross Kirby	Jack S. Dillard, Sr.	Walter W. Gresham
1965	Henry B. Clower, Sr.	William Ross Kirby	T. W. Briscoe	Walter W. Gresham
1966	Thomas W. Briscoe	William Ross Kirby	J.F. Phillips/Mitchel	F. Leon Phillips/ Jay C. Sager
1967	Thomas W. Briscoe		W. Mike Mitchell	Jay C. Sager
1968	Thomas W. Briscoe	Arnold Stancil	W. Mike Mitchell	Jay C. Sager

Snellville City Officials

Year	Mayor	Council Member	Council Member	Council Member
1969	Thomas W. Briscoe	Arnold Stancil	Floyd H. Cannon	Jay C. Sager
1970	Jay C. Sager	Arnold Stancil	Cannon/Mitchell	Sager/Briscoe
1971	Jay C. Sager	Arnold Stancil	Preston H. Mitchell, Jr.	T. W. Briscoe
1972	Thomas W. Briscoe	Arnold Stancil	Preston H. Mitchell, Jr.	Emmett W. Clower
1973	Thomas W. Briscoe	Stancil/Vira E. Cobb	Preston H. Mitchell, Jr.	Emmett W. Clower
1974	W. Emmett Clower	Wayne T. Sikes	Preston H. Mitchell, Jr.	Joseph B. Neighbors
1975	W. Emmett Clower	Wayne T. Sikes	Franklin W. Banks	Joseph B. Neighbors
1976	W. Emmett Clower	Wayne T. Sikes	Franklin W. Banks	Joseph B. Neighbors
1977	W. Emmett Clower	Wayne T. Sikes	Franklin W. Banks	Joseph B. Neighbors
1978	W. Emmett Clower	Wayne T. Sikes	S. Courtland Williams	Joseph B. Neighbors
1979	W. Emmett Clower	Wayne T. Sikes	S. Courtland Williams	Joseph B. Neighbors
1980	W. Emmett Clower	Wayne T. Sikes	S. Courtland Williams	Judy A. Waters
1981	W. Emmett Clower	Ronald J. Christopher	S. Courtland Williams	Judy A. Waters
1982	W. Emmett Clower	Ronald J. Christopher	S. Courtland Williams	Judy A. Waters
1983	W. Emmett Clower	Ronald J. Christopher	S. Courtland Williams	Waters/Yarbrough
1984	W. Emmett Clower	Ronald J. Christopher	S. Courtland Williams	Mack Q. Yarbrough
1985	W. Emmett Clower	Roger T. Lane	S. Courtland Williams	Mack Q. Yarbrough
1986	W. Emmett Clower	Roger T. Lane	S. Courtland Williams	Mack Q. Yarbrough
1987	W. Emmett Clower	Roger T. Lane	S. Courtland Williams	Mack Q. Yarbrough
1988	W. Emmett Clower	Roger T. Lane	S. Courtland Williams	Mack Q. Yarbrough
1989	W. Emmett Clower	Richard M. Staley	Leonard T. Martin	Mack Q. Yarbrough
1990	W. Emmett Clower	Richard M. Staley	Leonard T. Martin	Mack Q. Yarbrough
1991	W. Emmett Clower	Richard M. Staley	Leonard T. Martin	Mack Q. Yarbrough
1992	W. Emmett Clower	Richard M. Staley	Leonard T. Martin	James E. Walters
1993	W. Emmett Clower	Richard M. Staley	Leonard T. Martin	James E. Walters
1994	W. Emmett Clower	Richard M. Staley	Leonard T. Martin	James E. Walters
1995	W. Emmett Clower	Richard M. Staley	Leonard T. Martin	James E. Walters
1996	W. Emmett Clower	Richard M. Staley	Leonard T. Martin	Troy G. Carter
1997	W. Emmett Clower	Richard M. Staley	Leonard T. Martin	Troy G. Carter
1998	W. Emmett Clower	Deborah L. Rich	Leonard T. Martin	Troy G. Carter
1999	W. Emmett Clower	Deborah L. Rich	Leonard T. Martin	Troy G. Carter
2000	Brett A. Harrell	Deborah L. Rich	Martin /Everson	Troy G. Carter
2001	Brett A. Harrell	Deborah L. Rich	Melvin Everson	Troy G. Carter
2002	Brett A. Harrell	Deborah L. Rich	Melvin Everson	Michael O. Smith
2003	Brett A. Harrell	Deborah L. Rich	Melvin Everson	Michael O. Smith
2004	Gerald F. Oberholtzer	Chad A. Smith	Everson/Åuld	Michael O. Smith
2005	Gerald F. Oberholtzer	Chad A. Smith	Auld/Bender	Michael O. Smith
2006	Gerald F. Oberholtzer	Smith/Kautz	Barbara Bender	Smith/Auld
2007	Gerald F. Oberholtzer	Kelly Kautz	Barbara Bender	D. Warren Auld
2008	Gerald F. Oberholtzer	Kelly Kautz	Barbara Bender	D. Warren Auld

**** Years Served = Unknown***
Source: City of Snellville

Snellville City Officials (cont.)			
Year	Council Member	Council Member	City Clerk
1923			
1940			
1941			
1942			
1943			
1944			
1945			
1946			
1947	James C. Knight	James D. Cofer, Sr.	F.C. Snell/Camp
1948	James C. Knight	James D. Cofer, Sr.	JeanneCamp/GC Brooks/Vera Nash
1949	James C. Knight	A. W. Peters	George C. Brooks
1950	James C. Knight	A. W. Peters	George C. Brooks
1951	James C. Knight	A. W. Peters	Walter W. Gresham
1952		A. W. Peters	
1953		A. W. Peters	
1954		A. W. Peters	
1955		A. W. Peters	
1956		A. W. Peters	
1962	James D. Mason		Dennis C. Williams
1963	James D. Mason	S. Wayne Odum	Dennis C. Williams
1964	James D. Mason	S. Wayne Odum	Williams/Dillard
1965	James D. Mason	S. Wayne Odum	Jack Dillard
1966	James D. Mason	S. Wayne Odum	Jack Dillard
1967	James D. Mason	S. Wayne Odum	Jack Dillard
1968	Nelson L. Williams, Sr.	S. Wayne Odum	Jack Dillard
1969	Nelson L. Williams, Sr.	S. Wayne Odum	Dillard/McMichael
1970	Nelson L. Williams, Sr.	S. Wayne Odum	Betty McMichael
1971	Nelson L. Williams, Sr.	S. Wayne Odum	Betty McMichael
1972	Nelson L. Williams, Jr.	S. Wayne Odum	Betty McMichael
1973	Nelson L. Williams, Jr.	S. Wayne Odum	Betty McMichael
1974	James D. Cofer, Jr.	S. Wayne Odum	Betty McMichael
1975	James D. Cofer, Jr.	S. Wayne Odum	Betty McMichael
1976	Cofer/Lindsay	S. Wayne Odum	Betty McMichael
1977	Keith S. Lindsay, Jr.	S. Courtland Williams	Betty McMichael
1978	Keith S. Lindsay, Jr.	S. Wayne Odum	Betty McMichael
1979	Keith S. Lindsay, Jr.	S. Wayne Odum	Betty McMichael
1980	Elise W. Cotter	S. Wayne Odum	Betty McMichael
1981	Elise W. Cotter	S. Wayne Odum	Betty McMichael
1982	Elise W. Cotter	S. Wayne Odum	Betty McMichael
1983	Elise W. Cotter	S. Wayne Odum	Betty McMichael

Snellville City Officials (cont.)			
Year	Council Member	Council Member	City Clerk
1984	Elise W. Cotter	S. Wayne Odum	Betty McMichael
1985	Elise W. Cotter	S. Wayne Odum	Betty McMichael
1986	Elise W. Cotter	S. Wayne Odum	Betty McMichael
1987	Elise W. Cotter	S. Wayne Odum	Betty McMichael
1988	Elise W. Cotter	S. Wayne Odum	Betty McMichael
1989	Elise W. Cotter	S. Wayne Odum	McMichael/Callaway
1990	Elise W. Cotter	S. Wayne Odum	Dixie B. Callaway
1991	Elise W. Cotter	Mike M. Chancey	Dixie B. Callaway
1992	Kurt F. Schulz	Mike M. Chancey	Dixie B. Callaway
1993	Kurt F. Schulz	Mike M. Chancey	Callaway/Lowery
1994	Kurt F. Schulz	G. Troy Carter	Sharon Lowery
1995	Kurt F. Schulz	G. Troy Carter	Sharon Lowery
1996	Deborah L. Rich	S. Wayne Odum	Sharon Lowery
1997	Deborah L. Rich	S. Wayne Odum	Sharon Lowery
1998	Brett A. Harrell	S. Wayne Odum	Sharon Lowery
1999	Brett A. Harrell	S. Wayne Odum	Sharon Lowery
2000	Gerald F. Oberholtzer	Joe Anderson	Sharon Lowery
2001	Gerald F. Oberholtzer	Joe Anderson	Sharon Lowery
2002	Gerald F. Oberholtzer	Joe Anderson	Sharon Lowery
2003	Gerald F. Oberholtzer	Anderson/Jenkins	Sharon Lowery
2004	Bruce Garraway	Robert Jenkins	Sharon Lowery
2005	Bruce Garraway	Robert Jenkins	Sharon Lowery
2006	Bruce Garraway	Robert Jenkins	Sharon Lowery
2007	Garraway/Warner	Robert Jenkins	Sharon Lowery
2008	Tod Warner	Robert Jenkins	Sharon Lowery
Source: City of Snellville			

Sugar Hill City Officials, 1939-2008						
Year	Mayor	Council Members				
1939-47	Alton Tucker					
1948	Nelson Brogdon	E.E. Camp	Carl Duncan	Paul Marshall	H.A. Bailey	George H. Michael
1949	Nelson Brogdon	E.E. Camp	Carl Duncan	Paul Marshall	H.A. Bailey	George H. Michael
1950	Nelson Brogdon	E.E. Camp	Carl Duncan	Paul Marshall	H.A. Bailey	George H, Michael
1951	Nelson Brogdon	E.E. Camp	Carl Duncan	Paul Marshall	H.A. Bailey	George H, Michael
1952	Nelson Brogdon	E.E. Camp	Carl Duncan	Paul Marshall	H.A. Bailey	George H. Michael
1953	Nelson Brogdon	E.E. Camp	Carl Duncan	Paul Marshall	H.A. Bailey	George H. Michael
1954	Nelson Brogdon	E.E. Camp	Carl Duncan	Paul Marshall	H.A. Bailey	George H. Michael
1955	Raymond H. Smith	Forest Breedlove	H.A. Bailey	Guy Franklin	Curtis B. Hudgins	Lloyd Smith
1956	Raymond H. Smith	Forest Breedlove	H.A. Bailey	Guy Franklin	Curtis B. Hudgins	Lloyd Smith
1957	James Wages	Forest Breedlove	Hinton Freeman	Dean Allin	Carl Kemp, Sr.	Lloyd Smith
1958	James Wages	E.E. Camp	Carl Duncan	H.A. Bailey	Curtis B. Hudgins	Guy C. Gober
1959	James Wages	D.L. Venable	Hinton Freeman	Clifford Cross	Carl Kemp	Leon Fields
1961	James Wages	D.L. Venable	Hinton Freeman	Clifford Cross	Carl Kemp	Leon Fields
1962	Leon Fields	D.L. Venable	Ryman Maddox	Marshall Bruce	Herman Johnson	W.C. Kemp
1963	Marshall Bruce	D.L. Venable	Harold T. Pass	Frank Grizzle	Herman Johnson	W.J. Dodd
1964	E.E. Camp	D.L. Venable	Harold T. Pass	Frank Grizzle	Herbert A. Roberts	W.J. Dodd
1965	E.E. Camp	D.L. Venable	Simon Johnson	Frank Grizzle	Herbert A. Roberts	Charles Wallace
1966	E.E. Camp	W.E. Southerland	Simon Johnson	Frank Grizzle	Jack Atkins	Charles Wallace
1967	E.E. Camp	W.E. Southerland	Simon Johnson	Frank Grizzle	Jack Atkins	Kenneth Martin
1968	E.E. Camp	W.E. Southerland	Simon Johnson	Frank Grizzle	Jack Atkins	Kenneth Martin
1969	E.E. Camp	W.E. Southerland	Simon Johnson	Frank Grizzle	Jack Atkins	Kenneth Martin
1970	E.E. Camp	Sidney Hayes	Simon Johnson	Frank Grizzle	Jack Atkins	Kenneth Martin
1971	E.E. Camp	Jack Atkins	Simon Johnson	Frank Grizzle	Sidney Hayes	Kenneth Martin
1972	E.E. Camp	Curtis Westbrooks	Simon Johnson	Frank Grizzle	Sidney Hayes	Kenneth Martin
1973	E.E. Camp	Curtis Westbrooks	Simon Johnson	Frank Grizzle	Sidney Hayes	George Hazzard
1974	E.E. Camp	Curtis Westbrooks	Simon Johnson	Frank Grizzle	Floyd Henderson	George Hazzard
1975	Simon Johnson	Curtis Westbrooks	M.W. Brogdon	Jack Atkins	Floyd Henderson	Billy Appling
1976	Simon Johnson	Byron Cronic	M.W. Brogdon	Jack Atkins	Floyd Henderson	Billy Appling
1977	George Haggard	Byron Cronic	M.W. Brogdon	Jack Atkins	Thomas Morris	Hilda Hayes
1978	George Haggard	Byron Cronic	M.W. Brogdon	Jack Atkins	Thomas Morris	Hilda Hayes
1979	George Haggard	Byron Cronic	M.W. Brogdon	Michael Smith	Thomas Morris	Hilda Hayes
1980	George Haggard	Byron Cronic	M.W. Brogdon	Michael Smith	Thomas Morris	Jack Atkins
1981	Simon Johnson	Byron Cronic	Floyd Henderson	Michael Smith	Tommy Yancy	Jack Atkins
1982	Simon Johnson	Tim Robinson	Floyd Henderson	Connie Wiggins	Tommy Yancy	Jack Atkins
1983	Simon Johnson	Tim Robinson	Floyd Henderson	Connie Wiggins	Wayne Dixon	Jack Atkins
1984	Simon Johnson	Bobbie Queen	Floyd Henderson	Connie Wiggins	Wayne Dixon	Dave Hawthorne
1985	Simon Johnson	Bobbie Queen	Floyd Henderson	Connie Wiggins	Thomas Morris	Dave Hawthorne
1986	Simon Johnson	Bobbie Queen	Floyd Henderson	Jackie Caldwell	Thomas Morris	Dave Hawthorne

Sugar Hill City Officials, 1939-2008

Year	Mayor	Council Members				
1987	George Haggard	Bobbie Queen	Bobby Fowler	Jackie Caldwell	Thomas Morris	Dave Hawthorne
1988	George Haggard	Bobbie Queen	Bobby Fowler	Reuben Davis	Thomas Morris	Dave Hawthorne
1989	George Haggard	Bobbie Queen	Bobby Fowler	Reuben Davis	Thomas Morris	Dave Hawthorne
1990	George Haggard	Bobbie Queen	Bobby Fowler	Reuben Davis	Thomas Morris	Dave Hawthorne
1991	George Haggard	Bobbie Queen	Roger Everett	Reuben Davis	Thomas Morris	Dave Hawthorne
1992	George Haggard	Steve Bailey	Roger Everett	Reuben Davis	Thomas Morris	Jim Stanley
1993	Gary Webster	Steve Bailey	Jon Wright	Reuben Davis	Charles Spradlin	Jim Stanley
1994	Gary Webster	Steve Bailey	Jon Wright	Reuben Davis	Charles Spradlin	Jim Stanley
1995	Gary Webster	Steve Bailey	W.J. Dodd	Reuben Davis	Charles Spradlin	Jim Stanley
1996	Gary Webster	Steve Bailey	Tim Pugh	Reuben Davis	Charles Spradlin	Dorland Baird
1997	Gary Webster	Steve Bailey	Tim Pugh	Reuben Davis	Charles Spradlin	Dorland Baird
1998	Roberta Crabb	Steve Bailey	Tim Pugh	Reuben Davis	Michael Mosley	Gary Pirkle
1999	Roberta Crabb	Steve Bailey	Chris Abbey	Reuben Davis	Michael Mosley	Gary Pirkle
2000	Roberta Crabb	Meg Avery	Chris Abbey	Kim Hall	Michael Mosley	Gary Pirkle
2001	Roberta Crabb	Meg Avery	Chris Abbey	Kim Hall	Michael Mosley	Gary Pirkle (resigned August - Thomas Rhodes appt.)
2002	Gary Pirkle	Meg Avery	Chris Abbey	Kim Hall	Ron Johnson	Thomas Rhodes, Jr.
2003	Gary Pirkle	Meg Avery	Chris Abbey (resigned August - Steve Edwards)	Kim Hall	Ron Johnson	Thomas Rhodes, Jr. (resigned - Nick Thompson - Special Election)
2004	Gary Pirkle	Marc Cohen	Steve Edwards	Clint Thompson	Ron Johnson	Nick Thompson
2005	Gary Pirkle	Marc Cohen	Steve Edwards	Clint Thompson	Ron Johnson	Nick Thompson
2006	Gary Pirkle	Marc Cohen	Steve Edwards	Clint Thompson	Mike Sullivan	Nick Thompson
2007	Gary Pirkle	Marc Cohen	Steve Edwards	Clint Thompson	Mike Sullivan	Nick Thompson
2008	Gary Pirkle	Marc Cohen	Steve Edwards	Susie Gajewski	Mike Sullivan	Nick Thompson

Source: City of Sugar Hill

Suwanee City Officials, 1962-2008, Mayor & Posts 1-3				
Year	Mayor	Post 1	Post 2	Post 3
1962	Fred Tallant	John Davis	Burl Braziel	R.J. McDaniel
1963	Fred Tallant	John Davis	Burl Braziel	J. L Thompson
1964	John S. Herndon	James Burnette	Raymond Terry	J. L Thompson
1965	John S. Herndon	James Burnette	Raymond Terry	J. L Thompson
1966	John S. Herndon	James Burnette	Ted DeLay	J. L Thompson
1967	John S. Herndon	James Burnette	Ted DeLay	J. L Thompson
1968	John S. Herndon	James Burnette	John H. Goss	J. L Thompson
1969	John S. Herndon	James Burnette	John H. Goss	J. L Thompson
1970	John S. Herndon	James Burnette	John H. Goss	J. L Thompson
1971	John S. Herndon	James Burnette	John H. Goss	James W. Camp
1972	John S. Herndon	James Burnette	John H. Goss	James W. Camp
1973	Herman C. Terry	James Burnette	John H. Goss	Grady Daniel
1974	Herman C. Terry	James Burnette	Willard T. Roberts	Grady Daniel
1975	Herman C. Terry	James Burnette	Willard T. Roberts	Donnie Thigpen
1976	Herman C. Terry	James Burnette	Willard T. Roberts	Donnie Thigpen
1977	Herman C. Terry	James Burnette	Willard T. Roberts	Donnie Thigpen
1978	Herman C. Terry	James Burnette	Willard T. Roberts	Donnie Thigpen
1979	Herman C. Terry	James Burnette	Willard T. Roberts	Charles C. Cherry
1980	Herman C. Terry	James Burnette	Edgar Lewis	Charles C. Cherry
1981	Herman C. Terry	James Burnette	Edgar Lewis	Charles C. Cherry
1982	Herman C. Terry	James Burnette	Edgar Lewis	Loretta Roberts
1983	Jerry L. Brown	James Burnette	Edgar Lewis	Loretta Roberts
1984	Jerry L. Brown	James Burnette	Edgar Lewis	Loretta Roberts
1985	Herman C. Terry	James Burnette	Edgar Lewis	Charles C. Cherry
1986	Herman C. Terry	James Burnette	Ty McDaniel	Charles C. Cherry
1987	Herman C. Terry	James Burnette	Ty McDaniel	James Theus
1988*	Herman C. Terry	James Burnette	Richard Trice	Tom Mitchell
1989	Herman C. Terry	James Burnette	Richard Trice	Tom Mitchell
1990	Richard Trice	James Burnette	Joe Holt	Tom Mitchell
1991	Richard Trice	James Burnette	Joe Holt	Tom Mitchell
1992	Richard Trice	James Burnette	Joe Holt	Tom Mitchell
1993	Richard Trice	James Burnette	Joe Holt	Tom Mitchell
1994	Richard Trice	James Burnette	Joe Holt	John Barrett
1995	Richard Trice	James Burnette	Joe Holt	John Barrett
1996	Richard Trice	Jimmy Burnette	Joe Holt	John Barrett
1997	Richard Trice	Jimmy Burnette	Holt/Rispin	John Barrett
1998	Richard Trice	Jimmy Burnette	Jeannine Rispin	Dave Williams
1999	Chris Yoder	Jimmy Burnette	Jeannine Rispin	Dave Williams
2000	Nick Masino	Jimmy Burnette	Jeannine Rispin	Dave Williams
2001	Nick Masino	Jimmy Burnette	Jeannine Rispin	Dave Williams

Suwanee City Officials, 1962-2008, Mayor & Posts 1-3				
Year	Mayor	Post 1	Post 2	Post 3
2002	Nick Masino	Jimmy Burnette	Jeannine Rispin	Alan Landers
2003	Nick Masino	Jimmy Burnette	Jeannine Rispin	Alan Landers
2004	Nick Masino	Jimmy Burnette	Jeannine Rispin	Alan Landers
2005	Nick Masino	Jimmy Burnette	Jeannine Rispin	Alan Landers
2006	Nick Masino	Jimmy Burnette	Jeannine Rispin	Alan Landers
2007	Nick Masino	Jimmy Burnette	Jeannine Rispin	Landers/McOmber
2008	Dave Williams	Jimmy Burnette	Jeannine Rispin	Kevin McOmber

**** First year Posts designated in the record***
Source: City of Suwanee

Suwanee City Officials, Posts 4-5, Clerk, City Manager				
Year	Post 4	Post 5	Clerk	City Manager
1962	Ray Puckett		Ralph Kennedy	
1963	Ray Puckett	John Pierce	Ralph Kennedy	
1964	Ray Puckett	John Pierce	F. R. Puckett	
1965	Willard T. Roberts	R. A. Heard	Puckett/Terry	
1966	Willard T. Roberts	R. A. Heard	Herman C. Terry	
1967	Willard T. Roberts	R. A. Heard	Herman C. Terry	
1968	Willard T. Roberts	R. A. Heard	Herman C. Terry	
1969	Willard T. Roberts	R. A. Heard	Herman C. Terry	
1970	Willard T. Roberts	R. A. Heard	Herman C. Terry	
1971	Willard T. Roberts	Charles C. Cherry	Herman C. Terry	
1972	Willard T. Roberts	Charles C. Cherry	Herman C. Terry	
1973	John S. Herndon	Charles C. Cherry	Horace R. Cook	
1974	John S. Herndon	Charles C. Cherry	Horace R. Cook	
1975	John S. Herndon	Charles C. Cherry	Horace R. Cook	
1976	John S. Herndon	Charles C. Cherry	Amy E. Johnsa	
1977	Howard Richardson	Floyd Thompson	Amy E. Johnsa	
1978	Howard Richardson	Floyd Thompson	Amy E. Johnsa	
1979	John S. Herndon	Floyd Thompson	Amy E. Johnsa	
1980	John S. Herndon	Floyd Thompson	Amy E. Johnsa	
1981	John S. Herndon	David Reed	Amy E. Johnsa	
1982	John S. Herndon	David Reed	Johnsa/Heard	
1983	Donald R. Daniel	David Reed	Doris T. Heard	
1984	Donald R. Daniel	David Reed	Doris T. Heard	
1985	Tom Mitchell	David E. Smith	Doris T. Heard	
1986	Tom Mitchell	David E. Smith	Doris T. Heard	
1987	Tom Mitchell	David E. Smith	Doris T. Heard	

Suwanee City Officials, Posts 4-5, Clerk, City Manager				
Year	Post 4	Post 5	Clerk	City Manager
1988*	David E. Smith	James B. Theus	Kathy Lewis	
1989	David E. Smith	James B. Theus	Kathy Lewis	
1990	David E. Smith	Amy Johnsa	Kathy Lewis	
1991	David E. Smith	Jeannine Rispin	Kathy Lewis	
1992	David E. Smith	Jeannine Rispin	Kathy Lewis	
1993	David E. Smith	Jeannine Rispin	Kathy Lewis	
1994	Chris Yoder	Eileen Regan	Kathy Lewis	
1995	Chris Yoder	Eileen Regan	Kathy Lewis	
1996	Chris Yoder	Eileen Regan	Kathy Lewis	
1997	Chris Yoder	Eileen Regan	Lewis/Pendley	Hardin Watkins
1998	Chris Yoder	Alex Stone	Lisa Pendley	Hardin Watkins
1999	Andrew Krieman	Alex Stone	Lisa Pendley	Hardin Watkins
2000	Andrew Krieman	Alex Stone	Lisa Pendley	Hardin Watkins
2001	Andrew Krieman	Alex Stone	Lisa Pendley	Hardin Watkins
2002	Andrew Krieman/ Jace Brooks	Carol Hassell	Diane Boone	Hardin Watkins
2003	Jace Brooks	Carol Hassell	Boone/Rogers	Hardin Watkins
2004	Jace Brooks	Carol Hassell	Elvira Rogers	Hardin Watkins
2005	Jace Brooks	Carol Hassell	Elvira Rogers	Hardin Watkins
2006	Jace Brooks	Dan Foster	Elvira Rogers	Hardin Watkins
2007	Jace Brooks	Dan Foster	Elvira Rogers	Watkins/Allen
2008	Jace Brooks	Dan Foster	Elvira Rogers	Marty Allen

First year Posts designated in the record
Source: City of Suwanee

Chairmen of the Gwinnett Chamber of Commerce, 1947-2008		
Year	Chairman	Organization
1947	Marvin Allison*	Attorney
1948	Marvin Allison*	Attorney
1949	Milton McLain*	Buford Builders Supply
1950	J. F. Brannan*	Ford Dealer, Lawrenceville
1951	J.F. Brannan*	Ford Dealer, Lawrenceville
1952	J.F. Brannan*	Ford Dealer, Lawrenceville
1953	Pete Sever*	General Motors
1954	Pete Sever*	General Motors
1955	Walter B. White	Georgia Power Company
1956	Walter B. White	Georgia Power Company
1957	Clyde J. Roberts*	Belk Department Store
1958	K.A. (Ken) McMillon	Georgia Power Company
1959	K.A. (Ken) McMillon	Georgia Power Company
1960	K.A. (Ken) McMillon	Georgia Power Company
1961	Glenn Smith and Earl Story*	
1962	David Kistner*	Berkmere Farm
1963	David Kistner*	Berkmere Farm
1964	W.S. (Bill) Carrington*	Southern Bell
1965	Harold Grumann*	
1966	Thomas Nash	Nash Chevrolet
1967	Don Carroll	Bank of Duluth
1968	Ralph Saul	Saul's Department Store
1969	Earle Simpson*	Simpson Drug Company
1970	J. Grady Coleman	Gwinnett Bank and Trust Company
1971	Robert S. (Bob) Eldridge	Norcross Supply Company
1972	Jones Webb	Webb, Fowler and Tanner, attorneys
1973	Earle Snell	E.R. Snell Contractors, Inc.
1974	J.D. Caswell	Caswell Properties
1975	Grant Hayes	Hayes, James & Associates
1976	Dwight L. Craig*	Gwinnett County Bank
1977	Leo L. Rainey, Jr.	First National Bank of Gwinnett
1978	Leo L. Rainey, Jr.	First National Bank of Gwinnett
1979	John F. (Jack) Sawyer*	Lilburn Insurance
1980	Paul F. Duke	Peachtree Corners
1981	Richard S. (Dick) Myrick, Sr.	The Myrick Company
1982	Glenn Harben	Homebuilder
1983	Charles R. (Charlie) Brown	Technology Park/Atlanta
1984	J.W. Benefield	Modern Electric Company
1985	Herb Hamby	Hamby Construction Company
1986	T. Michael (Mike) Tennant	Alston & Bird
1987	Stephen Rogers	Arthur Andersen & Company
1988	John Schwab	Peachtree World of Tennis
1989	J. Leonard Cyphers*	Blockbuster Video
1990	Tom Morris	SunTrust Bank

Chairmen of the Gwinnett Chamber of Commerce, 1947-2008

Year	Chairman	Organization
1991	Thomas D. (Tom) Jones	Gwinnett Daily News
1992	Gene L. Ussery, Jr.	Georgia Power Company
1993	Glenn S. White	The Bank of Gwinnett County
1994	Peter F. Boyce	Attorney at Law
1995	Rick Porter	Richport Properties
1996	Roger Willis	Jackson Electric Membership Corporation
1997	David Nicholson	Rock-Tenn Company
1998	Forrest Robinson	Weeks Corporation
1999	Thomas J. (Tom) Andersen	Andersen, Tate, Mahaffey & McGarity, PC
2000	David Seago	Georgia Power Company
2001	Sharon Rigsby	Gwinnett Technical College
2002	David Snell	E.R. Snell Contractors, Inc.
2003	Rick Chandler	Chandler & Britt, LLC
2004	Bill Russell	Russell Landscape Group, Inc.
2005	Richard Tucker	Arlington Capital, LLC
2006	Wayne Shackelford	Gresham Smith & Partners
2007	Tom Martin	Gwinnett Community Bank
2008	Bill McCargo	Scientific Atlanta, a Cisco Company
2009	Kerry Armstrong	Duke Realty Corporation

***** deceased**

Source: Gwinnett Chamber of Commerce

Gwinnett Chamber Executive Officials

Year	Name
April 1947 - February 1948	Marvin Allison (founder)*
February 1948 - September 1948	H. Ross Holt*
September 1948 - January 1949	L.D. "Dutch" Ewing*
February 1949 - April 1952	no information
May 1952 - December 1953	Pete Sever*
January 1954 - December 1958	Mrs. Jean Jones
January 1959 - August 1960	William J. (Bill) Mosley*
September 1960 - December 1961	No record
January 1962 - November 1963	James M. Matthews
January 1964 - 1969	Robert L. Vansant*
1969 - December 1972	Golden A. Pirkle*
July 1972 - October 1980	Leonard A. Gilbert* (first full time president)
October 1980 - March 1981	John F. (Jack) Sawyer* (interim)
March 1981 - December, 1992	John F. (Jack) Sawyer*
January, 1993 - May, 1993	J.W. Benefield (interim)
May 1993 - January 1994	John W. (Jack) Talley, Jr.
February 1994 - October 1995	John F. Schraudenbach
May 1996 - September 2003	Richard L. Tucker
September 2003 -	Jim Maran

***** deceased**
Source: Gwinnett Chamber of Commerce

Gwinnett Chamber of Commerce Citizen of the Year Award Winners		
Year	Winner	Representing
1977	Rev. W.C. Corley	First Baptist Church, Lawrenceville
1978	E. R. Snell **	E.R. Snell Contractors Inc.
1979	J.W. Benefield	Gwinnett School Superintendent
1980	Jesse C. Long	Greater Atlanta Christian School
1981	Dr. Alton C. Crews **	Gwinnett School Superintendent
1982	Calvin Parsons **	Parsons Store, Duluth
1983	T.W. (Tom) Briscoe **	Former Snellville Mayor
1984	Faye B. Moore	Lilburn Woman's Club
1985	Paul A. Duke	Peachtree Corners Inc.
1986	D. Scott Hudgens Jr. **	Hudgens Company, Developer
1987	Robert D. Fowler **	Gwinnett Daily News
1988	Leo L. Rainey Jr.	First National Bank of Gwinnett
1989	Louise Radloff	Gwinnett School Board
1990	Sen. Steve Reynolds **	Reynolds Oil Company
1991	Charles R. Brown	Technology Park/Atlanta
1992	J.D. Caswell	Caswell Realty
1993	Connie Wiggins	Gwinnett Clean and Beautiful
1994	Elliott Brack	Atlanta Journal-Constitution
1995	Jim Cowart	Jim Cowart Realty
1996	Francis "Sonny" McDaniel	Delta Air Lines (ret.)
1997	Homer Stark	Gwinnett Superior Court Judge
1998	T. Michael Tennant	Alston and Bird
1999	Wayne H. Mason	Madison Enterprises
2000	Wayne Shackelford	Gresham, Smith and Partners
2001	Phylecia Wilson	American Cancer Society
2002	Jones Webb	Webb, Fowler and Tanner
2003	F. Wayne Hill	Gwinnett County Commission
2004	J. Alvin Wilbanks	Gwinnett School Superintendent
2005	Dr. Miles Mason	Duluth Physician
2006	John D. Stephens	Contractor
2007	Wayne Sikes	Gwinnett Medical Center
***** deceased***		
Source: Gwinnett Chamber of Commerce		

Public Service Award Winners of Gwinnett Chamber

Year	Winners
1977	John Crunkleton, Uhland F. Freeman, Sr., Ray Mattison, Lillian Webb, Marion Allison Webb
1978	B. B. Harris, Charles Hollifield, Mildred Martin, Charles Pittard, Wayne Shackelford, Ray Gunnin
1979	Fred Banks, L. D. (Dutch) Ewing, Vinnie Lowrey, Clarence Monfort, Clyde Roberts
1980	Cecil Gober, Gwinnett Daily News, Thomas Livsey, Steve Reynolds, Grace Snell
1981	Minor Corley, Carolyn Vance Foreman, Mickey Glasco, Mary Kay Jordan, Charles Martin
1982	Reinette Fortune Hyer, Dave H. Keever, Sr., Henry Peevy, Jimmy D. Puckett, Judge Alton Tucker
1983	Emmett Clower, III, Gwinnett County Homebuilders Association, Lloyd Harris, Louise Radloff, Troy Sharpton
1984	Maron Buice, J D. Caswell, Avery Graves, Gartrell Nash, George Pierce, Sr., Carvis P. Williams
1985	T. Carl Buice, Carey Cash, Florentine (Tine) Liegerot, Judge Reid Merritt, Robert Powell
1986	Boyd Q. Baggett, Charlotte M. Dispain, Mary Louise Stark, Tim Szymanski, Janice West
1987	Colonel John Adams, Jeanine Gullett, Chief Ron Houck (City of Lilburn), Dr. Cecil Miller, Kent A. Ryan
1988	Beauty Baldwin, Elliott Brack, Robert F. (Bob) Duncan, H. Rhodes Jordan (City of Lawrenceville), K. A. (Ken) McMillon
1989	Bill Baughman, George Black, Betty McMichael (City of Snellville), Vic Verdi, Connie Wiggins
1990	Gerald Davidson, Jr., J. T. (Shorty) Howell, Francis (Sonny) McDowall, A. W. Peters, Ann Smiley
1991	Jim Cowart, Dr. Jim Crutcher, Grace Harris, Betty Mauldin (City of Norcross)
1992	Earley Biffle (City of Buford), Winnie Guthrie Cain Corley (Civic Ctr), Bronnie Maxey, Hugh Frederick Snell, Kathryn Parsons Willis
1993	Dr. Brooks Coleman, Jean Cole (City of Lilburn), Jack Gantz, Dr. Laurence Lesser, The Quinn House
1994	Judge Handsel Morgan, Pastor William Sheals, Sherry Tennant, Russell (Russ) Weaver
1995	Polly Branan, Bartow Jenkins (City of Lawrenceville), Carolyn Collins, O. Millard Peevy, Glenn S. White
1996	Selma Medlock Cheeley, Rich Panyik, Jim Steele, Dr. Preston (Jack) Wall, Phylecia Wilson
1997	Phillip Beard, Charlotte Lousie Brinkley Gardner, Lorena Pharr, Chief Carl D. White, Richard Sikes
1998	Norman Baggs, Carolyn Hil, Edwin Richard Snell, Jr., Helen Tapp
	Legacy Award - Jimmy Mason
1999	Margaret Parsons Andrews, Nancy Chandler, L. E. "Sonny" Deavours, James F. "Jim" Pack, Forrest Robinson
2000	James Freeman, Tommy Hughes, Loretta Roberts, Rufus Tipton, Judy Waters
	Legacy Award - Calvin Fitchett
2001	Donnis Bowman, Jim Hinshaw, Sr., Charlotte Nash, J. Alvin Wilbanks, Roger Willis
2002	Millard Bowen, Barbara King, Tommy Melton, Rick O'Brien, Judge Jim Oxendine, John D. Stephens
2003	Wayne Sikes, Ruth Strickland, Tom Wheeler, Charles Wilder, Preston Williams
	Legacy Award - Ray Nash, D. Scott Hudgens Humanitarian Award - Peachtree Christian Hospice
2004	Tom Martin, Bill McCargo, Monte Nichols, Marina Peed, Sharon Rigsby, David Seago
	Legacy Award - Henry Howard, D. Scott Hudgens Humanitarian Award - Govenor George Busbee
2005	Roddy Sturdivant, Pat Brown, Joyce Ogletree, Rudy Bowen, Tom Andersen, David Snell
	Legacy Award - Warren Hendrix, D. Scott Hudgens Humanitarian Award - Hi Hope Service Center
2006	Stephen K. Hill, Jim Hinkle, Barbara Howard, Kerry Armstrong, Mike Hayes, Sue Morris
	Legacy Award - Clyde Roberts, D. Scott Hudgens Humanitarian Award - Gwinnett Children's Shelter
2007	Miguel Candelaria, Butch Conway, Karen C. Hill, Herman Pennamon Jr., Clyde and Sandra Strickland, Richard Chandler, Dr. Bill Russell
	Legacy Award- Bobby Sikes; D. Scott Hudgens Humanitarian Award: Annandale at Suwanee.

Source: Gwinnett Chamber of Commerce

Hospital System and Related Boards Members, 2008	
System Name	
Hospital Authority of Gwinnett County	Board of Directors Wayne Sikes, chair; Scott Batterton, Roy Beaty, Keith Carnes, Dr. Gale Hey, David Peterson, Edward W. Radford, Gay Wiley Shook and Bruce Still.
Gwinnett Health Systems Inc.	Board of Directors Steven Boyd, chair; Wayne Sikes, Kathryn P. Willis, Willard C. Hearin, MD, Chung H. Lee, JD, Jay Desai, MD, Miles H. Mason III, MD, Joseph Finley, MD, Tom Martin, Carolyn Hill, Eric Kreimer, David McCleskey, Edward Radford, Ph. D, Jock Connell, Manfred Sandler, MD.
Gwinnett Hospital System, Inc.	Board of Directors Steven Boyd, chair, Miles H. Mason III MD, Chung H. Lee, JD, Edward Radford, Manfred Sandler, MD.
Gwinnett Managed Care, Inc.	Board of Directors Jay Desai, MD, chair; David McCleskey, Edward Radford, Manfred Sandler, MD, Steve Boyd
Gwinnett Medical Services, Inc.	Board of Directors Joseph Finley, MD, chair, Chung H. Lee, JD, Kathryn P. Willis, Steven Boyd.
Gwinnett Medical Properties, Inc.	Board of Directors Edward Radford, chair, Willard C. Hearin MD, Kathryn P. Willis, Steven Boyd.
Gwinnett Hospital System Foundation	Board of Trustees Manfred Sandler, MD, chair; Ethel and Tom Anderson, chairs, Board Development; Beth Philips and Kerry Armstrong,co-chairs, Community Affairs; Bartow Morgan, chair, Development; Hector Baro, Lori Carnes, Jim Ellis, Carolyn Hill, Stephen K. Hill, Barbara Howard, Tom Martin, Wayne Mason, Bill Russell, Wayne Sikes, David Snell, Bruce Still, Clyde Strickland, Richard Tucker, Kathryn Willis, Phil Wolfe.
Source: Hospital Authority of Gwinnett County	

Gwinnett Medical Center Auxiliary Presidents, 1961-2008

Year	Person
1984-85	Anne Ranwater
1985-87	Diane Bayless
1987-89	Jackie Tadsen
1989-91	Vicki Brandt
1991-93	Martha (Marty) Henck
1993-95	Betty Walls
1995-96	Janfra Alexander
1996-97	Del Podsiadlo
1997-98	Bernice Johnson
1998-99	Angeline Holmes
1999-00	Ruth Ann Chapin
2000-01	Del Podsiadlo
2001-02	Cheryl Gifford
2002-03	Bernice Johnson
2003-04	Maureen O'Rourke
2004-05	Peggy Britt
2005-06	Ruth Ann Chapin
2006-07	Carole Martin
2007-08	Phyllis Patterson
2008-09	Carol Bullock

Source: Gwinnett Medical Center

Leaders of Council for Quality Growth	
Year	Chairman
1986	Alvin Ray Weeks Jr.
1987	Alvin Ray Weeks Jr.
1988	Frank B. McGowan
1989	Thomas W. Wheeler Jr.
1990	Allen M. Richardson
1991	Richard L. Porter
1992	Bryan Cohen
1993	Roger C Willis
1994	Michael K. Dominy
1995	Alfred F. Shiba
1996	Thomas J. Andersen
1997	Glenn S. White
1998	Forrest L. Adair
1999	J. Dennis Billew
2000	J.R. Connolly
2001	Streve Gualtney
2002	Jim Braden
2003	Mike Guynn
2004	T. Michael Tennant
2005	Kerry Armstrong
2006	Woody Snell
2007	David Seago
2008	Wade Beavers
Title changed from president to chairman in 2003.	
Source: Council for Quality Growth	

Button Gwinnett - Four Pillar Winners of Council for Quality Growth	
Year	Recipient
1990	Steve Reynolds
1991	Wayne Shackelford
1992	J.W. Benefield
1993	D. Scott Hudgens
1994	Wayne H. Mason
1995	Virgil R. Williams
1996	Paul D. Duke
1997	Jim Cowart
1998	J.D. Caswell
1999	A. Ray Weeks
2000	Louise Radloff
2001	F. Wayne Hill
2002	George Busbee
2003	Richard L. Tucker
2004	Charlie Brown
2005	Johnny Isakson
2006	John Wieland
2007	John A. Williams
Source: Council for Quality Growth	

Gwinnett Bar Association Presidents, 1961-2009

Term	President	Term	President
1961-62	Edward L. Owens	1985-86	Dennis T. Still
1962-63	Edward L. Owens	1986-87	David S. Lipscomb
1963-64	Edward L. Owens	1987-88	Alan Mulinax
1964-65	Handsel G. Morgan	1988-89	Barbara Bishop
1965-66	R.F.Duncan	1989-90	Mike Greene
1966-67	Jones Webb	1990-91	Robert Mock
1967-68	H. Rhodes Jordan	1991-92	Lee Washburn
1968-69	G. Hughel Harrison	1992-93	Larry Duttweiler
1969-70	Gene Reeves	1993-94	Phyllis Miller
1970-71	Gene Reeves	1994-95	Margaret Washburn
1971-72	Bryant Huff	1995-96	Kathy Schrader
1972-73	William G. Tanner	1996-97	Keith Miles
1973-74	George Gibson Dean, II	1997-98	Judy King
1974-75	James A. Henderson	1998-99	Ronnie Batchelor
1975-76	James W. Garner	1999-00	Jessica Towne
1976-77	Joseph E. Cheeley, Jr.	2000-01	Lyle Porter
1977-78	Joseph E. Cheeley, Jr.	2001-02	Melanie Williams
1978-79	William J. Porter, Jr.	2002-03	Pat O'Kelley
1979-80	T. Michael Tennant	2003-04	Sherriann Hicks
1980-81	J. L. Edmondson	2004-05	Mike Sheffield
1981-82	Gerald Davidson	2005-06	Francis Kuo
1982-83	Howard E. Cook	2006-07	Jeff Hicks
1983-84	Claira Mitcham Zellers	2007-08	Jorgia Northrup
1984-85	J. Michael McGarity	2008-09	Carole Cox

Source: Gwinnett Bar Association

Gwinnett Historical Society Presidents, 1966-2008

Year	President	Year	President
1966	Marvin Nash Worthy	1988	Marvin Hughes
1967	Marvin Nash Worthy	1989	Marvin Hughes
1968	Marvin Nash Worthy	1990	Phyllis Hughes
1969	Annette Williams Tucker	1991	Phyllis Hughes
1970	John Hood	1992	Wanda Burney McHann
1971	John Hood	1993	John W. "Bill" Baughman
1972	Hiram Plunkett	1994	John W. "Bill" Baughman
1973	James M. Edwards	1995	Betty Dixon
1974	James M. Edwards	1996	Betty Dixon
1975	Roy E. Hutchens	1997	Frances Huff Johnson
1976	Roy E. Hutchens	1998	Frances Huff Johnson
1977	Charles L. Pentecost	1999	Phyllis Garner Davis
1978	John W. Chatham	2000	Phyllis Garner Davis
1979	John W. Chatham	2001	Elaine Conner Roberts
1980	John W. Chatham	2002	Elaine Conner Roberts
1981	W. Dorsey Stancil	2003	Lucas Harsh
1982	W. Dorsey Stancil	2004	Lucas Harsh
1983	John W. "Bill" Baughman	2005	Terry Manning
1984	John W. "Bill" Baughman	2006	Steven P. Starling
1985	Alice Smythe McCabe	2007	Steven P. Starling
1986	Jon McDaniel	2008	Spencer Roberts
1987	Jon McDaniel	***Source: Gwinnett Historical Society***	

Gwinnett Historical Society Trustees

Five trustees govern the Gwinnett Historical Society. They are appointed by the president for staggered terms, and approved by the Executive Board.
Three trustees were initially named in 1977: Mildred Martin, Jay Summerour and John Hood.
The following have served as trustees at these dates:

Mildred Martin, 1977-1979	Alice McCabe, 1990-2001	Spence Roberts, 1997 – 2001
John Hood, 1977-1981	Wanda McHann, 1990	Vivian Coogler, 1998
Jay Summerour, 1977-1983	Marvin Hughes, 1990–1994	Jane Edwards, 1999 – 2000
Bill Baughman, 1977-92, 1996-2010	Joye Quinn, 1991-1992; 1997-2008	Tom Ewing, 2000 – 2004
Phyllis Hughes, 1987-90	Jon McDaniel, 1992–1995	Rachel Bronnum, 2001 – 2007
Frazier Duke, 1987-1988	Carla Rapp, 1992	Terry Manning, 2002 – 2003
Charles Bagwell, 1987	Lynn Moon, 1993 – 1994	Paula McGee, 2004
Janis Sawyer, 1987	Jean Todd, 1993 – 1995	Elaine Roberts, 2006 – 2009
Bill Dalton, 1989	Joel Fletcher, 1995 – 1996	Rick Lux, 2006-2007
James Cobb, 1989-91	Kathy Woodcock, 1995 – 1997	Vicki Watkins, 2008
Susan Frazier, 1989	Phyllis Davis, 1996, 2005, 2008 – 2009	***Source: Gwinnett Historical Society***

Officers of Northeast Georgia Foundation

Year	President	End of Year Assets	Executive Director
1985	Charles R. Brown	$170,700	Patricia M. Brown
1986	Ray Weeks	$919,487	Patricia M. Brown
1987	Paul Duke	$2,189,285	Patricia M. Brown
1988	Mike Tennant	$2,820,246	Brown/Roberts
1989	Mike Tennant	$2,792,185	Deborah H. Roberts
1990	J.D. Caswell	$2,800,000	Deborah H. Roberts
1991	J.D. Caswell	$3,182,852	Deborah H. Roberts
1992	William E. McLendon	$4,015,640	Deborah H. Roberts
1993	William E. McLendon	$4,340,704	Joseph J. Estafen
1994	Thomas W. Wheeler, Jr.	$4,076,029	Joseph J. Estafen
1995	Thomas W. Wheeler, Jr.	$5,137,310	Joseph J. Estafen
1996	Thomas D. Jones	$6,257,976	Joseph J. Estafen
1997	Thomas D. Jones	$7,655,432	Joseph J. Estafen
1998	Jeff D. Manry	$9,751,057	Joseph J. Estafen
1999	Jeff D. Manry	$10,512,043	Joseph J. Estafen
2000	Donald W. Dawson	$11,365,900	Joseph J. Estafen
2001	Donald W. Dawson	$12,098,961	Joseph J. Estafen
2002	Bill Russell	$11,199,800	Joseph J. Estafen
2003	Bill Russell	$14,539,984	Joseph J. Estafen
2004	Ethel D. Andersen	$14,138,549	Judy Waters
2005	Ethel D. Andersen	$16,374,290	Judy Waters
2006	Bartow Morgan, Jr.	$17,727,031	Judy Waters
2007	Bartow Morgan, Jr.	$32,223,967	Judy Waters
2008	Joe McCart		Judy Waters

Note: In 2001, the name was changed from the Gwinnett Foundation to the Community Foundation of Northeast Georgia

Source: Community Foundation of Northeast Georgia

Gwinnett Convention and Visitors Bureau Board Members

Year	Chairman	Members	Director
1990	John Schwab	Willie Bentley, Mike Berg, Chuck Button, Scott Ferguson, Mike Huff, Kevin Regan, Jack Sawyer, Tom Wheeler.	Brenda Branch
1991	John Schwab	Willie Bentley, Mike Berg, Chuck Button, Curtis McGill, Kevin Regan, Jack Sawyer, Lillian Webb, Tom Wheeler.	Brenda Branch
1992	John Schwab	Willie Bentley, Mike Berg, Sam Brownlee, Nancy Gullickson, Mike Lowery, Curtis McGill, Kevin Regan, Jack Sawyer, Lillian Webb.	Brenda Branch
1993	John Schwab	Willie Bentley, Mike Berg, Nancy Gullickson, Tommy Hughes, Mike Lowery, Kevin Regan, Jack Sawyer, Lillian Webb, Doug Williamson.	Brenda Branch
1994	John Schwab	J.W. Benefield, Willie Bentley, Nancy Gullickson, Tommy Hughes, Mike Lowery, Bill Northquest, Kevin Regan, Bill Short, Doug Williamson.	Susan Cohen
1995	John Schwab	J.W. Benefield, Betsy Canari, Nancy Gullickson, Tommy Hughes, Bob Lamar, Kevin Regan, John Schraudenbach, Natalie Shoaf, Richard Tucker, Judy Waters.	Susan Cohen
1996	Richard Tucker	J.W. Benefield, Betsy Canari, Joe Fidelibus, Nancy Gullickson, Tommy Hughes, Bob Lamar, John Schwab, Judy Waters, Kevin Regan	Susan Cohen; Christopher Walters
1997	Joe Fidelibus	J.W. Benefield, Jeff Fuller, Nancy Gullickson, Ed Hauptmann, Ray Hobbs, Tommy Hughes, Bob Lamar, Tom Martin, Richard Tucker, Judy Waters.	Christopher Walters; Bob Harris
1998	Joe Fidelibus	J.W. Benefield, Jeff Fuller, Nancy Gullickson, Ray Hobbs, Tommy Hughes, Bob Lamar, Tom Martin, Richard Tucker, Judy Waters.	Bob Harris
1999	Joe Fidelibus	J.W. Benefield, Nancy Gullickson, Tommy Hughes, Bob Lamar, Tom Martin, Meredith Mason, Richard Tucker, Judy Waters.	Bob Harris
2000	Tom Martin	J.W. Benefield, Erick Collazo, Joe Fidelibus, Nancy Gullickson, Tommy Hughes, Bob Lamar, Meredith Mason, Richard Tucker, Judy Waters.	Bob Harris
2001	Tommy Hughes	J.W. Benefield, Joe Fidelibus, Nancy Gullickson, Tim Huffman, Kevin Kenerly, Robert A. Lamar, Meredith Mason, Tom Martin, Octavio Ortiz, Patti Muise, Richard Tucker.	Caryn McGarity
2002	Tommy Hughes	J.W. Benefield, Joe Fidelibus, Nancy Gullickson, Tim Huffman, Craig Hillyard, Kevin Kenerly, Tom Martin, Meredith Mason, Marcia Neaton-Griggs, Art Rilling, Richard Tucker.	Caryn McGarity
2003	Tommy Hughes	J.W. Benefield, Joe Fidelibus, Nancy Gullickson, Craig Hillyard, Kevin Kenerly, Jim Maran, Meredith Mason, Tom Martin, Marcia Neaton, Art Rilling, Richard Tucker.	Caryn McGarity
2004	Tom Martin	J.W. Benefield, Joe Fidelibus, Nancy Gullickson, Craig Hillyard, Tommy Hughes, Kevin Kenerly, Meredith Mason, Jim Maran, Marcia Neaton, Art Riling, Richard Tucker.	Caryn McGarity
2005	Tom Martin	J.W. Benefield, Ernie Catanzaro, Joe Fidelibus, Lorraine Green, Nancy Gullickson, Tommy Hughes, Kevin Kenerly, Meredith Mason, Jim Maran, Frank Quallen, Art Rilling, Richard Tucker.	Caryn McGarity
2006	Tom Martin	J.W. Benefield, Joe Fidelibus, Lorraine Green, Nancy Gullickson, Tommy Hughes, Dave Kaplan, Kevin Kenerly, Meredith Mason, Jim Maran, Frank Quallen, Art Rilling, Richard Tucker.	Caryn McGarity
2007	Richard Tucker	J.W. Benefield, Lorraine Green, Nancy Gullickson, Tommy Hughes, Dave Kaplan, Bert Nasuti, Meredith Mason, Jim Maran, Frank Quallen, Art Rilling, Richard Tucker, Tom Martin.	Caryn McGarity
2008	Richard Tucker	J.W. Benefield, Lorraine Green, Tommy Hughes, Dave Kaplan, Bert Nasuti, Meredith Mason, Jim Maran, Art Rilling, Jeannine Rispin, Richard Tucker and Tom Martin. Vacancies are from the Arts Center and hospitality industry.	Caryn McGarity

Source: Gwinnett Convention and Visitors Bureau

Gwinnett Realtors Presidents, 1970-2008

Officially known as the Northeast Atlanta Metro Assoc of Realtors, Inc.

Organized Nov . 12, 1969 with 31 members

Year	President	End of Year Membership
1970	Boyd Duncan	79
1971	Thomas E. Howell	124
1972	Jim Hood	198
1973	C. Arnold Huff	334
1974	Elbert C. Durden	535
1975	Shelba J. Holmes	491
1976	Bob Wood	509
1977	David Nix	708
1978	Sadie Shaffer	875
1979	Carl Abbott	1,054
1980	Fancy Pritchett	1,351
1981	Joe Anziano	1,235
1982	Ron Taylor	1,078
1983	J. Lamar Frazier	1,247
1984	James Robinson	1,570
1985	Bill Lawson	1,791
1986	Jim Pollock	2,100
1987	Joan Johnson	2,417
1988	Bob Jones	2,484
1989	Dana Dean Bauguss	2,470
1990	David LeCraw	2,243
1991	Garland Smith	2,034
1992	John McCrory	1,900
1993	Donna Traylor	1,929
1994	Kathy Taylor	1,987
1995	Art Robinson	2,010
1996	Becky Bicknell	2,117
1997	Jan Baker	2,239
1998	Robert Stedeford	2,392
1999	Maureen Crean	2,353
2000	William Lewis	2,604
2001	Norma Santana	2,762
2002	Andrew Willis	3,352
2003	Garnett Nash	3,504
2004	Bob Hartwell	4,002
2005	Dina Pinard	4,232
2006	Mike Small	5,496
2007	Peggy Slappey	5,909
2008	Timothy McFadden	

Note: name change came in 1996

Source: Northeast Atlanta Metro Association of Realtors, Inc.

Chairs of Gwinnett Relay-for-Life, 1994-2009			
Year	Chair	Firm	Raised
1994	Phylecia Wilson	Volunteer	$119,926
1995	Phylecia Wilson	Volunteer	$242,242
1996	Phylecia Wilson	Volunteer	$304,699
1997	Phylecia Wilson	Volunteer	$552,653
1998	Lisa Tully		$901,839
1999	Paula Hill		$1,151,343
2000	Barbara Verzyl Linda Story	GC Public Schools	$1,458,295
2001	Barbara Verzyl Linda Story	GCPS	$1,881,299
2002	Nancy Stanberry-Kellam Joslyn Bacalis	GC Public Library Dan Cook Associates	$2,006,697
2003	Joslyn Bacalis Diane Fahring	Dan Cook Associates GCPS	$1,828,114
2004	Diane Fahring Mary Root	GCPS Volunteer	$2,107,998
2005	Mary Root Duane Downs	Volunteer Retired	$2,216,021
2006	Duane Downs Diana Preston	Retired GCPS	$2,409,697
2007	Diana Preston Phil Hoskins	GCPS Gwinnett County	$2,571,681
2008	Phil Hoskins Diane Fahring	Gwinnett County GCPS	*$2,500,000
2009	Diane Fahring Chuck Button	GCPS JJ&G	
Estimate as of June 1, 2008			
Source: Gwinnett Unit, American Cancer Society			

Presidents of Gwinnett Children's Shelter	
Year	Persons
1986-1988	Sherri Hague
1988-1989	Rob Waller
1989-1990	Paul Steckenrider
1990-1992	Marty Shaw
1992-1994	Roger Willis
1994-1996	Jesse Long
1996-1998	Richard Myrick
1998-2000	David Seago
2000-2002	Susie Hite
2002-2004	Jim Hinshaw
2004-2006	Tom Andersen
2006-2008	Lynn Price
Source: Gwinnett Children's Shelter	

Leadership Gwinnett Alumni

Year	Class Members
1986	Peter Boyce, Phil Boyd, Gary Cobb, Pat Corleto, Jim Crawford, Melita Easters, Lee Genson, Mary Kay Jordan, Julie Keeton, Ann Maize, Charles Mason, Don McEnery, Maribeth Minschwarner, Tom Morgan, Charotte Nash, Matthew Nichols, Emily Powell, Diana Preston, Forrest Robinson, Kent Ryan, Robbie Stedeford, Wayne Tanner, Lee Thompson, Russ Weaver, Connie Wiggins, Alvin Wilbanks, Roland Williams, Sheldon Zimmerman.
1987	Thie Autry, Mike Ayers, Scott Batterton, Karen Black, Darrell Chaney, Jerry Colley, Leonard Cyphers, David Fincher, Gwen Ganntt, Gary Gettis, Kay Harvey, Frances Hesser, Charles Hudson, Paul Kelman, Jonathan Ledford, Ed Loomis, Terry McCready, Faye B. Moore, Jann W. Moore, Janice Nevins, Bill Sanders, Wayne Sikes, Linda H. Sims, Richard Sissom, Sarah Strelitz, Vicki Sweeny, Helen Tapp, Gordon Van Mol, Jean White.
1988	David Crews, Janet Dickinson, Barbara Donald, Ed Driver, Fraser Duke, Sherry Hague, Susie Hite, Michael Huff, Otis P. Jones, Jane Karwoski, George Kerns, Jeff Moore, Joyce Ogletree, Richard Panyik, Grant Reed, Frances Rees, John Sawyer, William Sheals, Beth Sikes, Lynda Smith, Sherry Tennant, Gene Ussery, Andrew and Carolyn Wheeler, Eric White, Peggy White Woods, Roger Willis.
1989	Jackie Addington, Ethel Andersen, Rita Carreno, Newell Edenfield, Marty Godfrey, Rebecca Gordon, Ed Grove, Mary Harry, Bruce Hoopes, Heyward Horton, Ralph Jckson, Linda McClain, David McCleskey, Dick Myrick, Eric Norwood, Patrick O'Brien, Stephen Odum, Joe Pearson, Herman Pennamon, David Reichard, Beth Rosser, Ari Russell, Bill Short, Jim St. John, Joe Stafferi, Kathleen Teare, Helen Thomas, Robert Waller, Steve Williams, Phylecia Wilson.
1990	Sandra Wood Alexander, Marsha Anderson-Bomar, Bill Barry, Casey Brogdon, Carol Burdges, Gary Cornell, Phil Cuthbertson, Carol Dew, Stephen Franzen, Ed Fuller, Mary Gordon, Mike Gordon, Karen Harper, Bill Hawkins, Tom Karr, Bill Kirby, Marnie McIntosh, William McLendon, Victor Moldovan, Rick O'Brien, Rick Porter, Louise Radloff, Allen Richardson, John Schraudenbach, Katherine Sherrington, Abby Shirley, Stanley Sonenshine, John Thibadeau, Vic Verdi, Janice West.
1991	Mike Barkhurst, Sabra Bowers, Carole Boyce, V. H. "Brad" Brady, Georgia Brogdon, Rachel Bronnum, Michael Bruce, Charles Button, Richard Carothers, Joseph Cegala, Julia Davis, Janice Fatzinger, Donna Fisher, Sylvester Ford, Phyllis Henderson, Wayne Hill, Tommy Hughes, Jesse Long, Donna Marietta, Fred Meyer, Alan Najjar, Michael Newman, Donna O'Neal, Bobby Robbins, Tito Sanjuro, Steve Spellman, Jim Steele, Elaine Still, Roy Stowe, Mychal Walker, Cindy Wright.
1992	Walter Anderson, Robert Baker, William Brogdon, Michael Dailey, Stephen Day, Marilyn Dochenetz, Betty Dominy, Morris Friedman, Martha Fullwood, Hal Greene, Patty Grove, George Hamilton, Carolyn Hill, Joe Hoffman, Lisa Johnsa, Helen Morriss, Becky Monteanu, Bill Northquest, Michael O'Neal, Jim Peters, Paige H. Powers, Dawn Ramsey, Ann Richardson, Dorothy Roberts, Mary Root, Larry Rubenstein, Susan Paalz Scally, Cass Smith, Thomas Tate, Lynn H. Williams, John Woodley.
1993	Peggy Boynston, Pat Brown, Jeannine Collins, Leigh Couch, Linda Danco, Leigh Diffenderfer, Ed Gulesserian, Nita Hallford, Patty Heitmuller, Rosalyn Joseph, Debbie King, Linda McGregor, Jack Moore, Jack Morris, Cindy Murphy, Barbara Myers, Tim Pakenham, Jo Ann Pinder, Robert Ponder, Carol Quinn, Cathy Redding, Sharon Rigsby, Tom Shepherd, Leslie Sibert, Paul Steckinrider, Greg Stroupe, Joel Taylor, Mary Thompson, Robert Troxler.
1994	Joe Allen, Steven Bailey, Edwin Bennett, Ann Brown, Kenneth Brown, LuAnn Chambers, Michel Champagne, Susan Cohen, Jock Connell, Kim Cox, John Elliott, Steve Gaultney, Gale Hulme, Ben Hulsey, Carl Jordan, Berney Kirkland, Beth Malanoski, Tim Mansour, Mark Merritt, Richard Mikola, Pat Mitchell, Bert Nasuti, Kathryn Schrader, David Seago, Cynthia Stedeford, Linda Story, Kevin Swanson, Connie Thompson, Nancy Ward, Judy Waters, Richard Winegarden.

Leadership Gwinnett Alumni

Year	Class Members
1995	Maurice Allen, Larry Askew, Javid Bagheri, Donna Potts Bergeson, Victoria Braden, Ron Brooks, John Campbell, Mike Couch, Dick Daneke, Chris Dendy, Gwen Dykes, Sasandra Fischer, Tom Forkner, Ellen Gerstein, Alan Golden, Angelo Harris, Angela Hicks, Freida Hill, Olivia Hodges, Al Hombroek, Gregory Jay, Jan Jordan, Jim Mallory, Tommy McBride, Elnor Melton, Elleene Morgan, Rob Rodatus, Caryl Sumner, Tom Waggoner, Sheila Woodruff.
1996	David Ball, David Barker, Lea Bay, James Braden, Butch Conway, Steve Dubose, Royce Duncan, Paul Ellingson, Alan Fisher, Nancy Friauf, Jennifer Guynn, Joan Harris, Shirley Jones, Stan Jones, Sylvia Kyle, Nita Meadows, Patti Muise, Marina Peed, Mitch Peevy, Mary Prebula, Steve Reilly, Anna Shackelford, Carol Ann Stough, Beth Thompson, Wanda Warner, Allen Waters, Michael Williams, Jack Wilson, Woody Woodruff, Corbitt Woods, Pete Wooten, Gloria Wright.
1997	Brenda Anderson, Robert Ashman, Dorothy Carrillo, Jim Carsten, Robert Clark, Randy Dellinger, Karen Eggers, Myrna Feldman, Keith Funderbunk, Michael Greene, Mike Guynn, Tonya Hare, Jackie Hoffman, Andrew LeBlanc, Rejena Lucas, John Lucht, Warren McClellan Judy McDaniel, Roy Miller, Nancy Minor, Bill Shaver, Tammy Shumate, Allen Sistrunk, Nancy Stanberry-Kellam, Joy Still, Marvin Willis, Scott Zanardo.
1998	Lavoska Barton, Gerald Blaney, Carla Brown, Nancy Chandler, Carla Conway, Sean Coughlin, Dan English, Kathy Fries, Sandra Gluck, Dorsey Grist, Phil Hoskins, Kevin Kenerly, Jim Kraus, Gail Macrenaris, Jeff Mahaffey, Caryn McCarity, Lisa McGinley, Jim McKenzie, Thomas Mitchell, Douglas Mundrick, Tommy Nix, Ben Robuck, Jacqueline Rosier, Bill Russell, David Snell, Laurice Tatum, Joanne Taylor, Victoria Thomas, Denise Townsend, Nancy Travis, Lisa Tully, John Upchurch, Vickie Watts.
1999	Brian Allen, Wade Beavers, Frank Berry, Elizabeth Blackwell, Renee Byrd-Lewis, Douglas Cotter, Terry Franzen, Yvonne Frey, Kelly Greer, Bob Harris, Mahuli Jakubek, Thad Joiner, Teresa Lynn, Ken Massaroni, Ed McCabe, Patrick Meehan, Bartow Morgan, Emory Morsberger, Rebecca Murphy, Steve North, Raymer Sale Jr., Janet Schwalbe, Nell Stevens, June Sweat, Tommy Terrell, Karen Gilpin Thomas, Michael S. Webb, Terra Bullock Winter.
2000	Laurie Anderson, Curt Beavers, Jack Bolton, Darron Britt, Mark Brock, Bruce Carter, Guy Chamberlain, Dave Cook, Nancy DeLoach, Chris Ellerbee, John Green, Maryann Grimes, Carol Hassell, Susan Kendrick Lauhoff, David Lowry, Patrick Mahon, Symone McClain, Andrew Mertz, Susan Murphy, Cathy Nichols, John Riddle, Frank Stephens, Brenda Stokes, Jean Walker, David Willey, Dave Williams, Lisa Williams, Philip Williams, Jill Willis.
2001	Tony Arakawa, Brad Carr, Carla Carraway, Kenneth Davis, Warren Davis, Ron Garrard, Sheldon Glorit, Nancy Hammond, Rena Hanson, Greg Hayes, Kelly Herndon, Peter Hill, Connie Hinson, David Jacobson, Deborah Johnson, Denise Jones, Chung Lee, Kelly Love, William McCargo, Theresa McDugald, Brand Morgan, Diane Murray, Allison W.Rooks, Gloria Seals, Donald Shillington, Doug Stacks, Vivian Stranahan, Brett Taylor, Ralph Taylor, Hardin Watkins.
2002	Kerry Armstrong, Pam Baxter, Neal Booth, Douglas Bridges, Sherry Bowen Britt, Mary Beth Byerly, Greg Cantrell, Tom Combiths, Mike Comer, Delane Cope, Rick Cost, Frances Davis, Sharyl Dawes, Sue Dennen, Suzanne Glenn, Bob Jackson, Jamie Jones, Brad Kendall, Leahdee Kilgore, Mark King, Jan McKinney, Ed Miller, Jimmy Norton, LaPincky Phillips, Donna Powers, Lynn Price, Randy Rich, Lois Salter, Joyce Spraggs, Van Stephens, Lee Wolfe, Jay Wolverton.
2003	Tony Appling, Toby Blackwell, Beth Bragg, Don Britt, JoAnn Brown, James Burnette, Alice Cunningham, Laura Grams, Lorraine Green, Jennifer Holmes, Dawson Jackson, Jamie Kennedy, Patrick Kien, Daniel King, J. Michael Levengood, Katie Lovett, Pedro Marin, Lois Martin, Meredith Mason, Mark Newton, Faye Patterson, Mary Ray, Harry Rice, Steve Rolader, Perry Tindol, Drew Tomlin, Lee Tucker, Charlie Walters, Louis Young.

Leadership Gwinnett Alumni	
Year	Class Members
2004	Debra Kaye Battle, Matt Benson, Brian Blough, Kip Buss, Sid Camp, Whitney Capps, Steve Chapman, Paul Cook, Dionitia Cornell, Dave Ehrhardt, Mariangel Flynt, Laurie Garrard, Suzanne Geske, Kathleen Guy, Rodney Harris, Gale Goff Hey, John Karnowski, Steve Logan, Lee Marchen, Schelly Tennant Marlatt, Alicia McCart, Marcia Neaton, Patrice Prevost, Jeannie Rispin, Bob Russell, Philip Schroeder, Lesli Seta, Berry Simmons, Scott Smith, Derik Taylor, Teresa Welborn, Jennifer Whitaker, Patti Williamson, Katrina Marie Winberg.
2005	Sheila Adcock, Laura Best-Moore, Harry Blessing, Denise Brinson, Connie Burch Whitford, Steve Cannon, Tanya Eades, Steve Edwards, Wayne Ellison, Karen Fine, Tom Fricano, Javier Galeano, Jim Hall, Paula Hastings, Lloyd Hofer, Alexis Jones, Art Karalexis, Slade Lail, Jane LeMaster, Colin Martin, David McCulloch, Dave McMullen, Pablo Pittaluga, Shane Sale, Don Sherrill, Pamela South, Michael Sweigart, Rosanna Szabo, Jody Vickery, Jason West, Greg Whitlock, Nancy Yancey, Lisa Zaken.
2006	Salmaan Ajani, Craig Barlow, Hector Barlo, Mike Beaudreau, Diane DeGaetano, Scott Duncan, Amy Emling, Jaime Espinosa, Bernard Ethridge, Todd Evans, Ted Fluri, Chris Hayes, Doug Haynie, Eddie Hazan, Terri Johndahl, Anna Jones, Victoria Rose Kidd, Pamela Kramer, Mani Krishnaswamy, Phyllis Lamme, Pam Ledbetter, Donna Ledford, Wayne Lloyd, Debbie McMinn, Gerald B. Mitchell, Lorri O'Brien, Mark Richardson, Maria Schiaffino, Sally Sherrington, Michael Shirley, Glenn Stephens, Linda Story, Chuck Warbington.
2007	Cara Alexander, T.J. Alvarado, Linda Anderson, Jace Brooks, Travis Burroughs, Rita Cantrell, Lisa Cauthen, Geri Gonzalez, Mark Grams, Julia Hall, George Hutchinson, Jim Joedecke, Kenneth Lee, Dick LoPresti, Owen Malcolm, Alfie Meek, Beatriz Mauersberg, Joy Parish, Jonathan Patterson, Ginger Patton-Schmitt, Jodi Pierce, Sharon Plunkett, Adam Pomeranz, Randy Redner, John Reynolds, Paul Sansone, Bron Gayna Schmit, Michael Tennant, Julianne Thompson, Calvin Watts, Tanisha Webb, Christopher Wilson, Randy Winfield, Tammie Zeigler
2008	Mike Boyd, Shawn Bratton, Lori Buckheister, Beth Chandler, Keith Chaney, David Cross, Benin Dakar, Leah Dryden, Steve Flynt, Jeff Forrestall, Amy Greiner, Debbie Harris, Tina Hgall, Clay Hunter, Kathy Jackson, Demetrius Jordan, Callie Kaiser, Susan Lee, Marian Lucia, David Marshall, Walt Martin, Cathy Maxwell, Donald May, Laurie McClain, Patrick McDonough, Kevin McOmber, Jason Mirabella, Debra Orr, Ross Powell, Jody Reeves, Mike Reonas, Bonnie Sale, Keith Shewbert, Katherine Smith, Joe Sorenson, Patti Stafford, David Will.
2009	Houston Bass, Ron Bingham, Krista Blum, John Bonanno, Thomas Boyce, Lisa Bradshaw, Dan Bruno, Leng Leng Chancey, Raymond Cobb, Dennis Daniel, Norwood Davis, Nancy Kiel Dustin Greene, Sarah Hathorn, Valeria Head, Kathy Holland, Eric Johansen, Bucky Johnson, Sharon King, Larry Larsen, Javier Lopez, P.J. Lynch, John Martin, Lesha Price, Ossie Randall, Connie Russell, Dot Schoeller, Davine Sparks, Kip Stokes, Michael Sullivan, Brandy Swanson, Jennifer Thilo, Mark Tibbets, Terry Ann Watlington, Maria Woods.
	Members of the Board of Trustees of Leadership Gwinnett Larry Askew, Beauty Baldwin, Carole Boyce, Peter Boyce, Elliott Brack, Renee Byrd-Lewis, Richard Carothers, Art Dana, Betty Dominy, Larry Edmundson, Angelo Harris, John Johnson, Jim Maran, Thomas Mitchell, Tom Mitchell, Rick O'Brien, Tammy Shumate, Robbie Stedeford, Jim Steele, Michael Tennant, Sherry Tennant, George Thompson, Connie Wiggins.
Source: Gwinnett Chamber of Commerce	

Leadership Gwinnett Committees

Year	General Chair	Steering Committee	Program Committee	Alumni Committee
1986	Elliott Brack	Carolyn Collins	Art Dana	
1987	Elliott Brack	Carolyn Collins	Eve Hoffman	
1988	Carolyn Collins	Art Dana	Peter Boyce Connie Wiggins	Connie Wiggins
1989	Art Dana	Beauty Baldwin	Carolyn Collins George Thompson	Helen Tapp Gordon Van Mol
1990	Beauty Baldwin	George Thompson	Vicky Sweeny	Jan Nevins Robbie Stedeford
1991	George Thompson	Connie Wiggins	Mike Huff Robbie Stedeford	Jan Nevins Richard Sissom
1992	Connie Wiggins	Peter Boyce	Lee Genson Robbie Stedeford	JanNevins David McClesky
1993	Peter Boyce	Robbie Stedeford	Steve Schildecker Sherry Tennant	Leonard Cyphers Mary Harry
1994	Robbie Stedeford	Sherry Tennant	Dick Carothers Rick O'Brien	Bobby Robbins Beth Rosser
1995	Sherry Tennant	Rick O'Brien	Dick Carothers Beth Rosser	Bobby Robbins Donna Marietta
1996	Rick O'Brien	Dick Carothers	Betty Dominy Bobby Robbins	Rick Herzel Donna Marietta
1997	Dick Carothers	Bobby Robbins	Betty Dominy Paige White	Nance Donaldson Lisa Johnsa
1998	Bobby Robbins	Betty Dominy	Jim Steele Carole Boyce	Rejena Lucas Steve Spellman Pat Mitchell
1999	Betty Dominy	Jim Steele	Carole Boyce Angelo Harris	Tom Tate Mike Guynn Sylvia Kyle
2000	Jim Steele	Carole Boyce	Larry Askew Pat Mitchell	Mike Guynn Caryn Bean Yvonne Frey
2001	Carole Boyce	Larry Askew	Angelo Harris Phylecia Wilson	Connie Wiggins
2002	Larry Askew	Angelo Harris	Phylecia Wilson Thomas Mitchell	Connie Wiggins
2003	Angelo Harris	Phylecia Wilson	Thomas Mitchell Tammy Shumate	Connie Wiggins
2004	Phylecia Wilson	Thomas Mitchell	Tammy Shumate Chuck Button	Connie Wiggins
2005	Thomas Mitchell	Tammy Shumate	Chuck Button Renee Byrd-Lewis	Connie Wiggins
2006	Tammy Shumate	Chuck Button	Renee Byrd-Lewis Raymer Sale	Connie Wiggins
2007	Chuck Button	Renee Byrd-Lewis	Raymer Sale Marina Peed	Thomas Mitchell
2008	Renee Byrd-Lewis	Raymer Sale	Marina Peed Carla Carraway	Thomas Mitchell

Source: Gwinnett Chamber of Commerce

Senior Leadership Gwinnett Alumni	
Year	Class Members
1999	Lois Allen, Donnis Bowman, Pauline Brown, Don Burt, James Davis Jr. , Mary Frances Greer, Russell Johnson, Phyllis Kravitz, Mary Long, Gene Lowry, Roy Miller, Ruel Morrison, Walt Thompson, Charlie Underwood, Wanda Van Tyle.
2000	Libby Anderson, Bill Atkinson, Jane Bowery, Marlene Caplan, Nancy Chilcoat, Shirley Cook, Bill Crosland, Tim Dunn, Daniel Fraro, Kathy Gestar, Joyce Howington, David Kee, Virginia McIntosh, Flo Perry, Regis Ruffing, Anna Shackelford, Bill Skelton, William Sommers, Ellen Tucker, Kathryn Willis, Joe Winter.
2001	Marshall Acree, Betty Atkinson, Bill Barry, Marie Beiser, Elise Cotter, Al Culbreth Jr., Pat Edwards, Roy Frost, Jean Gulley, Walker Kendrick, Jo Ann Nelson, Joyce Ogletree, Patsy Rooks, Janis Sawyer, Daniel Sims, Alan Smiley, Fred Stokes, Ruth Strickland, Joyce Todman, Eugene Waterfall, Leo Wilde.
2002	Denny Arrington, Barbara Brack, Jimmie Clower, Rastus Franklin, Ethel Gentry, Edith Kemp, Parks Mann, Bill McCann, Nonnie McClellan, Joan Myers, Bette Noggle, Nona Patterson, Sandy Ray, Von Starkey, James Thompson, Sandra Webb, John Winters.
2003	Emily Breland, Martha Byrd, David Daniel Jayaprakash Desai, Beverly Dryden, Mary Lou Dykes, Kent Evans, James Henderson, Faye Hill, Jim Hinkle, Belva Jenkins, Frances Johnson, Cheryl Jones, Al Karnitz, Janet Kennedy, Gerald Littleton, James Magill, Peg Murray-Lowman, Barb Sekowski, Pat Swan, Dianne Templeton, Jack Tester, Tom Travis, Linda Turner, Judy Waters.
2004	Gloria Berry, Jean Bowen, Pat Brannon, Linda Busby, James Chisholm, Annie Copeland, Gay Gober, Ray Huebschmann, Mabel Kincheloe, Alberto Leyva, Barbara Mahaffey, Martha Perdue, Jose Perez, Pat Port, Larry Reed, Don Segars, Bettie Stoneking, Judy Wilson.
2005	Cheryl Barry, Brenda Bigham, Grace Cain, Dick Deason, Sybil Deacon, Susan Eyring, Mary Fergus, Edmond Floyd, Shirley Guinn, Bill Lavigno, David Leonard, Terry Manning, Sunny Ramsay, Peggy Reedy, JoAnn Shipley, Spencer Snedecor, Wally Speed, Linda Strange, Joseph Whitwell, Doug Wren.
2006	Taher Bagheri, Mamie Beam, Kay Bennett, Myron Bullock, Sue Cabreath, Sylvia Clower, James Freeman, Judy Greene, Velma Hinton, Larry Johnson, L.C. Johnson, Al Kates, Randy Meacham, Helen Morriss, Robert Post, Sonny Rader, Ann Richardson, Michael Runyan, Gail Trapnell.
2007	Lori Christopher, Julian Davis, Rekha Desai, John Forrestall, Craig Goebel, Barbara Grastat, Linda Harrison, Thor Johnson, Sue Kelley, Bill Kingsbury, Ellis Lamme, Mark Limmer, John McCauslan, Van Sewell, Patti Jo Shapiro, Michael Taylor, Hugh Wilkerson.
2008	No class held ending Spring 2008
2009	Roger Blais, Margaret Cain, Larry Christopher, Sal DeGaetano, Zack Doppel, Gary Galloway, Herbert George, James Gillespie, Margo Gribinich-Hunt, Richard Gray, Joanne Johnson, Carol Lee, Tom Long, Joe Markham, Debbie Mason, Gloria McGuire, Margaret Morgan, Julia Nash, Brenda Pruitt, Ann Sechrist, Navin Shah, Donald Smith, Tom Stratton, Jackie Thornberry, Ron Weber, Charles Whitehead.
Trustees of Senior Leadership Gwinnett	
Betty Atkinson, Bill Atkinson, Bill Barry, Donnis Bowman, Elliott Brack, Tim Dunn, Carolyn Hill, Anna Shackelford, Wayne Shackelford, Pat Swan, Mike Tennant and Connie Wiggins	
Source: Senior Leadership Gwinnett Records	

Senior Leadership Gwinnett Committees

Year	General Chair	Steering Committee	Program Committee
1999	Elliott Brack	Connie Wiggins	Jesse Long, Sherry Tennant, Russ Weaver
2000	Connie Wiggins	Sherry Tennant	Jack Gantz, Carolyn Hill
2001	Jesse Long	Carolyn Hill	Donnis Bowman, Charlie Underwood
2002	Carolyn Hill	Donnis Bowman	Tim Dunn, Anna Shackelford
2003	Donnis Bowman	Anna Shackelford	Bill Berry, Betty Atkinson
2004	Anna Shackelford	Betty Atkinson	Bill Barry, Pat Swan
2005	Betty Atkinson	Billy Barry	Pat Swan, Tom Travis
2006	Bill Barry	Pat Swan	Linda Strange, Sunny Ramsey
2008	Pat Swan	Tom Travis	Thor Johnson

Note: the program was not held in 2007-2008

Source: Senior Leadership Gwinnett Records

Teachers as Leaders Alumni, 1991-2009

Class	Teacher's Name
1991	Lila Adair, Beverly Askew, Dave Averyt, Bunny Bagley, Susan Bridwell, Sally Brizzolara, Betty Bruce, Beth Cacchioli, Barb Gebert, Craig Hanson, Patsy Huey, Edna Isaacs, Diane Jimerson, Debbie King, Linda Koch, Russ LaPlume, Sharon Mahan, Doris Mann, Marlene Melvin, Jackie Okolo, Marla Panyik, Joyce Parks, Jean Robinson, Donna Scott, Susan Turner, Nancy Ward, Jeff White, Bard Williams.
1992	Susan Amason, Barbara Blasch, Suzanne Bosarge, Tom Collins, Jone Cross, Nancy Fairchild, Jim Fincher, Wylene Hayes, Roberta Romeo Heron, Janice Justice, Bill Leathers, Margaret Leeper, Page Loyd, RoseMarie Mason, Sandy McAdams, Nancy Morrison, Linda Muray, Theresa Nicholson, Gaye Quick, Diane Rankin, Debbie Roberts, Linda Sery, Lane Shuttt, Chip Thompson, Rita Van Fleit.
1993	Gayle Adkinson, Sallie Barrett, Linda Bartling, Katie Bell, Janet Burris, Pat Carpenter, Judy Cook, Cyndi Darsch, Brad Denslow. Linda Elson, Carol Ann Fulgham, Jude Gregoire, Meg Grennan, Bob Izzo, Judy Johnson, Melissa Kinard, Johon LaMattina, Trissa Luftig, Florence Magee, Mary Mason, Sandy Miller, Bonnie Reavis, Barbara Reed, Anna Rinaldi, Marion Sebastian, Vivian Stranahan, Barbara Tillman, Deborah White, Laura West, Linda Williams, Connie Wright.
1994	Lita Tipton Barnette, Carol Birdsong, Cissy Brandt-Nichols, Christine Dailey, Chris Diffley, Michael Edwardy, Mary Lou Enright, J. Raul Fernandez, Laurie Fletcher, Claudia Gage, Marlynn Gaines, Ann Gleason, Sharon Grahn, Don Henderson, Todd Kearney, Linda Lamb, June Leneski, Marie Lelsey, Greta Loeber, Joe Long, Sarah Ann Mason, Carol Rappold, Sonia Rojales, Pat Saulson, Susan Scheer, Gloria Sill, Patsy Thompson, Bar West, Cindy Westaway, Maffie Winfrey Gene Ziegler.
1995	Rachel Adams, Deborah Riley Allgood, Terry Anderson, Carolyn Becker, Mary Hunkin Beem, Rand Bissel, Elizabeth Boucher, Linda Calhoun, David Cline, Jolinda Collins, Carla Collins, Marilyn Davis, Jo Dinnan, Jackie Elett, Clara Ann Foucht, Leigh Ann Fowler, Chris Freidenstein, Pat Griffin, Nita Hallford, Tony Harrison, Ren Hullender, Marcia Jenkins, Valerie Joiner, Tom Kolb, Cheryl Laine, Kathy Lucia, Anne Newhouse, Pam Poppe, Evelyn Schneider, Denna Serafin, Richard Shivers, Jim Small, Tammy Snyder, Merrilyn Vogtner, Doug Wagner, Anna Jo Wilhoite, Denise Young.
1996	Tony Aguirre, Pam Autrey, Joyce Berube, Lucy Biemiller, Ernie Blankenship, Karen Brown, Jill Brunham, Gaye Busbee, Fran Coyle, Landis King Dekle, Jan Eakin, Sandy Ewanowski, Liz Gembecki, Carol Grady, Diane Hall, Pam Hartley, Renee Head, Nancy Hightower, Bronwyn Hogan, Diane Hughes, Helen Love, Joan Mulderick, Jenny Nall, Katharine Newman, Edna Palombo, Millie Patterson, Cynthia Predmore, Jane Scott, Pricilla Sena, Lois Ann Shorter, Elizabeth Tarver, Dale Willard.
1997	Donna Ahlswede, Leslie Aiken, Robin Bowling, Bonnie Craft, Tammy Curti, Carol Ferguson, Priscilla Focks, Elizabeth Goldwire, Marisa Grant, Stephanie Hall, Nancy Haman, Roger Ivey, Gloria James, Mary Anne Jones, Shari LaComb, Wanda Law, Debbie Longshore, Dodie Magill, Angela Matheny, Mary Ann Meeks, Leslie Meiere, Cheryl Nakahata, Hollie Queen, Lori Schaefer, Pat Sharpton, Rebecca Sledd, Ed Stone, Kay Tichelaar, Kathy Upton, Susan Verell.
1998	Tere Aleman, Stephanie Arnette, Linda Bell, Cindy Brooks, Christie Brown, Amy Bryan, Nancy Childers, Cindy Conner, Cheryl Cutchin, Jana Czerwonky, Cristy Edwards, Sharon Green, Kathy Henry, Luis Hernandez, Kim Jackson, Patte James, Mary Klamer, Betsy Lilliston, Mary Lord, Susan Moccia, Pat Moore, Miffy Moore, Debbie Pearce, Jane Radman, Debbie Roberts, Susan Robirds, Cary Sell, Denise Skeels, Lisa Stark, Kathy Thomas, Lisa Wagner, Karen Walker.

Teachers as Leaders Alumni, 1991-2009

Class	Teacher's Name
1999	Robert Barnes, Colleen Blankenship, Stacy Byous, Beverly Evans, Millie Fuss, Mimi Gaines, Joan Gearhart, Ann Graham, Debbi Hadaway, Kathy Hocevar, Elaine Homestead, Krista Hunter, Lisa M. Johnson, Terri McCrary, Elizabeth McLean, Joanne Matricardi, Candace Perkola, Paulette Raus, Amanda Roach, JoEllyn, Robinson, Niki Ross, Kelly Rutledge, Pam Smith, Holly Watkins, Dawn White, Pat Williams.
2000	Vicky Arnette, Marlee Bettis, Katrina Blankenship, Kelly Cobb, Janet Davis, Ann Follett, Debra Giles, Julie Griggs, Sandy Grizzard, Tara Hayes, Amy Horn, Wanda Ireland, Cynthia Johnston, Cathy Karlick, Meg Kerr, Sue Kliefoth, Mark Leviton, LaTease Long, Michelle McCorkle, Bobby Moore, Demetria Neal, Lisa Newhouse, Gigi O'Shea, Francine Root, Marcia Rucks, Anita Saunders, Patty Stephens, Kirsten Stiles, Joy Straner, Karla Swafford, Gina Vines, Janice Warren, Pam Webb, Teresa White.
2001	Kristin Bartholomew, Kathy Blondheim, Kitty Bowers, Hope Cabot, Barbara Caldwell, Karen Carpenter, Paula Enayati, Denise Forbes, Debra Hall-Griffin, Ann Hince, Theresa Jarrell, Mark Jones, Fern LeMaster, Janet Lewis, Terry McGonigle, Audrey Miller, Bobby Jean Moore, Joyce Nelson, Susan Opferman, Bernice Parrott, Susan Strickler, Susan Thompson. Marsha Watts, Debi West, Carla Whitehead, Barbara Wilson, Julie Wilson, Ethel Wynn, Christina Zakis.
2002	Elizabeth Alday, Joe Bader, Gabby Bray, Wanda Cain, Lawanna Caudle, Angela Cheek, Charisse Deramus, Robin Dillard, Carrie Doker, Lynn Dunn, Janet Endenfield Rick Frey, Jane Frobose, Jeni Greeson, Iris Harris, Alexis Harsh, Nancy Jukins, Patty Kambiss, Nancy Knight, Jane T. Lindenfield, Lynn Loo, Kathy Martin, Kayshella Mitchell, Angie Muntan, Jay Polak, Madeline Realmuto, Jane Rogers, Penny Rogers, Janice Smith, Stephanie Twitty and Lydia Wright.
2003	Regina Allen, Kim Arakawa, Kelley Bailey, Karen Berry, Jennifer Blodgett, Rick Creed, Tammy Davis, Monice DeBarr, Diane Eberhaart, Linda Emerick, Tara Entrekin, Janet Faulkner, Toni Ferguson, Jenny Fornek, Ellie Kaple, Rynna Kidd, Susan Levinson, Brian Lucy, Leanne Luttrell, Brandon Manders, Pamela McRae, Donna Power, Missy Purcell Joanna Root, Pat Salter, Suzanne Skeen, Teri Snyder, Amanda Stewart, Christi Stout, Lisa Tilley, Julie Van Soelen.
2004	Marcia Arnold, Kimberly Baldwin, Rose Bulau, Michelle Burroughs, Nancy Chrisman, Alicia Cochran, Stuart Egan, Sonja Fox, Janet Fulkner, Susan Garber, Tina Gay, Michael Herring, Amy Jenkins, Chris Kendrick, Melissa Lawley, Shanon Lutz, Nina Mackellar, Tammy Murphree, Candice Noyes, Pam Papciak, T. C. Parker, Tamara Perkins, Claudia Rios, Sherri Rodgers, Lisa Rudowitz, Karen Sanders, Deborah Stanfield, Marsha Stroud, Kim Thames, Anne Thompson, Linza Todd, Gina Towler, Lori Wismans.
2005	Sophia Barton, Sarah Black, Elisa Brown, Cheri Carter, Belinda Chancey, Cheryl Cole, Stacey Cummings, Mary Edelberg, Lynne Franks, Bob Fryman, Marilyn Gates, Vernay Gilliard, Mary Ruth Hambrick, Anne Hawkins, Adrianne Hayes, Susan Headley, Emily Heck, Chrissy Hilfiger, Nancy Johnson, Linda King, Leslie Livaditis, Kirsten Mixter, Vernita Moore, Denise Newman, Julia Owens, Rosie Pacek, Cathy Payne, Terri Poffenberger, Brian Segool, Steve Straughan, Cathy Valiquette-Systsma, Madrey Worthy
2006	Kathi Abraham, Traci Baldwin, Rose Ball, Lisa Braby, Jill Bryson, Marketa Bullard, Lacy Byerly, Brad Callahan, Lisa Carlton, Tiffany Coleman, Sharon Coleman, Andie Derricho, Kimberly Fye, Beth Granger, Amie Gravitt, Todd Hamilton, Wendy Harben, Krista Herron, Angela Hoffman, Tammy Hullender, Janet Jonas, Felicia Jones, Pam Kern, Susan Kramer, Debbie Lifsey, Linda Nichols, Jasmine Nye, Deborah Obenschain, Ann Schintzius, Christina Spivey, Kimberly Stewart, Lucy Strother Diane Treuman, Kellie Wall, Sara Weeks, Katherine Wentworth.
2007	Lindsey Allen, Colby Bross, Kelly Buchanan, Katie Callahan, Kallie Clack, Amanda Dewhurst, Jennifer Dionne, Nicole Esswein, Terressa Ewing, Amanda Hall, Troy Henson, Suzanne Hood, Sandy Hughes, Rob Hutcheson, Melanie Hutsell, Jennifer Jankauskas, Krista Johnson, Beth Martinez, Jamie Page, Pam Perry, Jackie Petree, Verna Ramdeen, Mike Reilly, Rhetta Roy, Aneila Sahaye, Debbie Sanders, Amanda Sparks, Ciatta-Mae Stubbiefield, Heather Tanner, Stephanie Wallace, Leigh Anne Wearne, Glenda Young.
2008	Cindy Apley Rose, Lisa Archer, Jonathan Bulloch, Derrick Burchette, Marianne Carney, Becky Chappelear, Penny Cruise, Emily Cunningham, Adria Daniels, Jonathan Day, Ismall El-Shaakir, Sara Forrester, Kim Griffin, Susan H. Harris, Catana Harris, Amy Hayes, Gloria Howard, Rob Izzo, Maya Kirk, Tawanda Lewis, Elizabeth Marsh, J. W. Mozley Lorin Murphy, Mary Oliver, Amy Perkins, Lauren Phillips, Janet Piver, Jaclyn Rodriquez, Bill Ruff, Carolyn Shoemaker, Cinda Skelton, Rhonda Stroud, Kathy Williams, Tim Yoder.
2009	Jackie Ashmore, Brian Baron, Blair Binion, Carla Bland, Suzanne Bross, Jennifer Burley, Christina Burns, Michelle Busby, Tracey Casey, Amanda Chanco, Hyun Cho, Andrea Colglazier, Chekquita Colllins, Jackie Corley, Debbie Cornelison, Jennifer Covington, Amy Crook, Nikole Davis, Danyel Dollard, Christina Garcia, James Glenn, Janet Graves, Gerin Hennebaul, Nicolle Higgins, Crystal Johnson, Marisa Kana, Jill Landtroop, Tori Loke, Andrea M. Fowler, Derrielle Morris, Joann Morse, Tom Myers, Kari Parlier, Lydia Patrick, Kerri Schmitz, Judy Stephenson, Kara Taylor, Adrienne Tedesco, Marie Vidai, Heather Watkins.

Source: Gwinnett County Public Schools

Neighborhood Leadership Institute Alumni

Year	Class Members
1996	Malcolm J. Arrington, Karen Walsh Asher, Bo Ballard, Virginia C. Carswell, Millie E. Croom, Carmen Bracero-Dorio, Tony Finelli, Victoria B. Fitzpatrick, Mary S. Foster, Sanita H. Frank, Loretta A. Garcia, Mary M. Gresham, Dick Grutzmacher, Abdi M. Issak, Catherine Levine, Jacquelyn A. Morgan, Vincent R. Pagliari, Edgar J. Perkerson, Gere Perry, Tracee Ragan, Raymond F. Virgin, Y Van Vo, Janet Weisman, Linda S. Waters, Tammie Zeigler.
1997	Yvonne Bethea Andall, David Christopher Cawthon, Frank C. Fisk, Victoria Fitzpatrick, Mary Burns Galardi, Angela Halse, Phyllis G. Hasty, Rosetta E. Irons, David Johns, Lisa D. Johnson, Vicki L. Jones, Theresa M. Livsey Lemons, Andrea Malone, Paula S. Masterson, Steve Steelman Nutt, Grace Robinson, Tenjurie V. Thomas, Jess Villegas, Ann Vines, Mary Ann Wetzel, Edna R. Williams, Michele Williams, Renea L. Smith.
1998	Dale S. Brock, Elizabeth C. Dougherty, Cherryl Gary, Catherine M. Greenman, Harriet H. Hankerson, Lance A. Hatfield, Karla R. Kuntze, Susan E. Kendrick-Lauhoff, Mirza Meghji, John D. Mirkle, Laura G. Mitchell, Clifton E. Moore, Keith Nabb, Jeffrey Alan Neal, Jessie A. Scott, Leslie Villegas, Leo F. Wilde, Dee A. Williams, Denny Wood, Bob Zorn.
1999	Marilyn S. Allen, Jill Barsody, Malcolm Birch, Mildred Brown, Cynthia Chaffin, Laurie Ann Chluda, Inita Hammond Davis, Randy B. Everette, Rodney S. Harris, Donald W. Heath, Mary Jane LaBonte, Angela Rabidoux, Mina Rivera, Brian Schlottmann, Donna Stamper, Randy Stamper.
2000	Jude Andall, Barbara Batailon, Gale Belton, Ardith Brackett, Rebecca Branstetter, Michael Burns, Frank Daniell, Diana Daring, Bejamin Doster, John Edwards, Travis Evans, Teresa Hauck, Andy Hendrix, Velma King, Lynn Lewis, Taunya Lowe, Sylvia McCullough, Charles McDaniel, Ivonne McNally, Robert McNulty, Vinka Merlino, Jennifer Nail, Diane Pardoe, Rosalia Rivera, Bill Roa, Gregory Smith, Vanessa Thomas, Janice Turner, Bess Walthour, Nazir Welji, Renee White, Chanda Womack.
2001	Bernice Bailey, Laura Beall, Darsell Blackwell, Geneva Bottley, Pattie Cagle, Ashley Cantrell, Jim Dugan, Norma Dukes, Ann Eagerton, Bobby Hanna, Susan Holland, John Irvine, Darryl Jackson, Mary Melton, Altaf Noomohmad, Zachery Pratt, Bessie Shavers, Angela Smith, Judy Smith, John Stewart, Wendy Stewart, Gayle Teare, Elva Trevino, Keith Troxell, Yvonne Washington, Warren Wilcox, Toni Wyman.
2002	Anita Egwin, Beatrice Karangwa, Derraine Wilson, Donald Pinkard, Helen Jenkins, Jamille Eldridge, Jerry Stedman, Jim Woolen, Katherine Fulmer, Linda Burton, Lori Edelkind, Mary Rogelstad, Melinda Allen, Patricia Lark, Paula Webb, Rony Delgarde, Sara Snyder, Sheila Jones, Sherron Martinez, Tina Edmondson, Tina Upchurch, Vivian Gaither, Rob Hines.
2003	Albert Fowler, Ann Rodriguez, Brenda Holmes, Chris Moder, David Williams, Dewey Long, Don Ortega, Donielle Mitchner, Donna Shah, Edward Czyz, Ines Beltran, Jim Kraus, Karen Young, Judy Saucerman, Katie McIlwain, Kerry Mitchell, Leslay Durant, Marsha Dickey, Michelle Carew, Myong Jo, Rebecca Uggla, Segerick Clemon, Shantal Castello, Steve Gill, Vivian Pollard.
2004	Antonio Philantrope, Barbara Grastat, Hulon Garmon, Jeff Allen, John Bips, Kate Maloney, Ladele Oyelami, Linda Anty, Lisa Weston, Lydia Wright, Martha Sosebee, Norwood Simmons, Sharon Cook, Shermeen Ajani, Tony Persaud.
2005	Aaron Whiting, Jerald Estime, Ann Neuheiri, Babara Kubitz, Benjamin Wu, Bradley Leavitt, Candace Jordan, Frances Smith, Italia Metts, Josef Fain, Judy Edens, Kathy Timmons, Kelly Ann Davis, Marvin Brotherton, Michelle Holmes Chaney, Ossie Randall, Pamela Bridgeman, Rajindra Sooknanan.
2006	Andrea Beacham, Bryan Simmons, Consuela Luna, Janita Fuller, Jashim Uddin, Javier Munoz, Jesse Munoz, John Jones, John Stewart, Julianne Thompson, Kathy Barker, Kyle Ross, Laura Hill, Mannai Ng, Marcus Kellum, Marlyn Tillmon, Norwood Davis, Mariela Bernal, Rodrigo Infante, Rodrigo Varela, Susan K. Baxley.
2007	Akilah Townsend, Bazil Clyne, Brandon Bizzell, Charles Lucas, Constance Smith, Diana Moore, Diana Curtis, Latreace Sankey, Laura Nero, Quentin Townsend, Sharon Spallone, Sherri Hancel, Travis Gatson, Yadi Romero, Young Huynh, Gladys Harris.
2008	Andrew Hixson, Evette McKenzie, Jeffrey Thomas, John Williams, Judy Middleton, LaKeisha Hull, Lysandra D'Souza, Marcia Husband, Mark Williams, Millie Linville, Oceanna Pappillion-Blount, Timothy Daly, William Mayfield.

Source: Neighborhood Leadership Institute

Members, Gwinnett Student Leadership Team, 1995-2010

Name	School	Year
Josh Pavel	Brookwood High	1995-1997
Brenda Williams	Brookwood High	1995-1997
Allison Abbott	Buford High	1995-1997
Wesley Davis	Buford High	1995-1997
Brianna Hall	Central Gwinnett	1995-1997
Anthony Spencer	Central Gwinnett	1995-1997
Stephanie Aitcheson	Collins Hill High	1995-1997
Michael Tiller	Collins Hill High	1995-1997
Josh Bray	Dacula High	1995-1997
Stephanie Glenn	Dacula High	1995-1997
Vince Hayes	Dacula High	1995-1997
Casey Kelly	Duluth High	1995-1997
Scott Streacker	Duluth High	1995-1997
Nirmit Desai	Maxwell	1995-1997
Erin Gardtner	Maxwell	1995-1997
Semil Choksi	Meadowcreek High	1995-1997
Millie Linville	Meadowcreek High	1995-1997
William Rachelson	Meadowcreek High	1995-1997
Ashley Cramer	Norcross High	1995-1997
Krissy Brown	North Gwinnett	1995-1997
Clint Buice	North Gwinnett	1995-1997
Carrie Dillon	Parkview High	1995-1997
Ashley Hunt	Parkview High	1995-1997
Robin Troncalli	Phoenix High	1995-1997
Susan Kennedy	Shiloh High	1995-1997
Ronald Shinault, Jr.	Shiloh High	1995-1997
John Wilhoite	Shiloh High	1995-1997
Stephanie Henefield	South Gwinnett	1995-1997
Melody Weinstein	South Gwinnett	1995-1997
Adrian Tyler	Berkmar High	1996-1998
Patricia Wilson	Berkmar High	1996-1998
Erin Payne	Brookwood High	1996-1998
Randy Powers	Brookwood High	1996-1998
Suzanne Kiener	Buford High	1996-1998
Alan Maltbie	Buford High	1996-1998
Katie Huckaby	Central Gwinnett	1996-1998
Sarah Olds	Central Gwinnett	1996-1998
Brad Roby	Central Gwinnett	1996-1998
Christina Luu	Collins Hill High	1996-1998
Erin Crysler	Dacula High	1996-1998

Name	School	Year
Callie Medley	Duluth High	1996-1998
Lisa Rundle	Duluth High	1996-1998
Chrissy Creel	Meadowcreek High	1996-1998
Thuy Hoang	Meadowcreek High	1996-1998
Amy Pearman	Meadowcreek High	1996-1998
Terry Byers	North Gwinnett	1996-1998
Amber Jarrard	North Gwinnett	1996-1998
Jennifer Crawford	Parkview High	1996-1998
Faith Nixon	Parkview High	1996-1998
Jennifer Seago	Parkview High	1996-1998
Moon Kim	Phoenix High	1996-1998
Candace Curry	Shiloh High	1996-1998
Tino Huynh	Shiloh High	1996-1998
Tanya Hayes	South Gwinnett	1996-1998
Amy Nobs	South Gwinnett	1996-1998
Derrick Burchette	Berkmar High	1996-1998
Terry Byers	North Gwinnett	1996-1998
Amber Jarrard	North Gwinnett	1996-1998
Jennifer Crawford	Parkview High	1996-1998
Faith Nixon	Parkview High	1996-1998
Jennifer Seago	Parkview High	1996-1998
Moon Kim	Phoenix High	1996-1998
Candace Curry	Shiloh High	1996-1998
Tino Huynh	Shiloh High	1996-1998
Tanya Hayes	South Gwinnett	1996-1998
Damian Jimenez	South Gwinnett	1997-1999
Amy Nobs	South Gwinnett	1997-1999
Derrick Burchette	Berkmar High	1997-1999
Sara Dewaay	Berkmar High	1997-1999
Adam Bagley	Buford High	1997-1999
Lydia Cunnington	Buford High	1997-1999
Sal Mian	Central Gwinnett	1997-1999
Sean O'Donnell	Central Gwinnett	1997-1999
Jordon Gilleland	Collins Hill High	1997-1999
Tyson Phips	Collins Hill High	1997-1999
Bobby Byrd	Dacula High	1997-1999
Cecilia Trotter	Dacula High	1997-1999
Susannah Haarmann	Duluth High	1997-1999
Emma Tatum	Duluth High	1997-1999

Members, Gwinnett Student Leadership Team, 1995-2010

Name	School	Year	Name	School	Year
Wesley Duke	Meadowcreek High	1997-1999	J.W. Mozley	Duluth High	1998-2000
Ami Patel	Meadowcreek High	1997-1999	Christine Haman	North Gwinnett	1999-2001
Jeff Hunt	Norcross High	1997-1999	Justin Sharrett	North Gwinnett	1999-2001
Sarah Nelson	Norcross High	1997-1999	Jane Brown	Parkview High	1999-2001
Zach Martin	North Gwinnett	1997-1999	Justin Burke	Parkview High	1999-2001
Ashley Mayfield	North Gwinnett	1997-1999	Greg Spellman	Parkview High	1999-2001
Kevin Carmichael	Parkview High	1997-1999	Billy Karwisch	Phoenix High	1999-2001
Joseph Tallent	Parkview High	1997-1999	Tiffany Reichenbach	Phoenix High	1999-2001
Beth Plummer	Phoenix High	1997-1999	Brittany Davis	Shiloh High	1999-2001
Clay McCullough	Shiloh High	1997-1999	Emily Purcell	Shiloh High	1999-2001
Katie McGarity	Shiloh High	1997-1999	Loren Elliott	South Gwinnett	1999-2001
Kristen McCutchen	South Gwinnett	1997-1999	Stephen Fell	South Gwinnett	1999-2001
Stevie Tabor	South Gwinnett	1997-1999	Kendra Allen	South Gwinnett	1999-2001
Robby Izzo	Brookwood High	1998-2000	Amanda Bales	South Gwinnett	1999-2001
Marianna Ray	Brookwood High	1998-2000	Corey Giessen	Berkmar High	1999-2001
Christian Sailor	Berkmar High	1998-2000	Stephanie McBride	Berkmar High	1999-2001
Elisha Waugh	Berkmar High	1998-2000	Margaret Childers	Brookwood High	1999-2001
Suzanne Perrow	Brookwood High	1998-2000	Ansely Dillehay	Brookwood High	1999-2001
Meg Rithmire	Brookwood High	1998-2000	George Green	Brookwood High	1999-2001
Nathan Bonick	Buford High	1998-2000	Martin Lawson	Brookwood High	1999-2001
Ginger Justice	Buford High	1998-2000	Trent Bagley	Buford High	1999-2001
Jennifer Smith	Central Gwinnett	1998-2000	Mickel Roy	Buford High	1999-2001
Sanja Veledar	Central Gwinnett	1998-2000	Jonathan Carter	Central Gwinnett	1999-2001
Sarah Abood	Collins Hill High	1998-2000	Angela Chu	Central Gwinnett	1999-2001
Tyler Gaines	Collins Hill High	1998-2000	Justin Carpenter	Collins Hill High	1999-2001
Chip Guy	Dacula High	1998-2000	Megan Duttenhofer	Collins Hill High	1999-2001
Haley Magness	Dacula High	1998-2000	Brandon Archer	Dacula High	1999-2001
Ana Florez	Duluth High	1998-2000	Beth Lambers	Dacula High	1999-2001
Lauren Bellamy	Meadowcreek High	1998-2000	Seema Ganatra	Duluth High	1999-2001
Larry Johnson	Meadowcreek High	1998-2000	Scott Hulme	Duluth High	1999-2001
Claire Carothers	Norcross High	1998-2000	Matt King	Duluth High	1999-2001
Rob Neuman	Norcross High	1998-2000	Dhruv Parekh	Meadowcreek High	1999-2001
Robby Culpepper	North Gwinnett	1998-2000	Elina Terushkin	Meadowcreek High	1999-2001
Laura Slade	North Gwinnett	1998-2000	Mary Adkins	Berkmar High	2000-2002
Will Bacon	Parkview High	1998-2000	Michelle Godfrey	Berkmar High	2000-2002
Kourtney Shaddix	Parkview High	1998-2000	Coty Ervin	Brookwood High	2000-2002
Danielle Hahne	Phoenix High	1998-2000	Ravi Shah	Brookwood High	2000-2002
Bethany Miller	Phoenix High	1998-2000	Amber Aiken	Buford High	2000-2002
Gretchen Freling	Shiloh High	1998-2000	George Tucker	Buford High	2000-2002
Warren Geller	Shiloh High	1998-2000	Jenni Bacon	Central Gwinnett	2000-2002

Members, Gwinnett Student Leadership Team, 1995-2010

Name	School	Year
Brad Westover	Central Gwinnett	2000-2002
Kristi Greer	Collins Hill High	2000-2002
Jesse Hinson	Collins Hill High	2000-2002
Nolan Peevy	Dacula High	2000-2002
Danielle Seckinger	Dacula High	2000-2002
Tana Over	Duluth High	2000-2002
Neill Webb	Duluth High	2000-2002
Sarah Moody	Grayson High	2000-2002
Erin Willbanks	Grayson High	2000-2002
Emanuel Istudor	Meadowcreek High	2000-2002
Tiana Johnson	Meadowcreek High	2000-2002
Matthew Ritter	Norcross High	2000-2002
Deondra Rose	Norcross High	2000-2002
Lesley Kesley	North Gwinnett	2000-2002
Katie Williamson	North Gwinnett	2000-2002
Anna Hamrick	Parkview High	2000-2002
Wallace Miller	Parkview High	2000-2002
Kerry Kramer	Phoenix High	2000-2002
Matt Adams	Norcross High	2000-2002
Mayson Thornton	Norcross High	2000-2002
Christina Warren	Phoenix High	2000-2002
Christina Abufaris	Shiloh High	2000-2002
Fenil Ghodadra	Shiloh High	2000-2002
Gayle Gilmore	South Gwinnett	2001-2003
Daniel Hwang	South Gwinnett	2001-2003
Alison Reed	Berkmar High	2001-2003
Bernie Richardson	Berkmar High	2001-2003
Nick Hussain	Brookwood High	2001-2003
Kelly Keevan	Brookwood High	2001-2003
Katie Boles	Buford High	2001-2003
Bobby McKee	Buford High	2001-2003
Lauren Fortner	Central Gwinnett	2001-2003
Claire Hudlow	Central Gwinnett	2001-2003
Bryan Langley	Central Gwinnett	2001-2003
Tara Heddinger	Collins Hill High	2001-2003
Amir Malayery	Collins Hill High	2001-2003
Thomas Boyce	Dacula High	2001-2003
Ashley Kolb	Dacula High	2001-2003
Ryan Plocher	Duluth High	2001-2003
Tina Termei	Duluth High	2001-2003

Name	School	Year
Jason Flanders	Grayson High	2001-2003
Jeanette Purvis	Grayson High	2001-2003
Lan Nguyen	Meadowcreek High	2001-2003
Elisa Savan	Meadowcreek High	2001-2003
Avis Johnson	Norcross High	2001-2003
Patrick Neuman	Norcross High	2001-2003
Cameron Clack	North Gwinnett	2001-2003
Justin Wong	North Gwinnett	2001-2003
A.F. Rodgers	Parkview High	2001-2003
Ope Sanjo	Parkview High	2001-2003
Paul Hartzog	Phoenix High	2001-2003
Kristina Raffalovich	Phoenix High	2001-2003
Kelley Kendrick	Shiloh High	2001-2003
Ben Smith	Shiloh High	2001-2003
Jon Dees	Berkmar High	2002-2004
Grace Mooken	Berkmar High	2002-2004
Christina Barrett	Brookwood High	2002-2004
Shuvro De	Brookwood High	2002-2004
Breanne Dawkins	Buford High	2002-2004
Daniel Gaddis	Buford High	2002-2004
Jordon Alford	Central Gwinnett	2002-2004
Heidi Bacon	Central Gwinnett	2002-2004
Eric Griffin	Central Gwinnett	2002-2004
Takashi Doscher	Collins Hill High	2002-2004
John Robert Boyce	Dacula High	2002-2004
Rachel Coy	Dacula High	2002-2004
Jay Moore	Duluth High	2002-2004
Yasamin Vojdani	Duluth High	2002-2004
Winston Herndon	Grayson High	2002-2004
Ann Marie Papasodero	Grayson High	2002-2004
Sravanti Kusuma	Meadowcreek High	2002-2004
Samir Patel	Meadowcreek High	2002-2004
Dominic Bruno	Norcross High	2002-2004
Laura Quesinberry	Norcross High	2002-2004
Rachel Bomholt	North Gwinnett	2002-2004
Brittany Mohler	North Gwinnett	2002-2004
Tyler Bridges	Parkview High	2002-2004
Allison Greenfield	Parkview High	2002-2004
Cassidy Selzer	Phoenix High	2002-2004

Members, Gwinnett Student Leadership Team, 1995-2010

Name	School	Year
Rashad Burroughs	Shiloh High	2002-2004
Callie Grady	Shiloh High	2002-2004
Steve Henderson	South Gwinnett	2002-2004
Amber Sligar	South Gwinnett	2002-2004
Charlotte Carlstrom	Berkmar High	2003-2005
Aneeth Geetha	Berkmar High	2003-2005
Mark Davis	Brookwood High	2003-2005
Will Green	Brookwood High	2003-2005
Brittany Hodge	Brookwood High	2003-2005
Adrian Kinsey	Buford High	2003-2005
Ashley Mengwasser	Buford High	2003-2005
Logan Christensen	South Gwinnett	2003-2005
Francesca Seta	South Gwinnett	2003-2005
Christian Fuller	Central Gwinnett	2003-2005
Michelle Mallory	Central Gwinnett	2003-2005
Kelsey Kopro	Collins Hill High	2003-2005
Kristina Stafford	Collins Hill High	2003-2005
Daniel Treuman	Collins Hill High	2003-2005
Emily Gaunt	Dacula High	2003-2005
Clay Turner	Dacula High	2003-2005
Stephen Kim	Duluth High	2003-2005
Camila Santiago	Duluth High	2003-2005
Brent Heeke	Grayson High	2003-2005
Christen Junker	Grayson High	2003-2005
Uniqueka Jenkins	Meadowcreek High	2003-2005
Said Saab	Meadowcreek High	2003-2005
Sara Beth Terry	Norcross High	2003-2005
Ronnie Zeidan	Norcross High	2003-2005
Emma Abel	North Gwinnett	2003-2005
Jaryd Green	North Gwinnett	2003-2005
Raj Parikh	North Gwinnett	2003-2005
Neal Housworth	Parkview High	2003-2005
Allison Will	Parkview High	2003-2005
Chelsea Feustel	Peachtree Ridge	2003-2005
Craig McClellan	Peachtree Ridge	2003-2005
Matt Toedtli	Phoenix High	2003-2005
Nick Kruskamp	Shiloh High	2003-2005
Melody Rhine	Shiloh High	2003-2005
Blair Fell	South Gwinnett	2003-2005
James Ford	Collins Hill High	2004-2006

Name	School	Year
Melissa Pitcher	Collins Hill High	2004-2006
Cataline Colvin	Dacula High	2004-2006
Nancy Gunzenhauser	Dacula High	2004-2006
Rhapsodi Douglas	Duluth High	2004-2006
David Wu	Duluth High	2004-2006
Samantha Graham	Grayson High	2004-2006
Michael Warren	Grayson High	2004-2006
Anish Bhatt	Meadowcreek High	2004-2006
Sagar Patel	Meadowcreek High	2004-2006
Jessica Compton	Mill Creek High	2004-2006
Brent Maddux	Mill Creek High	2004-2006
Michael Dermer	Norcross High	2004-2006
Lindsay Eierman	Norcross High	2004-2006
Stephen Crawford	North Gwinnett	2004-2006
Katherine Park	North Gwinnett	2004-2006
Bobby Allred	Parkview High	2004-2006
Elizabeth Wilson	Parkview High	2004-2006
Matthew Newcomb	Peachtree Ridge	2004-2006
Anna Scott	Peachtree Ridge	2004-2006
Kevin Donegan	Phoenix High	2004-2006
Brian Ely	Shiloh High	2004-2006
Rachel Ledford	Shiloh High	2004-2006
Amanda Cole	South Gwinnett	2004-2006
Michael Springer	South Gwinnett	2004-2006
Greg Lockett	South Gwinnett	2004-2006
Amanda Pack	South Gwinnett	2004-2006
Kemah George	Berkmar High	2004-2006
Scott Johnson	Berkmar High	2004-2006
Andrea Barrett	Brookwood High	2004-2006
Russ Kanner	Brookwood High	2004-2006
Scotti Cline	Buford High	2004-2006
Trent Payne	Buford High	2004-2006
Tonya Mitchell	Berkmar High	2005-2007
Chip Stanford	Berkmar High	2005-2007
Marie Agnello	Brookwood High	2005-2007
Joseph Moore	Brookwood High	2005-2007
Chase Burnette	Buford High	2005-2007
Anna Cleveland	Buford High	2005-2007
John Overton	Buford High	2005-2007

Members, Gwinnett Student Leadership Team, 1995-2010

Name	School	Year
Ruth Levy	Central Gwinnett	2005-2007
Cory McCart	Central Gwinnett	2005-2007
Sam Whitehead	Central Gwinnett	2005-2007
Sarah Groth	Collins Hill High	2005-2007
David Johnson	Central Gwinnett	2005-2007
Jackie Mullen	Central Gwinnett	2005-2007
David Mathews	Collins Hill High	2005-2007
Robert Jenkins	Dacula High	2005-2007
Paige Pipes	Dacula High	2005-2007
Ronald Shultis	Dacula High	2005-2007
Joy Hung	Duluth High	2005-2007
Steven Lau	Duluth High	2005-2007
Gloria Lu	Duluth High	2005-2007
Chaney Moon	Grayson High	2005-2007
Madhuri Patel	Grayson High	2005-2007
Chip Tyndale	Grayson High	2005-2007
Keegan Nicodemus	Meadowcreek High	2005-2007
Ami Patel	Meadowcreek High	2005-2007
Emily Clayton	Mill Creek High	2005-2007
Alex Knight	Mill Creek High	2005-2007
Bethany Ullrich	Mill Creek High	2005-2007
Dana Lupuloff	Norcross High	2005-2007
Sam Snider	Norcross High	2005-2007
Philip Crawford	North Gwinnett	2005-2007
Ashley Ingram	North Gwinnett	2005-2007
Aaron Parkman	North Gwinnett	2005-2007
Jennifer Lanier	Parkview High	2005-2007
Darin McKenna	Parkview High	2005-2007
Drew Butler	Peachtree Ridge	2005-2007
Kelly Jones	Peachtree Ridge	2005-2007
Katherine Tison	Peachtree Ridge	2005-2007
Andrew Carlone	Shiloh High	2005-2007
Ayshea Khan	Shiloh High	2005-2007
Michael Clanahan	South Gwinnett	2005-2007
T.J. Flowers	Buford High	2006-2008
Jennifer Tucker	Buford High	2006-2008
Amy Gu	Central Gwinnett	2006-2008
Matt Jackson	Central Gwinnett	2006-2008
Antonela Kljajic	Central Gwinnett	2006-2008
Tyler Cromey	Collins Hill High	2006-2008

Name	School	Year
Derek Phillips	Collins Hill High	2006-2008
Olivia Boyce	Dacula High	2006-2008
Melissa Harward	Dacula High	2006-2008
Tony Hotle	Dacula High	2006-2008
Muneeb Ahmed	Duluth High	2006-2008
Caterina Li	Duluth High	2006-2008
Immanuel Phillips	Duluth High	2006-2008
Spencer Brady	Grayson High	2006-2008
Greg Schatell	Grayson High	2006-2008
Alysse Whatley	Grayson High	2006-2008
Emily Aune	Meadowcreek High	2006-2008
La'Sha Burney	Meadowcreek High	2006-2008
Anh-Vu Do	Meadowcreek High	2006-2008
Danielle Bryant	Mill Creek High	2006-2008
Ben Evans	Mill Creek High	2006-2008
Heather Gieseking	Mill Creek High	2006-2008
Emily Hackett	Norcross High	2006-2008
Jessica McPhail	Norcross High	2006-2008
Chris Tanner	Norcross High	2006-2008
Collin Jones	North Gwinnett	2006-2008
Kameon Prather	North Gwinnett	2006-2008
Vivian Yu	North Gwinnett	2006-2008
Jason Cole	Parkview High	2006-2008
Lauren Crean	Parkview High	2006-2008
Ryan Smith	Parkview High	2006-2008
Orlando Silva, Jr.	Phoenix High	2006-2008
Tyler Pate	Peachtree Ridge	2006-2008
Matt Upchurch	Peachtree Ridge	2006-2008
Sarah Vakili	Peachtree Ridge	2006-2008
Daniel Helena	Shiloh High	2006-2008
Calley Mersmann	South Gwinnett	2006-2008
Kelundra Smith	South Gwinnett	2006-2008
Megan Cook	Berkmar High	2006-2008
Joanna Pak	Berkmar High	2006-2008
Neka Goka	Brookwood High	2006-2008
Coco Keevan	Brookwood High	2006-2008
Lindsay Mushett	Brookwood High	2006-2008
Ashley Clark	Buford High	2006-2008
Matthew McCurdy	Shiloh High	2006-2008
Danyelle Reynolds	Shiloh High	2006-2008

Members, Gwinnett Student Leadership Team, 1995-2010

Name	School	Year	Name	School	Year
Kathryn Hedden	South Gwinnett	2006-2008	Brandon Patrick	Parkview High	2007-2009
Cameron Bullock	Berkmar High	2007-2009	Emily Peng	Parkview High	2007-2009
Jeffrey Kimble	Berkmar High	2007-2009	Ariel Ford	Peachtree Ridge	2007-2009
Anu Laxmi	Berkmar High	2007-2009	Tommy King	Peachtree Ridge	2007-2009
Kyle Remley	Berkmar High	2007-2009	Megan Lane	Peachtree Ridge	2007-2009
Sydney Brunelle	Brookwood High	2007-2009	Katelyn Fields	Phoenix High	2007-2009
JiSu (Jenny) Kim	Brookwood High	2007-2009	Stephany Flannery	Phoenix High	2007-2009
Patrick Starr	Brookwood High	2007-2009	Chibueze Ihenacho	Shiloh High	2007-2009
Adrian Hall	Buford High	2007-2009	Roxanne Rahbar	Shiloh High	2007-2009
Ryan Reed	Buford High	2007-2009	Stephanie Travis	Shiloh High	2007-2009
Jessica Wilson	Buford High	2007-2009	Makenzie Delegram	South Gwinnett	2007-2009
Meghan Jackson	Central Gwinnett	2007-2009	Brandon Lewis	South Gwinnett	2007-2009
Rachel Johnson	Central Gwinnett	2007-2009	Clay Mersmann	South Gwinnett	2007-2009
Matthew Ricciardi	Central Gwinnett	2007-2009	Amy Kierath	South Gwinnett	2007-2009
Mandi Corriveau	Collins Hill High	2007-2009	Luke Leonard	South Gwinnett	2007-2009
Matthew Davis	Collins Hill High	2007-2009	Iman Ahmed	Berkmar	2008-2010
Shivani Shah	Collins Hill High	2007-2009	Vu Hoang	Berkmar	2008-2010
Alejandro Velez	Collins Hill High	2007-2009	Alessandra Scarcia	Berkmar	2008-2010
Sarah Bentley	Dacula High	2007-2009	Nolan Alexander	Buford	2008-2010
Alex Sweatt	Dacula High	2007-2009	Jeb Dills	Buford	2008-2010
Bryson Turner	Dacula High	2007-2009	Jamie Pridemore	Buford	2008-2010
Scott Cummins	Duluth High	2007-2009	Brian Bloch	Brookwood	2008-2010
Taylor Lepera	Duluth High	2007-2009	Andrea Byrnes	Brookwood	2008-2010
Mary Thumaty	Duluth High	2007-2009	Jessica Martini	Brookwood	2008-2010
Mallory Davis	Grayson High	2007-2009	Akwasi Brefo	Central Gwinnett	2008-2010
Jeremy Knight	Grayson High	2007-2009	Zack Davis	Central Gwinnett	2008-2010
India Pender	Grayson High	2007-2009	Vanessa Gallegos	Central Gwinnett	2008-2010
Marisol Leal	Meadowcreek High	2007-2009	Matt Benson	Collins Hill	2008-2010
Quan Tyia Lewis	Meadowcreek High	2007-2009	Emma Jaggears	Collins Hill	2008-2010
Chad Charoenlap	Meadowcreek High	2007-2009	Robert Sosebee	Collins Hill	2008-2010
Linda Chen	Mill Creek High	2007-2009	Sara Valencia	Collins Hill	2008-2010
Valerie Mock	Mill Creek High	2007-2009	Kamyron Jordan	Dacula	2008-2010
Laura Nuta	Mill Creek High	2007-2009	Lauren Phillips	Dacula	2008-2010
Christina Jundt	Norcross High	2007-2009	Rachel Wall	Dacula	2008-2010
Peter Ngo	Norcross High	2007-2009	Daniel Espinel	Duluth	2008-2010
Sally Snider	Norcross High	2007-2009	Sahra Jabbehdari	Duluth	2008-2010
Allison Belfield	North Gwinnett	2007-2009	Abhishek Thumaty	Duluth	2008-2010
Eugene Chang	North Gwinnett	2007-2009	Jake Hannon	Grayson	2008-2010
Candace Crawford	North Gwinnett	2007-2009	Benjamin McDaniel	Grayson	2008-2010
Elizabeth Lukens	Parkview High	2007-2009	Alison McIntosh	Grayson	2008-2010

Members, Gwinnett Student Leadership Team, 1995-2010

Name	School	Year	Name	School	Year
Alexandra Dezii	Mill Creek	2008-2010	Manprett Kaur	Phoenix	2008-2010
Blake J. Elston	Mill Creek	2008-2010	Zach Beebe	Peachtree Ridge	2008-2010
Steven Zwick	Mill Creek	2008-2010	Amy Boudreau	Peachtree Ridge	2008-2010
Ken Ho	Meadowcreek	2008-2010	Michael Kersh	Peachtree Ridge	2008-2010
Shinal Patel	Meadowcreek	2008-2010	Nick Eberhart	Parkview	2008-2010
Palvi Walia	Meadowcreek	2008-2010	Stephen Scott	Parkview	2008-2010
David Buterbaugh	Norcross	2008-2010	Maggie Smith	Parkview	2008-2010
Brandon Hoover	Norcross	2008-2010	Jessica Bilz	South Gwinnett	2008-2010
Molly Kirksey	Norcross	2008-2010	Shaughnessy Flint	South Gwinnett	2008-2010
Seo Kim	North Gwinnett	2008-2010	Megan Willis	South Gwinnett	2008-2010
Wyatt McCausland	North Gwinnett	2008-2010	Alexandria Ayers	Shiloh	2008-2010
Niara Wright	North Gwinnett	2008-2010	Corbyn Nchako	Shiloh	2008-2010
Elizabeth Cuarenta	Phoenix	2008-2010	Brandon Williams	Shiloh	2008-2010

Source: Gwinnett Student Leadership

United Way Campaigns in Gwinnett

Year	Chairman	Firm	Dollar Goal
1986	Glenn White	First Atlanta Bank	$858,000
1987	J. W. Benefield	Modern Electric Co.	915,593
1988	Leo Rainey, Jr.	First National Bank of Gwinnett	1,109,936
1989	Elliott Brack	Atlanta Journal Constitution	1,343,142
1990	Newell Edenfield	Southeastern Mortgage	1,515,803
1991	Gene Ussery	Georgia Power Company	1,902,633
1992	Philip Reed	Southern Bell	2,078,560
1993	Marty Shaw	Rock Tenn Corp.	2,249,275
1994	Susie Hite	Commercial Bank of Gwinnett	2,527,000
1995	Tom Balsman	NCR Corporation	3,148,000
1996	Becky Munteanu	Georgia Power Co.	3,227,040
1997	Alan Golden	Georgia Power Co.	3,543,924
1998	Steve Spellman	Gwinnett Public Schools	3,690,000
1999	Phylecia Wilson	American Cancer Society	3,788,280
2000	Alan Golden & Phylecia Wilson	Georgia Power Company American Cancer Society	3,925,000
2001	Bill McCargo	Scientific Atlanta	3,768,906
2002	Chuck Button	Jordan, Jones and Goulding	3,491,888
2003	Kerry Armstrong	Duke Realty	3,771,631
2004	Sharon Rigsby	Gwinnett Technical College	4,022,695
2005	Al Hansen	EMS Technologies	4,243,257
2006	Mike Guynn	Guynn Properties	4,535,770
2007	Herman Pennaman	Georgia Power Company	4,705,783
2008	Marsha Bomar	Street Smarts	*4,728,752

**** = Anticipated Goal***
Source: United Way of Metropolitan Atlanta

FINANCIAL DATA

Gwinnett Budget Comparisons

Year	Budget*	Number of Employees	April 1 Estimate of County Population
1971	$3.5 million	245	72,349
1980	$27.1 million	1,128	166,903
1990	$580 million	2,874	352,910
2000	$1.27 billion	3,659	588,488
2005	$1,503 bilion	4,405	726,273
2006	$1.543 billion	4,586	757.104
2007	$1.675 billion	4,797	776,380
2008	$1.532 billion	4,893	**797,422

**** Amounts include operating and capital budgets***

***** 2008 Estimate from Gwinnett Economic Development Office***

Source: Gwinnett County Finance Dept.; Census.

Gwinnett Millage Rate, 1994-2008

Year	1994	1995	1996	1997	1998	1999	2000	2001	2002	2003	2004	2005	2006	2007	2008(*)
General Fund	10.10	10.10	10.10	9.30	9.40	8.65	8.48	8.43	8.30	8.29	8.27	10.14	10.00	9.81	9.81
Fire Fund	2.90	2.90	2.90	2.40	2.30	2.10	2.06	1.90	1.87	1.87	1.87	-	-	-	-
Recreation Fund	1.00	1.00	1.00	1.00	1.00	0.90	0.88	0.86	0.85	0.85	0.84	0.84	0.82	0.80	0.80
G.O. Bond Fund	0.95	0.95	0.95	0.75	0.75	0.60	0.57	0.30	0.30	0.24	0.24	0.24	0.23	0.23	0.23
G.O. Bond Fund II	-	-	-	-	-	-	-	-	-	0.25	0.25	0.25	0.25	0.24	0.24
Total County Tax	14.95	14.95	14.95	13.45	13.45	12.25	11.99	11.49	11.32	11.50	11.47	11.47	11.30	11.08	11.08
School M&O	17.10	17.10	17.10	17.10	18.10	17.45	17.12	18.62	18.62	18.87	18.87	19.25	19.25	19.25	19.25
School Bonds	4.75	4.75	3.65	3.65	2.65	2.30	2.05	1.80	1.68	1.43	1.43	1.30	1.30	1.30	1.30
Total School Tax	21.85	21.85	20.75	20.75	20.75	19.75	19.17	20.42	20.30	20.30	20.30	20.55	20.55	20.55	20.55
State Government	0.25	0.25	0.25	0.25	0.25	0.25	0.25	0.25	0.25	0.25	0.25	0.25	0.25	0.25	0.25
Total Property Tax	37.05	37.05	35.95	34.45	34.45	32.25	31.41	32.16	31.87	32.05	32.02	32.27	32.10	31.88	31.88

(*) This millage rate is a projection.
The actual rate may be different upon adoption due to possible changes in values that occur in 2008.

Source: Gwinnett County Government

Gwinnett Tax Digest of 2007

Type of Property	Count	Acres	40 Percent Valuation
Residential	408,396	256,164	$15,621,509,371
Transitional	2	3	95,960
Agricultural	452	1,244	40,557,656
Conservation Use	1,298	20,131	221,401,408
Environmentally Sensitive	1	8	105,440
Commercial	34,851	21,532	6,889,506,329
Industrial	2,321	4,479	975,749,855
Public Utility	65	66	282,616,500
Motor Vehicles	465,121		1,733,929,490
Mobile Homes	2,552		14,621,112
Total	915,059	303,627	25,780,093,067

Source: Gwinnett County Tax Assessor's Office

Gwinnett City Government Budgets and Registered Voters

City	2008 Budget *	2008 Millage	4/1/2007 Population Estimate	Voters Registered†	% of Voters Registered
Auburn	$3,823,425	4.796 (07)	7,474	159	50
Berk. Lake	$1,864,362	3.662	1,685	1,129	67
Braselton	$2,348,299	0	3,503	1,419	74
Buford	$101,054,095	13.25	10,857	4,669	47
Dacula	$3,083,055	4.311	4,344	2,304	53
Duluth	$43,986,732	5.191	24,340	13,048	54
Grayson	$1,359,873	2.5	2,215	1,306	59
Lawrenceville	$96,805,169	2.16	27,230	11,555	42
Lilburn	$6,531,260	4.26	11,285	5,293	47
Loganville	$16,361,123	9.00	8,390	1,270	63
Norcross	$32,072,706	6.027 (07)	9,914	3,401	34
Rest Haven	$29,250	0	148	19	18
Snellville	$21,190,865	4.15	19,608	11,183	57
Sugar Hill	$24,212,919	3.8	15,399	8,704	57
Suwanee	$15,449,900	5.77	12,936	8,148	63
County Budget	$1.532 billion	9.72	776,380	262,998	45.36

***Includes funds from all sources, property tax, SPLOST, enterprise funds**
† Includes registered voters in Gwinnett portion of city only.
Note also: Braselton and Rest Haven have no property tax.
Sources: Gwinnett governments and Atlanta Region Commission*

Top Ten Taxpayers in Gwinnett County for 2006				
Rank	Taxpayer	Type of Business	Assessed Valuation	Tax Paid*
1	BELLSOUTH TELECOMMUNICATIONS	Media/Utility	131,761,870	$4,107,898.90
2	PUBLIX SUPERMARKETS INC	Retail/Distrubution	106,715,300	$3,425,560.99
3	WAL-MART	Retail	101,931,690	$3,272,007.20
4	GEORGIA POWER CO	Utility	92,950,890	$3,036,604.81
5	MALL OF GEORGIA LLC	Retail	78,227,906	$2,511,115.79
6	SCIENTIFIC ATLANTA INC	Manufacturing	71,380,762	$2,244,372.91
7	JACKSON E M C	Utility	54,709,360	$1,756,170.43
8	SUGARLOAF MILLS LTD PTNSHIP	Retail	49,600,000	$1,592,160.00
9	GWINNETT PRADO L P	Retail	41,062,196	$1,318,096.51
10	CINGULAR WIRELESS LLC	Media	40,585,590	$1,302,797.42
Source: Gwinnett County Tax Department				

Top Ten Taxpayers in Gwinnett County for 2007				
Rank	Taxpayer	Type of Business	Assessed Valuation	Tax Paid*
1	AT&T COMMUNICATIONS	Media/Utility	136,554,000	$4,258,778.25
2	PUBLIX	Retail	112,863,747	$3,671,633.79
3	WAL-MART	Retail	112,057,860	$3,382,758.79
4	GEORGIA POWER CO	Utility	107,709,140	$3,181,192.29
5	MALL OF GEORGIA LLC	Retail	89,551,066	$2,863,064.57
6	SCIENTIFIC ATLANTA INC	Manufacturing	66,983,010	$2,135,418.34
7	JACKSON E M C	Utility	63,804,380	$1,981,981.30
8	FOURTH QUARTER PROP LLC	Retail	53,383,800	$1,581,152.98
9	INLAND SOUTHEAST	Retail	49,489,880	$1,545,857.37
10	SUGARLOAF PROERTIES INC	Retail	46,000,000	$1,466,480.00
***Amount includes County, School and State levy only - City taxes, Stormwater Fees, etc. are not included.**				
Source: Gwinnett County Tax Department				

Gwinnett County Special Purpose Local Option Sales Tax (SPLOST)		
Election	Question	Result
June 4, 1985 Special Election	"Shall a special 1 percent sales and use tax be imposed in Gwinnett County for a period of time not to exceed five years and for the raising of not more than $56,515,214.00 for the purpose of funding a capital outlay project consisting of a courthouse and administration building?"	YES - 18,188 88.46% NO - 2,372 11.54%
November 3, 1987 Special Election	"Shall a special 1 percent sales and use tax be imposed in Gwinnett County for a period of four (4) years, for road, street, and bridge purposes, and for the purchase of funding capital outlay projects consisting of a pretrial detention center, a civic center, and the renovation and preservation of the historic century-old county courthouse?"	YES - 14,711 66.47% NO - 7,420 33.53%
November 5, 1991 Special Election	"Shall a special one percent (1%) sales and use tax be imposed for road, street, and bridge purposes, in Gwinnett County for a period of four (4) years?"	YES - 16,321 52.74% NO - 14,627 47.26%
November 7, 1995 Special Election	"Shall a special one percent (1%) sales and use tax be imposed for road, street, and bridge purposes, in Gwinnett County for a period of time not to exceed five (5) years and for the raising of not more than $675,000,000?"	YES - 18,042 49.55% NO - 18,371 50.45%
November 5, 1996 General Election	"Shall a special one percent (1%) sales and use tax be imposed in Gwinnett County for a period of time not to exceed four (4) years and for the raising of not more than $120,000,000 for the purposes of public safety facilities and recreational facilities and for road, street, and bridge purposes for a period of time not to exceed four (4) years and for the raising of not more than $320,000,000?"	YES - 84,928 53.24% NO - 74,577 46.76%
November 7, 2000 General Election	"Shall a special 1 percent sales and use tax be imposed in Gwinnett county for a period of time not to exceed four years and for the raising of not more than $429,375,000 for the purposes of libraries, public safety facilities and parks and recreation facilities, and for road, street, and bridge purposes for a period of time not to exceed four years and for the raising of not more than $320,625,000?"	YES - 100,838 55.05% NO – 82,345 44.95%
November 2, 2004 General Election	"Shall a special one percent sales and use tax be imposed in the Special District of Gwinnett County for a period of time not to exceed four years and for the raising of an estimated amount of $550,000,000 for the purposes of recreational facilities, public safety facilities and equipment, libraries, roads, streets, and bridges, City administrative buildings, and city parking facilities?"	YES – 155,612 65.17% NO – 83,150 34.83%

Source: Gwinnett County Government

Banks with Headquarters in Gwinnett in 2008

Name of Bank	Date Founded	Initial Capital	Current Chairman	*Assets as of June 30, 2008	Board members in 2008
Brand Bank Lawrenceville	1905	$$35,000	Bartow Morgan, Jr.	$1,104,908,503	Patricia M. Thomas, Brand Morgan, Homer Stark, Harold Craig, Mack Meeks, Jim Henderson, Richard Tucker, Bartow Morgan Jr., Chris Smith, Jim Birts
The Community Bank Loganville	1946		Stanley Kelley Jr.	$625,058,758	Stanley Kelley Jr., Coy Baker, Katie Kelley Franklin, Neil Kelley, Donald Myers, Richard Norton, James Towler
Fidelity Bank Norcross	1973	$2 million	James B. Miller Jr.	$1,727,738,000	James B. Miller Jr., H. Palmer Proctor Jr., Maj. Gen. (Ret) David R. Bockel, Edward M. Bowen, M.D., Kevin S. King, James H. Miller III, Robert J. Rutland. W. Clyde Shepherd III, Rankin M. Smith Jr.
People's Bank and Trust Buford	1983	$2 million	Rotate every 3 yrs	$457,502,611	Larry Bailey, Clayton Bartlett, Phillip Beard, Robert Bowman, Larry Cheek, Wayne Hill, Douglas Nichols, George Page, Donn Peevy, Garrett Reed, Garland Roberts
First Security Bank Norcross	1985	$3 million	Ralph Barber Sr.	$147,037,235	Ralph Barber Sr., Ralph Barber Jr. Jerry Gardner, Jim Ellis, John Adams, John Smith, Lilllian Webb, Carl Howington, Tom Phillips, Jack Conway, Dan Baker
Quantum National Bank Suwanee	1995	$5 million	Dr. Narasimhulu Neelagaru	$346,824,000	Dr. Narasimhulu Neelagaru, Doug Wren (president), Doug Bridges, Newell Edenfield, Jim Maran, Warren Wheeler.
Gwinnett Community Bank Duluth	1999	$8.5 million	Thomas J. Martin	$485,819,714	Thomas Martin, Frank W. Bell Jr., Myles H. Mason III, J. Terry Gordon, Don F. Phillips Jr., Daniel E. Reeves, Franklin M. Rinker, John G. Martin, James H. Braden.
Security Bank of Gwinnett Suwanee	2003	$12 million	W.Thomas WheelerJr.	$357,839,000	Hank Baker, Jon Been, Tony Collins, Heyward Horton, Scott Hudgins, Jim Pope, Rob Jordan, Tom Wheeler, Roy Zellars.
American United Bank Lawrenceville	2004	$10 Million	P.I.Joy	$102,931,163	P.I. Joy, T. Glenn Thompson, James Jett, Naresh Parikh, Palamalai Mahizhnan, Surinder Bahl, Kati Patel, Gursharan S. Pannu, William F. Rubin, David B. Poythress.
Georgia Trust Bank Buford	2005	$18 million	William E. Smith	$138,695,920	William E. Smith, Ronald D. Adamson; J. Michael Allen (president and CEO), L. Myron Cantrell; Michael L. Jordan, C. Dean Robinson, Marvin O. Tibbetts III, James J. Tidwell; Michael E.Townsend
Legacy State Bank Loganville	2005	$18 million	Larry Garner	$113,942,000	J. Pat McGoldrick, C. Larry Garner, Robert E. Boss, Mack Ivey, Rob Kiser, Don McCullers, Mark Myers, Renzo Wiggins, W. Michael Strickland, Mark Streifert, William J. Williams, Robert Von Itter, Sanjay Patel, Charles B. Davis.
First Covenant Bank Norcross	2006	$16 million	Joe E. McCart	$182,909,000	James F. Bailey, William R. Blanton, Wydeen Cruikshank, Beverly Guthrie, Joe E. McCart, William C. Stem, Neil H. Strickland, Robert Williamson.

Banks with Headquarters in Gwinnett in 2008

Name of Bank	Date Founded	Initial Capital	Current Chairman	*Assets as of June 30, 2008	Board members in 2008
Republic Bank of Georgia Lawrenceville	2006	$24 million	Robert Ratliff	$129,981,551	Scott Reed (CEO), Wayne Bloodworth, Bill Brantley, Gary Byrd, Mike Buckman, Bill Eason, Charlotte Nash, George Oelschig, Robert Ratliff, Jim Stephenson and Mike Tennant
Embassy National Bank Lawrenceville	2007	$18 million	Nitin Shah	$35,452,000	Chris Fluehr (president and CEO), Nitin Shah, Chuck Thakkar, Steve King, Larry Johnson, Navin Shah, Phillip White.
Touchmark National Bank Norcross	2008	$31.25 million	Tom Persons	$38,336,686	Bill Short (CEO), Edgerton Burroughs, Bill Butler, Dan Cowart, Barry Culbertson, Howard Greenfield, Yuling Hayter, John Johnson, Dan Kaufman, Moon Kim, Hiluard Kitchens, Sudhirkamar Patel, Tom Persons, H.P. Rama, J.J. Shah, Meena Shah, Bill Williams, Vivian Wong.

Source: Individual banks

Gwinnett Revenue from Alcoholic Beverages, 1990-1997

	1990	1991	1992	1993
Category	Dollar Amounts	Dollar Amounts	Dollar Amounts	Dollar Amounts
Beer	2,372,976	2,406,288	2,575,188	2,695,641
Wine	*	*	*	*
Mixed Drink	322,110	330,761	347,946	358,488
Distilled Spirits	56,481	51,803	47,306	48,305
Licenses & Permits				
Beer & Wine Retail	155,000	172,329	164,960	164,500
Beer & Wine Pouring	185,720	190,748	214,234	212,531
Distilled Spirits Pouring	478,050	194,500	555,854	557,555
Alcohol - Wholesale	2,675	3,300	4,050	5,875
Alcohol Beverage Appeal Fee	200	400	2,700	1,800
Alcoholic Beverage Application Fee	15,600	15,900	18,360	12,900
Total Dollars	3,588,812	3,366,029	3,930,598	4,057,595

	1994	1995	1996	1997
Category	Dollar Amounts	Dollar Amounts	Dollar Amounts	Dollar Amounts
Beer	2,860,597	2,981,097	3,158,780	3,440,512
Wine	*	*	*	*
Mixed Drink	358,838	378,105	512,283	456,101
Distilled Spirits	59,361	55,948	61,841	61,163
Licenses & Permits				
Beer & Wine Retail	175,900	177,609	200,150	211,622
Beer & Wine Pouring	223,136	250,146	293,966	327,468
Distilled Spirits Pouring	568,350	593,652	733,570	779,857
Alcohol - Wholesale	3,300	5,550	5,050	5,750
Alcohol Beverage Appeal Fee	1,900	1,200	1,850	600
Alcoholic Beverage Application Fee	15,000	25,442	33,203	25,500
Total Dollars	4,266,382	4,468,749	5,000,693	5,308,573

Gwinnett Revenue from Alcoholic Beverages, 1998-2007

	1998	1999	2000	2001	2002
Category	Dollar Amounts	Dollar Amounts	Dollar Amounts	Dollar Amounts	Dollar Amounts
Beer	3,416,941	3,982,661	3,710,859	3,735,634	3,632,353
Wine	*	*	535,252	533,990	505,895
Mixed Drink	802,793	579,145	354,796	686,802	710,848
Distilled Spirits	66,030	72,196	76,747	77,222	100,692
Licenses & Permits					
Beer & Wine Retail	235,850	269,950	245,606	248,804	257,000
Beer & Wine Pouring	323,516	349,612	379,943	388,942	403,704
Distilled Spirits Pouring	790,561	896,786	972,797	980,765	1,011,370
Alcohol - Wholesale	3,150	5,325	4,025	7,550	9,400
Alcohol Beverage Appeal Fee	1,300	2,400	2,250	3,050	2,150
Alcoholic Beverage Application Fee	26,500	29,800	30,013	30,300	35,400
Total Dollars	5,666,641	6,187,875	6,312,288	6,693,059	6,668,812

	2003	2004	2005	2006	2007
Category	Dollar Amounts	Dollar Amounts	Dollar Amounts	Dollar Amounts	Dollar Amounts
Beer	3,677,775	4,144,716	3,834,726	3,789,932	4,145,425
Wine	581,122	644,658	538,541	497,888	749,933
Mixed Drink	743,177	840,952	745,762	756,838	903,515
Distilled Spirits	79,678	99,486	108,667	102,424	136,525
Licenses & Permits					
Beer & Wine Retail	277,912	273,413	271,636	341,221	341,320
Beer & Wine Pouring	440,565	460,046	474,321	746,667	795,895
Distilled Spirits Pouring	1,040,265	1,085,504	1,160,889	1,509,795	1,625,701
Alcohol - Wholesale	9,500	7,375	6,350	22,000	17,425
Alcohol Beverage Appeal Fee	1,000	3,150	3,500	2,100	1,250
Alcoholic Beverage Application Fee	40,262	49,800	48,000	77,600	92,000
Total Dollars	6,891,256	7,609,100	7,192,392	7,846,465	8,808,989

Source: Gwinnett County Financial Services Department

Industrial Development Authority Financing, 1967 - 2007			
Project/Borrower	Date of Issuance	Amount	Number of Employees
*Dolco Packaging Corporation	11/1/67	$3,500,000	220
*Dolco Packaging Corporation	5/1/69	$1,000,000	
*The Lovable Company	7/1/69	$1,200,000	470
*Georgia-Pacific Corporation	11/1/69	$300,000	
*AmBus Properties, Inc.	5/1/70	$300,000	25
*Blue Ridge Industries	1/1/72	$3,800,000	140
Whirlpool Corporation	12/1/72	$1,400,000	70
Ryder System, Inc.	6/1/74	$1,000,000	100
Mead Corporation	6/1/76	$1,800,000	25
U. S. Shoe Corporation	5/1/77	$3,000,000	80
Michelin Tire Corporaton	12/28/77	$3,000,000	20
*AmBus Properties, Inc.	3/1/78	$750,000	70
Falcons Nest 1, Ltd.	7/1/78	$4,000,000	
Nordson Corporation	11/1/78	$2,000,000	80
Carolina Freight Carriers Corporation	11/1/78	$825,000	25
Tempglass Eastern, Inc.	1/1/79	$1,000,000	60
Falcons Nest 1, Ltd.	1/1/79	$1,000,000	65
Scientific-Atlanta, Inc.	4/1/79	$3,000,000	60
Micromeritics Instrument Corporation	5/18/79	$750,000	100
Marmon/Keystone Corporation	6/14/79	$3,500,000	50
Leco Corporation	7/1/79	$1,000,000	37
J. J. Finnigan Industries	12/1/79	$1,150,000	100
Trammell Crow Distribution Corporation	12/1/79	$4,250,000	100
Mighty Distributing System of America, Inc.	12/14/79	$775,000	
National Steel Service Center, Inc.	3/1/80	$6,000,000	40
*Dolco Packaging Corporation	5/1/80	$1,500,000	
Crown Zellerbach Corporation	7/1/80	$1,800,000	
Phoenix Corporation	10/1/80	$500,000	55
Sampo Corporation of America	10/1/80	$5,300,000	250
Plant Improvement Company, Inc.	2/1/81	$1,000,000	15
McFadden Business Publications, Inc.	3/1/81	$500,000	40
Plastics Packaging, Inc.	3/20/81	$930,000	40
American Institute of Industrial Engineers, Inc.	4/1/81	$850,000	125
Plaid Enterprises, Inc.	5/1/81	$1,400,000	20
Makro Self-Service Wholesale Cororation	8/1/81	$7,000,000	300
Northeast Sales Distributing, Inc.	8/11/81	$1,200,000	25
Electromagnetic Sciences, Inc.	9/14/81	$2,100,000	
Graco, Inc.	10/1/81	$1,100,000	16
Williams Contracting, Inc.	10/29/81	$1,950,000	87
Williams Contracting, Inc.(Amendment)	10/29/81	$1,950,000	

Industrial Development Authority Financing, 1967 - 2007

Project/Borrower	Date of Issuance	Amount	Number of Employees
Wayne Watson Company	1/18/82	$1,500,000	85
Suzanna's Kitchen, Inc.	3/1/82	$800,000	25
BBL Industries, Inc.	3/10/82	$1,500,000	65
Interstate Distributors, Inc.	5/1/82	$2,500,000	125
Permag Dixie Corporation	5/1/82	$600,000	35-40
Waffle House, Inc.	6/29/82	$3,000,000	140-150
Georgia Industries, Inc.	7/15/82	$5,000,000	100-125
Continental Foodservice Company (CFS)	8/30/82	$1,500,000	50
Weyerhaeuser Company	10/1/82	$2,150,000	12
Nix & Miller, Inc.	11/1/82	$1,000,000	35-40
United Stationers Supply Company	11/1/82	$7,500,000	260
Scientific & Business Minicomputers, Inc.	12/1/82	$1,000,000	16
Mayer Electric Supply Company, Inc.	12/22/82	$1,000,000	
GIF Corporation	12/22/82	$3,500,000	150
Okabashi (U.S.) Corporation	12/22/82	$2,000,000	70
Humphries Ready-Mix Company	12/31/82	$1,000,000	20-35
Evans Transportation Company	2/1/83	$1,900,000	85
ODC, Inc.	3/1/83	$2,000,000	50
Binks Manufacturing Company	6/1/83	$1,000,000	25-30
H&M Realty Ventures	6/23/83	$600,000	30-40
Southern Copy Machines, Inc.	7/1/83	$550,000	35
German Auto Parts, Inc.	8/31/83	$1,050,000	20
Phoenix Corporation	9/1/83	$1,200,000	
Precision Processing Company	9/1/83	$1,000,000	3-5
Univar Corporation	11/1/83	$4,500,000	32
Marconi Avionics, Inc.	12/1/83	$4,350,000	400
Connecticut Valley Arms, Inc.	12/1/83	$1,000,000	40
Ulbrich of Georgia, Inc.	12/1/83	$1,000,000	20
Hughes Supply, Inc.	12/1/83	$900,000	12-50
Merck & Company, Inc.	12/1/83	$2,400,000	35-40
Micro Mart, Inc.	12/1/83	$1,700,000	33
J. R. Hobbs Company - Atlanta, Inc.	12/1/83	$330,000	90
Metro Materials, Inc.	12/13/83	$1,000,000	5
J.G.A. Corporation	12/21/83	$1,375,000	23-30
Stockholder Systems, Inc.	4/1/84	$3,600,000	58
Magbee Bros. Lumber & Supply Company, Inc.	4/1/84	$1,500,000	90
Mingledorff's, Inc.	5/1/84	$2,400,000	100
Kuranoff & Chary	5/22/84	$600,000	15
Engraph, Inc.	6/1/84	$3,800,000	75
Kawneer Company, Inc.	6/1/84	$5,250,000	100

Industrial Development Authority Financing, 1967 - 2007

Project/Borrower	Date of Issuance	Amount	Number of Employees
The Winko-Matic Signal Company	6/1/84	$3,200,000	100
OKI America, Inc.	7/1/84	$7,000,000	40
Paul Barrow Company, Inc.	7/11/84	$1,000,000	
Rock-Tenn Company	8/1/84	$3,000,000	20
Plastics/Packaging, Inc.	9/1/84	$900,000	20
Plastics/Packaging, Inc.	9/1/84	$415,000	
Heracus Amersil, Inc.	9/1/84	$7,000,000	44
Dryden Oil Company	9/1/84	$950,000	10-15
B&W Mechanical Contractors, Inc.	10/1/84	$660,000	25
K. C. Coatings, Inc.	10/1/84	$1,000,000	20
Williams Brothers Concrete, Inc.	10/1/84	$2,400,000	
Southern Business Communications, Inc.	10/1/84	$700,000	38
Ewing Brothers, Inc.	10/1/84	$950,000	20-30
Blue Ridge Industries, Inc.	10/1/84	$2,785,000	
Brainard-Kilman Drill Company	11/1/84	$1,500,000	48-53
Makita Corporation of America	12/1/84	$7,000,000	200
Kato Spring of Georgia, Inc.	12/1/84	$5,000,000	60
Sewell Plastics, Inc.	12/1/84	$1,500,000	250
Humphries Concrete Block Company	12/11/84	$4,000,000	
Analyst Maintenance Laboratories, Inc.	12/27/84	$1,000,000	17
Graybar Electric Company, Inc.	1/1/85	$2,100,000	80
Chambers Lumber Company	4/1/85	$400,000	40
Allergo Services, Inc.	5/14/85	$2,227,000	100
Miami Circle Associates, Ltd. Spotswood Parker Company	6/1/85	$2,400,000	
Southern Gwinnett, Ltd.	6/1/85	$3,200,000	100
John Wieland Homes, Inc.	8/1/85	$950,000	20
Interstate Distributors, Inc.	10/1/85	$1,000,000	20
Valentine Enterprises, Inc.	10/1/85	$600,000	25
Makro, Inc.	11/1/85	$7,000,000	
Weeks Super Partnership, Ltd.	11/1/85	$1,000,000	100
Dixie Plywood Company	12/1/85	$1,700,000	18
Kubota Tractor Corporation	12/1/85	$4,800,000	48
A&B Gwinnett, Inc.	12/1/85	$1,500,000	60
Distributors International, Inc.	12/1/85	$2,000,000	24
Best Friends Partners, Ltd.	12/1/85	$3,400,000	23
The Climatic Corporation	12/1/85	$1,000,000	32
Dean Cooper Company, Inc.	12/1/85	$500,000	25
The Lovable Company, L.P.	12/10/85	$1,000,000	16
Joe Powell & Associates, Inc.	2/1/86	$410,000	10
Morris E. Harrison and Associates, Inc.	4/1/86	$720,000	18

Industrial Development Authority Financing, 1967 - 2007

Project/Borrower	Date of Issuance	Amount	Number of Employees
Johnson, Frazier & Wright	4/1/86	$810,000	20
Selasco Corporation	4/14/86	$2,700,000	63
Volvo North America Corporation	11/1/86	$5,800,000	40
Plastics/Packaging, Inc.	5/1/88	$8,225,000	95
Mancurop, Inc.	4/1/89	$3,000,000	
Nordson Corporation	11/1/89	$6,000,000	
Brainard-Kilman Drill Company	6/1/90	$2,000,000	
United Stationers Supply Company	10/1/90	$7,500,000	
Rehrig Pacific Company	10/15/91	$8,000,000	
Suzanna's Kitchen, Inc.	12/1/91	$3,500,000	
Rohrer Properties	4/1/94	$5,500,000	
New Hermes, Inc.	8/1/94	$3,500,000	
Medical Packaging Technologies, Inc.	4/1/95	$6,000,000	
Klockner Namasco Corporation	6/1/95	$5,000,000	
Price Companies, Inc.	6/1/95	$3,000,000	
O'Neal	6/1/95	$3,000,000	
Suzanna's Kitchen, Inc.	11/1/95	$2,250,000	
Curtis 1000	5/1/96	$6,460,000	
Peachtree Packaging, Inc.	5/1/96	$1,800,000	
Sidel, Inc.	11/1/96	$3,300,000	
Virgil R. Williams Jr.	2/1/97	$630,000	
Shephard Construction Company	4/1/97	$2,200,000	
Wesleyan Schools, Inc.	3/26/97	$8,600,000	
Network Publications, Inc.	3/27/97	$6,000,000	
Providence Christian Academy, Inc.	10/9/97	$6,400,000	
Barco Inc.	11/26/97	$6,000,000	
Engleman Baking Co. Inc.	3/1/98	$3,390,000	
Network Publications Inc.	3/27/98	$6,000,000	
Pace Manufacturing Inc.	6/18/98	$2,200,000	
Newel Recycling of Atlanta, Inc.	8/4/98	$7,600,000	
Price Companies Inc.	12/10/98	$2,500,000	
Wesleyan School Inc.	11/4/99	$18,000,000	
Color Image Inc.	6/24/98	$4,100,000	
Lucent Technologies Inc.	5/25/00	$16,700,000	
The Peter R. Maltese Revocable Trust	2/2/00	$3,000,000	
Maltese Signs Inc.	2/10/00	$3,800,000	
TUFF Gwinnett Center LLC	12/1/00	$10,000,000	
Wesleyan School Inc.	3/22/01	$17,500,000	
Suzanna's Kitchns Inc.	4/26/01	$12,050,000	
Gwinnett Convention & Visitors Bureau	5/10/01	$65,000,000	

Industrial Development Authority Financing, 1967 - 2007			
Project/Borrower	Date of Issuance	Amount	Number of Employees
Ole' Mexican Foods Inc.	5/31/01	$7,700,000	
Hopewell Christian Academy	1/4/02	$6,500,000	
Greater Atlanta Christian Schools Inc.	5/16/02	$14,000,000	
CBD Management LLC	9/26/02	$2,500,000	
TUFF Gwnnett Cnter LLC	10/1/02	$1,619,113	
Barco View LLC	7/9/03	$3,700,000	
Pak-Lite Inc.	5/27/04	$3,100,000	
Gwinnett County School District (Lease/purchase financing of various educational facilities for the benefit of Gwinnett County School District)	4/1/04	$284,400,000	
Wesleyan School, Inc.		$22,500,000	
Civic & Cultural Center Expansion Project (Relating to the 65,000,000 Variable Rate Revenue Bonds), Series 2001.	5/3/06		
Hewlett Packard Co. - Pilot Agreement	6/16/06	$243,000,000	
Gwinnett County Public Schools (Partial refunding of Development Authority of Gwinnett County Certificates of Participation, Series 2004)	12/1/06	$23,625,000	
Alexus Enterprises, Inc.	1/31/07	$3,600,000	
KMD Group, LLC	4/18/07	$4,040,000	
Greater Atlanta Christian Schools, Inc.	4/26/07	$15,000,000	
Gwinnett Center Parking Deck	8/3/07	$12,000,000	
Notre Dame Academy, Inc.	9/13/07	$7,500,000	
Barco, Inc.	11/1/07	$9,375,000	
Commercial Truck & Van Equipment, Inc.	12/20/07	$3,500,000	
Satterfield Realty, LLC	12/28/07	$4,000,000	
Greater Atlanta Christian Schools, Inc.		$6,500,000	
Gwinnett Acquisitions, LLC		$12,000,000	
Winthrop Retirement Center of Tucker/McNabb Group, LLC		$6,750,000	
Gwinnett Title Holdings, LLC		$8,000,000	
Norcross Centurion I Corporation		$9,500,000	
Norcross Centurion II Corporation		$4,000,000	

***Bonds were financed by the Gwinnett Industrial Building Authority, which financed no other bonds after 1980.**
Source: Gwinnett Industrial Development Authority

Gwinnett Public Schools

Enrollment by Decade

Year	Students	# Schools
1960	10,836	19
1970	19,152	26
1980	35,957	39
1990	64,943	58
2000	110,075	87
2005	144,627	106
2006	152,044	106
2007	156,338	110
2008	158,336	114

Source: Gwinnett Board of Education

Enrollment at Gwinnett Public Schools

As of end of school, May 21, 2008

Elementary Schools

School	Enrollment
Alcova	986
Alford	951
Annistown	551
Arcado	885
Beaver Ridge	1,062
Benefield	1,205
Berkeley Lake	1,079
Bethesda	1,134
Britt	958
Brookwood	1,115
Camp Creek	1,046
Cedar Hill	1,364
Centerville	822
Chattahoochee	1,142
Chesney	814
Cooper	1,397
Corley	1,241
Craig	1,244
Dacula	1,712
Duncan Creek	1,700
Dyer	672
Early Childhood	483
Fort Daniel	1,213
Freemans Mill	1,130
Grayson	1,559

Elementary Schools

School	Enrollment
Gwin Oaks	1,017
Harbins	1,051
Harmony	661
Harris	726
Head	676
Hopkins	1,745
Ivy Creek	1,353
Jackson	1,745
Kanoheda	1,204
Knight	685
Lawrenceville	979
Level Creek	1,145
Lilburn	1,345
Lovin	501
Magill	1,704
Mason	1,428
McKendree	1,084
Meadowcreek	1,068
Minor	1,189
Monarch	300
Mountain Park	647
Mulberry	524
Nesbit	1,459
New Life Academy	201
Norcross	970

Elementary Schools	
School	Enrollment
Norton	1,964
Oakland Meadow	189
Parsons	1,151
Partee	772
Patrick	792
Peachtree	1,373
Pharr	1,442
Riverside	1,478
Rock Springs	1,184
Rockbridge	885
Shiloh	815
Simonton	1,545
Simpson	1,024
Stripling	988
Sugar Hill	1,132
Suwanee	944
Sycamore	1,274
T. Carl Buice	351
Taylor	1,113
Walnut Grove	1,004
Winn Holt	1,569

Middle Schools	
School	Enrollment
Berkmar	1,006
Creekland	2,808
Crews	1,356
Dacula	2,135
Duluth	1,863
Five Forks	1,161
Give East	148
Give West	210
Hooper Renwick	54
Hull	2,300
Jones	1,389
Lanier	2,584
Lilburn	1,163
McConnell	2,539
Osborne	2,011
Pinckneyville	1,247
Radloff	1,058
Richards	2,410
Shiloh	1,618
Snellville	2,240
Summerour	1,030
Sweetwater	1,723
Trickum	1,909

High Schools	
School	Enrollment
Berkmar	2,881
Brookwood	3,400
Central Gwinnett	2,561
Collins Hill	3,547
Dacula	2,207
Duluth	2,115
Give East	205
Give West	168
Grayson	3,151
Hooper Renwick	71
Math, Science & Tech	172
Meadowcreek	2,155
Mill Creek	3,824
Norcross	2,748
North Gwinnett	2,909
Parkview	2,577
Peachtree Ridge	3,046
Phoenix	397
Shiloh	1,948
South Gwinnett	2,611
Source: Gwinnett Board of Education	

Buford City Schools	
School	Enrollment
Buford Academy	627
Buford Elementary	716
Buford High	758
Buford Middle	701
May 23, 2008 Total = 2,802 ***Source: Buford City Schools***	

Superintendents of Gwinnett Public Schools, 1871-2008

Year	Name	Year	Name
1871	J.W. Glenn	1933-1941	R.C. Simonton
1871-1872	J. L. King	1941-1948	Howard Pool
1872-1873	No state funds, school suspended	1949-1956	R.C. Wilbanks
1873-1875	J.L. King	1956-1967	B.B. Harris
1876-1890	Thomas E. Winn	1967-1977	J.W. Benefield
1890-1900	W.T. Tanner	1977-1990	Alton C. Crews
1900-1907	J.A. Bagwell	1990-1994	George G. Thompson
1907-1920	C.R. Ware	January-July 1995	David O. Crews (Interim)
1921-1924	H.D. Meriweather.	1995-1996	Dr. Sidney Faucette
1925-1932	K.E. Taylor	1996-	J. Alvin Wilbanks

Source: Gwinnett County Board of Education

Gwinnett School Bond Referendums since 1971

Date		Amount	What For	Outcome	Voting Yes	Voting No	Percent Turnout
May 19 1971		$6 million	Classrooms	Won	4,486	3,072	22%
Jun 6 1973		$6 million	Classrooms	Won	2,588	1,936	11%
May 4 1976		$2 million	Classrooms	Won	11,624	7,911	32%
			2 Stadiums	Lost	7,658	11.667	32%
Feb 27 1979		$20 million	Classrooms	Won	7,808	4,518	18%
Feb 9 1982		$10 million	Classrooms	Won	7,795	4,837	17%
Jun 24 1984		$15 million	Classrooms	Won	8,046	3,110	12%
Feb. 11, 1986		$44 million	Classrooms	Won	7,932	2,420	10%
Feb 9 1988		$70 million	Classrooms	Won	8,974	2,633	11%
Feb 13 1990		$75 million	Classrooms	Lost	9,901	12,603	17%
Nov. 1990	$135 Million	$121 milliion	Classrooms	Won	59,524	33,965	12.50%
		$6 million	OpenCampus	Lost	44.315	47.806	
		$5 million	Computers	Won	54,988	37,230	
		$3 million	Gwin. Tech	Won	49,344	42,704	
Nov. 2, 1993	$225 million	$190 million	Classrooms	Won	24,958	15.473	23.20%
		$25 million	Computers	Won	24,079	16,241	
		$10 million	Gwin.Tech	Won	22,075	18,171	
Nov. 7, 2006	***	$425 million	Frontloading	Won	100,288	50,851	48.78%
Feb. 5, 2008		$750 million	Classrooms, technology, land	Won	106,688	38,958	46%

****** Gave authority to School Board to "frontload" sales tax receipts to build schools quicker.***

Source: Gwinnett County Board of Education

Naming Source for Gwinnett Schools

School	Named for...	Date School Opened	Comments
Alcova ES	The location is near the site of the old Alcova School, which is near the Alcovy River, originally spelled Alcova which is believed to come from a Native American tribe.	August 2004	
Alford (J.A.) ES	A former chairman of the Board of Education. Mr. Alford and his father donated land and materials for Bethesda ES.	August 2003	
Annistown ES	area of school (formerly known as Annie's Town after millowner's daughter, Annie)	September 1981	
Arcado ES	road that leads to the school-- road was originally named for three Gwinnett commissioners who served at the time road was paved-- Archer, Cain, and Dover	September 1981	
Beaver Ridge ES	old Beaver Ruin School that served community in 1896	September 1979	
Benefield ES	former Gwinnett County Superintendent of Schools J.W. Benefield	September 1982	
Berkeley Lake ES	community school resides in	September 1983	
Berkmar HS	combination of the voting districts' names (Berkshire and Martins)	September 1966	
Berkmar MS	This name represents the Berkmar Cluster.	August 2004	
Bethesda ES	location (Bethesda Church Road)	September 1940	
Britt (W.C.) ES	educator William Clifford Britt (longtime principal of Snellville HS)	September 1969	
Brookwood ES	proximity to Brookwood HS	September 1985	
Brookwood HS	location near the intersection of Hollybrook and Dogwood roads	September 1981	
Buchanan HS of Technology	Named for Edward Buchanan, an early Norcross industrialist and philanthropist, who manufactured the Norex automobile in the early 1900s, established several businesses in the Norcross area, and financed the first library in Gwinnett.	August 2001	Old Norcross HS
Buice (T. Carl) Pre-K School	Dedicated to Thompson Carl Buice (1905-1989), an educator in Gwinnett County for 40 years. Mr. Buice was principal at Sugar Hill School from 1935 to 1955.	August 1995	Old Sugar Hill ES
Camp Creek ES	nearby Camp Creek	September 1972	
Cedar Hill ES	old Cedar Hill school that was established during 1800s	August 1988	
Centerville ES	old Centerville School that was erected in late 1930s	September 1973	
Central Gwinnett-Lawrenceville HS	as part of consolidation efforts combined Lawrenceville and Bethesda high schools	September 1957	
Chattahoochee ES	Chattahoochee River	August 1989	
Chesney (Charles Brant) ES	Brant Chesney was killed in the line of duty on December 27, 1996, while fighting a fire on Lake Lanier. He was responsible for teaching hundreds of school children in Gwinnett County about fire safety and burn prevention.	August 2004	

Naming Source for Gwinnett Schools

School	Named for...	Date School Opened	Comments
Collins Hill HS	Named for the Collins Hill community in which the school is located.	August 1994	
Cooper (W.J.) ES	Mr. Cooper served the Grayson community on the Board of Education.	August 2003	
Corley ES	The Corley family is a prominent area family. The school replaces Corley's Store, a community landmark.	August 2003	
Craig ES	Named for Robert W. Craig, a local plantation owner. The school stands on property that was once part of this plantation. A prominent citizen, Mr. Craig was road commissioner and established the road that would become Hwy. 78. After the Civil War, he used his stores of reserve grain and seed to help others rebuild their farming operations.	August 1993	
Creekland MS	Based on research conducted by a group of gifted students, the name was recommended primarily because this area was once referred to as creek land because of the number of waterways that intersected on or near the school location.School also has a creek running on two sides of the property. Students further tied this general location to settlements of Creek Indians.	August 1996	Lawrenceville MS Replacement
Crews (Alton C.) MS	Named in memory of Dr. Alton C. Crews (1924-1996), long-time educator, who served as GCPS superintendent of schools from 1977 to 1989. Dr. Crews was a leader in education reform in the South throughout his career.	August 1997	
Dacula ES	Shares a name with the cluster HS. Named for the community, which was named by the first postmaster, who took letters from "Decatur" and "Atlanta" to form "Dacula."	August 1990	Replacement/New
Dacula ES		September 1940	
Dacula HS	community	September 1973	
Dacula MS	community	September 1965	
Duluth HS	community	September 1959	
Duluth MS	community	September 1970	
Duluth MS (replacement)		August 2004	Replacement/New
Duncan Creek ES	An old three-room school in the area that once served 110 students in seven grades.	August 2003	
Dyer (J.G.) ES	educator J.G. Dyer-- principal of Suwanee HS and Grayson HS also served as an assistant superintendent	September 1970	
Five Forks MS	named after its predecessor the old Five Forks School and the community of Five Forks	July 1979	
Fort Daniel ES	Named after a fort located in the area during the War of 1812. The fort was built by settlers as protection from the Indians. Fort Daniel is the first school located in the Hog Mountain community.	August 1994	
Freeman's Mill ES	Bears the name by which Dacula was once known.	August 1999	

Naming Source for Gwinnett Schools

School	Named for...	Date School Opened	Comments
GIVE Center East	Gwinnett InterVention Educational Center, housed in the Hooper-Renwick Center, serving MS and HS students.		
GIVE Center West		August 2004	Located in Buchanan HS of Technology
Grayson ES	community	September 1940	
Grayson HS	Named for the former Grayson HS, which served the community from 1913 to 1957. The community was founded by James P. McConnell and named Tripp. Years later, the community was renamed "Grayson" by postmaster John E. Jacobs.	August 2000	
Gwin Oaks ES	county of Gwinnett and for the beautiful oak trees surrounding the site	September 1976	
Gwinnett Technical College		August 1984	
Harbins ES	Named for the community, which took its name from John Harbin. Harbin was a militia district captain, leading Harbin's militia district. The apostrophe was later dropped. Harbin served as Justice of the Peace for the community from 1849-1853.	August 1995	
Harmony ES	community	September 1957	
Harris (B.B.) ES	Superintendent B.B. Harris	September 1967	
Head (R.D.) ES	long-time Gwinnett school administrator Ralph David Head	September 1979	
Holt (Margaret Winn)	Margaret Holt was a lifelong resident of Lawrenceville and a descendent of Elisha Winn. She taught Spanish and English at Lawrenceville High School. She helped establish the PTA at Lawrenceville Elementary School in the 1950's and was active in many volunteer organizations in Gwinnett.	August 2004	
Hooper Renwick	Named for Marshall M. Hooper, a teacher and principal, and for Lillie Renwick, a teacher. Hooper-Renwick School was the name of the high school for black students in Lawrenceville during segregation. The student bodies from Hooper-Renwick and Central Gwinnett HS were consolidated into one integrated school in the late 1960s and the students were housed at Central. Today, Hooper-Renwick houses the districts alternative program-- The GIVE Center-- as well as those students served through the North Metro program for students with profound learning and behavioral disorders.	August 1995	
Hopkins (G.H.) ES	educator George Harrison Hopkins-- first schoolmaster in the Pinckneyville militia district	September 1984	
Hull (Richard) MS	Dedicated to Richard L. Hull (1903-1953), a successful Atlanta businessman and civic leader, who worked with Duluth citizens to build Gwinnett's first hospital, the Joan Glancy Memorial Hospital and helped establish a school in Duluth.	August 1996	
Ivy Creek ES	A former school by the same name.	August 2003	

Naming Source for Gwinnett Schools

School	Named for...	Date School Opened	Comments
Jackson ES	Jackson family, Dedicated to Andrew and C.P. Jackson, who built Jackson Academy, an early Gwinnett school for poor children, in 1907.	August 1994	
Jones (Glenn C.) MS	A principal who served the K-12 school in the Harmony area for 35 years.	August 2004	
Kanoheda ES	Honors the cultural contributions of the Cherokee in Gwinnett County. "Kanoheda" is a Cherokee word meaning "truths passed through the generations."	August 1994	
Knight ES	Gwinnett educator Victor H. Knight-- principal of South Gwinnett HS	September 1975	
Lanier MS	close proximity to Lake Sidney Lanier	September 1973	
Lawrenceville East		July 1996	
Lawrenceville ES	community	September 1963	
Lawrenceville MS		September 1970	Replaced by Creekland MS
Lawrenceville West			
Level Creek ES	Level Creek was one of the old schools in this area and defines the geographical area where the school is being built.	August 2004	
Lilburn ES	town of Lilburn	September 1970	
Lilburn MS	town of Lilburn	September 1963	
Louise Radloff MS	longtime School Board member Louise Radloff	August 2004	
Magill (J.C.) ES	Named in memory of Gwinnett County Police Officer J.C. Magill, who was killed in the line of duty on May 23, 1993, by a drunk driver.	August 1996	
Mason (Dr. M.H.) Jr. ES	Dedicated to Miles H. Mason, Jr., MD, who served as a physician in the Duluth community for 43 years.	August 1997	
Maxwell HS of Technology	Named after Howard Maxwell, he was a longtime educator, serving as principal of the county's Vocational Education Center at Oakland	1993-- name of school chaged from GVEC-Oakland to Maxwell	
McConnell (J.P.) MS	Named after James P. McConnell (1854-1925), founder of Grayson, a state legislator, and the founder of the community's first school.	August 1996	
McKendree ES	old McKendree School that was built in 1884 adjacent to McKendree United Methodist church	August 1988	
Meadowcreek ES	Shares a name with the cluster HS. Named after the Meadows Family School and the Creek Indians who lived in the area.	August 1998	
Meadowcreek HS	Meadows Family School and the Creek Indians, both once located near the site of the school	August 1986	
Mill Creek HS	The many mills and creeks in the area.	August 2004	
Minor (Rebecca) ES	teacher Rebecca Minor	August 1987	
Monarch School	Special Ed/Pre-K	August 2004	Old Duluth MS

Naming Source for Gwinnett Schools

School	Named for...	Date School Opened	Comments
Mountain Park ES	community	September 1966	
Nesbit ES	educator Clara Nesbit, Honors Miss Clara Nesbit, who taught in Gwinnett schools from the 1920s until her death in 1989. Miss Clara was the granddaughter of slaves. Her first teaching jobs were in black schools as Gwinnett was segregated until the 1960s.	August 1993	
Norcross ES	community/town of Norcross	September 1957	
Norcross HS	community/town of Norcross	September 1956	Buchanan HS of Technology 2001
Norcross HS		August 2001	Replacement/New
North Gwinnett HS	location in the northern part of the county	August 2001	
Norton (R.L.) ES	Gwinnett County Board of Education member Robert Lee Norton	August 1986	
Oakland Center	named for old Oakland School	September 1977	
Osborne (Frank N.) MS	A longtime educator who started the first visiting teacher program in Gwinnett in 1945.	August 2004	
Parkview HS	location-- once enjoyed a direct view of Stone Mountain Park	September 1976	
Parsons ES	The Parsons family, which has a long history of community activism in Duluth.	August 2003	
Partee (Henry) ES	Named in honor of Henry "Sonny" Partee (1932-1989), a lifelong resident of Snellville and an educator in that community for 34 years until his retirement from Snellville MS, the county's first middle school.	August 1997	
Peachtree ES	Indian trail called Peachtree Path along which the school is built	September 1970	
Peachtree Ridge HS	The location (Old Peachtree Road) and for topography.	August 2003	
Pharr ES	educator Lorena Pharr who taught in Snellville for 30 years.	August 1990	
Phoenix HS	Named for the mythical bird that rose from the ashes to live again. Known as Open Campus High School until it was renamed in 1993-94, the school building was rededicated in 1997-98 after renovations.	August 1997	
Pinckneyville MS	community	September 1985	
Richards (J.E.) MS	educator James Everett Richards-- principal of Norcross HS and Lawrenceville MS	August 1987	
Riverside ES	Named for its proximity to the Chattahoochee River, which runs along the county's border.	August 1999	
Rock Springs ES	Named for former one-room school house that had been located in the general area of the new school.	August 1999	
Rockbridge ES	location near Rockbridge Road	September 1966	
Shiloh ES	Shares a name with the cluster HS. Named after the Shiloh community, which took its name from Shiloh Baptist Church, one of the congregations established by freed slaves during Reconstruction.	August 1990	

Naming Source for Gwinnett Schools

School	Named for...	Date School Opened	Comments
Shiloh HS	Shiloh Baptist Church and the community that has grown up around it.	September 1984	
Shiloh MS		September 1982	
Simonton (R.C.) ES	Dedicated to R.C. Simonton, born in Gwinnett County in 1893. Mr. Simonton was a teacher before being elected school superintendent in 1932. He served two terms, lost a third election, then returned to the classroom as a teacher until retirement.	August 1993	
Simpson ES	Honors Anna Louise Simpson-- Miss Ludie-- a longtime educator. She taught at West Gwinnett HS, now Norcross HS, between 1958 and 1962. She retired from teaching in her 70s.	August 1993	
Snellville MS	community	September 1974	
South Gwinnett HS	location in county	September 1957	
Stripling (Susan) ES	educator, Dedicated to respected teacher and yearbook sponsor at Norcross HS between 1979 and 1994. Mrs. Stripling passed away in February 1994, after battling cancer.	August 1999	
Sugar Hill ES	community	August 1995	Replacement/New
Sugar Hill ES		September 1957	Pre-K Center (Buice) 1995
Summerour MS	Lalah Simpson Summerour who gave land for Norcross HS	September 1963	
Suwanee ES	community which was originally named for location on Suwanee Creek	August 1988	Replacement/New
Sweetwater MS	community	September 1976	
Sycamore ES	The location-- Sycamore Road.	August 2003	
Taylor ES	Named after Kope Elise (K.E.) Taylor (1876-1933), who served Gwinnett schoolchildren as a teacher and school superintendent.	August 1997	
Trickum MS	proximity to Five Forks-Trickum Road	September 1975	
Trickum MS		August 2006	Replacement/New
Walnut Grove ES	This school's namesake, Walnut Grove School, was one of the early one-room schools that dotted the county during the late 1800s. Consolidation closed many of these community schools. The old building stands on the Winn House grounds today.	August 1992	

Source: Gwinnett County Board of Education

Proposed Names for New Gwinnett Schools 2007

Suggested recommendations are based on input received from the Naming Schools Committees for the twelve new schools. The Naming Schools Committees met with and received input from community members, educators, and staff of affected schools. Committees reviewed a variety of materials including research, petitions, and letters.

Working Name	Suggested Recommendation	Rationale
Mill Creek/Collins Hill/Dacula Relief Cluster HS Sunny Hill Rd	Mountain View High School	Historical and geographic
Grayson/Dacula Relief Cluster HS New Hope Rd	Archer High School (Benjamin Vernon)	Benjamin Vernon Archer taught and coached basketball in Gwinnett County for thirty five years.
Grayson Cluster MS Cooper Rd	Bay Creek Middle School	Geographic name
Grayson Cluster MS Grayson Hwy	Couch Middle School	The Couch family consisted of 11 children; all attended GCPS. All were achievers in both academics and sports. Eight of eleven of the Couch children graduated from Grayson High School. Eight members of the Couch family have been GCPS employees; the family is still active in GHSAA. The Couch family has invested over seventy-five years in GCPS.
Mill Creek/Collins Hill/Dacula Relief Cluster MS Braselton Hwy	Twin Rivers Middle School	Geographic name
North Gwinnett Cluster MS Peachtree Industrial Blvd.	North Gwinnett Middle School	Geographic name
Grayson Cluster ES Cooper Rd	Trip Elementary School	Geographic name; Trip Academy was the first school in Grayson.
Grayson Cluster ES Grayson Hwy	Starling Elementary School (Ann Cooper)	Mrs. Starling's family dates back to Gwinnett County in 1813 before Gwinnett was created. She taught in the Grayson Elementary School for 25 years. She died in 2004.
Lanier Cluster ES Suwanee Dam Rd	White Oak Elementary School	Historical reference to the one room school house of the early 1900's located at the corner of Suwanee Dam Road and Buford Dam Road.
Mill Creek Cluster ES S. Pucketts Mill Rd	Puckett's Mill Elementary School	Historical reference to Mr. Puckett's Mill – a mill ran for grinding corn and wheat.
Mill Creek/Collins Hill/Dacula Relief Cluster ES Buford Drive	Woodward Mill Elementary School	Woodward's Mill is a privately held landmark gristmill located close to the I-85 interchange at Georgia 20. Merchants came from surrounding counties to have their grain milled at Woodward's Mill in the early 20th century.
South Cluster ES Rosebud Road	Rosebud Elementary School	The location of the new school is across the street from the former Rosebud Elementary where many community members attended from 1903 to 1938.

Source: Gwinnett Board of Education

E-SPLOST I, II, and III Comparison of Results

Description/Category	E-SPLOST I (3-18-97)	E-SPLOST II (11-06-01)	E-SPLOST III (11-07-06)
# Registered Voters	249,808	242,222	315,626
# Votes Cast on E-SPLOST	42,909	34,530	151,139
Percent Voter Turnout	17.17%	13.58%	47.88%
YES Votes for E-SPLOST	30,344	27,121	100,288
% of YES Votes	70.72%	78.73%	66.35%
NO Votes for E-SPLOST	12,565	7,327	50,851
% of NO Votes	29.28%	21.27%	33.65%
E-SPLOST Revenue Project	$560M/545M	$995M/967M	$1.1B/1.081B

Note: The E-SPLOST referendums in 1997 and 2001 were special elections and the 2006 referendum was in the general election.

Source: Gwinnett County Board of Education

Size, Classrooms of Gwinnett Elementary Schools

Elementary Schools	Original Year	Sq. Footage	Current Sq. Footage	Classrooms
Alcova ES	2004	90,453	90,453	37
Alford ES	2004	90,453	134,078	56
Annistown ES	1981	51,014	70,516	35
Arcado ES	1981	52,138	101,800	38
Beaver Ridge ES	1979	52,604	129,108	53
Benefield ES	1982	43,051	82,439	43
Berkeley Lake ES	1983	59,303	102,142	49
Bethesda ES	1932	10,358	136,162	49
Britt ES	1969	26,918	70,110	32
Brookwood ES	1985	52,497	153,326	63
Camp Creek ES	1972	41,728	112,225	47
Cedar Hill ES	1988	78,583	112,979	58
Centerville ES	1973	37,175	82,214	37
Chattahoochee ES	1989	63,594	145,642	67
Chesney ES	2004	90,453	90,453	37
Cooper ES	2003	90,453	189,893	82
Corley ES	2003	90,453	134,078	56
Craig ES	1993	81,333	149,491	67
Dacula ES	1990	73,986	192,540	82
Duncan Creek ES	2003	90,453	162,135	67
Dyer ES	1970	37,860	85,991	36
Ft. Daniel ES	1994	93,933	103,472	49
Freeman's Mill ES	1999	109,410	109,410	49
Grayson ES	1940	9,649	106,534	49

Size, Classrooms of Gwinnett Elementary Schools

Elementary Schools	Original Year	Sq. Footage	Current Sq. Footage	Classrooms
Gwin Oaks ES	1976	45,847	87,766	47
Harbins ES	1995	105,600	152,460	65
Harmony ES	1957	15,427	98,242	35
Harris ES	1967	18,756	75,860	45
Head ES	1979	50,985	64,357	28
Hopkins ES	1984	59,100	175,098	77
Ivy Creek ES	2003	90,453	162,135	67
Jackson ES	1994	101,400	167,895	79
Kanoheda ES	1994	86,086	114,514	63
Knight ES	1975	45,847	52,007	25
Lawrenceville ES	1963	12,814	104,972	49
Level Creek ES	2004	131,656	131,656	53
Lilburn ES	1970	47,728	176,787	73
Magill ES	1996	90,509	180,416	72
Mason ES	1997	88,666	132,940	62
McKendree ES	1988	64,716	135,806	63
Meadowcreek ES	1998	115,696	115,696	46
Minor ES	1987	64,716	121,129	56
Mountain Park ES	1966	30,794	69,881	24
Nesbit ES	1993	93,933	165,792	73
Norcross ES	1957	15,778	91,082	40
Norton ES	1986	64,716	149,511	60
Parsons ES	2003	90,453	90,453	37
Partee ES	1997	100,036	100,036	41
Peachtree ES	1970	41,728	130,241	65
Pharr ES	1990	86,083	106,994	52
Riverside ES	1999	90,453	132,127	62
Rock Springs ES	1999	90,453	152,891	71
Rockbridge ES	1966	20,753	82,574	47
Shiloh ES	1990	87,157	87,157	41
Simonton ES	1992	109,860	134,500	58
Simpson ES	1993	83,648	144,772	62
Stripling ES	1999	110,282	128,122	50
Sugar Hill ES	1995	113,970	113,970	49
Suwanee ES	1988	60,947	82,997	43
Sycamore ES	2003	90,453	126,860	52
Taylor ES	1998	141,376	141,376	67
Walnut Grove ES	1992	87,984	152,076	70
Winn Holt ES	2004	150,871	150,871	64
TOTAL		4,515,582	7,631,210	3,371

Source of Square Footage Tables: Gwinnett County Board of Education

Size, Classrooms of Gwinnett Middle Schools

Middle Schools	Original Year	Sq. Footage	Current Sq. Footage	Classrooms
Berkmar MS	2004	160,018	160,018	45
Creekland MS	1994	275,904	275,904	95
Crews MS	1997	140,037	140,037	41
Dacula MS	1940	16,023	315,281	93
Duluth MS	1957	12,000	217,537	80
Five Forks MS	1979	84,350	130,472	46
Hull MS	1996	141,200	202,800	80
Jones MS	2004	153,154	153,154	45
Lanier MS	1973	39,700	189,149	80
Lilburn MS	1955	14,000	208,449	80
McConnell MS	1996	141,200	198,019	85
Osborne MS	2004	217,537	217,537	80
Pinkneyville MS	1985	84,105	156,626	55
Radloff MS	2004	177,380	177,380	45
Richards MS	1987	94,908	215,575	86
Shiloh MS	1982	81,827	164,888	71
Snellville MS	1974	59,760	191,524	72
Summerour MS	1963	41,480	129,270	44
Sweetwater MS	1976	84,350	209,725	74
Trickum MS	1975	40,095	241,350	72
TOTAL		2,059,028	3,894,695	1,369

Size, Classrooms of Gwinnett High Schools

High Schools	Original Year	Sq. Footage	Current Sq. Footage	Classrooms
HIGH SCHOOLS	YEAR	Sq. Footage	Sq. Footage	Classrooms
Berkmar HS	1966	38,904	429,704	120
Brookwood HS	1981	155,273	403,538	120
Central Gwinnett HS	1957	54,154	351,667	106
Collins Hill HS	1994	261,500	391,560	120
Dacula HS	1973	37,416	391,839	120
Duluth HS	1959	16,422	412,263	120
Grayson HS	2000	354,867	354,867	100
Meadowcreek HS	1986	150,916	469,338	120
Mill Creek HS	2004	423,800	423,800	130
Norcross HS	1956	58,490	416,000	120
North Gwinnett HS	1958	42,002	339,741	100
Parkview HS	1976	138,913	430,244	112
Peachtree Ridge HS	2003	416,000	416,000	120
Shiloh HS	1984	150,916	312,663	76
South Gwinnett HS	1957	42,735	382,681	96
TOTAL		2,342,308	5,925,905	1,680

Teachers of the Year in Gwinnett Public Schools, 1980-2009			
Year	Name	School	Subject
1980	Henry Janowski	Norcross High	
1981	Steve Spellman	Central Gwinnett High	World History/Geography
1982	Wendell Jackson	North Gwinnett High	Science
1983	Mike Strickland	Central Gwinnett High	Social Studies
1984	Dr. Kay Harvey **	Norcross High	Math/Computer Science
1985	Martha Brodrick	Sugar Hill Elementary	Fifth Grade
1986	Nita Hallford	Shiloh High	Language Arts
1987	Steve Spellman	South Gwinnett High	World History/Geography
1988	Mary Mason	Central Gwinnett High	Social Studies
1989	Kathy Rivas	Suwanee Elementary	Kindergarten
1990	Donna Gordon	Benefield Elementary	Second Grade
1991	Jeff White **	Berkmar High	Science
1992	Cindy Kennedy	Five Forks Middle	Seventh Grade Math/Science
1993	Patsy Huey	Shiloh High	Language Arts
1994	RoseMarie Mason	Berkmar High	Language Arts
1995	Ernie Blankenship	Meadowcreek High	Science
1996	Nancy Ward	Shiloh High	Ninth Grade Language Arts
1997	Cynthia Johnson	Parkview HS	Spanish
1998	Vickie McCrary	Collins Hill High	Special Education
1999	Suttiwan Cox	J. E. Richards Middle	ESOL
2000	Christina Starkey	B.B. Harris Elementary	Reading Recovery
2001	Dana Lowe	Duluth High	Orchestra
2002	Dr. Rick Creed	Parkview HS	Mathematics
2003	Dr. Terry J. Burns	Rock Springs ES	First Grade
2004	Judson Bridges	Collins Hill High	Spanish
2005	Deborah D. West	Level Creek Elementary	K-5 Visual Arts
2006	Dr. Mai Yin Tsoi	Collins Hill High	College Prep/Honors Chemistry
2007	Tiffany English	Sugar Hill Elementary	Music
2008	Mandy Collins	McKendree Elementary	Gifted Program
2009	Aimee Burgamy	Trickum Middle School	Art
***** Denotes Georgia Techer of the Year Winner***			
Sources: Gwinnett Board of Education			

Teachers of the Year in Buford City Schools, 1983-2009

Year	Name	School	Subject
1983	Susan Amason	Buford High	Art
1984	Willie Mae Brookins	Buford High	Business Education
1985	Nancy Clark Johnson	Buford Elementary	Third Grade
1986	Nancy Clark Johnson	Buford Elementary	Third Grade
1987	Gaye McNeil	Buford Middle	Art
1988	Elizabeth Puckett	Buford High	Home Economics
1989	Frances Scales	Buford Elementary	Special Education
1990	Jan Masingill	Buford Elementary	Second Grade
1991	Susan Amason	Buford High	Art
1992	Linda Murray	Buford Middle	Physical Education
1993	Kim Goodridge	Buford Elementary	Art
1994	Roger Jessup	Buford High	Technical Education
1995	Lois Shorter	Bufford Middle	Special Education
1996	Gerald Hopper	Buford High	Mathematics
1997	Bonita Burel	Buford Middle	Mathematics
1998	Roger West	Buford Elementary	Fourth Grade
1999	Tara Prince	Buford Elementary	Kindeergarten
2000	Jill Anderson	Buford Elementary	Fourth Grade
2001	Lacrecia Smith	Buford Elementary	Second Grade
2002	Anna Misley	Buford Academy	English Language Learners
2003	Amy Clark	Buford Elementary	First Grade
2004	Teacher of the Year Not Chosen		
2005	Kim Staples	Buford High	Theatre
2006	Karin Manis	Buford Elementary	First Grade
2007	Jacob Travis	Buford Middle	English
2008	Gina Wood	Buford Academy	Special Education
2009	Sara Lingerfelt	Buford Middle	Math

Source: Buford City Schools

Buford City School Superintendents

Years	Name
1909-1939	William N. Nunn
1939-1942	Lovick S. Adams
1942-1960	A.L. Clark
1960-1969	J.R. Callison
1969-1972	Joseph C. Avery
1972-1977	Aaron Looper
1977-1984	Jimmy D. Puckett
1984-1994	Beauty Baldwin
1994-1998	Andy Henderson
1999-2001	Tom Wilson
2001-2006	Sue Morris
2006-	Geye Hamby

Source: Buford City Schools

School Board Members, Gwinnett Public Schools, 1906-2008

Year	Chair	Member	Member	Member	Member
1906	C. D. Jacobs	E. G. McDaniel	C. A. McDaniel	M. T. Verner	M. R. Maynard
1907	C. D. Jacobs	E. G. McDaniel	C. A. McDaniel	M. T. Verner	M. R. Maynard
1908	C. D. Jacobs	E. G. McDaniel	C. A. McDaniel	M. T. Verner	M. R. Maynard
1909	C. D. Jacobs	J. M. Wilson	C. A. McDaniel	M. T. Verner	T. H. Evans
1910	C. D. Jacobs	J. M. Wilson	C. A. McDaniel	M. T. Verner	T. H. Evans
1911	C. A. McDaniel	J. M. Wilson	C. D. Jacobs	M. T. Verner	T. H. Evans
1912	C. A. McDaniel	J. M. Wilson	C. D. Jacobs	M. T. Verner	T. H. Evans
1913	C. D. Jacobs	J. M. Wilson	T. E. Johnson	M. T. Verner	T. H. Evans
1914	M. T. Verner	J. M. Wilson	H. B. Harmon	J.W. McElvaney	T. H. Evans
1915	M. T. Verner	J. M. Wilson	H. B. Harmon	J.W. McElvaney	C. D. Jacobs
1916	M. T. Verner	W. T. Hinton	H. B. Harmon	J.W. McElvaney	J. W. Ford
1917	M. T. Verner		H. B. Harmon	J.W. McElvaney	J. W. Ford
1918	M. T. Verner	W. T. Hinton	H. B. Harmon	J.W. McElvaney	J. W. Ford
1919	M. T. Verner	W. T. Hinton	H. B. Harmon	J. K. Jackson	J. W. Ford
1920	J. K. Jackson	W. T. Hinton	H. B. Harmon	J. C. Byrdf	J. W. Ford
1921	H. B. Harmon	T. S. Garner	Sam Craig, Jr.	J. W. Ford	J. C. Byrd
1922	H. B. Harmon	T. S. Garner	Sam Craig, Jr.*	J. W. Ford	J. C. Byrd
1923	H. B. Harmon	T. S. Garner	J. C. Pool	J. W. Ford	J. C. Byrd
1924	H. B. Harmon	F. M. Moore	J.T. Jones	J. W. Ford	E. C. Hays
1925	H. B. Harmon	F. M. Moore	J. T. Jones	J. W. Ford	Edwin Hays
1926	J. W. Ford	F. M. Moore	Cecil Pharr	T. E. Johnson	J. T. Jones
1927	J. W. Ford	F. M. Moore	C. S. Pharr	T. E. Johnson	J. T. Jones
1928	J. W. Ford	F. M. Moore	C. S. Pharr	Heard Summerour	J. T. Jones
1929	J. W. Ford	T. E. Johnson	C. S. Pharr	Heard Summerour	J. T. Jones
1930	J. W. Ford	T. E. Johnson	A. D. Moore	Heard Summerour	J. T. Jones
1931	J. W. Ford	T. E. Johnson	A. D. Moore	Heard Summerour	J. T. Jones
1932		Unavailable			
1933	J. E. Johnson				
1934					
1935					
1936					
1937					
1938					
1939					
1940					
1941	J. A. Alford	A. W. Tucker	W. J. Cooper	C. A. Garner	C. S. Pharr
1942	J. A. Alford	A. W. Tucker	W. J. Cooper	C. A. Garner	C. S. Pharr
1943	R. P. Pickens	C. A. Garner	C. F. Griswell	H. V. Kilgore	C. S. Pharr
1944	R. P. Pickens	C. A. Garner	C. F. Griswell	H. V. Kilgore	C. S. Pharr
1945	R. P. Pickens	C. F. Griswell	W. C. Britt	H. V. Kilgore	M. B. Verner
1946	R. P. Pickens	C. F. Griswell	H. V. Kilgore	W. C. Britt	M. B. Verner

School Board Members, Gwinnett Public Schools, 1906-2008					
Year	Chair	Member	Member	Member	Member
1947	R. P. Pickens	M. B. Verner	W. C. Britt	C. F. Griswell	H. V. Kilgore
1948	R. P. Pickens	M. B. Verner	W. C. Britt	H. V. Kilgore	C. F. Griswell
1949	R. P. Pickens	M. B. Verner	C. F. Griswell	H. V. Kilgore	R. L. Norton
1950	R. P. Pickens	H. V. Kilgore	M. B. Verner	Powell Smith	R. L. Norton
1951	R. P. Pickens	M. B. Verner	Ross Still	Powell Smith	R. L. Norton
1952	M. B. Verner	C. A. Garner	Ross Still	Powell Smith	R. L. Norton
1953	M. B. Verner	C. A. Garner	Ross Still	Powell Smith	R. L. Norton
1954	M. B. Verner	C. A. Garner	Ross Still	Powell Smith	R. L. Norton
1955	M. B. Verner	C. A. Garner	Ross Still	Powell Smith	R. L. Norton
1956	M. B. Verner	C. A. Garner	Ross Still	Powell Smith	R. L. Norton
1957	M. B. Verner	W. R. Still	W. M. Wells	Powell Smith	R. L. Norton
1958	M. B. Verner	W. R. Still	W. M. Wells	Powell Smith	R. L. Norton
1959	J. F. Brannan	Elizabeth Mason	A. W. Peters	Carey Cash	Ralph Kennedy
1960	J. F. Brannan	Elizabeth Mason	A. W. Peters	Carey Cash	Ralph Kennedy
1961	J. F. Brannan	Elizabeth Mason	A. W. Peters	Carey Cash	Ralph Kennedy
1962	J. F. Brannan	Elizabeth Mason	A. W. Peters	Carey Cash	Ralph Kennedy
1963	Elizabeth Mason	Ferris Hutchins	A. W. Peters	Carey Cash	Ralph Kennedy
1964	Elizabeth Mason	Ferris Hutchins	A. W. Peters	Carey Cash	Ralph Kennedy
1965	Ferris Hutchins	W. S. Dee	A. W. Peters	Carey Cash	Cecil Gober
1966	Ferris Hutchins	W. S. Dee	A. W. Peters	Carey Cash	Cecil Gober
1967	W. S. Dee, Jr.	Ferris Hutchins	Ronald Chadwick***	Carey Cash	Cecil Gober
1968	W. S. Dee, Jr.	Ferris Hutchins	Ronald Chadwick	Carey Cash	Cecil Gober
1969	Carey Cash	Howard Greene	Ronald Chadwick	Hollis Britt	Cecil Gober
1970	Carey Cash	Howard Greene	Ronald Chadwick	Hollis Britt	Cecil Gober
1971	Cecil Gober	Howard Greene	Earle Snell	Hollis Britt	Carey Cash
1972	Cecil Gober	Howard Greene	Earle Snell	Hollis Britt	Carey Cash
1973	Howard Greene	Cecil Gober	Earle Snell	Louise Radloff	Elizabeth Alford
1974	Earle Snell	Howard Greene	Ceil Gober	Louise Radloff	Elizabeth Alford
1975	Louise Radloff	Howard Greene	Ronald Chadwick	Cecil Gober	Elizabeth Alford
1976	Cecil Gober	Howard Greene	Ronald Chadwick	Louise Radloff	Elizabeth Alford
1977	Louise Radloff	Cecil Gober	Ronald Chadwick	Carrie Maloney	Martha Ashworth
1978	Ronald Chadwick	Cecil Gober	Carrie Maloney	Louise Radloff	Martha Ashworth
1979	Martha Ashworth	Cecil Gober	Carrie Maloney	Louise Radloff	Dr. David Richardson
1980	Carrie Maloney	Cecil Gober	Dr. David Richardson	Louise Radloff	Martha Ashworth
1981	Cecil Gober	Ellis Britt	Dr. David Richardson	Louise Radloff	Eve Hoffman
1982	Louise Radloff	Ellis Britt	Dr. David Richardson	Cecil Gober	Eve Hoffman
1983	Ellis Britt	Louise Radloff	Dr. David Richardson	Cecil Gober	Eve Hoffman
1984	Eve Hoffman	Cecil Gober	Ellis Britt	Louise Radloff	Stan Jones
1985	Cecil Gober	Bob Wood	Jeff Moore	Louise Radloff	Stan Jones
1986	Stan Jones	Cecil Gober	Jeff Moore	Bob Wood	Louise Radloff
1987	Louise Radloff	Bob Wood	Stan Jones	Jeff Moore	Daniel Parks

School Board Members, Gwinnett Public Schools, 1906-2008

Year	Chair	Member	Member	Member	Member
1988	Bob Wood	Stan Jones	Louise Radloff	Jeff Moore	Daniel Parks
1989	Daniel Parks	Stan Jones	Louise Radloff	Julie Duke	Thomas L. Harris
1990	Stan Jones	Daniel Parks	Louise Radloff	Julie Duke	Thomas L. Harris
1991	Thomas L. Harris	Pat Mitchell	Louise Radloff	Dr. Jim Fisher	Julie Duke
1992	Louise Radloff	Pat Mitchell	Thomas L. Harris	Louise Radloff	Julie Duke
1993	Julie Duke	Pat Mitchell	Dr. Jim Fisher	Joel Taylor	Louise Radloff
1994	Pat Mitchell	Joel Taylor	Julie Duke	Louise Radloff	Dr. Jim Fisher
1995	Joel Taylor	Louise Radloff	Daniel D. Seckinger	Dr. Robert McClure	Julie Duke
1996	Louise Radloff	Daniel D. Seckinger	Dr. Robert McClure	Julie Duke	Joel Taylor**
1997	Daniel D. Seckinger	Dr. Robert McClure	Louise Radloff	Dr. Billy Britt	Dr. Mary Kay Murphy
1998	Dr. Robert McClure	Louise Radloff	Daniel D. Seckinger	Dr. Billy Britt	Dr. Mary Kay Murphy
1999	Dr. Mary Kay Murphy	Louise Radloff	Daniel D. Seckinger	Dr. Billy Britt	Dr. Robert McClure
2000	Dr. Billy Britt	Louise Radloff	Daniel D. Seckinger	Dr. Robert McClure	Dr. Mary Kay Murphy
2001	Louise Radloff	Dr. Mary Kay Murphy	Daniel D. Seckinger	Dr. Billy Britt	Dr. Robert McClure
2002	Daniel D. Seckinger	Dr. Mary Kay Murphy	Louise Radloff	Dr. Billy Britt	Dr. Robert McClure
2003	Dr. Robert McClure	Dr. Mary Kay Murphy	Louise Radloff	Dr. Billy Britt	Daniel D. Seckinger
2004	Dr. Mary Kay Murphy	Dr. Robert McClure	Louise Radloff	Dr. Billy Britt	Daniel D. Seckinger
2005	Daniel D. Seckinger	Dr. Robert McClure	Carole Boyce	Louise Radloff	Dr. Mary Kay Murphy
2006	Dr. Robert McClure	Louise Radloff	Carole Boyce	Daniel D. Seckinger	Dr. Mary Kay Murphy
2007	Louise Radloff	Daniel D. Seckinger	Carole Boyce	Dr. Robert McClure	Dr. Mary Kay Murphy
2008	Carole Boyce	Daniel D. Seckinger	Dr. Robert McClure	Dr. Mary Kay Murphy	Louise Radloff

**** James C. Pool elected to replace Sam Craig Jr. who moved to another county.***
***** Mary Root replaced Joel Taylor in Dist. 1 July 9-December 31.***
****** Ronald Chadwick to fulfill unexpired term of Jimmie A. Johnson (June 1967).***

Source: Gwinnett County Board of Education

Buford City School Board Members, 1912-2008

Year	Superintendent	Member	Member	Member	Member	Member
1912	W. N. Nunn	W. B. Shadburn	John Q. Allen	Idus Bowden	J. M. Sewell	
1913	W. N. Nunn					
1914	W. N. Nunn	S. J. Busha	John Q. Allen	Bona Allen, Jr.	J. M. Sewell	C. I. White
1915	W. N. Nunn	S. J. Busha	John Q. Allen	Bona Allen, Jr.	J. M. Sewell	C. I. White
1916	W. N. Nunn	S. J. Busha	D. A. Irwin	J. L. Shadburn	V. H. Allen	W. M. Prater
1917	W. N. Nunn	W. L. Shadburn	D. A. Irwin	J. L. Shadburn	V. H. Allen	John Q. Allen
1918	W. N. Nunn	W. L. Shadburn	L. P. Pattillo	J. L. Shadburn	C. I. White	John Q. Allen
1919	W. N. Nunn	W. L. Shadburn	L. P. Patillo	J. L. Shadburn	C. I. White	Bona Allen, Jr.
1920	W. N. Nunn	W. L. Shadburn	N. W. Buice	J. L. Shadburn	J. M. Sewell	Bona Allen, Jr.
1921	W. N. Nunn	W. L. Shadburn	N. W. Buice	J. L Shadburn	J. M. Sewell	Bona Allen, Jr.
1922	W. N. Nunn	W. L. Shadburn	N. W. Buice	Bona Allen, Jr.	John Q. Allen	J. M. Sewell
1923	W. N. Nunn	D. A. Irwin	N. W. Buice	J. M. Sewell	S. J. Busha	S. J. Busha
1924	W. N. Nunn	D. A. Irwin	N. W. Buice	V. M. Beard	L. P. Patillo	S. J. Busha
1925	W. N. Nunn	John Q. Allen	N. W. Buice	V. M. Beard	L. P. Patillo	S. J. Busha
1926	W. N. Nunn	John Q. Allen	Bona Allen, Jr.	V. M. Beard	L. P. Patillo	S. J. Busha
1927	W. N. Nunn	John Q. Allen	J. L. Shadburn	V. M. Beard	L. P. Patillo	S. J. Busha
1928	W. N. Nunn	John Q. Allen	J. L. Shadburn	V. M. Beard	L. P. Patillo	S. J. Busha
1929	W. N. Nunn	John Q. Allen	Bona Allen, Jr.	V. M. Beard	L. P. Patillo	S. J. Busha
1930	W. N. Nunn	John Q. Allen	Bona Allen, Jr.	W. L. Shadburn	Kate Allen Shadburn	S. J. Busha
1931	W. N. Nunn	Paul T. Bagwell	Bona Allen, Jr.	W. L. Shadburn	Kate Allen Shadburn	G. T. Tapp
1932	W. N. Nunn	Paul T. Bagwell	Bona Allen, Jr.	W. L. Shadburn	Kate Allen Shadburn	G. T. Tapp
1933	W. N. Nunn	P. L. Royal	Bona Allen, Jr.	W. L. Shadburn	Kate Allen Shadburn	G. T. Tapp
1934	W. N. Nunn	P. L. Royal	Bona Allen, Jr.	W. L. Shadburn	Kate Allen Shadburn	G. T. Tapp
1935	W. N. Nunn	P. L. Royal	Bona Allen, Jr.	W. L. Shadburn	Kate Allen Shadburn	D. A. Irwin
1936	W. N. Nunn	P. L. Royal	Bona Allen, Jr.	W. L. Shadburn	Kate Allen Shadburn	D. A. Irwin
1937	W. N. Nunn	P. L. Royal	Bona Allen, Jr.	W. L. Shadburn	Kate Allen Shadburn	Carl Pirkle
1938	W. N. Nunn	P. L. Royal	G. R. Wallace	D. S. Ivey	Kate Allen Shadburn	Carl Pirkle
1939	L. S. Adams	P. L. Royal	G. R. Wallace	D. S. Ivey	Bona Allen, Jr.	
1940	L. S. Adams	John Q. Allen	G. R. Wallace	D. S. Ivey	Bona Allen, Jr.	P. L. Royal
1941	L. S. Adams	John Q. Allen	G. R. Wallace	D. S. Ivey	Bona Allen, Jr.	P. L. Royal
1942	A. L. Clark	M. E. McLain	G. R. Wallace	D. S. Ivey	Bona Allen, Jr.	John Q. Allen
1943	A. L. Clark	M. E. McLain	G. R. Wallace	D. S. Ivey	Bona Allen, Jr.	John Q. Allen
1944	A. L. Clark	M. E. McLain	G. R. Wallace	Golden Knight	Bona Allen, Jr.	John Q. Allen
1945	A. L. Clark	M. E. McLain	G. R. Wallace	Golden Knight	Bona Allen, Jr.	John Q. Allen
1946	A. L. Clark	M. E. McLain	G. R. Wallace	Golden Knight	Bona Allen, Jr.	John Q. Allen
1947	A. L. Clark	M. E. McLain	G. R. Wallace	Golden Knight		
1948	A. L. Clark	M. E. McLain	G. R. Wallace	Golden Knight	Harley Kimmel	J. E. Simpson
1949	A. L. Clark	M. E. McLain	G. R. Wallace	Golden Knight	Harley Kimmel	E. E. Robinson
1950	A. L. Clark	M. E. McLain	Benson Jones	Golden Knight	Harley Kimmel	E. E. Robinson
1951	A. L. Clark	M. E. McLain	Benson Jones	Stanley Allen	Mrs. W. V. Boling	Chief Garner
1952	A. L. Clark	L. A. Wilson	Dr. Harry Hutchins	Stanley Allen	Mrs. W. V. Boling	E. E. Robinson

Buford City School Board Members, 1912-2008

Year	Superintendent	Member	Member	Member	Member	Member
1953	A. L. Clark	L. A. Wilson	Handsel Morgan	W. N. Shadburn, Jr.	Chief Garner	Lionel Drake
1954	A. L. Clark	L. A. Wilson	Handsel Morgan	W. N. Shadburn, Jr.	Chief Garner	Lionel Drake
1955	A. L. Clark	L. A. Wilson	H. Carson Smith	M. E. McClain	Chief Garner	E. E. Robinson
1956	A. L. Clark	Dr. Harry Hutchins	H. Carson Smith	George Kelley	Chief Garner	Lionel Drake
1957	A. L. Clark	Dr. Harry Hutchins	H. Carson Smith	George Kelley	Chief Garner	Stanley Allen
1958	A. L. Clark	Charles Garrett	Joseph E. Cheeley, Jr.	John R. Roberts	Robert Perkins	E. E. Robinson
1959	A. L. Clark	Charles Garrett	Billy R. Cain	John R. Roberts	M. E. McLain	Lionel Drake
1960	J. Roy Callison	Arnold Hammer	Billy R. Cain	George Kelley	M. E. McLain	Stanley Allen
1961	J. Roy Callison	Arnold Hammer	J. E. Gober	George Kelley	Ed Brogdon	E. E. Robinson
1962	J. Roy Callison	Arnold Hammer	J. E. Gober	George Kelley	Ed Brogdon	Loss Sears
1963	J. Roy Callison	Arnold Hammer	Joseph E. Cheeley, Jr.	George Kelley	Frank Greer	Stanley Allen
1964	J. Roy Callison	Samuel Stancil	Joseph E. Cheeley, Jr.	Harry Hutchins	Frank Greer	E. E. Robinson
1965	J. Roy Callison	Samuel Stancil	Hubert Higgins	Harry Hutchins	Marion Williams	Stanley Allen
1966	J. Roy Callison	Glen Gasaway	Hubert Higgins	Reid Merritt	Marion Williams	Loss Sears
1967	J. Roy Callison	Glen Gasaway	Dr. Cecil Miller	Reid Merritt	Marion Williams	E. E. Robinson
1968	J. Roy Callison	Billy R. Cain	Dr. Cecil Miller	Edwin Wood	Marion Williams	E. E. Robinson
1969	Joe Avery	Billy R. Cain	Tom Moss	Edwin Wood	Joseph E. Cheeley, Jr.	Loss Sears
1970	Joe Avery	James W. Cain	Tom Moss	Edwin Wood	Joseph E. Cheeley, Jr.	E. E. Robinson
1971	Joe Avery	James W. Cain	Tom Moss	Edwin Wood	Joseph E. Cheeley, Jr.	Noah Herrington
1972	Aaron Looper	James W. Cain	Tom Moss	Edwin Wood	Joseph E. Cheeley, Jr.	Stanley Allen
1973	Aaron Looper	James W. Cain	Tom Moss	Edwin Wood	Selma Cheeley	E. E. Robinson
1974	Aaron Looper	Ed Merritt	Tom Moss	Edwin Wood	Selma Cheeley	Bob Joseph
1975	Aaron Looper	Ed Merritt	Rudolph Born	Edwin Wood	Paul Jones	Charles Martin
1976	Aaron Looper	Ed Merritt	Rudolph Born	Martha Moss	Paul Jones	Hubert Higgins
1977	Jim D. Puckett	Ed Merritt	Rudolph Born	Martha Moss	Robert Perkins	Phillip Beard
1978	Jim D. Puckett	Ed Merritt	Rudolph Born	Martha Moss	Robert Perkins	Charles Martin
1979	Jim D. Puckett	Ed Merritt*	Rudolph Born	Martha Moss	W. C. Greer	Robert Bell
1980	Jim D. Puckett	Robert Bell	Rudolph Born	Martha Moss	W. C. Greer	Hubert Higgins
1981	Jim D. Puckett	Robert Bell	Rudolph Born	Martha Moss	W. C. Greer	Robert Perkins
1982	Jim D. Puckett	Robert Bell	Rudolph Born	Priscilla K. Edwards	W. C. Greer	Phillip Beard
1983	Jim D. Puckett	Robert Bell	Gene Kimbro	Priscilla K. Edwards	J. Wyman Wilborn	Tommy Hughes
1984	Beauty P. Baldwin	Robert Bell	Gene Kimbro	Priscilla K. Edwards	J. Wyman Wilborn	Tommy Hughes
1985	Beauty P. Baldwin	Robert Bell	Gene Kimbro	Priscilla K. Edwards	J. Wyman Wilborn	Phillip Beard
1986	Beauty P. Baldwin	Robert Bell	Gene Kimbro	Barbara H. Fricks	J. Wyman Wilborn	Tommy Hughes
1987	Beauty P. Baldwin	Robert Bell	Gene Kimbro	Barbara H. Fricks	J. Wyman Wilborn	William Wiley
1988	Beauty P. Baldwin	Robert Bell	Gene Kimbro	Barbara H. Fricks	J. Wyman Wilborn	Phillip Beard

Buford City School Board Members, 1912-2008						
Year	Superintendent	Member	Member	Member	Member	Member
1989	Beauty P. Baldwin	Robert Bell	Gene Kimbro	Barbara H. Fricks	J. Wyman Wilborn	Tommy Hughes
1990	Beauty P. Baldwin	Robert Bell	Gene Kimbro	Barbara H. Fricks	J. Wyman Wilborn	William Wiley
1991	Beauty P. Baldwin	Robert Bell	Gene Kimbro	Barbara H. Fricks	Phillip Beard	Robert Boggs
1992	Beauty P. Baldwin	Robert Bell	Gene Kimbro	Barbara H. Fricks	William Wiley	Robert Boggs
1993	Beauty P. Baldwin	Robert Bell	Gene Kimbro	Barbara H. Fricks	Phillip Beard	Robert Boggs
1994	Andy Henderson	Robert Bell	Gene Kimbro	Barbara H. Fricks	Phillip Beard	Pat Pirkle
1995	Andy Henderson	Robert Bell	Gene Kimbro	Barbara H. Fricks	Chris Burge	Pat Pirkle
1996	Andy Henderson	Robert Bell	Gene Kimbro	Barbara H. Fricks	Phillip Beard	Pat Pirkle
1997	Andy Henderson	Robert Bell	Gene Kimbro	Barbara H. Fricks	Chris Burge	Pat Pirkle
1998	Andy Henderson	Robert Bell	Gene Kimbro	Barbara H. Fricks	Phillip Beard	Pat Pirkle
1999	Tom Wilson	Robert Bell	Gene Kimbro	Barbara H. Fricks	Phillip Beard	Pat Pirkle
2000	Tom Wilson	Robert Bell	Gene Kimbro	Phillip Perkins	Phillip Beard	Pat Pirkle
2001	Sue Morris	Robert Bell deceased)	Gene Kimbro	Phillip Perkins	Phillip Beard	Pat Pirkle
2002	Sue Morris	Leon Johnson	Gene Kimbro	Phillip Perkins	Phillip Beard	Pat Pirkle
2003	Sue Morris	Leon Johnson	Gene Kimbro	Phillip Perkins	Phillip Beard	Pat Pirkle
2004	Sue Morris	Leon Johnson	Gene Kimbro (deceased)	Steve Merritt	Phillip Beard	Pat Pirkle
2005	Sue Morris	Leon Johnson	Bruce Fricks	Steve Merritt (deceased)	Phillip Beard	Pat Pirkle
2006	Geye Hamby	Leon Johnson	Bruce Fricks	Daren Perkins	Phillip Beard	Pat Pirkle
2007	Geye Hamby	Leon Johnson	Bruce Fricks	Daren Perkins	Phillip Beard	Pat Pirkle
2008	Geye Hamby	Leon Johnson	Bruce Fricks	Daren Perkins	Phillip Beard	Pat Pirkle

**** Mr. Merritt died in office; replaced for balance of year by Philip Beard***
Source: Buford City Schools

Educational Foundations of Gwinnett Schools, Colleges

Foundation Name	Date Founded	Corpus Size at start	Corpus Size in 2007	Grants Since Inception	Total Contributors	Director
Berkmar Cluster Schools Foundation	September 17, 2008	$1,000	$10,000	5 = $12,000	2	Marc Cain, president
Brookwood Cluster Schools Foundation	June 25, 1909	$25,000	$94,000	49 = $74,000	500+	Denise Duch Widzgowski
Collins Hill Education Foundation		$11,000	$11,000	$15,771	83	Patti Stafford
Central Gwinnett High	No Foundation					
Dacula Academic Community Foundation	April 15, 2008	$3,000	$16,944	$8,302	14	Darby Coy Teresa Cantrell
Grayson Cluster Schools Foundation	June 23, 1909	$55,000	$187,000+	$88,000+	800+	Diane Schatell
Gwinnett Cunty Public School Foundation	June 29, 1909		$300,000	12	80	Vacant
Meadowcreek High School	No Foundation					
Mill Creek Cluster Education Foundation	February, 2005	$24,000	$62,000	12 = $10,065	100+	Lisa Daenen
Norcross High School Foundation for Excellenece	2001	0	$96,000	$250,000	300+	Jenny and Bob Chapin, co-presidents
North Gwinnett Education Foundation	March 22, 2001	$25,000	$256,000	$179,249	600+	Kathleen Bradshaw
Peachtree Ridge Education Foundation	February, 2007	0	$47,371	$244,000	1029	Lynn Brunatti
Shiloh Community Foundation	June 1, 2005	$53,000	$20,813	$0	1	Tom Marley
South Gwinnett Cluster Foundation	November 17, 2007	$2,000	$2,000	0	5	Glenn Williams Greg Bender
Georgia Gwinnett Foundation	March 8, 2006	0	$28,812	$266,262	218	Gordon Harrison
Gwinnett Tech Foundation	March, 1994	$80,000*	$7.3 million	$4.8 million	2,043 gifts; 921 donors	Mary Beth Byerly

**** Note Gwinnett Tech original corpus came by borrowing $80,000 from SunTrust, backed by board member's guarantee.***
Source: Individual Foundations

Private Schools in Gwinnett

Name of School	Date Started	Grades	Enrollment Elementary	Enrollment Middle	Enrollment High School	Faculty Number	Accredited?	Campus Value	Endowment
Greater Atlanta Christian School	1961	K4-12	K4-5th 787	504	646	146	SACS, SAIS ACSI	$162 million	$30 million
Wesleyan School	1963	K-12	299	353	429	134	SCS; SAIS, AAAIS, NAIS	$95 million	$7.2 million
Killian Hill Christian	1972	K5-12	263	146	116	32	GPSAC	$10 million	none
St John Neumann School	1986	K-8	398	169	0	40	SACS, SAIS	$8 million	In Process
Providence Christian Academy	1991	K-12	248	211	360	70	GAC; SACS; ACSI	$19 million	$15,000*
Hopewell Christian Academy	1997	K-12	169	26	3	26	GAC	$10 million	none
Hebron Christian Academy	1999	K-12	502	248	200	70	SACS, ACSI	$7 million	none
Notre Dame Academy	2005	PreK-8	475	0	0	45	SACS	$9 million	$150,000

**** Began in 2008***

Sources: Individual Schools

Private School Enrollment by Years in Gwinnett

School	Year	# Enrolled	# Graduating High School
Hebron Christian Academy	1999-2000	386	9
	2000-2001	497	16
	2001-2002	600	14
	2002-2003	660	15
	2003-2004	750	18
	2004-2005	825	34
	2005-2006	884	39
	2006-2007	956	37
	2007-2008	1015	50
Killian Hill Christian School	1999-2000	577	28
	2000-2001	526	26
	2001-2002	545	27
	2002-2003	515	25
	2003-2004	496	24
	2004-2005	498	24
	2005-2006	532	25
	2006-2007	528	21
	2007-2008	545	29

Private School Enrollment by Years in Gwinnett

School	Year	# Enrolled	# Graduating High School
Providence Christian Academy	1991-1992	363	19
	1992-1993	424	40
	1993-1994	456	36
	1994-1995	548	36
	1995-1996	584	37
	1996-1997	661	49
	1997-1998	707	53
	1998-1999	772	60
	1999-2000	852	76
	2000-2001	887	71
	2001-2002	925	77
	2002-2003	868	74
	2003-2004	873	104
	2004-2005	795	67
	2005-2006	793	66
	2006-2007	853	83
	2007-2008	850	95
Notre Dame Academy	2005-2006	212	0
	2006-2007	396	0
	2007-2008	503	0
Greater Atlanta Christian School	1968-1969	150	0
	1969-1970	240	17
	1970-1971	300	43
	1971-1972	370	48
	1972-1973	412	54
	1973-1974	500	67
	1974-1975	515	60
	1975-1976	530	68
	1976-1977	550	66
	1977-1978	600	70
	1978-1979	710	71
	1979-1980	740	52
	1980-1981	792	86
	1981-1982	782	74
	1982-1983	783	68
	1983-1984	833	82
	1984-1985	850	75

Private School Enrollment by Years in Gwinnett

School	Year	# Enrolled	# Graduating High School
Greater Atlanta Christian School (cont.)	1985-1986	842	85
	1986-1987	832	88
	1987-1988	934	101
	1988-1989	907	92
	1989-1990	916	63
	1990-1991	1005	92
	1991-1992	1015	86
	1992-1993	1003	88
	1993-1994	1025	72
	1994-1995	1065	77
	1995-1996	1090	85
	1996-1997	1129	88
	1997-1998	1199	103
	1998-1999	1273	99
	1999-2000	1418	118
	2000-2001	1489	107
	2001-2002	1623	146
	2002-2003	1741	113
	2003-2004	1799	145
	2004-2005	1819	135
	2005-2006	1879	135
	2006-2007	1953	154
	2007-2008	1946	153
St. John Neumann Regional Catholic School	1986-1987	160	0
	1987-1988	269	0
	1988-1989	363	0
	1989-1990	438	0
	1990-1991	518	0
	1991-1992	546	0
	1992-1993	570	0
	1993-1994	588	0
	1994-1995	614	0
	1995-1996	591	0
	1996-1997	574	0
	1997-1998	573	0
	1998-1999	572	0
	1999-2000	568	0
	2000-2001	543	0
	2001-2002	547	0
	2002-2003	575	0

Private School Enrollment by Years in Gwinnett

School	Year	# Enrolled	# Graduating High School
St John Neumann Regional Catholic School (cont.)	2003-2004	559	0
	2004-2005	566	0
	2005-2006	578	0
	2006-2007	585	0
	2007-2008	567	0
Hopewell Christian School	1997-1998	60	0
	1998-1999	133	0
	1999-2000	207	0
	2000-2001	247	0
	2001-2002	251	0
	2002-2003	246	0
	2003-2004	217	0
	2004-2005	290	0
	2005-2006	253	1
	2006-2007	241	3
	2007-2008	212	0
Wesleyan School	1996-1997	556	0
	1997-1998	770	17
	1998-1999	868	24
	1999-2000	939	40
	2000-2001	1017	80
	2001-2002	1036	80
	2002-2003	1058	93
	2003-2004	1063	105
	2004-2005	1056	95
	2005-2006	1074	102
	2006-2007	1074	94
	2007-2008	1081	106

Sources: individual schools

State High School Champions from Gwinnett, 1938-2007			
Sport	Year	Team	Classification
Baseball	1951	Duluth	Class C
	1963	Norcross	Class B
	1975	Greater Atlanta Christian	Class B
	1977	Buford	Class B
	1982	Greater Atlanta Christian	Class A
	1986	Brookwood	Class AAAA
	1987	Shiloh	Class AA
	1996	Parkview	Class AAAA
	2001	Parkview	Class AAAAA
	2002	Parkview	Class AAAAA
	2008	Wesleyan	Class AA
		Loganville	Class AAAA
		Brookwood	Class AAAAA
Boys Basketball	1938	Dacula	Class C
	1945	Dacula	Class B
	1951	Braselton	Class C
	1962	Central Gwinnett	Class A
	1971	Greater Atlanta Christian	Class C
	1972	Greater Atlanta Christian	Class C
	1977	Greater Atlanta Christian	Class B
	1979	Dacula	Class A
	2000	Berkmar	Class AAAA
	2001	Berkmar	Class AAAAA
	2004	South Gwinnett	Class AAAAA
	2006	Norcross	Class AAAAA
	2007	Norcross	Class AAAAA
	2008	Norcross	Class AAAAA
		Wesleyan	Class AA
Girls Basketball	1946	Bethesda	Class C
	1954	Dacula	Class C
	1972	Greater Atlanta Christian	Class C
	1973	Loganville	Class B
	1974	Greater Atlanta Christian	Class B
	1975	Greater Atlanta Christian	Class B
	1982	Greater Atlanta Christian	Class A
	1983	Greater Atlanta Christian	Class A
	1995	South Gwinnett	Class AAAA

State High School Champions from Gwinnett, 1938-2007			
Sport	Year	Team	Classification
Girls Basketball (cont.)	2001	Greater Atlanta Christian	Class AA
		Central Gwinnett	Class AAA
		Collins Hill	Class AAAAA
	2002	Wesleyan	Class A
		Greater Atlanta Christian	Class AA
		Collins Hill	Class AAAAA
	2003	Parkview	Class AAAAA
	2004	Wesleyan	Class AA
	2005	Wesleyan	Class AA
		Collins Hill	Class AAAAA
	2006	Wesleyan	Class AA
		Collins Hill	Class AAAAA
	2007	Greater Atlanta Christian	Class AA
		Collins Hill	Class AAAAA
	2008	Wesleyan	Class AA
Football	1952	Loganville	Class B
	1978	Buford	Class A
	1996	Brookwood	Class AAAA
	1997	Parkview	Class AAAA
	2000	Parkview	Class AAAAA
	2001	Buford	Class A
		Parkview	Class AAAAA
	2002	Buford	Class AA
		Parkview	Class AAAAA
	2003	Buford	Class AA
	2006	TIE: Peachtree Ridge and Roswell	Class AAAAA
	2007	Buford	Class AA
Girls Golf	2007	Greater Atlanta Christian	Class AA
	2008	Mill Creek	Class AAAAA
Boys Golf		None	

State High School Champions from Gwinnett, 1938-2007

Sport	Year	Team	Classification
Boys Soccer	1993	Parkview	Open
	1994	TIE: Parkview-Heritge	Class AAAA
	1997	Parkview	Class AAAA
	1998	Parkview	Class AAAA
	2000	TIE: Greater Atlanta Christian-Athens Acad.	Class AA/A
	2001	TIE: Parkview-Brookwood	Class AAAAA
	2003	Shiloh	Class AAAAA
	2004	TIE: Grayson and Richmond Academy	Class AAA
		Brookwood	Class AAAAA
	2005	Parkview	Class AAAAA
	2007	Greater Atlanta Christian	Class AA/A
Girls Soccer	1997	Parkview	Class AAAA
	1998	Brookwood	Class AAAA
	1999	Providence	Class AA/A
		TIE: Parkview-Pope	Class AAAA
	2003	TIE: Parkview-Brookwood	Class AAAAA
	2005	Parkview	Class AAAAA
	2007	Grayson/Parkview (tie)	Class AAAAA
		Providence	Class AA/A
GIrls Slow Pitch Softball	1984	Greater Atlanta Christian	Class A
	1985	Greater Atlanta Christian	Class A
		North Gwinnett	Class AA
	1987	Greater Atlanta Christian	Class A
	1988	North Gwinnett	Class AAA
	1989	Greater Atlanta Christian	Class A
		North Gwinnett	Class AAA
	1991	Brookwood	Class AAAA
	1995	Greater Atlanta Christian	Class A

State High School Champions from Gwinnett, 1938-2007

Sport	Year	Team	Classification
Girls Fast Pitch Softball	1997	South Gwinnett	Class AAAA
	1999	Duluth	Class AAAA
	2000	Providence	Class AA
	2001	Loganville	Class AAA
		Central Gwinnett	Class AAAA
	2002	Grayson	Class AAA
	2003	Grayson	Class AAA
	2005	Collins Hill	Class AAAAA
	2007	Buford	Class AA
Boys Swimming	1992	Shiloh	
	1994	Shiloh	
	1995	Parkview	
	1998	Parkview	
	2000	Parkview	Class AAAA
	2001	Parkview	Class AAAAA
	2002	Parkview	Class AAAAA
	2003	Parkview	Class AAAAA
	2004	Collins Hill	Class AAAAA
	2005	Collins Hill	Class AAAAA
	2006	Parkview	Class AAAAA
	2007	Parkview	Class AAAAA
	2008	Brookwood	Class AAAAA
Girls Swimming	1997	Parkview	Open
	1998	Parkview	Open
	2001	Brookwood	Class AAAAA
	2002	Brookwood	Class AAAAA
	2003	Brookwood	Class AAAAA
	2004	Brookwood	Class AAAAA
Boys Tennis	1991	Brookwood	Class AAAA
	1994	Shiloh (singles)	Class AAAA
	1996	Brookwood	Class AAAA
	1997	Brookwood	Class AAAA
	1998	Brookwood	Class AAAA
	2000	Brookwood	Class AAAA
	2001	Greater Atlanta Christian	Class AA
	2003	Greater Atlanta Christian	Class AA
	2005	Greater Atlanta Christian	Class AA
	2006	Greater Atlanta Christian	Class AA
	2007	Greater Atlanta Christian	Class AA

State High School Champions from Gwinnett, 1938-2007

Sport	Year	Team	Classification
Girls Tennis	1980	TIE: Parkview/Milton/Dalton	Class AAA
	2000	Brookwood	Class AAAA
	2001	Wesleyan	Class A
Boys Track	1964	Buford	Class C
	1967	Loganville	Class C
	1981	TIE: Greater Atlanta Christian/Metter	Class A
	1982	Buford	Class A
Girls Track	1984	Brookwood	Class AAA
	1985	Brookwood	Class AAAA
	1990	Brookwood	Class AAAAA
	1991	Brookwood	Class AAAAA
	1992	Brookwood	Class AAAAA
	1994	Brookwood	Class AAAAA
	2003	Collins Hill	Class AAAAA
	2005	Greater Atlanta Christian	Class AA
	2006	Collins Hill	Class AAAAA
	2007	Collins Hill	Class AAAAA
	2008	Collins Hill	Class AAAAA
Girls Volleyball	2004	Wesleyan	Class AA/A
	2005	Wesleyan	Class AA/A
	2006	Wesleyan	Class AA/A
	2007	Wesleyan	Class AA/A
Wrestling	1993	TIE: Dacula/Macon Co.	Class A
	2002	Collins Hill	Class AAAAA
	2004	Parkview	Class AAAAA
	2005	Collins Hill	Class AAAAA
	2006	Parkview	Class AAAAA
	2007	Wesleyan	Class AA
	2008	Collins Hill	Class AAAAA
Dual Wresting	2003	Parkview	Class AAAAA
	2004	Collins Hill	Class AAAAA
	2005	Collins Hill	Class AAAAA
	2006	Parkview	Class AAAAA
	2007	Wesleyan	Class AA
	2008	Collins Hill	Class AAAAA

State High School Champions from Gwinnett, 1938-2007

Sport	Year	Team	Classification
Literary	1975	TIE: Greater Atlanta Christian/Bremen	Class B
	1976	Buford	Class B
		North Gwinnett	Class A
	1981	Greater Atlanta Chiristian	Class A
	1982	TIE: Buford/Oak Mountain Academy	Class A
	1983	Greater Atlanta Christian	Class A
	1984	Greater Atlanta Christian	Class A
		Parkview	Class AAAA
	1985	Buford	Class A
		Parkview	Class AAAA
	1986	Parkview	Class AAAA
	1988	Parkview	Class AAAA
	1990	TIE: Greater Atlanta Christian/Pace Academy	Class A
	1993	TIE: Greater Atlanta Christian/ Calhoun	Class A
	1997	Greater Atlanta Christian	Class A
	1999	Brookwood	Class AAAA
	2005	Buford	Class AA
		Collins Hill	Class AAAAA
Debate	2006	Brookwood	AAAAA/AAAA
One Act Play	2000	Greater Atlanta Christian	Class AA
	2001	Collins Hill	Class AAAAA
	2002	Greater Atlanta Christian	Class AA
		Grayson	Class AAA
	2003	Greater Atlanta Christian	Class AA
	2004	Greater Atlanta Christian	Class AA
	2005	Greater Atlanta Christian	Class AA
	2006	Greater Atlanta Christian	Class AA
	2007	Greater Atlanta Christian	Class AA

Note: Debate and One Act Play were included in Literary Prior to 2000.

State High School Champions from Gwinnett, 1938-2007			
Sport	Year	Team	Classification
Cheerleading	1996-97	Parkview	Class AAAA
	1999-00	North Gwinnett	Class AAA
	2001-02	Shiloh	Class AAAAA
	2003-04	Duluth	Class AAAAA
	2005-06	Peachtree Ridge	Class AAAAA
	2006-07	Peachtree Ridge	Class AAAAA
	2007-08	Peachtree Ridge	Class AAAAA
Co-ed Cheerleading	2004-05	Duluth	Open
	2007-08	Duluth	Open
Cross Country Boys	1977	Greater Atlanta Christian	Class A-B-C
	1979	Greater Atlanta Christian	Class A
	1981	Greater Atlanta Christian	Class A
	1983	Greater Atlanta Christian	Class A
	1984	Greater Atlanta Christian	Class A
		Parkview	Class AAAA
	1985	Parkview	Class AAAA
	1986	Shiloh	Class AA
	1987	Shiloh	Class AA
		Parkview	Class AAAA
	1989	Brookwood	Class AAAA
	1990	Parkview	Class AAAA
	1992	South Gwinnett	Class AAAA
	1993	Parkview	Class AAAA
	1994	Brookwood	Class AAAA
	1995	Brookwood	Class AAAA
	1997	Greater Atlanta Christian	Class A
		Brookwood	Class AAAA
	1998	Brookwood	Class AAAA
	2000	Collins Hill	Class AAAAA
	2001	Wesleyan	Class A
		Brookwood	Class AAAAA
	2002	Wesleyan	Class AA
		Brookwood	Class AAAAA
	2003	Brookwood	Class AAAAA
	2004	Parkview	Class AAAAA
	2005	Wesleyan	Class AA
		Parkview	Class AAAAA
	2006	Wesleyan	Class AA
		Parkview	Class AAAAA
	2007	Wesleyan	Class AA
		Collins Hill	Class AAAAA

State High School Champions from Gwinnett, 1938-2007			
Sport	Year	Team	Classification
Cross Country Girls	1978	Greater Atlanta Chiristian	Class A
	1979	Greater Atlanta Christian	Class A
	1982	Greater Atlanta Christian	Class A
	1983	Brookwood	Class AAA
	1985	Brookwood	Class AAAA
Cross Country Girls (cont.)	1988	Parkview	Class AAAA
	1989	Brookwood	Class AAAA
	1990	Brookwood	Class AAAA
	1991	Brookwood	Class AAAA
	2001	Wesleyan	Class A
	2003	Wesleyan	Class A
		Collins Hill	Class AAAAA
	2004	Collins Hill	Class AAAAA
	2005	Collins Hill	Class AAAAA
	2006	Collins Hill	Class AAAAA
	2007	Collins Hill	Class AAAAA

Source: Georgia High School Association

Kiwanis Clubs in Gwinnett and Presidents

	Lawrenceville	North Gwinnett	Duluth	Suwanee	Lilburn (Greater Gwinnett)/Nor-cross
Charter Date	May 4, 1923	May 3, 1939	July 11, 1984	May 9, 1996	Mar. 28, 2006
1923	F. Q. Sammon				
1924	F. Q. Sammon				
1925	F.Q. Sammon	See below	See below	See below	See below
1926	D.C. Kelley				
1927	L.E. Smith to April 30				
	John J. Kelley to Dec. 31				
1928	Hervy H. Pharr				
1929	F. Q. Sammon				
1930	Victor L. Hegood				
1931	Charles Monfort				
1932	J.J. Baggett				
1933	J. W. Nicholson				
1934	C. E. Huff				
1935	Marvin A. Allison				
1936	Hope D. Stark				
1937	John M. Langley				
1938	R.H. Sims				
1939	Harold J. Campbell	Wallace Cecil Ford			
1940	F.F. Dowis	Garland R. Wallace			
1941	F. Q. Sammon Jr.	Chief P. Garner			
1942	Jesse A. Richardson	Lovie S. Adams			
1943	W.B. Alford	Emmett O. Dobbs Jr.			
1944	A. G. Robison	Emmett O. Dobbs Jr.			
1945	R. F. Duncan	Emmett O. Dobbs Jr.			
1946	T. L. Harris	Albert Lee Clark			
1947	L.E. Harper	Milton E. McClain			
1948	Jack O. Beggett	J. Earle Simpson			
1949	Hubert E. Tucker	H. Weldon Gardner			
1950	H. Rhodes Jordan	John O'Connor			
1951	Harry F. Wages	J. Ray Merritt			
1952	Alvin R. Sammon	Truman Hamilton			
1953	J. Floyd Hannon	Lester M. James			
1954	B. Q. Baggett	Carl Kelly			
1955	W. L. Stevenson	Joseph E. Cheeley Jr.			
1956	Earl P. Story	Thomas M. Moss			
1957	Clyde J. Roberts	Emmett L. Cook			
1958	Macon M. Ogletree Jr.	James C. Dover			
1959	Herman Tanner	Freeman L. Kilpatrick			

Kiwanis Clubs in Gwinnett and Presidents

	Lawrenceville	North Gwinnett	Duluth	Suwanee	Lilburn (Greater Gwinnett)/Norcross
Charter Date	May 4, 1923	May 3, 1939	July 11, 1984	May 9, 1996	Mar. 28, 2006
1960	Glenn Edge	Paul Cain			
1961	Harry W. Braselton	Kyle Clark			
1962	John B. Wilson	H. Weldon Gardner			
1963	J.W. Benefield Jr.	James B. Robinson			
1964	K.A. McMillon	Glen P. Gasaway			
1965	Fred Craig	Reid Merritt			
1966	Dr. W. A. Elinburg Jr.	Billy R. Cain			
1967	Ralph H. Landress	James B. Mathis Jr.			
1968	George E. Anderson	Edward M. Wood			
1969	Dr. Charles B. Teal	G. Gibson Dean II			
1970	G. Hughel Harrison	G. Gibson Dean II			
1971	D. L. Hitchcock	James. W. Cain			
1972	Thomas Huff	C. L. Daniel			
1973	Thomas E. Couch	W.J. Dodd			
1974	R. H. Thomas Jr.	C. Lamar Nash			
1975	Hubert Tucker Jr.	Golden A. Pirkle			
1976	Robert J. McGarity	Walter E. Stevens			
1977	Mickey Wages	Neal Davies			
1978	Hill Jordan	Dan Cole			
1979	T. Michael Tennant	Rick Chandler			
1980	Alton W. Tucker	Jerry Hughes			
1981	Richard Sissom	Jim Davis			
1982	Charles H. Allen	Joe Baughman			
1983	Perrin Walker	John Forrestall			Chris Chrisman*
1984	Mike Appling; Dr. Ray Harvey	William Crosland	Bill Williamson		Chris Chrisman
1985	Roger C. Willis	Grant Reed	Chip Smllwood		John Mahan
1986	Anthony O.L. Powell	Frank Lewis	Jim Sandlin		Woody Woodruff
1987	Louis T. Camerio Jr.	John Pless	Jim Sandlin		Guy Howell
1988	Michael D. Ayers	Scott Pryor	David Seay		Andy McClung
1989	Dennis Wall	David Hawthorne	Charles Summerour		Bill Austin
1990	Mark D. Merritt	David Hawthorne	Martin Putney		Jim Clarke
1991	David R. Still	David Hawthorne	Shirley Lasseter		C.E. Crissman
1992	Jeffrey B. Mahaffey	Paul Ranck	Jeff Bell		Bob Baugass
1993	Tim E. Hayes	Kathy Williamson	Beverly Blair		Kim Rowell
1994	Randy L. Dellinger	Bill Lamberson	Bill Lamberson		Al Hancock
1995	Sterling O. Ulrich	John Mardis; John Cann	James Johnson		Glenda Arthur
1996	Christopher T. Adams	Scott Snedecor	Jim McKenzie	Steve Agee	Bob Schmidgall
1997	Dr. Hubert E. Tucker Jr.	Adam Blackwell	Dave Robertson	Steve Agee	Bob Oglesby

Kiwanis Clubs in Gwinnett and Presidents

	Lawrenceville	North Gwinnett	Duluth	Suwanee	Lilburn (Greater Gwinnett)/Norcross
Charter Date	May 4, 1923	May 3, 1939	July 11, 1984	May 9, 1996	Mar. 28, 2006
1998	Greg Cantrell	Jay Asgari	Bill Lamberson	David Whitten	Steve Wilson
1999	Patrick Putnam	Thomas J. Crosby	Donnie Houston	Toby Blackwell	Sue Harthan
2000	Glenn Martin	Mike Phelan	Don Morris	Cathy McNally	Bill Alston
2001	Tony Appling	John Green	Bill Lamberson	Donna Schmid	Disbanded and Rechartered in 2006 as Norcross Club
2002	Walter J. Clarke	Frederick Kross	Deborah Hicks	Hardin Watkins	
2003	Mike Scheidrich	Scott Snedecor	Jim Barnes	Glenda Arthur	
2004	Carol Buffington	Sue Kelley	Tracy Wilkinson	Clay Eggleston	
2005	Margaret Washburn	Dawn P. Gober	Frank Gulia	Chip Randall	
2006	Ray Rumble	Charles J. Alford III	Elizabeth Lewis	Kevin O'Brien	Amy Greiner
2007	Jason West	Chales J. Lail Jr.	Mark Baker	Andrew Rodgers	Sandy Richardson
2008	Michael Stewart	Scott Hanlon	Jim Johnson	Denise Bradley	Bill Converse

Hamilton Mill Club was organized July, 2007, with Erica Kitchens as president; Chester Walden followed in 2008.
**** Lilburn organized in 1983 as "Greater Gwinnett" Kiwanis***
Source: State Kiwanis Office in Macon

Kiwanis Lieutenant Governors from Gwinnett	Kiwanis Lieutenant Governors from Gwinnett
Marvin A. Allison 1937 (Lawrenceville)	Hughel Harrison 1974-1975 (Lawrenceville)
William O. Austin, Jr. 1991-92 (Growing Gwinnett)	Deborah Hicks 2004-2005 (Duluth)
Glenda M Arthur 1998 - 1999 (Growing Gwinnett)	Steve T. Higgins 1995 -1996 (Duluth)
Jack O Baggett 1950 (Lawrenceville)	Donnie J. Houston 2001-2002 (Duluth)
Lewis Camerio - 1990-1991 (Lawrencville)	James Johnson 1996-1997 (Duluth)
Greg Cantrell 1999-2000 (Lawrenceville)	John E. Mahan 1988-1989 (Growing Gwinnett)
Richard Chandler Jr. -1979-1980 (Buford)	John Pitts 1990-1991 (Norcross)
Joe E. Cheeley 1957 (Buford)	Martin Putney 1992-1993 (Duluth)
Walter J. Clarke 2003-2004 (Lawrenceville)	Pete Sever 1954 (Lawrenceville)
Thomas J. Crosby 2000-2001 (Suwanee)	James Simpson 1972-1973 (Buford)
Randy L. Dellinger 1994-1995 (Lawrenceville)	Earl Story 1960 (Lawrenceville)
Randy L. Dellinger 1997-1998 (Lawrenceville)	Hubert E. Tucker 1968 (Lawrenceville)
John M. Forrestall 1986-1987 (Buford)	Dr. Hubert E. Tucker 1983-1984 (Lawrenceville)
Glen P. Gasaway 1965 (Buford)	William C. Ward 1987-1988 (Duluth)
Victor L. Hagood 1932 (Lawrenceville)	Margaret Gettle Washburn 2006-2007 (Lawrenceville)
Agnes B. Hamilton 1993-1994 (North Gwinnett)	W. Jason West 2007-2008 (Lawrenceville)

Source: State Kiwanis Office in Macon

Lions Clubs and Leaders of Gwinnett

Club	Lawrenceville	Snellville	Buford	Loganville
Charter Date	Feb. 19, 1946	Sept. 25, 1952	Feb. 14, 1953	April 19, 1965
Note: at one time, there were clubs also in Lilburn (started Oct. 1, 1948) and at Mountain Park (started Sept. 23, 1993), but both clubs have since folded.				
Note: Norcross Lions organized March 14, 1944. Presidents are unavailable.				
Year				
1946	R.P. Smith			
1947	T.T. McGee			
1947	Jim McGee			
1948	R.M. Gunter			
1949	R. B. Whitworth			
1950	Floyd Cofer			
1951	R.E. Whitworth			
1952	R.D. Johnson	Jimmie J. Powell		
1953	C.M. Higginbotham	Emmett Clower Jr.		
1954	R.L. Norton Jr.	A.W. Peters	Russell Phillips	
1955	Jones Webb	Earnest Williams	Thomas Riden	
1956	S.F. Fields	Lewis F. Bird	Roscoe Hartley	
1957	L.L. Bray	W. R. Williams	Ralph C. Dalton	
1958	H.R. Norton	James D. Cofer	Leon Allen	
1959	Ferris Hutchins	R D. Head	L.A. Wilson	
1960	J.V. Patton	Gerald Rawlins	James E. Gover	
1961	C.H. Brand	Jimmie Johnson	Glyndon C. Pruitt	
1962	Robert Fuqua	H.R. Hewatt	Winfred R.Pruitt	
1963	D. Ray Sosbee	Charles E. Nash	J. Edwin Johnson	
1964	Adison Starnes	Charles E. Nash	Harold Hannah	
1965	Virgil Thompson	Gerald Rawlins	Edward Wallace	
1966	P. D. Ellison	Richard Norton	Norris E. Vickery	L.L. James Jr.
1967	G. T. Young	Ray Roberts	Robert Bowman	Clifford Byrd
1968	G. C. Norris	Ray Roberts	Hubert S. Higgins	Rev. Shelby Cook
1968	Rev. Douglas Gibson			
1969	Douglas Edwards	Gerald Rawlins	James D. Wilson	Winston Byrd
1970	James Henderson	W.J. Britt	John W. Savage	Neal Byrd
1971	Robert "Bob" Powell	Randy Moore	O. Millard Peevy	Charles Ivey
1972	John Thomas	Don Lassahn	Harold Hannah	John King
1973	T.L. Williford Jr.	Jay Sager	Arthur Invester	Harold Tribble
1974	H.G. Lindstrom	Mike A. Royston	Leon Kimbro	Raymond Thrasher
1975	Fred Webb	Raymond L. Odom	Kenneth E. Martin	Howard Sweat
1976	Fred Webb	Hal M. Walls	Verlon C. Southerland	Wayne Morris
1977	Bob Biggers	Bill Crawford	William R. Wiley	Alvin Ruark

Lions Clubs and Leaders of Gwinnett

Club	Lawrenceville	Snellville	Buford	Loganville
1978	John Childs	Dr. Joe E. Snell	Jimmy House	Richard Woodall
1979	Larry Janney	Bob Allen	Edward L. Owens*	Joe Johnson
1980	Larry Janney	Cary Strickland	Maron Buice	Marion Williams
1981	Frank Gruber	Clyde Hopper	Kenneth R. Adams	Dewey Moody
1982	G.T. Young	Garvice Williams	J.W. Henderson	Boyce Petty
1983	Robert Bolan	Cecil Nash	Frank Free	Wendell Geiger
1984	Dan Gladney	Bruce Maney	Ken Martin	John T. McMillion
1985	Robert Rodatus	Carl McClung	Bob Bensinger	Jerry McElroy
1986	Donald Cash	John Adams/ James Hobson	Frank Free	Chris Gallman
1987	Bob Justin	Wayne Cain	Maron Buice	Keith Griffith
1988	Scott McEwen	Wayne Cain	Larry Henderson	Bill Jones
1989	Ellis Britt	Jimmy Kerlin	Jimmy & Jean Kilgore	Harry Hinton
1990	Ellis Britt	Norm Masters	Bill Hardman	David Carithers
1991	Chuck Reyner	W. "Mac" McCluskey	Jean Kilgore	Tom Polston
1992	Jack Etheridge	Calvin Gee	Jean Kilgore	Bob Swortz
1993	Judy Gladney	L.C. "Bud" Gee	Jean Kilgore	Neal Byrd
1994	Dan Gladney	W. "Mac" McCluskey	Gene Drummond	Bud McElhannon
1995	Ruth Britt	Bob Hadaway	Gene Drummond	Wendell Geiger
1996	Ellis Britt	Bill Miles	Gene Drummond	Bruce Howell
1997	Mark Sander	Bill Jarmon	Jean Kilgore	Neal Byrd
1998	Mark Sander	Bill Jarmon	Jean Kilgore	Doug Cathy
1999	Donald Sheppard	Ed Hald	Jean Kilgore	Brad Johnson
2000	Donald Sheppard	Bob Lawson	Jean Kilgore	Steve Mullins
2001	Pete Stamsen	Wayne Cain	Bill Hardman	Danny Byrd
2002	Pete Stamsen	Hinton Bailey	Jean Kilgore	Lee Garrett
2003	Loyd McHargue	Grace Clower	Bill Rappe	Richard Woodall
2004	Loyd McHargue	Joe Roth	Giri Peterson	Brad Johnson
2005	Pete Stamsen	Don Hanna	Giri Peterson	Layman Brannon
2006	Bruce Mercora	Leon Taylor	Holly Neyman	Steve Bowers
2007	Bruce Mercora	Jimmy Dallas	Kenny Jacobs	Ron Torre
2008	Bill Phyfer	Jimmy Dallas	Jean Kilgore	Thomas Summers

*** Past District Governor***

Source: Individual Lions Clubs

Presidents of Rotary Clubs in Gwinnett

Club	Gwinnett County	Peachtree Corners	South Gwinnett
Charter Date	June 29, 1973	June 11, 1981	Sept. 17, 1982
Year	President	President	President
1973-74	Troy Chatham		
1974-75	Hugh Ragsdale		
1975-76	Jim Wrath		
1976-77	Larry Laster		
1977-78	James Wilkerson		
1978-79	Jerry Ashworth		
1979-80	Julian Franklin		
1980-81	Ed Heys		
1981-82	Buck Lindsay	Henry Howard	
1982-83	Jim Steele	Rans Black	Dr. James St. John
1983-84	Wallace Lail	Gordon Kay	Dr. James St. John
1984-85	Frank Sledge	Jim Smulian	Thomas Andersen
1985-86	Wallace Odum Jr.	Mike McCarthy	Rich Panyik
1986-87	Terry Gordon	Brooks Coleman	David Hopkins
1987-88	Coy Dillard	John Wells	Hartwell B. Wash
1988-89	Willard Swanson	Carl Lusted	J.H. Crawford Jr.
1989-90	Jim Hinshaw	J.P. Harrington	Robert Andrews
1990-91	Bill Robinson	Bruce Morine	William Sanders
1991-92	Wayne Sikes	Larry Smith	Doug Langley
1992-93	Bernie Governale	Chip Mohme	Mike Hayes
1993-94	Bill Brogdon	Roy Threatt	Rob Ponder
1994-95	John Atwell	Von Starkey	Robert Huttman
1995-96	Ed Radford	Ron Toms	Jack Moore
1996-97	Terry Evans	Ed Poitras	Bill Cooper
1997-98	Jim Maughon	John Johnson	Susie Hite
1998-99	Herb Hamby	John Johnson/Becky Munteanu*	Scott LeCraw
1999-2000	Frank Rinker	Joe Daniels	Joe Allen
2000-01	Connie Wiggins	Robbie Stedeford	Raymer Sale
2001-02	Scott Zanardo	Harvey Snider	Tom Tate
2002-03	Roger Willis	Mike Sweigart	Vicki Sweeny
2003-04	Leonard Cyphers	Bill McCargo	Ed Hanley
2004-05	Bartow Morgan Jr.	Ranjan Raj	Bill Cox
2005-06	Perry Tindol	Carolyn Collins	Victoria Thomas
2006-07	Andy McClung	Bud Mingledorff	Curtis Law
2007-08	Tracey Mason Blasi	Debbie Sutton	Al Karnitz
2008-09 pres-elect	Slade Lail	Larry Reed	Joel Taylor

**** Norcross and Peachtree Corners combined in 1997-98***

Presidents of Rotary Clubs in Gwinnett

Club Year	Duluth President	Snellville President	Lawrenceville President	Buford President	Norcross President
1973-74					
1974-75					
1975-76					
1976-77					
1977-78					
1978-79					
1979-80					
1980-81					
1981-82					
1982-83					
1983-84					
1984-85					
1985-86					
1986-87	Tom Martin				
1987-88	Tom Martin				
1988-89	Russ Weaver				
1989-90	Clayton Preble				
1990-91	Eric Norwood	Dennis Still			
1991-92	Kent Evans	Dennis Still			
1992-93	Jesse Long	Mike Berg			Michael Pound
1993-94	Jackie Bradford	Larry Anderson			Marvin Cosgray
1994-95	Casey Brogdon	Dale Rich		Carolyn Hill	Sharon Rigsby
1995-96	Dave Rosenquist	Beth Sikes		Rick Pruett	Jerry Patterson
1996-97	Katherine Sherrington	Art O'Neill		David Lowry	Lisa Williams
1997-98	Mike Lowrey	Tom Shepherd	Jo Ann Pinder	Keith Pugh	Becky Munteanu*
1998-99	Randy Foster	Greg Brayfield	Bob Cowan	Andy Henderson	
1999-00	Dave McCulley	Brad Kendall	Jackie Hoffman	Steve Cannon	
2000-01	Mark Tyrrell	Mary Fergus	Al Hombroek	Brandy Swanson	
2001-02	Joanne Taylor	Gloria Berry	Judy McDaniel	Carolyn Hill	
2002-03	Jef Fincher	Buddy Watts	Nancy Friauf	Karen Eggers	
2003-04	Phillip Williams	Glenn Campbell	Randy Dellinger	Brent Cochran	
2004-05	Roy Miller	Joe Gilkey	Jim Eyler	Todd Adams	
2005-06	Laura Dennison	Scott Henle	Phil Hoskins	Bobby Robinett	
2006-07	Bob Dickinson	Don Britt	Beatty McCaleb	Rick Baldwin	
2007-08	Herman Pennamon	Don Britt	Otis Jones	Steve Cannon	
2008-09	Linda Storey	Joe Roth	David Freeman	Valerie Dirksen	

Source: Individual Rotary Clubs

Governors of Rotary District 6910 from Gwinnett	
Years	Governor
1986-87	Jim Smulian (Peachtree Corners)
1991-92	Buck Lindsay (Gwinnett)
1996-97	Jim Hinshaw (Gwinnett)
2000	Rick Panyik (South Gwinnett)
2005	Jimmy Maughon (Gwinnett)

Source: Rotary District 6910

Duluth Civitan Club	
Chartered May 20, 2003	
Year	President
2002-2003	Bob Watson
2003-2004	Scott Jordan
2004-2005	Loren Brown
2005-2006	Don Tew
2006-2007	Erica Dumpel
2007-2008	Melvin Buchanan

Source: Individual Clubs

Woman's Club Officers in Gwinnett

Club	Lawrenceville	Lilburn	Snellville
Charter Year	1970	1973	1980
Year	President	President	
1970-71	Barbara Bohne		
1971-72	Barbara Bohne		
1972-73	Melna Henderson		
1973-74	Melna Henderson	Faye Moore	
1974-75	Joyce Pack	Faye Moore	
1975-76	Margaret Hamilton	Doris Mann	
1976-77	Cynthia Tanner	Betty McMahon	
1977-78	Nancy Gullickson	Karen Bradford	
1978-79	Florentine Liegerot	Felicia Tanzosch	
1979-80	Mary Kay Jordan	Jenny Nall	Carol Bagheri
1980-81	Vonda Mercora	Sally Baker	
1981-82	Cathy Redding	Diane Young	
1982-83	Sherry Tennant	Diana Glymph	Others
1983-84	Cyndae Sims	Judy Garner	Unavailable
1984-85	Melna Henderson	Joan Borges	
1985-86	Joan Rushing	Nan Jackson	
1986-87	Marilyn Reed	Jean Beck	
1987-88	Kathie Fedyk	Schan Brown	
1988-89	Pam Autry-Sandra Strickland	Pat Swan	
1989-90	Mary Root-Sandra Strickland	Diane Bronk	
1990-91	Joanne Giel	Cheryl Barnhart	
1991-92	Donna Cameron	Jan Jewett	
1992-93	Monica Smith-Donna Walters	Janet Barnett	
1993-94	Judy Holland-Donna Walters	Faye Moore	
1994-95	Carrie Sheehan	Diane Ellis	
1995-96	Diane Borchers-Pat Johnson	Carol Mamey	
1996-97	Janice Lutz	Nadine Bily	
1997-98	Anita Solty	Doris Hutchins	
1998-99	Anita Solty	Pat Swan	
1999-2000	Lori Kendal-Tracy Clark	Debbie Slappey	

Woman's Club Officers in Gwinnett

Club	Lawrenceville	Lilburn	Snellville
Charter Year	1970	1973	1980
Year	President	President	
2000-01	Carrie Sheehan	Diane Bronk	
2001-02	Carie Sheehan	Sandra Langston	
2002-03	Theresa Bullock/ Terri Stikeleather	Catherine Anderson/ Sandra Langston	
2003-04	Sharon Britt	Christine Peredney	
2004-05	Sandra Strickland	Laura Byrd	
2005-06	Stacyu Bluse	Jackie Thornberry	
2006-07	Theresa Bullock	Jackie Thornberry	
2007-08	Carrie Sheehan	Barbara Brooks	

Source: *Local Club Records*

Buford-Lanier Woman's Club Presidents

Club began in 1922 and became a Woman's Club in 1932

Year	President	Year	President
1922-27	Miss Lizzie Hamilton	1970-72	Mrs. William H. Booth III
1927-28	Mrs. Horace Garner	1972-74	Mrs. Golden Pirkle
1928	Mrs. Edwina P. Royal	1974-76	Mrs. John Bearden
1929-31	Mrs. C.A. Stringer	1976-78	Mrs. Joe Cheeley Jr.
1932	Mrs. Edwina P. Royal	1978-80	Mrs. Harold B. Pass
1932	Mrs. W.V. Bolding	1980-81	Mrs. Edward W. Radford
1933	Mrs. J.W. Paret	1981-82	Mrs. Robert Neyman
1934	Mrs. W.L. Shadburn	1982-84	Mrs. Ralph Engle
1935	Mrs. H. K. Bowman	1984-85	Mrs. Edward W. Radford
1936-38	Mrs. John D. Carter	1985-86	Mrs. Harold B. Pass
1938-40	Mrs. D.S. Ivey	1986-87	Mrs. Robert Neman
1940-42	Mrs. P.L. Royal	1987-88	Mrs. Hal Scott (part year)
1942-44	Mrs. Glyndon P. Tapp	1987-88	Miss Earline Cooke
1944-46	Mrs. J.A. Bradley	1988-89	Mrs. Ace Gilbert
1946-48	Mrs. W.F. Moore	1989-90	Mrs. Ralph Engle
1948-50	Mrs. A.R. Truslow	1990-91	Mrs. O. D. Cain Jr.
1950-52	Mrs. F. C. Street	1991-92	Mrs. Frank O'Neal
1952-54	Mrs. A.R. Truslow	1992-94	Mrs. Jack Schiveree
1954-56	Mrs. W.F. Moore	1994-96	Mrs. William Hess
1956-58	Mrs. Kyle Clark	1996-98	Mrs. Martin Perry
1958-60	Mrs. Jesse Wheeler	1998-2000	Mrs. Alan Smiley
1960-62	Mrs. Kyle Clark	2000-2004	Mrs. Donald Hayes
1962-64	Mrs. Paul Cain	2004-2006	Mrs. Wirt McCreary
1964-66	Mrs. E.A. Wilbanks	2006-2008	Mrs. Robert Fitzsimmons
1966-68	Mrs. Joe Cheeley Jr.	2008-2010	Mrs. Jack Huff
1968-70	Mrs. Kyle Clark		

Source: *Buford-Lanier Woman's Club*

Norcross Woman's Club Presidents

Club first met in 1905, and was chartered in 1906

Year	President		Year	President
1906-08	Mrs. Homer V. Jones		1947-49	Miss Lola Key
1909-10	Mrs. W. A. Webster		1950-51	Mrs. S.O. Johnson
1911	Mrs. C. A. McDaniel		1951-52	Mrs. C.A. Garner Sr.
1912	Mrs. Homer Christian		1952-54	Mrs. H.J. Reynolds
1913	Mrs. J.E. McElroy		1954-55	Mrs. W.J. Ferguson
1914	Mrs. H.J. Reynolds		1955-56	Mrs. H.L. Baker
1915	Miss Lola Key		1956-57	Mrs. R. J. Broyles
1916	Mrs. H.V. Jones		1957-58	Mrs. C. P. Trice
1916-17	Mrs. R.A. Myers		1958-60	Mrs. C.A. Garner Sr.
1917-18	Mrs. C.A. McDaniel		1960	Mrs. M. L. Baker
1919-20	Mrs. W.M. Keady		1960-62	Mrs. C.A. Garner Sr.
1920-21	Mrs. B.F. Summerour		1962-64	Mrs. Charles Honour
1921-22	Mrs. J. E. McElroy		1964-66	Mrs. Walter Clapp
1922-23	Mrs. T.D. McDaniel		1966-68	Mrs. L.D. Ewing
1923-24	Mrs. L. deJarnete		1968-70	Mrs. C.A. Garner Sr.
1924-25	Mrs. T.D. McDaniel		1970-72	Mrs. E.M. Walden
1926	Mrs. M.C. Rhodes		1972-74	Mrs. L.D. Ewing
1927	Mrs. H.H. Miller		1974-76	Mrs. C.A. Garner Sr.
1928	Mrs. W.H. Keady		1976-78	Mrs. John A. Adams
1929-30	Mrs. Homer V. Jones		1978-80	Mrs. William L. Parker
1930-31	Mrs. A.A. O'Kelley		1980-81	Mrs. C. T. Chappas
1931-32	Mrs. T. D. McDaniel		1981-82	Mrs. Norman Briggs
1932-34	Mrs. C.A. Garner Sr.		1983-86	Mrs. Richard Lillie
1934-35	Mrs. T.D. McDaniel		1986-88	Mrs. W.H. Brownell
1935-37	Mrs. H.L. Sudderth		1988-90	Mrs. J.D. Caswell
1937-38	Mrs. R.H. Reynolds		1990-94	Mrs. John A. Adams
1939-41	Mrs. M.C. Rhodes Jr.		1994-96	Mrs. Robert Chaapel
1941-42	Mrs. A.A. O'Kelley		1996-02	Mrs. John A. Adams
1943-45	Mrs. H.L. Sudderth		2002-06	Mrs. Jesse R. Crapo
1945-47	Mrs. J.A. Davenport		2006-08	Mrs. Robert Chaapel

Source: Norcross Woman's Club

Loganville Woman's Club Presidents

Club was first organized in 1939

Year	President		Year	President
1939-43	Mrs. S. A. Boland		1978-80	Mrs. Lawrence Stevens
1941-43	Mrs. H.H. Brand		1980-82	Mrs. James Dorsey
1943-45	Mrs. R.H. Hodges		1982-84	Mrs. Bruce Howell
1945-47	Mrs. L.B. Whitworth		1984-86	Mrs. Dean King
1947-49	Mrs. L.B. Hodges		1986-88	Mrs. Charles Hazeligs
1949-51	Mrs. W.S. Tuck		1988-90	Mrs. Raymond Ashe
1951-54	Mrs. S.A. Boland		1990-91	Mrs. Marc Unterman
1954-56	Mrs. W. E. Sanders		1991-92	Mrs. Raymond Ashe
1956-58	Inactive		1992-94	Mrs. Gobel Berry
1958-60	Mrs. Willie D. O'Kelly		1994-96	Mrs. Benjamin Johnson
1960-62	Mrs. H.H. Dial		1996-98	Mrs. Arthur Marriott
1962-66	Mrs. J.M. Brooks		1998-00	Mrs. Spencer Baxley
1966-68	Inactive		2000-02	Mrs. Charles Hazlerigs
1968-70	Mrs. J.M. Brooks		2002-04	Mrs. Geran Dodson
1970-74	Mrs. R. W. Couch		2004-06	Mrs. Peter Goerissen
1974-78	Mrs. Talbot Phillips		2006-08	Mrs. Steve Bass

Source: Loganville Woman's Club

Stonehedge Garden Club Presidents

Year	President		Year	President
1970-71	Mrs. Cecil Miller		1988-91	Mrs. Robert Bowman
1971-72	Mrs. Larry Burel		1991-93	Mrs. Don Sherwood
1972-74	Mrs. Carson Smith III		1993-95	Mrs. Robert Hennig
1974-76	Mrs. W.H. Booth III		1995-97	Mrs. Richard Chandler
1976-77	Mrs. T.E. Kennedy		1997-99	Mrs. Richard Chandler
1978-79	Mrs. T.E. Kennedy		1999-01	Mrs. James Hinshaw
1979-81	Mrs. Carson Smith III		2001-03	Mrs. Wayne McWard
1981-83	Mrs. E.L. Stanley		2003-05	Mrs. Charles Anglin
1983-85	Mrs. J.E. Cheely		2005-07	Mrs. Robert Hennig
1985-87	Mrs. W.H. Booth III		2007-08	Mrs. Wayne Hill
1987-88	Mrs. J.E. Bradley		2008-09	Mrs. Alan Smiley

Source: Stonehedge Garden Club

"Miss Gwinnett" Winners, 1955-2008

Winner Selected During Gwinnett County Fair

Year	Winner
1955	Shirley Wheeler
1956	Linda Hodges
1957	Mima Pittard
1958	Judy Jones
1959	Carol Grogan
1960	Jeann Hunt
1961	Terri Tuggle
1962	Gale Alewine
1963	Margaret Smith
1964	Betty Pirtrard
1965	Beverly Reynolds
1966	Sandra Hickman
1967	Janiie Webb
1969	Beth Sharpton
1970	Janice Teal
1971	Denise Buice
1972	Diane Lindsay
1973	Kim Brown
1974	Susan Haney
1975	Lynn Eaton
1976	Susan Sikes
1977	Joanie Morgan
1978	Sue Angelyn Provost
1979	Angela Mauldin
1980	Robin Bradley
1981	Karen Thacker
1982	Debbie Atkinson
1983	Lisa Frankum
1984	Lori Freeman
1985	Donna Nichols
1986	Anne Poore
1987	Anglie Edwards
1988	Laura Spence
1989	Tamara Tesch
1990	Lani Barnes
1991	Shea Oliff
1992	Elizabeth Barron
1993	Jody Rhodes
1994	Rebecca Pietrowski
1995	Amy Robach
1996	Beth Williams
1997	Jennifer Ford
1998	Jessica Riley
1999	Natalie Roberts
2000	Christine Zimmerman
2001	Kelly Wells
2002	Tanaya Greer
2003	Lauren Jolley
2004	Allison Hutto
2005	Kate Michael
2006	Erinaq Patterson
2007	Caitlin Andrews
2008	Jessica Black

Source: Gwinnett County Fair

Miss Gwinnett 1955
Shirley Wheeler

Museums Within Gwinnett

Name	Address	City	Date Founded
Southeastern Rail Museum	3595 Buford Highway	Duluth	1970
Gwinnett History Museum	Female Seminary	Lawrenceville	1974
Gwinnett Fine Arts Center	6500 Sugarloaf Parkway	Duluth	1983
Buford History Museum	95 B East Main Street	Buford	1986
Norcross Baseball Museum	Norcross City Hall	Norcross	1993
Gwinnett Historical Society	Historic Courthouse	Lawrenceville	1996
Duluth Museum	3582 W. Lawrenceville St.	Duluth	2000
Hudgens Children's Museum *(Renamed Jackqueline Casey Hudgens Center for the Arts)*	6500 Sugarloaf Parkway	Duluth	2000
Veteran's Museum	Historic Gwinnett Courthouse	Lawrenceville	2004
Environmental Heritage Center	2020 Clean Water Drive	Buford	2006
Grayson Arts & History Center	2070 Rosebud Road	Grayson	2007
Norcross Fire Truck Muesum	Lawrenceville Street	Norcross	2008

Source: Individual museums

Southeastern Railway Museum Officials

Presidents of the Atlanta Chapter of the National Railway Historical Society which operates the Southeastern Railway Museum in Duluth

Year	Name	Year	Name
1959	Dave Austin	1981-91	Charles E. Srike
1960	George Rice	1992-95	Robert Zimmerman
1961	Thad McCleskey	1996	Del Kittendorf
1962	Wiliam Price	1997	Bob Herrington
1963	George Rice	1998-99	Randy Minter
1964-67	David W. Salter	2000	Fred Dobbs
1967	Col. James G. Bogle	2001-03	Jamie D. Reid
1968-73	William J. Purdie	2004	Randy Minter
1974-77	James M. Dykes Jr.	2004-06	Randy Pirkle
1977-80	Jerry Jarrett	2007-08	John Pollock

Source: Chapter Records

Properties on National Register of Historic Places in Gwinnett

Date Placed On Register	Property and Location
1970	Lawrenceville Female Seminary - Lawrenceville
1977	Wynn/Russell Home – Lilburn
1979	Elisha Winn Home and Grounds - Dacula
1980	Gwinnett Historic Courthouse – Lawrenceville
1980	Mechanicsville School – Doraville
1980	Downtown Historic District, Norcross
1982	Clarence Ware House – Lawrenceville
1982	William Terrell Home – Lawrenceville [destroyed by fire 1987].
1983	Bona Allen Home – Buford
1984	John Quincy Allen Home – Buford
1989	Parks-Strickland Archaeological Site – Dacula
1990	Robert Craig House "Little Egypt Plantation" – Lawrenceville
1990	Thomas P. Hudson Property & Yellow River Post Office – Lawrenceville
1998	Alcovy Mill – Lawrenceville
1999	"The Superb" Railroad Car – S. E. Railway Museum – Duluth
2000	Isaac Adair Home – Lawrenceville
2005	Bona Allen Shoe & Horse Collar Factory – Buford

Source: Gwinnett Historical Society

Visitors To Lake Lanier Islands

Year	Fee Paying Automobiles	Season Passes Sold	Admission for Magic Nights Of Lights
2002	118,965	6,341	39,038
2003	121,464	7,041	40,115
2004	116,233	6,582	44,005
2005	102,586	5,681	41,215
2006	89,550	5,125	39,136
2007	77,054	3,767	31,775

Source: Lake Lanier Islands Authority

Golf Courses in Gwinnett

Name	City	Begun	Yards	Holes	Other Information
Sawnee Golf Club *	Buford	1928	?	18	Had greens of compacted cottonseed hulls; closed about 1943
Windy Hill Golf Course *	Lawrenceville	1961	3,000	9	Designed by Perrin Walker and Doyle Johnson; Known as Perrin Country Club
Northwoods Country Club	Lawrenceville	1962	6,800	18	Willard Byrd and George Cobb, designers
Berkeley Hills Golf Club#	Duluth	1964	6,577	27	Designed by Davis Kirby and Ken Player Built by Larry McClure and Miles Mason Jr.
Collins Hill Golf Club**	Lawrenceville	1966	6,453	18#	Built by Perrin Walker Originally Pine Ridge Country Club
Summit Chase Country Club	Snellville	1973	6,780	18	Ward Northrupt design
Chateau Elan golf courses***	Braselton				
Chateau course		1989	7,030	18	First Course at Chateau Designed by Dennis Griffith
Legends course		1993	6,935	18	Designed by Sam Snead Gene Sarazan and Kathy Whitworth
Woodlands course		1996	6,735	18	Dennis Griffith design
Par 3			1,066	9	Dennis Griffith design
Sugar Hill Golf Club**	Sugar Hill	1992	6,522	18	Willard Byrd design
Country Club of Gwinnett	Snellville	1993	6,429	18	Steve Melnyk design
Peachtree Masters	Duluth	1993	2,600	18	Bob Henderson design
Trophy Club of Apalachee	Dacula	1994	6,620	18	Steve Melnyk design
Hamilton Mill Golf Club	Dacula	1995	6,843	18	Fred Couples design
Heritage Golf Club ##	Tucker	1996	9.904	27	Mike Young design
Sugarloaf Country Club	Duluth	1997	7,259	27	Greg Norman Design; Home of ATT Classic
The Hootch Golf Club **	Duluth	1998	4,200	18	Executive course designed by D.J. Johnson with extensive driving range
Bear's Best Golf Club	Suwanee	2002	7,034	18	Jack Nicklaus design
River Club	Suwanee	2005	7,200	18	Greg Norman design

**** No longer in operation***
***** Public Course***
****** All of the Legends course is in Gwinnett; three holes of Chateau and two of Woodlands in Gwinnett.***
 # First nine holes opened 1966; second nine opened in 1971.
21 of 27 holes are in Gwinnett.

Source: Individual clubs

Classic PGA Championship at Sugarloaf Country Club

Year	Winner	$$$ Share	4 Day Score	Second Place	Proceeds to Charity
1997	Scott McCarron	270,000	70-69-66-69=274	David Duval, Lee Janzen, Brian Henninger (277)	$942,672
1998	Tiger Woods	324,000	69-67-63-72=271	Jay Don Blake (272)	$1,019,696
1999	David Duval	450,000	66-69-68-67=270	Stewart Cink (272)	$846,066
*2000	**Phil Mickelson	504,000	67-69-69 = 205	Gary Nicklaus (205)	$763,290
2001	Scott McCarron	594,000	68-67-72-73=280	Mike Weir (283)	$604,883
2002	Retief Goosen	684,000	68-66-68-70=272	Jesper Parnevik (276)	$835,872
2003	Ben Crane	720,000	73-72-64-63=272	Bob Tway (276)	$796,414
2004	Zach Johnson	810,000	69-66-68-72=275	Mark Hensby (276)	$793,733
*2005	**Phil Mickelson	900,000	74-65-69 = 208	Arjun Atwal, Brandt Jobe, Rich Beem, Jose Maria Olazabal (208)	$971,949
2006	Phil Mickelson	954,000	63-65-67-65=260	Zach Johnson, Jose Maria Olazabal (273)	$1,717,188
2007	**Zach Johnson	972,000	71-66-69-67=273	Ryuji Imada (273)	$1,491,204
2008	** Ryuji Imada	999,000	71-69-66-67=273	Kenny Perry (273)	$1,250,000

Rain shortened   ** Won in playoff
Source: Classic Golf championship records

Index

A

A.G. Edwards Financial 283
A. Worley Brown Boys and Girls Club 407
A.A. Dyer Farm 31
Abplanalp, Glen 181
Abundant Life 555
Ackerman, Olive P. 188
Ackerman, Sonny 463
Adams, Betty 368
Adams, Cheryl 534
Adams, John xv, 459, 463, 521, 529
Adams, Martha Miller 545
Adams, Scooter 211
Adams, Venoy 211
Adamson, Ronald D. 463
Aderhold, Joel 130
Aderholt, John 459
Adopt-a-Highway 533
Adopt-A-Family 548
Agee, Steve 422
Aggarwal, Shiv 449
Agnes, Lynn 371
Aikman, Leo 523
Air Center Gwinnett 68, 271
Aircraft Specialist Jet Center 273
Airport Authority 268, 269, 270, 272, 273, 274
Airport Renewal and Extension Fund 273
AJC 243, 245
AJC Gwinnett 243
Akers, Curtis 368
Alabama National Bank of Birmingham 466
Alba, Jaime 198
Albert, Phil 375
Alcovy Grist Mill 152
Alexander, J.T. 76
Alexander, Mark 384
Alexander, T.W. 112
Alford, Alvin 72
Alford, Don 519
Alford, Eleanor (Lynn) 368
All Saints Lutheran 555
Allen, Bob and Kate 518
Allen, Sr., Bonaparte (Bona) 116, 117
Allen, Ernestine (Teeny) 85
Allen, J. Michael 463
Allen, Joe 442, 448
Allen, John 575, 577
Allen, Jr., Bona 117
Allen, Kate 455, 518
Allen, Mike 463
Allen, Robert H. 116
Allen, Stanley 139
Allen, Victor 120, 386
Alliance Plow Boy 240, 247
Allison, Marvin 240, 241, 247, 344, 455, 495, 575
Allison, Mrs. Marvin 241
Allison, Willela 29
Alumax Corporation 283
Amazing Grace Lutheran Church 424, 426
Amazing Graces 574
Amberfield 235
Ambrose, B. 458
American Association of Christian Schools 488
American Business Women's Association 87
American Cancer Society 328, 387, 500, 533, 547
American Institute of Architects 261
American Legion (Post 262) 30
American Medicorp Inc. 321
American Osteopathic Association 433, 434
American United Bank 465
Anderson, Elijah 99
Anderson, Lib 547
Anderson, Raymond 4
Anderson-McGriff Lumber Company 3, 4
Andrews, Agnew (Andy) 72, 324
Andrews, Bill 72
Andrews, Calvin 383
Andrews, Margaret Parsons 72, 369
Andrews, Miss Myra 114
Angarita, Roberto 562
Anheuser-Busch 283
Annandale Arts and Academics Villagers 402
Annandale at Suwanee, Inc. 16, 17, 186, 401
Annandale Village 401, 531, 545
Annestown Cotton Mill Corporation 99
Annistown Road Baptist Church 422
Antique Car Show 529
Appling, John 110
Arabic Baptist 557
ARC xv, 171, 363
Arcado Road 582
Archer, B.B. 215
Archer, Julian 40, 164, 203, 209
Archer, Luke 209
Archer, Weldon 139, 181, 183, 582
Ard, Paul 71, 424
Arenz, David 373
ARMPC 171
Armstead, Mildred 406
Armstrong, Kerry 171
Arnall, Ellis 316, 565
Arnold, Julie Keeton 171
Arp, Bill 112
Arsenault, Don 118, 387
Artists of Berkeley Lake 73
Arts Facility Authority 369
Ashworth, Charles 171, 258, 307, 350, 354, 355
Ashworth, Don 422
Ashworth, Martha 368
Asian Indian Baptist Community 557
Association of the Mentally Retarded 528
AT&T Classic 210, 217, 218, 287
Atkinson, Betty 371
Atkinson, Bill 39, 171, 182, 203, 205, 236, 238, 266, 513
Atlanta and Richmond Air-Line Railroad 124
Atlanta Athletic Club 9, 576, 577
Atlanta Baptist Association 328
Atlanta Church of Christ - Gwinnett 418
Atlanta Constitution 27, 84, 160, 170, 174, 242, 243, 301, 523
Atlanta Falcons 61, 209, 299, 300, 302, 371
Atlanta Jet 273
Atlanta Love Korean Baptist 557
Atlanta Metropolitan Planning Commission 173
Atlanta Precision Moulding 313
Atlanta Region Metropolitan Planning Commission 171, 363
Atlanta Vineyard Church 418
Atlas Manufacturing Company 52
Attaway, Laurie 308, 385
Auburn 67, 123, 124, 240, 255, 261, 486, 540
Aurora Theatre 147, 148, 151, 374, 375, 376, 377, 379, 541, 547
Austin, Dave 525
Austins 210
Aviation Division 272

B

Baggett, Baybe Oakes 542
Baggett, Jess 139, 142, 455
Bagheri, Carolyn 371, 547
Bagheri, M.T. 320
Bagwell Drug Store 210
Bagwell, Dorothy 124
Bagwell, Everett 461
Bagwell, Harris 461
Bagwell, J.A. 247
Bagwell, J.C. 461
Bagwell, Paula 367, 368, 371
Bahl, Surinder 465
Bailey, Courtney Lynn 325
Bailey, Glenn 325
Bailey, Larry 351, 353, 386
Bailey, Ray 270
Baker, Lloyd 441
Baldwin, Beauty Poole 85, 86, 504, 507
Balfour, Don 369
Ball, Alessandra 372
Ballard, Jim 465
Ballenger, Michael J. 406
Bank of America 57, 59, 68, 455
Bank of Buford 454, 455, 461
Bank of Duluth 454, 461, 464
Bank of Gwinnett 39, 113, 148, 349, 458, 459, 461, 465, 466
Bank of Loganville 460
Bank of Norcross 454, 458, 459
Bank of Suwanee 455, 465
Banks, Fred 160
BankSouth 57, 59, 455
Bannister, Charles 171, 261, 338, 354
BAPS Shri Swaminarayan Mandir 560
Baranto, Brenda 518
Barber, Ralph 313, 463
Barker, Ann 521
Barker, Bob 215
Barker, Leonel E. (Stud) 215
Barnes, Roy 525, 565
Barnett, Mike 303, 304
Baro, Hector C. 308
Baroni, Bob xv, 150, 151
Barrett, Lonice 63, 224
Barrington Industries 118
Barron, David I. (Red) 213, 214
Barrow County 116, 124, 575
Barrow, David Crenshaw "Uncle Dave" 576
Barry, Bill 513
Bartels, Sharon Rigsby 337
Bartlett, Clayton 462
Baughman, Bill 118, 153, 518
Baxter Cotton Manufacturing Company 100
Baxter, Mark 230
Bay Creek Park 531, 533
BBA 539
Beacon Award 331
Beall, Laura 361
Bear's Best 218
Beard, Les 323
Beard, Phillip 374, 421, 422
Beaudreau, Mike 540
Beaver Ruin Estates 231
Beaver, Jimmy 82
Beavers, Robert 413
Beckman Instruments 283
Behning, Eric 538
Beiser, Marie 364
Belk 10, 11, 12, 13, 14, 146
Bell Labs 287
Bell Telephone System 289
Bell, Woody 461, 520
BellSouth Classic 210, 218
Ben Summerour Farm 9
Benefield, J.W. 177, 476, 501
Bennett, Glenn 173, 211
Bentley, Mrs. William 514
Berg, Mike 338, 350, 352, 353, 388
Berkeley Dozen 196
Berkeley Hills Country Club 195, 217
Berkeley Lake 9, 73, 124, 163, 253, 381, 438, 564, 579
Berkeley Realty andÿInvestment Company 124
Berkmar Methodist Church 419
Berkmere Farms 173
Berkshire, Edna 521, 539
Best Friend Park 261, 264
Bethany Baptist 319, 421
Bethesda High 195
Bethesda United Methodist Church 426
Big Creek 191
Big Shoe 121
Biggers, Ann 34
Billew, Dennis 50
Billew, Dorris (Dot) 472
Billew, Hazel 472
Bird, F. W. 9
Birts, Jon D. 456
Bishop, E.M. (Skip) 459
Black Knights 211
Black, George 360
Blackburn, Matt 427
Blackmon, Luther 309
Blaha, Lana 378
Blasi, Ron 44
Blatchford, Pamela 544
Bloodworth, Wayne 465
Blue, Sondra 415
Bly, Chris 85
Bnhole, Dr. Sunil 327
Boat, Paul 519
Boeing Integrated Defense Systems 582
Bogan Park 263
Bogan, Shadrack 152
Bohne, Barbara 546
Bolding, Mrs. W.V. 455
Boles, Jerry 465
Bolton, Jack 442
Bomhoff, Lee 383
Bona Allen Company (Inc.) 116, 210, 383, 386
Bono, Pastor Guillremo 562
Borders, William Holmes 226
Borglum, Gutzon 225
Bottoms, I.G. 529
Boucher, Vern 529
Boully, Dennis 247
Bowden, Bob 384
Bowen Family Builders 408
Bowen, Courtney 547
Bowen, Dr. Edward 319
Bowers, Michael 352
Bowland, Mrs. S.A. 546
Bowling, David 63
Bowman Pirkle House 535
Bowman, Lynn 386, 523

Boy Scouts 34, 54, 87, 528, 533
Boyce, Peter 506
Boyd, Dr. James E. 297
Boyd, Stephen 326
Boyle, Stephen 442
Boys and Girls Clubs 305, 306, 307, 308
Bozeman, Rev. Jack 316
Brack, Barbara 368
Brack, Elliott xv, 301, 306, 313, 504, 505, 512, 513, 580
Bradberry, Raymond 211
Bradbury, J.T. 209
Braden, Jim 462
Bradford, Jackie 487
Bradley, Larry 192
Bradley, Russell 123
Bragg, Beth 519
Bramblett, Sybil 212
Branch Bank and Trust Company (BB&T) 461
Branch, Brenda 306
Brand Banking Company 30, 112, 455, 457
Brand Partners 469, 470
Brand Properties 470
Brand, C.H. 456
Brand, Charles 145
Brand, Dot 145
Brand, E.M. 456
Brand, Joe 50, 303
Brand, L.M. 113, 456
Brandon Mill 152
Brannan, James F. 145
Brannen, Jimmy 34
Brannon, Colbert 318
Bransby, Joe 309
Branscome, Curtis 228
Brantley, Bill 465
Braselton 46, 49, 124, 185, 217, 239, 255, 409, 457, 539, 555, 579
Braselton Business Association 539
Braselton Community Center 539
Braselton, Harry 39, 42, 457
Braselton, John O. 124
Breast Health Education and Resource Center 328
Breedlove, Mildred 75
Brent, Eon 414
Brewster, John 110
Brickton 122
Bridge Church 427
Brinkley, Lewis 309
Briscoe, Thomas 155, 271
Britt, Billy 214
Britt, Butch 211
Britt, Carson 214
Britt, Clark 319
Britt, Ellis 177
Britt, Harold 318
Britt, Hugh 268
Britt, Jack 210, 211, 212, 214
Britt, Tony 319
Britt, Van 217
Britt, W.C. 317
Britt, W.H. 465
Brock, Elizabeth 224
Brock, Mark 177, 178
Brock, Tony 542
Brogdon, Georgia 103, 154
Brogdon, William F. 313
Bronnum, Rachel 367, 368
Brooks, Dorsey 211
Brooks, Pascal 111
Brooks, Paul 211
Brooks, Rev. Mary Lane 420
Brosnan, D.W. 524
Brown Bank and Trust 112
Brown, Brent 230
Brown, Charles (Charlie) 274, 275, 277, 280, 281, 282
Brown, Geoffrey 377
Brown, Jerome 177
Brown, Loren 534
Brown, Pat 364, 366
Brown, Randy 310, 312, 314
Brown, Sam 112, 414
Bruce, George 529
Bruschini, Pat 536
Brush, Edgar 364
Buchanan, Edward 343
Buckman, Mike 465
Buford Academy 574
Buford Advertiser 241, 247, 248
Buford, Algernon Sidney 124
Buford Business Alliance 537
Buford Church of God 421
Buford City Commission 482
Buford City Hall 421
Buford City Schools 474
Buford Commercial Bank 462
Buford Dam 142, 143, 179, 182, 219, 222, 526, 535
Buford Enterprise 240, 247
Buford Fine Arts Theatre 510
Buford First United Methodist Church 422
Buford Gazette 240, 247
Buford General Hospital 136, 137, 317, 320
Buford Herald 240, 247
Buford High School 210, 317, 386, 523, 533
Buford Journal 240, 241, 247
Buford Kiwanis 141, 421
Buford Mall 382, 462
Buford Ministerial Association 421, 422
Buford Museum 386, 522
Buford Performing Arts Center 374
Buford Post Office 421
Buford Presbyterian Church 198
Buford Rock Quarry Prison for Incorrigibles 159
Buford School of Art 386
Buford Shoemakers 120, 121, 209, 210
Buford Tannery 382
Buford/Sugar Hill Library 546
Buford-Lanier Woman's Club 421
Buice, Maron 164, 165, 166, 203, 237, 252, 260
Buis, Jean 377
Buis, Kirk 378
Bullock, Carol 331
Bullock, Janice 241, 313
Bullock, Theresa 375
Bunton Road Park 74
Burdges, Carol 307, 308
Burel, Willis 455
Burnett, Alice and Henry 132
Burnett, Henry 132
Burnham, Hank 224
Burns, Dorothy 224
Burroughs, Edgerton 464
Burslem, Rick 492
Burson, Roy 220, 223
Burton, Howard 529
Busbee, George 16, 17, 52, 301, 463, 496
Busbee, Mary Beth 303

Bush, Allen 383, 384, 385, 387
Bush, Bill 351, 358
Bush, Marty 529
Bush, Warren 266
Butler, Bill 464
Button Gwinnett 90, 92, 94, 95, 96, 97, 515
Button Gwinnett Award 52, 361
Button Gwinnett Hospital 137, 267, 317, 318, 319, 325, 328, 330, 335
Button Gwinnett Hotel 115
Button Gwinnett Savings and Loan 41
Button, Chuck 351
Byerly, John 542
Byrd, Gary 465
Byrd, Willard 216

C

C.A. Kelly Park 546
C.W. Summerour Farm 9
Cabe, Jim 416
Cabe, Shirley 417
Cadillac Fairview Shopping Centers 12
Cady, Paula 414
Cain, Dr. Sylvester (Jack) 132
Cain, O.D. 181, 183, 582
Calder, Aggie 309
Caldwell, Ed A. 240, 247
Caldwell, Lantz 384
Callaway, Howard (Bo) 236, 565
Calvary Christian Church 380
Calvary Christian Fellowship 426
Camp Creek Baptist Church 103, 552, 557
Camp Sunshine 546
Camp, James 155, 156
Campbell High School 3
Campbell, Lane 522
Campbell, Patrick 377
Campbell, Tom 292, 296
Campus Church of Christ 418
Canaday, Frank 488
Cantrell, L. Myron 463
Cantrell, Teresa 442
Cardillo, Harry 308
Cardinal Lake Estates 231
Carlsen, Carol 424
Carlyle, Roy 522, 529
Carothers, Richard (Dick) 351, 360
Carroll, Donald 461
Carroll, Michael 379
Carroll, Tanya 379
Carson, Fiddling John 128
Carter Martin Classic 491
Carter Samuel Martin Experimental Therapy Research Fund 491
Carter, Ben 1, 15, 334, 335
Carter, Jimmy 43, 160, 194, 206, 207, 231, 232, 260, 278, 284, 285, 286, 441, 442, 443, 449, 459, 460, 563, 564, 566
Carville, James 63
Casco Forest 232
Casey, James 4, 19, 23, 25
Cash, Catherine 521
Cash, Karen 544
Cash, Mrs. P.D. 528
Castleview Golf and Country Club 216
Caswell Real Estate 232
Caswell, Carl 233
Caswell, J.D. 233, 235, 236, 356, 365
Cates, Geraldine 421, 422
Cates, Jonathan 378
Cates, Milton 211
Centerville 31, 32, 33, 37, 98, 99, 100, 102, 103, 106, 328, 345, 542, 555
Centerville Business Association 542
Central Baptist 426
Central Christian 424
Central Gwinnett High 86, 145, 211, 212, 528, 533
CEO Council 499
Chabad Enrichment Center 556
Chacon, Victoria 564
Chairman's Club 497
Chan, Wayne 442
Chandler, Cynthia 331
Chandler, Matt 427
Chandler, Nancy Smith 442
Chandler, Rick 171
Chapin, Bob 442
Chapin, Ruth Ann 331
Chappas, Charles 529
Chappell, Rev. Davis 425
Chappell, William 230
Charles W. Henson Garment Manufacturing Company 115
Charles W. Summerour Farm 1
Chastain Air Service 269
Chastain, Dr. J.B. 134
Chastain, Warren 269
Chateau Elan 185, 217, 239, 579
Chatham, Troy 530
Chattahoochee River 9, 10, 11, 53, 89, 91, 98, 101, 124, 126, 127, 132, 137, 138, 143, 167, 170, 179, 189, 191, 215, 217, 218, 219, 223, 235, 252, 262, 277, 314, 409, 527, 536, 554, 576
Checker, Chubby 365
Cheeley, Joe 198
Chernecky, Louise 313
Chestnut Grove Baptist 319
Chicopee Industries 118
Children's Museum 370, 371, 396
Choice's Store 106
Christ Church Episcopal 404, 406, 418, 567
Christ the King Lutheran Church 418
Christ the Lord Lutheran Church 424, 426
Christianomics Mall 558
Christiansen, Pastor Gary 555
Christmas in Braselton 539
Christopher, Lorri 513
Chrobak, Donna 422
Church of the Hills Presbyterian Church 426, 427
Circle K Club 527
Cisco Systems 282, 297, 298, 299
Citizens and Southern National Bank (C&S) 39, 50, 59, 196, 217, 232, 280, 459
Citizens Bank of Gwinnett 461
Citizens for New Suwanee Revenue 186
Civitan 421, 525, 534
Civitan International's Honor Club Award 534
Clack, David 378
Clark, Bob 441
Clark, John (June) 269
Clark, Kevin 223
Clay, Jim 218
Clay, Mark 313
Cleghorn, Gwen Michael 485
Clower Jr., W. Emmett 34, 171, 319
Coalition for Health and Human Services 342, 400, 404, 413
Coan, Mike 197
Coan, Sandra 195
Cobb, Gary 529
Cobb, George 216

Cochrane Jr., Eugene 328
Cockcroft, Dr. W.B. 198
Cofer, J.W. 518
Cofer-Adams Building Materials 115
Coggins, Frank 124
Coggins, Mrs. Howard 514
Cohen, Susan 501
Cohron, Terry 422
Cole, Dan 161
Cole, Mode 455
Cole, Shelley 538
Coleman, Brooks 525
Coleman, Darryl 308
Coleman, Grady 459
Collins Hill Baptist 426
Collins Hill Golf Club 216
Collins Hill High School 434
Collins Hill Library 216
Collins, Carolyn 504, 505, 507, 532
Collins, Dr. Jim 409
Collins, Stacy N. 415
Collins, Stephens 380
Colonial Bank 466
Combs, Rich 465
Commerce Club 503, 536
Commercial Bank of Gwinnett 466
Committee for Quality Hotels and Restaurants 192
CommScope 288
Community Concern 547
Community Connections 499
Community Foundation of Northeast Georgia 74, 365, 387, 500
Community Improvement Districts (CIDs) 363, 441, 443, 444, 445, 446, 447, 448, 449, 450, 569
Community of Grace Lutheran Church 423
Computer Intelligence Square Aviation Inc. 273
Concordia Association 282
Congregational Health Ministry 328
Conley, Gus 39
Connecticut General 181, 182
Connell, Jock 206
Consumer Credit Counseling 405
Contemporary International Museum of Art 384
Conti, Mary Carolyn 381
Conway, Butch 307
Conway, Jack 463
Cook, Marybeth 427
Cooley, Joe 270
Cooper, H. L. 145
Cooper, John 139
Cooper, Maurice 211
Cooper, Terrilee 442
Cooper, Travis 211
Corbin, Dickie 211
Corbin, Horace 211
Corbin, Marsha 309
Corley, A.J. 128
Corley, Minor M. xii, 128, 169, 183, 184, 185, 198
Cornerstone Church of Christ 427
Cornett Hotel 114, 115
Cornith Baptist 319
Corporate Property Investors 15, 334, 335
Corpus Christi Catholic 328
Costabile, Muriel 540
Couch, Edgar 40
Couch, Michelle 544
Council for Quality Growth 52, 355, 356, 357, 360, 361, 387
Council For Seniors 112
Country Club of Gwinnett 217
County Seat Players 381
Cousins REIT 284
Cowart, Dan 313, 464, 485
Cowart, Jim 2, 8, 10, 17, 233, 234, 312, 313, 314
Cowsert, Cliff 460
Cox, DiAnn Bruce 518
Cox, Doug 540
Cox, Mrs. Flora 520
Craig, Jack 211
Craig, Robert 550
Craigdale Estates 232
Crane, Stephanie 422
Crapo, Irene Ewing 545
Crawford, Jim 306
Crescent Resources 235
Crews, Alton 336, 364, 365, 477
Crews, David 476
Crews, Jeanette 368
Crock, Chris 536
Crooked Creek Water Reclamation Plant 257
Cross Pointe Church 558, 582
Crossroads Community Church 559
Crosstown 144, 145, 146
Crouch, Terry 534
Crowe, Nelson 211
Crowe, Scrappy 183
Crowson, Bobby 510
Crump, Randy 308
Crunkleton, John 163, 164, 165, 166
Crutcher, Dr. Jim 412
Csuka, Lynn 309
CSX 49, 108, 109, 111, 115, 269
Culbertson, Barry 464
Culvern, Joanne 407
Curley Tennis Courts 486
Currey Jr., Bradley 313
Currey, Bradley 307, 313, 496
Curry, Dan 542
Cyclic Environmental Maintenance Plan (CEMP) 57
Cyphers, Leonard 306, 307

D

D. Scott Hudgens Jr. Humanitarian Award 404
D.C. Hayes Associates Inc. 291
Dacula 75, 92, 108, 124, 128, 129, 130, 150, 177, 209, 213, 214, 215, 217, 262, 317, 345, 348, 361, 414, 424, 426, 458, 466, 492, 493, 515, 538, 558, 579
Dacula Banking Company 458
Dacula Business Association 538
Dacula High 214, 466
Dacula Memorial Day Parade 538
Dana, Art 504, 505
Daniel, Billy 215
Daniel, Fort 101
Darien Baptist 559
Davenport, Edward 559
David Kistner Center 406
David Weekley Homes 406
Davidson Natatorium 485
Davidson, Virginia and Gerald 310, 313
Davis, Ben and Clarissa 71
Davis, Cheri 421
Davis, Dawn 380
Davis, Dr. Jim 271
Davis, Joe Ben 70
Davis, Millard 211
Davis, Ralph 421
Davis, Rev. Joel 422

Davis, Richard 215
Davis, Thomas O. 528
Day, Brad 465
Day, Cecil 5, 8, 9
Deacon, Sybil Pate 518, 519
Dean, Christina 416, 417
Deardorff, Tom xi
Deganian, Javad 320
DeKalb College 450
Deleon, Dodger 521
Dellinger, Randy 510, 527
Deming, Michael 449
Democrats 110, 232, 337, 338, 352, 565, 566
Dennison, Laura 375, 376
Denny, Helen 213
Department of Family and Children Services 342
Department of Housing and Urban Development 10, 517
Development Authority of Lawrenceville 364
Development Authority of Snellville 363, 364
Dierdorf, Michael 383
Dingler, Charles 383
Discover Mills 48, 334, 335, 388, 437, 438, 439, 440, 579
Dispain, Charlotte 519
Dixon, Randall 356
Dodd, W.J. 352, 390
Dodson, Freddie 211
Dodson, W.M. 27
Don and Ida Yancey Gymnasium 486
Donga Daily News 564
Donohue, Bill 223
Doran, John 492
Doublestein, Barry 433
Dove, Dr. Donald 145
Dover, Paul 181, 183, 582
Dowdin, Debbie 420
Dowdy, Craig 224
Down Right Theatre 374, 375
Downtown Development Authority 361, 363, 542
Dr. and Mrs. Maxwell Berry 401
Drake Furniture Company 383
Drake, Laura 424
Dream House for Medically Fragile Children 533, 538, 547
Dubai Aerospace Enterprises 272
Duke Endowment 328
Duke Enterprises 257
Duke, Frank 39
Duke, Fraser 310
Duke, Paul 101, 257, 260, 275, 276, 279, 286, 459, 535, 536
Dukes, Rev. John 555
Duluth Church of God 426, 427
Duluth City Hall 74
Duluth Fall Festival 73, 534, 537
Duluth Festival Center 73
Duluth First Baptist Church 426, 427
Duluth First United Methodist Church 406, 426, 427
Duluth High School 28, 168, 195, 214, 215, 545
Duluth Historical Society 519
Duluth History Museum 519
Duluth Interact Club 533
Duluth Masonic Lodge 426
Duluth Merchant's Association 537
Duluth News Dispatch 241
Duluth Seventh Day Adventist 426, 427
Duluth Town Green 73
Duncan Creek Church 422
Duncan, Boyd 306
Duncan's Creek Park 345
Dunn, Bill 151
Dunn, Glancy 135, 136
Dunn, Richard 135
Dunn, Tim 513
Dunnigan, Rev. Ron 426
Dunwoody, Janet 371
Durden, Lu 309
Durrett, III, James F. (Jim) 442
Duvall, Junior 260

E

E.R. Snell, Contractor 155
Eason, Bill 465
East Lake Country Club 9
Easters, Melita 293
Eastside Medical Center 322, 323
Ebasco Services 275, 283
Economic Development office 276
Edge, Glenda 212
Edgemoor North 232, 233
Edmonds, Dr. H.P. 269
Edmundson, James L. 532
Edmundson, Larry 504
Edwards, Philip 320
Edwards, Shannon 519
EHCA, LLC. 322
Elam, Beth 378
Electromagnetic Sciences Inc. 275, 277
Elinburg, Dr. W.A. 183, 198
Elisha Winn House 515, 516
Elizabeth Williams Library 519
Elliott, Ted 306
Ellis, Mr. and Mrs. Jim 417, 463
Embassy National Bank 465
Embracing Hospice 323, 410
Emerald Point Hotel 62, 222
Emerson, Mrs. James 514
Emory Eastside Hospital 322, 323, 411
Encore Aviation 272
Environmental Health 342
Environmental Heritage Center 264
Environmental Protection Division (EPD) 63, 223, 356, 359, 360
Epic Faith Church 427
Epiphany Lutheran Church 421
Episcopal Charities Foundation 422
Eplan, Gary 447
Ernest Communications 374
Ernest, Pam 373
Ernst, Pastor Matthew 555
Erving, Julius 217
E-SPLOST 341, 342, 474, 476, 583
Estafan, Madeline 411
Estes, Mrs. R.C. 140
Estes, R.C. 140
Eternal Hills Cemetery 578
Etheridge, Lonnie 209
Etheridge, Roy 209
Evangel Community Church 423
Evangelical Lutheran Church of America 555
Evans, Paul 434
Everett, Clinton 209
Evergreen Conference Center 228, 229
Evermore Community Improvement District (CID) 363, 445, 446, 447, 540
Everson, Melvin 419, 420
Ewing Hotel 114, 115, 148
Ewing, A.E. 114
Ewing, Harvey 34

Ewing, L.D. 529
Ewing, Linda Mason 32
Ewing, Lottie 454
Ewing, Mrs. Hubert 114
Ewing, Thomas 518, 519
Executive Business Council 544
Exxon Mobil 283
Ezzard Charles Boxing Club 306
Ezzard, Dr. George 112
Ezzard, Dr. W.P. 112
Ezzard, Virginia 29, 424

F

FAA Airport Development and Aid program 271
Fairview Presbyterian Church 93, 103
Falcon Complex 186, 302
Family Aquatic Center 263
Fanning Leadership Institute 509
Farmer, William 521
Farmers and Merchants Bank 461
Farr, Arthur 540
Farrior, Patricia McLaurin 457
Faucette, Sidney 476
Faulkner, Beth 519
Faulkner, Glen 519
Faulkner, Gloria 541
Faulkner, Roy 227
Feldt, Jim 442
Female Seminary 131, 367, 368, 517, 547
Ferguson, John 274
Ferguson, Scott 350
Ferguson, W. H. 529
Ferrell, Sandra 427
Field of Dreams 533
Fifth Third Bank 465
Figliolini, Rico 442, 579
Fincher, Dr. David 449, 487
Fincher, Kathy 73
Findley, Sr., Mrs. Guy (Clare) 132
Findley, Guy Ben 28
Findley, Guy Washington 461
Fire Training Center 261
First Atlanta Bank 458, 466
First Bank of the South 41
First Baptist Church of Lawrenceville 30, 214
First Baptist Church of Lilburn 419, 557
First Baptist Church of Snellville 558, 559
First Baptist Church of Mountain Park 419
First Charter Corporation of Charlotte 465
First Christian Church 424
First Commercial Bank of Buford 461, 462
First Financial Management Corp 67, 463
First United Methodist of Church of Lawrenceville 426
First United Methodist of Dacula 426
Fishback, Carrie 545
Fisher Scientific 283
Fisher, Donna 354, 419, 424
Fisher, Sandra 422
Flanigan, James Cicero (J.C.) 92, 240, 247, 513, 526
Flanigan, Miss Annie Frances 514
FLASH 359
Fleagle, David and Madeleine 562
Fleischmann, John 434
Flint Hill Methodist Church 103
Fluehr, Chris 464, 465
Foote, Mark 542
Ford, Ronnie 371
Forde, Andy 579
Forrestall, Jeff 421, 422
Forrester, Jack 160
Fortune, Bill 29, 149, 150, 171, 209, 211, 212
Fortune, Donna 212
Fortune, Frances 179
Foster, David 306, 308
Foster, Randy 375, 377
Fountain, Myrna 212
Four Corners Primary Care Center 415
Four Pillar Award 361
Four Winds Farm 216
Fourtain, Dr. Greg 412
Fowler, Bob 146, 241, 301, 305, 310, 311, 312, 313, 314, 369, 370
Fowler, Chris 374
Fowler, Doris 419
Fowler, Judy 241, 406
Fowler, Red 574
Fowler, Robert 211, 314, 365
Frances Wood Wilson Foundation 308, 370
Franchisuer, Gordon 183
Francis, Allen Philip 545
Franklin, Julian 146
Franklin, Katherine 460
Frech, Bill 372
Free, Donald 224
Freeman, David 225
Freeman, Marie 212
Freeman, Uhland 183, 185, 198
Freeman's Mill 152
Freid, Norman 320
Freund, Linda 425
Friauf, Nancy 408
Friendship Church 33
Friendship Exchanges 531
Friendship Primitive Baptist 319
Frix, Dianne 421
Front Porch Gallery 382
Fry, Rev. Dave 406
Frye, Susan 427
Fuller, Scott xv, 272
Furukawa Electric Company, Inc. 288

G

GACS 487
Gaddess Sr., John 111
Gadlage, Robert 320
Gage, Barry 512
Gainesville/Hall County Chamber of Commerce 138
Galardi, Mary 308
GALILEO 346
Gallow, Margaret 519
Ganaway, Brenda 415
Gannett Foundation 365
Gant, R. A. (Junior) 522
Gantz 512
GA-PCOM 434
Gardner, Jerry 463
Gardner, Weldon 198
Garner, Carl 253, 459, 522, 528, 529
Garner, Chief 317
Garner, Ellis 529
Garner, James 368
Garner, Larry 460
Garner, Maxine 519, 520
Garner, Pat 386
Garner, Richard 253
Garran, Peter 198
Garrard's Raid 106

Garrett, Franklin 75, 101
Garrett, John W. 570
Garris, Eric S. 142
Garvin, Jeff 422
Gaskill, Marlene 536
Gaultney, Steve E. 364, 442
Gazaway, Dr. Hoyt 414
GBT Scholarship Program 372
GC&B 346, 347, 348, 349
Gee, Cheryl 372, 395
GEFA 176
General Electric 282, 283
General Shoe Company 115
Genesco 115
Genuine Parts 313
George Pierce Park 264
George, Nick 313
Georgia Association of Christian Schools 488, 493
Georgia Baptist Convention 388, 394, 553
Georgia Camp for the Blind 528
Georgia Cities Foundation 362
Georgia Community Development 368
Georgia Community Papers 241
Georgia Council for the Arts 377
Georgia Department of Community Affairs 171, 362
Georgia Department of Family and Children Services 342
Georgia Department of Technical and Adult Education 337
Georgia Department of Transportation 77, 237, 445, 535
Georgia Environmental Facilities Authority 63, 176
Georgia Force 61, 69, 209, 392, 393, 394
Georgia Greenspace Program 264
Georgia Gwinnett College 69, 453
Georgia High School Association 209, 393, 394, 490, 493
Georgia High Tech Alliance 293
Georgia Jet 273
Georgia Lighthouse for the Blind 528
Georgia Lions Lighthouse 529
Georgia Nonpublic Postsecondary Education Commission 433
Georgia Old-Time Fiddlers 130
Georgia Osteopathic Medical Association 433
Georgia Perimeter College 450
Georgia Poultry Federation 199
Georgia Power 54, 56, 149, 282, 309, 325, 348, 404, 510, 511, 571
Georgia Recordings for the Blind 529
Georgia Regional Transit Authority 438
Georgia Research Alliance 64
Georgia Rotary Student Program 531, 532
Georgia Safe Dam Act 177
Georgia Soil and Water Conservation Commission 177
Georgia State University 3
Georgia Tech Foundation 69, 274, 280, 281
Georgia Trust Bank 462
Georgia, Carolina and Northern Railroad 111
Gerstein, Ellen 400, 418
Gibb, John 224
Gibbs, John 273
Gilbert, J.B. 209
Gilbert, Leonard A. (Len) 495, 496
Gilbreth, Frank and Lillian 278
Gilleland, J. Paul 518
G-JAC 339, 340, 341, 342, 368
Glancy Outpatient Center 134, 329
Glancy Rehabilitation Center 134
Glancy, Gen. A.R. 132
Glenn, Jan 539
Global Forum 49
Gloster 72, 108
Gober, Dawn P. 364
Goe, Charles 450
Good Samaritan Clinic 413
Good Shepherd Presbyterian 419
GOP 84, 337, 565
Gordon, J. Terry 372, 406, 461
Gormally, Nancy 427
Gosta, Predrag 372
Governor's Comm. on Effectiveness and Economy in Government 64
Gower, Bill 446
Grace Church 418
Grace Harris Garden 545
Grady Holt Homes 145
Grams, Laura 372
Grant, James C. 269
Gravely, Aliza 380
Gravely, Martin 380
Graves, Rev. Avery 521
Gray, Dick 284
Grayson 50, 52, 71, 124, 148, 150, 155, 231, 261, 345, 361, 364, 381, 382, 423, 433, 434, 450, 460, 520, 521, 531, 543, 544, 555
Grayson Art and History Center 520
Grayson Chamber of Commerce 543
Grayson Historic Preservation Society 521
Greater Atlanta Christian School 87, 372, 486, 487
Greater Atlanta Vedic Temple Society, Inc. 561
Greater Grayson Chamber of Commerce 543
Green, Ambrose T. 115
Green, Edith 75
Green, Howard 454
Green, John 144, 510
Green, Lorraine 501
Greenbrier Mall 8
Greenfield, Howard 464
Greenwood, Hugh B. 111
Greer, Margaret 232
Greg Ellis Center 417
Gresham, Carl 529
Griffin, B.J. 425
Griffin, Charles 297
Griffin, Marvin 141, 160, 227
Griffin, Tom 253
Grizzel, Joe 368
Grogan, Bill 529
Group Study Exchanges 531
GRTA 437, 438, 439, 440, 441
GSLT 510, 511
GTC 337
Gullickson, Nancy 368, 369, 370
Gundy, B.J. Van 444
Gunnin, Ray 82, 164, 182, 202, 203, 207, 208, 237, 251, 252, 260
Gunter, Larry 211, 514
Gunter, Mrs. Larry 514
Gunter, Roy 153
Gunter, Shirley 211
Guthrie, Kelly 211
Guynn, Michael 308
Guyre, Marion and Michael 381
Gwinnett Airport Authority 268
Gwinnett Animal Shelter 509
Gwinnett Arena 61, 209, 393, 394, 395, 396, 397, 402, 469, 501, 569
Gwinnett Arts Center 80, 83, 387
Gwinnett Arts Council 80, 83, 387
Gwinnett Atlas 240, 247
Gwinnett Ballet School 372
Gwinnett Ballet Theatre 372

Gwinnett Bank and Trust 84, 459, 460
Gwinnett Board of Education 145, 575
Gwinnett Braves 209, 469, 471, 472, 569
Gwinnett C&B 348, 349
Gwinnett Chamber 17, 79, 80, 84, 87, 145, 156, 173, 198, 202, 239, 268, 302, 364, 387, 404, 444, 447, 448, 450, 451, 453, 458, 496, 498, 499, 500, 504, 505, 506, 510, 512, 513, 526, 536, 539, 553, 577
Gwinnett Church of Christ 426
Gwinnett Citizen of the Year 79
Gwinnett Civic and Cultural Center 388
Gwinnett Civic Center 387, 390, 392, 468, 501, 535
Gwinnett Clean and Beautiful 342, 346, 347, 348, 349, 480, 532, 546
Gwinnett Coalition 400, 413, 418
Gwinnett Commerce Center 503
Gwinnett Community Bank 427, 461
Gwinnett Community Clinic 323, 411, 412
Gwinnett Community Foundation 83, 422
Gwinnett Community Health Clinic 319
Gwinnett Community Hospital 318, 321, 322
Gwinnett Convention and Visitors Bureau (GCVB) 387, 391, 397, 398, 467, 469, 470, 500, 501
Gwinnett Correctional Facility 160
Gwinnett Council for the Arts 73, 367, 373, 546
Gwinnett County Airport 268, 269, 270, 274
Gwinnett County Bank 40, 41, 57, 65, 66, 303, 304, 463
Gwinnett County Bank of Snellville 57
Gwinnett County Board of Commissioners 433, 445, 447, 448
Gwinnett County Building and Loan Association 455
Gwinnett County Commission 12, 111, 203, 232, 266, 329, 350, 388, 390, 429, 442
Gwinnett County Development Authority 396
Gwinnett County Hospital Authority 134
Gwinnett County Parks and Recreation Department 263
Gwinnett County Public Library 246, 342, 343, 344, 345, 346, 377, 518, 532, 541, 568
Gwinnett County Public Schools 480, 508
Gwinnett County Recreation Authority 259
Gwinnett County Relay for Life 546
Gwinnett County School Board 171, 233
Gwinnett County Transit System 436
Gwinnett County Water and Sewer Authority 258
Gwinnett Daily News 3, 146, 202, 241, 242, 243, 244, 245, 246, 247, 248, 265, 267, 279, 285, 301, 305, 315, 365, 370, 481
Gwinnett Daily Post 244, 245, 246, 247, 248, 249, 387, 579
Gwinnett Development Association 356, 357
Gwinnett Downtown Development Authorities 364
Gwinnett Environmental and Heritage Center 533, 535
Gwinnett EXTRA 16, 243, 245
Gwinnett Federal Bank 82, 455
Gwinnett Federal Savings and Loan 309, 455, 459
Gwinnett Foundation Inc. 364
Gwinnett Girls Club 307
Gwinnett Gladiators 209, 393, 394
Gwinnett Great Day of Service 533
Gwinnett Health Department 411
Gwinnett Herald 105, 240, 247
Gwinnett Historic Courthouse 113
Gwinnett Historical Society 74, 76, 92, 113, 118, 142, 428, 513, 514, 515, 550
Gwinnett History Center 515
Gwinnett History Museum 264, 517, 518
Gwinnett Home Weekly 248, 579
Gwinnett Hospital Authority 63, 73, 134, 317, 320, 323, 331, 546
Gwinnett Hospital System, Inc. 326
Gwinnett Industrial Development Authority 300, 470, 577
Gwinnett Journal 240, 247, 344
Gwinnett Justice and Administrative Center (G-JAC) 104, 113, 427, 431
Gwinnett Managed Care Inc. 326
Gwinnett Medical Center Foundation 73, 326
Gwinnett Medical Center-Duluth 134, 329
Gwinnett Medical Properties Inc. 326
Gwinnett Medical Services Inc. 326
Gwinnett Merit Board 577
Gwinnett Neighborhood Leadership Institute 509
Gwinnett News 245
Gwinnett Park System 265
Gwinnett Philharmonic 372, 373, 374
Gwinnett Place CID 444, 447, 448
Gwinnett Place Mall 12, 13, 77, 264, 334, 335, 438, 439, 447, 537, 563, 581
Gwinnett Planning Commission 535
Gwinnett Police Academy 165
Gwinnett Post-Tribune 245, 248
Gwinnett Pregnancy Center 491
Gwinnett Public Schools 477, 479, 482, 510, 551
Gwinnett Recreation Authority 470
Gwinnett Recreational District 265
Gwinnett Rotary Club 530, 531, 532
Gwinnett School Board 336, 337, 342, 450, 474, 507, 576
Gwinnett Student Leadership 504, 510, 569
Gwinnett Technical College 336, 337, 345, 438, 450, 494, 496, 497, 512, 513, 531, 533, 547
Gwinnett Town Business Connection 539
Gwinnett Transit 436, 437, 438, 439, 440
Gwinnett Transportation Committee 79
Gwinnett United in Drug Education 510
Gwinnett University Center 450, 451, 452
Gwinnett Village CID 444, 448, 449
Gwinnett Water Authority 190
Gwinnett Water Park 535
Gwinnett Water System xii, 40, 49, 178, 179, 181, 188
Gwinnett Writer's Club 75
Gwinnett YMCA 310
Gwinnett Youth Symphony Orchestra 374
Gwinnoters 518

H

Haas, Elliot 401
Habitat for Humanity 419, 533
Haden, C.J. 99
Hagan Lodge 316
Hagler, Connie 224
Hagood, Victor 527
Hague, Sherry 407
Hahn, Rev. Bert 416
Hail, Bob 422
Hale, Thomas 518
Hales, Robert 434
Hall, Julia 539
Hall, Stan 372
Hall, Warren 485
Hamby, Herb 408
Hames, Luther 163
Hamilton Mill 102, 217, 235, 239, 252, 345, 422, 426, 462, 527, 555, 560, 579
Hamilton Mill Presbyterian 422
Hamilton Mill United Methodist Church 426
Hamilton, Frank 529
Hamilton, Lionel 211
Hamilton, Otis 128
Hamrick, Bud 529
Hanberry, Rev. Donald 555
Hancock, Walker 227
Hands of Christ Duluth Cooperative Ministry 426

Hansard, Charles 215
Hansard, Lamar 186, 215
Hansard, Rev. Lamar 215
Hanson, Bob 90
Hanson, Rev. Edward 555
Harbins 203, 261, 262, 265
Hardin, Audrey 309
Hardy Jr., Charlie 217
Hardy, Oliver 114
Harley, Shawn 272
Harmony Grove Estates 232
Harmony Grove United Methodist Church 419
Harold Hannah Civic Center 530
Harper, Judy 424
Harrell, Brett 444, 447, 540
Harriman, John 434
Harris, B.B. 403, 475
Harris, Bob 501
Harris, Buckner 103, 154
Harris, Cleve 573, 574
Harris, David 321, 411
Harris, Gerald 373
Harris, Grace 545, 573, 574
Harris, Leola 424
Harris, Lloyd 175, 177
Harris, Peggy 420
Harris, T. L. 144
Harris, Will 240
Harrison, Dwight 441
Harrison, Hughel 177
Hartman, Chuck 534
Hartman, Mary Ann 309
Hartmann, Dr. W.A. 173
Hartsfield, William B. 139, 142
Hartwell Wash 306
Harvest Table 129
Harvey, Carol 177
Hashbarger, Ed 529
Hatch, Sarah 383
Hatfield, Lance 442
Haun, David 308
Havens and Emerson of New York 181
Hawkins, Barbara 375
Hawkins, Bishop Gary 559
Hawkins, Trip 291
Hawthorne Aviation 271
Hay, Jim 301
Hayes Communications 296
Hayes Corporation 296
Hayes Microcomputer 49, 276, 291, 292, 293, 294, 295, 296, 297
Hayes Smartmodem 295
Hayes, Dennis 289, 290, 293, 296
Hayes, Grant 465
Hayes, Mike 306
Haynes Creek Primitive Baptist Church 98, 102
Hayter, Yuling 464
Haywood, Walker 403
HCA 322, 491
Head Elementary School 31
Head, Bill 537
Head, Ralph 318
Hearn, George 198
Heatherington, Dale 289, 295
Heathman, Don 304
Hebron Baptist Church 414, 492, 493, 558
Hebron Christian Academy 492, 493
Hebron Clinic 414
Hechenberger, Pat 309
Hecht, Petra and Deitrich 383
Heckman, George 398, 471
Heitmuller, Dr. Patty 508
Henderson, Jim 457
Hendrix, Arnie 241, 247
Hendrix, Will 247
Henning, Pastor Matthew 555
Hensley, Tonya 378
Henson, Arthur 116
Heritage Bank 57, 59, 66, 67, 363, 463
Heritage Golf Club 217
Heritage Savings Bank 57, 66, 463
Herman, Bob 529
Herman, Martha 529
Herndon, Al 518
Herndon, Kelly K. 442
Herndon, Winifred Mason 32
Heron, Bill 529
Herrington, Faye 425
Herron, H.B. 27
Herron, H.G. 132
Herschend Family Entertainment Corporation 227
Hetzel, Rick 510
Hewatt, Ralph 529
Hewell, James 463
Hewett, Carl 318
Heys, Ed 368
HFEC 228, 229
Hicks, George 309
Hightower Indian Trail 98
Highway 78 CID 443, 444, 446
Hi-Hope Center 402, 533, 546, 547
Hi-Hope Service Center 17, 404, 528, 547
Hill, Carolyn 421, 422, 512, 513
Hill, Faye 513
Hill, Paula 308
Hill, Wayne 171, 181, 223, 239, 257, 265, 268, 354, 389, 390, 398, 429, 436, 451
Hill-Burton Hospital 319
Hillcrest Lodge 25
Hillyard, Craig 447
Hinkle, Barbara 521
Hinkle, Jim 520
Hinshaw, Faye 369
Hinshaw, Jim 323, 327, 408, 532
Hinson, David 177
Hinton, L.O. 317
Hinze, Keith 377
Hirsch, David 442
Hispanic Baptist of Lilburn 557
Historic Register 517
Hitchcock, Tom 368
Hite, Susie 408
Hoch, Amy Lynn 442
Hofer, Dr. Lloyd 415
Hoffman, Eve Parker 171
Hoffman, Pam 512
Hog Mountain 92, 93, 101, 263, 264, 515
Hogan, Carson 209
Hogg, Brian 277
Holbrook, Robert 463
Holcomb, Eric Russell 322
Holcomb, George 577
Holcomb, Mary and Larry 322
Holcomb, Noel 230
Holder Construction Company 201, 397
Holder Sr., Robert 199

Holland, Cora W. 346
Holland, E.J. 574
Holland, Grace Reed 573
Holloway, Dr. Harold 463
Holstad, Michelle 413
Holt, James 211
Home Weekly 244, 246, 248, 579
Homestead Bank of Suwanee 465
Honer, Robert 297
Honest Alley 153
Hood, Allen 458
Hood, Jim 211, 212, 235
Hood, Jim Vic 194, 458, 466
Hood, Mr. and Mrs. John 74, 514
Hood, Ken 211
Hooper-Renwick Girls Club 306
Hoover Student Activities Center 485
Hope and Life Fellowship 103, 542
Hope Clinic 412, 413
Hopewell Baptist Church 87, 328, 491, 558, 559
Hopewell Christian Academy 88, 491, 492, 558
Hopkin's Mill 152
Hopper, Jeff 539
Horizon Theatre 380
Horton, Heyward 313, 465
Hosch, Lester 139
Hoschton 15, 17, 18, 25, 402
Hoskins, Phil xv, 265, 431
Hospital Authority of Gwinnett County 69, 136, 317
Hospital Corporation of America 322
Houten, Tom Van 2, 9, 12
Hover, Paul 139
Howard, Barbara 376
Howard, Ed 459
Howard, Jim 303
Howard, Lynette 536
Howard, Shelly 380
Howell Station 11
Howell, Evin 550
Howell, Leslie 308
Howell, O. J. 574
Howell's Landing 124
Howington, Carl 463
Howse, Jim 309
HUD 10
Hudgens Family Foundation 1
Hudgens Foundations 313
Hudgens Jr., Dallas Scott 3
Hudgens Sr., Dallas 3
Hudgens, Jackie 1, 5
Hudgens, Laura Scarborough 3
Hudgens, Scott iii, 1, 2, 3, 5, 6, 7, 9, 10, 13, 16, 17, 18, 19, 25, 77, 169, 311, 333, 334, 335, 369, 370, 404, 407, 409, 467, 472, 494, 496, 497, 498, 576
Hudson, Connie 368
Hudson, Rev. Joel P. 555
Hudson, Thomas J.P. 105
Huff, Bryant 144, 145, 267
Hughes, Jerry D. 462
Hughes, Tommy 390, 394, 398, 399, 451, 468, 497, 501
Hughes, Von 421
Hughey, Lucille and Arnold 316
Hull, Gary 135
Hull, Richard 132, 135
Hulme, Gale 532
Hulsey, Harold 529
Hulsey, Julius 84
Humana Hospital 321
Humphries, E.R. 529
Humphries, Harold 254, 260, 459
Hunt, David 445
Hunter, Tommy 258
Hussey, Lee McClure 194
Huston, Hoke 162
Hutchins Guards of the 35th Regiment 105
Hutchins Jr., William Jackson 136
Hutchins Memorial Clinic 136
Hutchins, Dr. William Jackson 136
Hutchins, Hubert 211
Hutchins, Jasper Dorsey 136
Hutchins, John xv, 136, 210, 455
Hutchins, Mike 504
Hutchins, Nathan L. 93, 112, 550
Hutchins, Robert 211
Huttman, Bob 306, 307

I

IBT 58, 59, 61, 463
Industrial Development Authority 300, 363, 470, 577
Ingbritsen, Sherry 380
Ingleside Presbyterian Church 382
Inside Gwinnett 74, 579
Intelligent Systems 275
Irvindale Farms 132, 135
Ivey, Gaines 317
Ivie, Benjamin 110, 115
Ivie, E.M. 523
Ivy Creek Church 426

J

J. Smith Lanier Insurance 283
J.M. Tull Foundation 312
J.M. Tull Metals 312
Jackson, Karen 415
Jackson, Mrs. J. Terrell 346
Jackson, Sylvia 424
Jacobs, George W. 514
Jacobs, John E. 124
Jacqueline Casey Hudgens Center for the Arts 73, 371
James F. Pack Teen Center 308
Jamestown Shopping Center 5
Jay, Esther 421
Jean Kirby Bowen Home 408
Jenkins, Bartow 151, 211, 213
Jenkins, Ed 322
Jennings, Leah 518
Jett, James 465
Jewett, Richard 368
Jim Cowart Inc. 233
Jimmy Carter Boulevard 160, 194, 206, 207, 231, 232, 284, 285, 286, 441, 442, 443, 449, 459, 460, 563, 564, 566
Joan Glancy Hospital 9, 26, 134, 136, 317, 318, 319, 327, 329, 335
Johannes, John 556
John Wesley United Methodist Church 418
Johns Creek United Methodist Church 418, 426
Johnson Controls 283
Johnson, Aaron 209
Johnson, Allen 71, 459
Johnson, Carl 132
Johnson, Clifton 233
Johnson, Doyle 216
Johnson, Ed 519
Johnson, Geoffrey 383
Johnson, Greer 230
Johnson, Jere 305

Johnson, Joanne 212
Johnson, John 386, 464, 504, 505
Johnson, L.C. 536
Johnson, Larry 465, 497
Johnson, Mrs. J. Walter 514
Johnson, Pat 315
Johnson, Rick 147, 376
Johnson, Rory 308
Johnson, T. Snell 319
Johnson, Thor 539
Joiner, Allen 536
Jondahl, Terri 376
Jones Bridge 10, 127, 128, 261, 262, 312, 554
Jones Bridge Park 127, 128, 261, 262
Jones, Cliff Jr. 487
Jones, Clifford Sr. 454, 459
Jones, Gladys and John 134
Jones, Helen 520
Jones, Melia Beth 518
Jones, Michael 543
Jones, Mollie James 459
Jones, Otis 414
Jones, Ralph 421
Jones, W.P. "Willie" 195
Jordan, Al 424
Jordan, Albert 29
Jordan, Demetrius L. 372
Jordan, Hill 347
Jordan, J.T. 33
Jordan, Maude Lee 29
Jordan, Michael L. 463
Jordan, Rhodes 29, 30, 150, 212, 307
Jordan, Sr., Hilliard Rhodes 29
Jordan, Will 29
Joseph, Jacqueline and Bob 562
Joy, P.I. 465
Jug Tavern 576
Juhan, Leon 319
Juhan, Mary Alice 69
Junior Civitan 421
Justice, James 273

K

Kaiser Permanente 405
Kaiser-Aetna Park 286
Kalaitzidis, Dr. Gina 415
Kaplan, Dave 218, 501
Karina Miller Nature Preserve 264
Karnowski, John 333
Kasbo, Barbara 416, 417
Kaufman, Daniel 452, 453, 464
Kawneer 283
Kay, Kerry 338
Kee, David 309
Keeton, Julie 171, 306
Kelley Sr., Dr. G.C. 458
Kelley, Charlie 460
Kelley, Lamar 215
Kelley, P. V. 145
Kelley, Stan 460
Kelley, Sumter 181
Kelly, Harold 461
Kelly, Paul 270
Kendall, Brad 408
Kendall, Carol 369
Kendall, David 370
Kennedy, Eugene 136, 137
Kennerly, T.T. "Doc" 520
Kennerly-Cox House 520
Kent, Jon 488
Kerlin, Bobby 385
Kesmodel, Paul 427
Key, Larry 465
Kidd, David 383
Kilgore, Jean 530
Killian Hill Baptist Church 488
Killian Hill Christian School 488
Killian, Daniel 517
Kim, Moon 464
Kimsey, John 529
King, Barbara 510
King, Dean 570
King, Gregory 308
King, Jim 529
King, Kenny 445
King, Silas 102
King, Steve 465
Kirkland, Carolyne 518, 519
Kirkman, Charles 424
Kistner, Byron 81
Kistner, David 80, 82, 173, 177, 318, 406
Kistner, Mary Straw 80, 83, 370
Kitchen, Houston W. 319
Kitchens, Hiluard 464
Kitchens, John 427
Kiwanis Clubs 526
Knight, Jamie 209
Knoff, Jerry 380
Knoff, Rebecca 380
Knox, Jr. Mr. and Mrs. Peter 316
Knox, Mr. and Mrs. Robert E. 316
Knox, Wayne 536
Koch, Harold 555
Koenning, Tim 538
Kohn, Elizabeth 84
Kolk, Margaret 537
Korean Community Presbyterian Church 231
Korean Daily News 564
Kornowa, Maureen 422
Kramer, Pam 411
Kramlich, Buzz 149
Kramlich's Supermarket 571
Kravitz, Rabbi Robert 556
Kresge Foundation 308
KSL Recreation Corp 62, 221
Ku Klux Klan 226
Kuharic, Kevin 519
Kukucka, Claudia Diaz 413
Kun K. Park 563

L

L&L Railroad 108, 124
LaBonte, Mary Jane 415
Lake Lanier 8, 37, 52, 62, 63, 64, 137, 138, 140, 141, 142, 182, 189, 190, 191, 199, 219, 220, 221, 222, 223, 236, 239, 252, 255, 257, 344, 346, 383, 385, 421, 506, 515, 546, 562, 568, 573
Lake Lanier Association 223, 546
Lake Lanier Islands 52, 62, 63, 64, 142, 219, 220, 221, 222, 223, 385, 573
Lake Lanier Islands Development Authority 62, 219, 220, 223
Lake Lanier Islands Resort 220
Lake Lanier Navy 142
Lake Lanier Regional Library 344, 346
Lake, J.B. Johnson 265
Lamb, Rev. Gene 416
Lamme, Ellis 177, 178

Lander, Jan 424
Landmark Aviation 271, 272
Landmark Church 417
Landress, Doug 130
Lane, Donna 408
Lane, Mills B. 196, 226
Langley, Doug 465
Langley, Morris 211
Langston, Jean 212
Lant, Michael 442
Larsen, Larry 381
LaSelva, Kathy 372
Lassiter, Shirley 28, 380
Laszlo, Sandy 536
Latimer, Frank 422
Latter Day Saints 553, 554
Laurel Baye Health Care 546
Lawler, Laine 415
Lawler, Tom 338
Lawrence, James 93, 110, 125
Lawrenceville Boys and Girls Club 307, 308
Lawrenceville Church of God 424
Lawrenceville City Hall 151
Lawrenceville City Schools 71
Lawrenceville Cooperative Ministry 424, 426, 526, 533
Lawrenceville Development Authority 363
Lawrenceville First United Methodist Church 424
Lawrenceville High School 112, 211
Lawrenceville Home Weekly 244
Lawrenceville Medical Center 335
Lawrenceville News 240, 246, 247, 248
Lawrenceville News Herald 246
Lawrenceville Presbyterian Church 70, 71, 345, 424, 426
Lawrenceville Public Housing Authority 144
Lawrenceville Tourism and Trade Association 540
Lazar, Richard 441
LeaderNext 511
Leadership Gwinnett 87, 504, 505, 506, 507, 510, 511, 512, 513, 569
Leadership Gwinnett Board of Trustees 506
League, Gloria 518
League, Wayne 519
Leah Morgan Scholarship Fund 533
Leather City 117
LeCraw, Scott 171
Lee, Bob 210
Lee, Chung 373
Lee, Kook-Ja "Cookie" 442
Lee, Troy 403
Leersen, Christopher 442
Legacy State Bank 460
Lehman, E.J. 544
Lenora and Alfred Glancy Foundation 135
Leroux, Mr. and Mrs. Robert L. 346, 514
Lesser, Dr. Lanny 319, 411
Lettie Pate Evans Foundation 370
Level Creek Methodist Church 103
Lewis, Barb 407
Lewis, Dr. John 368
Lewis, Pat 231, 232
Liable, Norm 427
Liegerot, Tine 348
Lilburn Business Association 419, 538
Lilburn Cooperative Ministries 547
Lilburn Daze Arts Festival 547
Lillian Webb Center 407
Lindemuth, John 198
Linder, John 434
Lindsay, Winford (Buck) 368, 531, 532
Link, Fred 85
Lionheart Theatre 379
Lisle, Wayne 217
Little Best Friend Park 264
Little Mulberry Park 263, 264
Little, Charles 522
Little, David 522
Little, Wayne 522
Livable Centers Initiative 363
Living Grace Lutheran Church 328
Livsey, Green 100
Livsey, Robert 100
Llorens, Carlos 539
Lockhart, Anne 381
Lockridge, Ray 232
Lockwood, Vince 380
Logan, James Harvie 125
Loganville Chamber of Commerce 542
Loganville International Airport 570
Loggins, Don 306, 308, 350, 370, 372
Long, Jesse 368, 408, 487, 512
Long, Rev. Nat 102
Looby, Tom 310
Lord, Tony 383
Lotz, Charles 447
Louise Radloff Middle School 246, 248
Love, Dr. Dwight 487
Love, Kelly 361
Loveless, John and Levi 152
Lovin, Joe 209
Lowery, Michael 447
Lowry, Mrs. Vinie 403
LOX 570
Loye, Babatunde T. 415
LTTA 540, 541, 542
Lucent Technologies 287
Lukeman, Augustus 226
Luther, Tim 488
Lyle, Dorothy 214
Lynch, John 537
Lynott, Dick 196
LZU 269, 274

M

Mabry, David 386
Mackle, Barbara 163
Macrenaris, Gail 510
Maddox, Cody Austin 325
Maddox, Lester 80, 120, 121, 227, 521, 564
Maddox, Runette and Gerald 325
Magill, Mrs. James W. 115
Maguire's Mill 99
Mahaffey, Betty Jo 212
Mahizhnan, Palamalai 465
Mahoney, Jan 420
Makizhnan, Dr. P. 464
Malcolm Baldrige Award 481
Mall of Georgia 12, 13, 15, 16, 97, 334, 335, 382, 439, 462, 471, 497
Maloney, Leon 252, 459
Maloof, Dr. Marion 537
Maloof, Kevin 214
Maltbie, William 93, 103, 110, 125, 154
Manby, Joel 228
Mancini, Rob 270, 271
Manley, Mary Ann 510
Manning, John 313

Mapp Jr, Erwin E. 346
Maran, Jim 444, 497, 499, 502
Marbury, John 422
Marchman Gymnasium 485
Mardis, Kathi 378
Markwalter, Jay 376, 541
MARTA 109, 110, 435, 436, 437, 438, 439, 496, 525
Martin, Carole 331
Martin, Desmond 519
Martin, Don 145, 149, 269
Martin, Dr. Bill 412, 413
Martin, Elaine 581
Martin, John 462, 514
Martin, John F. 127
Martin, L.R. 145
Martin, Mrs. John 514
Martin, Pam 413
Martin, Rich 144
Martin, Sam 270, 271
Martin, Tom 42, 461, 462, 468, 502, 537
Martinez, Armando 539
Mary Our Queen 556
Mary Straw Kistner Fund 83
Mason Clinic 415
Mason III, Dr. Miles 45, 331, 461
Mason Jr, Dr. Miles 193, 195, 197, 217, 415
Mason, Bill 195, 196, 197
Mason, Claude 195
Mason, Daddy 415
Mason, Doris 43, 44
Mason, Dr. Miles 45, 193, 195, 197, 217, 331, 415, 461
Mason, Dr. Tina 44
Mason, Ellery J. 99
Mason, Ida Belle Moore 32
Mason, J.P. 31, 33
Mason, James Winston 32
Mason, Jimmy 32, 41, 42, 120, 205, 252, 266, 267, 463, 498
Mason, Keith 45, 46
Mason, Meredith 501
Mason, Mike 536
Mason, Tracey 44, 45
Mason, Wayne 31, 32, 33, 36, 38, 39, 41, 46, 48, 57, 63, 163, 165, 171, 182, 183, 184, 187, 189, 205, 208, 232, 265, 266, 267, 305, 319, 356, 365, 368, 496, 498, 506, 559
Mason-Todd House 32
Massey, Abit 198, 199
Massey, Amy 313
Mast, Rev. Michael 555
Masters, Venita 382
Matlock, Glenn 579
Mattison, Frank 132, 571
Mattison, Ray 253, 260
Maughon, Jimmy 532
Mauldin, Betty 522
Mayes, Ernest 215
McBride, Tom 308
McCabe, Alice 74
McCallum, Vic 383
McCarthur, Celia 406
McClure, Bill 194, 195, 196, 197
McClure, James 110, 111
McClure, Larry 70, 197, 217
McClure, Myrtice Burrell 197
McConnell, Rev. James Patterson 124
McCullers, Betty 543
McCurdy, Doug 266
McCurdy, Kathy 532
McDaniel Farm 264
McDaniel, Judy 466
McDaniel, Julian 130
McDevitt and Street 325
McDonald Transit Associates 439
McEnery, Don 306
McGarity, Bob 562
McGarity, Caryn 372, 501
McGee, J.H. 115, 146, 458
McGill, Curtis 307, 352, 390
McGloin, Paul W. 434
McGoldrick, J. Patrick 460
McGowan, Frank 356
McGregory, Thomas 315
McGuire, Thomas 99, 106
McGuirk, Terry 469
McHaffey, Robert 211
McIntosh, Lynne 383
McIntyre, Sue 427
McIver, Julie 424
McKelvey, Victor 211
McKendree United Methodist Church 406, 424, 426
McKisley, Nancy 554
McKoy, Bill 314
McLaughlin, Joe 338
McLemore, Phil 380
McLendon, William E. 313
McMichen, Clayton 129
McMillian, Horace 209
McMillon, Ken 198
McMullan, Steve 301
McMullen, David 372
McNally, Carl 338
McNally, Cathy 526
McOmber, Kevin 258
McQuaig, Gerald 210
Meals on Wheels 547
Means, Jeremy 177
Medical/Health Care Council 499
Medieval Fair 335
Medina, Oscar 320
Medlock, Harold 463, 529
Meek, Alfie 239
Mentz, Pastor Marlin 555
Menzies, Gary 373
Merchandise Mart and Industrial Park 182
Mercier, James 575
Merrill, Hugh 3, 5
Merritt, Reid 163, 164, 165, 261
Merritt, Rev. James 558
Mertz, Carl 309
Messiah Korean Church 555
Metropolitan Arts Fund 374
Mezzullo, Art 445
Michko, Patricia 380
Mill Creek 15, 239
Miller, Bill 380
Miller, Bobby 529
Miller, Carol 532
Miller, Cecil 136
Miller, Mr. and Mrs. James
Miller, Joan 536
Miller, Monroe 459
Miller, Reps 459
Miller, Shirley 232
Miller, Zell 1, 14, 42, 44, 52, 63, 69, 77, 219, 221, 232, 325, 451, 506, 529
Mimms, Malon 17
Mingledorff, L.N. (Bud) 313

Minish, Dr. Al 202
Mitchell, Billy 196
Mitchell, J.W. 482
Mitchell, Jack 215
Mitchell, John 413
Mitchell, Pat 508
Mitchell, Thomas 504
Mobley, John xii, 181, 184, 354
Mobley, Mary Lynn 421
Monfort, Clarence 145
Moon, Bill 211
Moore, Birdie 134
Moore, Charles 232
Moore, Eron 307, 308
Moore, Faye 368, 547
Moore, Hill 266
Moore, Jeff 338
Moore, Katie 136
Moore, Lisa 406
Moore, Lloyd 121
Moore, Oscar 33
Moore-Huie, Gail 544
Morcock, D.C. 247
Morgan III, Bartow 38, 39, 40, 69, 456, 457
Morgan Jr, Bartow 38, 40, 46, 456, 457
Morgan, Bartow 38, 39, 40, 46, 69, 456, 457
Morgan, Brand 39, 456, 457
Morgan, Candace 520
Morgan, Gerald 211
Morgan, Hansel 118, 216, 240, 256, 455, 484
Morgan, Louise Brand 39, 456
Morgan, Nick 217
Morgan, Ray 185, 514
Morgan, Tony 542
Morris, Grover 529
Morrison, Cline 424
Morsberger, Emory 144, 146, 147, 376, 442, 445, 449
Mortin, Gordon 351
Morton, Gus 522
Morton, Rozelle 383, 387
Moser, Len 471
Moses, Deana 421, 422
Moses, Nell 403
Mount Carmel Cemetery 315
Mount Tabor Baptist 426, 427
Mountain Park 50, 105, 106, 107, 219, 221, 224, 227, 228, 262, 303, 304, 305, 345, 382, 419, 420, 525, 530, 543, 555
Mountain Park United Methodist Church 419
Mt. Moriah Baptist 102
Mt. Zion Baptist 319
Munteanu, Becky 308
Murphy, Mike 536
Murrain, William A. 415
Museum of Buford 386
Music on Main 538
Muyskens, Dr. James 450
Muyskens, Jim 452
Myers, Lilburn Trigg 125
Myers, Rev. Kevin 559
Myrick, Dick 356
Myrick, Jr, Richard 408

N

Nash, Charlotte 351, 353, 465
Nash, Gartrell 50, 572
Nash, Hollis 318
Nash, Lamar 562
Nash, Norman 364
Nash, Norris 37, 120, 205, 252, 266, 267, 465
Nash, Tom 146
Nasuti, Bert 442, 467, 468, 472, 501
National Bank of Georgia 462
National Data Corp 289
National Railway Historical Society 523
NationsBank 59, 68, 455
NCM 416, 417, 418
NCR 282
Neal, Rubye 307, 308
Neelagaru, Dr. Narasimhulu 464
Neely, Frank 170
Neighborhood Leadership Institute 508, 509, 569
Neighborhood News 579
Neighborhood Service Leadership 504
Nelems, James H. 313
Nelson, Pat 406
Nesbit, Joe 454
Nesbit, Noye H. 179
New Bethany Baptist 421
New Dawn Theater 380
New Hope Christian 426
New Life Worship Center 427
New London 31, 125, 377, 378, 379
New Prospect 421
News of Gwinnett 241, 248
News-Herald 27, 113, 115, 134, 146, 162, 240, 241, 246, 247, 248, 450, 482, 577
Newton, Craig L. 441
Nichol, Ridley 5, 6, 7
Nichols, Doug 462
Nichols, Matthew 354
Nichols, Monte 372
Nicholson, David 307, 308
Nickelson, Rev. Victor 555
Nixon, J.C. 519
Nobis, Tommy 302
Norcross Baseball Association 521
Norcross Baseball Hall of Fame 521, 522
Norcross Baseball Museum 521
Norcross Boys and Girls Club 308
Norcross Business Association 539
Norcross Community and Cultural Arts Center 379
Norcross Cooperative Ministry 413, 416, 417, 418, 421, 533, 545, 558
Norcross Fire Museum 252, 521
Norcross First Baptist Church 418
Norcross First United Methodist Church 406, 416, 418
Norcross Garden Club 581
Norcross High School 98, 314, 521, 528, 533, 534
Norcross History Center 521
Norcross News Reporter 241
Norcross Presbyterian Church 379, 418
Norcross Wesleyan 417
Norcross Woman's Club 343, 521, 544, 545
Norcross, Jonathan 125
Nordsen 283
Norfolk Southern 108, 109, 199, 206, 382, 524
Norman, Greg 218
Norman, Ms. Freddie 306
Norris, Don 520
Norris, Fate 129
Norris, Joy 520
North Georgia Church of God 554
North Georgia Conference (UMC) 314, 316, 317, 554
North Gwinnett Business Alliance 539, 540
North Gwinnett Cooperative Ministry 420, 422
North Gwinnett High School 428, 484, 510
North Metro Baptist 426

North River Community 426
North, Jimmy 364
Northeast Atlanta Christian School 492
Northeast Atlanta Metro Association of Realtors 235
Northeast Foundation 365
Northeast Georgia Civil War Roundtable 518
Northeast Georgia Community Foundation 313
Northside Wesleyan 416
Northwoods Country Club 216
Norton Jr., Frank 239
Norton Jr., R.L. 145
Norton, Hulon R. 458
Norton, Jimmy 364, 536
Norton, Richard 319
Notre Dame Academy 494
Novartis 283
Nugent, Dr. Jeffrey 17

O

O'Brien, Kevin 364
O'Brien, Rick 277, 280, 281, 283, 498
O'Kane, John 498
O'Kelley, Horace 233
O'Kelley, Mark 44
O'Kelley, William Clark 83
O'Neill, Jim 338
Oakbrook Technology Park 59, 284
Oakes, Eddie 153
Oakes, John Henry Hansford 153
Oakes, Ray 211, 212
Odum, Ann Parsons 72
Odum, Ken 364
Odum, Wally 72
Oelschig, George 465
Old Academy 256, 482, 483
Old Peachtree Presbyterian 426, 427
One Heart Church 418
Open Hands 420
Orkin, Billy 261
Ortloff, Ann 80, 82
Osborn, Teresa 381
Osborne, Barron 211
Otwell, John 368
Otwell, Roy 139, 241
Outlet, Mamie 414
Owens, Ed 529
Owens, Walter 529
Ownby, Eric 308

P

Pack, Jim 407, 455
Padgett, Pastor Nancy 555
Pakenham, Timothy J. 407
Pannu, Gursharan S. 465
Panos, Pastor Jim 555
Panyik, Rich 171, 307, 532
Pardee, Lewis 524
Parikh, Naresh 465
Paris, Michael 361
Parish Nurse Program 328
Park Place Association 540
Parker, Bobby 215
Parker, Gordon 165
Parkview High School 213, 365, 469
Parkway Baptist 426, 427
Parsons Andrews Building Supply 525
Parsons, Calvin 72, 461
Parsons, Kate Alford 72
Partnership Gwinnett 499, 536, 569
Patel, Chandra 464
Patel, Kati 465
Patel, Nancy 445
Patel, Ramon 445
Patel, Sudhirkamar 464
Patillo, John and Wayne 211
Patricia M. Brown Center 401
Patterson, J.T. 529
Patterson, Phyllis 331
Patterson, R.T. 254
Paul Duke Parkway 535, 536
Paul Harris Fellows of Rotary International 533
Paul, Chuck 539
Paynik, Rick 306
Payton, Rev. Bill 424
Peachtree Bank of Fulton County 466
Peachtree Bank, Gwinnett 466
Peachtree Christian Church 409, 410
Peachtree Christian Hospice 16, 17, 18, 407, 409
Peachtree Corners 58, 101, 127, 193, 208, 233, 234, 235, 239, 257, 260, 275, 276, 277, 278, 279, 286, 289, 296, 305, 312, 313, 314, 316, 317, 345, 373, 418, 439, 459, 464, 485, 486, 502, 526, 531, 532, 533, 535, 536, 539, 555, 579, 580
Peachtree Corners Baptist 373, 418
Peachtree Corners Christian Church 418
Peachtree Corners Church of Christ 418
Peachtree Corners Overlay District 535
Peachtree Corners Presbyterian 418
Peachtree Corners YMCA 312, 313, 314
Peachtree Industrial Boulevard 101, 199
Peachtree Road 101
Peachtree Station 235
Peachtree Street 101
Peachtree World of Tennis 192, 365
Peavy, Mary 306, 307
Peed, Marina 442
Peeples, Tyler M. 247
Peevy, Mitch 356, 357
Pence, Ann-Carol 375, 376
Penn, Irven 383
Pentecost, Hal W. 145
Pentecost, John 308
Pentecost, Michael 230
Peoples Bank and Trust Company 462
Perdue, Sonny 453, 565
Perimeter Church 406, 418, 426, 427, 554
Perimeter College 450
Perkin Elmer Corp 275, 283
Perlman, John 449
Perrin Country Club 216
Perry, Carl 455
Perry, J.A. 240, 247
Persons, Tom 464
Peters, A.W. 318
Peters, Beth 380
Pharr, Keith 211
Pharr, Willie 209
Pharr, Yulee 318
Phillips, Helen Elizabeth 34
Phillips, Mrs. Elfrieda 534
Phillips, Rev. A.A. 133
Phillips, Russell 529
Phillips, Tom 463
Pickwick, Ralph 309
Piedmont Hawthorne 271
Pilgrimage Presbyterian Church 416, 419
Pinckney, Charles 97

Pinckney, Charles Cotesworth 97
Pinckneyville 97, 98, 101, 202, 207, 208, 252, 253, 255, 261, 262, 264, 265, 381
Pinckneyville Community Association 202
Pinckneyville Community Center 381
Pinckneyville militia district 98
Pinder, Jo Ann 346, 532
Pine Ridge Country Club 216
PineIsle Hotel 220, 222
Pinetree Road 101
Pinion, George 211
Piper, Mrs. Robert 514
Pippin, Dr. John 277, 278
Pitchtree Road 101
Pitt, Mark 380
Pittard, Charles 164
Pittard, Charles C. 164, 268, 514
Pittard, Crawford 195
Pittard, Mrs. Mack (Martha) 132
Pittman, John Wesley 317
Plane, Helen 225
Platt, Marvin 427
Pleasant Hill Baptist Church 425
Pleasant Hill Presbyterian 426, 427
Plunkett, Bobby 338
Poole, Doris 421, 422
Poole, Jerry 273
Poole, Ted 421
Pope, Mike 504
Poplar Hill Baptist 574
Porter, Joan 536
Porter, Rick 171
Poss, Barbara 100
Powell, Bob 178, 403, 528
Powell, Jimmy 529
Powell, Joe 465
Powell, Robert 177
Power, Myrt 121, 122
Poythress, David B. 465
PPG Industries 437
Prater, Dr. Gretchen 412
Pratt, Mary 383
Preble, Clayton H. 313
Premji, Mark 563
Presbyterian Church of the Redeemer 328
Price, Lynn 408
Price, Maxie 267
Prieto Communications 562
Prieto, Filiberto 562
Primm, Dennis 384
Prince of Peace Church 553, 556
Project Safe Place 408
Prospect United Methodist 424, 426
Providence Christian Academy 489, 490
Pruitt, Dudge 164, 185, 205, 232, 284
Pruitt, Glyndon 121
Pruitt, W.R. 171
Puckett, Larry 164, 211
Puckett, Riley 129, 130
Puckett, V. H. 317
Puckett, Wiley 268
Pugh, Robert 417
Purvis, David 488
Pyburn, Jack 114
Pyron, Jeannie 132

Q

Quail, Pastor William 555
Quality Growth Council 500
Quantum National Bank 464
Quinn House 547
Quinn, Sheron 415

R

Raab, Leslie 378
Rabon, Sherrie 518
Radio Korea 563
Radio Mex 562
Radio Uncion 562
Radloff Middle School 246, 248, 308, 481
Radloff, Louise 246, 248, 337, 338, 449, 565
Rainbow Village, Inc. 404, 405, 406, 533
Rainey, Leo 348, 458
Rama, H.P. 464
Ramirez, Ana L. 442
Raney, Jane 212
Ratliff, Robert 465
Rauschenberg, Robert 384
Rawlins, Dr. George 319
Ray, Rev. John 555
RBC Bank 466
Recycling Bank 349, 569
Red Clay Theatre and Arts Center 379, 380
Red Land Baptist 102
Reddy, Dr. Srinivas K. 464
Reddy, Narender 464
Redeemer Presbyterian Church 542
Reed, Philip 348
Reed, Rev. Ken 426
Reed, Scott 465
Reedy, Mike 364
Reepe, Betty Jo 212
Reeves, Dan 302, 462
Reeves-Tullis, Christi 372
Regan, Kevin 373
Regional Organized Crime Information Center 166
Reid, George 92
Relay for Life 379, 533, 546, 547
Republic Bank of Georgia 465
Republicans 110, 254, 337, 338, 352, 565, 566, 575
Resource Conservation and Development Council 176
Rest Haven 125, 261
Reynolds, Steve 236, 246, 248, 348, 448, 564
Rhodes Jordan Park 30, 150, 212
Rhodes, Garry M. 441
Rich, Deborah 518
Rich, Dick 8, 11, 12, 13, 528
Richards, Jon 441
Richardson, Gerald 441
Richardson, Howard 186
Richardson, Rev. Larry 426
Richardson, Sharon 424
Riddett, Mary 421
Riden, Tom 210
Ridgedell, Cindy 423
Riehm, Edie 521
Rigsby, Sharon 337, 512
Rilling, Art 445, 502
Rinker, Frank 63, 324, 328, 406, 462
Rispin, Jeannine 502
River Green Business Park 169
River Green Industrial Park 11
Roark, Dr. John 198
Robert D. Fowler Family YMCA 312
Robert Woodruff Foundation 371
Roberts, Claude 171
Roberts, Clyde 146

Roberts, Deb 308
Roberts, Elaine 519
Roberts, Mary 427
Roberts, Ronda 420
Robertson, Frank 522
Robertson, John 307
Robinson Aviation Inc 273
Robinson, Brent 542
Robinson, C. Dean 463
Robinson, Dean 463
Robinson, Forrest W. 313, 372, 498
Robinson, George 211
Robinson, Harold 215
Robinson, J. Mack 40, 41, 57, 245, 463
Robinson, Terry 539
Robison, John 390
Robson, Lisa Sheppard 372
Rock Tenn Corp 313
Rockbridge Baptist Church 98, 102, 103
Rockwell International 582
Rocquemore Cotton Gin 571
Rodriguez, Anthony 375, 376
Rogers, George 214, 215
Rolfe, Mrs. Ethlyn R. 346
Rolling Hills Baptist Church 422
Rollins Center 316
Rollins, Gerald 319
Roman Aviation 270
Ronald Reagan Park 264
Rooks, Patsy xiv, 496
Rosa, Ferdinand 383
Rosenbaum, Art 130
Rosenblum, Celia 381
Rosenblum, I.J. 381
Ross, Ray 374
Rosselle, Dave 444
Rosselot, Gerald 297
Rotary Club 302, 421, 525, 530, 531, 532, 533
Rouse, Colleen and Dennis 557
Rovetta, Joyce 75
Rowe, Mr. and Mrs. Frank 371
Rowe, Johnnie A. 371
Rudert, John 529
Rudert, Trudy 529
Rupert, Georgia 410
Rusk, Parks 186
Russell, Ari 510
Russell, Herman 2, 10, 42, 43, 44
Russell, Sen. Richard 142, 220, 236
Rutherford, Mike 510
Ryan, Kent 306
Ryan, Kimberly 323
Rydell, Pat 424

S

Sailors, Brenda 488
Salvation Army 284, 285, 532, 533, 558
Salzano, Loretta 406
Sammon Jr., Frank Quill 162
Sammon, F.Q. 526
Sams, Mrs. R.H. 343
Sanders, Carl 80, 137, 268, 317, 524
Sanders, Eugene 528
Sanders, Mariah Jackson 315
Sandler, Dr. Manfred 326
Saul, Ralph 403
Sawnee Golf Club 216
Sawyer, Gordon 167
Sawyer, Jack 41, 268, 495, 498, 504
Sawyer, James 31, 125
Scarborough, Frank 3
Schaffer, Harry 233
Schickedanz, J.C. 309
SCHRAM 6
Schure, Dr. Matthew 433
Schwab, John 192, 500
Scientific-Atlanta 49, 277, 282, 297, 298, 299, 313, 374, 510, 533
Scott Builders 5
Scott Development Company 5
Scott Hudgens Company 7
Scott Hudgens Mortgage 7
Scott Hudgens Realty and Mortgage 6, 7, 9
Scott, John 375
Seago, David 313, 408, 510, 511
Sears, Mrs. Bertha P. 346
Security Bank of Gwinnett County 465
Seeley, Merv 260
Seibenhener, Ron 360
Selvam, Sri Sri 561
Semerjian, Jonathan 177
Senior Golden Olympics 264
Senior Leadership Gwinnett 504, 512, 513, 569
Sexton, John W. 442
Shaafer, Jenell 488
Shackelford, Anna Nolan 79
Shackelford, Wayne xv, 76, 77, 79, 80, 164, 187, 189, 203, 205, 259, 260, 305, 506, 513
Shadburn Banking Company of Buford 455
Shadburn, Kate Allen 455
Shafer, Pat 424
Shaffer, Nancy 383
Shah, J.J. 464
Shah, Meena 464
Shah, Navin 465
Shah, Nitin 465
Shaw, G. Martin 313
Shaw, Marty 408
Shay, Jim 275, 277
Sheals, Rev. Dr. William 373, 558, 559
Sheffer, Rev. George Washington 210
Sheldon, Art 441
Sheltering Arms 308, 406, 407
Shelton, John 346, 368
Shepherd, Dan 459
Shepherd, Tom 327
Sherrington, Katherine 338
Sherrington-Haggard, Sally 415
Shiloh Baptist Church 98
Shook, Gay 536
Shore, Jimmy 529
Short, William 313, 464
Shorty Howell Park 531
Sikes, Beth 547
Sikes, Bobby 147
Sikes, Richard 39, 323, 324, 458, 466, 467
Sikes, Wayne xv, 323, 324, 326, 331, 368, 532
Simmons, James P. 105, 112
Simmons, James T. 105
Simmons, Mayor F.Q. 115
Simon Property Group 15, 334, 335
Simonis, Kyle 378
Simpson, Elizabeth Jane Sanders 314
Simpson, Frank 522
Simpson, J.T. 314
Simpson, Ludie 314, 315, 317

Simpson, Marjean 425
Simpson, Randolph 211
Simpson, Randy 70, 338, 518
Simpsonwood 314, 316, 317, 406, 416, 418, 536, 554
Simpsonwood United Methodist Church 317, 406, 416, 418
Sims, Cyndae 368
Sims, Susie Dunnigan 581
Sirkis, Glenn 290
Skillet Lickers 128, 129, 130
Skin Alley 153
Slattery, Celia 419
Sloan, Boyd 162
Smallwood, Gloria 331
Smartmodem 290, 292, 295
Smith III, Ray S. 230
Smith, Arnold 461
Smith, Carson 317
Smith, Charles H. 112
Smith, Christopher 456
Smith, Cleveland 191
Smith, Doug 211
Smith, E.H. 247
Smith, Elizabeth 581
Smith, Frances 540
Smith, Garland 258
Smith, George 311
Smith, Jane 13
Smith, Jimmy 215
Smith, Jodi 331
Smith, John 463, 529
Smith, John Clay 111
Smith, John Owen 315
Smith, Larry 266
Smith, Lee 223
Smith, Matthew 274
Smith, Michael 261
Smith, Powell 211
Smith, Quill (Smitty) 211
Smith, R.P. 528
Smith, Rankin 300, 302, 371
Smith, Ruben E. 456
Smith, Scott 492
Smith, Wayne 421
Smith, William E. 463
Smithgall, Charlie 241
Smulian, Jim 532
Snedecor, Scott 422
Sneezer 99
Snell, Bill 157
Snell, Bryant 157
Snell, Chris 82, 156
Snell, David 156
Snell, E.R. 155, 157, 212
Snell, Ferle 518
Snell, G.F. (Gladstone Frederick) 155
Snell, Hugh 37
Snell, Richard 83, 156
Snell, Robin 156
Snell, Thomas 31, 125
Snellville Baptist Church 559
Snellville Cemetery 35
Snellville Citizen 579
Snellville City Council 32, 37, 320
Snellville Commerce Club 536
Snellville Community Health Association 318
Snellville Community Health Trust 319
Snellville Consolidated School 519
Snellville First United Methodist Church 423
Snellville High School 32, 519
Snellville Historical Cemetery 319
Snellville Historical Society 518, 519
Snellville Merchant's Association 536
Snellville Woman's Club 547
Snider, Harvey 313
Snipes, Lynn 372
Snodon 576
Soesbe, Amanda 540
Sola Fide Lutheran 424
Soloman, Dr. Mike 309
Soracco, Marie 532
Sorrels, Charles 165
Sosebee, Martha 380
South Gwinnett High School 50, 81, 88, 213, 377, 378, 533
Southeast Gwinnett Cooperative Ministry 422, 423, 424
Southeastern Gwinnett Food Ministry 533
Southeastern Merchandise Mart 198, 199, 200
Southeastern Railway Museum 523
Spalding Corners 234, 235
Special Needs Children's School 533
Special Purpose Option Local Sales Tax (SPLOST) 47, 125, 261, 263, 265, 339, 340, 341, 342, 345, 388, 394, 474, 476, 483, 568,
Spence, J.D. 113
Spence, John 529
Spice Radio 563
Springbrook Golf Course 263
St Marguerite D'youville 556
St. Edwards Episcopal 424
St. James Lutheran 416, 418
St. John Neumann Regional Catholic School 488, 489
St. Lawrence Catholic 75, 424
St. Martha of Bethany Episcopal Church 421
St. Mary and Martha of Bethany 555
St. Monica 556
St. Oliver Plunkett 556
St. Patrick's Catholic Church 416
St. Pius X Catholic 328
St. Stephen, the Martyr 556
St. Vincent de Paul Society 416
Stanley, Fleet 130
Stanley, Roba 130, 131
Stanley, Robert Morland 130
Stansbery-Kellam, Nancy 346
Stansell, Jeff 308
Stanton, Bill 465
Stark, Homer 182
Stark, Hope 182, 514
Stark, Mary Louise 367, 368
Starling, Steve 521
Steckenrider, Paul 408
Stedeford, Robert 313
Steele, Jim 178, 347, 349, 477, 479, 480
Steinbaum, Kelley 427
Stephens, Betsy 421
Stephens, Dovie 49
Stephens, Gerald 313
Stephens, John D. 32, 41, 42, 49, 50, 188, 266, 496, 498
Stephens, Nick and Dovie 49
Stephenson, Jim 465
Stevens, Ellen 385
Stevens, Mavis 383
Stewart, Anita 386
Still, Bernard 209
Still, Bruce 241, 244, 246, 248
Stilo, Al 377
Stingley-Seals, Dr. Gloria 415
Stokes, Guy 165

Stone Mill Church 427
Stone Mountain Airport 219
Stone Mountain Inn 228
Stone Mountain Confederate Memorial Association 219, 225, 226, 227, 228, 230
Stone, Alex 364
Stonehedge Garden Club 534
Storey, Carol 212
Story, Earl 202, 212
Stouffer's PineIsle 220
Stough, Carol Ann 381
Straughan and Company 284
Straughan, C.L. 284
Strickland Jr., Henry 26, 28
Strickland, Alice 26, 27, 28
Strickland, Harrell 26, 27, 28
Strickland, M. B. 442
Strickland, Ruth 373
Strother, Renekia 308
Sturdivant, Robby 41
Sturgis, Nancy 520
Suffridge, Ken 350, 352, 353
Sugar Hill Baptist Church 420, 421
Sugar Hill Militia District 119, 120
Sugar Hill United Methodist Church 420, 421
Sugarloaf 217, 218, 235, 239, 282, 298, 310, 334, 336, 387, 388, 389, 392, 406, 426, 427, 437, 450, 451, 496, 497, 498, 502, 503, 553, 554, 579
Sugarloaf Community Church 426
Sugarloaf Country Club 217, 218, 579
Sugarloaf Golf Classic 218
Sugarloaf United Methodist Church 406, 426
Sullivan, Michael 258
Summerour, Ben 9
Summerour, Charles A. 576
Summerour, Charles William 576
Summerour, Harrison 9
Summerour, John Heard 132, 133, 344, 576, 577
Summerour, Heinrich 576
Summerour, Jay 27, 577
Summerour, John 461
Summerour, Knox 576
Summers, Chappell 277
Summerville, James 22, 25
Summit Chase Country Club 35, 48, 217, 265, 321, 381
Summit Ridge 137, 328, 330, 335, 547
Sumner, Sandra (Sandy) 522
Sunrise Baptist Church 424, 426
Surowiec, Judith 383
Sussman, Michael 321
Sutt, Cynthia 376
Sutt, Randy 375, 376
Sutton, Debbie 314
Suwanee Business Alliance 538
Suwanee Parish Methodist 421
Swaim, Terry 534
Swan, Pat 372, 513
Swann, Dr. Lewis 152
Swann's Mill 152, 264
Swanson, Warren 211
Swanson, Willard 211
Sweetbottom Plantation 11, 16
Sweetwater Primitive Baptist 103
Swift, Commodore Lamar 142

T

TAL, Inc 508
Tanner, Gordon 129
Tanner, James Gideon (Gid) 128, 129, 130
Tanner, Phil 129, 130
Tannery Row Cultural Arts Center 387
Tapp, Helen 357, 361
Taylor, Dr. Roy 554
Taylor, Joanne 381
Teachers as Leaders 504, 507, 508, 569
Technology Park 59, 275, 276, 277, 278, 279, 280, 281, 282, 283, 284, 286, 293, 296, 298, 299, 349, 364, 439, 464, 498
Temple Beth David 556
Tennant, Mike 465, 504, 505, 513
Tennant, Sherry 368
Tennant, Shirley 512
Terrell, Thurman 522
Terry, Bill 419
Thakkar, Chuck 465
Thayer, Edward A. 313
The Atlanta Constitution 160, 170, 174, 242, 301, 523
The Atlanta Journal 16, 132, 159, 170, 242, 243, 248, 249, 294, 301, 526
The Atlanta Journal and Constitution 243
The Atlanta Times 564
The Bank of the South-Gwinnett 461
The Buford Gazette 240
The Church of the Way 426
The Community Bank 460
The Community Foundation of Northeast Georgia 500
The Daily News 244, 246
The Duffer's Club 195
The Falcon Inn 299, 301, 302, 495
The Heritage 142, 517
The Hootch 217
The Jimmy Powell Scholarship 529
The Korea Daily 564
The Lawrenceville News 240, 247
The Mills Corporation 334, 335
The Morsberger Group 146
The New York Times 243, 244, 248
The Parc at Duluth 494
Thomas, Benjamin 550
Thomas, Jacqueline J. 518
Thomas, Joan 230
Thomas, Patricia Bowden 457
Thomas, Steffan 370
Thomas, Walter 311, 459
Thompson Theatre 70
Thompson, Brian 413
Thompson, Curt 449
Thompson, Felton 185, 514
Thompson, George 504, 507, 508
Thompson, Glenn 465
Thompson, Harry 171
Thompson, Lewis 20, 22, 23, 25
Thompson, T. Glenn 465
Thrasher Park 125, 343, 545, 581
Thrasher, J.J. "Cousin John" 125, 545
Threadwell, John 92
Three Winds Farm 214
Tibbetts III, Marvin O. 463
Tidwell, James J. 463
Tillman, April 415
Tinsley, Virginia 417
Tisdale, Donna 308
Todd, Martha and Bill 409, 410
Topol, Sid 297
Topolski, Fran 309
Touchmark National Bank 464
Towers, William 92, 93, 110

Townsend, Denise 308
Townsend, Michael E. 463
TP/A 277, 280, 283
Transportation History Museum of Georgia 525
Travelers Insurance 282
Tribble Mill Park 82, 176, 263, 264, 349
Tribble, Janice 543
Tri-City Realty 5
Trickum Crossroads 107
Trigg, Angela 518
Trinity Lutheran Church 419, 423, 534, 555
Trinity United Methodist Church 426, 427
Truhe, Christina 537, 538
Tucker High School 211
Tucker Jr., Dr. Hubert 527
Tucker, Alton 121, 337, 565, 575
Tucker, Annette W. 518
Tucker, Hubert E. 317, 514, 517, 518, 527
Tucker, Lee 372
Tucker, Mrs. Hubert (Annette) 514, 515, 517
Tucker, Richard 41, 42, 45, 391, 451, 468, 469, 496, 499, 500, 501, 502, 510, 512
Tucker, Woodrow 121
Tuggle, Paul 413
Tull Foundation 311, 312
Tull YMCA 75, 312, 533
Tull, J.M. 312
Turkey Gizzard 98
Turner, Audrey 574
Turner, H.J.B. 209
Turner, Jack 139
Turner, Jerry 215
Turner, Mrs. Esther 403
Turner, Murlene 212
Twiggs, Ralph 197
Tyler, Curtis 414
Tyrrell, Mark 376

U

U.S. Highway 78 Corridor Improvement Association 445
UDC 225
Underwood, Charlie 216, 308
Underwood, Robert 268
UNICEF 547
Unisys Corporation 283
United Hospice of Atlanta 409
United Methodist Homeless Council 422
United Peachtree Corners Civic Association 526, 535, 536
United Way 60, 61, 305, 306, 307, 308, 406, 407, 422, 458, 500, 533
Unity Place 533
Unterman, Renee 151, 390
UPCCA 535, 536
Upchurch, John 510
Upper Chattahoochee Development Association 141, 198
Upper Ocmulgee River Resource Conservation and Development Council, Inc. 176
Urban Redevelopment Agency of the City of Duluth 363, 364
Ussery, Gene 306

V

Valezquez, Jaime 415
Vandiver, Ernest 80, 198, 317
Vanishing Gwinnett 75, 115, 515, 516, 517
Vanishing Gwinnett II 516, 517
Vann Tavern 140
Vann, Cherokee Chief James 140
Vann, Naomi 427
Vansant, R.L. 177
Vantress Farms 168, 269
Vantress, Charles 167, 168, 269
Varghese, Dr. Jacob 414
Varner, Jay 427
Vaughan III, Woodrow 354
Venable, Samuel H. 225
Veolia Transportation 440
Veterans Museum 113
Vickers, Billy 529
Vickery, Amy 417
Victor Allen House 386
Victory World Church 418, 557
Vietnamese Baptist Church 557
Village Blue 449
Vines Botanical Gardens 263, 381, 547
Voices of Faith 559
Vulcan Rock Quarry 195

W

W.S. (Winfield Scott) Freeman 152
Wachovia Bank 458, 460
Wages Field 270
Wages, Emory "Red" 270
Wages, Marlon 209
Wages, Mickey 211, 313
Wages, Peggy 212
Wages, Tom 136, 578
Wagner, Dick 308
Walker Golf Club 216
Walker, David 554
Walker, Inez 527
Walker, Jean 308
Walker, Jim 306
Walker, Perrin 216, 527
Walker, Sandra 512
Walker-Little, Deborah 521
Wall Aviation 271
Wall, Edmund J. 351
Wall, Jack 531
Wall, Marlon 211
Wall, Robert 271
Wallace, Buice 383
Wallace, Garland 455
Waller, Robert 408
Walls, Betty 331
Walsh, Dorothy 331
Walter Alford Sunday School class 30
Walters, Christopher 501
Walton EMC 82, 529
Ward, Nancy xv, 508, 510, 511
Wardlaw, James 92, 110, 111
Warren, Cy 416
Washington Academy 98
Water and Sewer Authority 37, 187, 190, 258, 259, 261, 350, 351, 353
Water Authority 183, 184, 189, 190
Waterfall, Gene 308
Waters, Gary 44
Waters, Judy 171, 366, 372, 390
Waters, Teresa 44
Waters, Thomas J. 550
Watkins, Elizabeth 531
Watson, Jim F. 313
Watson, Monty 313, 464
Watson, Tom 146, 202, 218
Weaver, Russ 348, 512
Webb, Anne 521

Webb, Bud 571
Webb, Jones xiv, 241, 268, 269, 570
Webb, Lillian xv, 15, 123, 171, 206, 339, 350, 351, 355, 357, 388, 390, 407, 463, 515
Webb, Marion 368
Webb, Mrs. Jones 241
Webb, Sandra 425
Webb, Tony 536
Weber, Ron 542
Webster, Gary 421
Weeks, A.R. 370
Weeks, Ray 356, 357, 361, 370, 503
Weilhiem, Lee 465
Wells, Jan 422
Wesleyan Day School 485
West Gwinnett Christian Church 426
West Gwinnett High 195
West Walton Park 546
Western Electric 207, 208, 235, 277, 285, 286, 287, 289
Westminster Presbyterian Church 380
Wetherington, Dave 421
Wheat Street Baptist Church 226
Wheelchair Sports Center 531
Wheeler, Tom 2, 12, 356, 369, 447
White, George 383
White, Glenn 450
White, Paige 368
White, Philip 465
Wickes, Betty 15
Widdle, Lamar 297
Wiener, Leo 447
Wienges, Cheryl 547
Wiggins, Connie xv, 178, 348, 506, 512, 513, 532
Wilbanks, Alvin 336, 476
Wilbanks, E.W. 241
Wilbanks, Early A. 241
Wilbanks, Emma Mae 241, 248
Wilbanks, Mrs. E.A. 241
Wilder, Charles 187, 351, 356
Wilderquist, Vernon 297
Wilkerson, Bob 364
Wilkerson, Doug 520
Williams Commission 64, 69
Williams, Andrew David 368
Williams, Barbara and Jim 53
Williams, Bill 464
Williams, Bobby 537
Williams, Bruce 2, 14, 447
Williams, Carvis 37, 164, 205, 266
Williams, Dave 171
Williams, George 368
Williams, Gertrude and Mercer 52, 53
Williams, Isham 93, 103, 154
Williams, Jim 55, 57, 61, 65, 67
Williams, Mark 442, 520
Williams, Paul 488
Williams, Preston xv, 391, 392, 393, 397, 398, 468, 501
Williams, Ralph 2, 9, 13, 14, 23
Williams, Raymond 319
Williams, Rev. J. Thornton 140
Williams, Rev. Joe 416
Williams, Sara and Virgil 53, 68
Williams, Sue 575
Williams, Virgil 41, 42, 47, 51, 52, 53, 61, 62, 63, 64, 68, 69, 222, 260, 271, 318, 324, 451, 463, 496, 559
Williams, William August Holmes 84
Williams, William Pittman 52
Williamson, Doug 390
Williamson, Kathy 421, 527
Williamson, Rick 261
Willis, Gene 72
Willis, Kathryn 17, 572
Willis, Roger 408
Wilson, A.M. 458
Wilson, Judy Ann 520
Wilson, Merrill P. 461
Wilson, Phylecia 547
Wilson, W.W. 240
Wiltshire, Judy 426
Winder 109, 130, 149, 211, 230, 240, 260, 387, 575, 576
Windy Hill Golf Course 216
Winegarden, Richard 510
Wingo, Absalom Holbrook (Red) 522
Wingo, Ivy Brown 522
Winn House 514, 515, 516
Winn, Elisha 75, 92, 93, 154, 515, 516
Winn, Philadelphia 92
Winn, Richard D. 105
Wolaver, Tommy 543
Wolfe, Phil 331
Women's Clubs 544, 545, 547
Women's Domestic Violence Center 534
Wong, Vivian 464
Woo, Angela 376
Wood, Bob 233, 354
Wood, Bobby (Bob) 338
Wood, Dr. Charles 45
Wood, Randy 382, 383, 385, 386
Woods, Corbitt 308
Woods, Peggy 372
Woodward Mill 382
Works Progress Administration 114
Worthy, Marvin Nash 514, 515, 517
Wozencraft, Oscar 240, 247
Wren, Douglas 465
Wynn, Elisha 103
Wynn, Larry 558
Wynn, Ron 396, 397
Wynne Russell House 547

Y

Yamasaki La Belle Verde 448
Yancey, Reverend Nancy 404
Yarbrough, Janice 519
Yates, Gary 338
Yates, Larry 309
Yeager, Bill 563
Yellow River Park 264
YMCA 75, 211, 305, 309, 310, 311, 312, 313, 314, 533
Yoest, Dan 424
Yohan, Yoel 308
Young Men's Christian Association 305, 309
Young, Joe 406
Young, Zach 485
Youth Leadership Summit 510
Yow, Mike 380

Z

Zahn, Pastor Larry 555
Zaken, Lisa 539
Zammeron, Sam 563
Zammit, Charlie 19, 22, 23, 24, 25
Zion Lutheran Church 555
Zoar Methodist Church 33, 98, 102, 319

Annual Calendar of Events in Gwinnett

	Date	Event	Location
January	Through Second Friday in January	Christmas Tree Recycling-Chipping	Most fire stations in the County
	Second Saturday in January	Kite Festival (Bring your own kite)	BAPS Shri Swanubarayan Mandir, Lilburn
February	February Second	Groundhog Day	Yellow River Game Ranch, Lilburn
	First weekend in February	Taste of Dacula	Dacula High Cafeteria
	Early February	Chinese New Year's Celebration	Lucky Shoals Park, Norcross
	Weekend prior to Valentine's Day	Valentine Dinner and Dance	Historic Gwinnett Courthouse
	Weekend closest to Valentine's Day	Romance on the Rails	Southeastern Railway Museum
	Valentine's Day, February 14	Renew Your Wedding Vows	Justice and Administrative Center
	Late February	Continuum Art Show	Tannery Row Art Colony
	Mid February	Annual "Run the Reagan"	Ronald Reagan Parkway
March	Mid March	Annual Hi-Hope Gala	Gwinnett Center, Duluth
	Easter Sunday (varying Sundays)	Annual Easter Sunrise Service	Stone Mountain Park
	Easter Sunrise Service	Sponsored by Shadowbrook Baptists	Town Center Park, Suwanee
April	First weekend in April	Caboose Days	Southeastern Railway Museum
	Mid April Saturday	Corners to Crossing Race	P'tree Corners to Downtown Norcross
	Mid April Saturday	Kudzu Paint the Town Art Show	Thrasher Park, Norcorss
	Third weekend in April	Barefoot in the Park Fine Arts Show	Duluth Town Green
	Third weekend in April	Alcovy Dist. Boy Scout Exposition	Gwinnett Fairgrounds, Lawrenceville
	Third weekend in April	Earth Day	Gwin. Environmental & Heritage Ctr.
	Last weekend in April	Relay for Life Road Race	Lilburn City Park
	Last Saturday in April	Grayson Day	Grayson Community Park
	Last Sunday in April	Lake Lanier Home Tour	By Buford-Lanier Woman's Club
May	First weekend in May	Snellville Days Festival	T.W. Briscoe Park, Snellville
	Second weekend in May	Gwinnett ACS Relay for Life	Gwinnett Fairgrounds, Lawrenceville
	Second Saturday in May	Old McDaniel Farm Day	McDaniel Farm Park, Duluth
	Second weekend in May	Art and Jazz Festival	Downtown Buford
	Third Saturday in May	Annual Old Car Show	Downtown Norcross
	Fourth weekend in May	Art on Historic Courthouse Square	Downtown Lawrenceville
	Some weekend in May	Jazz Festival	Downtown Buford
	A few days before Memorial Day	Flags Placed in Town Honoring Vets	Near Downtown Duluth
	Memorial Day Saturday	Memorial Day Service	Duluth Town Green
	Memorial Day Weekend	American Indian Festival	Gwinnett Fairgrouds, Lawrenceville
	Memorial Day	Memorial Day Parade	Downtown Dacula
June	First Saturday in June	Trail Mix Celebration	Alternating at Gwinnett Park Locations
July	July 3 Prelude to the Fourth	Dramatic Presentation, Activities	Historic Courthouse Square, L'ville
	July 3 Prelude to the Fourth	Fireworks, Local Activities	Downtown Norcross
	July 3 Sparks in the Park	Fireworks, Local Activities	E.E. Robinson Park, Sugar Hill
	July 3 Duluth Celebrates America	Fireworks, Local Activities	Scott Hudgens Park, Duluth

Annual Calendar of Events in Gwinnett

	Date	Event	Location
July (cont.)	July 4 Celebration	Fourth of July Festival	Downtown Auburn
	July 4 in Lawrenceville	Gwinnett Glows Festival	Historic Courthouse Square, L'ville
August	It's HOT in August—No events of record except the return to school		
September	First weekend in September	Yellow Daisy Festival	Stone Mountain Park
	11 days, beginning second Thursday	Gwinnett County Fair	Gwinnett Fairgrounds, Lawrenceville
	Third weekend in September	Suwanee Day Festival	Town Center Park, Suwanee
	Last weekend in September	Duluth Fall Festival	Duluth Town Green
	Last week of Sept. First week of Oct.	Gwinnett Corporate Challenge	Gwinnett Park sites
October	First weekend in October	Elisha Winn Fair	Elisha Winn House, Dacula
	First weekend in October	Norcross Art Fest	Main Street, Norcross
	First weekend in October	American Indian Festival	Gwinnett Fairgrounds, Lawrenceville
	Second weekend in October	Lilburn Daze Fall Festival	Lilburn City Park
	Third weekend in October	Highland Games	Stone Mountain Park
	Third Saturday in October	OctoberFest	City of Auburn
	Third Saturday in October	Sugar Hill Fall Festival	E.E. Robinson Park, Sugar Hill
	Third Saturday in October	Gwinnett Reading Festival	Gwinnett Fairgrounds, Lawrenceville
	Third Saturday in October	Festival of Leaves	Historic Courthouse, Lawrenceville
November	First weekend in November	Hamfest, Alfred Memorial Radio Club	Gwinnett Fairgrounds, Lawrenceville
	Sunday and Tuesday after T-giving	The Nutcracker Ballet	Gwinnett Center, Duluth
	Thanksgiving Night	Yule Tree Lighting and Santa Arrival	Historic Courthouse, Lawrenceville
	Late November through December 30	Magic Night of Lights	Lake Lanier Islands
	Last Saturday in November	Sounding Off the Christmas Season	Auburn City Hall
	First Monday following Thanksgiving	Christmas Tree Lighting	Historic Second Avenue, Dacula
December	Friday prior to First Saturday	Tree Lighting	Thrasher Park, Norcross
	First weekend in December	Holiday Festival, Lighting and Santa	Town Green, Duluth
	First Saturday in December	Christmas Parade	Downtown Buford
	First Saturday in December	Historic Tour of Norcorss Homes	Downtown Norcross
	First Saturday in December	Tree Lighting and Christmas Parade	Downtown Loganville
	First Saturday in December	Christmas Tour of Homes	Grayson
	First Saturday in December	Christmas Parade	Downtown Lilburn
	Friday after T-giving until Dec. 23	Christmas Canteen Musical	Aurora Theatre, Lawrenceville
	First Friday in December	Tree Lighting and Christmas Concert	First Baptist Church, Lilburn
	First Sunday in December	Tour of Historic Homes	Downtown Lilburn
	Second Sunday in December	Placing Luminaries on Tombstones	City Cemetery, Norcross
	Weekends Before Christmas	Santa Visits, Crafts, Carriage Rides	Historic Courthouse, Lawrenceville
	Begins Day after Christmas	Christmas Tree Recycling-Chipping	Most fire stations in the County
	New Year's Eve	Lawrenceville Rings	Historic Courthouse, Lawrenceville

Source: Event organizers

Sites of Facilities of the Gwinnett Parks and Recreation Department

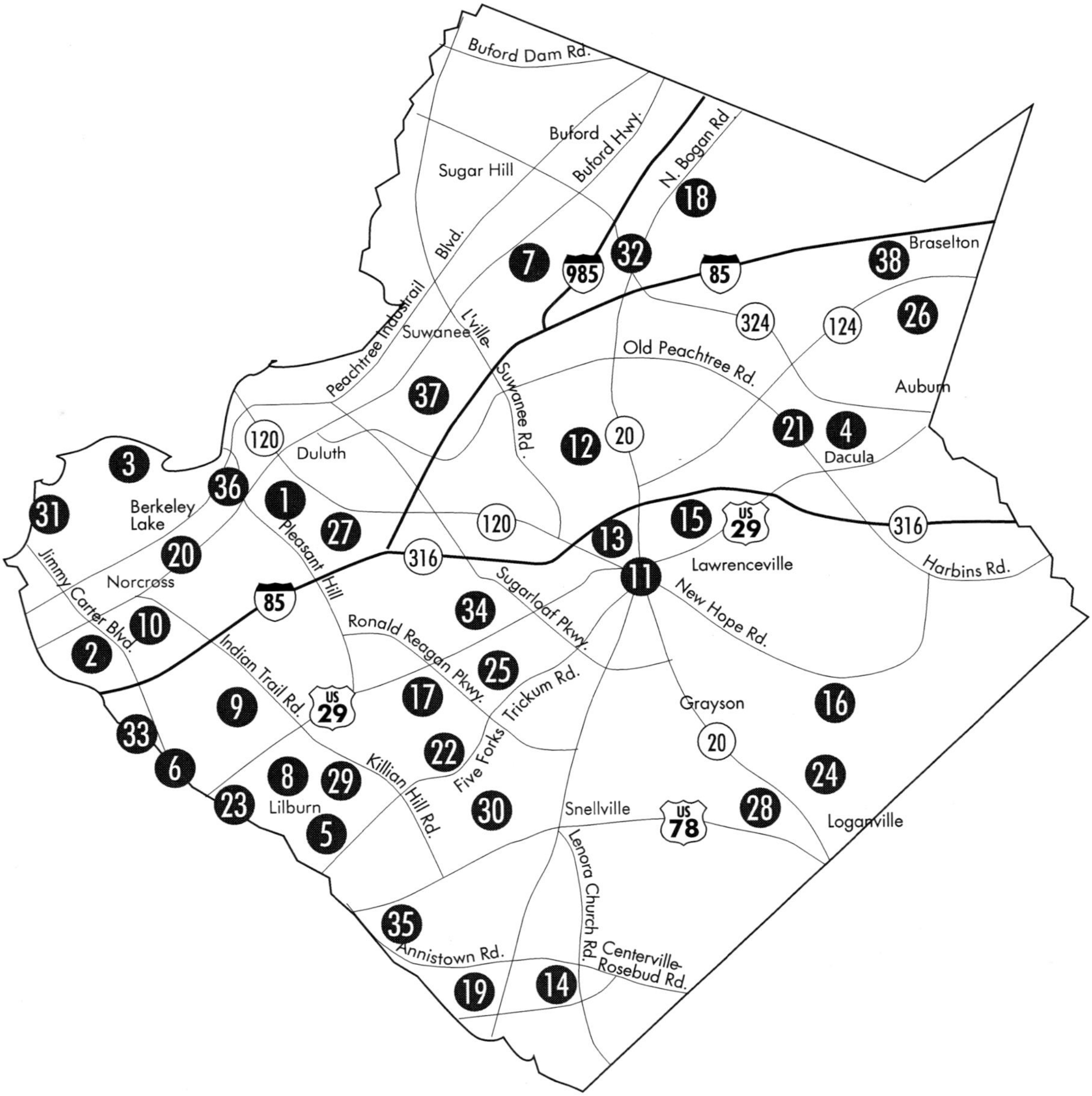